2012 Novel & Short Story Writer's MARKET®

Includes a 1-year online subscription to **Novel & Short Story Writer's Market** on

THE ULTIMATE MARKET RESEARCH TOOL FOR WRITERS

To register your *2012 Novel & Short Story Writer's Market* and **start your 1-year online fiction subscription**, scratch off the block below to reveal your activation code, then go to WritersMarket.com. Click on "Sign Up Now" and enter your contact information and activation code. It's that easy!

UPDATED MARKET LISTINGS FOR YOUR INTEREST AREA

EASY-TO-USE SEARCHABLE DATABASE • RECORD-KEEPING TOOLS

PROFESSIONAL TIPS & ADVICE • INDUSTRY NEWS

Your purchase of *Novel & Short Story Writer's Market* gives you access to updated listings related to this genre of writing (valid through 12/31/12). For just $9.99, you can upgrade your subscription and get access to listings from all of our best-selling Market books. Visit **WritersMarket.com** for more information.

31ST ANNUAL EDITION

2012 Novel & Short Story Writer's MARKET

Adria Haley, Editor

WRITER'S DIGEST BOOKS
WritersDigest.*com*
Cincinnati, Ohio

Publisher & Editorial Director, Writing Community: Phil Sexton

Managing Editor, Writer's Digest Market Books: Adria Haley

Writer's Market website: www.writersmarket.com

Writer's Digest website: www.writersdigest.com

Distributed in Canada by Fraser Direct
100 Armstrong Avenue
Georgetown, Ontario, Canada L7G 5S4
Tel: (905) 877-4411

Distributed in the U.K. and Europe by F&W Media International
Brunel House, Newton Abbot, Devon, TQ12 4PU, England
Tel: (+44) 1626-323200, Fax: (+44) 1626-323319
E-mail: postmaster@davidandcharles.co.uk

Distributed in Australia by Capricorn Link
P.O. Box 704, Windsor, NSW 2756 Australia
Tel: (02) 4577-3555

ISSN: 0897-9812
ISBN 13: 978-1-59963-228-5 (pbk:alk.paper)
ISBN 10: 1-59963-228-4 (pbk:alk.paper)

Attention Booksellers: This is an annual directory of F+W Media, Inc.
Return deadline for this edition is December 31, 2012.

Edited by: Adria Haley
Cover designed by: Jessica Boonstra
Interior designed by: Claudean Wheeler
Production coordinated by: Greg Nock
Cover illustration by: Emily Keafer

CONTENTS

MANAGING WORK

RESOURCES

MARKETS

INDEX

FROM THE EDITOR

Many have called this past year the "Year of the e-Book." For the first time in history, many e-books are beginning to outsell printed books. This is especially true for fiction. E-books are now available in various formats for a selection of devices including the Kindle, the Nook, the iPad, and iPhones and iPods. More than ever, it is essential to learn how to market and position your novels or freelance work in a rapidly changing industry.

In the *2012 Novel & Short Story Writer's Market*, I tried to focus on building upon the fantastic articles included in the previous edition by continuing to emphasize the importance of developing your craft and technique: learning the skill of fine-tuning authentic dialogue, improving in your particular fiction genre, and learning how to move beyond creation into sharing your work (i.e. managing your writing career like a business).

In addition to the e-Book revolution that happened this year, many more authors are also considering the DIY route. The rise of self-publishers has widened the options for novelists. To learn the skills needed to get a start in this arena, check out the piece "Self-Publishing Strategies."

Per usual, this book is also packed with numberous markets and opportunities to get paid for your writing—whether you're on the hunt for an agent, book publishers, magazines, or contests.

Keep honing your craft, learning the business, and enjoying the journey!

Adria Haley
Managing Editor, Writer's Digest Market Books
http://www.writersmarket.com
adriahaley@fwmedia.com

Follow me on Twitter @adria_haley (http://twitter.com/adria_haley)

PHOTO: Brooke Morgan Photography

HOW TO USE *NSSWM*

To make the most of *Novel & Short Story Writer's Market*, you need to know how to use it. And with more than five hundred pages of fiction publishing markets and resources, a writer could easily get lost amid the information. This quick-start guide will help you wind your way through the pages of *Novel & Short Story Writer's Market*, as well as the fiction publishing process, and emerge with your dream accomplished—to see your work in print.

1. READ, READ, READ. Read numerous magazines, fiction collections and novels to determine if your fiction compares favorably with work currently being published. If your fiction is at least the same caliber as what you're reading, then move on to step two. If not, postpone submitting your work and spend your time polishing your fiction. Writing and reading the work of others are the best ways to improve craft.

For help with craft and critique of your work: You'll find advice and inspiration from best-selling authors and top fiction editors in the articles found in the first few sections of this book (**Finding Work**, **Craft & Technique**, **Fiction Genres**, and **Managing Work**). You'll find contest listings in the **Contests & Awards** section and even more listings to help you locate various events where you can hone your craft in the **Conferences & Workshops** section.

2. ANALYZE YOUR FICTION. Determine the type of fiction you write to best target markets most suitable for your work. Do you write literary, genre, mainstream or one of many other categories of fiction? For definitions and explanations of genres and subgenres, check out the **Glossary** and the **Genre Glossary** in the **Resources** section of the book. There are magazines and presses seeking specialized work in each of these areas as well as numerous others.

For editors and publishers with specialized interests, see the **Category Index** in the back of the book.

3. LEARN ABOUT THE MARKET. Read *Writer's Digest* magazine (F+W Media, Inc.); *Publishers Weekly*, the trade magazine of the publishing industry; and *Independent Publisher*, which contains information about small- to medium-sized independent presses. And don't forget the Internet. The number of sites for writers seems to grow daily, and among them you'll find www.writersmarket.com and www.writersdigest.com.

4. FIND MARKETS FOR YOUR WORK. There is a variety of ways to locate markets for fiction. The periodical section in bookstores and libraries is a great place to discover new journals and magazines that might be open to your type of short stories. Read writing-related magazines and newsletters for information about new markets and publications seeking fiction submissions. Also, frequently browse bookstore shelves to see what novels and short story collections are being published and by whom. Check acknowledgment pages for names of editors and agents, too. Online journals often have links to the websites of other journals that may publish fiction. And last but certainly not least, read the listings found here in *Novel & Short Story Writer's Market*.

Also, don't forget to utilize the various category **Indexes** at the back of this book to help you target the market for your fiction.

5. SEND FOR GUIDELINES. In the listings in this book, we try to include as much submission information as we can get from editors and publishers. Over the course of the year, however, editors' expectations and needs may change. Therefore, it is best to request submission guidelines by sending a self-addressed stamped envelope (SASE). You can also check each magazine's and press's website—which usually contains a page with guideline information. And for an even more comprehensive and continually updated online markets list, you can obtain a subscription to www.writersmarket.com.

6. BEGIN YOUR PUBLISHING EFFORTS WITH JOURNALS AND CONTESTS OPEN TO BEGINNERS. If this is your first attempt at publishing your work, your best bet is to begin with local publications or those you know are open to beginning writers. Then, after you have built a publication history, you can try the more prestigious and nationally distributed magazines. For markets most open to beginners, look for the ○ symbol preceding listing titles. Also, look for the ◐ symbol that identifies markets open to exceptional work from beginners as well as work from experienced, previously published writers.

7. SUBMIT YOUR FICTION IN A PROFESSIONAL MANNER. Take the time to show editors that you care about your work and are serious about publishing. By following a publication's or book publisher's submission guidelines and practicing standard submission etiquette, you can increase your chances that an editor will want to take the time to read your work and consider

- ⊕ market new to this edition
- Ⓐ market accepts agented submissions only
- ⊘ market does not accept unsolicited submissions
- award-winning market
- Canadian market
- market located outside of the U.S. and Canada
- $ market pays (in magazine sections)
- comment from the editor of *Novel & Short Story Writer's Market*
- ○ actively seeking new writers
- ◐ seeks both new and established writers
- ● prefers working with established writers, mostly referrals
- ◎ market has a specialized focus
- imprint, subsidiary or division of larger book publishing house (in book publishers section)
- publisher of graphic novels or comics

it for publication. Remember, first impressions last; a carelessly assembled submission packet can jeopardize your chances before your story or novel manuscript has had a chance to speak for itself.

8. KEEP TRACK OF YOUR SUBMISSIONS. Know when and where you have sent fiction and how long you need to wait before expecting a reply. If an editor does not respond by the time indicated in his or her market listing or guidelines, wait a few more months and then follow up with a letter (and SASE) asking when the editor anticipates making a decision. If you still do not receive a reply from the editor within a month or two, send a letter withdrawing your work from consideration and move on to the next market on your list.

9. LEARN FROM REJECTION. Rejection is the hardest part of the publication process. Unfortunately, rejection happens to every writer, and every writer needs to learn to deal with the negativity involved. On the other hand, rejection can be valuable when used as a teaching tool rather than a reason to doubt yourself and your work. If an editor offers suggestions with his or her rejection slip, take those comments into consideration. You don't have to automatically agree with an editor's opinion of your work. It may be that the editor has a different perspective on the piece than you do. Or, you may find that the editor's suggestions give you new insight into your work and help you improve your craft.

10. DON'T GIVE UP. The best advice for you as you try to get published is be persistent, and always believe in yourself and your work. By continually reading other writers' work, constantly working on the craft of fiction writing, and relentlessly submitting your work, you will eventually find that magazine or book publisher that's the perfect match for your fiction. *Novel & Short Story Writer's Market* will be here to help you every step of the way.

GUIDE TO LISTING FEATURES

Below is an example of the market listings contained in *Novel & Short Story Writer's Market* with callouts identifying the various format features of the listings. (For an explanation of the icons used, see the sidebar on the opposite page).

THE SOUTHERN REVIEW

Old President's House, Louisiana State University, Baton Rouge, LA 70803-5001. (225)578-5108. Fax: (225)578-5098. E-mail: southernreview@lsu.edu (**Website:** www.lsu.edu/thesouthernreview/.

Contact Jeanne Leiby, editor. Magazine: 6 ¼ × 10; 240 pages; 50 lb. Glatfelter paper; 65 lb. #1 grade cover stock. Quarterly. Circ. 3,000.

- Several stories published in The Southern Review were Pushcart Prize selections.

NEEDS Literary. "We select fiction that conveys a unique and compelling voice and vision." Receives approximately 300 unsolicited mss/month. Accepts 4-6 mss/issue. Reading period: September-June. Publishes ms 6 months after acceptance. Agented fiction 1%. Publishes 10-12 new writers/year. Recently published work by Jack Driscoll, Don Lee, Peter Levine, and Debbie Urbanski. Also publishes literary essays, literary criticism, poetry and book reviews.

HOW TO CONTACT Mail hard copy of ms with cover letter and SASE. No queries. ("Prefer brief letters giving author's professional information, including recent or notable publications. Biographical info not necessary." Responds within 10 weeks to mss. Sample copy for $8. Writer's guidelines online. Reviews fiction, poetry.

PAYMENT/TERMS Pays $30/page. Pays on publication for first North American serial rights. Sends page proof to author via e-mail. Sponsors awards/contests.

TIPS "Careful attention to craftsmanship and technique combined with a developed sense of the creation of story will always make us pay attention."

EASY-TO-USE REFERENCE ICONS

E-MAIL AND WEBSITE INFORMATION

SPECIFIC CONTACT NAMES

DETAILED SUBMISSION GUIDELINES

EDITOR'S COMMENTS

Don't forget your webinar!

To access the webinar that is included with your book, go to writersmarket.com/2012nsswm and learn how to write query letters that get results.

DON'T TAKE NO FOR AN ANSWER

Dealing with Rejection

by Tania Casselle

If you're reading this book, you are no doubt all fired up to submit your fiction to the many great literary journals featured here, or to hit 'send' on queries for your novel. May the writing gods smile on you to receive an acceptance first time out, but if you're in the writing game for any amount of time, sooner or later you'll receive a heart-sinking "Sorry, this isn't for us." As you rip up the letter and kick the nearest object that won't kick back, THIS is the time to remember the real secret to publishing success: Only one thing differentiates between decent writers who are published, and decent writers who are not published, and that is perseverance. You can't send one story to one journal and, if it's rejected, throw your hands in the air and stop submitting. Well, you can of course, but then you'll join the long line of other decent but unpublished writers who did the same thing. And to persevere on the writer's path, you need to be able to handle rejection.

"That's no secret," you say, citing examples of best-selling writers now hallowed in the literary canon who were rejected umpteen times before some blessed editor or agent saw their potential. And you're right; everyone talks about rejection as part of the publishing biz. (Just hang out with authors at the bar, and the conversation soon turns to this sorry subject.)

But being told rejection is a normal part of the process, and dealing with it when it happens to you are two different things. Rejection stings if you have a thin skin, and the discouragement (or even the fear of rejection in advance) has stopped many a talented writer in their tracks. They give up far too soon and remain unpublished. You don't plan to be one of those writers, do you? Good. So let's put the realities of rejection into perspective. (While we mainly refer here to short story submissions for simplicity, the same applies to queries to agents or publishing houses.)

DON'T TAKE IT PERSONALLY

Please don't take rejection personally—it's not about YOU. If your story is refused, there may be a hundred explanations. Perhaps this editor just accepted a story with a similar theme; maybe she needs a very short work to complete the next issue so she can't take your 8,000-word piece; or perhaps she has a phobia about cats and your story is jam-packed with cats. You could drive yourself crazy trying to figure it out. Editors reject a lot of perfectly good stories. They might know your story is well crafted, but it's simply not to their taste. Or they like it a lot, but they have to cull submissions to a small proportion to publish, so somebody has to get a rejection. It's all part and parcel of the creative life, and any writer submitting work for publication can wear his or her letters of rejection like badges of honor. So pat yourself on the back for every rejection. It means you put your work out there; you are living a writer's life. Then eat ice cream. Then send to the next place on your list.

IT'S A NUMBERS GAME

It's important to know that success in publishing is a numbers game. Publishers receive far more submissions than they can publish, and it's normal for the majority to be rejected, including work from stunningly accomplished writers. So you're in good company. However, to maximize your chances, you must keep a steady flow of work in the mail. This doesn't mean flooding every editor in this book. Of course you'll research suitable markets and ensure your manuscript or query is polished to its shiny best before letting it fly. But there are many publishers to submit to, and while one editor says no, another editor out there may love your work. Your job is to find that editor.

If you've ever participated in a writing workshop, you've seen the bafflingly diverse responses given to the same story, right? Some reviewers want a different ending to a story that another reviewer gets all lit up and glowy about. Editors are only human, too (that's their excuse, anyway), so you need to find the lit-up and glowy ones. That's where market research comes in, plus perseverance, and a sprinkling of luck . . . remembering that every rejection brings you one step closer to the person who'll really "get" your work. I can guarantee one thing: If it's not on an editor's desk, it doesn't stand a chance. They aren't going to come knocking at your door asking if you have a masterpiece hidden away somewhere.

95 TIMES LUCKY

Clifford Garstang, author of the linked story collection *In an Uncharted Country* (Press 53, 2009) and editor of *Prime Number* magazine, with fiction credits including *Baltimore Review, Tampa Review,* and *Los Angeles Review,* collected ninety-five rejections on one story before finding a good home. *"Savage Source"* was one of his first stories, and in 2003 he submitted it to thirty publications. "I did not do a very good job of researching markets, so the reason I collected so many rejections is that I wasn't sending it to the right places," says Garstang. He kept workshopping the piece, and the version finally accepted was his sixth or seventh rewrite. "Originally the story was told from two points of view, in some cases covering the same ground. I was convinced by a very famous workshop teacher to choose between the two. It bothered me at first but I eventually decided he was right." "*Savage Source*" was accepted by *Ashé Journal* in November 2008 ("It's one that I should have thought of earlier"), and a version is also in his book.

"I don't believe in giving up," says Garstang. "I think that stories are either good and haven't found the right place yet, or I can make them better. So much of the editorial process of magazines is subjective, and eventually there's an editor who's going to like it. Rejection is a good thing in the sense that it is evidence that you are a real writer. It means that you're participating in the process."

EDITORS ARE NOT THE ENEMY

Editors don't enjoy sending rejections. They are in the job because they love fiction and are eager to find work they're excited to publish. And it's in your own interest to work with editors who are enthusiastic to work with you too. Note that I said work WITH you. If you experience the submissions process as a collaborative effort for mutual benefit rather than feeling further down the food chain than the folk on the other side of the transom, you'll feel much more empowered and it'll be easier to receive a rejection. And if you think editors can't possibly understand a writer's angst, it's worth noting that many editors are writers too.

THE EDITOR'S TALE

It took Joseph Levens, editor of *the **Summerset Review***, six years and fifty submissions to place his story "*Back to Rosemary Farm.*" Levens (a Bakeless Prize finalist, whose fiction has appeared in *Florida Review, AGNI, Swink, Other Voices)* started submitting the story in 2003, mostly to high-end literary publications. Although rejection notes were garnished with nice comments, nobody bit. On the fiftieth submission, it was accepted by *Cream City Review* for the fall 2010 issue. He'd revised the story during those years, including changing the ending. "I'm a tweaker," says Levens. "I can't leave a story that's not been published alone." Why did he persevere? "I believed in the story. I read a lot of literary magazines, and I felt it was of the same caliber as the stories I'm reading. I think you just have to do the math. There are so many submissions to the higher-end literary magazines . . . it's a needle in a haystack."

He knows this well from the editor's side of the desk at *the Summerset Review.* "We get five prose submissions a day and only accept five in a quarter. You've got about 1 percent chance of being published. It's easier to stomach rejection when you know the odds."

Levens advises writers to read one or more issues of any target market. While *the Summerset Review* rarely publishes fiction that is violent, graphic, or about death or serious illness, "we still get many submissions that heavily carry one or more of those themes. Those stories, we never finish reading. It's our own particular taste. There are many other topics and themes to be explored and those are the ones we're looking for."

THE WORST THEY CAN SAY

Some writers are intimidated from submitting for fear of a hurtful rejection. But even if an editor hates your story, so what? The rejection slip will say something like: *"Thank you for your submission; it's not a good fit for us at this time"* and that's as bad as it gets. (Usually! On a rare occasion an editor might be acerbic, so if you chance on one of those and there's nothing useful in his or her comments, just thank your lucky stars that you're not married to that editor, ball up the rejection slip, and give it to the dog to chew.)

FEEDBACK . . . OR SILENCE

A personalized response, rather than a standard rejection, should be seen as encouraging. Busy editors and agents usually only send a personal note if they see promise in the work. If they kindly take time to provide feedback, listen and learn. You don't have to follow slavishly, but these professionals see tons of the best and worst writing and have a good sense of what works. If several say the same thing, really take note! If you don't hear back in the time frame indicated by the guidelines—follow up! A polite query on whether a manuscript is still under consideration is quite acceptable. Don't assume it's rejected; it could just have gone astray.

COMFORT IN COMMUNITY

Connect with other fiction writers in local or online groups. Writing is inherently an isolated pursuit, and it makes a big difference to compare notes with others who are also marketing their work—for moral support, tips, and a reality check to prove that you are not personally being singled out for rejections.

IT'S IN THE JOB DESCRIPTION

Take heart from knowing that even well-published writers are not immune to rejection—they, too, are vulnerable to feelings of inadequacy or frustration. Their first book is published; can they write a second one? They received terrific reviews, but they didn't win the

Pulitzer. Or an Amazon customer left a disparaging remark. There's always another ego hurdle to overcome as you climb the publishing ladder, and you can't please all the people all of the time. Growing a thicker skin now stands you in good stead for the long haul.

SETTING YOUR SIGHTS

Aim high, but balance that with realistic expectations, especially on your first time out. I've read stories I'm confident could be published in nice mid-level journals, but the writer only sends them to star publications like the *New Yorker*, or leading literary journals, which might receive 40,000 submissions a year. Yes, you could be pulled from the slush pile, but odds are long. If these are the only places you submit to, it's especially important not to be discouraged. Try aiming at a broader range of mid-level publications, as an acceptance will boost your morale and start building your writer's bio.

DON'T REJECT YOURSELF

Consider revising the piece after a while if you haven't had any positive feedback. We're always growing as writers, and we can always finesse our work. So if something isn't hitting, take another look at it, solicit critiques from writing peers and mentors, keep reading, and check out your target publishers again to ensure your submissions are in the vein of the work they feature—in writing standard, subject matter, and style. (A "no" is guaranteed if you send a realistic story to a venue that only publishes surrealism.) You are effectively rejecting yourself if you don't keep expanding your skills, or keep current on market requirements. You're also rejecting yourself if you don't send out at all.

THE GOOD NEWS

Although discussing rejection might seem depressing in our "can do" culture, it's actually liberating once you realize it's par for the course. This is both bad news (rejection is inevitable) and good news (rejection is inevitable, so why take it personally?). Forewarned is forearmed, and ensures that you don't crumple in the face of your first rejection.

In other words: You have more control about your writing fate than you think, if you keep honing your craft, submitting steadily, and don't get fazed by rejection slips. Have faith, and remember: you just need to find the right editor at the right time. That could be the first editor, the fifteenth, or the fiftieth.

The only reason we can tell inspiring anecdotes today about writers who were repeatedly rejected before an editor saw the light is because those writers didn't give up. If they'd taken rebuffs personally, if they'd stormed off in a huff feeling misunderstood, or hidden their manuscript in a shoebox under the bed, we would never have heard of them. So when you receive rejection slips (as you surely will, as many good writers always have), don't stop. There's no failure in rejection; the only loss is in giving up on a short story or novel that is worth trying at another twenty places, until it finds its home. At the very least you'll know you did your best and have no regrets on this one (and you'll have learned something to take forward into your next round of submissions). And at the highest end of the rainbow, maybe you'll become one of the authors quoted anecdotally by a future generation of writers.

SPECULATE TO ACCUMULATE

Laura DiSilverio retired from the Air Force in 2004 to write mystery novels. "In my hubris and ignorance, I figured I'd have a book on the shelves within a couple of years." She finished a manuscript, researched agents, and began querying. "Eighty some-odd rejections later, I had worked my way up from 'Dear Author' responses on slips of paper to agents who used my name on the rejection letter. Then I started getting actual feedback." She kept revising, and working on other novels, and after another twenty-four rejections secured an agent. Still, it took over 20 more rejections from publishers before DiSilverio's first book sold, and then she had seven novels under contract by the end of the year. Her latest is the PI novel *Swift Edge* (St. Martin's Minotaur, 2011). "Obviously, I think perseverance and a 'never quit' attitude was key to my eventual sales, but the critical thing was that I became a better observer and writer," says DiSilverio. "Just sending out the same query and manuscript 190 times and not changing anything falls more into the definition of insanity: doing the same thing over and over again and expecting a different result." Finally—just keep writing. "It's very helpful to me to have several projects going, so if something comes back with a rejection, it's not your only iron in the fire; your whole professional identity is not tied up in one project."

TANIA CASSELLE's fiction has appeared in *New York Stories, the Saint Ann's Review, South Dakota Review, the Bitter Oleander, Carve Magazine*, etc., and she's contributed to the anthologies *Harlot Red* (Serpent's Tail Press), *Online Writing: The Best of the First Ten Years* (Snowvigate Press), and *Now Write! Fiction Writing Exercises from Today's Best Writers and Teachers* (Tarcher). Tania is a freelance writer for consumer and business publications, author of *Insiders' Guide to Albuquerque* (Globe Pequot, 2010), and the award-winning host of the SOMOS *Writers on Radio* show broadcast on stations in New Mexico and Colorado. She leads writing workshops online and for arts organizations. Visit www.WriteOnDeadline.com.

THE EDITOR RELATIONSHIP

by Leigh Hamrick

Creating a relationship with an editor begins long before you submit your first query letter or manuscript to him, before she reads your name printed on your cover letter, typed in the address line of an e-mail or scribbled on the outside of an envelope, and certainly way before he or she reads your submission and makes a decision on it.

The roots of that relationship are put down the moment you bend intently over this book and begin researching the publication and the editor you want to send your work to.

BUT I JUST WANT TO HIT SEND!

All writers suffer from "hurry up and query" syndrome. We spend so much precious time crafting our work—choosing each word with loving care, agonizing over plot complications, pulling out our hair over whether or not our heroine should be named Melanie or Melissa—and yet the moment we've put the final touch on it, we instantly fling it out to every "To Whom it May Concern" we can get an e-mail address for. Editors of fantasy magazines are getting our light romance. Editors of nonfiction magazines are getting our Star Wars epic. Editors of children's magazines are getting our blood-drenched horror.

It's difficult enough to get published. Mindlessly sending out query letters without thoroughly scoping both the publication and a specific editor first makes your work falling into the right hands as likely as tossing it out the window and hoping for the same results.

Many of us feel that we aren't doing a day's work if we aren't sending out ten queries before five o'clock, myself included. However, getting an editor in your crosshairs is a far better and more efficient way of spending your time. Instead of making it your goal to get your story on the desks of ten faceless editors before dinner, limit yourself to one query a

TURN PREVIOUS PUBLISHERS INTO FANS

For an editor to accept and publish your work means he or she liked it. When you're published again by another editor, why not use this unique opportunity to create a new fan: your previous editor?

Use these simple steps to make a regular reader out of your previous editor, but remember never to be heavy-handed and always send editors something within the same lines as your previous submission to them. For example, don't send your new story on dysfunctional families to a magazine that published your science fiction comedy.

- Stay in touch with a brief e-mail offering your previous editor a chance to read your new work.
- Make use of social networking by sending your previous editor a link to your Facebook or Twitter account that is literary minded. He or she probably doesn't want to know who you're dating at the moment so make sure it's as devoid of personal matters as possible.
- Offer your new book or story for review. Editors who enjoy your writing will take an interest in incorporating their thoughts on your work into the review section of their magazine or newsletter.
- Send a signed copy of your new book to them.
- If you get a good response, offer (tactfully) to sit for an interview on your new work for their publication. Don't be pushy; however, this is a great opportunity for both the editor and yourself. The editor gets a great article for free, and you get good publicity.
- Err on the side of brevity. A bad impression is much more difficult to alter than a good one. Keep it brief, keep it tasteful, and keep it professional.

day, or even every other day, and spend that time putting a face, a name, a personality and a publishing preference to your target editor.

WHAT'S IN A NAME?

"Everyone loves being addressed by name," points out Colin Meldrum, editor of the literary magazine *A cappella Zoo*. "We're tuned to perk up at the sight or sound of our names."

This seemingly obvious notion, this basis for human interaction, is very often overlooked during the submission process. Whether it's by not addressing an editor by name or by not addressing the right editor, this omission not only causes us to see "editor" rather than person, it causes an editor to see "just another query" instead of a writer who stands out.

This is especially true if the editor's name isn't readily available online. "Since my name isn't included with our submission guidelines," continues Meldrum, "addressing me by name suggests that a writer has explored our website beyond looking up our address."

If you've ever received a standard rejection letter, you know what a sting that carries. You're offended and disappointed by the obvious lack of personal attention; you toss it away with a snort and wonder privately if they even took the time to read your query thoroughly.

The same feelings apply to the person on the other side of the desk. An editor sees your query—either minus his/her name, directed to the wrong person, or with his/her name misspelled—and even though he or she is hoping to find an original writer with an original idea, an editor can't help but feel annoyed that you didn't even take the five minutes needed to find out who your letter was going to. The impression you're making just went down a notch.

Another tip? Don't guess at a gender. Ever. I've had an editor mistake my own name for a masculine one—an editor with the *Washington Post*, no less—and my opinion of him quickly nosedived. It didn't matter that he was with one of the most distinguished newspapers in the country or that his salary surely tripled mine. It's instinctual; we can't help it. So do your homework and find out which Terrys and Shanes wear skirts and which ones don't and avoid that quick frown altogether.

KNOW THE PUBLICATION

"What makes a writer stand out to me is if it's clear she has done the research to target her article to my publication," states Kristen Page-Kirby, editor of *Chesapeake Family Magazine*. "Saying things like 'I notice you like to cover local travel, so that's why I thought this article would be a good fit' or 'with this issue big in your area', with an issue that is, in fact, newsworthy, makes me feel like the writer has done at least some research."

Meldrum agrees. "Any detail that shows that we are a unique publication to the writer helps that writer stand out as unique to us. Referring to past works we've published, our aesthetic, a review or mentioning why we in particular might consider publishing a specific submission all opens doors for human-to-human connection. This immediately puts a submitter above the masses."

As writers, we read advice like this constantly, and yet every newspaper and magazine editor, every book publisher, and every literary agent I've spoken to has told me that the majority of queries are sent to the rejection pile for one thing: clear misdirection.

Being serious about writing, being passionate about the craft itself and tenaciously determined to be successful, means being responsible for taking a step that is often neatly sidestepped simply because of the time it takes. It isn't enough to look up a magazine or publisher in this book. Keep going. Visit the magazine's website and take some time getting a feel for its atmosphere.

Don't stop there. Make a drive to your local bookstore or library and pick up a copy of the magazine. Buy yourself a cup of coffee and read the magazine from cover to cover. Isolate which section could be a proper fit for your own work and then look up the editor of that particular section. Once you've got the name of an editor who publishes writing similar to your own, narrow your beam on that person. Look him or her up on the internet. Find his or her personal website, if that editor has one, or search for articles the individual has written, seminars he or she has participated in, classes he or she may have given.

When you do sit down to the business of creating the query letter, you'll not only have the face and personality of the person you're writing to in mind, but you'll also know what he or she has already published. This familiarity will bring noticeable focus to your letter and will catch the attention of an editor. Instead of being one of the "masses," as Colin Meldrum said, your correspondence will stand out for the fact that it wasn't written to "an editor"—it was written to that person. For someone who may be receiving hundreds of submissions a month, this means a great deal.

REJECTION DOESN'T NEED TO BE THE END

What do you do if your work is ultimately rejected? "A writer who responds after getting a rejection stands out on his or her own. So often I say no and people disappear," Kristen Page-Kirby comments. "I still want to work with talented, driven people even if the first pitch didn't work out."

Don't let everything you did to create a relationship with this editor vanish simply because you didn't get published right away. If his or her magazine and criteria still suit the work you do, don't drop the ball at this key point.

What's nice about putting so much effort into crafting a personalized query letter is that if you do get rejected, you're less likely to receive a standard, cookie-cutter "no," in which case you'll be able to identify why your work didn't make the grade. Was it something technical like word count or timing? Could your grammar have stood some brushing up? Was the story itself not to the editor's taste? Isolate the reason and, while continuing to submit your work to other editors, write a reply to your rejection.

Keep records, be dilligent, know what you've sent to that editor, and track his or her answers. Your next submission needs to be aimed closer to the bull's-eye.

Something as simple as "Thank you for responding so quickly" or "I appreciate the comments you made and I'll take them into consideration" followed by a line stating your earnest interest in continuing to submit to the magazine are all that are needed to create another personal touch and enhance a relationship that has made it beyond the usual anonymity. The next time you submit, that editor will recognize your name and will be much more likely to open your letter or e-mail ahead of others.

Additionally, make sure that your next submission addresses the points that caused your last one to be rejected. Was your story too long? Send a more succinct one this time. Was your story too graphic? Next time send a more mellow one. Did you tell the story too exclusively from one point of view? Open the story up to several of your characters' viewpoints.

Being responsive is absolutely necessary—mandatory, even. "If a writer responds to a rejection with more ideas," Page-Kirby tells us, "great. It's even better if the response is tailored to the reason I gave for the rejection." Going to all of this trouble to set your sights specifically on an editor and then not following through is a complete waste of your time.

Keep records, be diligent, know what you've sent to that editor, and track his or her answers. Your next submission needs to be aimed closer to the bull's-eye. Doing so will begin an entirely new form of communication from your editor, one you've been holding your breath for: the acceptance letter.

DON'T QUERY STALK—THAT'S A NO-NO

Never lose sight of what you're doing. "I appreciate tenacity," adds Nancy Luse, editor for both the *Frederick News-Post* newspaper and *Elegant Living* magazine. "If one story proposal doesn't work, that's not to say another won't. But," she cautions, "don't overdo it."

Editors don't have a great deal of time on their hands. Even smaller magazines, such as *Button: New England's Tiniest Magazine of Poetry, Fiction, and Gracious Living*, get flooded with submissions. "We publish only once a year," states editor and founder Sally Cragin, "but around 400 submissions come in over the transom annually." That doesn't leave a lot of time for chitchat.

While it's important to cultivate a relationship with your editor, remember it's a professional relationship you're after. You aren't trying to become best friends or pen pals. An editor is going to appreciate a writer who has been thorough and dedicated to research; an editor is not going to appreciate being bombarded with e-mail after e-mail. "What about this idea? Well, what about this idea?" or "Hey, I liked your speech from the 2007 writer's convention; it reminded me of my cat, and let me tell you about her" types of correspondence are going to get you noticed, all right—enough to get your name flagged for the junk folder.

Colin Meldrum puts it perfectly: "The key is to stay relevant and professional. Keep conversation within the realm of the literary relationship." Page-Kirby is a little more blunt, but just as easy to understand. "It's important not to be annoying," she says. "If I seem disinterested in starting an e-mail conversation, it's probably because I am."

SOME RELATIONSHIPS JUST WEREN'T MEANT TO BE

It took me nearly a year of rejections, a year of frustration and angst, to start following these rules. Then I began to be pleasantly surprised: instead of standard "no thank you's" I began getting real correspondence. Editors began taking the time to make suggestions that would improve my chance of getting published. I'll never forget when I received three requests for my work in one day, followed by an offer mentioning pay that was far above anything I'd made to date. I sat at my desk and giggled through tears for all of thirty minutes. Luckily no one else was home or they would have thought I'd truly lost it.

However, I've also experienced "relationships" that had issues. I've received e-mails from a few editors that were full of enthusiasm and interest, even an offer of work, that ended in prolonged silence on their part and utter confusion on my part. A follow-up query would be eagerly responded to, but then silence would reign again for months. You can choose either to keep playing this odd game of ball or move on. I decided to move on. Just as with our personal relationships, some professional relationships simply aren't going to make it to the publication altar. Quietly pack your literary bags and move on.

DON'T FORGET TO SAY THANK YOU

I wouldn't recommend sending a teddy bear through the mail, but when a publisher or editor has seriously come through for you—dedicated themselves to honing your story until it was worth publishing or taken time to participate in an interview you've written—you need to show your appreciation. It could be a well-written letter of thanks or even a card. Keep it simple and keep it honest. By doing so you'll be putting the finishing touch on a relationship that can last your entire writing career.

LEIGH HAMRICK is a freelance writer in Maryland whose work has appeared in magazines such as *Sacramento Parent, Pregnancy & Newborn, Writers' Forum,* and more. When she isn't writing fantastic magazine articles, she locks herself in her study to furiously pound away at short stories and epic novels that have a tendency to get out of hand. She's a wife, a mother of two, and a servant to two luxuriously spoiled kitties, Triton and Hercules. If you'd like to get in touch with her, visit her website at www.leighhamrick.com.

DEVELOPING YOUR PROSE STYLE:

Form Following Function

by Jack Smith

HOW MUCH DETAIL?

Prose style. It's the language of the story, involving such varied elements as diction, tone, and rhythm. Style can be formal or informal. It can be edged with irony and sarcasm, or it can be straightforward and direct. It can be opaque or accessible. It can be lyrical or jarring.

But there's certainly another way to think of style, and that is the extent to which it is "dense" (without the pejorative connotations) or *spare* in terms of detail. *Dense* here meaning full-bodied, richly textured. *Spare* meaning lean, sometimes cut almost to the bone.

DENSE: James, Faulkner, Bellow.

SPARE: Hemingway and Carver. Cormac McCarthy's work can be provocatively spare.

Certainly prose style is often a writer's signature, yet beyond this, we do need to keep in mind that style, like any element of fiction, is not separable from the various other story elements. "The notion of appropriate prose," states Sven Birkerts, editor of *Agni*, "assumes that all elements are integral, organically interconnected." Robert Stewart, editor, *New Letters*, states the matter categorically: "A writer should put nothing into a story that does not have its own role in the overall impact." Every word, that is, and every device used in the creation of the story, must somehow contribute to the whole—and relate to each part. Style, says Grant Tracey, fiction editor, *North American Review*, "always relates to character. A lean prose can suggest inarticulateness, repression, hard-boiled sentiment. Violence hovers. A more heavily textured prose invites a closer proximity to the character and a sense of things being shared, confessed. I know that's simplifying things somewhat, but those are some possible moods created by these choices. Of course there are others too."

Or, in other words, regardless of the style, dense or spare, prose style is expressive of what's happening at all levels of the story. "Form must follow function," as Caitlin McGuire, managing editor, *Berkeley Fiction Review*, points out—which is another way of speaking of organic unity.

EDITORIAL PREFERENCE

As a writer, you probably have a preference when it comes to prose style—at least you lean more toward one style than another. Readers often have preferences. What about editors?

For some literary magazine editors, organic unity is all that's important. Each story dictates its own style. Brock Clarke, fiction editor, *Cincinnati Review*, emphasizes the different demands and needs of each story, pointing out that editors have "to recognize those needs and demands and adjust accordingly: some stories are surrealistic, some premise driven, some realistic, some intensely devoted to details of the natural world, etc. We love them all, as long as they're well done." And "well done" is judged by appropriateness to subject, character, etc.

> "Quality is all, and quality (aside from appropriate spelling, grammar, and word choice) is a result of the style supporting and crystalizing the content: characters, setting, action."
>
> —Francine Ringold, editor-in-chief, *Nimrod International Journal*

The same standard applies at Pocol Press. J. Thomas Hetrick, editor, states that his press accepts "both thoroughly descriptive authors such as Brian Ames (*As Many Hands as God*) and Thomas Sheehan (*From the Quickening*) and the sparser prose styles of Paul Perry (*Street People, Lost People*) and Robert Garner McBrearty (*Episode*). The commonality of each of these authors," says Hetrick, "is that every one of them are expert storytellers."

Nimrod International Journal has absolutely no preference at all, states Francine Ringold, editor-in-chief: "Through the 52 years of *Nimrod*'s history we have published stories and prose poems that demonstrate our openness to many different styles. We neither prefer a heavily textured style, nor a severely spare approach. Quality is all, and quality (aside from appropriate spelling, grammar, and word choice) is a result of the style supporting and crystallizing the content: characters, setting, action."

Grant Tracey, *NAR*, can also appreciate both prose styles. "I like lyrical prose full of poetry, and harder, crisp prose full of Anglo-Saxon words. I probably prefer the latter, but realize that is more of a 'scene-driven' Hemingway and Carver style. Lately, in my own work," says Tracey, "I've been interested in summary and voice and the art of telling. Lyricism and details of the heart (what a character thinks and feels) lends itself more to that voice. So I'm waffling here. I like both."

Some magazines are not as open; they do have distinct stylistic preferences. *Agni*, for instance, goes for a "rich, textured presentation." For Sven Birkerts, prose style "represents something of the complexity of the character's psyche/thought process, and while we respect and admire many writers who prefer a more pared-down Carveresque mode, we don't feature it as part of our 'vision.'" A magazine can do "only so much," says Birkerts, and thus "it must strive for a certain distinctiveness."

"There's a danger in being too lean, in losing readers by leaving out clarifying details, or losing the heart of the story by being too terse. There's no vivid world where every character speaks in one-line, three-word sentences."

New Letters, says Robert Stewart, doesn't generally publish minimal fiction, though he points out that all fiction today "in some way probably has been influenced by Hemingway." While the range of fiction published by *New Letters* is "unusually wide," including the traditional, the short-short, and "tightly satirical fiction," the prose style isn't likely to be the Carver type.

For some editors, like Fred Schepartz at *Mobius*, "less is more." He adds to this a concern about prose that gets too detailed, that becomes "overwrought, overdone, or just flat-out pretentious." Some writers tend to believe that the more detail, the better. Schepartz is concerned about where this thinking might lead: "I just want to stress that elegant, beautifully written prose need not be wordy."

Mary Wharff, fiction editor, *Coal City Review*, also prefers a spare style. She admits that this preference may be due to the fact that she herself writes "lean prose." That fact aside, Wharff does believe that "the right details can make a great bare-bones story much more satisfying for readers." Yet writers should be careful to leave some flesh on the bones, cautions Wharff: "There's a danger in being too lean, in losing readers by leaving out clarifying details, or losing the heart of the story by being too terse. There's no vivid world where every character speaks in one-line, three-word sentences." On the whole, what Wharff looks for are "stories that are sparely vivid, where details are few, but are so right-on that each one interests me."

The matter of preference could depend on the editor who considers the story—this is true at the *Bellevue Literary Review*. Three different editors, working in democratic fashion, make final choices. Danielle Ofri, editor-in-chief, tends to "favor narrative detail over minimalism," though she does "shy away from stories in which the author's hand (or author's thesaurus) is too heavily felt." Ronna Wineberg, senior fiction editor, is more open. For Wineberg, "it's a question of whether a story with a minimal style develops character sufficiently and also has narrative movement. This is my consideration for a denser style, too."

EDITORIAL CRITIQUING OF STYLE

It is highly unlikely that an editor will take a well-wrought Carveresque piece and try to turn it into a Faulknerian one—or vice versa. If the magazine or press tends not to take the lean, spare kind of writing, they will simply reject the work as "not right for us" because it doesn't fit with the taste or vision of the editors. Suggestions about style—about cutting, adding, or rethinking the language in some way—come either as a final condition for acceptance, or as final editing for an accepted piece. Prose style editing at this stage is one of chopping "excessiveness," on the one hand; or, on the other, adding necessary material to make the writing clear.

So what can you expect?

At *Agni*, says Sven Birkerts, any editorial changes on prose style are handled in a "a case by case process, and we do both, but always in close consultation with the author." Barbara Pezzopane, foreign editor, *Storie*, writes: "In terms of editing, we are more interested in the dramatic syntax than in doing a lot of scissors-work. Much more than each word the writer uses, we're concerned with the overall composition of the story."

Grant Tracey, *NAR*, states: "I rarely mess with a writer's prose. I think writing is sacred and I don't want to impose my will or aesthetic to a writer's craft. That being said, I will on occasion challenge writers to make language more striking when I feel they've resorted to clichés or stock expressions. And I have, now and then, suggested cutting a paragraph (usually at the end of the story) that I feel 'sells' too much."

Suggestions about style—about cutting, adding, or rethinking the language in some way—come either as a final condition for acceptance, or as final editing for an accepted piece.

The ending is also fair game for Brock Clarke, *Cincinnati Review*: "Writers, despite some evidence to the contrary, are like most other humans in that they tend to go on too long, and when this happens, I often suggest cutting the ending. And sometimes, although not as often, I suggest additions that might add what the excised material lacked."

At the *Bellevue Literary Review*, final editing is fairly routine. "Sometimes," says Ronna Wineberg, "we ask an author to condense parts of a story, take out paragraphs or words, to make the prose leaner. And sometimes we ask a writer to add more description, to anchor a story in time, or to work on the dialogue. This, of course, depends on what we believe a piece needs. So we may ask for cutting in one story and expanding in another story." An editor "works closely," says Wineberg, "with the author on revisions. If an author objects to some of the changes, we try to respect the author's wishes." But editing can also be a requirement for acceptance. "There are times we accept a piece with the understanding that certain revisions must be made before the story can be published."

At *Berkeley Fiction Review*, editing is mainly a matter of meeting a condition for acceptance: "Typically," says Caitlin McGuire, "the only stories that we have any follow-up correspondence on in the way of workshopping are the stories that get a divided vote from the staff. Sometimes, we accept the submission if one section is cut; other times, we need additions to the story to make it flow better."

Robert Stewart states the policy at *New Letters*: "I frequently suggest cutting words when working with prose writers, especially writing that I want to accept for publication. William Zinsser says that clutter is the disease of the American language; and even when an essay or story has good material, it often contains redundancy or other clutter. Most of the time, the cutting takes the form of individual words or short phrases that slow down the pace and bore the reader." As to making the writing more descriptive, that's an entirely different matter, says Stewart: "If I need to suggest that more descriptive writing would be helpful, the story or essay probably is not close to being accepted. Most of the work I would do as editor occurs with writing that is already mostly complete."

P.T. McNiff, editor-in-chief, *Southern California Review*, makes the same point about stories under consideration: "At our journal, we don't heavily edit the material before publishing it—if we feel that the story needs either paring down or beefing up, we end up passing. If that's the only hold-up, we include a note when we return the story encouraging the author to continue working on the piece."

PROSE STYLE THAT WORKS

As we've seen, some editors have their own stylistic preferences. Other editors do not—if the style performs its function, that's enough. But, as we've also seen, outside of this question of preference, prose style issues may come up for editors in the acceptance or final editing process. Editors may suggest cutting or adding. Whatever stylistic changes are made, the final governing principle for style is that which governs short story composition as a whole: the organic interrelationship between all elements of the story. Different stories make different demands.

Character is, of course, a key element.

Francine Ringold recalls two prize-winning stories published by *Nimrod* that were radically different in style. Ann Forer's "Adolescence," which won a Nimrod/Katherine Anne Porter prize, was one sentence only, "as breathless and complex as the speaker. Oh, of course, the reader (aloud or in the theatre of her mind) knew when to stop or pause just from the lilt of the language, but the overall effect was to wind the reader into the mind of the narrator." The second award-winning story, "Verge," by Laura Louis, consisted of "spare, short sentences, and words that you hit and drop." Style is closely related to character, says Ringold, as a Chinese mother "chopping, always chopping vegetables, fruit, meat" gives "abrupt commands to her daughter: do this, do that!"

The lesson here? Style must relate to character, as Grant Tracey has pointed out. Organically. Form following function.

DEVELOPING YOUR OWN STYLE

To develop your own style, read and study good fiction, both contemporary and classic. Study both styles closely: the richly textured, full-bodied style; and the lean, spare one. Which style works best for you? Be open to change as you develop your style over time. Be open to change with each story you write.

That is, for each story, be sure your style works at all levels as the language of character, place, action, mood, and idea. If you go for a richly textured style, is this right for the story you're now working on? Or is a leaner style better? And what about other stylistic features? Should the language be ironic or direct? Should it be somewhat elliptical, or should it be plainspoken, accessible? What about the rhythm or pacing? As you consider the specific elements of your story, you'll wonder about these stylistic features—and more. Working in this manner, with your vision of the story as an organic unit, you'll be well on your way to developing a strong prose style, regardless of the kind you choose.

JACK SMITH has published a dozen articles in *Novel & Short Story Writer's Market*. His novel *Hog to Hog* won the 2007 George Garrett Fiction Prize and was published by Texas Review Press in 2008. He has published stories in a number of literary magazines, including *Southern Review, North American Review, Texas Review, X-Connect, In Posse Review,* and *Night Train*. His reviews have appeared widely in such publications as *Ploughshares, Georgia Review, American Book Review, Prairie Schooner, Mid-American Review, Pleiades, the Missouri Review,* and *Environment* magazine. His coauthored nonfiction environmental book entitled *Killing Me Softly* was published by Monthly Review Press in 2002. Besides his writing, Smith coedits *the Green Hills Literary Lantern*, an online literary magazine published by Truman State University.

AVOIDING CLICHÉS

Recognizing Them & Getting Beyond Them

by Jack Smith

If there's one criticism most writers have received at one time or another in their writing careers, it's that their work is clichéd—in some way. It might be their story's premise, or it might be a character or two, even the protagonist. Whatever happens to be clichéd is old, well-tilled soil, the road we've been on before, old hat—all clichés to describe clichés. In a word, a cliché lacks freshness or originality, and even the word *novel* means new, different—not the same old thing we've seen and heard over and over. So of course if writers want their work appreciated, valued, and accepted for publication, they must find ways to avoid clichés of various kinds.

CLICHÉD PLOTS

Plot is an important fictional element and one that is subject to cliché. Certain topics garner a lot of attention at different times. They're in the news, so to speak. Cliff Garstang, author of the award-winning *In an Uncharted Country* and editor of *Prime Number* magazine, tries to stay away from some plots that turn on topics that are "just too familiar," and among these he lists "senile parents, cancer victims, cheating spouses, partner dying of AIDS." Even so, as he points out, these human ills and problems do certainly make up real life, so why should a writer "completely ignore them?" And in addition, "all of them are useful metaphors for other aspects of life." So if Garstang tends to avoid plots that turn on these overused topics, he does believe writers shouldn't utterly avoid them—yet to handle them well is clearly a challenge: "The trick, I think, is to layer stories effectively. Okay, so someone in your story has cancer. That can't be all that story is about, but perhaps the cancer is in the background and what's really happening is . . . something else."

Robert Garner McBrearty is a recipient of the Sherwood Anderson Foundation Fiction Award. McBrearty's solution to "predictable" plots, akin to Garstang's, is "to take the story elsewhere, not to deliver the expected trajectory or ending." This mustn't be done, though, at the expense of "internal consistency and authenticity." For McBrearty, surprise is the key element, but this comes with a caveat: "Merely being surprising for surprise's sake is almost its own cliché. The surprise has to be earned; it has to feel right."

Tikvah Feinstein, editor of *Taproot Literary Review*, has tired of coming across two predictable plots: the "long estranged and then reunited" one and the "I fell in love again plot, often after a long pulling apart and a sudden maturing." Feinstein explains her antipathy toward these two plotlines: "At *Taproot* we read a lot of stories with hospitals and nursing home settings where the 'end of life' drama is played out by a survivor who has lost a last chance to say something he/she should have said long before." This plot becomes too reductive, Feinstein suggests: "Writers should keep in mind that it's easy to fall into a let's-fix-it story line. But conflict in the reality of relationships, unpredictability and surprising resolution is the plot and story line we seek." Like Garstang, Feinstein doesn't rule out using such plots, but she does emphasize that they "are hard to write in an unpredictable style." The payoff is that when the writer freshens them up, "they can be fantastic."

> "Writers should keep in in mind that it's easy to fall into a let's-fix-it story line. But conflict in the reality of relationships, unpredictability and surprising resolution is the plot and story line we seek."
>
> —Tikvah Feinstein, editor, *Taproot Literary Review*

Ronna Wineberg is senior fiction editor of the *Bellevue Literary Review* and author of *Second Language*, a story collection that won the New Rivers Press Many Voices Project Literary Competition. Wineberg points out that "almost any situation can seem clichéd"—typically tied to the "great topics" that writers so often turn to: "love, sex, betrayal, cruelty, death—to name a few." To avoid clichéd treatment of these topics, what the writer must do, says Wineberg, is make the situation "unique and surprising, give the characters depth, create authentic individuals on the page."

CLICHÉD CHARACTERS

If it's difficult to avoid clichéd plots, it's also difficult to avoid clichéd characters—or one-dimensional stereotypes. "Sometimes one can play with stereotypes," says Garstang, "but it's a dangerous game." The dilemma the writer faces is this: "On the one hand, characters should be recognizable, but characters who are too familiar will fail to surprise."

As with clichéd plots, there is a list of overused character types editors reject and writers try to avoid. Lydia Dishman, editor, *Emrys Journal* says: "We've run the gamut including hooker with a heart of gold, abused wife, surly teenager, etc." Barrett Bowlin, editor, *Harpur Palate*, sees as especially risky those characters having "difficulties with disease (especially cancer); male characters as alcoholics, and female characters with eating and/or body-image disorders." These character types themselves are not deal breakers for publication, says Bowlin, but authors must find ways to "push past" such ready-made clichés. Some of Bowlin's favorite stories have, in fact, worked with these very character types. "I love stories about disease. I love characters who wrestle with alcoholism, eating disorders, and problems with self-image." Bowlin loves writers who "find a way to kill the cliché while simultaneously working within it." But how do you do this? Bowlin's answer: "I'd encourage authors to be extremely careful in areas in which they feel comfortable. If your writing feels safe, or if your plot or characters or settings or images feel reliable, get rid of them. The people who read your stories want you to surprise them."

Stated simply: with character, as with plot, if you settle for clichés, you won't surprise. And you must find ways to surprise your reader, or your work will fall flat. Overworked character types are off-putting if that's all you have, but writers who are somehow able to "push past" the cliché can delight readers with their insights and creativity.

But it's not just the overused character types that present traps. Gary Fincke, winner of the Flannery O'Connor Award for Short Fiction and author of many books of fiction, believes that avoiding the typical character clichés like the "drunk daddy" really isn't all that hard. What is hard, says Fincke, is "to avoid the clichés that form because they're so personally accessible from the writer's experience." Fincke has found ways to avoid these in his own work. "One of my revision steps is always to try to complicate characters and working to vary situations."

"I'd encourage authors to be extremely careful in areas in which they feel comfortable. If your writing feels safe, or if your plot or characters or settings or images feel reliable, get rid of them. The people who read your stories want you to surprise them."

—BARRETT BOWLIN, editor, *Harpur Palate*

Robert Garner McBrearty can speak to the problem of avoiding clichés related to what's "personally accessible"—in his case, it's the university scene. "Maybe because I teach, I have to think about avoiding clichés about teachers and academia"— which means the potential for both a clichéd plot and clichéd characters. A typically comic writer, McBrearty states: "One always wants to do a certain 'take' on academia, to reduce it to an absurdity. Because much of it really is absurd, one is in the precarious position of trying to depict the very real absurdity of academia while simultaneously trying to avoid reducing it to a cliché about academia." Clichéd treatment equals one-dimensional characters—characters that seem cartoonish, not fully alive or real. To deal with this problem, McBrearty struggles "to get inside the character, to sense the character almost like a living human being." Don't "impose characterizations," McBrearty cautions: "I will now create a hard-boiled detective who has a kind spot for dogs and orphans." This strategy of working from the outside, of artificially rigging things, won't work to create multidimensional, real-to-life characters, asserts McBrearty. Instead, you need to reach down to a "much more subliminal level."

"If you cannot imagine yourself and your character sharing similar types of concerns with love and family, personal and occupational goals, fears and secrets, your story has probably not yet found its footing."

—BARRY KITTERMAN, author

Linda B. Swanson-Davies, co-editor of *Glimmer Train*, is also troubled by one-dimensional characters. She states: "I suppose, because we publish literary fiction, we are most aware of character-related clichés. We see stories with pimply runaways, used-car salesmen, diner waitresses with Southern drawls, and people described only by nationality, as though those descriptions are all we need to understand who the labeled person is." She doesn't believe writers deliberately set out to "diminish their characters in this way"—such stereotypes result instead from a lack of knowing "anything of consequence about them." And this kind of knowing does take time. Swanson-Davies suggests this litmus test for clichéd characters: "To help figure out if your character is a cliché, imagine that someone you personally know and care about actually matches the description of your character. If you cannot imagine yourself and your character sharing similar types of concerns with love and family, personal and occupational goals, fears and secrets, your story has probably not yet found its footing."

Not knowing characters well enough to avoid clichés may stem from a lack of direct personal experience, believes Barry Kitterman, author of two story collections. "Sometimes, the problem arises from our only knowing a subject through stories we've read, movies we watched, or worst of all, television. So we can't easily rise above cliché." Kitterman's solution is to choose protagonists who are closer to us in terms of their basic background and knowledge so that we are able to write about them with authority and believability.

OTHER CLICHÉS

Clichéd language is, of course, a big offender. In fact, clichéd phrases are often one of the first things writers are cautioned about, and many writers work on clichéd words and phrases even if they never get beyond clichéd plots and characters. Even so, clichéd language does persist, as Michael G. Czyzniejewski, author of *Elephants in Our Bedroom*, and editor at *Mid-American Review*, can tell you, and clichéd language absolutely kills a story's chance for publication at MAR. Writers better shun "dead as a doornail" and "green with envy," says Czyzniejewski, but, in more general terms, they need to watch out for "any set of words commonly found together." Put another way, writers need to be careful about depending on "commonspeak." Czyzniejewski attributes this dependence on predictable phrasing partly to laziness, but partly also to not knowing that clichés make for bad writing—that good writing has to be "original, not to mention musical, persuasive, and full of life."

> "If . . . I sense the author has a limited worldview or a limited inner integrity I find myself rejecting his or her work in its entirety as a cliché."
>
> —Karl Harshbarger

"Shock openers," "blatant cleverness," and "open endings" are three story features that Barrett Bowlin, at *Harpur Palate*, says are currently on the rise in the submissions he receives—and rapidly becoming stock clichés. He attributes this to the workshopping of stories, which, on the whole, does produce better submissions but paradoxically carries with it certain problems. "What I mean by this is the act of being clever for cleverness's sake in the story, or the author feeling the need to start off with an attempt at being shocking (so as to catch the attention of the editor) and then failing to earn the value of that shock factor for the remainder of the story, and so on." Clearly, the lesson here is not to depend on special effects and arty devices but instead on solid, well-developed plots and genuine characters.

RETHINKING THE CLICHÉ

There's still another way of thinking about clichés—not, in this case, as a specific story weakness or problem as we've seen so far. To Karl Harshbarger, whose many stories have appeared in high-profile literary magazines, including the *Atlantic Monthly*, it's the clichés that go to the core of the story's very premise that are the most off-putting. When Harshbarger begins to read a story or novel, he says, "I sense (or at least believe I sense) whether this author has a legitimate world view, or, perhaps I should say, an inner integrity, which can teach me something about this universe I live in. When I find this quality I will accept whatever particular approach the writer decides to use: flowery language, simple language; bizarre characters, run-of-the-mill characters; wild, improbable plots, old, exhausted plots, and so forth. If, on the other hand, I sense the author has a limited worldview or a limited inner integrity I find myself rejecting his or her work in its entirety as a cliché."

> "I tried to give the character very particular voices, dimension and their own struggles, so the frailty of the mother wouldn't overwhelm the story."
>
> —Ronna Wineberg, author of *Second Language*

Harshbarger's concern is not, then, with clichéd plots, clichéd characters, clichéd language, or any other story element that might be clichéd. His concern goes to the heart of the matter, to the story's fundamental ideas or themes—and whether this work can "teach" him something about this universe he lives in. Harshbarger's view here is akin to a poet-priest kind of view of literature versus a more aesthetic one. This may not be a viewpoint that has a lot of currency today, but it is certainly something to reflect on if one considers how it's the basic conception of the story that is the wheelhouse that governs the whole. If Harshbarger finds the story's core itself stale, he doesn't care how good the execution is. Technical performance plays a supporting role, at best, in Harshbarger's concept of a story or novel's primary function. While one may reject his belief that if a story or novel doesn't enlighten us somehow, it's clichéd, it does seem reasonable to consider to what end the criteria Harshbarger mentions, if met, might have possible payoffs for a story or novel's success with readers, agents, and publishers.

HOVERING ON THE BRINK . . . YET AVOIDING THE CLICHÉ

As we've noted, fiction can hover on the brink of plot and character clichés, and yet still avoid them. This takes a skillful maneuver or two, a new emphasis, a re-shifting of the story's focus from a hackneyed plot or character to new, fresh ground. Seasoned writers report battle successes on various cliché fronts.

The Dying Mother

Ronna Wineberg's story "Second Language," the title story of her prize-winning collection, deals with a woman and her dying mother. The problem Wineberg faced was how to keep this topic from being utterly predictable. A writer friend gave her some helpful advice: "You have to make this different from all the other stories that people write about dying parents." As she revised, she "decided the daughter would be married, have an affair, and think about this while she was visiting her mother in the hospital." She also found other ways—namely, humor—to shift the attention away from the obsession with dying. She made the hospital experience absurd in places: "a doctor wanting to perform an operation he'd already done, the difficulty of getting a nurse to come into a patient's room." These humorous plot developments weren't all, though, says Wineberg: "I tried to give the characters very particular voices, dimension and their own struggles, so the frailty of the mother wouldn't overwhelm the story." With her added story devices, Wineberg's story was now much more than a Dying Mother story.

The Bipolar Disorder

Robert Garner McBrearty considers his story "Episode" (from his prize-winning *Episode*, Pocol Press, 2009) a good example of a story avoiding the Bipolar Disorder cliché. The story's basic plot is about a younger brother intervening in one of his brother's many bipolar episodes. "I wanted to show that the brother having the episode is actually being fairly logical at times, rather than presenting him as a raving maniac." Further, McBrearty wanted to cast the bipolar brother as "more than his illness," and in doing so he believes he was able to beat the cliché: "I think too often writers overplay illnesses like depression, bipolar disorder, alcoholism. They reduce their characters to representative of the disease." McBrearty, on the other hand, wanted to create "a fully-individualized character, suffering from his disease, but not consumed by his disease." He believes because he put the emphasis on the family's struggle "with the disorder at this particular time," he was able to avoid making the older brother merely a specimen of bipolar disorder.

The Bully

In "Someone like Me" (from *From the San Joaquin*, SMU Press, 2010), Barry Kitterman was struggling to create a character "very similar to a kid who bullied me when I was a boy." The problem to overcome, says Kitterman, is that "bullies can easily be cartoonish." To avoid the cliché, he needed to make sure his character, like all good characters, was three-dimensional. Kitterman offers a general guideline for character creation, based on the principle of difference: "A beautiful woman needs an ugly character trait; a striving self-centered stock broker needs a butterfly collection. A bully needs a weakness of his own." Kitterman overcame the clichéd bully problem by giving his character something you wouldn't normally associate with a bully—"a speech impediment." The result? "He started to seem halfway human."

Angry, Cold Father, & Smart, but Passive Son

Gary Fincke says: "At a recent reading, I was fifteen pages into a story called 'A Room of Rain,' which has an angry, cold father and a smart, but passive son, when I arrived at a scene where the father admits to heartbreak and the desire to hold on to sentiment." Fincke was pretty well into the revision process when he wrote this scene, and once he'd read it out loud, he realized that it alone made a great difference in helping him avoid the cliché: "the father is more than what the son believes he is, and now there is more at stake if the son chooses to dismiss him—there's ambivalence, which lies at the center of every solid story."

A FINAL REMINDER

If it's a subject or story line that everyone's familiar with, if it's a character type we all recognize, if it's an expression on everyone's lips, be careful. Don't necessarily steer clear of potentially clichéd plots and characters entirely, but do find ways to freshen or liven them up—to make your fiction as fresh and as original as you can make it, but at the same time believable. This is certainly a hard balancing act to perform, but certainly well worth it when you are successful at it.

KEEPING A JOURNAL

What's It Worth?

by Jack Smith

Keeping a journal is a typical writerly thing to do. After all, writers are absorbing the world around them, noting things of interest for their work: odd and intriguing things, funny things, human traits, distinguishing characteristics, mannerisms. These things find their way into stories, maybe a bit later, maybe years hence. And if writers don't record ideas and details as they occur, they'll probably forget them. Valuable material could be lost forever. But saving important stuff for later use is only one purpose of keeping a journal. There are a number of other good reasons, as writers have discovered. And the payoffs can be substantial.

DIFFERENT JOURNAL TYPES, DIFFERENT CONTENTS

What writers put in their journals depends on their needs as well as how they conceive of the function of a journal.

Some writers keep a journal mostly as a storehouse of information—for later use.

John Flynn, author of a travel novel, *Heaven Is a Place Where Your Language Isn't Spoken*, has kept a journal "at varying times, and at varying intensities." His journals have been all-encompassing in detail, including "thoughts, descriptive passages, lists of books, authors, movies, philosophers, dates in history, quotations, all sorts of information that I may find useful in the future." But in addition to all this he will "scribble little notes" to himself and later organize them for use in poems, stories, or a novel.

Kristen-Paige Madonia, whose debut novel will be published by Simon and Schuster Books for Young Readers in 2012, uses her journal to work out plot and characters for current projects as well as to generate ideas for future ones. She also keeps her journal handy to eavesdrop in public places. "I've mined countless coffee shop conversations for character, dialogue and plot ideas!" Madonia also lists books she wants to read as well as book reviews. She takes notes at writers' conferences and readings, jotting down "inspiring quotes or writing and industry advice."

If writers use their journals to record ideas for both works in progress and future ones, they also find them a good place for storing revision ideas. Ronna Wineberg, author of the prize-winning *Second Language*, states: "I sometimes have an idea for how to revise a piece. I write this in the journal—a quick idea, some dialogue, description, or a whole scene or scenes. Then I go back to it when I have time to work on the story or novel."

I try to spill the ideas out, without worrying about how they look or sound. It's a more fertile, intimate, private space, as close to my mind as I can come in words.

A journal can also be a place to think out your thoughts—a kind of private sounding board. Harriet Scott Chessman, author of *Lydia Cassatt Reading the Morning Paper*, among other novels, sees her journal "primarily as a space in which I can be free to 'talk' to myself. I try to spill the ideas out, without worrying about how they look or sound. It's a more fertile, intimate, private space, as close to my mind as I can come in words." Overall, this private space helps prepare Chessman for writing her stories.

Author of several works of fiction, most recently *Heidegger's Glasses*, Thaisa Frank keeps what she calls a "writer's log," which departs from any standard kind of journal—radically, she believes. She explains the difference: "That is—I jot down numerous words, phrases and spontaneous outpourings that come from my voice, rather than from socialized language." Her log is a place of risk versus record keeping of any kind. "I don't keep a journal in the sense of 'journaling'—i.e. talking about my day, my feelings. This sort of journal is death to my writing, because fiction writing is about what I don't know rather than what I already know." If Frank does write about a real event, she goes "into a reverie and a few concrete images appear (a red coat, a conversation, the way potatoes looked on a blue plate)." These are not images observed in the regular manner. "These images," she says, "have nothing to do with the running narrative of my day, which I know about and can't surprise me. They're what I don't know about my day or don't even want to remember." Above all, her writer's log needs to be "dangerous."

If the use and contents of a journal vary, so does the method of keeping one. Some writers keep several notebooks going at a time instead of what we might think of as the traditional journal look—that is, all in one volume. How writers use these notebooks varies, of course.

Dennis Must, author of two collections of short fiction, enters "bits and pieces in several small notebooks," which he keeps "deposited" in his most frequented places throughout the house. Says Must: "The one alongside my bed I write in frequently while awaiting sleep and pondering the scribbling I'd done earlier that day. Also I always carry one with me when away from the house." What Must keeps are the fairly traditional kinds of things to store up for future use—but in his case, in abbreviated form. "What gets entered are seldom more than a couple words, a sentence or two that I often work off of the following day. There might be a story idea, a bit of dialogue I've overheard, say, in a restaurant, the ending of a story that I've been worrying over for several days, a snippet of a dream, etc. The entries function in a manner like pods which when opened or explored often have the potential to lead to full narratives." Dennis Must thinks of his short, scattered journal entries as "found objects." When he enters them they tend to "excite the mind as to what they may fully reveal later."

Midge Raymond, author of the prize-winning collection *Forgetting English*, is also a devoted keeper of notebooks—as many as a half dozen notebooks at a time. She keeps morning pages, for which she thanks Julia Cameron and *The Artist's Way*, but the notebooks she values the most are her travel-themed notebooks, which she carries to "record anything new or unusual," whether she's "going to another city or another country." In these notebooks she records useful material for story ideas, including "a description of an unusual person, a strange sign at the side of the road, or part of a juicy conversation I've overheard."

> "The entries function in a manner like pods which when opened or explored often have the potential to lead to full narratives."
>
> —Dennis Must, author

We should probably think of a journal in very broad terms—as Harriet Chessman makes clear: "It could be that your best ideas come to you in emails to friends, or in off-the-cuff rants, or Facebook messages." Chessman herself keeps a computer file of emails called "Inspiration." She states: "These can be forms of journals too, if you can figure out how to collect them for a bit, so that they can inspire contemplation about your current and future projects." By the same token, Flynn supplements his journal with "select paper ephemera such as brochures, maps and business cards." These materials, says Flynn, "stir memories and re-orient myself back into the past."

LONGHAND OR COMPUTER?

One might think that in this computer age, most writers would abandon longhand entirely. But just as some writers still draft stories in longhand, they also prefer longhand over the computer when keeping a journal.

Harriet Chessman herself prefers paper. "I often use both a large blank book and separate sheets of good, heavy stock paper. Sometimes I open a file on my computer desktop too, although I like paper best, because of the intimacy and the sense of freedom." She enjoys the tactile experience of turning the pages of the book as she reflects on her ideas. The computer screen, she says, "is largely the place of writing with a capital 'W.'"

Midge Raymond prefers longhand period, both for her notebooks and for her drafts of stories. "I've found that my creative energy can get sapped at the computer, where I also spend a lot of time on the day job, so getting away from it helps." Raymond enjoys writing in longhand more than she once did, and she makes sure she has a notebook with her when she stops at a café or sits in the park.

Something about the act of writing alone, either on a train, or in a café, especially when I'm traveling, is a comfort.

To Kristen-Paige Madonia "the physical act of scratching notes on paper" feels both "organic and inspiring" when she's in the early stages of a new project. She also finds a notebook convenient to carry with her to record memorable ideas before they're lost. While an idea may seem quite memorable at the time, "it's crucial," says Madonia, "to write it down while it's still vivid and fresh." Writing in longhand in a notebook makes this easy to do.

John Flynn also enjoys keeping a journal in longhand. "Something about the act of writing alone, either on a train, or in a café, especially when I'm traveling, is a comfort." But Flynn also uses a computer. "Even when I am not keeping a journal, I keep a file on my computer which is a repository of story ideas."

Thaisa Frank is geared toward the computer entirely. "I always use my computer, since I work on a laptop that's almost always with me. And this technique works well if I print things out right away so I can look at them from time to time. I find notebooks cumbersome and my handwriting is awful!"

THE BENEFITS, THE PAYOFF

If writers commit time to keeping a journal, in whatever form, and for whatever purpose, what's the payoff? Is it merely busywork? Does it sidetrack you from your regular writing? Writers report several distinct benefits based on their particular journal uses:

A Storehouse of Useful Material

Certainly not everything stored up in a journal—all the plot ideas, character ideas, overheard conversations, and details of all kinds—will prove useful to a writer looking to mine

it for potential story material. But some of it might. John Flynn credits his journal for the descriptive passages in his novel. He also drew on his journal for "specific tidbits of information, such as street names and hotel names." Kristen-Paige Madonia states: "For me, knowing that I have a notebook full of ideas, character sketches, dialogue, and anecdotes makes returning to the blank screen a lot less scary."

Anthony Varallo, winner of the prestigious Drue Heinz Literature Prize, states: "I can't imagine writing without my journal. Many of my stories have come from some small observation I jotted down, forgot about, and later came back to, using it for a story." Varallo does, however, mention a downside he's noticed: "The journal is instructive in reminding me that a good story doesn't necessarily arise from good notes—in fact the opposite is often true: how many mediocre stories of mine arose from pages and pages of 'notes,' perhaps robbing the actual story of mystery and interest. (Sometimes the notes are better than the story, alas.)" Still, having said this, Varallo does believe that a journal can certainly assist the writer: "If keeping a journal helps you get to the next page, then by all means, please keep a journal. That seems purpose enough."

A Direction for Your Novel

Getting to the next page is one distinct benefit of a journal for Harriet Chessman. In addition to her private forum, she uses her journal to work out story problems and story structure. "I'm someone who thinks quite visually, so it's helpful to have rows and circles and arrows to conceptualize a story's arc or architecture." For those with novel projects, Chessman believes the journal can be a friend indeed. "I think of these pages as my companion during the writing of a book. A novel is so long, and can ask for so much patience and self-confidence as you go down dead ends and find fresh spots to start. It can be enormously discouraging and daunting, especially in the middle, as you're trying to find your way." For

Chessman, the journal contains the various "sign posts" the writer needs—as well as "the encouraging notion that you WILL find your way."

DNA for a Novel

Thaisa Frank reports a startling success regarding her writer's log: "Most strikingly: 16 pages that I wrote over 16 years ago, printed out and then put away, turned out to be the DNA for my new novel, *Heidegger's Glasses*. I'd ignored those 16 pages because I knew they belonged to a novel and I was sure I'd never write one. But they kept appearing—under tax returns, lists from my child's school—as if on springs." When she wrote her novel, she didn't actually look at those pages, but she did have a "dim memory of them." When she received her galley copy, Frank says, "the 16 pages popped out again. I read them over and realized that they were, in fact, the DNA for this novel." This isn't the only time keeping her writer's log has benefited Frank. She credits it with helping her write successful short stories as well as prose poems.

An Off-Place from the Real Writing

Besides using his journal to store up potentially useful information, John Flynn also views his journal as a place to take a breather from the hard, committed writing of fiction. "A journal helps me clear the slate, so to speak, during times when I've much on my mind, when there is a lot of upheaval going on in my life and I still wish to keep to my writing regimen." Flynn does offer one caveat about this breathing space: "I don't think a journal should be a substitute for the created work." He sees it as "ancillary" to one's regular work—providing a special function: "It's a good way to keep one's attic organized, so to speak."

Midge Raymond's morning pages serve a similar function of renewal. "These pages are sometimes useful to my writing, often not—but they're always useful for clearing my head and creating the necessary mental space to write." Anjali Banerjee, author of both commercial press literary and YA fiction, appreciates this "warm-up" function of a journal because "it can help you to be honest with yourself without the intrusion of the editorial/critical mind."

A Place to Explore Your Ideas in Writing

For Chessman, one of the primary benefits of a journal is the rich, "fertile" field it provides for exploring ideas in writing. "I think all writing is experimentation. You try this, you try that—the important thing is, you have to hold yourself open and listen carefully to what you're thinking, how you're conceiving of something. A journal—in any form—can be a lively part of this wonderfully rich experiment called writing." Exploration can mean surprises, as Ronna Wineberg has discovered. As writers write, "surprising things may appear on the page"—things useful for later.

STARTING YOUR JOURNAL

You might delay starting a journal because you think there's a "right" way to keep a journal, calling for some basic, bottom-line commitment. Some writers, after all, do follow a given routine. For instance, Ronna Wineberg tries to write a little the first thing each morning, "even if it's brief." Wineberg says: "I enjoy writing in a journal and starting the day this way." But she does stress this: "It would be counterproductive to view a journal as a chore to be accomplished every day. This would make keeping a journal oppressive."

Harriet Chessman purposely shuns any form of "organized" approach to keeping her journal—whether it's keeping a daily journal or committing herself to recording specific things in it. To Chessman, this practice feels "too self-conscious and stilted," and she would rather "travel more lightly." She states: "I'm not a hoarder, but more of a bird making a nest in a certain season; once I have no more need of this particular nest, I'm happy to move on."

Some writers have kept journals their whole lives. Others are less committed. And they may write in their journals only occasionally when they do keep one. Anjali Banerjee writes in her journal, on average, two times a week and writes only a couple pages. At the most, she may write in it twenty minutes a day—when she feels "compelled" to, when the "blank page calls to me."

Keeping a journal is a fluid kind of thing. It's also a private one. As Banerjee says, "it's for your eyes only." And the benefits are many.

WRITING AUTHENTIC DIALOGUE

Handling Dialect & Jargon—and Getting Outside Your Own Language Background

by Jack Smith

Great fiction almost always includes great dialogue. As with drama, we get to know characters by what they say and by what others say about them. If the dialogue is flat, the characters will be flat. If the dialogue seems off, or not believable or real, we won't trust the characters as authentic beings. Grant Tracey, author of three story collections and editor of the *North American Review*, emphasizes the importance of dialogue in solid character development: "Dialogue is about giving characters space to breathe, to step out from the author's controlling voice to speak from a real authentic place of their own. Through dialogue characters are at their most autonomous and free." It's this distinct speaking voice, in the larger context of the story's narrative voice, that fiction writers need to master

Writing dialogue of course presents many challenges, especially to authors whose characters tend to come from diverse backgrounds. Speech patterns vary from region to region of the country—and the world. Characters from different ethnic groups and social classes speak differently. Different trades have their own jargon. To create authentic characters and authentic-sounding dialogue, writers can sometimes depend on their own background or experience, at other times on research of various kinds, and imaginative powers.

REGION AND CULTURE

Robert Garner McBrearty, winner of the Sherwood Anderson Foundation Fiction Award, likes "doing 'Texans.'" He grew up with that language on his "ear and mind" and has a feel for handling the regional speech patterns. Still, he emphasizes, there's some skill involved—you have to make sure you don't overdo it. As an example he cites his story "Episode," the title story of his winning collection, which has a "distinct Texas flavor in the dialogue." The language is "fairly subtle," says McBrearty. "They don't sound like a bunch of hicks."

When it comes to handling regional dialect, Catherine Brady, cowinner of the 2002 Flannery O'Connor Award for Short Fiction and author of *Story Logic* and the *Craft of Fiction*, emphasizes that the writer has "to develop an ear—to be alert for the idiosyncratic qualities of speech and to respect them." She warns against such variant spellings as "I lak to be goin'" for "I like to be going"—word corruptions that are "implicitly condescending" as well as "sloppy." What's needed instead, says Brady, is a close attention to "the syntax and expressions that characterize a particular dialect or slang."

Steven Wingate, winner of the Bakeless Prize for his collection *Wifeshopping*, spots one thing writers tend to ignore about dialect—overall characterization: For one thing, says Wingate, writers need to attend to "body language, which can reveal a great deal about how a character communicates." And they should keep this principle in mind: "If a character is rendered well overall, dialect or jargony speech patterns will be easier to do—and more effective in small doses—because characterization doesn't depend so much on them."

"When I'm trying to learn a new voice, I try every possible way to first hear those voices. I'll rent movies where the characters speak that dialect. I'll find YouTube videos with characters from that world."

Handling dialect well is one thing; making it fully accessible to your readers is another. Josh Weil, like McBrearty, has a close familiarity with his subject—the Appalachian South—along with the speech patterns or dialect of its inhabitants. Yet the challenge for Weil has been how to make the Appalachian dialect harmonize well with the rest of the narrative. In the first two novellas of *The New Valley*, which won the Sue Kaufman Prize for First Fiction, Weil connects dialect and speech inflections tonally with narrative voice. "So the rhythms and patterns and musicality of the way people speak in the mountains crept organically into the voice in the narration." At first glance, this may not seem all that important, says Weil, yet it is: "It creates a subtle connection between the music of the narrator and the musicality of the characters' speech." This tonal harmony between character speech and narrative voice "eases the reader into a more easy acceptance of the dialect in dialogue."

The writer's challenge may be how to handle dialect in another country, in a completely different culture. Midge Raymond, author of the prize-winning *Forgetting English*, drew on her experience living in Taiwan to write her title story, which required a strong sense for Chinese speech patterns. Had she not lived and traveled throughout Asia, she wouldn't have known, for instance, which English words native Chinese speakers have problems with pronouncing and which articles (*a*, *the*, etc.), they regularly leave out of English sentences.

Since she was learning Chinese at the time, Raymond says, this enhanced her understanding of Chinese speech patterns.

Yet authors sometimes have neither direct experience—at least not the sustained kind that Midge Raymond had—nor geographical or cultural roots to draw on. Yet a particular character they're introducing requires that they write outside their own language background. Doing this will take "comprehensive research," Catherine Brady states, "but it comes in the form of talking and listening rather than reading." Ellen Sussman, author of both nonfiction and fiction, most recently the novel *French Lessons*, says: "When I'm trying to learn a new voice, I try every possible way to first hear those voices. I'll rent movies where the characters speak that dialect. I'll find YouTube videos with characters from that world." David Hubbard, a short story writer from Carlsbad, California, even makes trips to different areas of the country to listen to the way people talk to each other. But as we've seen, getting a sense of the regional dialect, while absolutely necessary, is only the beginning. The rest is putting it into play—and not overdoing it.

ETHNICITY

Carolina De Robertis, author of the prize-winning *The Invisible Mountain*, speaks of the "added challenges" writers face in writing outside their own cultural or ethnic background. "There is the potential danger of falling into stereotypes—especially when the cultural group we're writing about is historically marginalized. There is plenty of bad writing, and even decent writing, that falls into this trap." Ethnic stereotypes need to be avoided, says De Robertis. "Stereotypes are not only sociopolitically problematic; they also bleed the vitality from fiction." This second result alone, De Robertis believes, should prompt writers to be sure their characters reflect as much "complex humanity as possible"—and dialogue plays a critical part in characterization.

"There is the potential danger of falling into stereotypes—especially when the cultural group we're writing about is historically marginalized. There is plenty of bad writing, and even decent writing, that falls into this trap."

—CAROLINA DE ROBERTIS, author, *The Invisible Moutain*

It's this complex humanity that Irina Reyn, the Russia-born author of *What Happened to Anna K*, respects as she writes ethnic characters, and in her case it means opting for "very little dialect." She wants to develop her characters fully as individuals. "I usually allow speech patterns, tone and voice to guide presentation of a character," says Reyn. "I am very sensitive to the dangers of representing otherness."

So is Joe Benevento, the author of *The Odd Squad*, a finalist for the John Gardner Fiction Book Award. Benevento believes that accurately representing slang, dialect, and words peculiar to a given ethnicity is quite important. He feels comfortable, he says, doing a Cuban store owner as well as an Italian-American grandmother but not a Cajun character since he lacks the sufficient firsthand experience to do so. But from what Benevento has seen, his own emphasis on verisimilitude is surprisingly not shared by a lot of agents, editors, and readers. For Italian-American language, for example, most people, says Benevento, seem to be ignorant of certain linguistic nuances, as when Mickey Rourke's supposedly Italian-American character in *The Pope of Greenwich Village* responds to the question *"Capisc?"* ("You understand?") with the ridiculous response *"Capisc"* ("You understand") instead of *"Capisco"* ("I understand"). As for fiction, "I've rarely seen working class dialogue done right—Italian Americans are always stereotyped, even though not all of us are Mafia wannabes, and the other dialects I also know about, Latino, black, Jewish, etc., are also usually botched. But it doesn't seem to matter." Why is this? Benevento explains that a "veneer of verisimilitude" is apparently enough if readers are sufficiently hooked by the characters and plot. Yet this is problematic for Benevento, who holds that writers who ignore verisimilitude create ethnic stereotypes and "botched" representations of ethnicity of several kinds.

Midge Raymond also believes dialogue should be accurately represented. She avoids writing dialogue for a given ethnic group unless she's sure she "can get it right." While extensive research might conceivably work, Raymond does believe the best way to capture the dialect of ethnic groups outside one's own is immersion: "hearing voices firsthand." But what if you can't gain such firsthand experience? There is one resource to consider, as a second option, says Raymond: the Library of Congress's Center for Applied Linguistics Collection has recorded 118 hours of audio documenting North American English dialects, and this is available online (http://memory.loc.gov/ammem/collections/linguistics).

One controversial issue that sometimes arises is whether or not a writer not of a given ethnicity even has a right to create a character from an ethnic background not the writer's own. Writers are sometimes criticized for doing this, just as male writers are sometimes criticized for creating women protagonists. Cliff Garstang, author of the award-winning *In an Uncharted Country* and editor of *Prime Number* magazine, calls such criticism "ridiculous." For him, "A fiction writer is free to assume any identity he or she needs to for the purpose of telling a story; the only obligation is to do it well, and that's a whole other challenge."

SOCIAL CLASS

DeWitt Henry, founder of Ploughshares, came from an upper-middle-class background, certainly not the working class that he wrote about in his novel *The Marriage of Anna Maye Potts*, winner of the inaugural Peter Taylor Prize for the Novel. Yet, growing up, Henry did have a good deal of exposure to different social classes and ethnic groups, including working-class idiom and speech patterns. For his novel he was able to draw on this fund of language experience. The question for Henry was how to do it well.

"A primary focus for me," says Henry, "in writing *The Marriage of Anna Maye Potts*, was to translate articulate perceptions into the vocabularies and idioms of my characters." Since each character was quite different, Henry found this to be "painstaking, slow work." He found himself initially writing speech/thought in his "own literary vocabulary," then struggling for a "translation, which was sometimes silence and gesture and sometimes vernacular and cliché." The right technique comes, Henry believes, from developing "an ear" or "an eye"—and this takes a regular regimen, which he likens to the rigors of an athlete's training.

"A primary focus for me . . . was to translate articulate perceptions into the vocabularies and idioms of my characters."

—DeWitt Henry, author, *The Marriage of Anna Maye Potts*

While Robert Garner McBrearty has sometimes depended on his Texas roots, he's also done informal "field research" such as watching movies, TV, and the news to create working-class characters. Working different jobs and eavesdropping on the way working-class people talk has been one avenue that has really paid off. Then the challenge is to get these characters down in writing. McBrearty tends to start from just a little and take it from there, relying on his imaginative powers. "The idea is sort of like if one gets a little piece of the character, then the writer goes to work filling the character out." Once McBrearty gets that first line down, he's usually able to "tap into the way the person speaks"—that is, if he writes from "inside the character" versus "planting dialogue in someone's mouth." On the whole, he does feel more comfortable creating characters he's familiar with, and yet he's seen successes with material gained from eavesdropping too.

HISTORICAL FICTION

The issue of realistic speech, along with dialect, naturally arises in historical fiction. But here the reach of years, when the writer goes deeply into the past, can present an additional problem. How does one obtain all the linguistic information one needs? And then, how does one handle it?

Edmund White is the author of many commercial press works of fiction, including *Fanny: A Fiction*, set in the pre–Civil War period, and based on the life of Fanny Trollope, mother of the famous novelist Anthony Trollope. In this work White includes a runaway black slave named Jupiter Higgins. To handle Higgins with authenticity, he did extensive research, read-

ing "slave narratives and fiction written before 1900 in which there were black characters." He didn't read "any technical linguistic studies on black speech of that period," but White says he would have if he'd come across them at the British Library, where he conducted his research. He did skim hundreds of books there. As far as Jupiter Higgins's speech patterns and dialect, White notes that he "had him quote from the Bible, from hymns and from the oratory of preachers." White did have one distinct advantage. He could draw on his growing up in the South, where he picked up the speech patterns of Southern blacks, including "their ways of emphasizing a word and many of their vocabulary choices."

As with contemporary regional dialect, handling dialect in historical fiction can be quite demanding. In *The Circus in Winter*, some of which takes place before the Civil War, Cathy Day sought to capture her characters' voices "accurately, but not literally"—a difficult balance to achieve. With her novel-in-progress, set in the Gilded Age, Day faces new challenges. "How did people of that cultural milieu speak?" For answers, she's been doing considerable research: reading *Edith Wharton*, the first edition of Emily Post's *Etiquette*, and the society pages of the *New York Times*. The tone, as well as the vocabulary of this Edwardian era, is quite different from our own, Day points out, and she hopes to get a firm handle on "the lilt and cadences and rhythms of those voices." Day doesn't believe she needs to cover every base, though, just a few "dated phrases, old-timey words"—just enough to make her characters' speech sound real.

Josh Weil has wrestled with black slave dialect in his new novella *Solarium*. He feels comfortable with white Southern dialect, picking this up from neighbors in Virginia. Handling slave dialect, however, has called for a lot of research. He finds this dialect "fascinating and wonderful and full of music." As a result, he says, "for a long time, I stuck to my guns, writing the first person slave sections in full-bore slave dialect." Yet this dialect led to problems:

first, the difficulty of reading it; second, the fact that it was so "overpowering" that it caused readers to focus "on the way the words sounded instead of what they were saying." So Weil reduced the amount of dialect and left just enough that the dialect now adds to, versus detracts from, the story. In the current version of his novella, it isn't used in first-person narration, but only "when a narrator is relaying the speech of others." This technique makes the slave dialect easier for the reader to accept, Weil believes.

WORKPLACE JARGON

Ellen Sussman has eavesdropped for a few days at a time at a garage in order to pick up "mechanic talk." To pick up jargon she believes you have to be in the language as much as possible: "The research is best when it's real immersion—then we can find our way to characters who really speak the language."

Once one's gathered the material, again the question is: how do you handle it? With jargon this means finding a way not to explain it.

> "Whatever job a character has let the dialogue reflect the milieu of their environment without worrying about explaining what they're talking about to readers outside that environment. Trust readers to get it through context."
>
> —Grant Tracey, editor of the *North American Review*

For Grant Tracey it has to be "real, natural sounding." To make sure this happens, Tracey says: "Whatever job a character has let the dialogue reflect the milieu of their environment without worrying about explaining what they're talking about to readers outside that environment. Trust readers to get it through context." John Yunker, author of *The Tourist Trail*, solved the issue of exposition in his environmental novel by introducing outsiders to the world of penguin naturalists and animal activists so that the characters pick up the jargon themselves. This technique helped him avoid "overtly painful exposition."

TAKING THE CHALLENGE

As we've seen, sometimes you can depend on your background or experience when writing regional or ethnic speech patterns, or dialect, or group jargon, but you may need to do research if you lack the needed background. But wouldn't you be wise simply to avoid dealing with characters outside your own ethnic, cultural, or language background? Wouldn't that be playing it safe? Why risk being "off"?

Catherine Brady urges writers to take the challenge: "It's actually hard for me to imagine an American writer whose social world is so insular that s/he never encounters other dialects or speech patterns, and I also think that dialect and slang and regional (or even generational) speech patterns enrich dialogue—they're its 'poetic rhythm.' So I would encourage any writer to try to render differences in speech pattern while always remembering that s/he's not trying to create a sociologically accurate composite but a believable individual."

Mark Wisniewski, author of *Confessions of a Polish Used Car Salesman*, also sees a problem with writerly insularity, especially when it leads to autobiographical fiction: "I recommend using dialect that's not your own. It forces you out of your own manner of speaking and encourages you to write about characters unlike yourself. Semi-autobiographical (and certainly autobiographical) work, as most fiction editors will tell you, is often mundane, probably because the ego clouds the writer's perception of what engages the average reader. Anyway the use of dialect can keep you from falling into the I'm-so-interesting trap."

Skip Horack, author of the historical novel *The Eden Hunter*, reminds us of an important truth: If writers had always avoided certain kinds of characters, there would be "a whole lot of great fiction that never would have been written."

UNDERSTANDING THREE-ACT STRUCTURE

by Jeff Gerke

Life is a moderately written play with a badly written third act.

—Truman Capote

Now we move to the structure of your plot. Here is where we actually build the framework for your novel. The genre, theme, era, villain, and the rest will inform and color what we do now, but this is the main work. It's like deciding whether to build a speedboat or a fishing boat: Function and design will vary, but certain structural principles will be the same no matter what.

There are as many definitions of what three-act structure is as there are definers. Experts differ on what the acts are, what they do, and where they divide. Some even say three-act structure is woefully outdated, or that novels that use it are formulaic.

If you find a structure that helps you tell your story and accomplish your goal, it's a win, in my opinion. Whether it has three acts or five or twenty, who's to know or mind? However, for those character-first novelists or anyone else hoping to seize upon a framework that makes readers breathlessly turn pages and leaves them feeling satisfied at the end, there's nothing wrong and everything right about working with the classic structure developed by storytellers across the millennia.

Essentially, three-act structure is a way of organizing your story. The simplest way to explain it is "beginning, middle, and end." I've also heard the three acts defined as river, rapids, and waterfall. That's helpful to understanding the increasing drama and speed of the story as it moves along. You may also have heard the acts described as setup, confrontation, and resolution. That description gets a little closer to how I see it but draws the line in the wrong place, in my opinion.

For our purposes we're going to use these terms:

- **ACT 1:** Introductions
- **ACT 2:** The Heart of the Matter
- **ACT 3:** Climax and Dénouement

And, as usual, I'm going to talk about them out of order. Explaining the heart of it first helps the other parts make sense, in my opinion. I'll start with Act 2, then move to Act 1, and finally to Act 3.

THREE-ACT STRUCTURE AT A GLANCE

I've created a new graphic for this. Here it is at its simplest:

Introduction	The Heart of the Matter	Climax & Dénouement
ACT 1	ACT 2	ACT 3

The heart of your story is Act 2. It's where the defining actions of the plot and your main character's inner journey takes place.

But you can't just start right there. You can't start with Frodo already on his quest to Mount Doom or none of it will make sense—and the reader won't care. You have to set up what's going on, who these people are, what the stakes are, who the bad guy is, and why it's all important. Those introductions are the stuff of Act 1.

When the conflicts of Act 2 come to a head, you're in Act 3 territory. Here, you show the final confrontation between the hero and his chief adversary. Act 3 also inlcudes the dénouement or "falling action," the fallout and tying off that constitute the end of a novel.

In terms of story movement, we've already talked about river, rapids, and waterfall. That shows the speed and danger of the story's progression. But it doesn't capture the feeling of heightened drama well enough for me. How about a graphical map of the three acts:

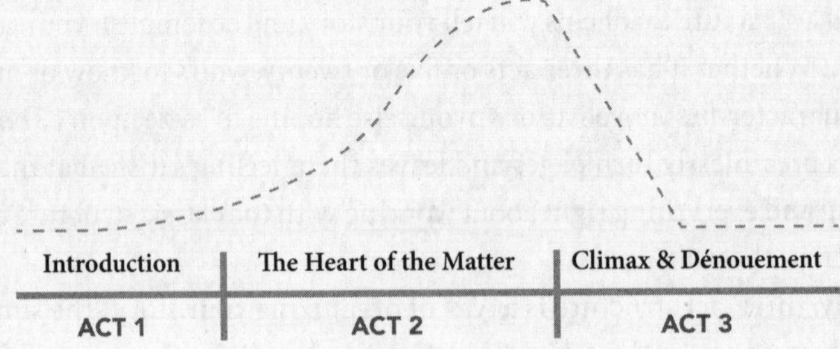

Everything rises to that diving board at the top—and the stuntman drop pad at the bottom. Maybe it's not a diving board. Maybe it's a yard high above the deck of *Hispaniola*. And depending on what happens in the climactic moment, the pit of pillows might become a pit of acid.

You can see that Act 1 is where we start to get acquainted with the situation and the characters. Act 2, is, as the title suggests, the heart of the matter. Everything but the big finish happens in Act 2. How we get from the hero in his resting state to the hero taking a flying leap off the diving board is what we're interested in as readers.

WHO NEEDS A PLOT?

Silly question, right? But think about it for a minute. Why do we need one?

The core of any novel built with *Plot Versus Character* is the main character's inner journey. It is, in essence, a psychological quest, a movement toward—or away from—transformation. That's what the real story is. But this is largely invisible. Internal. Because we always want to show and not tell, and because we don't want a novel that is nothing more than a stream of consciousness monologue, we seek to play that out somehow with characters, settings, and scenes. We want a story, something that could be depicted onstage. Or, we always hope, made into a movie.

The trick is to make visible that which is invisible. To externalize that which is internal. To incarnate a spiritual truth into a physical, observable form.

That's what your plot is. It's the "body host" for the ephemeral truism of a character in transition. It's also the thing that makes it interesting to watch your story unfold.

Just as words are the vehicles for ideas, so a plot is the vehicle for your protagonist's transformation. Without words, no one would be able to comprehend your amazing revelation. Without a plot, no one would be able to experience the meaning of your character's journey to change. The more articulate a speaker, the better his original concept can cross the void and reconstruct itself in your mind in a form as close as possible to what it was in the speaker's mind.

An artist may have an idea for an image or song. It may be fully formed in her mind's eye. But until she can translate it into some observable form—painting, sculpture, song—it remains trapped and unexpressed. So it is with plot. Your novel's plot is the form you give to this incredible internal conflict and resolution you have in mind. It is the way we detect and internalize the idea you want to express.

So let's start getting this marvelous story out of your mind and into reality.

JEFF GERKE is an editor and author of fiction and nonfiction including such books as the Operation: Firebrand novels. He is the founder of Marcher Lord Press, an indie publishing company dedicated to producing Christian science fiction and fantasy.

CRAFTING SHORT STORIES

Letting Plot Guide Your Narrative

by John Dufresne

The short story is the art of abbreviation. We aren't dealing with the panorama of life as we might be in a novel. We're focused. If the novel is the art of the gaze, the short story is the art of the glance. The short story's illumination must be sudden and should *suggest* an ongoing life, not present it in full. A short story must immediately pull the reader out of her world and drop her into the world of the story. There's little time for setup. We begin when everything but the action is over—at the edge of the cliff.

If crafting such an engaging world in so few words seems intimidating, begin by grounding yourself in the fundamentals of good storytelling. We read stories to make sense of our lives, to be entertained, and to feel something. We read them to be transported to another more lucid and compelling world, to learn about ourselves, what it's like to be human, and to "meet" someone we can care about. We read stories in order to imagine and to create, and so we ask the writer to tell us a story. And when we say story, we mean *plot*.

Plots, Aristotle told us, have beginnings, middles and ends, and they proceed through a series of reversals and recognitions, a reversal being a shift in a situation to its opposite, and a recognition being a change from ignorance to awareness. The basic plot of every story—regardless of length or complexity—is: A central character wants something intensely, goes after it despite opposition and, as a result of a struggle, comes to either win or lose.

Many aspiring short-story writers shun plot and instead focus on the other elements that make up a snapshot of a story—characters, descriptions, setting and the like. But no matter how luminous your prose or how fascinating your characters, if you have no plot—no narrative shape—if the characters have nothing meaningful to accomplish, the reader will lose interest in even a short piece. Plot is your weapon of suspense. Wield it wisely, and the reader will want to know what happens next.

So in crafting a short story, let's begin by taking our definition of plot and letting it guide us, quite naturally, to considerations of characterization, theme, tone, point of view, setting and so on. This approach can guide you in composing a short story that creates the emotional and intellectual experience your reader hopes for.

TENSION AND SCENE

Because it is more interesting to write about people at the ends of their ropes, let's begin our plot with a husband and wife, Grady and Alice Bell, who have lost their 20-year-old daughter, Hope. (We don't need to use an allegorical first name, and we may decide that doing so is a bit heavy-handed. If so, we'll revise. After all, we're writing a first draft, and nothing is carved in stone.) The Bells are home alone after the burial and the distressing but obligatory reception for family and friends at their house. Alice is slumped in a corner of the sofa, a sweater draped over her shoulders. She's blotting her swollen eyes with tissues. Grady's sitting in a ladder-back chair, elbows on his knees, staring at his folded hands. He believes that if he had been listened to, Hope would still be alive. He wants Alice to accept her responsibility for what happened.

If the novel is the art of the gaze, the short story is the art of the glance.

We've decided our short story will follow this event, its aftermath, and its transformative effect on these characters. Even though it's just the start of an idea, we've laid out the force that will drive this plot forward: How will the Bells survive this loss? We've also hinted at the tension that will complicate the trajectory of the plot: Grady blames Alice for their daughter's death. This tension will keep our opening scene interesting and will lead us to the next one.

Each scene is an uninterrupted unit of dramatic action. It shows, illustrates and presents. In scene, the reader becomes emotionally involved with the characters. Everything important in a story should happen in a scene, and this is especially true in the short story, where there is little room to discuss backstory at length.

In our example, Grady's looming expression of resentment is certainly an important twist in the plot: Can their marriage survive Grady's resentment? When deciding which path your story should take, remember that the struggle of your story needs to be dramatized, not summarized, and begin to plan your scenes accordingly.

EXERCISES: 4 WAYS TO MAKE EACH WORD COUNT

Getting the full value out of every word you write is especially important when it comes to the short story. The key is to recognize the power of a single well-chosen word, and trust it to do its work. As a rule, the more economically you use language, the more powerfully you will deliver your message. Here are four techniques to help you make each word count.

DELETE REDUNDANT MODIFIERS

Both Mark Twain and Ernest Hemingway cautioned writers against the careless use of modifiers. The challenge in eliminating redundant modifiers, however, is that familiarity breeds complacence. The more we hear and read certain word combinations, the more acceptable they begin to sound—and the more likely we are to use them unknowingly.

Here are some commonly used redundant modifiers:

climb up	consensus of opinion
end result	future plan
important essentials	past memories
sudden crisis	terrible tragedy

When editing, look closely at your modifiers and make certain they don't repeat the meanings of the words they modify. If they do, delete them. There's no point in repeating the same idea twice.

ELIMINATE UNNECESSARY CATEGORIES

When a word implies a category, you don't need to write both the word and the category. Common redundant categories include:

at an early time	heavy in weight
of a strange type	round/square in shape
odd in appearance	unusual in nature

We know that *round* is a *shape,* just as *heavy* is a *weight,* so avoid including the categories of descriptors like these.

CONSOLIDATE REDUNDANT WORD PAIRINGS

We English speakers operate in a language that is extraordinarily rich in both quantity of words and in synonyms. We can choose, for example, to offer someone either *a hearty welcome* or *a cordial reception.* The wording we choose depends on the tone and nuance we want to convey.

The problem with having such a plethora of choices is that we tend to pile words on rather than choosing one and sticking with it. Availing ourselves of too many of these possibilities when expressing a simple thought can lead to wordiness.

The following pairings are common in speech, where rhythm plays an especially important role in how we perceive language, but they should be avoided in most forms of writing:

any and all	first and foremost
hope and desire	one and only
over and done with	peace and quiet
true and accurate	various and sundry

It's worth noting that legal writing has its own idioms of word pairs, such as *aid and abet, cease and desist, full faith and credit* and *pain and suffering.* But try not to use them outside of a legal context.

STEER CLEAR OF INDIRECT STATEMENTS

To be *not* unlike something is to resemble it. To be *not* in agreement is to disagree. To be *not* pleased is to be displeased. Avoid indirect statements using the word *not.* Instead, use it to express denial ("I did *not* do it") or to create antithesis ("Do this, *not* that").

CHANGE THIS: The alterations were *not significant.*

TO THIS: The alterations were *insignificant*.

CHANGE THIS: We did*n't* break any laws.

TO THIS: We broke *no* laws.

CHANGE THIS: She was*n't very nice* to us.

TO THIS: She was *rude* to us.

As is often the case, however, emphasis depends as much on the sound of language as on a particular principle of economy. Of the following statements, which sounds more emphatic to you? "I am not happy about your coming home so late." "I am unhappy about your coming home so late." To my ear, the first statement is more emphatic and may be more practical.

SETTING AND CHARACTERIZATION

The details we choose to depict the characters and setting should be vivid and consequential, expressing a theme or advancing the plot while revealing character. So before you can craft your opening scene, you'll need to look closer at the stage you've begun to set—in this case, at the bereaved Bells in their living room. When people talk, they also act, and when characters act, the reader sees them. (When I wrote that Alice blotted her tears, could you see her red-rimmed eyes and the wad of tissue balled up in her fist?) We want to know what our couple can do in this room. And we also understand that every detail in the room will tell us something about the people who live there.

In a short story, it's especially important for every detail to express a character's personality and motivation. We may picture Grady with a scar on his left wrist, but is the background story of this scar relevant to the story at hand? If not, leave it out. A better detail may be two tiny silver eyes pinned to his lapel. Perhaps he bought the silver charm, thought to possess healing powers, from an elderly woman outside a church in Mexico. He has, we decide, glaucoma. When he told the woman he wanted a *milagro*, a miracle, for his daughter as well, she asked him what was wrong with the girl. He said, "Everything!"

What did Grady mean by "Everything!"? Perhaps this gives you a chance to discover that Hope was a drug addict who had robbed Grady and Alice blind while they were in Mexico. This incident reveals something about Hope's character and the desperation she faced, but it also reveals more about Grady and how he saw his daughter: He was aware of her problems, but he still had "hope" that something would help his daughter overcome them.

In this way, let your plot lead you to begin asking the kinds of questions that will lead to the revelations of such details in your work. Explore as many possibilities as you need to until you've chosen setting and character descriptors that do much more than just set the scene.

MOTIVATION AND ACTION

Next, you must continually raise the stakes to keep your plot moving forward and your readers interested. Sometimes the key to moving ahead can be found in looking back. In our example, a brief digression into backstory can illuminate Grady's current motivation and the anger and resentment he feels. He has already lost his daughter, but we can raise the stakes further by having him lose someone else—his wife.

When we begin by looking back, Grady reminds Alice that he'd been against throwing Hope out of the house after her last relapse: "You wanted her to hit bottom and she did!" Alice, who is also grieving, does not take this lightly. Perhaps she picks up a teacup and throws it at Grady, calling him a monster. Alice weeps until she can't catch her breath. Grady knows he should go to her, but he's frozen with anger and overcome with shame. He apologizes profusely. Alice heads for the door. Grady tries to stop her. She runs to the driveway. When he tries to calm her, she screams—the neighbors peek out of their open windows. She storms off. In this scene, Grady's anger motivates what he says and what he does—or doesn't do. It also provides a convenient way to reveal Grady's ultimate character motivation—to accept his daughter's death and heal his marriage.

Motivation provokes action. In our story, Grady's desire to win Alice back must be considerable. In being confronted with her absence, he is forced to realize that he loves Alice and can't imagine living without her. He needs her forgiveness. Now he has reason to act. Every time he tries to save the marriage, we'll write a scene, right up to the climactic moment. Do the same as your own character takes steps through the plot toward her goal.

POINT OF VIEW

In a short story, it's best to keep the focus on one central character who dominates most of the action. Choose the character who has the most to lose, as we've done with Grady. Through his point of view, the high stakes and strong emotions will be conveyed at their most compelling as he seeks redemption.

In choosing your POV, consider where the real drama of your story lies. In our example, it's not just what Grady and Alice say and do, but what's going on in their minds. First-person POV affords us a look at one but not the other, which can build suspense. This is an especially effective choice if you're considering an unreliable narrator. What if Grady isn't telling us the whole truth? All first-person narrators can be unreliable because they have a stake in the outcome. This can also help readers connect with the narrating character; if Grady continues to be a sympathetic figure, readers will identify with his internal thoughts and struggles.

OBSTACLES AND REVERSALS

So we have a central character, and we know what he wants and why he wants it. Now he has to struggle toward his goal despite opposition. Say we leap ahead to an evening when Grady arrives at Alice's sister's apartment to persuade Alice to come home. She refuses, saying her home was with Hope. Again, he accuses Alice of throwing Hope out when she needed them most. The argument escalates, and we see Aristotle's reversal clearly illustrated: Grady came to win Alice back, but instead drove her further away. He can't stop trying, however, or we have no story. Struggle implies protracted effort, impassioned conflict.

Grady's obstacle so far has been Alice, but adding other obstacles would continue to raise the stakes and drive the plot forward. Other obstacles might include circumstances beyond the protagonist's control, or even other characters. Say in our next scene, Alice comes by to pick up her clothes and some furniture. This time, Grady is helpful and understanding, but Alice arrives with her pals and Grady never gets a moment alone with her.

Obstacles can also be internal. For example, our next scene could find him at his kitchen table, poring over photos in the family album, trying to discern the moment when his daughter decided, *To hell with ballet and tennis—I'm going to be a derelict*. His heart is broken and his resolve is wearing thin. Grady thinks: *Maybe I should let Alice get on with her life, and I should do the same with mine.* Now Grady has to struggle against himself, as well.

He decides he won't let his despair stop him. He calls Alice and leaves a message begging her to try couples' counseling (and now we've discovered the next scene we'll write). He wonders if she's listening to him as he speaks, and so are we. He's wondering if she's alone. We suspect she's not, and the plot thickens. At counseling, Grady makes it clear he's here to save the marriage. But Alice says she wants a divorce, a new life. She tells Grady she loves him but can no longer live with him.

CLIMAX AND FALLING ACTION

Our story can end one of many ways. But no matter how it ends, our central character will be changed, and so, we hope, will our reader. The conflict must be resolved. Grady can fail and Alice can move in with her new boyfriend. Or Grady can succeed and Alice can come home, deciding that after so many years, she owes Grady the effort at least.

For your lead character, nothing will ever be the same again. To continue the emotional impact of a short story, close with scene rather than summary.

Alice sits on the couch reading by lamplight, but she's been on the same page for an hour. When Grady looks at her in the light, he sees a halo around her head (the glaucoma) and thinks: *St. Alice.* He notices that the baby photo isn't on the coffee table and realizes she's holding the photo behind the book, punishing herself with the image of her loss.

In that moment Grady understands that time will heal some wounds, but also that in other ways time will make no difference, and he will never recover from the loss of his child. Bringing Alice home has shown Grady the futility of their decision to live together. We have our simultaneous reversal and recognition—and thus, a satisfying end for our readers.

The plot led, and we followed, and now we have our causal sequence of events; our requisite beginning, middle and end; and we can go back and add the connective tissue of exposition, flesh out our existing scenes, and write the others we've discovered on our way. The hard part's done; the fun is just beginning.

JOHN DUFRESNE is a fiction writer and teacher whose most recent book is *Is Life Like This? A Guide to Writing Your First Novel in Six Months.* He also is the author of *The Lie That Tells a Truth: A Guide to Writing Fiction,* as well as several novels and short-story collections. He lives in south Florida.

Excerpted from the March/April 2011 issue of *Writer's Digest.* Used with the kind permission of *Writer's Digest,* a publication of F+W Media Inc. Visit writersdigestshop.com or call (800)448-0915 to subscribe.

CRAFT & TECHNIQUE

IS YOUR BOOK A MOVIE?

A Crash Course in Book-to-Screen Adaptation

by John Robert Marlow

Is your book a movie? Should it be? How do you get there from here—and what's in it for you? Here's the deal . . .

THE AWFUL TRUTH

Being an author is a noble profession, but reaching the financial pinnacle of our chosen profession requires more than the ability to put brilliant words on paper. *Forbes* magazine recently published a list of the top ten highest-earning authors. All have heavy film/TV involvement. And while one could argue that films are simply based on books that are already massive bestsellers, this fails to account for the many bestsellers that are not made into movies, even when written by the same authors. (Michael Crichton's *Prey* and *State of Fear*, for example).

Then there are stories whose performance is poor to middling or genre-specific, which gain widespread recognition only after adaptation (*Bladerunner, Total Recall, Minority Report*—all based on short stories by Philip K. Dick).

Hollywood does like to base movies on existing bestsellers, but there's something more going on here. And so the most important question for the book or short story author may be this: Why are some books made into movies, and others not—and what can I do to make my book more attractive to Hollywood?

WHAT HOLLYWOOD WANTS

Like publishers, film studios and production companies look for a good story, well told with interesting characters. But they also look for other things, some of which simply don't matter to publishers. Which is why it's possible to have a great book with little film appeal. Hollywood wants . . .

A CONCEPT that can be communicated in one to three sentences. Agents and studio execs are among the busiest people on the planet. They need to get ideas across to other busy people—quickly. If this cannot be done, it suggests that the story is not sharply focused, and that conveying the concept to its potential audience in a thirty-second trailer is going to be a problem.

STRONG VISUAL POTENTIAL. A novel can go anywhere, even inside the characters' heads. And it can stay there for 300 pages. Film is a visual medium, and interesting things must pass before the camera. When not carefully adapted, introspective books make lousy movies. (When brilliantly adapted, they win Academy Awards.)

A TWO-HOUR LIMIT, of sorts: if a story cannot be told in two hours or less (120 script pages), it may be too costly to shoot. Film is an extraordinarily expensive medium, and when you're footing a bill that could run a million dollars per minute of screen time, you don't want to hear that some rookie screenwriter thinks his story should run long. Seasoned veterans with proven track records warrant occasional exceptions; newcomers do not.

A RELATABLE HERO that a large segment of the population can relate to, root for, sympathize or empathize with. If moviegoers aren't likely to care about what happens to your hero, Hollywood doesn't care about your story.

A THREE-ACT STRUCTURE. The overwhelming majority of commercially successful films are "classically structured" into three acts. Even those with additional acts (*Star Wars*, for example) have three major acts, with the other acts falling within that framework.

A REASONABLE BUDGET. In the book world, the publisher's cost-per-page is the same, whether your characters are sipping tea or blowing up a planet. This is not true of film, where shooting two characters sipping tea might cost $200,000, and filming a major battle sequence could run $10 million. If the story seems prohibitively expensive to film, it will not become a movie unless someone very powerful pushes the project very hard.

LOW FAT. Because of time and budgetary constraints, there's little room for anything not absolutely essential to the story. Novelists can spend ten pages describing a room and its furnishings. A screenwriter might do this in a sentence; going on for more than a paragraph will mark him/her as an amateur.

SEQUEL POTENTIAL. Can a film based on your book be sequeled and prequeled? If so, that's a big point in your favor. If the first movie hits, it's a safer bet to release a sequel to your film than it is to risk vast sums on something new and untried.

"FOUR QUADRANT" APPEAL. The moviegoing public is composed of four large sections, or quadrants: young male, older male, young female, older female. The greater the number of quadrants your project appeals to, the better. Four-quadrant appeal is the primary reason for the huge success of animated films—and of *Avatar* and *Titanic*, the two biggest-grossing films of all time.

Four-quadrant appeal is not a strict necessity (the more people you pull from one quadrant, the fewer you need to pull from others)—but it's nice to have.

MERCHANDISING POTENTIAL. Film studios make more money from film-related merchandising than they do from the films themselves. A lot more. And while films with low or no merchandising potential continue to be made, the tidal wave is moving the other way, favoring projects with strong merchandising appeal.

Generally speaking, big-budget action and animation films are merchandising bonanzas, while dramas, thrillers, and comedies have considerably less appeal.

MAKING YOUR STORY FILM-FRIENDLY

Most books are not movies. Some books will never be movies. The majority, however, *could* be movies, if carefully adapted. There are several routes to take here.

If your tale is still in manuscript form, you can alter the story to render it more cinematic by incorporating or emphasizing the elements Hollywood is looking for. (*Booklist*'s review of my first novel read: "Reads like a big-budget summer blockbuster.")

If you'd rather see your manuscript published the way it is, or if your book has already been published—you can adapt your story by writing (or commissioning) a screenplay based on the book. You might want to consider this option even if your story is already film-friendly.

When approaching Hollywood, it's essential that your story be as much like a movie as possible—and the best way to do that is to present it as a screenplay. Books raise questions screenplays don't.

The purpose of a book is to be read and enjoyed for what it is. The purpose of a screenplay is to play a movie in the reader's head so vividly that he says: "I want to make this movie, I want to see it on the screen, and I will pay money to make that happen."

Chris Lockhart is story editor at William Morris/Endeavor, one of the few Hollywood super-agencies. His job is to read and consult on scripts intended for top-end clients, including Mel Gibson, Denzel Washington, Steve Martin, and others. In his experience, every player in Hollywood asks one question after reading a script: "Is this a movie?" If the answer is yes, you've got a shot at selling your tale.

When approaching Hollywood, it's essential that your story be as much like a movie as possible—and the best way to do that is to present it as a screenplay. Books raise questions screenplays don't:

Can we really make this work onscreen? How do we compress 400 pages into two hours? Half the book is spent inside the hero's head—how do we fix that? This would cost $300 million to shoot—how can we make it less expensive? Can we streamline the plot, make it three acts, strengthen character arcs? If we buy the rights, who do we get to do the adaptation? How much is that going to cost? And, at the end of all that—will this be a movie?

By presenting a screenplay instead of a book, you avoid such complications, allowing the prospective buyer to focus on that one, all-important question: is this a movie? Another thing to consider is . . .

MONEY, MONEY, MONEY

The average advance on a first novel is in the neighborhood of $15–20,000. The average selling price of a spec screenplay by an unsold writer hovers somewhere between $300,000 and $600,000—with some first scripts topping the $1 million mark.

Novels run 300 to 500 pages of densely written text. Screenplays run 100 to 120 pages of fairly light text. Do the math—but also be aware that screenplay earnings have a cap; regardless of how successful the film or television series may be, you will be paid the purchase price, bonuses etc. After that, the well runs dry. (For you; the studio makes money forever.)

In the book world, there is no ceiling: every copy sold puts more money in your pocket. If the book does insanely well, you make an insane amount of money. This is why there are no pure screenwriters on *Forbes*' list of the world's highest-earning writers. But remember, there are no authors without film involvement, either. Because to reach those rarefied heights, you need . . .

SYNERGY

Having both a book and a screenplay opens up new possibilities. Interest in either will bump up interest in the other. The actual sale of either will make sale of the other more likely. If things go astonishingly well, a savvy agent might play studio interest against publisher interest and jack up the price on book and screenplay to ridiculous heights.

If the book is published and does well, the screenplay is more likely to be produced (even if it's already been purchased and has stalled at the studio). If the book didn't sell, but the screenplay does, publishers will suddenly become interested in the book. (The reverse is also true: if the script doesn't sell, and the book sells high or becomes popular, the screenplay may get a second life.)

A successful movie will resurrect poor book sales and push brisk sales higher. Because of the cap on screen-side earnings, a hit film can cause your book to make you more money than the screenplay ever will. But you need the screenplay to make that happen.

ADAPTING YOUR BOOK

Once you've decided to adapt your book, you have three choices: write the screenplay yourself, get some help, or hire someone to write it for you . . .

Write It Yourself

This costs you nothing but time. But don't let that 120 pages fool you—a screenplay can be every bit as difficult to write as a novel. And it can take even longer to write. The challenge of the screenwriter's art is to say more with less, using fewer words to convey greater meaning. For those unaccustomed to the format, this takes a surprising amount of time.

The most difficult transition of all is going from novelist to screenwriter. Novelists tend to write long, and overly descriptive writing is the surest mark of an amateur scriptwriter. How long does it take to become a good screenwriter? In most cases, the answer is years. You can speed that up if you . . .

Consult with an Experienced Screenwriter

Or, better yet, screenwriter/novelist. The consultant can review your story with a practiced eye toward screen potential, and tell you where things stand. He or she can also suggest specific changes to consider during the adaptation.

The trick is to find the right person (see below) and work with him or her on a detailed outline for the screenplay. Given professional input and some flexibility on your part, this should provide you with a solid three-act structure, proper pacing, a relatable hero, and good character arcs.

Of course, it's still up to you to make all of that work. Check in with your consultant every thirty pages or so to see how you're doing.

Working this way can accelerate your learning curve tremendously. Still, if it takes you a long time to become a good screenwriter, those consulting fees can add up—quite possibly to the point where it would have been cheaper to . . .

Hire a Screenwriter

Hiring someone who knows their way around a screenplay is the fastest way to ensure quality results. WGA members are out, unless you have $50,000 or more to put on the table (WGA members [whose ranks include most produced screenwriters] are contractually forbidden to work for less; those at the top of the heap often ask—and receive—$1 million or more, typically from studios). So how can you be sure that a probably unproduced scriptwriter knows his (or her) stuff?

Look for someone who's been optioned by a real producer or company, or someone who's been in development with a real company or filmmaker. If genuine industry professionals have shown strong interest in your writer's work, that puts him/her very far above the cast of thousands of would-be screenwriter/consultants.

Another thing to look for is someone who's placed very highly in a prestigious screenwriting competition. And be aware that there are many bozo script contests, designed more to fatten the wallets of their creators than anything else. Placing highly, even winning one of these, may mean little. As Lockhart says: "Somebody's gotta win."

The Nicholl Fellowships in Screenwriting program, on the other hand, is run by the same organization that hands out the Academy Awards. If there's one competition that matters, this is it. Those who've placed in the top 10 have gone on to write scripts like *Air Force One*, *Erin Brockovitch*, *Transformers 2*, *Pocahontas*, *Arlington Road*, *28 Days*, and the *Castle* TV series.

Be open to changes—but know when to say enough is enough, that this is no longer the story you want to tell.

Ideally, you want someone who also knows what it's like to write (and adapt) a book, because he/she'll have a better understanding of where you're coming from, and what it takes to get your story from 300-plus pages to 120. A published novelist or nonfiction book author who is also an accomplished screenwriter is ideal, if somewhat difficult to find.

Also look for someone who sees the story as you do, and wants to keep the story's "heart" alive and beating strongly in the new medium. Be open to changes—but know when to say enough is enough, that this is no longer the story you want to tell. Again, work with the screenwriter to create a detailed outline before the writing begins. Major deviations from the outline should be approved in advance.

Check in every thirty pages or so to be sure things are going as planned, and consult again at the end, before the "polish." You'll find that seeing screenwriting principles applied to your own work is a powerful learning experience.

Keep in mind that, like everyone else, screenwriters have bills to pay. The classic amateur move is asking a writer to work for nothing up front, and a percentage of the sale price if the script sells. L.A. papers and online classifieds are littered with such offers.

As Rocky Balboa once said, "it's simple mathematics." If the screenwriter does his own script and sells it, he gets 100 percent of the money. So why should he put his fabulous idea aside to work on yours?

Great ideas are more common than you might think. Doing those ideas justice for the duration of a screenplay (or novel) is rare. That's what good writers are paid to do.

SUMMING UP

When clients approach me for a consultation or adaptation, I tell them this: There are no guarantees, and it's tougher to sell a screenplay or TV series than a book.

On the other hand, having both increases your chances of selling. The average first screenplay sells for ten to thirty times what the average first book does, and a movie or series will bring your story to a global audience. Not everyone reads, but everyone watches.

So whether you're looking to maximize your chances of a sale, or become a household name—you should at least consider adapting your work for the screen.

JOHN ROBERT MARLOW is a published novelist, screenwriter, editor, and consultant. In the twenty-five-year history of the Acacdemy Nicholl Fellowships Program, he is the only screenwriter (among 50,000+) to make finalist (top 10) twice—both times with adaptations. John specializes in adapting books and short stories for the screen. His adapted screenplay *Nano* recently went into development with director-producer Jan De Bont (*Speed, Twister, Minority Report*). John's online *Self-Editing Blog* (http://selfeditingblog.com) provides free advice and industry interviews for authors and screenwriters.

DENISE HILDRETH JONES

Southern Voices

by Annie Downs

"I feel like I'm just a storyteller." That's quite an oversimplified statement coming from Denise Hildreth Jones. Author of seven fiction novels, including the popular Savannah series, Denise has repeatedly crafted characters and stories that perfectly exemplify a section of Southern American culture. If you live in the South, you feel like Denise's novels could happen on your street. If you don't live in the South, her books make you feel like you do.

Writing her first novel, *Savannah from Savannah*, in 2002, Denise entered the Southern fiction/inspiration market and has left an indelible mark. Full of Southern charm, these books have filed out, one by one, over the last decade. In 2011, Denise released two books—*Flying Solo*, a nonfiction memoir of her first year after a painful divorce, and her seventh novel, *The First Gardener*. As a prominent voice in this genre, Denise uses her personal experiences, research, and faith to craft stories that reveal the depth of beauty, humor, and heartbreak found in the South.

What is Southern fiction to you? Why did you choose to write it?

When I sat on my back porch and got the idea for my very first book (*Savannah from Savannah*), I thought back to once hearing that you should write what you know. So I asked myself the question, *What do I know?* All my nonfiction had been rejected hundreds of times. So what did I know? I know the South, I know crazy people, and I know rigged beauty pageants. And out came Savannah. It was all I knew. If you made me write a book set in New York, you would throw it across the room, saying I had blasphemed all the Northern states.

What makes for a strong Southern fiction book?

First, it's the characters. Their characters run so deep and so wide that you just can get lost in them. There is an element of crafting to them. I'm very visual, so I see my characters before I begin writing them. When I wrote Savannah, she just took a life of her own. I had never written before; I just like to read books. I had never studied writing. I had written songs before, but never a story. She just came to life for me on the page. And Victoria [Savannah's mother] came to life for me on the page. And once I got into them, they just kind of crafted themselves. I would fine-tune them as I went, and sometimes when I start they're nowhere near as fleshed out as they will be by the end.

And because I'm partial to it, there is an element of food in the South that is so relational and fellowship oriented, it drives Southern stories. I mean, how many Southern books have you read where there is some kind of dinner scene? It is what we know. There are elements of the South that you can't find in other stories. But that is true of any region. I'm sure if something is set in Alaska, the author can tell me something and express something in a way that I would never be able to do.

You aren't going to want to read a book I write about somewhere I don't live. I think the beauty of regional fiction is that you get to know this area that you are not familiar with from the palate of someone who knows it so well. I love to read books set in places I have never been and when I know the author is from that area, there is an authenticity to that—you take them as an expert and they bring a flavor to that story, using real places. Sure, that is researchable, but there is something about writing the true experience and the true places. It is a different read. A different mentality.

But what if you want to write about a different place than the exact city limits in which you live? What does that research look like?

For my first Savannah book (*Savannah from Savannah*) I spent ten days in Savannah by myself and I consumed every piece of those twenty-two squares. I ate in the restaurants; I documented the atmosphere; I took walking tours, carriage tours; I stayed at bed-and-breakfasts. I did everything I could in the physical realm to absorb how I would feel if I was that character. I wanted any reader to feel like she had set foot on those squares. I picked the house that I wanted to be Savannah's, I knew exactly the one. I defined her world.

I did that with *The Will of Wisteria*. I picked a plantation out on Edisto Island. I made it come to life that way.

The First Gardener, because I have lived here [in Tennessee] so long, more of that is internal. I just knew those places well. But giving a reader the opportunity to feel like they are really there is my job—so I take the research of that really seriously.

For *Hurricanes in Paradise*, I went to Atlantis. The trip was a gift. I spent four days there consuming that place. And everything from photographing it (so I have those

photos when I get home) to touching the place, hearing it, smelling it—it all makes for a better book.

When it comes to taking time to research locations, I had to ask myself if I believed in this story enough to invest in it. And with Savannah, I felt like I had something worth investing in and it was a huge leap of faith. I didn't know if it would work. Unless you are willing to risk something, you may never know.

Your three-book Savannah series is hugely popular. Are you finished writing about Savannah?

Publishers say I am done. Readers beg me not to be. My head tells me there are two more. But I have no idea when I will write them. The biggest challenge for me now would be going back into that brain space. Capturing her voice.

Because it has been a while since *Savannah by the Sea* came out, right?

I started writing her in 2002, and *Savannah by the Sea* came out in 2006. So it's been five years. But I've also changed so much as a person, so to get back in her brain space now would take a lot of research.

Do you see yourself writing another series?

I don't see it. But I never saw writing stand-alones. All I thought I was capable of writing was Savannah. The story decides whether it is one book or three books. Which is interesting, because I have had readers tell me they want sequels to my stand-alone books and I always have to say, "There's not one there." But for me as an author, I feel like I know when the story is finished. The rest is for the reader to explore in their own imagination to decide what they think is going to happen next.

Do you like leaving your readers wanting more like that? Or would you rather them feel satisfied?

I think you know that the reader has become invested in the characters when they ask for sequels. As an author, you can't ask for more than that. If they aren't invested, you aren't going to hear from them and the story you wrote didn't impact. I've had people call me after they finished *Will of Wisteria* and say, "You've got to be kidding me! You've got to rewrite this ending!" I was like, "First of all, these are not real people! It is just a story!"

But every time you write a book, you are risking it being torn apart, rejected, maybe adored, dissected, and on top of that, you might still have to have a second job. So when someone e-mails you and says, "You've got to write another book with these characters," it makes that year (or however long it took you to write that story and develop those characters) worth it. Because there are some things you can't put a price on. It's not about the money. The true heart of a storyteller is that you just can't NOT tell your story.

In 2011, you have both a fiction book, *The First Gardener,* and a nonfiction book, *Flying Solo,* releasing. Is this a good definition of who you are as an author?

It is very indicative of this journey of life that I am on right now. Even in the middle of living some of the most traumatic moments, God still allowed me the beauty of sensing His pleasure. And I sense His pleasure when I write. I went for a year with no story—I didn't write anything.

I think my writing has changed a little—with *Hurricanes in Paradise* and *The First Gardener*, I'm dealing with topics that are thematically heavier—grief in both of them (in different measures). I think that is parallel with my journey.

I tried for so many years to get nonfiction published—that was my dream. But if that would have happened, I would have never written fiction. I would have never even thought to try. And I think it was such a sweet closed door that allowed me to realize there was a fiction/storytelling gift inside of me. Now, if I had to choose, I wouldn't want to!

What is *The First Gardener* about?

This novel centers around Jeremiah Williams, who has been tending the gardens of the Tennessee governor's mansion for over twenty-five years. The first family of Tennessee, Mackenzie and her husband, Governor Gray London, have struggled for ten years to have a child and are now enjoying a sweet season of life—anticipating the coming reelection and sending their precious daughter, Maddie, off to kindergarten—when a tragedy tears their world apart. As the entire state mourns, Mackenzie falls into a grief that threatens to swallow her whole. Though his heart is also broken, Jeremiah realizes that his gift of gardening is about far more than pulling weeds and planting flowers. It's about tending hearts as well. As he uses the tools that have been placed in his hands, he gently begins to cultivate the hard soil of Mackenzie's heart, hoping to help her realize what it took him years to discover.

THE FIRST TOP 10 BEST-SELLING FICTION E-BOOKS LIST (FEB. 13TH, 2011):

1. *Tick Tock*, by James Patterson and Michael Ledwidge (Little, Brown)
2. *The Girl with the Dragon Tattoo*, by Stieg Larsson (Knopf Doubleday)
3. *The Girl Who Played with Fire*, by Stieg Larsson (Knopf Doubleday)
4. *The Girl Who Kicked the Hornet's Nest*, by Stieg Larsson (Knopf Doubleday)
5. *Water for Elephants*, by Sara Gruen (Algonquin)
6. *The Confession*, by John Grisham (Knopf Doubleday)
7. *Cutting for Stone*, by Abraham Verghese (Knopf Doubleday)
8. *The Help*, by Kathryn Stockett (Penguin Group)
9. *Room*, by Emma Donoghue (Little, Brown)
10. *Cross Fire*, by James Patterson (Little, Brown)

How do you think creativity and faith work together?

I think creativity and faith are vital to each other. For me, one does not work without the other. I am incapable of writing a story separate of my faith. But I never let faith dictate where the story is going to go. I have some books where faith is just a footnote, it's ingrained in the decisions they make, but you don't hear Jesus' name in every chapter. I have other books, like *The First Gardener* (releases August 1, 2011), where there is a huge element of the Lord in that book. But the story would be incapable of being told without it. So I let the story drive the faith component.

Since you've been doing this career for about ten years, do you have a daily schedule? What does a typical writing day look like for you?

If I am in a season where I'm writing the first draft, that book is my job. So it is the first thing I do every morning. After my quiet time, I sit down and work. And I know it is work. Still, how many people get to work in their pajamas and do what they love? I am so blessed and I can't complain. The beauty of my work is that I never know where I am going, but I take it serious.

I don't have huge expectations on myself. I'm also not delivering three books a year like some people do. I usually do one a year. And I write a scene a day. That scene may be 1,000 words or 2,000 words. It may take me an hour, an hour and a half, or three hours. But when it is done, it's done.

I reread what I wrote the day before, tweak it, then get into today's writing.

Do you outline a novel before you write it?

I'm not an outliner. I know the ending, but I don't know what is going to happen from the middle to the end. I love it! I never know, when I sit down, what is going to happen.

Every now and then when I'm praying in the mornings, and I'm in the middle of the book, I'll spend some time walking and a scene will play out in my mind. It might not be the next scene. It may be a scene that is going to happen in the middle of the book somewhere, but that is the extent to which I know where we're headed.

The Will of Wisteria is the only book I've ever had to chart out because it happened over four disctint seasons with four distinct characters and I knew specific things were going to have to happen in their journeys to get to the end point; I knew the end point. So that's the only book I've ever had to craft that way. For that book, it was essential. It forced me, because of the timeline. Up to then my books had happened over a day or a week, so for a year span, I didn't know how I was going to do that. So I had to chart it out.

What is the editing process like?

You have about a month to six weeks lull until you get that phone call from your editor. And then you cry. And cry. *The First Gardener* had the most work that I've had to do in a long time—probably since *Savannah*. Lots of work. So I had a huge meltdown.

Sometimes that editing process is substantial. Sometimes it is not. It just depends on what you are trying to tackle. Then you do those edits and you walk away from it for a while; then you do a line edit. Then you get a final read-through and you are done.

ANNIE DOWNS is a freelance writer in Nashville, Tennessee. With several Bible studies and many articles under her literary belt, Annie also writes books for teen girls and women braving college and the years after. Her first book, *From Head to Foot,* released in 2010. She is a huge fan of the Internet, singer/songwriters, waffles with peanut butter, and sports of all kinds, especially four square. Read more at annieblogs.com.

FICTION GENRES

ROMANTIC AUTHOR ROUNDUP

by I.J. Schecter

Other genres come and go, but romantic fiction soldiers on with the hopefulness of Emma Bovary, the resilience of Scarlett O'Hara, and the charm of Jo March. Here, romance authors at three different stages of their literary careers talk about the writing urge, the trials and tribulations of authorship, and whether or not they'd take sex over the perfect sentence.

CAT LINDLER's (catlindler.com) first historical romance novel, *Kiss of a Traitor* (Medallion Press), garnered raves for its portrayal of the Revolutionary War in South Carolina. Her second romance, *Starlight & Promises* (Medallion Press), based on the search for a living saber-toothed tiger among the islands off Tasmania during the Victorian Age, was released in April 2010. In 2012, Medallion Press will publish her novel *Shot Through the Heart*, a western romance set in Mexico in 1885.

TINA DONAHUE (tinadonahue.com) is a multi-published novelist in contemporary and historical romance. *Booklist*, *Publishers Weekly*, and *Romantic Times* have praised her work, and she has reached the finals and/or placed in numerous RWA-sponsored contests. Tina was the editor of an award-winning Midwestern newspaper, has worked in story direction for a Hollywood production company and is currently the managing editor for a global business document concern.

JENNIFER BLAKE (jenniferblake.com) has been called a "pioneer of the romance genre" and an "icon of the romance industry." A *New York Times* and international best-selling author, she is a charter member of Romance Writers of America, member of the RWA Hall of Fame, and recipient of the RWA Lifetime

Achievement RITA. She has written over sixty books with translations in twenty languages and more than thirty million copies in print worldwide.

When did you first feel the writing bug inside you? What did you do to feed it?

JENNIFER BLAKE: A teacher told me at thirteen that I had talent. I loved the thought of it, but was too in awe of great writers to try anything beyond school assignments. Then at nineteen I had a particularly vivid dream set in Scotland, which I wrote out in story form. That was so satisfying that I tried other small things, mostly stream-of-consciousness pieces and poetry. I subscribed to *Writer's Digest*, bought *Writer's Market*, took a correspondence course on writing. Over the next few years, I sold a poem or two, a short story, and a few newspaper articles. Having been paid for my work, I was considered a professional, so became eligible to join the National League of American Penwomen. The members of the local branch were writing a book on Louisiana landmarks at the time. We were each required to research and write essays on two historical landmarks. It was while walking through an old plantation house that it occurred to me what a wonderful setting it would make for a Gothic novel. The manuscript was returned unread because I hadn't sent a query letter, something that was just being required. Since I had no idea how to write a query, I sent the manuscript to publisher number two, Fawcett Gold Medal. Two months later I received a letter saying it was too short for their list, but if I could add thirty pages, they would buy it. The book was published in 1970 as *The Secret of Mirror House.*

CAT LINDLER: When I was ten, I wrote an essay on what it meant to be an American, which won a contest. Two years later I started writing my first romance. A girl stows away in the hold of a Viking ship—this is before I found out Viking ships don't have holds—meets and falls in love with a horse and a Viking. I've written ever since, but didn't really start writing fiction in earnest until about ten years ago.

TINA DONAHUE: I can't remember not wanting to write. I wrote my first series of stories when I was nine—children's stuff called *Dimples the Adventurous Flea* and *The Musical World of the FaLaLas.* I illustrated my stories and sold them to my friends' parents. After that, I was hooked. During college, my poetry evolved into short stories and then into novellas and, finally, my first novel.

How would you fare as the protagonist of one of your own books?

DONAHUE: Pretty well, I believe. I always make my heroines strong with the ability to solve their own problems. Same for my heroes.

BLAKE: Reasonably well, I suppose, if you're asking whether my life has been romantic. I met my husband when I was thirteen and he was seventeen. Since I was dating one of his friends, he didn't intrude but sent me a series of anonymous poems. We're still married, more than fifty years later.

LINDLER: My heroines are always strong, independent, sassy, and competent. I resemble only two of those. I leave it to you to decide which two.

Are your friends fascinated by what you do? Despite your success, do others still talk to you about writing like it's just a hobby?

LINDLER: Friends are fascinated, yes, not necessarily because I'm published, but that I've even written a book. Most believe that publishing comes naturally from writing. People who aren't in the business think all you have to do is sell one book and you're knee-deep in money. They don't understand that it doesn't work that way, except for the very few.

DONAHUE: Since most of my friends are writers, they aren't all that fazed by my work. In the beginning, before I'd sold any of my novels, family members would generally treat my writing as though it was a hobby. Once I sold, and kept selling, even my family members came around and recognized it as a career.

BLAKE: My friends appreciate my job, but have heard too much about it to be fascinated. One of the great benefits of longevity in the field, however, is that people finally realize you're serious about it so they leave you alone while you're working. My mother is the only person who still thinks I can drop what I'm doing anytime she calls. Of course, she's usually right.

Are you big on outlines and prework, or do you prefer to see what direction the story will take?

BLAKE: For every book, I brainstorm possible events for the story, then create a synopsis and fill in a Chapter Chart with events taken from it. I create a Character Chart as well, establishing conflicts, goals, and motivations as well as basic appearances and descriptions. I sometimes outline important scenes, and now and then outline points to be made through dialogue. If I know where I'm going with my story, then I'm free to be creative with language, atmosphere, movements, internal monologues, and all the other elements.

DONAHUE: I research fully and outline every detail of the story before I write anything. To me, it's easier to get to the end of a book if you know where you're going. That's not to say that my plots haven't veered into other directions at times.

LINDLER: I never used to start with anything but a title and an idea, but now my publisher requires a synopsis for a proposal. So I've been forcing myself to think more in depth sooner. However, the characters often take their own directions contrary to my dictates, so an early synopsis doesn't always reflect the completed book.

What's the best part of authorship? The most challenging part?

DONAHUE: The best part: reading what I've written. The most challenging: a plot that won't gel.

BLAKE: The best part of authorship is those rare times when everything clicks and you write at such a swift, smooth pace it's like magic. The most challenging part is the need to change on demand from a solitary, introverted writer into an extroverted, book-promoting author.

LINDLER: The best part is immersing myself in the writing itself. The most challenging part is having to work for a living and pay bills while I write.

Why is the romance genre so enduringly popular?

LINDLER: Everyone wants perfect love, and perfect sex, and seeing as life doesn't usually work out that way, reading romance is a way to fulfill our most basic needs.

DONAHUE: To be wanted, loved, cherished, and protected is one of the most basic human needs.

BLAKE: They are stories about that most basic human drive: finding a mate and procreating. They are also tales designed to engage the emotions of female readers, as opposed to thriller and action-adventure stories created to excite male readers. Beyond this, romances, like all commercial fiction, are morality tales where good is rewarded, evil is set aside, and all turns out right in the end.

Is part of the definition of a true writer someone who loves revising and being revised?

DONAHUE: Absolutely. If you're not willing to revise, you'll never sell. And if you can't take constructive criticism, your work will never improve.

BLAKE: No. Anyone who loves revising and being revised is more interested in the process than in the story. Revising is necessary, as it lends greater clarity to the text and allows a writer to come closer to saying what was originally intended. Otherwise, spending weeks second-guessing every word is a painful exercise if not downright drudgery.

LINDLER: Revising is certainly necessary; seldom are our first attempts perfect, even in our eyes. But revising is tedious and frustrating. So does anyone love it? I don't think so. As to being revised, that's even harder. Anne Rice never allowed her manuscripts to be edited, much less revised. Unfortunately, most of us don't have that option.

What's your favorite moment in the manuscript process?

BLAKE: Starting.

DONAHUE: The first revision after I've finished the story.

LINDLER: Typing THE END.

Give me three pieces of advice for aspiring writers.

DONAHUE: Read everything you can get your hands on, not only the genre you're planning to write. Dissect the books you've most loved to learn about story structure, dialogue, emotional build, etc. Write as much as you can, and never, ever give up.

BLAKE: One: Think of writing as a profession and understand that the training period for it may be as long and difficult as for a medical or legal career. Two: Learn the craft by reading constantly as well as studying books on writing in general. Three: Practice writing with no thought of selling. Write for the fun of it, to entertain yourself or for the joy of putting thoughts on paper. Nothing you write is ever wasted; every single word is another stroke toward honing your craft.

LINDLER: Read your genre, not just your favorite writers. Learn the craft of writing. Enter contests for feedback (and don't automatically discard all comments from judges who don't "get" you).

What's the most unusual research you've done for a story?

LINDLER: I had to calculate the length of time it would take a steamship to sail from Boston to Tasmania, given size of ship, knots under sail, knots when under steam, stops along the way, currents, etc. It truly strained my ability.

BLAKE: While researching *Tigress* in the mid-1980s, I toured the back reaches of the Mississippi River docks in New Orleans with a U.S. Customs agent as my guide. We boarded a rusting Liberian freighter after hailing the captain for permission, as I wanted to see the ship's layout and hold. Since my presence made such good camouflage for the boarding, the agent conducted a surprise search of the vessel for contraband. It was a nervous few minutes, as anything could go down. Nothing was found, so it turned out fine.

DONAHUE: Early in my career, I visited a prison in California to use it as the backdrop for one of my novels. Unfortunately, the novel never sold.

Can you remember the first moment you decided, "THIS is the kind of stuff I want to write"?

DONAHUE: When I first read *The Exorcist*, I wanted to be a horror writer. Then, I read *Sea Trial* and wanted to do suspense. Then I read *Shanna* and wanted to write romance. I've had a lot of those lightbulb moments.

BLAKE: It's actually happened twice, once when I suddenly envisioned a Southern Gothic while walking through that old plantation house, then again when historical romances began. I'd written three or four Gothic novels in 1972 when *The Flame and the Flower* by Kathleen Woodiwiss came out. I loved the concept and, since I'd always enjoyed mainstream historical romance and my Gothics had historical backgrounds and sexual tension, it seemed a perfect match. I contacted my former agent, suggesting the change. His reply was, "The historical romance is as dead as the dodo." I was disappointed but accepted his evaluation; he was in New York, after all, so should know more than I did in the backcountry of Louisiana. It was a good two years before New York publishing houses finally caught up, and I was asked to do a proposal for a historical romance. The book was released in January of 1977 as *Love's Wild Desire*, becoming my first *New York Times* best seller.

LINDLER: I don't know that I ever had that moment, as a genuine moment. I first wrote horror, but after three books, I had an idea for a romance based on the search for a living saber-toothed tiger in Tasmania. That became *Starlight & Promises*. It took me two years to write it. Then the urge came over me to write a Revolutionary War romance set in South Carolina, and that became *Kiss of a Traitor*. I wrote it in only a month but spent another two years editing and obsessing over it. As it turns out, *Kiss of a Traitor* sold first. Since then, I've been hooked.

Say I'm about to tackle my first romance novel. What advice do you have?

LINDLER: Just write! Get actual words down. I've had literally hundreds of people tell me they have a great idea, want to write a book. "Why don't you?" I ask. "I don't know anything about writing," they say, or "I don't have the time—work, kids, etc." If you truly want to write, you will find the time.

BLAKE: Try something unusual but not ridiculously bizarre for your first scene—and for heaven's sake, bring your hero onstage in the middle of it!

DONAHUE: Study the genre and subgenres carefully to determine what serves your talent best. And always remember: It's not about the sex; it's about the emotional build—what I like to call heat with heart.

Complete the following sentence. To make it in this business, you need:

BLAKE: Intelligence, imagination, perseverance, guts, and a guardian angel.

LINDLER: A thick skin, determination, and a love of words.

DONAHUE: Desire and persistence.

What's better: sex, or nailing a sentence?

DONAHUE: Nailing a sentence, hands down.

LINDLER: Sex.

BLAKE: As with most things in a writer's life, that depends on who, what, where, when, and how.

I.J. SCHECTER (www.ijschecter.com) is an award-winning writer, interviewer, and essayist based in Toronto. His best-selling collection, *Slices: Observations from the Wrong Side of the Fairway* (John Wiley & Sons), is available in bookstores and online. Schecter is also the author of *102 Ways to Earn Money Writing 1,500 Words or Less* (Writer's Digest Books). Schecter provides corporate, creative, and technical writing services to a diverse range of clients spanning the globe.

CATHERINE ASARO

Taking Readers on Trips to Other Worlds

by Deborah Bouziden

Catherine Asaro blends science and art to create one-of-a-kind reading experiences. She says the science comes from her dad and the art (literature) comes from her mother. She was raised with both and from an early age she began creating new worlds and putting stories together in her head.

"I started making the Skolian Empire up as a child. As I matured, so did the characters and the complexity of the universe. When I wrote the stories as an adult, I filled in the details and fleshed out the plots. I have a lot of notes now, but the framework for the stories is still in my head."

Continued interest in the arts led her to become involved in ballet, study classical piano and of course, read books. She enrolled in the University of California, Los Angeles (UCLA), to study dance, but after reading a chapter on quantum theory for chemistry, she was drawn to a scientific area of study. Asaro graduated with a bachelor of science degree from UCLA, and then continued on to earn a masters in physics and a PhD in chemical physics, both from Harvard.

From there the blend of science and writing became second nature to Asaro. She wrote stories in college and continued writing afterwards.

"The first full-length book I finished was *The Last Hawk*. I wrote it in graduate school as a way to unwind from writing my doctoral thesis. When I was postdoc, I sent it to a publisher. They returned it saying, "No thanks on this one, but try another."

So she did. During a year she and her husband spent in Germany, she wrote *Primary Inversion*. Although she had two novelette sales prior, *Primary Inversion* was her first book sale. Most authors recall exactly where they were when they receive the good news. Asaro is no exception.

"I remember it well. I was standing in the kitchenette of the apartment where we were living at the time. The phone rang. I answered it while eating a donut. When my editor from Tor made the offer for *Primary Inversion*, I jumped! It was great. The hardcover came out in 1995 and the paperback in 1996."

"I've always made up the stories in my mind, all my life, since I was three or four, old enough to create imaginary places and people."

Today, Asaro's works include thirteen science-fiction books, five fantasy books, four near-future books, contributions to numerous anthologies, essays and articles for science publications, and lyrics for CDs. Her novel, *The Quantum Rose*, won the Nebula Award. She has been nominated for the Romance Writers' of America RITA award, and the Nebula and Hugo Awards for her novellas. In addition, her science fiction novels have been compared to Frank Herbert's Dune series.

"I'm quite flattered. It's an honor to be compared to one of the best-selling science fiction universes of all time.

"I suspect it's because my Ruby Dynasty series and the Dune series both deal with complex cultures spread across many worlds. Both have intricate connections between the many story arcs and a large cast of characters, including interstellar empires with a powerful dynasty and noble houses."

Her readers will tell you simply it's because "Asaro writes darn good books."

With everything you were involved in (college, career, etc.), what prompted you to try your hand at writing fiction?

I've always made up the stories in my mind, all my life, since I was three or four, old enough to create imaginary places and people. When I was older, writing them seemed a natural progression. It also provided stress relief while I was in graduate school. For a time, I lived in a little one-room apartment with almost no food or furniture because I had no money. But I had my Heath-Zenith computer with 48K of memory (a dinosaur!). So I wrote.

How did your family react to your first book sale?

My husband was excited for me and glad to see my work paying off, figuratively and literally. He's always been supportive of my writing, and does things like the dishes and grocery shopping to give me more time to write.

My daughter was about four at the time. She was happy because I was happy. She also liked to read picture books, so hearing that Mommy would have a book come out was fun for her.

I remember when the hardcover of *Christmas Forever* came in the mail. I danced around the living room, showing it to my family. My daughter took it in her small hands and looked it over very carefully. She studied the pictures of Christmas ornaments on the cover, then opened it up and looked at all the words. Then she looked up at me with this sweet, concerned expression on her angelic face and spoke very gently, saying, "Don't worry, Mommy. Someday you'll get to be in a book with pictures." It was delightful.

Define the difference between science fiction and fantasy for readers.

Fantasy draws on mythology and folklore, whereas science fiction draws on science and technology. Many cultures developed mythologies to explain natural phenomena before they understood the scientific causes. So, for example, the gods caused volcanoes and earthquakes. Within that framework, the mythology answered questions about how people lived, explored their emotions, and analyzed moral judgments. Fantasy continues that tradition.

Science fiction is an extrapolation of what we know is possible. Given the geological reasons for the volcano or earthquake, we ask, "What would happen if we took the idea further?" But it's more than theories or gadgets. It's about how the creations of our intellect affect us as human beings, how they change our lives and dreams.

"The magic in fantasy may be anything from known mythology, such as the Greek pantheon, to a system the author makes up."

Both science fiction and fantasy seek to take the reader beyond our mundane lives. Although both also tackle the question of what it means to be human, they approach it from different directions. Fantasy may look at good and evil as imposed from the outside. The actions of gods or the granting of magic are often beyond our control. Science fiction looks at how we use the creations of our intellects. The choice to do good or evil with that knowledge comes from within the characters.

The magic in fantasy may be anything from known mythology, such as the Greek pantheon, to a system the author makes up. In my book *The Night Bird*, I used a system based on geometry and the optical spectrum. Shapes and colors. Many authors base their world-building in historical research. Good fantasy is as demanding to write as good science fiction. The magic system has to be consistent and coherent, and often includes allegories that comment on themes in our culture, such as the allegories to Christianity in the Narnia books.

Soft science fiction keeps science in the background, whereas in hard science fiction it's explicitly part of the story. I've done both. *Diamond Star,* my book about a rock star in the future, assumes new technologies but doesn't explain how they work. In contrast, *Spherical Harmonic* has equations, math puzzles, diagrams of quantum orbitals, and prose poems written in the form of sine waves.

At its best, literature transcends genre and becomes a door into our visions of what it means to be human, with all our frailties, strengths, passions, struggles, and triumphs.

You have won awards from both the science fiction and romance communities. In your books there is romance woven throughout. Do you consciously lean one direction or the other, or does it just happen?

I write science fiction. My work is published by a science fiction house and marketed that way, but I also enjoy the romantic subplots. I didn't start out to do crossover fiction. I just wrote the stories. I didn't even know romance existed as a genre; my first book was marketed as hard science fiction. But I soon discovered I had readers from both genres, for which I'm grateful.

The importance of the romantic subplots varies from story to story. For example, in *Diamond Star* my focus was on the hero's journey. As the story progressed, though, I realized his producer had her own issues to work through, and that her interaction with him strengthened the story. Although their relationship isn't a major plot point, it ended up being more integral to the book than I expected.

I find it intriguing that romance is the aspect of my fiction most often singled out for discussion. My work has many aspects, most of them more integral to the books. The stories have been used in university programs as an example of good science in fiction, many reviews talk about the characterization, world-building, and military subplots, they come up in feminist discussions of books with strong female characters, and so on. Yet romance gets the attention. I suspect it's because romance isn't traditionally associated with science fiction, whereas most science fiction readers take the science, technology, math, and military themes for granted.

Romance, like science fiction, has many stereotypes associated with it. If I can help show those are wrong for either genre, I'm all for it.

How has your background in physics and dance helped/prepared/assisted you in writing your books?

I've always enjoyed solving math problems. I love puzzles. Similarly in science, the gathering of data, analyzing it, solving equations, and finding answers fascinates me. So researching the science and world-building for my fiction is always fun.

A paper about some of the physics ideas in my books appeared in the *American Journal of Physics*. It's a math trick I came up with for circumventing the speed of light. Basically, you add an imaginary component to your speed, making it a complex number. The singularity in the equations of special relativity goes away and life is great. Of course, no known physical analog exists for complex speed, so it's really just a math game. The paper did get me invited to participate in the Breakthrough Physics Propulsion program at NASA, though, which explores new theories of physics that might make interstellar travel feasible.

"I've always enjoyed solving math problems. I love puzzles. Similarly in science, the gathering of data, analyzing it, solving equations, and finding answers fascinates me. So searching the science and world-building for my fiction is always fun."

It's hard to say how dancing or singing influences my writing. I've always been able to imagine dance that I choreograph in full moving action and color. The same is true for the scenes in my books. I "choreograph" my favorite scenes to music before I write them.

Ballet is actually quite mathematical. It involves geometry, spatial perception, algorithms, and pattern recognition. I doubt it is coincidence that the percentage of ballet dancers who do well at math is larger than the percentage in the general population. I don't think the separation our culture puts between "analytic" and "artistic" pursuits is real. Both are aspects of human creativity.

How do you create your worlds—planets and kingdoms?

I do a lot of world-building, with notes, diagrams, equations, tables. For example, I worked out a history of the Skolian Empire. The background is this: an unknown race took humans from Mesoamerica, North Africa, and India in the Stone Age, left them on another planet, and vanished. That's the mystery: who were the aliens and why did they relocate humans? The stranded humans eventually developed space travel and set up an interstellar empire.

That gave me a lot to work with. I could create different worlds, and I had rich Earth cultures to draw on. For example, many names in my stories have Mayan roots. Languages evolve, so the words aren't exactly Mayan, but the similarities remain. For *Catch the Lightning* especially, I read a great deal about the Maya and used a Maya-English-Spanish dictionary.

For planets and star systems, I calculate as much as I can, including the orbit of the planet, length of the day, length of the year, how much light the planet receives, its axial tilt, the luminosity of its star. All of that. It's fun working out the details.

For *Diamond Star*, you wrote songs for your character, Del, to sing. How is writing lyrics different from writing narrative and dialogue? How is it similar?

Lyrics are similar to prose in the sense that a song often tells a story. Even if it doesn't you still have to put them together in a way that makes your audience care about what they add to the song. The songs I wrote for *Diamond Star* were all designed to fit Del's life.

Lyrics are different from poetry in that they often rhyme, at least with assonance, whereas modern poetry rarely does. They need a rhythm that fits the music. It really helps me to listen to the music, if it's written, either by me or the musicians I work with. For me, music is inspiration.

I love writing music. I do it on the computer so I'm not limited by any technical inability to play what I hear in my head. But a computer program doesn't give the best sound. When the musicians I work with turn my music into full-fledged songs, it's an incredible gift. I listen and think, "Good Lord, I wrote that. How can that be?"

How has the industry changed since you started writing?

It has become even more competitive as publishers consolidate, bookstores close, and the economy struggles. At the same time, new opportunities have opened up. My interest in finding creative ways to promote my fiction is what took *Diamond Star* from a manuscript to the recording studio. With modern technology, we can catapult storytelling to a new level, creating a multimedia experience. And that's exciting.

Please offer some advice to those who are interested in writing a book. What should they pursue? Stay away from?

Write, write, write! Finish one story; send it out, start the next. That middle step is important. If you would like to be published, you need publishers and agents to see your work. Be willing to risk rejection. It happens to us all. It hurts, yes, absolutely, but it's worth the trouble. If you don't send the story out, that's the same as a rejection: no publication. At least if you send it out, the possibility exists that it will find a home.

Remember that publishers pay you. If someone wants to charge you for publishing your work, that's not a professional publication, it's a vanity press or self-publishing. Before you go to self-publishing, try to place your work with a professional house. They will pay you and get you book distribution that you can rarely achieve on your own.

Also, be willing to listen to criticism (*thoughtful* criticism). A good critique is valuable. The hard part is learning to separate the good from the chaff. Also, a critique should never comment on the writer, only the writing. The person doing the critique should seek to help you write what you want, not what they want.

Most importantly, believe in yourself. Don't give up. The passion you bring to your story comes through to the reader, and that is what makes the tales we create special.

What are you working on now?

Besides writing *Carnelians*, I'm doing a story for a paranormal anthology, a chapter in a textbook on science fiction, and for something completely new, a story for *Dungeons and Dragons*. I also released a new CD with jazz musician Donald Wolcott, and we've been touring with a show. You can find our schedule of signings, readings, concerts, and conventions at www.tinyurl.com/Asaro-Wolcott. Information about the book *Diamond Star* and my other most recent books is at www.tinyurl.com/Asaro-Baen.

DEBORAH BOUZIDEN has been writing and publishing books and articles since 1983. During that time she has had hundreds of articles published in such magazines as *Woman's Day, Writer's Digest, Oklahoma Today, Living with Children, Fate,* and others. In the fall of 2011, her eleventh book, *How to Start a Home Painting Business,* will be released. She has spoken at conferences across the Southwest and held several writing workshops. To learn more about Bouziden, visit her website at www.deborahbouziden.com.

JULIA QUINN

Author Finds Niche & Loves It

by Deborah Bouziden

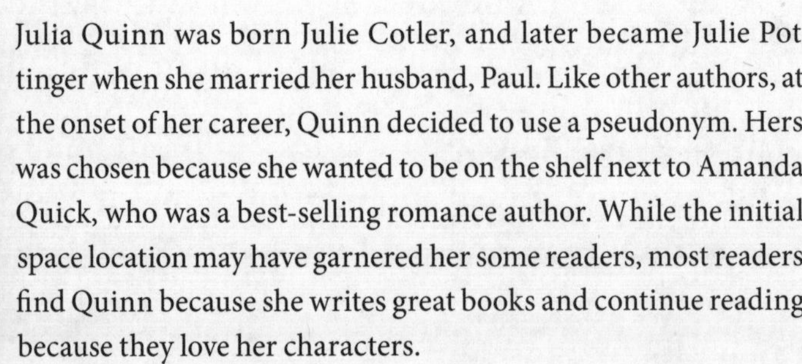

Julia Quinn was born Julie Cotler, and later became Julie Pottinger when she married her husband, Paul. Like other authors, at the onset of her career, Quinn decided to use a pseudonym. Hers was chosen because she wanted to be on the shelf next to Amanda Quick, who was a best-selling romance author. While the initial space location may have garnered her some readers, most readers find Quinn because she writes great books and continue reading because they love her characters.

Quinn began writing at an early age. She loved to read, and her favorites at the time were any books in the Sweet Dreams and Sweet Valley High series, much to her father's chagrin. He told her she could read them if she could show they were good for her. To get by her father's disapproval, she told him she was reading these books because she wanted to write them.

"Today, he's my biggest fan," Quinn said. "In fact, he's a novelist now, too, writing young reader fiction."

Three years following that initial confrontation, Quinn completed her first book. She sent it to *Sweet Dreams* and was rejected. But Quinn's dream didn't die; it was just shelved for a while.

After Quinn received her degree in art history from Harvard, she decided to pursue a career in the medical field. While working on completing her science prerequisites, she started writing again. She chose the Regency time period because that is the period of books she had been reading. By the time she had been accepted and entered Yale medical school, three of her books had been published. After a couple months of med school, Quinn decided she'd much rather be writing than anything else, so she dropped out of school and headed back to her computer to pursue her writing career full-time.

As of May 2010, Quinn had twenty novels, four novellas, and six short stories published. Her books have been translated into nineteen languages. While all of her books are good reads, her most popular seem to be the eight Bridgerton Family series books. Six of those eight, *An Offer from a Gentleman*; *Romancing Mr. Bridgerton*; *To Sir Phillip, with Love*; *When He Was Wicked*; *It's In His Kiss*; *On the Way to the Wedding*; as well as *The Secret Diaries of Miss Miranda Cheever*; *The Lost Duke of Wyndham*; and *Mr. Cavendish, I Presume*; have been on the *New York Times* Best Seller List. *Publishers Weekly* named *To Sir Phillip, With Love*, a best original novel of 2002. In that same year, the Romance Writers of America (RWA) membership voted *Romancing Mr. Bridgerton* one of the top ten books of the year. In 2003, *Time* magazine wrote a profile piece about Quinn, something not commonly done for romance writers. In 2007, *On the Way to the Wedding* won the RWA RITA Award for Best Long Historical Romance and in 2008, Quinn walked away with another RITA for Best Regency Historical Romance for *The Secret Diaries of Miss Miranda Cheever.*

While Quinn continues to write in the Regency time period and at times her characters show up in different stories, every one of her books is different. She works hard at keeping her plots original and her characters engaging.

"I write fairly detailed outlines, but usually the stories end up being as much about characterization as they do about plot. And of course the story frequently veers off course. Most of my favorite scenes, in fact, have come out of the actual writing process as opposed to the outlining process."

According to what is happening in Quinn's life at the time, each book takes about four to six months to write.

"I can be zooming along with a manuscript and then get an e-mail from my editor asking if I can write the back cover copy for a different book. Or perhaps I'll have a conference I've agreed to attend, so the manuscript gets set aside. And the longer you're away from a manuscript, the longer it takes to get back into it."

So what does Quinn do to get back *into* it?

"Panic and caffeine seem to do the trick."

You started your career in 1994. How has your writing changed? How has your career changed?

I approach books differently now than I did when I first started. My initial question was: "What is going to happen?" Now it's: "Who are these people?" Even if I am starting the process with a particular plot-hook in mind, I go immediately to the characters and work from there. I have to know who they are. Not just character traits such as shy, clumsy, musical, etc. I need to know their histories. What happened in their childhoods that made them the way they are? I spend weeks on this, and I often end up with details that never make it into the book. But even if the reader never learns about some random event that occurred when the hero was nine, I know about it, and it helps me to build a three-dimensional character.

"I work very hard to make sure I'm not writing the same book over and over again."

My career has obviously changed, too. I've hit the top of the best-seller lists. On the one hand, this gives the writer greater power. I can get away with things a newer writer can't. But on the other hand, I now must approach each book with the weight of reader expectations. Writing genre fiction can be quite a balancing act. Readers expect a certain kind of story when they pick up a book with my name on it, and I want to deliver that. But at the same time, I have to keep it fresh and interesting for me, too. I work very hard to make sure I'm not writing the same book over and over again.

You have been compared to Jane Austen. How does that make you feel? Did you read Jane Austen before you started writing? Do you read her now? What do you think of her work?

I can't imagine any writer not being flattered by a comparison to Austen. I was recently asked to write an afterword for the new Penguin Classics edition of *Mansfield Park*, and it was fascinating to read her work with a critical eye. I have to say, writing that afterword was one of the hardest things I've done in years. It hadn't occurred to me that I had not done that type of academic writing since college. You use a completely different part of your brain. It also gave me the opportunity to reflect on what makes a specific author or book resonate with readers. *Mansfield Park* is the least popular Jane Austen novel, and there's a reason for that. It's not that it's any less well written. But it does not meet reader expectations for an Austen novel, and thus many readers are disappointed. This is something writers of genre fiction face every day. A romance must end happily. A mystery must be solved. And perhaps most critically, a certain author must deliver a book written in a certain voice.

Why did you choose to write in the Regency time period? What about this time period attracts you?

Regencies were my favorite books to read, so it was only natural that when I sat down to write my first book that would be the setting I'd choose. Now that I understand the novel-writing process much better, though, I can see that the time period is tailor-made for a writer of my particular strengths. I'm great with dialogue, less so with description. The witty repartee of the Regency time period is a natural fit.

What is your favorite thing about your writing career? What do you dislike about it?

Flexibility! For both. I love being able to set my own schedule. It makes balancing work and family so much easier. On the other hand, if you're not terribly disciplined (and I'm not), that same flexibility can be your worst enemy. I am constantly trying to learn how to work more productively when I don't have a deadline breathing down my neck. I have friends who keep rigorous writing schedules and I am just in awe of them.

In the past, you've given workshops on writing dialogue. Please give readers some tips about writing dialogue for their own books.

My number one tip is to read the dialogue out loud. You will know instantly if it does not feel natural, or a particular speech has gone on too long. Also, it's important to remember that your characters are talking to each other, not to the reader. It can be extremely difficult to get all of the necessary expository information into the beginning of a book, but you cannot have one of your characters saying to her sister, "Remember how Mom and Dad died in that plane crash when I was ten and you were eight? And then we went to live with our great-aunt, and she was so mean, and as soon as I was old enough, we left, and it's been such a struggle since then but we're still glad we did it?" That information might be critical to the book, but dialogue is probably not the way to get it out there. There is nothing there that both of these characters don't already know. They would never say that to each other.

Some of your books include list making, writing in diary, a guidebook, etc. Besides the obvious (you're a writer, make lists, etc.), what gave you the idea to include these in your books?

It started in my sixth novel, *To Catch an Heiress.* I was almost halfway through the book, and something wasn't quite clicking. I finally figured out that I didn't have a good enough sense of the heroine. Then one day, I was doing my usual procrastination-through-e-mail routine, and I received one from the Word-a-Day listserv, which my father had subscribed me to. I don't recall what the word was that day, but it gave me the idea to have the heroine write a personal dictionary. Each chapter opened with a definition of a word, followed by a sentence (written by the character) using the word in context. I felt electrified. Suddenly I had all these opportunities to write in the first person, which allowed me to explore the character in ways that had previously been impossible. The whole book fell into place after that, and I fell in love with "epigraphical" writing. I should add that I was extremely annoyed when my father signed me up for a listserv without telling me, but he said, "You'll thank me later." He was right.

A few years back you posted your year's goals. Do you set goals for your writing every year? If you do, why do you think goals are important?

I do think goals are important. But I have always felt strongly that writers should have attainable goals. For example, most every writer of commercial fiction would love to hit the *New York Times* list. I think that's a terrific goal, and certainly one that I set for myself from day one. But I knew that I wasn't going to hit the list with my first book. Or my second. Or my third. For those earlier books, I always made sure that I had other goals, ones that I actually had a chance of reaching. I did finally hit the New York Times list with my tenth book, at which point I immediately readjusted my "pie-in-the-sky" goal to hitting #1. I did that with my eighteenth book and have now reset the goal to an all-expenses-paid international book tour. Strangely enough, I have yet to convince any of my publishers that this is a good idea.

You have said you like to travel. If you could pick your ideal travel spot, where would you go?

I'll travel almost anywhere. If I have friends living abroad, I'm always the first to say, "We'll come visit!" We went to Bangalore that way, and I'm currently planning a trip to Paris to visit my fellow author Eloisa James, who will be finishing up a year there. I have cousins in Namibia, so that's also high on the list. I've never been to Africa, and to an inveterate traveler like me, that just seems wrong.

You choose music and put together soundtracks for your books. How do you choose the songs? Do they come along as the book comes along, or do you choose them beforehand?

I didn't develop the soundtracks until I was working on my sixteenth novel, so for my earlier books, I chose songs that I remembered listening to a lot when I was writing or that somehow seemed to connect with the story. Now I come up with the soundtracks as I'm writing. I'll hear a song and suddenly realize it might as well be written about one of the characters. Or I'll look at the play count in iTunes and see that I've listened to a certain song over a hundred times in the previous month.

How do you think the Internet assists writers in their marketing efforts?

It allows us unprecedented interaction with our readers. This can sometimes be overwhelming, but for the most part, it's terrific. A well-designed, comprehensive website is an author's best marketing tool, period. If a new reader wants to find out more about me and my books, my website can give her all the information she needs. If a reader wants to take it a step further, she can become a fan of my Facebook page, where I try to read and respond to all of the comments. This creates a sense of community, and readers who feel connected to a favorite author are more likely to buy her books the moment they hit the stores or to recommend them to fans. Plus, I enjoy it. I don't write in a vacuum, and part of what I perceive as the writing experience is knowing that my words are read. So I like hearing what my fans have to say.

"A well-designed, comprehensive website is an author's best marketing tool, period."

What are you working on now? (And what about Sebastian from *What Happens in London*? Is he next? Surely he can't have fallen and dislocated his shoulder for nothing.)

Sebastian's book, *Ten Things I Love About You*, comes out May 25, 2010. After that is *The List: A Novel in Three Parts*, a collaboration with Eloisa James and Connie Brockway. Both of those are completely written, though. I'm about to get started on the final two Bridgerton 2nd Epilogues, and then after that on my next novel. I think I'm actually going to go back in time a bit to the Georgian period, and write about an earlier generation of Bridgertons. I'm excited! It'll be new and different but still something I think my readers will love.

LAURA KINSALE

Romance Author Knows Her Limits & Does It Her Way

by Deborah Bouziden

New York Times Bestseller and Romance Writers of America RITA award winner Laura Kinsale may not pump out a book every year or even every two or three years, but her readers don't care and neither does she.

"I began to write because I loved to write. That is still the only way."

Kinsale wrote her first story in third grade. In high school, she had a story published in the school paper and then as an adult, she picked up a pen and legal pad and started writing stories while she was enmeshed in her full-time career as a petroleum geologist. Sitting on drilling rigs and pulling all-night shifts in the middle of nowhere in Texas, Kinsale decided enough was enough and traded in her hard hat for an office chair.

Even though she had no formal training in writing, her characters' emotions and motivations were so deeply revealed that Kinsale drew a devoted readership with the release of her first book, *Hidden Heart*, in 1986. Writing ten books in twelve years took an emotional toll, and by the time she finished her tenth manuscript, it was as if her creative energy had packed its bags and deserted her. She tried to write by determination and perseverance, but by this time thoughts of even turning on her computer sent her into a crying heap.

While the industry demanded she turn out a certain number of books every year or so, Kinsale couldn't force her heart and mind to do what every fiber of her being was screaming not to do. Kinsale believes writing a book takes time. For her, the characters and plot need time to ferment like a fine wine and without that time the finished product will end up flat and not worth presenting to the world. So instead of bowing to the gods of industry and their ever-increasing hunger for product, Kinsale decided to take her time, coax her Muse gently, and write the stories she wanted to write, how she wanted to write them.

Known for her dark, intense books, when Kinsale writes she doesn't see her books in that vein. She writes characters that portray real life with real-life issues and problems. She creates her character-driven stories because she wants to reach her readers in a deep and memorable way.

Kinsale's readers say her books grab them by the heartstrings and pull them in. When they start reading her books, they're difficult to put down and will keep them up late into the night because they've got to read one more scene.

Catering to her love for animals, Kinsale gives her readers little extras by including special creatures in her stories. She's woven a horse, hedgehog, penguin, domesticated wolf, to name a few animals, into her stories, and her most recent release, *Lessons in French*, has a prizewinning bull named Hubert taking center stage.

Lessons in French is Kinsale's twelfth book and comes six years after the release of *Shadowheart* in 2004. This book is a departure from her previous works in that it is a lighthearted romp. The heroine, Lady Callista, jilted three times, has resigned herself to her unmarried status. Her current goal is to win the silver cup with her bull, Hubert, at the agricultural fair. Life is simple until Trev d'Augustin, a suitor from her past, reappears. This book had been written for a number of years before it was picked up by Sourcebooks. Kinsale believes that other publishers were put off because of her change in style; however, she says *Lessons in French* is still filled with that deep emotion her readers have come to expect and love. As her new publisher, Sourcebook Casablanca is in the process of reprinting many of her earlier books. Kinsale is not only excited about the prospect of her books finding new readers, but because she loves color knows the new covers will be exciting and lovely.

There is a lot of buzz in conjunction with the release of this new highly anticipated book. Kinsale has been on the road doing book signings, she is featured in the February 2010 issue of *Romantic Times*, and her readers are flocking to stores in person and online to get their hands on a copy. In addition, Kinsale launched her new website, www.laurakinsale.com in January 2010. From here, she updates where she'll be making personal appearances, announcing new projects and keeping in touch with her readers on a more personal level through her message board format.

Please share with readers how your first book, *Hidden Heart*, came about and got published.

Through a bit of a fluke, I was lucky enough to sell my first manuscript on proposal. Avon had returned my initial proposal and three chapters to me, suggesting some revisions and asking me to resubmit it. I did so, but in the meantime, a new editor, Ellen Edwards arrived. She was looking for new authors, and called me, asking if I could provide her with a sample of a love scene I'd written. I'd never written one! So I had to jump far forward mentally in the book (I only had about ten chapters at that point) and write the scene. It was very difficult! But then that scene became a sort of beacon for me, and I "wrote to it" to finish the book after Avon bought it. I'd never finished a novel before, so it was my lighthouse scene to guide me through writing my first book, *The Hidden Heart*.

How did your husband react to your decision to write?

My husband has always been my biggest supporter, and I can truly say without him I would never have finished a book. He says one day he'll write a book himself, called *The Care and Feeding of the Romance Writer*.

How do you write your books? Outline the plot or plot as you go? Do you focus on character or plot? Why? How long does it normally take you to write a book?

I am a character-driven writer. Over the years I've gotten somewhat better at plotting through a great deal of effort and trying to train myself. But it's always a struggle. Characters are easy. Plotting is hard. How long the book takes usually depends on how long it takes me to figure out what happens next.

Your books are filled with historical and it seems medical/equestrian/etc. detail. How do you do your research? How do you keep it all organized?

I love doing research. I find all sorts of things interesting, but I'm particularly interested in reading contemporary historical sources, or scholarly research about social history. I tend to buy a lot of books from university book sales, on odd topics, like the banking system in medieval Venice. I guess my organization is fairly organic—Firefox bookmarks and grouping books together on shelves as it seems they relate to me!

All the time writers hear, "Write what you know." What do you think that means?

Sometimes I've used "what I know" with a twist. When I wrote my medievals, I knew religion permeated the characters' lives in ways I found hard to imagine myself, until I realized that it could be equated with "health" today. It's something that brings out a lot of visceral emotions, has a "right" and a "wrong" (but the right and wrong varies with the "health expert/priest" you listen to). With cookies, as with minor sins, we often tend to say, "Oh, I'll be bad today, and make up for it tomorrow." This gave me a template of sorts to imagine how people related to an all-pervasive medieval religion.

Please share some writing tips for beginning writers. What lessons have you learned over the span of your career?

Read, read, read, and read. Then go back and analyze anything that really moved you, and figure out how the writer did it.

What writers' groups do you belong to? Do you belong to a critique group? Have you belonged in the past? How do you think writers' groups/organizations benefit writers?

I've never belonged to a formal critique group. I think a writer has to be very wise about whom to trust with their work-in-progress. My husband and several close friends work with me while I'm writing.

I belong to the Authors Guild and Romance Writers of America. I think both are highly beneficial to writers, who all start out naive and alone in a difficult industry. The education and camaraderie of these organizations is invaluable.

You've been nominated for awards, been on best-seller lists, won RITA awards. How does it feel to be rewarded for your hard work?

I'm very honored by the awards I've received. I think of them as hugs; they connect me to my readership. The time between the work and the awards is so long that there isn't really a strong connection in terms of a sense of reward for hard work. The writing itself is independent of any external motivation, and that includes awards, reviews, and money.

With the book marketplace being in such flux these days, what advice can you give writers about marketing their books?

Elizabeth Law, publisher of Egmont Books, said, "Just write your heart out. I promise you that's what matters. I would much, much, much rather find a great, unusual, distinctive book by a phobic writer covered in oozing sores who lives in a closet than a decent but not amazingly original book by the world's best promoter. I could sell the former a lot better, too."

I would advise writers to take that to heart.

Lessons in French was released in January 2010. Please share with readers how this book came about.

Lessons in French is a feel-good book. I'm known for writing dark, intense books. But I love to read Georgette Heyer's light Regencies. I enjoy a writing challenge, and I gave myself the challenge to do a book that would be funny and very romantic. After I finished it, several years ago, I didn't feel that the publishers were quite ready to do it justice at the time, as it wasn't in the style of my "bigger books." So I decided to put it away for a while. Sourcebooks came to me and asked to publish it. Their enthusiasm was just what I hoped for, and it's a very good fit.

In an interview on "Goodreads" you said about *Lessons in French,* "What this book returned to me was my joy in writing." What happened to take the joy away? Did you get burned-out? Too much pressure to produce? What can the rest of us learn from your experiences?

I personally put a lot of pressure on myself to write the best and most original book I can each time. That took me longer than the publishing schedule I had agreed to on a particular multi-book contract, one book a year. I had to learn this through experience; I couldn't have predicted it. Every writer is different, and many can write faster than I do, so I don't really have any advice for other writers about it. I would not accept a deadline schedule I was worried about meeting now, but some people have the ability to continue to produce in those circumstances.

I'm not sure any of us know until we try.

I did learn that the most important thing to me about writing is actually doing it. There's quite a bit of research that indicates creative work flows the best when it's detached from external motivations, and that's been my experience of it. But of course, deadlines are real and necessary in the publishing industry, so there's a bit of mental jiu-jitsu required.

If you could change one thing about your writing career, what would you change and why?

I wish I had been more proactive in suggesting to Berkley that they publish my later books, *Shadowheart* and *The Dream Hunter*, with an eye to a mainstream market. I think that would have broadened the readership and also alerted romance readers that the books, while definitely romances, were not entirely typical of the genre. Which is not to say I would be right! I'm no expert on marketing.

LISA GARDNER

Creating the Diabolical Villain (& Other Great Characters)

by Janice Gable Bashman

Lisa Gardner creates great characters that grab the reader's attention and don't let go. Gardner states that "before you get to the what, you must make your reader care about the who." It doesn't matter if it's the diabolical villain, the hero or the heroine, or the mother of a missing kid. And when it comes to creating the diabolical villain, she believes the villain should possess charisma and principles, must persevere when faced with adversity, and must have something important to fight for, all characteristics that make him (or her) a chilling and memorable villain. Gardner's ability to create great characters and make them come alive quickly draws the readers into the story and keeps them hanging on to every chapter, every scene, every word.

Twelve of Lisa Gardner's books have hit the *New York Times* Best Seller list, and she has over 20 million copies of her books in print, including her latest novel, *Live to Tell.* The fifth book in her Detective D.D. Warren series, *Love You More*, was released in March 2011. She is the 2010 Thriller award winner for best hardback novel for *The Neighbor.*

Why is it so important for an author to make readers "care about the who" before they "get to the what"?

There's an adage in writing that there are only seven stories in the world, and they've all been told. Basically, readers know the "what" of any novel—been there, done that. Thus, it's the characters in a book that really make it stand out. For example, Thomas Harris's *Silence of the Lambs.* On the one hand, another serial killer novel in an overcrowded suspense marketplace. On the other hand, Hannibal Lecter. Here's a character that broke all the molds. A serial killer with charm. A serial killer so brilliant, you couldn't help but respect him. Readers connected with that. Readers were mesmerized by that. Then Harris paired Hannibal with an equally compelling heroine, newbie FBI agent Clarice Starling. Suddenly, readers had something more than a "serial killer novel." Readers had a battle of wits between two worthy opponents, both of whom captured the imagination. And a little bit of success ensued.

How do you accomplish this quickly in your thrillers?

Beware TMI [too much information]. Crafting a complicated character is a matter of establishing layers, which most writers get. Where we screw up is crafting interesting characters with interesting backstories, then throwing it all in the reader's face in the first three pages. Dole out your characters. Seed your opening pages with basic information—what would you politely share at a cocktail party? Hint at more interesting things to come. Then walk away. Character revelations should happen naturally over the next four hundred pages and not be force-fed in chapter 1.

Also, craft characters that can evolve with the story. When I first wrote *The Neighbor*, the wife, Sandy Jones, was supposed to be evil. But then I fell in love with her daughter, Ree, and I couldn't give Ree a terrible mom. So, instead, Sandy's story became one of redemption (with a twist, I suppose), but it happened organically. I didn't have to change the character I started; Sandy simply made different choices when it came to key turning points in the novel. She learned from her past mistakes instead of repeating them. That's when characters feel natural to readers. They are people, doing the best they can, and some of their choices are better than others, but we relate to their desire to be a better parent, spouse, neighbor, even as danger looms just outside their front door.

When it comes to the diabolical villain, how do you get the reader to care about him or her?

Villains need a moral code and balancing influences. When I was writing *Alone*, I crafted one of my most vicious villains, Mr. Bosu, a man who'd once held a young girl captive in an underground pit as his personal plaything. But hating a villain is too easy. So I gave Mr. Bosu a puppy, which he genuinely loved and adored. Then, as the story unfolded, the reader learned of a man who's not just a stone-cold killer, but who's also socially awkward, a hulking misfit. The kind of guy who kidnapped a girl because he didn't know how to approach one any other way. The kind of person who's more comfortable with the unconditional love of a dog, because he doesn't understand his fellow man. He's still a psychopath, but now he's more relatable, and that makes him more interesting and the story more compelling.

Why must the villain possess charisma, principles, perseverance, and have something to fight for in order to make him a great villain?

Think of it this way: the hero of the story is only as good as the obstacles he/she overcomes. A stupid villain doesn't make for a great contest then. Plus, you want your reader to get into the story. The toughest novel I ever wrote was *Say Goodbye*, where in flashback scenes, you watch the villain, Dinchara (an anagram for arachnid), basically be "made" through the violence done to him. You see how he starts to identify with spiders, even consider them a sort of talisman to keep him safe, because once he was weak and hurt and victimized and he never wants to feel that way again. Now, those are goals we can all relate to. Unfortunately, as often happens in real life, the difference between the hero and the villain isn't the goal; it's how they approach it. Dinchara's solution to achieving his goal is to be the worst predator in town, the top of the homicidal food chain. And yet, part of him remembers the boy he used to be, the dreams he used to have, the person he could've been before life twisted him. He can't change, but he recognizes his own corruption, and that gives him poignancy, a self-awareness that is much more powerful than a dude who simply likes to collect spiders and murder women. Once, he might have been a better person. Now, he doesn't know how.

You stated you don't like to nail down characters but watch how they develop throughout the writing of the book. What happens when a "good" character turns "bad" or vice versa, and how do you deal with it?

One of my favorite books to write was *Alone*, where I crafted a character Catherine Gagnon, who was either the most tragic woman in Boston, or the most deadly. I didn't even know the answer. I played it out just like we see in the media, with one chapter portraying how heroic she was, and the next stating how evil she was. We see this dichotomy all the time in real life, and it fascinates me. A man goes postal at work and inevitably you get one neighbor talking about what a "normal" guy he was, while the next raves he was a total creep. One person, two very different impressions. As a writer, I think it's fun to create that kind of duality, a character that can go either way, then see how it plays out. In the case of *Alone*, I was waiting to see how much I'd like Catherine; then I'd make my decision whether she was good or evil or maybe both. You'll have to read the book to find out!

So, how do you create a realistic duality of character?

This is a matter of layering. Everyone has duality. There is the "external" person—the aspects of ourselves we carefully wrap up and present to the public. Perhaps even the person we see ourselves to be. Then there is the "internal" person—the person deep down, we truly are, the parts of ourselves we don't even want to always know. For some people, there is little disconnect between the two. But for complex people, this disconnect is larger, perhaps even shocking. For example, in *Love You More* I crafted a highly respected female police officer, Tessa Leoni, an admirable state trooper and mom. Yet,

by halfway through the book, she's broken out of prison, is on the run from her fellow officers, and is committed to a course of violence. Basically, her dire situation has stripped off her "external" character, revealing an internal core of coldhearted determination she didn't even know she had. And under these situations, she can do things she didn't know she could do, including lie, maim, and kill. It's the two halves of love: sometimes, you nurture the one you love, and sometimes, you kill for them. Duality.

What makes Sergeant Detective D.D. Warren such a fascinating character, and how do you keep her interesting for the reader?

Detective D.D. Warren is that great character who says all the things you'd never be bold enough to say, makes that intuitive leap you'd never be smart enough to make, and eats all the chocolate you'd feel too guilty to devour. She's the person we're too polite to be, but she carries a gun, so she can get away with it. Her natural "instinct for action" ensures that she'll never be boring and certainly keeps me on my toes. Let me say there's a scene toward the end of *Love You More* between her and a fellow officer I never saw coming! But I figure if I'm having fun writing D.D. Warren, chances are you'll have fun reading about her.

Character development over the course of a series can be tricky. Readers want the protagonist to remain the same protagonist they fell in love with, yet the protagonist must also grow and change to maintain the reader's interest. How do you accomplish this?

The joy of writing thrillers it that you can use plot to evolve your characters. I married off Detective D.D. Warren's love interest, the man she let go but could never get over. Any woman will tell you, when your first love ends up happily married and you still aren't, it messes with your head. Suddenly, naturally, my workaholic homicide detective can start having second thoughts about domestic bliss. And yet, she's still a workaholic. Meaning, I have even more conflict to play with. Meaning, it was really a lot of fun to totally ruin D.D.'s life in the first ten pages of *Love You More*. Life should change for series characters. How they adapt—or fight—those changes, makes for great writing and great reading!

You stated you are "driven by dark questions" and that you "want to know what is the nature of evil." How do you explore those themes through your characters and their actions?

Like a lot of people, I'm fascinated by the psychology of crime. Why do some men kill their wives instead of divorcing them (*The Neighbor*)? Why do some fathers think the best solution to life's hardship is to murder their entire families (*Live to Tell*)? What would drive a mother to harm her own child (*Love You More*)? And conversely, as a parent and a spouse, how far would you go to save your family (all of the above)? This classic battle between one person's instinct to destroy, and one person's desperate desire to save, makes for great characterization. It's war, where each setback breaks down the characters bit by bit, until they hit the black moment, where all seems lost. How the person responds to this moment, giving up or digging deep, is the stuff great fiction is made of. Let your characters battle it out, and evolution will naturally occur. And hopefully a few surprises as well. It's a great moment as a writer when your character does something you didn't expect, but in hindsight, makes perfect sense. Those are the days you can feel good about this job, versus all the other days, when I highly recommend brownies.

What advice can you give to other writers about building solid characters and creating the diabolical villain?

Think balance; think universal needs; think relatable goals. Then trust yourself to dole out the relevant information over time, instead of data dumping all at once. You'll know you've achieved magic when your characters are telling you what they need to do, and you're simply along for the ride. Be open to fresh techniques. I have a tendency to try to capture the "essence" of my character and let things evolve from there. One friend turns all of her characters into flavors of Ben & Jerry's. Hey, if it works for you, go for it!

JANICE GABLE BASHMAN is coauthor (with Jonathan Maberry) of *Wanted Undead or Alive* (Citadel Press, 2010), nominated for a 2010 Bram Stoker Award, and managing editor of the *Big Thrill* (International Thriller Writers' newsletter and e-zine). Her short fiction has been published in various anthologies, including the upcoming *Bigfoot Among Us* and *Rhonny Reapers Roadkill Cafe*. She is an active member of the International Thriller Writers, the Horror Writers Association, and Mystery Writers of America.

MICHAEL SWANWICK

Weaving Science Fiction into Present-Day Scenarios & Vice Versa

by Janice Gable Bashman

One of the most respected fantasy and science fiction writers of his generation, Michael Swanwick is a master at weaving science fiction into present-day scenarios and vice versa. He ensures his inventions are believable, his characters "behave in a way that's recognizably human," and the universes he creates serve a unique purpose to his stories.

Swanwick's work has won the Nebula, Hugo, Theodore Sturgeon, and World Fantasy Awards. He is the author of nine novels, including *The Dragons of Babel*, *Bones of the Earth*, *Jack Faust*, *Vacuum Flowers*, and *Stations of the Tide*, and six collections including, *The Dog Said Bow-Wow*, *The Periodic Table of Science Fiction*, and *The Best of Michael Swanwick*. He's published over a hundred short stories in magazines such as *Asimov's Science Fiction*, *Fantasy & Science Fiction*, and *Analog*; has been translated into a dozen languages; and appears frequently in best-of-the-year anthologies.

You mix the past with the present and the future to create worlds that seem familiar yet are so different than what readers have experienced. What kind of latitude does this give you as a writer, and how does it help you achieve your story objectives?

The freedom is limitless. I think of science fiction and fantasy as being not so much genres as a set of tools. With those tools, you can undo past actions, read minds, fly on griffin-back, sail worlds through the galaxies like so many galleons. I wrote a story called "Foresight," in which consciousness had been reversed in time, so that you'd know everything that was going to happen to you up until the instant you die . . . but not what you did a second ago, or who that person you woke up beside this morning might be. If you tried that in a non-genre story, the reader could only assume that either the protagonist was mad or else the author was just goofing around. But since it was science fiction, I was able to seriously explore questions of whether it's possible to have free will in a predetermined universe, and what love might actually mean under such conditions. That's an extraordinary privilege.

But it's also an extraordinary responsibility. When God gives you a set of burglar tools, you're not expected to use them to putter about making repairs around the house. It's your job to go out and ransack the secrets of the human soul.

When weaving science fiction into the historical past or real-life present day, what things must you keep in mind to make these scenarios seem plausible?

You have to be careful not to keep piling invention upon invention to the detriment of the story. There must be consequences and those consequences must be in keeping both with the universe as you understand it to be and with the universe as you've altered it for the story. The characters must behave in a way that's recognizably human. And you have to be sure that the payoff justifies the extraordinary liberties you've taken to get there. If you set a story on a planet-sized grasshopper and populate it with wizards and immortals and all it leads to is a quiet moment in which the protagonist reflects that life is good, then the reader is going to feel cheated. "I believed in all that stuff for this?" That same resolution could be achieved with two estranged friends meeting unexpectedly in a 7-Eleven.

You also have to do your homework. If you're writing about rocket travel to one of the moons of Jupiter, you must know how long that's going to take and how much shielding you need to protect yourself from the ambient radiation there. If your hero is a knight, you must know about weapons, armor, horses, tactics. But, having done your homework, you should keep your exposition to an absolute minimum. The reader trusts you the writer, and will continue to do so as long as that trust is not violated.

Here's an example. An elephant cannot get all four feet off the ground at the same time. When writing about elephants, you must know this. It's not necessary to have one of your characters say, "As you know, Fred, an elephant cannot . . ." But if you have your elephant effortlessly leap over a ravine to escape a pack of pursuing wolves, you'll lose every knowledgeable elephant-fancier in your audience. And there are always more of them than you'd expect.

Do you find this process easy or difficult, and why?

All writing is hard work, even bad writing. But good writing is exhilarating.

Well . . . it is after the fact, anyway.

In order to write fantastic literature you must believe in it literally. Which may sound disingenuous coming from a man who put Merlin in an oil refinery and a tiny civilization in a refrigerator freezer. But it's true. When I come up with a fantastic idea, I carry it around in my mind, studying its implications and playing with its possibilities until it finally makes sense to me. Then I begin writing. There are ideas that I've been carrying around for decades that still haven't won me over. But every so often, I take them out and look at them again. Someday they will.

What about when you weave elements from today's world or the past into a fantastic world? How do you make that work well?

In *The Dragons of Babel*, I wrote a scene in which the young hero, Will Le Fey, is crossing Faerie Minor by train to the Tower of Babel. Just as he sees his destination, somebody switches on a radio and he hears Duke Ellington's "Take the A Train" for the first time. That was a magical moment for me. I didn't know why an invented land full of elves and giants and night-gaunts might have such specific commonalities with our own universe. I only knew that it felt right, and so I ran with it. I wrote, "It sounded like something that might have been sung by the stars just before dawn on the very first morning of the world." Which is very much in the rhetorical tradition of twentieth-century high fantasy. C. S. Lewis might have written that line. But once it was applied to Duke Ellington, the falseness of the vague, misty, airy-fairy music those words would have previously evoked was revealed and, paradoxically, the original intent of such rhetoric was restored. "Take the A Train" really is that good. If you had to choose a sound track for Creation, you could hardly do better.

I constantly hold my inventions up against reality, to make sure they can stand the comparison. When I wrote *The Iron Dragon's Daughter*, I taped a picture of the Sex Pistols to my computer monitor, to remind myself that the fairy creatures had to be at least as threatening as they were.

You stated that you "hate to describe the same thing the same way twice . . . This is a shortcoming, not a virtue, and one [you're] trying to overcome." Why do you see this as a shortcoming?

Let's say you stand in a snowstorm at night and the flakes swirl about you like great white feathers, which, when you extend a hand, inexplicably melt on your skin. That's vivid and the reader sees it. If, in another work, you're describing the exact same sort of snow, why waste time trying to put it into radically different words? That's just novelty for the sake of novelty. The reader wants you to get on with business, move the plot along, break her flinty little heart, move him to tears.

Sitting all alone in a room with a keyboard, it's easy to lose sight of the fact that it's not just about arranging words beautifully. Half of our chore lies in knowing how those words will be received, and composing them accordingly.

You often use the fantastic world to critique the real world. How do you accomplish this in your writing?

Estrangement is a wonderfully underrated and uncannily effective tool. When you've replaced the extremely wealthy with elves and strike-breakers with ogres and orphan children with changelings, the cruelty and strangeness of the world shines out. We've grown so used to reality that it seems ordinary to us! G. K. Chesterton observed that every tree is a miracle, if only we could look at it clearly.

If you are as honest as possible and treat your invented world as seriously as you do the one you live in, what you say cannot help but be a critique of the real world. It's as simple (and as hard) as that.

You stated, "the real challenge, the Great Game, is to come up with genuinely original ideas. The writer who invents the time machine or the generation ship or cyberspace wins big." That writer is rare, so what does your statement mean for the rest of the writers out there?

Most of us will be forgotten. Worse, most of the best of us will be forgotten. That's a harsh and terrible truth, but it's just the way things are.

If you're hoping your work will outlast you (as opposed to the perfectly respectable ambition of simply making money and having fun while you're alive), you have to discover what you can do that nobody else can. It might be big ideas, like H. G. Wells, or a quirky sense of humor like P. G. Wodehouse. Finding out is a lifelong process of discovery which, ironically enough, can be enormous fun.

But if you only want to write better-written versions of stories that have already been told, you've failed before you've ever begun.

You've also stated that "simply writing well is not enough. You've got to come up with something new, some reason why somebody might want to read your work rather than using the same time to (say) re-read Proust." How do you accomplish this time and time again? What's your process like?

I write. I rewrite. I rerewrite. And I keep doing that until everything that seems false or cheap or easy in what I've written has been burned away. I've been published for almost thirty years, and I'd still be ashamed to let anybody see my first drafts. They're that bad. But I keep improving them and replacing lame ideas with more interesting ones until the only way to make them any better is to first become a better writer. Then I send them out for publication.

And then I try to become a better writer. A lot of this consists of reading as widely and appreciatively as possible. After a while, you begin to recognize which of the hundreds of fleeting ideas everybody has every day has the potential to become something interesting.

What advice can you give to other writers about weaving science fiction into present-day scenarios and vice versa?

The best and easiest advice I can give is to remember that research consists of more than simply going to the library for books. Going out and looking at things counts too. One of my stories began with a man dying in a parking lot. So I turned off my computer, went to a nearby lot, and lay down on the asphalt. From that vantage, I saw a rusted spark plug that had been driven over so many times it was almost flat, the Styrofoam sleeve of a soda bottle rocking in the breeze, thorns and weeds at the verge of the lot, a galaxy of broken glass . . . in just a couple of moments I had all the convincing detail I needed.

It's fun, too. I've gone to shopping malls in order to picture what space stations would look like, and rambled about old factories, imagining them being used to manufacture mechanical war-dragons. My neighborhood straddles the fall-line between the Piedmont and Tidewater regions of the East Coast, and there are iron-and-concrete steps down the cliff face separating them. I wrote a story in which three army brats in the Middle East go to the edge of the world and discover a stairway down; all three descend it, and only two return. Before I began writing, I spent an entire day climbing up and down all the stairs in my neighborhood. It was a wonderful experience, like spending a day in a children's book, and again it gave me more detail than I could use: There were small flowers growing in the cracks of the rock. Teenagers had cut the names of heavy-metal bands into the paint of the railings. Somebody had thrown a car door halfway down the cliff, and somebody else had thrown a shopping cart after it. I let the universe do my writing for me, copied down everything I saw in my notebook, and simply chose the best.

What other advice do you have for writers of science fiction and fantasy?

Don't try writing science fiction and fantasy unless you actually enjoy reading it yourself—and not just the classics, but the works that are being written today, particularly by new writers. Those people are your peers and your best way to find out what's currently happening in your chosen field. I also recommend subscribing to at least two short fiction magazines—but, again, only those you actually enjoy reading.

In short—and this is the oldest and best writing advice there is—write what you love best.

KEVIN J. ANDERSON

Crossing Techniques Over Genres

by Janice Gable Bashman

International best seller Kevin J. Anderson draws writing techniques from across genres to shape the reader's experiences and draw the reader into a story. He's used suspense/thriller/horror techniques in his science fiction novels, big science in his mysteries, and historical epic techniques (multiple story lines, huge canvases, etc.) in his fantasy and science fiction epics, techniques he says are "drawn directly from historical epics like *Pillars of the Earth* and *Shōgun*." He likes to read "widely outside of the genres in which [he] write[s], so [he] can add new and unexpected ingredients to keep the story fresh. Too many genre writers read only the types of novels that they write, and so it's like they're in a creative hamster-wheel."

Anderson is the author of more than one hundred novels, forty-eight of which have appeared on national or international best seller lists. He has over 20 million books in print in thirty languages. Anderson has coauthored with Brian Herbert both the science fiction original *Hellhole* and twelve books in Frank Herbert's classic Dune series, and he has also coauthored with Dean Koontz a major best seller, *Prodigal Son*. Anderson is also the author of the Star Wars Jedi Academy books, the highly popular epic science fiction series The Saga of Seven Suns, and the sailing-ships-and-sea-monsters fantasy trilogy Terra Incognita (along with two companion rock CDs). He has won or been nominated for numerous prestigious awards, including the Nebula Award, the Bram Stoker Award, the SFX Reader's Choice Award, the American Physics Society's Forum Award, and *New York Times* Notable Book. He and his wife, best-selling author Rebecca Moesta, have cowritten a middle-readers series, Star Challengers, in conjunction with the Challenger Centers for Space Science Education.

Why is it important for writers to reach beyond their genre and use techniques from other genres in their work?

A good story is a good story, but certain genres tend to use particular techniques (sometimes clichés). If a writer reads only fantasy, or only romance, or only mysteries, then his or her work may end up being self-referential, even derivative. It's like cooking with leftovers—try adding new ingredients instead; stretch your imagination. Larry McMurtry (westerns) and John D. MacDonald (mysteries) are two of the absolute best character writers I've ever read, and I would never have experienced them if I'd read only inside science fiction and fantasy. It's like a treasure hunt, finding shiny objects from far afield and bringing them back to add to your own pile of goodies.

How do you use techniques from other genres to draw your readers into your stories?

Science fiction and fantasy is my first love, but I also read horror, thrillers, mysteries, historicals, even mainstream that's highly recommended. When I write a big science fiction epic, I can follow the rules that my readers expect, but I also intensify it with a few extra colors from an expanded palette. I've also read widely in nonfiction history (I have a college minor in Russian history, as well as classes in Japanese history, history of medicine, history of science), and I can apply broad historical comparisons. Studying real historical wars, movements of peoples, grand stories of monarchs and religious leaders provides great inspiration for big fictional plots. My Terra Incognita fantasy series is based on the myth of Prester John from the Middle Ages, with a heavy dose of the history of the Crusades as well as the Age of Discovery, Prince Henry the Navigator, and the great sailing-ship explorers.

When authors write science fiction, most don't consider using suspense, thriller, or horror techniques, yet you feel it's key in helping to shape a reader's experience. Explain the techniques you use from these genres and how you use them in your science fiction.

My first novel, Resurrection, Inc., was a hard science-fiction, gothic-horror, murder mystery, nominated for the Bram Stoker Award. I was able to draw from horror and mystery tropes to tell an innovative science fiction story. I've learned a great deal from Dean Koontz in my development as a writer—he's a master at suspense scenes, especially chase scenes. I remember in particular one chase in his novel *Dragon Tears* that seems to go on forever (in a good way) . . . I had never seen an author who could milk so much suspense from a scene. I have used those techniques to "Koontz up" many of my own suspense scenes in a science fiction or fantasy story. Even if a novel doesn't fit in the thriller genre, there have to be suspenseful scenes—so why not learn how to do them by studying the masters of suspense?

How has using multiple story lines and huge canvases, techniques most often used in historical epics, helped you in creating your fantasy and science fiction epics?

I've written many novels with Frank Herbert's son Brian in the Dune universe, and Dune is one of the original sprawling SF epics. I've also written many Star Wars novels and my own seven-volume epic, The Saga of Seven Suns. I have read and studied James Clavell's big historical novels (especially *Shōgun*, *Tai-Pan*, and *Noble House*), amazed by how such a huge cast of characters can drive such a complex plot. In those books, the story itself is practically a main character. I also like *Gone with the Wind*, Ken Follett's *The Pillars of the Earth*, and the wonderful *Lonesome Dove* by Larry McMurtry. When plotting the seven volumes of Seven Suns, start to finish, I drew up a comparably huge canvas—the saga of a galactic war between several empires and alien races. I have characters from emperors and captains of industry, military leaders and regular soldiers, down to lowly street kids, romances, political clashes, personal feuds with grand implications, all told through a kaleidoscope of points of view, which lets me show the whole story from all angles. And that comes from studying historical epics.

What about the use of big science in writing mysteries? How do you use that to your advantage?

Doug Beason and I wrote three high-tech mysteries featuring the same FBI special agent, Craig Kreident. *Virtual Destruction* is set inside the nuclear-weapons design facility, the Lawrence Livermore National Laboratory (where both of us have worked); *FALLOUT* is set at the Nevada Nuclear Test Facility and Nellis Air Force Base (again, where we've both worked); and *Lethal Exposure* is set at the Fermilab particle accelerator, which I've toured and we both know people there. We crafted mysteries, but the unique aspect to those novels is the absolute veracity of the setting, exotic high-tech places that most readers never get to see. We added our big-science experience to make our mystery novels stand out.

You stated you "like to view [your] best novels as literary widescreen CinemaScope productions." Explain.

When writing a novel, I have an unlimited special-effects budget—I can create the wildest, most exotic landscapes, strange aliens, spectacular scenes that even James Cameron couldn't afford to film. I am limited only by the reader's imagination . . . so I bear that in mind when I'm writing, to make my scenes broad and epic. I have no constraints.

Unlike most writers, who use either a computer or a pen and paper to write, you do most of your writing with a handheld digital recorder while out hiking in the Colorado Rocky mountains. Why does this work so well for you, and what's next in the process once you have the raw material in audio format?

I love being surrounded by real-world scenery that's as spectacular as the worlds in my imagination. I have hiked over 300 miles on the Colorado Trail, climbed all 54 of the state's peaks over 14,000 feet; I have checked off trail lists in numerous hiking books. I love to walk out for miles and miles, allowing myself just to sink into the story, the characters, the setting, and I dictate the chapters. It's the same process as typing, actually—I think of the next sentence, but instead of moving my fingers to capture the words via the keyboard, I move my lips and speak the same words out loud. It allows for clean dialogue, and a straightforward flow of the story—just like an old storyteller around a campfire. When I get back home, I e-mail the digital files to my typist, who transcribes the chapters and returns a Word file to me. Then I edit the chapters five-ten times until it's clean and polished.

I have written many chapters set on the desert planet Dune while climbing the Great Sand Dunes or exploring the arid canyons around Moab, Utah, or out in Death Valley. I have written stories about adventurers on an icy planet while snowshoeing through a blizzard in the Sierra Nevada mountains. It helps me live the story in my imagination.

What advice can you give to other writers about crossing techniques over genres?

Don't get in a rut: read enough to keep up with your own field, but don't read that exclusively. Add something from a different shelf. You'll discover new ingredients to add to your fiction.

For instance, in my Star Wars novel *Darksaber*, I was supposed to write the story of the great love of Luke Skywalker's life. Now, I had read all the Star Wars novels, but I wanted a new approach, so I read the three greatest romances I could think of—*Gone with the Wind*, *The Thorn Birds*, and *Somewhere in Time*. Those books gave me the right perspective to add a deep romance story line to a science fiction adventure.

You bought a typewriter at age eight because you knew you wanted to be a writer and sold your first short story as a freshman in high school after receiving eighty rejection slips. Since then you've become one of the most prolific writers of your generation and you've also collected over eight hundred rejection slips along the way. Explain your approach to your writing career and how this has helped you achieve your great success.

I love to write, and I'm even a little obsessive about it (okay, maybe very obsessive), but I've never understood why a full-time writer should expect to put in any less time "at work" than anyone else with a challenging full-time job. A teacher is expected to be at school before the buses arrive, teach classes all day, stay until after the students have gone (sometimes coaching after-school sports), and grade papers, often into the night. A doctor sees patients all day long, usually eight hours or more. A lawyer spends the entire day (and more) writing briefs, researching cases, meeting with clients, filing papers, appearing in court. Why shouldn't a writer put in a full day of work?

I spend a lot of hours, and I'm quite productive, but I wouldn't say it's much different than, say, a corporate executive, the owner of a busy restaurant, or a hospital administrator. A successful author doesn't get to just write for an hour or two and then dink around the rest of the time.

This is my job. This is my career. This is how I make a living. And like anyone else who has a freelance occupation, if I don't do work, I don't get paid. If I don't deliver what I promised in a contract, I'm not likely to get work again. A professional writer treats a day at work like a day on the job—it's the difference between a career and a hobby.

Any last tidbits of wisdom about crossing techniques over genres?

It's an old creative writing adage, "Write about what you know about." So, the more a writer knows, and reads, the more you can add to your writing. Explore the landscape, see what you can learn from other genres, and add it to your skill set.

BECOME A SNATCHER OF TIME . . .

and maybe you'll hit 700 books, too

by James Scott Bell

Isaac Asimov wrote more than 700 books. He had no other life, of course (he admitted as much), but that's still quite a haul.

How'd he do it?

One thing he copped to was snatching time to peck away at his typewriter. If he had a free fifteen minutes before dinner, rather than use that in casual conversation or watching the tube, or doing anything else for that matter, he saw it as an opportunity to get some writing in.

He had several typewriters around his apartment, each with a different project sitting in it. He'd pick one and type for fifteen minutes.

I'd like to snatch time. I've written a number of chapters on an AlphaSmart Neo, a nifty little dedicated word processor that fires up in one second and runs forever on AA batteries. For pure input of words, it's a lot more convenient than a laptop. It weighs about a pound. I hardly know I'm carrying it.

Use pads and pencils if you like, but find ways to snatch the occasional chunk of writing time. It all adds up.

Just remember not to snatch so much time you become a social pariah, an ingrate, or a hermit. "One may achieve remarkable writerly success while flunking all the major criteria for success as a human being," says Michael Bishop. "Try not to do that."

Try this exercise:

Print out a blank calendar of your typical week. Divide it up by the hour as illustrated in the sample on the next page.

WEEKLY TIME SHEET

	SUN	MON	TUE	WED	THU	FRI	SAT
6:00							
7:00							
8:00							
9:00							
10:00							
11:00							
12:00							
1:00							
2:00							
3:00							
4:00							
5:00							
6:00							
7:00							
8:00							
9:00							
10:00							

	MON	TUE	WED	THU	FRI
6:00					
7:00					
8:00					
9:00					
10:00					
11:00					
12:00					
1:00					
2:00					
3:00					
4:00					
5:00					
6:00					
7:00					
8:00					
9:00					
10:00					

Now, go through and darken every cell where you have a daily obligation, as illustrated on the sample. (You can do separate sheets for your weekends.)

You should see that there are many more blank cells than dark ones.

These represent potential "snatch writing" times. Plan for a few of these, just as you would an appointment.

Then be ready to take advantage of others that arise.

You will be amazed the awards of this system.

> If, in the midst of difficulties, we are always ready to seize an advantage, we may extricate ourselves from misfortune.
>
> —Sun Tzu

JAMES SCOTT BELL is a best-selling novelist and popular writing teacher. His books for the Write Great Fiction series, *Plot & Structure* and *Revision & Self-Editing*, have become standards of the fiction craft. He lives in Los Angeles. His website is www.jamesscottbell.com.

Excerpted from *The Art of War for Writers* © 2009 by James Scott Bell. Used with the kind permission of Writer's Digest Books, an imprint of F+W Media Inc. Visit writersdigestshop.com or call (800)448-0915 to obtain a copy.

AGENTS

Building a Breakout Career

by Donald Maass

How many hundreds of hours did you spend writing your last novel? How many thousands of hours have you spent on your writing career? Work it out; the sum is probably quite high. The time invested by full-time professional novelists is staggering. It astonishes me that having invested so heavily most novelists then spend so little time choosing an agent.

Now hold on, you say, I spent ages searching for an agent. I sweated. I agonized. Don't tell me that I ducked that process!

Maybe not, but for many novelists, the agony is mostly that of waiting for replies. What about the rest of it? A true search involves not only finding names and checking reputations, but making a full comparison based on a broad range of factors. Not many authors go to such trouble. Most spend as much time choosing an agent as they would choosing a coat.

For new writers, that is understandable. They have already experienced a lot of rejection. They do not want more. Their dearest wish to find an agent who will say yes, and as soon as they do, the search is over. Who can blame them? New writers feel, with some justification, they are not choosing but being chosen.

You would think mid-career writers would be more savvy. They have been published. The pressure is off. What they should be after is a better agent. Amazingly, though, writers in this position often give themselves no more choice than beginners. Again, the reasons are not difficult to understand. If mid-career writers are thinking of a switch, it is probably because things are not going well. They feel neglected and in need. They are looking for a champion. Consequently, they may automatically narrow their choices to one: the agent who appears to have the most "clout." Again, who can blame them?

Well-established writers do not often search for a new agent. They have long since learned their needs and have usually settled down with the agent that best suits them. Anything wrong with that? Perhaps not, but the comfortable old marriage of author and agent can have its drawbacks. We imagine that well-established authors are successful, if not rich, but many are not. Careers can slide, advances can decline, reviews can become mixed, characters and stories can grow old-fashioned.

Given that, why do some well-established writers stay in place? Perhaps because they are comfortable doing business in an old-fashioned way. The old rules were easy to understand. The new world of publishing, on the other hand, is cold and corporate. To these writers, an old-fashioned agent may feel like an ally in a hostile world. They want to hold change at bay. That's a shame. Not only are such writers holding back their careers, they may also be depriving us of their best stories.

So, you ask, how do you actually give yourself a choice? Is it really possible? And what criteria should you use in evaluating agents.

CHECK THE MENU

The first point to grasp is that agents come in many varieties. I am not talking about the obvious difference that everyone knows about: big shops versus boutiques; New York versus elsewhere. I'm talking about factors like background, business style, editorial skill, accessibility, and comprehensiveness.

To illustrate these factors, I have created a roster of fictitious agents. These amalgams are inspired by my colleagues, but none is a roman-a-clef portrait of any particular agent.

The King Maker

Formerly an entertainment attorney, this guy is one of the biggest names in the business. His client roster reads like The New York Times best-seller list. Known for getting his clients astronomical advances, few realize that he does so by selling all rights. A sharp dresser, he can be seen most lunchtimes at the Grill Room at the Four Seasons, publishing's number-one power scene. However, his clients speak with him far less often than publishers do. It is said that he takes calls only from clients whose books are hot. Unknown to them, all but his top-grossing clients are actually handled by subordinates. The results are mixed. As for editorial help, his clients receive none; that, he feels, is the editor's job.

The Celebrity Agent

This agent earned her nickname not because of the many movie stars whose autobiographies she has sold, but because of the appearance of her picture so often in the trade magazines. Seen at all the right publishing parties, she is the industry's gossip queen. She has made some huge deals, too. No wonder: At her mega-agency, status depends solely on the dollar value of an agent's last deal. While she does represent some fiction writers, they tend to be young and trendy. Her biggest bestsellers have been authors of glitzy nonfiction books. Editorially, she is strictly hands off. If a novelist needs help, she will send him to an independent editor—whom he will pay separately.

The Rights Broker

Once the subsidiary rights director of a small publishers, this agent is addicted to deals. She is especially good at selling subsidiary rights. Nothing gets her blood going like an audiocassette offer. Her phone is glued to her ear, and her clients love that. Some, though, wish that she was a little more helpful editorially. Career planning? She does not indulge. Her motto: Who knows? One day you're hot, the next you're not.

The Discounter

A talented self-promoter, this agent's name is well known. His list of clients is long; his sales volume is enormous. Some publishers privately complain about his business practices, but most cannot seem to stop doing business with him. Why should they? His prices are the lowest in town. Most clients believe that the Discounter personally handles their work, but he, too, has a legion of helpers who handle the majority of tasks. He boasts of his clout, but what his clients really get is safety in numbers.

The Trend Guru

This agent's motto is *Give the editors what they want*. She gathers tips over lunch then quickly phones her clients, who churn out quickie proposals. Because she is ahead of every trend, she has obtained a few six-figure advances for writers. This usually happens only once; after that, her clients flounder and fade.

The Editor

Eighteen months ago, he was an in-house editor but was fired during an industry downtorn. Since then, he has loaded his list with newbies and mid-career novelists in his area of specialty: suspense. His clients get plenty of editorial advice. He knows his way around the business but doesn't much like to negotiate. What he most loves to do is to edit.

The Start-Up

A new agent, this former real estate broker knows how to hustle. Though her clients' average income is low, her website lists her motto as *deals, deals, deals*. Her proudest moment was selling *Two-Minute Weight Loss*. Because she more clients than she can handle, she is constantly frazzled and apologetic. She'll be out of the business in a couple of years when her mother takes ill and she moves back home.

The Part-Timer

This former English professor lives in the Midwest. Looking for a part-time career to keep himself busy in retirement, he decided to become an agent. His list is small, less than a dozen clients. Needless to say, he is easy to get on the phone. One of his clients is successful; the rest have not sold. He travels to New York twice a year to meet editors and see Broadway shows. The rest of the year he mails in manuscripts with a "selling" cover letter.

The Mail Drop

This former actor has been an agent for three decades. Indiscriminate in picking clients, he is famous among editors for the low quality of his submissions. Even more amazing, he fails to market 40 percent of the material his clients send him. (When asked, he tells them he is "testing the market.") Even so, there is one area in which his record is superior: the sale of movie rights. His name often appears in Paul Nathan's column "Rights" in *Publishers Weekly*. He travels annually to the Cannes Film Festival.

I could go on, but you get the picture. When you get an agent, what you are getting is a person with strong points and weak points. Those strengths and weaknesses will affect the course of your writing career, and I am not talking only about income. They will affect the books you write (or do not), how well you write them, and how smoothly (or not) your career goes.

THE BIG ISSUES

Specialists vs. Generalists

It is a rare author indeed whose ambitions are limited to one type of book. For the truly versatile author, a generalist can make sense. Here, though, you must be honest with yourself: Do you regularly write and sell in a variety of markets? If so, a well-rounded agent with wide contacts will be useful to you. And if not?

Most novelists write primarily one type of book—science fiction, say—and only sometimes make excursions into other areas. Is this is you, you may be better off finding an agent who has a strong track record in your primary field. That is obvious, you would think, but you would be surprised. When genre authors call me, many open the conversation asking, Do you also handle mainstream? I do. That reassures them—but not necessarily me.

It's not that I think authors shouldn't stretch themselves creatively. In fact, it's important. But a switch to a different type of novel means learning a whole new set of skills. Many genre authors haven't grasped them and, in fact, may be poorly read in the category they're seeking to enter. A horror writer who wants to write a political satire is in for a shock. It's an extremely difficult story form. Only a mere handful of novelists have mastered it.

So how do you know what a prospective agent handles? Once upon a time you had to ask—but today, directories, the agents' websites, and the deal reporting done on the industry website Publishers Marketplace will tell you what you want to know. How do your prospective agents handle career development? Do they recommend a focused approach or writing a variety of things to see what works? What about formats like hardcover or original paperback? Which is the best idea for you? Should you shoot for a big advance or something modest and safer? What sort of expectations do your prospective agents have, and what expectations do they suggest that you adopt?

It's a bother to ask such questions, I'll admit, but do ask and listen carefully to what you hear. The right agent for you may not necessarily be telling you what you want to hear, but what they say will make perfect sense.

Big Shops vs. Boutiques

You are a human being, not a number. Naturally, then, you expect a high level of personal service from your agent, something small independent agencies can surely provide. But don't large agencies have more clout?

And how about sub-rights? Large agencies have wide reach, true, but aren't independent agents better motivated to get all the small deals done? Actually, neither big nor small guarantees getting all the jobs done and done right. Big agencies may take better care of their big clients, but small agencies don't necessarily shine on sub-rights sales, either.

In mega-agencies—those bicoastal behemoths that handle not just literary properties, but film and TV talent and more—books can be a backwater. Such agencies do package film projects, and books can be an integral part of that, but if packaging is done only inter-agency, then you may wonder whose interests are being best served when a package is assembled. Big agencies can also be deal driven with agents' compensation set up to reward high revenues rather than smart career management.

Are boutique agencies then the better choice? Not automatically. Boutiques are only as good as the agents who run them. Their strengths may be your strengths; their weaknesses may be your weaknesses. Today, there are a number of midsized agencies with two, three, twelve, or more agents on staff. Many are strong players, but again it is not an agency that is representing you, but an individual agent. A good match is the goal, no matter what size of agency you're with.

New York vs. Out of Town

Once upon a time, it was felt that New York agents automatically had the edge over out-of-towners. That's not necessarily true anymore. There are agents with outstanding reputations working in Boston, Washington, Atlanta, Dallas, Minneapolis, and Portland, among other places. There are plenty in New York, too. The point is that geographic location is no longer the most important item on an agent's résumé.

Far more important is how a particular agent got started. When shopping, ask about your prospects' backgrounds. While most reputable agents belong to the AAR (Association of Authors' Representatives, Inc.), the business itself is unlicensed and unregulated by any government agencies, except in California. Anyone can call himself or herself a literary agent, so it pays to know exactly with whom you are dealing.

The majority of literary agents started as in-house editors. Some have legal backgrounds. Nowadays, it's not unusual for young college graduates seeking a career in book publishing to skip working for publishers and go straight into the agency realm. That's perhaps because there are more agencies of a size to hire assistants, and possibly also because word has gotten out that agency work is more fun than the cubicle farm. You can move up faster, too.

There are also more agencies around, period. As publishers' editorial staffs have downsized, the number of agencies has grown. Authors have seized on this; indeed, there are websites that will alert you to new agents on the scene. *Pounce!* Or maybe not. In addition to an agent's background, temperament, specialization, business style, and approach to career development, you might also want to weigh experience.

That, not ZIP code, is the more important issue. A start-up or junior agent may be easier to get, but there's something to be said for savvy. Only years on the inside can give you that.

Market-Timers vs. Fundamentalists

In the stock market, a *market-timer* is a trader who moves with the trends. Market-timers pay little attention to the merits of individual stocks, and lots of attention to momentum and other technical weather vanes. *Fundamentalists*, in contrast, ignore the ups and downs of the market, and stalwartly buy and sell stocks based on their merits, such as the company's outlook, earnings, or cash value.

Literary agents have similar characteristics. Some believe in meeting the market's needs. They closely track the movement of editors from publisher to publisher, monitor genre trends, glean tips over lunch, and race to capitalize on the latest trends. They can rack up impressive sales totals in hot sub-genres but can also be quick to drop clients when they stumble.

Fundamentalist literary agents are not concerned with jumping onto bandwagons. Their clients write the stories that they must write, and that is fine with the fundamentalists. If a client can't say what her next novel will be, so be it. Such agents can be especially well suited to literary fiction and may exhibit more loyalty than their fleet-footed peers. They also can be less proactive since the focus here is art not commerce.

How do you know which type you need? Here are some questions to ask yourself: *Do I want to know what's "hot"? Do I comb through deals on Publishers Marketplace to see what's selling? Do I tailor my fiction to take advantage of genre trends?* If your answer to any of these questions is yes, then you probably need an agent with a healthy dose of the market-timer in him.

Now ask yourself: *Do I ignore trends and write books that I have no choice but to write? Do I see my market more as readers than as editors? Am I mostly clueless about the industry, editors, and contracts?* If your answer to any of these questions is yes, then your agent should probably be a fundamentalist.

If you are agent shopping, you may need to be crafty in order to discover what sorts of agents to whom you are talking. Being salespeople, agents are very good at finding out what you want to hear and telling it to you. Here are some useful questions: *What is your position on writing for packagers? What is hot right now? How many books a year do you think I should write?*

The tone of the answers will tell you a lot about your prospects. Trust your instincts. It pays to make the right match.

THE INFLUENCE OF ANXIETY

If you are a new author, the first thing to realize as you search for the right agent is that you probably feel anxious. Oh, there may be moments when you feel that your work is at least as good as anything out there. Then there are the bad moments when you remember what you're heard about the odds, slush piles, and imperial agents. Maybe you have heard that it is easier to get a contract than to get an agent. Or that without an agent no decent publisher will read your work.

The truth is that you have a choice of agents. You may not feel like that, but you do. Understanding it, believing it, is your first challenge. To help you, here are three common feelings that block the empowerment I am talking about:

OKAY, JUST ONE MORE REWRITE AND IT WILL BE PERFECT. A reluctance to let go is a common experience. The problem is that most novels probably *could* use another rewrite. Where does it end? Authors with manuscripts on submission are forever sending me replacement pages, chapters, and even whole new manuscripts with panicky notes like, *DISREGARD THE EARLIER VERSION!* How different are the rewritten pages? Usually not much. After a while, the process seems a bit silly.

The answer is to cultivate objectivity about your writing, even though at the end of a year or two or five of writing, that may be the last thing you feel. But try. Step back. Put the manuscript aside for a while. Read it again with a fresh eye. When you're sure you feel good about it, the novel is done. Time to submit. Let it go. Last-minute changes, especially light polishing, will not improve your chances of success. If you are tempted to send a new version, then you weren't really done to begin with.

OH, WHAT DOES IT MATTER? NO ONE'S GOING TO WANT IT ANYWAY. You are no fool. You know the score. If you are extremely lucky, you might land a decent agent, but the odds are against it, right? If this describes you, you are also having a common experience.

The problem with this defense mechanism is that it leads authors to feel that the process is out of their hands. Why discriminate? Why push? Why feel anything but shock and job when some randomly chosen agent finally says yes. No reason. And so begins many a woeful publishing tales.

I DON'T KNOW WHERE TO BEGIN. Help! There's too much information! All these lists! How do I know which agency would be best?

There's no panic worse than that of beginning a scary task. One way to cope is to put if off. Another is to rush. Obviously, neither strategy works. Similarly, throwing up your hands at the array of choices among potential agents is not going to help. It's like throwing up your hands because there are too many car models from which to choose.

You have to start somewhere. Where? Deciding on your criteria is probably a good place to begin. What do you want in an agent besides acceptance and anxiety relief? Reread the sections above. In those I discuss six large issues that distinguish agencies from each other. Where do you stand on those issues?

WHEN TO LOOK

When should you approach agents? After you've sold a few stories? When you've finished your first novel? When you've got a publisher interested in it, perhaps even an offer on the table?

Working backward through these options, it should be obvious that approaching agents with an offer in hand is going to produce powerful results. Agents are drawn to commissions like bees to honey. Expect to hear some highly flattering buzz. But how deep is that enthusiasm? To find out, you will have to listen hard and filter much. It is wise to begin this scenario with a strong idea of what you want in an agent.

Most authors do not wait so long. Of the eight thousand queries I receive each year, most come from writers who have finished a novel. But must you necessarily have completed a manuscript to make contact?

The truth is that it is difficult to the point of impossible to sell a first novel that is not finished. These days, it can even be difficult to move an established author from one house to another with only a partial manuscript to show. Hence, for me there is little point in reading an unfinished manuscript by a first-time novelist. I can't sell it until it's done.

Short story sales are useful credits to have. Sales to national magazines never fail to catch my eye. In and of themselves, such credits don't guarantee a brilliant novel. Nor does their absence necessarily mean anything bad. But they do suggest that an author is serious about her craft. Sell some short stories if you can. It's not critical, but it helps.

Last word: The time not to contact an agent is before you have written any fiction at all. You're not going to get very far.

WHERE TO LOOK

Some authors actually enjoy being seduced by the aura of power and secrecy that surrounds agents. They don't want to know how agents do their work. They are romantics. They would rather believe in magic. Good for them, but you can do better.

As an author, you are a consumer. The service you will be buying is quite expensive. You have a right to information, but if you want it, you may have to look beyond source books. One good way to start is to join a writers' organization. Its officers and members may be helpful. So may its national and regional newsletter. Agents' names, clients, and recent sales often turn up in their pages. So do interviews with agents.

To develop a more refined feel for agents' styles and effectiveness, talk to their clients. Here, both writers' organizations and writers' conferences can be helpful. Head for the bar. That's where writers most often hang out, and where you will hear the most candid talk about agents. Be discerning, though; frank talk is one thing, gossip is another.

Network around online. Your goal is to learn not merely who handles whom, or which agents are looking for what. You need a sense of agents as people. Today, a number of agents blog. Agents websites also can be informative. There also are sites that track agents, their interests, and even their response times to queries; all useful, but mostly as starting points.

Recognize that you will probably work with your agent for a long time. You owe it to yourself to choose one you like and enjoy, whose business style fits with yours, who's experienced with your type of fiction, and who lets you feel creatively free.

WHAT TO ASK

The most urgent question is not, *How much do you charge?* But *What you do you think of my novel?* The first thing you want from the answer is enthusiasm. For agents, handling new novelists often means taking a loss. It is a rough road. It can take years to swing that first sale. Even then, problems may abound and commissions may be meager. What sustains an agent through that? I will tell you: passion.

By passion, I mean an irrational love of your writing and an unshakeable faith in your future. Without that, you are sunk. I've lost count of how many calls I've gotten from authors who've been dropped by their agents shortly after an option book was dropped, sometimes before. It makes me mad. What kind of commitment is that? Don't let that happen to you.

The second thing you need from the answer is a sense of your prospective agent's editorial vocabulary and approach. What is good editorial advice? That depends. If you are a facile, outline-handy, trend-watching sort of author, then you probably want an agent to advise you how to tailor your fiction to what's selling. If you are a trend-ignoring type of author, then you probably want an agent who nurtures your own unique voice. Above all, you want an agent who gets your type of fiction.

That leads to the second most important question: *How much of my type of writing do you handle?* A lot? Exactly how would this agent describe your work? Which leads to another crucial question: *What plans do you have for marketing my work?*

The answer should be detailed and logical. Today, there are many more strategies to choose from than in years past. Once, the best possible hardcover deal was always the top objective; not so anymore. Hard and soft deals with large commercial houses are good for many novels, but others may be best served by original paperback publication. What about yours and why?

Next vital question: *Are you a member of the AAR (Association of Authors' Representatives, Inc.)?* While membership does not guarantee you will get brilliant representation, it does mean that your prospect has met minimum performance standards and abides by a Canon of Ethics that addresses the handling of funds, the availability of information, confidentiality, expenses, conflicts of interest, reading fees, and other issues of real importance to authors.

More questions to ask: *How many people work at your company? How many are agents? Who will actually handle my work? How are overseas sales and movie/TV sales accomplished? Will you consult with me before closing every deal? Will you ever sign agreements on my behalf? When you receive money, how quickly will you turn around my share? What happens if you die or are incapacitated? How will I receive moneys due to me?*

Aren't you glad you are asking these questions now?

THE AGENCY AGREEMENT

I used to work with my clients on a handshake basis. I liked the old-fashioned and trusting feel of that. Times change, though, and today like most agents, I ask clients to sign an agency agreement. This contract cements the author-agent relationship and governs its terms. Most such agreements are simple and straightforward, but there are issues to consider.

Commission rates should of course be in writing. Although agents do compete, 15 percent on domestic sales and 20 percent overseas is the almost universal standard. What works are covered by the agreement—everything you write, or only part of your output? If you want to exclude some of your writing (say, your regular gig as a columnist for a golf magazine), then ask. Also, how long does the agreement last? Some agreements are renewable and some are open-ended. The renewable plan is a problem only when you may want to get out early.

Thus, a significant issue is the procedure for ending the relationship. How much notice is needed? What happens to control of unsold sub-rights? (A great many agency agreements do not cover that.) In most cases, contracts that were negotiated by an agent will continue to be administered by that agent; he will collect royalties and commissions until the contract terminates. Don't stress too much about that. If you're moving on, that probably wasn't the main irritant.

WORKING WITH YOUR AGENT

If you have chosen well, you are probably paired with an agent whose experience, temperament, and business style are well suited to your needs. But even author-agent relationships have a honeymoon; after that comes the bumpy breaking-in period.

The important thing here is to accurately identify what you need and communicate it clearly to your agent. That is not always easy. It can be tough to separate, say, a need for reporting on submissions from feelings of anxiety if a novel is not selling. Here, you must know yourself and your agent. Be patient.

As you go forward, you will probably come to rely more and more on your agent for advice and counsel. Some of this is mere "hand-holding" while waiting for offers, contracts, and checks. However, some of the comments you hear may change the way you write. Some may even change the entire direction of your career.

Given clear goals, hard work, good communication, and a bit of luck, the author-agent relationship is usually happy and mutually profitable. Sometimes, though, it does not work out so well. Oddly enough, the reason may not be so much in your relationship with your agent as in your relationship to your writing. Marriages can go stale. So can friendships. So can your engagement with your own fiction if you do not strive to keep it fresh.

When that happens, you will see it in your sales. You will feel it in a level of frustration with your publisher. You will want to fix what's wrong—and, believe me, you will want to believe that the problem is your agent. Is that true? Sometimes. More often, though, the root problem is in your writing. How do I know? I read.

MOVING ON

How do you know when it is time to leave your agent? That's a tough one. Having taken over many authors from other agencies, I can tell you that the level of problems authors experience varies. Some problems are simmering, others are so sudden and big that they boggle the mind, but generally the issues are long term.

Breakdown of communication is one warning sign. Do your calls go unreturned? Is there no follow-through on routine requests? If so, examine the situation. Are you being unreasonable? Are there differences or disagreements causing bad feelings? Lack of progress is another worry, but again, it is wise to study the situation before making any moves. Say that your advances have hit a plateau—is this your agent's fault or yours? Maybe it's your writing that has hit a plateau.

Certainly there are problems for which only your agent is to blame: blown deals, lost manuscripts, misunderstandings with your publishers. That kind of thing is just bad business. Once you do decide to move on, try to maintain a businesslike demeanor. You will thank yourself later. Dignity is a precious possession.

When you hook up with your new agent, you begin a new honeymoon . . . and soon thereafter the bumpy part. But if you have taken my advice, you will have learned a lot about yourself during the divorce. That self-knowledge should serve you well as you move forward.

DONALD MAASS heads the Donald Maass Literary Agency in New York City, which represents more than 150 novelists and sells more than 150 novels every year to publishers in America and overseas. He is a past president of the Association of Authors Representatives, Inc., and is the author of several books of interest to fiction writers: *The Career Novelist* (now available as a free download from his agency's website), *Writing the Breakout Novel, and The Fire in Fiction.* HIs website is www.maassagency.com.

SELF-PUBLISHING STRATEGIES

Publishing Through a POD Print Service Provider

by April L. Hamilton

There are differences among POD (Print-on-Demand) print service providers, but the overall process of working with them is essentially the same. I'll begin by presenting some introductory material about POD service providers, followed by answering some commonly asked questions about working with them. Next, I'll go through the process of setting up a book with a service provider in more detail, listing the specific pieces of information you'll be asked to provide, and highlighting areas to which you'll want to pay special attention. Finally, I'll talk about what to do after the book is released for sale.

ADVANTAGES OF POD

POD technologies allow a print service provider to keep a digital copy of a work on file, and then create physical copies of that work only as needed to fill individual orders. This is a departure from the old business model of publishing, in which the provider would try to estimate how many copies of a given title would sell, pay tens to hundreds of thousands of dollars to have that many copies manufactured in advance of the title going on sale, then fulfill orders for the title from a large warehoused stockpile of copies. For most titles, inevitably a certain amount of the stockpile would not sell and the provider would have to dispose of them. That waste is one reason traditional publishers have such high overhead costs.

From the indie author's perspective, the advantage of POD is that you don't have to order a minimum print run up front, you don't have to store a bunch of books in your home or garage, and you don't have to sell books by hand if you don't want to. Customers can order your book from various on- and off-line booksellers; the order goes directly to your service provider; the book is printed, bound, and shipped to the purchaser; and your only involvement is in collecting your royalty payment from the sale.

QUESTIONS AND ANSWERS ABOUT POD PRINT SERVICE PROVIDERS

Do I need special tools to work with a POD print service provider?

You need a word processing program to create your manuscript, a graphics editing program to create your cover art (unless your provider offers an online book cover design tool), and a program that can convert both your completed manuscript and your cover art (if applicable) into PDF files.

In general, how does it work?

POD providers generally use a heavily automated staging system to manage your book production project. You begin by setting up an account and creating a piece that may be called a "project," "book," "title," or "file" on the provider's website. After entering and saving details about your book, such as title, category (meaning book type or genre), author name(s), keywords, description, you upload your manuscript and cover art (if applicable), usually in PDF format.

File type (DOC, PDF, TXT, to name a few) and size requirements vary among the different providers, and I can't address the specific requirements of every provider here. . . . Be sure to check the file type and file size requirements of your chosen provider before you submit, as they are subject to change at any time.

Some service providers offer easy-to-use book cover design tools on their sites. If you don't already have a cover prepared, it's definitely worthwhile to experiment with these tools. You'll be surprised at the level of quality you can achieve with them, and they allow for a great deal of customization so there's no worry that your cover will be cookie-cutter.

Following file uploads, your provider's staffers review them to ensure the files meet with their specifications for your chosen project type. If the files are acceptable, you receive an e-mail confirmation inviting you to order a proof copy of the book. If not, you receive an e-mail detailing any problems with the files, inviting you to make corrections and upload new PDF files as needed.

After you've received your proof copy, review it to ensure it meets with your approval prior to formal release of the book for sale on your provider's site and on any sales channels, such as Amazon.com or Barnesandnoble.com, you've selected. If you find any problems, you can make corrections to your files, generate new PDFs, reupload the files, wait for the confirmation e-mail, and order a new corrected proof.

When you've received a proof which you're satisfied, approve the proof for release. If you've specified a desire to offer the book for sale when you first set up the project, the book will show for sale on your provider's site shortly. Depending on your provider, your book may be offered on the provider's site via a personalized product page to which you must link from your own website or blog directly, or via a searchable site catalog which points to such a page on the site. It can take up to six weeks for your book to be listed through various other sales channels, though listings on Amazon's U.S. site generally show up within three weeks.

With a true POD print service provider (as opposed to a vanity or subsidy publisher) there is no minimum number of author copies you must buy, and in fact, apart from the proof(s), you don't have to buy any copies at all.

What does it cost?

Some providers charge nothing to open an account or set up a basic project, which may even include free ISBN and EAN-13 number assignment, if you haven't already purchased your own. With such a provider's basic project package, the first time you're asked to pay anything is when you order a proof copy of your book. Others will charge an up-front fee for project setup or offer various publishing packages for a fee. In my experience, there are enough quality service providers out there who don't require setup fees that it shouldn't be necessary for you to shoulder this cost. Publishing packages are also to be avoided, since they typically include bundled services you either don't need or can get at a better price elsewhere.

> It's not usually worth paying the provider's fee for U.S. copyright/Library of Congress registration, as this is a service you can provide for yourself very easily and at minimal expense.

Some providers allow you to upgrade your book project for a flat fee at the time of project setup and possibly an additional annual fee per year. Depending on the provider, paying for an upgraded project can get you any or all of the following: ISBN/EAN assignment, lower per-page and per-copy production costs, use of enhanced cover design tools, an enhanced or featured listing in the provider's online bookstore, listings with online booksellers like Amazon and Barnes and Noble, expanded distribution options (for instance, listings in book wholesaler catalogs used by libraries and booksellers within the United States or globally), conversion of your manuscript to one or more e-book formats to be offered for sale, U.S. copyright/Library of Congress registration, purchase of author copies at a greater discount than standard. See your provider's website for more information about pricing and available upgrades.

It can be be worthwhile to upgrade for the sake of lower per-copy and per-page production costs, since reducing those expense will enable you to reduce the retail price of your book while still earning a healthy royalty.

Online bookseller listings and expanded distribution options are also worth paying extra for, as they may be your only means of getting your book listed with booksellers other than the provider's own online bookstore. Use of enhanced cover design tools may be worth the extra cost, but it's up to you to decide whether the price tag is reasonable.

If you're paying a fee in exchange for ISBN/EAN assignment, you'll want to be sure the ISBN/EAN will be registered in your name (or that of any imprint you've formed), not the name of the service provider. Remember that only the registered owner of the ISBN/EAN can list the associated book with wholesaler catalogs, so if you're paying for the ISBN/EAN, you want to be sure you'll benefit from all it has to offer. Verify ISBN/EAN ownership with your provider, and if it turns out you will not be the registered owner of the ISBN, you're better off purchasing your own directly from Bowker (www.bowker.com).

It's not usually worth paying the provider's fee for U.S. copyright/Library of Congress registration, as this is a service you can provide for yourself very easily and at minimal expense. To register your own U.S. copyright online for a nominal fee, go to www.copyright.gov. Works registered with the U.S. Copyright office are automatically listed in the U.S. Library of Congress's register. Paying extra for e-book conversion is also a mistake since it's free to publish your book in various e-book formats through numerous e-book service providers.

How long does it take?

It takes about fifteen minutes to set up an account with a service provider. Assuming your manuscript is complete and properly formatted . . . it takes another five to ten minutes to enter the specific details of your project and upload the manuscript. Assuming your cover art is complete and properly formatted, it takes only a few minutes to upload that file.

The matter of how long it takes to design your own book cover using on-site design tools offered by your provider is really up to you. If you already have your design and text for the front and back cover sketched out, the provider's design tools allow you to easily duplicate your sketch and paste in your prepared text, it need not take longer than twenty minutes or so. On the other hand, if you begin the process without a set design in mind, or if you're a hopeless tinkerer of perfectionist, it may take you many hours over a span of days to prepare your cover.

Delays in the process which are beyond your control include waiting for your service provider to confirm receipt and acceptance of your files, and then waiting for receipt of your snail-mailed proof copy. If you decide to make changes after viewing the proof, release of your book will be delayed further since you'll have to upload revised files, wait for your provider's acceptance, order another proof and wait for its arrival.

What rights do I give up with a POD print service provider?

None. A POD print service provider is essentially manufacturing a book on your behalf; you (or the imprint you've formed) will be the publisher of record.

Does my book need to have a preassigned ISBN?

Not necessarily. As stated above, some services will provide an ISBN/EAN as part of your project setup and others will offer to see you an ISBN/EAN.

Also note, there is no legal or regulatory requirement that a book produced in the United States must have an ISBN/EAN. An ISBN/EAN is required by some service providers (such as LSI) and most booksellers, and is also needed for registration with wholesale book catalogs. But if your provider doesn't require one and you only intend to sell your book by hand or give copies as gifts, an ISBN/EAN is optional.

What will my author royalty be on sales of my book?

Your net royalty per copy sold depends on three factors: your per-copy production cost, whether the book was sold by hand or sold through a retail outlet, and the retail price at which the book was sold. The general formula for calculating your royalty is this:

Author Royalty = Retail Price–Per-Copy
Production Cost–Bookseller Percentage (if any)

Per-copy production costs are the sum of a per-copy flat fee (for cover printing and binding) plus a per-page printing fee. Note that for purposes of these calculations, "per page" means "per page side." In other words, the front side of a page counts as one page, and the back side of a page counts as a second page. Any project setup fees, site membership fees, or optional upgrade fees are all part of your up-front costs, which do not impact royalty calculations. Per-copy production cost calculations are as follows:

Per-Copy fee + Per-Page Fee = Production
Cost For One Copy of Your Book

If you're going to buy some author copies, here's how much you'll pay for them:

Total Production Cost + Shipping Fee =
Cost Per Author Copy Purchased

If you're hand selling your books, the additional costs you must take into account are the cost to have copies shipped from the service provider to you, the cost of any packaging materials you must use to ship books to your buyers, and the postage expense for shipping the books to buyers. You must also pay sales tax on every copy sold, but so long as you charge the customers the correct rate for your geographic region at the time of sale, that expense is covered.

Author Copy Cost + Packaging Materials

Cost + Postage = CostPerCopyHandSold

If your books are sold through a retail outlet (such as Amazon, Barnes and Noble, Borders, Costco, and Target), the seller will generally keep a 40 percent cut of the retail price on every sale.

Refer to your service provider's website for its per-copy and per-page production costs.

When looking over pricing information on your provider's site, note that a color book is a book that has a full-color cover and includes color on its interior pages. A black-and-white book has a full-color cover and interior pages that are black and white.

How hard is it, really?

The more and better your computer skills are, the easier it is to do a professional job. Even with only intermediate word processor skills and beginner skills in your graphics or photo editing program (to create cover art), you will be able to manage without much difficulty.

Can you answer my ten million other questions?

No, but your service provider can. Check your provider's help file, FAQ, terms of use, user guides, tutorials, and support, and community forums to get more information, and if you don't find what you need in any of those resources, use the site's contact form or e-mail address to pose your question.

PREPARING YOUR MANUSCRIPT

This chapter assumes you have a complete, final copy of your manuscript formatted according to the instruction in the Formatting for POD chapter. Open your manuscript and Save As to create a duplicate copy for your service provider.

Save in PDF Format

Some service providers require your manuscript to be uploaded in PDF format, while it's optional for others. I strongly recommend you submit in PDF format because a PDF file is a WYSIWIG (What You See Is What You Get) version of your eventual book. If you submit a PDF file, no further file conversion is required on the part of the service provider, and the pages of your eventual book will look exactly the same as the fie you submitted. If you submit a word processor, InDesign, or other type of file, the provider's file conversion process will likely make some formatting changes to your manuscript.

Use your PDF-maker program or utility to save a PDF version of your manuscript. . . . Open the PDF version and look through it to ensure it's complete and all your desired formatting has been preserved.

Verify that the page numbers shown in the table of contents match up with the page numbers printed on the corresponding pages of the PDF file. Bear in mind that the document page numbers reflect the page count, but will not match the page numbers printed on your book's pages because none of the pages in Section I of your manuscript are numbered.

If you are satisfied with the PDF version, make a note of the document page count (which includes unnumbered front and back matter pages), save the file and close it. If not, delete the PDF version, make any desired changes in the word processing version of the file, update the Table of Contents if needed, save as a PDF, and again make note of the document page count.

SET UP YOUR BOOK

Now that you've got your manuscript ready, you need to register for an account with your provider and enter all the details about yourself and your project.

First, you'll be asked to provide your e-mail address, and first and last name. Enter your legal name here, not a pen name or imprint name.

You may be asked to create a password, or the provider may assign one to you. In that case, you should be able to change your password to whatever you'd like after your account is set up.

When your registration is complete, log in to your provider's site to view your user "control panel" or "dashboard." Here is where you will set up your book project and enter all the details about it.

Complete Your Profile

Account information you'll be asked to provide includes your (legal) name, e-mail address, password, and possibly an e-mail advertising preferences check box (for example, Are you willing to receive a monthly e-mail newsletter from your provider?).

If your provider has an online bookstore in which your book may be listed, or you've signed up for a bookseller distribution plan through your provider, you'll also be asked to provide a tax I.D. number for purposes of royalty payments and tax reporting. In the United States, if you've set up your publishing business as a sole proprietor, your tax I.D. number is either your social security number or the tax identification number (ITIN) assigned to you as a resident alien. Otherwise, it's the tax identification number assigned to your publishing business entity (a corporation or partnership).

Additionally, you will be required to state your royalty payment preferences. Most providers allow you to choose between electronic funds transferred directly into your bank account or payment via snail-mailed checks. There's usually a handling fee for payments made by check. Note that there may be a minimum threshold amount you must earn before any royalty payment will be made ($25 or more per quarter, for example).

You may also be asked to provide a default shipping address for receipt of author copy orders, and billing information for payment on author copy orders.

Create Your Project/File/Title

After you're finished setting up your account and completing all your profile information, it's time to set up your project. Most of the fields on the setup form are self-explanatory, and those that aren't generally have an About or ? link you can click to get more information. However, there are certain fields that require special attention. Here are the fields you are likely to encounter and information on how to complete each one.

TITLE—enter the title of your book. Remember that your book may come to be published in multiple editions (trade paperback, Kindle book, audiobook) and you must be certain the title you enter here is consistent across all editions so that retailers will recognize them as different editions of the same book. In my case, I published Kindle editions prior to trade paperback editions, so I was careful to copy my titles exactly as I'd entered them for the Kindle editions. This may seem like a no-brainer, but in my case I'd used the subtitle, "A Novel by April L. Hamilton" for both of my Kindle editions and had to make sure I used the same subtitle for the trade paperbacks.

SUBTITLE—enter the subtitle of your book, if applicable. If your book doesn't have a subtitle, leave this field blank. Do not make up a subtitle just for the form.

VOLUME NUMBER—if your book is part of a series (such as is often the case in sets of reference books), enter your book's volume number in the series. Again, if your book has no volume number, leave this field blank.

DESCRIPTION—enter the brief description you've prepared previously. This description will be used in catalog and bookseller listings (if applicable).

ISBN/EAN—some providers allow you to leave this field blank, some require you to enter an ISBN/EAN you've previously purchased, some allow you the option to purchase an ISBN/EAN in this part of the form, and some allow you to opt for a free ISBN/EAN to be assigned by the provider here.

CATEGORY OR TYPE—general category for your book (fiction, nonfiction, reference).

GENRE—you'll usually be allowed to select one or more genres from a pick list based on the category or type you've specified for your book.

PREVIOUSLY PUBLISHED DATE—if this is a new, revised, or updated edition of a previously published book, whether that means self-published or mainstream published, enter the year the previous edition was published.

PUBLISHED IN/COUNTRY OF PUBLICATION—list the country in which you are publishing the book. This will usually be the country in which you reside, but if you've set up an offshore company to run your imprint, you should list that country.

LANGUAGE—the language in which the book is written.

KEYWORDS—search terms and search phrases you'd like to have included as part of your book's catalog and bookseller listings, to make it easier for buyers to find your book. For example, this book's keywords might include manuscript formatting, manuscript editing, publishing, and indie author.

AUTHOR(S)/CONTRIBUTOR(S)—enter the names of all authors who contributed to the book; here is where you will list pen name(s), where applicable, instead of legal names. Author name(s) must be consistent not only across all editions of a given book, but across all books you want to be associated with the author name(s) you're using. Some authors use a single pen name for all of their works, some use different pen names for different types of works, and still others use some version of their real name.

AUTHOR BRIEF BIOGRAPHY—enter the brief author biography you've prepared previously, for use on bookseller websites and possibly in catalog listings.

AUTHOR WEBSITE URL—enter the Web address of your author website or blog, again, for use on bookseller websites and possibly in catalog listings. If you don't have a website or blog, leave this field blank.

NUMBER OF PAGES—page count, including unnumbered front and back matter, and taking into account both the front and reverse of each physical page. Some providers require an even number while others will include a blank page at the end of any odd-numbered manuscript to even the page count.

INTERIOR TYPE—choose black and white or color.

TRIM SIZE—select the trim size for the dimensions of your book (for example, 6" x 9" [metrics] for a trade paperback).

BINDING—select your desired binding type. If your provider offers many options, you may have to do an Internet search on each one to decide which you'd like. The most common options are *perfect bound* for trade paperbacks with a glued binding, and *saddle stitched* for hardcover books with a stitched binding. Note that there may be per-copy cost differences for different binding types.

PAPER COLOR/TYPE—select your desired paper color and type. Colors are typically limited to variations of white and cream/buff. Type specifies a weight, or thickness, of paper, and may also specify a type of page edging. *Deckled edging*, for example, is an irregular type of edge that gives each page the appearance of having been hand torn from a larger sheet. Note that there may be per-page cost differences for different paper colors and types.

OPTIONAL UPGRADES SELECTED—here is where you specify any upgrades you've selected, such as expanded distribution, setup grade fee in exchange for lower per-copy and per-page production costs, e-book conversion service, and so on.

SALES CHANNEL CHOICES—if your provider has on online bookstore, here's where you can specify whether you'd like to have your book listed in that store and whether you're opting for paid upgrades to your listing in that store.

Your provider may also allow you to password-protect your book's page in its online store, so that your book will not be available for sale to the general public but you can still allow anyone to whom you've given the password to buy your book from your provider's online store.

Yet another option you may find here is the ability to create discount codes for use in provider's online store. You may be allowed to specify a discount percent or specific dollar amount, as well as an expiration date for the discount code. Once you've created a discount code, you can post it on your website/blog, share it on Twitter or Facebook, or distribute it through other means as a promotional tool to help drive more book buyers to your listing. If this option is available, see your provider's on-site help for more information about how to set it up.

LIST PRICE—here is where you set your book's retail price.

LOCKED FIELDS—be on the lookout for any fields marked, "cannot be changed after you submit the book for publication," or something similar. Recall after you've uploaded your content and cover art (if applicable) you will receive a notification from your provider indicating whether your files meet their specifications; if your files are approved, your next step is to order a proof copy of the book for review.

When you order the proof copy, you are submitting the book for production/manufacture and those specially marked fields will most likely be locked down, meaning no further changes allowed.

Add Files

After completing all the information about your book, the author(s) and related information, you'll be ready to upload your "interior" and (if applicable) "cover" files. The "interior" file is your manuscript file, ideally in PDF format. The "cover" file may be something you've prepared off-line and must now upload (again, ideally in PDF format unless your provider requires a different file type), or it may be a file you created on the service provider's site using a cover design tool.

REVIEW SETUP

After you're done entering all required information and uploading your files, the last step before ordering a proof is to review your project. Review everything very carefully. If you've entered all of the information in a single setting, consider taking a break for an hour or more before doing this final review. After you're satisfied that everything is correct and to your liking, submit your project for publication/production.

Verification Message

Your provider will review your uploaded files and other information. If they find everything has been entered correctly and your uploaded files meet their specifications, you will receive a message inviting you to order a proof copy of your book.

If There Are Problems . . .

If your provider finds any problems with the information you entered, or with your uploaded files, they will send a notification detailing what problems exist and what steps you need to take to correct the problems. When you're done, you will need to submit for publication/production again.

THE REVIEW PROOF

If your files are approved and you are also satisfied that all the information you entered is correct, the next step is to order a proof copy of your book. Since the purpose of a proof copy is to verify that the book meets your approval, you need to order just one copy. You will be asked to pay for this order and there may also be tax and shipping costs, just as if you were ordering a regular book from any retailer.

When you receive your proof, inspect it carefully. Remember that if you approve this proof, the book your customers receive will be an identical copy of the proof. Examine every page, check the alignment of the cover art and cover text, and if possible, have someone else examine the proof as well since a fresh pair of eyes will catch things that have escaped your notice.

If you are happy with the proof, follow your provider's directions to approve the proof, thereby approving your book for release. These directions may be on the provider's website, they may have been e-mailed to you when you ordered the proof, or they may be included in the package with your proof copy.

If There Are Problems . . .

If there are any problems with your proof copy, you will need to log back in to your account/dashboard to make any necessary corrections, upload new files if the problems were in the body of your manuscript or the body of your cover, submit for publication, wait for your provider's confirmation that your files and information are acceptable, and submit for publication/production again. When you're done, assuming your provider accepts your revised files/project information changes, you will need to order a new proof.

Most print service providers operate online bookstores to offer their customers' books for sale to the public, and some of them allow authors to customize their books' listing pages in the online store.

Note that your provider may have locked all the details of your book when you submitted it for publication last time. In that case, you will have to unlock the title (from within your account/dashboard) before you will be allowed to make changes.

When you receive your new proof, go over it just as carefully as you did the first one. If you are happy with the new proof, follow the directions to approve the proof, thereby approving your book for release.

The book will usually appear in your provider's online bookstore immediately if you've opted for that sales channel, but it may take up to six weeks to show up in other online booksellers' listings and up to three months to appear in wholesale catalogs.

CUSTOMIZE YOUR BOOK'S PAGE ON YOUR PROVIDER'S BOOKSTORE SITE

Most print service providers operate online bookstores to offer their customers' books for sale to the public, and some of them allow authors to customize their books' listing pages in the online store. Don't miss this opportunity to make your book stand out from the crowd. Any or all of the following options may be offered:

REVIEWS: Enter blurbs from positive reviews your book has received.

BUZZ: Enter links to online articles about you or the book or to author interviews.

LINKS: Enter links to your author website, blog, and any other pages that highlight you as an author or this specific book.

CUSTOM COLORS: Select custom colors for your book's listing page.

CUSTOM BANNER: Create and upload a custom banner for your book's listing page. In Figure 8-1 you can see how I've created a custom banner using the same design elements employed in the cover of my novel, *Snow Ball.*

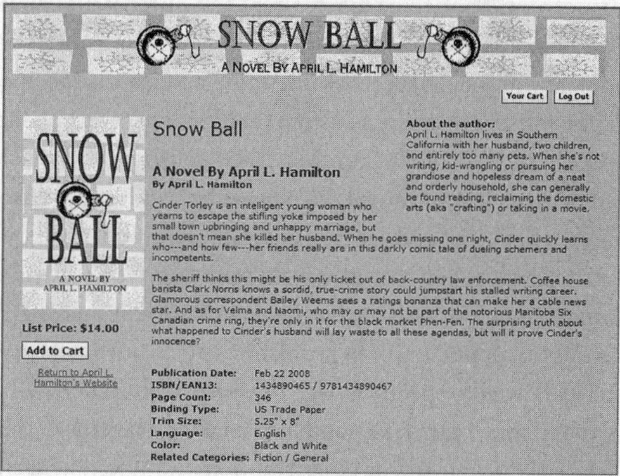

As in the example, your banner should echo your book cover. Use the same background image or color used on your book cover, as well as the same font and text color. If possible, also incorporate a graphic element from your book cover, as I've done in my banner.

When you're finished creating the banner, save it in the native file format of your graphics editor (usually PSD or PNG). If you intend to size down the banner, be sure to save this native copy before you downsize the file, since it will be the highest-quality version of the image. You'll need this native copy for any future edits or changes if you're not completely happy with the banner once you've seen it in place on your book's listing page.

Now use the Save for E-mail or Web option in your graphics editor program to save a JPG version of the file with dimensions matching those specified by your service provider's requirements for banner files. Saving this way compresses the file to reduce its byte size, which is helpful because most providers strictly limit file size.

BOOK COVER THUMBNAIL IMAGE: Some providers will automatically insert a thumbnail image taken from the cover you uploaded or created on the provider's site, while others require the author to create and upload a separate thumbnail image. If you created your own book cover . . . you should already have a thumbnail image prepared. If you used an online cover creation tool from your service provider, the provider will most likely pull a thumbnail off the cover you created and insert it here.

CONTINUE SHOPPING/YOUR PURCHASE IS COMPLETE LINK: Some providers don't have searchable storefront but provide a listing page for each book, to which the author can provide links on his website or blog. When visitors to the author's site or blog click the link, they are taken to the book's listing page on the provider's site.

In this situation, the provider may allow you to specify a Web address for where you'd like any purchasers of your book to be taken after their purchase is complete. Unless you have the Web development skills to create a "thanks for your purchase" type of page on your author website or blog, you should accept whatever default page is specified here.

Otherwise, it's a good idea to create a custom thank you page on your author site or blog and specify that page here. If you do so, purchasers will return to your site or blog following a purchase instead of being left on your service provider's site. The thank you page should thank the customer for her order and provide instructions or links for how to return to the main part of your site or blog. You may also want to include your provider's customer service e-mail or phone number for purchasers to use in the event there's any problems with their order. Never miss an opportunity to provide excellent customer service.

You may also be allowed to specify a page to which Web visitors will be taken if they decide not to buy your book. Agan, it's a good idea to take advantage of this opportunity to bring those visitors back to your site or blog. You won't want to take them to the "thanks for your order" page if they haven't purchased the book, but you can specify your site or blog's home page instead.

WATCH FOR YOUR BOOK LISTING(S)

If you've opted to sell your book through your provider's online store or through other online booksellers such as Amazon, beginning three weeks after you've released your book for sale start checking those websites for the appearance of your book. If any listings are missing after six weeks, notify your service provider.

MONITORING SALES AFTER YOUR BOOK IS RELEASED

Some service providers allow authors to monitor sales of their books right on the provider's site via electronic reports. If your provider offers this service, you can log in to your account/dashboard at any time after the book is released for sale to view your sales' reports, and you will probably also be allowed to download copies of them. If downloading is permitted, be sure to take advantage of it so you can keep copies of all your sales reports on file for later reference and tax reporting purposes.

Other providers e-mail or snail mail sales reports on a periodic basis. If this is the case with your provider, keep an eye out for your reports and notify your provider immediately if any fail to arrive.

Either way, read your sales reports closely and use them to compare against any royalty payments you receive from your service provider. Mistakes happen, so don't assume the reports and your royalty payments are in agreement. Verify it.

STILL UNCLEAR ON SOMETHING

Check your provider's site help, FAQ, terms of use, user guides, tutorials, support, and community forums to get more information, and if you don't find what you need in those resources, use the site's contact form or e-mail address to pose your question(s).

APRIL L. HAMILTON is an author, blogger, *Technorati* BlogCritic, leading advocate and speaker for the indie author movement, and founder of Publetariat.com, the premiere online news hub and community for indie authors and small imprints. She's spoken at the O'Reilly Tools of Change conference, the Writer's Digest Business of Getting Published conference, and has judged self-published books for competitions run by Writer's Digest and the Next Generation Indie Book Awards. Find out more at www.aprilhamilton.com.

PRACTICAL TIPS FOR THE NIGHTTIME NOVELIST

by Joseph Bates

The purpose of this section is to offer some further advice on novel writing that doesn't really fit into easy categorization, though I'm hesitant to call this advice purely practical. Some of it is—you'll need a good place to work that meets your individual needs, and you should absolutely set goals and deadlines for yourself as you go—but other bits of wisdom you find here will seem more off-topic. Or superstitious. Or weird.

Of course that's fine. Take what's useful and feel free to disregard the rest. But don't forget this section is here; there might come a time when you're stuck in the work and find yourself thinking, *What the heck! I'll go take a shower.* Maybe you'll find yourself out at dinner somewhere, about to spill the secrets of your novel writing, and will suddenly find yourself thinking, *Wait, maybe I shouldn't discuss it. I might jinx it.* Maybe you'll find yourself feeling a bit guilty for spending so much of your time locked away in a little room, separate from the world, and will need someone to tell you that your family and friends understand that what you're doing means something to you; it's okay. Maybe you'll need some of the advice in the chapter after all, no matter how rational or irrational you find it, to help make it through as a Nighttime Novelist. And if that's the case, then who cares if any of these seem rational? As John Lennon reminds us: Whatever gets you through the night, it's alright.

I couldn't agree more.

Here, then, presented in no particular order, are some tips that might help you get your novel written. I hope these do the trick.

And one last thing: I wish you all the best in your writing.

- **FIND A WORKSPACE THAT MEETS ALL YOUR NEEDS.** Most writers require the following: privacy, quiet, access to the Internet, a bathroom, and few distractions. Figure out what you'd add or subtract from the list, and make sure your environment meets your needs. If it doesn't, see how you can change it, or find a new workspace that'll be available any time you need it.

- **DON'T CHECK YOUR E-MAIL WHEN YOU WORK.** Or surf the Internet. Or read the news. You should have access to the Internet just in case you need to check a fact, or conduct quick research, or look for inspiration, but try to imagine the Internet has glass around it like a fire extinguisher. In case of emergency . . .
- **DISCOVER YOUR BEST WORKING HABITS AND CONDITIONS, AND THEN MAKE THEM ROUTINE.** Routine can help you access the state of mind you need, becoming more automatic (or as automatic as creativity can be). Try to stick to it.
- **WHEN THE ROUTINE STOPS WORKING, CHANGE THE ROUTINE.** That coffee shop really did the trick for a month, but now you're sick of it. So find a new coffee shop and make a new routine. When routine becomes rut, it's outlived its usefulness.
- **SET GOALS AND MEET THEM.** Some writers like achieving a daily word count—say, 1,000 words total, no matter how quickly they come or how long they take. Others like a weekly word or page count, so if they have one bad day they can make it up the next. Find what works for you as a goal, and then meet it consistently.
- **DELEGATE REAL-WORLD RESPONSIBILITIES.** If you have a family or a partner, ask them to help you take care of the practical things that need to get done: bill paying, dinner, taking out the trash, whatever. Again, if they understand your writing is important to you, they'll be happy to help. (And you can return the favor sometime if they'd like to take on some project of their own . . .)
- **TAKE CARE OF YOURSELF.** Don't get so wrapped up in the project that you forget to eat, sleep, recharge, and TCB. Taking care of yourself is taking care of your novel.
- **KEEP A BOOK YOU LOVE NEARBY.** When you get stuck, or need to be inspired, open it up to a good passage and read. Let it jumpstart your creative brain.
- **KEEP MUSIC YOU CAN WRITE TO.** This is different for every writer. Personally I need ambient music—no words, nothing too loud or fast-moving. Find out what kind of music you write best to and then get a lot of it. Make a playlist called "Writing Music" and keep some headphones at your desk.
- **HAVE SOME MINDLESS ACTIVITY AT HAND.** Sometimes getting out of your head for a few moments is the best way to solve a problem. Play solitaire for a minute. Play with a slinky. Get a little squeeze ball designed to release tension, and squeeze the life out of it.
- **HAVE MINDLESS ACTIVITIES ELSEWHERE.** Take a shower. Get out and take a drive or a walk. Wash the dishes. Do something that requires handiwork but no concentration.
- **KEEP SEVERAL KINDS OF YOUTUBE VIDEOS BOOKMARKED.** Save those that make you laugh, those that inspire you, and those that require no thought whatsoever, for when you need to quit thinking. Use as needed (but only as needed).

- **FILL YOUR WORKSPACE WITH ART AND OBJECTS THAT MAKE YOU THINK OF YOUR STORY.** Choose things from the time period of your novel, or associated with your characters , or reminiscent of the book's mood, or what have you. If you work out in public, then change your laptop's wallpaper to something related.
- **DON'T DISCUSS A WORK IN PROGRESS.** You don't need any external pressures or expectations on when you write, not even those by well-meaning friends. If you get asked about the novel, simply say, "I'm working on something, but I'm not exactly sure what." That will confuse them long enough for you to change the subject.
- **KEEP A TAPE RECORDER OR JOURNAL NEARBY AT ALL TIMES.** In the car, at your bedside, in your personal bag, everywhere. As soon as you stop thinking about the novel, something will come to you. Make sure you have a way of recording it. (Don't try to scribble while driving, of course. And don't take your tape recorder into the shower.)
- **WHEN THE PERFECT IMAGE OR IDEA COMES TO YOU AS SOON AS YOU'VE GONE TO BED, GET OUT OF BED.** Don't tell yourself that you'll remember when you wake up. You won't.
- **DON'T READ WHILE YOU WRITE.** This is maybe personal preference, but I find that whatever I'm reading while working on a novel inevitably begins corrupting the novel; I start writing like whomever I'm reading. So by all means read often and read well—good writers are, obviously, good readers—but be careful about anything that might contaminate the creative process.
- **BE RITUALISTIC AND SUPERSTITIOUS.** If you realize that your best writing days come when you've eaten chicken, then by all means: Eat chicken. Every day.
- **CAST OFF A BAD RITUAL.** The moment chicken stops working for you, try pork. Or go vegetarian. Or change your socks. Or take on whatever ritual gets you going again. It doesn't matter if this is just the placebo effect. Placebos occasionally save lives.
- **WORK QUICKLY.** Especially on a first draft. Don't spend your energy fretting about what you just wrote, or what's still to come. Write with your focus on the words right now, and get them onto the page without overthinking.
- **CUT YOURSELF SOME SLACK.** There will be days when you're the worst writer who ever lived. Everyone has those days. Tell yourself it's okay, and then keep going.
- **WRITE THE SCENE THAT'S COMING TO YOU, EVEN IF IT'S OUT OF SEQUENCE.** If you're working on Act II, and suddenly an Act III scene pops into your head and comes to life, write it.
- **DON'T THROW ANYTHING AWAY.** Even if that chapter or subplot isn't right for this novel, it might be right for the next. (Or, you might realize in another month that it did fit after all.) Keep versions and drafts and cut material.
- **KEEP YOUR FILES ORGANIZED ON YOUR COMPUTER.** Make folders with versions and dates, so you'll know which draft is which. And clearly mark the draft you're currently working on so you can find it easily.

- **CELEBRATE MILESTONES AND VICTORIES.** Go out to dinner with your significant other, who'll be glad to see you. Buy yourself some small luxury item. Take a night off and have fun, then get right back to it the next day.
- **DON'T BEAT YOURSELF UP OVER FAILURES.** The next victory will make them all worthwhile.
- **DON'T FEEL GUILTY FOR BEING SO ISOLATED AND SECRETIVE.** You're doing something important, something that means a lot to you. Your loved ones and friends understand. They do.
- **FINISH YOUR WRITING DAY IN THE MIDDLE OF A SENTENCE.** Finishing at the end of a section or chapter can make the next day's start a slow one. Stopping in mid-sentence, as goofy as it sounds, allows you to jump right back in the next day.
- **BE PREPARED FOR FALSE STARTS.** Everyone false-starts in big and small ways. It's just part of the process, but eventually it'll lead you to the right entry point into the story, or even into your day's work. Don't get discouraged by it.
- **ENJOY YOUR WORK.** Enjoy your work. Enjoy your work.

> I type in one place, but I write all over the house.
>
> —Toni Morrison

JOSEPH BATES's fiction and nonfiction have appeared in *the South Carolina Review, Identity Theory, Lunch Hour Stories, the Cincinnati Review*, and *Shenandoah*. He holds a PhD in comparative literature and fiction writing from the University of Cincinnati and currently teaches in the creative writing program at Miami University in Oxford, Ohio. Find out more at www.nighttimenovelist.com.

WRITING CALENDAR

The best way for writers to achieve success is by setting goals. Goals are usually met by writers who give themselves or are given deadlines. Something about having an actual date to hit helps create a sense of urgency in most writers (and editors, for that matter). This writing calendar is a great place to keep your important deadlines.

Also, this writing calendar is a good tool for recording upcoming writing events you'd like to attend or contests you'd like to enter. Or use this calendar to block out time for yourself—to just write.

Of course, you can use this calendar to record other special events, especially if you have a habit of remembering to write but of forgetting birthdays or anniversaries. After all, this calendar is now yours. Do with it what you will.

AUGUST 2011

SUN	MON	TUE	WED	THURS	FRI	SAT
	1	2	3	4	5	6
7	8	9	10	11	12	13
14	15	16	17	18	19	20
21	22	23	24	25	26	27
28	29	30	31			

Start a blog and make at least one post per week.

SEPTEMBER 2011

SUN	MON	TUE	WED	THU	FRI	SAT
				1	2	3
4	5	6	7	8	9	10
11	12	13	14	15	16	17
18	19	20	21	22	23	24
25	26	27	28	29	30	

Try sending out one targeted query per day during September.

OCTOBER 2011

SUN	MON	TUE	WED	THU	FRI	SAT
						1
2	3	4	5	6	7	8
9	10	11	12	13	14	15
16	17	18	19	20	21	22
23	24	25	26	27	28	29
30	31					

Are you on Twitter? Try leaving a meaningful tweet daily.

NOVEMBER 2011

SUN	MON	TUE	WED	THU	FRI	SAT
		1	2	3	4	5
6	7	8	9	10	11	12
13	14	15	16	17	18	19
20	21	22	23	24	25	26
27	28	29	30			

Write a novel during November as part of NaNoWriMo!

DECEMBER 2011

SUN	MON	TUE	WED	THU	FRI	SAT
				1	2	3
4	5	6	7	8	9	10
11	12	13	14	15	16	17
18	19	20	21	22	23	24
25	26	27	28	29	30	31

Evaluate your 2011 accomplishments and make 2012 goals.

JANUARY 2012

SUN	MON	TUE	WED	THU	FRI	SAT
1	2	3	4	5	6	7
8	9	10	11	12	13	14
15	16	17	18	19	20	21
22	23	24	25	26	27	28
29	30	31				

Make 2012 your best year freelancing yet!

FEBRUARY 2012

SUN	MON	TUE	WED	THU	FRI	SAT
			1	2	3	4
5	6	7	8	9	10	11
12	13	14	15	16	17	18
19	20	21	22	23	24	25
26	27	28	29			

Use the extra day in February to submit your writing.

MARCH 2012

SUN	MON	TUE	WED	THU	FRI	SAT
				1	2	3
4	5	6	7	8	9	10
11	12	13	14	15	16	17
18	19	20	21	22	23	24
25	26	27	28	29	30	31

Don't wait until April to file your 2011 taxes.

APRIL 2012

SUN	MON	TUE	WED	THU	FRI	SAT
1	2	3	4	5	6	7
8	9	10	11	12	13	14
15	16	17	18	19	20	21
22	23	24	25	26	27	28
29	30					

Write a poem a day for National Poetry Month.

MAY 2012

SUN	MON	TUE	WED	THU	FRI	SAT
		1	2	3	4	5
6	7	8	9	10	11	12
13	14	15	16	17	18	19
20	21	22	23	24	25	26
27	28	29	30	31		

Plan to attend a writing conference this summer.

JUNE 2012

SUN	MON	TUE	WED	THU	FRI	SAT
					1	2
3	4	5	6	7	8	9
10	11	12	13	14	15	16
17	18	19	20	21	22	23
24	25	26	27	28	29	30

Develop one story or article idea each week.

JULY 2012

SUN	MON	TUE	WED	THU	FRI	SAT
1	2	3	4	5	6	7
8	9	10	11	12	13	14
15	16	17	18	19	20	21
22	23	24	25	26	27	28
29	30	31				

Don't forget to keep accurate records for next tax season.

AUGUST 2012

SUN	MON	TUE	WED	THU	FRI	SAT
			1	2	3	4
5	6	7	8	9	10	11
12	13	14	15	16	17	18
19	20	21	22	23	24	25
26	27	28	29	30	31	

Most successful writers read as much as (or more than) they write.

SEPTEMBER 2012

SUN	MON	TUE	WED	THU	FRI	SAT
						1
2	3	4	5	6	7	8
9	10	11	12	13	14	15
16	17	18	19	20	21	22
23	24	25	26	27	28	29
30						

Try an unfamiliar writing style to help you grow as a writer.

OCTOBER 2012

SUN	MON	TUE	WED	THU	FRI	SAT
	1	2	3	4	5	6
7	8	9	10	11	12	13
14	15	16	17	18	19	20
21	22	23	24	25	26	27
28	29	30	31			

Remember to hit the save button when you're writing

NOVEMBER 2012

SUN	MON	TUE	WED	THU	FRI	SAT
				1	2	3
4	5	6	7	8	9	10
11	12	13	14	15	16	17
18	19	20	21	22	23	24
25	26	27	28	29	30	

Write a novel during November for NaNoWriMo!

DECEMBER 2012

SUN	MON	TUE	WED	THU	FRI	SAT
						1
2	3	4	5	6	7	8
9	10	11	12	13	14	15
16	17	18	19	20	21	22
23	24	25	26	27	28	29
30	31					

If you don't have it yet, find a copy of *2013 Novel & Short Story Writer's Market.*

PUBLISHERS & THEIR IMPRINTS

The publishing world is in constant transition. With all the buying, selling, reorganizing, consolidating, and dissolving, it's hard to keep publishers and their imprints straight. To help make sense of these changes, here's a breakdown of major publishers (and their divisions)—who owns whom and which imprints are under each company umbrella. Keep in mind that this information changes frequently. The website of each publisher is provided to help you keep an eye on this ever-evolving business.

HACHETTE BOOK GROUP USA

www.hachettebookgroupusa.com

CENTER STREET

FAITHWORDS

GRAND CENTRAL PUBLISHING

- Business Plus
- 5-Spot
- Forever
- Springboard Press
- Twelve
- Vision
- Wellness Central

HACHETTE BOOK GROUP DIGITAL MEDIA

- Hachette Audio

LITTLE, BROWN AND COMPANY

- Back Bay Books
  - Bulfinch
- Reagan Arthur Books

LITTLE, BROWN BOOKS FOR YOUNG READERS

- LB Kids
- Poppy

ORBIT

YEN PRESS

HARLEQUIN ENTERPRISES

www.eharlequin.com

HARLEQUIN

- Harlequin American Romance
- Harlequin Bianca

Harlequin Blaze
Harlequin Deseo
Harlequin eBooks
Harlequin Historical
Harlequin Historical Undone
Harlequin Intrigue
Harlequin Medical Romance
Harlequin NASCAR
Harlequin Nonfiction
Harlequin Presents
Harlequin Romance
Harlequin Special Releases
Harlequin Superromance
Harlequin Teen
Harlequin Tiffany

HQN BOOKS

HQN eBooks

KIMANI PRESS

Kimani Press Arabesque
Kimani Press eBooks
Kimani Press Kimani Romance
Kimani Press Kimani TRU
Kimani Press New Spirit
Kimani Press Sepia
Kimani Press Special Releases

LUNA

Luna eBooks

MIRA

Mira eBooks

RED DRESS INK

Red Dress eBooks

SILHOUETTE

Silhouette Desire
Silhouette eBooks
Silhouette Nocturne
Silhouette Nocturne Bites
Silhouette Romantic Suspense
Silhouette Special Edition

SPICE

SPICE Books
SPICE Briefs

STEEPLE HILL

Steeple Hill Café©
Steeple Hill eBooks
Steeple Hill Love Inspired
Steeple Hill Love Inspired Historical
Steeple Hill Love Inspired Suspense
Steeple Hill Women's Fiction

WORLDWIDE LIBRARY

Rogue Angel
Worldwide Library eBooks
Worldwide Mystery

HARLEQUIN CANADA

HARLEQUIN U.K.

Mills & Boon

HARPERCOLLINS

www.harpercollins.com

HARPERMORROW

Amistad
Avon
  Avon A
  Avon Inspire
  Avon Red
Collins Design
Ecco
Eos
Harper
  Harper Business
  HarperLuxe
  Harper Paperbacks
  Harper Perennial

HarperAudio
HarperBibles
HarperCollins e-Books
HarperOne
ItBooks
Rayo
William Morrow

HARPERCOLLINS CHILDREN'S BOOKS

Amistad
Balzer + Bray
Children's Audio
Greenwillow Books
HarperCollins
HarperCollins e-Books
Harper Festival
HarperTeen
Katherine Tegen Books
Rayo
TOKYOPOP

HARPERCOLLINS U.K.

Fourth Estate
The Friday Project
HarperCollins Childrens Books
Collins
Collins Education
Collins Geo
Collins Language
HarperFiction
Angry Robot
Avon U.K.
Blue Door
Voyager
HarperNonfiction
HarperPerennial
HarperPress
HarperThorsons/Element
HarperSport
HarperTrue

HARPERCOLLINS CANADA

Collins Canada
HarperCollinsPublishers
HarperPerennial Canada
HarperTrophyCanada
Phyllis Bruce Books

HARPERCOLLINS AUSTRALIA

Angus & Robertson
Collins
Fourth Estate
HarperCollins
Harper Perennial
HarperSports
Voyager

HARPERCOLLINS INDIA

HARPERCOLLINS NEW ZEALAND

Flamingo
HarperCollins
HarperSports
Perennial
Voyager

ZONDERVAN

Editorial Vida
Youth Specialties
Zonderkids

MACMILLAN US (HOLTZBRINCK)

http://us.macmillan.com

MACMILLAN

Faber and Faber, Inc.
Farrar, Straus
Farrar, Straus & Giroux
Hill & Wang

HENRY HOLT & CO.

Henry Holt Books for Young Readers
Holt Paperbacks
Metropolitan
Times

MACMILLAN CHILDREN'S

Feiwel & Friends
Farrar, Straus and Giroux Books for Young Readers
First Second
Holt Books for Young Readers
Kingfisher
Priddy Books
Roaring Brook Press
Square Fish

PICADOR

PALGRAVE MACMILLAN

TOR/FORGE BOOKS

Forge
Orb
Tor
Tor/Seven Seas

ST. MARTIN'S PRESS

Minotaur Press
Thomas Dunne Books

BEDFORD, FREEMAN & WORTH PUBLISHING GROUP

BEDFORD/ST. MARTIN'S

HAYDEN-MCNEIL

W.H. FREEMAN

WORTH PUBLISHERS

MACMILLAN KIDS

YOUNG LISTENERS

MACMILLAN AUDIO

PENGUIN GROUP (USA), INC.

www.penguingroup.com

PENGUIN ADULT DIVISION

Ace
Alpha
Amy Einhorn Books/Putnam
Avery
Berkley
Current
Dutton
G.P. Putnam's Sons
Gotham
HPBooks
Hudson Street Press
Jeremy P. Tarcher
Jove
NAL
Pamela Dorman Books
Penguin
Penguin Press
Perigree
Plume
Portfolio
Prentice Hall Press

PUFFIN BOOKS

Razorbill
Speak
Viking Books for Young Readers

RIVERHEAD

Price Stern Sloan
Sentinel
Tarcher
Viking Press

YOUNG READERS DIVISION

Dial Books for Young Readers
Dutton Children's Books

Firebird
Frederick Warne
Grosset & Dunlap
Philomel

RANDOM HOUSE, INC. (BERTELSMANN)

www.randomhouse.com

CROWN TRADE GROUP

Amphoto Books
Backstage Books
Billboard Books
Broadway Business
Crown
Crown Business
Crown Forum
Clarkson Potter
Doubleday Religion
Harmony
Monacelli Press
Potter Craft
Potter Style
Shaye Areheart Books
Ten Speed Press
Three Rivers Press
Tricycle Press
Waterbrook Multnomah
Watson-Guptill

KNOPF DOUBLEDAY PUBLISHING GROUP

Alfred A. Knopf
Anchor Books
Doubleday
Everyman's Library
Nan A. Talese
Pantheon Books
Schocken Books
Vintage/Anchor

RANDOM HOUSE PUBLISHING GROUP

Ballantine Books
Bantam
Dell
Del Rey
Del Rey/Lucas Books
The Dial Press
The Modern Library
One World
Presidio Press
Random House Trade Group
Random House Trade Paperbacks
Spectra
Spiegel and Grau
Villard Books

RANDOM HOUSE AUDIO PUBLISHING GROUP

Listening Library
Random House Audio

RANDOM HOUSE CHILDREN'S BOOKS

Bantam Books
David Fickling Books
Delacorte Press Books for Young Readers
Delacorte Press Trade Paperbacks
Disney Books for Young Readers
Doubleday Books for Young Readers
Dragonfly
Golden Books
Kids@Random
Laurel-Leaf
Picturebacks
Robin Corey Books
Schwartz and Wade Books
Wendy Lamb Books
Yearling

RANDOM HOUSE INFORMATION GROUP

Fodor's Travel
Living Language

Prima Games

Princeton Review

RH Puzzles & Games

RH Reference Publishing

Sylvan Learning

RANDOM HOUSE INTERNATIONAL

Arete

McClelland & Stewart Ltd.

Plaza & Janes

RH Australia

RH of Canada Limited

RH Mondadori

RH South America

RH United Kingdom

Transworld UK

Verlagsgruppe RH

SIMON & SCHUSTER

www.simonandschuster.com

SIMON & SCHUSTER ADULT PUBLISHING

Atria Books/Beyond Words

Beach Lane Books

Folger Shakespeare Library

Free Press

Gallery Books

Howard Books

Pocket Books

Pimsleur

Scribner

Simon & Schuster

Simon & Schuster Audioworks

Strebor

The Touchstone & Fireside Group

SIMON & SCHUSTER CHILDREN'S PUBLISHING

Aladdin Paperbacks

Atheneum Books for Young Readers

Libros Para Niños

Little Simon®

Margaret K. McElderry Books

Simon & Schuster Books for Young Readers

Simon Pulse

Simon Spotlight®

SIMON & SCHUSTER INTERNATIONAL

Simon & Schuster Australia

Simon & Schuster Canada

Simon & Schuster UK

CANADIAN WRITERS TAKE NOTE

While much of the information contained in this section applies to all writers, here are some specifics of interest to Canadian writers:

POSTAGE: When sending an SASE from Canada, you will need an International Reply Coupon ($3.50). Also be aware: a GST tax is required on postage in Canada and for mail with postage under $5 going to destinations outside the country. Since Canadian postage rates are voted on in January of each year (after we go to press), contact a Canada Post Corporation Customer Service Division (located in most cities in Canada) or visit www.canadapost.ca for the most current rates.

COPYRIGHT: For information on copyrighting your work and to obtain forms, write Canadian Intellectual Property Office, Industry Canada, Place du Portage I, 50 Victoria St., Room C-114, Gatineau, Quebec K1A 0C9 or call (866)997-1936. website: www.cipo.gc.ca.

THE PUBLIC LENDING RIGHT: The Public Lending Right Commission has established that eligible Canadian authors are entitled to payments when a book is available through a library. Payments are determined by a sampling of the holdings of a representative number of libraries. To find out more about the program and to learn if you are eligible, write to the Public Lending Right Commission at 350 Albert St., P.O. Box 1047, Ottawa, Ontario K1P 5V8 or call (613)566-4378 or (800)521-5721 for information. website: www.plr-dpp.ca. The Commission, which is part of the Canada Council, produces a helpful pamphlet, *How the PLR System Works*, on the program.

GRANTS AVAILABLE TO CANADIAN WRITERS: Most province art councils or departments of culture provide grants to resident writers. Some of these, as well as contests for Canadian writers, are listed in our Contests and Awards section. For national programs, contact The Canada Council, Writing and Publishing Section, 350 Alberta St., P.O. Box 1047, Ottawa, Ontario K1P 5V8 or call (613)566-4414 or (800)263-5588 for information. Fax: (613)566-4410. website: www.canadacouncil.ca.

FOR MORE INFORMATION: Contact The Writer's Union of Canada, 90 Richmond St. E, Suite 200, Toronto, Ontario M5C 1P1; call them at (416)703-8982 or fax them at (416)504-9090. E-mail: info@writersunion.ca. website: www.writersunion.ca. This organization provides a wealth of information (as well as strong support) for Canadian writers, including specialized publications on publishing contracts; contract negotiations; the author/editor relationship; author awards, competitions and grants; agents; taxes for writers, libel issues and access to archives in Canada.

PRINTING & PRODUCTION TERMS DEFINED

In most of the magazine listings in this book, you will find a brief physical description of each publication. This material usually includes the number of pages, type of paper, type of binding, and whether or not the magazine uses photographs and/or illustrations.

Although it is important to look at a copy of the magazine to which you are submitting, these descriptions can give you a general idea of what the publication looks like. This material can provide you with a feel for the magazine's financial resources and prestige. Do not, however, rule out small, simply produced publications, as these may be the most receptive to new writers. Watch for publications that have increased their page count or improved their production from year to year. This is a sign the publication is doing well and may be accepting more fiction.

You will notice a wide variety of printing terms used within these descriptions. We explain here some of the more common terms used in our listing descriptions. We do not include explanations of terms such as *Mohawk* and *Karma*, which are brand names and refer to the paper manufacturer.

PAPER

A5: An international paper standard; 148 × 210 mm or 5.8 × 8.3 in.

ACID-FREE: Paper that has low or no acid content. This type of paper resists deterioration from exposure to the elements. More expensive than many other types of paper, publications done on acid-free paper can last a long time.

BOND: Bond paper is often used for stationery and is more transparent than text paper. It can be made of either sulphite (wood) or cotton fiber. Some bonds have a mixture of both wood and cotton (such as "25 percent cotton" paper). This is the type of paper most often used in photocopying or as standard typing paper.

COATED/UNCOATED STOCK: *Coated* and *uncoated* are terms usually used when referring to book or text paper. More opaque than bond, it is the paper most used for offset printing. As the name implies, uncoated paper has no coating. Coated paper is coated with a layer of clay, varnish, or other chemicals. It comes in various sheens and surfaces depending on the type of coating, but the most common are dull, matte, and gloss.

COVER STOCK: Cover stock is heavier book or text paper used to cover a publication. It comes in a variety of colors and textures and can be coated on one or both sides.

CS1/CS2: Most often used when referring to cover stock, *CS1* means paper that is coated only on one side; *CS2* is paper coated on both sides.

NEWSPRINT: Inexpensive absorbent pulp wood paper often used in newspapers and tabloids.

TEXT: Text paper is similar to book paper (a smooth paper used in offset printing), but it has been given some texture by using rollers or other methods to apply a pattern to the paper.

VELLUM: Vellum is a text paper that is fairly porous and soft.

SOME NOTES ABOUT PAPER WEIGHT AND THICKNESS: Often you will see paper thickness described in terms of pounds, such as 80 lb. or 60 lb. paper. The weight is determined by figuring how many pounds in a ream of a particular paper (a ream is 500 sheets). This can be confusing, however, because this figure is based on a standard sheet size, and standard sheet sizes vary depending on the type of paper used. This information is most helpful when comparing papers of the same type. For example, 80 lb. book paper versus 60 lb. book paper. Since the size of the paper is the same, it would follow that 80 lb. paper is the thicker, heavier paper.

Some paper, especially cover stock, is described by the actual thickness of the paper. This is expressed in a system of points. Typical paper thicknesses range from 8 points to 14 points thick.

PRINTING

There are many other printing methods, but these are the ones most commonly referred to in our listings.

LETTERPRESS: Letterpress printing is printing that uses a raised surface, such as type. The type is inked and then pressed against the paper. Unlike offset printing, only a limited number of impressions can be made, as the surface of the type can wear down.

OFFSET: Offset is a printing method in which ink is transferred from an image-bearing plate to a "blanket" and from the blanket to the paper.

SHEET-FED OFFSET: Offset printing in which the paper is fed one piece at a time.

WEB OFFSET: Offset printing in which a roll of paper is printed and then cut apart to make individual sheets.

BINDING

CASE BINDING: In case binding, signatures (groups of pages) are stitched together with thread rather than glued together. The stitched pages are then trimmed on three sides and glued into a hardcover or board "case" or cover. Most hardcover books and thicker magazines are done this way.

COMB BINDING: A comb is a plastic spine used to hold pages together with bent tabs that are fed through punched holes in the edge of the paper.

PERFECT BINDING: Used for paperback books and heavier magazines, perfect binding involves gathering signatures (groups of pages) into a stack, trimming off the folds so the edge is flat, and gluing a cover to that edge.

SADDLE STITCHED: Publications in which the pages are stitched together using metal staples. This fairly inexpensive type of binding is usually used with books or magazines that are under 80 pages.

SMYTHE-SEWN: Binding in which the pages are sewn together with thread. Smythe is the name of the most common machine used for this purpose.

SPIRAL BINDING: A wire spiral that is wound through holes punched in pages is a spiral bind. This is the binding used in spiral notebooks.

GLOSSARY

ADVANCE. Payment by a publisher to an author prior to the publication of a book, to be deducted from the author's future royalties.

ADVENTURE STORY. A genre of fiction in which action is the key element, overshadowing characters, theme, and setting. The conflict in an adventure story is often man against nature. A secondary plot that reinforces this kind of conflict is sometimes included. In Allistair MacLean's *Night without End*, for example, the hero, while investigating a mysterious Arctic air crash, also finds himself dealing with espionage, sabotage and murder.

ALL RIGHTS. The rights contracted to a publisher permitting a manuscript's use anywhere and in any form, including movie and book club sales, without additional payment to the writer.

AMATEUR SLEUTH. The character in a mystery, usually the protagonist, who does the detection but is not a professional private investigator or police detective.

ANTHOLOGY. A collection of selected writings by various authors.

ASSOCIATION OF AUTHORS' REPRESENTATIVES (AAR). An organization for literary agents committed to maintaining excellence in literary representation.

AUCTION. Publishers sometimes bid against each other for the acquisition of a manuscript that has excellent sales prospects.

BACKLIST. A publisher's books not published during the current season but still in print.

BIOGRAPHICAL NOVEL. A life story documented in history and transformed into fiction through the insight and imagination of the writer. This type of novel melds the elements of biographical research and historical truth into the framework of a novel, complete with dialogue, drama, and mood. A biographical novel resembles historical fiction, save for one aspect: Characters in a historical novel may be fabricated and then placed into an authentic setting; characters in a biographical novel have actually lived.

BOOK PRODUCER/PACKAGER. An organization that may develop a book for a publisher based upon the publisher's idea or may plan all elements of a book, from its initial concept to writing and marketing strategies, and then sell the package to a book publisher and/or movie producer.

CLIFFHANGER. Fictional event in which the reader is left in suspense at the end of a chapter or episode, so that interest in the story's outcome will be sustained.

CLIP. Sample, usually from a newspaper or magazine, of a writer's published work.

CLOAK-AND-DAGGER. A melodramatic, romantic type of fiction dealing with espionage and intrigue.

COMMERCIAL. Publishers whose concern is salability, profit, and success with a large readership.

CONTEMPORARY. Material dealing with popular current trends, themes, or topics.

CONTRIBUTOR'S COPY. Copy of an issue of a magazine or published book sent to an author whose work is included.

COPUBLISHING. An arrangement in which the author and publisher share costs and profits.

COPYEDITING. Editing a manuscript for writing style, grammar, punctuation and factual accuracy.

COPYRIGHT. The legal right to exclusive publication, sale, or distribution of a literary work.

COVER LETTER. A brief letter sent with a complete manuscript submitted to an editor.

"COZY" (OR "TEACUP") MYSTERY. Mystery usually set in a small British town, in a bygone era, featuring a somewhat genteel, intellectual protagonist.

CYBERPUNK. Type of science fiction, usually concerned with computer networks and human-computer combinations, involving young, sophisticated protagonists.

ELECTRONIC RIGHTS. The right to publish material electronically, either in book or short story form.

ELECTRONIC SUBMISSION. A submission of material by e-mail or on computer disk.

ETHNIC FICTION. Stories and novels whose central characters are black, Native American, Italian-American, Jewish, Appalachian, or members of some other specific cultural group. Ethnic fiction usually deals with a protagonist caught between two conflicting ways of life: mainstream American culture and his ethnic heritage.

EXPERIMENTAL FICTION. Fiction that is innovative in subject matter and style; avant-garde, non-formulaic, usually literary material.

EXPOSITION. The portion of the story line, usually the beginning, where background information about character and setting is related.

E-ZINE. A magazine that is published electronically.

FAIR USE. A provision in the copyright law that says short passages from copyrighted material may be used without infringing on the owner's rights.

FANZINE. A noncommercial, small-circulation magazine usually dealing with fantasy, horror or science-fiction literature and art.

FICTIONAL BIOGRAPHY. The biography of a real person that goes beyond the events of a person's life by being fleshed out with imagined scenes and dialogue. The writer of fictional biographies strives to make it clear that the story is, indeed, fiction and not history.

FIRST NORTH AMERICAN SERIAL RIGHTS. The right to publish material in a periodical before it appears in book form, for the first time, in the United States or Canada.

FLASH FICTION. See short short stories.

GALLEYS. The first typeset version of a manuscript that has not yet been divided into pages.

GENRE. A formulaic type of fiction such as romance, western, or horror.

GOTHIC. This type of category fiction dates back to the late 18th and early 19th centuries. Contemporary gothic novels are characterized by atmospheric, historical settings and feature young, beautiful women who win the favor of handsome, brooding heroes—simultaneously dealing successfully with some life-threatening menace, either natural or supernatural. Gothics rely on mystery, peril, romantic relationships, and a sense of foreboding for their strong, emotional effect on the reader. A classic early gothic novel is Emily Bronte's *Wuthering Heights*. The gothic writer builds a series of credible, emotional crises for his ultimately triumphant heroine. Sex between the woman and her lover is implied rather than graphically detailed; the writer's descriptive talents are used instead to paint rich, desolate, gloomy settings in stark mansions and awesome castles. He composes slow-paced, intricate sketches that create a sense of impending evil on every page.

GRAPHIC NOVEL. A book (original or adapted) that takes the form of a long comic strip or heavily illustrated story of 40 pages or more, produced in paperback. Though called a novel, these can also be works of nonfiction.

HARD-BOILED DETECTIVE NOVEL. Mystery novel featuring a private eye or police detective as the protagonist; usually involves a murder. The emphasis is on the details of the crime, and the tough, unsentimental protagonist usually takes a matter-of-fact attitude toward violence.

HARD SCIENCE FICTION. Science fiction with an emphasis on science and technology.

HIGH FANTASY. Fantasy with a medieval setting and a heavy emphasis on chivalry and the quest.

HISTORICAL FICTION. A fictional story set in a recognizable period of history. As well as telling the stories of ordinary people's lives, historical fiction may involve political or social events of the time.

HORROR. Howard Phillips (H.P.) Lovecraft, generally acknowledged to be the master of the horror tale in the 20th century and the most important American writer of this genre since Edgar Allan Poe, maintained that "the oldest and strongest emotion of mankind is fear, and the oldest and strongest kind of fear is fear of the unknown. These facts few psychologists will dispute, and their admitted truth must establish for all time the genuineness and dignity of the weirdly horrible tale as a literary form." Lovecraft distinguishes horror literature from fiction based entirely on physical fear and the merely gruesome. "The true weird tale has something more than secret murder, bloody bones or a sheeted form clanking chains according to rule. A certain atmosphere of breathless and unexplainable dread of outer, unknown forces must be present; there must be a hint, expressed with a seriousness and portentousness becoming its subject, of that most terrible concept of the human brain—a malign and particular suspension or defeat of the fixed laws of Nature which are our only safeguards against the assaults of chaos and the daemons of unplumbed space." It is that atmosphere—the creation of a particular sensation or emotional level—that, according to Lovecraft, is the most important element in the creation of horror literature. Contemporary writers enjoying considerable success in horror fiction include Stephen King, Robert Bloch, Peter Straub, and Dean Koontz.

HYPERTEXT FICTION. A fictional form, read electronically, which incorporates traditional elements of storytelling with a nonlinear plot line, in which the reader determines the direction of the story by opting for one of many author-supplied links.

IMPRINT. Name applied to a publisher's specific line (e.g. Owl, an imprint of Henry Holt).

INTERACTIVE FICTION. Fiction in book or computer-software format where the reader determines the path the story will take by choosing from several alternatives at the end of each chapter or episode.

INTERNATIONAL REPLY COUPON (IRC). A form purchased at a post office and enclosed with a letter or manuscript to an international publisher, to cover return postage costs.

JUVENILES, WRITING FOR. This includes works intended for an audience usually between the ages of 2 and 18. Categories of children's books are usually divided in this way: (1) picture books and storybooks (ages 2 to 8); (2) young readers or easy-to-read books (ages 5 to 8); (3) middle readers or middle grade (ages 9 to 11); (4) young adult books (ages 12 and up).

LIBEL. Written or printed words that defame, malign, or damagingly misrepresent a living person.

LITERARY AGENT. A person who acts for an author in finding a publisher or arranging contract terms on a literary project.

LITERARY FICTION. The general category of fiction that employs more sophisticated technique, driven as much or more by character evolution than action in the plot.

LITERARY FICTION VS. COMMERCIAL FICTION. To the writer of literary, or serious, fiction, style and technique are often as important as subject matter. Commercial fiction, however, is written with the intent of reaching as wide an audience as possible. Commercial fiction is sometimes called *genre fiction* because books of this type often fall into categories, such as western, gothic, romance, historical, mystery, and horror.

MAINSTREAM FICTION. Fiction that appeals to a more general reading audience, versus literary or genre fiction. Mainstream is more plot-driven than literary fiction and less formulaic than genre fiction.

MALICE DOMESTIC NOVEL. A mystery featuring a murder among family members, such as the murder of a spouse or a parent.

MANUSCRIPT. The author's unpublished copy of a work, usually typewritten, used as the basis for typesetting.

MASS MARKET PAPERBACK. Softcover book on a popular subject, usually around 4×7, directed to a general audience and sold in drugstores and groceries as well as in bookstores.

MIDDLE READER. Also called *middle grade*. Juvenile fiction for readers aged 9 to 11.

MS(S). Abbreviation for *manuscript(s)*.

MULTIPLE SUBMISSION. Submission of more than one short story at a time to the same editor. Do not make a multiple submission unless requested.

MYSTERY. A form of narration in which one or more elements remain unknown or unexplained until the end of the story. The modern mystery story contains elements of the serious novel: a convincing account of a character's struggle with various physical and psychological obstacles in an effort to achieve his goal, good characterization, and sound motivation.

NARRATION. The account of events in a story's plot as related by the speaker or the voice of the author.

NARRATOR. The person who tells the story, either someone involved in the action or the voice of the writer.

NEW AGE. A term including categories such as astrology, psychic phenomena, spiritual healing, UFOs, mysticism, and other aspects of the occult.

NOIR. A style of mystery involving hard-boiled detectives and bleak settings.

NOM DE PLUME. French for "pen name"; a pseudonym.

NONFICTION NOVEL. A work in which real events and people are written [about] in novel form, but are not camouflaged, as they are in the roman à clef. In the nonfiction novel, reality is presented imaginatively; the writer imposes a novelistic structure on the actual events, keying sections of narrative around moments that are seen (in retrospect) as symbolic. In this way, he creates a coherence that the actual story might not have had. *The Executioner's Song*, by Norman Mailer, and *In Cold Blood*, by Truman Capote, are notable examples of the nonfiction novel.

NOVELLA (ALSO NOVELETTE). A short novel or long story, approximately 20,000-50,000 words.

#10 ENVELOPE. 4×9½ envelope, used for queries and other business letters.

OFFPRINT. Copy of a story taken from a magazine before it is bound.

ONETIME RIGHTS. Permission to publish a story in periodical or book form one time only.

OUTLINE. A summary of a book's contents, often in the form of chapter headings with a few sentences outlining the action of the story under each one; sometimes part of a book proposal.

OVER THE TRANSOM. A phrase referring to unsolicited manuscripts, or those that come in "over the transom."'

PAYMENT ON ACCEPTANCE. Payment from the magazine or publishing house as soon as the decision to print a manuscript is made.

PAYMENT ON PUBLICATION. Payment from the publisher after a manuscript is printed.

PEN NAME. A pseudonym used to conceal a writer's real name.

PERIODICAL. A magazine or journal published at regular intervals.

PLOT. The carefully devised series of events through which the characters progress in a work of fiction.

POLICE PROCEDURAL. A mystery featuring a police detective or officer who uses standard professional police practices to solve a crime.

POPULAR FICTION. Generally, a synonym for category or genre fiction; i.e., fiction intended to appeal to audiences for certain kinds of novels. Popular, or category, fiction is defined as such primarily for the convenience of publishers, editors, reviewers, and booksellers who must identify novels of different areas of interest for potential readers.

PRINT ON DEMAND (POD). Novels produced digitally one at a time, as ordered. Self-publishing through print on demand technology typically involves some fees for the author. Some authors use POD to create a manuscript in book form to send to prospective traditional publishers.

PROOFREADING. Close reading and correction of a manuscript's typographical errors.

PROOFS. A typeset version of a manuscript used for correcting errors and making changes, often a photocopy of the galleys.

PROPOSAL. An offer to write a specific work, usually consisting of an outline of the work and one or two completed chapters.

PROTAGONIST. The principal or leading character in a literary work.

PSYCHOLOGICAL NOVEL. A narrative that emphasizes the mental and emotional aspects of its characters, focusing on motivations and mental activities rather than on exterior events. The psychological novelist is less concerned about relating what happened than about exploring why it happened. The term is most often used to describe 20th-century works that employ techniques such as interior monologue and stream of consciousness. Two examples of contemporary psychological novels are Judith Guest's *Ordinary People* and Mary Gordon's *The Company of Women*.

PUBLIC DOMAIN. Material that either was never copyrighted or whose copyright term has expired.

PULP MAGAZINE. A periodical printed on inexpensive paper, usually containing lurid, sensational stories or articles.

QUERY. A letter written to an editor to elicit interest in a story the writer wants to submit.

READER. A person hired by a publisher to read unsolicited manuscripts.

READING FEE. An arbitrary amount of money charged by some agents and publishers to read a submitted manuscript.

REGENCY ROMANCE. A subgenre of romance, usually set in England between 1811 and 1820.

REMAINDERS. Leftover copies of an out-of-print book, sold by the publisher at a reduced price.

REPORTING TIME. The number of weeks or months it takes an editor to report back on an author's query or manuscript.

REPRINT RIGHTS. Permission to print an already published work whose rights have been sold to another magazine or book publisher.

ROMAN À CLEF. French "novel with a key." A novel that represents actual living or historical characters and events in fictionalized form.

ROMANCE NOVEL. A type of category fiction in which the love relationship between a man and a woman pervades the plot. The story is often told from the viewpoint of the heroine, who meets a man (the hero), falls in love with him, encounters a conflict that hinders their relationship, then resolves the conflict. Romance is the overriding element in this kind of story: The couple's relationship determines the plot and tone of the book. The theme of the novel is the woman's sexual awakening. Although she may not be a virgin, she has never before been so emotionally aroused. Despite all this emotion, however, characters and plot both must be well developed and realistic. Throughout a romance novel, the reader senses the sexual and emotional attraction between the heroine and hero. Lovemaking scenes, though sometimes detailed, are not generally too graphic, because more emphasis is placed on the sensual element than on physical action.

ROYALTIES. A percentage of the retail price paid to an author for each copy of the book that is sold.

SAE. Self-addressed envelope.

SASE. Self-addressed stamped envelope.

SCIENCE FICTION [VS. FANTASY]. It is generally accepted that, to be science fiction, a story must have elements of science in either the conflict or setting (usually both). Fantasy, on the other hand, rarely utilizes science, relying instead on magic, mythological and neo-mythological beings, and devices and outright invention for conflict and setting.

SECOND SERIAL (REPRINT) RIGHTS. Permission for the reprinting of a work in another periodical after its first publication in book or magazine form.

SELF-PUBLISHING. In this arrangement, the author keeps all income derived from the book, but he pays for its manufacturing, production, and marketing.

SEQUEL. A literary work that continues the narrative of a previous, related story or novel.

SERIAL RIGHTS. The rights given by an author to a publisher to print a piece in one or more periodicals.

SERIALIZED NOVEL. A book-length work of fiction published in sequential issues of a periodical.

SETTING. The environment and time period during which the action of a story takes place.

SHORT SHORT STORY. A condensed piece of fiction, usually under 1,000 words.

SIMULTANEOUS SUBMISSION. The practice of sending copies of the same manuscript to several editors or publishers at the same time. Some editors refuse to consider such submissions.

SLANT. A story's particular approach or style, designed to appeal to the readers of a specific magazine.

SLICE OF LIFE. A presentation of characters in a seemingly mundane situation that offers the reader a flash of illumination about the characters or their situation.

SLUSH PILE. A stack of unsolicited manuscripts in the editorial offices of a publisher.

SOCIAL FICTION. Fiction written with the purpose of bringing positive changes in society.

SOFT/SOCIOLOGICAL SCIENCE FICTION. Science fiction with an emphasis on society and culture versus scientific accuracy.

SPACE OPERA. Epic science fiction with an emphasis on good guys versus bad guys.

SPECULATION (OR SPEC). An editor's agreement to look at an author's manuscript with no promise to purchase.

SPECULATIVE FICTION (SPECFIC). The all-inclusive term for science fiction, fantasy, and horror.

SPLATTERPUNK. Type of horror fiction known for its very violent and graphic content.

SUBSIDIARY. An incorporated branch of a company or conglomerate (e.g. Alfred Knopf, Inc., a subsidiary of Random House, Inc.).

SUBSIDIARY RIGHTS. All rights other than book publishing rights included in a book contract, such as paperback, book club, and movie rights.

SUBSIDY PUBLISHER. A book publisher who charges the author for the cost of typesetting, printing, and promoting a book. Also called a *vanity publisher*.

SUBTERFICIAL FICTION. Innovative, challenging, nonconventional fiction in which what seems to be happening is the result of things not so easily perceived.

SUSPENSE. A genre of fiction where the plot's primary function is to build a feeling of anticipation and fear in the reader over its possible outcome.

SYNOPSIS. A brief summary of a story, novel or play. As part of a book proposal, it is a comprehensive summary condensed in a page or page and a half.

TABLOID. Publication printed on paper about half the size of a regular newspaper page (e.g. the *National Enquirer*).

TEARSHEET. Page from a magazine containing a published story.

TECHNO-THRILLER. This genre utilizes many of the same elements as the thriller, with one major difference. In techno-thrillers, technology becomes a major character. In Tom Clancy's *The Hunt for Red October*, for example, specific functions of the submarine become crucial to plot development.

THEME. The dominant or central idea in a literary work; its message, moral, or main thread.

THRILLER. A novel intended to arouse feelings of excitement or suspense. Works in this genre are highly sensational, usually focusing on illegal activities, international espionage, sex, and violence. A thriller is often a detective story in which the forces of good are pitted against the forces of evil in a kill-or-be-killed situation.

TRADE PAPERBACK. A softbound volume, usually around 5x8, published and designed for the general public, available mainly in bookstores.

TRADITIONAL FANTASY. Fantasy with an emphasis on magic, using characters with the ability to practice magic, such as wizards, witches, dragons, elves, and unicorns.

UNSOLICITED MANUSCRIPT. A story or novel manuscript that an editor did not specifically ask to see.

URBAN FANTASY. Fantasy that takes magical characters, such as elves, fairies, vampires, or wizards, and places them in modern-day settings, often in the inner city.

VANITY PUBLISHER. See subsidy publisher.

VIEWPOINT. The position or attitude of the first- or third-person narrator or multiple narrators, which determines how a story's action is seen and evaluated.

WESTERN. Genre with a setting in the West, usually between 1860 and 1890, with a formula plot about cowboys or other aspects of frontier life.

WHODUNIT. Genre dealing with murder, suspense, and the detection of criminals.

WORK-FOR-HIRE. Work that another party commissions you to do, generally for a flat fee. The creator does not own the copyright and therefore cannot sell any rights.

YOUNG ADULT. The general classification of books written for readers 12 and up.

ZINE. Often one- or two-person operations run from the home of the publisher/editor. Themes tend to be specialized, personal, experimental, and often controversial.

GENRE GLOSSARY

Definitions of Fiction Subcategories

The following were provided courtesy of The Extended Novel Writing Workshop, created by the staff of Writers Online Workshops (www.writersonlineworkshops.com).

MYSTERY SUBCATEGORIES

The major mystery subcategories are listed below, each followed by a brief description and the names of representative authors, so you can sample each type of work. Note that we have loosely classified "suspense/thriller" as a mystery category. While these stories do not necessarily follow a traditional "whodunit" plot pattern, they share many elements with other mystery categories. In addition, many traditional mysteries are marketed as suspense/thriller because of this category's current appeal in the marketplace. Since the lines between categories are frequently blurred, it seems practical to include them all here.

AMATEUR DETECTIVE. As the name implies, the detective is not a professional detective (private or otherwise), but is almost always a professional something. This professional association routinely involves the protagonist in criminal cases (in a support capacity), gives him or her a special advantage in a specific case, or provides the contacts and skills necessary to solve a particular crime. (Jonathan Kellerman, Patricia Cornwell, Jan Burke)

CLASSIC MYSTERY (WHODUNIT). A crime (almost always a murder or series of murders) is solved. The detective is the viewpoint character; the reader never knows any more or less about the crime than the detective, and all the clues to solving the crime are available to the reader.

COURTROOM DRAMA. The action takes place primarily in the courtroom; the protagonist is generally a defense attorney out to prove the innocence of his or her client by finding the real culprit. (Scott Turow, Steve Martini, Richard North Patterson, John Grisham)

COZY. A special class of the amateur detective category that frequently features a female protagonist. (Agatha Christie's Miss Marple stories are the classic example.) There is less onstage violence than in other categories, and the plot is often wrapped up in a final scene where the detective identifies the murderer and explains how the crime was solved. In contemporary stories, the protagonist can be anyone from a chronically curious housewife to a mystery-buff clergyman to a college professor, but he or she is usually quirky, even eccentric. (Susan Isaacs, Andrew Greeley, Lillian Jackson Braun)

ESPIONAGE. The international spy novel is less popular since the end of the cold war, but stories can still revolve around political intrigue in unstable regions. (John le Carré, Ken Follett)

HEISTS AND CAPERS. The crime itself is the focus. Its planning and execution are seen in detail, and the participants are fully drawn characters that may even be portrayed sympathetically. One character is the obvious leader of the group (the ``brains"); the other members are often brought together by the leader specifically for this job and may or may not have a previous association. In a heist, no matter how clever or daring the characters are, they are still portrayed as criminals, and the expectation is that they will be caught and punished (but not always). A caper is more lighthearted, even comedic. The participants may have a noble goal (something other than personal gain) and often get away with the crime. (Eric Ambler, Tony Kenrick, Leslie Hollander)

HISTORICAL. May be any category or subcategory of mystery, but with an emphasis on setting, the details of which must be diligently researched. But beyond the historical details (which must never overshadow the story), the plot develops along the lines of its contemporary counterpart. (Candace Robb, Caleb Carr, Anne Perry)

JUVENILE/YOUNG ADULT. Written for the 8-12 age group (Middle Grade) or the 12 and up age group (Young Adult), the crime in these stories may or may not be murder, but it is serious. The protagonist is a kid (or group of kids) in the same age range as the targeted reader. There is no graphic violence depicted, but the stories are scary and the villains are realistic. (Mary Downing Hahn, Wendy Corsi Staub, Cameron Dokey, Norma Fox Mazer)

MEDICAL THRILLER. The plot can involve a legitimate medical threat (such as the outbreak of a virulent plague) or the illegal or immoral use of medical technology. In the former scenario, the protagonist is likely to be the doctor (or team) who identifies the virus and procures the antidote; in the latter he or she could be a patient (or the relative of a victim) who uncovers the plot and brings down the villain. (Robin Cook, Michael Palmer, Michael Crichton, Stanley Pottinger)

POLICE PROCEDURALS. The most realistic category, these stories require the most meticulous research. A police procedural may have more than one protagonist since cops rarely work alone. Conflict between partners, or between the detective and his or her superiors, is a common theme. But cops are portrayed positively as a group, even though there may be a couple of bad or ineffective law enforcement characters for contrast and conflict. Jurisdictional disputes are still popular sources of conflict as well. (Lawrence Treat, Joseph Wambaugh, Ridley Pearson, Julie Smith)

PRIVATE DETECTIVE. When described as "hard-boiled," this category takes a tough stance. Violence is more prominent, characters are darker, the detective—while almost always licensed by the state—operates on the fringes of the law, and there is often open resentment between the detective and law enforcement. More "enlightened" male detectives and a crop of contemporary females have brought about new trends in this category. (For female P.I.s—Sue Grafton, Sara Paretsky; for male P.I.s—John D. MacDonald, Lawrence Sanders, Robert Parker)

SUSPENSE/THRILLER. Where a classic mystery is always a whodunit, a suspense/thriller novel may deal more with the intricacies of the crime, what motivated it, and how the villain (whose identity may be revealed to the reader early on) is caught and brought to justice. Novels in this category frequently employ multiple points of view and have a broader scope than a more traditional murder mystery. The crime may not even involve murder—it may be a threat to global economy or regional ecology; it may be technology run amok or abused at the hands of an unscrupulous scientist; it may involve innocent citizens victimized for personal or corporate gain. Its perpetrators are kidnappers, stalkers, serial killers, rapists, pedophiles, computer hackers, or just about anyone with an evil intention and the means to carry it out. The protagonist may be a private detective or law enforcement official, but is just as likely to be a doctor, lawyer, military officer, or other individual in a unique position to identify the villain and bring him or her to justice. (James Patterson, John J. Nance, Michael Connelly)

TECHNO-THRILLER. These are replacing the traditional espionage novel, and feature technology as an integral part of not just the setting, but the plot as well. (Tom Clancy, Stephen Coonts)

WOMAN IN JEOPARDY. A murder or other crime may be committed, but the focus is on the woman (and/or her children) currently at risk, her struggle to understand the nature of the danger, and her eventual victory over her tormentor. The protagonist makes up for her lack of physical prowess with intellect or special skills, and solves the problem on her own or with the help of her family (but she runs the show). Closely related to this category is the Romantic Suspense. But, while the heroine in a romantic suspense is certainly a "woman in jeopardy,"' the mystery or suspense element is subordinate to the romance. (Mary Higgins Clark, Mary Stewart, Jessica Mann)

ROMANCE SUBCATEGORIES

These categories and subcategories of romance fiction have been culled from the *Romance Writer's Sourcebook* (Writer's Digest Books) and Phyllis Taylor Pianka's *How to Write Romances* (Writer's Digest Books). We've arranged the "major" categories below with the subcategories beneath them, each followed by a brief description and the names of authors who write in each category, so you can sample representative works.

CATEGORY OR SERIES. These are published in "lines" by individual publishing houses (such as Harlequin and Silhouette); each line has its own requirements as to word length, story content, and amount of sex. (Debbie Macomber, Nora Roberts, Glenda Sanders)

CHRISTIAN. With an inspirational, Christian message centering on the spiritual dynamic of the romantic relationship and faith in God as the foundation for that relationship; sensuality is played down. (Janelle Burnham, Ann Bell, Linda Chaikin, Catherine Palmer, Dee Henderson, Lisa Tawn Bergen)

GLITZ. So called because they feature (generally wealthy) characters with high-powered positions in careers that are considered to be glamorous—high finance, modeling/acting, publishing, fashion—and are set in exciting or exotic (often metropolitan) locales, such as Monte Carlo, Hollywood, London, or New York. (Jackie Collins, Judith Krantz)

HISTORICAL. Can cover just about any historical (or even prehistorical) period. Setting in the historical is especially significant, and details must be thoroughly researched and accurately presented. For a sampling of a variety of historical styles, try Laura Kinsell (*Flowers from the Storm*), Mary Jo Putney (*The Rake and the Reformer*) and Judy Cuevas (*Bliss*). Some currently popular periods/themes in historicals are:

- **GOTHIC:** historical with a strong element of suspense and a feeling of supernatural events, although these events frequently have a natural explanation. Setting plays an important role in establishing a dark, moody, suspenseful atmosphere. (Phyllis Whitney, Victoria Holt)
- **HISTORICAL FANTASY:** with traditional fantasy elements of magic and magical beings, frequently set in a medieval society. (Amanda Glass, Jayne Ann Krentz, Kathleen Morgan, Jessica Bryan, Taylor Quinn Evans, Carla Simpson, Karyn Monk)

- **EARLY AMERICAN:** usually Revolution to Civil War, set in New England or the South, but "frontier" stories set in the American West are quite popular as well. (Robin Lee Hatcher, Elizabeth Lowell, Heather Graham)
- **NATIVE AMERICAN:** where one or both of the characters are Native Americans; the conflict between cultures is a popular theme. (Carol Finch, Elizabeth Grayson, Karen Kay, Kathleen Harrington, Genell Dellim, Candace McCarthy)
- **REGENCY:** set in England during the Regency period from 1811 to 1820. (Carol Finch, Elizabeth Elliott, Georgette Heyer, Joan Johnston, Lynn Collum)

MULTICULTURAL. Most currently feature African-American or Hispanic couples, but editors are looking for other ethnic stories as well. Multiculturals can be contemporary or historical, and fall into any subcategory. (Rochelle Alers, Monica Jackson, Bette Ford, Sandra Kitt, Brenda Jackson)

PARANORMAL. Containing elements of the supernatural or science fiction/fantasy. There are numerous subcategories (many stories combine elements of more than one) including:

- **TIME TRAVEL:** One or more of the characters travels to another time—usually the past—to find love. (Jude Devereaux, Linda Lael Miller, Diana Gabaldon, Constance O'Day Flannery)
- **SCIENCE FICTION/FUTURISTIC:** S/F elements are used for the story's setting: imaginary worlds, parallel universes, Earth in the near or distant future. (Marilyn Campbell, Jayne Ann Krentz, J.D. Robb [Nora Roberts], Anne Avery)
- **CONTEMPORARY FANTASY:** From modern ghost and vampire stories to "New Age" themes such as extraterrestrials and reincarnation. (Linda Lael Miller, Anne Stuart, Antoinette Stockenberg, Christine Feehan)

ROMANTIC COMEDY. Has a fairly strong comic premise and/or a comic perspective in the author's voice or the voices of the characters (especially the heroine). (Jennifer Crusie, Susan Elizabeth Phillips)

ROMANTIC SUSPENSE. With a mystery or psychological thriller subplot in addition to the romance plot. (Mary Stewart, Barbara Michaels, Tami Hoag, Nora Roberts, Linda Howard, Catherine Coulter)

SINGLE TITLE. Longer contemporaries that do not necessarily conform to the requirements of a specific romance line and therefore feature more complex plots and nontraditional characters. (Mary Ruth Myers, Nora Roberts, Kathleen Gilles Seidel, Kathleen Korbel)

YOUNG ADULT. Focus is on first love with very little, if any, sex. These can have bittersweet endings, as opposed to the traditional romance happy ending, since first loves are often lost loves. (YA historical—Nancy Covert Smith, Louise Vernon; YA contemporary—Mary Downing Hahn, Kathryn Makris)

SCIENCE FICTION SUBCATEGORIES

Peter Heck, in his article "Doors to Other Worlds: Trends in Science Fiction and Fantasy," which appears in the 1996 edition of *Science Fiction and Fantasy Writer's Sourcebook* (Writer's Digest Books), identifies some science fiction trends that have distinct enough characteristics to be defined as categories. These distinctions are frequently the result of marketing decisions as much as literary ones, so understanding them is important in deciding where your novel idea belongs. We've supplied a brief description and the names of authors who write in each category. In those instances where the author writes in more than one category, we've included titles of appropriate representative works.

ALTERNATE HISTORY. Fantasy, sometimes with science fiction elements, that changes the accepted account of actual historical events or people to suggest an alternate view of history. (Ted Mooney, *Traffic and Laughter*; Ward Moore, *Bring the Jubilee*; Philip K. Dick, *The Man in the High Castle*)

CYBERPUNK. Characters in these stories are tough outsiders in a high-tech, generally near-future society where computers have produced major changes in the way society functions. (William Gibson, Bruce Sterling, Pat Cadigan, Wilhelmina Baird)

HARD SCIENCE FICTION. Based on the logical extrapolation of real science to the future. In these stories the scientific background (setting) may be as, or more, important than the characters. (Larry Niven)

MILITARY SCIENCE FICTION. Stories about war that feature traditional military organization and tactics extrapolated into the future. (Jerry Pournelle, David Drake, Elizabeth Moon)

NEW AGE. A category of speculative fiction that deals with subjects such as astrology, psychic phenomena, spiritual healing, UFOs, mysticism, and other aspects of the occult. (Walter Mosley, *Blue Light*; Neil Gaiman)

SCIENCE FANTASY. Blend of traditional fantasy elements with scientific or pseudoscientific support (genetic engineering, for example, to "explain" a traditional fantasy creature like the dragon). These stories are traditionally more character driven than hard science fiction. (Anne McCaffrey, Mercedes Lackey, Marion Zimmer Bradley)

SCIENCE FICTION MYSTERY. A cross-genre blending that can either be a more-or-less traditional science fiction story with a mystery as a key plot element, or a more-or-less traditional whodunit with science fiction elements. (Philip K. Dick, Lynn S. Hightower)

SCIENCE FICTION ROMANCE. Another genre blend that may be a romance with science fiction elements (in which case it is more accurately placed as a subcategory within the romance genre) or a science fiction story with a strong romantic subplot. (Anne McCaffrey, Melanie Rawn, Kate Elliot)

SOCIAL SCIENCE FICTION. The focus is on how the characters react to their environments. This category includes social satire. (George Orwell's *1984* is a classic example.) (Margaret Atwood, *The Handmaid's Tale*; Ursula K. Le Guin, *The Left Hand of Darkness*; Marge Piercy, *Woman on the Edge of Time*)

SPACE OPERA. From the term "horse opera," describing a traditional good-guys-versus-bad-guys western, these stories put the emphasis on sweeping action and larger-than-life characters. The focus on action makes these stories especially appealing for film treatment. (The Star Wars series is one of the best examples; also Samuel R. Delany.)

STEAMPUNK. A specific type of alternate history science fiction set in Victorian England in which characters have access to 20th-century technology. (William Gibson; Bruce Sterling, *The Difference Engine*)

YOUNG ADULT. Any subcategory of science fiction geared to a YA audience (12-18), but these are usually shorter novels with characters in the central roles who are the same age as (or slightly older than) the targeted reader. (Jane Yolen, Andre Norton)

FANTASY SUBCATEGORIES

Before we take a look at the individual fantasy categories, it should be noted that, for purposes of these supplements, we've treated fantasy as a genre distinct from science fiction. While these two are closely related, there are significant enough differences to warrant their separation for study purposes. We have included here those science fiction categories that have strong fantasy elements, or that have a significant amount of crossover (these categories appear in both the science fiction and the fantasy supplements), but "pure" science fiction categories are not included below. If you're not sure whether your novel is fantasy or science fiction, consider this definition by Orson Scott Card in *How to Write Science Fiction and Fantasy* (Writer's Digest Books):

"Here's a good, simple, semi-accurate rule of thumb: If the story is set in a universe that follows the same rules as ours, it's science fiction. If it's set in a universe that doesn't follow our rules, it's fantasy.

Or in other words, science fiction is about what could be but isn't; fantasy is about what couldn't be."

But even Card admits this rule is only "semi-accurate." He goes on to say that the real boundary between science fiction and fantasy is defined by how the impossible is achieved:

"If you have people do some magic, impossible thing [like time travel] by stroking a talisman or praying to a tree, it's fantasy; if they do the same thing by pressing a button or climbing inside a machine, it's science fiction."

Peter Heck, in his article "Doors to Other Worlds: Trends in Science Fiction and Fantasy," which appears in the 1996 edition of the *Science Fiction and Fantasy Writer's Sourcebook* (Writer's Digest Books), does note some trends that have distinct enough characteristics to be defined as separate categories. These categories are frequently the result of marketing decisions as much as literary ones, so understanding them is important in deciding where your novel idea belongs. We've supplied a brief description and the names of authors who write in each category, so you can sample representative works.

ARTHURIAN. Reworking of the legend of King Arthur and the Knights of the Round Table. (T.H. White, *The Once and Future King*; Marion Zimmer Bradley, *The Mists of Avalon*)

CONTEMPORARY (ALSO CALLED "URBAN") FANTASY. Traditional fantasy elements (such as elves and magic) are incorporated into an otherwise recognizable modern setting. (Emma Bull, *War for the Oaks*; Mercedes Lackey, *The SERRAted Edge*; Terry Brooks, the Knight of the Word series)

DARK FANTASY. Closely related to horror, but generally not as graphic. Characters in these stories are the "darker" fantasy types: vampires, witches, werewolves, demons, etc. (Anne Rice; Clive Barker, *Weaveworld*, *Imajica*; Fred Chappell)

FANTASTIC ALTERNATE HISTORY. Set in an alternate historical period (in which magic would not have been a common belief) where magic works, these stories frequently feature actual historical figures. (Orson Scott Card, *Alvin Maker*)

GAME-RELATED FANTASY. Plots and characters are similar to high fantasy, but are based on a particular role-playing game. (Dungeons and Dragons; Magic: The Gathering; Dragonlance Chronicles; Forgotten Realms; Dark Sun)

HEROIC FANTASY. The fantasy equivalent to military science fiction, these are stories of war and its heroes and heroines. (Robert E. Howard, the Conan the Barbarian series; Elizabeth Moon, *Deed of Paksenarion*; Michael Moorcock, the Elric series)

HIGH FANTASY. Emphasis is on the fate of an entire race or nation, threatened by an ultimate evil. J.R.R. Tolkien's Lord of the Rings trilogy is a classic example. (Terry Brooks, David Eddings, Margaret Weis, Tracy Hickman)

HISTORICAL FANTASY. The setting can be almost any era in which the belief in magic was strong; these are essentially historical novels where magic is a key element of the plot and/

or setting. (Susan Schwartz, *Silk Road and Shadow*; Margaret Ball, *No Earthly Sunne*; Tim Powers, *The Anubis Gates*)

JUVENILE/YOUNG ADULT. Can be any type of fantasy, but geared to a juvenile (8-12) or YA audience (12-18); these are shorter novels with younger characters in central roles. (J.K. Rowling, Christopher Paolini, C.S. Lewis)

SCIENCE FANTASY. A blend of traditional fantasy elements with scientific or pseudoscientific support (genetic engineering, for example, to "explain" a traditional fantasy creature like the dragon). These stories are traditionally more character driven than hard science fiction. (Anne McCaffrey, Mercedes Lackey, Marion Zimmer Bradley)

HORROR SUBCATEGORIES

Subcategories in horror are less well defined than in other genres and are frequently the result of marketing decisions as much as literary ones. But being familiar with the terms used to describe different horror styles can be important in understanding how your own novel might be best presented to an agent or editor. What follows is a brief description of the most commonly used terms, along with names of authors and, where necessary, representative works.

DARK FANTASY. Sometimes used as a euphemistic term for horror in general, but also refers to a specific type of fantasy, usually less graphic than other horror subcategories, that features more ``traditional" supernatural or mythical beings (vampires, werewolves, zombies, etc.) in either contemporary or historical settings. (Contemporary: Stephen King, *Salem's Lot*; Thomas Tessier, *The Nightwalker*. Historical: Brian Stableford, *The Empire of Fear*; Chelsea Quinn Yarbro, *Werewolves of London*.)

HAUNTINGS. "Classic" stories of ghosts, poltergeists, and spiritual possessions. The level of violence portrayed varies, but many writers in this category exploit the reader's natural fear of the unknown by hinting at the horror and letting the reader's imagination supply the details. (Peter Straub, *Ghost Story*; Richard Matheson, *Hell House*)

JUVENILE/YOUNG ADULT. Can be any horror style, but with a protagonist who is the same age as, or slightly older than, the targeted reader. Stories for middle grades (eight to 12 years old) are scary, with monsters and violent acts that might best be described as "gross," but stories for young adults (12-18) may be more graphic. (R.L. Stine, Christopher Pike, Carol Gorman)

PSYCHOLOGICAL HORROR. Features a human monster with horrific, but not necessarily supernatural, aspects. (Thomas Harris, *The Silence of the Lambs, Hannibal*; Dean Koontz, *Whispers*)

SPLATTERPUNK. Very graphic depiction of violence—often gratuitous—popularized in the 1980s, especially in film. (*Friday the 13th*, *Halloween*, *Nightmare on Elm Street*, etc.)

SUPERNATURAL/OCCULT. Similar to the dark fantasy, but may be more graphic in its depiction of violence. Stories feature satanic worship, demonic possession, or ultimate evil incarnate in an entity or supernatural being that may or may not have its roots in traditional mythology or folklore. (Ramsey Campbell; Robert McCammon; Ira Levin, *Rosemary's Baby*; William Peter Blatty, *The Exorcist*; Stephen King, *Pet Sematary*)

TECHNOLOGICAL HORROR. "Monsters" in these stories are the result of science run amok or technology turned to purposes of evil. (Dean Koontz, *Watchers*; Michael Crichton, *Jurassic Park*)

PROFESSIONAL ORGANIZATIONS

AGENTS' ORGANIZATIONS

ASSOCIATION OF AUTHORS' AGENTS (AAA), David Higham Associates Ltd., 5-8 Lower John Street, Golden Square, London W1F 9HA. (020) 7434 5900. E-mail: anthonygoff@davidhigham.co.uk. Website: www.agentsassoc.co.uk.

ASSOCIATION OF AUTHORS' REPRESENTATIVES (AAR). E-mail: info@aar-online.org. Website: www.aar-online.org.

ASSOCIATION OF TALENT AGENTS (ATA), 9255 Sunset Blvd., Suite 930, Los Angeles CA 90069. (310)274-0628. Fax: (310)274-5063. E-mail: shellie@agentassociation.com. Website: www.agentassociation.com.

WRITERS' ORGANIZATIONS

ACADEMY OF AMERICAN POETS 584 Broadway, Suite 604, New York NY 10012-5243. (212)274-0343. Fax: (212)274-9427. E-mail: academy@poets.org. Website: www.poets.org.

AMERICAN CRIME WRITERS LEAGUE (ACWL), 17367 Hilltop Ridge Dr., Eureka MO 63205. Website: www.acwl.org.

AMERICAN MEDICAL WRITERS ASSOCIATION (AMWA), 30 West Gude Drive, Suite 525, Rockville MD 20850-4347. (301)294-5303. Fax: (301)294-9006. E-mail: amwa@amwa.org. Website: www.amwa.org.

AMERICAN SCREENWRITERS ASSOCIATION (ASA), 269 S. Beverly Dr., Suite 2600, Beverly Hills CA 90212-3807. (866)265-9091. E-mail: asa@goasa.com. Website: www.asascreenwriters.com.

AMERICAN TRANSLATORS ASSOCIATION (ATA), 225 Reinekers Lane, Suite 590, Alexandria VA 22314. (703)683-6100. Fax: (703)683-6122. E-mail: ata@atanet.org. Website: www.atanet.org.

EDUCATION WRITERS ASSOCIATION (EWA), 2122 P St., NW, Suite 201, Washington DC

20037. (202)452-9830. Fax: (202)452-9837. E-mail: ewa@ewa.org. Website: www.ewa.org.

GARDEN WRITERS ASSOCIATION (GWA), 10210 Leatherleaf Ct., Manassas VA 20111. (703)257-1032. Fax: (703)257-0213. E-mail: info@gardenwriters.org. Website: www.gardenwriters.org.

HORROR WRITERS ASSOCIATION (HWA), 244 Fifth Ave., Suite 2767, New York NY 10001. E-mail: hwa@horror.org. Website: www.horror.org.

THE INTERNATIONAL WOMEN'S WRITING GUILD (IWWG),P.O. Box 810, Gracie Station, New York NY 10028-0082. (212)737-7536. Fax: (212)737-9469. E-mail: dirhahn@aol.org. Website: www.iwwg.com.

MYSTERY WRITERS OF AMERICA (MWA), 1140 Broadway, Suite 1507, New York NY 10001. (212)888-8171. Fax: (212)888-8107. E-mail: mwa@mysterywriters.org. Website: www.mysterywriters.org.

NATIONAL ASSOCIATION OF SCIENCE WRITERS (NASW), P.O. Box 7905, Berkeley, CA 94707. (510)647-9500. E-mail: LFriedmann@nasw.org. website: www.nasw.org.

NATIONAL ASSOCIATION OF WOMEN WRITERS (NAWW), 24165 IH-10 W., Suite 217-637, San Antonio TX 78257. Phone/Fax: (866)821-5829. Website: www.naww.org.

ORGANIZATION OF BLACK SCREENWRITERS (OBS). Golden State Mutual Life Insurance Bldg., 1999 West Adams Blvd., Rm. Mezzanine Los Angeles, CA 90018. Website: www.obswriter.com.

OUTDOOR WRITERS ASSOCIATION OF AMERICA (OWAA), 121 Hickory St., Suite 1, Missoula MT 59801. (406)728-7434. Fax: (406)728-7445. E-mail: krhoades@owaa.org. Website: www.owaa.org.

POETRY SOCIETY OF AMERICA (PSA), 15 Gramercy Park, New York NY 10003. (212)254-9628. website: www.poetrysociety.org. Poets & Writers, 90 Broad St., Suite 2100, New York NY 10004. (212)226-3586. Fax: (212)226-3963. Website: www.pw.org.

ROMANCE WRITERS OF AMERICA (RWA), 114615 Benfer Road, Houston TX 77069. (832)717-5200. Fax: (832)717-5201. E-mail: info@rwanational.org. Website: www.rwanational.org.

SCIENCE FICTION AND FANTASY WRITERS OF AMERICA (SFWA), P.O. Box 877, Chestertown MD 21620. E-mail: execdir@sfwa.org. Website: www.sfwa.org.

SOCIETY OF AMERICAN BUSINESS EDITORS & WRITERS (SABEW), University of Missouri, School of Journalism, 30 Neff Annex, Columbia MO 65211. (602) 496-7862. E-mail: sabew@sabew.org. Website: www.sabew.org.

SOCIETY OF AMERICAN TRAVEL WRITERS (SATW), 7044 S. 13 St., Oak Creek WI 53154. (414)908-4949. Fax: (414)768-8001. E-mail: satw@satw.org. Website: www.satw.org.

SOCIETY OF CHILDREN'S BOOK WRITERS & ILLUSTRATORS (SCBWI), 8271 Beverly Blvd., Los Angeles CA 90048. (323)782-1010. Fax: (323)782-1892. E-mail: scbwi@scbwi.org. Website: www.scbwi.org.

AMERICAN INDEPENDENT WRITERS (AIW), 1001 Connecticut Ave. NW, Suite 701, Washington DC 20036. (202)775-5150. Fax: (202)775-5810. E-mail: info@aiwriters.org. Website: www.americanindependentwriters.org.

WESTERN WRITERS OF AMERICA (WWA). E-mail: spiritfire@kc.rr.com. Website: www.westernwriters.org.

INDUSTRY ORGANIZATIONS

AMERICAN BOOKSELLERS ASSOCIATION (ABA), 200 White Plains Rd., Suite 600, Tarrytown NY 10591. (914)591-2665. Fax: (914)591-2720. E-mail: info@bookweb.org. Website: www.bookweb.org.

AMERICAN SOCIETY OF JOURNALISTS & AUTHORS (ASJA), 1501 Broadway, Suite 302, New York NY 10036. (212)997-0947. Fax: (212)937-2315. E-mail: director@asja.org. Website: www.asja.org.

ASSOCIATION FOR WOMEN IN COMMUNICATIONS (AWC), 3337 Duke St., Alexandria VA 22314. (703)370-7436. Fax: (703)342-4311. E-mail: info@womcom.org. Website: www.womcom.org.

ASSOCIATION OF AMERICAN PUBLISHERS (AAP), 71 Fifth Ave., 2nd Floor, New York NY 10003. (212)255-0200. Fax: (212)255-7007. Or, 50 F St. NW, Suite 400, Washington DC 20001. (202)347-3375. Fax: (202)347-3690. Website: www.publishers.org.

THE ASSOCIATION OF WRITERS & WRITING PROGRAMS (AWP), Mail Stop 1E3, George Mason University, Fairfax VA 22030. (703)993-4301. Fax: (703)993-4302. E-mail: services@awpwriter.org. website: www.awpwriter.org.

THE AUTHORS GUILD, INC., 31 E. 32nd St., 7th Floor, New York NY 10016. (212)563-5904. Fax: (212)564-5363. E-mail: staff@authorsguild.org. website: www.authorsguild.org.

CANADIAN AUTHORS ASSOCIATION (CAA), P.O. Box 581, Stn. Main Orilla ON L3V 6K5 Canada. (705)653-0323. Fax: (705)653-0593. E-mail: admin@canauthors.org. Website: www.canauthors.org.

CHRISTIAN BOOKSELLERS ASSOCIATION (CBA), P.O. Box 62000, Colorado Springs CO 80962-2000. (800)252-1950. Fax: (719)272-3510. E-mail: info@cbaonline.org. website: www.cbaonline.org.

THE DRAMATISTS GUILD OF AMERICA, 1501 Broadway, Suite 701, New York NY 10036. (212)398-9366. Fax: (212)944-0420. Website: www.dramatistsguild.com.

NATIONAL LEAGUE OF AMERICAN PEN WOMEN (NLAPW), 1300 17th St. NW, Washington DC 20036-1973. (202)785-1997. Fax: (202)452-8868. E-mail: nlapw1@verizon.net. Website: www.americanpenwomen.org.

NATIONAL WRITERS ASSOCIATION (NWA), 10940 S. Parker Rd., #508, Parker CO 80134. (303)841-0246. Fax: (303)841-2607. E-mail: natlwritersassn@hotmail.com. Website: www.nationalwriters.com

NATIONAL WRITERS UNION (NWU), 256 West 38th Street, Suite 703, New York, NY 10018. (212)254-0279. Fax: (212)254-0673. E-mail: nwu@nwu.org. Website: www.nwu.org.

PEN AMERICAN CENTER, 588 Broadway, Suite 303, New York NY 10012-3225. (212)334-1660. Fax: (212)334-2181. E-mail: pen@pen.org. Website: www.pen.org.

THE PLAYWRIGHTS GUILD OF CANADA (PGC), 215 Spadina Ave., Suite #210, Toronto ON M5T 2C7 Canada. (416)703-0201. Fax: (416)703-0059. E-mail: info@playwrightsguild.ca. Website: www.playwrightsguild.com.

VOLUNTEER LAWYERS FOR THE ARTS (VLA), One E. 53rd St., 6th Floor, New York NY 10022. (212)319-2787. Fax: (212)752-6575. Website: www.vlany.org.

WOMEN IN FILM (WIF), 6100 Wilshire Blvd., Suite 710, Los Angeles CA 90048. (323)935-2211. Fax: (323)935-2212. E-mail: info@wif.org. Website: www.wif.org.

WOMEN'S NATIONAL BOOK ASSOCIATION (WNBA), P.O. Box 237, FDR Station, New York NY 10150. (212)208-4629. Fax: (212)208-4629. E-mail: publicity@bookbuzz.com. Website: www.wnba-books.org.

WRITERS GUILD OF ALBERTA (WGA), 11759 Groat Rd., Edmonton AB T5M 3K6 Canada. (780)422-8174. Fax: (780)422-2663. E-mail: mail@writersguild.ab.ca. Website: writers-guild.ab.ca.

WRITERS GUILD OF AMERICA-EAST (WGA), 555 W. 57th St., Suite 1230, New York NY 10019. (212)767-7800. Fax: (212)582-1909. e-mail: info@wgaeast.org. Website: www.wgaeast.org.

WRITERS GUILD OF AMERICA-WEST (WGA), 7000 W. Third St., Los Angeles CA 90048. (323)951-4000. Fax: (323)782-4800. Website: www.wga.org.

WRITERS UNION OF CANADA (TWUC), 90 Richmond St. E., Suite 200, Toronto ON M5C 1P1 Canada. (416)703-8982. Fax: (416)504-9090. E-mail: info@writersunion.ca. Website: www.writersunion.ca.

LITERARY AGENTS

Many publishers are willing to look at unsolicited submissions, but most feel having an agent is in the writer's best interest. In this section, we include agents who specialize in or represent fiction.

The commercial fiction field is intensely competitive. Many publishers have small staffs and little time. For that reason, many book publishers rely on agents for new talent. Some publishers are even relying on agents as "first readers" who must wade through the deluge of submissions from writers to find the very best. For writers, a good agent can be a foot in the door—someone willing to do the necessary work to put your manuscript in the right editor's hands.

It would seem today that finding a good agent is as hard as finding a good publisher. Yet those writers who have agents say they are invaluable. Not only can a good agent help you make your work more marketable; an agent also acts as your business manager and adviser, protecting your interests during and after contract negotiations.

Still, finding an agent can be very difficult for a new writer. If you are already published in magazines, you have a better chance than someone with no publishing credits. (Some agents read periodicals, searching for new writers.) Although many agents do read queries and manuscripts from unpublished authors without introduction, referrals from their writer clients can be a big help. If you don't know any published authors with agents, attending a conference is a good way to meet agents. Some agents even set aside time at conferences to meet new writers.

Almost all the agents listed here have said they are open to working with new, previously unpublished writers as well as published writers. They do not charge a fee to cover the time and effort involved in reviewing a manuscript or a synopsis and chapters, but their time is still extremely valuable. Only send an agent your work when you feel it is as complete and polished as possible.

USING THE LISTINGS

It is especially important that you read individual listings carefully before contacting these busy agents. The first information after the company name includes the address and phone, fax, e-mail address (when available) and website. **Member Agents** gives the names of individual agents working at that company. (Specific types of fiction an agent handles are indicated in parentheses after that agent's name.) The **Represents** section lists the types of fiction the agency works with. Reading the **Recent Sales** gives you the names of writers with whom an agent is currently working and, very important, publishers with whom the agent has placed manuscripts . **Writers' Conferences** identifies conferences an agent attends (and where you might possibly meet that agent). **Tips** presents advice directly from the agent to authors.

Also, look closely at the openness to submissions icons that precede most listings. They will indicate how willing an agency is to take on new writers.

AITKEN ALEXANDER ASSOCIATES

18-21 Cavaye Place, London England SW10 9PT UK. (44)(207)373-8672. Fax: (44)(207)373-6002. E-mail: reception@aitkenalexander.co.uk. Website: www.aitkenalexander.co.uk. **Contact:** Submissions Department. Estab. 1976. Represents 300+ clients. 10% of clients are new/unpublished writers.

MEMBER AGENTS Gillon Aitken, agent; Clare Alexander, agent; Andrew Kidd, agent.

REPRESENTS nonfiction books, novels. **Considers these fiction areas:** historical, literary.

"We specialize in literary fiction and nonfiction." Does not represent illustrated children's books, poetry, or screenplays.

HOW TO CONTACT Query with SASE. Submit synopsis, first 30 pages, and SASE. Aitken Alexander Associates. You can either address your submission to an individual agent, or simply to the Submissions Department. Responds in 6-8 weeks to queries. Obtains most new clients through recommendations from others, solicitations.

TERMS Agent receives 15% commission on domestic sales. Agent receives 20% commission on foreign sales. Offers written contract; 28-day notice must be given to terminate contract. Charges for photocopying and postage.

RECENT SALES Sold 50 titles in the last year. *My Life with George*, by Judith Summers (Voice); *The Separate Heart*, by Simon Robinson (Bloomsbury); *The Fall of the House of Wittgenstein*, by Alexander Waugh (Bloomsbury); *Shakespeare's Life*, by Germane Greer (Picador); *Occupational Hazards*, by Rory Stewart.

TIPS "Before submitting to us, we advise you to look at our existing client list to establish whether your work will be of interest. Equally, you should consider whether the material you have written is ready to submit to a literary agency. If you feel your work qualifies, then send us a letter introducing yourself. Keep it relevant to your writing (e.g., tell us about any previously published work, be it a short story or journalism; you may be studying or have completed a post-graduate qualification in creative writing; when it comes to nonfiction, we would want to know what qualifies you to write about the subject)."

ALIVE COMMUNICATIONS, INC.

7680 Goddard St., Suite 200, Colorado Springs CO 80920. (719)260-7080. Fax: (719)260-8223. E-mail: submissions@alivecom.com. Website: www.alivecom.com. **Contact:** Rick Christian. Member of AAR. Other memberships include Authors Guild. Represents 100+ clients. 5% of clients are new/unpublished writers. Currently handles nonfiction books (50%), novels (40%), juvenile books (10%).

MEMBER AGENTS Rick Christian, president (blockbusters, bestsellers); Lee Hough (popular/commercial nonfiction and fiction, thoughtful spirituality, children's); Andrea Heinecke (thoughtful/inspirational nonfiction, women's fiction/nonfiction, popular/commercial nonfiction and fiction); Joel Kneedler popular/commercial nonfiction and fiction, thoughtful spirituality, children's).

REPRESENTS nonfiction books, novels, short story collections, novellas. **Considers these fiction areas:** adventure, contemporary issues, crime, family saga, historical, humor, inspirational, literary, mainstream, mystery, police, religious, satire, suspense, thriller.

This agency specializes in fiction, Christian living, how-to, and commercial nonfiction. Actively seeking inspirational, literary, and mainstream fiction, and work from authors with established track records and platforms. Does not want to receive poetry, scripts, or dark themes.

HOW TO CONTACT Query via e-mail. "Be advised that this agency works primarily with well-established, best-selling, and career authors. Always looking for a breakout, blockbuster author with genuine talent." New clients come through recommendations from others.

TERMS Agent receives 15% commission on domestic sales. Offers written contract; 2-month notice must be given to terminate contract.

RECENT SALES Sold 300+ titles in the last year. *A spiritual memoir* by Eugene Peterson (Viking); *A Biography of Rwandan President Paul Kagame*, by Stephen Kinzer (St. Martin's Press); *Ever After*, by Karen Kingsbury (Zondervan); *A Hole in our Gospel*, by Rich Stearns (Nelson); *My Life outside the Ring*, by Hulk Hogan (St. Martin's Press), Tim Pawlenty (Tyndale).

TIPS Rewrite and polish until the words on the page shine. Endorsements and great connections may help, provided you can write with power and passion. Network with publishing professionals by making contacts, joining critique groups, and attending writers' conferences in order to make personal connections and to get feedback. Alive Communications, Inc., has established itself as a premiere literary agency. We serve an elite group of authors who are critically acclaimed and commercially successful in both Christian and general markets.

AMBASSADOR LITERARY AGENCY

P.O. Box 50358, Nashville TN 37205. (615)370-4700. E-mail: wes@ambassadoragency.com; info@ambassadoragency.com. Website: www.AmbassadorAgency.com. **Contact:** Wes Yoder. Represents 25-30 clients. 10% of clients are new/unpublished writers.Currently handles nonfiction books (95%), novels (5%).

Prior to becoming an agent, Mr. Yoder founded a music artist agency in 1973; he established a speakers bureau division of the company in 1984.

REPRESENTS nonfiction books, novels.

"This agency specializes in religious market publishing dealing primarily with A-level publishers." Actively seeking popular nonfiction themes, including the following: practical living; Christian spirituality; literary fiction. Does not want to receive short stories, children's books, screenplays, or poetry.

HOW TO CONTACT Ambassador Literary's department represents a growing list of best-selling authors. We represent select authors and writers who are published by the leading religious and general market publishers in the United States and Europe, and represent television and major motion picture rights for our clients. Authors should e-mail a short description of their manuscript with a request to submit their work for review. Guidelines for submission will be sent if we agree to review a manuscript. Accepts simultaneous submissions. Responds in 2-4 weeks to queries. Obtains most new clients through recommendations from others.

TERMS Agent receives 15% commission on domestic sales. Agent receives 20% commission on foreign sales. Offers written contract.

RECENT SALES Sold 20 titles in the last year. *The Death and Life of Gabriel Phillips*, by Stephen Baldwin (Hachette); *Amazing Grace: William Wilberforce and the Heroic Campaign to End Slavery*, by Eric Mataxas (Harper San Francisco); *Life@The Next Level*, by Courtney McBath (Simon and Schuster); *Women, Take Charge of Your Money*, by Carolyn Castleberry (Random House/Multnomah).

MARCIA AMSTERDAM AGENCY

41 W. 82nd St., Suite 9A, New York NY 10024-5613. (212)873-4945. **Contact:** Marcia Amsterdam. Signatory of WGA. Currently handles nonfiction books (15%), novels (70%), movie scripts (5%), TV scripts (10%).

Prior to opening her agency, Ms. Amsterdam was an editor.

REPRESENTS novels, movie scripts, feature film, sitcom. **Considers these fiction areas:** adventure, detective, horror, mainstream, mystery, romance (contemporary, historical), science, thriller, young adult.

HOW TO CONTACT Query with SASE. Responds in 1 month to queries.

TERMS Agent receives 15% commission on domestic sales. Agent receives 20% commission on foreign sales. Agent receives 10% commission on film sales. Offers written contract, binding for 1 year. Charges clients for extra office expenses, foreign postage, copying, legal fees (when agreed upon).

RECENT SALES *Hidden Child* by Isaac Millman (FSG); *Lucky Leonardo*, by Jonathan Canter (Sourcebooks).

TIPS "We are always looking for interesting literary voices."

BETSY AMSTER LITERARY ENTERPRISES

6312 SW Capitol Hwy #503, Portland OR 97239. Website: www.amsterlit.com. **Contact:** Betsy Amster. Estab. 1992. Member of AAR. Represents more than 65 clients. 35% of clients are new/unpublished writers.Currently handles nonfiction books (65%), novels (35%).

Prior to opening her agency, Ms. Amster was an editor at Pantheon and Vintage for 10 years, and served as editorial director for the Globe Pequot Press for 2 years.

REPRESENTS nonfiction books, novels. **Considers these fiction areas:** ethnic, literary, women's, high quality.

"Actively seeking strong narrative nonfiction, particularly by journalists; outstanding literary fiction (the next Richard Ford or Jhumpa Lahiri); witty, intelligent commerical women's fiction (the next Elinor Lipman or Jennifer Weiner); mysteries that open new worlds to us; and high-profile self-help and psychology, preferably research based." Does not want to receive poetry, children's books, romances, western, science fiction, action/adventure, screenplays, fantasy, techno-thrillers, spy capers, apocalyptic scenarios, or political or religious arguments.

HOW TO CONTACT For adult titles: b.amster.assistant@gmail.com. See submission requirements online at website. The requirements have changed and only e-mail submissions are accepted. Accepts simultaneous submissions. Responds in 1 month to queries. Responds in 2 months to mss. Obtains most new clients through recommendations from others, solicitations, conferences.

TERMS Agent receives 15% commission on domestic sales. Agent receives 20% commission on foreign sales. Offers written contract, binding for 1 year; 3-month notice must be given to terminate contract. Charges for photocopying, postage, long distance phone calls, messengers, galleys/books used in submissions to foreign and film agents and to magazines for first serial rights.

WRITERS CONFERENCES USC Masters in Professional Writing; San Diego State University Writers' Conference; UCLA Extension Writers' Program; Los Angeles Times Festival of Books; The Loft Literary Center; Willamette Writers Conference.

ARTISTS AND ARTISANS INC.

244 Madison Ave., Suite 334, New York NY 10016. Website: www.artistsandartisans.com. **Contact:** Adam Chromy and Jamie Brenner. Represents 70 clients. 80% of clients are new/unpublished writers. Currently handles nonfiction books (50%), fiction 50%.

MEMBER AGENTS Adam Chromy (fiction and narrative nonfiction); Jamie Brenner (thrillers, commercial and literary fiction, memoir, narrative nonfiction, Young Adult); Gwendolyn Heasley (Young Adult).

REPRESENTS nonfiction books, novels. **Considers these fiction areas:** confession, family, humor, literary, mainstream.

"My education and experience in the business world ensure that my clients' enterprise as authors gets as much attention and care as their writing." Working journalists for nonfiction books. No scripts, photo, or childrens' books.

HOW TO CONTACT Query by e-mail only. Start subject line with "query." No unsolicted submissions. All fiction queries must include a brief author's bio, and the setup or premise for the book. Accepts simultaneous submissions. Responds to queries only if interested. Obtains most new clients through recommendations from others, solicitations, conferences.

TERMS Agent receives 15% commission on domestic sales. Agent receives 25% commission on foreign sales. Offers written contract; 1-month notice must be given to terminate contract. "We only charge for extraordinary expenses (e.g., client requests check via FedEx instead of regular mail)."

RECENT SALES *New World Monkeys*, (Shaye Areheart); *World Made by Hand* (Grove Atlantic); *House of Cards*, by David Ellis Dickerson (Penguin).

WRITERS CONFERENCES ASJA Writers Conference, Pacific Northwest Writers Conference, Newbury Port Writers Conference.

TIPS "Please make sure you are ready before approaching us or any other agent. If you write fiction, make sure it is the best work you can do and get objective criticism from a writing group. If you write nonfiction, make sure the proposal exhibits your best work and a comprehensive understanding of the market."

AVENUE A LITERARY

419 Lafayette St., Second Floor, New York NY 10003. Fax: (212)228-6149. E-mail: submissions@avenuealiterary.com. Website: www.avenuealiterary.com. **Contact:** Jennifer Cayea. Represents 20 clients. 75% of clients are new/unpublished writers.Currently handles nonfiction books (40%), novels (45%), story collections (5%), juvenile books (10%).

Prior to opening her agency, Ms. Cayea was an agent and director of foreign rights for Nicholas Ellison, Inc., a division of Sanford J. Greenburger Associates. She was also an editor in the audio and large print divisions of Random House.

REPRESENTS nonfiction books, novels, short story collections, juvenile. **Considers these fiction areas:** contemporary issues, family saga, feminist, historical, literary, mainstream, thriller, young adult women's/chick lit.

"Our authors are dynamic and diverse. We seek strong new voices in fiction and nonfiction, and are fiercely dedicated to our authors." We are actively seeking new authors of fiction and nonfiction.

HOW TO CONTACT Query via e-mail only. Submit synopsis, publishing history, author bio, full contact info. Paste info in e-mail body. No attachments. Include all information *in the body of your* *e-mail*: submissions sent as attachments will *not* be read. Accepts simultaneous submissions. Responds in 6-8 weeks to queries. Obtains most new clients through recommendations from others, solicitations, conferences.

TERMS Agent receives 15% commission on domestic sales. Agent receives 15% commission on foreign sales. Offers written contract; 30-day notice must be given to terminate contract.

RECENT SALES *Gunmetal Black*, by Daniel Serrano.

TIPS "Build a résumé by publishing short stories if you are a fiction writer."

BAKER'S MARK LITERARY AGENCY

P.O. Box 8382, Portland OR 97207. (503)432-8170. E-mail: info@bakersmark.com. Website: www.Bakersmark.com. **Contact:** Bernadette Baker-Baughman or Gretchen Stelter. Currently handles nonfiction books (35%), novels (25%), (40% graphic novels).

REPRESENTS nonfiction books, novels, scholarly books, graphic novels. **Considers these fiction areas:** cartoon, comic books, contemporary issues, crime, detective, erotica, ethnic, experimental, fantasy, feminist, gay, glitz, historical, horror, humor, lesbian, literary, mainstream, mystery, police, psychic, regional, satire, supernatural, suspense, thriller, women's chick literature.

"Baker's Mark specializes in graphic novels and popular nonfiction with an extremely selective taste in commercial fiction." Actively seeking graphic novels, nonfiction, fiction (YA/Teen and magical realism in particular). Does not want to receive westerns, poetry, sci-fi, novella, high fantasy, or children's picture books.

HOW TO CONTACT Query with 1 page with no attachments and no chapters in the e-mail. Queries sent with attachments will be deleted unread. Send SASE if mailing by post. "If interested, we will request representative materials from you." Accepts simultaneous submissions. Responds in 4-6 weeks. Obtains most new clients through recommendations from others, solicitations.

TERMS Agent receives 15% commission on domestic sales. Agent receives 20% commission on foreign sales. Offers written contract, binding for 18 months; 30-day notice must be given to terminate contract.

RECENT SALES *Never After*, by Dan Elconin (Simon Pulse); *Boilerplate: History's Mechanical Marvel* by Paul Guinan and Anina Bennet (Abrams Image); *War Is Boring*, by David Axe, with illustration by Matt Bors (New American Library); *The Choyster Generation*, by Amalia mcGibbon, Claire Williams, and Lara Vogel (Seal Press).

WRITERS CONFERENCES New York Comic Convention, BookExpo of America, San Diego Comic Con, Stumptown Comics Fest, Emerald City Comic Con.

TIPS "Baker's Mark is also looking to help pioneer new media models for books, and is especially interested in books that experiment with social media, open source software (and other digital technologies) as we help establish new business paradigms for the ebook revolution."

BARER LITERARY, LLC

270 Lafayette St., Suite 1504, New York NY 10012. (212)691-3513. E-mail: submissions@barerliterary.com. Website: www.barerliterary.com. **Contact:** Julie Barer. Estab. 2004. Member of AAR.

Before becoming an agent, Julie worked at Shakespeare & Co. Booksellers in New York City. She is a graduate of Vassar College.

MEMBER AGENTS Julie Barer.

REPRESENTS nonfiction books, novels, short story collections. Julie Barer is especially interested in working with emerging writers and developing long-term relationships with new clients. **Considers these fiction areas:** contemporary issues, ethnic, historical, literary, mainstream.

This agency no longer accepts young adult submissions. No Health/Fitness, Business/Investing/Finance, Sports, Mind/Body/Spirit, Reference, Thrillers/Suspense, Military, Romance, Children's Books/Picture Books, Screenplays.

HOW TO CONTACT Query with SASE; no attachments if query by e-mail. We do not respond to queries via phone or fax.

TERMS Agent receives 15% commission on domestic sales. Agent receives 20% commission on foreign sales. Offers written contract. Charges for photocopying and books ordered.

RECENT SALES *The Unnamed*, by Joshua Ferris (Reagan Arthur Books); *Tunneling to the Center of the Earth*, by Kevin Wilson (Ecco Press); *A Disobedient Girl*, by Ru Freeman (Atria Books); *A Friend of the Family*, by Lauren Grodstein (Algonquin); *City of Veils*, by Zoe Ferraris (Little, Brown).

LORELLA BELLI LITERARY AGENCY (LBLA)

54 Hartford House, 35 Tavistock Crescent, Notting Hill, London England W11 1AY United Kingdom. (44)(207)727-8547. Fax: (44)(870)787-4194. E-mail: info@lorellabelliagency.com. Website: www.lorellabelliagency.com. **Contact:** Lorella Belli. Other memberships include AAA.

REPRESENTS nonfiction books, novels. **Considers these fiction areas:** historical, literary genre fiction; women's; crime.

"We are interested in first-time novelists, journalists, multicultural and international writing, and books about Italy." Does not want children's books, fantasy, science fiction, screenplays, short stories, or poetry.

HOW TO CONTACT For fiction, send query letter, first 3 chapters, synopsis, brief CV, SASE. For nonfiction, send query letter, full proposal, chapter outline, 2 sample chapters, SASE.

TERMS Agent receives 15% commission on domestic sales. Agent receives 20% commission on foreign sales.

TIPS "Please send an initial inquiry letter or e-mail before submitting your work to us."

THE BENT AGENCY

204 Park Place, Number 2, Brooklyn NY 11238. E-mail: info@thebentagency.com. Website: www.thebentagency.com. Contact: Jenny Bent, Susan Hawk. Estab. 2009.

Prior to forming her own agency, Ms. Bent was an agent and vice president at Trident Media.

MEMBER AGENTS Jenny Bent (all adult fiction except for science fiction); Susan Hawk (young adult and middle grade books; within the realm of kids stories, she likes fantasy, science fiction, historical fiction and mystery).

REPRESENTS Considers these fiction areas: commercial, crime, historical, horror, mystery, picture books, romance, suspense, thriller, women's, young adult literary.

HOW TO CONTACT E-mail queries@thebentagency.com, or if you're writing for children or teens, kidsqueries@thebentagency.com. "Tell us briefly who you are, what your book is, and why you're the one to write it. Then include the first ten pages of your material in the body of your e-mail. We respond to all queries, please resend your query if you haven't had a response within 4 weeks." Accepts simultaneous submissions.

RECENT SALES *Worst Laid Plans*, by Laura Kindred and Alexandra Lydon; *The Dark Ink Chronicles*, by Elle Jasper; *What We Don't Tell*, by Desiree Washington; *Bent Road*, by Lori Roy; *The Art of Saying Goodbye*, by Ellyn Bache; *Through Her Eyes*, by Jenny Archer; *You Don't Sweat Much for a Fat Girl*, by Celia Rivenbark; *When Harry Met Molly*, by Kieran Kramer.

BLEECKER STREET ASSOCIATES, INC.

217 Thompson St., #519, New York NY 10012. (212)677-4492. Fax: (212)388-0001. E-mail: bleeckerst@hotmail.com. **Contact:** Agnes Birnbaum. Member of AAR. Other memberships include RWA, MWA. Represents 60 clients. 20% of clients are new/unpublished writers.Currently handles nonfiction books (75%), novels (25%).

Prior to becoming an agent, Ms. Birnbaum was a senior editor at Simon & Schuster, Dutton/Signet, and other publishing houses.

REPRESENTS nonfiction books, novels. **Considers these fiction areas:** ethnic, historical, literary, mystery, romance, thriller, women's.

"We're very hands-on and accessible. We try to be truly creative in our submission approaches. We've had especially good luck with first-time authors." Does not want to receive science fiction, westerns, poetry, children's books, academic/scholarly/professional books, plays, scripts, or short stories.

HOW TO CONTACT Query with SASE. No e-mail, phone, or fax queries. Accepts simultaneous submissions. Responds in 2 weeks to queries. Responds in 1 month to mss. "Obtains most new clients through recommendations from others, solicitations, conferences, plus, I will approach someone with a letter if his/her work impresses me."

TERMS Agent receives 15% commission on domestic sales. Agent receives 25% commission on foreign sales. Offers written contract; 1-month notice must be given to terminate contract. Charges for postage, long distance, fax, messengers, photocopies (not to exceed $200).

RECENT SALES Sold 14 titles in the last year. *Following Sarah*, by Daniel Brown (Morrow); *Biology of the Brain*, by Paul Swingle (Rutgers University Press); *Santa Miracles*, by Brad and Sherry Steiger

(Adams); *Surviving the College Search*, by Jennifer Delahunt (St. Martin's).

TIPS "Keep query letters short and to the point; include only information pertaining to the book or background as a writer. Try to avoid superlatives in description. Work needs to stand on its own, so how much editing it may have received has no place in a query letter."

BOOKENDS, LLC

136 Long Hill Rd., Gillette NJ 07933. Website: www.bookends-inc.com; bookendslitagency.blogspot.com. **Contact:** Jessica Faust, Kim Lionetti, Jessica Alvarez. Member of AAR. RWA, MWA. Represents 50+ clients. 10% of clients are new/unpublished writers. Currently handles nonfiction books (50%), novels (50%).

MEMBER AGENTS Jessica Faust (fiction: romance, erotica, women's fiction, mysteries and suspense; nonfiction: business, finance, career, parenting, psychology, women's issues, self-help, health, sex); Kim Lionetti (Kim is only currently considering romance, women's fiction, and young adult queries. If your book is in any of these 3 categories, please be sure to specify "Romance," "Women's Fiction," or "Young Adult" in your e-mail subject line. Any queries that do not follow these guidelines will not be considered); Jessica Alvarez.

REPRESENTS nonfiction books, novels. **Considers these fiction areas:** detective, cozies, mainstream, mystery, romance, thriller, women's.

"BookEnds is currently accepting queries from published and unpublished writers in the areas of romance (and all its subgenres), erotica, mystery, suspense, women's fiction, and literary fiction. We also do a great deal of nonfiction in the areas of self-help, business, finance, health, pop science, psychology, relationships, parenting, pop culture, true crime, and general nonfiction." BookEnds does not want to receive children's books, screenplays, science fiction, poetry, or technical/military thrillers.

HOW TO CONTACT Review website for guidelines, as they change. BookEnds is no longer accepting unsolicited proposal packages or snail mail queries. Send query in the body of e-mail to only one agent.

BOOKS & SUCH LITERARY AGENCY

52 Mission Circle, Suite 122, PMB 170, Santa Rosa CA 95409. E-mail: representation@booksandsuch.biz. Website: www.booksandsuch.biz. **Contact:** Janet Kobobel Grant, Etta Wilson, Rachel Kent, Mary Keeley. Member of AAR. Member of CBA (associate), American Christian Fiction Writers. Represents 150 clients. 5% of clients are new/unpublished writers.Currently handles nonfiction books (50%), novels (50%).

Prior to becoming an agent, Ms. Grant was an editor for Zondervan and managing editor for Focus on the Family; Ms. Lawton was an author, sculptor, and designer of porcelein dolls. Ms. Zurakowski concentrates on material for 20-something or 30-something readers. Ms. Keeley accepts both nonfiction and adult fiction. She previously was an acquisition editor for Tyndale publishers.

REPRESENTS nonfiction books, novels. **Considers these fiction areas:** contemporary, family, historical, mainstream, religious, romance.

This agency specializes in general and inspirational fiction, romance, and in the Christian booksellers market. Actively seeking well-crafted material that presents Judeo-Christian values, if only subtly.

HOW TO CONTACT Query via e-mail only, no attachments. Accepts simultaneous submissions. Responds in 1 month to queries. "If you don't hear from us asking to see more of your writing within 30 days after you have sent your e-mail, please know that we have read and considered your submission but determined that it would not be a good fit for us." Obtains most new clients through recommendations from others, conferences.

TERMS Agent receives 15% commission on domestic sales. Agent receives 20% commission on foreign sales. Offers written contract; 2-month notice must be given to terminate contract. No additional charges.

RECENT SALES Sold 125 titles in the last year. *One Perfect Gift*, by Debbie Macomber (Howard Books); *Greetings from the Flipside*, by Rene Gutteridge and Cheryl Mckay (B&H Publishing); *Key on the Quilt*, by Stephanie Grace Whitson (Barbour Publishing); *Annotated Screwtape Letters, Annotations*, by Paul Mccusker, (Harper One). Other clients include: Lauraine Snelling, Lori Copeland, Rene Gutteridge, Dale Cramer, BJ Hoff, Diann Mills.

WRITERS CONFERENCES Mount Hermon Christian Writers' Conference; Writing for the Soul; American Christian Fiction Writers' Conference; San Francisco Writers' Conference.

TIPS "The heart of our agency's motivation is to develop relationships with the authors we serve, to do what we can to shine the light of success on them, and to help be a caretaker of their gifts and time."

BRADFORD LITERARY AGENCY

5694 Mission Center Rd., #347, San Diego CA 92108. (619)521-1201. E-mail: query@bradfordlit.com; laura@bradfordlit.com. Website: www.bradfordlit.com. **Contact:** Laura Bradford. Member of AAR. RWA Represents 35 clients. 20% of clients are new/unpublished writers. Currently handles nonfiction books (10%), novels (90%).

Ms. Bradford started with her first literary agency straight out of college and has 14 years of experience as a bookseller in parallel.

REPRESENTS nonfiction books, novels, novellas, stories within a single author's collection anthology. **Considers these fiction areas:** adventure, detective, erotica, ethnic, historical, humor, mainstream, mystery, romance, thriller psychic/supernatural.

Actively seeking romance (including category), romantica, women's fiction, mystery, thrillers, and young adult. Does not want to receive poetry, short stories, children's books (juvenile), or screenplays.

HOW TO CONTACT Query with SASE. Submit cover letter, first 30 pages of completed ms., synopsis, and SASE. Send no attachments via e-mail; only send a query letter with "query" in the subject line. Accepts simultaneous submissions. Responds in 2-4 weeks to queries. Responds in 10 weeks to mss. Obtains most new clients through solicitations.

TERMS Agent receives 15% commission on domestic sales. Agent receives 20% commission on foreign sales. Offers written contract, nonbinding for 2 years; 45-day notice must be given to terminate contract. Charges for photocopies, postage, extra copies of books for submissions.

RECENT SALES Sold 53 titles in the last year. *Tempting Eden*, by Margaret Rowe (Berkley Heat); *Princess Poltergeist*, by Stacey Kade (Hyperion Children's); *Ruthless Heart*, by Emma Lang (Kensington Brava); *Deadly Fear*, by Cynthia Eden (Grand Central); *Precious and Fragile Things*, by Megan Hart (Mira Books); *Cruel Enchantment*, by Anya Bast (Berkley Sensation); *Razorland*, by Elisabeth Naughton (Dorchestser); *His Darkest Craving*, by Juliana Stone (Avon).

WRITERS CONFERENCES RWA National Conference; Romantic Times Booklovers Convention.

BROWN LITERARY AGENCY

410 Seventh St. NW, Naples FL 34120. E-mail: broagent@aol.com. Website: www.brownliteraryagency.com. **Contact:** Roberta Brown. Member of AAR. Other memberships include RWA, Author's Guild. Represents 45 clients. 5% of clients are new/unpublished writers.

REPRESENTS novels. **Considers these fiction areas:** erotica, romance, women's single title and category. The agency specializes in women's fiction, erotica, single title and category romance. We have eclectic tastes and enjoy romantic comedies to sizzling erotica. Historicals to category romances. We look for unique voices and page-turning plots. We also represent young adult novels and mystery cozies.

"This agency is selectively reading material at this time."

HOW TO CONTACT ****At this time, the agency is closed to submissions, except by NY published authors seeking new representation.**** Query via e-mail only. Send synopsis and two chapters in Word attachment. Response time varies.

TERMS Agent receives 15% commission on domestic sales. Agent receives 20% commission on foreign sales. Offers written contract; 30-day notice must be given to terminate contract.

WRITERS CONFERENCES RWA National Conference.

TIPS "Polish your manuscript. Be professional."

CURTIS BROWN, LTD.

10 Astor Place, New York NY 10003-6935. (212)473-5400. E-mail: gknowlton@cbltd.com. Website: www.curtisbrown.com. **Contact:** Ginger Knowlton. Alternate address: Peter Ginsberg, president at CBSF, 1750 Montgomery St., San Francisco CA 94111. (415)954-8566. Member of AAR. Signatory of WGA.

MEMBER AGENTS Ginger Clark; Katherine Fausset; Holly Frederick, VP; Emilie Jacobson; Elizabeth Hardin; Ginger Knowlton, Exec. VP; Timothy Knowlton, CEO; Laura Blake Peterson; Mitchell Waters. San Francisco Office: Peter Ginsberg (President).

REPRESENTS nonfiction books, novels, short story collections, juvenile. **Considers these fiction areas:** contemporary, glitz, New Age, psychic, adventure, comic, confession, detective, erotica, ethnic, experimental, family, fantasy, feminist, gay, gothic, hi lo, historical, horror, humor, juvenile, literary, mainstream, military, multicultural, multimedia, mystery, occult, picture books, plays, poetry, regional, religious, romance, science, short, spiritual, sports, thriller, translation, western, young women's.

HOW TO CONTACT Prefers to read materials exclusively. *No unsolicited mss.* Responds in 3 weeks to queries. Responds in 5 weeks to mss. Obtains most new clients through recommendations from others, solicitations, conferences.

TERMS Offers written contract. Charges for some postage (overseas, etc.).

RECENT SALES This agency prefers not to share information on specific sales.

TRACY BROWN LITERARY AGENCY

P.O. Box 772, Nyack NY 10960. (914)400-4147. Fax: (914)931-1746. E-mail: tracy@brownlit.com. **Contact:** Tracy Brown. Represents 35 clients. Currently handles nonfiction books (90%), novels (10%).

Prior to becoming an agent, Mr. Brown was a book editor for 25 years.

REPRESENTS nonfiction books, novels anthologies. **Considers these fiction areas:** contemporary issues, feminist, literary, mainstream, women's.

Specializes in thorough involvement with clients' books at every stage of the process from writing to proposals to publication. Actively seeking serious nonfiction and fiction. Does not want to receive YA, sci-fi or romance.

HOW TO CONTACT Submit outline/proposal, synopsis, author bio. Accepts simultaneous submissions. Responds in 2 weeks to queries. Obtains most new clients through referrals.

TERMS Agent receives 15% commission on domestic sales. Agent receives 20% commission on foreign sales. Offers written contract.

RECENT SALES *Why Have Kids?* by Jessica Valenti (HarperCollins); *Hotel Notell: A Novel*, by Daphne Uviller (Bantam); *Healing Sexual Pain*, by Deborah Coady, MD, and Nancy Fish, MSW, MPH (Seal Press).

BROWNE & MILLER LITERARY ASSOCIATES

410 S. Michigan Ave., Suite 460, Chicago IL 60605-1465. (312)922-3063. E-mail: mail@browneandmiller.com. Website: www.browneandmiller.com. **Contact:** Danielle Egan-Miller. Estab. 1971. Member of AAR. Other memberships include RWA, MWA, Author's Guild. Represents 150 clients. 2% of clients are new/unpublished writers.Currently handles nonfiction books (25%), novels (75%).

REPRESENTS nonfiction books, most genres of commercial adult fiction and nonfiction, as well as select young adult projects. **Considers these fiction areas:** contemporary issues, crime, detective, erotica, ethnic, family saga, glitz, historical, inspirational, literary, mainstream, mystery, police, religious, romance, sports, suspense, thriller paranormal.

"We are partial to talented newcomers and experienced authors who are seeking hands-on career management, highly personal representation, and who are interested in being full partners in their books' successes. We are editorially focused and work closely with our authors through the whole publishing process, from proposal to after publication." "We are most interested in commercial women's fiction, especially elegantly crafted, sweeping historicals; edgy, fresh teen/chick/mom/lady lit; and CBA women's fiction by established authors. We are also very keen on literary historical mysteries and literary YA novels. Topical, timely nonfiction projects in a variety of subject areas are also of interest, especially prescriptive how-to, self-help, sports, humor, and pop culture." Does not represent poetry, short stories, plays, original screenplays, articles, children's picture books, software, horror, or sci-fi novels.

HOW TO CONTACT Only accepts e-mail queries. Inquiring authors may initially submit one chapter and a synopsis. *No unsolicited mss.* Prefers to read material exclusively. Put submission in the subject line. Send no attachments. Also has online submission form. Responds in 2-4 months to queries. Obtains most new clients through referrals, queries by professional/marketable authors.

TERMS Agent receives 15% commission on domestic sales. Agent receives 20% commission on foreign sales. Offers written contract, binding for 2 years. Charges clients for photocopying, overseas postage.

WRITERS CONFERENCES BookExpo America; Frankfurt Book Fair; RWA National Conference; ICRS; London Book Fair; Bouchercon, regional writers conferences.

TIPS "If interested in agency representation, be well informed."

PEMA BROWNE, LTD.

11 Tena Place, Valley Cottage NY 10989. E-mail: ppbltd@optonline.net. Website: www.pemabrowneltd.com. **Contact:** Pema Browne. Signatory of WGA. Other memberships include SCBWI, RWA. Represents 30 clients. Currently handles nonfiction books (25%), novels (50%), juvenile books (25%).

Prior to opening her agency, Ms. Browne was an artist and art buyer.

REPRESENTS nonfiction books, novels, juvenile reference books. **Considers these fiction areas:** contemporary, glitz, adventure, feminist, gay, historical, juvenile, literary, mainstream, commercial, mystery, picture books, religious, romance, contemporary, gothic, historical, regency, young.

"We are not accepting any new projects or authors until further notice."

HOW TO CONTACT Query with SASE. No attachments for e-mail.

TERMS Agent receives 20% commission on domestic sales. Agent receives 20% commission on foreign sales.

RECENT SALES *The Champion*, by Heather Grothaus (Kensington/Zebra); *The Highlander's Bride*, by Michele Peach (Kensington/Zebra); *The Daring Harriet Quimby*, by Suzanne Whitaker (Holiday House); *One Night to Be Sinful*, by Samantha Garver (Kensington); *Taming the Beast*, by Heather Grothaus (Kensington/Zebra); *Kisses Don't Lie* by Alexis Darin (Kensington/Zebra).

TIPS "We do not review manuscripts that have been sent out to publishers. If writing romance, be sure to receive guidelines from various romance publishers. In nonfiction, one must have credentials to lend credence to a proposal. Make sure of margins, double-space, and use clean, dark type."

KIMBERLEY CAMERON & ASSOCIATES

1550 Tiburon Blvd., #704, Tiburon CA 94920. Fax: (415)789-9177. E-mail: info@kimberleycameron.com. Website: www.kimberleycameron.com. **Contact:** Kimberley Cameron. Member of AAR. 30% of clients are new/unpublished writers.Currently handles nonfiction books 50%; fiction 50%.

Kimberley Cameron & Associates (formerly The Reece Halsey Agency) has had an illustrious client list of established writers, including the estate of Aldous Huxley, and has represented Upton Sinclair, William Faulkner, and Henry Miller.

MEMBER AGENTS Kimberley Cameron, Amy Burkhardt.

REPRESENTS nonfiction, fiction,. **Considers these fiction areas:** adventure, contemporary issues, ethnic, family saga, historical, horror, mainstream, mystery, interlinked short story collections, thriller, women's, and sophisticated/crossover young adult.

"We are looking for a unique and heartfelt voice that conveys a universal truth."

HOW TO CONTACT Query via e-mail. See our website for submission guidelines. Obtains new clients through recommendations from others, solicitations.

TERMS Agent receives 15% on domestic sales; 10% on film sales. Offers written contract, binding for 1 year.

WRITERS CONFERENCES Pacific Northwest Writers Association Conference, Aspen Summer Words, Willamette Writers Conference, San Diego State University Writers Conference, San Francisco Writers Conference, Killer Nashville, Left Coast Crime, Bouchercon, Book Passage Mystery and Travel Writers Conferences, Antioch Writers Workshop, Florida Writers Association Conference, and others.

TIPS "Please consult our submission guidelines and send a polite, well-written query to our e-mail address."

CAROL MANN AGENCY

55 Fifth Ave., New York NY 10003. (212)206-5635. Fax: (212)675-4809. Website: www.carolmannagency.com/. **Contact:** Eliza Dreier. Member of AAR. Represents roughly 200 clients. 15% of clients are new/unpublished writers.Currently handles nonfiction books (90%), novels (10%).

MEMBER AGENTS Carol Mann (health/medical, religion, spirituality, self-help, parenting, narrative nonfiction, current affairs); Laura Yorke; Gareth Esersky; Myrsini Stephanides (nonfiction areas of interest: pop culture and music, humor, narrative nonfiction and memoir, cookbooks; fiction areas of interest: offbeat literary fiction, graphic works, and edgy YA fiction). Joanne Wyckoff (nonfiction areas of interest: memoir, narrative nonfiction, personal narrative, psychology, women's issues, education, health and wellness, parenting, serious self-help, natural history); fiction.

REPRESENTS nonfiction books, novels. **Considers these fiction areas:** commercial, literary.

8→ This agency specializes in current affairs, self-help, popular culture, psychology, parenting, and history. Does not want to receive genre fiction (romance, mystery, etc.).

HOW TO CONTACT Please see website for submission guidelines. Responds in 4 weeks to queries.

TERMS Agent receives 15% commission on domestic sales. Agent receives 20% commission on foreign sales. Offers written contract.

CASTIGLIA LITERARY AGENCY

1155 Camino Del Mar, Suite 510, Del Mar CA 92014. (858)755-8761. Fax: (858)755-7063. E-mail: deborah@castigliaagency.com; win@castiglioagency.com. Website: home.earthlink.net/~mwgconference/id22.html. Member of AAR. Other memberships include PEN. Represents 65 clients. Currently handles nonfiction books (55%), novels (45%).

MEMBER AGENTS Julie Castiglia; Winifred Golden (science fiction, ethnic, commercial and thriller novels, plus narrative nonfiction and some health books—prefers referrals); Sally Van Haitsma (actively looking for good proposals by way of query letters, and her wish list covers literary and women's fiction, current affairs, architecture, pop culture, and science fiction); Deborah Ritchken (narrative nonfiction, food/cook books, design, France, literary fiction, no genre fiction).

REPRESENTS nonfiction books, novels. **Considers these fiction areas:** contemporary issues, ethnic, literary, mainstream, mystery, suspense, women's.

8→ Does not want to receive horror, screenplays, poetry or academic nonfiction.

HOW TO CONTACT No unsolicited submissions. Query with SASE. No e-mail submissions accepted. Obtains most new clients through recommendations from others, solicitations, conferences.

TERMS Agent receives 15% commission on domestic sales. Agent receives 25% commission on foreign sales. Offers written contract; 6-week notice must be given to terminate contract.

RECENT SALES *Germs Gone Wild*, by Kenneth King (Pegasus); *The Insider* by Reece Hirsch (Berkley/Penguin); *The Leisure Seeker*, by Michael Zadoorian (Morrow/HarperCollins); *Beautiful: The Life of Hedy Lamarr*, by Stephen Shearer (St. Martin's Press); *American Libre*, by Raul Ramos y Sanchez (Grand Central); *The Two Krishnas*, by Ghalib Shiraz Dhalla (Alyson Books).

WRITERS CONFERENCES Santa Barbara Writers' Conference; Southern California Writers' Conference; Surrey International Writers' Conference; San Diego State University Writers' Conference; Willamette Writers' Conference.

TIPS "Be professional with submissions. Attend workshops and conferences before you approach an agent."

CHERRY WEINER LITERARY AGENCY

28 Kipling Way, Manalapan NJ 07726-3711. (732)446-2096. Fax: (732)792-0506. E-mail: cherry8486@aol.com. **Contact:** Cherry Weiner. Represents 40 clients. 10% of clients are new/unpublished writers.Currently handles nonfiction books (10-20%), novels (80-90%).

REPRESENTS nonfiction books, novels. **Considers these fiction areas:** action, adventure, contemporary issues, crime, detective, family saga, fantasy, frontier, historical, mainstream, mystery, police, psychic, romance, science fiction, supernatural, thriller, westerns.

8→ *This agency is currently not accepting new clients except by referral or by personal contact at writers' conferences.* Specializes in fantasy, science fiction, westerns, mysteries (both contemporary and historical), historical novels, Native-American works, mainstream, and all genre romances.

HOW TO CONTACT Query with SASE. Prefers to read materials exclusively. Responds in 1 week to queries. Responds in 2 months to mss that I have asked for.

TERMS Agent receives 15% commission on domestic sales. Agent receives 15% commission on foreign sales. Offers written contract. Charges clients for extra copies of mss, first-class postage for author's copies of books, express mail for important documents/mss.

RECENT SALES Sold 70 titles in the last year. This agency prefers not to share information on specific sales.

TIPS "Meet agents and publishers at conferences. Establish a relationship, then get in touch with them and remind them of the meeting and conference."

CRICHTON & ASSOCIATES

6940 Carroll Ave., Takoma Park MD 20912. (301)495-9663. Fax: (202)318-0050. E-mail: query@crichton-associates.com. Website: www.crichton-associates.com. **Contact:** Sha-Shana Crichton. 90% of clients are new/unpublished writers.Currently handles nonfiction books 50%, fiction 50%.

Prior to becoming an agent, Ms. Crichton did commercial litigation for a major law firm.

REPRESENTS nonfiction books, novels. **Considers these fiction areas:** ethnic, feminist, inspirational, literary, mainstream, mystery, religious, romance, suspense chick lit.

Actively seeking women's fiction, romance, and chick lit. Looking also for multicultural fiction and nonfiction. Does not want to receive poetry, children's, YA, science fiction, or screenplays.

HOW TO CONTACT In the subject line of e-mail, please indicate whether your project is fiction or nonfiction. Please do not send attachments. Your query letter should include a description of the project and your biography. If you wish to send your query via snail mail, please include your telephone number and e-mail address. We will respond to you via e-mail. For fiction, include short synopsis and first 3 chapters with query. For nonfiction, send a book proposal. Responds in 3-5 weeks to queries.

TERMS Agent receives 15% commission on domestic sales. Agent receives 20% commission on foreign sales. Offers written contract, binding for 45 days. Only charges fees for postage and photocopying.

RECENT SALES *The African American Entrepreneur*, by W. Sherman Rogers (Praeger); *The Diversity Code*, by Michelle Johnson (Amacom); *Secret & Lies*, by Rhonda McKnight (Urban Books); *Love on the Rocks*, by Pamela Yaye (Harlequin). Other clients include Kimberley White, Beverley Long, Jessica Trap, Altonya Washington, Cheris Hodges.

WRITERS CONFERENCES Silicon Valley RWA; BookExpo America.

D4EO LITERARY AGENCY

7 Indian Valley Rd., Weston CT 06883. (203)544-7180. Fax: (203)544-7160. E-mail: d4eo@optonline.net. Website: http://www.d4eo.com. **Contact:** Bob Diforio. Represents more than 100 clients. 50% of clients are new/unpublished writers.Currently handles nonfiction books (70%), novels (25%), juvenile books (5%).

Prior to opening his agency, Mr. Diforio was a publisher.

MEMBER AGENTS Kristin Miller, Weronika Janczuk.

REPRESENTS nonfiction books, novels. **Considers these fiction areas:** adventure, detective, erotica, historical, horror, humor, juvenile, literary, mainstream, mystery, picture books, romance, science, sports, thriller, western, young adult.

HOW TO CONTACT Query with SASE. Accepts and prefers e-mail queries. Prefers to read material exclusively. Responds in 1 week to queries. Obtains most new clients through recommendations from others.

TERMS Agent receives 15% commission on domestic sales. Agent receives 25% commission on foreign sales. Offers written contract, binding for 2 years; 60-day notice must be given to terminate contract. Charges for photocopying and submission postage.

DANIEL LITERARY GROUP

1701 Kingsbury Dr., Suite 100, Nashville TN 37215. (615)730-8207. E-mail: submissions@danielliterarygroup.com. Website: www.danielliterarygroup.com. **Contact:** Greg Daniel. Represents 45 clients. 30% of clients are new/unpublished writers. Currently handles nonfiction books (85%), novels (15%).

Prior to becoming an agent, Mr. Daniel spent 10 years in publishing—six at the executive level at Thomas Nelson Publishers.

REPRESENTS nonfiction books, novels. **Considers these fiction areas:** action, adventure, contemporary issues, crime, detective, family saga, historical, humor, inspirational, literary, mainstream, mystery, police, religious, satire, suspense, thriller.

The agency currently accepts all fiction topics, except for children's, romance and sci-fi. "We take pride in our ability to come alongside our authors and help strategize about where they want their writing to take them in both the near and long term. Forging close relationships with our authors, we help them with such critical factors as editorial refinement, branding, audience, and marketing." The agency is open to submissions in almost every popular category of nonfiction, especially if authors are recognized experts in their fields. No screenplays, poetry, science fiction/fantasy, romance, children's, or short stories.

HOW TO CONTACT Query via e-mail only. Submit publishing history, author bio, brief synopsis of work, key selling points. E-queries only. Send no attachments. For fiction, send first 5 pages pasted in e-mail. Check Submissions Guidelines before querying or submitting. Please do not query via telephone. Responds in 2-3 weeks to queries.

DARHANSOFF & VERRILL LITERARY AGENTS

236 W. 26th St., Suite 802, New York NY 10001. (917)305-1300. Fax: (917)305-1400. E-mail: chuck@dvagency.com. Website: www.dvagency.com. Member of AAR. Represents 120 clients. 10% of clients are new/unpublished writers.Currently handles nonfiction books (25%), novels (60%), story collections (15%).

MEMBER AGENTS Liz Darhansoff; Chuck Verrill, Michele Mortimer.

REPRESENTS novels, juvenile books narrative nonfiction, literary fiction, mystery & suspense, young adult.

HOW TO CONTACT Queries welcome via website or with SASE. Obtains most new clients through recommendations from others.

DAVIS WAGER LITERARY AGENCY

419 N. Larchmont Blvd., #317, Los Angeles CA 90004. E-mail: submissions@daviswager.com. Website: www.daviswager.com. **Contact:** Timothy Wager. Estab. 2004. Represents 12 clients.

Prior to his current position, Mr. Wager was with the Sandra Dijkstra Literary Agency, where he worked as a reader and associate agent.

REPRESENTS nonfiction books, novels. **Considers these fiction areas:** literary.

Actively seeking: literary fiction and general-interest nonfiction. "I do not handle screenplays, children's books, romance, or science fiction. Memoirs and most genre fiction (other than crime or noir) are a serious long shot, too."

HOW TO CONTACT Query with SASE. Submit author bio, synopsis for fiction, book proposal or outline for nonfiction. Query via e-mail. No author queries by phone.

DEFIORE & CO.

47 E. 19th St., 3rd Floor, New York NY 10003. (212)925-7744. Fax: (212)925-9803. E-mail: info@defioreandco.com; submissions@defioreandco.com. Website: www.defioreandco.com. **Contact:** Lauren Gilchrist. Member of AAR. Represents 75 clients. 50% of clients are new/unpublished writers. Currently handles nonfiction books (70%), novels (30%).

Prior to becoming an agent, Mr. DeFiore was publisher of Villard Books (1997-1998), editor-in-chief of Hyperion (1992-1997), and editorial director of Delacorte Press (1988-1992).

MEMBER AGENTS Brian DeFiore (popular nonfiction, business, pop culture, parenting, commercial fiction); Laurie Abkemeier (memoir, parenting, business, how-to/self-help, popular science); Kate Garrick (literary fiction, memoir, popular non-fiction); Debra Goldstein (health and diet, wellness); Laura Nolan (cookbooks, memoir, nonfiction); Matthew Elblonk (young adult, popular culture, narrative nonfiction); Karen Gerwin (popular culture, memoir); Caryn Karmatz-Rudy (popular fiction, self-help, narrative nonfiction).

REPRESENTS nonfiction books, novels. **Considers these fiction areas:** ethnic, literary, mainstream, mystery, suspense, thriller.

"Please be advised that we are not considering children's picture books, poetry, adult science fiction and fantasy, romance, or dramatic projects at this time."

HOW TO CONTACT Query with SASE or e-mail to submissions@defioreandco.com. Please include the word "Query" in the subject line. All attachments will be deleted; please insert all text in the body of the e-mail. For more information about our agents, their individual interests, and their query guidelines, please visit our "About Us" page. Accepts simultaneous submissions. Responds in 3 weeks to queries. Responds in 2 months to mss. Obtains most new clients through recommendations from others.

TERMS Agent receives 15% commission on domestic sales. Agent receives 20% commission on foreign sales. Offers written contract; 10-day notice must be given to terminate contract. Charges clients for photocopying and overnight delivery (deducted only after a sale is made).

WRITERS CONFERENCES Maui Writers Conference; Pacific Northwest Writers Conference; North Carolina Writers' Network Fall Conference.

DHS LITERARY, INC.

10711 Preston Road, Suite 100, Dallas TX 75230. (214)363-4422. Fax: (214)363-4423. Website: www.dhsliterary.com. **Contact:** David Hale Smith, president. Represents 35 clients. 15% of clients are new/unpublished writers. Currently handles nonfiction books (60%), novels (40%).

Prior to opening his agency, Mr. Smith was an agent at Dupree/Miller & Associates.

REPRESENTS nonfiction books, novels. **Considers these fiction areas:** crime, detective, ethnic, frontier, literary, mainstream, mystery, police, suspense, thriller, westerns.

This agency is not actively seeking clients and usually takes clients on by referral only.

HOW TO CONTACT We accept new material by referral only. Only responds if interested. *No unsolicited mss.*

TERMS Agent receives 15% commission on domestic sales. Agent receives 25% commission on foreign sales. Offers written contract; 10-day notice must be given to terminate contract. This agency charges for postage and photocopying.

RECENT SALES *So Cold the River*, by Michael Koryta; *In The Shadow of Gotham*, by Stefanie Pintoff; *The Body Scoop for Girls*, by Jennifer Ashton, MD; *The Prosperity Plan*, by Laura Berman Fortgang .

TIPS "Remember to be courteous and professional, and to treat marketing your work and approaching an agent as you would any formal business matter. If you have a referral, always query first via e-mail. Sorry, but we cannot respond to queries sent via mail, even with a SASE. Visit our website for more information."

DONALD MAASS LITERARY AGENCY

121 W. 27th St., Suite 801, New York NY 10001. (212)727-8383. E-mail: info@maassagency.com. Website: www.maassagency.com. Member of AAR. Other memberships include SFWA, MWA, RWA. Represents more than 100 clients. 5% of clients are new/unpublished writers. Currently handles novels (100%).

Prior to opening his agency, Mr. Maass served as an editor at Dell Publishing (New York) and as a reader at Gollancz (London). He also served as the president of AAR.

MEMBER AGENTS Donald Maass (mainstream, literary, mystery/suspense, science fiction, romance); Jennifer Jackson (commercial fiction, romance, science fiction, fantasy, mystery/suspense); Cameron McClure (literary, mystery/suspense, urban, fantasy, narrative nonfiction and projects with multicultural, international, and environmental themes, gay/lesbian); Stacia Decker (fiction, memoir, narrative nonfiction, pop-culture [cooking, fashion, style, music, art], smart humor, upscale erotica/erotic memoir and multicultural fiction/nonfiction); Amy Boggs (fantasy and science fiction, especially urban fantasy, paranormal romance, steampunk, YA/children's, and alternate history. historical fiction, multi-cultural fiction, westerns).

REPRESENTS novels. **Considers these fiction areas:** crime, detective, fantasy, historical, horror, literary, mainstream, mystery, police, psychic, science fiction, supernatural, suspense, thriller, women's romance (historical, paranormal, and time travel).

This agency specializes in commercial fiction, especially science fiction, fantasy, mystery and suspense. Actively seeking to expand in literary fiction and women's fiction. We are fiction specialists. All genres are welcome. Does not want to receive nonfiction, picture books, prescriptive nonfiction, or poetry.

HOW TO CONTACT Query with SASE. Returns material only with SASE. Accepts simultaneous submissions. Responds in 2 weeks to queries. Responds in 3 months to mss.

TERMS Agent receives 15% commission on domestic sales. Agent receives 20% commission on foreign sales.

RECENT SALES *Codex Alera 5: Princep's Fury*, by Jim Butcher (Ace); *Fonseca 6: Bright Futures*, by Stuart Kaimsky (Forge): *Fathom*, by Cherie Priest (Tor); *Gospel Grrls 3: Be Strong and Curvaceous*, by Shelly Adina (Faith Words); *Ariane 1: Peacekeeper*, by Laura Reeve (Roc); *Execution Dock*, by Anne Perry (Random House).

WRITERS CONFERENCES Donald Maass: World Science Fiction Convention; Frankfurt Book Fair; Pacific Northwest Writers Conference; Bouchercon. Jennifer Jackson: World Science Fiction Convention; RWA National Conference.

TIPS We are fiction specialists, also noted for our innovative approach to career planning. Few new clients are accepted, but interested authors should query with a SASE. Works with subagents in all principle foreign countries and Hollywood. No prescriptive nonfiction, picture books, or poetry will be considered.

DON CONGDON ASSOCIATES INC.

156 Fifth Ave., Suite 625, New York NY 10010-7002. (212)645-1229. Fax: (212)727-2688. E-mail: dca@doncongdon.com. **Contact:** Don Congdon, Michael Congdon, Susan Ramer, Cristina Concepcion, Maura Kye-Casella, Katie Kotchman, Katie Grimm. Member of AAR. Represents 100 clients. Currently handles nonfiction books (60%), other (40% fiction).

REPRESENTS nonfiction books fiction. **Considers these fiction areas:** action, adventure, contemporary issues, crime, detective, literary, mainstream, mystery, police, short story collections, suspense, thriller, women's.

8→ Especially interested in narrative nonfiction and literary fiction.

HOW TO CONTACT Query with SASE or via e-mail (no attachments). Responds in 3 weeks to queries. Responds in 1 month to mss. Obtains most new clients through recommendations from other authors.

TERMS Agent receives 15% commission on domestic sales. Agent receives 19% commission on foreign sales. Charges client for extra shipping costs, photocopying, copyright fees, book purchases.

TIPS "Writing a query letter with a SASE is a must. We cannot guarantee replies to foreign queries via standard mail. No phone calls. We never download attachments to e-mail queries for security reasons, so please copy and paste material into your e-mail."

● DOYEN LITERARY SERVICES, INC.

1931 660th St., Newell IA 50568-7613. (712)272-3300. Website: www.barbaradoyen.com. **Contact:** (Ms.) B.J. Doyen, president. Represents over 100 clients. 20% of clients are new/unpublished writers. Currently handles nonfiction books (100%).

Prior to opening her agency, Ms. Doyen worked as a published author, teacher, guest speaker, and wrote and appeared in her own weekly TV show airing in 7 states. She is also the coauthor of *The Everything Guide to Writing a Book Proposal* (Adams 2005) and *The Everything Guide to Getting Published* (Adams 2006).

REPRESENTS nonfiction for adults, no children's.

8→ This agency specializes in nonfiction. Actively seeking business, health, science, how-to, self-help—all kinds of adult nonfiction suitable for the major trade publishers. Does not want to receive pornography, screenplays, children's books, fiction, or poetry.

HOW TO CONTACT Send a **query letter** initially. Do not send us any attachments. Your text must be in the body of the e-mail. Prefer e-mail query through our website, using the contact button. Please read the website before submitting a query. Include your background information in a bio. Send no unsolicited attachments. Accepts simultaneous submissions. Responds immediately to queries. Responds in 3 weeks to mss.

TERMS Agent receives 15% commission on domestic sales. Agent receives 20% commission on foreign sales. Offers written contract, binding for 2 years.

RECENT SALES *Stem Cells For Dummies*, by Lawrence S.B. Goldstein and Meg Schneider; *The Complete Idiot's Guide to Country Living*, by Kimberly Willis; *The Complete Illustrated Pregnancy Companion* by Robin Elise Weiss; *The Complete Idiot's Guide to Playing the Fiddle*, by Ellery Klein; *Healthy Aging for Dummies*, by Brent Agin, MD, and Sharon Perkins, RN.

TIPS "Our authors receive personalized attention. We market aggressively, undeterred by rejection. We get the best possible publishing contracts. We are very interested in nonfiction book ideas at this time and will consider most topics. Many writers come to us from referrals, but we also get quite a few who initially approach us with query letters. Do not call us regarding queries. It is best if you do not collect editorial rejections prior to seeking an agent, but if you do, be upfront and honest about it. Do not submit your manuscript to more than 1 agent at a time—querying first can save you (and us) much time. We're open to established or beginning writers—just send us a terrific letter!"

◐ DUNHAM LITERARY, INC.

156 Fifth Ave., Suite 625, New York NY 10010-7002. (212)929-0994. Website: www.dunhamlit.com. **Contact:** Jennie Dunham. Member of AAR. SCBWI represents 50 clients. 15% of clients are new/unpublished writers. Currently handles nonfiction books (25%), novels (25%), juvenile books (50%).

Prior to opening her agency, Ms. Dunham worked as a literary agent for Russell & Volkening. The Rhoda Weyr Agency is now a division of Dunham Literary, Inc.

MEMBER AGENTS Blair Hewes. Represents authors of literary and commercial fiction, narrative nonfiction, and books for children of all ages. She is interested in representing authors of nonfiction books in the categories of pop culture, historical biography, lifestyle, and women's issues. She is not interested in westerns, hard-boiled crime fiction, or political or medical thrillers.

REPRESENTS nonfiction books, novels, short story collections, juvenile. **Considers these fiction areas:** ethnic, juvenile, literary, mainstream, picture books, young adult.

HOW TO CONTACT Query with SASE. Responds in 1 week to queries. Responds in 2 months to mss. Obtains most new clients through recommendations from others, solicitations.

TERMS Agent receives 15% commission on domestic sales. Agent receives 20% commission on foreign sales.

RECENT SALES Sold 30 books for young readers in the last year. *Peter Pan*, by Robert Sabuda (Little Simon); *Flamingos on the Roof*, by Calef Brown (Houghton); *Adele and Simon in America*, by Barbara McClintock (Farrar, Straus & Giroux); *Caught Between the Pages*, by Marlene Carvell (Dutton); *Waiting for Normal*, by Leslie Connor (HarperCollins), *The Gollywhopper Games*, by Jody Feldman (Greenwillow). *America the Beautiful* by Robert Sabuda; *Dahlia*, by Barbara McClintock; *Living Dead Girl* by Tod Goldberg; *In My Mother's House* by Margaret McMulla; *Black Hawk Down* by Mark Bowden; *Look Back All the Green Valley* by Fred Chappell; *Under a Wing* by Reeve Lindbergh; *I Am Madame X* by Gioia Diliberto.

◐ DUPREE/MILLER AND ASSOCIATES INC. LITERARY

100 Highland Park Village, Suite 350, Dallas TX 75205. (214)559-BOOK. Fax: (214)559-PAGE. Website: www.dupreemiller.com. **Contact:** Submissions Department. Other memberships include ABA. Represents 200 clients. 20% of clients are new/unpublished writers. Currently handles nonfiction books (90%), novels (10%).

MEMBER AGENTS Jan Miller, president/CEO; Shannon Miser-Marven, senior executive VP; Annabelle Baxter; Nena Madonia; Cheri Gillis.

REPRESENTS nonfiction books, novels, scholarly, syndicated religious.inspirational/spirituality. **Considers these fiction areas:** action, adventure, crime, detective, ethnic, experimental, family saga, feminist, glitz, historical, humor, inspirational, literary, mainstream, mystery, picture books, police, psychic, religious, satire, sports, supernatural, suspense, thriller.

This agency specializes in commercial fiction and nonfiction.

HOW TO CONTACT Submit 1-page query, summary, bio, how to market, SASE through U.S. postal service. Obtains most new clients through recommendations from others, conferences, lectures.

TERMS Agent receives 15% commission on domestic sales. Offers written contract.

WRITERS CONFERENCES Aspen Summer Words Literary Festival.

TIPS "If interested in agency representation, it is vital to have the material in the proper working format. As agents' policies differ, it is important to follow their guidelines. Work on establishing a strong proposal that provides sample chapters, an overall synopsis (fairly detailed), and some biographical information on yourself. Do not send your proposal in pieces; it should be complete upon submission. Your work should be in its best condition."

⊘ DWYER & O'GRADY, INC.

Agents for Writers & Illustrators of Children's Books, P.O. Box 790, Cedar Key FL 32625-0790. (352)543-9307. Fax: (603)375-5373. Website: www.dwyerogrady.com. **Contact:** Elizabeth O'Grady. Estab. 1990. Other memberships include SCBWI. Represents 30 clients. Currently handles juvenile books (100%).

Prior to opening their agency, Mr. Dwyer and Ms. O'Grady were booksellers and publishers.

MEMBER AGENTS Elizabeth O'Grady; Jeff Dwyer.

REPRESENTS juvenile. **Considers these fiction areas:** juvenile, picture books, young.

"We are not accepting new clients at this time. This agency represents only writers and illustrators of children's books."

HOW TO CONTACT Do not send unsolicited material. We are not adding new clients. Check website to see if policy changes. Obtains most new clients through recommendations from others, direct approach by agent to writer whose work they've read.

TERMS Agent receives 15% commission on domestic sales. Agent receives 20% commission on foreign sales. Offers written contract; 1-month notice must be given to terminate contract. This agency charges clients for photocopying of longer mss or mutually agreed-upon marketing expenses.

WRITERS CONFERENCES BookExpo America; American Library Association Annual Conference; SCBWI.

TIPS "This agency previously had an address in New Hampshire. Mail all materials to the new Florida address."

● EAST/WEST LITERARY AGENCY, LLC

1158 26th St., Suite 462, Santa Monica CA 90403. (310)573-9303. Fax: (310)453-9008. E-mail: dwarren@eastwestliteraryagency.com; mgjames@eastwestliteraryagency.com; rpfeffer@eastwestliteraryagency.com. Estab. 2000. Represents 100 clients. 70% of clients are new/unpublished writers.Currently handles juvenile books (80%), adult books 20%.

MEMBER AGENTS Deborah Warren, founder; Mary Grey James, partner literary agent (special interest: Southern writers and their stories, literary fiction); Rubin Pfeffer, partner content agent and digital media strategist.

HOW TO CONTACT By referral only. Submit proposal and first 3 sample chapters, table of contents (2 pages or fewer), synopsis (1 page). For picture books, submit entire ms. Requested submissions should be sent by mail as a Word document in Courier, 12-pt., double-spaced with 1.20-inch margin on left, ragged right text, 25 lines per page, continuously paginated, with all your contact info on the first page. Only responds if interested, no need for SASE. Responds in 60 days. Obtains new clients through recommendations from others.

TERMS Agent receives 15% commission on domestic sales. Agent receives 25% commission on foreign sales. Offers written contract; 30-day notice must be given to terminate contract. Charges for out-of-pocket expenses, such as postage and copying.

EDITE KROLL LITERARY AGENCY, INC.

20 Cross St., Saco ME 04072. (207)283-8797. Fax: (207)283-8799. E-mail: ekroll@maine.rr.com. **Contact:** Edite Kroll. Represents 45 clients. 20% of clients are new/unpublished writers.Currently handles nonfiction books (40%), novels (5%), juvenile books (40%), scholarly books (5%), other.

Prior to opening her agency, Ms. Kroll served as a book editor and translator.

REPRESENTS nonfiction books, novels, very selective, juvenile, scholarly. **Considers these fiction areas:** juvenile, literary, picture books, young adult middle grade, adult.

"We represent writers and writer-artists of both adult and children's books. We have a special focus on international feminist writers, women writers and artists who write their own books (including children's and humor books)." Actively seeking artists who write their own books and international feminists who write in English. Does not want to receive genre (mysteries, thrillers, diet, cookery, etc.), photography books, coffee table books, romance, or commercial fiction.

HOW TO CONTACT Query with SASE. Submit outline/proposal, synopsis, 1-2 sample chapters, author bio, entire ms if sending picture book. No phone queries. Responds in 2-4 weeks to queries. Responds in 4-8 weeks to mss. Obtains most new clients through recommendations from others.

TERMS Agent receives 15% commission on domestic sales. Agent receives 20% commission on foreign sales. Offers written contract; 30-day notice must be given to terminate contract. Charges clients for photocopying and legal fees with prior approval from writer.

RECENT SALES Sold 12 domestic/30 foreign titles in the last year. This agency prefers not to share information on specific sales. Clients include Shel Silverstein estate, Suzy Becker, Geoffrey Hayes, Henrik Drescher, Charlotte Kasl, Gloria Skurzynski, Fatema Mernissa.

TIPS "Please do your research so you won't send me books/proposals I specifically excluded."

THE ELAINE P. ENGLISH LITERARY AGENCY

4710 41st St. NW, Suite D, Washington DC 20016. (202)362-5190. Fax: (202)362-5192. E-mail: queries@elaineenglish.com. E-mail: elaine@elaineenglish.com; naomi@elaineenglish.com. Website: www.elaineenglish.com/literary.php. **Contact:** Elaine English; Naomi Hackenberg. Member of AAR. Represents 20 clients. 25% of clients are new/unpublished writers. Currently handles novels (100%).

Ms. English has been working in publishing for more than 20 years. She is also an attorney specializing in media and publishing law.

MEMBER AGENTS Elaine English (novels); Naomi Hackenberg (Young Adult fiction).

REPRESENTS novels. **Considers these fiction areas:** historical, multicultural, mystery, suspense, thriller, women's romance (single title, historical, contemporary, romantic, suspense, chick lit, erotic), general women's fiction. The agency is slowly but steadily acquiring in all mentioned areas.

Actively seeking women's fiction, including single-title romances, and young adult fiction. Does not want to receive any science fiction, time travel, or picture books.

HOW TO CONTACT Generally prefers e-queries sent to queries@elaineenglish.com or YA sent to naomi@elaineenglish.com. If requested, submit synopsis, first 3 chapters, SASE. Please check website for further details. Responds in 4-8 weeks to queries; 3 months to requested submissions. Obtains most new clients through recommendations from others, conferences, submissions.

TERMS Agent receives 15% commission on domestic sales. Agent receives 20% commission on foreign sales. Offers written contract; 30-day notice must be given to terminate contract. Charges only for shipping expenses; generally taken from proceeds.

RECENT SALES Have been to Sourcebooks, Tor, Harlequin.

WRITERS CONFERENCES RWA National Conference; Novelists, Inc.; Malice Domestic; Washington Romance Writers Retreat, among others.

THE NICHOLAS ELLISON AGENCY

Affiliated with Sanford J. Greenburger Associates, 55 Fifth Ave., 15th Floor, New York NY 10003. (212)206-5600. Fax: (212)463-8718. E-mail: nellison@sjga.com. Website: www.greenburger.com. **Contact:** Nicholas Ellison. Represents 70 clients. Currently handles nonfiction books (50%), novels (50%).

Prior to becoming an agent, Mr. Ellison was an editor at Minerva Editions and Harper & Row, and editor-in-chief at Delacorte.

MEMBER AGENTS Nicholas Ellison; Sarah Dickman; Chelsea Lindman;.

REPRESENTS nonfiction books, novels literary, mainstream children's books. **Considers these fiction areas:** literary, mainstream.

HOW TO CONTACT Query with SASE. Responds in 6 weeks to queries.

TERMS Agent receives 15% commission on domestic sales. Agent receives 20% commission on foreign sales.

●◎ ELYSE CHENEY LITERARY ASSOCIATES, LLC

78 Fifth Avenue, 3rd Floor, New York NY 10011. Website: www.cheneyliterary.com. **Contact:** Elyse Cheney, Nicole Steen.

Prior to her current position, Ms. Cheney was an agent with Sanford J. Greenburger Associates.

REPRESENTS nonfiction, novels. **Considers these fiction areas:** upmarket commercial fiction, historical fiction, literary, suspense, upmarket women's fiction, and YA novels.

HOW TO CONTACT Query this agency with a referral. Include SASE or IRC. No fax queries. Snail mail or e-mail (submissions@cheneyliterary.com) only.

RECENT SALES *Moonwalking with Einstein: The Art and Science of Remembering Everything*, by Joshua Foer; *The Possessed: Adventures with Russian Books and the People Who Read Them*, by Elif Batuman (Farrar, Strauss & Giroux); *The Coldest Winter Ever*, by Sister Souljah (Atria); *A Heartbreaking Work of Staggering Genius*, by Dave Eggers (Simon and Schuster).

◐ FAIRBANK LITERARY REPRESENTATION

P.O. Box 6, Hudson NY 12534-0006. (617)576-0030. Fax: (617)576-0030. E-mail: queries@fairbankliterary.com. Website: www.fairbankliterary.com. **Contact:** Sorche Fairbank. Member of AAR. Represents 45 clients. 20% of clients are new/unpublished writers. Currently handles nonfiction books (60%), novels (22%), story collections (3%), other (15% illustrated).

MEMBER AGENTS Sorche Fairbank (narrative nonfiction, commercial and literary fiction, memoir, food and wine); Matthew Frederick (scout for sports nonfiction, architecture, design).

REPRESENTS nonfiction books, novels, short story collections. **Considers these fiction areas:** action, adventure, feminist, gay, lesbian, literary, mainstream, mystery, sports, suspense, thriller, women's Southern voices.

"I have a small agency in Harvard Square, where I tend to gravitate toward literary fiction and narrative nonfiction, with a strong interest in women's issues and women's voices, international voices, class and race issues, and projects that simply teach me something new about the greater world and society around us. We have a good reputation for working closely and developmentally with our authors and love what we do." Actively seeking literary fiction, international and culturally diverse voices, narrative nonfiction, topical subjects (politics, current affairs), history, sports, architecture/design and pop culture. Does not want to receive romance, poetry, science fiction, pirates, vampire, young adult, or children's works.

HOW TO CONTACT Query with SASE. Submit author bio. Accepts simultaneous submissions. Responds in 6 weeks to queries. Responds in 10 weeks to mss. Obtains most new clients through recommendations from others, solicitations, conferences, ideas generated in-house.

TERMS Agent receives 15% commission on domestic sales. Agent receives 20% commission on foreign sales. Offers written contract, binding for 12 months; 45-day notice must be given to terminate contract.

WRITERS CONFERENCES San Francisco Writers' Conference, Muse and the Marketplace/Grub Street Conference, Washington Independent Writers' Conference, Murder in the Grove, Surrey International Writers' Conference.

TIPS "Be professional from the very first contact. There shouldn't be a single typo or grammatical flub in your query. Have a reason for contacting me about your project other than I was the next name listed on some website. Please do not use form query software! Believe me, we can get a dozen or so a day that look identical—we know when you are using a form. Show me that you know your audience—and your competition. Have the writing and/or proposal at the very, very best it can be before starting the querying process. Don't assume that if someone likes it enough they'll 'fix' it. The biggest mistake new writers make is starting the querying process before they—and the work—are ready. Take your time and do it right."

FARRIS LITERARY AGENCY, INC.

P.O. Box 570069, Dallas TX 75357. (972)203-8804. E-mail: farris1@airmail.net. Website: www.farrisliterary.com. **Contact:** Mike Farris, Susan Morgan Farris. Represents 30 clients. 60% of clients are new/unpublished writers. Currently handles nonfiction books (40), novels (60).

Both Mr. Farris and Ms. Farris are attorneys.

REPRESENTS nonfiction books, novels. **Considers these fiction areas:** action, adventure, crime, detective, frontier, historical, humor, inspirational, mainstream, mystery, police, religious, romance, satire, sports, suspense, thriller, westerns.

"We specialize in both fiction and nonfiction books. We are particularly interested in discovering unpublished authors. We adhere to AAR guidelines." Does not want to receive science fiction, fantasy, gay and lesbian, erotica, young adult, or children's.

HOW TO CONTACT Query with SASE or by e-mail. Accepts simultaneous submissions. Responds in 2-3 weeks to queries. Responds in 4-8 weeks to mss. Obtains most new clients through recommendations from others, solicitations, conferences.

TERMS Agent receives 15% commission on domestic sales. Agent receives 20% commission on foreign sales. Offers written contract; 30-day notice must be given to terminate contract. Charges clients for postage and photocopying.

RECENT SALES *The Yard Dog* and The Insane Train, by Sheldon Russell (St. Martin's Press); *Eurostorm*, by Payne Harrison (Variance Publishing); *Relative Chaos*, by Kay Finch (Avalon Books); *Call Me Lucky: A Texan in Hollywood*, by Robert Hinkle and Mike Farris (University of Oklahoma Press); *Sketch Me If You Can* (the first book in a three-book deal for the A Portrait of Crime mystery series), by Sharon Pape (Berkley Books); film rights options for *Balaam Gimble's Gumption*, by Mike Nichols (John M. Hardy Publishing).

WRITERS CONFERENCES The Screenwriting Conference in Santa Fe; La Jolla Writers Conference; East Texas Christian Writers Conference.

FAYE BENDER LITERARY AGENCY

19 Cheever Place, Brooklyn NY 11231. E-mail: info@fbliterary.com. Website: www.fbliterary.com. **Contact:** Faye Bender. Estab. 2004. Member of AAR.

MEMBER AGENTS Faye Bender.

REPRESENTS nonfiction books, novels, juvenile. **Considers these fiction areas:** commercial, literary, women's, young adult (middle-grade).

"I choose books based on the narrative voice and strength of writing. I work with previously published and first-time authors." Faye does not represent picture books, genre fiction for adults (western, romance, horror, science fiction, fantasy), business books, spirituality, or screenplays.

HOW TO CONTACT Query with SASE and 10 sample pages via mail or e-mail (no attachments). Guidelines online. "Please do not send queries or submissions via registered or certified mail, or by FedEx or UPS requiring signature. We will not return unsolicited submissions weighing more than 16 ounces, even if an SASE is attached. We do not respond to queries via phone or fax."

TIPS "Please keep your letters to the point, include all relevant information, and have a bit of patience."

FELICIA ETH LITERARY REPRESENTATION

555 Bryant St., Suite 350, Palo Alto CA 94301-1700. (650)375-1276. Fax: (650)401-8892. E-mail: felicia-eth@aol.com. **Contact:** Felicia Eth. Member of AAR. Represents 25-35 clients. Currently handles nonfiction books (75%), novels (25% adult).

REPRESENTS nonfiction books, novels. **Considers these fiction areas:** literary, mainstream.

This agency specializes in high-quality fiction (preferably mainstream/contemporary) and provocative, intelligent, and thoughtful nonfiction on a wide array of commercial subjects.

HOW TO CONTACT Query with SASE. Accepts simultaneous submissions. Responds in 3 weeks to queries. Responds in 4-6 weeks to mss.

TERMS Agent receives 15% commission on domestic sales. Agent receives 20% commission on foreign sales. Agent receives 20% commission on film sales. Charges clients for photocopying and express mail service.

RECENT SALES Sold 70-10 titles in the last year. *Bumper Sticker Philosophy*, by Jack Bowen (Random House); *Boys Adrift* by Leonard Sax (Basic Books); *A War Reporter*, by Barbara Quick (HarperCollins); *Pantry*, by Anna Badkhen (Free Press/S&S).

WRITERS CONFERENCES "Wide Array—from Squaw Valley to Mills College."

TIPS "For nonfiction, established expertise is certainly a plus—as is magazine publication—though not a prerequisite. I am highly dedicated to those projects I represent, but highly selective in what I choose."

DIANA FINCH LITERARY AGENCY

116 W. 23rd St., Suite 500, New York NY 10011. E-mail: diana.finch@verizon.net. Website: dianafinchliteraryagency.blogspot.com/. **Contact:** Diana Finch. Member of AAR. Represents 40 clients. 20% of clients are new/unpublished writers.Currently handles nonfiction books (85%), novels (15%), juvenile books (5%), multimedia (5%).

Seeking to represent books that change lives. Prior to opening her agency in 2003, Ms. Finch worked at Ellen Levine Literary Agency for 18 years.

REPRESENTS nonfiction books, novels, scholarly. **Considers these fiction areas:** action, adventure, crime, detective, ethnic, historical, literary, mainstream, police, thriller, young adult.

Actively seeking narrative nonfiction, popular science, memoir, and health topics. "Does not want romance, mysteries, or children's picture books."

HOW TO CONTACT Query with SASE or via e-mail (no attachments). Accepts simultaneous submissions. Obtains most new clients through recommendations from others.

TERMS Agent receives 15% commission on domestic sales. Agent receives 20% commission on foreign sales. Offers written contract. "I charge for photocopying, overseas postage, galleys, and books purchased, and try to recoup these costs from earnings received for a client, rather than charging outright."

RECENT SALES *Heidegger's Glasses*, by Thaisa Frank; *Genetic Rounds*, by Robert Marion, MD (Kaplan); *Honeymoon in Tehran*, by Azadeh Moaveni (Random House); *Darwin Slept Here* by Eric Simons (Overlook); *Black Tide*, by Antonia Juhasz (HarperCollins); *Stalin's Children*, by Owen Matthews (Bloomsbury); *Radiant Days*, by Michael Fitzgerald (Shoemaker & Hoard); *The Queen's Soprano*, by Carol Dines (Harcourt Young Adult); *What to Say to a Porcupine*, by Richard Gallagher (Amacom); *The Language of Trust*, by Michael Maslansky et al.

TIPS "Do as much research as you can on agents before you query. Have someone critique your query letter before you send it. It should be only 1 page and describe your book clearly—and why you are writing it—but also demonstrate creativity and a sense of your writing style."

FINEPRINT LITERARY MANAGEMENT

240 West 35th St., Suite 500, New York NY 10001. (212)279-1282. E-mail: stephany@fineprintlit.com. Website: www.fineprintlit.com. Member of AAR.

MEMBER AGENTS Peter Rubie, CEO (nonfiction interests include narrative nonfiction, popular science, spirituality, history, biography, pop culture, business, technology, parenting, health, self help, music, and food; fiction interests include literate thrillers, crime fiction, science fiction and fantasy, military fiction and literary fiction); Stephany Evans, president (nonfiction interests include health and wellness—especially women's health, spirituality, lifestyle, home renovating/decorating, entertaining, food and wine, popular reference, and narrative nonfiction; fiction interests include stories with a strong and interesting female protagonist, both literary and upmarket commercial—including chick lit, romance, mystery, and light suspense); June Clark (nonfiction: entertainment, self-help, parenting, reference/how-to books, teen books, food and wine, style/beauty, and prescriptive business titles); Diane Freed (nonfiction: health/fitness, women's issues, memoir, baby boomer trends, parenting, popular culture, self-help, humor, young adult, and topics of New England regional interest); Meredith Hays (both fiction and nonfiction: commercial and literary; she is interested in sophisticated women's fiction such as urban chick lit, pop culture, lifestyle, animals, and absorbing nonfiction accounts); Janet Reid (mysteries and offbeat literary fiction); Colleen Lindsay; Marissa Walsh; Ward Calhoun; Laura Wood.

REPRESENTS nonfiction books, novels. **Considers these fiction areas:** crime, detective, fantasy, literary, military, mystery, police, romance, science fiction, suspense, war, women's, young adult.

HOW TO CONTACT Query with SASE. Submit synopsis and first two chapters for fiction; proposal for nonfiction. Do not send attachments or manuscripts without a request. See contact page onilne at website for e-mails. Obtains most new clients through recommendations from others, solicitations.

TERMS Agent receives 15% commission on domestic sales. Agent receives 20% commission on foreign sales.

FOUNDRY LITERARY + MEDIA

33 West 17th St., PH, New York NY 10011. (212)929-5064. Fax: (212)929-5471. Website: www.foundrymedia.com.

MEMBER AGENTS Peter H. McGuigan (smart, offbeat nonfiction, particularly works of narrative nonfiction on pop culture, niche history, biography, music and science; fiction interests include commercial and literary, across all genres, especially first-time writers); Yfat Reiss Gendell (favors nonfiction books focusing on all manners of prescriptive: how-to, science, health and well-being, memoirs, adventure, travel stories and lighter titles appropriate for the gift trade genre. Yfat also looks for commercial fiction highlighting the full range of women's experiences—young and old—and also seeks science fiction, thrillers and historical fiction); Stéphanie Abou (in fiction and nonfiction alike, Stéphanie is always on the lookout for authors who are accomplished storytellers with their own distinctive voice, who develop memorable characters, and who are able to create psychological conflict with their narrative. She is an across-the-board fiction lover, attracted to both literary and smart upmarket commercial fiction. In nonfiction she leans towards projects that tackle big topics with an unusual approach. Pop culture, health, science, parenting, women's and multicultural issues are of special interest); Chris Park (memoirs, narrative nonfiction, Christian nonfiction and character-driven fiction); David Patterson (outstanding narratives and/or idea-driven works of nonfiction); Hannah Brown Gordon (fiction, YA, memoir, narrative nonfiction, history, current events, science, psychology and pop culture); Lisa Grubka; Mollie Glick (literary fiction, narrative nonfiction, YA, and a bit of practical nonfiction); Stephen Barbara (all categories of books for young readers in addition to servicing writers for the adult market); Brandi Bowles (idea and platform-driven nonfiction in all categories, including music and pop culture, humor, business, sociology, philosophy, health, and relationships. Quirky, funny, or contrarian proposals are always welcome in her in-box, as are big-idea books that change the way we think about the world. Brandi also represents fiction in the categories of literary fiction, women's fiction, urban fantasy, and YA).

REPRESENTS Considers these fiction areas: literary, religious.

HOW TO CONTACT Query with SASE. Should be addressed to one agent only. Submit synopsis, 3 sample chapters, author bio, For nonfiction, submit query, proposal, sample chapter, TOC, bio. Put "submissions" on your snail mail submission.

FOX LITERARY

168 Second Ave., PMB 180, New York NY 10003. E-mail: submissions@foxliterary.com. Website: www.foxliterary.com.

REPRESENTS Considers these fiction areas: erotica, fantasy, literary, romance, science, young adult, science fiction, thrillers, historical fiction, literary fiction, graphic novels, commercial fiction, women's fiction, gay and lesbian, erotica historical romance.

Does not want to receive screenplays, poetry, category westerns, horror, Christian/inspirational, or children's picture books.

HOW TO CONTACT E-mail query and first 5 pages in body of e-mail. E-mail queries preferred. For snail mail queries, must include an e-mail address for response. Do not send SASE.

SARAH JANE FREYMANN LITERARY AGENCY

59 W. 71st St., Suite 9B, New York NY 10023. (212)362-9277. E-mail: sarah@sarahjanefreymann.com; Submissions@SarahJaneFreymann.com. Website: www.sarahjanefreymann.com. **Contact:** Sarah Jane Freymann, Steve Schwartz. Represents 100 clients. 20% of clients are new/unpublished writers. Currently handles nonfiction books (75%), novels (23%), juvenile books (2%).

MEMBER AGENTS Sarah Jane Freymann; (nonfiction books, novels, illustrated books); Jessica Sinsheimer, Jessica@sarahjanefreymann.com (young adult fiction); Steven Schwartz, steve@sarahjanefreymann.com; Katharine Sands.

REPRESENTS **Considers these fiction areas:** ethnic, literary, mainstream.

HOW TO CONTACT Query with SASE. Responds in 2 weeks to queries. Responds in 6 weeks to mss. Obtains most new clients through recommendations from others.

TERMS Agent receives 15% commission on domestic sales. Agent receives 20% commission on foreign sales. Offers written contract. Charges clients for long distance, overseas postage, photocopying. 100% of business is derived from commissions on ms sales.

RECENT SALES *How to Make Love to a Plastic Cup: And Other Things I Learned While Trying to Knock Up My Wife*, by Greg Wolfe (Harper Collins); *I Want to Be Left Behind: Rapture Here on Earth*, by Brenda Peterson (a Merloyd Lawrence Book); *That Bird Has My Name: The Autobiography of an Innocent Man on Death Row*, by Jarvis Jay Masters with an Introduction by Pema Chodrun (HarperOne); *Perfect One-Dish Meals*, by Pam Anderson (Houghton Mifflin); *Birdology*, by Sy Montgomery (Simon & Schuster); *Emptying the Nest: Launching Your Reluctant Young Adult*, by Dr. Brad Sachs (Macmillan); *Tossed & Found*, by Linda and John Meyers (Steward, Tabori & Chang); *32 Candles*, by Ernessa Carter; *God and Dog*, by Wendy Francisco.

TIPS "I love fresh, new, passionate works by authors who love what they are doing and have both natural talent and carefully honed skill."

FREDRICA S. FRIEDMAN AND CO., INC.

136 E. 57th St., 14th Floor, New York NY 10022. (212)829-9600. Fax: (212)829-9669. E-mail: info@fredricafriedman.com; submissions@fredricafriedman.com. Website: www.fredricafriedman.com/agency.htm. **Contact:** Ms. Chandler Smith. Represents 75+ clients. 50% of clients are new/unpublished writers.Currently handles nonfiction books (95%), novels (5%).

REPRESENTS nonfiction books, novels anthologies. **Considers these fiction areas:** literary.

"We represent a select group of outstanding nonfiction and fiction writers. We are particularly interested in helping writers expand their readership and develop their careers." Does not want poetry, plays, screenplays, children's books, sci-fi/fantasy, or horror.

HOW TO CONTACT Submit e-query, synopsis; be concise, and include any pertinent author information, including relevant writing history. If you are a fiction writer, we also request a one-page sample from your manuscript to provide its voice. We ask that you keep all material in the body of the e-mail. Accepts simultaneous submissions. Responds in 4-6 weeks to queries. Responds in 4-6 weeks to mss. Obtains most new clients through recommendations from others.

TERMS Agent receives 15% commission on domestic sales. Agent receives 25% commission on foreign sales. Offers written contract. Charges for photocopying and messenger/shipping fees for proposals.

RECENT SALES *A World of Lies: The Crime and Consequences of Bernie Madoff*, by Diana B. Henriques (Times Books/Holt); *Polemic and Memoir: The Nixon Years* by Patrick J. Buchanan (St. Martin's Press); *Angry Fat Girls: Five Women, Five Hundred Pounds, and a Year of Losing It . . . Again*, by Frances Kuffel (Berkley/Penguin); *Life with My Sister Madonna*, by Christopher Ciccone with Wendy Leigh (Simon & Schuster Spotlight); *The World Is Curved: Hidden Dangers to the Global Economy*, by David Smick (Portfolio/Penguin); *Going to See the Elephant*, by Rodes Fishburne (Delacorte/Random House); *Seducing the Boys Club: Uncensored Tactics from a Woman at the Top*, by Nina DiSesa (Ballantine/Random House); *The Girl from Foreign: A Search for Shipwrecked Ancestors, Forgotten Histories, and a Sense of Home*, by Sadia Shepard (Penguin Press).

TIPS "Spell the agent's name correctly on your query letter."

FULL CIRCLE LITERARY, LLC

7676 Hazard Center Dr., Suite 500, San Diego CA 92108. E-mail: submissions@fullcircleliterary.com. Website: www.fullcircleliterary.com. **Contact:** Lilly Ghahremani, Stefanie Von Borstel. Represents 55 clients. 60% of clients are new/unpublished writers. Currently handles nonfiction books (70%), novels (10%), juvenile books (20%).

Before forming Full Circle, Ms. Von Borstel worked in both marketing and editorial capacities at Penguin and Harcourt; Ms. Ghahremani received her law degree from UCLA, and has experience in representing authors on legal affairs.

MEMBER AGENTS Lilly Ghahremani (Lilly is only taking referrals: young adult, pop culture, crafts, "green" living, narrative nonfiction, business, relationships, Middle Eastern interest, multicultural); Stefanie Von Borstel (Latino interest, crafts, parenting, wedding/relationships, how-to, self help, middle grade/teen fiction/YA, green living, multicultural/bilingual picture books); Adriana Dominguez (fiction areas of interest: children's books—picture books, middle grade novels, and [literary] young adult novels; on the adult side, she is looking for literary, women's, and historical fiction. Nonfiction areas of interest: multicultural, pop culture, how-to, and titles geared toward women of all ages).

REPRESENTS nonfiction books, juvenile. **Considers these fiction areas:** ethnic, literary, young adult.

"Our full-service boutique agency, representing a range of nonfiction and children's books (limited fiction), provides a one-stop resource for authors. Our extensive experience in the realms of law and marketing provide Full Circle clients with a unique edge." "Actively seeking nonfiction by authors with a unique and strong platform, projects that offer new and diverse viewpoints, and literature with a global or multicultural perspective. We are particularly interested in books with a Latino or Middle Eastern angle and books related to pop culture." Does not want to receive "screenplays, poetry, commercial fiction or genre fiction (horror, thriller, mystery, Western, sci-fi, fantasy, romance, historical fiction)."

HOW TO CONTACT Agency accepts e-queries. See website for fiction guidelines, as they are in flux. For nonfiction, send full proposal. Accepts simultaneous submissions. Responds in 1-2 weeks to queries. Responds in 4-6 weeks to mss. Obtains most new clients through recommendations from others, solicitations, conferences.

TERMS Agent receives 15% commission on domestic sales. Agent receives 20% commission on foreign sales. Offers written contract; up to 30-day notice must be given to terminate contract. Charges for copying and postage.

TIPS "Put your best foot forward. Contact us when you simply can't make your project any better on your own, and please be sure your work fits with what the agent you're approaching represents. Little things count, so copyedit your work. Join a writing group and attend conferences to get objective and constructive feedback before submitting. Be active about building your platform as an author before, during, and after publication. Remember this is a business and your agent is a business partner."

GELFMAN SCHNEIDER LITERARY AGENTS, INC.

250 W. 57th St., Suite 2122, New York NY 10107. (212)245-1993. Fax: (212)245-8678. E-mail: mail@gelfmanschneider.com. Website: www.gelfmanschneider.com. **Contact:** Jane Gelfman, Deborah Schneider. Member of AAR. Represents 300+ clients. 10% of clients are new/unpublished writers.

REPRESENTS fiction and nonfiction books. **Considers these fiction areas:** literary, mainstream, mystery, women's.

Does not want to receive romance, science fiction, westerns, or children's books.

HOW TO CONTACT Query with SASE. Send queries via snail mail only. No unsolicited mss. Please send a query letter, a synopsis, and a SAMPLE CHAPTER ONLY. Responds in 1 month to queries. Responds in 2 months to mss.

TERMS Agent receives 15% commission on domestic sales. Agent receives 20% commission on foreign sales. Agent receives 15% commission on film sales. Offers written contract. Charges clients for photocopying and messengers/couriers.

BARRY GOLDBLATT LITERARY, LLC

320 Seventh Ave., #266, Brooklyn NY 11215. Fax: (718)360-5453. Website: www.bgliterary.com. **Contact:** Barry Goldblatt. Member of AAR. SCBWI.

MEMBER AGENTS Barry Goldblatt, Joe Monti, Beth Fleisher (kids work and graphic novels; she is particularly interested in finding new voices in middle grade and young adult fantasy, science fiction, mystery, historicals and action adventure).

REPRESENTS juvenile books. **Considers these fiction areas:** picture books, young adult middle grade, all genres.

This agency specializes in children's books of all kinds from picture books to young adult novels, across all over genres.

HOW TO CONTACT E-mail queries query@bgliterary.com, and include the first 5 pages and a synopsis of the novel pasted into the text of the e-mail. No attachments or links.

Recent Sales *Prophecy: The Dragon King Chronicles*, by Ellen Oh; *Kiss Number Eight*, by Colleen Af Venable; The Mysterious Four Series, by Dan Poblocki

THE SUSAN GOLOMB LITERARY AGENCY

875 Avenue of the Americas, Suite 2302, New York NY 10001. Fax: (212)239-9503. E-mail: susan@sgolombagency.com; eliza@sgolombagency.com. **Contact:** Susan Golomb. Represents 100 clients. 20% of clients are new/unpublished writers. Currently handles nonfiction books (50%), novels (40%), story collections (10%).

MEMBER AGENTS Susan Golomb (accepts queries); Sabine Hrechdakian (accepts queries); Kim Goldstein (no unsolicited queries).

REPRESENTS nonfiction books, novels, short story collections, novellas. **Considers these fiction areas:** ethnic, historical, humor, literary, mainstream, satire, thriller, women's, young adult chick lit.

"We specialize in literary and upmarket fiction and nonfiction that is original, vibrant and of excellent quality and craft. Nonfiction should be edifying, paradigm-shifting, fresh and entertaining." Actively seeking writers with strong voices. Does not want to receive genre fiction.

HOW TO CONTACT Query with SASE. Submit outline/proposal, synopsis, 1 sample chapter, author bio, SASE. Query via mail or e-mail. Responds in 2 week to queries. Responds in 8 weeks to mss. Obtains most new clients through recommendations from others, solicitations.

TERMS Agent receives 15% commission on domestic sales. Agent receives 20% commission on foreign sales. Offers written contract.

RECENT SALES Sold 20 titles in the last year. *Sunnyside*, by Glen David Gold (Knopf); *How to Buy a Love of Reading*, by Tanya Egan Gibson (Dutton); *Telex from Cuba*, by Rachel Kushner (Scribner); *The Imperfectionists* by Tom Rachman (Dial).

GOUMEN & SMIRNOVA LITERARY AGENCY

Nauki pr., 19/2 fl. 293, St. Petersburg 195220 Russia. E-mail: info@gs-agency.com. Website: www.gs-agency.com. **Contact:** Julia Goumen, Natalia Smirnova. Represents 20 clients. 10% of clients are new/unpublished writers. Currently handles nonfiction books (10%), novels (80%), story collections (5%), juvenile books (5%).

Prior to becoming agents, both Ms. Goumen and Ms. Smirnova worked as foreign rights managers with an established Russian publisher selling translation rights for literary fiction.

MEMBER AGENTS Julia Goumen (translation rights, Russian language rights, film rights); Natalia Smirnova (translation rights, Russian language rights, film rights).

REPRESENTS nonfiction books, novels, short story collections, novellas, movie, TV, TV movie, sitcom. **Considers these fiction areas:** adventure, experimental, family, historical, horror, literary, mainstream, mystery, romance, thriller, young, womens.

"We are the first full-service agency in Russia, representing our authors in book publishing, film, television, and other areas. We are also the first agency, representing Russian authors worldwide, based in Russia. The agency also represents international authors, agents and publishers in Russia. Our philosophy is to provide an individual approach to each author, finding the right publisher both at home and across international cultural and linguistic borders, developing original marketing and promotional strategies for each title." Actively seeking manuscripts written in Russian, both literary and commercial; and foreign publishers and agents with the high-profile fiction and general nonfiction lists to represent in Russia. Does not want to receive unpublished manuscripts in languages other than Russian, or any information irrelevant to our activity.

HOW TO CONTACT Query with SASE. Submit synopsis, author bio. Accepts simultaneous submissions. Responds in 14 days to mss. Obtains most new clients through recommendations from others, solicitations.

TERMS Agent receives 20% commission on domestic sales. Agent receives 20% commission on foreign sales. Offers written contract, binding for 1 year; 2-month notice must be given to terminate contract.

● SANFORD J. GREENBURGER ASSOCIATES, INC.

55 Fifth Ave., New York NY 10003. (212)206-5600. Fax: (212)463-8718. E-mail: queryHL@sjga.com. Website: www.greenburger.com. Member of AAR. Represents 500 clients.

MEMBER AGENTS Heide Lange; Faith Hamlin; Dan Mandel; Matthew Bialer; Courtney Miller-Callihan, Michael Harriot, Brenda Bowen (authors and illustrators of children's books for all ages as well as graphic novelists); Lisa Gallagher.

REPRESENTS nonfiction books and novels. **Considers these fiction areas:** action, adventure, crime, detective, ethnic, family saga, feminist, gay, glitz, historical, humor, lesbian, literary, mainstream, mystery, police, psychic, regional, satire, sports, supernatural, suspense, thriller.

No Westerns. No screenplays.

HOW TO CONTACT Submit query, first 3 chapters, synopsis, brief bio, SASE. Accepts simultaneous submissions. Responds in 2 months to queries and mss. Responds to mss. Obtains most new clients through recommendations from others.

TERMS Agent receives 15% commission on domestic sales. Agent receives 20% commission on foreign sales. Charges for photocopying and books for foreign and subsidiary rights submissions.

◐ KATHRYN GREEN LITERARY AGENCY, LLC

250 West 57th St., Suite 2302, New York NY 10107. (212)245-2445. Fax: (212)245-2040. E-mail: query@kgreenagency.com. **Contact:** Kathy Green. Other memberships include Women's Media Group. Represents approximately 20 clients. 50% of clients are new/unpublished writers.Currently handles nonfiction books (50%), novels (25%), juvenile books (25%).

Prior to becoming an agent, Ms. Green was a book and magazine editor.

REPRESENTS nonfiction books, novels, short story collections, juvenile, middle grade and young adult only). **Considers these fiction areas:** crime, detective, family saga, historical, humor, juvenile, literary, mainstream, mystery, police, romance, satire, suspense, thriller, women's, young adult women's.

Keeping the client list small means that writers receive my full attention throughout the process of getting their project published. Does not want to receive science fiction or fantasy.

HOW TO CONTACT Query to query@kgreenagency.com. Send no samples unless requested. Accepts simultaneous submissions. Responds in 1-2 months to mss. Obtains most new clients through recommendations from others, solicitations, conferences.

TERMS Agent receives 15% commission on domestic sales. Agent receives 20% commission on foreign sales. No written contract.

RECENT SALES The Touch Series by Laurie Stolarz; *How Do You Light a Fart*, by Bobby Mercer; *Creepiosity*, by David Bickel; *Hidden Facets: Diamonds for the Dead* by Alan Orloff; *Don't Stalk the Admissions Officer*, by Risa Lewak; *Designed Fat Girl*, by Jennifer Joyner.

TIPS "This agency offers a written agreement."

◐ GREGORY & CO. AUTHORS' AGENTS

3 Barb Mews, Hammersmith, London W6 7PA England. (44)(207)610-4676. Fax: (44)(207)610-4686. E-mail: info@gregoryandcompany.co.uk. E-mail: maryjones@gregoryandcompany.co.uk. Website: www.gregoryandcompany.co.uk. **Contact:** Jane Gregory. Other memberships include AAA. Represents 60 clients. Currently handles nonfiction books (10%), novels (90%).

MEMBER AGENTS Stephanie Glencross.

REPRESENTS nonfiction books, novels. **Considers these fiction areas:** crime, detective, historical, literary, mainstream, police, thriller contemporary women's fiction.

As a British agency, we do not generally take on American authors. Actively seeking well-written, accessible modern novels. Does not want to receive horror, science fiction, fantasy, mind/body/spirit, children's books, screenplays, plays, short stories or poetry.

HOW TO CONTACT Query with SASE. Submit outline, first 10 pages by e-mail or post, publishing history, author bio. Send submissions to Mary Jones, submissions editor: maryjones@gregoryandcompany.co.uk. Accepts simultaneous submissions. Returns materials only with SASE. Obtains most new clients through recommendations from others, conferences.

TERMS Agent receives 15% commission on domestic sales. Agent receives 20% commission on foreign sales. Offers written contract; 1-month notice must be given to terminate contract. Charges clients for photocopying of whole typescripts and copies of book for submissions.

RECENT SALES *Ritual*, by Mo Hader (Bantam UK/Grove Atlantic); *A Darker Domain*, by Val McDermid (HarperCollins UK); *The Chameleon's Shadow*, by Minette Walters (Macmillan UK/Knopf Inc); *Stratton's War*, by Laura Wilson (Orion UK/St. Martin's).

WRITERS CONFERENCES CWA Conference; Bouchercon.

◐ HALSTON FREEMAN LITERARY AGENCY, INC.

140 Broadway, 46th Floor, New York NY 10005. E-mail: queryhalstonfreemanliterary@hotmail.com. **Contact:** Molly Freeman, Betty Halston. Currently handles nonfiction books (65%), novels (35%).

Prior to becoming an agent, Ms. Halston was a marketing and promotion director for a local cable affiliate; Ms. Freeman was a television film editor and ad agency copywriter.

MEMBER AGENTS Molly Freeman, Betty Halston.

REPRESENTS nonfiction books, novels. **Considers these fiction areas:** action, adventure, crime, detective, ethnic, feminist, frontier, historical, horror, humor, literary, mainstream, mystery, police, romance, satire, science fiction, suspense, thriller, westerns, women's.

"We are a hands-on agency specializing in quality nonfiction and fiction. As a new agency, it is imperative that we develop relationships with good writers who are smart, hardworking and understand what's required of them to promote their books." Does not want to receive children's books, textbooks or poetry. Send no e-mail attachments.

HOW TO CONTACT Query with SASE. For nonfiction, include sample chapters, synopsis, platform, bio and competitive titles. For fiction, include synopsis, bio and three sample chapters. No e-mail attachments. Accepts simultaneous submissions. Responds in 2-6 weeks to queries. Responds in 1-2 months to mss. Obtains most new clients through recommendations from others, solicitations, conferences.

TERMS Agent receives 15% commission on domestic sales. Agent receives 20% commission on foreign sales. This agency charges clients for copying and postage directly related to the project.

● HARTLINE LITERARY AGENCY

123 Queenston Dr., Pittsburgh PA 15235-5429. (412)829-2483. Fax: (412)829-2432. E-mail: joyce@hartlineliterary.com. Website: www.hartlineliterary.com. **Contact:** Joyce A. Hart. Represents 40 clients. 20% of clients are new/unpublished writers. Currently handles nonfiction books (40%), novels (60%).

MEMBER AGENTS Joyce A. Hart, principal agent; Terry Burns: terry@hartlineliterary.com; Tamela Hancock Murray: tamela@hartlineliterary.com; Diana Flegal: diana@hartlineliterary.com.

REPRESENTS nonfiction books, novels. **Considers these fiction areas:** action, adventure, contemporary issues, family saga, historical, inspirational, literary, mystery, regional, religious, suspense, thriller amateur sleuth, cozy, contemporary, gothic, historical, and regency romances.

"This agency specializes in the Christian bookseller market." Actively seeking adult fiction, self-help, nutritional books, devotional, and business. Does not want to receive erotica, gay/lesbian, fantasy, horror, etc.

HOW TO CONTACT Submit summary/outline, author bio, 3 sample chapters. Accepts simultaneous submissions. Responds in 2 months to queries. Responds in 3 months to mss. Obtains most new clients through recommendations from others.

TERMS Agent receives 15% commission on domestic sales. Offers written contract.

RECENT SALES *Aurora, An American Experience in Quilt, Community and Craft*, and *A Flickering Light*, by Jane Kirkpatrick (Waterbrook Multnomah); *Oprah Doesn't Know My Name* by Jane Kirkpatric (Zondervan); *Paper Roses, Scattered Petals, and Summer Rains*, by Amanda Cabot (Revell Books); *Blood Ransom*, by Lisa Harris (Zondervan); *I Don't Want a Divorce*, by David Clark (Revell Books); *Love Finds You in Hope, Kansas*, by Pamela Griffin (Summerside Press); Journey to the Well, by Diana Wallis Taylor (Revell Books); *Paper Bag Christmas, The Nine Lessons* by Kevin Milne (Center Street); *When Your Aging Parent Needs Care* by Arrington & Atchley (Harvest House); *Katie at Sixteen* by Kim Vogel Sawyer (Zondervan); *A Promise of Spring*, by Kim Vogel Sawyer (Bethany House); *The Big 5-OH!* by Sandra Bricker (Abingdon Press); A *Silent Terror & A Silent Stalker*, by Lynette Eason (Steeple Hill); Extreme Devotion series, by Kathi Macias (New Hope Publishers); *On the Wings of the Storm*, by Tamira Barley (Whitaker House); Tribute, by Graham Garrison (Kregel Publications); *The Birth to Five Book*, by Brenda Nixon (Revell Books); *Fat to Skinny Fast and Easy*, by Doug Varrieur (Sterling Publishers).

JOHN HAWKINS & ASSOCIATES, INC.

71 W. 23rd St., Suite 1600, New York NY 10010. (212)807-7040. Fax: (212)807-9555. E-mail: jha@jhalit.com. Website: www.jhalit.com. **Contact:** Moses Cardona (moses@jhalit.com). Member of AAR. Represents over 100 clients. 5-10% of clients are new/unpublished writers.Currently handles nonfiction books (40%), novels (40%), juvenile books (20%).

MEMBER AGENTS Moses Cardona; Anne Hawkins (ahawkins@jhalit.com); Warren Frazier (frazier@jhalit.com); William Reiss (reiss@jhalit.com).

REPRESENTS nonfiction books, novels young adult. **Considers these fiction areas:** action, adventure, crime, detective, ethnic, experimental, family saga, feminist, frontier, gay, glitz, hi-lo, historical, inspirational, lesbian, literary, mainstream, military, multicultural, multimedia, mystery, police, psychic, religious, short story collections, sports, supernatural, suspense, thriller, translation, war, westerns, women's, young adult.

HOW TO CONTACT Submit query, proposal package, outline, SASE. Accepts simultaneous submissions. Responds in 1 month to queries. Obtains most new clients through recommendations from others.

TERMS Agent receives 15% commission on domestic sales. Agent receives 20% commission on foreign sales. Charges clients for photocopying.

RECENT SALES *Celebration of Shoes*, by Eileen Spinelli; *Chaos*, by Martin Gross; *The Informationist*, by Taylor Stevens; *The Line*, by Olga Grushin.

RICHARD HENSHAW GROUP

22 West 23rd Street, 5th Floor, New York NY 10010. E-mail: submissions@henshaw.com. Website: http://www.richh.addr.com. **Contact:** Rich Henshaw. Member of AAR. Other memberships include SinC, MWA, HWA, SFWA, RWA. 20% of clients are new/unpublished writers. Currently handles nonfiction books (35%), novels (65%).

Prior to opening his agency, Mr. Henshaw served as an agent with Richard Curtis Associates, Inc.

REPRESENTS nonfiction books, novels. **Considers these fiction areas:** action, adventure, crime, detective, ethnic, family saga, historical, humor, literary, mainstream, mystery, police, psychic, romance, satire, science fiction, sports, supernatural, suspense, thriller.

This agency specializes in thrillers, mysteries, science fiction, fantasy and horror.

HOW TO CONTACT Query with SASE. Accepts multiple submissions. Responds in 3 weeks to queries. Responds in 6 weeks to mss. Obtains most new clients through recommendations from others, solicitations, conferences.

TERMS Agent receives 15% commission on domestic sales. Agent receives 20% commission on foreign sales. No written contract. Charges clients for photocopying and book orders.

Recent Sales *Though Not Dead*, by Dana Stabenow; *The Perfect Suspect*, by Margaret Coel; *City of Ruins*, by Kristine Kathryn Rusch; *A Dead Man's Tale*, by James D. Doss, *Wickedly Charming*, by Kristine Grayson, History of the World series by Susan Wise Bauer; *Notorious Pleasures*, by Elizabeth Hoyt.

TIPS "While we do not have any reason to believe that our submission guidelines will change in the near future, writers can find up-to-date submission policy information on our website. Always include a SASE with correct return postage."

HIDDEN VALUE GROUP

1240 E. Ontario Ave., Ste. 102-148, Corona CA 92881. (951)549-8891. Fax: (951)549-8891. Website: www.hiddenvaluegroup.com. **Contact:** Nancy Jernigan. Represents 55 clients. 10% of clients are new/unpublished writers.

MEMBER AGENTS Jeff Jernigan, jjernigan@hiddenvaluegroup.com (men's nonfiction, fiction, Bible studies/curriculum, marriage and family); Nancy Jernigan, njernigan@hiddenvaluegroup.com (nonfiction, women's issues, inspiration, marriage and family, fiction).

REPRESENTS nonfiction books and adult fiction no poetry. **Considers these fiction areas:** action, adventure, crime, detective, fantasy, frontier, inspirational, literary, police, religious, thriller, westerns, women's.

"The Hidden Value Group specializes in helping authors throughout their publishing career. We believe that every author has a special message to be heard and we specialize in getting that message out." Actively seeking established fiction authors, and authors who are focusing on women's issues. Does not want to receive poetry or short stories.

HOW TO CONTACT Query with SASE. Submit synopsis, 2 sample chapters, author bio, and marketing and speaking summary. Accepts queries to bookquery@hiddenvaluegroup.com. No fax queries. Responds in 1 month to queries. Responds in 1 month to mss. Obtains most new clients through recommendations from others, solicitations.

TERMS Agent receives 15% commission on domestic sales. Agent receives 15% commission on foreign sales. Offers written contract.

WRITERS CONFERENCES Glorieta Christian Writers' Conference; CLASS Publishing Conference.

HOPKINS LITERARY ASSOCIATES

2117 Buffalo Rd., Suite 327, Rochester NY 14624-1507. (585)352-6268. **Contact:** Pam Hopkins. Member of AAR. Other memberships include RWA. Represents 30 clients. 5% of clients are new/unpublished writers. Currently handles novels (100%).

REPRESENTS novels. **Considers these fiction areas:** mostly women's genre romance, historical, contemporary, category, women's.

This agency specializes in women's fiction, particularly historical, contemporary, and category romance, as well as mainstream work.

HOW TO CONTACT Regular mail with synopsis, 3 sample chapters, SASE. Accepts simultaneous submissions. Responds in 2 weeks to queries. Responds in 1 month to mss. Obtains most new clients through recommendations from others, solicitations, conferences.

TERMS Agent receives 15% commission on domestic sales. Agent receives 20% commission on foreign sales. No written contract.

RECENT SALES Sold 50 titles in the last year. *The Wilting Bloom Series* by Madeline Hunter (Berkley); *The Dead Travel Fast*, by Deanna Raybourn; *Baggage Claim*, by Tanya Michna (NAL).

WRITERS CONFERENCES RWA National Conference.

● INTERNATIONAL TRANSACTIONS, INC.

P.O. Box 97, Gila NM 88038-0097. (845)373-9696. Fax: (845)373-7868. E-mail: submissions@intltrans.com; submission-fiction@intltrans.com; submission-nonfiction@intltrans.com. Website: www.intltrans.com. **Contact:** Peter Riva. Represents 40+ clients. 10% of clients are new/unpublished writers.Currently handles nonfiction books (60%), novels (25%), story collections (5%), juvenile books (5%), scholarly books (5%).

MEMBER AGENTS Peter Riva (nonfiction, fiction, illustrated; television and movie rights placement); Sandra Riva (fiction, juvenile, biographies); JoAnn Collins (fiction, women's fiction, medical fiction).

REPRESENTS nonfiction books, novels, short story collections, juvenile, scholarly illustrated books, anthologies. **Considers these fiction areas:** action, adventure, crime, detective, erotica, experimental, family saga, feminist, gay, historical, humor, lesbian, literary, mainstream, mystery, police, satire, spiritual, sports, suspense, thriller, women's, young adult chick lit.

"We specialize in large and small projects, helping qualified authors perfect material for publication." Actively seeking intelligent, well-written innovative material that breaks new ground. Does not want to receive material influenced by TV (too much dialogue); a rehash of previous successful novels' themes, or poorly prepared material.

HOW TO CONTACT First, e-query with an outline or synopsis. E-queries only! Responds in 3 weeks to queries. Responds in 5 weeks to mss. Obtains most new clients through recommendations from others, solicitations.

TERMS Agent receives 15% (25% on illustrated books) commission on domestic sales. Agent receives 20% commission on foreign sales. Offers written contract; 120-day notice must be given to terminate contract.

TIPS "'Book'—a published work of literature. That last word is the key. Not a string of words, not a book of (TV or film) 'scenes,' and never a stream of consciousness unfathomable by anyone outside of the writer's coterie. A writer should only begin to get 'interested in getting an agent' if the work is polished, literate and ready to be presented to a publishing house. Anything less is either asking for a quick rejection or is a thinly disguised plea for creative assistance—which is often given but never fiscally sound for the agents involved. Writers, even published authors, have difficulty in being objective about their own work. Friends and family are of no assistance in that process either. Writers should attempt to get their work read by the most unlikely and stern critic as part of the editing process, months before any agent is approached. In another matter: the economics of our job have changed as well. As the publishing world goes through the transition to e-books (much as the music industry went through the change to downloadable music)—a transition we expect to see at 95% within 10 years—everyone is nervous and wants 'assured bestsellers' from which to eke out a living until they know what the new e-world will bring. This makes the sales rate and, especially, the advance royalty rates, plummet. Hence, our ability to take risks and take on new clients' work is increasingly perilous financially for us and all agents."

◐ IRENE GOODMAN LITERARY AGENCY

27 W. 24th Street, Suite 700B, New York NY 10010. E-mail: queries@irenegoodman.com. Website: www.irenegoodman.com. **Contact:** Irene Goodman, Miriam Kriss. Member of AAR.

MEMBER AGENTS Irene Goodman; Miriam Kriss; Barbara Poelle; Jon Sternfeld.

REPRESENTS nonfiction books, novels. **Considers these fiction areas:** historical, intelligent literary, modern urban fantasies, mystery, romance, thriller, women's.

⊶ "Specializes in the finest in commercial fiction and nonfiction. We have a strong background in women's voices, including mysteries, romance, women's fiction, thrillers, suspense. Historical fiction is one of Irene's particular passions and Miriam is fanatical about modern urban fantasies. In nonfiction, Irene is looking for topics on narrative history, social issues and trends, education, Judaica, Francophilia, Anglophilia, other cultures, animals, food, crafts, and memoir." Barbara is looking for commercial thrillers with strong female protagonists; Miriam is looking for urban fantasy and edgy sci-fi/young adult. No children's picture books, screenplays, poetry, or inspirational fiction.

HOW TO CONTACT Query. Submit synopsis, first 10 pages. E-mail queries only! See the website submission page. No e-mail attachments. Responds in 2 months to queries.

RECENT SALES *The Ark*, by Boyd Morrison; *Isolation*, by C.J. Lyons; *The Sleepwalkers*, by Paul Grossman; *Dead Man's Moon*, by Devon Monk; *Becoming Marie Antoinette*, by Juliet Grey; *What's Up Down There*, by Lissa Rankin; *Beg for Mercy*, by Toni Andrews; *The Devil Inside*, by Jenna Black.

TIPS "We are receiving an unprecedented amount of email queries. If you find that the mailbox is full, please try again in two weeks. Email queries to our personal addresses will not be answered. Emails to our personal in-boes will be deleted."

◐ JABBERWOCKY LITERARY AGENCY

P.O. Box 4558, Sunnyside NY 11104-0558. (718)392-5985. Website: www.awfulagent.com. **Contact:** Joshua Bilmes. Other memberships include SFWA. Represents 40 clients. 15% of clients are new/unpublished writers. Currently handles nonfiction books (15%), novels (75%), scholarly books (5%), other (5% other).

MEMBER AGENTS Joshua Bilmes; Eddie Schneider.

REPRESENTS novels. **Considers these fiction areas:** action, adventure, contemporary issues, crime, detective, ethnic, family saga, fantasy, gay, glitz, historical, horror, humor, lesbian, literary, mainstream, police, psychic, regional, satire, science fiction, sports, supernatural, thriller.

⊶ This agency represents quite a lot of genre fiction and is actively seeking to increase the amount of nonfiction projects. It does not handle children's or picture books. Book-length material only—no poetry, articles, or short fiction.

HOW TO CONTACT We are currently closed to unsolicited queries. No e-mail queries, please. Query with SASE. Please check our website, as there may be times during the year when we are not accepting queries. Query letter only; no manuscript material unless requested. Accepts simultaneous submissions. Responds in 3 weeks to queries. Obtains most new clients through solicitations, recommendation by current clients.

TERMS Agent receives 15% commission on domestic sales. Agent receives 20% commission on foreign sales. Offers written contract, binding for 1 year. Charges clients for book purchases, photocopying, international book/ms mailing.

RECENT SALES Sold 30 US and 100 foreign titles in the last year. *Dead in the Family*, by Charlaine Harris; *The Way of Kings*, by Brandon Sanderson; *The Desert Spear*, by Peter V. Brett; *Oath of Fealty*, by Elizabeth Moon. Other clients include Tanya Huff, Simon Green, Jack Campbell, Kat Richardson, and Jon Sprunk.

WRITERS CONFERENCES World SF Convention, September 2009; World Fantasy, October 2009; Boucheron, September 2009; full schedule of appearances can be found on our website.

TIPS "In approaching with a query, the most important things to us are your credits and your biographical background to the extent it's relevant to your work. I (and most agents) will ignore the adjectives you may choose to describe your own work."

JET LITERARY ASSOCIATES

2570 Camino San Patricio, Santa Fe NM 87505. (505)474-9139. E-mail: etp@jetliterary.com. Website: www.jetliterary.com. **Contact:** Liz Trupin-Pulli. Represents 75 clients. 35% of clients are new/unpublished writers.

MEMBER AGENTS Liz Trupin-Pulli (adult and YA fiction/nonfiction; romance, mysteries, parenting); Jim Trupin (adult fiction/nonfiction, military history, pop culture); Jessica Trupin, associate agent based in Seattle (adult fiction and nonfiction, children's and young adult, memoir, pop culture).

REPRESENTS nonfiction books, novels, short story collections. **Considers these fiction areas:** action, adventure, crime, detective, erotica, ethnic, gay, glitz, historical, humor, lesbian, literary, mainstream, mystery, police, romance, suspense, thriller, women's, young adult.

"JET was founded in New York in 1975, so we bring a wealth of knowledge and contacts, as well as quite a bit of expertise to our representation of writers." Actively seeking women's fiction, mysteries and narrative nonfiction. JET represents the full range of adult and YA fiction and nonfiction, including humor and cookbooks. Does not want to receive sci-fi, fantasy, horror, poetry, children's, or religious.

HOW TO CONTACT An e-query only is accepted. Responds in 1 week to queries. Responds in 8 weeks to mss. Obtains most new clients through recommendations from others, solicitations, conferences.

TERMS Agent receives 15% commission on domestic sales. Agent receives 10% commission on foreign sales. Offers written contract, binding for 3 years. This agency charges for reimbursement of mailing and any photocopying.

RECENT SALES Sold 22 books in 2009 including several ghostwriting contracts. *Mom-in-chief*, by Jamie Woolf (Wiley, 2009); *Dangerous Games* by Charlotte Mede (Kensington, 2009); *So You Think You Can Spell!* by David Grambs and Ellen Levine (Perigee, 2009); *Cut, Drop & Die*, by Joanna Campbell Slan (Midnight Ink, 2009).

WRITERS CONFERENCES Women Writing the West; Southwest Writers Conference; Florida Writers Association Conference.

TIPS Do not write cute queries—stick to a straightforward message that includes the title and what your book is about, why you are suited to write this particular book, and what you have written in the past (if anything), along with a bit of a bio.

CAREN JOHNSON LITERARY AGENCY

132 East 43rd St., No. 216, New York NY 10017. E-mail: caren@johnsonlitagency.com. Website: www.johnsonliterary.com. **Contact:** Caren Estesen, Elana Roth. Represents 20 clients. 50% of clients are new/unpublished writers. Currently handles nonfiction books 35%, juvenile books 35%, romance/women's fiction 30%.

Prior to her current position, Ms. Estesen was with Firebrand Literary and the Peter Rubie Agency.

MEMBER AGENTS Caren Estesen, Elana Roth, Katie Shea.

REPRESENTS nonfiction books, novels. **Considers these fiction areas:** detective, erotica, ethnic, romance, young adult middle grade, women's fiction.

Does not want to receive poetry, plays, or screenplays/scripts. Elana Roth will consider picture books but is very selective of what she takes on.

HOW TO CONTACT Query via e-mail only, "directing your query to the appropriate person; responds in 12 weeks to all materials sent. Include 4-5 sample pages within the body of your e-mail when pitching us. Accepts simultaneous submissions. Responds in 4-6 weeks to queries. Responds in 6-8 weeks to mss. Obtains most new clients through recommendations from others.

TERMS Agent receives 15% commission on domestic sales. Agent receives 20% commission on foreign sales. Offers written contract; 30-day notice must be given to terminate contract. This agency charges for postage and photocopying, though the author is consulted before any charges are incurred.

RECENT SALES Please check out website for a complete client list.

WRITERS CONFERENCES RWA National; BookExpo America; SCBWI.

◐ HARVEY KLINGER, INC.

300 W. 55th St., Suite 11V, New York NY 10019. (212)581-7068. E-mail: queries@harveyklinger.com. Website: www.harveyklinger.com. **Contact:** Harvey Klinger. Member of AAR. Represents 100 clients. 25% of clients are new/unpublished writers. Currently handles nonfiction books (50%), novels (50%).

MEMBER AGENTS David Dunton (popular culture, music-related books, literary fiction, young adult, fiction, and memoirs); Sara Crowe (children's and young adult authors, adult fiction and nonfiction, foreign rights sales); Andrea Somberg (literary fiction, commercial fiction, romance, sci-fi/fantasy, mysteries/thrillers, young adult, middle grade, quality narrative nonfiction, popular culture, how-to, self-help, humor, interior design, cookbooks, health/fitness).

REPRESENTS nonfiction books, novels. **Considers these fiction areas:** action, adventure, crime, detective, family saga, glitz, literary, mainstream, mystery, police, suspense, thriller.

This agency specializes in big, mainstream, contemporary fiction and nonfiction.

HOW TO CONTACT Use online e-mail submission form, or query with SASE. No phone or fax queries. Don't send unsolicited manuscripts or e-mail attachments. Responds in 2 months to queries and mss. Obtains most new clients through recommendations from others.

TERMS Agent receives 15% commission on domestic sales. Agent receives 25% commission on foreign sales. Offers written contract. Charges for photocopying mss and overseas postage for mss.

RECENT SALES *Woman of a Thousand Secrets*, by Barbara Wood; *I Am Not a Serial Killer*, by Dan Wells; untitled memoir, by Bob Mould; *Children of the Mist*; by Paula Quinn; *Tutored*, by Allison Whittenberg; *Will You Take Me As I Am*, by Michelle Mercer. Other clients include: George Taber, Terry Kay, Scott Mebus, Jacqueline Kolosov, Jonathan Maberry, Tara Altebrando, Alex McAuley, Eva Nagorski, Greg Kot, Justine Musk, Alex McAuley, Nick Tasler, Ashley Kahn, Barbara De Angelis.

◐ KRAAS LITERARY AGENCY

E-mail: irenekraas@sbcglobal.net. Website: www.kraasliteraryagency.com. **Contact:** Irene Kraas. Represents 35 clients. 75% of clients are new/unpublished writers. Currently handles novels 100%.

MEMBER AGENTS Irene Kraas, principal.

REPRESENTS novels. **Considers these fiction areas:** literary, thriller, young adult.

This agency is interested in working with published writers, but that does not mean self-published writers. "The agency is ONLY accepting new manuscripts in the genre of adult thrillers and mysteries. Submissions should be the first ten pages of a completed manuscript embedded in an email. I do not open attachments or go to websites." Does not want to receive short stories, plays, or poetry. This agency no longer represents adult fantasy or science fiction.

HOW TO CONTACT Query and e-mail the first 10 pages of a completed ms. Requires exclusive read on mss. Accepts simultaneous submissions.

TERMS Offers written contract.

TIPS "I am interested in material—in any genre—that is truly, truly unique."

○ KT LITERARY, LLC

9249 S. Broadway, #200-543, Highlands Ranch CO 80129. (720)344-4728. Fax: (720)344-4728. E-mail: contact@ktliterary.com. Website: http://ktliterary.com. **Contact:** Kate Schafer Testerman. Member of AAR. Other memberships include SCBWI. Represents 20 clients. 60% of clients are new/unpublished writers. Currently handles nonfiction books (5%), novels (5%), juvenile books (90%).

Prior to her current position, Ms. Schafer was an agent with Janklow & Nesbit.

REPRESENTS nonfiction books, novels, juvenile books. **Considers these fiction areas:** action, adventure, fantasy, historical, juvenile, romance, science fiction, women's, young adult.

"I'm bringing my years of experience in the New York publishing scene, as well as my lifelong love of reading, to a vibrant area for writers, proving that great work can be found, and sold, from anywhere." "Actively seeking brilliant, funny, original middle grade and young adult fiction, both literary and commercial; witty women's fiction (chick lit); and pop-culture, narrative nonfiction. Quirky is good." Does not want picture books, serious nonfiction, and adult literary fiction.

HOW TO CONTACT E-mail queries only. Ms. Testerman is closed to submissions until June of 2011. Keep an eye on the KT Literary blog for updates. Responds in 2 weeks to queries. Responds in 2 months to mss. Obtains most new clients through recommendations from others, solicitations, conferences.

TERMS Agent receives 15% commission on domestic sales. Agent receives 20% commission on foreign sales. Offers written contract; 30-day notice must be given to terminate contract.

WRITERS CONFERENCES Various SCBWI conferences, BookExpo.

TIPS "If we like your query, we'll ask for (more). Continuing advice is offered regularly on my blog 'Ask Daphne,' which can be accessed from my website."

KT PUBLIC RELATIONS & LITERARY SERVICES

1905 Cricklewood Cove, Fogelsville PA 18051. (610)395-6298. Fax: (610)395-6299. Website: www.ktpublicrelations.com; Blog: http://newliteraryagents.blogspot.com. **Contact:** Jon Tienstra. Represents 12 clients. 75% of clients are new/unpublished writers. Currently handles nonfiction books (50%), novels (50%).

Prior to becoming an agent, Kae Tienstra was publicity director for Rodale, Inc. for 13 years and then founded her own publicity agency; Mr. Tienstra joined the firm in 1995 with varied corporate experience and a master's degree in library science.

MEMBER AGENTS Kae Tienstra (health, parenting, psychology, how-to, women's fiction, general fiction); Jon Tienstra (nature/environment, history, cooking/foods/nutrition, war/military, automotive, health/medicine, gardening, general fiction, science fiction/contemporary fantasy, popular fiction).

REPRESENTS nonfiction books, novels. **Considers these fiction areas:** action, adventure, crime, detective, family saga, historical, literary, mainstream, mystery, police, romance, science fiction, suspense, thriller contemporary fantasy (no swords or dragons).

"Wehaveworkedwithavarietyofauthorsand publishers over the years and have learned what individual publishers are looking for in terms of new acquisitions. We are both mad about books and authors and we look forward to finding publishing success for all our clients. Specializes in parenting, history, cooking/foods/nutrition, war, health/medicine, psychology, how-to, gardening, science fiction, contemporary fantasy, women's fiction, and popular fiction." Does not want to see unprofessional material.

HOW TO CONTACT Query with SASE. Prefers snail mail queries. Will accept e-mail queries. Responds in 3 months to chapters; 6-9 months for mss. Accepts simultaneous submissions. Responds in 4 weeks to queries.

TERMS Agent receives 15% commission on domestic sales. Agent receives 20% commission on foreign sales. Offers written contract. Charges clients for long-distance phone calls, fax, postage, photocopying (only when incurred). No advance payment for these out-of-pocket expenses.

PETER LAMPACK AGENCY, INC.

551 Fifth Ave., Suite 1613, New York NY 10176-0187. (212)687-9106. Fax: (212)687-9109. E-mail: alampack@verizon.net. **Contact:** Andrew Lampack. Represents 50 clients. 10% of clients are new/unpublished writers. Currently handles nonfiction books (20%), novels (80%).

MEMBER AGENTS Peter Lampack (president); Rema Delanyan (foreign rights); Andrew Lampack (new writers).

REPRESENTS nonfiction books, novels. **Considers these fiction areas:** adventure, crime, detective, family saga, literary, mainstream, mystery, police, suspense, thriller contemporary relationships.

"Thisagencyspecializesincommercialfiction and nonfiction by recognized experts." Actively seeking literary and commercial fiction, thrillers, mysteries, suspense, and psychological thrillers. Does not want to receive horror, romance, science fiction, westerns, historical literary fiction, or academic material.

HOW TO CONTACT Query via e-mail. *No unsolicited mss.* Responds within 2 months to queries. Obtains most new clients through referrals made by clients.

TERMS Agent receives 15% commission on domestic sales. Agent receives 20% commission on foreign sales.

RECENT SALES *Spartan Gold*, by Clive Cussler with Grant Blackwood; *The Wrecker*, by Clive Cussler with Justin Scott; *Medusa*, by Clive Cussler and Paul Kemprecos; *Silent Sea* by Clive Cussler with Jack Dubrul; *Summertime*, by J.M. Coetzee; *Dreaming in French*, by Megan McAndrew; *Time Pirate*, by Ted Bell.

WRITERS CONFERENCES BookExpo America; Mystery Writers of America.

TIPS "Submit only your best work for consideration. Have a very specific agenda of goals you wish your prospective agent to accomplish for you. Provide the agent with a comprehensive statement of your credentials—educational and professional accomplishments."

◐ LAURA LANGLIE, LITERARY AGENT

63 Wyckoff St., Brooklyn NY 11201. (718)855-8102. Fax: (718)855-4450. E-mail: laura@lauralanglie.com. **Contact:** Laura Langlie. Represents 25 clients. 50% of clients are new/unpublished writers. Currently handles nonfiction books (15%), novels (58%), story collections (2%), juvenile books (25%).

Prior to opening her agency, Ms. Langlie worked in publishing for 7 years and as an agent at Kidde, Hoyt & Picard for 6 years.

REPRESENTS nonfiction books, novels, short story collections, novellas, juvenile. **Considers these fiction areas:** crime, detective, ethnic, feminist, historical, humor, juvenile, literary, mainstream, mystery, police, suspense, thriller, young adult mainstream.

"I'm very involved with and committed to my clients. I also employ a publicist to work with all my clients to make the most of each book's publication. Most of my clients come to me via recommendations from other agents, clients and editors. I've met very few at conferences. I've often sought out writers for projects, and I still find new clients via the traditional query letter." Does not want to receive how-to, children's picture books, science fiction, poetry, men's adventure, or erotica.

HOW TO CONTACT Query with SASE. Accepts queries via fax. Accepts simultaneous submissions. Responds in 1 week to queries. Responds in 1 month to mss. Obtains most new clients through recommendations, submissions.

TERMS Agent receives 15% commission on domestic sales. Agent receives 20% commission on foreign and dramatic sales. No written contract.

RECENT SALES Sold 15 titles in the last year. *Autobiography of Mrs. Tom Thumb*, by Melanie Benjamin (Delacorte Press); *A Body of Water*, by Sarah Dooley (Feiwel & Friends/Macmillan); *Miss Dimple Rallies to the Cause*, by Mignon F. Ballard (St. Martin's Press); *Abandon* by Meg Cabot (Scholastic, Inc.); *Overbite*, by Meg Cabot (William Morrow); *Huntress*, by Malinda Lo (Little, Brown & Co Books for Young Readers); *Everybody Bugs Out*, by Leslie Margolis (Bloomsbury); *The Elite Gymnasts*, by Dominique Moceanu and Alicia Thompson (Disney/Hyperion); *Safe from the Sea*, by Peter Geye (Unbridled Books).

TIPS "Be complete, forthright and clear in your communications. Do your research as to what a particular agent represents."

LANGTONS INTERNATIONAL AGENCY

124 West 60th St., #42M, New York NY 10023. (646)344-1801. E-mail: langton@langtonsinternational@com; llangton@langtonsinternational.com. Website: www.langtonsinternational.com. **Contact:** Linda Langton, President.

Prior to becoming an agent, Ms. Langton was a co-founding director and publisher of the international publishing company, The Ink Group.

REPRESENTS nonfiction books and literary fiction. **Considers these fiction areas:** literary, political thrillers, young adult, and middle grade books.

"Langtons International Agency is a multimedia literary and licensing agency specializing in nonfiction, inspirational, thrillers and children's middle grade and young adult books as well as the the visual world of photography."

HOW TO CONTACT Please submit all queries via hard copy to the address aove or e-mail outline/proposal, synopsis, publishing history, author bio. Only published authors should query this agency. Accepts simultaneous submissions.

RECENT SALES *Talking with Jean-Paul Sartre: Conversations and Debates*, by Professor John Gerassi (Yale University Press); *The Obama Presidency and the Politics of Change*, by Professor Stanley Renshon (Routledge Press); *I Would See a Girl Walking*, by Diana Montane and Kathy Kelly (Berkley Books); *Begin 1913-1992*, by Avi Shilon (Yale University Press); *This Borrowed Earth*, by Robert Emmet Hernan (Palgrave McMillan); *The Perfect Square*, by Nancy Heinzen (Temple Uni Press); *The Honey Trail* by Grace Pundyk (St. Martin's Press); *Dogs of Central Park* by Fran Reisner (Rizzoli/Universe Publishing).

THE STEVE LAUBE AGENCY

5025 N. Central Ave., #635, Phoenix AZ 85012. (602)336-8910. E-mail: krichards@stevelaube.com. Website: www.stevelaube.com. **Contact:** Steve Laube. Other memberships include CBA. Represents 60+ clients. 5% of clients are new/unpublished writers. Currently handles nonfiction books (48%), novels (48%), novella (2%), scholarly books (2%).

Prior to becoming an agent, Mr. Laube worked 11 years as a Christian bookseller and 11 years as editorial director of nonfiction with Bethany House Publishers.

REPRESENTS nonfiction books, novels. **Considers these fiction areas:** religious.

Primarily serves the Christian market (CBA). Actively seeking Christian fiction and religious nonfiction. Does not want to receive children's picture books, poetry, or cookbooks.

HOW TO CONTACT Submit proposal package, outline, 3 sample chapters, SASE. No e-mail submissions. Consult website for guidelines. Accepts simultaneous submissions. Responds in 6-8 weeks to queries. Obtains most new clients through recommendations from others, solicitations, conferences.

TERMS Agent receives 15% commission on domestic sales. Agent receives 20% commission on foreign sales. Offers written contract; 30-day notice must be given to terminate contract.

RECENT SALES Sold 80 titles in the last year. Other clients include Deborah Raney, Allison Bottke, H. Norman Wright, Ellie Kay, Jack Cavanaugh, Karen Ball, Tracey Bateman, Susan May Warren, Lisa Bergren, John Rosemond, Cindy Woodsmall, Karol Ladd, Judith Pella, Michael Phillips, Margaret Daley, William Lane Craig, Tosca Lee, Ginny Aiken.

WRITERS CONFERENCES Mount Hermon Christian Writers' Conference; American Christian Fiction Writers' Conference.

ROBERT LECKER AGENCY

4055 Melrose Ave., Montreal QC H4A 2S5 Canada. (514)830-4818. Fax: (514)483-1644. E-mail: leckerlink@aol.com. Website: www.leckeragency.com. **Contact:** Robert Lecker. Represents 20 clients. 20% of clients are new/unpublished writers. Currently handles nonfiction books (80%), novels (10%), scholarly books (10%).

Prior to becoming an agent, Mr. Lecker was the cofounder and publisher of ECW Press and professor of English literature at McGill University. He has 30 years of experience in book and magazine publishing.

MEMBER AGENTS Robert Lecker (popular culture, music); Mary Williams (travel, food, popular science).

REPRESENTS nonfiction books, novels, scholarly syndicated material. **Considers these fiction areas:** action, adventure, crime, detective, erotica, literary, mainstream, mystery, police, suspense, thriller.

RLA specializes in books about popular culture, popular science, music, entertainment, food, and travel. The agency responds to articulate, innovative proposals within 2 weeks. Actively seeking original book mss only after receipt of outlines and proposals.

HOW TO CONTACT Query first. Only responds to queries of interest. Discards the rest. Accepts simultaneous submissions. Responds in 2 weeks to queries. Responds in 1 month to mss. Obtains most new clients through recommendations from others, conferences, interest in website.

TERMS Agent receives 15% commission on domestic sales. Agent receives 15-20% commission on foreign sales. Offers written contract, binding for 1 year; 6-month notice must be given to terminate contract.

LESCHER & LESCHER, LTD.

346 E. 84th St., New York NY 10028. (212)396-1999. Fax: (212)396-1991. E-mail: cl@lescherltd.com. **Contact:** Carolyn Larson, agent. Member of AAR. Represents 150 clients. Currently handles nonfiction books (80%), novels (20%).

REPRESENTS nonfiction books, novels. **Considers these fiction areas:** commercial, literary, mystery, suspense.

Does not want to receive screenplays, science fiction, or romance.

HOW TO CONTACT Query with SASE. Obtains most new clients through recommendations from others.

TERMS Agent receives 15% commission on domestic sales. Agent receives 10% commission on foreign sales.

LEVINE GREENBERG LITERARY AGENCY, INC.

307 Seventh Ave., Suite 2407, New York NY 10001. (212)337-0934. Fax: (212)337-0948. E-mail: submit@levinegreenberg.com. Website: www.levinegreenberg.com. Member of AAR. Represents 250 clients. 33% of clients are new/unpublished writers. Currently handles nonfiction books (70%), novels (30%).

Prior to opening his agency, Mr. Levine served as vice president of the Bank Street College of Education.

MEMBER AGENTS James Levine, Daniel Greenberg, Stephanie Kip Rostan, Lindsay Edgecombe, Danielle Svetcov, Elizabeth Fisher, Victoria Skurnick.

REPRESENTS nonfiction books, novels. **Considers these fiction areas:** literary, mainstream, mystery, thriller, psychological, women's.

This agency specializes in business, psychology, parenting, health/medicine, narrative nonfiction, spirituality, religion, women's issues, and commercial fiction.

HOW TO CONTACT See website for full submission procedure at "How to Submit." Or use our e-mail address if you prefer, or online submission form. Do not submit directly to agents. Prefers electronic submissions. Cannot respond to submissions by mail. Obtains most new clients through recommendations from others.

TERMS Agent receives 15% commission on domestic sales. Agent receives 20% commission on foreign sales. Offers written contract. Charges clients for out-of-pocket expenses—telephone, fax, postage, photocopying—directly connected to the project.

WRITERS CONFERENCES ASJA Writers' Conference.

TIPS "We focus on editorial development, business representation, and publicity and marketing strategy."

PAUL S. LEVINE LITERARY AGENCY

1054 Superba Ave., Venice CA 90291-3940. (310)450-6711. Fax: (310)450-0181. E-mail: paul@paulslevinelit.com. Website: www.paulslevinelit.com. **Contact:** Paul S. Levine. Other memberships include the State Bar of California. Represents over 100 clients. 75% of clients are new/unpublished writers. Currently handles nonfiction books (60%), novels (10%), movie scripts (10%), TV scripts (5%), juvenile books 5%.

MEMBER AGENTS Paul S. Levine (children's and young adult fiction and nonfiction, adult fiction and nonfiction except sci-fi, fantasy, and horror); Loren R. Grossman (archaeology, art/photography/architecture, gardening, education, health, medicine, science).

REPRESENTS nonfiction books, novels, episodic drama, movie, TV, movie scripts, feature film, TV movie of the week, sitcom, animation, documentary, miniseries syndicated material, reality show. **Considers these fiction areas:** action, adventure, comic books, confession, crime, detective, erotica, ethnic, experimental, family saga, feminist, frontier, gay, glitz, historical, humor, inspirational, lesbian, literary, mainstream, mystery, police, regional, religious, romance, satire, sports, suspense, thriller, westerns.

Does not want to receive science fiction, fantasy, or horror.

HOW TO CONTACT Query with SASE. Accepts simultaneous submissions. Responds in 1 day to queries. Responds in 6-8 weeks to mss. Obtains most new clients through conferences, referrals, listings on various websites, and in directories.

TERMS Agent receives 15% commission on domestic sales. Offers written contract. Charges for postage and actual, out-of-pocket costs only.

RECENT SALES Sold 8 books in the last year.

WRITERS CONFERENCES Willamette Writers Conference; San Francisco Writers Conference; Santa Barbara Writers Conference and many others.

TIPS "Write good, sellable books."

LINDSTROM LITERARY MANAGEMENT, LLC

871 N. Greenbrier St., Arlington VA 22205. Fax: (703)527-7624. E-mail: submissions@lindstromliterary.com; kristin@lindstromliterary.com. Website: www.lindstromliterary.com. **Contact:** Kristin Lindstrom. Other memberships include Author's Guild. Represents 9 clients. 30% of clients are new/unpub-

lished writers. Currently handles nonfiction books (30%), novels (70%).

Prior to her current position, Ms. Lindstrom started her career as an editor of a monthly magazine in the energy industry, and was employed as a public relations manager for a national software company before becoming an independent marketing and publicity consultant.

REPRESENTS nonfiction books, novels. **Considers these fiction areas:** action, adventure, crime, detective, erotica, inspirational, mainstream, mystery, police, religious, suspense, thriller, women's.

"In 2006, I decided to add my more specific promotion/publicity skills to the mix in order to support the marketing efforts of my published clients." Actively seeking commercial fiction and narrative nonfiction. Does not want to receive young adult or children's books, or books of poetry.

HOW TO CONTACT Query via e-mail only. Submit author bio, synopsis and first four chapters if submitting fiction. For nonfiction, send the first 4 chapters, synopsis, proposal, outline and mission statement. *You will only hear from us again if we decide to ask for a complete manuscript or further information.* Accepts simultaneous submissions. Responds in 6 weeks to queries. Responds in 8 weeks to requested mss. Obtains most new clients through referrals and solicitations.

TERMS Agent receives 15% commission on domestic sales. Agent receives 20% commission on performance rights and foreign sales. Offers written contract. This agency charges for postage, UPS, copies and other basic office expenses.

RECENT SALES A memoir by Agathe von Trapp (It Books/Harper). Two book deal for Alice Wisler (Bethany House); a thriller by J.C. Hutchins (St. Martin's Press).

TIPS "Do your homework on accepted practices; make sure you know what kind of book the agent handles."

LINN PRENTIS LITERARY

155 East 116th St., #2F, New York NY 10029. Fax: (212)875-5565. E-mail: ahayden@linnprentis.com; linn@linnprentis.com. Website: www.linnprentis.com. **Contact:** Amy Hayden, acquisitions director; Linn Prentis, agent; Jordana Frankel assistant. Represents 18-20 clients. 25% of clients are new/unpublished writers. Currently handles nonfiction books (5%), novels (65%), story collections (7%), novella (10%), juvenile books (10%), scholarly books (3%).

Prior to becoming an agent, Ms. Prentis was a nonfiction writer and editor, primarily in magazines. She also worked in book promotion in New York. Ms. Prentis then worked for and later ran the Virginia Kidd Agency. She is known particularly for her assistance with manuscript development.

REPRESENTS nonfiction books, novels, short story collections, novellas (from authors whose novels I already represent), juvenile (for older juveniles), scholarly anthology. **Considers these fiction areas:** adventure, ethnic, fantasy, feminist, gay, glitz, historical, horror, humor, juvenile, lesbian, literary, mainstream, mystery, thriller.

"Because of the Virginia Kidd connection and the clients I brought with me at the start, I have a special interest in sci-fi and fantasy, but, really, fiction is what interests me. As for my nonfiction projects, they are books I just couldn't resist." Actively seeking hard science fiction, family saga, mystery, memoir, mainstream, literary, women's. Does not want to "receive books for little kids."

HOW TO CONTACT Query with SASE. Submit synopsis. No phone or fax queries. No snail mail. E-mail queries to ahayden@linnprentis.com. Include first 10 pages and synopsis as either attachment or as text in the e-mail. Accepts simultaneous submissions. Obtains most new clients through recommendations from others, solicitations.

TERMS Agent receives 15% commission on domestic sales. Agent receives 20% commission on foreign sales. Offers written contract; 60-day notice must be given to terminate contract.

RECENT SALES Sold 15 titles in the last year. *The Sons of Heaven*, *The Empress of Mars*, and *The House of the Stag*, by Kage Baker (Tor); the last has also been sold to Dabel Brothers to be published as a comic book/graphic novel; *Indigo Springs* and a sequel, by A.M. Dellamonica (Tor); Wayne Arthurson's debut mystery plus a second series book; *Bone Crossed* and *Cry Wolf* for *New York Times* #1 best-selling author Patricia Briggs (Ace/Penguin). "The latter is the start of a new series."

TIPS "Consider query letters and synopses as writing assignments. Spell names correctly."

LIPPINCOTT MASSIE MCQUILKIN

27 West 20th Street, Suite 305, New York NY 10011. Fax: (212)352-2059. E-mail: info@lmqlit.com. Website: www.lmqlit.com.

MEMBER AGENTS Maria Massie (fiction, memoir, cultural criticism); Will Lippincott (politics, current affairs, history); Rob McQuilkin (fiction, history, psychology, sociology, graphic material); Jason Anthony (young adult, pop culture, memoir, true crime, and general psychology).

REPRESENTS nonfiction books, novels, short story collections, scholarly graphic novels. **Considers these fiction areas:** action, adventure, cartoon, comic books, confession, family saga, feminist, gay, historical, humor, lesbian, literary, mainstream, regional, satire.

"LMQ focuses on bringing new voices in literary and commercial fiction to the market, as well as popularizing the ideas and arguments of scholars in the fields of history, psychology, sociology, political science, and current affairs. Actively seeking fiction writers who already have credits in magazines and quarterlies, as well as nonfiction writers who already have a media platform or some kind of a university affiliation." Does not want to receive romance, genre fiction, or children's material.

HOW TO CONTACT "We accepts electronic queries only. Only send additional materials if requested." Accepts simultaneous submissions. Responds in 1 week to queries. Responds in 1 month to mss. Obtains most new clients through recommendations from others, solicitations, conferences.

TERMS Agent receives 15% commission on domestic sales. Agent receives 20% commission on foreign sales. Offers written contract; 30-day notice must be given to terminate contract. Only charges for reasonable business expenses upon successful sale.

RECENT SALES Clients include: Peter Ho Davies, Kim Addonizio, Natasha Trethewey, Anne Carson, David Sirota, Katie Crouch, Uwen Akpan, Lydia Millet, Tom Perrotta, Jonathan Lopez, Chris Hayes, Caroline Weber.

LITERARY MANAGEMENT GROUP, INC.

(615)812-4445. E-mail: brucebarbour@literarymanagementgroup.com; brb@brucebarbour.com. Website: http//:literarymanagementgroup.com; www.brucebarbour.com. **Contact:** Bruce Barbour.

Prior to becoming an agent, Mr. Barbour held executive positions at several publishing houses, including Revell, Barbour Books, Thomas Nelson, and Random House.

REPRESENTS nonfiction books, novels.

"Although we specialize in the area of Christian publishing from an Evangelical perspective, we have editorial contacts and experience in general interest books as well." Does not want to receive gift books, poetry, children's books, short stories, or juvenile/young adult fiction. No unsolicited mss or proposals from unpublished authors.

HOW TO CONTACT Query with SASE. E-mail proposal as an attachment.

TERMS Agent receives 15% commission on domestic sales.

LORETTA BARRETT BOOKS, INC.

220 E. 23rd St., 11th Floor, New York NY 10010. (212)242-3420. E-mail: query@lorettabarrettbooks.com. Website: www.lorettabarrettbooks.com. **Contact:** Loretta A. Barrett, Nick Mullendore, Gabriel Davis. Estab. 1990. Member of AAR. Currently handles nonfiction books (50%), novels (50%).

Prior to opening her agency, Ms. Barrett was vice president and executive editor at Doubleday and editor-in-chief of Anchor Books.

MEMBER AGENTS Loretta A. Barrett; Nick Mullendore.

REPRESENTS nonfiction books, novels. **Considers these fiction areas:** contemporary, psychic, adventure, detective, ethnic, family, historical, literary, mainstream, mystery, thriller, young adult.

"The clients we represent include both fiction and nonfiction authors for the general adult trade market. The works they produce encompass a wide range of contemporary topics and themes including commercial thrillers, mysteries, romantic suspense, popular science, memoirs, narrative fiction and current affairs." No children's, juvenile, cookbooks, gardening, science fiction, fantasy novels, historical romance.

HOW TO CONTACT See guidelines online. Use e-mail (no attachments) or if by post, query with SASE. For hardcopy queries, please send a 1-2 page query letter and a synopsis or chapter outline for your project. In your letter, please include your contact information, any relevant background information on yourself or your project, and a paragraph of description of your project. If you are submitting electronically, then all of this material may be included in the body of your e-mail. Accepts simultaneous submissions. Responds in 3-6 weeks to queries.

TERMS Agent receives 15% commission on domestic sales. Agent receives 20% commission on foreign sales. Offers written contract. Charges clients for shipping and photocopying.

● LOWENSTEIN ASSOCIATES INC.

121 W. 27th St., Suite 601, New York NY 10001. (212)206-1630. Fax: (212)727-0280. E-mail: assistant@bookhaven.com. Website: www.lowensteinassociates.com. **Contact:** Barbara Lowenstein. Member of AAR. Represents 150 clients. 20% of clients are new/unpublished writers. Currently handles nonfiction books (60%), novels (40%).

MEMBER AGENTS Barbara Lowenstein, president (nonfiction interests include narrative nonfiction, health, money, finance, travel, multicultural, popular culture, and memoir; fiction interests include literary fiction and women's fiction); Kathleen Ortiz, associate agent and foreign rights manager at Lowenstein Associates. She is seeking children's books (chapter, middle grade, and young adult) and young adult nonfiction.

REPRESENTS nonfiction books, novels. **Considers these fiction areas:** crime, detective, erotica, ethnic, fantasy, feminist, historical, literary, mainstream, mystery, police, romance, suspense, thriller, young adult.

8—ᴥ "Thagenspyecialhealth,business, creative nonfiction, literary fiction and commercial fiction—especially suspense, crime and women's issues. We are a full-service agency, handling domestic and foreign rights, film rights and audio rights to all of our books." Barbara Lowenstein is currently looking for writers who have a platform and are leading experts in their field, including business, women's issues, psychology, health, science and social issues, and is particularly interested in strong new voices in fiction and narrative nonfiction.

HOW TO CONTACT Please send us a 1-page query letter, along with the first 10 pages pasted in the body of the message (if fiction; for nonfiction, please send only a query letter), by e-mail. Please put the word QUERY and the title of your project in the subject field of your e-mail and address it to the agent of your choice. Please do not send an attachment. We reply to all queries and generally send a response within 2-4 weeks. By mail: For Fiction: Mail a query letter, short synopsis, first chapter and a SASE For Nonfiction: Mail a query letter, proposal, if available, or else a project overview and a SASE. Responds in 4 weeks to queries. Obtains most new clients through recommendations from others, solicitations, conferences.

TERMS Agent receives 15% commission on domestic sales. Agent receives 20% commission on foreign sales. Offers written contract. Charges for large photocopy batches, messenger service, international postage.

WRITERS CONFERENCES Malice Domestic

TIPS "Know the genre you are working in and read! Also, please see our website for details on which agent to query for your project."

LYNN C. FRANKLIN ASSOCIATES, LTD.

1350 Broadway, Suite 2015, New York NY 10018. (212)868-6311. Fax: (212)868-6312. **Contact:** Lynn Franklin, President; Claudia Nys, Foreign Rights; Michelle Andelman, Agent/Children's. Other memberships include PEN America. Represents 30-35 clients. 50% of clients are new/unpublished writers. Currently handles nonfiction books (90%), novels (10%).

REPRESENTS nonfiction books, novels. **Considers these fiction areas:** literary, mainstream, commercial; juvenile, middle-grade, and young adult.

8—ᴥ "This agency specializes in general nonfiction with a special interest in self-help, biography/memoir, alternative health, and spirituality."

HOW TO CONTACT Query via e-mail to agency@franklinandsiegal.com. No unsolicited mss. No attachments. For nonfiction, query letter with short outline and synopsis. For fiction, query letter with short synopsis and a maximum of 10 sample pages (in the body of the e-mail). Please indicate "query adult" or "query children's) in the subject line. Accepts simultaneous submissions. Responds in 2 weeks to queries. Responds in 6 weeks to mss. Obtains most new clients through recommendations from others, solicitations.

TERMS Agent receives 15% commission on domestic sales. Agent receives 20% commission on foreign sales. Offers written contract.

RECENT SALES Adult: *Made for Goodness*, by Archbishop Desmond Tutu and Reverend Mpho Tutu (HarperOne); *Children of God Storybook Bible*, by Archbishop Desmond Tutu (Zondervan for originating publisher Lux Verbi); *Playing Our Game: Why China's Economic Rise Doesn't Threaten the West*, by Edward Steinfeld (Oxford University Press); *The 100 Year Diet*, by Susan Yager (Rodale); Children's/YA: *I Like Mandarin*, by Kirsten Hubbard (Delacorte/Random House); *A Scary Scene in a Scary Movie*, by Matt Blackstone (Farrar, Straus & Giroux).

LYONS LITERARY, LLC

27 West 20th St., Suite 10003, New York NY 10011. (212)255-5472. Fax: (212)851-8405. E-mail: info@lyonsliterary.com. Website: www.lyonsliterary.com. **Contact:** Jonathan Lyons. Member of AAR. Other memberships include the Author's Guild, American Bar Association, New York State Bar Associaton, New York State Intellectual Property Law Section. Represents 37 clients. 15% of clients are new/unpublished writers.Currently handles nonfiction books (60%), novels (40%).

REPRESENTS nonfiction books, novels. **Considers these fiction areas:** contemporary issues, crime, detective, fantasy, feminist, gay, historical, humor, lesbian, literary, mainstream, mystery, police, psychic, regional, satire, science fiction, sports, supernatural, suspense, thriller, women's chick lit.

"With my legal expertise and experience selling domestic and foreign language book rights, paperback reprint rights, audio rights, film/TV rights and permissions, I am able to provide substantive and personal guidance to my clients in all areas relating to their projects. In addition, with the advent of new publishing technology, Lyons Literary, LLC is situated to address the changing nature of the industry while concurrently handling authors' more traditional needs."

HOW TO CONTACT Only accepts queries through online submission form. Accepts simultaneous submissions. Responds in 8 weeks to queries. Responds in 12 weeks to mss. Obtains most new clients through recommendations from others.

TERMS Agent receives 15% commission on domestic sales. Agent receives 20% commission on foreign sales. Offers written contract.

WRITERS CONFERENCES Agents and Editors Conference.

TIPS "Please submit electronic queries through our website submission form."

MACGREGOR LITERARY INC.

2373 N.W. 185th Ave., Suite 165, Hillsboro OR 97124. (503)277-8308. E-mail: submissions@macgregorliterary.com. Website: www.macgregorliterary.com. **Contact:** Chip MacGregor. Signatory of WGA. Represents 40 clients. 10% of clients are new/unpublished writers.Currently handles nonfiction books (40%), novels (60%).

Prior to his current position, Mr. MacGregor was the senior agent with Alive Communications. Most recently, he was associate publisher for Time-Warner Book Group's Faith Division, and helped put together their Center Street imprint.

MEMBER AGENTS Chip MacGregor, Sandra Bishop, Amanda Luedeke.

REPRESENTS nonfiction books, novels. **Considers these fiction areas:** crime, detective, historical, inspirational, mainstream, mystery, police, religious, romance, suspense, thriller, women's chick lit.

"My specialty has been in career planning with authors—finding commercial ideas, then helping authors bring them to market, and in the midst of that assisting the authors as they get firmly established in their writing careers. I'm probably best known for my work with Christian books over the years, but I've done a fair amount of general market projects as well." Actively seeking authors with a Christian worldview and a growing platform. Does not want to receive fantasy, sci-fi, children's books, poetry or screenplays.

HOW TO CONTACT Query with SASE. Accepts simultaneous submissions. Responds in 3 weeks to queries. Obtains most new clients through recommendations from others. Not looking to add unpublished authors except through referrals from current clients.

TERMS Agent receives 15% commission on domestic sales. Agent receives 15% commission on foreign sales. Offers written contract; 30-day notice must be given to terminate contract. Charges for exceptional fees after receiving authors' permission.

WRITERS CONFERENCES Blue Ridge Christian Writers' Conference; Write to Publish.

TIPS "Seriously consider attending a good writers' conference. It will give you the chance to be face-to-face with people in the industry. Also, if you're a novelist, consider joining one of the national writers' organizations. The American Christian Fiction Writers (ACFW) is a wonderful group for new as well as established writers. And if you're a Christian writer of any kind, check into The Writers View, an online writing group. All of these have proven helpful to writers."

MANUS & ASSOCIATES LITERARY AGENCY, INC.

425 Sherman Ave., Suite 200, Palo Alto CA 94306. (650)470-5151. Fax: (650)470-5159. E-mail: manuslit@manuslit.com. Website: www.manuslit.com. **Contact:** Jillian Manus, Jandy Nelson, Penny Nelson. Member of AAR. Represents 75 clients. 30% of clients are new/unpublished writers. Currently handles nonfiction books (70%), novels (30%).

Prior to becoming an agent, Ms. Manus was associate publisher of two national magazines and director of development at Warner Bros. and Universal Studios; she has been a literary agent for 20 years.

MEMBER AGENTS Jandy Nelson, jandy@manuslit.com (self-help, health, memoirs, narrative nonfiction, women's fiction, literary fiction, multicultural fiction, thrillers). Nelson is currently on sabbatical and not taking on new clients. Jillian Manus, jillian@manuslit.com (political, memoirs, self-help, history, sports, women's issues, Latin fiction and nonfiction, thrillers); Penny Nelson, penny@manuslit.com (memoirs, self-help, sports, nonfiction); Dena Fischer (literary fiction, mainstream/commercial fiction, chick lit, women's fiction, historical fiction, ethnic/cultural fiction, narrative nonfiction, parenting, relationships, pop culture, health, sociology, psychology); Janet Wilkens Manus (narrative fact-based crime books, religion, pop psychology, inspiration, memoirs, cookbooks); Stephanie Lee (not currently taking on new clients).

REPRESENTS nonfiction books, novels. **Considers these fiction areas:** literary, mainstream, multicultural, mystery, suspense, thriller, women's quirky/edgy fiction.

"Our agency is unique in the way that we not only sell the material, but we edit, develop concepts, and participate in the marketing effort. We specialize in large, conceptual fiction and nonfiction, and always value a project that can be sold in the TV/feature film market." Actively seeking high-concept thrillers, commercial literary fiction, women's fiction, celebrity biographies, memoirs, multicultural fiction, popular health, women's empowerment and mysteries. No horror, romance, science fiction, fantasy, western, young adult, children's, poetry, cookbooks, or magazine articles.

HOW TO CONTACT Query with SASE. If requested, submit outline, 2-3 sample chapters. All queries should be sent to the California office. Accepts simultaneous submissions. Responds in 3 months to queries. Responds in 3 months to mss. Obtains most new clients through recommendations from others, solicitations, conferences.

TERMS Agent receives 15% commission on domestic sales. Agent receives 20-25% commission on foreign sales. Offers written contract, binding for 2 years; 60-day notice must be given to terminate contract. Charges for photocopying and postage/UPS.

RECENT SALES *Nothing Down for the 2000s* and *Multiple Streams of Income for the 2000s*, by Robert Allen; *Missed Fortune 101*, by Doug Andrew; *Cracking the Millionaire Code*, by Mark Victor Hansen and Robert Allen; *Stress Free for Good*, by Dr. Fred Luskin and Dr. Ken Pelletier; *The Mercy of Thin Air*, by Ronlyn Domangue; *The Fine Art of Small Talk*, by Debra Fine; *Bone Men of Bonares*, by Terry Tamoff.

WRITERS CONFERENCES Maui Writers' Conference; San Diego State University Writers' Conference; Willamette Writers' Conference; BookExpo America; MEGA Book Marketing University.

TIPS "Research agents using a variety of sources."

THE EVAN MARSHALL AGENCY

6 Tristam Place, Pine Brook NJ 07058-9445. (973)882-1122. Fax: (973)882-3099. E-mail: evanmarshall@optonline.net. **Contact:** Evan Marshall. Member of AAR. Other memberships include MWA, Sisters in Crime. Currently handles novels (100%).

REPRESENTS novels. **Considers these fiction areas:** action, adventure, erotica, ethnic, frontier, historical, horror, humor, inspirational, literary, mainstream, mystery, religious, satire, science fiction, suspense, western romance (contemporary, gothic, historical, regency).

HOW TO CONTACT Do not query. Currently accepting clients only by referal from editors and our own clients. Responds in 1 week to queries. Responds in 3 months to mss. Obtains most new clients through recommendations from others.

TERMS Agent receives 15% commission on domestic sales. Agent receives 20% commission on foreign sales. Offers written contract.

RECENT SALES *Watch Me Die*, by Erica Spindler (St. Martin's Press); *The First Day of the Rest of My Life*, by Cathy Lamb (Kensington); *Highland Protector*, by Hannah Howell (Zebra); *Devoured by Darkness*, by Alexandra Ivy (Kensington).

● THE MARTELL AGENCY

1350 Avenue of the Americas, Suite 1205, New York NY 10019. Fax: (212)317-2676. E-mail: afmartell@aol.com. **Contact:** Alice Martell.

REPRESENTS nonfiction. **Considers these fiction areas:** commercial Novels include mystery, thriller/suspense.

HOW TO CONTACT Query with SASE. Submit sample chapters. Submit via snail mail. No e-mail or fax queries.

RECENT SALES *Peddling Peril: The Secret Nuclear Arms Trade* by David Albright and Joel Wit (Five Press); *America's Women: Four Hundred Years of Dolls, Drudges, Helpmates, and Heroines*, by Gail Collins (William Morrow). Other clients include Serena Bass, Janice Erlbaum, David Cay Johnston, Mark Derr, Barbara Rolls, PhD.

◐ MAX AND CO., A LITERARY AGENCY AND SOCIAL CLUB

3929 Coliseum St., New Orleans LA 70115. (504)377-7745; (201)704-2483. E-mail: mmurphy@maxlit.com. Website: www.maxliterary.org. **Contact:** Michael Murphy.

Max & Co. was established in the Fall of 2007 by Michael Murphy. Prior to the literary agency, Michael began in book publishing in 1981 at Random House. He left in '95 as a vice president and later ran William Morrow as their publisher. Co-agent Jack Perry joined publishing in 1994 and has been a vice president in Sales & Marketing for Random House, Source Books, and Scholastic.

MEMBER AGENTS Michael Murphy, Nettie Hartsock (literary and commercial fiction, business books and popular nonfiction, and the occasional Southern fiction book), Jack Perry (nonfiction books with a foundation in history, sports, business, politics, narrative nonfiction, math, and science).

REPRESENTS **Considers these fiction areas:** commercial, literary.

Seeking work in literary or eclectic fiction. In nonfiction, seeks narrative or creative nonfiction. Does not represent romance, science fiction, fantasy, tea-cozy or whodunnit mysteries. Does not represent self-help or prescriptive (how-to) nonfiction. Represents no children's or YA work.

HOW TO CONTACT Agency desires e-mailed submissions and will not accept nor respond to mailed submissions. There are four agents—two in New York, one in Austin, Texas, and Michael Murphy in New Orleans.

◐ MARGRET MCBRIDE LITERARY AGENCY

P.O. Box 9128, La Jolla CA 92038. (858)454-1550. Fax: (858)454-2156. E-mail: staff@mcbridelit.com. Website: www.mcbrideliterary.com. **Contact:** Michael Daley, submissions manager. Other address: 7744 Fay Ave., Suite 201, La Jolla, CA 92037. Member of AAR. Other memberships include Authors Guild. Represents 55 clients.

Prior to opening her agency, Ms. McBride worked at Random House, Ballantine Books, and Warner Books.

REPRESENTS nonfiction books, novels. **Considers these fiction areas:** action, adventure, crime, detective, ethnic, frontier, historical, humor, literary, mainstream, mystery, police, satire, suspense, thriller, westerns.

This agency specializes in mainstream fiction and nonfiction. Does not want to receive screenplays, romance, poetry, or children's/young adult.

HOW TO CONTACT The agency is only accepting new clients by referral at this time. Query with synopsis, bio, SASE. No e-mail or fax queries. Accepts simultaneous submissions. Responds in 4-6 weeks to queries. Responds in 6-8 weeks to mss.

TERMS Agent receives 15% commission on domestic sales. Agent receives 25% commission on foreign sales. Charges for overnight delivery and photocopying.

THE MCCARTHY AGENCY, LLC

7 Allen St., Rumson NJ 07660. Phone/Fax: (732)741-3065. E-mail: McCarthylit@aol.com; ntfrost@hotmail.com. **Contact:** Shawna McCarthy. Member of AAR. Currently handles nonfiction books (25%), novels (75%).

MEMBER AGENTS Shawna McCarthy, Nahvae Frost.

REPRESENTS nonfiction books, novels. **Considers these fiction areas:** fantasy, juvenile, mystery, romance, science, womens.

HOW TO CONTACT Query via e-mail or regular mail to The McCarthy Agency, c/o Nahvae Frost, 101 Clinton Avenue, Apartment #2, Brooklyn, NY 11205 Accepts simultaneous submissions.

MCCARTHY CREATIVE SERVICES

625 Main St., Suite 834, New York NY 10044-0035. (212)832-3428. Fax: (212)829-9610. E-mail: paulmccarthy@mccarthycreative.com. Website: www.mccarthycreative.com. **Contact:** Paul D. McCarthy. Other memberships include the Authors Guild, American Society of Journalists & Authors, National Book Critics Circle, Authors League of America. Represents 5 clients. 0% of clients are new/unpublished writers.Currently handles nonfiction books (95%), novels (5%).

Prior to his current position, Mr. McCarthy was a professional writer, literary agent at the Scott Meredith Literary Agency, senior editor at publishing companies (Simon & Schuster, HarperCollins and Doubleday) and a public speaker. Learn much more about Mr. McCarthy by visiting his website.

MEMBER AGENTS Paul D. McCarthy.

REPRESENTS nonfiction books, novels. **Considers these fiction areas:** glitz, adventure, confession, detective, erotica, ethnic, family, fantasy, feminist, gay, historical, horror, humor, literary, mainstream, mystery, regional, romance, science, sports, thriller, western, young, women's.

"I deliberately founded my company to be unlimited in its range. That's what I offer, and the world has responded. My agency was founded so that I could maximize and build on the value of my combined experience for my authors and other clients, in all of my capacities and more. I think it's *very* important for authors to know that because I'm so exclusive as an agent, I may not be able to offer representation on the basis of the manuscript they submit. However, if they decide to invest in their book and lifetime career as authors, by engaging my professional, near-unique editorial services, there is the possibility that at the end of the process, when they've achieved the very best, most salable and competitive book they can write, I may see sufficient potential in the book and their next books, that I do offer to be their agent. Representation is never guaranteed." Established authors of serious and popular nonfiction, who want the value of being one of MCS's very exclusive authors who receive special attention, and of being represented by a literary agent who brings such a rich diversity and depth of publishing/creative/professorial experience, and distinguished reputation. No first novels. "Novels by established novelists will be considered very selectively."

HOW TO CONTACT Submit outline, one chapter (either first or best). Queries and submissions by e-mail only. Send as e-mail attachment. Responds in 3-4 weeks to queries. Obtains most new clients through recommendations from others.

TERMS Agent receives 15% commission on domestic sales. Agent receives 20% commission on foreign sales. Offers written contract; 30-day notice must be given to terminate contract. "All reading done in deciding whether or not to offer representation is free. Editorial services are available. Mailing and postage expenses that incurred on the author's behalf are always approved by them in advance."

TIPS "Always keep in mind that your query letter/proposal is only one of hundreds and thousands that are competing for the agent's attention. Therefore, your presentation of your book and yourself as author has to be immediate, intense, compelling, and concise. Make the query letter one-page, and after short, introductory paragraph, write a 150-word KEYNOTE description of your manuscript."

MENDEL MEDIA GROUP, LLC

115 W. 30th St., Suite 800, New York NY 10001. (646)239-9896. Fax: (212)685-4717. E-mail: scott@

mendelmedia.com. Website: www.mendelmedia.com. Member of AAR. Represents 40-60 clients.

Prior to becoming an agent, Mr. Mendel was an academic. "I taught American literature, Yiddish, Jewish studies, and literary theory at the University of Chicago and the University of Illinois at Chicago while working on my PhD in English. I also worked as a freelance technical writer and as the managing editor of a healthcare magazine. In 1998, I began working for the late Jane Jordan Browne, a long-time agent in the book publishing world."

REPRESENTS nonfiction books, novels, scholarly, with potential for broad/popular appeal. **Considers these fiction areas:** action, adventure, contemporary issues, crime, detective, erotica, ethnic, feminist, gay, glitz, historical, humor, inspirational, juvenile, lesbian, literary, mainstream, mystery, picture books, police, religious, romance, satire, sports, thriller, young adult Jewish fiction.

"I am interested in major works of history, current affairs, biography, business, politics, economics, science, major memoirs, narrative nonfiction, and other sorts of general nonfiction." Actively seeking new, major or definitive work on a subject of broad interest, or a controversial, but authoritative, new book on a subject that affects many people's lives. I also represent more light-hearted nonfiction projects, such as gift or novelty books, when they suit the market particularly well." Does not want "queries about projects written years ago that were unsuccessfully shopped to a long list of trade publishers by either the author or another agent. I am specifically not interested in reading short, category romances (regency, time travel, paranormal, etc.), horror novels, supernatural stories, poetry, original plays, or film scripts."

HOW TO CONTACT Query with SASE. Do not e-mail or fax queries. For nonfiction, include a complete, fully edited book proposal with sample chapters. For fiction, include a complete synopsis and no more than 20 pages of sample text. Responds in 2 weeks to queries. Responds in 4-6 weeks to mss. Obtains most new clients through recommendations from others.

TERMS Agent receives 15% commission on domestic sales. Agent receives 20% commission on foreign sales.

WRITERS CONFERENCES BookExpo America; Frankfurt Book Fair; London Book Fair; RWA National Conference; Modern Language Association Convention; Jerusalem Book Fair.

TIPS "While I am not interested in being flattered by a prospective client, it does matter to me that she knows why she is writing to me in the first place. Is one of my clients a colleague of hers? Has she read a book by one of my clients that led her to believe I might be interested in her work? Authors of descriptive nonfiction should have real credentials and expertise in their subject areas, either as academics, journalists, or policy experts, and authors of prescriptive nonfiction should have legitimate expertise and considerable experience communicating their ideas in seminars and workshops, in a successful business, through the media, etc."

MICHAEL LARSEN/ELIZABETH POMADA, LITERARY AGENTS

1029 Jones St., San Francisco CA 94109-5023. (415)673-0939. E-mail: larsenpoma@aol.com. Website: www.larsen-pomada.com. **Contact:** Mike Larsen, Elizabeth Pomada. Member of AAR. Other memberships include Authors Guild, ASJA, PEN, WNBA, California Writers Club, National Speakers Association. Represents 100 clients. 40-45% of clients are new/unpublished writers. Currently handles nonfiction books (70%), novels (30%).

Prior to opening their agency, Mr. Larsen and Ms. Pomada were promotion executives for major publishing houses. Mr. Larsen worked for Morrow, Bantam, and Pyramid (now part of Berkley); Ms. Pomada worked at Holt, David McKay and Dial Press. Mr. Larsen is the author of the 4th edition of *How to Write a Book Proposal* and *How to Get a Literary Agent* as well as the coauthor of *Guerilla Marketing for Writers: 100 Weapons for Selling Your Work*, which was republished in September 2009.

MEMBER AGENTS Michael Larsen (nonfiction); Elizabeth Pomada (fiction & narrative nonfiction).

REPRESENTS **Considers these fiction areas:** action, adventure, contemporary issues, crime, detective, ethnic, experimental, family saga, feminist, gay, glitz, historical, humor, inspirational, lesbian, literary, mainstream, mystery, police, religious, romance, satire, suspense chick lit.

We have diverse tastes. We look for fresh voices and new ideas. We handle literary, commercial and genre fiction, and the full range of nonfiction books. Actively seeking commercial, genre and literary fiction. Does not want to receive children's books, plays, short stories, screenplays, pornography, poetry or stories of abuse.

HOW TO CONTACT Query with SASE. **Elizabeth Pomada** handles literary and commercial fiction, romance, thrillers, mysteries, narrative non-fiction and mainstream women's fiction. If you have completed a novel, **please e-mail the first 10 pages and 2-page synopsis to larsenpoma@aol.com**. Use 14-point typeface, double-spaced, as an e-mail letter with no attachments. For nonfiction, please read Michael's *How to Write a Book Proposal* book—available through your library or bookstore, and through our website—so you will know exactly what editors need. Then, before you start writing, send him the title, subtitle, and your promotion plan via conventional mail (with SASE) or e-mail. If sent as e-mail, please include the information in the body of your email with NO attachments. Please allow up to two weeks for a response. Responds in 8 weeks to pages or submissions.

TERMS Agent receives 15% commission on domestic sales. Agent receives 20% (30% for Asia) commission on foreign sales. May charge for printing, postage for multiple submissions, foreign mail, foreign phone calls, galleys, books, legal fees.

RECENT SALES Sold at least 15 titles in the last year. *Secrets of the Tudor Court*, by D. Bogden (Kensington); *Zen & the Art of Horse Training*, by Allan Hamilton, MD (Storey Pub.); *The Solemn Lantern Maker* by Merlinda Bobis (Delta); *Bite Marks*, the fifth book in an urban fantasy series by J.D. Rardin (Orbit/Grand Central); *The Iron King*, by Julie Karawa (Harlequin Teen).

WRITERS CONFERENCES This agency organizes the annual San Francisco Writers' Conference (www.sfwriters.org).

TIPS "We love helping writers get the rewards and recognition they deserve. If you can write books that meet the needs of the marketplace and you can promote your books, now is the best time ever to be a writer. We must find new writers to make a living, so we are very eager to hear from new writers whose work will interest large houses, and nonfiction writers who can promote their books. For a list of recent sales, helpful info, and three ways to make yourself irresistible to any publisher, please visit our website."

MORTIMER LITERARY AGENCY

41769 Enterprise Circle N., Suite 107, Temecula CA 92590. (951)208-5674. E-mail: kmortimer@mortimerliterary.com. E-mail: queries@mortimerliterary.com. Website: www.mortimerliterary.com. **Contact:** Kelly Gottuso Mortimer. Romance Writers of America. Represents 16 clients. 80% of clients are new/unpublished writers. Currently handles nonfiction books (40%), novels (40%), young adult books (20%).

Prior to becoming an agent, Ms. Mortimer was a freelance writer and the CFO of Microvector, Inc. She has a degree in contract law, finance, and is a winner of the American Christian Fiction Writers Literary Agent of the Year Award in 2008 and the OCC-RAW Volunteer of the Year award. Was Top 5: Publishers marketplace Top 100 Dealmakers—Romance category, 2008.

REPRESENTS nonfiction books, novels, young adult. **Considers these fiction areas:** Please refer to submissions page on website, as the list changes.

"I keep a short client list to give my writers personal attention. I edit my clients' manuscripts as necessary. I send manuscripts out to pre-selected editors in a timely fashion, and send my clients monthly reports. I only sign writers not yet published, or not published in the last 3 years. Those are the writers who need my help the most."

HOW TO CONTACT See website for submission guidelines. Accepts simultaneous submissions. Responds in 3 months to mss. Obtains most new clients through query letters.

TERMS Agent receives 15% commission on domestic sales. Agent receives 20% commission on foreign sales. Offers written contract. "I charge for postage-only the amount I pay and it comes out of the author's advance. The writer provides me with copies of their manuscripts if needed."

WRITERS CONFERENCES RWA, several conference. See schedule on website.

TIPS "Follow submission guidelines on the website, submit your best work and don't query unless your manuscript is finished. Don't send material or mss that I haven't requested."

DEE MURA LITERARY

269 West Shore Dr., Massapequa NY 11758-8225. (516)795-1616. Fax: (516)795-8797. E-mail: query@deemuraliterary.com. Website: http://deemuraliterary.com/. **Contact:** Dee Mura. Signatory of WGA. 50% of clients are new/unpublished writers.

Prior to opening her agency, Ms. Mura was a public relations executive with a roster of film and entertainment clients and worked in editorial for major weekly news magazines.

MEMBER AGENTS Dee Murá, Karen Roberts, Bobbie Sokol, David Brozain.

REPRESENTS **Considers these fiction areas:** action, adventure, contemporary issues, crime, detective, ethnic, experimental, family saga, fantasy, feminist, gay, glitz, historical, humor, juvenile, lesbian, literary, mainstream, military, mystery, psychic, regional, romance, science fiction, sports, thriller, westerns, young adult political.

"Some of us have special interests and some of us encourage you to share your passion and work with us." Does not want to receive "ideas for sitcoms, novels, films, etc., or queries without SASEs."

HOW TO CONTACT Query with SASE. Accepts e-mail queries (no attachments). If via e-mail, please include the type of query and your genre in the subject line. If via regular mail, you may include the first few chapters, outline, or proposal. Mark envelope "Attn: Query Dept. No fax queries. Accepts simultaneous submissions. Only responds if interested; responds as soon as possible. Obtains most new clients through recommendations from others, queries.

TERMS Agent receives 15% commission on domestic sales. Agent receives 20% commission on foreign sales. Offers written contract. Charges clients for photocopying, mailing expenses, overseas/long-distance phone calls/faxes.

RECENT SALES Sold more than 40 titles and 35 scripts in the last year.

TIPS "Please include a paragraph on your background, even if you have no literary background, and a brief synopsis of the project."

MUSE LITERARY MANAGEMENT

189 Waverly Place, #4, New York NY 10014-3135. (212)925-3721. E-mail: museliterarymgmt@aol.com. Website: www.museliterary.com/. **Contact:** Deborah Carter. Associations: NAWE, International Thriller Writers, Historical Novel Society, Associations of Booksellers for Children, The Authors Guild, Children's Literature Network, and American Folklore Society. Represents 5 clients. 80% of clients are new/unpublished writers.

Prior to starting her agency, Ms. Carter trained with an AAR literary agent and worked in the music business and as a talent scout for record companies in artist management. She has a BA in English and music from Washington Square University College at NYU.

REPRESENTS novels, short story collections, poetry books. **Considers these fiction areas:** adventure, detective, juvenile, mystery, picture books, suspense, thriller, young adult espionage; middle-grade novels; literary short story collections, literary fiction with popular appeal.

Specializes in manuscript development, the sale and administration of print, performance, and foreign rights to literary works, and post-publication publicity and appearances. Actively seeking "writers with formal training who bring compelling voices and a unique outlook to their manuscripts. Those who submit should be receptive to editorial feedback and willing to revise during the submission process in order to remain competitive." Does not want "manuscripts that have been worked over by book doctors (collaborative projects ok, but writers must have chops); category romance, chick lit, sci-fi, fantasy, horror, stories about cats and dogs, vampires or serial killers, fiction or nonfiction with religious or spiritual subject matter."

HOW TO CONTACT Query with SASE. Query via e-mail (no attachments). Discards unwanted queries. Responds in 2 weeks to queries. Responds in 2-3 weeks to mss. Obtains most new clients through recommendations from others, conferences.

TERMS Agent receives 15% commission on domestic sales. Agent receives 20% commission on foreign sales. One-year contract offered when writer and agent agree that the manuscript is ready for submission; manuscripts in development are not bound by contract. Sometimes charges for postage and photocopying. All expenses are preapproved by the client.

TIPS "I give editorial feedback and work on revisions on spec. Agency agreement is offered when the writer and I feel the manuscript is ready for submission to publishers. Writers should also be open to doing revisions with editors who express serious interest in their work, prior to any offer of a publishing contract. All aspects of career strategy are discussed with writers, and all decisions are ultimately theirs. I make multiple and simultaneous submissions when looking for rights opportunities, and share all correspondence. All agreements are signed by the writers. Reimbursement for expenses is subject to client's approval, limited to photocopying (usually press clips) and postage. I always submit fresh manuscripts to publishers printed in my office with no charge to the writer."

NELSON LITERARY AGENCY

1732 Wazee St., Suite 207, Denver CO 80202. (303)292-2805. E-mail: query@nelsonagency.com. Website: www.nelsonagency.com. **Contact:** Kristin Nelson, president and senior literary agent; Sara Megibow, associate literary agent. Member of AAR. RWA, SCBWI, SFWA.

Prior to opening her own agency, Ms. Nelson worked as a literary scout and subrights agent for agent Jody Rein.

REPRESENTS novels select nonfiction. **Considers these fiction areas:** commercial, literary, mainstream, women's chick lit (includes mysteries), romance (includes fantasy with romantic elements, science fiction, fantasy, young adult).

NLA specializes in representing commercial fiction and high-caliber literary fiction. Actively seeking Latina writers who tackle contemporary issues in a modern voice (think *Dirty Girls Social Club*). Does not want short story collections, mysteries (except chick lit), thrillers, Christian, horror, or children's picture books.

HOW TO CONTACT Query by e-mail only.

RECENT SALES *New York Times* Best-selling author of *I'd Tell You I Love You, But Then I'd Have to Kill You*, Ally Carter's fourth novel in the Gallagher Girls series; *Hester* (historical fiction), by Paula Reed; *Proof by Seduction* (debut romance), by Courtney Milan; *Soulless* (fantasy debut), by Gail Carriger; *The Shifter* (debut children's fantasy), by Janice Hardy; *Real Life & Liars* (debut women's fiction), by Kristina Riggle; *Hotel on the Corner of Bitter and Sweet* (debut literary fiction), by Jamie Ford.

NORTHERN LIGHTS LITERARY SERVICES, LLC

2323 State Rd. 252, Martinsville IN 46151. (888)558-4354. Fax: (208)265-1948. E-mail: queries@northernlightsls.com. Website: www.northernlightsls.com. **Contact:** Sammie Justesen. Represents 25 clients. 35% of clients are new/unpublished writers.Currently handles nonfiction books (90%), novels (10%).

MEMBER AGENTS Sammie Justesen (fiction and nonfiction); Vorris Dee Justesen (business and current affairs).

REPRESENTS nonfiction books, novels. **Considers these fiction areas:** action, adventure, crime, detective, ethnic, family saga, feminist, glitz, historical, inspirational, mainstream, mystery, police, psychic, regional, religious, romance, supernatural, suspense, thriller, women's.

"Our goal is to provide personalized service to clients and create a bond that will endure throughout the writer's career. We seriously consider each query we receive and will accept hardworking new authors who are willing to develop their talents and skills. We enjoy working with healthcare professionals and writers who clearly understand their market and have a platform." Actively seeking general nonfiction—especially if the writer has a platform. Does not want to receive fantasy, horror, erotica, children's books, screenplays, poetry, or short stories.

HOW TO CONTACT Query with SASE. Submit outline/proposal, synopsis, 3 sample chapters, author bio. E-queries preferred. No phone queries. All queries considered, but the agency only replies if interested. If you've completed and polished a novel, send a query letter, a one-or-two page synopsis of the plot, and the first chapter. Also include your biography as it relates to your writing experience. Do not send an entire mss unless requested. If you'd like to submit a nonfiction book, send a query letter, along with the book proposal. Include a bio showing the background that will enable you to write the book. Accepts simultaneous submissions. Responds in 2 months to queries. Responds in 2 months to mss. Obtains most new clients through solicitations, conferences.

TERMS Agent receives 15% commission on domestic sales. Agent receives 20% commission on foreign sales. Offers written contract; 30-day notice must be given to terminate contract.

RECENT SALES *Intuitive Parenting*, by Debra Snyder, PhD (Beyond Words); *The Confidence Trap* by Russ Harris (Penguin); *The Never Cold Call Again Toolkit* by Frank Rumbauskas Jr. (Wiley); *Thank You for Firing Me*, by Candace Reed and Kitty Martini (Sterling); *The Wal-Mart Cure: Ten Lifesaving Supplements for Under $10* (Sourcebooks).

TIPS "If you're fortunate enough to find an agent who answers your query and asks for a printed manuscript, always include a letter and cover page containing your name, physical address, e-mail address and phone number. Be professional!"

● KATHI J. PATON LITERARY AGENCY

P.O. Box 2236 Radio City Station, New York NY 10101. (212)265-6586. E-mail: KJPLitBiz@optonline.net. Website: www.PatonLiterary.com. **Contact:** Kathi Paton. Currently handles nonfiction books (85%), novels (15%).

REPRESENTS nonfiction books, novels, short story collections book-based film rights. **Considers these fiction areas:** literary, mainstream, multicultural short stories.

This agency specializes in adult nonfiction.

HOW TO CONTACT Accepts e-mail queries only. Accepts simultaneous submissions. Accepts new clients through recommendations from current clients.

TERMS Agent receives 15% commission on domestic sales. Agent receives 20% commission on foreign sales. Offers written contract. Charges clients for photocopying.

WRITERS CONFERENCES Attends major regional panels, seminars and conferences.

ALISON J. PICARD, LITERARY AGENT

P.O. Box 2000, Cotuit MA 02635. Phone/Fax: (508)477-7192. E-mail: ajpicard@aol.com. **Contact:** Alison Picard. Represents 48 clients. 30% of clients are new/unpublished writers. Currently handles nonfiction books (40%), novels (40%), juvenile books (20%).

Prior to becoming an agent, Ms. Picard was an assistant at a literary agency in New York.

REPRESENTS nonfiction books, novels, juvenile. **Considers these fiction areas:** action, adventure, contemporary issues, crime, detective, erotica, ethnic, family saga, feminist, gay, glitz, historical, horror, humor, juvenile, lesbian, literary, mainstream, multicultural, mystery, New Age, picture books, police, psychic, romance, sports, supernatural, thriller, young adult.

"Many of my clients have come to me from big agencies, where they felt overlooked or ignored. I communicate freely with my clients and offer a lot of career advice, suggestions for revising manuscripts, etc. If I believe in a project, I will submit it to a dozen or more publishers, unlike some agents who give up after four or five rejections." No science fiction/fantasy, westerns, poetry, plays or articles.

HOW TO CONTACT Query with SASE. Accepts simultaneous submissions. Responds in 2 weeks to queries. Responds in 4 months to mss. Obtains most new clients through recommendations from others, solicitations.

TERMS Agent receives 15% commission on domestic sales. Agent receives 20% commission on foreign sales. Offers written contract, binding for 1 year; 1-week notice must be given to terminate contract.

RECENT SALES *Zitface*, by Emily Ormand (Marshall Cavendish); *Totally Together*, by Stephanie O'Dea (Running Press); *The Ultimate Slow Cooker Cookbook*, by Stephanie O'Dea (Hyperion); Two Untitled Cookingbooks, by Erin Chase (St. Martin's Press); *A Journal of the Flood Year*, by David Ely (Portobello Books – United Kingdom, L'Ancora – Italy); *A Mighty Wall* by John Foley (Llewellyn/Flux); *Jelly's Gold*, by David Housewright (St. Martin's Press).

TIPS "Please don't send material without sending a query first via mail or e-mail. I don't accept phone or fax queries. Always enclose an SASE with a query."

◐ PROSPECT AGENCY, LLC

Attn: Submissions, 285 Fifth Ave., PMB 445, Brooklyn NY 11215. (718)788-3217. E-mail: esk@prospectagency.com. Website: www.prospectagency.com. **Contact:** Becca Stumpf, Emily Sylvan Kim. Represents 15 clients. 50% of clients are new/unpublished writers. Currently handles novels (66%), juvenile books (33%).

Prior to starting her agency, Ms. Kim briefly attended law school and worked for another literary agency.

MEMBER AGENTS Emily Sylvan Kim; Becca Stumpf (adult and YA literary, mainstream fiction; nonfiction interests include narrative nonfiction, journalistic perspectives, fashion, film studies, travel, art, and informed analysis of cultural phenomena.

She has a special interest in aging in America and environmental issues); Rachel Orr (fiction and nonfiction, particularly picture books, beginning readers, chapter books, middle-grade, YA novels); Teresa Kietlinski (artists who both write and illustrate).

REPRESENTS nonfiction books, novels, juvenile. **Considers these fiction areas:** action, adventure, detective, erotica, ethnic, frontier, juvenile, literary, mainstream, mystery, picture books, romance, suspense, thriller, westerns, young adult.

🗝 "We are currently looking for the next generation of writers to shape the literary landscape. Our clients receive professional and knowledgeable representation. We are committed to offering skilled editorial advice and advocating our clients in the marketplace." Actively seeking romance, literary fiction, and young adult submissions. Does not want to receive poetry, short stories, textbooks, or most nonfiction.

HOW TO CONTACT Upload outline and 3 sample chapters to the website. Accepts simultaneous submissions. Responds in 3 weeks to queries. Responds in 1 month to mss. Obtains most new clients through recommendations from others, conferences, unsolicited mss.

TERMS Agent receives 15% commission on domestic sales. Agent receives 20% commission on foreign sales. Offers written contract.

RECENT SALES *BADD* by Tim Tharp (Knopf); *Six* by Elizabeth Batten-Carew (St. Martin's); *Rocky Road*, by Rose Kent (Knopf); *Mating Game*, by Janice Maynard (NAL); *Golden Delicious*, by Aaron Hawkins (Houghton Mifflin Harcourt); *Damaged*, by Pamela Callow (Mira); *Seduced by Shadows*, by Jessica Slade (NAL); *Identity of Ultraviolet*, by Jake Bell (Scholastic); *Quackenstein*, by Sudipta Bardhan-Quallen (Abrams); *Betraying Season*, by Marissa Doyle (Holt); *Sex on the Beach*, by Susan Lyons (Berkley), more.

WRITERS CONFERENCES "Please see our website for a complete list of attended conferences."

P.S. LITERARY AGENCY

20033 - 520 Kerr St., Oakville ON L6K 3C7 Canada. E-mail: query@psliterary.com. Website: http://www.psliterary.com. **Contact:** Curtis Russell, principal agent. Estab. 2005. Currently handles nonfiction books (50%), novels (50%).

REPRESENTS nonfiction, novels, juvenile books. **Considers these fiction areas:** action, adventure, detective, erotica, ethnic, family saga, historical, horror, humor, juvenile, literary, mainstream, mystery, picture books, romance, sports, thriller, women's, young adult biography/autobiography, business, child, guidance/parenting, cooking/food/nutrition, current affairs, government/politics/law, health/medicine, history, how-to, humor, memoirs, military/war, money/finance/economics, nature/environment, popular culture, science/technology, self-help/personal improvement, sports, true crime/investigative, women's issues/women's studies.

🗝 "What makes our agency distinct: We take on a small number of clients per year in order to provide focused, hands-on representation. We pride ourselves in providing industry-leading client service." Actively seeking both fiction and nonfiction. Seeking both new and established writers. Does not want to receive poetry or screenplays.

HOW TO CONTACT Accepts queries by e-mail/mail, but prefer e-mail. Submit query, synopsis, and bio. Accepts simultaneous submissions. Responds in 4-6 weeks to queries/proposals; mss 4-8 weeks. Obtains most new clients through solicitations.

TERMS Agent receives 15% commission on domestic sales. Agent receives 25% commission on foreign sales. We offer a written contract, with 30-days notice terminate. Fees for postage/messenger services only if project is sold. "This agency charges for postage/messenger services only if a project is sold."

TIPS "Please review our website for the most up-to-date submission guidelines. We do not charge reading fees. We do not offer a critique service."

QUICKSILVER BOOKS: LITERARY AGENTS

508 Central Park Ave., #5101, Scarsdale NY 10583. Phone/Fax: (914)722-4664. E-mail: quicksilverbooks@hotmail.com. Website: www.quicksilverbooks.com. **Contact:** Bob Silverstein. Represents 50 clients. 50% of clients are new/unpublished writers. Currently handles nonfiction books (75%), novels (25%).

Prior to opening his agency, Mr. Silverstein served as senior editor at Bantam Books and managing editor at Dell Books/Delacorte Press.

REPRESENTS nonfiction books, novels. **Considers these fiction areas:** action, adventure, glitz, mystery, suspense, thriller.

This agency specializes in literary and commercial mainstream fiction and nonfiction, especially psychology, New Age, holistic healing, consciousness, ecology, environment, spirituality, reference, self-help, cookbooks, and narrative nonfiction. Does not want to receive science fiction, pornography, poetry, or single-spaced mss.

HOW TO CONTACT Query with SASE. Authors are expected to supply SASE for return of ms and for query letter responses. Accepts simultaneous submissions. Responds in 2 weeks to queries. Responds in 1 month to mss. Obtains most new clients through recommendations, listings in sourcebooks, solicitations, workshop participation.

TERMS Agent receives 15% commission on domestic sales. Agent receives 20% commission on foreign sales. Offers written contract.

RECENT SALES *Simply Mexican*, by Lourdes Castro (Ten Speed Press); *Indian Vegan Cooking*, by Madhu Gadia (Perigee/Penguin); *Selling Luxury*, by Robin Lent & Genevieve Tour (Wiley); *Get the Job You Want, Even When No One's Hiring*, by Ford R. Myers (Wiley); *Matrix Meditations*, by Victor & Kooch Daniels (Inner Traditions Bear & Co.); *Macrobiotics for Dummies* (Wiley); *The Power of Receiving* (Tarcher); *Eat, Drink, Think in Spanish* (Ten Speed Press); *Nice Girls Don't Win at Life* (Broadway).

WRITERS CONFERENCES National Writers Union.

TIPS "Write what you know. Write from the heart. Publishers print, authors sell."

RAINES & RAINES

103 Kenyon Rd., Medusa NY 12120. (518)239-8311. Fax: (518)239-6029. **Contact:** Theron Raines (member of AAR); Joan Raines; Keith Korman. Member of AAR. Represents 100 clients.

REPRESENTS nonfiction books, novels. **Considers these fiction areas:** action, adventure, crime, detective, fantasy, frontier, historical, mystery, picture books, police, science fiction, suspense, thriller, westerns, whimsical.

HOW TO CONTACT Query with SASE. Responds in 2 weeks to queries.

TERMS Agent receives 15% commission on domestic sales. Agent receives 20% commission on foreign sales. Charges for photocopying.

THE REDWOOD AGENCY

474 Wellesley Ave., Mill Valley CA 94941. (415)381-2269, ext. 2. E-mail: info@redwoodagency.com. E-mail: query@redwoodagency.com. Website: www.redwoodagency.com. **Contact:** Catherine Fowler, founder. Adheres to AAR canon of ethics. Currently handles nonfiction books (100%).

Prior to becoming an agent, Ms. Fowler was an editor, subsidiary rights director and associate publisher for Doubleday, Simon & Schuster and Random House for her 20 years in New York Publishing. Content exec for web start-ups Excite and WebMD.

REPRESENTS nonfiction books, novels. **Considers these fiction areas:** literary, mainstream, suspense, women's quirky.

"Along with our love of books and publishing, we have the desire and commitment to work with fun, interesting and creative people, to do so with respect and professionalism, but also with a sense of humor." Actively seeking high-quality, nonfiction works created for the general consumer market, as well as projects with the potential to become book series. Does not want to receive fiction. Do not send packages that require signature for delivery.

HOW TO CONTACT Query via e-mail only. While we redesign website, submit "quick query" to: query@redwoodagency.com. See all guidelines online. Obtains most new clients through recommendations from others, solicitations.

TERMS Offers written contract. Charges for copying and delivery charges, if any, as specified in author/agency agreement.

HELEN REES LITERARY AGENCY

14 Beacon St., Suite 710, Boston MA 02108. (617)227-9014. Fax: (617)227-8762. E-mail: reesagency@reesagency.com. Website: http://reesagency.com. **Contact:** Joan Mazmanian, Ann Collette, Helen Rees, Lorin Rees. Estab. 1983. Member of AAR. Other memberships include PEN. Represents more than 100 clients. 50% of clients are new/unpublished writers. Currently handles nonfiction books (60%), novels (40%).

MEMBER AGENTS Ann Collette (literary, mystery, thrillers, suspense, vampire, and women's fiction; in nonfiction, she prefers true crime, narrative non-fiction, military and war, work to do with race and class, and work set in or about Southeast Asia. Ann can be reached at: Agent10702@aol.com). Lorin Rees (literary fiction, memoirs, business books, self-help, science, history, psychology, and narrative nonfiction. lorin@reesagency.com).

REPRESENTS nonfiction books, novels. **Considers these fiction areas:** historical, literary, mainstream, mystery, suspense, thriller.

HOW TO CONTACT Query with SASE, outline, 2 sample chapters. No unsolicited e-mail submissions. No multiple submissions. Responds in 3-4 weeks to queries. Obtains most new clients through recommendations from others, conferences, submissions.

TERMS Agent receives 15% commission on domestic sales. Agent receives 20% commission on foreign sales.

RECENT SALES Sold more than 35 titles in the last year. *Get Your Ship Together*, by Capt. D. Michael Abrashoff; *Overpromise and Overdeliver*, by Rick Berrara; *Opacity* by Joel Kurtzman; *America the Broke*, by Gerald Swanson; *Murder at the B-School*, by Jeffrey Cruikshank; *Bone Factory*, by Steven Sidor; *Father Said*, by Hal Sirowitz; *Winning*, by Jack Welch; *The Case for Israel*, by Alan Dershowitz; *As the Future Catches You*, by Juan Enriquez; *Blood Makes the Grass Grow Green*, by Johnny Rico; *DVD Movie Guide*, by Mick Martin and Marsha Porter; *Words That Work*, by Frank Luntz; *Stirring It Up*, by Gary Hirshberg; *Hot Spots*, by Martin Fletcher; *Andy Grove: The Life and Times of an American*, by Richard Tedlow; *Girls Most Likely To*, by Poonam Sharma.

JODY REIN BOOKS, INC.

7741 S. Ash Ct., Centennial CO 80122. (303)694-9386. Website: www.jodyreinbooks.com and www.bookproposalpro.com. **Contact:** Winnefred Dollar. Member of AAR. Resigned to design software for writers. Other memberships include Authors' Guild. Currently handles nonfiction books (100%).

Prior to opening her agency, Ms. Rein worked for 13 years as an acquisitions editor for Contemporary Books and as executive editor for Bantam/Doubleday/Dell and Morrow/Avon.

REPRESENTS nonfiction books, novels. **Considers these fiction areas:** literary, mainstream.

This agency is no longer actively seeking new clients.

TERMS Agent receives 15% commission on domestic sales. Agent receives 25% commission on foreign sales. Agent receives 20% commission on film sales. Offers written contract. Charges clients for express mail, overseas expenses, photocopying mss.

RECENT SALES *How to Remodel a Man*, by Bruce Cameron (St. Martin's Press); *8 Simple Rules for Dating My Teenage Daughter*, by Bruce Cameron (ABC/Disney); *Unbound* and *Skeletons on the Zahara*, by Dean King (Little, Brown); *Halfway to Heaven* and *The Big Year*, by Mark Obmascik (Free Press); *The Rhino with Glue-On Shoes*, by Dr. Lucy Spelman (Random House); *See You in a Hundred Years*, by Logan Ward (Bantam).

TIPS Jody Rein's new software, Book Proposal Pro, can be found at bookproposalpro.com. "Do your homework before submitting. Make sure you have a marketable topic and the credentials to write about it. Agents and editors seek well-written books on fresh and original nonfiction topics that have broad appeal, as well as novels written by authors who have spent years developing their craft. Authors must be well established in their fields and have strong media experience."

JODIE RHODES LITERARY AGENCY

8840 Villa La Jolla Dr., Suite 315, La Jolla CA 92037-1957. Website: jodierhodesliterary.com. **Contact:** Jodie Rhodes, president. Member of AAR. Represents 74 clients. 60% of clients are new/unpublished writers. Currently handles nonfiction books (45%), novels (35%), juvenile books (20%).

Prior to opening her agency, Ms. Rhodes was a university-level creative writing teacher, workshop director, published novelist, and vice president/media director at the N.W. Ayer Advertising Agency.

MEMBER AGENTS Jodie Rhodes; Clark McCutcheon (fiction); Bob McCarter (nonfiction).

REPRESENTS nonfiction books, novels. **Considers these fiction areas:** ethnic, family saga, historical, literary, mainstream, mystery, suspense, thriller, women's, young adult.

"Actively seeking witty, sophisticated women's books about career ambitions and relationships; edgy/trendy YA and teen books; narrative nonfiction on groundbreaking scientific discoveries, politics, economics, military and important current affairs by prominent scientists and academic professors." Does not want to receive erotica, horror, fantasy, romance, science fiction, religious/inspirational, or children's books (does accept young adult/teen).

HOW TO CONTACT Query with brief synopsis, first 30-50 pages, SASE. Do not call. Do not send complete ms unless requested. This agency does not return unrequested material weighing a pound or more that requires special postage. Include e-mail address with query. Accepts simultaneous submissions. Responds in 3 weeks to queries. Obtains most new clients through recommendations from others, agent sourcebooks.

TERMS Agent receives 15% commission on domestic sales. Agent receives 20% commission on foreign sales. Offers written contract; 1-month notice must be given to terminate contract. Charges clients for fax, photocopying, phone calls, postage. Charges are itemized and approved by writers upfront.

RECENT SALES Sold 42 titles in the last year. *The Ring*, by Kavita Daswani (HarperCollins); *Train to Trieste*, by Domnica Radulescu (Knopf); *A Year with Cats and Dogs*, by Margaret Hawkins (Permanent Press); *Silence and Silhouettes*, by Ryan Smithson (HarperCollins); *Internal Affairs*, by Constance Dial (Permanent Press); *How Math Rules the World*, by James Stein (HarperCollins); *Diagnosis of Love*, by Maggie Martin (Bantam); *Lies, Damn Lies, and Science*, by Sherry Seethaler (Prentice Hall); *Freaked*, by Jeanne Dutton (HarperCollins); *The Five Second Rule*, by Anne Maczulak (Perseus Books); *The Intelligence Wars*, by Stephen O'Hern (Prometheus); *Seducing the Spirits*, by Louise Young (Permanent Press), and more.

TIPS "Think your book out before you write it. Do your research, know your subject matter intimately, and write vivid specifics, not bland generalities. Care deeply about your book. Don't imitate other writers. Find your own voice. We never take on a book we don't believe in, and we go the extra mile for our writers. We welcome talented, new writers."

● ANN RITTENBERG LITERARY AGENCY, INC.

15 Maiden Lane, Suite 206, New York NY 10038. Website: www.rittlit.com. **Contact:** Ann Rittenberg, president, and Penn Whaling, associate. Member of AAR. Currently handles fiction 75%, nonfiction (25%).

REPRESENTS Considers these fiction areas: literary, thriller upmarket fiction.

⚷ This agent specializes in literary fiction and literary nonfiction. Does not want to receive screenplays, straight genre fiction, poetry, self-help.

HOW TO CONTACT Query with SASE. Submit outline, 3 sample chapters, SASE. Query via postal mail *only*. Accepts simultaneous submissions. Responds in 6 weeks to queries. Responds in 2 months to mss. Obtains most new clients through referrals from established writers and editors.

TERMS Terms: Agent receives 15% commission on domestic sales. Agent receives 20% commission on foreign sales. Offers written contract. This agency charges clients for photocopying only.

RECENT SALES *The Given Day*, by Dennis Lehane; *My Cat Hates You*, by Jim Edgar; *Never Wave Goodbye*, by Doug Magee; *House and Home*, by Kathleen McCleary; *Nowhere to Run*, by C.J. Box; and *Daughter of Kura*, by Debra Austin.

◐ RLR ASSOCIATES, LTD.

Literary Department, 7 W. 51st St., New York NY 10019. (212)541-8641. Fax: (212)262-7084. E-mail: sgould@rlrassociates.net. Website: www.rlrassociates.net. **Contact:** Scott Gould. Member of AAR. Represents 50 clients. 25% of clients are new/unpublished writers. Currently handles nonfiction books (70%), novels (25%), story collections (5%).

REPRESENTS nonfiction books, novels, short story collections, scholarly. **Considers these fiction areas:** action, adventure, cartoon, comic books, crime, detective, ethnic, experimental, family saga, feminist, gay, historical, horror, humor, lesbian, literary, mainstream, multicultural, mystery, police, satire, sports, suspense.

⚷ "We provide a lot of editorial assistance to our clients and have connections." Actively seeking fiction, current affairs, history, art, popular culture, health and business. Does not want to receive screenplays.

HOW TO CONTACT Query by either e-mail or mail. Accepts simultaneous submissions. Responds in 4-8 weeks to queries. Obtains most new clients through recommendations from others.

TERMS Agent receives 15% commission on domestic sales. Agent receives 20% commission on foreign sales. Offers written contract.

RECENT SALES Clients include Shelby Foote, The Grief Recovery Institute, Don Wade, Don Zimmer, The Knot.com, David Plowden, PGA of America, Danny Peary, George Kalinsky, Peter Hyman, Daniel Parker, Lee Miller, Elise Miller, Nina Planck, Karyn Bosnak, Christopher Pike, Gerald Carbone, Jason Lethcoe, Andy Crouch.

TIPS "Please check out our website for more details on our agency."

B.J. ROBBINS LITERARY AGENCY

5130 Bellaire Ave., North Hollywood CA 91607-2908. E-mail: Robbinsliterary@gmail.com. E-mail: amy.bjrobbinsliterary@gmail.com. **Contact:** (Ms.) B.J. Robbins, or Amy Maldonado. Member of AAR. Represents 40 clients. 50% of clients are new/unpublished writers. Currently handles nonfiction books (50%), novels (50%).

REPRESENTS nonfiction books, novels. **Considers these fiction areas:** crime, detective, ethnic, literary, mainstream, mystery, police, sports, suspense, thriller.

HOW TO CONTACT Query with SASE. Submit outline/proposal, 3 sample chapters, SASE. Accepts e-mail queries (no attachments). Accepts simultaneous submissions. Responds in 2-6 weeks to queries. Responds in 6-8 weeks to mss. Obtains most new clients through conferences, referrals.

TERMS Agent receives 15% commission on domestic sales. Agent receives 20% commission on foreign sales. Offers written contract; 3-month notice must be given to terminate contract. This agency charges clients for postage and photocopying (only after sale of ms).

RECENT SALES Sold 15 titles in the last year. *The Sweetness of Tears*, by Nafisa Haji (William Morrow); *Paper Dollhouse: A Memoir*, by Dr. Lisa M. Masterson; *The Sinatra Club*, by Sal Polisi and Steve Dougherty (Gallery Books); *Getting Stoned with Savages*, by J. Maarten Troost (Broadway); *Hot Water*, by Kathryn Jordan (Berkley); *Between the Bridge and the River*, by Craig Ferguson (Chronicle); *I'm Proud of You* by Tim Madigan (Gotham); *Man of the House*, by Chris Erskine (Rodale); *Bird of Another heaven*, by James D. Houston (Knopf); *Tomorrow They Will Kiss* by Eduardo Santiago (Little, Brown); *A Terrible Glory*, by James Donovan (Little, Brown); *The Writing on My Forehead*, by Nafisa Haji (Morrow); *Seen the Glory*, by John Hough Jr. (Simon & Schuster); *Lost on Planet China*, by J. Maarten Troost (Broadway).

WRITERS CONFERENCES Squaw Valley Writers Workshop; San Diego State University Writers' Conference.

JANE ROTROSEN AGENCY LLC

318 E. 51st St., New York NY 10022. (212)593-4330. Fax: (212)935-6985. Website: www.janerotrosen.com. Estab. 1974. Member of AAR. Other memberships include Authors Guild. Represents over 100 clients. Currently handles nonfiction books (30%), novels (70%).

MEMBER AGENTS Jane R. Berkey; Andrea Cirillo; Annelise Robey; Meg Ruley; Christina Hogrebe; Peggy Gordijn, director of rights.

REPRESENTS nonfiction books, novels. **Considers these fiction areas:** crime, family saga, historical, mystery, police, romance, suspense, thriller, women's.

HOW TO CONTACT Query with SASE to the attention of "Submissions." Find appropriate agent contact/e-mail on website. Responds in 2 weeks to writers who have been referred by a client or colleague. Responds in 2 months to mss. Obtains most new clients through recommendations from others.

TERMS Agent receives 15% commission on domestic sales. Agent receives 20% commission on foreign sales. Offers written contract, binding for 3 years; 2-month notice must be given to terminate contract. Charges clients for photocopying, express mail, overseas postage, book purchase.

RUSSELL & VOLKENING

50 W. 29th St., Suite 7E, New York NY 10001. (212)684-6050. Fax: (212)889-3026. Website: www.randvinc.com. **Contact:** Jesseca Salky (adult, general fiction and nonfiction, memoirs: jesseca@randvinc.com); Carrie Hannigan (children's and YA), Josh Getzler (mysteries, thrillers, literary and commercial fiction, young adult and middle grade, particularly adventures and mysteries for boys; e-mail queries only with cover letter and first 5 pages: josh@randvinc.com); Joy Azmitia (chick-lit, multicultural fiction, romance, humor, and nonfiction in the areas of travel, pop culture, and philosophy: joy@randvinc.com). Member of AAR. Represents 140 clients. 20% of clients are new/unpublished writers. Currently handles nonfic-

tion books (45%), novels (50%), story collections (3%), novella (2%).

REPRESENTS nonfiction books, novels, short story collections. **Considers these fiction areas:** action, adventure, crime, detective, ethnic, literary, mainstream, mystery, picture books, police, sports, suspense, thriller.

This agency specializes in literary fiction and narrative nonfiction. Actively seeking novels.

HOW TO CONTACT Query only with SASE to appropriate person. Responds in 4 weeks to queries.

TERMS Agent receives 15% commission on domestic sales. Agent receives 20% commission on foreign sales. Charges clients for standard office expenses relating to the submission of materials.

TIPS "If the query is cogent, well written, well presented, and is the type of book we'd represent, we'll ask to see the manuscript. From there, it depends purely on the quality of the work."

VICTORIA SANDERS & ASSOCIATES

241 Avenue of the Americas, Suite 11 H, New York NY 10014. (212)633-8811. Fax: (212)633-0525. E-mail: queriesvsa@hotmail.com. Website: www.victoriasanders.com. **Contact:** Victoria Sanders, Diane Dickensheid. Estab. 1992. Member of AAR. Signatory of WGA. Represents 135 clients. 25% of clients are new/unpublished writers. Currently handles nonfiction books (30%), novels (70%).

MEMBER AGENTS Tanya McKinnon, Victoria Sanders, Chris Kepner (open to all types of books as long as the writing is exceptional. Include the first three chapters in the body of the e-mail. At the moment, he is especially on the lookout for quality nonfiction).

REPRESENTS nonfiction books, novels. **Considers these fiction areas:** action, adventure, contemporary issues, ethnic, family saga, feminist, gay, lesbian, literary, thriller.

HOW TO CONTACT Query by e-mail only.

TERMS Agent receives 15% commission on domestic sales. Agent receives 20% commission on foreign sales. Offers written contract. Charges for photocopying, messenger, express mail. If in excess of $100, client approval is required.

RECENT SALES Sold 20+ titles in the last year.

TIPS "Limit query to letter (no calls) and give it your best shot. A good query is going to get a good response."

SCHIAVONE LITERARY AGENCY, INC.

236 Trails End, West Palm Beach FL 33413-2135. (561)966-9294. Fax: (561)966-9294. E-mail: profschia@aol.com. Website: www.publishersmarketplace.com/members/profschia; blog site: www.schiavoneliteraryagencyinc.blogspot.com. **Contact:** Dr. James Schiavone. CEO, corporate offices in Florida; Jennifer DuVall, president, New York office. New York office: 3671 Hudson Manor Terrace, No. 11H, Bronx, NY, 10463-1139, phone: (718)548-5332; fax: (718)548-5332; e-mail: jendu77@aol.com Other memberships include National Education Association. Represents 60+ clients. 2% of clients are new/unpublished writers. Currently handles nonfiction books (50%), novels (49%), textbooks (1%).

Prior to opening his agency, Dr. Schiavone was a full professor of developmental skills at the City University of New York and author of 5 trade books and 3 textbooks. Jennifer DuVall has many years of combined experience in office management and agenting.

REPRESENTS nonfiction books, novels, juvenile, scholarly, textbooks. **Considers these fiction areas:** ethnic, family saga, historical, horror, humor, juvenile, literary, mainstream, science fiction, young adult.

This agency specializes in celebrity biography and autobiography and memoirs. Does not want to receive poetry.

HOW TO CONTACT Query with SASE. Do not send unsolicited materials or parcels requiring a signature. Send no e-attachments. Accepts simultaneous submissions. Responds in 2 weeks to queries. Responds in 6 weeks to mss. Obtains most new clients through recommendations from others, solicitations, conferences.

TERMS Agent receives 15% commission on domestic sales. Agent receives 20% commission on foreign sales. Offers written contract. Charges clients for postage only.

WRITERS CONFERENCES Key West Literary Seminar; South Florida Writers' Conference; Tallahassee Writers' Conference, Million Dollar Writers' Conference; Alaska Writers Conference.

TIPS "We prefer to work with established authors published by major houses in New York. We will consider marketable proposals from new/previously unpublished writers."

SUSAN SCHULMAN LITERARY AGENCY

454 West 44th St., New York NY 10036. (212)713-1633. Fax: (212)581-8830. E-mail: schulmanqueries@yahoo.com. **Contact:** Susan Schulman. Estab. 1980. Member of AAR. Signatory of WGA. Other memberships include Dramatists Guild. 10% of clients are new/unpublished writers. Currently handles nonfiction books (50%), novels (25%), juvenile books (15%), stage plays (10%).

MEMBER AGENTS Linda Kiss, director of foreign rights; Katherine Stones, theater; Emily Uhry, submissions editor.

REPRESENTS **Considers these fiction areas:** action, adventure, crime, detective, feminist, historical, humor, inspirational, juvenile, literary, mainstream, mystery, picture books, police, religious, suspense, women's, young adult.

"We specialize in books for, by and about women and women's issues including nonfiction self-help books, fiction and theater projects. We also handle the film, television and allied rights for several agencies as well as foreign rights for several publishing houses." Actively seeking new nonfiction. Considers plays. Does not want to receive poetry, television scripts or concepts for television.

HOW TO CONTACT Query with SASE. Submit outline, synopsis, author bio, 3 sample chapters, SASE. Accepts simultaneous submissions. Responds in 6 weeks to queries. Responds in 6 weeks to mss. Obtains most new clients through recommendations from others, solicitations, conferences.

TERMS Agent receives 15% commission on domestic sales. Agent receives 20% commission on foreign sales. Offers written contract; 30-day notice must be given to terminate contract.

RECENT SALES Sold 50 titles in the last year; hundred of subsidiary rights deals.

WRITERS CONFERENCES Geneva Writers' Conference (Switzerland); Columbus Writers' Conference; Skidmore Conference of the Independent Women's Writers Group.

TIPS "Keep writing!"

SCRIBBLERS HOUSE, LLC LITERARY AGENCY

P.O. Box 1007, Cooper Station, New York NY 10276-1007. (212)714-7744. E-mail: query@scribblershouse.net. Website: www.scribblershouse.net. **Contact:** Stedman Mays, Garrett Gambino. 25% of clients are new/unpublished writers.

MEMBER AGENTS Stedman Mays, Garrett Gambino.

REPRESENTS nonfiction books, novels, occasionally. **Considers these fiction areas:** crime, historical, literary, suspense, thriller, women's.

HOW TO CONTACT "Query via e-mail. Put 'nonfiction query' or 'fiction query' in the subject line followed by the title of your project (send to our submissions e-mail on our website). Do not send attachments or downloadable materials of any kind with query. We will request more materials if we are interested. Usually respond in 2 weeks to 2 months to e-mail queries if we are interested (if we are not interested, we will not respond due to the overwhelming amount of queries we receive). We are only accepting e-mail queries at the present time." Accepts simultaneous submissions.

TERMS Agent receives 15% commission on domestic sales. Charges clients for postage, shipping and copying.

TIPS "If you must send by snail mail, we will return material or respond to a U.S. Postal Service-accepted SASE. (No international coupons or outdated mail strips, please.) Presentation means a lot. A well-written query letter with a brief author bio and your credentials is important. For query letter models, go to the bookstore or online and look at the cover copy and flap copy on other books in your general area of interest. Emulate what's best. Have an idea of other notable books that will be perceived as being in the same vein as yours. Know what's fresh about your project and articulate it in as few words as possible. Consult our website for the most up-to-date information on submitting."

SCRIBE AGENCY, LLC

5508 Joylynne Dr., Madison WI 53716. E-mail: whattheshizzle@scribeagency.com. E-mail: submissions@scribeagency.com. Website: www.scribeagency.com. **Contact:** Kristopher O'Higgins. Represents 11 clients. 18% of clients are new/unpublished writers. Currently handles novels (98%), story collections (2%).

"We have 17 years of experience in publishing and have worked on both agency and editorial sides in the past, with marketing expertise to boot. We love books as much or more than anyone you know. Check our website to see what we're about and to make sure you jive with the Scribe vibe."

MEMBER AGENTS Kristopher O'Higgins; Jesse Vogel.

REPRESENTS nonfiction books, novels, short story collections, novellas anthologies. **Considers these fiction areas:** detective, erotica, experimental, fantasy, feminist, gay, horror, humor, lesbian, literary, mainstream, mystery, psychic, science fiction, thriller.

Actively seeking excellent writers with ideas and stories to tell.

HOW TO CONTACT E-queries only: submissions@scribeagency.com. See the website for submission info, as it may change. Responds in 3-4 weeks to queries. Responds in 5 months to mss.

TERMS Agent receives 15% commission on domestic sales. Agent receives 20% commission on foreign sales. Offers written contract. Charges for postage and photocopying.

RECENT SALES Sold 3 titles in the last year.

WRITERS CONFERENCES BookExpo America; The Writer's Institute; Spring Writer's Festival; WisCon; Wisconsin Book Festival; World Fantasy Convention.

SECRET AGENT MAN

P.O. Box 1078, Lake Forest CA 92609-1078. (949)698-6987. E-mail: scott@secretagentman.net. E-mail: query@secretagentman.net. Website: www.secretagentman.net. **Contact:** Scott Mortenson.

REPRESENTS novels. **Considers these fiction areas:** detective, mystery, religious, suspense, thriller, westerns.

Actively seeking selective mystery, thriller, suspense and detective fiction. Does not want to receive scripts or screenplays.

HOW TO CONTACT Query with SASE. Query via e-mail or snail mail; include sample chapter(s), synopsis and/or outline. Prefers to read the real thing rather than a description of it. Obtains most new clients through recommendations from others, solicitations.

LYNN SELIGMAN, LITERARY AGENT

400 Highland Ave., Upper Montclair NJ 07043. (973)783-3631. **Contact:** Lynn Seligman. Other memberships include Women's Media Group. Represents 32 clients. 15% of clients are new/unpublished writers. Currently handles nonfiction books (60%), novels (40%).

Prior to opening her agency, Ms. Seligman worked in the subsidiary rights department of Doubleday and Simon & Schuster, and served as an agent with Julian Bach Literary Agency (which became IMG Literary Agency). Foreign rights are represented by Books Crossing Borders, Inc.

REPRESENTS nonfiction books, novels. **Considers these fiction areas:** detective, ethnic, fantasy, feminist, historical, horror, humor, literary, mainstream, mystery, romance, contemporary, gothic, historical, regency, science fiction.

"This agency specializes in general nonfiction and fiction. I also do illustrated and photography books and have represented several photographers for books."

HOW TO CONTACT Query with SASE. Prefers to read materials exclusively. Accepts simultaneous submissions. Responds in 2 weeks to queries. Responds in 2 months to mss. Obtains most new clients through referrals from other writers and editors.

TERMS Agent receives 15% commission on domestic sales. Agent receives 25% commission on foreign sales. Charges clients for photocopying, unusual postage, express mail, telephone expenses (checks with author first).

RECENT SALES Sold 15 titles in the last year. Lords of Vice series, by Barbara Pierce; Untitled series, by Deborah Leblanc.

THE SEYMOUR AGENCY

475 Miner St., Canton NY 13617. (315)386-1831. E-mail: marysue@twcny.rr.com; nicole@theseymouragency.com. Website: www.theseymouragency.com. **Contact:** Mary Sue Seymour, Nicole Resciniti. Member of AAR. Signatory of WGA. Other memberships include RWA, Authors Guild. Represents 50 clients. 5% of clients are new/unpublished writers. Currently handles nonfiction books (50%), other (50% fiction).

Ms. Seymour is a retired New York State certified teacher.

MEMBER AGENTS Mary Sue Seymour (accepts queries in Christian, inspirational, romance, and nonfiction; Nicole Resciniti (accepts queries in same categories as Mary Sue in addition to action/suspense/thriller, mystery, sci-fi, fantasy, and YA/children's).

REPRESENTS nonfiction books, novels. **Considers these fiction areas:** action, fantasy, mystery, religious, romance, science fiction, suspense, thriller, young adult.

HOW TO CONTACT Query with SASE, synopsis, first 50 pages for romance. Accepts e-mail queries. Accepts simultaneous submissions. Responds in 1 month to queries. Responds in 3 months to mss.

TERMS Agent receives 12-15% commission on domestic sales.

RECENT SALES Dinah Bucholz's *The Harry Potter Cookbook* to Adams Media.com; Vannetta Chapman's *A Simple Amish Christmas* to Abingdon Press; Shelley Shepard Gray's current book deal to Harper Collins; Shelley Galloway's multibook deal to Zondervan; Beth Wiseman's Christmas two novellas and multibook deal to Thomas Nelson; Mary Ellis's multibook deal to Harvest House, Barbara Cameron's novellas to Thomas Nelson and multibook deal to Abingdon Press.

SHEREE BYKOFSKY ASSOCIATES, INC.

PO Box 706, Brigantine NJ 08203. E-mail: shereebee@aol.com. E-mail: submitbee@aol.com. Website: www.shereebee.com. **Contact:** Sheree Bykofsky. Member of AAR. Other memberships include ASJA, WNBA. Currently handles nonfiction books (80%), novels (20%).

Prior to opening her agency, Ms. Bykofsky served as executive editor of Stonesong Press and managing editor of Chiron Press. She is also the author or coauthor of more than 20 books, including *The Complete Idiot's Guide to Getting Published*. Ms. Bykofsky teaches publishing at NYU and SEAK, Inc.

MEMBER AGENTS Janet Rosen, associate.

REPRESENTS nonfiction books, novels. **Considers these fiction areas:** contemporary issues, literary, mainstream, mystery, suspense.

This agency specializes in popular reference nonfiction, commercial fiction with a literary quality, and mysteries. "I have wide-ranging interests, but it really depends on quality of writing, originality, and how a particular project appeals to me (or not). I take on fiction when I completely love it—it doesn't matter what area or genre." Does not want to receive poetry, material for children, screenplays, westerns, horror, science fiction, or fantasy.

HOW TO CONTACT We only accept e-queries now and will only respond to those in which we are interested. E-mail short queries to submitbee@aol.com. Please, no attachments, snail mail, or phone calls. One-page query, one-page synopsis, and first page of manuscript in the body of the e-mail. Nonfiction: One-page query in the body of the e-mail. We cannot open attached Word files or any other types of attached files. These will be deleted. Accepts simultaneous submissions. Responds in 1 month to requested mss. Obtains most new clients through recommendations from others.

TERMS Agent receives 15% commission on domestic sales. Agent receives 20% commission on foreign sales. Offers written contract, binding for 1 year. Charges for postage, photocopying, fax.

RECENT SALES *Red Sheep: The Search for My Inner Latina*, by Michele Carlo (Citadel/Kensington); *Bang the Keys: Four Steps to a Lifelong Writing Practice*, by Jill Dearman (Alpha, Penguin); *Signed, Your Student: Celebrities on the Teachers Who Made Them Who They Are Today*, by Holly Holbert (Kaplan); *The Five Ways We Grieve*, by Susan Berger (Trumpeter/Shambhala).

WRITERS CONFERENCES ASJA Writers Conference; Asilomar; Florida Suncoast Writers' Conference; Whidbey Island Writers' Conference; Florida First Coast Writers' Festival; Agents and Editors Conference; Columbus Writers' Conference; Southwest Writers' Conference; Willamette Writers' Conference; Dorothy Canfield Fisher Conference; Maui Writers' Conference; Pacific Northwest Writers' Conference; IWWG.

TIPS "Read the agent listing carefully and comply with guidelines."

WENDY SHERMAN ASSOCIATES, INC.

27 W. 24th St., New York NY 10010. (212)279-9027. E-mail: wendy@wsherman.com. E-mail: submissions@wsherman.com. Website: www.wsherman.com. **Contact:** Wendy Sherman. Member of AAR. Represents 50 clients. 30% of clients are new/unpublished writers.

Prior to opening the agency, Ms. Sherman served as vice president, executive director, associate publisher, subsidiary rights director, and sales and marketing director for major publishers.

MEMBER AGENTS Wendy Sherman (board member of AAR), Kim Perel.

REPRESENTS Considers these fiction areas: mainstream Mainstream fiction that hits the sweet spot between literary and commercial.

"We specialize in developing new writers, as well as working with more established writers. My experience as a publisher has proven to be a great asset to my clients."

HOW TO CONTACT Query via e-mail Accepts simultaneous submissions. Responds in 1 month to queries. Obtains most new clients through recommendations from others.

TERMS Agent receives 15% commission on domestic sales; 20% commission on foreign and film sales. Offers written contract.

RECENT SALES *Exposure*, by Therese Fowler, *It's All Relative*, by Wade Rouse. *In Stitches*, by Dr. Tony Youn, *Daughters of the Witching Hill*, by Mary Sharratt; *The Sweet By and By*, by Todd Johnson; *Supergirls Speak Out*, by Liz Funk; *Love in 90 Days* and *Sealing the Deal*, by Dr. Diana Kirschner; *A Long Time Ago* and *Essentially*, by Brigid Pasulka; *Changing Shoes*, by Tina Sloan.

TIPS "The bottom line is: Do your homework. Be as well prepared as possible. Read the books that will help you present yourself and your work with polish. You want your submission to stand out."

JEFFREY SIMMONS LITERARY AGENCY

15 Penn House, Mallory St., London NW8 8SX England. (44)(207)224-8917. E-mail: jasimmons@unicombox.co.uk. **Contact:** Jeffrey Simmons. Represents 43 clients. 40% of clients are new/unpublished writers.Currently handles nonfiction books (65%), novels (35%).

Prior to becoming an agent, Mr. Simmons was a publisher. He is also an author.

REPRESENTS nonfiction books, novels. **Considers these fiction areas:** action, adventure, confession, crime, detective, family saga, literary, mainstream, mystery, police, suspense, thriller.

"This agency seeks to handle good books and promising young writers. My long experience in publishing and as an author and ghostwriter means I can offer an excellent service all around, especially in terms of editorial experience where appropriate." Actively seeking quality fiction, biography, autobiography, showbiz, personality books, law, crime, politics, and world affairs. Does not want to receive science fiction, horror, fantasy, juvenile, academic books, or specialist subjects (e.g., cooking, gardening, religious).

HOW TO CONTACT Submit sample chapter, outline/proposal, SASE (IRCs if necessary).Prefers to read materials exclusively. Responds in 1 week to queries. Responds in 1 month to mss. Obtains most new clients through recommendations from others, solicitations.

TERMS Agent receives 10-15% commission on domestic sales. Agent receives 15% commission on foreign sales. Offers written contract, binding for lifetime of book in question or until it becomes out of print.

TIPS "When contacting us with an outline/proposal, include a brief biographical note (listing any previous publications, with publishers and dates). Preferably tell us if the book has already been offered elsewhere."

BEVERLEY SLOPEN LITERARY AGENCY

131 Bloor St. W., Suite 711, Toronto ON M5S 1S3 Canada. (416)964-9598. Fax: (416)921-7726. E-mail: beverly@slopenagency.ca. Website: www.slopenagency.ca. **Contact:** Beverley Slopen. Represents 70 clients. 20% of clients are new/unpublished writers. Currently handles nonfiction books (60%), novels (40%).

Prior to opening her agency, Ms. Slopen worked in publishing and as a journalist.

REPRESENTS nonfiction books, novels, scholarly, textbooks, college. **Considers these fiction areas:** literary, mystery, suspense.

"This agency has a strong bent toward Canadian writers." Actively seeking serious nonfiction that is accessible and appealing to the general reader. Does not want to receive fantasy, science fiction, or children's books.

HOW TO CONTACT Query with SAE and IRCs. Returns materials only with SASE (Canadian postage only). Accepts simultaneous submissions. Responds in 2 months to queries.

TERMS Agent receives 15% commission on domestic sales. Agent receives 10% commission on foreign sales. Offers written contract, binding for 2 years; 3-month notice must be given to terminate contract.

RECENT SALES *Solar Dance*, by Modris Eksteins (Knopf Canada); *God's Brain*, by Lionel Tiger &

Michael McGuire (Prometheus Books); *What They Wanted*, by Donna Morrissey (Penguin Canada, Premium/DTV Germany); *The Age of Persuasion*, by Terry O'Reilly & Mike Tennant (Knopf Canada, Counterpoint US); *Prisoner of Tehran*, by Marina Nemat (Penguin Canada, Free Press US, John Murray UK); *Race to the Polar Sea*, by Ken McGoogan (HarperCollins Canada, Counterpoint US); *Transgression*, by James Nichol (HarperCollins US, McArthur Canada, Goldmann Germany); *Vermeer's Hat*, by Timothy Brook (HarperCollins Canada, Bloomsbury US); *Distantly Related to Freud*, by Ann Charney (Cormorant).

TIPS "Please, no unsolicited manuscripts."

VALERIE SMITH, LITERARY AGENT

1746 Route 44-55, Box 160, Modena NY 12548. **Contact:** Valerie Smith. Represents 17 clients. Currently handles nonfiction books (2%), novels (75%), story collections (1%), juvenile books (20%), scholarly books (1%), textbooks (1%).

REPRESENTS nonfiction books, novels, juvenile, textbooks. **Considers these fiction areas:** fantasy, historical, juvenile, literary, mainstream, mystery, science, young women's/chick lit.

"This is a small, personalized agency with a strong long-term commitment to clients interested in building careers. I have strong ties to science fiction, fantasy and young adult projects. I look for serious, productive writers whose work I can be passionate about." Does not want to receive unsolicited mss.

HOW TO CONTACT Query with synopsis, bio, 3 sample chapters, SASE. Contact by snail mail only. Obtains most new clients through recommendations from others.

TERMS Agent receives 15% commission on domestic sales. Agent receives 20% commission on foreign sales. Offers written contract; 6-week notice must be given to terminate contract.

SPECTRUM LITERARY AGENCY

320 Central Park W., Suite 1-D, New York NY 10025. Fax: (212)362-4562. Website: www.spectrumliteraryagency.com. **Contact:** Eleanor Wood, president. Estab. 1976. SFWA Represents 90 clients. Currently handles nonfiction books (10%), novels (90%).

MEMBER AGENTS Eleanor Wood, Justin Bell.

REPRESENTS nonfiction books, novels. **Considers these fiction areas:** fantasy, historical, mainstream, mystery, romance, science fiction, suspense.

Justin is actively seeking submissions in mysteries and a select amount of nonfiction

HOW TO CONTACT Query with SASE. Submit author bio, publishing credits. No unsolicited mss will be read. Queries and submissions by snail mail only. Eleanor and other agents have different addresses—see the website for full info. Responds in 1-3 months to queries. Obtains most new clients through recommendations from authors.

TERMS Agent receives 15% commission on domestic sales. Deducts for photocopying and book orders.

TIPS "Spectrum's policy is to read only book-length manuscripts that we have specifically asked to see. Unsolicited manuscripts are not accepted. The letter should describe your book briefly and include publishing credits and background information or qualifications relating to your work, if any."

SPENCERHILL ASSOCIATES

P.O. Box 374, Chatham NY 12037. (518)392-9293. Fax: (518)392-9554. E-mail: submissions@spencerhillassociates.com. Website: www.spencerhillassociates.com. **Contact:** Karen Solem or Jennifer Schober (please refer to their website for the latest information). Member of AAR. Represents 96 clients. 10% of clients are new/unpublished writers.

Prior to becoming an agent, Ms. Solem was editor-in-chief at HarperCollins and an associate publisher.

MEMBER AGENTS Karen Solem; Jennifer Schober.

REPRESENTS novels. **Considers these fiction areas:** crime, detective, historical, inspirational, literary, mainstream, police, religious, romance, thriller, young adult.

"We handle mostly commercial women's fiction, historical novels, romance (historical, contemporary, paranormal, urban fantasy), thrillers, and mysteries. We also represent Christian fiction only—no nonfiction." No nonfiction, poetry, science fiction, children's picture books, or scripts.

HOW TO CONTACT Query submissions@spencerhillassociates.com with synopsis and first three chapters attached as a .doc or .rtf file. "Please note we no longer accept queries via the mail." Responds in 6-8 weeks to queries "if we are interested in pursuing."

TERMS Agent receives 15% commission on domestic sales. Agent receives 20% commission on foreign sales. Offers written contract; 3-month notice must be given to terminate contract.

NANCY STAUFFER ASSOCIATES

1540 Boston Post Rd., P.O. Box 1203, Darien CT 06820. (203)202-2500. Fax: (203)655-3704. E-mail: StaufferAssoc@optonline.net. Website: publishersmarketplace.com/members/nstauffer. **Contact:** Nancy Stauffer Cahoon. Other memberships include Authors Guild. 5% of clients are new/unpublished writers.Currently handles nonfiction books (15%), novels (85%).

REPRESENTS **Considers these fiction areas:** contemporary, literary, regional.

HOW TO CONTACT Obtains most new clients through referrals from existing clients.

TERMS Agent receives 15% commission on domestic sales. Agent receives 20% commission on foreign sales. Agent receives 15% commission on film sales.

RECENT SALES *The Magic and Tragic Year of My Broken Thumb*, by Sherman Alexie; *Bone Fire*, by Mark Spragg; *Claiming Ground*, by Laura Bell; *The Best Camera Is the One That's with You*, by Chase Jarvis.

STEELE-PERKINS LITERARY AGENCY

26 Island Ln., Canandaigua NY 14424. (585)396-9290. Fax: (585)396-3579. E-mail: pattiesp@aol.com. **Contact:** Pattie Steele-Perkins. Member of AAR. Other memberships include RWA. Currently handles novels (100%).

REPRESENTS novels. **Considers these fiction areas:** romance, women's All genres: category romance, romantic suspense, historical, contemporary, multicultural, and inspirational.

HOW TO CONTACT Submit synopsis and one chapter via e-mail (no attachments) or snail mail. Snail mail submissions require SASE. Accepts simultaneous submissions. Responds in 6 weeks to queries. Obtains most new clients through recommendations from others, queries/solicitations.

TERMS Agent receives 15% commission on domestic sales. Offers written contract, binding for 1 year; 1-month notice must be given to terminate contract.

RECENT SALES Sold 130 titles last year. This agency prefers not to share specific sales information.

WRITERS CONFERENCES RWA National Conference; BookExpo America; CBA Convention; Romance Slam Jam, Romantic Times.

TIPS "Be patient. E-mail rather than call. Make sure what you are sending is the best it can be."

STERNIG & BYRNE LITERARY AGENCY

2370 S. 107th St., Apt. #4, Milwaukee WI 53227-2036. (414)328-8034. Fax: (414)328-8034. E-mail: jackbyrne@hotmail.com. Website: www.sff.net/people/jackbyrne. **Contact:** Jack Byrne. Other memberships include SFWA, MWA. Represents 30 clients. 10% of clients are new/unpublished writers.Currently handles nonfiction books (5%), novels (90%), juvenile books (5%).

REPRESENTS nonfiction books, novels, juvenile. **Considers these fiction areas:** fantasy, horror, mystery, science fiction, suspense.

"Our client list is comfortably full and our current needs are therefore quite limited." Actively seeking science fiction/fantasy and mystery by established writers. Does not want to receive romance, poetry, textbooks, or highly specialized nonfiction.

HOW TO CONTACT Query with SASE. Prefers e-mail queries (no attachments); hard copy queries also acceptable. Responds in 3 weeks to queries. Responds in 3 months to mss.

TERMS Agent receives 15% commission on domestic sales. Agent receives 20% commission on foreign sales. Offers written contract; 2-month notice must be given to terminate contract.

TIPS "Don't send first drafts, have a professional presentation (including cover letter), and know your field. Read what's been done—good and bad."

STRACHAN LITERARY AGENCY

P.O. Box 2091, Annapolis MD 21404. E-mail: query@strachanlit.com. Website: www.strachanlit.com. **Contact:** Laura Strachan.

Prior to becoming an agent, Ms. Strachan was (and still is) an attorney.

REPRESENTS nonfiction books, novels. **Considers these fiction areas:** literary and upmarket commercial.

"This agency specializes in literary fiction and narrative nonfiction."

HOW TO CONTACT Email queries only with brief synopsis and bio; no attachments or samples unless requested.

RECENT SALES *The Interventionist* (Hazelden); The Golden Bristled Boar (UVA Press); *Poser* (Walker).

THE STROTHMAN AGENCY, LLC

197 Eighth St., Flagship Wharf - 611, Charlestown MA 02129. (617)742-2011. Fax: (617)742-2014. E-mail: strothmanagency@gmail.com. Website: www.strothmanagency.com. **Contact:** Wendy Strothman, Lauren MacLeod. Member of AAR. Other memberships include Authors' Guild. Represents 50 clients. Currently handles nonfiction books (70%), novels (10%), scholarly books (20%).

Prior to becoming an agent, Ms. Strothman was head of Beacon Press (1983-1995) and executive vice president of Houghton Mifflin's Trade & Reference Division (1996-2002).

MEMBER AGENTS Wendy Strothman; Lauren MacLeod.

REPRESENTS nonfiction books, novels, scholarly young adult and middle grade. **Considers these fiction areas:** literary, young adult middle grade.

"Because we are highly selective in the clients we represent, we increase the value publishers place on our properties. We specialize in narrative nonfiction, memoir, history, science and nature, arts and culture, literary travel, current affairs, and some business. We have a highly selective practice in literary fiction, young adult and middle grade fiction, and nonfiction. We are now opening our doors to more commercial fiction but ONLY from authors who have a platform. If you have a platform, please mention it in your query letter." "The Strothman Agency seeks out scholars, journalists, and other acknowledged and emerging experts in their fields. We are now actively looking for authors of well written young-adult fiction and nonfiction. Browse the Latest News to get an idea of the types of books that we represent. For more about what we're looking for, read Pitching an Agent: The Strothman Agency on the publishing website www.strothmanagency.com." Does not want to receive commercial fiction, romance, science fiction or self-help.

HOW TO CONTACT Accepts queries only via e-mail at strothmanagency@gmail.com. See submission guidelines online. Accepts simultaneous submissions. Responds in 4 weeks to queries. Responds in 6 weeks to mss. Obtains most new clients through recommendations from others.

TERMS Agent receives 15% commission on domestic sales. Agent receives 20% commission on foreign sales. Offers written contract; 30-day notice must be given to terminate contract.

EMMA SWEENEY AGENCY, LLC

245 East 80th St., Suite 7E, New York NY 10075. E-mail: queries@emmasweeneyagency.com. Website: www.emmasweeneyagency.com. Member of AAR. Other memberships include Women's Media Group. Represents 80 clients. 5% of clients are new/unpublished writers. Currently handles nonfiction books (50%), novels (50%).

Prior to becoming an agent, Ms. Sweeney was director of subsidiary rights at Grove Press. Since 1990, she has been a literary agent.

MEMBER AGENTS Emma Sweeney, president; Eva Talmadge, rights manager and agent (Represents literary fiction, young adult novels, and narrative nonfiction. Considers these nonfiction areas: popular science, pop culture and music history, biography, memoirs, cooking, and anything relating to animals. Considers these fiction areas: literary (of the highest writing quality possible), young adult. eva@emmasweeneyagency.com); Justine Wenger, junior agent/assistant (justine@emmasweeneyagency.com).

REPRESENTS nonfiction books, novels.

"We specialize in quality fiction and nonfiction. Our primary areas of interest include literary and women's fiction, mysteries and thrillers; science, history, biography, memoir, religious studies and the natural sciences." Does not want to receive romance and westerns or screenplays.

HOW TO CONTACT Send query letter and first 10 pages in body of e-mail (no attachments) to queries@emmasweeneyagency.com. No snail mail queries.

TERMS Agent receives 15% commission on domestic sales. Agent receives 10% commission on foreign sales.

WRITERS CONFERENCES Nebraska Writers' Conference; Words and Music Festival in New Orleans.

TALCOTT NOTCH LITERARY

2 Broad St., Second Floor, Suite 10, Milford CT 06460. (203)876-4959. Fax: (203)876-9517. E-mail: editorial@talcottnotch.net. Website: www.talcottnotch.net.

Contact: Gina Panettieri, President. Represents 35 clients. 25% of clients are new/unpublished writers. Currently handles nonfiction books (50%), novels (20%), story collections (5%), juvenile books (20%), scholarly books (10%).

Prior to becoming an agent, Ms. Panettieri was a freelance writer and editor.

MEMBER AGENTS Gina Panettieri (nonfiction, mystery); Rachel Dowen (children's fiction, mystery).
REPRESENTS nonfiction books, novels, juvenile, scholarly, textbooks. **Considers these fiction areas:** action, adventure, crime, detective, fantasy, juvenile, mystery, police, romance, suspense, thriller, young adult.
HOW TO CONTACT Query via e-mail (preferred) with first 10 pages of the ms within the body of the e-mail, not as an attachment, or with SASE. Accepts simultaneous submissions. Responds in 1 week to queries. Responds in 4-6 weeks to mss.
TERMS Agent receives 15% commission on domestic sales. Agent receives 20% commission on foreign sales. Offers written contract, binding for 1 year.
RECENT SALES Sold 36 titles in the last year. *Delivered from Evil*, by Ron Franscell (Fairwinds) and *Sourtoe* (Globe Pequot Press); *Hellforged*, by Nancy Holzner (Berkley Ace Science Fiction); *Welcoming Kitchen*; *200 Allergen- and Gluten-Free Vegan Recipes*, by Kim Lutz and Megan Hart (Sterling); *Dr. Seteh's Love Prescription*, by Dr. Seth Meyers (Adams Media); *The Book of Ancient Bastards*, by Brian Thornton (Adams Media); *Hope in Courage*, by Beth Fehlbaum (Westside Books) and more.
TIPS "Know your market and how to reach them. A strong platform is essential in your book proposal. Can you effectively use social media/ Are you a strong networker: Are you familiar with the book bloggers in your genre? Are you involved with the interest-specific groups that can help you? What can you do to break through the 'noise' and help present your book to your readers? Check our website for more tips and information on this topic."

● PATRICIA TEAL LITERARY AGENCY

2036 Vista Del Rosa, Fullerton CA 92831-1336. Phone/Fax: (714)738-8333. **Contact:** Patricia Teal. Member of AAR. Other memberships include RWA, Authors Guild. Represents 20 clients. Currently handles nonfiction books (10%), other (90% fiction).

REPRESENTS nonfiction books, novels. **Considers these fiction areas:** glitz, mainstream, mystery, romance, suspense.

This agency specializes in women's fiction, commercial how-to, and self-help nonfiction. Does not want to receive poetry, short stories, articles, science fiction, fantasy, or regency romance.

HOW TO CONTACT Published authors only may query with SASE. Accepts simultaneous submissions. Responds in 10 days to queries. Responds in 6 weeks to mss. Obtains most new clients through conferences, recommendations from authors and editors.
TERMS Agent receives 10-15% commission on domestic sales. Agent receives 20% commission on foreign sales. Offers written contract, binding for 1 year. Charges clients for ms copies.
RECENT SALES Sold 30 titles in the last year. *Texas Rose* by Marie Ferrarella (Silhouette); *Watch Your Language*, by Sterling Johnson (St. Martin's Press); *The Black Sheep's Baby*, by Kathleen Creighton (Silhouette); *Man with a Message*, by Muriel Jensen (Harlequin).
WRITERS CONFERENCES RWA Conferences; Asilomar; BookExpo America; Bouchercon; Maui Writers Conference.
TIPS "Include SASE with all correspondence. I am taking on published authors only."

⊙ ANN TOBIAS: A LITERARY AGENCY FOR CHILDREN'S BOOKS

520 E. 84th St., Apt. 4L, New York NY 10028. E-mail: AnnTobias84@hotmail.com. **Contact:** Ann Tobias. Estab. 1988. Represents 25 clients. 10% of clients are new/unpublished writers.Currently handles juvenile books (100%).

Prior to opening her agency, Ms. Tobias worked as a children's book editor at Harper, William Morrow and Scholastic.

REPRESENTS juvenile and young adult. **Considers these fiction areas:** picture books, poetry, poetry in translation, young adult illustrated mss; mid-level novels.

This agency specializes in books for children.

HOW TO CONTACT For all age groups and genres: Send a one-page letter of inquiry accompanied by a one-page writing sample, double-spaced. No attachments will be opened. Other Responds in 2 months to mss. Obtains most new clients through recommendations from editors.

TERMS Agent receives 15% commission on domestic sales. Agent receives 20% commission on foreign sales. This agency charges clients for photocopying, overnight mail, foreign postage, foreign telephone.

WRITERS CONFERENCES 3LiteraryAgents.com. For questions contact info@3literaryagents.com.

TIPS "Read at least 200 children's books in the age group and genre in which you hope to be published. Follow this by reading another 100 children's books in other age groups and genres so you will have a feel for the field as a whole."

TRANSATLANTIC LITERARY AGENCY

2 Bloor St., Suite 3500, Toronto ON M4W 1A8 Canada. E-mail: info@tla1.com. Website: www.tla1.com. Represents 250 clients. 10% of clients are new/unpublished writers. Currently handles nonfiction books (30%), novels (15%), juvenile books (50%), textbooks (5%).

MEMBER AGENTS Lynn Bennett, Lynn@tla1.com, (juvenile and young adult fiction); Shaun Bradley, Shaun@tla1.com (literary fiction and narrative nonfiction); Marie Campbell, Marie@tla1.com (literary juvenile and young adult fiction); Andrea Cascardi, Andrea@tla1.com (literary juvenile and young adult fiction); Samantha Haywood, Sam@tla1.com (literary fiction, narrative nonfiction and graphic novels); Don Sedgwick, Don@tla1.com (literary fiction and narrative nonfiction).

REPRESENTS nonfiction books, novels, juvenile. **Considers these fiction areas:** juvenile, literary, mainstream, mystery, suspense, young adult.

"In both children's and adult literature, we market directly into the United States, the United Kingdom and Canada." Actively seeking literary children's and adult fiction, nonfiction. Does not want to receive picture books, poetry, screenplays or stage plays.

HOW TO CONTACT Submit e-query with synopsis, 2 sample chapters, bio. Always refer to the website, as guidelines will change. Also refer to website for appropriate agent contact info to send e-query. Responds in 2 weeks to queries. Obtains most new clients through recommendations from others.

TERMS Agent receives 15% commission on domestic sales. Agent receives 20% commission on foreign sales. Offers written contract; 45-day notice must be given to terminate contract. This agency charges for photocopying and postage when it exceeds $100.

RECENT SALES Sold 250 titles in the last year.

TRIADA U.S. LITERARY AGENCY, INC.

P.O. Box 561, Sewickley PA 15143. (412)401-3376. E-mail: uwe@triadaus.com. Website: www.triadaus.com. **Contact:** Dr. Uwe Stender. Member of AAR. Represents 65 clients. 20% of clients are new/unpublished writers.

REPRESENTS fiction, nonfiction. **Considers these fiction areas:** action, adventure, crime, detective, ethnic, historical, horror, juvenile, literary, mainstream, mystery, occult, police, romance, women's especially young adult, women's fiction, and mysteries.

"We are looking for great writing and story platforms. Our response time is fairly unique. We recognize that neither we nor the authors have time to waste, so we guarantee a 5-day response time. We usually respond within 24 hours. " Actively looking for both fiction and nonfiction in all areas.

HOW TO CONTACT E-mail queries preferred; otherwise query with SASE. Accepts simultaneous submissions. Responds in 1-5 weeks to queries. Responds in 2-6 weeks to mss. Obtains most new clients through recommendations from others, conferences.

TERMS Agent receives 15% commission on domestic sales. Agent receives 20% commission on foreign sales. Offers written contract; 30-day notice must be given to terminate contract.

RECENT SALES *The Man Whisperer*, by Samantha Brett and Donna Sozio (Adams Media); *Whatever Happened to Pudding Pops*, by Gael Fashingbauer Cooper and Brian Bellmont (Penguin/Perigee); *86'd*, by Dan Fante (Harper Perennial); *Hating Olivia*, by Mark SaFranko (Harper Perennial); *Everything I'm Not Made Me Everything I Am*, by Jeff Johnson (Smiley Books).

TIPS "I comment on all requested manuscripts that I reject."

UPSTART CROW LITERARY

P.O. Box 25404, Brooklyn NY 11202. E-mail: info@upstartcrowliterary.com. E-mail: chris.submission@gmail.com. Website: www.upstartcrowliterary.com. **Contact:** Chris Richman. Estab. 2009.

MEMBER AGENTS Michael Stearns; Chris Richman (special interest in books for boys, books with unforgettable characters, and fantasy that doesn't take itself too seriously); Danielle Chiotti (books ranging from contemporary women's fiction to narrative nonfiction, from romance to relationship stories, humorous tales and young adult fiction); Ted Malawer (accepting queries only through conference submissions and client referrals).

REPRESENTS Considers these fiction areas: women's, young adult middle grade.

HOW TO CONTACT This agency likes submissions sent via e-mails to Chris Richman or Danielle Chiotti.

VENTURE LITERARY

2683 Via de la Valle, G-714, Del Mar CA 92014. (619)807-1887. Fax: (772)365-8321. E-mail: submissions@ventureliterary.com. Website: www.ventureliterary.com. **Contact:** Frank R. Scatoni. Represents 50 clients. 40% of clients are new/unpublished writers. Currently handles nonfiction books (80%), novels (20%).

Prior to becoming an agent, Mr. Scatoni worked as an editor at Simon & Schuster.

MEMBER AGENTS Frank R. Scatoni (general nonfiction, biography, memoir, narrative nonfiction, sports, serious nonfiction, graphic novels, narratives).

REPRESENTS nonfiction books, novels graphic novels, narratives. **Considers these fiction areas:** action, adventure, crime, detective, literary, mainstream, mystery, police, sports, suspense, thriller, women's.

Specializes in nonfiction, sports, biography, gambling, and nonfiction narratives. Actively seeking nonfiction, graphic novels and narratives. Does not want fantasy, sci-fi, romance, children's picture books, and westerns.

HOW TO CONTACT Considers e-mail queries only. *No unsolicited mss* and no snail mail whatsoever. See website for complete submission guidelines. Obtains most new clients through recommendations from others.

TERMS Agent receives 15% commission on domestic sales. Agent receives 20% commission on foreign sales. Offers written contract.

RECENT SALES *The 9/11 Report: A Graphic Adaptation*, by Sid Jacobson and Ernie Colon (FSG); *Having a Baby* by Cindy Margolis (Perigee/Penguin); *Phil Gordon's Little Blue Book*, by Phil Gordon (Simon & Schuster); *Atomic America*, by Todd Tucker (Free Press); *War as They Knew It*, by Michael Rosenberg (Grand Central); *Game Day*, by Craig James (Wiley); *The Blueprint* by Christopher Price (Thomas Dunne Books).

BETH VESEL LITERARY AGENCY

80 Fifth Ave., Suite 1101, New York NY 10011. (212)924-4252. E-mail: mlindley@bvlit.com. **Contact:** Julia Masnik, assistant. Represents 65 clients. 10% of clients are new/unpublished writers.Currently handles nonfiction books (75%), novels (10%), story collections (5%), scholarly books (10%).

Prior to becoming an agent, Ms. Vesel was a poet and a journalist.

REPRESENTS nonfiction books, novels. **Considers these fiction areas:** crime, detective, literary, police Francophone novels.

"My specialties include serious nonfiction, psychology, cultural criticism, memoir, and women's issues." Actively seeking cultural criticism, literary psychological thrillers, and sophisticated memoirs. No uninspired psychology or run-of-the-mill first novels.

HOW TO CONTACT Query with SASE. Accepts simultaneous submissions. Responds in 2 weeks to queries. Responds in 1 month to mss. Obtains most new clients through referrals, reading good magazines, contacting professionals with ideas.

TERMS Agent receives 15% commission on domestic sales. Agent receives 20% commission on foreign sales. Offers written contract.

RECENT SALES Sold 10 titles in the last year. *Life with Pop*, by Janis Spring, Ph.D (Avery); *American Scandal*, by Laura Kipnis (Metropolitan); *Bird in Hand*, by Christina Baker Kline (William Morrow); *Reimagining the South*, by Tracy Thompson (Simon & Schuster); *Are Fathers Necessary*, by Raul Raeburn (Simon & Schuster); *Blind Date*, by Virginia Vitzhum (Workman); *Bipolar Breakthrough*, by Ron Fieve (Rodale).

WRITERS CONFERENCES Squaw Valley Writers Workshop, Iowa Summer Writing Festival.

TIPS "Try to find out if you fit on a particular agent's list by looking at his/her books and comparing yours. You can almost always find who represents a book by looking at the acknowledgements."

VIRGINIA KIDD AGENCY, INC.

538 E. Harford St., P.O. Box 278, Milford PA 18337. (570)296-6205. Fax: (570)296-7266. Website: www.vk-agency.com. Other memberships include SFWA, SFRA. Represents 80 clients.

MEMBER AGENTS Christine Cohen.

REPRESENTS novels. **Considers these fiction areas:** fantasy, historical, mainstream, mystery, science fiction, suspense, women's speculative.

This agency specializes in science fiction and fantasy.

HOW TO CONTACT *This agency is not accepting queries from unpublished authors at this time.* Submit synopsis (1-3 pages), cover letter, first chapter, SASE. Snail mail queries only. Responds in 6 weeks to queries.

TERMS Agent receives 15% commission on domestic sales. Agent receives 20-25% commission on foreign sales. Agent receives 20% commission on film sales. Offers written contract; 2-month notice must be given to terminate contract. Charges clients occasionally for extraordinary expenses.

RECENT SALES *Sagramanda*, by Alan Dean Foster (Pyr); *Incredible Good Fortune*, by Ursula K. Le Guin (Shambhala); *The Wizard and Soldier of Sidon*, by Gene Wolfe (Tor); *Voices and Powers*, by Ursula K. Le Guin (Harcourt); *Galileo's Children*, by Gardner Dozois (Pyr); *The Light Years Beneath My Feet* and *Running From the Deity*, by Alan Dean Foster (Del Ray); *Chasing Fire*, by Michelle Welch. Other clients include Eleanor Arnason, Ted Chiang, Jack Skillingstead, Daryl Gregory, Patricia Briggs, and the estates for James Tiptree, Jr., Murray Leinster, E.E. "Doc" Smith, R.A. Lafferty.

TIPS "If you have a completed novel that is of extraordinary quality, please send us a query."

IRENE WEBB LITERARY

551 W. Cordova Rd. #238, Santa Fe NM 87505. (505)988-1817. E-mail: webblit@gmail.com. Website: www.irenewebb.com. **Contact:** Irene Webb.

REPRESENTS nonfiction books, novels. **Considers these fiction areas:** commercial, crime, horror, mystery, suspense, thriller, women's, young adult middle grade, literary and commercial fiction.

"Irene Webb Literary is known as one of the top boutique agencies selling books to film and TV. We have close relationships with top film producers and talent in Hollywood." Does not want to receive unsolicited manuscripts or screenplays.

HOW TO CONTACT Query via e-mail only. Obtains most new clients through recommendations from others, solicitations.

RECENT SALES *Secrets of a Soap Opera Diva*, by Victoria Rowell (Atria); *Now I Can See the Moon*, by Elaine Hall (Harper Studio); *Dead Write*, by Sheila Low (NAL); *East to the Dawn*, by Susan Butler (Fox Studio for the Amelia Earhart Story starring Hilary Swank).

THE WEINGEL-FIDEL AGENCY

310 E. 46th St., 21E, New York NY 10017. (212)599-2959. **Contact:** Loretta Weingel-Fidel. Currently handles nonfiction books (75%), novels (25%).

Prior to opening her agency, Ms. Weingel-Fidel was a psychoeducational diagnostician.

REPRESENTS nonfiction books, novels. **Considers these fiction areas:** literary, mainstream.

This agency specializes in commercial and literary fiction and nonfiction. Actively seeking investigative journalism. Does not want to receive genre fiction, self-help, science fiction, or fantasy.

HOW TO CONTACT Accepts writers by referral only. *No unsolicited mss.*

TERMS Agent receives 15% commission on domestic sales. Agent receives 20% commission on foreign sales. Offers written contract, binding for 1 year with automatic renewal. Bills sent back to clients are all reasonable expenses, such as UPS, express mail, photocopying, etc.

TIPS "A very small, selective list enables me to work very closely with my clients to develop and nurture talent. I only take on projects and writers about which I am extremely enthusiastic."

LARRY WEISSMAN LITERARY, LLC

526 8th St., #2R, Brooklyn NY 11215. E-mail: lwsubmissions@gmail.com. **Contact:** Larry Weissman. Represents 35 clients. Currently handles nonfiction books (80%), novels (10%), story collections (10%).

REPRESENTS nonfiction books, novels, short story collections. **Considers these fiction areas:** literary.

"Very interested in established journalists with bold voices. Interested in anything to do with food. Fiction has to feel 'vital' and short stories are accepted, but only if you can sell us on an idea for a novel as well." Nonfiction, including food and lifestyle, politics, pop culture, narrative, cultural/social issues, journalism. No genre fiction, poetry or children's.

HOW TO CONTACT "Send e-queries only. If you don't hear back, your project was not right for our list."

TERMS Agent receives 15% commission on domestic sales. Agent receives 20% commission on foreign sales.

O WHIMSY LITERARY AGENCY, LLC

New York/Los Angeles E-mail: whimsynyc@aol.com. Website: http://whimsyliteraryagency.com/. **Contact:** Jackie Meyer. Other memberships include Center for Independent Publishing Advisory Board. Represents 30 clients. 20% of clients are new/unpublished writers. Currently handles nonfiction books (100%).

Prior to becoming an agent, Ms. Meyer was with Warner Books for 19 years; Ms. Vezeris and Ms. Legette have 30 years' experience at various book publishers.

MEMBER AGENTS Jackie Meyer; Olga Vezeris (fiction and nonfiction); Nansci LeGette, senior associate in LA.

REPRESENTS nonfiction books. **Considers these fiction areas:** mainstream, religious, thriller, women's.

"Whimsy looks for projects that are concept- and platform-driven. We seek books that educate, inspire and entertain." Actively seeking experts in their field with good platforms.

HOW TO CONTACT Send a query letter via e-mail. Send a synopsis, bio, platform, and proposal. No snail mail submissions. Responds "quickly, but only if interested" to queries. *Does not accept unsolicited mss.* Obtains most new clients through recommendations from others, solicitations.

TERMS Agent receives 15% commission on domestic sales. Agent receives 20% commission on foreign sales. Offers written contract. Charges for posting and photocopying.

● WM CLARK ASSOCIATES

186 Fifth Ave., Second Floor, New York NY 10010. (212)675-2784. Fax: (347)-649-9262. E-mail: general@wmclark.com. Website: www.wmclark.com. Estab. 1997. Member of AAR. 50% of clients are new/unpublished writers. Currently handles nonfiction books (50%), novels (50%).

Prior to opening WCA, Mr. Clark was an agent at the William Morris Agency.

REPRESENTS nonfiction books, novels. **Considers these fiction areas:** contemporary issues, ethnic, historical, literary, mainstream Southern fiction.

William Clark represents a wide range of titles across all formats to the publishing, motion picture, television, and new media fields on behalf of authors of first fiction and award-winning, best-selling narrative nonfiction, international authors in translation, chefs, musicians, and artists. Offering individual focus and a global presence, the agency undertakes to discover, develop, and market today's most interesting content and the talent that create it, and forge sophisticated and innovative plans for self-promotion, reliable revenue streams, and an enduring creative career. Referral partners are available to provide services including editorial consultation, media training, lecture booking, marketing support, and public relations. Agency does not respond to screenplays or screenplay pitches. It is advised that before querying you become familiar with the kinds of books we handle by browsing our Book List, which is available on our website.

HOW TO CONTACT Accepts queries via online form only at www.wmclark.com/queryguidelines.html. We respond to all queries submitted via this form. Responds in 1-2 months to queries.

TERMS Agent receives 15% commission on domestic sales. Agent receives 20% commission on foreign sales. Offers written contract.

TIPS "WCA works on a reciprocal basis with Ed Victor Ltd. (UK) in representing select properties to the US market and vice versa. Translation rights are sold directly in the German, Italian, Spanish, Portuguese, Latin American, French, Dutch, and Scandinavian territories in association with Andrew Nurnberg Associates Ltd. (UK); through offices in China, Bulgaria, Czech Republic, Latvia, Poland, Hungary, and Russia; and through corresponding agents in Japan, Greece, Israel, Turkey, Korea, Taiwan, and Thailand."

O WOLFSON LITERARY AGENCY

P.O. Box 266, New York NY 10276. E-mail: query@wolfsonliterary.com. Website: www.wolfsonliterary.com/. **Contact:** Michelle Wolfson. Other memberships include Adheres to AAR canon of ethics.

Currently handles nonfiction books (70%), novels (30%).

Prior to forming her own agency, Michelle spent two years with Artists & Artisans, Inc. and two years with Ralph Vicinanza, Ltd.

REPRESENTS nonfiction books, novels. **Considers these fiction areas:** mainstream, mystery, romance, suspense, thriller, women's, young adult.

Actively seeking commercial fiction, mainstream, mysteries, thrillers, suspense, women's fiction, romance, YA, practical nonfiction (particularly of interest to women), advice, medical, pop culture, humor, business.

HOW TO CONTACT E-queries only! Accepts simultaneous submissions. Responds only if interested. Positive response is generally given within 2-4 weeks. Responds in 3 months to mss. Obtains most new clients through recommendations from others, solicitations.

TERMS Agent receives 15% commission on domestic sales. Agent receives 25% commission on foreign sales. Offers written contract; 30-day notice must be given to terminate contract.

WRITERS CONFERENCES SDSU Writers' Conference; New Jersey Romance Writers of America Writers' Conference; American Independent Writers Conference in Washington DC.

TIPS "Be persistent."

WRITERS' REPRESENTATIVES, LLC

116 W. 14th St., 11th Floor, New York NY 10011-7305. Fax: (212)620-0023. E-mail: transom@writersreps.com. Website: www.writersreps.com. Represents 130 clients. 10% of clients are new/unpublished writers. Currently handles nonfiction books (90%), novels (10%).

Prior to becoming an agent, Ms. Chu was a lawyer; Mr. Hartley worked at Simon & Schuster, Harper & Row, and Cornell University Press.

MEMBER AGENTS Lynn Chu; Glen Hartley; Christine Hsu.

REPRESENTS nonfiction books, novels. **Considers these fiction areas:** literary.

Serious nonfiction and quality fiction. No motion picture or television screenplays.

HOW TO CONTACT Query with SASE. Prefers to read materials exclusively. Considers simultaneous queries, but must be informed at time of submission.

TERMS Agent receives 15% commission on domestic sales. Agent receives 20% commission on foreign sales.

TIPS "Always include a SASE; it will ensure a response from the agent and the return of your submitted material."

YATES & YATES

1100 Town & Country Road, Suite 1300, Orange CA 92868. E-mail: email@yates2.com. Website: www.yates2.com. Represents 60 clients.

REPRESENTS nonfiction books.

RECENT SALES *No More Mondays*, by Dan Miller (Doubleday Currency).

HELEN ZIMMERMANN LITERARY AGENCY

3 Emmy Lane, New Paltz NY 12561. (845)256-0977. Fax: (845)256-0979. E-mail: Helen@ZimmAgency.com. Website: www.zimmermannliterary.com. **Contact:** Helen Zimmermann. Estab. 2003. Represents 25 clients. 50% of clients are new/unpublished writers. Currently handles nonfiction books (80%), other (20% fiction).

Prior to opening her agency, Ms. Zimmermann was the director of advertising and promotion at Random House and the events coordinator at an independent bookstore.

REPRESENTS nonfiction books, novels. **Considers these fiction areas:** family saga, historical, literary, mystery, suspense.

"As an agent who has experience at both a publishing house and a bookstore, I have a keen insight for viable projects. This experience also helps me ensure every client gets published well, through the whole process." Actively seeking memoirs, pop culture, women's issues, and accessible literary fiction. Does not want to receive horror, science fiction, poetry or romance.

HOW TO CONTACT Accepts e-mail queries only. E-mail should include a short description of project and bio, whether it be fiction or nonfiction. Accepts simultaneous submissions. Responds in 2 weeks to queries. Responds in 1 month to mss. Obtains most new clients through recommendations from others, solicitations.

TERMS Agent receives 15% commission on domestic sales. Offers written contract; 30-day notice must be given to terminate contract. Charges for photocopying and postage (reimbursed if project is sold).

RECENT SALES *She Bets Her Life: Women and Gambling*, by Mary Sojourner (Seal Press); *Seeds: One Man's Quest to Preserve the Trees of America's Most Famous People*, by Rick Horan (HarperCollins); *Saddled*, by Susan Richards (Houghton Mifflin Harcourt); *Final Target*, by Steven Gore (HarperPerennial); *Liberated Body, Captive Mind: A WWII POW Memoir*, by Normal Bussel (Pegasus Books).

WRITERS CONFERENCES BEA/Writer's Digest Books Writers' Conference, Portland, ME Writers Conference, Berkshire Writers and Readers Conference.

LITERARY MAGAZINES

This section contains markets for your literary short fiction. Although definitions of what constitutes "literary" writing vary, editors of literary journals agree they want to publish the best fiction they can acquire. Qualities they look for in fiction include fully developed characters, strong and unique narrative voice, flawless mechanics, and careful attention to detail in content and manuscript preparation. Most of the authors writing such fiction are well read and well educated, and many are students and graduates of university creative writing programs.

Please also review our Online Markets section, page 354, for electronic literary magazines. At a time when paper and publishing costs rise while funding to small and university presses continues to be cut or eliminated, electronic literary magazines are helping generate a publishing renaissance for experimental as well as more traditional literary fiction. These electronic outlets for literary fiction also benefit writers by eliminating copying and postage costs and providing the opportunity for much quicker responses to submissions. Also notice that some magazines with Web sites give specific information about what they offer online, including updated writer's guidelines and sample fiction from their publications.

STEPPING-STONES TO RECOGNITION

Some well-established literary journals pay several hundred or even several thousand dollars for a short story. Most, though, can only pay with contributor's copies or a subscription to their publication. However, being published in literary journals offers the important benefits of experience, exposure and prestige. Agents and major book publishers regularly read literary magazines in search of new writers. Work from these journals is also selected for inclusion in annual prize anthologies.

You'll find most of the well-known prestigious literary journals listed here. Many, including the *Southern Review* and *Ploughshares*, are associated with universities, while others like the *Paris Review* are independently published.

Selecting the Right Literary Journal

Once you have browsed through this section and have a list of journals you might like to submit to, read those listings again carefully. Remember this is information editors provide to help you submit work that fits their needs. How to Use *NSSWM*, starting on page 2, will guide you through the process of finding markets for your fiction.

Note that you will find some magazines that do not read submissions all year long. Whether limited reading periods are tied to a university schedule or meant to accommodate the capabilities of a very small staff, those periods are noted within listings (when the editors notify us). The staffs of university journals are usually made up of student editors and a managing editor who is also a faculty member. These staffs often change every year. Whenever possible, we indicate this in listings and give the name of the current editor and the length of that editor's term. Also be aware that the schedule of a university journal usually coincides with that university's academic year, meaning that the editors of most university publications are difficult or impossible to reach during the summer.

Furthering Your Search

It cannot be stressed enough that reading the listings for literary journals is only the first part of developing your marketing plan. The second part, equally important, is to obtain fiction guidelines and to read with great care the actual journal you'd like to submit to. Reading copies of these journals helps you determine the fine points of each magazine's publishing style and sensibility. There is no substitute for this type of hands-on research.

Unlike commercial periodicals available at most newsstands and bookstores, it requires a little more effort to obtain some of the magazines listed here. The super-chain bookstores are doing a better job these days of stocking literaries, and you can find some in independent and college bookstores, especially those published in your area. The Internet is an invaluable resource for submission guidelines, as more and more journals establish an online presence. You may, however, need to send for a sample copy. We include sample copy prices in the listings whenever possible. In addition to reading your sample copies, pay close attention to the **Advice** section of each listing. There you'll often find a very specific description of the style of fiction the editors at that publication prefer.

Another way to find out more about literary magazines is to check out the various prize anthologies and take note of journals whose fiction is being selected for publication in them. Studying prize anthologies not only lets you know which magazines are publishing award-winning work, but it also provides a valuable overview of what is considered to be the best fiction published today. Those anthologies include:

- *Best American Short Stories*, published by Houghton Mifflin.
- *New Stories from the South: The Year's Best*, published by Algonquin Books of Chapel Hill.
- *The O. Henry Prize Stories*, published by Doubleday/Anchor.
- *Pushcart Prize: Best of the Small Presses*, published by Pushcart Press.

At the beginnings of listings, we include symbols to help you narrow your search. Keys to those symbols can be found on the inside covers of this book.

ACM (ANOTHER CHICAGO MAGAZINE)

P.O. Box 408439, Chicago IL 60640. Website: www.anotherchicagomagazine.net. **Contact:** Jacob S. Knabb, editor-in-chief. Estab. 1977. **Contact:** Jacob S. Knabb, Managing/Fiction editor. Magazine: $5\frac{1}{2}\times8\frac{1}{2}$; 200-220 pages; "art folio each issue." Biannual. Estab. 1977. Circ. 2,000.

Work published in *ACM* has been included frequently in *The Best American Poetry* and *The Pushcart Prize.*

NEEDS ethnic/multicultural, experimental, feminist, gay, lesbian, literary, translations, contemporary, prose poem. No religious, strictly genre or editorial. Receives 300 unsolicited mss/month. Reads mss from February 1 to August 31. Publishes ms 6-12 months after acceptance. **Publishes 10 new writers/year.** Recently published work by Stuart Dybek and Steve Almond.

HOW TO CONTACT "Please include the following contact information in your cover letter and on your ms: Byline (name as you want it to appear if published), mailing address, phone number, and e-mail. Include a self-addressed stamped envelope (SASE). If a SASE is not enclosed, you will only hear from us if we are interested in your work. Include the genre (e.g., fiction, et al.) of your work in the address." Responds in 3 months to queries; 6 months to mss. Accepts simultaneous, multiple submissions. Sample copy for $8 ppd. Writer's guidelines online.

PAYMENT/TERMS Pays small honorarium when possible, contributor's copies and 1 year subscription. Acquires first North American serial rights.

TIPS "Support literary publishing by subscribing to at least one literary journal—if not ours, another. Get used to rejection slips, and don't get discouraged. Keep introductory letters short. Make sure manuscript has name and address on every page, and that it is clean, neat and proofread. We are looking for stories with freshness and originality in subject angle and style, and work that encounters the world."

THE ALLEGHENY REVIEW

Allegheny College Box 32, Meadville PA 16335. Website: http://webpub.allegheny.edu/group/review. Estab. 1983. **Contact:** Senior editor. Magazine: 6×9; 100 pages; illustrations; photos. "*The Allegheny Review* is one of America's only nationwide literary magazines exclusively for undergraduate works of poetry, fiction and nonfiction. Our intended audience is persons interested in quality literature." Annual. Estab. 1983.

NEEDS Adventure, ethnic/multicultural, experimental, family saga, fantasy, feminist, gay, historical, horror, humor/satire, lesbian, literary, mainstream, military/war, mystery/suspense, New Age, psychic/supernatural/occult, religious/inspirational (general), romance, science fiction, western. No "fiction not written by undergraduates—we accept nothing but fiction by currently enrolled undergraduate students. We consider anything catering to an intellectual audience." Receives 50 unsolicited mss/month. Accepts 3 mss/issue. Publishes ms 2 months after deadline. **Publishes roughly 90% new writers/year.** Recently published work by Dianne Page, Monica Stahl, and DJ Kinney. Publishes short shorts (up to 20 pages). Also publishes literary nonfiction and poetry.

HOW TO CONTACT Send complete mss with a cover letter. Accepts submissions on disk. Responds in 2 weeks to queries; 4 months to mss. Send disposable copy of ms and #10 SASE for reply only. Sample copy for $4. Writer's guidelines for SASE, by e-mail, or on website.

PAYMENT/TERMS Pays 1 contributor's copy; additional copies $3. Sponsors awards/contests; reading fee of $5.

TIPS "We look for quality work that has been thoroughly revised. Unique voice, interesting topic and playfulness with the English language. Revise, revise, revise! And be careful how you send it—the cover letter says a lot. We definitely look for diversity in the pieces we publish."

AMERICAN LITERARY REVIEW

University of North Texas, P.O. Box 311307, Denton TX 76203-1307. (940)565-2755. E-mail: americanliteraryreview@gmail.com; bond@unt.edu. Website: www.engl.unt.edu/alr/. Estab. 1990. Magazine: 6×9; 128 pages; 70 lb. Mohawk paper; 67 lb. Wausau Vellum cover. "Publishes quality, contemporary poems and stories." Semi-annual. Circ. 1,200. Ph.: (940)565-2755; Fax: (940)565-4355. Web site: www.engl.unt.edu/alr/

NEEDS Literary, mainstream. "No genre works." Receives 150-200 unsolicited mss/month. Accepts 5-6 mss/issue; 12-16 mss/year. Reading period: October 1-May 1. Publishes ms within 2 years after acceptance. Recently published work by Marylee MacDonald, Michael Isaac Shokrian, Arthur Brown, Roy Bentley, Julie Marie Wade, and Karin Forfota Poklen. Also publishes creative nonfiction, poetry. Critiques or comments on rejected mss.

HOW TO CONTACT Send complete ms with cover letter. Responds in 2-4 months to mss. Accepts simultaneous submissions. Sample copy for $8. Writer's guidelines for #10 SASE.

PAYMENT/TERMS Pays in contributor's copies. Acquires onetime rights.

TIPS "We encourage writers and artists to examine our journal. The *American Literary Review* publishes semiannually. If you would like to subscribe to our journal, subscription rates run $14 for a 1-year subscription, $26 for a 2 year subscription, and $36 for a 3-year subscription. You may also obtain a sample copy of the *American Literary Review* for $7 plus $1 per issue for shipping and handling in the U.S. and Canada ($2 for postage elsewhere)."

AMERICAN SHORT FICTION

Badgerdog Literary Publishing, P.O. Box 301209, Austin TX 78703. (512) 538-1305. Fax: (512) 538-1306. E-mail: editors@americanshortfiction.org. E-mail: submissions@americanshortfiction.org. Website: www.americanshortfiction.org. **Contact:** Jill Myers, editor. Estab. 1991. Literary magazine/journal. 6x9.5, 140 pages. Contains illustrations. Includes photographs. Member CLMP.

ASF has had two stories included in *Best American Short Stories* 2009. ASF has had a selection included in *Best Nonrequired Reading*, 2007 and *New Stories from the Southwest*, 2008. Awards from the previous incarnation of ASF (when published by the University of Texas, 1991-1998) include selections in *Best American Short Stories, The O. Henry Prize Stories,* the *Graywolf Annual*, the *Pushcart Prize* anthology, and two time finalist for the National Magazine Award.

NEEDS experimental, literary, translations. Does not want young adult fiction or genre fiction. "However, we are open to publishing mystery or speculative fiction if we feel it has literary value." Receives 300-400 mss/month. Accepts 5-6 mss/issue; 20-25 mss/year. Manuscript published 3 months after acceptance. Agented fiction 20%. **Publishes 2-3 new writers/year.** Published Joice Carol Oates, Maud Casey, Chris Bachelder, Vendela Vida, Benjamin Percy, Jack Pendarvis, Paul Yoon, and Dagoberto Gilb. Also publishes literary essays, literary criticism. Sometimes comments on/critiques rejected mss.

HOW TO CONTACT Submit complete ms electronically on website. Include estimated word count, brief bio. Responds to queries in 2 weeks. Responds to mss in 4-5 months. Guidelines available for SASE, via e-mail, on website. Regular submissions are open. **"To help defray the administrative costs of this new system, we ask that our submitters pay a submission fee of $2 per story.** Submitters should visit our publisher's online store to pay the submission fee. When the transaction is complete, submitters will be directed to our Submission Manager, where they can upload their stories. Our **Submission Manager requires that uploaded files be less than 500 KB**. Send complete ms."

PAYMENT/TERMS Writers receive $250-500, 2 contributor's copies, free subscription to the magazine. Additional copies $5. Pays on publication. Acquires first North American serial rights, electronic rights. Sends galleys to author. Publication is copyrighted. Sponsors Short Story Contest. See separate listing or website.

TIPS "We publish fiction that speaks to us emotionally, uses evocative and precise language, and takes risks in subject matter and/or form. Try to read an issue or two of *American Short Fiction* to get a sense of what we like. Also, to be concise is a great virtue."

AMOSKEAG, THE JOURNAL OF SOUTHERN NEW HAMPSHIRE UNIVERSITY

2500 N. River Rd., Manchester NH 03106. E-mail: m.brien@snhu.edu. Website: www.amoskeagjournal.com. **Contact:** Michael J. Brien, editor. Estab. 1983; literary journal since 2005. Magazine has revolving editor and occasional themes (see website). Editorial term: 3 yrs. Literary magazine/journal. 6×9, 105-130 pages. Contains photographs. "We select fiction, creative nonfiction and poetry that appeals to general readers, writers, and academics alike. We accept work from writers nationwide, but also try to include New England writers. We tend not to accept much experimental work, but the language of poetry or prose must nevertheless be dense, careful and surprising." Annual.

NEEDS Ethnic/multicultural (general), experimental, feminist, gay, humor/satire, literary. Does not want genre fiction. Receives 200 mss/month. Accepts 10 prose mss and 20-25 poems/issue. Does not read December-July. Reading period is Aug-Dec. Ms published in late April. Published Ann Hood, Donald Hall, Craig Childs, Diane Les Becquets, Maxine Kumin, Jonathan Blake, Philip Dacey, Charles Harper Webb. Fiction and Creative Nonfiction. Publishes short shorts. Also publishes poetry. Sometimes comments on/critiques rejected mss.

HOW TO CONTACT Send complete ms with cover letter. Include brief bio, list of publications. Responds to queries in 1 month. Responds to mss in 4-5 months. Send either SASE (or IRC) for return of ms or disposable copy of ms and #10 SASE or e-mail address for reply only. Considers simultaneous submissions, multiple submissions. Sample copy available for $6. Guidelines on website.

PAYMENT/TERMS Writers aren't paid, but receive 2 contributor's copies. Additional copies $7. Acquires onetime rights. Publication is copyrighted.

TIPS "We're looking for quality and pizzazz. Stories need good pacing, believable characters and dialogue, as well as unusual subjects to stand out. Most stories we get are 'domestic fiction;' middle-class family dramas. Read the news, live an exciting life. Write about remarkable people."

◐ APALACHEE REVIEW

Apalachee Press, P.O. Box 10469, Tallahassee FL 32302. (850)644-9114. E-mail: arsubmissions@hotmail.com (for queries outside of the U.S.). Website: http://apalacheereview.org/index.html. **Contact:** Michael Trammell, editor; Mary Jane Ryals, fiction editor. Estab. 1976. Literary magazine/journal: trade paperback size, 100-140 pages. Includes photographs. "At *Apalachee Review*, we are interested in outstanding literary fiction, but we especially like poetry, fiction, and nonfiction that addresses intercultural issues in a domestic or international setting/context." Annual. Circ. 500. Member CLMP.

NEEDS ethnic/multicultural, edgy, experimental, fantasy/sci-fi (with a literary bent), feminist, historical, humor/satire, literary, mainstream, mystery/suspense, New Age with a literary bent, translations. Does not want cliché-filled genre-oriented fiction. Receives 60-100 mss/month. Accepts 5-10 mss/issue. Manuscript published 1 yr after acceptance. Agented fiction 0.5%. **Publishes 1-2 new writers/year.** Recently published Lu Vickers, Joe Clark, Joe Taylor, Jane Arrowsmith Edwards, Vivian Lawry, Linda Frysh, Charles Harper Webb, Reno Raymond Gwaltney. Length: 600 words (min)-5,500 words (max). Average length: 3,500 words. Publishes short shorts. Average length of short shorts: 250 words. Also publishes literary essays, book reviews, poetry. Send review copies to Michael Trammell, editor. Sometimes comments on/critiques rejected mss.

HOW TO CONTACT Send complete ms with cover letter. Include brief bio, list of publications. Responds to queries in 4-6 weeks. Responds to mss in 3-14 months. Send either SASE (international authors should see website for "international" guidelines, no IRCs, please) for return of ms or disposable copy of ms and #10 SASE for reply only. Considers simultaneous submissions. Sample copy available for $8 (current issue), $5 (back issue). Guidelines available for SASE, or check the website.

PAYMENT/TERMS Writers receive 2 contributors copies. Additional copies $5/each. Pays on publication. Acquires onetime rights, electronic rights. Publication is copyrighted.

◐ APPALACHIAN HERITAGE

CPO 2166, Berea KY 40404. (859)985-3699. Fax: (859)985-3903. E-mail: george_brosi@berea.edu; appalachianheritage@berea.edu. Website: http://community.berea.edu/appalachianheritage. **Contact:** George Brosi. Estab. 1973. Magazine: 6×9; 104 pages; 60 lb. stock; 10 pt. Warrenflo cover; drawings; b&w photos. "*Appalachian Heritage* is a Southern Appalachian literary magazine. We try to keep a balance of fiction, poetry, essays, scholarly works, etc., for a general audience and/or those interested in the Appalachian mountains." Quarterly.

NEEDS historical, literary, regional. "We do not want to see fiction that has no ties to Southern Appalachia." Receives 60-80 unsolicited mss/month. Accepts 2-3 mss/issue; 12-15 mss/year. Publishes ms 3-6 months after acceptance. **Publishes 8 new writers/year.** Recently published work by Wendell Berry, Sharyn Mcrumb, Jayne Anne Phillips, Silas House, Ron Rash, and Jim Wayne Miller. Publishes short shorts. Occasionally comments on rejected mss.

HOW TO CONTACT Send complete ms. Send SASE for reply, return of ms or send a disposable copy of ms. Responds in 1 month to queries; 6 weeks to mss. Sample copy for $8. Writer's guidelines online.

PAYMENT/TERMS Pays 3 contributor's copies; $8 charge for extras. Acquires first North American serial rights.

TIPS "Get acquainted with *Appalachian Heritage*, as you should with any publication before submitting your work."

APPARATUS MAGAZINE

2013 W. Farragut Ave., Unit #2, Chicago IL 60625. E-mail: submissions@apparatusmagazine.com; editor@apparatusmagazine.com. Website: www.apparatusmagazine.com. **Contact:** Adam W. Hart, publisher/editor. Estab. 2009. Accepts adventure, ethnic, experimental, fantasy, horror, humorous, mystery, science fiction, suspense, gay, lesbian, feminist, psychic/supernatural, regional, literary, mainstream. "No overtly inspirational fiction, fiction aimed at children, or confessional fiction. Avoid work that is overly sexist, racist, violent, homophobic, discriminatory, pornographic, or otherwise in questionable taste. Each issue has a specific theme. Work submitted can address the themes, or not. General work will also be accepted. Themes are listed in the writer's guidelines, available online or via e-mail at guidelines@apparatusmagazine.com." Acquires first rights, first North American serial rights, electronic rights, including the right to archive work online, option for possible inclusion in print anthology with writer's permission. Publication is copyrighted.

Online monthly magazine which "strives to bring readers poetry and fiction from around the world that explores the mythos of 'man (or woman) vs. machine,' that conjures up words from the inner machine, and more." Each issue of apparatus magazine features work from around the world, bringing the reader literary updates from the internal machine. Fiction consists of short fiction/flash fiction (500 words or less), and each issue of the magazine has a specific theme.

HOW TO CONTACT Send complete ms with a cover letter including estimated word count, brief bio, list of publications to submissions@apparatusmagazine.com. Accepts submissions by e-mail. Label subject line with "fiction submission." Responds in 2-3 months. Accepts multiple submissions; no simultaneous or previously published submissions. Sample copy on website.

TIPS "Be sure to read the guidelines as posted. Themes for each issue are typically posted 3 months (or more) in advance. Include cover letter and bio with e-mail submissions. Submit more than just one poem, so I can get a feel for your work. Be sure to read back issues of the magazine. The journal tends to select work that focuses on specific themes, and usually tries to pick work that will compliment/contrast with other pieces selected for the issue. Send your best work and don't be afraid of trying again. I often suggest other publications/markets if a piece is not a good match for the journal."

ARTFUL DODGE

College of Wooster, Department of English, Wooster OH 44691. (330)263-2577. E-mail: artfuldodge@wooster.edu. Website: www.wooster.edu/artfuldodge. **Contact:** Daniel Bourne, editor; Marcy Campbell, associate fiction editor. Magazine: 180 pages; illustrations; photos. "There is no theme in this magazine, except literary power. We also have an ongoing interest in translations from Central/Eastern Europe and elsewhere." Annual. Circ. 1,000.

NEEDS Experimental, literary, translations, prose poem. "We judge by literary quality, not by genre. We are especially interested in fine English translations of significant prose writers. Translations should be submitted with original texts." Receives 50 unsolicited mss/month. Accepts 5 mss/year. **Publishes 1 new writer/year.** Recently published work by Nin Andres, Vénus Khoury-Ghata, Eva Marie Ginsburg, Philip Metres, and Daniel Tobin. Average length: 2,500 words. Also publishes literary essays, literary criticism, poetry. Occasionally comments on rejected mss.

HOW TO CONTACT Send complete ms with SASE. Do not send more than 30 pages at a time. Responds in 1 year to mss. Accepts simultaneous submissions if contacted immediately after being accepted elsewhere. Sample copy/1-year subscription for $7; 2-year subscriptions are $14. Writer's guidelines for #10 SASE.

PAYMENT/TERMS Pays 2 contributor's copies and honorarium of $5/page, "thanks to funding from the Ohio Arts Council." Acquires first North American serial rights.

TIPS "If we take time to offer criticism, do not subsequently flood us with other stories no better than the first. If starting out, get as many *good* readers as possible. Above all, read contemporary fiction and the magazine you are trying to publish in."

ARTS & LETTERS

Georgia College & State University, Campus Box 89, Milledgeville GA 31061. (478)445-1289. E-mail: al.journal@gcsu.edu. Website: http://al.gcsu.edu. Estab. 1999. **Contact:** Martin Lammon, editor. Literary magazine: 7×10; 200 pages; 60 lb.; some photos. "The journal features the mentors interview series, the world poetry translation series, and color reproductions of original artistic prints. Also, it is the only journal nationwide to feature authors and artists that represent such an eclectic range of creative work." Semiannual. Estab. 1999. Circ. 1,500.

NEEDS Literary. No genre fiction. Receives 50 unsolicited mss/month. Accepts 5 mss/issue; 10 mss/year. Reads mss September 1-April 1. Publishes ms 6-12 months after acceptance. **Publishes 1-2 new writers/year.** Recently published work by Bret Lott, Heather Sellers, Edith Pearlman, and Austin Ratner. Length: 3,000-7,500 words; average length: 6,000 words. Sometimes comments on rejected mss.

HOW TO CONTACT Send complete ms with cover letter. Include estimated word count, brief bio and list of publications. Send disposable copy of ms and #10 SASE for reply only. Responds in 4-8 weeks to mss. Sample copy for $5, plus $1 for postage. Writer's guidelines online.

PAYMENT/TERMS Pays $10 minimum or $50/published page. Pays on publication. Rights revert to author after publication. Sends galleys to author.

TIPS "An obvious, but not gimmicky, attention to and fresh usage of language. A solid grasp of the craft of story writing. Fully realized work."

BARBARIC YAWP

BoneWorld Publishing, 3700 County Rt. 24, Russell NY 13684-3198. Website: www.boneworldpublishing.com. (315)347-2609. **Contact:** Nancy Berbrich, fiction editor. Estab. 1997. Magazine: digest-size; 60 pages; 24 lb. paper; matte cover stock. "We publish what we like. Fiction should include some bounce and surprise. Our publication is intended for the intelligent, open-minded reader." Quarterly. Estab. 1997. Circ. 120.

NEEDS Adventure, experimental, fantasy (science, sword and sorcery), historical, horror, literary, mainstream, psychic/supernatural/occult, regional, religious/inspirational, science fiction (hard, soft/sociological). "We don't want any pornography, gratuitous violence or whining." Wants more suspense and philosophical work. Receives 30-40 unsolicited mss/month. Accepts 10-12 mss/issue; 40-48 mss/year. Publishes ms up to 6 months after acceptance. **Publishes 4-6 new writers/year.** Recently published work by Francine Witte, Jeff Grimshaw, Thaddeus Rutkowski and Holly Interlandi. Length: 1,500 words; average length: 600 words. Publishes short shorts. Also publishes literary essays, literary criticism, poetry. Often comments on rejected mss.

HOW TO CONTACT Send SASE for reply, return of ms or send a disposable copy of ms. Responds in 2 weeks to queries; 4 months to mss. Accepts simultaneous, multiple submissions and reprints. Sample copy for $4. Writer's guidelines for #10 SASE.

PAYMENT/TERMS Pays 1 contributor's copy; additional copies $3. Acquires onetime rights.

TIPS "Don't give up. Read much, write much, submit much. Observe closely the world around you. Don't borrow ideas from TV or films. Revision is often necessary—grit your teeth and do it. Never fear rejection."

BELLEVUE LITERARY REVIEW

NYU Langone Medical Center, Department of Medicine, 550 First Ave., OBV-A612, New York NY 10016. (212)263-3973. E-mail: info@BLReview.org. E-mail: stacy.bodziak@nyumc.org. Website: www.blreview.org. **Contact:** Stacy Bodziak, managing editor. Estab. 2001. A Journal of Humanity and Human Experience. Magazine: 6×9; 160 pages. "The *BLR* is a literary journal that examines human existence through the prism of health and healing, illness and disease. We encourage creative interpretations of these themes." Semiannual. Member CLMP.Literary. No genre fiction. Publishes ms 3-6 months after acceptance. Agented fiction 1%. **Publishes 3-6 new writers/year.** Recently published work by Amy Hempel, Sheila Kohler, Martha Cooley. Sample copy for $7. Writer's guidelines for SASE, e-mail or on website.

Work published in *Bellevue Literary Review* has appeared in *The Pushcart Prize*.

NEEDS Publishes short shorts. Also publishes literary essays, poetry. Sometimes comments on rejected mss

HOW TO CONTACT Submit online at www.blreview.org (preferred). Also accepts mss via regular mail. Send complete ms. Send SASE (or IRC) for return of ms or disposable copy of the ms and #10 SASE for reply only. Responds in 3-6 months to mss. Accepts simultaneous submissions.

PAYMENT/TERMS Pays 2 contributor's copies, 1-year subscription and 1 year gift subscription; additional copies $6. Pays on publication for first North American serial rights. Sends galleys to author.

BELLOWING ARK

P.O. Box 55564, Shoreline WA 98155. E-mail: bellowingark@bellowingark.org. Website: www.bellowingark.org. **Contact:** Robert R. Ward, editor. Estab. 1984. Tabloid: $11\frac{1}{2}\times17\frac{1}{2}$; 32 pages; electro-brite paper and cover stock; illustrations; photos. "We publish material we feel addresses the human situation in an affirmative way. We do not publish academic fiction." Bimonthly. Circ. 650.

Work from *Bellowing Ark* appeared in the *Pushcart Prize* anthology. Work from *Bellowing Ark* appeared in the *Pushcart Prize* anthology.

NEEDS literary, mainstream, serialized novels. "No science fiction or fantasy." Receives 30-70 unsolicited mss/month. Accepts 2-5 mss/issue; 700-1,000 mss/year. Publishes ms 6 months after acceptance. **Publishes 6-10 new writers/year**. Recently published work by Tom Cook, Tanyo Ravicz, Jan Johnson, Jane Lawless, and E.R. Romaine. Also publishes literary essays, literary criticism, poetry. Sometimes comments on rejected mss.

HOW TO CONTACT Send complete ms and SASE. Responds in 6 weeks to mss. No simultaneous submissions. Sample copy for $4, 9½×12½ SAE and $1.43 postage.

PAYMENT/TERMS Pays in contributor's copies. Acquires onetime rights.

TIPS "*Bellowing Ark* began as (and remains) an alternative to the despair and negativity of the workshop/academic literary scene; we believe that life has meaning and is worth living—the work we publish reflects that belief. Learn how to tell a story before submitting. Avoid 'trick' endings; they have all been done before and better. *Bellowing Ark* is interested in publishing writers who will develop with the magazine, as in an extended community. We find good writers and stick with them. This is why the magazine has grown from 12 to 32 pages."

BELOIT FICTION JOURNAL

Box 11, Beloit, 700 College St., Beloit WI 53511. (608)363-2079. E-mail: bfj@beloit.edu. Website: www.beloit.edu/english/fictionjournal/. **Contact:** Chris Fink, editor-in-chief. Estab. 1985. Literary magazine: 6×9; 250 pages; 60 lb. paper; 10 pt. C1S cover stock; illustrations; photos on cover; ad-free. "We are interested in publishing the best contemporary fiction and are open to all themes except those involving pornographic, religiously dogmatic or politically propagandistic representations. Our magazine is for general readership, though most of our readers will probably have a specific interest in literary magazines." Annual.

Work first appearing in *Beloit Fiction Journal* has been reprinted in award-winning collections, including the Flannery O'Connor and the Milkweed Fiction Prize collections, and has won the Iowa Short Fiction award.

NEEDS Literary, mainstream, contemporary. Wants more experimental and short shorts. Would like to see more "stories with a focus on both language and plot, unusual metaphors and vivid characters. No pornography, religious dogma, science fiction, horror, political propaganda or genre fiction." Receives 200 unsolicited mss/month. Accepts 20 mss/year. Publishes ms 9 months after acceptance. **Publishes 3 new writers/year.** Recently published work by Dennis Lehane, Silas House and David Harris Ebenbach. Length: 250-10,000 words; average length: 5,000 words. Sometimes comments on rejected mss.

HOW TO CONTACT "Our reading period is from August 1-December 1 only. " No fax, e-mail, or disk submissions. Responds in 2 weeks to queries; 2 months to mss. Accepts simultaneous submissions if identified as such. Please send one story at a time. Always include SASE. Sample copy for $ 10 (new issue), $8 (back issue, double issue), $ 6 (back issue, single issue). Writer's guidelines for #10 SASE or on website.

PAYMENT/TERMS Buys first North American serial rights only. Payment in copies.

TIPS "Many of our contributors are writers whose work we had previously rejected. Don't let one rejection slip turn you away from our—or any—magazine."

BERKELEY FICTION REVIEW

10B Eshleman Hall, University of California, Berkeley CA 94720. (510)642-2892. E-mail: bfictionreview@yahoo.com. Website: www.ocf.berkeley.edu/~bfr. **Contact:** Caitlin McGuire, editor. Estab. 1981. Magazine: 5½×8½; 180 pages; perfect-bound; glossy cover; some b&w art; photographs. "The mission of Berkeley Fiction Review is to provide a forum for new and emerging writers as well as writers already established. We publish a wide variety of contemporary short fiction for a literary audience." Annual. Circ. 1,000.

NEEDS Experimental, literary, mainstream. "Quality, inventive short fiction. No poetry or formula fiction." Receives 100 unsolicited mss/month. Accepts 10-15 mss/issue. **Publishes 10-15 new writers/year.** Publishes short shorts. Occacionally comments on rejected mss.

HOW TO CONTACT Responds in 2-4 months to mss. Accepts simultaneous, multiple submissions. Sample copy for $10. Writer's guidelines for SASE and online. Accepts e-mail submissions in PDF or Word attachments.

PAYMENT/TERMS Pays one contributor's copy. Acquires first rights. Sponsors awards/contests.

TIPS "Our criteria is fiction that resonates. Voices that are strong and move a reader. Clear, powerful prose (either voice or rendering of subject) with a point. Unique ways of telling stories—these capture the editors. Work hard, don't give up. Ask an honest person to point out your writing weaknesses, and then work on them. We look forward to reading fresh new voices."

BIG MUDDY: A JOURNAL OF THE MISSISSIPPI RIVER VALLEY

MS2650 English Dept., Southeast MO State Universit, Cape Girardeau MO 63701. Website: www6.semo.edu/universitypress/bigmuddy. **Contact:** Susan Swartwout, publisher/editor. Estab. 2001. Magazine: $8^1{}_2 \times 5^1{}_2$ perfect-bound; 150 pages; acid-free paper; color cover stock; layflat lamination; illustrations; photos. "*Big Muddy* explores multidisciplinary, multicultural issues, people, and events mainly concerning, but not limited to, the 10-state area that borders the Mississippi River. We publish fiction, poetry, historical essays, creative nonfiction, environmental essays, biography, regional events, photography, art, etc." Semiannual. Circ. 500.

NEEDS Adventure, ethnic/multicultural, experimental, family saga, feminist, historical, humor/satire, literary, mainstream, military/war, fiction, nonfiction, poetry, mystery/suspense, regional (Mississippi River Valley; Midwest), translations. "No romance, fantasy or children's." Receives 50 unsolicited mss/month. Accepts 20-25 mss/issue. Publishes ms 6-12 months after acceptance.

HOW TO CONTACT Send SASE for return of ms or send a disposable copy of ms and #10 SASE for reply only. Responds in 12 weeks to mss. Accepts multiple submissions. Sample copy for $6. Writer's guidelines for SASE, e-mail, fax or on website. Reviews fiction, poetry, nonfiction.

PAYMENT/TERMS Pays 2 contributor's copies; additional copies $5. Acquires first North American serial rights.

TIPS "We look for clear language, avoidance of clichés except in necessary dialogue, a fresh vision of the theme or issue. Find some excellent and honest readers to comment on your work-in-progress and final draft. Consider their viewpoints carefully. Revise if needed."

BLACK WARRIOR REVIEW

P.O. Box 862936, Tuscaloosa AL 35486. (205)348-4518. E-mail: bwr@ua.edu; blackwarriorreview@gmail.com. Website: www.bwr.ua.edu. **Contact:** Jenny Gropp Hess, editor. Estab. 1974. Magazine: 6×9; 160 pages; color artwork. "We publish contemporary fiction, poetry, reviews, essays and art for a literary audience. We publish the freshest work we can find." Semiannual. Circ. 2,000.

Work that appeared in the *Black Warrior Review* has been included in the *Pushcart Prize* anthology, *Harper's Magazine, Best American Short Stories, Best American Poetry* and *New Stories from the South.*

NEEDS literary, contemporary, short and short-short fiction. Wants "work that is conscious of form and well crafted. We are open to good experimental writing and short-short fiction. No genre fiction, please." Receives 300 unsolicited mss/month. Accepts 5 mss/issue; 10 mss/year. Unsolicited novel excerpts are not considered unless the novel is already contracted for publication. Publishes ms 6 months after acceptance. **Publishes 5 new writers/year.** Recently published work by Lily Hoang, Brian Evenson, Peter Markus, Aimee Bender, Lance Olson, Laird Hunt, Pamela Ryder, Michael C. Boyko, James Grinwis. Length: 7,500 words; average length: 2,000-5,000 words. Occasionally comments on rejected mss.

HOW TO CONTACT Now takes online submissions exclusively. Responds in 4 months to mss. Accepts simultaneous submissions if noted. Sample copy for $10. Writer's guidelines online.

PAYMENT/TERMS Pays up to $100, copies, and a 1-year subscription. Pays on publication for first rights.

TIPS "We look for attention to language, freshness, honesty, a convincing and sharp voice. Send us a clean, well-printed, proofread manuscript. Become familiar with the magazine prior to submission."

BLUELINE

120 Morey Hall, Dept. of English and Communication, Postdam NY 13676. (315)267-2043. E-mail: blueline@potsdam.edu. Website: www2.potsdam.edu/blueline. **Contact:** Donald McNutt, editor. Estab. 1979. Magazine: 6×9; 200 pages; 70 lb. white stock paper; 65 lb. smooth cover stock; illustrations; photos. "*Blueline* is interested in quality writing about the Adirondacks or other places similar in geography and spirit. We pub-

lish fiction, poetry, personal essays, book reviews and oral history for those interested in Adirondacks, nature in general, and well-crafted writing." Annual.

PROOFREAD ALL SUBMISSIONS. It is difficult for our editors to get excited about work containing typographical and syntactic errors.

NEEDS Adventure, humor/satire, literary, regional, contemporary, prose poem, reminiscences, oral history, nature/outdoors. We also welcome short essays or creative nonfiction that interpret the literature or culture of the region, including New York State, New England, and eastern Canada. No urban stories or erotica. Receives 8-10 unsolicited mss/month. Accepts 6-8 mss/issue. Does not read January-August. Publishes ms 3-6 months after acceptance. **Publishes 2 new writers/year.** Recently published work by Joan Connor, Laura Rodley and Ann Mohin. Length: 500-3,000 words; average length: 2,500 words. Also publishes literary essays, poetry. Occasionally comments on rejected mss.

HOW TO CONTACT Accepts simultaneous submissions. Sample copy for $7.

PAYMENT/TERMS Pays 1 contributor's copy; charges $7 each for 3 or more copies. Acquires first rights.

TIPS "We look for concise, clear, concrete prose that tells a story and touches upon a universal theme or situation. We prefer realism to romanticism but will consider nostalgia if well done. Pay attention to grammar and syntax. Avoid murky language, sentimentality, cuteness or folkiness. We would like to see more good fiction related to the Adirondacks and more literary fiction and prose poems. If manuscript has potential, we work with author to improve and reconsider for publication. Our readers prefer fiction to poetry (in general) or reviews. Write from your own experience, be specific and factual (within the bounds of your story) and if you write about universal features such as love, death, change, etc., write about them in a fresh way. Triteness and mediocrity are the hallmarks of the majority of stories seen today."

BLUESTEM

English Dept., Eastern Illinois University, Website: bluestem.submishmash.com. **Contact:** Olga Abella, editor. Estab. 1966. "*Bluestem*, formerly known as *Karamu*, produces a quarterly online issue (December, March, June, September) and an annual print issue. Please submit no more than 5 poems at one time, or one short story, or one creative nonfiction essay, or 5 black & white drawings. Fiction / prose / essays should be no longer than 5,000 words. Query for writing longer than 5,000 words. Please include a brief (no more than 100 words) bio with your submission. All work is considered for both print and online publication. We will not read work for print only. All genres are welcome. We only accept submissions via our online submission manager, which can be accessed at bluestem.submishmash.com. No previously published work is accepted. Simultaneous submissions are fine. If your work is accepted elsewhere, please withdraw your work via the submission manager. Submissions are accepted year-round. Response times will be significantly longer during the summer. Expect a response in 6-8 weeks. The wait will be longer if we are seriously considering your work. Print contributors receive a complimentary copy of the issue containing their work, and may purchase extra copies at a discounted price. There is no compensation for online contributors but we will promote your work enthusiastically and widely. Sample back issues of *Bluestem (KARAMU)* are available for $4 for each issue you would like. The current issue is $8.00. Click here for subscription information. Watch for announcements of future themes or contests in Sept/Oct issue of POETS & WRITERS. Past issues have included themes such as: The Humor Issue, The Music Issue, The Millennium."

BOGG

422 N. Cleveland St., Arlington VA 22201-1424. E-mail: boggmag@aol.com. Estab. 1968. A Journal of Contemporary Writing Bogg Publications. **Contact:** John Elsberg, editor. Magazine: 6×9; 72 pages; 70 lb. white paper; 70 lb. cover stock; line illustrations. "Poetry (to include prose poems, haiku/tanka and experimental forms), experimental short fiction, reviews." Published 2 times a year. Circ. 800.

NEEDS Very short experimental fiction and prose poems. Receives 25 unsolicited prose mss/month. Accepts 4-6 mss/issue. Accepts for either of next two issues. Publishes ms 3-18 months after acceptance. **Publishes 40-80 new writers/year.** Recently published work by Linda Bosson, Ann Menebroker, J. Wesley Clark, Karen Rosenberg, Carla Mayfield, and Elizabeth Bernays. Also occasionally publishes interviews and essays on small press history. Rarely comments on rejected mss.

HOW TO CONTACT Responds in 1 week to queries; 2 weeks to mss. Sample copy for $5 or $8 (current issue). Reviews poetry and fiction. Does not consider e-mail or simultaneous submissions.

PAYMENT/TERMS Pays 2 contributor's copies; reduced charge for extras. Acquires onetime rights.

TIPS "We look for voice and originality. Read magazine first. Bogg is mainly a poetry journal, but we also look for innovative short fiction that works well with the poetry."

BOOK WORLD MAGAZINE

2 Caversham Street, London En SW3 4AH United Kingdom. 0207 351 4995. E-mail: leonard.holdsworth@btopenworld.com. **Contact:** James Hughes. Estab. 1971. Magazine: 64 pages; illustrations; photos. "Subscription magazine for serious book lovers, book collectors, librarians and academics." Monthly. Circ. 6,000.

NEEDS Also publishes literary essays, literary criticism.

HOW TO CONTACT Query. Send IRC (International Reply Coupon) for return of ms. Responds in 3 months to queries; 3 months to mss. Accepts simultaneous submissions. Sample copy for $7.50. Writer's guidelines for IRC.

PAYMENT/TERMS Pays on publication for onetime rights.

TIPS "Always write to us before sending any mss."

THE BRIAR CLIFF REVIEW

3303 Rebecca St., Sioux City IA 51104-0100. (712)279-5477. E-mail: curranst@briarcliff.edu. E-mail: jeanne.emmons@briarcliff.edu (poetry). Website: www.briarcliff.edu/bcreview. **Contact:** Phil Hey or Tricia Currans-Sheehan, fiction editors. Estab. 1989. Magazine: 8½×11; 120 pages; 70 lb. 100# Altima Satin Text; illustrations; photos. "The *Briar Cliff Review* is an eclectic literary and cultural magazine focusing on (but not limited to) Siouxland writers and subjects. We are happy to proclaim ourselves a regional publication. It doesn't diminish us; it enhances us." Annual. Circ. 1,000.

NEEDS ethnic/multicultural, feminist, historical, humor/satire, literary, mainstream, regional. "No romance, horror or alien stories." Accepts 5 mss/year. Reads mss only between August 1 and November 1. Publishes ms 3-4 months after acceptance. **Publishes 10-14 new writers/year.** Recently published work by Siobhan Fallon, Shelley Scaletta, Jenna Blum, Brian Bedard, Rebecca Tuch, Scott H. Andrews, and Josip Novakovich. Length: 2,500-5,000 words; average length: 3,000 words. Also publishes literary essays, literary criticism, poetry. Sometimes comments on rejected mss.

HOW TO CONTACT Send SASE for return of ms. Does not accept electronic submissions (unless from overseas). Responds in 4-5 months to mss. Accepts simultaneous submissions. Sample copy for $15 and 9×12 SAE. Writer's guidelines for #10 SASE. Reviews fiction.

PAYMENT/TERMS Pays 2 contributor's copies; additional copies available for $12. Acquires first rights.

TIPS "So many stories are just telling. We want some action. It has to move. We prefer stories in which there is no gimmick, no mechanical turn of events, no moral except the one we would draw privately."

BRILLANT CORNERS

Lycoming College, Williamsport PA 17701. (570) 321-4279. Fax: (570) 321-4090. E-mail: feinstein@lycoming.edu. **Contact**: Sascha Feinstein, editor. Estab. 1996. Journal: 6×9; 90 pages; 70 lb. Cougar opaque, vellum, natural paper; photographs. "We publish jazz-related literature—fiction, poetry and nonfiction." Semiannual. Estab. 1996. Circ. 1,200.

NEEDS Condensed novels, ethnic/multicultural, experimental, literary, mainstream, romance (contemporary). Receives 10-15 unsolicited mss/month. Accepts 1-2 mss/issue; 2-3 mss/year. Does not read mss May 15-September 1. Publishes ms 4-12 months after acceptance. Publishes short shorts. Also publishes literary essays, literary criticism, poetry. Rarely comments on rejected mss.

HOW TO CONTACT SASE for return of ms or send a disposable copy of ms. Accepts unpublished work only. Responds in 2 weeks to queries; 1-2 months to mss. Sample copy for $7. Reviews fiction.

PAYMENT/TERMS Acquires first North American serial rights. Sends galleys to author when possible.

TIPS "We look for clear, moving prose that demostrates a love of both writing and jazz. We primarily publish established writers, but we read all submissions carefully and welcome work by outstanding young writers."

THE BROADKILL REVIEW

Broadkill Publishing Associates c/o John Milton & Company, 104 Federal St., Milton DE 19968. E-mail: the_broadkill_review@earthlink.net. Website: www.thebroadkillreview.blogspot.com. **Contact:** Jamie Brown, editor. Estab. 2005. PDF Literary magazine/journal. Bimonthly. Contains illustrations, photographs. "Quality is the most important factor. Your stories and poems should not rely on the unusual circumstance in place of actually having work which is finely crafted, insightful of the human condition, or which manages to make the reader continue to think about it after they have finished reading it. We are fans of John Gardner's *On Becoming a Novelist*, and firmly believe in establishing 'the waking dream' as the responsibility of the author." Member CLMP, Delaware Press Assn. Does not want anything gratuitous; no theme issues. Receives 8-20 mss/month. Accepts 1-4 mss/issue; 16-20 mss/year. Manuscript published 1-3 months after acceptance. **Publishes 30 new writers/year.** Published Thom Wade Myers, Chad Clifton, Tina Hession, Joshua D. Isard, Maryanne Khan, Richard Myers Peabody, H. A. Maxson, Bob Yearick, Gaylene Carbis, Louise D'Arcy, and Andee Jones. Length: 6,000 words (max). Average length: 3,300 words. Publishes short shorts. Also publishes literary essays, literary criticism, book reviews, poetry. Send two review copies to Editor, The Broadkill Review, 104 Federal Street, Milton, DE 19968.

"*The Broadkill Review* accepts the best fiction, poetry and nonfiction by new and established writers. We have published Pushcart nominated fiction and poetry."

HOW TO CONTACT Send complete ms with cover letter—preferably by e-mail. Include estimated word count, brief bio, list of publications. Responds to queries in 1 week. Responds to mss in 4-26 weeks. Send either SASE (or IRC) for return of ms or disposable copy of ms and #10 SASE for reply only. Considers simultaneous submissions, multiple submissions. Sample copy delivered electronically free upon request. Guidelines available via e-mail.

PAYMENT/TERMS Sometimes comments on/critiques rejected mss, if requested by the author. Writers receive contributor's copy. Pays on publication. Acquires first rights. Publication is copyrighted.

TIPS "Query the editor first. Visit our website to familiarize yourself with the type of material we publish. Request and read copy of magazine first!"

CAIRN: THE ST. ANDREWS REVIEW

1700 Dogwood Mile, Laurinburg NC 28352. (910)277-5310. Fax: (910)277-5020. E-mail: pressemail@sapc.edu. Website: www.sapc.edu/sapress.html. Estab. 1969. Magazine: 50-60 lb. paper. "*CAIRN* is a non-profit, national/international literary magazine which publishes established as well as emerging writers." Member CLMP and AWP.

NEEDS Poetry, essays, literary, short stories and short-short fiction. "We're looking for original, well-crafted work with style and insight." **Publishes 10-15 new writers/year.**

HOW TO CONTACT Send a recyclable copy of ms. by postal mail. Include SASE for reply only. Submissions are accepted September through December only. Accepts simultaneous submissions with notice. Responds in 3-4 months.

PAYMENT/TERMS Pays 2 contributor copy.

CALLALOO

TAMU 4212, Texas A&M University, College Station TX 77843-4227. (979)458-3108. Fax: (979)458-3275. E-mail: callaloo@tamu.edu. Website: http://callaloo.tamu.edu. Estab. 1976. **Contact:** Charles H. Rowell, editor. Magazine: 7X10; 300 pages. "Devoted to publishing fiction, poetry, drama of the African diaspora, including North, Central and South America, the Caribbean, Europe and Africa. Visually beautiful and well-edited, the journal publishes 3-5 short stories in all forms and styles in each issue." Quarterly. Estab. 1976. Circ. 2,000.

One of the leading voices in African-American literature, Callaloo has received NEA literature grants. Several pieces every year are chosen for collections of the year's best stories, such as Beacon's Best John Wideman's "Weight" from Callaloo won the 2000 O. Henry Award.

NEEDS Ethnic/multicultural (black culture), feminist, historical, humor/satire, literary, regional, science fiction, serialized novels, translations, contemporary, prose poem. "No romance, confessional. Would like to see more experimental fiction, science fiction and well-crafted literary fiction particularly dealing with the black middle class, immigrant communities and/or the black South." Accepts 3-5 mss/issue; 10-20 mss/year. **Publishes 5-10 new writers/year.** Recently published work by Charles Johnson, Edwidge Danticat, Thomas Glave, Nallo Hopkinson, John Edgar Wideman, Jamaica Kincaid, Percival Everett and Patricia Powell. Also publishes poetry.

HOW TO CONTACT Generally accepts unpublished work, rarely accepts reprints. Responds in 2 weeks to queries; 6 months to mss. Accepts multiple submissions. Sample copy for $15. Writer's guidelines online.

PAYMENT/TERMS Pays in contributor's copies. Acquires some rights. Sends galleys to author do not send galley copies.

TIPS "We look for freshness of both writing and plot, strength of characterization, plausibilty of plot. Read what's being written and published, especially in journals such as *Callaloo*."

○ CC&D, CHILDREN, CHURCHES & DADDIES MAGAZINE: THE UNRELIGIOUS, NONFAMILY-ORIENTED LITERARY AND ART MAGAZINE

Scars Publications and Design, 829 Brian Court, Gurnee IL 60031-3155. (847)281-9070. E-mail: ccandd96@scars.tv. Website: scars.tv. **Contact:** Janet Kuypers. Estab. 1993. Literary magazine/journal: 5.5x8.5 perfect-bound, 84-page book. Contains illustrations & photographs as well as short stories, essays, and poetry. Monthly.

NEEDS "Our biases are works that relate to issues such as politics, sexism, society, and the like, but are definitely not limited to such. We publish good work that makes you think, that makes you feel like you've lived through a scene instead of merely reading it. If it relates to how the world fits into a person's life (political story, a day in the life, coping with issues people face), it will probably win us over faster. We have received comments from readers and other editors saying that they thought some of our stories really happened. They didn't, but it was nice to know they were so concrete, so believable people thought they were nonfiction. Do that to our readers." Interested in many topics including adventure, ethnic/multicultural, experimental, feminist, gay, historical, lesbian, literary, mystery/suspense, new age, psychic/supernatural/occult, science fiction. Does not want religious or rhyming or family-oriented material. Manuscript published 1 yr after acceptance. Published Mel Waldman, Kenneth DiMaggio, Pat Dixon, Robert William Meyers, Troy Davis, G.A. Scheinoha, Ken Dean. Average length: 1,000 words. "Contact us if you are interested in submitting very long stories, or parts of a novel (if you are accepted, it would appear in parts in multiple issues)." Publishes short shorts, essays and stories. Also publishes poetry. Always comments on/critiques rejected mss if asked.

HOW TO CONTACT Send complete ms with cover letter or query with clips of published work. Prefers submissions by e-mail. "If you have email and send us a snail-mail submission, we will accept writing only if you email it to us." Responds to queries in 2 weeks; mss in 2 weeks. "Responds much faster to e-mail submissions and queries." Send either SASE (or IRC) for return of ms or disposable copy of ms and #10 SASE for reply only, but if you have e-mail PLEASE send us an electronic submission instead. (If we accept your writing, we'll only ask for you to e-mail it to us anyway.) Considers simultaneous submissions, previously published submissions, multiple submissions. Sample copy available of issues before 2010 for $6. Guidelines available for SASE, via e-mail, on website. Reviews fiction, essays, journals, editorials, short fiction.

◐ CENTER

202 Tate Hall, University of Missouri-Columbia, Columbia MO 65211-1500. (573)884-7773. E-mail: cla@missouri.edu. Website: center.missouri.edu. **Contact:** Managing editor. Estab. 2000. Magazine: 6×9; 150-250 pages; perfect bound, with 4-color card cover. "*Center* publishes poetry, fiction, creative nonfiction, and occasionally, translations. We publish work from a broad range of aesthetic categories and privilege work that is deliberately crafted, engaging, and accessible." Annual. Circ. 500.

NEEDS Ethnic/multicultural, experimental, humor/satire, literary. Receives 40-60 unsolicited mss/month. Accepts 2-4 mss/year. Reads mss from July 1-December 1 only. Publishes ms 6 months after acceptance. **Publishes 35% new writers/year.** Recently published work by Kim Chinquee, William Eisner, and April Ayers Lawson. Publishes short shorts. Also publishes literary essays, poetry. Sometimes comments on rejected mss. **Send submissions July 1-December 1.**

HOW TO CONTACT Send SASE (or IRC) for return of ms or send a disposable copy of ms and #10 SASE for reply only. Responds in 1 month to queries; 3-4 months to mss. Accepts simultaneous, multiple submissions. Sample copy for $3.50, current copy $7. Writer's guidelines online.

PAYMENT/TERMS Pays 2 contributor's copies; additional copies $3.50. Pays on publication for one-time rights.

CHA

Hong Kong E-mail: editors@asiancha.com; j@asiancha.com. E-mail: submissions@asiancha.com. Website: www.asiancha.com. **Contact:** Eddie Tay, reviews editor. Estab. 2007. (Specialized: Asian) **Contact:** Tammy Ho Lai-ming and Jeff Zroback, editors. Online magazine. "*Cha* is the first and currently the only Hong Kong-based online literary quarterly journal dedicated to publishing creative works from and about Asia, primarily in English."

"Please read the guidelines on our website carefully before you submit work to us."

NEEDS creative works from and about Asia, primarily in English. List of upcoming themes available on website. Length: 100 words (min)-3,000 words (max). Publishes short shorts. Also publishes poetry.
HOW TO CONTACT Accepts submissions by e-mail at submissions@asiancha.com. Responds to queries in 3 months. Considers simultaneous submissions. Guidelines available on website.
PAYMENT/TERMS Cannot pay contributors.
TIPS "Do not send attachments in your e-mail. Include all writing in the body of -email. Include a brief biography (100 words)."

CHAFFIN JOURNAL

English Department, Eastern Kentucky University, C, Richmond KY 40475-3102. (859)622-3080. E-mail: robert.witt@eku.edu. Website: www.english.edu/chaffin_journal. **Contact:** Robert Witt, editor. Estab. 1998. Magazine: 8×5½; 120-130 pages; 70 lb. paper; 80 lb. cover. "We publish fiction on any subject; our only consideration is the quality." Annual. Circ. 150.
NEEDS Ethnic/multicultural, historical, humor/satire, literary, mainstream, regional (Appalachia). "No erotica, fantasy." Receives 20 unsolicited mss/month. Accepts 6-8 mss/year. Does not read mss October 1 through May 31. Publishes ms 6 months after acceptance. **Publishes 2-3 new writers/year.** Recently published work by Meridith Sue Willis, Marie Manilla, Raymond Abbott, Marjorie Bixler, Chris Helvey. Length: 10,000 words per submission period; average length: 5,000 words.
HOW TO CONTACT Send SASE for return of ms. Responds in 1 week to queries; 3 months to mss. Accepts simultaneous, multiple submissions. Sample copy for $6.
PAYMENT/TERMS Pays 1 contributor's copy; additional copies $6. Pays on publication for onetime rights.
TIPS "All manuscripts submitted are considered."

CHICAGO QUARTERLY REVIEW

517 Sherman Ave., Evanston IL 60202. Website: www.chicagoquarterlyreview.com. **Contact:** Syed Afzal Haider and Elizabeth McKenzie, editors. Estab. 1994. Magazine: 6×9; 125 pages; illustrations; photos. Annual. Estab. 1994. Circ. 300.
NEEDS literary. Receives 60-80 unsolicited mss/month. Accepts 8-10 mss/issue; 16-20 mss/year. Publishes ms 6 months-1 year after acceptance. Agented fiction 5%. **Publishes 8-10 new writers/year.** Length: 5,000 words; average length: 2,500 words. Publishes short shorts. Also publishes literary essays, poetry. Sometimes comments on rejected mss.
HOW TO CONTACT Send a disposable copy of ms and #10 SASE for reply only. Responds in 2 months to queries; 6 months to mss. Accepts simultaneous submissions. Up to 5 poems in a single submission; does not accept multiple short story submissions. Sample copy for $9.
PAYMENT/TERMS Pays 2 contributor's copies; additional copies $9. Pays on publication for one-time rights.
TIPS "The writer's voice ought to be clear and unique and should explain something of what it means to be human. We want well-written stories that reflect an appreciation for the rhythm and music of language, work that shows passion and commitment to the art of writing."

CHICAGO REVIEW

5801 S. Kenwood Ave., Chicago IL 60637. E-mail: chicago-review@uchicago.edu. Website: humanities.uchicago.edu/orgs/review. **Contact:** P. Genesius Durica. Estab. 1946. Magazine for a highly literate general audience: 6×9; 128 pages; offset white 60 lb. paper; illustrations; photos. Quarterly. Circ. 3,500.
NEEDS experimental, literary, contemporary. Receives 200 unsolicited mss/month. Accepts 2 mss/issue; 8 mss/year. Recently published work by Harry Mathews, Tom House, Viet Dinh and Doris Doörrie. Also publishes literary essays, literary criticism, poetry. Does not generally publish pieces more than 5,000 words.
HOW TO CONTACT Submit ms with SASE. Does not accept e-mail or fax submissions. Responds in 3-6 months to mss. No simultaneous submissions. Sample copy for $15. Guidelines via website or SASE.
PAYMENT/TERMS Pays 3 contributor's copies and subscription.
TIPS "We look for innovative fiction that avoids clicheé."

CHROMA, AN INTERNATIONAL QUEER LITERARY JOURNAL

P.O. Box 44655, London N16 0WQ England. (44)(0)20-3287-6335. E-mail: submissions@chromajournal.co.uk. Website: www.chromajournal.co.uk. **Contact:** Shaun Levin, founding editor. Literary magazine/journal. 52 pages. Contains illustrations. Includes photographs. "*Chroma* is the only international queer literary and arts journal based in Europe. We publish poetry, short prose and artwork by lesbian, gay, bisexual and transgendered writers and artists. We are always looking for new work and encourage work in translation. Each issue is themed, so please check the website for details. Past themes have included: Foreigners, Beauty, Islands, and Tormented." Semiannual. Estab. 2004. Circ. 1,000.

NEEDS Comics/graphic novels, erotica, ethnic/multicultural, experimental, feminist, gay, lesbian, literary. Receives 100 mss/month. Accepts 12 mss/issue; 24 mss/year. Ms published 3 months after acceptance. **Publishes 20 new writers/year.** Length: 2,000 words (min)-5,000 words (max). Average length: 3,000 words. Publishes short shorts. Average length of short shorts: 1,000 words. Also publishes book reviews, poetry. Send review copies to Eric Anderson, books editor. Sometimes comments on/critiques rejected mss.

HOW TO CONTACT Send complete ms with cover letter to submissions@chromajournal.co.uk. Include brief bio. Responds to queries in 1 month via e-mail. Considers simultaneous submissions, multiple submissions. Guidelines available on website.

PAYMENT/TERMS Writers receive up to $150. Additional copies $7. Pays on publication. Acquires first rights. Publication is copyrighted. "The *Chroma* International Queer Writing Competition runs every two years. The first was in 2006. Check guidelines on our website."

TIPS "We look for a good story well told. We look for writers doing interesting things with language, writers who are not afraid to take risks in the stories they tell and the way they tell them. Read back issues. If you like what we do, send us your work."

O COAL CITY REVIEW

Coal City Press, University of Kansas, Lawrence KS 66045. E-mail: coalcity@sunflower.com. E-mail: briandal@ku.edu. Website: www.coalcityreview.com. **Contact:** Mary Wharff, fiction editor. Literary magazine/journal: 8½ X 5½, 124-150 pages, heavy cover. Includes b&w photographs. Annual.

NEEDS Experimental, literary, contemporary. Does not want erotica, horror, romance, mystery. Receives 20-30 mss/month. Accepts 8-12 mss/issue. Reads year-round. Manuscript published up to 1 year after acceptance. Agented fiction 0%. **Publishes new writers every year.** Published Catherine Bell, Tasha Haas, Bill Church, Aimee Parkison, Thomas Zurwellen, John Talbird. Length: 50 words (min)—4,000 words (max). Average length: 2,000 words. Also publishes literary criticism, poetry. Sometimes comments on/critiques rejected manuscripts.

HOW TO CONTACT Submit via e-mail to coalcity@sunflower.com. Attach Word file. Include estimated word count, brief bio, list of publications. Responds to mss in 4 months. Send disposable copy of ms and #10 SASE for reply only. Considers simultaneous submissions. Guidelines available via e-mail.

PAYMENT/TERMS Writers receive 2 contributor's copies. Additional copies $5. Pays on publication. Acquires onetime rights. Publication is copyrighted.

TIPS "We are looking for artful stories—with great language and great heart. Please do not send work that has not been thoughtfully and carefully revised or edited."

CONTE, AN ONLINE JOURNAL OF NARRATIVE WRITING

E-mail: poetry@conteonline.net. E-mail: prose@conteonline.net. Website: http://www.conteonline.net. **Contact:** Adam Tavel, poetry editor. Estab. 2005. Biannual online magazine. "We aim to publish narrative writing of all kinds. Relating a sequence of events is a primary method of human communication; we are interested in the narrative form as a means of relating ideas, experiences, and emotions, and we love how the act of telling a story unites the perspectives of listeners and speakers. We are dedicated to the concept of disseminating fresh, stellar writing to as many people as possible, as quickly and as often as possible, hence our online basis. We are enthusiastic about publishing the latest works of writers from all backgrounds and of varying experience. We hope *Conte* will be a mechanism not only for publication, but communication among writers as well as between readers and authors, and above all that we continue the ancient and perhaps sacred tradition of telling a good yarn." "We'll consider fiction on essentially any topic; our primary focus is the effective use of narrative." Agented fiction <5%. Responds to queries in 3-4 weeks. Responds to mss in 8-10 weeks. **Publishes 4 new writers/year.** Also publishes poetry. Sometimes comments on/critiques rejected mss. Considers simultaneous submissions. Guidelines available via e-mail, on website. Acquires electronic rights. Sends galleys to author. Publication is not copyrighted.

NEEDS narrative writing of all kinds.

HOW TO CONTACT Send complete ms with cover letter. Accepts submissions by e-mail only. Include estimated word count, brief bio. Email: poetry@conteonline.net; prose@conteonline.net. Website: http://www.conteonline.net.

TIPS "Submit poems in the body of an email to: poetry@conteonline.net, with subject line 'Poetry Submission' followed by the title. We are averse to rhyme schemes and attachments. Submit prose to: prose@conteonline.net, with subject line 'Prose Submission' followed by title. Rich Text (.rtf) attachments are preferred but submissions in the body of an email are acceptable."

COTTONWOOD

1301 Jayhawk Blvd. Room 400, Kansas Union, University of Kansas, Lawrence KS 66045. E-mail: tlorenz@ku.edu. Website: www.cottonwoodmagazine.org/read. **Contact:** Tom Lorenz, fiction editor. Estab. 1965. Magazine: 6×9; 100 pages; illustrations; photos. "Cottonwood publishes high quality prose, poetry and artwork and is aimed at an audience that appreciates the same. We have a national scope and reputation while maintaining a strong regional flavor." Semiannual. Circ. 500.

NEEDS "We publish literary prose and poetry." Receives 25-50 unsolicited mss/month. Accepts 5-6 mss/issue; 10-12 mss/year. Publishes ms 6-18 months after acceptance. Agented fiction 10%. **Publishes 1-3 new writers/year.** Recently published work by Connie May Fowler, Oakley Hall, Cris Mazza. Length: 1,000-8,000 words; average length: 2,000-5,000 words. Publishes short shorts. Also publishes literary essays, literary criticism, poetry.

HOW TO CONTACT SASE for return of ms. Responds in 6 months to mss. Accepts simultaneous submissions. Sample copy for $8.50, 9×12 SAE and $1.90. Reviews fiction.

PAYMENT/TERMS Acquires onetime rights.

TIPS "We're looking for depth and/or originality of subject matter, engaging voice and style, emotional honesty, command of the material and the structure. *Cottonwood* publishes high quality literary fiction, but we are very open to the work of talented new writers. Write something honest and that you care about and write it as well as you can. Don't hesitate to keep trying us. We sometimes take a piece from a writer we've rejected a number of times. We generally don't like clever, gimmicky writing. The style should be engaging but not claim all the the attention itself."

CUTTHROAT, A JOURNAL OF THE ARTS

P.O. Box 2414, Durango CO 81302. (970) 903-7914. E-mail: cutthroatmag@gmail.com. Website: www.cutthroatmag.com. **Contact:** William Luvaas, fiction editor. Literary magazine/journal and "one separate online edition of poetry, translations, short fiction, and book reviews yearly. 6×9, 180+ pages, fine cream paper, slick cover. Includes photographs. "We publish only high quality fiction and poetry. We are looking for the cutting edge, the endangered word, fiction with wit, heart, soul and meaning." Annual. Estab. 2005. Member CCLMP.

NEEDS ethnic/multicultural, experimental, feminist, humor/satire, literary, mainstream. Does not want romance, horror, historical, fantasy, religious, teen, juvenile. List of upcoming themes available on website. Receives 100+ mss/month. Accepts 6 mss/issue; 10-12 mss/year. Does not read from October 1st-March 1st and from June 1st-July 15th. **Publishes 5-8 new writers/year.** Published Michael Schiavone, Rusty Harris, Timothy Rien, Summer Wood, Peter Christopher, Jamey Genna, Doug Frelke, Sally Bellerose, Marc Levy. Length: 500 words (min)-5,000 words (max). Publishes short shorts. Also publishes book reviews. Send review copies to Pamela Uschuk. Sometimes comments on/critiques rejected mss.

HOW TO CONTACT Send complete ms with cover letter. Accepts submissions by e-mail for online edition and from authors living overseas only. Include estimated word count, brief bio. Responds to queries in 1-2 weeks. Responds to mss in 6-8 months. Send either SASE (or IRC) for return of ms or disposable copy of ms and #10 SASE for reply only. Considers simultaneous submissions, multiple submissions. Sample copy available for $10. Guidelines available for SASE, on website.

PAYMENT/TERMS Writers receive contributor's copies. Additional copies $10. Pays on publication. Acquires first North American serial rights. Sends galleys to author. Publication is copyrighted. "Sponsors the Rick DeMarinis Short Fiction Prize ($1250 first prize). See separate listing and website for more information."

TIPS "Read our magazine and see what types of stories we've published. The piece must have heart and soul, excellence in craft. "

DESCANT

TCU Box 297270, Ft. Worth TX 76129. (817)257-6537. Fax: (817)257-6239. E-mail: descant@tcu.edu. Website: www.descant.tcu.edu. **Contact:** David Kuhne, editor. Estab. 1956. Magazine: 6×9; 120-150 pages; acid-free paper; paper cover. "*Descant* seeks high quality poems and stories in both traditional and innovative form." Annual. Circ. 500-750. Member CLMP.

Offers four cash awards: The $500 Frank O'Connor Award for the best story in an issue; the $250 Gary Wilson Award for an outstanding story in an issue; the $500 Betsy Colquitt Award for the best poem in an issue; the $250 Baskerville Publishers Award for outstanding poem in an issue. Several stories first published by *Descant* have appeared in *Best American Short Stories.*

NEEDS Literary. "No horror, romance, fantasy, erotica." Receives 20-30 unsolicited mss/month. Accepts 25-35 mss/year. Publishes ms 1 year after acceptance. **Publishes 50% new writers/year.** Recently published work by William Harrison, Annette Sanford, Miller Williams, Patricia Chao, Vonesca Stroud, and Walt McDonald. Length: 1,000-5,000 words; average length: 2,500 words. Publishes short shorts. Also publishes poetry.

HOW TO CONTACT Send complete ms with cover letter. Include estimated word count and brief bio. Responds in 6-8 weeks to mss. Accepts simultaneous submissions. Sample copy for $10. SASE, e-mail or fax.

PAYMENT/TERMS 2 Contributor's copies, additional copies $6. Pays on publication for onetime rights. Sponsors awards/contests.

TIPS "We look for character and quality of prose. Send your best short work."

DISLOCATE

University of Minnesota English Department, the Edelstein-Keller Endowment, and Adam Lerner of the Lerner Publishing Group, 1 Lind Hall, 207 Church St. SE, Minneapolis MN 55455. Website: http://dislocate.umn.edu. **Contact:** Shantha Susman. Magazine has a revolving editor. Literary magazine/journal: 5½ x 8½, 128 pages. Annual. Estab. 2005. Circ. 2,000. The print journal covers literary writing that bends genres and otherwise pushes the envelope; the submission period for issue 7 is July 15 to November 15. See print journal submission guidelines. The online magazine publishes content of interest to writers and readers: Writing-related content may include articles, essays, interviews, and book reviews. Our culture-related content encompasses everything from arts to entertainment to fashion to "lifestyle" pieces. See online content submission guidelines. dislocate.umn.edu also runs a monthly Short Forms Contest; winners are published on the website and awarded prizes that vary from month to month. See contest submission guidelines and prize details.

Reading period currently closed.

NEEDS literary fiction. Receives 25-50 mss/month. Accepts 2-3 mss/year. Publishes short shorts. Also publishes literary essays, poetry.

HOW TO CONTACT We are now using Submishmash for all submissions. (Submissions will become available when the reading period begins.) We will not consider or respond to submissions or by post or e-mail. Send complete ms with cover letter. Considers simultaneous submissions, multiple submissions. Guidelines available on website.

PAYMENT/TERMS Pays on publication.

TIPS "Looking for excellent writing that rearranges the world."

ECHO INK REVIEW

E.I. Publishing Services, Published by Sildona Creative, 5920 Nall Ave., Suite 301, Mission KS 66202. E-mail: editor@echoinkreview.com. Website: www.echoinkreview.com. **Contact:** Don Balch, editor. Estab. 1997.

TIPS "Please use our Online Submission Manager: the $2.00 submission fee helps support our journal—please support us instead of the post office. Other submission option: free postal submissions to office address. Read the online guidelines. Surprising, precise language + dynamic character arcs and character-driven plots that resonate = you have our attention. We publish quite a few stories by established writers, but we want to discover the best new talent out there. To that end, we reserve 50% of each issue to stories by new and moderately established writers. Additionally, we support our writers by paying them professional rates. Tips on judging your work: If you want to know where your writing stands in relation to that of your peers, compare your stories to those published by your favorite literary journal. If you don't have a favorite literary journal, get one. Entering our contests will also give you an idea of where your writing stands; in addition to posting winners (top 3), we post finalists (top 10), semifinalists (top 25), and quarter-finalists (top 25% of mss received). Stay positive; be persistent; keep writing."

ECLIPSE

Glendale College, 1500 N. Verdugo Rd., Glendale CA 91208. (818)240-1000. Fax: (818)549-9436. E-mail: eclipse@glendale.edu. Magazine: 8½×5½; 150-200 pages; 60 lb. paper. "Eclipse is committed to publishing outstanding fiction and poetry. We look for compelling characters and stories executed in ways that provoke our readers and allow them to understand the world in new ways." Annual. Circ. 1,800. CLMP.

"*Eclipse* is committed to publishing outstanding fiction and poetry. We look for compelling characters and stories executed in ways that provoke our readers and allow them to understand the world in new ways." Annual. Circ. 1,800. Receives 50-100 unsolicited mss/month. Accepts 10 mss/year. Publishes ms 6-12 months after acceptance. **Publishes 8 new writers/year.** Recently published work by Amy Sage Webb, Ira Sukrungruang, Richard Schmitt, George Rabasa. Length: 6,000 words; average length: 4,000 words. Publishes short shorts. Also publishes poetry. Sometimes comments on rejected mss. Send complete ms. Responds in 2 weeks to queries; 4-6 weeks to mss. Accepts simultaneous submissions. Sample copy for $8. Writer's guidelines for #10 SASE or by e-mail. Pays 2 contributor's copies; additional copies $7. Pays on publication for first North American serial rights.

NEEDS ethnic/multicultural, experimental, literary. "Does not want horror, religious, science fiction or thriller mss." Receives 50-100 unsolicited mss/month. Accepts 10 mss/year. Publishes ms 6-12 months after acceptance. **Publishes 8 new writers/year.** Recently published work by Amy Sage Webb, Ira Sukrungruang, Richard Schmitt, George Rabasa. Length: 6,000 words; average length: 4,000 words. Publishes short shorts. Also publishes poetry. Sometimes comments on rejected mss.

HOW TO CONTACT Send complete ms. Responds in 2 weeks to queries; 4-6 weeks to mss. Accepts simultaneous submissions. Sample copy for $8. Writer's guidelines for #10 SASE or by e-mail.

PAYMENT/TERMS Pays 2 contributor's copies; additional copies $7. Pays on publication for first North American serial rights.

TIPS "We look for well crafted fiction, experimental or traditional, with a clear unity of elements. A good story is important, but the writing must transcend the simple act of conveying the story."

ELLIPSIS MAGAZINE

Westminster College of Salt Lake City, 1840 S. 1300 E., Salt Lake City UT 84105. (801)832-2321. E-mail: ellipsis@westminstercollege.edu. Website: www.westminstercollege.edu/ellipsis. **Contact:** Stephanie Peterson (revolving editor; changes every year). Estab. 1967. Magazine: 6×9; 110-120 pages; 60 lb. paper; 15 pt. cover stock; illustrations; photos. *Ellipsis Magazine* needs good literary poetry, fiction, essays, plays and visual art. Annual. Estab. 1967. Circ. 2,000.

Reads submissions August 1 – November 1.

NEEDS Receives 110 unsolicited mss/month. Accepts 4 mss/issue. Does not read mss November 1-July 31. Publishes ms 3 months after acceptance. **Publishes 2 new writers/year.** Length: 6,000 words; average length: 4,000 words. Also publishes poetry. Rarely comments on rejected mss.

HOW TO CONTACT Send complete ms. Send SASE (or IRC) for return of ms or send disposable copy of the ms and #10 SASE for reply only. Responds in 6 months to mss. Accepts simultaneous submissions. Sample copy for $7.50. Writer's guidelines online.

PAYMENT/TERMS Pays $50 per story and one contributor's copy; additional copies $3.50. Pays on publication for first North American serial rights. Not copyrighted.

ESSAYS & FICTIONS

209 Cascadilla St., Ithaca NY 14850. (914)572-7351. E-mail: essaysandfictions@gmail.com. Website: http://essaysandfictions.com; **Contact:** David Pollock and Danielle Winterton, co-founding editors. Literary magazine. Magazine: 5.5x8.25; 100 pages; laminated card stock cover with illustrations. "*Essays & Fictions* is an online journal of literature and criticism. Publishes fictional essay, reflective essay, academic rhetorical essay, literary narrative essay, lyric essay, linear fiction, non-linear fiction, essayistic fiction, fictionalized memoir, questionable histories, false historical accounts, botched accounts, cultural analysis, criticism or commentary, compositional analysis, criticism or commentary, or any blend thereof. We do not differentiate between essay and fiction in the table of contents because we consciously challenge the validity of genre boundaries and definitions. We believe language is not fixed and neither is truth. As art, forms of literature have varying degrees of truth value. Many writers have recently chosen to compose works that blend or subvert the genres of short fiction and essay. We are particularly interested in publishing these kinds of writers. We encourage writers to experiment with hybrid forms that lead to literary transcendence."

Semiannual. Receives 10-20 mss/month, accepts approx 3/month, 6/year. Reading periods are February 1-May 31 for October issue, and September 1-December 31 for May issue. Time between acceptance and publication is 1-4 months. **Publishes 3-4 new writers each year**. Has published: Karl Parker, John Taylor, Myronn Hardy, Stephen Poleskie, Margot Berwin, Melita Schaum. Length: up to 10,000 words. Average length: 3,000 words. Publishes short shorts. Also publishes literary essays, literary criticism, and poetry, and reviews. Send copy of reviews to David and Danielle. Rarely comments on rejected mss.

NEEDS Ethnic/multicultural, experimental, feminist, gay, historical, humor/satire, lesbian, literary, translations. Does not want "genre writing, American Realism, or straight, formulaic reflective memoir."

HOW TO CONTACT Send complete ms with cover letter. Accepts submissions by e-mail. Responds to mss in 1-3 months. Accepts multiple submissions; no simultaneous or previously published submissions. Guidelines available by e-mail or on website. Acquires first and electronic rights. Publication is copyrighted. Sends prepublication galleys to author. See website or e-mail for more information. Sample copy: $15.

PAYMENT/TERMS Contributors get one free copy and 15% off additional copies of the issue in which they are published.

TIPS "We look for confident work that uses form/structure and voice in interesting ways without sounding overly self-conscious or deliberate. We encourage rigorous excellence of complex craft in our submissions and discourage bland reproductions of reality. Read the journal. Be familiar with the *Essays & Fictions* aesthetic. We are particularly interested in writers who read theory and/or have multiple intellectual and artistic interests, and who set high intellectual standards for themselves and their work."

EUREKA LITERARY MAGAZINE

300 E. College Ave., Eureka College, Eureka IL 61530. E-mail: elm@eureka.edu. Website: www.eureka.edu/arts/literary/literary.htm. Estab. 1992. (309)467-6591. **Contact:** Zeke Jarvis, editor. Magazine: 6×9; 120 pages; 70 lb. white offset paper; 80 lb. gloss cover; photographs (occasionally). "We seek to be open to the best stories that are submitted to us. Our audience is a combination of professors/writers, students of writing and literature, and general readers." Semiannual. Estab. 1992. Circ. 500.

NEEDS ethnic/multicultural, experimental, fantasy (science), feminist, historical, humor/satire, literary, mainstream, mystery/suspense (private eye/hardboiled, romantic), science fiction (soft/sociological), translations. Would like to see more "good literary fiction stories, good magical realism, historical fiction. We try to achieve a balance between the traditional and the experimental. We look for the well-crafted story, but essentially any type of story that has depth and substance to it is welcome." Receives 100 unsolicited mss/month. Accepts 10-12 mss/issue; 20-30 mss/year. Does not accept mss in summer (May-August). **Publishes 5-6 new writers/year.** Recently published work by Jane Guill, Sarah Strickley, Ray Bradbury, Patrick Madden, Virgil Suarez, Cynthia Gallaher, Wendell Mayo, Tom Noyes, and Brian Doyle. Length: 4,000-6,000 words; average length: 5,000 words. Also publishes short shorts, flash fiction and poetry.

HOW TO CONTACT Accepts submissions by e-mail. Send SASE for reply, return of ms or send disposable copy of ms. Responds in 2 weeks to electronic queries; 4 months to mss. Accepts simultaneous submissions. Sample copy for $7.50.

TIPS "Do something that hasn't been done a thousand times already. Give us unusual but believable characters in unusual but believable conflicts—clear resolution isn't always necessary, but it's nice. We don't hold to hard and fast rules about length, but most stories could do with some cutting. Make sure your title is relevant and eye-catching. Please do not send personal gifts or hate mail. We're a college-operated magazine, so we do not actually exist in summer. If we don't take a submission, that doesn't automatically mean we don't like it—we try to encourage authors who show promise to revise and resubmit. Order a copy if you can."

EVANSVILLE REVIEW

University of Evansville English Dept., 1800 Lincoln Ave., Evansville IN 47722. (812)488-1402. E-mail: evansvillereview@evansville.edu. Website: http://evansvillereview.evansville.edu. **Contact:** Editor. Estab. 1990. **Contact:** Fiction editor. Magazine: 6×9; 180 pages; 70 lb. white paper; glossy full-color cover; perfect bound. Annual. Circ. 1,000.

NEEDS Does not want erotica, fantasy, experimental or children's fiction. "We're open to all creativity. No discrimination. All fiction, screenplays, nonfiction, poetry, interviews, and anything in between." Receives 70 unsolicited mss/month. Does not read mss December-

August. Agented fiction 2%. **Publishes 20 new writers/year.** Recently published work by John Updike, Arthur Miller, X.J. Kennedy, Jim Barnes, Rita Dove. Also publishes literary essays, poetry.

HOW TO CONTACT Send SASE for reply, or send a disposable copy of ms. Responds in 1 month to queries; 3 months to mss. Accepts simultaneous, multiple submissions and reprints. Sample copy for $5. Writer's guidelines free.

PAYMENT/TERMS Pays 2 contributor's copies. Pays on publication for onetime rights. Not copyrighted.

TIPS "Because editorial staff rolls over every 1-2 years, the journal always has a new flavor."

EVENING STREET REVIEW

Evening Street Press, Inc., 7652 Sawmill Rd. #352, Dublin OH 43016-9296. E-mail: editor@eveningstreetpress.com. Website: www.eveningstreetpress.com. **Contact:** Gordon Grigsby, editor. Estab. 2007. Circ. 300.

NEEDS "Intended for a general audience, *Evening Street Press*, published semiannually, is centered on Elizabeth Cady Stanton's 1848 revision of the Declaration of Independence: 'that all men—and women—are created equal,' with equal rights to 'life, liberty, and the pursuit of happiness.' It focuses on the realities of experience, personal and historical, from the most gritty to the most dreamlike, including awareness of the personal and social forces that block or develop the possibilities of this new culture."

HOW TO CONTACT Send complete ms. by mail or e-mail. Wants confession, ethnic, experimental, mainstream, and novel excerpts. Does not want "male chauvinism."

PAYMENT/TERMS Pays contributor copies. Rights revert to author upon publication.

TIPS "Does not want to see male chauvinism. Mss are read year round. See website for chapbook and book competitions."

FAULTLINE

Dept. of English and Comparative Literature, University of California at Irvine, Irvine CA 92697-2650. (949) 824-1573. E-mail: faultline@uci.edu. Website: www.humanities.uci.edu/faultline. **Contact:** Editors change in September each year. Estab. 1992. Literary magazine: 6×9; 200 pages; illustrations; photos. "We publish the very best of what we receive. Our interest is quality and literary merit." Annual.

Reading period is September 15-February 15. Submissions sent at any other time will not be read.

NEEDS translations, literary fiction, nonfiction up to 20 pages. Receives 150 unsolicited mss/month. Accepts 6-9 mss/year. Does not read mss April-September. Publishes ms 9 months after acceptance. Agented fiction 10-20%. **Publishes 30-40% new writers/year.** Recently published work by Maile Meloy, Aimee Bender, David Benioff, Steve Almond, Helen Maria Viramontes, Thomas Keneally. Publishes short shorts. Also publishes literary essays, poetry.

HOW TO CONTACT Send SASE for reply, return of ms or send a disposable copy of ms. Responds in 2 weeks to queries; 4 months to mss. Accepts simultaneous submissions. Sample copy for $5. Writer's guidelines for business-size envelope.

PAYMENT/TERMS Pays 2 contributor's copies. Pays on publication for onetime rights. **Tips:** "Our commitment is to publish the best work possible from well-known and emerging authors with vivid and varied voices."

THE FIDDLEHEAD

University of New Brunswick, Campus House, 11 Garland Court, Box 4400, Fredericton NB E3B 5A3 Canada. (506)453-3501. Fax: (506) 453-5069. E-mail: fiddlehd@unb.ca; scl@unb.ca. Website: www.thefiddlehead.ca. **Contact:** Kathryn Taglia, Managing Editor. Estab. 1945. Magazine: 6×9; 128-180 pages; ink illustrations; photos. "No criteria for publication except quality. For a general audience, including many poets and writers." Quarterly.

NEEDS literary. Receives 100-150 unsolicited mss/month. Accepts 4-5 mss/issue; 20-40 mss/year. Publishes ms within 1 year after acceptance. Agented fiction: small percentage. **Publishes high percentage of new writers/year.** Recently published work by Marjorie Celona, Wasela Hiyate, Alexander MacLeod, and Erika Van Winden. Average length: 3,000-6,000 words. Publishes short shorts. Occasionally comments on rejected mss.

HOW TO CONTACT Send SASE and *Canadian* stamps or IRCs for return of mss. Responds in 6 months to mss. No e-mail submissions. Simultaneous submissions only if stated on cover letter; must contact immediately if accepted elsewhere. Sample copy for $15 (US).

PAYMENT/TERMS Pays up to $40 (Canadian)/published page and 2 contributor's copies. Pays on publication for first or onetime serial rights.

TIPS "If you are serious about submitting to *The Fiddlehead*, you should subscribe or read an issue or two to get a sense of the journal. Contact us if you would to order sample back issues ($10-$15 plus postage)."

FIRST CLASS

P.O. Box 86, Friendship IN 47021. E-mail: christopherm@four-sep.com. Website: www.four-sep.com. **Contact:** Christopher M, editor. Estab. 1995. Magazine: 4¼×11; 48-60+ pages; 24 lb./60 lb. offset paper; craft cover; illustrations; photos. "First Class features short fiction and poetics from the cream of the small press and killer unknowns—mingling before your very hungry eyes. I publish plays, too." Biannual. Circ. 200-400.

NEEDS Erotica, literary, science fiction (soft/sociological), satire, drama. "No religious or traditional poetry, or 'boomer angst'—therapy-driven self loathing." Receives 50-70 unsolicited mss/month. Accepts 12-17 mss/issue; 20-30 mss/year. Publishes ms 1 month after acceptance. **Publishes 10-15 new writers/year.** Recently published work by Alan Catlin, Gary Every, John Bennet, B.Z. Niditch. Length: 5,000-8,000; average length: 2,000-3,000 words. Publishes short shorts. Also publishes poetry. Sometimes comments on rejected mss.

HOW TO CONTACT Send SASE or send a disposable copy of ms and #10 SASE for reply only. Responds in 4-8 week to queries. Accepts simultaneous submissions and reprints. Sample copy for $6. Writer's guidelines for #10 SASE. Reviews fiction.

PAYMENT/TERMS Pays 1 contributor's copy; additional copies $5. Acquires onetime rights.

TIPS "Don't bore me with puppy dogs and the morose/sappy feeling you have about death. Belt out a good, short, thought-provoking, graphic, uncommon piece."

THE FIRST LINE

P.O. Box 250382, Plano TX 75025-0382. (972)824-0646. E-mail: submission@thefirstline.com. Website: www.thefirstline.com. **Contact:** Robin LaBounty, manuscript coordinator. Estab. 1999. Magazine: 8×5; 64-72 pages; 20 lb. bond paper; 80 lb. cover stock. "We only publish stories that start with the first line provided. We are a collection of tales—of different directions writers can take when they start from the same place. Quarterly.

NEEDS adventure, ethnic/multicultural, fantasy, gay, humor/satire, lesbian, literary, mainstream, mystery/suspense, regional, romance, science fiction, western. Receives 200 unsolicited mss/month. Accepts 12 mss/issue; 48 mss/year. Publishes ms 1 month after acceptance. **Publishes 6 new writers/year.** Length: 300-3,000 words; average length: 1,500 words. Publishes short shorts. Also publishes literary essays, literary criticism. Often comments on rejected mss.

HOW TO CONTACT Send complete ms. Accepts submissions by e-mail. Send SASE for return of ms or disposable copy of the ms and #10 SASE for reply only. Responds in 1 week to queries; 3 months to mss. Accepts multiple submissions. No simultaneous submissions. Sample copy for $4.00. Writer's guidelines for SASE, e-mail or on website. Reviews fiction.

PAYMENT/TERMS Pays $20 maximum and contributor's copy; additional copy $2. Pays on publication.

TIPS "Don't just write the first story that comes to mind after you read the sentence. If it is obvious, chances are other people are writing about the same thing. Don't try so hard. Be willing to accept criticism."

FLINT HILLS REVIEW

Dept. of English, Box 4019, Emporia State University, Emporia KS 66801-5087. Website: www.emporia.edu/fhr/. **Contact:** Editors. Estab. 1996. E-mail: webbamy@emporia.edu. Magazine: 9×6; 115 pages; 60 lb. paper; glossy cover; illustrations; photos. "FHR seeks work informed by a strong sense of place or region, especially Kansas and the Great Plains region. We seek to provide a publishing venue for writers of the Great Plains and Kansas while also publishing authors whose work evidences a strong sense of place, writing of literary quality, and accomplished use of language and depth of character development." Annual. Circ. 300. CLMP.

NEEDS Ethnic/multicultural, gay, historical, regional (Plains), translations. "No religious, inspirational, children's." Want to see more "writing of literary quality with a strong sense of place." List of upcoming themes online. Receives 5-15 unsolicited mss/month. Accepts 2-5 mss/issue; 2-5 mss/year. Does not read mss April-December. Publishes ms 4 months after acceptance. **Publishes 4 new writers/year.** Recently published work by Kim Stafford, Elizabeth Dodd, Bart Edelman, and Jennifer Henderson. Length: 1 page-5,000; average length: 3,000 words. Publishes short shorts. Also publishes literary essays, literary criticism, poetry.

HOW TO CONTACT Send a disposable copy of ms and #10 SASE for reply only. Responds in 5 weeks to queries; 6 months to mss. Accepts simultaneous, multiple submissions. Sample copy for $5.50. Writer's guidelines for SASE, by e-mail, fax, or on website. Reviews fiction.

PAYMENT/TERMS Pays 2 contributor's copies; additional copies $5.50. Acquires onetime rights.

TIPS "Strong imagery and voice, writing that is informed by place or region, writing of literary quality with depth of character development. Hone the language down to the most literary depiction that is possible in the shortest space that still provides depth of development without excess length."

◐ FLORIDA REVIEW

Dept. of English, University of Central Florida, Suite P, P.O. Box 161346, Orlando FL 32816-1346. (407) 823-5329. E-mail: flreview@mail.ucf.edu. Website: http://floridareview.cah.ucf.edu/. **Contact:** Jocelyn Bartkevicius, editor. Magazine: 6×9; 185 pages; semi-gloss full color cover, perfect bound. "We publish fiction of high 'literary' quality—stories that delight, instruct and take risks. Our audience consists of avid readers of fiction, poetry and creative nonfiction." Semiannual. Estab. 1972.

NEEDS experimental, literary. "We aren't particularly interested in genre fiction (sci-fi, romance, adventure, etc.) but a good story can transcend any genre." Receives over 500 unsolicited mss/month. Accepts 5-7 mss/issue; 10-14 mss/year. Publishes 3-5 new writers/year. Recently published work by Gerald Vizenor, Billy Collins, Sherwin Bitsui, Kelly Clancy, Denise Duhamel, Tony Hoagland, Baron Wormser, Marcia Aldrich, and Patricia Foster. Length: 2,000-8,000 words; average length: 5,000 words. Publishes short shorts. Also publishes creative nonfiction, poetry, and graphic narrative. Rarely comments on rejected mss. Accepts simultaneous submissions if notified promptly when accepted elsewhere. Rights held by The Florida Review, revert to author after publication.

HOW TO CONTACT Send complete ms. Send SASE (or IRC) for return of the ms or send disposable copy of the ms and #10 SASE for reply only. Responds in 2 weeks to queries; 3 months to mss. Accepts simultaneous submissions. Sample copy for $8. Writer's guidelines for #10 SASE or online.

PAYMENT/TERMS Rights held by UCF, revert to author after publication.

TIPS "We're looking for writers with fresh voices and original stories. We like risk."

◐ FLYWAY

Iowa State University, 206 Ross Hall, Ames IA 50011. (515)294-8273. Fax: (515)294-6814. E-mail: flyway@iastate.edu. Website: www.flyway.org. **Contact:** Stephen Pett, editor. Estab. 1995. Literary magazine: 6×9; 120 pages; quality paper; cover stock; some illustrations; photos. "We publish quality fiction, creative nonfiction, and poetry with a particular interest in place as a component of 'story,' or with an 'environmental' sensibility. Accepted works are accompanied by brief commentaries by their authors, the sort of thing a writer might say introducing a piece at a reading." Biannual. Circ. 500.

NEEDS literary. Receives 50 unsolicited mss/month. Accepts 2-5 short story and creative nonfiction mss/issue; 10-12 poetry mss/issue. Reads mss September 1-May 1. Publishes ms 6-8 months after acceptance. **Publishes 7-10 new writers/year.** Recently published work by Linda Hasselstrom, Ann Pancake, Ted Kooser, Michael Martone. Length: 5,000; average length: 3,500 words. Publishes short shorts. Often comments on rejected mss.

HOW TO CONTACT Send SASE. Sample copy for $8. Writer's guidelines with SASE.

PAYMENT/TERMS Pays 2 contributor's copies; additional copies $8. Acquires onetime rights.

TIPS "Quality, originality, voice, drama, tension. Make it as strong as you can."

O FOLIATE OAK LITERARY MAGAZINE

University of Arkansas-Monticello, P.O. Box 3460, Monticello AR 71656. (870)460-1247. E-mail: foliateoak@uamont.edu. Website: www.Foliateoak.Uamont.edu. **Contact:** Online Submission Manager. Estab. 1973. Magazine: 6×9; 80 pages. Monthly.

NEEDS Adventure, comics/graphic novels, ethnic/multicultural, experimental, family saga, feminist, gay, historical, humor/satire, lesbian, literary, mainstream, science fiction (soft/sociological). No religious, sexist or homophobic work. Receives 80 unsolicited mss/month. Accepts 20 mss/issue; 160 mss/year. Does not read mss May-August. Publishes ms 1 month after acceptance. Publishes 130 new writers/year. Recently published work by David Barringer, Thom Didato, Joe Taylor, Molly Giles, Patricia Shevlin, Tony Hoagland. Length: 50-2,500 words; average length: 1,500 words. Publishes short shorts. Also publishes literary essays, literary criticism, poetry. Rarely comments on rejected mss.

HOW TO CONTACT Use our online submission manager to submit work. Postal submissions will not be read. Responds in 4 weeks. Only accepts submissions August through April. Accepts simultaneous submissions and multiple submissions. Please contact ASAP if work is accepted elsewhere. Sample copy with SASE and 6×8 envelope. Read writer's guidelines online. Reviews fiction.

PAYMENT/TERMS Pays contributor's copy if included in the annual print anthology. Acquires electronic rights. Sends galleys to author. Not copyrighted.

TIPS "We're open to honest, experimental, offbeat, realistic and surprising writing, if it has been edited. Limit poems to five per submission, and one short story or creative nonfiction (less than 2,500 words. You may send up to three flash fictions. Please put your flash fiction in one attachment. Please don't send more writing until you hear from us regarding your first submission. We are also looking for artwork sent as.jpg or.gif files."

FOLIO

Department of Literature, American University, Washington DC 20016. E-mail: folio.editors@gmail.com. Website: www.american.edu/cas/literature/folio/. **Contact:** Greta Schuler. Estab. 1984. Magazine: about 70 pages; illustrations; photos. "*Folio* is a journal of poetry, fiction and creative nonfiction; illustrations; photos. *Folio* is a nationally recognized literary journal sponsored by the College of Arts and Sciences at American University in Washington, D. C. Since 1984, we have published original creative work by both new and established authors. Past issues have included work by Michael Reid Busk, Billy Collins, William Stafford, and Bruce Weigl, and interviews with Michael Cunningham, Charles Baxter, Amy Bloom, Ann Beattie, and Walter Kirn. We look for well-crafted poetry and prose that is bold and memorable." Does not read submissions May-July. Publishes 2-3 new writers/year. Length: 5,000 words; average length: 2,500 words. Publishes short shorts. How to submit. Send a SASE for reply only. Responds in 3-4 months to submission. Accepts simultaneous submissions. Sample copy for $6. "Visit our website and read the journal for more information." We look for work that ignites and endures, is artful and natural, daring and elegant." Semiannual.

NEEDS literary. Does not want anything that is sexually offensive. Receives 50-60 unsolicited mss/month.

HOW TO CONTACT Send complete ms. Send a SASE (or IRC) for reply only.

PAYMENT/TERMS Pays 2 contributor's copies. Pays on publication for first North American serial rights.

FOLIO

10 Gate St., Lincoln's Inn Fields London WC2A-3P England. +44 0207 242 9562. Fax: +44 0207 242 1816. E-mail: info@folioart.co.uk. Website: www.folioart.co.uk.

FOURTEEN HILLS

Dept. of Creative Writing, San Francisco State Univ., 1600 Holloway Ave., San Francisco CA 94132-1722. E-mail: hills@sfsu.edu. Website: www.14hills.net. Estab. 1994. Editors change each year. Magazine: 6×9; 200 pages; 60 lb. paper; 10-point C15 cover. "*Fourteen Hills* publishes the highest quality innovative fiction and poetry for a literary audience." Semiannual. Circ. 700.

NEEDS ethnic/multicultural, experimental, gay, humor/satire, literary, mainstream, translations. Receives 300 unsolicited mss/month. Accepts 8-10 mss/issue; 16-20 mss/year. Does not usually read mss during the summer. Publishes ms 2-4 months after acceptance. Recently published work by Terese Svoboda, Peter Rock and Stephen Dixon, Adam Johnson. Publishes short shorts. Also publishes literary essays, flash fiction, creative nonfiction, poetry, and art. Sometimes comments on rejected mss.

HOW TO CONTACT SASE for return of ms. Responds in 5 months to mss. Sample copy for $9. Submission guidelines online at website.

PAYMENT/TERMS Pays 2 contributor's copies. Acquires onetime rights.

TIPS "Please read an issue of *Fourteen Hills* before submitting."

FREEFALL MAGAZINE

Freefall Literary Society of Calgary, 922 Ninth Ave. SE, Calgary AB T2G 0S4 Canada. E-mail: freefallmagazine@yahoo.com. Website: www.freefallmagazine.ca. **Contact:** Lynn S. Fraser, managing editor. Estab. 1990. Freefall Literary Society of Calgary. *Freefall* Magazine: $8\frac{1}{2}$×$5\frac{3}{4}$; 100 pages; bond paper; bond stock; b&w illustrations; photos. "*FreeFall* features the best of new, emerging writers and gives them the chance to get into print along with established writers. Magazine published biannually containing fiction, poetry, creative nonfiction, essays on writing, interviews, and reviews. Submit up to 5 poems at once. We are looking for exquisite writing with a strong narrative." Circ.: 1,000. Buys first North American serial rights (ownership reverts to author after onetime publication). Pays on publication. 100% freelance.

NEEDS fiction

PAYMENT/TERMS Pays $25 per poem and one copy of the issue poems appeear in. Wants prose of all types, up to 3,000 words; pays $10/page to a maximum of $100 per piece and one copy of issue piece appears in.

TIPS "We look for thoughtful word usage, craftmanship, strong voice and unique expression coupled with clarity and narrative structure. Professional, clean presentation of work is essential. Carefully read *FreeFall* guidelines before submitting. Do not fold manuscript, and submit 9×11 envelope. Include SASE/IRC for reply and/or return of manuscript. You may contact us by e-mail after initial hardcopy submission. For accepted pieces a request is made for disk or e-mail copy. Strong Web presence attracts submissions from writers all over the world."

FRONT & CENTRE

573 Gainsborough Ave., Ottawa ON K2A 2Y6 Canada. (613)729-8973. E-mail: firth@istar.ca. Website: www.blackbilepress.com. **Contact:** Matthew Firth, editor. Estab. 1998. Magazine: half letter-size; 40-50 pages; illustrations; photos. "We look for new fiction from Canadian and international writers—bold, aggressive work that does not compromise quality." Three issues per year. Circ. 500.

NEEDS literary ("contemporary realism/gritty urban"). "No science fiction, horror, mainstream, romance or religious." Receives 20 unsolicited mss/month. Accepts 6-7 mss/issue; 10-20 mss/year. Publishes ms 6 months after acceptance. Agented fiction 10%. **Publishes 8-9 new writers/year.** Recently published work by Len Gasparini, Katharine Coldiron, Salvatore Difalco, Gerald Locklin, Amanda Earl, Tom Johns. Length: 50-4,000 words; average length: 2,500 words. Publishes short shorts. Always comments on rejected mss.

HOW TO CONTACT Send SASE (from Canada) (or IRCs from USA) for return of ms or send a disposable copy of ms with #10 SASE for reply only. Responds in 2 weeks to queries; 4 months to mss. Accepts multiple submissions. Sample copy for $5. Writer's guidelines for SASE or by e-mail. Reviews fiction.

PAYMENT/TERMS Acquires first rights. Not copyrighted.

TIPS "We look for attention to detail, unique voice, not overtly derivative, bold writing, not pretentious. We should like to see more realism. Read the magazine first—simple as that!"

FUGUE LITERARY MAGAZINE

200 Brink Hall, University of Idaho P.O. Box 44110, Moscow ID 83844-1102. E-mail: fugue@uidaho.edu. Website: http://www.uiweb.uidaho.edu/fugue/. **Contact:** Jennifer Yeatts, Managing Editor. Estab. 1990. Magazine: 6×9; 175 pages; 70 lb. stock paper. By allowing the voices of established writers to lend their authority to new and emerging writers, *Fugue* strives to provide its readers with the most compelling stories, poems, essays, interviews and literary criticism possible. Semiannual.

Work published in *Fugue* has won the Pushcart Prize and has been cited in *Best American Essays.*

NEEDS ethnic/multicultural, experimental, humor/satire, literary. Receives 80 unsolicited mss/month. Accepts 6-8 mss/issue; 12-15 mss/year. Does not read mss May 1-August 31. Publishes ms 6 months after acceptance. **Publishes 4-6 new writers/year.** Recently published work by Kent Nelson, Marilyn Krysl, Cary Holladay, Padgett Powell, Dean Young, W.S. Merwin, Matthew Vollmer. Publishes short shorts. Also publishes literary essays, literary criticism, poetry. Sometimes comments on rejected mss.

HOW TO CONTACT Send complete ms. Send SASE (or IRC) for return of the ms or disposable copy of the ms and #10 SASE for reply only. Responds in 3-4 months to mss. Accepts simultaneous submissions. Sample copy for $8. Writer's guidelines for SASE or on website.

PAYMENT/TERMS All contributors receive payment and 2 complimentary copies of the journal. Pays on publication for first North American serial, electronic rights.

TIPS "The best way, of course, to determine what we're looking for is to read the journal. As the name *Fugue* indicates, our goal is to present a wide range of literary perspectives. We like stories that satisfy us both intellectually and emotionally, with fresh language and characters so captivating that they stick with us and invite a second reading. We are also seeking creative literary criticism which illuminates a piece of literature or a specific writer by examining that writer's personal experience."

GARGOYLE

Paycock Press, 3819 N. 13th St., Arlington VA 22201. (703)525-9296. E-mail: hedgehog2@erols.com. Website: www.gargoylemagazine.com. **Contact:** Richard Peabody, co-editor, Lucinda Ebersole, co-editor. Estab. 1976. Literary magazine: 5½×8½; 200 pages; illustrations; photos. "*Gargoyle* Magazine has always been a scallywag magazine, a maverick magazine, a bit too academic for the underground and way too underground for the academics. We are a writer's magazine in that we are read by other writers and have never worried about reaching the masses." Annual. Circ. 2,000.

NEEDS erotica, ethnic/multicultural, experimental, gay, lesbian, literary, mainstream, translations. "No romance, horror, science fiction." Wants "edgy realism or experimental works. We run both." Wants to see more Canadian, British, Australian and Third World fiction. Receives 50-200 unsolicited mss/month. Accepts 10-15 mss/issue. Accepts submissions during June, July, and Aug. Publishes ms 6-12 months after acceptance. Agented fiction 5%. **Publishes 2-3 new writers/year.** Recently published work by Stephanie Allen, Tom Carson, Susaan Cokal, Ramola D., Janice Eidus, James Grady, Susan Smith Nash, Zena Polin, Wena Poon, Elisabeth Sheffield, and Daniel Stola. Length: 30 pages maximum; average length: 5-10 pages. Publishes short shorts. Also publishes literary essays, literary criticism, poetry. Sometimes comments on rejected mss.

HOW TO CONTACT "We prefer electronic submissions. Please use submission engine online." For snail mail, send SASE for reply, return of ms or send a disposable copy of ms. Responds in 2 weeks to queries; 3 months to mss. Accepts simultaneous submissions. Sample copy for $12.95.

PAYMENT/TERMS Pays 10% of print run and so-so split (after/if) we break even. Acquires first North American serial, and first British rights. Sends galleys to author.

TIPS "We have to fall in love with a particular fiction."

GEORGETOWN REVIEW

Box 227, 400 East College St., Georgetown KY 40324. (502)863-8308. Fax: (502)868-8888. E-mail: gtownreview@georgetowncollege.edu. Website: http://georgetownreview.georgetowncollege.edu. **Contact:** Steven Carter, editor. Estab. 1993. Literary magazine/journal: 6×9, 192 pages, 20 lb. paper, four-color 60 lb. glossy cover. Email: gtownreview@georgetowncollege.edu. "We publish the best fiction we receive, regardless of theme or genre." Annual. Estab. 1993. Circ. 1,000. Member CLMP.

NEEDS Ethnic/multicultural (general), experimental, literary. Receives 100-125 mss/month. Accepts 8-10 mss/issue; 15-20 mss/year. Does not read January 1-August 31. Manuscript published 1 month-2 years after acceptance. Agented fiction 0%. **Publishes 3-4 new writers/year.** Published Andrew Plattner, Sallie Bingham, Alison Stine. Average length: 4,000 words. Publishes short shorts. Average length of short shorts: 500-1,500 words. Also publishes literary essays, poetry. Sometimes comments on/critiques rejected mss. Does not want adventure, children's, fantasy, romance.

HOW TO CONTACT Send complete ms with cover letter. Include brief bio, list of publications. Responds to queries in 1 month. Responds to mss in 1-3 months. Send either SASE (or IRC) for return of ms or disposable copy of ms and #10 SASE for reply only. Considers simultaneous submissions. Sample copy available for $7. Make checks payable to Georgetown College. Guidelines available on website.

PAYMENT/TERMS Writers receive 2 contributor's copies, free subscription to the magazine. Additional copies $5. Pays on publication. Acquires first North American serial rights. Publication is copyrighted. "Sponsors annual contest with $1,000 prize. Check website for guidelines."

TIPS "We look for fiction that is well written and that has a story line that keeps our interest. Don't send a first draft, and even if we don't take your first, second, or third submission, keep trying."

GERTRUDE

P.O. Box 83948, Portland OR 97283. E-mail: editor@gertrudepress.org. Website: www.gertrudepress.org. Estab. 1999. PO Box 83948, Portland OR 97283. E-mail: editor@gertrudepress.org. Website:www.gertrudepress.org. **Contact:** Eric Delehoy, editor. Magazine: 5×8½; 64-72 pages; perfect bound; 60 lb. paper; glossy card cover; illustrations; photos. *Gertrude* is an "annual publication featuring the voices and visions of the gay, lesbian, bisexual, transgender and supportive community." Estab. 1999. Circ. 400.

NEEDS ethnic/multicultural, feminist, gay, humor/satire, lesbian, literary, mainstream. "No romance, pornography or mystery." Wants more multicultural fiction. "We'd like to publish more humor and positive portrayals of gays—steer away from victim roles, pity." Receives 15-20 unsolicited mss/month. Accepts 4-8 mss/issue; 4-8 mss/year. Publishes ms 1-2 months after acceptance. **Publishes 4-5 new writers/year.** Recently published work by Carol Guess, Demrie Alonzo, Henry Alley and Scott Pomfret. Length: 200-3,000 words; average length: 1,800 words. Publishes short shorts. Also publishes poetry.

HOW TO CONTACT Send SASE for reply to query and a disposable copy of ms. Responds in 6-9 months to mss. Accepts multiple submissions Simultaneous submissions okay. Sample copy for $5, 6×9 SAE and 4 first-class stamps. Writer's guidelines for #10 SASE. Also can submit via online subission form on website.

PAYMENT/TERMS Pays 1-2 contributor's copies; additional copies $4. Pays on publication. Author retains rights upon publication. Not copyrighted.

TIPS "We look for strong characterization, imagery and new, unique ways of writing about universal experiences. Follow the construction of your work until the ending. Many stories start out with zest, then flipper and die. Show us, don't tell us."

GRASSLIMB

P.O. Box 420816, San Diego CA 92142. E-mail: editor@grasslimb.com. Website: www.grasslimb.com. **Contact:** Valerie Polichar, editor. Estab. 2002. Magazine: 14×20; 8 pages; 60 lb. white paper; illustrations. "*Grasslimb* publishes literary prose, poetry and art. Fiction is best when it is short and avant-garde or otherwise experimental." Semiannual. Circ. 200.

NEEDS experimental, literary, mystery/suspense (crime), regional, thriller/espionage, translations. Does not want romance or religious writings. Accepts 2-4 mss/issue; 4-8 mss/year. Publishes ms 3-6 months after acceptance. **Publishes 4 new writers/year.** Recently published work by Kuzhali Manickavel, Amanda Lyell. Length: 500-2,000 words; average length: 1,500 words. Publishes short shorts. Also publishes poetry. Rarely comments on rejected mss.

HOW TO CONTACT Send complete ms. Send SASE for return of ms or disposable copy of ms and #10 SASE for reply only. Responds in 4 months to mss. Accepts simultaneous and reprints, multiple submissions. Sample copy for $2.50. Writer's guidelines for SASE, e-mail or on website. Reviews fiction.

PAYMENT/TERMS Writers receive $10 minimum; $70 maximum, and 2 contributor's copies; additional copies $3. Pays on acceptance for first print publication serial rights.

TIPS "We publish brief fiction work that can be read in a single sitting over a cup of coffee. Work is generally 'literary' in nature, rather than mainstream. Experimental work welcome. Remember to have your work proofread and to send short work. We cannot read over 2,500 and prefer under 2,000 words. Include word count."

THE GREENSBORO REVIEW

MFA Writing Program, 3302 HHRA Building, UNC Greensboro, Greensboro NC 27402-6170. (336)334-5459. E-mail: jlclark@uncg.edu. Website: www.greensbororeview.org. **Contact:** Jim Clark, editor. Magazine: 6×9; approximately 128 pages; 60 lb. paper; 80 lb. cover. Literary magazine featuring fiction and poetry for readers interested in contemporary literature. Semiannual. Circ. 1,000.

Stories for the *Greensboro Review* have been included in *Best American Short Stories, The O. Henry Awards Prize Stories,* and *New Stories from The South*and *Pushcart Prize.*

NEEDS Accepts 6-8 mss/issue; 12-16 mss/year. Unsolicited manuscripts must arrive by September 15 to be considered for the spring issue and by February 15 to be considered for the fall issue. Manuscripts arriving after those dates may be held for the next consideration. **Publishes 10% new writers/year.** Has published work by Renee Ashley, Michael Cadnum, Carl Dennis, Jack Gilbert, Chard diNiord, Curtis Smith, and Kevin Wilson.

HOW TO CONTACT Responds in 4 months to mss. Accepts simultaneous submissions. No e-mail submissions. Submit manuscripts by regular or by submission form on website. Sample copy for $8.

PAYMENT/TERMS Pays in contributor's copies. Acquires first North American serial rights.

TIPS "We want to see the best being written regardless of theme, subject or style."

THE GRIFFIN

Gwynedd-Mercy College, 1325 Sumneytown Pike, P.O. Box 901, Gwynedd Valley PA 19437-0901. (215)641-5518. Fax: (215)641-5552. E-mail: allego.d@gmc.edu. Website: www.gmc.edu/students/clubsorganizations/thegriffin.php. **Contact:** Dr. Donna M. Allegro, editor. Estab. 1999. Literary magazine: 8.5 × 5.5; 112 pages. "*The Griffin* is an annual literary journal sponsored by Gwynedd-Mercy College. Its mission is to enrich society by nurturing and promoting creative writing that demonstrates a unique and intelligent voice. We seek writing which accurately reflects the human condition with all its intellectual, emotional and ethical challenges."

NEEDS short stories, essays, and poetry. Open to genre work. "No slasher, graphic violence or sex." Accepts mss depending on the quality of work submitted. Receives 20-30 unsolicited mss/month. Publishes ms 6-9 months after acceptance. Publishes 10-15 new writers/year. Length: 2,500 words; average length: 2,000 words. Publishes short shorts. Also publishes literary essays, poetry.

HOW TO CONTACT Send complete ms. All submissions must be on disk and include a hard copy. Send disposable copy of ms, disk and #10 SASE for reply only. Responds in 2-3 months to queries; 6 months to mss. Accepts simultaneous submissions "if notified." Sample copy for $10. Change to $10. The *Griffin* will be published online.

TIPS "Looking for well-constructed works that explore universal qualities, respect for the individual and community, justice and integrity. Check our description and criteria. Rewrite until you're sure every word counts. We publish the best work we find regardless of industry needs."

GUERNICA

A Magazine of Art and Politics, Attn: Michael Archer, 165 Bennett Ave., 4C, New York NY 10040. E-mail: editors@guernicamag.com; art@guernicamag.com (art/photography); poetry@guernicamag.com; publisher@guernicamag.com. Website: www.guernicamag.com. **Contact:** Erica Wright, poetry; Dan Eckstein, art/photography. Estab. 2005.

Received Caine Prize for African Writing, Best of the Net, cited by Esquire as a "great literary magazine."

NEEDS Literary, preferably with an international approach. No genre fiction.

HOW TO CONTACT Submit complete ms with cover letter Attn: Meakin Armstrong to fiction@guernicamag.com. In subject line (please follow this format exactly): "fiction submission."

TIPS "Please read the magazine first before submitting. Most stories that are rejected simply do not fit our approach. Submission guidelines available online."

GULF STREAM MAGAZINE

Florida International Univ., English Dept., Biscayne Bay Campus, 3000 N.E. 151st St., N. Miami FL 33181-3000. (305)919-5599. E-mail: gulfstreamfiu@yahoo.com. Website: www.gulfstreamlitmag.com. Estab. 1989. **Contact:** fiction editor. Magazine: 5½×8½; 124 pages; recycled paper; 80 lb. glossy cover; cover illustrations. "We publish good quality fiction, nonfiction and poetry for a predominately literary market." Semiannual. Estab. 1989. Circ. 300.

"Submit online only. Please read guidelines on website in full. Submissions that do not conform to our guidelines will be discarded. We do not accept emailed or mailed submissions. We read from Sept 15- Dec 15; Jan 15 - Mar 15." Does not pay writers' expenses.

NEEDS literary, mainstream, contemporary. Does not want romance, historical, juvenile or religious work. Receives 250 unsolicited mss/month. Accepts 5 mss/issue; 10 mss/year. Does not read mss during the summer. Publishes ms 3-6 months after acceptance. **Publishes 2-5 new writers/year.** Past contributors include Sherman Alexie, Steve Almond, Jan Beatty, Lee Martin, Robert Wrigley, Dennis Lehane, Liz Robbins, Stuart Dybek, David Kirby, Ann Hood, Ha Jin, B.H. Fairchild, Naomi Shihab Nye, F. Daniel Rzicznek, and Connie May Fowler. Length: 7,500 words; average length: 5,000 words. Publishes short shorts. Also publishes poetry.

HOW TO CONTACT Responds in 6 months to mss. Accepts simultaneous submissions "if noted." Sample copy for $5. Writer's guidelines for #10 SASE.

PAYMENT/TERMS Pays in gift subscriptions and contributor's copies. Acquires first North American serial rights.

TIPS "Looks for fresh, original writing—well plotted stories with unforgettable characters, fresh poetry and experimental writing. Usually longer stories do not get accepted. There are exceptions, however."

HAWAI'I PACIFIC REVIEW

1060 Bishop St., Honolulu HI 96813. (808)544-1108. Fax: (808)544-0862. E-mail: pwilson@hpu.edu. E-mail: hprsubmissions@hpu.edu. Website: www.hpu.edu/hpr. **Contact:** Dr. Patrice M. Wilson, editor. Magazine: 6×9; 100 pages; glossy coated cover. "*Hawai'i Pacific Review* is looking for poetry, short fiction and personal essays that speak with a powerful and unique voice. We encourage experimental narrative techniques and poetic styles, and we welcome works in translation." Annual.

NEEDS ethnic/multicultural (general), experimental, fantasy, feminist, historical (general), humor/satire, literary, mainstream, regional (Pacific), translations. "Open to all types as long as they're well done. Our audience is adults, so nothing for children/teens." Receives 30-50 unsolicited mss/month. Accepts 5-10 mss/year. Reads mss September- December each year. Publishes ms 10 months after acceptance. **Publishes 2-4 new writers/year.** Recently published work by Wendell Mayo, Elizabeth Crowell, Janet Flora, Mary Ann Cain, and Jean Giovanetti. Publishes short shorts. Also publishes literary essays, poetry. Sometimes comments on rejected mss.

HOW TO CONTACT Send SASE for return of ms or send a disposable copy of ms and SASE for reply only. Responds in 2 weeks to queries; 15 weeks to mss. Accepts simultaneous submissions but must be cited in the cover letter. Sample copy for $5.

PAYMENT/TERMS Pays 2 contributor's copies; additional copies $5. Pays on publication for first North American serial rights.

TIPS "We look for the unusual or original plot; prose with the texture and nuance of poetry. Character development or portrayal must be unusual/original; humanity shown in an original insightful way (or characters); sense of humor where applicable. Be sure it's a draft that has gone through substantial changes, with supervision from a more experienced writer, if you're a beginner. Write about intense emotion and feeling, not just about someone's divorce or shaky relationship. No soap-opera-like fiction."

HAYDEN'S FERRY REVIEW

c/o Virginia G. Piper Center for Creative Writing, Arizona State University, P.O. Box 875002, Tempe AZ 85287-5002. (480)965-1337. E-mail: HFR@asu.edu. Website: www.haydensferryreview.org. **Contact:** Beth Staples, managing editor. Estab. 1986. Editors change every 1-2 years. Magazine: $6\frac{3}{4}\times9\frac{3}{4}$; 150 pages; fine paper; illustrations; photos. "*Hayden's Ferry Review* publishes best quality fiction, poetry, translations, and creative nonfiction from new, emerging and established writers." Semiannual. Circ. 1,300.

Work from *Hayden's Ferry Review* has been selected for inclusion in *Pushcart Prize* anthologies, *Best of the West*, and *Best Creative Nonfiction*.

NEEDS ethnic/multicultural, experimental, humor/satire, literary, regional, slice-of-life vignettes, contemporary, prose poem. Possible special issue. Receives 250 unsolicited mss/month. Accepts 5 mss/issue; 10 mss/year. Publishes ms 6 months after acceptance. Recently published work by Joseph Heller, Ron Carlson, Norman Dubie, John Updike, Richard Ford, Yusef Komunyakaa, Joel-Peter Witkin, Ai, David St. John, Gloria Naylor, Tess Gallagher, Ken Kesey, Naomi Shihab Nye, Allen Ginsberg, T.C. Boyle, Raymond Carver, Rita Dove, Chuck Rosenthal, Rick Bass, Charles Baxter, Pam Houston, Mary Ruefle, and Denise Duhamel. Publishes short shorts.

HOW TO CONTACT Accepts submissions online. Responds in 2-3 days to queries; 2-4 months to mss. Accepts simultaneous submissions. Sample copy for $7.50. Writer's guidelines online.

PAYMENT/TERMS Pays $50-100, 2 copies, and 1-year subscription. Pays on publication for first North American serial rights. Sends galleys to author.

THE HELIX

Central Connecticut State University English Dept., E-mail: helixmagazine@gmail.com. Website: http://helixmagazine.org.

HOME PLANET NEWS

P.O. Box 455, High Falls NY 12440. (845)687-4084. E-mail: homeplanetnews@yahoo.com. Website: www.homeplanetnews.org. **Contact:** Donald Lev, editor. Estab. 1979. Tabloid: $11\frac{1}{2}\times16$; 24 pages; newsprint; illustrations; photos. "*Home Planet News* publishes mainly poetry along with some fiction, as well as reviews (books, theater and art) and articles of literary interest. We see *HPN* as a quality literary journal in an eminently readable format and with content that is urban, urbane and politically aware." Triannual. Circ. 1,000.

HPN has received a small grant from the Puffin Foundation for its focus on AIDS issues.

NEEDS ethnic/multicultural, experimental, feminist, gay, historical, lesbian, literary, mainstream, science fiction (soft/sociological). No "children's or genre stories (except rarely some science fiction)." Publishes special fiction issue or anthology. Receives 12 unsolicited mss/month. Accepts 1 mss/issue; 3 mss/year. Publishes ms 1 year after acceptance. Recently published work by Hugh Fox, Walter Jackman, Jim Story. Length: 500-2,500 words; average length: 2,000 words. Publishes short shorts. Also publishes literary criticism.

HOW TO CONTACT Send complete ms. Send SASE for reply, return of ms or send a disposable copy of the ms. Responds in 6 months to mss. Sample copy for $4. Writer's guidelines for SASE.

PAYMENT/TERMS Pays 3 contributor's copies; additional copies $1. Acquires one-time rights.

TIPS "We use very little fiction, and a story we accept just has to grab us. We need short pieces of some complexity, stories about complex people facing situations which resist simple resolutions."

HYCO REVIEW ARTS AND LITERARY JOURNAL

Piedmont Community College, P.O. Box 1197, Roxboro NC 27573. (336)599-1181, ext. 428. E-mail: reflect@piedmontcc.edu. Website: www.piedmontcc.edu. **Contact:** Dawn Langley, editor. Estab. 1999. Online magazine. 100-150 pages.

NEEDS literary. "Accepts mss from Person and Caswell counties, NC or Piedmont Community college student or alumni authors only (residents or natives). If time and space permit, we'll consider submissions from other North Carolina authors." Publishes mss 6-10 months after acceptance. **Publishes 3-5 new writers/year.** Recently published work by Maureen Sherbondy, Dainiel Green, Betty Moffett, Lian Gouw, Sejal Badani Ravani, Donna Conrad. Max Length: 4,000 words; average length: 2,500 words. Publishes short shorts. Also publishes poetry and essays, photographs, videos, digital animation, and artwork.

HOW TO CONTACT Send SASE for return of ms or #10 SASE for reply only. Sample copy for $5. Writer's guidelines for SASE or by e-mail.

PAYMENT/TERMS Publication is online. Acquires first North American serial rights. Sponsors awards/contests.

TIPS "We look for good writing with a flair, which captivates an educated lay audience. Don't take rejection letters personally. We turn away many submissions simply because we don't have room for everything we like or because the author is not from our region. For that reason, we're more likely to accept shorter well-written stories than longer stories of the same quality. Also, stories containing profanity that doesn't contribute to the plot, structure or intended tone are rejected immediately."

THE IDAHO REVIEW

Boise State University, English Dept., 1910 University Dr., Boise ID 83725. (208)426-1002. Fax: (208)426-4373. E-mail: mwieland@boisestate.edu. **Contact:** Mitch Wieland, editor. Estab. 1998. Magazine: 6×9; 180-200 pages; acid-free accent opaque paper; coated cover stock; photos. "A literary journal for anyone who enjoys good fiction." Annual. Circ. 1,000. Member CLMP.

Recent stories reprinted in *The Best American Short Stories, The O. Henry Prize Stories, The Pushcart Prize*, and *New Stories from the South*.

NEEDS experimental, literary. "No genre fiction of any type." Receives 150 unsolicited mss/month. Accepts 5-7 mss/issue; 5-7 mss/year. "We do not read from May 1-August 31." Publishes ms 1 year after acceptance. Agented fiction 5%. **Publishes 3 new writers/year.** Recently published work by Ann Beattie, Pam Houston, Rick Bass, Edith Pearlman, Joy Williams, Richard Bausch. Length: open; average length: 7,000 words. Publishes short shorts. Also publishes literary essays, poetry. Sometimes comments on rejected mss.

HOW TO CONTACT Send SASE for return of ms or send a disposable copy of ms and #10 SASE for reply only. Responds in 3-5 months to mss. Accepts simultaneous, multiple submissions. Sample copy for $8.95. Writer's guidelines for SASE. Reviews fiction.

PAYMENT/TERMS Pays $100 when funds are available plus 2 contributor's copies; additional copies $5. Pays on publication for first North American serial rights. Sends galleys to author.

TIPS "We look for strongly crafted work that tells a story that needs to be told. We demand vision and intlligence and mystery in the fiction we publish."

ILLUMINATIONS

Dept. of English, College of Charleston, 66 George St., Charleston SC 29424-0001. (843)953-1920. Fax: (843)953-3180. E-mail: lewiss@cofc.edu. Website: www.cofc.edu/illuminations. **Contact:** Simon Lewis, editor. Estab. 1982. Magazine: 5×8; 80 pages; illustrations. "*Illuminations* is one of the most challengingly eclectic little literary magazines around, having featured writers from the United States, Britain and Romania, as well as Southern Africa." Annual. Circ. 500.

NEEDS Literary. Receives 5 unsolicited mss/month. Accepts 1 mss/year. **Publishes 1 new writer/year.** Recently published work by John Michael Cummings.

Also publishes poetry. Sometimes comments on rejected mss.

HOW TO CONTACT Send SASE for reply, return of ms or send a disposable copy of ms. Responds in 2 weeks to queries; 2 months to mss. No simultaneous submissions. Sample copy for $10 and 6×9 envelope. Writer's guidelines free.

PAYMENT/TERMS Pays 2 contributor's copies of current issue; 1 of subsequent issue. Acquires one-time rights.

IMAGE

3307 Third Ave. W., Seattle WA 98119. (206)281-2988. Fax: (206)281-2979. E-mail: gwolfe@imagejournal.org. Website: www.imagejournal.org. **Contact:** Gregory Wolfe, publisher/editor. Estab. 1989. Magazine: 7×10; 136 pages; glossy cover stock; illustrations; photos. "*Image* is a showcase for the encounter between religious faith and world-class contemporary art. Each issue features fiction, poetry, essays, memoirs, reviews, an in-depth interview and articles about visual artists, film, music, etc. and glossy 4-color plates of contemporary visual art." Quarterly. Circ. 4,500. Member CLMP.

NEEDS Literary, essays. Receives 100 unsolicited mss/month. Accepts 2 mss/issue; 8 mss/year. Publishes ms 1 year after acceptance. Agented fiction 5%. Has published work by Annie Dillard, David James Duncan, Robert Olen Butler, Bret Lott, Melanie Rae Thon. Length: 4,000-6,000 words; average length: 5,000 words.

HOW TO CONTACT Send SASE for reply, return of ms or send disposable copy of ms. Responds in 1 month to queries; 3 months to mss. Sample copy for $16. Reviews fiction.

PAYMENT/TERMS Pays $10/page and 4 contributor's copies; additional copies for $6. Pays on acceptance. Sends galleys to author.

TIPS "Fiction must grapple with religious faith, though the settings, and subjects need not be overtly religious."

THE IOWA REVIEW

308 EPB, The University of Iowa, Iowa City IA 52242. (319)335-0462. Website: iowareview.org. **Contact:** Russell Scott Valentino, editor. Estab. 1970. Magazine: 5½×8½; 200 pages; first-grade offset paper; Carolina CS1 10-pt. cover stock. "Stories, essays, poems for a general readership interested in contemporary literature." Tri-annual magazine. Circ. 2,500.

"This magazine uses the help of colleagues and graduate assistants. Its reading period for unsolicited work is September 1-December 1. From January through April, we read entries to our annual Iowa Awards competition. Check our website for further information."

NEEDS "We are open to a range of styles and voices and always hope to be surprised by work we then feel we need." Receives 600 unsolicited mss/month. Accepts 4-6 mss/issue; 12-18 mss/year. Does not read mss January-August. Publishes ms an average of 12-18 months after acceptance. Agented fiction less than 2%. **Publishes some new writers/year.** Recently published work by Benjamin Chambers, Pierre Hauser, Stellar Kim. Also publishes literary essays, literary criticism, poetry.

HOW TO CONTACT Send complete ms with cover letter. "Don't bother with queries." SASE for return of ms. Responds in 3 months to queries; 3 months to mss. "We discourage simultaneous submissions." Sample copy for $9 and online; subscription $25. Writer's guidelines online. Reviews fiction.

PAYMENT/TERMS Pays $.08 per word with a $100 minimum, plus 2 contributor's copies; additional copies 30% off cover price. Pays on publication for first North American serial, nonexclusive anthology, classroom, online serial rights.

TIPS "We publish essays, reviews, novel excerpts, stories, and poems, and would like for our essays not always to be works of academic criticism. We have no set guidelines as to content or length, but strongly recommend that writers read a sample issue before submitting. **Buys 65-80 unsolicited ms/year.** Submit complete ms with SASE. **Pays $25 for the first page and $15 for each subsequent page of poetry or prose.**"

JABBERWOCK REVIEW

Department of English, Mississippi State University, Drawer E, Mississippi State MS 39762. E-mail: jabberwockreview@english.msstate.edu. Website: www.msstate.edu/org/jabberwock. **Contact:** Michael Kardos, editor. Estab. 1979. Literary magazine/journal: 6x9; 120 pages; 60 lb paper; 80 lb cover.

NEEDS ethnic/multicultural, experimental, feminist, gay, literary, mainstream, regional, translations. "No science fiction, romance." Receives 150 unsolicited mss/month. Accepts 7-8 mss/issue; 15 mss/year. "We do not read March 15 to September 1." Publishes ms 4-6 months after acceptance. **Publishes 1-5 new writers/year.** Recently published work by Robert Morgan, Charles Harper Webb, Ted Kooser, Alison Baker, Alyce Miller, Lorraine Lopez, J.D. Chapman. Length: 250-5,000 words; average length: 4,000 words. Publishes short shorts. Also publishes literary essays, poetry. Sometimes comments on rejected mss.

HOW TO CONTACT Send SASE (or IRC) for return of ms. Does not accept e-mail submissions. Responds in 5 months to mss. Accepts simultaneous submissions "with notification of such." Sample copy for $6. Writer's guidelines for SASE.

PAYMENT/TERMS Pays 2 contributor's copies. Sponsors awards/contests.

TIPS "It might take a few months to get a response from us, but your manuscript will be read with care. Our editors enjoy reading submissions (really!) and will remember writers who are persistent and committed to getting a story 'right' through revision."

J JOURNAL: NEW WRITING ON JUSTICE

619 West 54th St., 7th Fl, New York NY 10019. (212) 327-8697. E-mail: jjournal@jjay.cuny.edu. Website: www.jjournal.org. **Contact:** Adam Berlin and Jeffrey Heiman, editors. Estab. 2008. Literary magazine/journal: 6x9; 120 pages; 60 lb paper; 80 lb cover. "*J Journal* publishes literary fiction, creative nonfiction and poetry on the subjects of crime, criminal justice, law and law enforcement. While the themes are specific, they need not dominate the work. We're interested in questions of justice from all perspectives." Semiannual. Estab. 2008.

NEEDS experimental, gay, historical (general), literary, military/war, regional. Receives 100 mss/month. Accepts 5 mss/issue; 10 mss/year. Ms. published 6 months after acceptance. Length: 750-6,000 words (max). Average length: 4,000 words. Also publishes poetry. Sometimes comments on/critiques rejected mss.

HOW TO CONTACT Send complete ms with cover letter. Include estimated word count, brief bio, list of publications. Responds to queries in 4 weeks; mss in 12 weeks. Send recyclable copy of ms and #10 SASE or email for reply only. Considers simultaneous submissions. Sample copy available for $10.

PAYMENT/TERMS Writers receive 2 contributor's copies. Additional copies $10. Pays on publication. Acquires first rights. Publication is copyrighted.

TIPS "We're looking for literary fiction/memoir/personal narrative poetry with a connection, direct or tangential, to the theme of justice."

KEREM

Jewish Study Center Press, 3035 Porter St. NW, Washington DC 20008. (202)364-3006. E-mail: langner@erols.com; kerem@simpatico.ca. Website: www.kerem.org. **Contact:** Gilah Langner, co-editor. Estab. 1992. Magazine: 6×9; 128 pages; 60 lb. offset paper; glossy cover; illustrations; photos. "Kerem publishes Jewish religious, creative, literary material—short stories, poetry, personal reflections, text study, prayers, rituals, etc." Estab. 1992.

NEEDS Jewish: feminist, humor/satire, literary, religious/inspirational. Receives 10-12 unsolicited mss/month. Accepts 1-2 mss/issue. Publishes ms 2-10 months after acceptance. **Publishes 2 new writers/year.** Also publishes literary essays, poetry.

HOW TO CONTACT Prefers submissions by e-mail. Send SASE for reply, return of ms or send disposable copy of ms. Responds in 2 months to queries; 5 months to mss. Accepts simultaneous, multiple submissions. Sample copy for $8.50. Writer's guidelines online.

PAYMENT/TERMS Pays free subscription and 2-10 contributor's copies. Acquires onetime rights.

TIPS "Should have a strong Jewish content. We want to be moved by reading the manuscript!"

LA KANCERKLINIKO

c/o Laurent Septier, 162 rue Paradis, P.O. Box 174, 13444 Marseille Cantini Cedex France. (33) 2-48-61-81-98. Fax: (33) 2-48-61-81-98. E-mail: lseptier@hotmail.com. **Contact:** Laurent Septier. "An Esperanto magazine which appears 4 times annually. Each issue contains 32 pages. La Kancerkliniko is a political and cultural magazine." Recently published work by Mao Zifu, Manuel de Seabra, Peter Brown, and Aldo de'Giorgi. Quarterly. Circ. 300.

NEEDS science fiction, short stories, or very short novels. "The short story (or the very short novel) must be written only in Esperanto, either original or translation from any other language." Wants more science fiction. **Publishes 2-3 new writers/year.**

HOW TO CONTACT Accepts submissions by e-mail, fax. Accepts disk submissions. Accepts multiple submissions. Sample copy for 3 IRCs from Universal Postal Union.

PAYMENT/TERMS Pays in contributor's copies.

LAKE EFFECT

4951 College Dr., Erie PA 16563-1501. (814)898-6281. Fax: (814)898-6032. E-mail: goL1@psu.edu. Website: www.pserie.psu.edu/lakeeffect. **Contact:** George Looney, editor-in-chief. Estab. 1978. Magazine: 5½×8½; 180-200 pages; 55 lb. natural paper; 12 pt. C1S cover. "In addition to seeking strong, traditional stories, *Lake Effect* is open to more experimental, language-centered fiction as well." Annual. Estab. as *Lake Effect*, 2001; as *Tempest*, 1978. Member CLMP.

NEEDS experimental, literary, mainstream. "No children's/juvenile, fantasy, science fiction, romance or young adult/teen." Receives 120 unsolicited mss/month. Accepts 5-9 mss/issue. Publishes ms 1 year after acceptance. **Publishes 6 new writers/year.** Recently published work by Edith Pearlman, Francois Camoin, Cris Mazza, Joan Connor, Aimee Parkison, Joanna Howard. Length: 4,500-5,000 words; average length: 2,600-3,900 words. Publishes short shorts. Also publishes literary essays, poetry.

HOW TO CONTACT Send SASE for return of ms or send a disposable copy of ms and #10 SASE for reply only. Responds in 3 weeks to queries; 2-6 months to mss. Accepts simultaneous submissions. Sample copy for $6. Writer's guidelines for SASE.

PAYMENT/TERMS Pays 2 contributor's copies; additional copies $2. Acquires first, onetime rights. Not copyrighted.

TIPS "We're looking for strong, well-crafted stories that emerge from character and language more than plot. The language is what makes a story stand out (and a strong sense of voice). Be sure to let us know immediately should a submitted story be accepted elsewhere."

LANDFALL/OTAGO UNIVERSITY PRESS

Otago University Press, P.O. Box 56, Dunedin New Zealand. Fax: (643)479-8385. E-mail: landfall@otago.ac.nz. **Contact:** Landfall Editor.

NEEDS Publishes fiction, poetry, commentary and reviews of New Zealand books.

HOW TO CONTACT Email your submission to landfall@otago.ac.nz. Submission guidelines are at www.otago.ac.nz/press/landfall.

TIPS "We concentrate on publishing work by New Zealand writers, but occasionally accept work from elsewhere."

LEAVES & FLOWERS

15409 Bear Creek Ct., Findlay OH 45840. (419)957-5133. E-mail: leavesandflowers@gmail.com. Website: www.leavesandflowers.webs.com. **Contact:** Bailey Shoemaker Richards, editor-in-chief. Estab. 2009. "*Leaves & Flowers* is unique in that it is focused on exploring the creative diversity of writers and artists. Each issue has a new, individual prompt. Each submission must use this shared prompt as its inspiration to be considered for publication. L&F is looking for new writers, established writers, and artists of all types. The website contains excerpts, writer's guidelines, editor blogs, author interviews, writing not included in the print version, the prompt for each issue, and other information about the journal and writing." 50-100 pages with illustrations and photographs. Triannual.

NEEDS adventure, comics and graphic novels, ethnic/multicultural, experimental, family saga, feminist, gay, lesbian, glitz, historical, horror, humor/satire, literary, mainstream, military/war, mystery/suspense, New Age, psychic/supernatural, romance, science fiction, thriller/espionage, YA. Does not publish erotica. See upcoming issue or website for prompts. Accepts up to 40 fiction mss/issue. Time between acceptance and publication is 1-3 months. **Publishes 5-20 new writers per year.** Has published work by Renda Dodge, Ryan Shoemaker, Jearl Rugh, Caleb Krause, Lydia Ondrusek. Maximum length: 10,000 words. Average length: 2,000 words. Publishes short shorts, minimum 500 words. Also publishes literary essays and poetry. Often comments on rejected mss.

HOW TO CONTACT Send complete ms with cover letter. Accepts submissions by e-mail. Include estimated word count, brief bio, and list of publications. Responds to mss. in 2 weeks. Does not accept submissions by mail. Considers simultaneous and previously published submissions. Guidelines and sample copy on website.

PAYMENT/TERMS Writers receive 1 pdf contributor's copy upon publication. Acquires onetime rights.

TIPS "Writers should strive to use the prompt in a unique way that demonstrates both their individual take on a shared prompt, as well as showcases their talent as a writer. L&F is looking for writers who can use language and prompts in unfamiliar and interesting ways. Read all the submissions guidelines on the website and follow them—improper submissions are rejected. Take some time to study the prompt before writing—find a way of utilizing the prompt that speaks to your own viewpoint and writing style."

THE LEDGE MAGAZINE

40 Maple Ave., Bellport NY 11713-2011. (631)219-5969. E-mail: info@theledgemagazine.com. Website: www.theledgemagazine.com. **Contact:** Tim Monaghan, Editor-in-Chief, tkmonaghan@aol.com. Estab. 1988. Literary magazine/journal: 6 x 9, 300 pages, offset paper, glossy stock cover. "The *Ledge Magazine* publishes cutting-edge contemporary fiction by emerging and established writers." Annual. Estab. 1988. Circ. 1,000.

NEEDS erotica, ethnic/multicultural (general), literary. Receives 120 mss/month. Accepts 9 mss/issue. Manuscript published 6 months after acceptance. Published Pia Chatterjee, Xujun Eberlein, Clifford Garstang, Richard Jespers, William Luvaas, Michael Thompson. Length: 2,500 words (min)-7,500 words (max). Average length: 6,000 words. Also publishes poetry. Rarely comments on/critiques rejected mss.

HOW TO CONTACT Send complete ms with cover letter. Include estimated word count, brief bio. Responds to queries in 6 weeks. Responds to mss in 8 months. Send SASE (or IRC) for return of ms. Considers simultaneous submissions. Sample copy available for $10. Subscription: $20 (2 issues), $36 (4 issues). Guidelines available for SASE.

PAYMENT/TERMS Writers receive 1 contributor's copy. Additional copies $6. Pays on publication. Acquires first North American serial rights. Sends galleys to author. Publication is copyrighted.

TIPS "We seek compelling stories that employ innovative language and complex characterization. We especially enjoy poignant stories with a sense of purpose. We dislike careless or hackneyed writing."

◐ LE FORUM

University of Maine, Franco American Center, Orono ME 04469-5719. (207)581-3764. Fax: (207)581-1455. E-mail: lisa_michaud@umit.maine.edu. Website: Francoamericanarchives.org. **Contact:** Lisa Michaud, managing editor. Estab. 1972. Magazine: 56 pages; illustrations; photos. Publication was founded to stimulate and recognize creative expression among Franco-Americans, all types of readers, including literary and working class. This publication is used in classrooms. Circulated internationally. Quarterly. Estab. 1972. Circ. 5,000.

NEEDS "We will consider any type of short fiction, poetry and critical essays having to do with Franco-American experience. They must be of good quality in French or English. We are also looking for Canadian writers with French-North American experiences." Receives 10 unsolicited mss/month. Accepts 2-4 mss/issue. **Publishes some new writers/year.** Length: 750-2,500 words; average length: 1,000 words. Occasionally comments on rejected mss.

HOW TO CONTACT Include SASE. Responds in 3 weeks to queries; 1 month to mss. Accepts simultaneous submissions and reprints. Sample copy not available.

PAYMENT/TERMS Pays 3 copies. Acquires onetime rights.

TIPS "Write honestly. Start with a strongly felt personal Franco-American experience. If you make us feel what you have felt, we will publish it. We stress that this publication deals specifically with the Franco-American experience."

◐ THE LISTENING EYE

Kent State University Geauga Campus, 14111 Claridon-Troy Rd., Burton OH 44021. (440)286-3840. E-mail: grace_butcher@msn.com. Website: http://reocities.com/Athens/3716/eye.htm. **Contact:** Grace Butcher, editor. Magazine: 5½×8½; 60 pages; photographs. "We publish the occasional very short stories (750 words/3 pages double spaced) in any subject and any style, but the language must be strong, unusual, free from cliché and vagueness. We are a shoestring operation from a small campus but we publish high-quality work." Annual. Estab. 1970. Circ. 250.

NEEDS literary. "Pretty much anything will be considered except porn." Reads mss January 1-April 15 only. Publishes ms 3-4 months after acceptance. Recently published work by Elizabeth Scott, Sam Ruddick, H.E. Wright. Publishes short shorts. Also publishes poetry. Sometimes comments on rejected mss.

HOW TO CONTACT Send SASE for return of ms or disposable copy of ms with SASE for reply only. Responds in 4 weeks to queries; 4 months to mss. Accepts reprint submissions. Sample copy for $3 and $1 postage. Writer's guidelines for SASE.

PAYMENT/TERMS Pays 2 contributor's copies; additional copies $3 with $1 postage. Pays on publication for onetime rights.

TIPS "We look for powerful, unusual imagery, content and plot in our short stories. In poetry, we look for tight lines that don't sound like prose; unexpected images or juxtapositions; the unusual use of language; noticeable relationships of sounds; a twist in viewpoint; an ordinary idea in extraordinary language; an amazing and complex idea simply stated; play on words and with words; an obvious love of language. Poets need to read the 'Big 3'—Cummings, Thomas, Hopkins—to see the limits to which language can be taken. Then read the 'Big 2'—Dickinson to see how simultaneously tight, terse, and universal a poem can be, and Whitman to see how sprawling, cosmic, and personal. Then read everything you can find that's being published in literary magazines today, and see how your work compares to all of the above."

LITERAL LATTE

200 E. 10th St., Suite 240, New York NY 10003. (212)260-5532. E-mail: litlatte@aol.com. Website: www.literal-latte.com. Estab. 1994. **Contact:** Jenine Gordon Bockman. "Publishes great writing in many flavors and styles. *Literal Latte* expanded the readership for literary magazines by offering free copies in New York coffeehouses and bookstores. Now online only and free to the world." Bimonthly. CLMP.

NEEDS experimental, fantasy, literary, science fiction. Receives 4,000 unsolicited mss/month. Accepts 5-8 mss/issue; 40 mss/year. Agented fiction 1%. **Publishes 6 new writers/year.** Length: 500-8,000 words; average length: 4,000 words. Publishes short shorts. Often comments on rejected mss.

HOW TO CONTACT Send SASE for return of mss or send a disposable copy of ms and e-mail for reply only. Responds in 6 months to mss. Accepts simultaneous, multiple submissions. Sample copy for $3. Writer's guidelines for SASE, e-mail or check website. Reviews fiction.

PAYMENT/TERMS Pays annual anthology. First rights. May request additional rights to put piece in annual anthology. Pays on publication for first, one-time rights. Sponsors awards/contests.

TIPS "Keeping free thought free and challenging entertainment are not mutually exclusive. Words make a manuscript stand out, words beautifully woven together in striking and memorable patterns."

THE LITERARY REVIEW

285 Madison Ave., Madison NJ 07940. (973)443-8564. Fax: (973)443-8364. E-mail: tlr@fdu.edu. Website: www.theliteraryreview.org. **Contact:** Minna Proctor, Editor-In-Chief. Estab. 1957. Magazine: 6×9; 200 pages; professionally printed on textpaper; semigloss card cover; perfect-bound. "Literary magazine specializing in fiction, poetry and essays with an international focus. Our audience is general with a leaning toward scholars, libraries and schools." Quarterly. Estab. 1957. Circ. 2,000.

Work published in the *Literary Review* has been included in *Editor's Choice, Best American Short Stories* and *Pushcart Prize* anthologies.

NEEDS Works of high literary quality only. Does not want to see "overused subject matter or pat resolutions to conflicts." Receives 90-100 unsolicited mss/month. Submit on line only; No paper mss.Accepts 20-25 mss/year. Does not read submissions June 1-September 1. Publishes ms 1-2 years after acceptance. Agented fiction 1-2%. **Publishes 80% new writers/year.** Recently published work by Irvin Faust, Todd James Pierce, Joshua Shapiro, Susan Schwartz Senstadt. Also publishes literary essays, literary criticism, poetry. Occasionally comments on rejected mss.

HOW TO CONTACT Responds in 6-12 months to mss. Submit online at www.theliteraryreview.org/submit.html only. Accepts multiple submissions. Sample copy for $8. Writer's guidelines for SASE. Reviews fiction.

PAYMENT/TERMS Pays 2 contributor's copies; $4 discount for extras. Acquires first rights.

TIPS "We want original dramatic situations with complex moral and intellectual resonance and vivid prose. We don't want versions of familiar plots and relationships. Too much of what we are seeing today is openly derivative in subject, plot and prose style. We pride ourselves on spotting new writers with fresh insight and approach."

THE LONG STORY

18 Eaton St., Lawrence MA 01843. (978)686-7638. E-mail: rpburnham@mac.com. Website: web.me.com/rpburnham/Site/LongStory.html. **Contact:** R.P. Burnham. Estab. 1983. Magazine: 5½×8½; 160 pages; 60 lb. cover stock; illustrations (b&w graphics). For serious, educated, literary people. Annual. Circ. 600.

NEEDS ethnic/multicultural, feminist, literary, contemporary. "No science fiction, adventure, romance, etc. We publish high literary quality of any kind but especially look for stories that have difficulty getting published elsewhere—committed fiction, working class settings, left-wing themes, etc." Receives 30-50 unsolicited mss/month. Accepts 6-7 mss/issue. Publishes ms 3 months to 1 year after acceptance. **Publishes 90% new writers/year.** Length: 8,000-20,000 words; average length: 8,000-12,000 words.

HOW TO CONTACT Include SASE. Responds in 2 months to mss. Accepts simultaneous submissions "but not wild about it." Sample copy for $7.

PAYMENT/TERMS Pays 2 contributor's copies; $5 charge for extras. Acquires first rights.

TIPS "Read us first and make sure submitted material is the kind we're interested in. Send clear, legible manuscripts. We're not interested in commercial success;

rather we want to provide a place for long stories, the most difficult literary form to publish in our country."

LOUISIANA LITERATURE

SLU Box 10792, Southeastern Louisiana University, Hammond LA 70402. E-mail: lalit@selu.edu; ngerman@selu.edu. Website: www.louisianaliterature.org. **Contact:** Jack B. Bedell, editor. Estab. 1984. Magazine: 6×9; 150 pages; 70 lb. paper; card cover; illustrations. "Essays should be about Louisiana material; preference is given to fiction and poetry with Louisiana and Southern themes, but creative work can be set anywhere." Semiannual. Circ. 600 paid; 750-1,000 printed.

NEEDS Literary, mainstream, regional. "No sloppy, ungrammatical manuscripts." Receives 100 unsolicited mss/month. May not read mss June-July. Publishes ms 6-12 after acceptance. **Publishes 4 new writers/year.** Recently published work by Anthony Bukowski, Aaron Gwyn, Robert Phillips, R.T. Smith. Length: 1,000-6,000 words; average length: 3,500 words. Sometimes comments on rejected mss.

HOW TO CONTACT Include SASE. Responds in 3 months to mss. Sample copy for $8. Reviews fiction.

PAYMENT/TERMS Pays usually in contributor's copies. Acquires one-time rights.

TIPS "Cut out everything that is not a functioning part of the story. Make sure your manuscript is professionally presented. Use relevant specific detail in every scene. We love detail, local color, voice and craft. Any professional manuscript stands out."

THE LOUISIANA REVIEW

Division of Liberal Arts, Louisiana State University at Eunice, P.O. Box 1129, Eunice LA 70535. (337)550-1315. E-mail: bfonteno@lsue.edu. Website: web.lsue.edu/la-review. **Contact:** Dr. Billy Fontenot, editor. Estab. 1999. Magazine: $8\frac{1}{2}$x$5\frac{1}{2}$ bound; 100-200 pages; b&w illustrations. "We are looking for excellent work by Louisiana writers as well as those outside the state who tell us their connection to it. Non-Louisiana material is considered, but Louisiana/Gulf Coast themed work gets priority." Annual. Circ. 300-600.

NEEDS Ethnic/multicultural (Cajun or Louisiana culture), historical (Louisiana-related or setting), regional (Louisiana, Gulf Coast). Receives 25 unsolicited mss/month. Accepts 5-7 mss/issue. Reads year-round. Publishes ms 6-12 months after acceptance. Recently published work by Ronald Frame, Tom Bonner, Laura Cario, Sheryl St. Germaine. Length: up to 9,000 words; average length: 2,000 words. Publishes short shorts. Also publishes poetry and b&w artwork. Sometimes comments on rejected mss.

HOW TO CONTACT Send SASE for return of ms. Responds in 5 weeks to queries; 10 weeks to mss. Accepts multiple submissions. Sample copy for $5.

PAYMENT/TERMS Pays 1 contributor's copy. Pays on publication for onetime rights. Not copyrighted but has an ISSN number.

TIPS "We do like to have fiction play out visually as a film would rather than static and undramatized. Louisiana or Gulf Coast settings and themes preferred."

THE MACGUFFIN

18600 Haggerty Rd., Livonia MI 48152-2696. (734)462-4400, ext 5327. E-mail: macguffin@schoolcraft.edu. Website: www.macguffin.org. **Contact:** Steven A. Dolgin, editor; Nicholle Cormier, managing editor; Elizabeth Kircos, fiction editor. Estab. 1984. Magazine: 6×9; 160 pages; 60 lb. paper; 110 lb. cover; b&w illustrations, photos. "*The MacGuffin* is a literary magazine which publishes a range of material including poetry, creative nonfiction, fiction, and art. Material ranges from traditional to experimental. Our periodical attracts a variety of people with many different interests." Triannual. Circ. 500.

NEEDS adventure, ethnic/multicultural, experimental, historical (general), humor/satire, literary, mainstream, translations, contemporary, prose poem. "No religious, inspirational, juvenile, romance, horror, pornography." Receives 80-100 unsolicited mss/month. Accepts 14-18 mss/issue; 42-54 mss/year. Publishes ms 6 months to 1.5 years after acceptance. Agented fiction 10-15%. **Publishes 30 new writers/year.** Recently published work by Thomas Lynch, Linda Nemec Foster, Jim Daniels, M. E. Parker, and Daniel Pearlman. Length: 100-5,000 words; average length: 2,000-2,500 words. Publishes short shorts. Also publishes literary essays. Occasionally comments on rejected mss.

HOW TO CONTACT Send SASE or e-mail. Responds in 4-6 months to mss. Sample copy for $6; current issue for $9. Writer's guidelines free on website or with SASE. Pays 2 contributor's copies. Acquires onetime rights.

TIPS "We strive to give promising new writers the opportunity to publish alongside recognized writers. Follow the submission guidelines, proofread your work, and be persistent. When we reject a story, we may accept the next one you send. When we make suggestions for a rewrite, we may accept the revision. Make your characters come to life. Even the most ordinary people become fascinating if they live for your readers."

THE MADISON REVIEW

University of Wisconsin, 600 N, Park St., 6193 Helen C. White Hall, Madison WI 53706. E-mail: madisonreview@gmail.com. Website: www.english.wisc.edu/madisonreview/. Estab. 1972. Magazine: 6×9; 180 pages. "We are an independent literary journal featuring quality fiction, poetry, artwork, and interviews. Both established and emerging writers are encouraged to submit." Semiannual.

"We do not publish unsolicited interviews or genre ficion."

NEEDS "Well-crafted, compelling fiction featuring a wide range of styles and subjects." Receives 300 unsolicited mss/period. Accepts 6 mss/issue. Does not read May-September. Publishes ms 4 months after acceptance. **Publishes 4 new writers/year.** Recently published work by Lori Rader Day and Ian Williams. Average length: 4,000 words. Also publishes poetry.

HOW TO CONTACT Accepts multiple submissions. Sample copy for $4 via postal service or e-mail.

PAYMENT/TERMS Pays 2 contributor's copies; $5 charge for extras. Acquires first North American serial rights.

TIPS "Our editors have very ecclectic tastes, so don't specifically try to cater to us. Above all, we look for original, high quality work."

MARGINALIA

Communication Arts, Language and Literature Department of Western State College of Colorado, P.O. Box 258, Pitkin CO 81241. (970) 642-0393. E-mail: marginaliajournal@gmail.com. Website: www.marginaliajournal.com. **Contact:** Alicita Rodriguez, editor. Estab. 2005. Annual literary magazine/journal. 6×9, 150 pages, 100 lb paper. "We like writing that pays close attention to the sentence. Language is not a means to an end. It should not be something that gets used solely to establish plot. We want gorgeous diction, unusual and striking imagery, reversed and playful syntax. We don't want to remember what the story or poem is about; we want to remember how it's told. We welcome any hybrid or unidentifiable genres, though we shun experimentation for experimentation's sake. We don't want work that depends on clever jokes or conceits. We like the odd but well-written traditional story, though we don't see too many of these. No gratuitous violence (especially against women and animals)."

NEEDS experimental, literary. Does not want mainstream or genre fiction. List of upcoming themes available on Web site. Receives 40 mss/month. Accepts 20 mss/issue; 20 mss/year. Ms published 6-9 months after acceptance. Publishes 15% new writers/year. Published Brian Evenson, Laird Hunt, Mark Irwin, Steve Katz, Alex Lemon, Harry Matthews, Gina Ochsner, Lance Olsen, George Singleton, Abdelkrim Tabal, Wendy Walker, and Tom Whalen. Average length: 2,000 words. Publishes short shorts. Also publishes literary essays, book reviews, poetry, visual art. Send review copies to P.O. Box 258, Pitkin CO 81241. Sometimes comments on/critiques rejected mss.

HOW TO CONTACT Submit full ms via e-mail to marginaliajournal@gmail.com or by mail to P.O. Box 258, Pitkin CO 81241. Include estimated word count, brief bio, list of publications. Responds to mss in 6-9 months. Considers simultaneous submissions, multiple submissions. Sample copy available for $9. Sample copy, guidelines available on Web Site: www.marginaliajournal.com. Payment/Terms: Writers receive 3 contributor's copies. Additional copies $5. Pays on acceptance. Acquires first rights. Sends galleys to author. Publication is copyrighted. No contests at this time.

TIPS "Beginning fiction writers should be professional. Do not write clever or long cover letters. Never explain what your story intends to do: the work should speak for itself. Do not write emails asking about the status of your submission—staff is unpaid and overworked. For verse, please make sure your line breaks are purposeful; for prose, please pay attention to syntax."

THE MARLBORO REVIEW

The Marlboro Review Inc., P.O. Box 243, Marlboro VT 05344. (802)254-4938. E-mail: editor@marlbororeview.org. Website: www.marlbororeview.org. **Contact:** Ellen Dudley, fiction editor. Estab. 1996. Magazine: 6×9; 80-120 pages; 60 lb. paper; photos. Wants material approached from a writer's sensibility. "Our only criterion for publication is strength of work." Semiannual. Estab. 1996. Circ. 1,000. Receives 400-500 unsolicited mss/month. "Accepts manuscripts September through May." Recently published work by Stephen Dobyns, Jean Valentine, Joseph Shuster, Chana Bloch, William Matthews and Alberto Rios. Length: 500-12,000 words; average length:

7,000 words. Publishes short shorts. Also publishes literary essays, literary criticism, poetry. Accepts 2-3 mss/issue; 4-6 mss/year. Accepts simultaneous, multiple submissions. Sample copy for $20. Writer's guidelines for SASE or on website. Reviews fiction. All rights revert to author on publication. Member CLMP, AWP.

Open to short fiction and poetry submissions. Include SASE with proper postage, otherwise your work will be discarded unread. Submissions received during the summer break will be returned unread.

NEEDS cultural, philosophical, scientific and literary issues material

HOW TO CONTACT Send SASE for return of ms or send a disposable copy of ms and #10 SASE for reply only. No summer or e-mail submissions.

PAYMENT/TERMS Pays 2 contributor's copies; additional copies $8.

TIPS "Check Guidelines for details and restrictions. Open to most themes. We are particularly interested in translation, as well as cultural, scientific, and philosophical issues approached from a writer's sensibility. If you are overseas and must submit electronically, consult with Ellen Dudley before sending any files."

MINNETONKA REVIEW

Minnetonka Review Press, LLC, P.O. Box 386, Spring Park MN 55384. E-mail: query@minnetonkareview.com. Website: www.minnetonkareview.com. **Contact:** Troy Ehlers, editor-in-chief. Literary magazine/journal. 6x9, 200 pages, recycled natural paper, glossy cover. Contains illustrations. Includes photographs. "We publish work of literary excellence. We are particularly attracted to fiction with careful prose, engaging and tension filled stories, and new perspectives, forms and styles." Semiannual. Estab. 2007. Circ. 1,000.

NEEDS literary, mainstream. Receives 100 mss/month. Accepts 7 mss/issue; 15 mss/year. Does not read during the summer between May 15th and October 15th. Ms published 6-8 months after acceptance. **Publishes 6 new writers/year.** Published Bev Jafek, Daniel DiStasio, Nathan Leslie, Robin Lippincott, Megan Cass, Arthur Saltzman, Gary Amdahl, and Arthur Winfield Knight. Length: 1,200 words (min)-6,000 words (best). Will accept up to 10,00 words but must be outstanding. Average length: 4,000 words. Publishes short shorts. Average length of short shorts: 1,200 words. Also publishes literary essays, poetry. Rarely comments on/critiques rejected mss.

HOW TO CONTACT Send complete ms with cover letter. Accepts submissions by mail or by submission manager online. Include brief bio. Responds to queries in 2 weeks. Responds to mss in 4 months. Send either SASE (or IRC) for return of ms or disposable copy of ms and #10 SASE for reply only. Considers simultaneous submissions. Sample copy available for $9. Guidelines available for SASE, via e-mail, on website.

PAYMENT/TERMS Writers receive 3 contributor's copies. Additional copies $7. Pays on publication. Acquires first North American serial rights. Publication is copyrighted. "Two authors from each issue receive a $150 Editor's Prize. Other contests with $1,000 prize are held from time to time. Details are available on our website."

TIPS "The trick seems to be holding our attention, whether via novelty, language, style, story, good descriptions or tension. Always be honing your craft, reading and writing. And when you read, it helps to be familiar with what we publish, but in general, you should be reading a number of literary journals and anthologies. Think of your work as a contribution to a greater literary dialogue."

MOBIUS

505 Christianson, Madison WI 53714. (608)242-1009. E-mail: fmschep@charter.net. Website: www.mobiusmagazine.com. **Contact:** Fred Schepartz, editor. Estab. 1989. No longer a print magazine. Strictly a web-based magazine, but with the same quarterly publication schedule. Magazine: 8½ ×11; 16-24 pages; 60 lb. paper; 60 lb. cover. "Looking for fiction which uses social change as either a primary or secondary theme. This is broader than most people think. Need social relevance in one way or another. For an artistically and politically aware and curious audience." Quarterly.

NEEDS ethnic/multicultural, experimental, fantasy, feminist, gay, historical, horror, humor/satire, lesbian, literary, mainstream, science fiction, contemporary, prose poem. "No porn, no racist, sexist or any other kind of -ist. No Christian or spirituality proselytizing fiction." Wants to see more science fiction, erotica "assuming it relates to social change." Receives 15 unsolicited mss/month. Accepts 3-5 mss/issue. Publishes ms 3-9 months after acceptance. **Publishes 10 new writers/year.** Recently published work by Margaret Karmazin, Benjamin Reed, John Tuschen, Ken Byrnes. Length:

500-5,000 words; average length: 3,500 words. Publishes short shorts. Always comments on rejected mss.

HOW TO CONTACT Include SASE. Responds in 4 weeks to mss. Accepts reprints, but no multiple or simultaneous submissions." Sample copy for $2, 9×12 SAE and 3 first class stamps. Writer's guidelines for SASE.

PAYMENT/TERMS Acquires onetime electronic rights as well as archival rights. All rights revert back to author after publication.

TIPS "Note that fiction and poetry may be simultaneously published in e-version of Mobius. Due to space constraints of print version, some works may be accepted in e-version, but not print version. We like high impact, we like plot and character-driven stories that function like theater of the mind. Looks for first and foremost, good writing. Prose must be crisp and polished; the story must pique my interest and make me care due to a certain intellectual, emotional aspect. Second, *Mobius* is about social change. We want stories that make some statement about the society we live in, either on a macro or micro level. Not that your story needs to preach from a soapbox (actually, we prefer that it doesn't), but your story needs to have *something* to say."

THE MOCHILA REVIEW

Missouri Western State University, 4525 Downs Dr., St. Joseph MO 64507. E-mail: church@missouriwestern.edu. Website: www.missouriwestern.edu/orgs/mochila/homepage.htm. **Contact:** Bill Church, editor. "Good readership, no theme." Annual. Estab. 2000.

NEEDS literary. Does not accept genre work, erotica. Receives 25 unsolicited mss/month. Accepts 5-10 mss/issue. Does not read mss December-July. Publishes ms 6 months after acceptance. **Publishes 2-3 new writers/year.** Length: 5,000 words (max); average length: 3,000 words. Publishes short shorts; average 500 words. Also publishes literary essays, poetry. Rarely comments on rejected mss.

HOW TO CONTACT Send complete disposable copy of ms with cover letter and #10 SASE for reply only. Include estimated word count, brief bio and list of publications. Responds in 3-5 months to mss. Accepts simultaneous submissions. Sample copy for $7. Writer's guidelines for SASE or on website.

PAYMENT/TERMS Pays 2 contributor's copies; additional copies $5. Acquires first rights. Publication not copyrighted.

TIPS "Manuscripts with fresh language, energy, passion and intelligence stand out. Study the craft and be entertaining and engaging."

NASSAU REVIEW

Nassau Community College, State University of New York, English Dept. Y9, 1 Education Dr., Garden City NY 11530-6793. (516)572-7792. E-mail: christina.rau@ncc.edu. **Contact:** Christina Rau, editor. Estab. 1964. "The *Nassau Review*, published annually, welcomes submissions of many genres, preferring work that is innovative, captivating, well-crafted, and unique, work that crosses boundaries of genres and tradition. New and seasoned writers are both welcome. All work must be in English. Simultaneous submission accepted. No children's lit, fan fiction, or previously published work (online included). Full guidelines will be available at www.ncc.edu. Email submissions in the body of the email only with the subject line indicating genre and your full name. No attachments. No hard copies. *Nassau Review* is about 190 pages, digest-sized, flat-spined. Press run is 1,100. Sample: free. Contact: Christina M. Rau, editor. Email: christina.rau@ncc.edu. Submit 3-5 poems with 50 lines max each or 1 prose piece with 3,000 words max. Reading period: September 1—February 1. Responds in up to 4 months. Pays 2 contributor's copies. Sponsors an annual aitjprs awards contest with two $250 awards. Check the website for announcements."

TIPS "We look for narrative drive, perceptive characterization and professional competence. Write concretely. Does not want over-elaborate details, and avoid digressions."

NATURAL BRIDGE

Dept. of English, University of Missouri–St. Louis, One University Blvd., St. Louis MO 63121. (314)516-7327. E-mail:natural@umsl.edu. Website: www.umsl.edu/~natural. **Contact:** Editor. Estab. 1999. Magazine: 6×9; 250 pages; 60 lb. opaque recycled paper; 12-pt. matte cover. "*Natural Bridge* is published by the UM–St. Louis MFA Program. Faculty and graduate students work together in selecting manuscripts, with a strong emphasis on originality, freshness, honesty, vitality, energy, and linguistic skill." Semiannual. CLMP.

NEEDS literary. List of upcoming themes available for SASE or online. Receives 900 unsolicited mss/submission period. Accepts 35 mss/issue; 70 mss/year. Submit only July 1-August 31 and November 1-December 31. Publishes ms 9 months after acceptance. **Publishes 12**

new writers/year. Recently published work by Tayari Jones, Steve Stern, Jamie Wriston Colbert, Lex Williford, and Mark Jay Mirsky. Also publishes literary essays, poetry. Sometimes comments on rejected mss.

HOW TO CONTACT Send SASE for return of ms or send a disposable copy of ms and #10 SASE for reply only. Responds in 6 months to mss. Accepts simultaneous submissions. Sample copy for $8. Writer's guidelines for SASE, e-mail, or on website. **Does not accept electronic submissions.**

PAYMENT/TERMS Pays 2 contributor's copies and a one-year subscription; additional copies $5. Acquires first North American serial rights.

TIPS "We look for fresh stories, extremely well written, on any subject. We publish mainstream literary fiction. We want stories that work on first and subsequent readings—stories, in other words, that both entertain and resonate. Study the journal. Read all of the fiction in it, especially in fiction-heavy issues like numbers 4 and 11."

NEW COLLAGE

New College of Florida, c/o WRC, 5800 Bayshore Rd., Sarasota FL 34243. E-mail: newcollagemag@gmail.com. Website: newcollagemag.wordpress.com. **Contact:** Alexis Orgera, editor. Estab. 1970.

NEEDS "We choose well-written, thought-provoking short fiction. A ms stands out if it interacts with the theme of *collage* and/or if it has a compelling voice all its own. We like to be surprised by voice and language." Do not send any genre fiction (fantasy, horror, religious, erotic, etc.).

HOW TO CONTACT *New CollAge is not currently accepting submissions as we take two months to recalibrate and organize our online submission system. If you have sent us work within the past several months, please consider resending when we've reopened submissions.* (1/17/11) E-mail no more than 1500 words in a single Word document. "Do not submit again until you've heard back." Note "submission" in the subject line, as well as the type of work you're submitting." Accepts simultaneous submissions. Reads September-May. Responds in 2-6 months.

PAYMENT/TERMS Acquires first serial rights, print and online. All rights revert to author upon publication. Author receives 2 contributor copies.

TIPS "Our website includes online exclusives such as Artattack and (Editor)ials, featuring interviews from artists and editors. Also posts artwork from the magazine, contributor's notes and excerpts from the current issue."

NEW MADRID

Murray State University, Department of English and Philosophy, 7C Faculty Hall, Murray KY 42071-3341. (270)809-4730. E-mail: msu.newmadrid@murraystate.edu. Website: http://newmadridjournal.org. **Contact:** Ann Neelon, editor. Literary magazine/journal: 160 pages. "*New Madrid* is the national journal of the low-residency MFA program at Murray State University. It takes its name from the New Madrid seismic zone, which falls within the central Mississippi Valley and extends through western Kentucky." Semiannual. Circ. 1,000.

NEEDS literary. See website for guidelines and upcoming themes. "We have two reading periods, one from August 15-October 15, and one from January 15-March 15." Also publishes poetry and creative nonfiction. Rarely comments on/critiques rejected mss.

HOW TO CONTACT Accepts submissions by Online Submissions Manager only. Include brief bio, list of publications. Considers multiple submissions. Guidelines available on website.

PAYMENT/TERMS Pays 2 contributor's copies on publication. Acquires first North American serial rights. Publication is copyrighted.

TIPS "Quality is the determining factor for breaking into *New Madrid*. We are looking for well-crafted, compelling writing in a range of genres, forms and styles."

NEW MILLENNIUM WRITINGS

New Messenger Writing and Publishing, P.O. Box 2463, Knoxville TN 37901. (865)428-0389. E-mail: donwilliams7@charter.net. Website: http://newmillennium-writings.com. **Contact:** Don Williams, editor. Estab. 1996. Annual anthology. 6×9, 204 pages, 50 lb. white paper, glossy 4-color cover. Contains illustrations. Includes photographs. "Superior writing is the sole criterion." Annual. Circ. 3,000. Received Golden Presscard Award from Sigma Delta Chi (1997)

NEEDS "While we only accept general submissions January-March, we hold four contests twice each year for all types of fiction, nonfiction, short-short fiction and poetry." Receives average of 200 mss/month. Accepts 60 mss/year. Manuscript published 6 months to one year after acceptance. Agented fiction 0%. Publishes 10 new writers/year. Published Charles Wright, Ted Kooser, Allen Wier, Lucille Clifton, John Updike, and Don Williams. Length: 200 words (min)-6,000 words (max). Average length: 4,000 words for fiction. Publishes short shorts. Also publishes literary essays, poetry. Rarely comments on/critiques rejected manuscripts.

HOW TO CONTACT Accepts ms through biannual *New Millennium Writing* Awards only. Visit website for more information.

PAYMENT/TERMS See listing for *New Millennium Writing* Awards in Contests & Awards section.

TIPS "Looks for originality, accessibility, musicality, psychological insight, moral sensibility. E-mail for list of writing tips or send SASE. No charge."

NEW OHIO REVIEW

English Department, 360 Ellis Hall, Ohio University, Athens OH 45701. (740)597-1360. E-mail: noreditors@ohio.edu. Website: www.ohiou.edu/nor. **Contact:** Jill Allyn Rosser, editor. Estab. 2007.

NEEDS *NOR*, published biannually in spring and fall, publishes fiction, nonfiction, and poetry. Wants "literary submissions in any genre. Translations are welcome if permission has been granted." Billy Collins, Stephen Dunn, Stuart Dybek, Eleanor Wilner, Yusef Komunyakaa, Kim Addonizio, William Olson. Single: $9; Subscription: $16. Member: CLMP.

HOW TO CONTACT Send complete ms online at www.newohioreview.com. "We accept literary submissions in any genre, however we do not accept unsolicited translations. Please do not send more than 6 poems in a single submission." Reading period is September 1-May 1, "but we will consider work year-round from subscribers. Please do not submit more than once every 6 months."

PAYMENT/TERMS $20/page, $50 minimum honorarium.

THE NEW ORPHIC REVIEW

New Orphic Publishers, 706 Mill St., Nelson BC V1L 4S5 Canada. (250)354-0494. E-mail: dreamhorsepress@yahoo.com. Website: www.dreamhorsepress.com; www3.telus.net/neworphicpublishers-hekkanen. **Contact:** Ernest Hekkanen, editor-in-chief. Magazine; $5\frac{1}{2}\times8\frac{1}{2}$; 120 pages; common paper; 100 lb. color cover. "In the traditional Orphic fashion, our magazine accepts a wide range of styles and approaches—from naturalism to the surreal, but, please, get to the essence of the narrative, emotion, conflict, state of being, whatever." Semiannual. Estab. 1998. Circ. 300.

Margrith Schraner's story, "Dream Dig" was included in *The Journey Prize Anthology*, 2001.

NEEDS ethnic/multicultural, experimental, fantasy, historical (general), literary, mainstream. "No detective or sword and sorcery stories." List of upcoming themes available for SASE. Receives 20 unsolicited mss/month. Accepts 10 mss/issue; 22 mss/year. Publishes ms 1 year after acceptance. **Publishes 6-8 new writers/year.** Recently published work by Eveline Hasler (Swiss), Leena Krohn (Finnish), Pekka Salmi. Length: 2,000-10,000 words; average length: 3,500 words. Publishes short shorts. Also publishes literary essays, literary criticism, poetry. Sometimes comments on rejected mss.

HOW TO CONTACT Send SASE (or IRC) for return of ms or send a disposable copy of ms and #10 SASE for reply only. Responds in 1 month to queries; 4 months to mss. Accepts simultaneous, multiple submissions. Sample copy for $17.50. Writer's guidelines for SASE. Reviews fiction.

PAYMENT/TERMS Pays 1 contributor's copy; additional copies $14. Pays on publication for first North American serial rights.

TIPS "I like fiction that deals with issues, accounts for every motive, has conflict, is well written and tackles something that is substantive. Don't be mundane; try for more, not less."

THE NEW YORKER

4 Times Square, New York NY 10036. (212) 286-5900. E-mail: beth_lusko@newyorker.com. E-mail: toon@cartoonbank.com. Website: www.newyorker.com; www.cartoonbank.com. **Contact:** Deborah Treisman, fiction editor. Estab. 1925. A quality magazine of interesting, well-written stories, articles, essays, and poems for a literate audience. Weekly.

The *New Yorker* receives approximately 4,000 submissions per month.

NEEDS Accepts 1 mss/issue.

HOW TO CONTACT Send complete ms as .pdf attachments via online e-mail manager. No more than 1 story or 6 poems should be submitted. No attachments. Responds in 3 months to mss. No simultaneous submissions. Writer's guidelines online.

PAYMENT/TERMS Payment varies. Pays on acceptance.

TIPS "Be lively, original, not overly literary. Write what you want to write, not what you think the editor would like. Send poetry to Poetry Department."

NIMROD

800 S. Tucker Dr., Tulsa OK 74104-3189. (918)631-3080. Fax: (918)631-3033. E-mail: nimrod@utulsa.edu. Website: www.utulsa.edu/nimrod/. **Contact:** Susan Mase, fiction editor. Estab. 1956.

PAYMENT/TERMS Magazine: 6×9; 192 pages; 60 lb. white paper; illustrations; photos. "We publish one thematic issue and one awards issue each year. A recent theme was 'Crossing Borders,' a compilation of poetry and prose from all over the world. We seek vigorous, imaginative, quality writing. Our mission is to discover new writers and publish experimental writers who have not yet found a 'home' for their work." Semiannual. Circ. 3,000."We accept contemporary poetry and/or prose. May submit adventure, ethnic, experimental, prose poem or translations. No science fiction or romance." Receives 120 unsolicited mss/month. **Publishes 5-10 new writers/year.** Recently published work by Felicia Ward, Ellen Bass, Jeanette Turner Hospital, Kate Small. Also publishes poetry. SASE for return of ms. Accepts queries by e-mail. Does not accept submissions by e-mail unless the writer is living outside the U.S. Responds in 5 months to mss. Accepts simultaneous, multiple submissions. Pays 2 contributor's copies.

TIPS "We have not changed our fiction needs: quality, vigor, distinctive voice. We have, however, increased the number of stories we print. See current issues. We look for fiction that is fresh, vigorous, distinctive, serious and humorous, unflinchingly serious, ironic—whatever. Just so it is quality. Strongly encourage writers to send #10 SASE for brochure for annual literary contest with prizes of $1,000 and $2,000."

NITE-WRITER'S INTERNATIONAL LITERARY ARTS JOURNAL

158 Spencer Ave., Suite 100, Pittsburgh PA 15227. (412)668-0691. E-mail: nitewritersliteraryarts@gmail.com. Website: http://nitewritersinternational.webs.com. **Contact:** John Thompson. Estab. 1994. An online literary arts journal. "*Nite-Writer's International Literary Arts Journal* is dedicated to the emotional intellectual with a creative perception of life." Quarterly.

NEEDS literary mainstream, historical, adventure, erotica, humor/satire, inspirational, senior citizen/retirement, sports. Average length: 2,500 words. Also publishes literary essays, literary criticism, photography, poetry, nonfiction, and haiku/senryu.

HOW TO CONTACT "If submitting by snail mail, enclose SASE for return of mss. Responds within 6 months to mss. Accepts simultaneous submissions and previously published work (let us know when & where). Send SASE for writer's guidelines or go to our website for guidelines. Does not pay at this time. Will offer a print on demand service quarterly. Copyright reverts to author upon publication. Retains First North American Serial rights."

TIPS "Read a lot of what you write—study the market. Don't fear rejection, but use it as learning tool to strengthen your work before resubmitting."

THE NORMAL SCHOOL

The Press at the California State University–Fresno, 5245 North Backer Ave., M/S PB 98, Fresno CA 93740-8001. E-mail: editors@thenormalschool.com; submissions@thenormalschool.com. Website: http://thenormalschool.com. **Contact:** Steven Church, editor. Estab. 2008. Semiannual magazine that accepts "outstanding work by beginning and established writers." Does not read mss. between May 1 and August 31. Acquires first North American serial rights. Publication is copyrighted. Accepts 50-75% unsolicited freelance material. 3-6 months from acceptance to published ms. Does not accept previously published stories. Responds to stories in 8 weeks. Sample copy available for $7 on website or via e-mail. For guidelines, send check and address or visit website. "The average length of stories in our publication is 6,000-10,000 words. We publish short shorts (fewer than 1,500 words). We sponsor The Normal Prizes in Fiction Contest and Creative Nonfiction Contest."

NEEDS Does not want any genre writing (fantasy, romance, western, etc.) or cat poems.

HOW TO CONTACT Send complete ms with a cover letter. No e-mail or fax submissions. Include estimated word count, brief bio, list of publications. Send disposable copy of the ms or #10 SASE for reply. One submission at a time.

PAYMENT/TERMS Writers receive 2 contributor's copies and a free subscription to the magazine. Charge for additional copies is $5 each. Pays on publication.

TIPS "We are looking for writers who are pushing the limits of writing and creativity. Please read a couple issues of our magazine to get an idea of what to submit.

NORTH DAKOTA QUARTERLY

Merrifeild Hall Room 110, 276 Centennial Drive Stop 7209, Grand Forks ND 58202-7209. (701)777-3322. E-mail: ndq@und.edu. Website: www.und.nodak.edu/org/ndq. Estab. 1911. **Contact:** Robert Lewis, editor. Magazine: 6×9; 200 pages; bond paper; illustrations; photos. "*North Dakota Quarterly* is a literary journal publishing essays in the humanities; some short stories, some poetry. Occasional special topic issues." General audience. Quarterly.

Work published in *North Dakota Quarterly* was selected for inclusion in *The O. Henry Prize Stories, The Pushcart Prize Series,* and *Best American Essays.*

NEEDS ethnic/multicultural, experimental, feminist, historical, literary, Native American. Receives 125-150 unsolicited mss/month. Accepts 4 mss/issue; 16 mss/year. Publishes ms 2 years after acceptance. **Publishes 4-5 new writers/year.** Recently published work by Louise Erdrich, Robert Day, Maxine Kumin and Fred Arroyo. Average length: 3,000-4,000 words. Also publishes literary essays and criticism. Sometimes comments on rejected mss.

HOW TO CONTACT SASE. Responds in 3 months to mss. Sample copy for $10. Reviews fiction.

PAYMENT/TERMS Pays 2-4 contributor's copies; 30% discount for extras. Acquires onetime rights. Sends galleys to author.

NORTHWEST REVIEW

5243 University of Oregon, Eugene OR 97403-5243. (541)346-3957. Fax: (541)346-0537. E-mail: nweditor@uoregon.edu. Website: http://nwr.uoregon.edu. **Contact:** Geri Doran, general editor. Estab. 1957. **Contact:** Geri Doran, general editor. Magazine: 6×9; 140-160 pages; high quality cover stock; illustrations; photos. "A general literary review featuring poems, stories, essays and reviews, circulated nationally and internationally. For a literate audience in avant-garde as well as traditional literary forms; interested in the important writers who have not yet achieved their readership." Triannual. Circ. 1,200.

Poetry published by *Northwest Review* has been included in *The Best American Poetry, Poetry Daily,* and *Verse Daily.*

NEEDS experimental, feminist, literary, translations, contemporary. Receives 150 unsolicited mss/month. Accepts 4-5 mss/issue; 12-15 mss/year. **Publishes some new writers/year.** Recently published work by Diana Abu-Jaber, Madison Smartt Bell, Maria Flook, Charles Marvin. Also publishes literary essays, literary criticism, poetry. Comments on rejected mss "when there is time."

HOW TO CONTACT Responds in 4 months to mss. No simultaneous submissions. Sample copy for $4. Reviews fiction.

PAYMENT/TERMS Pays 3 contributor's copies and 1-year subscription; 40% discount on extras. Acquires first rights.

TIPS "Our advice is to persist."

OBSIDIAN III

North Carolina State University, Department of English, Box 8105, Raleigh NC 27695-8105. (919)515-4153. E-mail: obsidian@gw.ncsu.edu. Website: www.ncsu.edu/chass/obsidian/. **Contact:** Sheila Smith McKoy, editor. Magazine: 130 pages. "Creative works in English by black writers, scholarly critical studies by all writers on black literature in English." Published 2 times/year (spring/summer, fall/winter). Estab. 1975.

NEEDS Ethnic/multicultural (Pan-African), feminist, literary. Accepts 7-9 mss/year. Publishes ms 4-6 months after acceptance. **Publishes 20 new writers/year.** Recently published work by R. Flowers Rivera, Terrance Hayes, Eugene Kraft, Arlene McKanic, Pearl Bothe Williams, Kwane Dawes, Jay Wright, and Octavia E. Butler.

HOW TO CONTACT Accepts submissions by e-mail. Responds in 4 months to mss. Sample copy for $10.

PAYMENT/TERMS Pays in contributor's copies. Acquires onetime rights. Sponsors awards/contests.

TIPS "Following proper format is essential. Your title must be intriguing and text clean. Never give up. Some of the writers we publish were rejected many times before we published them."

OHIO TEACHERS WRITE

644 Overlook Dr., Columbus OH 45601. E-mail: rmcclain@bright.net; ohioteacherswrite@gmail.com. Website: www.octela.org/OTW.html. Estab. 1995. Editors change every 3 years. Magazine: $8\frac{1}{2}$×11; 50 pages; 60 lb. white offset paper; 65-lb. blue cover stock; illustrations; photos. "The purpose of the magazine is three fold: (1) to provide a collection of fine literature for the reading pleasure of teachers and other adult readers; (2) to encourage teachers to compose literary works along with their students; (3) to provide the literate citizens of Ohio a window into the world of educators

not often seen by those outside the teaching profession." Annual. Circ. 1,000. Submissions are limited to Ohio Educators.

NEEDS Adventure, ethnic/multicultural, experimental, fantasy (science fantasy), feminist, gay, historical, humor/satire, lesbian, literary, mainstream, regional, religious/inspirational, romance (contemporary), science fiction (hard science, soft/sociological), western (frontier, traditional), senior citizen/retirement, sports, teaching. Receives 2 unsolicited mss/month. Accepts 7 mss/issue. "We read only in May when editorial board meets." Recently published work by Lois Spencer, Harry R. Noden, Linda J. Rice, June Langford Berkley. Publishes short shorts. Also publishes poetry. Often comments on rejected mss.

HOW TO CONTACT Send SASE with postage clipped for return of ms or send a disposable copy of ms. Accepts multiple submissions. Sample copy for $6.

PAYMENT/TERMS Pays 2 contributor's copies; additional copies $6. Acquires first rights.

OPEN WIDE MAGAZINE

40 Wingfield Road, Lakenheath, Brandon SK Ip27 9HR UK. E-mail: contact@openwidemagazine.co.uk. Website: www.openwidemagazine.co.uk. **Contact:** Liz Roberts. Estab. 2001. Online literary magazine/journal: Quarterly.

NEEDS Short fiction and poetry journal enjoys adventure, ethnic/multicultural, experimental, feminist, humor/satire, mainstream, mystery/suspense, principle beat. Receives 100 mss/month. Accepts 25 mss/issue. Manuscript published 3 months after acceptance. Publishes 30 new writers/year. Length: 500-4,000. Average length: 2,500. Publishes short shorts. Also publishes poetry, reviews (music, film, art) and interviews. Rarely comments on/critiques rejected mss.

HOW TO CONTACT Accepts submissions by e-mail and online. Include estimated word count, brief bio. Send either SASE (or IRC) for return of ms or disposable copy of ms and #10 SASE for reply only. The magazine costs just £1.00 for a PDF copy that is mailed to you at the e-mail address you provide us with via your Paypal account, unless you specify otherwise.

PAYMENT/TERMS Acquires onetime rights. Publication is copyrighted.

OXFORD MAGAZINE

356 Bachelor Hall, Miami University, Oxford OH 45056. (513) 529-1279. E-mail: oxmag@muohio.edu. Website: www.oxfordmagazine.org. Estab. 1984. **Contact:** Fiction editor, oxmagfictioneditor@muohio.edu. Annual. Circ. 1,000.

National literary magazine edited by students in the graduate program in the English department. Historically, these students have largely been M.A. students in creative writing. The magazine has featured both celebrated and new writers working in fiction, poetry, and creative nonfiction. Interviews, photography, and other visual art have also occasionally appeared in the journal, and the possibility of including literary criticism and reviews is currently on the table. *Oxford* has been awarded two Pushcart Prizes.

NEEDS Wants quality fiction and prose, genre is not an issue, but nothing sentimental. Receives 150 unsolicited mss/month. **Publishes some new writers/year.** Recently published work by Stephen Dixon, Andre Dubus and Stuart Dybek. Publishes short shorts. Also publishes poetry.

HOW TO CONTACT Responds in 2 months, depending upon time of submissions; mss received after December 31 will be returned. Accepts simultaneous submissions if notified. Sample copy for $5.

PAYMENT/TERMS Acquires onetime rights.

TIPS "*Oxford Magazine* accepts fiction, poetry, and essays (this last genre is a catch-all, much like the space under your couch cushions, and includes creative nonfiction, critical work exploring writing, and the like). Appearing once a year, *OxMag* is a Web-based journal that acquires first North American serial rights, onetime anthology rights and online serial rights. Simultaneous submissions are okay if you would kindly let us know if and when someone beats us to the punch."

OYEZ REVIEW

Roosevelt University, Dept. of Literature & Languages, 430 S. Michigan Ave., Chicago IL 60605-1394. (312)341-3500. E-mail: oyezreview@roosevelt.edu. Website: legacy.roosevelt.edu/roosevelt.edu/oyezreview. Estab. 1965. Literary magazine/journal. "*Oyez Review* publishes fiction, creative nonfiction, poetry and art. There are no restrictions on style, theme, or subject matter."

Reading period is August 1-October 1. Responds by mid-December.

NEEDS Publishes short stories and flash fiction from established authors and newcomers. Literary excellence is our goal and our primary criterion. Send us your best work, and you will receive a thoughtful, thorough reading. Recently published J. Weintraub, Lori Rader Day, Joyce Goldenstern, Norman Lock, Peter Obourn, Jotham Burrello.

HOW TO CONTACT Accepts art and international submissions by e-mail. Sample copy available for $5. Guidelines available on website.

PAYMENT/TERMS Writers receive 2 contributors copies. Acquires first North American serial rights.

OYSTER BOY REVIEW

P.O. Box 1483, Pacifica CA 94044. E-mail: email_2010@oysterboyreview.com. Website: www.oysterboyreview.com. **Contact:** Damon Suave, editor/publisher. Estab. 1993. Electronic and print magazine. "We publish kick-ass, teeth-cracking stories." Published 4 times a year.

NEEDS No genre fiction. "Fiction that revolves around characters in conflict with themselves or each other; a plot that has a beginning, a middle, and an end; a narrative with a strong moral center (not necessarily 'moralistic'); a story with a satisfying resolution to the conflict; and an ethereal something that contributes to the mystery of a question, but does not necessarily seek or contrive to answer it." Submissions closed for 2009. **Publishes 4 new writers/year.** Recently published work by Todd Goldberg, Ken Wainio, Elisha Porat, Kevin McGowan.

HOW TO CONTACT Accepts multiple submissions. Sample copy not available.

TIPS "Keep writing, keep submitting, keep revising."

PACIFIC REVIEW

Dept. of English and Comparative Literature, San Diego State University, 5500 Campanile Dr., MC6020, San Diego CA 92182-6020. E-mail: pacificreview_sdsu@yahoo.com. Website: http://pacificREVIEW.sdsu.edu. **Contact:** Lester O'Connor, fiction editor. Magazine: 6×9; 200 pages; book stock paper; paper back, extra heavy cover stock; b&w illustrations, b&w photos. "*Pacific REVIEW* publishes the work of emergent literati, pairing their efforts with those of established artists. It is available at West Coast independent booksellers and university and college libraries and is taught as text in numerous university literature and creative writing classes." Circ. 2,000.

NEEDS "We welcome submissions of previously published poems, short stories, translations, and creative nonfiction, including essays and reviews." For information on theme issues see website. **Publishes 15 new writers/year.** Recently published work by Ai, Alurista, Susan Daitch, Lawrence Ferlinghetti, William T. Vollmann.

HOW TO CONTACT Responds in 3 months to mss. Sample copy for $10.

PAYMENT/TERMS Pays 2 contributor's copies. Acquires first serial rights. All other rights revert to author.

TIPS "We welcome all submissions, especially those created in or in the context of the West Coast/California and the space of our borders."

PACKINGTOWN REVIEW

The University of Illinois at Chicago, English Department, UH 2027 MC 162, 601 S. Morgan, Chicago IL 60607. (908)745-1547. E-mail: editors@packingtownreview.com. Website: www.packingtownreview.com. **Contact:** Editor. Estab. 2008. Magazine has revolving editor. Editorial term: 2 years. Next term: 2013. Literary magazine/journal. 8½x11, 250 pages. "*Packingtown Review* publishes imaginative and critical prose by emerging and established writers. We welcome submissions of poetry, scholarly articles, drama, creative nonfiction, fiction, and literary translation, as well as genre-bending pieces." Annual.

NEEDS comics/graphic novels, ethnic/multicultural (general), experimental, feminist, gay, glitz, historical (general), literary, mainstream, military/war, translations. Does not want to see uninspired or unrevised work. "We also would like to avoid fantasy, science fiction, overtly religious, or romantic pieces." Ms published max of one year after acceptance. Length: 3,000 words (min)-8,000 words (max). Publishes short shorts. Also publishes literary essays, literary criticism, book reviews, poetry. Send review copies to Jennifer Moore and Matthew Corey Editor. Sometimes comments on/critiques rejected mss.

HOW TO CONTACT Send complete ms with cover letter. Include estimated word count, brief bio. Responds to queries in 3 weeks. Responds to mss in 3 months. Considers simultaneous submissions. See website for price guidelines. Guidelines available for SASE, via e-mail.

PAYMENT/TERMS Writers receive 2 contributor's copies. Pays on publication. Acquires first North American serial rights. Sends galleys to author. Publication is copyrighted.

TIPS "We are looking for well-crafted prose. We are open to most styles and forms. We are also looking for prose that takes risks and does so successfully. We will consider articles about prose."

PADDLEFISH

1105 W. 8th St., Yankton SD 57078. (605)688-1362. E-mail: james.reese@mtmc.edu. Website: www.mmc-paddlefish.com. **Contact:** Dr. Jim Reese, Editor. Estab. 2007. Literary magazine/journal. 6x9, 200 pages. Includes photographs. "We publish unique and creative pieces." Annual. Estab. 2007.

NEEDS adventure, comics/graphic novels, erotica, ethnic/multicultural, experimental, family saga, fantasy, feminist, gay, glitz, historical, horror, humor/satire, lesbian, literary, mainstream, military/war, mystery, new age, psychic/supernatural/occult, religious, romance, science fiction, thriller/espionage, translations, western, young adult/teen. Does not want excessive or gratuitous language, sex or violence. Receives 300 mss/month. Accepts 30 mss/year. Submission period is Nov 1-Feb 28. Ms published 3-9 months after acceptance. **Publishes 5-10 new writers/year.** Published David Lee, William Kloefkorn, David Allen Evans, Jack Anderson and Maria Mazziotti Gillan. Length: 2,500 words (max). Publishes short shorts. Also publishes literary essays, poetry. Rarely comments on/critiques rejected mss.

HOW TO CONTACT Send complete ms with cover letter. Include estimated word count, brief bio, list of publications. Send disposable copy of ms and #10 SASE for reply only. Guidelines available for SASE.

PAYMENT/TERMS Writers receive 1 contributor's copy. Additional copies $8. Acquires onetime rights. Sends galleys to author. Publication is copyrighted. "Cash prizes are award to Mount Marty students."

PAINTED BRIDE QUARTERLY

Drexel University, Dept. of English and Philosophy, 3141 Chestnut St., Philadelphia PA 19104. E-mail: pbq@drexel.edu. Website: http://webdelsol.com/pbq. Estab. 1973. "PBQ seeks literary fiction, experimental and traditional." Publishes online each quarter and a print annual each spring. Estab. 1973.

NEEDS ethnic/multicultural, experimental, feminist, gay, lesbian, literary, translations. "No genre fiction." "Publishes theme-related work, check website; holds annual fiction contests. **Publishes 24 new writers/year.** Length: 5,000 words; average length: 3,000 words. Publishes short shorts. Also publishes literary essays, literary criticism, poetry. Occasionally comments on rejected mss.

HOW TO CONTACT Send complete ms. No electronic submissions. Responds in 6 months to mss. Sample copy online. Writer's guidelines online. Reviews fiction.

PAYMENT/TERMS Acquires first North American serial rights.

TIPS "We look for freshness of idea incorporated with high-quality writing. We receive an awful lot of nicely written work with worn-out plots. We want quality in whatever—we hold experimental work to as strict standards as anything else. Many of our readers write fiction; most of them enjoy a good reading. We hope to be an outlet for quality. A good story gives, first, enjoyment to the reader. We've seen a good many of them lately, and we've published the best of them."

PANK

PANK, Department of Humanities, 1400 Townsend Dr., Houghton MI 49931-1200. Website: www.pankmagazine.com. **Contact:** M. Bartley Seigel, Editor. Estab. 2007.

To read *PANK* is to know *PANK*. Or, read a lot within the literary magazine and small press universe—there's plenty to choose from. Unfortunately, we see a lot of submissions from writers who have clearly read neither *PANK* nor much else. Serious writers are serious readers. Read. Seriously."

PASSAGES NORTH

Northern Michigan University, Department of English, Marquette MI 49855. (906)227-2711. Fax: (906)227-1096. E-mail: passages@nmu.edu. Website: www.nmu.edu/passagesnorth. Estab. 1979. **Contact:** Kate Myers Hanson, Editor-in-Chief. Magazine: 7×10; 200-300 pages; 60 lb. paper. "*Passages North* publishes quality fiction, poetry and creative nonfiction by emerging and established writers." Annual. Estab. 1979. Circ. 1,500.

NEEDS ethnic/multicultural, literary, short-short fiction. No genre fiction, science fiction, "typical commercial press work." Receives 200 unsolicited mss/month. Accepts 12-15 mss/year. Reads mss September 1-April 15. **Publishes 10% new writers/year.** Recently published work by John McNally, Steve Almond, Tracy Winn and Midege Raymond. Length: 5,000 words (max). Average length 3,000 words. Publishes short shorts. Average length: 1,000 words. Also publishes literary essays, poetry. Comments on rejected mss when there is time.

HOW TO CONTACT Send complete ms with cover letter. Responds in 2-4 months to mss. Accepts simultaneous submissions. Sample copy for $3-7. Guidelines for SASE, e-mail, on website.

PAYMENT/TERMS Pays 2 contributor's copies. Rights revert to author upon publication. Publication is copyrighted. Occasionally sponsors contests; check website for details.

TIPS "We look for voice, energetic prose, writers who take risks. We look for an engaging story in which the author evokes an emotional response from the reader through carefully rendered scenes, complex characters, and a smart, narrative design. Revise, revise. Read what we publish."

PASSION

Crescent Moon Publishing, P.O. Box 393, Maidstone Kent ME14 5XU United Kingdom. (44)(162)272-9593. E-mail: cresmopub@yahoo.co.uk. Website: www.crescentmoon.org.uk. Estab. 1988. **Contact:** Jeremy Robinson, editor. *Passion*, published quarterly, features poetry, fiction, reviews, and essays on feminism, art, philosophy, and the media. Wants "thought-provoking, incisive, polemical, ironic, lyric, sensual, and hilarious work." Does not want "rubbish, trivia, party politics, sport, etc." Has published poetry by Jeremy Reed, Penelope Shuttle, Alan Bold, D.J. Enright, and Peter Redgrove. Single copy: £2.50 ($4 USD); subscription: £10 ($17 USD). Make checks payable to Crescent Moon Publishing.

THE PATERSON LITERARY REVIEW

Passaic County Community College, Cultural Affairs Dept., One College Blvd., Paterson NJ 07505-1179. (973)684-6555. Fax: (973)523-6085. E-mail: mGillan@pccc.edu. Website: www.pccc.edu/poetry. **Contact:** Maria Mazziotti Gillan, editor/executive director. Magazine: 6×9; 400 pages; 60 lb. paper; 70 lb. cover; illustrations; photos. Annual.

Work for *PLR* has been included in the *Pushcart Prize* anthology and *Best American Poetry.*

NEEDS ethnic/multicultural, literary, contemporary. "We are interested in quality short stories, with no taboos on subject matter." Receives 60 unsolicited mss/month. Publishes ms 6-12 months after acceptance. **Publishes 5% new writers/year.** Recently published work by Robert Mooney and Abigail Stone. Also publishes literary essays, literary criticism, poetry.

HOW TO CONTACT Send SASE for reply or return of ms. "Indicate whether you want story returned." Accepts simultaneous submissions. Sample copy for $13 plus $1.50 postage. Reviews fiction.

PAYMENT/TERMS Pays in contributor's copies. Acquires first North American serial rights.

TIPS Looks for "clear, moving and specific work."

PENNSYLVANIA ENGLISH

Penn State DuBois, College Place, DuBois PA 15801-3199. (814)375-4785. Fax: (814)375-4785. E-mail: ajv2@psu.edu. Website: www.english.iup.edu/pcea. **Contact:** Antonio Vallone, editor. Estab. 1985. Magazine: $5^1{}_4$×$8^1{}_4$; up to 200 pages; perfect bound; full-color cover featuring the artwork of a Pennsylvania artist. "Our philosophy is quality. We publish literary fiction (and poetry and nonfiction). Our intended audience is literate, college-educated people." Annual. Circ. 300.

NEEDS literary, mainstream, contemporary. "No genre fiction or romance." Reads mss during the summer. Publishes ms up tp 12 months after acceptance. **Publishes 4-6 new writers/year.** Recently published work by Dave Kress, Dan Leone and Paul West. Publishes short shorts. Also publishes literary essays, literary criticism, poetry. Sometimes comments on rejected mss.

HOW TO CONTACT SASE. Does not accept electronic submissions. "We are creating Pennsylvania English Online—www.pennsylvaniaenglish.com—for electronic submissions and expanded publishing opportunities." Responds in up to 12 months to mss. Accepts simultaneous submissions. Does not accept previously published work. Sample copy for $10.

PAYMENT/TERMS Pays in 2 contributor's copies. Acquires first North American serial rights.

TIPS "Quality of the writing is our only measure. We're not impressed by long-winded cover letters detailing awards and publications we've never heard of. Beginners and professionals have the same chance with us. We receive stacks of competently written but boring fiction. For a story to rise out of the rejection pile, it takes more than the basic competence."

PEREGRINE

Amherst Writers & Artists Press, P.O. Box 1076, Amherst MA 01004. (413)253-3307. Fax:(413)253-7764. E-mail: peregrine@amherstwriters.com. Website: www.

amherstwriters.com. **Contact:** Nancy Rose, editor. Estab. 1983. Magazine: 6x9; 100 pages; 60 lb. white offset paper; glossy cover. "Peregrine has provided a forum for national and international writers since 1983, and is committed to finding excellent work by emerging as well as established writers. We welcome work reflecting diversity of voice. We like to be surprised. We look for writing that is honest, unpretentious, and memorable. We like to be surprised. All decisions are made by the editors." Annual. Member CLMP.

NEEDS poetry and prose. "No previously published work. No children's stories." Short pieces have a better chance of publication. No electronic submissions. Accepts 6-12 mss/issue. Reads January-April. Publishes ms 4 months after acceptance. **Publishes 8-10 new writers/year.** Recently published work by Douglas Andrew, Brad Buchanan, Krikor N. Der Hohannesian, Myron Ernst, Laura Hogan, Lucy Honig, Dana Kroos, M.K. Meder, Pat Schneider, John Surowiecki, Edwina Trentham, Sacha Webley, Fred Yannantuono. Publishes short shorts.

HOW TO CONTACT Enclose sufficiently stamped SASE for return of ms; if disposable copy, enclose #10 SASE (use Forever stamp) for response. Accepts manuscripts postmarked March 15-May 15. Accepts simultaneous submissions. Sample copy for $12. Writer's guidelines for #10 SASE or website.

PAYMENT/TERMS Pays contributor's copies. All rights return to writer upon publication.

TIPS "Check guidelines before submitting your work. Familiarize yourself with Peregrine. We look for heart and soul as well as technical expertise. Trust your own voice."

◐ PERMAFROST: A LITERARY JOURNAL

c/o English Dept., Univ. of Alaska Fairbanks, P.O. Box 755720, Fairbanks AK 99775. Website: www.uaf.edu/english/permafrost. Estab. 1977. *Permafrost: A Literary Journal*, published in May/June, contains poems, short stories, creative nonfiction, b&w drawings, photographs, and prints. "We survive on both new and established writers, hoping and expecting to see the best work out there. We publish any style of poetry provided it is conceived, written, and revised with care. While we encourage submissions about Alaska and by Alaskans, we also welcome poems about anywhere, from anywhere. We have published work by E. Ethelbert Miller, W. Loran Smith, Peter Orlovsky, Jim Wayne Miller, Allen Ginsberg, and Andy Warhol." *Permafrost* is about 200 pages, digest-sized, professionally printed, flat-spined. Subscription: $9/year, $16/2 years, $22/3 years. Back-issues $5.

PAYMENT/TERMS Pays 1 contributor copy; reduced contributor rate on additional copies.

◐ PHILADELPHIA STORIES

Fiction/Art/Poetry of the Delaware Valley, 93 Old York Road, Suite 1/#1-753, Jenkintown PA 19046. (215) 551-5889. Fax: (215) 635-0195. E-mail: christine@philadelphiastories.org; info@philadelphiastories.org. Website: www.philadelphiastories.org. **Contact:** Christine Weiser, co-publisher/managing editor; Carla Spataro, fiction editor/co-publisher. Literary magazine/journal. $8\frac{1}{2}$×11; 24 pages; 70# matte text, all four-color paper; 70# Matte Text cover. Contains illustrations., photographs. "*Philadelphia Stories* magazine publishes fiction, poetry, essays and art written by authors living in, or originally from, Pennsylvania, Delaware, or New Jersey." Estab. 2004. Quarterly. Circ. 10,000. Member CLMP.

NEEDS experimental, literary, mainstream. "We will consider anything that is well written but are most inclined to publish literary or mainstream fiction. We are NOT particularly interested in most genres (sci fi/fantasy, romance, etc.)." List of upcoming themes available for SASE, on website. Receives 45-80 mss/month. Accepts 3-4 mss/issue for print, additional 1-2 online; 12-16 mss/year for print, 4-8 online. Ms published 1-2 months after acceptance. **Publishes 50% new writers/year.** Published katherine Hill, Jenny Lentz, Tom Larsen, Liz-Abrams-Morley, and Mitchell Sommers. Length: 5,000 words (max). Average length: 4,000 words. Publishes short shorts. Average length of short shorts: 800 words. Also publishes literary essays, book reviews, poetry. Send review queries to: info@philadelphiastories.org. Rarely comments on/critiques rejected mss.

HOW TO CONTACT Send complete ms with cover letter via online submission form only. Include estimated word count, list of publications, affiliation to the Philadelphia area. Responds to mss in 12 weeks. Considers simultaneous submissions. Sample copy available for $5, on website. Guidelines available on website.

PAYMENT/TERMS Writers receive 2+ contributor's copies. Pays on publication. Acquires onetime rights. Publication is copyrighted. "Launched First National Fiction contest in 2009 with $1,000 prize and plans another one for 2010. Visit our website for opportunities."

TIPS "All work is screened by 3 editorial board members, who rank the work. These scores are processed at the end of the quarterly submission period, and then the board meets to decide which pieces will be published in print and online. We look for exceptional, polished prose, a controlled voice, strong characters and place, and interesting subjects. Follow guidelines. We cannot stress this enough. Read every guideline carefully and thoroughly before sending anything out. Send out only polished material. We reject many quality pieces for various reasons; try not to take rejection personally. Just because your piece isn't right for one publication doesn't mean it's bad. Selection is an extremely subjective process."

◐ PHOEBE: A JOURNAL OF LITERATURE AND ART

George Mason Univ., 4400 University Dr., Fairfax VA 22030. E-mail: phoebe@gmu.edu. Website: www.phoebejournal.com. Estab. 1972. Phoebe. George Mason University, MSN 2C5, 4400 University Dr., Fairfax VA 22030. (703)993-2915. **Contact:** Editors change every year. Recently published work by Blake Butler, Kim Chinquee, Beth Staples, and more. Accepts simultaneous submissions. Sample copy for $6.

HOW TO CONTACT SASE.

PAYMENT/TERMS Pays 2 contributor's copies or one- year subscription. Acquires onetime rights. All rights revert to author on publication.

◐ THE PINCH

Dept. of English, The University of Memphis, Memphis TN 38152. (901)678-4591. E-mail: editor@thepinchjournal.com. Website: www.thepinchjournal.com. **Contact:** Kristen Iverson, editor-in-chief. Estab. 1980. (Formerly *River City*) Magazine: 7×10; 168 pages. Semiannual.

NEEDS short stories, poetry, creative nonfiction, essays, memoir, travel, nature writing, photography, art. **Publishes some new writers every year.** Recently published work by Chris Fink, George Singleton, Stephen Dunn, Denise Duhamel, Floyd Skloot, and Beth Ann Fennelly.

HOW TO CONTACT Send complete ms. Responds in 2 months to mss. Sample copy for $12.

PAYMENT/TERMS Pays 2 contributor's copies. Acquires first North American serial rights.

TIPS "We have a new look and a new edge. We're soliciting work from writers with a national or international reputation as well as strong, interesting work from emerging writers. The Pinch Literary Award (previously River City Writing Award) in Fiction offers a $1,500 prize and publication. Check our website for details."

◐ PINYON

Mesa State College, Languages, Literature and Mass Communications, Mesa State College, 1100 North Ave., Grand Junction CO 81501-3122. E-mail: pinyonpoetry@hotmail.com. Website: www.mesastate.edu/english/publications.html. **Contact:** Managing editor. Estab. 1995. Literary magazine/journal: $8\frac{1}{2}\times5\frac{1}{2}$, 120 pages, heavy paper. Contains illustrations and photographs. Annual.

NEEDS literary. Receives 16-20 mss/month. Accepts 3-4 mss/issue; 3-4 mss/year. Does not read mss January-August. Manuscript published 6 months after acceptance. Length: 1,500 words (min)-5,000 words (max). Average length: 2,500 words. Publishes short shorts. Average length of short shorts: 500 words. Also publishes poetry.

HOW TO CONTACT Send complete ms with cover letter. Include brief bio. Responds to queries in 1 month. Responds to mss in 6 months. Send either SASE (or IRC) for return of ms or disposable copy of ms and #10 SASE for reply only. Considers simultaneous submissions, multiple submissions. Sample copy available for $5. Send SASE for guidelines.

PAYMENT/TERMS Writers receive 2 contributor's copies. Acquires onetime rights. Publication is copyrighted.

TIPS "Ask yourself if the work is something you would like to read in a publication."

O PISGAH REVIEW

Division of Humanities, Brevard College, 400 N. Broad St., Brevard NC 28712. (828)884-8349. E-mail: tinerjj@brevard.edu. Website: www.pisgahreview.com. **Contact:** Jubal Tiner, editor. Estab. 2005. Literary magazine/journal: $5\frac{1}{2}$ x $8\frac{1}{2}$, 120 pages. Includes cover artwork. "*Pisgah Review* publishes primarily literary short fiction, creative nonfiction and poetry. Our only criteria is quality of work; we look for the best." Semiannual. Circ. 200.

NEEDS Ethnic/multicultural, experimental, literary, mainstream. Special interests: stories rooted in the theme of place—physical, psychological, or spiritual. Does not want genre fiction or inspirational stories.

Receives 85 mss/month. Accepts 6-8 mss/issue; 12-15 mss/year. Manuscript published 6 months after acceptance. **Publishes 5 new writers/year.** Published Ron Rash, Thomas Rain Crowe, Joan Conner, Gary Fincke, and Steve Almond. Length: 2,000 words (min)-7,500 words (max). Average length: 4,000 words. Publishes short shorts. Average length of short shorts: 1,000 words. Also publishes poetry and creative nonfiction. Sometimes comments on/critiques rejected mss.

HOW TO CONTACT Send complete ms with cover letter. Accepts submissions by e-mail and online submission form on website. Responds to mss in 4-6 months. Send either SASE (or IRC) for return of ms or disposable copy of ms and #10 SASE for reply only. Considers simultaneous submissions. Sample copy available for $7. Guidelines available on website.

PAYMENT/TERMS Writers receive 2 contributor's copies. Additional copies $7. Pays on publication. Acquires first North American serial rights. Sends galleys to author. Publication is copyrighted.

TIPS "We select work only of the highest quality. Grab us from the beginning and follow through. Engage us with your language and characters. A clean manuscript goes a long way toward acceptance. Stay true to the vision of your work, revise tirelessly, and submit persistently."

PLAIN SPOKE

Amsterdam Press, 6199 Steubenville Road SE, Amsterdam OH 43903. (740) 543-4333. E-mail: plainspoke@gmail.com. Website: www.plainspoke.net. **Contact:** Cindy Kelly, editor; Shaun M. Barcalow, fiction editor. Estab. 2007. Magazine: digest-sized; 36-52 pages; heavy paper; card cover. "We publish work that has a sense of word economy, strong voice, Americana appeal, tightness, and shies away from the esoteric and expositional. We like to be surprised." Quarterly.

NEEDS comics, experimental, folksy, humor/satire, literary, mainstream, western (frontier saga), Americana, flash fiction, metafiction. Does not want science fiction, furry, cliché, plot-driven, formulaic. Receives 80 mss/month. Accepts 2-3 mss/issue; 10-12 mss/year. Length: 1,500-3,000 words. Average length: 1,750 words. Publishes short shorts. Average length of short shorts: fewer than 1,000 words. Also publishes literary essays, literary criticism, book reviews, poetry. Send review copies with cover letter to reviews editor. Often comments on/critiques rejected manuscripts.

HOW TO CONTACT Send complete ms with cover letter. Accepts submissions by e-mail and on disk. Include estimated word count, brief bio in third person, list of publications. "Limit publication credits to 6." Responds to mss in 1-4 months. Send disposable copy of ms and #10 SASE for reply only. Considers simultaneous submissions, multiple submissions. Guidelines available for SASE, via e-mail, on website.

PAYMENT/TERMS Writers receive 1 contributor copy; additional copies $4. Pays on publication. Acquires first North American serial rights. Publication is copyrighted.

TIPS "Work that surprises us stands out. We don't like the predictable. We don't want to feel like we're reading a story, pull us in. Make every word count and don't rely on adverbs."

PMS POEMMEMOIRSTORY

University of Alabama at Birmingham, HB 217, 1530 3rd Ave. South, Birmingham AL 35294-1260. (205)934-8578. E-mail: kmadden@uab.edu. Website: www.pms-journal.org/submissions-guidelines. **Contact:** Kerry Madden, Editor-in-Chief. Literary magazine/journal: 6x9; 120 pages; recycled white; matte paper; cover photos. "We print one issue a year, our cover price is $7, and our journal publishes fine creative work by women writers from across the nation (and beyond) in the three genres listed in the title." Circ. 1,500. Member Council of Literary Magazines and Presses and the Council of Editors of Learned Journals." Receives 30 mss/month. Accepts 4-6 mss/issue. As of 2009, reading period is January 1 - March 30. Ms published within 6 months after acceptance. Publishes 5 new writers/year. Published Vicki Covington, Kim Aubrey, Patricia Brieschke, Gaines Marsh. Length: 4,500 words (max). Average length: 3,500-4,000 words. Publishes short shorts. Average length of short shorts: 300-350 words. Also publishes literary essays, poetry. Rarely comments on/critiques rejected mss.

Work from PMS has been reprinted in a number of award anthologies: *New Stories from the South 2005, The Best Creative Nonfiction 2007* and *2008, Best American Poetry 2003* and *2004*, and *Best American Essays 2005* and *2007*.

NEEDS comics/graphic novels, ethnic/multicultural (general), experimental, feminist, literary, translations. "We don't do erotic, mystery work, and most popular forms. We publish short stories and essays including memoirs and other brands of creative nonfiction.

HOW TO CONTACT Send complete ms with cover letter. Include list of publications. Responds to queries in 1 month. Responds to mss in 1-4 months. Send disposable copy of ms and #10 SASE for reply only. Considers simultaneous submissions, multiple submissions. Sample copy available for $7. Guidelines available for SASE, on website.

PAYMENT/TERMS Writers receive 2 contributor's copies. Additional copies $7. Pays on publication. Acquires onetime rights. Publication is copyrighted.

TIPS "We seek unpublished original work that we can recycle. Include cover letter, brief bio with SASE. All mss should be typed on 1-side of 8 x 11 white paper with author's name, address, phone no. and email address on front of each submission." Reading period runs Jan. 1-Mar. 31. Submissions received at other times of the year will be returned unread. Best way to make contact is through e-mail.

◐ POINTED CIRCLE

Portland Community College–Cascade, 705 N. Killing, Portland OR 97217. E-mail: lutgarda.cowan@pcc.edu. **Contact:** Lutgarda Cowan, English instructor, faculty advisor. Estab. 1980. Magazine: 80 pages; b&w illustrations; photos. "Anything of interest to educationally/culturally mixed audience." Annual.

NEEDS ethnic/multicultural, literary, regional, contemporary, prose poem. "We will read whatever is sent, but encourage writers to remember we are a quality literary/arts magazine intended to promote the arts in the community. No pornography, nothing trite. Be mindful of deadlines and length limits." Accepts submissions only October 1-March 1, for July 1 issue.

HOW TO CONTACT Accepts submissions by e-mail, mail. Prose up to 3,000 words; poetry up to 6 pages; artwork in high-resolution digital form. Submitted materials will not be returned; SASE for notification only. Accepts multiple submissions.

PAYMENT/TERMS Pays 2 copies. Acquires onetime rights.

O POLYPHONY H.S., AN INTERNATIONAL STUDENT-RUN LITERARY MAGAZINE FOR HIGH SCHOOL WRITERS AND EDITORS

Polyphony High School, 1514 Elmwood Ave., #2, Chicago IL 60201. (847) 910-3221. E-mail: polyphonyhs@gmail.com. Website: www.polyphonyhs.com. Estab. 2005. **Contact:** Billy Lombardo, Managing Editor at polyphonyhs@gmail.com, or Beth Keegan, Executive Editor at beth@polyphonyhs@gmail.com, or phone (847)910-3221. Literary magazine/journal: 9x6, 70-120 pages, silk finish 80 lb. white paper, silk finish 100 lb. cover. "We are a 501(c) 3 organization. Our goal is to work directly with all of our submitting authors in an attempt to help them grow as writers, to publish the best of the year's submissions on our web edition, and to publish the best of those in our annual print edition. Every submission sent in before our early deadline (March 15) is edited, commented upon, by at least 3 high school editors from around the country. Polyphony H.S. invites high school students to serve as readers and editors, and hosts summer workshops for National Editors. We manage the Claudia Ann Seaman Awards for Young Writers; cash awards for the best poem, best story, best work of creative nonfiction. See website for details." Annual. Estab. 2005. To be considered for CAS awards, entries must be accompanied by student name, address, e-mail address, high school, high school address, and name and e-mail address of your high school English teacher. Circ. 2,000. **Advice:** "We think this is the most important literary magazine in the world. Inherent in it is the collective value of every other magazine in circulation. If you're a high school teacher, you should have us in your classroom. If you teach in a university you should be paying attention to our writers."

NEEDS poetry, fiction, and creative nonfiction.

HOW TO CONTACT See website. Online submission process. Deadline April 15. Responds in 6-8 weeks. Considers simultaneous submissions. Sample copy available for $7.50 + $2.50 shipping/handling.

PAYMENT/TERMS Writers receive 2 contributor's copies. Pays on publication. Acquires first rights.

◐ POST ROAD

P.O. Box 600725, Newtown MA 02460. E-mail: postroad@bc.edu; ricco@postroadmag.com. Website: www.postroadmag.com. **Contact:** Ricco Siasoco, managing editor. Literary magazine/journal. 8½x11½, 240 pages, 60 lb. opaque paper, gloss cover. "*Post Road* is a nationally distributed literary magazine based out of New York and Boston that publishes work in the following genres: art, criticism, fiction, nonfiction, and poetry. *Post Road* also features two innovations: the Recommendations section, where established writers write 500-1,000 words on a favorite book(s) or author(s); and the Etcetera section, where we publish interviews, profiles, translations, letters, classic reprints, documents, topical essays, travelogues, etc." Estab. 2000. Circ. 2,000.

Work from *Post Road* has received the following honors: honorable mention in the 2001 O. Henry Prize Issue guest-edited by Michael Chabon, Mary Gordon, and Mona Simpson; the Pushcart Prize; honorable mention in *The Best American Nonfiction* series; and inclusion in the *Best American Short Stories* 2005.

NEEDS literary. Receives 100 mss/month. Accepts 4-6 mss/issue; 8-12 mss/year. See website for reading periods. Manuscript published 6 months after acceptance. Published Brian Booker, Louis E. Bourgeois, Becky Bradway, Adam Braver, Ashley Capps, Susan Choi, Lisa Selin Davis, Rebecca Dickson, Rick Moody. Average length: 5,000 words. Average length of short shorts: 1,500 words. Also publishes literary essays, literary criticism, poetry. Sometimes comments on/critiques rejected manuscripts.

HOW TO CONTACT Accepts submissions by online submissions manager only. Include brief bio. Responds to mss in 1 months. Send SASE (or IRC) for return of ms. Considers simultaneous submissions. Guidelines available on website.

PAYMENT/TERMS Writers receive 2 contributor's copies. Pays on publication. Acquires first North American serial rights. Sends galleys to author. Publication is not copyrighted.

TIPS "Looking for interesting narrative, sharp dialogue, deft use of imagery and metaphor. Be persistent and be open to criticism."

POSTSCRIPTS: THE A TO Z OF FANTASTIC FICTION

PS Publishing LTD., Grosvenor House, 1 New Road, Hornsea East Yorkshire HU18 1P9 England. 0-11-44-1964 537575. Fax: 0-11-44-1964 537535. E-mail: editor@pspublishing.co.uk. Website: www.pspublishing.co.uk. **Contact:** Peter Crowther, editor/publisher. Estab. 2004. Literary magazine/journal: digest, 144 pages. Contains illustrations and photographs. "Science fiction, fantasy, horror and crime/suspense. We focus on the cerebral rather than the visceral, with an emphasis on quality literary fiction within the specified areas." Quarterly. Circ. around 1,000.

PS Publishing has received 5 British Fantasy Awards, a World Fantasy Award, an International Horror Guild Award, and a Horror Writers Association Award.

NEEDS fantasy (space fantasy, sword and sorcery), horror (dark fantasy, futuristic, psychological, supernatural), mystery (amateur sleuth, cozy, police procedural, private eye/hard-boiled), science fiction (hard science/technological, soft/sociological), List of upcoming themes available on website. Receives 20-50 mss/month. Accepts 10 mss/issue; 50 mss/year. Manuscript published up to 2 years after acceptance. Agented fiction less than 10%. **Publishes 4-8 new writers/year.** Length: 3,000 words (min)–8,000 words (max). Average length: 5,000 words. Publishes short shorts. Average length of short shorts: 1,000 words. Rarely comments on/critiques rejected mss.

HOW TO CONTACT Send complete ms with cover letter. Accepts submissions by mail, e-mail. Include estimated word count, brief bio, list of publications. Responds to queries in 2 weeks; mss in 4 weeks. Send either SASE (or IRC) for return of ms or disposable copy of ms and #10 SASE for reply only. Sample copy available for $10 (and $5 IRCs). Guidelines available on website.

PAYMENT/TERMS Writers receive 4–7¢/word, 2 contributor's copies. Additional copies $10 (inc. postage). **Pays on acceptance.** Acquires first worldwide English rights. Publication is copyrighted.

TIPS "Read the magazine."

POTOMAC REVIEW

Montgomery College, 51 Mannakee St., MT/212, Rockville MD 20850. (301)251-7417. Fax: (301)738-1745. E-mail: zachary.benavidez@montgomerycollege.edu. Website: www.montgomerycollege.edu/potomacreview. **Contact:** Zachary Benavidez, editor. Estab. 1994. Magazine: 5½×8½; 175 pages; 50 lb. paper; 65 lb. color cover. *Potomac Review* "reflects a view of our region looking out to the world, and in turn, seeks how the world views the region." Biannual.

NEEDS "Stories and poems with a vivid, individual quality that get at 'the concealed side' of life." Flash fiction accepted. Essays and creative nonfiction pieces welcome. No themes. Receives 300+ unsolicited mss/month. Accepts 40-50 mss/issue. Publishes ms within 1 year after acceptance. Recently published work by Jennine Capo Crucet, T.J. Forrester, Irene Keliher, Myfanwy Collins, Tiger D. Quinn, and Julee Newberger. Length: 5,000 words; average length: 2,000 words.

HOW TO CONTACT Send SASE with adequate postage for reply and/or return of ms. Responds in 3-6 months to mss. Accepts simultaneous submissions. Sample copy for $10. Writer's guidelines on website.

PAYMENT/TERMS Pays 2 or more contributor's copies; additional copies for a 40% discount.

TIPS "Send us interesting, well crafted stories. Have something to say in an original, provocative voice. Read recent issue to get a sense of the journal's new direction."

THE PUCKERBRUSH REVIEW

English Dept., University of Maine, 413 Neville Hall, Orono ME 04469. E-mail: sanphip@aol.com. Website: http://puckerbrushreview.com. **Contact:** Sanford Phippen, Editor. Estab. 1971. Magazine: 9×12; 80-100 pages; illustrations. "We publish interviews, fiction, reviews, poetry for a literary audience." Semiannual. Estab. 1979. Circ. 500. "Wants to see more original, quirky and well-written fiction. No genre fiction. Nothing cliché, nothing overly sensational except in its human interest." Receives 30 unsolicited mss/month. Accepts 6 mss/issue; 12 mss/year. Publishes ms 1 year after acceptance. Recently published work by John Sullivan, Beth Thorpe, Chenoweth Hall, Merle Hillman, Wayne Burke. Publishes short shorts. Also publishes literary essays, literary criticism, poetry. Sometimes comments on rejected mss. Include SASE. Responds in 2 months to mss. Accepts simultaneous, multiple submissions. Sample copy for $3. Writer's guidelines for SASE. Reviews fiction and poetry. Pays in contributor's copies.

"Please submit your poetry, short stories, literary essays and reviews through our website link. Hard-copy submissions will no longer be accepted."

NEEDS belles lettres

TIPS "Just write the best and freshest poetry you can."

PUERTO DEL SOL

New Mexico State University, English Department, P.O. Box 30001, MSC 3E, Las Cruces NM 88003. (505)646-3931. E-mail: contact@puertodelsol.org. Website: www.puertodelsol.org. **Contact:** Carmen Giménez Smith, editor-in-chief. Estab. 1964. Magazine: 7×9; 200 pages; 60 lb. paper; 70 lb. cover stock. "We publish innovative work from emerging and established writers and artists. Poetry, fiction, nonfiction, drama, theory, artwork, interviews, reviews, and interesting combinations thereof." Semiannual. Circ. 1,500.

NEEDS literary, experimental, theory, drama, work in translation. Accepts 8-12 mss/issue; 16-24 mss/year. Does not accept mss April 1-September 14. **Publishes 8-10 new writers/year.** Recently accepted and published work by Kim Chinquee, Grace Krilanovich, Robert Lopez, Peter Markus, Shya Scanlon. Responds in 3-6 months to mss. Accepts simultaneous submissions. Sample copy for $10.

HOW TO CONTACT Submit 1 short story, 2-4 short short stories, or 5 poems at a time through online submission manager. Responds in 3-6 months to mss. Accepts simultaneous submissions. Sample copy for $8. Email: contact@puertodelsol.org.

PAYMENT/TERMS Pays 2 contributor's copies. Acquires one-time print and electronic rights and anthology rights. Rights revert to author after publication.

TIPS "We are especially pleased to publish emerging writers who work to push their art form or field of study in new directions."

THE RAVEN CHRONICLES: A JOURNAL OF ART, LITERATURE, & THE SPOKEN WORD

A Journal of Art, Literature, & the Spoken Word, 12346 Sand Point Way NE, Seattle WA 98125. (206)941-2955. E-mail: editors@ravenchronicles.org. Website: www.ravenchronicles.org. Estab. 1991. Magazine: 8½×11; 88-100 pages; 50 lb. book; glossy cover; b&w illustrations; photos. "The *Raven Chronicles* is designed to promote transcultural art, literature and the spoken word." Biannual. Circ. 2,500-5,000.

NEEDS ethnic/multicultural, literary, regional, political, cultural essays. "No romance, fantasy, mystery or detective." Receives 300-400 unsolicited mss/month. Accepts 35-60 mss/issue; 105-150 mss/year. Publishes ms 12 months after acceptance. **Publishes 50-100 new writers/year.** Recently published work by David Romtvedt, Sherman Alexie, D.L. Birchfield, Nancy Redwine, Diane Glancy, Greg Hischak, Sharon Hashimoto. Length: 2,500 words (but negotiable); average length: 2,000 words. Publishes short shorts. Also publishes literary essays, literary criticism, poetry. Sometimes comments on rejected mss.

HOW TO CONTACT Send complete ms with SASE. Does not accept unsolicited submissions by e-mail (except foreign submissions). Responds in 3 months to mss. Does not accept simultaneous submissions. Sample copy for $5.19-10.19. Writer's guidelines for #10 SASE.

PAYMENT/TERMS Pays $10-40 and 2 contributor's copies; additional copies at half cover cost. Pays on publication for first North American serial rights. Sends galleys to author. See website for submission deadlines.

TIPS Looks for "clean, direct language, written from the heart, and experimental writing. Read sample copy, or look at *Before Columbus* anthologies and *Greywolf Annual* anthologies."

THE READER

19 Abercromby Square, Liverpool, Merseyside LG9 7ZG United Kingdom. E-mail: magazine@thereader.org.uk; info@thereader.org.uk. Website: www.thereader.org.uk. **Contact:** Philip Davis, editor. Estab. 1997. Literary magazine/journal: 216 x 138 mm, 130 pages, 80 gsm (Silver Offset) paper. Includes photographs. "The Reader is a quarterly literary magazine aimed at the intelligent 'common reader'—from those just beginning to explore serious literary reading to professional teachers, academics and writers. As well as publishing short fiction and poetry by new writers and established names, the magazine features articles on all aspects of literature, language, and reading; regular features, including a literary quiz and 'Our Spy in NY', a bird's-eye view of literary goings-on in New York; reviews; and readers' recommendations of books that have made a difference to them. The *Reader* is unique among literary magazines in its focus on reading as a creative, important and pleasurable activity, and in its combination of high-quality material and presentation with a genuine commitment to ordinary but dedicated readers." Quarterly. Estab. 1997.

NEEDS Literary. Receives 10 mss/month. Accepts 1-2 mss/issue; 8 mss/year. Manuscript published 16 months after acceptance. Publishes 4 new writers/year. Published Karen King Arbisala, Ray Tallis, Sasha Dugdale, Vicki Seal, David Constantine, Jonathan Meades, Ramesh Avadhani. Length: 1,000 words (min)-3,000 words (max). Average length: 2,300 words. Publishes short shorts. Average length of short shorts: 1,500 words. Also publishes literary essays, literary criticism, poetry. Sometimes comments on/critiques rejected mss.

HOW TO CONTACT No e-mail submissions. Send complete ms with cover letter. Include estimated word count, brief bio, list of publications. Responds to queries in 2 months; mss in 2 months. Send SASE (or IRC) for return of ms. Considers simultaneous submissions, multiple submissions. Guidelines available for SASE.

PAYMENT/TERMS Additional copies $14. Pays on publication. Sends galleys to author.

TIPS "The style or polish of the writing is less important than the deep structure of the story (though of course, it matters that it's well written). The main persuasive element is whether the story moves us—and that's quite hard to quantify—it's something to do with the force of the idea and the genuine nature of enquiry within the story. When fiction is the writer's natural means of thinking things through, that'll get us. "

THE RED CLAY REVIEW

Dr. Jim Elledge, Director, M. A. in Professional Writing Program, Department of English, Kennesaw State University, 1000 Chastain Rd., #2701, Kennesaw GA 30144-5591. E-mail: redclayreview@gmail.com. Website: http://redclayreview.com. **Contact:** Dr. Jim Elledge, director, M.A. in Professional Writing Program. Magazine has revolving editor. Editorial term: 1 year. Literary magazine/journal. $8\frac{1}{2} \times 5\frac{1}{2}$; 80-120 pages, 60# white paper, 10-pt matte lam. cover. "*The Red Clay Review* is dedicated to publishing only the most outstanding graduate literary pieces. It has been established by members of the Graduate Writers Association at Kennesaw State University. It is unique because it only includes the work of graduate writing students. We publish poems (must be limited to 300 words, double spaced, 12 pt. font, 3-5 poems per submission), fiction/non-fiction pieces (must not exceed 10 pages, double spaced, 12 pt. font), and 10 minute plays/scenes (should be limited to 11 total pages since the first page will usually be mostly taken up by character listing/setting description.)" Annual. Estab. 2008.

NEEDS "We do not have any specific themes or topics, but keep in mind that we are a literary publication. We will read whatever is sent in. We will publish whatever we deem to be great literary writing. So in essence, every topic is open to submission, and we are all interested in a wide variety of subjects. We do not prohibit any topic or subject matter from being submitted. As long as submissions adhere to our guidelines, we are open to reading them. However, subject matter in any area that is too extreme may be less likely to be published because we want to include a broad collection of literary graduate work, but on the other hand, we cannot morally reject great writing." Receives 12 mss/month. Does not read November 1-June 1. Ms published 6 months after acceptance. Length: 2,500 words (min)-8,000 words (max). Publishes short shorts. Also publishes literary essays, poetry. Never comments on/critiques rejected mss.

HOW TO CONTACT Send complete ms with cover letter. Include brief bio, list of publications, and an e-mail address must be supplied for the student, as well as the student's advisor's contact information (to verify student status). Responds to mss in 12-16 weeks. Considers simultaneous submissions, multiple submissions. Guidelines available on website.

PAYMENT/TERMS Writers receive 2 contributor's copies. Pays on publication. Acquires first rights. Publication is copyrighted.

TIPS "Because the editors of *RCR* are graduate student writers, we are mindful of grammatical proficiency, vocabulary, and the organizational flow of the submissions we receive. We appreciate a heightened level of writing from fellow graduate writing students; but we also hold it to a standard to which we have learned in our graduate writing experience. Have your submission(s) proofread by a fellow student or professor."

REDIVIDER

Department of Writing, Literature, and Publishing, Emerson College, 120 Boylston St., Boston MA 02116. E-mail: fiction@redividerjournal.com; poetry@redividerjournal.com. Website: www.redividerjournal.org. Estab. 1986. Editors change each year. Magazine: $5\frac{1}{2}\times8\frac{1}{2}$; 160 pages; 60 lb. paper. *Redivider*, a journal of literature and art, is published twice a year by students in the graduate writing, literature and publishing department of Emerson College. Biannual.

NEEDS literary. Receives 100 unsolicited mss/month. Accepts 6-8 mss/issue; 10-12 mss/year. Publishes ms 3-6 months after acceptance. Publishes short shorts. Also publishes poetry. Sometimes comments on rejected mss.

HOW TO CONTACT "We are taking electronic submissions solely through our online submissions manager. Hard copy submissions and inquiries may be sent to the appropriate genre editor through postal mail. Send disposable copy of ms." Accepts simultaneous submissions with notification. Sample copy for $6 with a #10 SASE. Writer's guidelines for SASE or online.

PAYMENT/TERMS Pays 2 contributor's copies; additional copies $6. Pays on publication for onetime rights. Sponsors awards/contests.

TIPS "Our deadlines are July 1 for the Fall issue, and December 1 for the Spring issue."

REED MAGAZINE

San Jose State University, Dept. of English, One Washington Square, San Jose CA 95192-0090. (408) 927-4458. E-mail: reed@email.sjsu.edu. Website: http://www.reedmag.org/drupal/. **Contact:** Nick Taylor, editor. Estab. 1944. Literary magazine/journal. 9×5.75, 200 pages, semi-gloss paper, card cover. Contains illustrations. Includes photographs. "Reed Magazine is one of the oldest student-run literary journals west of the Mississippi. We publish outstanding fiction, poetry, nonfiction and art as a service to the South Bay literary community." Annual. Circ. 3500. Member CLMP.

NEEDS Ethnic/multicultural (general), experimental, feminist, gay, historical (general), humor/satire, lesbian, literary, mainstream, regional (northern California). Does not want children's, young adult, fantasy, or erotic. Receives 30 mss/month. Accepts 5-7 mss/issue. Does not read Nov 2-May 31. Ms published 6 months after acceptance. Publishes 3-4 new writers/year. Published Tommy Mouton, Alan Soldofsky, Gwen Goodkin and Al Young. Length: 2,000 words (min)-6,000 words (max). Average length: 3,500 words. Also publishes literary essays, book reviews, poetry. Send review copies to Nick Taylor, Editor. Never comments on/critiques rejected mss.

HOW TO CONTACT Submit online. Include estimated word count, brief bio. Responds to mss in 6 months. Considers simultaneous submissions, multiple submissions. Sample copy available for $8. Guidelines available on website.

PAYMENT/TERMS Writers receive free subscription to the magazine. Additional copies $5. Pays on publication. Acquires first North American serial rights. Sends galleys to author. Publication is copyrighted. "Sponsors the Steinbeck Award, given annually for the best short story. The prize is $1,000 and there's a $15 entry fee."

TIPS "Well-writen, original, clean grammatical prose is essential. Keep submitting! The readers are students and change every year."

THE REJECTED QUARTERLY

P.O. Box 1351, Cobb CA 95426. E-mail: bplankton@yahoo.com. Website: www.rejectedq.com. **Contact:** Daniel Weiss, fiction editor. Estab. 1998. Magazine: $8\frac{1}{2}\times11$; 36-44 pages; 60 lb. paper; 10-pt. coated cover stock; illustrations. "We want the best literature possible, regardless of genre. We do, however, have a bias toward the unusual and toward speculative fiction. We aim for a literate, educated audience. *The Rejected Quarterly* believes in publishing the highest quality rejected fiction and other writing that doesn't fit anywhere else. We strive to be different, but will go for quality every time, whether conventional or not." Semiannual.

NEEDS experimental, fantasy, historical, humor/satire, literary, mainstream, mystery/suspense, romance (futuristic/time travel only), science fiction (soft/sociological), sports. Accepts poetry about being rejected. Receives 30 unsolicited mss/month. Accepts 3-6 mss/issue; 8-12 mss/year. Publishes ms 1-12 months after acceptance. **Publishes 2- 4 new writers/year.** Recently published work by Sharon Ellis, C. Marcus Parr, Adam Fuller, Tim Kissell, Hannah Gersen and John C. Carter. Length: 8,000 words. Publishes short shorts (literature related), literary criticism, rejection-related poetry. Often comments on rejected mss.

HOW TO CONTACT Send SASE for reply, return of ms or send a disposable copy of ms. No longer accepting e-mail submissions. Responds in 2-4 weeks to queries; 1-9 months to mss. Accepts reprint submissions. Sample copy for $7.50 (IRCs for foreign requests). Reviews fiction.

PAYMENT/TERMS Pays $20 and 1 contributor's copy; additional copies $5. Pays on acceptance for first rights.

TIPS "Beginning in June 2010, we will be reading manuscripts from June through August only. We are looking for high-quality writing that tells a story or expresses a coherent idea. We want unique stories, original viewpoints and unusual slants. We are getting far too many inappropriate submissions. Please be familiar with the magazine. Be sure to include your rejection slips! Send out quality rather than quantity."

◐ RIVER OAK REVIEW

Elmhurst College, 190 Prospect Ave., Elmhurst IL 60126-3296. (630) 617-3137. Fax: (630) 617-3609. E-mail: riveroak@elmhurst.edu. Website: www.riveroakreview.org. **Contact:** Ron Wiginton, fiction editor, ronw@elmhurst.edu. Literary magazine/journal: 6×9, 195 pages; perfect bound paper; glossy, 4 color cover. "We try with each issue to showcase many voices of America, loud and soft, radical and sublime. Each piece we publish, prose or poetry, is an attempt to capture a part of 'us', with the notion that it is through our art that we are defined as a culture." Estab. 1993. Circ. 500.

NEEDS ethnic/multicultural (general), experimental, literary, mainstream, translations. Does not want genre fiction or "lessons of morality; 'idea' driven stories usually do not work." Receives 50-75 mss/month. Accepts 7-8 mss/issue; 14-16 mss/year. Ms published 3 months after acceptance. Agented fiction 1%. **Publishes 2-3 new writers/year.** Published Adam Lichtenstein, Robert Moulthrop, J. Malcom Garcia and Laura Hope-Gill. Length: 250 words (min)-7,000 words (max). Average length: 3,000 words. Publishes short shorts. Average length of short shorts: 750 words. Also publishes literary essays, book reviews, poetry. Send review copies to Ron Wiginton, Editor. Sometimes comments on/critiques rejected mss.

HOW TO CONTACT Send complete ms with cover letter. Accepts submissions by e-mail. Include list of publications. Responds to mss in 6 months. Send disposable copy of ms and #10 SASE for reply only. Considers simultaneous submissions. Sample copy available for $5. Guidelines available for SASE, via e-mail, on website, via fax.

PAYMENT/TERMS Writers receive 2 contributor's copies. Additional copies $10. Pays on publication. Acquires first North American serial rights. Publication is copyrighted.

TIPS "The voice is what we notice first. Is the writer in command of the language? Secondly, does the story have anything to say? It's not that 'fluff' cannot be good, but we note our favorites stories tend to have meaning beyond the surface of the plot. Thirdly, the story must by populated by 'real' peoples who are also interesting, characters, in other words, who have lives underneath the storyline. Finally, look before you leap."

◐ RIVERWIND

3301 Hocking Park Way, Nelsonville OH 45764. (740)753-3591. E-mail: williams_k@hocking.edu. Magazine: 7×7; 125-150 pages; 60 lb. offset paper; illustrations; photos. *Riverwind* is an established magazine that prints fiction, poetry, black-and-white photos and prints, drawings, creative nonfiction, book reviews, and plays. Special consideration is given to writers from the Appalachian region. Annual. Estab. 1976. Circ. 200-400.

NEEDS adventure, ethnic/multicultural (Appalachian), humor/satire, literary, mainstream, regional. DOES NOT WANT erotica, fantasy, horror, experimental, religious, children's/juvenile. Receives 25 unsolicited mss/month. Does not read mss June-September. Publishes ms 6-9 months after acceptance. **Publishes many new writers/year.** Recently published work by Gerald Wheeler, Wendy McVicker, Roy Bentley, Perry A. White, Tom Montag, Beau Beadreaux. Length: 500-2,500 words; average length: 1,750 words. Publishes short shorts. Also publishes literary essays, literary criticism, poetry. Rarely comments on rejected mss.

HOW TO CONTACT Send complete ms. Accepts submissions by e-mail, disk. Send disposable copy of ms and #10 SASE for reply only. Responds in 4 weeks to queries; 8-16 weeks to mss. Accepts simultaneous, multiple submissions. Sample copy for $5. Writer's guidelines for #10 SASE or by e-mail.

PAYMENT/TERMS Pays 2 contributor's copies. Pays on publication for first North American serial rights.

TIPS "Avoid stereotypical plots and characters. We tend to favor realism but not sentimentality."

ROANOKE REVIEW

Roanoke College, 221 College Lane, Salem VA 24153-3794. E-mail: review@roanoke.edu. Website: http://roanokereview.wordpress.com. **Contact:** Paul Hanstedt, editor. Magazine: 6×9; 200 pages; 60 lb. paper; 70 lb. cover. "We're looking for fresh, thoughtful material that will appeal to a broader as well as literary audience. Humor encouraged." Annual. Estab. 1967. Circ. 500.

NEEDS feminist, gay, humor/satire, lesbian, literary, mainstream, regional. Receives 150 unsolicited mss/month. Accepts 5-10 mss/year. Does not read mss February 1-September 1. Publishes ms 6 months after acceptance. **Publishes 1-5 new writers/year.** Has published work by Siobhan Fallon, Jacob M. Appel, and JoeAnn Hart. Length: 1,000-5,000 words; average length: 3,000 words. Publishes short shorts. Also publishes poetry. Sometimes comments on rejected mss.

HOW TO CONTACT Send SASE for return of ms or send a disposable copy of ms and #10 SASE for reply only. Responds in 1 month to queries; 6 months to mss. Sample copy for 8×11 SAE with $2 postage. Writer's guidelines for SASE.

PAYMENT/TERMS Pays $10-50/story (when budget allows) and 2 contributor's copies; additional copies $5. Pays on publication for one-time rights.

TIPS "Pay attention to sentence-level writing—verbs, metaphors, concrete images. Don't forget, though, that plot and character keep us reading. We're looking for stuff that breaks the MFA story style." "Be real. Know rhythm. Concentrate on strong images."

THE ROCKFORD REVIEW

The Rockford Writers Guild, P.O. Box 858, Rockford IL 61105. E-mail: editors@rockfordwritersguild.com. Website: www.rockfordwritersguild.com. **Contact:** Connie Kluntz, Managing Editor. Estab. 1947. Magazine: 100 pages; perfect bound; color illustrations; b&w photos. Rockford Writers' Guild is a nonprofit corporation established in 1947 with the mission to promote the literary arts in Rockford, IL, and beyond. Monthly meetings, interaction with other writers, writers groups, editorial support, current information and useful resources through the website, discounts on book production, and other benefits are just part of what RWG offers to its members. Semiannual.

Poetry 50 lines or less, prose 1,300 words or less.

NEEDS ethnic/multicultural, experimental, fantasy, humor/satire, literary, regional, science fiction (hard science, soft/sociological). "No graphic sex, translations or overly academic work." Recently published work by James Bellarosa, Sean Michael Rice, John P. Kristofco, L.S. Sedishiro. Also publishes literary essays.

HOW TO CONTACT Please go online and follow the rules for submission: www.rockfordwritersguild.com/submit.html. Please note that submissions rules may change from time to time and for each edition there is a different theme to write about. So, check the website regularly. Be sure your mss conform to the rules, or they may not be considered. Pays 1 contributor's copy and pays 2 editor's choice awards of $25 each: one for prose and one for poetry. 1,300 words or less for prose.

PAYMENT/TERMS If published in the winter-spring edition of the *Rockford Review*, payment is one copy of magazine and $5 per published piece. Pays on publication.

TIPS "We're wide open to new and established writers alike—particularly short satire."

ROOM

P.O. Box 46160, Station D, Vancouver BC V6J 5G5 Canada. E-mail: contactus@roommagazine.com. Website: www.roommagazine.com. **Contact:** Growing Room Collective. Estab. 1975. Magazine: 112 pages; illustrations; photos. "*Room of One's Own* is Canada's oldest feminist literary journal. *ROOM* is Canada's oldest literary journal by and for women. Since 1975, ROOM has been a forum in which women can share their unique perspectives on the world, each other and themselves." Quarterly. Estab. 1975.

NEEDS Accepts literature that illustrates the female experience—short stories, creative nonfiction, poetry—by, for and about women. Receives 100-120 unsolicited mss/month. Accepts 18-20 mss/issue; 75-80 mss/year. Publishes ms 1 year after acceptance. **Publishes 15-20 new writers/year.**

HOW TO CONTACT We accept e-mail submissions with some guidelines—see our full guidelines at our website. Or, send complete ms with a cover letter. Include estimated word count and brief bio. Do not send a SASE. Responds in 6 months to mss. Sample copy for $13 or online. Writer's guidelines online. Reviews fiction.

PAYMENT/TERMS Pays $50 (Canadian), 2 contributor's copies, and a 1-year subscription. Pays on publication for first North American serial rights.

SALMAGUNDI

Skidmore College, 815 North Broadway, Saratoga Springs NY 12866. (518)580-5000 ext. 4495. Fax: (518)580-5188. E-mail: salmagun@skidmore.edu. Website: cms.skidmore.edu/salmagundi/index.cfm. Estab. 1965. Magazine: 8×5; 200-300 pages; illustrations; photos. "*Salmagundi* publishes an eclectic variety of materials, ranging from short-short fiction to novellas from the surreal to the realistic. Authors include Nadine Gordimer, Russell Banks, Steven Millhauser, Gordon Lish, Clark Blaise, Mary Gordon, Joyce Carol Oates and Cynthia Ozick. Our audience is a generally literate population of people who read for pleasure." Quarterly. Circ. 4,800. Member CLMP.

Salmagundi authors are regularly represented in *Pushcart* collections and *Best American Short Story* collections.

NEEDS ethnic/multicultural (multicultural), experimental, family saga, gay, historical (general), literary, poetry. Receives 300-500 unsolicited mss/month. Accepts 2 mss/year. Read unsolicited mss October 1-May 1 "but from time to time close the doors even during this period because the backlog tends to grow out of control." Publishes ms up to 2 years after acceptance. Agented fiction 10%. Also publishes literary essays, literary criticism, poetry.

HOW TO CONTACT *Currently not accepting unsolicited mss.* Send complete ms by e-mail (pboyes@skidmore.edu). Responds in 6 months to mss. Sample copy for $5. Writer's guidelines for #10 SASE.

PAYMENT/TERMS Pays 6-10 contributor's copies and subscription to magazine. Acquires first, electronic rights.

TIPS "I look for excellence and a very unpredictable ability to appeal to the interests and tastes of the editors. Be brave. Don't be discouraged by rejection. Keep stories in circulation. Of course, it goes without saying: Work hard on the writing. Revise tirelessly. Study magazines and send only to those whose sensibility matches yours."

SANDY RIVER REVIEW

University of Maine at Farmington, 238 Main St., Farmington ME 04938. E-mail: srreview@gmail.com. Website: http://studentorgs.umf.maine.edu/~srreview. **Contact:** Emma Deans, editor (changes each semester); Kelsey Moore, assistant editor. "*The Sandy River Review* seeks prose, poetry and art submissions twice a year for our Spring and Fall issues. Prose submissions may be either Fiction or Creative Non-Fiction and should be 15 pages or fewer in length, 12 pt., Times Roman font, double-spaced. Most of our art is published in black & white, and must be submitted as 300 dpi quaity, CMYK color mode, and saved as a .TIF file. We publish a wide variety of work from students as well as professional, established writers. Your submission should be polished and imaginative with strongly drawn characters and an interesting, original narrative. The review is the face of the University of Maine at Farmington's venerable BFA Creative Writing program, and we strive for the highest quality prose and poetry standard."

TIPS "We recommend that you take time with your piece. As with all submissions to a literary journal, submissions should be fully-completed, polished final drafts that require minimal to no revision once accepted. Double-check your prose pieces for basic grammatical errors before submitting."

SANTA MONICA REVIEW

1900 Pico Blvd., Santa Monica CA 90405. Website: www.smc.edu/sm_review/. Estab. 1989. Magazine: 250 pages. "The editors are committed to fostering new talent as well as presenting new work by established writers. There is also a special emphasis on presenting and promoting writers who make their home in Southern California." Circ. 4,000.

NEEDS experimental, literary, memoirs. "No crime and detective, mysogyny, footnotes, TV, dog stories. We want more self-conscious, smart, political, humorous, digressive, meta-fiction." Receives 250 unsolicited mss/month. Accepts 10 mss/issue; 20 mss/year. Agented fiction 10%. **Publishes 5 new writers/year.** Recently published work by Charles Baxter, Greg Bills, John Cage, Bernard Cooper, Mary Jeselnik-Koral, Amy Gerstler, Judith Grossman, Peter Handke, Jim Krusoe, Michelle Latiolais, and Deena Metzger. Also publishes literary essays.

HOW TO CONTACT Send complete ms. Send disposable copy of ms. Responds in 3 months to mss. Accepts simultaneous, multiple submissions. Sample copy for $7.

PAYMENT/TERMS Pays 5 contributor's copies. Acquires first North American serial rights. Sends galleys to author.

THE SARANAC REVIEW

CVH, Department of English, SUNY Plattsburgh, 101 Broad St., Plattsburgh NY 12901. (518)564-2414. Fax: (518)564-2140. E-mail: saranacreview@plattsburgh.edu. Website: http://research.plattsburgh.edu/saranacreview. **Contact:** Fiction Editor. Estab. 2004. Magazine: 5½×8½; 180 pages; 80 lb. cover/70 lb. paper; glossy cover stock; illustrations; photos. "*The Saranac Review* is committed to dissolving boundaries of all kinds, seeking to publish a diverse array of emerging and established writers from Canada and the U.S. *The Saranac Review* aims to be a textual clearing in which a space is opened for cross-pollination between American and Canadian writers. In this way the magazine reflects the expansive bright spirit of the etymology of its name, Saranac, meaning 'cluster of stars.'" Annual.

NEEDS ethnic/multicultural, historical, literary, flash fiction. Publishes ms 8 months after acceptance. Also publishes poetry and literary/creative nonfiction. Sometimes comments on rejected mss.

HOW TO CONTACT Send complete ms. Send SASE (or IRC) for return of ms or send disposable copy of the ms and #10 SASE for reply only. Responds in 4 months to mss. Accepts simultaneous submissions. Sample copy for $6. Writer's guidelines online, or by e-mail. "Please send one story at a time." Maximum length: 7,000 words.

PAYMENT/TERMS Pays 2 contributor's copies; discount on extras. Pays on publication for first North American serial, first rights.

TIPS "We publish serious, generous fiction."

SHORT STORY AMERICA

Short Story America, LLC, 66 Thomas Sumter St., Beaufort SC 29907. (843)597-3220. E-mail: tim@shortstoryamerica.com;sarah@shortstoryamerica.com. Website: www.shortstoryamerica.com. **Contact:** Tim Johnston or Sarah Turocy, Acquisitions. Estab. 2010.

PAYMENT/TERMS "Pays $100 per story ($50 for flash), new or reprint, and authors also share in anthology and audio royalties as well."

TIPS "We want stories which readers will remember and want to read again. If your story entertains from the first page forward, and the pacing and conflict engages the reader's interest from plot, character and thematic standpoints, then please submit your story today! If the reader genuinely wants to know what eventually happens in your story, and is still thinking about it 10 minutes after finishing, then your story works."

SNOWY EGRET

The Fair Press, P.O. Box 9265, Terre Haute IN 47808. Website: www.snowyegret.net. Estab. 1922. **Contact:** Editors. Magazine: 8½×11; 60 pages; text paper; heavier cover; illustrations. "We publish works which celebrate the abundance and beauty of nature and examine the variety of ways in which human beings interact with landscapes and living things. Nature writing from literary, artistic, psychological, philosophical and historical perspectives." Semiannual. Estab. 1922. Circ. 400.

NEEDS "No genre fiction, e.g., horror, western, romance, etc." Receives 25 unsolicited mss/month. Accepts up to 6 mss/issue; up to 12 mss/year. Publishes ms 6 months after acceptance. **Publishes 20 new writers/year.** Recently published work by James Hinton, Ron Gielgun, Tom Noyes, Alice Cross, Maeve Mullin Ellis. Length: 500-10,000 words; average length: 1,000-3,000 words. Publishes short shorts. Sometimes comments on rejected mss.

HOW TO CONTACT Send complete ms with SASE. Cover letter optional: do not query. Responds in 2 months to mss. Accepts simultaneous submissions if noted. Sample copy for 9×12 SASE and $8. Writer's guidelines for #10 SASE.

PAYMENT/TERMS Pays $2/page plus 2 contributor's copies. Pays on publication for first North American serial, onetime anthology rights, or reprint rights. Sends galleys to author.

TIPS Looks for "honest, freshly detailed pieces with plenty of description and/or dialogue which will allow the reader to identify with the characters and step into the setting; fiction in which nature affects character development and the outcome of the story."

SO TO SPEAK: A FEMINIST JOURNAL OF LANGUAGE AND ART

George Mason University, 4400 University Dr., MSN 2C5, Fairfax VA 22030-4444. E-mail: sts@gmu.edu (inquiries only). Website: http://sotospeakjournal.org. **Contact:** Jen Daniels, editor-in-chief. Estab. 1993. **Contact:** Lisa Hill-Corley, fiction editor; Jen Daniels, editor-in-chief. Magazine: 5½×8½; approximately 100 pages. "We are a feminist journal of language and art." Semiannual. Circ. 1,000.

NEEDS ethnic/multicultural, experimental, feminist, lesbian, literary, mainstream, regional, translations. "No science fiction, mystery, genre romance." Receives 100 unsolicited mss/month. Accepts 3-5 mss/issue; 6-10 mss/year. Publishes ms 6 months after acceptance. **Publishes 7 new writers/year.** Length: For fiction, up to 5,000 words; for poetry, 3-5 pages per submission; average length: for fiction, up to 5,000 words; for poetry, 3-5 pages per submission. Publishes flash and short fiction, creative nonfiction, poetry, and visual art.

HOW TO CONTACT Accepts submissions only via submissions manager on website. Does not accept paper or e-mail submissions. "Fiction submitted during the August 1–October 15 reading period will be considered for our Spring Issue and requires no reading fee. Fiction submitted during the January 1–March 15 reading period will be considered for our Fall annual fiction contest and must be accompanied by a $15 reading fee. See contest guidelines. Contest entries will not be returned." Responds in 6 months to mss. Accepts simultaneous submissions. Sample copy for $7. Reviews fiction.

PAYMENT/TERMS Pays contributor copies. Acquires first North American serial rights. Sponsors awards/contests.

TIPS "We do not read between March 15 and August 15. Every writer has something they do exceptionally well; do that and it will shine through in the work. We look for quality prose with a definite appeal to a feminist audience. We are trying to move away from strict genre lines. We want high quality fiction, nonfiction, poetry, art, innovative and risk-taking work."

SOUTH CAROLINA REVIEW

Clemson University, Strode Tower Room 611, Box 340522, Clemson SC 29634-0522. (864) 656-5399. Fax: (864) 656-1345. E-mail: cwayne@clemson.edu. Website: www.clemson.edu/cedp/cudp/scr/scrintro.htm. **Contact:** Wayne Chapman, editor. Magazine: 6×9; 200 pages; 60-lb. cream white vellum paper; 65-lb. color cover stock. Semiannual. Estab. 1967. Circ. 500.

NEEDS literary, mainstream, poetry, essays, reviews. Does not read mss June-August or December. Receives 50-60 unsolicited mss/month. Recently published work by Ronald Frame, Dennis McFadden, Dulane Upshaw Ponder, and Stephen Jones. Rarely comments on rejected mss.

HOW TO CONTACT Send complete ms. Requires text on disk upon acceptance in WordPerfect or Microsoft Word in PC format. Responds in 2 months to mss. Sample copy for $16 includes postage inside the U.S. Reviews fiction.

PAYMENT/TERMS Pays in contributor's copies.

THE SOUTHEAST REVIEW

Florida State University, Tallahassee FL 32306-1036. Website: southeastreview.org. **Contact:** Katie Cortese, editor. Estab. 1979. Magazine: 6×9; 160 pages; 70 lb. paper; 10 pt. Krome Kote cover; photos. The *Southeast Review* publishes literary fiction, poetry, and nonfiction. Biannual. Circ. 1,000.

"The mission of *The Southeast Review* is to present emerging writers on the same stage as well-established ones. In each semi-annual issue, we publish literary fiction, creative nonfiction, poetry, interviews, book reviews and art. With nearly 60 members on our editorial staff who come from throughout the country and the world, we strive to publish work that is representative of our diverse interests and aesthetics, and we celebrate the eclectic mix this produces. We receive approximately 400 submissions per month and we accept less than 1-2% of them. We will comment briefly on rejected mss when time permits. Publishes ms 2-6 months after acceptance." **Publishes 4-6 new writers/year.** Recently published work by Elizabeth Hegwood, Anthony Varallo, B.J. Hollars, Tina Karelson, John Dufresne, and more.

HOW TO CONTACT Submit complete ms through online manager only up to 7,500 words. Does not accept e-mail or paper. No previously published submissions. Accepts submissions year-round, though please be advised that the response time is slower during the summer months. Response time is usually between 2-4 months.

PAYMENT/TERMS Pays 2 contributor's copies. Acquires first North American serial rights, which then revert to author.

TIPS The *Southeast Review* accepts regular submissions for publication consideration year-round exclusively through the **online Submission Manager**. Any breaks, hiatuses, or interruptions to the reading period will be announced online, and are more likely to occur during the summer months. *SER* does not, under any circumstances, accept work via e-mail. **Except during contest season, paper submissions sent through regular postal mail will not be read or returned.** Please note that, during contest season, entries to our World's Best Short Short Story, Poetry, and Creative Nonfiction competitions must still be sent through regular postal mail. "Avoid trendy experimentation for its own sake (present-tense narration, observation that isn't also revelation). Fresh stories, moving, interesting characters and a sensitivity to language are still fiction mainstays. We also publish the winner and runners-up of the World's Best Short Story Contest, Poetry Contest, and Creative Nonfiction Contest."

● SOUTHERN CALIFORNIA REVIEW

3501 Trousdale Pkwy., Mark Taper Hall, THH 355J, University of Southern California, Los Angeles CA 90089-0355. E-mail: scr@college.usc.edu. Website: http://usc.edu/scr. **Contact:** Fiction Editor. Estab. 1982. Magazine: 150 pages; semiglosss cover stock. "Formerly known as the *Southern California Anthology, Southern California Review* (*SCR*) is the literary journal of the Master of Professional Writing program at the University of Southern California. It has been publishing fiction and poetry since 1982 and now also accepts submissions of creative nonfiction, plays, and screenplays. Printed every fall and spring with original cover artwork, every issue contains new, emerging, and established authors." Semiannual. Circ. 1,000.

NEEDS "We accept short shorts but rarely use stories more than 8,000 words. Novel excerpts are acceptable if they can stand alone. We do consider genre work (horror, mystery, romance, sci-fi) if it transcends the boundaries of the genre." Receives 120 unsolicited mss/month. Accepts 10-15 mss/issue. Publishes ms 4 months after acceptance. **Publishes 20-30 new writers/year.** Has published work by Judith Freeman, Gary Fincke David Francis, Gerald Locklin, Seth Greenland, and interviews with Nathan Englander, Steve Almond, Danzy Senna. Publishes short shorts.

HOW TO CONTACT Send complete, typed, double-spaced ms. Cover letter should include list of previous publications. Address to the proper editor (Fiction, Poetry, etc.). Please include a cover letter. Be sure your full name and contact information (address, phone, and email) appear on the first page of the manuscript. Response time for submissions is 3 to 6 months. No electronic or e-mail submissions are accepted. Every submission must include a self-addressed stamped envelope (SASE). Sample copy for $10. Writer's guidelines for SASE and on website.

PAYMENT/TERMS Pays in 2 contributor copies. Acquires first rights.

◐ SOUTHWESTERN AMERICAN LITERATURE

Center for the Study of the Southwest, Brazos Hall, Texas State University-San Marcos, San Marcos TX 78666-4616. (512)245-2224. Fax: (512)245-7462. E-mail: swpublications@txstate.edu. Website: http://swrhc.txstate.edu/cssw/. **Contact:** Twister Marquiss, assistant editor; Mark Busby, co-editor; Dick Maurice Heaberlin, co-editor. Estab. 1971. Magazine: 6x9; 125 pages; 80 lb. cover stock. "We publish fiction, nonfiction, poetry, literary criticism and book reviews. Generally speaking, we want material covering the Greater Southwest or material written by Southwest writers." Biannual.

NEEDS Ethnic/multicultural, literary, mainstream, regional. "No science fiction or romance." Receives 10-15 unsolicited mss/month. Accepts 1-2 mss/issue; 4-5 mss/year. Publishes ms 6 months after acceptance. **Publishes 1-2 new writers/year.** Recently published work by Sherwin Bitsui, Alison Hawthorne Deming, Keith Ekiss, Sara Marie Ortiz, Karla K. Morton, Lowell Mick White, John Blanchard, Jeffrey C. Alfier, Carol Hamilton, and Larry D. Thomas. Length: 6,250 words; average length: 4,000 words. Also publishes literary essays, literary criticism, poetry. Sometimes comments on rejected mss.

HOW TO CONTACT Send complete ms. Include cover letter, estimated word count, 2-5 line bio and list of publications. Accepts e-mail submissions: swpublications@txstate.edu. Include bio and list of publications in e-mail. Responds in 3-6 months to mss. Sample copy for $10. Writer's guidelines free.

PAYMENT/TERMS Pays 2 contributor copies. Acquires first rights.

TIPS "We look for crisp language, an interesting approach to material; a regional approach is desired but not required. Read widely, write often, revise carefully. We are looking for stories that probe the relationship between the tradition of Southwestern American literature and the writer's own imagination in creative ways. We seek stories that move beyond stereotype and approach the larger defining elements and also ones that, as William Faulkner noted in his Nobel Prize acceptance speech, treat subjects central to good literature—the old verities of the human heart, such as honor and courage and pity and suffering, fear and humor, love and sorrow."

◐ SOUTHWEST REVIEW

P.O. Box 750374, Dallas TX 75275-0374. (214)768-1037. Fax: (214)768-1408. E-mail: swr@smu.edu. Website: www.smu.edu/southwestreview. **Contact:** Jennifer Cranfill, senior editor. Magazine: 6×9; 150 pages. "The majority of our readers are well read adults who wish to stay abreast of the latest and best in contemporary fiction, poetry, and essays in all but the most specialized disciplines." Quarterly. Estab. 1915. Circ. 1,600.

NEEDS "High literary quality; no specific requirements as to subject matter, but cannot use sentimental, religious, western, poor science fiction, pornographic, true confession, mystery, juvenile or serialized or condensed novels." Receives 200 unsolicited mss/month. Publishes ms 6-12 months after acceptance. Recently published work by Alice Hoffman, Sabina Murray, Alix Ohlin. Also publishes literary essays, poetry. Occasionally comments on rejected mss.

HOW TO CONTACT Mail complete ms to P.O. Box or submit online. Please note that online submissions require a $2.00 administrative fee. Responds in 1-4 months to mss. Accepts multiple submissions. Sample copy for $6. Writer's guidelines for #10 SASE or on website.

PAYMENT/TERMS Pays negotiable rate and 3 contributor copies. Acquires first North American serial rights. Sends galleys to author.

TIPS "Despite the title, we are not a regional magazine. Before you submit your work, it's a good idea to take a look at recent issues to familiarize yourself with the magazine. We strongly advise all writers to include a cover letter. Keep your cover letter professional and concise and don't include extraneous personal information, a story synopsis, or a resume. When authors ask what we look for in a strong story submission the answer is simple regardless of graduate degrees in creative writing, workshops, or whom you know. We look for good writing, period."

●◐$ STORIE

Leconte Press, Via Suor Celestina Donati 13/E, Rome 00167 Italy. (+39) 06 614 8777. Fax: (+39) 06 614 8777. E-mail: storie@tiscali.it. Website: www.storie.it. **Contact**: Gianluca Bassi, editor; Barbara Pezzopane, assistant editor; George Lerner, foreign editor. Magazine: 186 pages; illustrations; photographs. "*Storie* is one of Italy's leading literary magazines. Committed to a truly crossover vision of writing, the bilingual (Italian/English) review publishes high quality fiction and poetry, interspersed with the work of alternative wordsmiths such as filmmakers and musicians. Through writings bordering on narratives and interviews with important contemporary writers, it explores the culture and craft of writing." Bimonthly. Estab. 1989. Circ. 20,000.

NEEDS Literary. Receives 150 unsolicited mss/month. Accepts 6-10 mss/issue; 30-50 mss/year. Does not read mss in August. Publishes ms 2 months after acceptance. Publishes 20 new writers/year. Recently published work by Joyce Carol Oates, Haruki Murakami, Paul Auster, Robert Coover, Raymond Carver, T.C. Boyle, Ariel Dorfman, Tess Gallagher. Length: 2,000-6,000 words; average length: 1,500 words. Publishes short shorts. Also publishes literary essays, literary criticism, poetry. Sometimes comments on rejected mss.

HOW TO CONTACT Accepts submissions by e-mail or on disk. Include brief bio. Send complete ms with cover letter. "Manuscripts may be submitted directly by regular post without querying first; however, we do not accept unsolicited manuscripts via e-mail. Please query via e-mail first. We only contact writers if their work has been accepted. We also arrange for and oversee a high-quality, professional translation of the piece." Responds in 1 month to queries; 6 months to mss. Accepts multiple submissions. Sample copy for $ 10. Writer's guidelines online.

PAYMENT/TERMS Pays $30-600 and 2 contributor's copies. Pays on publication for first (in English and Italian) rights.

TIPS "More than erudite references or a virtuoso performance, we're interested in the recording of human experience in a genuine, original voice. *Storie* reserves the right to include a brief review of interesting submissions not selected for publication in a special column of the magazine."

STRAYLIGHT

UW-Parkside, English Dept., 900 Wood Rd., P.O. Box 2000, Kenosha WI 53141. (262)595-2139. Fax: (262)595-2271. E-mail: straylight@litspot.net. Website: www.straylightmag.com. **Contact:** Fiction Editor. Magazine has revolving editor. Editorial term: 1 years. Literary magazine/journal: 6x9 115 pages, quality paper, uncoated index stock cover. Contains illustrations. Includes photographs. "*Straylight* publishes high quality, character-based fiction of any style. We tend not to publish strict genre pieces, though we may query them for future special issues. We do not publish erotica." Biannual with special issues. Estab. 2005.

NEEDS Ethnic/multicultural (general), experimental, gay, lesbian, literary, mainstream, regional. Special interests: genre fiction in special theme issues. Accepts 3-5 mss/issue; 6-10 mss/year. Does not read May-August. Manuscript published 6 months after acceptance. Agented fiction 10%. Length: 2,500 words (min)-6,000 words (max). Average length: 2,500 words. Publishes short shorts. Also publishes poetry. Rarely comments on/critiques rejected mss.

HOW TO CONTACT Send complete ms with cover letter. Accepts submissions by e-mail. Include brief bio, list of publications. Responds to queries in 2 weeks. Responds to mss in 2 months. Send either SASE (or IRC) for return of ms or disposable copy of ms and #10 SASE for reply only. Sample copy available for $10. Guidelines available for SASE, on website.

PAYMENT/TERMS Writers receive 2 contributor's copies. Additional copies $3. Pays on publication. Acquires first North American serial rights. Publication is copyrighted.

TIPS "We tend to publish character-based and inventive fiction with cutting-edge prose. We are unimpressed with works based on strict plot twists or novelties. Read a sample copy to get a feel for what we publish."

STRUGGLE: A MAGAZINE OF PROLETARIAN REVOLUTIONARY LITERATURE

P.O. Box 28536, Detroit MI 48228. (313)273-9039. E-mail: timhall11@yahoo.com. Website: www.strugglemagazine.net. **Contact:** Tim Hall, Editor. Estab. 1985. Magazine: 512×812; 36-72 pages; 20 lb. white bond paper; colored cover; illustrations; occasional photos. Publishes short shorts. Normally comments on rejected mss. Recently published work by Billie Louise Jones, Stephen Graf, Juan H. Rodriguez, Paris Smith, Gregory Alan Norton.

HOW TO CONTACT E-mail.

PAYMENT/TERMS Pays 1 contributor's copy. No rights acquired. Not copyrighted.

SUBTERRAIN

Strong Words for a Polite Nation, P.O. Box 3008, MPO, Vancouver BC V6B 3X5 Canada. (604)876-8710. Fax: (604)879-2667. E-mail: subter@portal.ca. Website: www.subterrain.ca. **Contact:** Fiction editor. Magazine: 8^{1}_{4}×10 7/8; 56 pages; gloss stock paper; color gloss cover stock; illustrations; photos. *subTerrain* magazine is published 3 times a year from modest offices just off of Main Street in Vancouver, BC. We strive to produce a stimulating fusion of fiction, poetry, photography, and graphic illustration from uprising Canadian, U.S., and international writers and artists. "Looking for unique work and perspectives from Canada and beyond." Triannual. Estab. 1988. Circ. 3,000.

NEEDS literary. Does not want genre fiction or children's fiction. Receives 100 unsolicited mss/month. Accepts 4 mss/issue; 10-15 mss/year. Publishes ms 4 months after acceptance. Recently published work by John Moore. Also publishes literary essays, literary criticism. Rarely comments on rejected mss.

HOW TO CONTACT Send complete ms. Include disposable copy of the ms and #10 SASE for reply only. Responds in 2-4 months to mss. Accepts multiple submissions. Sample copy for $5. Writer's guidelines online.

PAYMENT/TERMS Pays $25 per page for prose. Pays on publication for first North American serial rights.

TIPS "Read the magazine first. Get to know what kind of work we publish."

TAKAHE

P.O. Box 13-335, Christchurch 8141, New Zealand. (03)359-8133. E-mail: fiction@takahe.org.nz. Website: http://takahe.org.nz. **Contact:** Fiction Editor. "*Takahe* is a hardcopy literary magazine which appears three times a year and publishes short stories, poetry, and artwork by both established and emerging writers. The publisher is Takahe Collective Trust, a non-profit organization formed by established writers to help new writers get into print."

NEEDS "Offer a new perspective; something a little different." **Publishes 20 new writers/year.** Recently published work by Raewyn Alexander, Simon Minto, Claire Baylis, Hayden Williams, Sarah Penwarden, Michael Botur, Doc Drumheller, Andrew McIntyre.

HOW TO CONTACT Send complete ms. by e-mail (poetry in hard copy). Include e-mail address, mailing address, 40 word bio and SASE (IRC for overseas submissions). See website for formatting. No simultaneous submissions. Copyright reverts to author on publication.

PAYMENT/TERMS NZ residents receive $30 (amount subject to change) and all contributors receive two hard copies of the issue in which their work appears. Overseas contributors receive a one-year subscription to *Takahe* in lieu of payment.

TIPS "We pay a flat rate to each writer/poet appearing in a particular issue regardless of the number/length of items. Editorials and literary commentaries are by invitation only."

◐ TALKING RIVER

Division of Literature and Languages, 500 8th Ave., Lewiston ID 83501. (208)792-2189. Fax: (208)792-2324. E-mail: talkingriver@lcmail.lcsc.edu. Website: www.lcsc.edu/talkingriverreview. **Contact:** Kevin Goodan, editorial advisor. Estab. 1994. Magazine: 6×9; 150-200 pages; 60 lb. paper; coated, color cover; illustrations; photos. "We look for new voices with something to say to a discerning general audience." Semiannual. Circ. 250.

NEEDS ethnic/multicultural, feminist, humor/satire, literary, regional. "Wants more well-written, character-driven stories that surprise and delight the reader with fresh, arresting yet unselfconscious language, imagery, metaphor, revelation." No stories that are sexist, racist, homophobic, erotic for shock value; no genre fiction. Receives 400 unsolicited mss/month. Accepts 5-8 mss/issue; 10-15 mss/year. Reads mss September 1-May 1 only. Publishes ms 1-2 years after acceptance. **Publishes 10-15 new writers/year.** Recently published work by X.J. Kennedy and Gary Fincke. Length: 4,000 words; average length: 3,000 words. Also publishes literary essays, poetry. Sometimes comments on rejected mss.

HOW TO CONTACT Send complete manuscript with cover letter. Include estimated word count, 2-sentence bio and list of publications. Send SASE for reply, return of ms or send disposable copy of ms. Responds in 3 months to mss. Does not accept simultaneous submissions. Sample copy for $6. Writer's guidelines for #10 SASE.

PAYMENT/TERMS Pays contributor's copies; additional copies $4. Acquires onetime rights.

TIPS "We look for the strong, the unique; we reject clicheéd images and predictable climaxes."

◐ TAPROOT LITERARY REVIEW

Box 204, Ambridge PA 15003. (724)266-8476. E-mail: taproot10@aol.com. **Contact:** Tikvah Feinstein, editor. Estab. 1987. Magazine: $5\frac{1}{2}$×$8\frac{1}{2}$; 93 pages; 20 lb. paper; hardcover; attractively printed; saddle-stitched. "We select on quality, not topic. Variety and quality are our appealing features." Annual. Circ. 500.

NEEDS Literary. "No pornography, religious, popular, romance fiction. Wants more stories with multicultural themes, showing intensity, reality and human emotions that readers can relate to, learn from, and most importantly—be interesting." The majority of ms published are received through annual contest. Receives 20 unsolicited mss/month. Accepts 6 mss/issue. **Publishes 2-4 new writers/year.** Recently published work by Bruce Mikkiff, Derrick Harrison Hurd, Faith Romeo Cataffa, B.Z. Niditch, Alicia Stakay, Alena Horowitz, Shirley Barasch, and Tikvah Feinstein. Publishes short shorts. Also publishes poetry. Sometimes comments on rejected mss.

HOW TO CONTACT Accepts submissions by e-mail. Send for guidelines first. Send complete ms with a cover letter. Include estimated word count and bio. Responds in 6 months to mss. No simultaneous submissions. "The best way for fiction writers to break into *Taproot* is through the annual contest. Send a SASE for guidelines. Sample copy for $5, 6×12 SAE with 5 first-class stamps. Writer's guidelines for #10 SASE.

PAYMENT/TERMS Awards $25 in prize money for first place fiction and poetry winners each issue; certificate for 2nd and 3rd place; 1 contributor's copy.

TIPS "*Taproot* is getting more fiction submissions, and every one is read entirely. This takes time, so response can be delayed at busy times of year. Our contest is a good way to start publishing. Send for a sample copy and read it through. Ask for a critique and follow suggestions. Don't be offended by any suggestions—just take them or leave them and keep writing. Looks for a story that speaks in its unique voice, told in a well-crafted and complete, memorable style, a style of signature to the author. Follow writer's guidelines. Research markets. Send cover letter. Don't give up."

TEXAS REVIEW

Texas Review Press, Department of English, Sam Houston State University, Box 2146, Huntsville TX 77341-2146. (936)294-1992. Fax: (936)294-3070. E-mail: eng_pdr@shsu.edu; cww006@shsu.edu. Website: www.shsu.edu/~www_trp. **Contact:** Dr. Paul Ruffin, editor/director; Claude Wolley, assistant to director. Magazine: 6×9; 148-190 pages; best quality paper; 70 lb. cover stock; illustrations; photos. "We publish top quality poetry, fiction, articles, interviews and reviews for a general audience." Estab. 1976. Semiannual. Circ. 1,200. A member of the Texas A&M University Press consortium.

NEEDS humor/satire, literary, mainstream, contemporary fiction. "We are eager enough to consider fiction of quality, no matter what its theme or subject matter. No juvenile fiction." Receives 40-60 unsolicited mss/ month. Accepts 4 mss/issue; 6 mss/year. Does not read mss May-September. Publishes ms 6-12 months after acceptance. **Publishes some new writers/year.** Recently published work by George Garrett, Ellen Gilchrist, Fred Chappell. Also publishes literary essays, literary criticism, poetry. Sometimes comments on rejected mss.

HOW TO CONTACT Send complete ms. No mss accepted via fax. Send disposable copy of ms and #10 SASE for reply only. Responds in 2 weeks to queries; 3-6 months to mss. Accepts multiple submissions. Sample copy for $5. Writer's guidelines for SASE and on website.

PAYMENT/TERMS Pays contributor's copies and one year-subscription. Pays on publication for first North American serial, onetime rights. Sends galleys to author.

THIRD WEDNESDAY: A LITERARY ARTS MAGAZINE

174 Greenside Up, Ypsilanti MI 48197. (734) 434-2409. E-mail: submissions@thirdwednesday.org; LaurenceWT@aol.com. Website: http://thirdwednesday.org. **Contact:** Laurence Thomas, editor. Estab. 2007. Literary magazine/journal. 60-65 pages. Contains illustrations. Includes photographs. "*Third Wednesday* publishes quality (a subjective term at best) poetry, short fiction and artwork by experienced writers and artists. We welcome work by established writers/artists, as well as those who are not yet well known, but headed for prominence." Quarterly. Estab. 2007.

NEEDS experimental, fantasy, humor/satire, literary, mainstream, romance, translations. Does not want "purely anecdotal accounts of incidents, sentimentality, pointless conclusions, or stories without some characterization or plot development." Receives 5-10 mss/ month. Accepts 3-5 mss/issue. Ms published 3 months after acceptance. Length: 1,500 words (max). Average length: 1,000 words. Publishes short shorts. Also publishes poetry. Sometimes comments on/critiques rejected mss.

HOW TO CONTACT Send complete ms with cover letter. Accepts submissions by e-mail. Include estimated word count, brief bio. Responds to mss in 6-8 weeks. Considers simultaneous submissions. Sample copy available for $8. Guidelines available for SASE, via e-mail.

PAYMENT/TERMS Writers receive $3, 1 contributor's copy. Additional copies $8. Pays on acceptance. Acquires first rights.

TIPS "Of course, originality is important along with skill in writing, deft handling of language and meaning which goes hand in hand with beauty, whatever that is. Short fiction is specialized and difficult, so the writer should read extensively in the field."

TICKLED BY THUNDER

14076-86A Ave., Surrey BC V3W 0V9 Canada. (604)591-6095. E-mail: info@tickledbythunder.com. Website: www.tickledbythunder.com. **Contact:** Larry Lindner, publisher. Estab. 1990. Magazine: digest-sized; 24 pages; bond paper; bond cover stock; illustrations; photos. "*Tickled By Thunder* is designed to encourage beginning writers of fiction, poetry and nonfiction." Quarterly. Estab. 1990.

NEEDS fantasy, humor/satire, literary, mainstream, mystery/suspense, science fiction, western. "No overly indulgent horror, sex, profanity or religious material." Receives 25 unsolicited mss/month. Accepts 3 mss/issue; 12 mss/year. Publishes ms 3-9 months after acceptance. **Publishes 5 new writers/year.** Recently published work by John Connors and J-Ann Godfrey. Length: 2,000 words; average length: 1,500 words. Also publishes literary essays, literary criticism, poetry.

HOW TO CONTACT Send complete ms. Include estimated word count and brief bio. Send SASE or IRC for return of ms; or send disposable copy of ms and #10 SASE for reply only. Only subscribers may send e-mail submissions online. Responds in 3 months to queries; 6 months to mss. Accepts simultaneous, multiple submissions and reprints. Writer's guidelines online.

PAYMENT/TERMS Pays on publication for first, second serial (reprint) rights.

TIPS "Allow your characters to breathe on their own. Use description with action."

TOAD SUCK REVIEW

Univ. of Central Arkansas, Dept. of Writing, Conway AR 72035. E-mail: toadsuckreview@gmail.com. Website: http://toadsuckreview.org. **Contact:** Mark Spitzer, Editor. Estab. 2011. 6 x 11 magazine, 150 pages, 70 lb. white. Illustrations and Photographs. Accepts outstanding work by beginning and established writers. Born from the legendary *Exquisite Corpse Annual*, the innovative *Toad Suck Review* is a cutting-edge mixture of poetry, fiction, creative nonfiction, translations, reviews, and artwork with a provocative sense of humor and an interest in diverse cultures and politics. Publishes short shorts; average length: 500 words. No themes planned for 2012 issues. Reads mss in the fall. Published Kevin Brockmeie, Teresa Bergen, Daniel Grandbois, William Lychack. Publishes 5 unpublished writers each year. Rarely comments on rejected mss. Responds to ms in 1 week to 9 months. Acquires one-time rights.

No agented submissions. Does not send prepublication galleys to author. Publication is copyrighted. Annual. 6 x 11. All forms and styles are welcome, especially those that take risks and shoot for something new. Has published poetry by Lawrence Ferlinghetti, Antler, Jack Hirschman, Jack Collom, Lyn Lifshin, Jacques Prevert. Professionally printed with perfect bound flat spine; full cover cardstock cover. Does not include ads. Press run is 1,000-2,000; goes to 10 libraries, 3 shelf sales; 333 distributed free to select reviewers. Single copy: $15 subscription (lifetime) $100. Make checks payable to UCA. Submit 1-10 poems at a time. Lines/poem: 1-111. Accepts e-mail submissions as attached document. Cover letter is required. Please send SASE with postal submissions. Reads in the fall. Does not charge reading fees. Sometimes publishes theme issues. Sometimes comments on rejected poems. Never sends prepublication galleys. Does not charge criticism fees. Reviews books of poetry, chapbooks of poetry, and other magazines/journals.

HOW TO CONTACT Send cover letter with complete disposable copy of ms, brief bio, and list of publications.

PAYMENT/TERMS Pays contributor's copies.

TIPS "See a recent issue or a back issue of the *Exquisite Corpse Annual* for an idea of our aesthetics." "Our guidelines are very open and ambiguous. Don't send us too much and don't make it too long. If you submit in an email, use rtf. We're easy. If it works, we'll be in touch." "It's a brutal world—wear your helmet."

TORCH: POETRY, PROSE AND SHORT STORIES BY AFRICAN AMERICAN WOMEN

3720 Gattis School Rd., Suite 800, Round Rock TX 78664. E-mail: info@torchpoetry.org (inquiries), poetry@torchpoetry.org (submissions). Website: www.torchliteraryarts.com. **Contact:** Amanda Johnston, editor. Estab. 2006. *TORCH: Poetry, Prose, and Short Stories by African American Women*, published semiannually online, provides "a place to publish contemporary poetry, prose, and short stories by experienced and emerging writers alike. We prefer our contributors to take risks, and offer a diverse body of work that examines and challenges preconceived notions regarding race, ethnicity, gender roles, and identity." Has published poetry by Sharon Bridgforth, Patricia Smith, Crystal Wilkinson, Tayari Jones, and Natasha Trethewey. Receives about 250+ submissions/year, accepts about 20. Number of unique visitors: 600+/month. Submit 3 poems at a time. No previously published poems or simultaneous submissions. Accepts e-mail submissions only (as one MS Word attachment). Send to poetry@torchpoetry.org with "Poetry Submission" in subject line. Cover letter is preferred (in the body of the e-mail). Reads submissions April 15-August 31 only. Time between acceptance and publication is 2-7 months. Sometimes comments on rejected poems. Guidelines available on website. Always sends prepublication galleys. No payment. Acquires rights to publish accepted work in online issue and in archives. Rights revert to authors upon publication. "Within *TORCH*, we offer a special section called Flame that features an interview, biography, and work sample by an established writer as well as an introduction to their Spark—an emerging writer who inspires them and adds to the boundless voice of creative writing by Black women." A free online newsletter is available; see website.

TRANSITION: AN INTERNATIONAL REVIEW

104 Mount Auburn St., 3R, Cambridge MA 02138. (617)496-2845. Fax: (617)496-2877. E-mail: transition@fas.harvard.edu. Website: www.transitionmagazine.com. **Contact:** Sara Bruya, managing editor. Estab. 1961. Magazine: $9^1{}_2 \times 6^1{}_2$; 150-175 pages; 70 lb. Finch Opaque paper; 100 lb. White Warren Lustro dull cover; illustrations; photos. "*Transition* Magazine is a trimestrial international review known for compelling and controversial writing from and about Africa and the Diaspora. This prestigious magazine is edited at the W.E.B. Du Bois Institute of Harvard Univ. by Tommie Shelby, Vincent Brown, and Glenda Carpio. The magazine attracts famous contributors such as Wole Soyinka, Jamaica Kincaid, and Carlos Fuentes, but is also committed to providing space for new voices; Transition recently made a capsule collection of Cape Verde's finest fiction available for the first time in English. In the words of our publisher, Henry Louis Gates Jr., Transition seeks to publish fiction, poetry, and criticism that wrestles with "the freshest, most compelling, most curious ideas about race—indeed, about what it means to be human—today." Quarterly. Circ. 3,000.

Essays first published in a recent issue of *Transition* were selected for inclusion in *Best American Essays 2008, Best American Nonrequired Reading 2008*, and *Best African American Writing 2009.* Four-time winner of the Alternative Press Award for international reporting (2001, 2000, 1999, 1995); finalist in the 2001 National Magazine Award in General Excellence category.

NEEDS fiction, poetry, creative nonfiction, and cultural and political criticism. Sometimes comments on rejected mss.

HOW TO CONTACT E-mail us to request the *Transition* Style Guide. E-mail submissions are preferred. If submitting by mail, please include a SASE to receive a response from *Transition.* Mss will not be returned. You will receive confirmation of receipt and notification of editorial decision after review of your work. We are not able to respond to requests for status updates. If your piece is longer than 20 pages, please also send a hard copy (in Times New Roman, font size 12, double spaced). For all submissions, please include the following information in your e-mail or cover letter and in the top left corner of the first page of all documents: name, address, e-mail address, word count, date of submission. Please also include a title with each work. Sara Bruya, Managing Editor.

PAYMENT/TERMS 1 contributor's copy.

TIPS "We look for a non-white, alternative perspective, dealing with issues of race, ethnicity and identity in an upredictable, provocative way."

UNMUZZLED OX

Unmuzzled Ox Foundation Ltd., 105 Hudson St., New York NY 10013. (212)226-7170. E-mail: mandreox@aol.com. **Contact:** Michael Andre, editor. Magazine: $5^1{}_2 \times 8^1{}_2$. "Magazine about life for an intelligent audience." Irregular frequency. Estab. 1971. Circ. 7,000.

Recent issues of this magazine have included art, poetry and essays only. Check before sending submissions. Recent issues of this magazine have included art, poetry and essays only. Check before sending submissions.

NEEDS literary, mainstream, translations, prose poetry. "No commercial fiction." Receives 20-25 unsolicited mss/month. Also publishes poetry. Sometimes comments on rejected mss.

HOW TO CONTACT "Please no phone calls and no e-mail submissions. Correspondence by *mail* only. Cover letter is significant." Responds in 1 month to queries; 1 month to mss. Sample copy not available.

PAYMENT/TERMS Pays in contributor's copies.

TIPS "You may want to check out a copy of the magazine before you submit."

THE VILLA

University of Wisconsin–Parkside, English Department, University of Wisconsin-Parkside, 900 Wood Rd., Box 2000, Kenosha WI 53414-2000. (262) 595-2139. Fax: (262) 595-2271. E-mail: villa@straylightmag.com. Website: http://straylightmag.com. **Contact:** Appropriate genre editor (revolving editors). Estab. 2008. "*The Villa* is the web counterpart to *Straylight Literary Arts Journal.* We publish some crossover print material, but the *Villa* is centered on publishing work suited to a biannual magazine." Acquires first North American serial rights. Copyrighted. Guidelines available on website.

NEEDS experimental, mainstream, science fiction, flash fiction, and serialized novelettes and novellas.

HOW TO CONTACT Send complete ms. by using submission form on website or by e-mail. Include a cover letter with a brief bio (25 words or so) with your submission.

TIPS "Please submit fiction and poetry through the website or by e-mail, and indicate you are submitting for the web magazine, and provide a short (25 word) bio with your submission. Query for reviews. We have publisher contacts and provide advanced copies."

WHITE FUNGUS: AN EXPERIMENTAL ARTS MAGAZINE

P.O. Box 6173, Wellington, Aotearoa, New Zealand. (64) 4 382 9113. E-mail: whitefungusmail@yahoo.com. Website: www.whitefungus.com. **Contact:** Ron Hanson, Editor. Literary magazine/journal. Oversize A5, 104 pages, matte paper, matte card cover. Contains illustrations, photographs. "*White Fungus* covers a range of experimental arts including literature, poetry, visual arts, comics and music. We are interested in material that is bold, innovative and well-researched. Independence of thought and meaningful surprises are a high priority." Semiannual. Estab. 2004. Circ. 2,000.

NEEDS comics/graphic novels, ethnic/multicultural, experimental, feminist, gay, historical (general), humor/satire, lesbian, literary, science fiction. "*White Fungus* considers submissions on the basis of quality rather than genre." Receives 20 mss/month. Accepts 3 mss/issue; 6 mss/year. Ms published 1-12 months after acceptance. **Publishes 2 new writers/year.** Published Hamish Low, Cyril Wong, Aaron Coyes, Hamish Wyn, Tim Bollinger, Kate Montgomery, Tessa Laird and Tobias Fischer. Average length: 1,200 words. Publishes short shorts. Average length of short shorts: 1,000 words. Also publishes literary criticism, poetry. Sometimes comments on/critiques rejected mss.

HOW TO CONTACT Query with clips of published work. Accepts submissions by e-mail, on disk. Include brief bio, list of publications. Responds to queries in 1 week. Responds to mss in 1 week. Send either SASE (or IRC) for return of ms or disposable copy of ms and #10 SASE for reply only. Considers simultaneous submissions, multiple submissions. Sample copy available for $10. Guidelines available via e-mail.

PAYMENT/TERMS Writers receive 10 contributor's copies, free subscription to the magazine. Additional copies $6. Pays on publication. Acquires first rights. Publication is copyrighted.

TIPS "We like writing that explores the world around it rather than being self-obsessed. We're not interested in personal fantasies or self-projections, just an active critical response to one's enviroment. Be direct, flexible and consider how your work might be considered in an international context. What can you contribute or shed light on?"

WILLARD & MAPLE

163 S. Willard Street, Freeman 302, Box 34, Burlington VT 05401. (802)860-2700 ext. 2462. E-mail: willardanddmaple@champlain.edu. **Contact:** Fiction Editor. Magazine: perfect bound; 125 pages; illustrations; photos. "*Willard & Maple* is a student-run literary magazine from Champlain College that publishes a wide array of poems, short stories, creative essays, short plays, pen and ink drawings, black and white photos, and computer graphics. We now accept color." Annual. Estab. 1996.

NEEDS "We accept all types of mss." Receives 20 unsolicited mss/month. Accepts 1 mss/year. Does not read mss March 31-September 1. Publishes ms within 1 year after acceptance. **Publishes 10 new writers/year.** Has published work by Ian Frisch, Mark Belair, Rachel Chalmers, Robin Gaines, W.J. Everts, and Shirley O. Length: 5,000 words; average length: 2,500 words. Publishes short shorts. Also publishes literary essays, poetry. Sometimes comments on rejected mss.

HOW TO CONTACT Send complete mss. Send SASE for return of ms or send disposable copy of mss and #10 SASE for reply only. Responds in 6 months to queries; 6 months to mss. Accepts simultaneous, multiple submissions. Sample copy for $10. Writer's guidelines for SASE or send e-mail. Reviews fiction.

PAYMENT/TERMS Pays 2 contributor's copies; additional copies $12. Pays on publication for onetime rights.

TIPS "The power of imagination makes us infinite."

WINDHOVER

A Journal of Christian Literature, University of Mary Hardin-Baylor, P.O. Box 8008, 900 College St., Belton TX 76513. (254)295-4561. E-mail: windhover@umhb.edu. **Contact:** D. Audell Shelburne, editor. Magazine: 6×9; white bond paper. "We accept poetry, short fiction, nonfiction, creative nonfiction. *Windhover* is devoted to promoting writers and literature with a Christian perspective and with a broad definition of that perspective." Annual. Estab. 1997. Circ. 500.

NEEDS ethnic/multicultural, experimental, fantasy, historical, humor/satire, literary. No erotica. Receives 30 unsolicited mss/month. Accepts 5 mss/issue; 5 mss/year. Publishes ms 1 year after acceptance. **Publishes 5 new writers/year.** Recently published work by Walt McDonald, Cleatus Rattan, Greg Garrett, Barbara Crooker. Length: 1,500-4,000 words; average length: 3,000 words. Publishes short shorts. Also publishes literary essays, poetry. Sometimes comments on rejected mss.

HOW TO CONTACT Send complete ms via regular mail; does not accept e-mailed submissions. Estimated word count, brief bio and list of publications. Include SASE postcard for acknowledgment. No submissions by e-mail. "Deadlines for submissions is June 1st for next issue. Editors read during summer months and notify writers in early September." Accepts simultaneous submissions. Sample copy for $10. Writer's guidelines by e-mail.

PAYMENT/TERMS Pays 2 contributor copies. Pays on publication for first rights.

TIPS "Be patient. We have an editorial board and it sometimes take s longer than I like. We particularly look for convincing plot and character development."

WISCONSIN REVIEW

University of Wisconsin Oshkosh, 800 Algoma Blvd., Oshkosh WI 54901. (920)424-2267. E-mail: wisconsinreview@uwosh.edu. Website: www.uwosh.edu/wisconsinreview. Estab. 1966. *Wisconsin Review*, published annually, is a "contemporary poetry, prose, and art magazine run by students at the University of Wisconsin Oshkosh." *Wisconsin Review* is 250 pages, digest-sized, perfect-bound, with 4-color glossy cover stock. Receives about 400 poetry submissions/year, accepts about 50; Press run is 2,000. Single copy: $10; subscription: $10 plus $3 extra per issue for shipments outside the U.S.

HOW TO CONTACT Send complete ms with cover letter and SASE. Sample copy and yearly subscription $10/year. Pays with 2 contributor copies. Acquires first rights. Simultaneous submissions are not accepted.

TIPS "We are open to any poetic form and style, and look for outstanding imagery, new themes, and fresh voices—poetry that induces emotions."

WITHERSIN MAGAZINE, DARK, DIFFERENT; PLEASANTLY SINISTER

Temecula CA 92591. (951) 795-5498. E-mail: withersin@hotmail.com. Website: withersin.com. **Contact:** Misty Gersley, editor-in-chief. Literary magazine/journal. 6×9, 100 pages. Contains illustrations. Includes photographs. "A literary chimera, Withersin explores the bittersweet stain of the human condition. Comprised of an impressive array of original razor wire fiction, oddments and incongruities, obscure historical footnotes, unconventional research articles, delectable interviews, highlights, reviews and releases in film, music and print; all sewn together with threads of deviant art." Triannual. Circ. 600.

NEEDS comics/graphic novels, experimental, historical (general), horror, literary, psychic/supernatural/occult, regional (specific and unique places; legends and lore). Does not want romance, erotica (read: pornography), or politically charged pieces. List of upcoming themes available for SASE, on website. Receives 100-300 mss/month. Accepts 3-5 mss/issue; 9-15 mss/year. Does not read July-March. Ms published 9-18 months after acceptance. **Publishes 5 new writers/year.** Published David Bain, Robert Heinze, Edward Morris, Michael Pignatella, M.W. Anderson, Sunil Sadanand, David Sackmyster, Mark Allan Gunnells and Chet Gottfried. Length: 500 words (min)-3,000 words (max). Average length: 2,000 words. Publishes short shorts. Average length of short shorts: 500 words. Also publishes literary essays, literary criticism, book reviews, poetry. Often comments on/critiques rejected mss.

HOW TO CONTACT Send complete ms with cover letter. Accepts submissions by e-mail, on disk. Include estimated word count, brief bio. Responds to queries in 2-3 weeks. Responds to mss in 4-6 weeks. Send either SASE (or IRC) for return of ms or disposable copy of ms and #10 SASE for reply only. Considers previously published submissions (reprints have different pay scale), multiple submissions. Sample copy available for $7.25, on website. Guidelines available for SASE, via e-mail, on website.

PAYMENT/TERMS Writers receive 1-5¢ per word, 3000 word payment cap, 1 contributor's copy. Additional copies $7.25. Pays on publication. Acquires first North American serial rights, onetime rights. Publication is copyrighted. Occasionally sponsors contests, check website for details. "We also sponsor videography contests on www.youtube.com/withersin."

TIPS "Beyond an interesting plot structure and ideology, we definitely look for 'complete' pieces i.e. short works that have a distinct beginning, middle and end—Emphasis on END. It is actually difficult to complete a work of short fiction with all of these elements present, and it is important to continue to work and rework your piece until this comes to fruition. Your work should be free of errors, and each sentence should flow well into the next. Stand out works feature looking at the world from an odd, oblique angle. Make us think. Look outside the box, and tell us what you see—Elements of horror can always be presented in a non-traditional, yet still somehow gut-wrenching and unsettling way. Stay away from cliché. Before turning in your manuscript, read it aloud. Then have someone else unfamiliar with the piece read it aloud to you. This will highlight any unintentional snafus in grammar, spelling, sentence structure and flow. It will also allow you some great feedback. Look for open endings and correct them. Remember, you must articulate your writing so the reader can understand your message."

THE WORCESTER REVIEW

1 Ekman St., Worcester MA 01607. (508)797-4770. E-mail: rodgerwriter@myfairpoint.net. Website: wreview.homestead.com. **Contact:** Rodger Martin, managing editor. Estab. 1972. Magazine: 6×9; 100 pages; 60 lb. white offset paper; 10 pt. CS1 cover stock; illustrations; photos. "We like high quality, creative poetry, artwork and fiction. Critical articles should be connected to New England." Annual. Circ. 1,000.

NEEDS literary, prose poem. "We encourage New England writers in the hopes we will publish at least 30% New England but want the other 70% to show the best of writing from across the U.S." Receives 20-30 unsolicited mss/month. Accepts 2-4 mss/issue. Publishes ms 11 months after acceptance. Agented fiction less than 10%. Recently published work by Robert Pinsky, Marge Piercy, Wes McNair, Ed Hirsch. Length: 1,000-4,000 words; average length: 2,000 words. Publishes short shorts. Also publishes literary essays, literary criticism, poetry. Sometimes comments on rejected mss.

HOW TO CONTACT Send complete ms. Responds in 1 year to mss. Accepts simultaneous submissions only if other markets are clearly identified. Sample copy for $8. Writer's guidelines free.

PAYMENT/TERMS Pays 2 contributor copies and honorarium if possible. Acquires onetime rights.

TIPS "Send only one short story—reading editors do not like to read two by the same author at the same time. We will use only one. We generally look for creative work with a blend of craftsmanship, insight and empathy. This does not exclude humor. We won't print work that is shoddy in any of these areas."

WORKERS WRITE!

Blue Cubicle Press, LLC, P.O. Box 250382, Plano TX 75005-0382. (972)824-0646. E-mail: info@workerswritejournal.com. E-mail: combat@workerswritejournal.com,. Website: www.workerswritejournal.com. **Contact:** David LaBounty, editor. Literary magazine/journal: 100-164 pages, 20 lb. bond paper paper, 80 lb. cover stock cover. "We publish stories that center on a particular workplace." Annual.

NEEDS ethnic/multicultural (general), humor/satire, literary, mainstream, regional. Receives 100 mss/month. Accepts 12-15 mss/year. Manuscript published 3-4 months after acceptance. **Publishes 1 new writer/year**. Length: 500 words (min)-5,000 words (max). Average length: 3,000 words. Publishes short shorts. Also publishes poetry. Often comments on rejected mss.

HOW TO CONTACT Send complete ms with cover letter. Accepts submissions by e-mail. Responds to queries in 1 weeks. Responds to mss in 2-3 months. Send either SASE (or IRC) for return of ms or disposable copy of ms and #10 SASE for reply only. Considers simultaneous submissions, previously published submissions, multiple submissions. Sample copy available for $8. Guidelines available for SASE, via e-mail, on website.

PAYMENT/TERMS Pays $50 maximum and contributor's copies. Additional copies $4. Pays on publication.

TIPS "We publish stories from the worker's point of view."

THE WRITE PLACE AT THE WRITE TIME

E-mail: submissions@thewriteplaceatthewritetime.org. Website: www.thewriteplaceatthewritetime.org. **Contact:** Nicole M. Bouchard, Editor-in-Chief. Estab. 2008.

"We encourage new and seasoned writers to send in submissions for the next issue, benefit from resources we provide, read the current issue and enjoy themselves. It's a supportive writers' environment dedicated to artistic expression, learning and living the written word. We are a quarterly publication and our writers range from previously unpublished to having written for *The New York Times, Newsweek*, HBO, and *Business Week* and they come from all over the US and Europe." Frequently comments on rejected mss.

HOW TO CONTACT Send complete ms with cover letter by e-mail. Include est. word count, brief bio. Accepts multiple submissions, up to 3 fiction/nonfiction stories or 5 poems at a time.

PAYMENT/TERMS We are not currently offering monetary compensation.

TIPS "We sponsor writer's contests—visit the website for details." Our publication is copyrighted. Sends prepublication galleys to author depending on whether the story underwent significant edits. We like to work closely with our writers. If the material is only slightly edited, then we don't.

THE WRITING DISORDER

P.O. Box 93613, Los Angeles CA 90093-0613. (323)336-5822. E-mail: submit@thewritingdisorder.com. Website: www.thewritingdisorder.com. **Contact:** C.E. Lukather, editor; Paul Garson, managing editor. Estab. 2009. Quarterly literary magazine featuring new and established writers. "*The Writing Disorder* is an online literary magazine devoted to literature, art, and culture. The mission of the magazine is to showcase new and emerging writers—particularly those in MFA writing programs—as well as established ones. The magazine also features original artwork, photography, and comic art. Although it strives to publish original and experimental work, *The Writing Disorder* remains rooted in the classic art of storytelling."

NEEDS ethnic, experimental, fantasy, historical, horror, humorous, mystery, novel excerpts, science fiction, serialized novels, short stories, slice-of-life vignettes, comic art. Does not want to see romance, religious, or fluff.

HOW TO CONTACT Query by mail or e-mail. Publishes ms an average of 3-6 months after acceptance. Submit seasonal material 6 months in advance. Accepts simultaneous submissions. Responds in 6-12 weeks to queries; 3-6 months to ms. Sample copy and guidelines available online.

PAYMENT/TERMS Accepts 1-3 mss/year. 7,500 words maximum. Acquires first North American serial rights. Pays contributor's a copy of anthology to writer's whose work has been selected for inclusion.

TIPS "We are looking for writers currently in writing programs—both students and faculty."

XAVIER REVIEW

Xavier University, 1 Drexel Dr., New Orleans LA 70125-1098. Website: www.xula.edu/review/. **Contact:** Dr. Nicole P. Green, editor. Estab. 1980. Magazine: 6×9; 75 pages; 50 lb. paper; 12 pt. CS1 cover; photographs. Magazine of "poetry/fiction/nonfiction/reviews (contemporary literature) for professional writers, libraries, colleges and universities." Semiannual. Circ. 500.

NEEDS ethnic/multicultural, experimental, historical, literary, mainstream, regional (Southern, Latin American), religious/inspirational, serialized novels, translations. Receives 40 unsolicited mss/month. Accepts 2 mss/issue; 4 mss/year. **Publishes 2-3 new writers/year.** Recently published work by Andrei Codrescu, Terrance Hayes, Naton Leslie, Patricia Smith. Also publishes literary essays, literary criticism. Occasionally comments on rejected mss.

HOW TO CONTACT Send complete ms. Include 2-3 sentence bio. Sample copy for $5.

PAYMENT/TERMS Pays 2 contributor copies.

SMALL CIRCULATION MAGAZINES

This section of *Novel & Short Story Writer's Market* contains general-interest, special-interest, regional, and genre magazines with circulations under 10,000. Although these magazines vary greatly in size, theme, format, and management, the editors are all looking for short stories. Their specific fiction needs present writers of all degrees of expertise and interests with an abundance of publishing opportunities. Among the diverse publications in this section are magazines devoted to almost every topic, every level of writing, and every type of writer. Some of the markets listed here publish fiction about a particular geographic area or by authors who live in that locale.

Although not as high-paying as the large-circulation consumer magazines, you'll find some of the publications listed here do pay writers 1-5¢/word or more. Also, unlike the big consumer magazines, these markets are very open to new writers and relatively easy to break into. Their only criterion is that your story be well written, well presented, and suitable for their particular readership.

In this section you will also find listings for zines. Zines vary greatly in appearance as well as content. Some paper zines are photocopies published whenever the editor has material and money, while others feature offset printing and regular distribution schedules. A few have evolved into very slick four-color, commercial-looking publications.

SELECTING THE RIGHT MARKET

First, zero in on those markets most likely to be interested in your work. Begin by looking at the Index starting on page **640**. If your work is more general—or conversely, very specialized—you may wish to browse through the listings, perhaps looking up those magazines published in your state or region. Also check the Online Markets section for other specialized and genre publications.

In addition to browsing through the listings and using the Index, check the openness icons at the beginning of listings to find those most likely to be receptive to your work. This is especially true for beginning writers, who should look for magazines that say they are especially open to new writers ○ and for those giving equal weight to both new and established writers ◐. For more explanation about these icons, see the inside covers of this book.

Once you have a list of magazines you might like to try, read their listings carefully. Much of the material within each listing carries clues that tell you more about the magazine. How to Use *Novel & Short Story Writer's Market*, starting on page 2, describes in detail the listing information common to all the markets in our book.

The physical description appearing near the beginning of the listings can give you clues about the size and financial commitment to the publication. This is not always an indication of quality, but chances are a publication with expensive paper and four-color artwork on the cover has more prestige than a photocopied publication featuring a clip-art cover. For more information on some of the paper, binding, and printing terms used in these descriptions, see Printing and Production Terms Defined on page 172.

FURTHERING YOUR SEARCH

It cannot be stressed enough that reading the listing is only the first part of developing your marketing plan. The second part, equally important, is to obtain fiction guidelines and read the actual magazine. Reading copies of a magazine helps you determine the fine points of the magazine's publishing style and philosophy. There is no substitute for this type of hands-on research.

Unlike commercial magazines available at most newsstands and bookstores, it requires a little more effort to obtain some of the magazines listed here. You may need to send for a sample copy. We include sample copy prices in the listings whenever possible. Above all, editors appreciate a professional presentation. Include a brief cover letter and send a self-addressed, stamped envelope for a reply. Be sure the envelope is large enough to accommodate your manuscript, if you would like it returned, and include enough stamps or International Reply Coupons (for replies from countries other than your own) to cover your manuscript's return. Many publishers today appreciate receiving a disposable manuscript, eliminating the cost to writers of return postage and saving editors the effort of repackaging manuscripts for return.

Most of the magazines listed here are published in the U.S. You will also find some English-speaking markets from around the world. These foreign publications are denoted with a icon at the beginning of listings. To make it easier to find Canadian markets, we include a symbol at the start of those listings

ALBEDO ONE

2 Post Rd., Lusk, Co Dublin Ireland. (353)1 8730 177. E-mail: bobn@yellowbrickroad.ie. Website: www.albedo.com. **Contact:** Editor. Estab. 1993. Magazine: A4; 64 pages. "We hope to publish interesting and unusual fiction by new and established writers. We will consider anything, as long as it is well written and entertaining, though our definitions of both may not be exactly mainstream. We like stories with plot and characters that live on the page. Most of our audience are probably committed genre fans, but we try to appeal to a broad spectrum of readers." Triannual. Circ. 900.

NEEDS experimental, fantasy, horror, literary, science fiction. Receives more than 80 unsolicited mss/month. Accepts 15-18 mss/year. Publishes ms 1 year after acceptance. Publishes 6-8 new writers/year. Length: 2,000-9,000 words; average length: 4,000 words. Also publishes literary criticism. Sometimes comments on rejected mss.

HOW TO CONTACT Responds in 3 months to mss. PDF—electronic—sample copies are available for download at a reduced price. Guidelines available by e-mail or on website. Reviews fiction.

PAYMENT/TERMS Pays €3 per 1,000 words, and 1 contributor's copy. Pays on publication for first rights.

TIPS "We look for good writing, good plot, good characters. Read the magazine, and don't give up."

ANY DREAM WILL DO REVIEW

250 Jeanell Dr., Carson City NV 89703. (775)786-0345. E-mail: cassjmb@intercomm.com. Website: www.willigocrazy.org/Ch08.htm. **Contact:** Dr. Jean M. Bradt, editor and publisher. Estab. 2001. Magazine: $5\frac{1}{2}$×$8\frac{1}{2}$; 52 pages; 20 lb. bond paper; 12-pt. Carolina cover stock. "The *Any Dream Will Do Review* showcases a new literary genre, Fiction In The Raw, which attempts to fight the prejudice against consumers of mental-health services by touching hearts, that is, by exposing the consumers' deepest thoughts and emotions. In the *Review*'s stories, accomplished authors honestly reveal their most intimate secrets. See website for detailed instructions on how to write Fiction In The Raw." Published every 4 or 5 years.

NEEDS adapted ethnic/multicultural, mainstream, psychic/supernatural/occult, romance (contemporary), science fiction (soft/sociological), all of which must follow the guidelines at website. Accepts 10 mss/issue; 5 mss/year. Publishes ms 12 months after acceptance. **Publishes 2 new writers/year.** Publishes short-shorts.

HOW TO CONTACT Send complete ms. Accepts submissions by e-mail (cassjmb@intercomm.com). Please submit by e-mail. If you must submit by hard copy, please send disposable copies. No queries, please. Responds in 8 weeks to mss. Sample copy for $4 plus postage. Writer's guidelines online.

PAYMENT/TERMS Pays in contributor's copies; additional copies $4 plus postage. Acquires first North American serial rights.

TIPS "Read several stories on website before starting to write. Proof your story many times before submitting. Make the readers think. Above all, present people (preferably diagnosed with mental illness) realistically rather than with prejudice."

THE APUTAMKON REVIEW: VOICES FROM DOWNEAST MAINE AND THE CANADIAN MARITIMES (OR THEREABOUTS)

The WordShed, LLC, P.O. Box 190, Jonesboro ME 04648. (207) 434-5661. Fax: (207) 434-5661. E-mail: thewordshed@tds.net. Website: http://thewordshed.com. **Contact:** Les Simon, Publisher. Magazine. Approx. 190 pages. Contains b&w illustrations. Includes photographs. "All age groups living in downeast Maine and the Canadian Maritimes, or thereabouts, are invited to participate. The *Aputamkon Review* will present a mismash of truths, half truths and outright lies, including but not limited to short fiction, tall tales, creative non-fiction, essays, (some) poetry, haiku, b&w visual arts, interviews, lyrics and music, quips, quirks, quotes that should be famous, witticisms, follies, comic strips, cartoons, jokes, riddles, recipes, puzzles, games. Stretch your imagination. Practically anything goes." Annual. Estab. 2006. Circ. 500. Member Maine Writers and Publishers Alliance.

NEEDS Adventure, children's/juvenile, comics/graphic novels, ethnic/multicultural, experimental, family saga, fantasy, glitz, historical, horror, humor/satire, literary, mainstream, military/war, mystery, psychic/supernatural/occult, religious, romance, science fiction, thriller/espionage, translations, western, young adult/teen. Does not want mss which are heavy with sex or religion. Receives 1-20 mss/month. Accepts 30-40 mss/year. Ms published max of 12 months after acceptance. Length: 50 words (min)-3,000 words (max). Average length: 500 words. Publishes short shorts. Also publishes literary essays, literary criticism, poetry. Rarely comments on/critiques rejected mss.

HOW TO CONTACT Send complete ms with cover letter. Accepts submissions in the body of an e-mail, on disk via USPS. Submission period is 12 months a year; reading January 1 through March 31. Responds only between Jan. 31 and April 31. Include age if under 18, and a bio will be requested upon acceptance of work. Responds to queries or submissions in 2-8 weeks. Send SASE (or IRC) for return of ms or a disposable copy of ms and #10 SASE for reply only. Considers simultaneous submissions, multiple submissions. Sample copy available for $12.85 US plus $2.75 US s/h. Guidelines available for SASE, via e-mail, via fax.

PAYMENT/TERMS Submissions receive $10-35 depending on medium, plus one copy. Pays on acceptance. Acquires first North American serial rights. Publication is copyrighted. All rights revert back to the contributors upon publication.

TIPS "Be colorful, heartfelt not mainstream. Write what you want and then submit."

BLACK LACE

P.O. Box 83912, Los Angeles CA 90083-0912. (310)410-0808. Fax: (310)410-9250. E-mail: newsroom@blk.com. Website: www.blacklace.org. **Contact:** Editor. Estab. 1991. Magazine: 8 1/8×10 5/8; 48 pages; book stock; color glossy cover; illustrations; photos. "*Black Lace* is a lifestyle magazine for African-American lesbians. Its content ranges from erotic imagery to political commentary." Quarterly.

NEEDS "*Black Lace* seeks erotic material of the highest quality, but it need not be written by professional writers. The most important thing is that the work be erotic and that it feature black men in the life or ITL themes. We are not interested in stories that demean black women or place them in stereotypical situations." Ethnic/multicultural, lesbian. Wants "full-length erotic fiction of 2,000-4,000 words detailing the exploits of black women in the life. Avoid interracial stories of idealized pornography." Accepts 4 mss/year. Recently published work by Nicole King, Wanda Thompson, Lynn K. Pannell, Sheree Ann Slaughter, Lyn Lifshin, JoJo and Drew Alise Timmens. Publishes short shorts. Also publishes literary essays, literary criticism, poetry.

HOW TO CONTACT Query with published clips or send complete ms by mail, e-mail, or fax. Send a disposable copy of ms. No simultaneous submissions. Accepts electronic submissions. Sample copy for $7. Writer's guidelines free.

PAYMENT/TERMS Pays $50 and 2 contributor's copies. Acquires first North American serial rights. Right to anthologize.

TIPS "*Black Lace* seeks erotic material of the highest quality. The most important thing is that the work be erotic and that it feature black lesbians or themes. Study the magazine to see what we do and how we do it. Some fiction is very romantic, other is highly sexual. Most articles in *Black Lace* cater to black lesbians between two extremes."

CHAFFIN JOURNAL

English Department, Eastern Kentucky University, C, Richmond KY 40475-3102. (859)622-3080. E-mail: robert.witt@eku.edu. Website: www.english.edu/chaffin_journal. **Contact:** Robert Witt, editor. Estab. 1998. Magazine: 8×5½; 120-130 pages; 70 lb. paper; 80 lb. cover. "We publish fiction on any subject; our only consideration is the quality." Annual. Circ. 150.

NEEDS ethnic/multicultural, historical, humor/satire, literary, mainstream, regional (Appalachia). "No erotica, fantasy." Receives 20 unsolicited mss/month. Accepts 6-8 mss/year. Does not read mss October 1 through May 31. Publishes ms 6 months after acceptance. **Publishes 2-3 new writers/year.** Recently published work by Meridith Sue Willis, Marie Manilla, Raymond Abbott, Marjorie Bixler, Chris Helvey. Length: 10,000 words per submission period; average length: 5,000 words.

HOW TO CONTACT Send SASE for return of ms. Responds in 1 week to queries; 3 months to mss. Accepts simultaneous, multiple submissions. Sample copy for $6.

PAYMENT/TERMS Pays 1 contributor's copy; additional copies $6. Pays on publication for one-time rights.

TIPS "All manuscripts submitted are considered."

CONCEIT MAGAZINE

P.O. Box 884223, San Francisco CA 94188-4223 or P.O. Box 761495, San Antonio, TX 78245, or P.O. Box 8544, Emeryville, CA 94662. (210)645-4943. Fax: (210)645-4943. E-mail: conceitmagazine2007@yahoo.com. Website: www.myspace.com/conceitmagazine; www.sites.google.com/site/conceitmagazine/home.

Contact: Perry Terrell, Editor. Also on Facebook, Twitter, LinkedIn, Goodreads, and Grouply. Magazine. 812×51₂, 44 pages, copy paper paper. Contains illustrations, photographs. "If it's on your mind, write it down and send it to Perry Terrell at *Conceit Magazine*. Writing is good therapy." Monthly. Estab. 2007. Circ. 900+.

NEEDS adventure, children's/juvenile, ethnic/multicultural, experimental, family saga, fantasy, feminist, gay, historical, horror (futuristic, psychological, supernatural), humor/satire, lesbian, literary, mainstream, military/war, mystery, new age, psychic/supernatural/occult, religious, romance (contemporary, futuristic/time travel, historical, regency, suspense), science fiction (soft/sociological), thriller/espionage, translations, western, young adult/teen (adventure, easy-to-read, fantasy/science fiction, historical, mystery/suspense, problem novels, romance, series, sports, western). Does not want profanity, porn, gruesomeness. List of upcoming themes available for SASE and on website. Receives 40-50 mss/month. Accepts 20-22 mss/issue; up to 264 mss/year. Ms published 3-10 months after acceptance. **Publishes 150 new writers/year.** Published D. Neil Simmers, Tamara Fey Turner, Eve J. Blohm, Barbara Hantman, David Body. Length: 100 words (min)-3,000 words (max). Average length: 1,500-2,000 words. Publishes short shorts. Average length of short shorts: 50-500 words. Also publishes literary essays, literary criticism, book reviews, poetry. Send review copies to Perry Terrell. Sometimes comments on/critiques rejected mss.

HOW TO CONTACT Query first or send complete ms with cover letter. Accepts submissions by e-mail, by fax and snail mail. Include estimated word count, brief bio, list of publications. Responds to queries in 2-3 weeks. Responds to mss in 4-6 months. Send either SASE (or IRC) for return of ms or disposable copy of ms and #10 SASE for reply only. Considers simultaneous submissions, previously published submissions, multiple submissions. Sample copy free with SASE. Guidelines available for SASE, via e-mail, on website, via fax.

PAYMENT/TERMS Writers receive 1 contributor copy. Additional copies $4.50. PayPal to conceitmagazine@yahoo.com. Pays writers through contests. Pays on publication. Acquires onetime rights. Publication is copyrighted. "Occasionally sponsors contests. Send SASE or check blog on website for details."

TIPS "Uniqueness and creativity make a manuscript stand out. Be brave and confident. Let me see what you created."

O CREATIVE WITH WORDS PUBLICATIONS

P.O. Box 223226, Carmel CA 93922. Fax: (831)655-8627. E-mail: geltrich@mbay.net. Website: creativewithwords.tripod.com. **Contact:** Brigitta Geltrich, publisher/editor. Estab. 1975.

NEEDS ethnic/multicultural, humor/satire, mystery/suspense (amateur sleuth, private eye), regional (folklore), young adult/teen (adventure, historical). "Do not submit essays." No violence or erotica, overly religious fiction, or sensationalism. "Twice a year we publish the Eclectics written by adults only (20 and older); throughout the year we publish thematic anthologies written by all ages." List of upcoming themes available for SASE. Limit poetry to 20 lines or less, 46 characters per line or less. Receives 50-200 unsolicited mss/month. Accepts 50-80 mss/anthology. Publishes ms 1-2 months after acceptance. Recently published work by Najwa Salam Brax, Sirock Brighton, Roger D. Coleman, Antoinette Garrick, and Maria Dickerhof. Sometimes comments on rejected mss.

HOW TO CONTACT Send complete ms with a cover letter with SASE. Include estimated word count. Responds in 2 weeks to queries; 1-2 months after a specific theme's due date to mss. Please request a list of themes with SASE before sending manuscript. Sample copy for $7. Make checks payable to Brigitta Ludgate. Writer's guidelines for #10 SASE.

PAYMENT/TERMS 20% reduction cost on 1-9 copies ordered, 30% reduction on 10 to 19 copies, 40% reduction on each copy on order of 20 or more. Acquires one-time rights. Does not accept previously published mss.

TIPS "We offer a great variety of themes. We look for clean family-type fiction/poetry. Also, we ask the writer to look at the world from a different perspective, research topic thoroughly, be creative, apply brevity, tell the story from a character's viewpoint, tighten dialogue, be less descriptive, proofread before submitting and be patient. We will not publish every manuscript we receive. It has to be in standard English, well written, proofread. We do not appreciate receiving manuscripts where we have to do the proofreading and the correcting of grammar."

DARK TALES

Dark Tales, 7 Offley Street, Worcester WR3 8BH United Kingdom. E-mail: sean@darktales.co.uk. Website: www.darktales.co.uk. **Contact:** Sean Jeffery, editor. Estab. 2003. Magazine: Contains illustrations. "We publish horror and speculative short fiction from anybody, anywhere, and the publication is professionally illustrated throughout." Circ. 350+.

NEEDS horror (dark fantasy, futuristic, psychological, supernatural), science fiction (soft/sociological). Receives 25+ mss/month. Accepts 10-15 mss/issue; 25-40 mss/year. Ms published 6 months after acceptance. **Publishes 20 new writers/year.** Published Davin Ireland, Niall McMahon, David Robertson, Valerie Robson, K.S. Dearsley, and Mark Cowley. Length: 500-3,500 words. Average length: 2,500 words. Publishes short shorts. Average length of short shorts: 500 words. Sometimes comments on/critiques rejected mss. Has occasional contests; see website for details.

HOW TO CONTACT Send complete ms with cover letter. Include estimated word count, list of publications. Responds to queries in 1 week. Responds to mss in 12 weeks. Send disposable copy of ms and #10 SASE for reply only. Sample copy available for $3. Guidelines available on website.

PAYMENT/TERMS Writers receive $5 per thousand words. Additional copies $7.10. Pays on publication. Acquires first British serial rights. Sends galleys to author. Publication is copyrighted.

TIPS "Have a believable but inspiring plot, sympathetic characters, an original premise, and a human heart no matter how technical or disturbing a story. Read a copy of the magazine! Make sure you get your writing basics spot-on. Don't rehash old ideas—if you must go down the werewolf/vampire route, put a spin on it."

DOWN IN THE DIRT

829 Brian Court, Gurnee IL 60031-3155. (847)281-9070. E-mail: alexrand@scars.tv. Website: scars.tv. **Contact:** Alexandria Rand, editor. Estab. 2000. Magazine: $5\frac{1}{2}\times8\frac{1}{2}$; perfect-bound 84-page book. Monthly.

NEEDS Adventure, ethnic/multicultural, experimental, fantasy, feminist, gay, historical, horror, lesbian, literary, mystery/suspense, New Age, psychic/supernatural/occult, science fiction. No religious or rhyming or family-oriented material. Publishes ms within 1 year after acceptance. Recently published work by Pat Dixon, Mel Waldman, Ken Dean Aeon Logan, Helena Wolfe. Average length: 1,000 words. Publishes short shorts. Also publishes poetry. "Contact us if you are interested in submitting very long stories, or parts of a novel (if accepted, it would appear in parts in multiple issues)." Always, if asked, comments on rejected mss.

HOW TO CONTACT Query editor with e-mail submission. "99.5% of all submissions are via e-mail only, so if you do not have electronic access, there is a strong chance you will not be considered. We recommend you e-mail submissions to us, either as an attachment or by placing it directly in the letter). For samples of what we've printed in the past, visit our website: http://scars.tv/dirt. Responds in 1 month to queries; 1 month to mss. Accepts simultaneous, multiple submissions and reprints. Sample copy for $6. Writer's guidelines for SASE, e-mail or on the website.

THE FIRST LINE

P.O. Box 250382, Plano TX 75025-0382. (972)824-0646. E-mail: submission@thefirstline.com. Website: www.thefirstline.com. **Contact:** Robin LaBounty, manuscript coordinator. Estab. 1999. Magazine: 8×5; 64-72 pages; 20 lb. bond paper; 80 lb. cover stock. "We only publish stories that start with the first line provided. We are a collection of tales—of different directions writers can take when they start from the same place." Quarterly.

NEEDS adventure, ethnic/multicultural, fantasy, gay, humor/satire, lesbian, literary, mainstream, mystery/suspense, regional, romance, science fiction, western. Receives 200 unsolicited mss/month. Accepts 12 mss/issue; 48 mss/year. Publishes ms 1 month after acceptance. **Publishes 6 new writers/year.** Length: 300-3,000 words; average length: 1,500 words. Publishes short shorts. Also publishes literary essays, literary criticism. Often comments on rejected mss.

HOW TO CONTACT Send complete ms. Accepts submissions by e-mail. Send SASE for return of ms or disposable copy of the ms and #10 SASE for reply only. Responds in 1 week to queries; 3 months to mss. Accepts multiple submissions. No simultaneous submissions. Sample copy for $4.00. Writer's guidelines for SASE, e-mail or on website. Reviews fiction.

PAYMENT/TERMS Pays $20 maximum and contributor's copy; additional copy $2. Pays on publication.

TIPS "Don't just write the first story that comes to mind after you read the sentence. If it is obvious, chances are other people are writing about the same thing. Don't try so hard. Be willing to accept criticism."

IRREANTUM

The Association for Mormon Letters, P.O. Box 1315, Salt Lake City UT 84110-1315. E-mail: editor@aml-pubs.org. Website: www.irreantum.org. Estab. 1999. Magazine or zine: $8^1{}_2 \times 7^1{}_2$; 100-120 pages; 20 lb. paper; 20 lb. color cover; illustrations; photos. "While focused on Mormonism, *Irreantum* is a cultural, humanities-oriented magazine, not a religious magazine. Our guiding principle is that Mormonism is grounded in a sufficiently unusual, cohesive, and extended historical and cultural experience that it has become like a nation, an ethnic culture. We can speak of Mormon literature at least as surely as we can of a Jewish or Southern literature. Irreantum publishes stories, one-act dramas, stand-alone novel and drama excerpts, and poetry by, for, or about Mormons (as well as author interviews, essays, and reviews). The magazine's audience includes readers of any or no religious faith who are interested in literary exploration of the Mormon culture, mindset, and worldview through Mormon themes and characters. *Irreantum* is currently the only magazine devoted to Mormon literature." Biannual. Circ. 300.

Also publishes short shorts, literary essays, literary criticism, and poetry.

NEEDS "high quality work that explores the Mormon experience, directly or by implication, through literature. We acknowledge a broad range of experience with Mormonism, both as a faith and as a culture—on the part of devoted multi-generation Mormons, ethnic Mormons, new converts, and people outside the faith and culture who interact with Mormons and Mormon culture. We are committed to respectful exploration of Mormonism through literature. Receives 5 unsolicited mss/month. Accepts 3 mss/issue; 6 mss/year. Publishes ms 3-12 months after acceptance. **Publishes 3 or more new writers/year.** Recently published work by Orson Scott Card, Terryl Givens, Jack Harrell, Eric Samuelsen, Michael Collins, Phyllis Barber, Paul Swenson. Length: 1,000-5,000 words; average length: 5,000 words. Publishes short shorts. Also publishes literary essays, literary criticism, poetry. Sometimes comments on rejected mss. Annual fiction contest and annual personal essay contest with cash prizes.

HOW TO CONTACT Accepts submissions by e-mail only in Microsoft Word or rich text files only. Accepts critical essays to criticalessaysubmissions@mormonletter.org. "The fiction and personal essay/creative nonfiction we publish is selected from the contest entries for the annual fiction contest and annual personal essay contest with offer cash prizes. There is a submission window—January 1-May 31st—for fiction and creative nonfiction submissions. All unsolicited fiction and creative nonfiction must be submitted according to contest rules which can be found on the website." Winner will receive a copy of the *Irreantum* issue in which his or her work appears. Send complete ms. with cover letter. Include a brief bio and list of publications. Responds in 2 weeks to queries, 2 months to mss. Accepts simultaneous and reprints, multiple submissions. Sample copy $15. Writer's guidelines on website. Reviews fiction.

PAYMENT/TERMS Pays $0-100. Pays on publication for onetime rights.

TIPS *Irreantum* is not interested in didactic or polemnical fiction that primarily attempts to prove or disprove Mormon doctrine, history, or corporate policy. We encourage beginning writers to focus on human elements first, with Mormon elements introduced only as natural and organic to the story. Readers can tell if you are honestly trying to explore human experience or if you are writing with a propagandistic agenda either for or against Mormonism. For conservative, orthodox Mormon writers, beware of sentimentalism, simplistic resolutions, and foregone conclusions.

ITALIAN AMERICANA

80 Washington St., Providence RI 02903-1803. E-mail: itamericana@yahoo.com. Website: www.italianamericana.com. **Contact:** C.B. Albright, editor-in-chief. Estab. 1974. Magazine: 6×9; 240 pages; varnished cover; perfect bound; photos. "*Italian Americana* contains historical articles, fiction, poetry and memoirs, all concerning the Italian experience in the Americas." Semiannual. Circ. 1,200.

NEEDS Literary, Italian American. No nostalgia. Wants to see more fiction featuring "individualized characters." Receives 10 unsolicited mss/month. Accepts 3 mss/issue; 6-7 mss/year. Publishes ms up to 1 year after acceptance. Agented fiction 5%. **Publishes 2-4 new writers/year.** Publishing 2 issues a year of historical articles, fiction, memoir, poetry and re-

SMALL CIRCULATION MAGAZINES

views. Seeking historical articles. Award-winning authors in all categories, such as Mary Caponegro, Sal La Puma, Dana Gioia (past poetry editor).

HOW TO CONTACT Send complete ms (in duplicate) with a cover letter. Include 3-5 line bio, list of publications. Responds in 1 month to queries; 2 months to mss. No simultaneous submissions. Subscription: $20/year; $35/2 years. Sample copy for $7. Writer's guidelines for #10 SASE. Reviews fiction.

PAYMENT/TERMS 1 contributor's copy; additional copies $7. Acquires first North American serial rights.

TIPS "Check out our new website supplement to the journal at www.italianamericana.com. Read *Wild Dreams: The Best of Italian Americana* (Fordham University Press), the best stories, poems and memoirs in the journal's 35-year history."

●◎ KELSEY REVIEW

P.O. Box B, Liberal Arts Division, Trenton NJ 08690. E-mail: kelsey.review@mccc.edu. Website: www.mccc.edu/community_kelsey-review.shtml. **Contact:** Holly-Katharine Matthews. Estab. 1988. Magazine: 7×14; 98 pages; glossy paper; soft cover. "Must live or work in Mercer County, NJ." Annual.

NEEDS regional (Mercer County, NJ only), open. Receives 10 unsolicited mss/month. Accepts 24 mss/issue. Reads mss only in May. **Publishes 10 new writers/year.** Recently published work by Thom Beachamps, Janet Kirk, Bruce Petronio. Publishes short shorts. Also publishes literary essays, poetry.

HOW TO CONTACT **The deadline for all submissions is May 15.** Submissions are limited to people who live, work, or give literary readings in Mercer County, NJ. Decisions on which material will be published are made by the four-person editorial board in June and July. Contributors will be notified of submission acceptance determination(s) by the second week of August. SASE for return of ms. Responds no later than September 1 to mss. Accepts multiple submissions. Sample copy free.

PAYMENT/TERMS 3 contributor's copies. Rights revert to author on publication.

TIPS Look for "quality, intellect, grace and guts. Avoid sentimentality, overwriting and self-indulgence. Work on clarity, depth and originality."

KRAX MAGAZINE

63 Dixon Lane, Leeds Yorkshire Br LS12 4RR United Kingdom. **Contact:** A. Robson, co-editor. "Krax publishes lighthearted, humorous and whimsical writing. It is for anyone seeking light relief at a gentle pace. Our audience has grown middle-aged along with us, especially now that we're annual and not able to provide the instant fix demanded by teens and twenties." "Contemporary light-hearted poetry from Britain, America and elsewhere. Currently over 68 pages of anything but stodgy poetry, short fiction and glowingly brilliant graphics. Usually there is and interview with a writer of interest and a sizeable review section covering a vast range of related books, magazines, pamphlets, audio tape and CD's."

NEEDS "No war stories, horror, space bandits, boy-girl soap opera. We publish mostly poetry of a light-hearted nature but use comic or spoof fiction, witty and humorous essays. Would like to see more whimsical items, trivia ramblings or anything daft." Accepts 1 mss/issue. **Publishes 1 new writer/year.** Recently published work by Aaron Dabrowski, Rovert L. Voss.

HOW TO CONTACT No specific guidelines but cover letter appreciated. Sample copy for $2.

TIPS "Look at what you enjoy in all forms of fiction—from strip cartoons to novels, movies to music lyrics—then try to put some of this into your own writing. Go for the idea first, then find the scenery to set it in. There are plenty of unreal worlds out there."

LADY CHURCHILL'S ROSEBUD WRISTLET

150 Pleasant St., #306, Easthampton MA 01027. E-mail: smallbeerpress@gmail.com. Website: www.smallbeerpress.com/lcrw. **Contact:** Gavin Grant, editor. Estab. 1996. Zine: half legal size; 60 pages; 60 lb. paper; glossy cover; illustrations; photos. Semiannual. Circ. 1,000.

NEEDS comics/graphic novels, experimental, fantasy, feminist, literary, science fiction, translations, short story collections. Receives 100 unsolicited mss/month. Accepts 4-6 mss/issue; 8-12 mss/year. Publishes ms 6-12 months after acceptance. **Publishes 2-4 new writers/year.** Recently published work by Ted Chiang, Gwenda Bond, Alissa Nutting, Charlie Anders. Length: 200-7,000 words; average length: 3,500 words. Also publishes literary essays, poetry. Sometimes comments on rejected mss.

HOW TO CONTACT Send complete ms with a cover letter. Include estimated word count. Send SASE (or IRC) for return of ms, or send a disposable copy of ms and #10 SASE for reply only. Responds in 4 weeks to queries; 3-6 months to mss. Sample copy for $5. Writer's guidelines online. Reviews fiction.

PAYMENT/TERMS Pays 1¢/word, $20 minimum and 2 contributor's copies; additional copies contributor's discount 40%. Pays on publication for first serial, nonexclusive anthology, and electronic rights.

TIPS "I like fiction that tends toward the speculative." "We recommend at least one rewrite for both our sanities. Please follow standard ms format: 12-pt Courier, double-spaced, numbered pages, and an SASE (with a Forever Stamp) for our reply."

THE LAKEVIEW REVIEW

301 Fremont St., P.O. Box 428, Wayland NY 14572. (585)645-2924. Fax: (585)219-5762. E-mail: editor@lakeviewreview.com. Website: www.lakeviewreview.com. **Contact:** Tanya Babcock, sr. ed. Estab. 2008.

TIPS "The *Lakeview Review* only accepts online submissions. Read the guidelines carefully and follow them."

LEFT CURVE

P.O. Box 472, Oakland CA 94604-0472. (510)763-7193. E-mail: editor@leftcurve.org. Website: www.leftcurve.org. **Contact:** Csaba Polony, editor. Estab. 1974. Magazine: 8½×11; 144 pages; 60 lb. paper; 100 pt. C1S gloss layflat lamination cover; illustrations; photos. "*Left Curve* is an artist-produced journal addressing the problem(s) of cultural forms emerging from the crises of modernity that strive to be independent from the control of dominant institutions, based on the recognition of the destructiveness of commodity (capitalist) systems to all life." Published irregularly. Circ. 2,000.

NEEDS ethnic/multicultural, experimental, historical, literary, regional, science fiction, translations, contemporary, prose poem, political. "No topical satire, religion-based pieces, melodrama. We publish critical, open, social/political-conscious writing." Receives 50 unsolicited mss/month. Accepts 3-4 mss/issue. Publishes ms 6-12 months after acceptance. Recently published work by Mike Standaert, Ilan Pappe, Terrence Cannon, John Gist. Length: 500-5,000 words; average length: 1,200 words. Publishes short shorts. Sometimes comments on rejected mss.

HOW TO CONTACT Send complete ms. Accepts submissions by e-mail (editor@leftcurve.org). Send complete ms with cover letter. Include "statement of writer's intent, brief bio and reason for submitting to *Left Curve*." Accepts electronic submissions and hard copy, though for accepted work we request e-mail copy, either in body of text or as attachments." For accepted longer work we prefer submission of final draft in digital form via disk or e-mail. Responds in 6 months to mss. Sample copy for $12; backcopies $10. Writer's guidelines available with SASE.

PAYMENT/TERMS Contributor's copies. Rights revert to author.

TIPS "We look for continuity, adequate descriptive passages, endings that are not simply abandoned (in both meanings). Dig deep; no superficial personalisms, no corny satire. Be honest, realistic and gouge out the truth you wish to say. Understand yourself and the world. Have writing be a means to achieve or realize what is real."

THE LONDON MAGAZINE

11 Queen's Gate, London En SW7 5ELU UK. +44 (0)20 7584 5977. E-mail: admin@thelondonmagazine.net; editorial@thelondonmagazine.net. Website: www.thelondonmagazine.net. **Contact:** Editor. Estab. 1732. **"We look for poetry and short fiction that startles and entertains us. We are obviously interested in writing that has a London focus, but not exclusively so, since London is a world city with international concerns.** Reviews, essays, memoir pieces and features should be erudite, lucid and incisive. Please look at *The London Magazine* before you submit work, so that you can see the type of material we publish. Nonfiction pieces should be between 800 and 2,000 words. Short fiction should address mature and sophisticated themes. Moreover, it should have an elegance of style, structure and characterisation. We do not normally publish science fiction or fantasy writing, or erotica. We will consider short stories of up to 4,000 words in length."

Abstraction is the enemy of good poetry. Poetry should display a commitment to the ultra specificities of language, and show a refined sense of simile and metaphor. The structure should be tight and exact. We do not normally publish long, loose poems.

THE LOS ANGELES REVIEW

Red Hen Press, P.O. Box 40820, Pasadena CA 91114. (626)356-4760. Fax: (626)356-9974. E-mail: lareviewеditor@gmail.com. Website: http://losangelesreview.org. **Contact:** Stefanie Freele, Fiction Editor.

Estab. 2003. We publish short shorts that average 500/ words and lengthier shorts up to 4,000 words—lively, vivid, excellent literary fiction; literary essays, literary criticism, and poetry. Reviews novels, short story collections, nonfiction books. Deadlines vary. Sends prepublication galleys to writer. Our publication is copyrighted. We sponsor Red Hen Press Short Story Award contest. Details at http://www.redhen.org.

- "Accepts outstanding work by beginning and established writers."

HOW TO CONTACT Submit mss through our Submissions Manager only. Questions to lareview.fiction@gmail.com

PAYMENT/TERMS Pays 1 contributor's copy on publication.

TIPS "Read a recent issue or two to see what we're about. Pay close attention to the submission guidelines. We like cover letters, but please keep them brief."

MAMAZINA

Mom Writer's Productions, LLC., Mamazina Magazine, PO Box 210, Hastings on Hudson NY 10706. (877)771-6667. E-mail: managingeditor@mamazina.com; mamazinamagazine@gmail.com. Website: http://mamazina.wordpress.com. **Contact:** Kris Underwood, Managing Editor. Mom Writer's Productions, LLC., P.O. Box 447, St. Johnsbury, VT 05719. (877)382-6771. Online and print literary magazine. Print: 8x10, 84 pages. Contains illustrations. Includes photographs. "*Mamazina*—formerly *Mom Writer's Literary Magazine*—is a publication written by moms for moms across the globe who come together to share their stories. We publish creative nonfiction essays, fiction, columns, book reviews, profiles about mom writers and visual art. *Mamazina* seeks writing that is vivid, complex and practical. We are not looking for 'sugar-coated' material. We believe the art of Motherhood is deserving of literary attention. We are a literary magazine for mothers with something to say. We're proud to have published essays that are emotionally moving, smart, raw and, sometimes, humorous. *Mamazina* honors the fulfilling and tedious work that women do by making their stories visible through print." Semiannual. Estab. 2005. Online, 2007. Print. Circ. 6,000. Member Mom Writers Publishing Cooperative.

- *Mom Writer's Literary Magazine* was picked by *Writer's Digest* magazine as one of the Best Web Sites for Writers in 2006, 2007, and 2008.

NEEDS adventure, ethnic/multicultural, family saga, feminist, literary, mainstream, romance (contemporary, suspense). Special interests: motherhood. Does not want children/juvenile, religious, horror, or western. Receives 20-30 mss/month. Accepts 2 mss/issue; 4 mss/year. Ms published 1-4 months after acceptance. **Publishes 2 new writers/year.** Length: 800-1,500 words. Average length: 1,400 words. Publishes short shorts. Average length of short shorts: 1,200 words. Also publishes literary essays, book reviews, poetry. Send review copies to Kathy Schlaeger, Reviews Editor, Mom Writer's Literary Magazine, 6224 Deer Run Road Liberty Township, OH 45044. Rarely comments on/critiques rejected mss.

HOW TO CONTACT *MAMAZINA* does not accept any submissions by snail mail. Please send all submissions via e-mail. Please *do not* send attachments. Send complete ms with cover letter. Include estimated word count, brief bio. For all essay and poetry submissions—we read submissions in January and July. All submissions carry a $12 reading fee, payable by using the PayPal on our website. Please read our letter explaining the new submission procedure. Responds to mss in 1-3 months. Considers simultaneous submissions. Guidelines available on website.

PAYMENT/TERMS Writers receive $100 max., 1 contributor's copy. Additional copies $10. Pays on publication. Acquires onetime rights. Publication is copyrighted.

TIPS "May be any genre. Story must flow smoothly and really get our attention (all editors). Must be within the word limits and submitted correctly. Also, please have a title for your story."

THE NOCTURNAL LYRIC

P.O. Box 542, Astoria OR 97103. E-mail: thenocturnallyric@rocketmail.com. Website: www.angelfire.com/ca/nocturnallyric. **Contact:** Susan Moon, editor. Estab. 1987. "Annual magazine. Magazine: 8½x11; 40 pages; illustrations. Fiction and poetry submitted should have a bizarre horror theme. Our audience encompasses people who stand proudly outside of the mainstream society."

NEEDS horror (dark fantasy, futuristic, psychological, supernatural, satirical). "No sexually graphic material—it's too overdone in the horror genre lately." Receives 25-30 unsolicited mss/month. Accepts 10-11 mss/issue; 10-11 mss/year. Publishes ms 1 year after acceptance. Publishes 20 new writers/year. Recently published work by Murphy Edwards, Tim Scott, Richard Grebe, Melissa S. Mutlu, and Jessica Brown. Length: 2,000 words maximum; average length: 1,500 words. Publishes short shorts. Also publishes literary essays, poetry. Rarely comments on rejected mss.

HOW TO CONTACT Send complete ms with cover letter. Include estimated word count. Responds in 3 month to queries; 8 months to mss. Accepts simultaneous, multiple submissions and reprints. Sample copy for $2 (back issue); $3 (current issue). Writer's guidelines online. Pays with discounts on subscriptions and discounts on copies of issue. Pays on acceptance. Not copyrighted. Any stories submitted now won't be read until Feb 2012. If you submit a story now, #72 is the soonest you will be printed if accepted. #72 will be out in the Fall of 2012. Any poetry sent after March 2011 won't be read until March 2012. If you submit a poem now, #72 is the soonest you will be printed if accepted. #72 will be out in the Fall of 2012.

TIPS "A manuscript stands out when the story has a very original theme and the ending is not predictable. Don't be afraid to be adventurous with your story. Mainstream horror can be boring. Surreal, satirical horror is what true nightmares are all about."

NOVA SCIENCE FICTION MAGAZINE

Nova Publishing Company, 17983 Paseo Del Sol, Chino Hills CA 91709-3947. (909)393-0806. **Contact:** Wesley Kawato, editor. Zine specializing in evangelical Christian science fiction: $8^1{}_2 \times 5^1{}_2$; 64 pages; cardstock cover. "We publish religious science fiction short stories, no fantasy or horror. One story slot per issue will be reserved for a story written from an evangelical Christian viewpoint." Biannual. Estab. 1999. Circ. 25.

"NOVA doesn't accept unsolicited manuscripts; writers must first query and in the query must indicate you've been published, attended Clarion Workshop or meet other requirements. **Pay:** Half a penny per word . **Word count (maximum):** 7,000 words. Does not **want:** Stories showing that man will one day outgrow his need for religion; in fact, makes a point of saying magazine isn controlled by Libertarians or the Secular Humanist. **Mail query to:** NOVA Science Fiction, C/O: Wesley Kawato, 17983 Paseo Del Sol, Chino Hills, CA 91709-3947."

NEEDS science fiction (hard science/technological, soft/sociological, religious). "No stories where the villain is a religious fanatic and stories that assume the truth of evolution." Accepts 6 mss/issue; 12 mss/year. Publishes ms 3 months after acceptance. **Publishes 7 new writers/year.** Recently published work by Jonathan Cooper, Lawrence Dagstine, Don Kerr, Gary Carter, Wesley Lambert, Susan Taylor, Erik Leinhart, David Baumann, Francis Alexander, Mark Galbert, Howard Bowman. Length: 250-7,000 words; average length: 4,000 words. Publishes short shorts. Sometimes comments on rejected mss.

HOW TO CONTACT Query first. Include estimated word count and list of publications. Responds in 3 months to queries and mss. Send SASE (or IRC) for return of ms. Accepts reprints, multiple submissions. Sample copy for $6. Guidelines free for SASE.

PAYMENT/TERMS Pays $1.25-35. Pays on publication for first North American serial rights. Not copyrighted.

TIPS "Make sure your plot is believable and describe your characters well enough so I can visualize them. If I like it, I buy it. I like happy endings and heroes with a strong sense of faith."

NTH DEGREE

3502 Fernmoss Ct., Charlotte NC 28269. E-mail: submissions@nthzine.com. Website: www.nthzine.com. **Contact:** Michael Pederson. Estab. 2002. 1211 Lauderdale Dr., Richmond, VA 23238. Magazine: Online downloadable ezine; illustrations; photos. "We print the best SF/Fantasy from the genre's newest writers and run artwork by the hottest new artists. Our goal is to help make it easier for new artists and writers to break into the field." Bimonthly. Circ. 3,500.

NEEDS Fantasy (space fantasy, sword and sorcery), historical (alternate history), horror (dark fantasy, futuristic, psychological, supernatural), humor/satire, science fiction (hard science/technological), young adult/teen (fantasy/science fiction), comic strips. Receives 3 unsolicited mss/month. Accepts 4 mss/issue; 6 mss/year. Publishes ms 6 months after acceptance. **Publishes 6 new writers/year.** Recently published work by Robert E. Waters, Scott D. Coon, and Helen Lloyd Montgomery. Length: 2,000-7,000 words; average length: 3,500 words. Publishes short shorts. Also publishes poetry. Always comments on rejected mss.

HOW TO CONTACT Send complete ms. Accepts submissions by e-mail, disk. Send SASE (or IRC) for return of ms, or send disposable copy of the ms and #10 SASE for reply only. Responds in 2 weeks to queries; 2 months to mss. Accepts simultaneous, multiple submissions. Writer's guidelines online, or by e-mail.

PAYMENT/TERMS Pays 5 contributor's copies and free subscription to the magazine. Pays on publication for onetime rights.

TIPS "Don't submit anything that you may be ashamed of ten years later."

◐ NUTHOUSE

Twin Rivers Press, P.O. Box 119, Ellenton FL 34222. www.nuthousemagazine.com. **Contact:** Dr. Ludwig "Needles" Von Quirk, chief of staff. Zine: digest-sized; 12-16 pages; bond paper; illustrations; photos. "Humor of all genres for an adult readership that is not easily offended." Published every 2-3 months. Estab. 1993. Circ. 100.

NEEDS humor/satire (erotica, experimental, fantasy, feminist, historical [general], horror, literary, mainstream/contemporary, mystery/suspense, psychic/supernatural/occult, romance, science fiction and westerns). Receives 30-50 unsolicited mss/month. Accepts 5-10 mss/issue; 50-60 mss/year. Publishes ms 6-12 months after acceptance. **Publishes 10-15 new writers/year.** Recently published work by Michael Fowler, Dale Andrew White, and Jim Sullivan. Length: 100-1,000 words; average length: 500 words. Publishes short shorts. Also publishes literary essays, literary criticism, poetry. Often comments on rejected mss.

HOW TO CONTACT Send complete ms with a cover letter. Include estimated word count, bio (paragraph) and list of publications. SASE for return of ms or send disposable copy of ms. Sample copy for $1. 50 (payable to Twin Rivers Press). Writer's guidelines for #10 SASE. "We consider prose submissions under 1,000 words and verse that is, preferably, no more than a dozen or so lines. The shorter, the better. Previously published submissions are acceptable, if so noted. No response without a SASE. No e-mail submissions, please. We publish all genres, from the homespun to the horrific. We don't automatically dismiss crudity or profanity. We're not prudes. Yet we consider such elements cheap and insulting unless essential to the gag. *NuTHOuSe* seeks submissions that are original, tightly written and laugh-out-loud funny."

PAYMENT/TERMS Pays 1 contributor's copy. Acquires onetime rights. Not copyrighted.

TIPS Looks for "laugh-out-loud prose. Strive for original ideas; read the great humorists—Saki, Woody Allen, Robert Benchley, Garrison Keillor, John Irving—and learn from them. We are turned off by sophomoric attempts at humor built on a single, tired, overworked gag or pun; give us a story with a beginning, middle and end."

O OPIUM MAGAZINE

Literary Humor for the Deliriously Captivated, 166 Albion St., San Francisco, CA 94110. (347)229-2443. E-mail: todd@opiummagazine.com. Website: www.opiumden.org. **Contact:** Todd Zuniga, editor-in-chief. Biannual magazine. Contains black-and-white cartoons, illustrations, and photographs. "*Opium* Magazine displays an eclectic mix of stories, poetry, reviews, cartoons, interviews and much more. It features 'estimated reading times' that precede each piece. While the focus is often humorous literature, we love to publish heartbreaking, serious work. Our rule is that all work must be well written and engaging from the very first sentence. While we publish traditional pieces, we're primarily engaged by writers who take risks." Updated daily. Estab. 2001. Circ. 25,000 hits/month. Member CLMP.

NEEDS comics/graphic novels, experimental, humor/satire, literary, mainstream. "Vignettes and first-person 'look at what a whacky time I had going to Spain' stories aren't going to get past first base with us." Receives 200 mss/month. Accepts 60 mss/year. Manuscript published 4 months after acceptance. Agented fiction 10%. **Publishes 10-12 new writers/year.** Published Etgar Keret, Art Spiegelman, Jack Handey, Terese Svoboda. Length: 50-1,200 words. Average length: 700 words. Publishes short shorts. Average length of short shorts: 400 words. Also publishes literary essays, literary criticism, poetry. Sometimes comments on/critiques rejected mss.

HOW TO CONTACT Send complete ms with cover letter by e-mail only at: opiumforthearts@gmail.com. Ms received via snail mail will not be read. Include estimated word count, brief bio, list of publications, and your favorite book. Responds to queries in 2 weeks. Responds to mss in 15 weeks. Considers simultaneous submissions. Guidelines available via e-mail or on website. http://opiummagazine.com.

PAYMENT/TERMS Acquires first North American serial rights. Publication is copyrighted.

TIPS "If you don't strike out in that first paragraph to expose something definitive or new, then you better by the second. We get scores of stories, and like the readers we want to attract, we demand to be engaged immediately. Tell us it's your first time, we'll be gentle, and our editors usually give thoughts and encouragement if a piece has promise, even if we reject it."

ORACLE STORY & LETTERS

7510 Lake Glen Drive, Glen Dale MD 20769. (301)352-2533. Fax: (301)352-2529. E-mail: hekwonna@aol.com. **Contact:** Obi H. Ekwonna, publisher. Estab. 1989. Magazine: $5\frac{1}{2} \times 8\frac{1}{2}$; 60 lb. white bound paper. Quarterly. Estab. 1989. Circ. 1,000.

NEEDS adventure, children's/juvenile (adventure, fantasy, historical, mystery, series), comics/graphic novels, ethnic/multicultural, family saga, fantasy (sword and sorcery), historical, literary, mainstream, military/war, romance (contemporary, historical, suspense), thriller/espionage, western (frontier saga), young adult/teen (adventure, historical). Does not want gay/lesbian or erotica works. Receives 10 unsolicited mss/month. Accepts 7 mss/issue. Publishes ms 4 months after acceptance. **Publishes 5 new writers/year.** Recently published work by Joseph Manco, I.B.S. Sesay. Publishes short shorts. Also publishes literary essays, literary criticism, poetry. Rarely comments on rejected mss.

HOW TO CONTACT Send complete ms. Accepts submissions by disk. Send SASE (or IRC) for return of the ms, or send a disposable copy of the ms and #10 SASE for reply only. Responds in 1 month to mss. Accepts multiple submissions. Sample copy for $10. Writer's guidelines for #10 SASE, or by e-mail.

PAYMENT/TERMS Pays 1 contributor's copy. Pays on publication for first North American serial rights.

TIPS "Read anything you can lay your hands on."

PARADOXISM

200 College Rd., Gallup NM 87301. Fax: (503)863-7532. E-mail: smarand@unm.edu. Website: www.gallup.unm.edu/~smarandache/a/paradoxism.htm. **Contact:** Dr. Florentin Smarandache. Estab. 1993. Magazine: $8\frac{1}{2} \times 11$; 100 pages; illustrations. "*Paradoxism* is an avant-garde movement based on excessive use of antinomies, antitheses, contraditions, paradoxes in the literary creations set up by the editor in the 1980s as an anti-totalitarian protest." Annual. Circ. 500.

NEEDS experimental, literary. "Contradictory, uncommon, experimental, avant garde." Plans specific themes in the next year. Publishes annual special fiction issue or anthology. Receives 5 unsolicited mss/month. Accepts 10 mss/issue. Recently published work by Mircea Monu, Doru Motoc and Patrick Pinard. Publishes short shorts. Also publishes literary essays, literary criticism, poetry. Sometimes comments on rejected mss. "Please send: a) paradoxist essays, criticism, poetry, short dramas, short prose, or b) outer-art essays, criticism, outer-paintings, outer-collages, outer-photos, respectively to: 'Paradoxism' journal (or 'Outer-Art' journal)."

HOW TO CONTACT Send a disposable copy of ms. Responds in 2 months to mss. Accepts simultaneous submissions. Sample copy for $19.95 and $8\frac{1}{2} \times 11$ SASE. Writer's guidelines online.

PAYMENT/TERMS Pays subscription. Pays on publication. Not copyrighted.

TIPS "We look for work that refers to the paradoxism or is written in the paradoxist style. The Basic Thesis of the paradoxism: everything has a meaning and a non-meaning in a harmony with each other. The Essence of the paradoxism: a) the sense has a non-sense, and reciprocally b) the non-sense has a sense. The Motto of the paradoxism: 'All is possible, the impossible too!' The Symbol of the paradoxism: a spiral—optic illusion, or vicious circle."

PAVEMENT SAW

Pavement Saw Press, 321 Empire Street, Montpelier OH 43543. E-mail: info@pavementsaw.org. Website: http://pavementsaw.org. **Contact:** David Baratier, editor. *Pavement Saw*, published annually in August, wants "letters and short fiction, and poetry on any subject, especially work." Does not want "poems that tell; no work by a deceased writer, and no translations." Dedicates 15-20 pages of each issue to a featured writer. Has published poetry by Simon Perchik, Sofia Starnes, Alan Catlin, Adrianne Kalfopoulou, Jim Daniels, and Mary Weems. *Pavement Saw* is 88 pages, digest-sized, perfect-bound. Receives about 9,000 poems/year, accepts less than 1%. Press run is 550. Single copy: $8; subscription: $14. Sample: $7. Make checks payable to Pavement Saw Press. Guidelines available in magazine or for SASE.

Responds in 4 months. Sometimes sends prepublication galleys. Pays at least 2 contributor's copies. Acquires first rights.

O PRAYERWORKS

P.O. Box 301363, Portland OR 97294-9363. (503)761-2072. E-mail: vannm1@aol.com. Website: www.prayerworksnw.org. **Contact:** V. Ann Mandeville, editor. Estab. 1988. Newsletter: 5½×8; 4 pages; bond paper. "Our intended audience is 70% retired Christians and 30% families. We publish 350-500 word devotional material—fiction, nonfiction, biographical, poetry, clean quips and quotes. Our philosophy is evangelical Christian serving the body of Christ in the area of prayer."

NEEDS religious/inspirational. "No nonevangelical Christian. Subject matter may include anything which will build relationship with the Lord—prayer, ways to pray, stories of answered prayer, teaching on a Scripture portion, articles that will build faith, or poems will all work." We even use a series occasionally. Publishes ms 2-6 months after acceptance. **Publishes 30 new writers/year.** Recently published work by Allen Audrey and Petey Prater. Length: 350-500 words; average length: 350-500 words. Publishes short shorts. Also publishes poetry. Often comments on rejected mss.

HOW TO CONTACT Submit online. Send complete ms with cover letter. Include estimated word count and a very short bio. Responds in 1 month to mss. Accepts simultaneous, multiple submissions and reprints. Writer's guidelines for #10 SASE.

PAYMENT/TERMS Pays free subscription to the magazine and contributor's copies. Pays on publication. Not copyrighted.

TIPS Stories "must have a great take-away—no preaching; teach through action. Be thrifty with words—make them count."

• THE PUCKERBRUSH REVIEW

English Dept., University of Maine, 413 Neville Hall, Orono ME 04469. E-mail: sanphip@aol.com. Website: http://puckerbrushreview.com. **Contact:** Sanford Phippen, Editor. Estab. 1971. Magazine: 9×12; 80-100 pages; illustrations. "We publish interviews, fiction, reviews, poetry for a literary audience." Semiannual. Estab. 1979. Circ. 500. "Wants to see more original, quirky and well-written fiction. No genre fiction. Nothing cliché, nothing overly sensational except in its human interest." Receives 30 unsolicited mss/month. Accepts 6 mss/issue; 12 mss/year. Publishes ms 1 year after acceptance. Recently published work by John Sullivan, Beth Thorpe, Chenoweth Hall, Merle Hillman, Wayne Burke. Publishes short shorts. Also publishes literary essays, literary criticism, poetry. Sometimes comments on rejected mss. Include SASE. Responds in 2 months to mss. Accepts simultaneous, multiple submissions. Sample copy for $3. Writer's guidelines for SASE. Reviews fiction and poetry. Pays in contributor's copies.

"Please submit your poetry, short stories, literary essays and reviews through our website link. Hard-copy submissions will no longer be accepted."

NEEDS belles lettres

TIPS "Just write the best and freshest poetry you can."

O SLATE & STYLE

2861 S. 93 Plaza APT 8, Omaha NE 68124. (402)350-1735. E-mail: bpollpeter@hotmail.com. Website: www.nfb-writers-division.org. **Contact:** Bridgit Pollpeter, editor. Estab. 1982. Quarterly magazine: 28-32 print/40 Braille pages; available by e-mail, cassette and in large print. "Accepts articles of interest to writers, and resources for blind writers."

NEEDS adventure, fantasy, humor/satire, contemporary, blindness. No erotica. "Avoid theme of death." Does not read mss in June or July. Publishes 2 new writers/year. Recently published work by Bruce Adkins, Patricia Hubschman, Kristen Diaz, and Amy Krout-horn. Accepts short stories up to 2,000 words. Publishes short shorts. Also publishes literary criticism, poetry. Sometimes comments on rejected mss. Accepts submissions by e-mail: bpollpeter@hotmail.com. Responds in 3-6 weeks to queries; 3-6 weeks to mss. Sample copy for $3. Pays in contributor's copies. Acquires onetime rights. Sponsors awards/contests.

TIPS "The best advice I can give is to send your work out; manuscripts left in a drawer have no chance at all."

SPACE AND TIME

458 Elizabeth Ave., Somerset NJ 08873. E-mail: nytebird45@aol.com. Website: www.spaceandtimemagazine.com. **Contact:** Linda D. Addison. Estab. 1966. Magazine. 8½x11, 48 pages, matte paper, glossy cover. Contains illustrations. "We love stories that blend elements—horror and science fiction, fantasy with SF elements, etc. We challenge writers to try something new and send us their unclassifiable works—what

other publications reject because the work doesn't fit in their 'pigeonholes.'" Quarterly. Circ. 2,000. Receives 250 mss/reading period. Accepts 8 mss/issue; 32 mss/year. Only open during announced reading periods. Check website to see if submissions are open. Ms published 3-6 months after acceptance. **Publishes 2-4 new writers/year.** Published PD Cacek, AR Morlan, Jeffrey Ford, Charles De Lint, and Jack Ketchum. Also publishes poetry, occasional book reviews. Sample copy available for $6.50. Guidelines available only on website. Additional copies $5. Pays on publication. Acquires first North American serial rights, onetime rights. Publication is copyrighted.

NEEDS fantasy (high, sword and sorcery, modern), horror (dark fantasy, futuristic, psychological, supernatural), romance (futuristic/time travel), science fiction (hard science/technological, soft/sociological). Does not want anything without some sort of speculative element.

HOW TO CONTACT Send review copies to Publisher Hildy Silverman, hildy@spaceandtimemagazine.com. Sometimes comments on/critiques rejected mss. Send complete ms with cover letter. Accepts submissions by e-mail only. Include estimated word count, brief bio, list of publications. Responds to queries in 4-6 weeks. Responds to mss in 4-6 weeks. Send disposable query letter and #10 SASE for reply only if unable to email submission.

PAYMENT/TERMS Payment made upon publication and is a flat $5.00 per poem plus 2 contributor's copies.

STEAMPUNK MAGAZINE, PUTTING THE PUNK BACK INTO STEAMPUNK

Strangers in a Tangled Wilderness, Wales. E-mail: readers@steampunkmagazine.com. Website: steampunkmagazine.com. **Contact:** Allegra Hawksmoor. "**We are currently not accepting submissions.** Please keep in mind before submitting that we publish under Creative Commons licensing, which means that people will be free to reproduce and alter your work for noncommercial purposes. We also, regretfully, are no longer able to offer payment to our contributors." Magazine/Online magazine. 8 ½ ×7", 80 pages, recycled paper. Contains illustrations. "*SteamPunk Magazine* is involved in supporting the SteamPunk subculture, a subculture that offers a competing vision of humanity's interaction with technology, a subculture that wears too many goggles." Quarterly. Estab. 2007. Circ. 1,000 print; 60,000 online.

NEEDS adventure, comics/graphic novels, ethnic/multicultural, experimental, fantasy (space fantasy), feminist, horror (dark fantasy, supernatural), humor/satire, literary, military/war, mystery, romance (gothic, historical), science fiction, western. Special interests: steampunk. "We are not interested in promoting misogynist, nationalistic, pro-colonial, monarchical, homophobic, or otherwise useless text." List of upcoming themes available on website. Receives 5-12 mss/month. Accepts 1-2 mss/issue; 3-6 mss/year. Manuscript published 2 months after acceptance. **Publishes 6-10 new writers/year.** Published John Reppion, Margaret Killjoy, GD Falksen, Will Strop, Catastraphone Orchestra, and Olga Izakson. Length: 500-6,000 words. Average length: 3,500 words. Publishes short shorts. Average length of short shorts: 800 words. Also publishes literary essays, literary criticism, book reviews. Send review copies to Magpie Killjoy. Sometimes comments on/critiques rejected mss.

HOW TO CONTACT Send complete ms with cover letter. Accepts submissions by e-mail only. Include brief bio, list of publications. Responds to queries in 2 weeks. Responds to mss in 2 months. Considers simultaneous submissions, previously published submissions, multiple submissions. Sample copy available for $3, on website. Guidelines available on website.

PAYMENT/TERMS Pays in contributor copies.

TIPS "We want work that does not simply repeat the stereotypical steampunk genre ideas; work that offers something tangible other than shiny brass thing-a-mabobs. Don't write about a steam-powered robot, unless you really have to."

O TRAIL OF INDISCRETION

Fortress Publishing, Inc., Lemoyne PA 17011. E-mail: fortresspublishinginc@yahoo.com; cosmicshark@comcast.net. Website: www.fortresspublishinginc.com. Fortress Publishing, Inc., 3704 Hartzdale Dr., Camp Hill PA 17011. (717) 350-8760. **Contact:** Brian Koscienski, editor in chief. Zine specializing in genre fiction: digest ($5^{1}{}_{2}\times 8^{1}{}_{2}$), 48 pages, 24 lb. paper, glossy cover. "We publish genre fiction—sci-fi, fantasy, horror, etc. We'd rather have a solid story containing great characters than a weak story with a surprise 'trick' ending." Quarterly. Estab. 2006. Circ. 100.

NEEDS *Trail of Indiscretion* accepts horror, sci fi, and fantasy short fiction (5000 words or less). No graphic sex or violence/no profanity. Submit story as a .doc to: fortresspublishinginc@yahoo.com. Adventure, fantasy (space fantasy, sword and sorcery), horror (dark fantasy, futuristic, psychological, supernatural), humor/satire, psychic/supernatural/occult, science fiction (hard science/technological, soft/sociological). Does not want "touchy-feely 'coming of age' stories or stories where the protagonist mopes about contemplating his/her own mortality." Accepts 5-7 mss/issue. Manuscript published 3-9 months after acceptance. **Publishes 2-10 new writers/year.** Published Cliff Ackman (debut), Roger Arnold, Susan Kerr (debut), Kristine Ong Muslim, Tala Bar, CJ Henderson, Danielle Ackley-McPhail. Length: 5,000 words (max). Average length: 3,000 words. Publishes short shorts. Sometimes comments on/critiques rejected mss.

HOW TO CONTACT Send complete ms with cover letter. Accepts submissions by e-mail. Include estimated word count, brief bio, list of publications. Responds to queries in 1-2 weeks. Responds to mss in 1-10 weeks. Send either SASE (or IRC) for return of ms or disposable copy of ms and #10 SASE for reply only. Considers simultaneous submissions, previously published submissions. Sample copy available for $4 or on website. Guidelines available for SASE, via e-mail, on website.

PAYMENT/TERMS Writers receive 1 contributor copy. Additional copies $2.50. Pays on publication. Acquires onetime rights. Publication is copyrighted.

TIPS "If your story is about a 13-year-old girl coping with the change to womanhood while poignantly reflecting the recent passing of her favorite aunt, then we *don't* want it. However, if your story is about the 13-year-old daughter of a vampire cowboy who stumbles upon a government conspiracy involving unicorns and aliens while investigating the grizzly murder of her favorite aunt, then we'll look at it. Please read the magazine to see what we want." "Love your story, but listen to advice."

TRANSITION: AN INTERNATIONAL REVIEW

104 Mount Auburn St., 3R, Cambridge MA 02138. (617)496-2845. Fax: (617)496-2877. E-mail: transition@fas.harvard.edu. Website: www.transitionmagazine.com. **Contact:** Sara Bruya, managing editor. Estab. 1961. Magazine: $9\frac{1}{2}\times6\frac{1}{2}$; 150-175 pages; 70 lb. Finch Opaque paper; 100 lb. White Warren Lustro dull cover; illustrations; photos. "*Transition* Magazine is a trimestrial international review known for compelling and controversial writing from and about Africa and the Diaspora. This prestigious magazine is edited at the W.E.B. Du Bois Institute of Harvard Univ. by Tommie Shelby, Vincent Brown, and Glenda Carpio. The magazine attracts famous contributors such as Wole Soyinka, Jamaica Kincaid, and Carlos Fuentes, but is also committed to providing space for new voices; Transition recently made a capsule collection of Cape Verde's finest fiction available for the first time in English. In the words of our publisher, Henry Louis Gates Jr., *Transition* seeks to publish fiction, poetry, and criticism that wrestles with "the freshest, most compelling, most curious ideas about race—indeed, about what it means to be human—today." Quarterly. Circ. 3,000.

Essays first published in a recent issue of *Transition* were selected for inclusion in *Best American Essays 2008*, *Best American Nonrequired Reading 2008*, and *Best African American Writing 2009*. Four-time winner of the Alternative Press Award for international reporting (2001, 2000, 1999, 1995); finalist in the 2001 National Magazine Award in General Excellence category.

NEEDS Publishes fiction, poetry, creative nonfiction, and cultural and political criticism. Sometimes comments on rejected mss.

HOW TO CONTACT E-mail us to request the *Transition* Style Guide. E-mail submissions are preferred. If submitting by mail, please include a SASE to receive a response from Transition. Mss will not be returned. You will receive confirmation of receipt and notification of editorial decision after review of your work. We are not able to respond to requests for status updates. If your piece is longer than 20 pages, please also send a hard copy (in Times New Roman, font size 12, double spaced). For all submissions, please include the following information in your e-mail or cover letter and in the top left corner of the first page of all documents: name, address, e-mail address, word count, date of submission. Please also include a title with each work. Sara Bruya, Managing Editor.

PAYMENT/TERMS 1 contributor's copy.

TIPS "We look for a non-white, alternative perspective, dealing with issues of race, ethnicity and identity in an unpredictable, provocative way."

WATERMAN MAGAZINE

Fine & Finer Graphic, 146 N. Gunston Dr., Los Angeles CA 90049. (310) 809-4048. E-mail: tomlockie@sbcglobal.net. Website: www.watermanmagazine.com. Magazine. 8.5×11, 32 pages. Contains illustrations. Includes photographs. "*Waterman* is a term referring to the lifequarding, bodysurfing, surfing, spearfishing, SCUBA diving lifestyle. The magazine is dedicated to the ocean lifestyle, arts, fashion and sports: diving, surfing, kayaking, paddleboating, underwater photography. We publish stories and articles dealing with adventure travel and above all ecological issues—protecting oceans and water health. Also publishes medical articles, travel articles, poems and short stories." Semiannual. Estab. 2006. Circ. Online.

NEEDS Adventure, humor/satire, literary, mainstream. Special interests: watersport stories. Receives 10-12 mss/month. Accepts 2-3 mss/issue; 4-6 mss/year. Ms published 1-5 months after acceptance. Agented fiction 10%. **Publishes 1-2 new writers/year.** Published Brian Donahue and Matteo Verna. Length: 500-1,500 words. Average length: 1,200 words. Publishes short shorts. Average length of short shorts: 400-500 words. Also publishes book reviews, poetry. Send review copies to Tom Lockie; has to be watersport based. Sometimes comments on/critiques rejected mss.

HOW TO CONTACT Accepts submissions by e-mail only. Please query first. Include brief bio. Responds to queries in 3 weeks. Responds to mss in 1 months. Sample copy free with 8½x11 SASE and $2.60 postage. Guidelines available via e-mail. Publishes new writers @ no charge; no monetary renumeration.

PAYMENT/TERMS Writers receive $20 per page. Additional copies $5 & $1.90 postage. Pays on publication. Acquires electronic rights, archive rights. Publication is not copyrighted.

TIPS "Writer must be seriously involved in watersports to stand out. Pay some heavy dues in the water."

WEIRD TALES

P.O. Box 38190, Tallahassee FL 32315. E-mail: weirdtales@gmail.com. Website: www.weirdtales.net. Estab. 1923. Magazine: 8½×11; 80-96 pages; white, newsprint paper; glossy 4-color cover; illustrations and comics. "We publish fantastic fiction, supernatural horror for an adult audience." Published 6 times a year. Circ. 5,000.

NEEDS fantasy (sword and sorcery), horror, psychic/supernatural/occult, translations. No hard science fiction or non-fantasy. "Looking for darkly fantastical fiction, work that is unique and unusual. Stories that are recognized as weird tales for the 21st Century." Receives 1,200 unsolicited mss/month. Accepts 8 mss/issue; 48 mss/year. Publishes ms 6-18 months after acceptance. Agented fiction 10%. **Publishes 8 new writers/year.** Recently published work by Michael Moorcock, Tanith Lee, Thomas Ligotti, Darrell Schweitzer, Sarah Monette and Michael Boatman. Length: up to 10,000 words, but very few longer than 8,000; average length: 4,000 words. Publishes short shorts.

HOW TO CONTACT Send complete ms via submissions manager online. Responds in 6-8 weeks to mss. Accepts simultaneous submissions. No multiple submissions. Also accepts e-mail submissions to weirdtales@gmail.com. For hardcopy submissions through the mail: provide an SASE with proper postage to ensure a response. If the postage is not enough to return the manuscript, it will be considered disposable. *Weird Tales* is not responsible for loss or damage to any unsolicited work Sample copy for $6. Writer's guidelines for #10 SASE or by e-mail. Reviews books of fantasy fiction.

PAYMENT/TERMS Pays 3-4¢/word and 2 contributor's copies on acceptance. Acquires First North American publication rights, covering all print and electronic versions of the magazine, plus nonexclusive rights to reprint stories for an additional fee in translated and collected editions drawn from the magazine.

TIPS "Traditional fantasy tropes are fine as long as it's a new and different take on the genre. Do not send any familiar story lines and do not send any pastiches of Lovecraft."

ONLINE MARKETS

As production and distribution costs go up and the number of subscribers falls, more and more magazines are giving up print publication and moving online. Relatively inexpensive to maintain and quicker to accept and post submissions, online fiction sites are growing fast in numbers and legitimacy. The benefit for writers is that your stories can get more attention in online journals than in small literary journals. Small journals have small print runs—500-1,000 copies—so there's a limit on how many people will read your work. There is no limit when your work appears online.

There is also no limit to the types of online journals being published, offering outlets for a rich and diverse community of voices. These include genre sites, particular those for science fiction/fantasy and horror, and mainstream short fiction markets. Online literary journals range from the traditional to those with a decidedly more quirky bent. Writers will also find online outlets for more highly experimental and multimedia work.

While the medium of online publication is different, the traditional rules of publishing apply to submissions. Writers should research the site and archives carefully, looking for a match in sensibility for their work. Follow submission guidelines exactly and submit courteously. True, these sites aren't bound by traditional print schedules, so your work theoretically may be published more quickly. But that doesn't mean online journals have larger staffs, so exercise patience with editors considering your manuscript.

Also, while reviewing the listings in this market section, notice they are grouped differently from other market listings. In our Literary Magazines section, for example, you'll find primarily publications searching for only literary short fiction. But online markets are grouped by medium, so you'll find publishers of mystery short stories listed next to those looking for horror next to those specializing in flash fiction, so review with care. In addition, online markets with print counterparts can be found listed in the print markets sections.

A final note about online publication: Like literary journals, the majority of these markets are either nonpaying or very low paying. In addition, writers will not receive print copies of the publications because of the medium. So in most cases, do not expect to be paid for your exposure.

5-TROPE

Website: www.5trope.com. Estab. 1999. E-mail: editor.5trope@gmail.com. Website: www.5trope.com. **Contact:** Gunnar Benediktsson, editor. Online literary journal. "We aim to publish the new and original in fiction, poetry and new media. We are seeking writers with a playful seriousness about language and form." Quarterly. Estab. 1999. Circ. 5,000.

NEEDS avant-garde prose, experimental, literary. "No religious, horror, fantasy, espionage." Receives 75 unsolicited mss/month. Accepts 6 mss/issue; 18 mss/year. Publishes ms 6-12 months after acceptance. **Publishes 5 new writers/year.** Recently published work by Cole Swensen, Carol Novack, Christopher Kennedy, Mike Topp, Norman Lock, Jeff Johnson, Peter Markus, Mandee Wright, and Jane Unrue. Length: 25-5,000 words; average length: 1,000 words. Publishes short shorts. Also publishes poetry. Sometimes comments on rejected mss.

HOW TO CONTACT Accepts submissions by e-mail. Send complete mss electronically. Sample copy online.

PAYMENT/TERMS Acquires first rights. Sends galleys to author.

TIPS "Before submitting, please visit our site, read an issue, and consult our guidelines for submission. Include your story within the body of an e-mail, not as an attachment. Include a descriptive subject line to get around spam filters. Experimental work should have a clarity about it, and should never be sentimental. Our stories are about the moment of rupture, not the moment of closure."

THE 13TH WARRIOR REVIEW

P.O. Box 5122, Seabrook NJ 08302-3511. E-mail: theeditor@asteriusonline.com. Website: www.asteriusonline.com/13thWR/. **Contact:** John C. Erianne, editor. Estab. 1997. Published 2-3 times/year.

NEEDS literary/mainstream, erotica, experimental, magical realism, meta-fiction. Receives 500 unsolicited mss/month. Accepts 4-8 mss/issue; 10-15 mss/year. Publishes ms 6 months after acceptance. **Publishes 1-2 new writers/year.** Recently published work by Cindy Rosmus, Jeff Blechle, Elizabeth Farren, and Andrew Hellem. Length: 500-6,000 words; average length: 1,800 words. Publishes short shorts. Also publishes literary essays, literary criticism, poetry, and book reviews. Sometimes comments on rejected mss.

HOW TO CONTACT Send complete ms. Include estimated word count, brief bio and address/e-mail. Send SASE or IRC for return of ms or send a disposable copy of ms and #10 SASE for reply only. Accepts submissions by e-mail (will accept file attachments, but prefers text in message body). Responds in 1 week to queries; 1-2 months to mss. Accepts simultaneous submissions. Sample copy online at www.13thwr.org. Reviews fiction.

PAYMENT/TERMS Acquires first rights, Internet archival rights.

THE ADIRONDACK REVIEW

Black Lawrence Press, P.O. Box 205619 c/o Diane Goettel Sunset Station, Brooklyn NY 11220-7619. E-mail: editors@theadirondackreview.com; angela@blacklawrencepress.com. Website: www.adirondackreview.homestead.com. **Contact:** Angela Leroux-Lindsey, Kara Christenson, Diane Goettel, editor. Estab. 2000. Online literary magazine/journal. Contains illustrations & photographs.

NEEDS adventure, experimental, family saga, gay, historical (general), psychological, translations. Does not want sci-fi, fantasy. Receives over 200 mss/month. Accepts 5-10 mss/issue; 20-30 mss/year. Manuscript published 1-5 months after acceptance. Agented fiction 5%. **Publishes 15% new writers/year.** Published Frank Haberle, Steve Gillis, Melinda Misrala, Kate Swoboda. Length: 700-8,000 words. Average length: 2,000 words. Publishes short shorts. Average length of short shorts: 800 words. Also publishes literary essays, literary criticism, book reviews, poetry. Rarely comments on/critiques rejected mss.

HOW TO CONTACT Send complete ms with cover letter. Accepts submissions by e-mail. Include estimated word count, brief bio, list of publications, and "how they learned about the magazine." Responds to queries in 1-2 months. Responds to mss in 2-4 months. Send either SASE (or IRC) for return of ms or disposable copy of ms and #10 SASE for reply only. Considers simultaneous submissions, multiple submissions.

PAYMENT/TERMS Acquires first rights. Sponsors contests. See website for details.

ALLEGORY

1225 Liberty Bell Dr., Cherry Hill NJ 08003. E-mail: submissions@allegoryezine.com. Website: www.allegoryezine.com. **Contact:** Ty Drago, editor. Estab. 1998. Online magazine specializing in science fiction, fantasy and horror. "We are an e-zine by writers for writers. Our articles focus on the art, craft and business of writing. Our links and editorial policy all focus on the needs of fiction authors." Triannual.

Peridot Books won the Page One Award for Literary Contribution.

NEEDS fantasy (space fantasy, sword and sorcery, sociological), horror (dark fantasy, futuristic, supernatural), science fiction (hard science/technological, soft/sociological). "No media tie-ins (*Star Trek*, Star Wars, etc., or space opera, vampires)." Receives 150 unsolicited mss/month. Accepts 8 mss/issue; 24 mss/year. Publishes ms 1-2 months after acceptance. Agented fiction 5%. **Publishes 10 new writers/year.** Length: 1,500-7,500 words; average length: 4,500 words. Also publishes literary essays, literary criticism. Often comments on rejected mss.

HOW TO CONTACT All submissions should be sent by e-mail (no letters or telephone calls please) in either text or RTF format. Please place "Submission [Title]-[first and last name]" in the subject line. Include the following in both the body of the e-mail and the attachment: your name, name to use on the story (byline), if different, your preferred e-mail address, your mailing address, the story's title and the story's word count. Responds in 8 weeks to mss. Accepts simultaneous submissions and reprints. Writer's guidelines online.

PAYMENT/TERMS $15/story-article. Pays on publication for onetime, electronic rights.

TIPS "Give us something original, preferably with a twist. Avoid gratuitous sex or violence. Funny always scores points. Be clever, imaginative, but be able to tell a story with proper mood and characterization. Put your name and e-mail address in the body of the story. Read the site and get a feel for it before submitting."

ANDERBO.COM

Anderbo Publishing, 270 Lafayette St., Suite 1412, New York NY 10012-3364. E-mail: editors@anderbo.com. Website: www.anderbo.com. **Contact:** Rick Rofihe, editor-in-chief. Online literary magazine/journal. "Quality fiction, poetry, 'fact' and photography on a website with 'print-feel' design." Member CLMP.

Received the Best New Online Magazine or Journal, *storySouth* Million Writers Award in 2005.

NEEDS literary. Does not want any genre literature. "We're interested only in literary fiction, poetry, and literary 'fact.'" Receives 200 mss/month. Accepts 20 mss/year. Ms published one month after acceptance. **Publishes 6 new writers/year.** Published Lisa Margonelli, Margot Berwin, Jeffrey Lent, and Susan Breen. Length: 3,500. Average length: 1,750 words. Publishes short shorts. Average length of short shorts: 1,400 words. Also publishes literary essays, poetry. Rarely comments on/critiques rejected mss.

HOW TO CONTACT Send complete ms with cover letter. Accepts submissions by e-mail. Include brief bio, list of publications. Responds to queries in 2 weeks. Responds to mss in 1-4 weeks. Considers simultaneous submissions. Guidelines available on website.

PAYMENT/TERMS Acquires first rights, first North American serial rights, onetime rights, electronic rights. Publication is copyrighted.

TIPS "We are looking for fiction that is unique, urgent, accessible and involving. Look at our site and read what we've already published."

AOIFE'S KISS

The Speculative Fiction Foundation, P.O. Box 782, Cedar Rapids IA 52406-0782. E-mail: aoifeskiss@yahoo.com. Website: www.samsdotpublishing.com. **Contact:** Tyree Campbell, Managing Editor. Estab. 2002. *Aoife's Kiss* (print version) is 54 pages, magazine-sized, offset-printed, saddle-stapled, perfect-bound, with color paper cover, includes ads. Receives about 300 poems/year, accepts about 50 (17%). Press run is 150; 5 distributed free to reviewers. Single copy: $7; subscription: $22/year, $40 for 2 years. Make checks payable to Sam's Dot Publishing.

HOW TO CONTACT Accepts e-mail submissions (pasted into body of message); no disk submissions. "Submission should include snail mail address and a short (1-2 lines) bio." Reads submissions year round.

APPLE VALLEY REVIEW, A JOURNAL OF CONTEMPORARY LITERATURE

Queen's Postal Outlet, Box 12, Kingston ON K7L 3R9 Canada. E-mail: editor@leahbrowning.net. Website: www.applevalleyreview.com. **Contact:** Leah Browning, editor. Estab. 2005. Online literary magazine. Includes photographs/artwork on cover. "Each issue features a selection of beautifully crafted poetry, short fiction and essays. We prefer work that has both mainstream and literary appeal. As such, we avoid erotica and very explicit work. Our audience includes teens and adults of all ages." Semiannual. Member CLMP.

NEEDS Ethnic/multicultural (general), experimental, humor/satire, literary, mainstream, regional (American South, Southwest), translations, literary women's fiction (e.g. Barbara Kingsolver, Anne Tyler, Lee Smith, Elinor Lipman, Perri Klass). Does not want strict genre fiction, erotica, work containing explicit language, or anything extremely violent or depressing. Receives 100+ mss/month. Accepts 1-3 mss/issue; 2-12 mss/year. Manuscript published 3-6 months after acceptance. Published Barry Jay Kaplan, Jenny Steele, Tai Dong Huai, Matthew Grice, Arrie Brown. Length: 100-3,000 words. Average length: 2,000 words. Publishes short shorts. Average length of short shorts: 1,200 words. Also publishes literary essays, poetry. Sometimes comments on/critiques rejected mss.

HOW TO CONTACT Send complete ms with cover letter. Accepts submissions only via e-mail. Include estimated word count, brief bio. Responds to mss in 1 week-2 months. No simultaneous submissions. Guidelines available on website. Sample copy on website.

PAYMENT/TERMS Acquires first rights, right to archive online. Publication is copyrighted.

TIPS "Excellent writing always makes a manuscript stand out. Beyond that, I look for stories and poems that I want to read again, and that I want to give to someone else to read—work so interesting for one reason or another that I feel compelled to share it. Please read at least some of the previously published work to get a feel for our style, and follow the submission guidelines as closely as possible. We accept submissions only via e-mail."

ASCENT ASPIRATIONS

1560 Arbutus Dr., Nanoose Bay BC C9P 9C8 Canada. E-mail: ascentaspirations@shaw.ca. Website: www.ascentaspirations.ca. **Contact:** David Fraser, Editor. Estab. 1997. E-zine specializing in short fiction (all genres) and poetry, essays, visual art: 40 electronic pages; illustrations; photos. Ascent publishes one additional issues in print each year. "*Ascent Aspirations* Magazine publishes monthly online and once in print. The print issues are operated as contests. Please refer to current guidelines before submitting. Ascent Aspirations is a quality electronic publication dedicated to the promotion and encouragement of aspiring writers of any genre. The focus however is toward interesting experimental writing in dark mainstream, literary, science fiction, fantasy and horror. Poetry can be on any theme. Essays need to be unique, current and have social, philosophical commentary." Monthly online.

NEEDS erotica, experimental, fantasy (space fantasy), feminist, horror (dark fantasy, futuristic, psychological, supernatural), literary, mainstream, mystery/suspense, New Age, psychic/supernatural/occult, science fiction (hard science/technological, soft/sociological). Receives 100-200 unsolicited mss/month. Accepts 40 mss/issue; 240 mss/year. Publishes ms 3 months after acceptance. **Publishes 10-50 new writers/year.** Recently published work by Taylor Graham, Janet Buck, Jim Manton, Steve Cartwright, Don Stockard, Penn Kemp, Sam Vargo, Vernon Waring, Margaret Karmazin, Bill Hughes. Length: 1,000 words or less. Publishes short shorts. Also publishes literary essays, literary criticism, poetry. Sometimes comments on rejected mss.

HOW TO CONTACT "Query by e-mail with Word attachment." Include estimated word count, brief bio and list of publications. If you have to submit by mail because it is your only avenue, provide a SASE with either International Coupons or Canadian stamps only. Responds in 1 week to queries; 3 months to mss. Accepts simultaneous, multiple submissions, and reprints. Guidelines by e-mail or on website. Reviews fiction and poetry collections.

PAYMENT/TERMS "No payment at this time. Rights remain with author."

TIPS "Short fiction should, first of all tell, a good story, take the reader to new and interesting imaginary or real places. Short fiction should use language lyrically and effectively, be experimental in either form or content and take the reader into realms where they can analyze and think about the human condition. Write with passion for your material, be concise and economical and let the reader work to unravel your story. In terms of editing, always proofread to the point where what you submit is the best it possibly can be. Never be discouraged if your work is not accepted; it may just not be the right fit for a current publication."

BABEL: THE MULTILINGUAL, MULTICULTURAL ONLINE JOURNAL AND COMMUNITY OF ARTS AND IDEAS

E-mail: submissions@towerofbabel.com. Website: http://towerofbabel.com. **Contact:** Malcolm Lawrence, Editor-in-Chief. Estab. 1995. Publishes regional reports from international stringers all over the planet, as well as features, round table discussions, fiction, columns, poetry, erotica, travelogues, and reviews of all the arts and editorials. Our bloggers include James Schwartz, the first out gay poet raised in the Old Order Amish community in Southwestern

Michigan and author of the book *The Literary Party*; Susanna Zaraysky, author of the book *Language Is Music: Making People Multilingual*; James Rovira, Assistant Professor of English and Program Chair of Humanities at Tiffin University and author of the book *Blake & Kierkegaard: Creation and Anxiety*; and Paul B. Miller, Assistant Professor Department of French and Italian at Vanderbilt University. We're interested in fiction, non-fiction and poetry from all over the world, including multicultural or multilingual work, as well as poetry that has been translated from or into another language, as long as it is also in English. We also appreciate gay/lesbian and bisexual poetry. Cover letter is required. Reviews books/chapbooks of poetry and other magazines, single- and multi-book format. Open to unsolicited reviews. Send materials for review consideration.

Babel is recognized by the UN as one of the most important social and human sciences onl ine periodicals.

NEEDS We are currently looking for WordPress bloggers in the following languages: Arabic, Bulgarian, Bengali, Catalan, Czech, Welsh, Danish, German, English, Esperanto, Spanish, Persian, Finnish, Faroese, French, Hebrew, Croatian, Indonesian, Italian, Japanese, Korean, Latvian, Malay, Dutch, Polish, Portuguese, Russian, Albanian, Serbian, Swedish, Tamil, Thai, Ukrainian, Urdu, Uzbek, Vietnamese, and Chinese.

HOW TO CONTACT Send queries/mss by email. "Please send submissions with a resumé/cover letter or biography attached to the email." Reviews novels and short story collections.

PAYMENT/TERMS Does not pay.

TIPS "We would like to see more fiction with first-person male characters written by female authors, as well as more fiction first-person female characters written by male authors. We would also like to see that dynamic in action when it comes to other languages, cultures, races, classes, sexual orientations and ages. Know what you are writing about and write passionately about it."

THE BARCELONA REVIEW

Correu Vell 12-2, Barcelona 08002 Spain. E-mail: editor@barcelonareview.com. Website: www.barcelonareview.com. **Contact:** Jill Adams, editor. "*TBR* is an international review of contemporary, cutting-edge fiction published in English, Spanish and Catalan. Our aim is to bring both new and established writers to the attention of a larger audience. Well-known writers such as Alicia Erian in the U.S., Michel Faber in the U.K., Carlos Gardini in Argentina, and Nuria Amat in Spain, for example, were not known outside their countries until appearing in *TBR*. Our multilingual format increases the audience all the more. Internationally known writers, such as Irvine Welsh and Douglas Coupland, have contributed stories that ran in small press anthologies available only in one country. We try to keep abreast of what's happening internationally and to present the best finds every two months. Our intended audience is anyone interested in high-quality contemporary fiction that often (but not always) veers from the mainstream; we assume that our readers are well read and familiar with contemporary fiction in general."

NEEDS short fiction. "Our bias is towards potent and powerful cutting-edge material; given that general criteria, we are open to all styles and techniques and all genres. No slice-of-life stories, vignettes or reworked fables, and nothing that does not measure up, in your opinion, to the quality of work in our review, which we expect submitters to be familiar with." **Publishes 20 new writers/year.** Recently published work by Niall Griffiths, Adam Haslett, G.K. Wuori, Adam Johnson, Mary Wornov, Emily Carter, Jesse Shepard, and Julie Orringer.

HOW TO CONTACT Send submissions by e-mail as an attached file. Hard copies accepted but cannot be returned. No simultaneous submissions. Reply takes 8 weeks.

PAYMENT/TERMS "In lieu of pay we sometimes offer a highly professional Spanish translation to English language writers and vice versa to Spanish writers. Work is showcased along with two or more known authors in a high quality literary review with an international readership. Author retains all rights although for the Internet only we ask for exclusive rights for the time period agreed upon."

TIPS "Send top drawer material that has been drafted two, three, four times—whatever it takes. Then sit on it for a while and look at it afresh. Keep the text tight. Grab the reader in the first paragraph and don't let go. Keep in mind that a perfectly crafted story that lacks a punch of some sort won't cut it. Make it new, make it different. Surprise the reader in some way. Read the best of the short fiction available in your area of writing to see how yours measures up. Don't send anything off until you feel it's ready and then familiarize yourself with the content of the review/magazine to which you are submitting."

BLACKBIRD

Virginia Commonwealth University Department of English, P.O. Box 843082, Richmond VA 23284. (804)827-4729. E-mail: blackbird@vcu.edu. Website: www.blackbird.vcu.edu. **Contact:** Mary Flinn, Gregory Donovan, senior editors. Estab. 2001. Online journal: 80+ pages if printed; illustrations; photos. "We strive to maintain the highest quality of writing and design, bringing the best things about a print magazine to the outside world. We publish fiction that is carefully crafted, thoughtful and suprising." Semiannual. Estab. 2001. Circ. 30,000 readers per month.

NEEDS literary, novel excerpts. Does not want science fiction, religious/inspirational, condensed novels, horror, romance, children's. Receives 400-600 unsolicited mss/month. Accepts 4-5 mss/issue; 8-10 mss/year. Does not read from April 15-November 1. Publishes ms 3-6 months after acceptance. **Publishes 1-2 new writers/year.** Length: 5,000-10,000 words; average length: 5,000-6,500 words. Also publishes literary essays, literary criticism, poetry. Sometimes comments on rejected mss.

HOW TO CONTACT Send complete ms online at www.blackbirdsubmissions.vcu.edu. Include cover letter, name, address, telephone number, brief biographical comment. Responds in 6 months to mss. Accepts simultaneous submissions. Sample copy online. Writer's guidelines online.

PAYMENT/TERMS Pays $200 for fiction, $40 for poetry. Pays on publication for first North American serial rights.

TIPS "We like a story that invites us into its world, that engages our senses, soul and mind."

THE CAFE IRREAL

E-mail: editors@cafeirreal.com. Website: www.cafeirreal.com. **Contact:** G.S. Evans, Alice Whittenburg, coeditors. Estab. 1998. E-zine: illustrations. "The *Cafe Irreal* is a webzine focusing on short stories and short shorts of an irreal nature." Quarterly.

NEEDS experimental, fantasy (literary), science fiction (literary), translations. "No horror or 'slice-of-life' stories; no genre or mainstream science fiction or fantasy." Accepts 8-10 mss/issue; 30-40 mss/year. Recently published work by Ignacio Padilla, Peter Cherches, Michal Ajvaz, Marianne Villanueva, and Bruce Holland Rogers. Length: 2,000 words (max). Publishes short shorts. Also publishes literary essays, literary criticism. Sometimes comments on rejected mss.

HOW TO CONTACT Accepts submissions by e-mail. "No attachments, include submission in body of e-mail. Include estimated word count." Responds in 2-4 months to mss. No simultaneous submissions. Sample copy online. Writer's guidelines online.

PAYMENT/TERMS Pays 1¢/word, $2 minimum. Pays on publication for first-time electronic rights. Sends galleys to author.

TIPS "Forget formulas. Write about what you don't know, take me places I couldn't possibly go, don't try to make me care about the characters. Read short fiction by writers such as Franz Kafka, Jorge Luis Borges, Donald Barthelme, Magnus Mills, Ana Maria Shua and Stanislaw Lem. Also read our website and guidelines."

ORSON SCOTT CARD'S INTERGALACTIC MEDICINE SHOW

Hatrack River Publications, P.O. Box 18184, Greensboro NC 27419. Website: InterGalacticMedicineShow.com; oscIGMS.com. **Contact:** Edmund R. Schubert, editor. Estab. 2005. E-zine specializing in science fiction and fantasy. Contains illustrations. "We like to see well-developed milieus and believeable, engaging characters. We also look for clear, unaffected writing. Asimov, Niven, Tolkien, Yolen and Hobb are more likely to be our literary exemplars than James Joyce." Bimonthly.

NEEDS fantasy (space fantasy, sword and sorcery), horror (dark fantasy, futuristic), science fiction (hard science/technological, soft/sociological), young adult/teen (fantasy/science fiction). Receives 300-400 mss/month. Accepts 7 mss/issue; 30+ mss/year. Ms published 4-9 months after acceptance. Agented fiction 5%. **Publishes 4-6 new writers/year.** Published Peter S. Beagle, Tim Pratt, Eugie Foster, James Maxey, Eric James Stone, Alethea Kontis, Steven Savile, and Cat Rambo. Length: 1,000 words (min)-10,000 words (max). Average length: 4,000-7,000 words. Publishes short shorts. Average length of short shorts: 750 words. Also publishes book reviews. Sometimes comments on/critiques rejected mss.

HOW TO CONTACT Submit ms via submission form on website. Include estimated word count, e-mail address. Responds to queries in 2 weeks. Responds to mss in 3-6 months. Considers simultaneous submissions, previously published submissions (if obscure publication). Guidelines available on website.

PAYMENT/TERMS Writers receive 6¢ per word for first 7,500 words, 5¢ per word beyond 7,500, contributor's copy. Pays on publication. Acquires first North American serial rights, electronic rights. Publication is copyrighted.

TIPS "Plain and simple, we want to see plots that go somewhere, filled with people we care about. Stories that show the author has a real undersanding of the subtleties of human nature. Proper manuscript formatting and up-to-date contact information are overlooked by more writers than you could imagine. Also, please bear in mind that all stories must be PG-13 suitable. Gratuitous sex, violence or language will get you rejected right away."

◐ CEZANNE'S CARROT, A LITERARY JOURNAL OF FRESH OBSERVATIONS

Spiritual, Transformational & Visionary Art, Inc., P.O. Box 6037, Santa Fe NM 87502-6037. E-mail: query@cezannescarrot.org. Website: www.cezannescarrot.org. **Contact:** Barbara Jacksha and Joan Kremer, editors. Online magazine. "*Cezanne's Carrot* publishes "high quality literary fiction and creative nonfiction that explores spiritual, metaphysical, transformational, visionary, or mind-expanding themes. We are most interested in stories that push us into a transcendent realm, that give us a higher understanding of our expanding, multi-dimensional selves."

Publishes 1-5 new writers/year. Published Bruce Holland Rogers, Tamara Kaye Sellman, Tantra Bensko, R. Virgil Ellis, Rebecca Hodgkins, Cheryl Wood Ruggiero, Corey Mesler, Christine Boyka Kluge, and Charles P. Ries. Length: 100 words (min)-3,000 words (max). Average length: 1,800 words. Publishes short shorts. Send complete ms with cover letter. Include estimated word count, brief bio, list of publications. Pays $10 per story upon publication.

NEEDS Experimental, fantasy (speculative), literary, new age, psychic/supernatural/occult, science fiction (soft/sociological), magical realism, irrealism, visionary, surrealism, metaphysical, spiritual, "and other genres, as long as the work is literary and embraces the journal's metaphysical mission and theme. Does not want horror, gore, murder, serial-killers, abuse stories, drug stories, vampires or other monsters, political stories, war stories, stories written for children, stories that primarily promote an agenda or a particular religion. We're not interested in dogma in any form." Receives 100-200 mss/month. Accepts 24-36 mss/issue; 40-60 mss/year. Manuscript published 1-9 months after acceptance.

HOW TO CONTACT Send complete ms with cover letter. Accepts submissions by e-mail only. Include estimated word count, brief bio, list of publications. Responds to mss in 1-6 months. Considers simultaneous submissions, previously published submissions. Guidelines available on website.

PAYMENT/TERMS Pays $10 per story upon publication. Acquires onetime rights, reprint rights.

TIPS "We only accept work with a strong tie to our journal's mission and theme. Read our guidelines and mission statement carefully. Read previous issues to understand the kind of work we're looking for. Only submissions sent to the correct e-mail address will be considered. Submissions sent as attachments or that exceed our maximum word count will not be read or responded to."

CHIZINE: TREATMENT OF LIGHT AND SHADE IN WORDS

Canada. Estab. 1997. E-mail: savory@rogers.com. **Contact:** Brett Alexander Savory, editor-in-chief. E-zine. "Subtle, sophisticated dark fiction with a literary bent." Quarterly. Estab. 1997.

Received Bram Stoker Award for Other Media in 2000.

NEEDS experimental, fantasy, horror (dark fantasy, futuristic, psychological, supernatural), literary, mystery, science fiction (soft/sociological), Does not want "tropes of vampires, werewolves, mummies, monsters, or anything that's been done to death." Receives 100 mss/month. Accepts 3-4 mss/issue; 12-16 mss/year. Does not read June, July, and August due to Chizine Short Story Contest. Length: 4,000 words (max). Publishes short shorts. Average length of short shorts: 500 words. Also publishes poetry. Send to savory@rogers.com to query. Always comments on/critiques rejected mss.

HOW TO CONTACT Send complete ms with cover letter. Accepts only submissions by e-mail. Include estimated word count, brief bio. Responds to queries in 1 week. Responds to mss within 3 months. Considers simultaneous submissions so long as we're told it is simultaneous. Guidelines available on website.

PAYMENT/TERMS Writers receive 7¢/word, with a $280 max. Pays on publication. Acquires all rights for 90 days, then archival rights for one year. Sends any edits to author. Publication is copyrighted. Sponsors the Chizine Short Story contest. Guidelines posted on website around May. See entry in Contests & Awards section.

CONTE, AN ONLINE JOURNAL OF NARRATIVE WRITING

E-mail: poetry@conteonline.net. E-mail: prose@conteonline.net. Website: http://www.conteonline.net. **Contact:** Adam Tavel, poetry editor. Estab. 2005. Biannual online magazine. "We aim to publish narrative writing of all kinds. Relating a sequence of events is a primary method of human communication; we are interested in the narrative form as a means of relating ideas, experiences, and emotions, and we love how the act of telling a story unites the perspectives of listeners and speakers. We are dedicated to the concept of disseminating fresh, stellar writing to as many people as possible, as quickly and as often as possible, hence our online basis. We are enthusiastic about publishing the latest works of writers from all backgrounds and of varying experience. We hope *Conte* will be a mechanism not only for publication, but communication among writers as well as between readers and authors, and above all that we continue the ancient and perhaps sacred tradition of telling a good yarn." "We'll consider fiction on essentially any topic; our primary focus is the effective use of narrative." Agented fiction <5%. Responds to queries in 3-4 weeks. Responds to mss in 8-10 weeks. **Publishes 4 new writers/year.** Also publishes poetry. Sometimes comments on/critiques rejected mss. Considers simultaneous submissions. Guidelines available via e-mail, on website. Acquires electronic rights. Sends galleys to author. Publication is not copyrighted.

NEEDS narrative writing of all kinds.

HOW TO CONTACT Send complete ms with cover letter. Accepts submissions by e-mail only. Include estimated word count, brief bio. Email: poetry@conteonline.net; prose@conteonline.net. Website: http://www.conteonline.net.

TIPS "Submit poems in the body of an email to: poetry@conteonline.net, with subject line 'Poetry Submission' followed by the title. We are averse to rhyme schemes and attachments. Submit prose to: prose@conteonline.net, with subject line 'Prose Submission' followed by title. Rich Text (.rtf) attachments are preferred but submissions in the body of an email are acceptable."

CONTRARY

3133 S. Emerald Ave., Chicago IL 60616-3299. E-mail: chicago@contrarymagazine.com (no submissions). Website: www.contrarymagazine.com. **Contact:** Jeff McMahon, editor. Estab. 2003. Online literary magazine/journal. Contains illustrations. "*Contrary* publishes fiction, poetry, literary commentary, and prefers work that combines the virtues of all those categories. Founded at the University of Chicago, it now operates independently and not-for-profit on the South Side of Chicago. We like work that is not only contrary in content, but contrary in its evasion of the expectations established by its genre. Our fiction defies traditional story form. For example, a story may bring us to closure without ever delivering an ending. We don't insist on the ending, but we do insist on the closure. And we value fiction as poetic as any poem." Quarterly. Circ. 38,000 unique readers. Member CLMP.

NEEDS literary. Receives 650 mss/month. Accepts 6 mss/issue; 24 mss/year. Ms published no more than 21 days after acceptance. **Publishes 1 new writer/year.** Published Sherman Alexie, Andrew Coburn, Amy Reed, Clare Kirwan, Stephanie Johnson, Laurence Davies, and Edward McWhinney. Length: 2,000 words (max). Average length: 750 words. Publishes short shorts. Average length of short shorts: 750 words. Also publishes literary essays, poetry. Rarely comments on/critiques rejected mss.

HOW TO CONTACT Accepts submissions through website only. www.contrarymagazine.com/Contrary/Submissions.html. Include estimated word count, brief bio, list of publications. Responds to queries in 2 weeks. Responds to mss in 3 months. Considers simultaneous submissions. Guidelines available on website.

PAYMENT/TERMS Pays $20-60. Pays on publication. Acquires first rights and perpetual archive and anthology rights. Publication is copyrighted.

TIPS "Beautiful writing catches our eye first. If we realize we're in the presence of unanticipated meaning, that's what clinches the deal. Also, we're not fond of expository fiction. We prefer to be seduced by beauty, profundity and mystery than to be presented with the obvious. We look for fiction that entrances, that stays the reader's finger above the mouse button. That is, in part, why we favor microfiction, flash fiction and short-shorts. Also, we hope writers will remember that most editors are looking for very particular species of work. We try to describe our particular species in our mission statement and our submission guidelines, but those descriptions don't always convey nuance. That's why many editors urge writers to read the publication itself; in the hope that they will intuit an understanding of its particularities. If you happen to write that particular species of work we favor, your submission may find a happy home with us. If you don't, it does not necessarily reflect on your quality or your ability. It usually just means that your work has a happier home somewhere else."

CONVERGENCE: AN ONLINE JOURNAL OF POETRY AND ART

An Online Journal of Poetry and Art, E-mail: clinville@csus.edu. E-mail: clinville@csus.edu. Website: www.convergence-journal.com. **Contact:** Cynthia Linville, managing editor. Estab. 2003. *Convergence* seeks to unify the literary and visual arts and draw new interpretations of the written word by pairing poems and flash fiction with complementary art. Quarterly. Estab. 2003. Circ. 200.

Deadlines are January 5 and June 5.

NEEDS Accepts 5 mss/issue. Publishes ms 1-6 months after acceptance. Recently published work by Oliver Rice, Simon Perchik, Mary Ocher. Publishes short shorts. Also publishes poetry.

HOW TO CONTACT Send complete ms. E-mail submissions only with "Convergence" in subject line. No simultaneous submissions. Responds in less than a week to queries; 6 months to mss. Writer's guidelines online.

PAYMENT/TERMS Acquires first rights.

TIPS "We look for freshness and originality and a mastery of the craft of flash fiction. Working with a common theme has a greater chance of being accepted."

THE COPPERFIELD REVIEW

E-mail: info@copperfieldreview.com. Website: www.copperfieldreview.com. **Contact:** Meredith Allard, executive editor. Estab. 2000. "We are an online literary journal that publishes historical fiction and articles, reviews and interviews related to historical fiction. We believe that by understanding the lessons of the past through historical fiction we can gain better insight into the nature of our society today, as well as a better understanding of ourselves." Quarterly.

NEEDS historical (general), romance (historical), western (frontier saga, traditional). "We will consider submissions in most fiction categories, but the setting must be historical in nature. We don't want to see anything not related to historical fiction." Receives 30 unsolicited mss/month. Accepts 7-10 mss/issue; 28-40 mss/year. Responds to mss during the months of January, April, July, and October. **Publishes "between 30 and 40 percent" new writers/year.** Publishes short shorts. Also publishes literary essays, literary criticism, poetry. Seldom comments on rejected mss.

HOW TO CONTACT Send complete ms. Accepts submissions by e-mail. Responds in 6 weeks to queries. Accepts simultaneous, multiple submissions and reprints. Sample copy online. Writer's guidelines online. Reviews fiction.

PAYMENT/TERMS Acquires onetime rights.

TIPS "We wish to showcase the very best in literary historical fiction. Stories that use historical periods and details to illuminate universal truths will immediately stand out. We are thrilled to receive thoughtful work that is polished, poised and written from the heart. Be professional, and only submit your very best work. Be certain to adhere to a publication's submission guidelines, and always treat your e-mail submissions with the same care you would use with a traditional publisher. Above all, be strong and true to your calling as a writer. It is a difficult, frustrating but wonderful journey. It is important for writers to review our online submission guidelines prior to submitting."

DARGONZINE

E-mail: dargon@dargonzine.org. Website: dargonzine.org. **Contact:** Jon Evans, editor. E-zine specializing in fantasy fiction. "*DargonZine* is an E-zine that prints original fantasy fiction by aspiring fantasy writers. The Dargon Project is a shared world anthology whose goal is to provide a way for aspiring fantasy writers to meet and improve their writing skills through mutual contact and collaboration as well as contact with a live readership via the Internet."

NEEDS fantasy. "Our goal is to write fantasy fiction that is mature, emotionally compelling, and professional. Membership in the Dargon Project is a requirement for publication." **Publishes 1-3 new writers/year.** Guidelines available on website. Sample copy online. "As a strictly noncommercial magazine, our writers' only compensation is their growth and membership in a lively writing community. Authors retain all rights to their stories."

TIPS "The Readers and Writers FAQs on our website provide much more detailed information about our mission, writing philosophy and the value of writing for *DargonZine*."

DISLOCATE

University of Minnesota English Department, the Edelstein-Keller Endowment, and Adam Lerner of the Lerner Publishing Group., Dept. of English, University of Minnesota, 1 Lind Hall, 207 Church St. SE, Minneapolis MN 55455. Website: http://dislocate.umn.edu. E-mail: dislocate.magazine@gmail.com. **Contact:** Shantha Susman. Magazine has revolving editor. Literary magazine/journal: 5½ x 8½, 128 pages. Annual. Estab. 2005. Circ. 2,000. The print journal covers literary writing that bends genres and otherwise pushes the envelope; the submission period for issue 7 is July 15 to November 15. See print journal submission guidelines. The online magazine publishes content of interest to writers and readers: Writing-related content may include articles, essays, interviews, and book reviews. Our culture-related content encompasses everything from arts to entertainment to fashion to "lifestyle" pieces. See online content submission guidelines. Dislocate.umn.edu also runs a monthly Short Forms Contest; winners are published on the website and awarded prizes that vary from month to month. See contest submission guidelines and prize details.

Reading period currently closed.

NEEDS literary fiction. Receives 25-50 mss/month. Accepts 2-3 mss/year. Publishes short shorts. Also publishes literary essays, poetry.

HOW TO CONTACT We are now using Submishmash for all submissions. (Submissions will become available when the reading period begins.) We will not consider or respond to submissions or by post or e-mail. Send complete ms with cover letter. Considers simultaneous submissions, multiple submissions. Guidelines available on website.

PAYMENT/TERMS Pays on publication.

TIPS "Looking for excellent writing that rearranges the world."

DUCTS

P.O. Box 3203, Grand Central Station, New York NY 10163. E-mail: fiction@ducts.org; essays@ducts.org. Website: http://ducts.org. **Contact:** Jonathan Kravetz. Estab. 1999. Semiannual. Estab. 1999. *DUCTS* is a webzine of personal stories, fiction, essays, memoirs, poetry, humor, profiles, reviews and art. "*DUCTS* was founded in 1999 with the intent of giving emerging writers a venue to regularly publish their compelling, personal stories. The site has been expanded to include art and creative works of all genres. We believe that these genres must and do overlap. *DUCTS* publishes the best, most compelling stories and we hope to attract readers who are drawn to work that rises above."

NEEDS ethnic/multicultural, humor/satire, literary, mainstream. "Please do not send us genre work, unless it is extraordinarily unique." Receives 50 unsolicited mss/month. Accepts 40 mss/issue; 80 mss/year. Publishes ms 1-6 months after acceptance. Publishes 10-12 new writers/year. Recently published work by Charles Salzberg, Mark Goldblatt, Richard Kostelanz, and Helen Zelon. Publishes short shorts. Also publishes literary essays, literary criticism, poetry. Sometimes comments on rejected mss.

HOW TO CONTACT Reading period is January 1-August 31. Send complete ms. Accepts submissions by e-mail to appropriate departments. Responds in 1-4 weeks to queries; 1-6 months to mss. Accepts simultaneous and reprints submissions. Writer's guidelines on ducts.org.

PAYMENT/TERMS $15. Acquires onetime rights.

TIPS "We prefer writing that tells a compelling story with a strong narrative drive."

THE EXTERNALIST: A JOURNAL OF PERSPECTIVES

c/o Larina Warnock, P.O. Box 2052, Corvallis OR 97339. E-mail: editor@theexternalist.com; fiction@theexternalist.com; poetry@theexternalist.com. Website: www.theexternalist.com. **Contact:** Larina Warnock. Online magazine, PDF format, 45-60 pages. "The *Externalist* embraces the balance between craft, entertainment and substance with a focus on subjects that are meaningful in human context. The externalist writer is the writer who is driven by a desire to write well while also writing in such a way that others can understand their perspective (even if they disagree or can't relate), and in this way, keeps an eye on the world outside of self. *Externalism* values craft and content equally. It recognizes there are still important lessons to be learned, there is still a need to understand and relate to the world around us, and differences are as important as similarities, and vice versa. The externalist believes there are significant human concerns across the globe and here in the United States, and that good literature has the power to create discussion around these concerns. The externalist also believes the multiplicity of perspectives found in today's quickly changing world can (and should) be valued as a means to comprehension—a way to change the things that do not work and give force to the things that do." Bimonthly. Estab. 2007. Circ. approx.1,000 unique visitors a month.

Work published in the the *Externalist* has received awards from "Best of the Web."

NEEDS adventure, ethnic/multicultural, family saga, fantasy, feminist, gay, historical, horror, humor/satire, lesbian, literary, mainstream, military/war, mystery, new age, psychic/supernatural/occult, religious, science fiction, thriller/espionage, and western, but "all fiction must have an externalist focus regardless of genre." Does not want children's or young adult literature, erotica or pornography, or standard romance. "We do not publish any work that is designed to inspire hate or violence against any population. Highly experimental work is strongly discouraged. Slice-of-life fiction that does not deal with a significant social issue will not be accepted." List of upcoming themes available on website. Receives 20-25 mss/month. Accepts 2-3 mss/issue; 12-18 mss/year. Ms published 4 months after acceptance. Publishes 10-15 new writers/year. Published Simon Perchik, Lois Shapley Bassen, and Shaul Hendel. Length: 500-5,000 words. Average length: 3,500 words. Publishes short shorts. Average length of short shorts: 750 words. Also publishes literary essays, literary criticism, poetry. Often comments on/critiques rejected mss.

HOW TO CONTACT E-mail submissions only. Include estimated word count, brief bio. Responds to queries in 2-3 weeks. Responds to mss in 3 months. Considers simultaneous submissions, previously published submissions. Guidelines available on website.

PAYMENT/TERMS Contributor's link on Web page (see website for details). Acquires first North American serial rights. Sends galleys to author. Publication is copyrighted. "All work published in *The Externalist* is eligible for Editor's Choice (each issue) and our annual Best of *The Externalist* anthology."

TIPS "The fiction that appears in *The Externalist* is well-crafted and speaks subtly about significant social issues in our world today. The more thought-provoking the story, the more likely we will accept it for publication. The editor has a soft spot for well written satire. However, read the work we publish before submitting. Familiarize yourself with externalism. This information is on our website free of charge, and even a brief look at the material we publish will improve your chances. Follow the guidelines! We do not open unsolicated attachments, and manuscripts that do not follow our e-mail formatting guidelines stand a good chance of hitting our junk mail folder and not being seen."

FAILBETTER.COM

2022 Grove Ave., Richmond VA 23221. E-mail: tdidato@failbetter.com; submissions@failbetter.com. Website: www.failbtetter.com. **Contact:** Thom Didato, publisher. Estab. 2000.

TIPS "Read an issue. Read our guidelines! We place a high degree of importance on originality, believing that even in this age of trends it is still possible. We are not looking for what is current or momentary. We are not concerned with length: One good sentence may find a home here, as the bulk of mediocrity will not. Most importantly, know that what you are saying could only come from you. When you are sure of this, please feel free to submit."

FANTASY WORLD GEOGRAPHIC

The best fiction on the web, Website: www.skaggsworld.com. **Contact:** Shawn Edwards, Submissions Editor. Estab. 2005. Published approximately 20 previously unpublished writers each year. Some include: Tom Arbino, Amy Keeley, Beth Woodzinski, Ivan Belacic, Jonathan Moeller. Average length of stories is 3,000 words. Publish short short (fewer than 1,500 words; average short short length is 1,000 words. Submit complete ms via website. Reviews novels. Send review copies to James Skaggs. Often comments on rejected mss. Accepts simultaneous, previously published, and multiple submissions. See our criteria on our website under guidelines, like uniqueness of story plot, well-developed characters and world, captivating storytelling. Sends prepublication galleys to the author; sometimes sends mark ups and artwork for approval. Publication is copyrighted. We sponsor contests for fiction writers; writers participate by submitting a story with a note stating the contest they are entering and paying the fees before acceptance.

HOW TO CONTACT Submit complete ms via website. Responds to queries in 1 month; mss in 2 months.

PAYMENT/TERMS Pays $2/min-$10/max. Pays upon acceptance. Acquires first rights.

TIPS See tips on website under submission guidelines.

FICKLE MUSES

315 Terrace Street SE, Albuquerque NM 87106. E-mail: fiction2@ficklemuses.com. Website: www.ficklemuses.com. Estab. *Fickle Muses* is an online journal ofpoetry and fiction engaged with myth and legend. Online magazine. Contains illustrations. Includes photographs. "We feature poetry and short stories that re-imagine old myths or reexamine mythic themes contemporarily." Weekly.

NEEDS literary. "Stories may cross over into any genre as long as the story is based in a myth or legend. Does not want stories that treat myth as a false belief or stereotype (e.g. the myth of beauty). No pure genre (romance, horror, mystery, etc.)." Receives 13-15 mss/month. Accepts 12-24 mss/year. Ms published up to 3 months after acceptance. **Publishes approx 10% new writers/year.** Published Neil de la Flor, Maureen Seaton, Virginia Mohlere, and M.M. De Voe. Length: 1,000-5,000 words. Average length: 2,000 words. Publishes short shorts. Average length of short shorts: 500 words. Also publishes literary essays, literary criticism, book reviews, poetry. Send review query to fiction@ficklemuses.com. Rarely comments on/critiques rejected mss.

HOW TO CONTACT Send complete ms with cover letter. Accepts submissions by e-mail only. Include estimated word count and "a brief description of the myth or legend your story is based on if it is not standard knowledge." Responds to queries in 3 weeks. Responds to mss in 3 weeks. Considers simultaneous submissions, previously published submissions. Guidelines available on website.

PAYMENT/TERMS Acquires onetime rights. Publication is not copyrighted.

TIPS "Originality. An innovative look at an old story. I'm looking to be swept away. Get a feel for our website."

FLASHQUAKE

P.O. Box 2154, Albany NY 12220-0154. E-mail: cbell@flashquake.org. Website: www.flashquake.org. **Contact:** Cindy Bell, publisher/editor-in-chief. E-zine specializing in flash literature. "*Flashquake* is a quarterly online literary journal featuring flash literature—flash fiction, flash nonfiction, and short poetry. Send us works that will leave readers thinking. We define flash as works less than 1,000 words, shorter pieces will impress us. Poetry can be up to 35 lines; prose poetry up to 300 lines. We want the best story you can tell us in the fewest words you need to do it! Move us, engage us, give us a complete story with characters, plot, and a beginning, middle and end."

NEEDS ethnic/multicultural (general), experimental, literary, flash literature of all types: fiction, memoir, creative nonfiction, poetry, and artwork. "Not interested in romance, graphic sex, graphic violence, gore, jokey humor, vampires, or work of a religious nature." Receives 200-250 unsolicited mss/month. Accepts 30 mss/issue. Publishes ms 1-3 months after acceptance. Publishes only short shorts. Comments on most rejected mss.

HOW TO CONTACT Accepts submissions online at http://flashquake.submishmash.com/Submit only. No land mail. Include brief bio, mailing address, and e-mail address. Guidelines and submission instructions on website.

PAYMENT/TERMS Pays $5-25 plus CD copy of site. Pays within two weeks of publication for electronic rights. Sponsors occasional awards/contests.

TIPS "Read our submission guidelines before submitting. Proofread your work thoroughly! We will instantly reject your work for spelling and grammar errors. Save your document as plain text and paste it into an e-mail message. We do not open attachments. We like experimental work, but that is not a license to forget narrative clarity, plot, character development or reader satisfaction."

FULLOSIA PRESS

P.O. Box 280, Ronkonkoma NY 11779. E-mail: deanofrpps@aol.com. Website: rpps_fullosia_press.tripod.com. **Contact:** J.D. Collins, editor; Geoff Jackson, associate editor. Estab, 1999. E-zine. "Part-time publisher of fiction and non-fiction. Our publication is right wing and conservative, leaning to views of Patrick Buchanan but amenable to the opposition's point of view. We promote an independent America. We are anti-global, anti-UN. Collects unusual news from former British or American provinces. Fiction interests include military, police, private detective, courthouse stories." Monthly. Circ. 175.

NEEDS historical (American), military/war, mystery/suspense, thriller/espionage. Christmas, St. Patrick's Day, Fourth of July. Publishes ms 1 week after acceptance. **Publishes 10 new writers/year.** Recently published work by Geoff Jasckson, "Awesome" Dave Lawrence, John Grey, James Davies, Andy Martin, and Michael Levy. Length: 500-2,000 words; average length: 750 words. Publishes short shorts. Also publishes literary essays. Always comments on rejected mss.

HOW TO CONTACT Query with or without published clips. Accepts submissions by e-mail. Include brief bio and list of publications. Mail submissions must be on 3¼ floppy disk. Responds in 1 month to mss. Please avoid mass mailings. Sample copy online. Reviews fiction.

PAYMENT/TERMS Acquires electronic rights.

TIPS "Make your point quickly. If you haven't done so, after five pages, everybody hates you and your characters."

THE FURNACE REVIEW

16909 N. Bay Rd. #305, Sunny Isles FL 33160. E-mail: editor@thefurnacereview.com. E-mail: submissions@thefurnacereview.com. Website: http://thefurnacereview.com. **Contact:** Ciara LaVelle, editor. Estab. 2004. "We reach out to a young, well-educated audience, bringing them new, unique, fresh work they won't find elsewhere." Quarterly. Estab. 2004.

NEEDS Experimental, literary, mainstream. Does not want children's, science fiction, or religious submissions. Receives 50-60 unsolicited mss/month. Accepts 1-5 mss/issue; 5-8 mss/year. **Publishes 10-20 new writers/year.** Recently published work by Amy Greene, Dominic Preziosi, and Sandra Soson. Length: 7,000 words; average length: 4,000 words. Publishes short shorts. Also publishes poetry.

HOW TO CONTACT Send complete ms. Accepts submissions only by e-mail at submissions@thefurnacereview.com or online at http://thefurnacereview.com/submit/. Responds in 4 month to queries. Accepts simultaneous submissions.

PAYMENT/TERMS Acquires first North American serial rights.

GULF STREAM MAGAZINE

Florida International University, English Dept., Biscayne Bay Campus, 3000 NE 151st St., N. Miami FL 33181-3000. (305)919-5599. E-mail: gulfstreamfiu@yahoo.com. **Contact:** fiction editor. Magazine: 5½×8½; 124 pages; recycled paper; 80 lb. glossy cover; cover illustrations. "We publish good quality fiction, nonfiction and poetry for a predominately literary market." Semiannual. Estab. 1989. Circ. 300.

"Submit online only. Please read guidelines on website in full. Submissions that do not conform to our guidelines will be discarded. We do not accept emailed or mailed submissions. We read from Sept 15-Dec 15; Jan 15-Mar 15." Does not pay writers' expenses.

NEEDS literary, mainstream, contemporary. Does not want romance, historical, juvenile, or religious work. Receives 250 unsolicited mss/month. Accepts 5 mss/issue; 10 mss/year. Does not read mss during the summer. Publishes ms 3-6 months after acceptance. **Publishes 2-5 new writers/year.** Past contributors include Sherman Alexie, Steve Almond, Jan Beatty, Lee Martin, Robert Wrigley, Dennis Lehane, Liz Robbins, Stuart Dybek, David Kirby, Ann Hood, Ha Jin, B.H. Fairchild, Naomi Shihab Nye, F. Daniel Rzicznek, and Connie May Fowler. Length: 7,500 words; average length: 5,000 words. Publishes short shorts. Also publishes poetry.

HOW TO CONTACT Responds in 6 months to mss. Accepts simultaneous submissions "if noted." Sample copy for $5. Writer's guidelines for #10 SASE.

PAYMENT/TERMS Pays in gift subscriptions and contributor's copies. Acquires first North American serial rights.

TIPS "Looks for fresh, original writing—well plotted stories with unforgettable characters, fresh poetry and experimental writing. Usually longer stories do not get accepted. There are exceptions, however."

HYCO REVIEW ARTS AND LITERARY JOURNAL

Piedmont Community College, P.O. Box 1197, Roxboro NC 27573. (336)599-1181, ext. 428. E-mail: reflect@piedmontcc.edu. Website: www.piedmontcc.edu. **Contact:** Dawn Langley, editor. Estab. 1999. Online magazine. 100-150 pages.

NEEDS Literary. "Accepts mss from Person and Caswell counties, NC or Piedmont Community college student or alumni authors only (residents or natives). If time and space permit, we'll consider submissions from other North Carolina authors." Publishes mss 6-10 months after acceptance. **Publishes 3-5 new writers/year.** Recently published work by Maureen Sherbondy, Dainiel Green, Betty Moffett, Lian Gouw, Sejal Badani Ravani, Donna Conrad. Max Length: 4,000 words; average length: 2,500 words. Publishes short shorts. Also publishes poetry and essays, photographs, videos, digital animation, and artwork.

HOW TO CONTACT Send SASE for return of ms or #10 SASE for reply only. Sample copy for $5. Writer's guidelines for SASE or by e-mail.

PAYMENT/TERMS Publication is online. Acquires first North American serial rights. Sponsors awards/contests.

TIPS "We look for good writing with a flair, which captivates an educated lay audience. Don't take rejection letters personally. We turn away many submissions simply because we don't have room for everything we like or because the author is not from our region. For that reason, we're more likely to accept shorter well-written stories than longer stories of the same quality. Also, stories containing profanity that doesn't contribute to the plot, structure or intended tone are rejected immediately."

IDEOMANCER

Wales. E-mail: publisher@ideomancer.com. Website: www.ideomancer.com. **Contact:** Leah Bobet, publisher. Estab. 2001. Online magazine. Contains illustrations. "*Ideomancer* publishes speculative fiction and poetry that explores the edges of ideas; stories that subvert, refute and push the limits. We want unique pieces from authors willing to explore non-traditional narratives and take chances with tone, structure and execution, balance ideas and character, emotion and ruthlessness. We also have an eye for more traditional tales told with excellence." Quarterly.

NEEDS fantasy (mythic, urban, historical, low, literary), horror (dark fantasy, futuristic, psychological, supernatural), science fiction (hard science/technological, soft/sociological). Special interests: slipstream, hyperfiction and poetry. Does not want fiction without a speculative element. Receives 160 mss/month. Accepts 3 mss/issue; 9-12 mss/year. Does not read February, May, August, and November. Ms published within 12 months of acceptance. **Publishes 1-2 new writers/year.** Published Sarah Monette, Ruth Nestvold, Christopher Barzak, Nicole Kornher-Stace, Tobias Buckell, Yoon Ha Lee, and David Kopaska-Merkel. Length: 7,000 words (max). Average length: 4,000 words. Publishes short shorts. Average length of short shorts: 1,000 words. Also publishes book reviews, poetry. *Requests only* to have a novel or collection reviewed should be sent to the publisher. Often comments on/critiques rejected mss.

HOW TO CONTACT Send complete ms with cover letter. Accepts submissions by e-mail only. Include estimated word count. Responds to queries in 1 week. Responds to mss in 4 weeks. Guidelines available on website.

PAYMENT/TERMS Writers receive 3¢ per word, max of $40. Pays on acceptance. Acquires electronic rights. Publication is copyrighted.

TIPS "Beyond the basics of formatting the fiction as per our guidelines, good writing and intriguing characters and plot, where the writer brings depth to the tale, make a manuscript stand out. We receive a number of submissions which showcase good writing, but lack the details that make them spring to life for us. Visit our website and read some of our fiction to see if we're a good fit. Read our submission guidelines carefully and use rtf formatting as requested. We're far more interested in your story than your cover letter, so spend your time polishing that."

MAD HATTERS' REVIEW: EDGY AND ENLIGHTENED ART, LITERATURE AND MUSIC IN THE AGE OF DEMENTIA

Carol Novack DBA Mad Hatters' Review, Wales. E-mail: madhattersreview@gmail.com. Website: www.madhattersreview.com. Queries re artworks, music, audios, collages, cartoons, reviews, interviews, and columns are welcome year-round. But please, not at this time, as we are only running reviews of books by our contributors. Online magazine. "*Mad Hatters' Review* is a socially aware/progressive, multimedia/literary journal, featuring original works of fiction, flash fiction, poetry, creative/literary nonfiction, whatnots, drama, collages, audios, book reviews, columns, contests and more. We also feature cartoons and comic strips, including the 'The Perils of Patriotic Polly' and 'Coconuts.' All of our contributing authors' writings are accompanied by original art created specifically for the material, as well as original, custom made music or recitations by authors. We are proud of our spectacular featured artists' galleries, as well as our mini-movies, parodies, and featured foreign sections. Our staff musicians and visual artists are wonderful." Semiannual. Member CLMP.

"*Mad Hatters' Review* has received an Artistry Award from Sixty Plus Design, 2006-7 Web Design Award from Invision Graphics, and a Gold Medal Award of Excellence for 2006-7 from ArtSpace2000.com."

NEEDS inventive works, mixed media, translations, humor, literary prose and poetry that demonstrate a unique, unconventional, intellectual, sophisticated and emotional perspective on the world and a delight in craft. Does not want mainstream prose/story that doesn't exhibit a love of language and a sophisticated mentality. No religious or inspirational writings, confessionals, boys sowing oats, sentimental, and coming-of-age stories. Accepts 3-6 mss/issue. Submissions are open briefly for each issue: check guidelines periodically for dates or subscribe free to newsletter. Ms published 5-6 months after acceptance. **Publishes 1 new writer/year.** Published Alastair Gray, Kass Fleisher, Vanessa Place, Harold Jaffe, Andrei Codrescu, Sheila Murphy, Simon Perchik, Terese Svoboda, Niels Hav, Martin, Nakell, and Juan Jose Millas (translated from the Spanish). Length: 3,000 words (max). Average length of fictions: 1,500-2,500 words. Publishes short shorts. Average length of short shorts: 500-800 words. Also publishes literary essays, literary criticism, book reviews, and interviews. Send review queries to: madhattersreview@gmail.com. Sometimes comments on/critiques rejected mss. "Our submissions period for Issue 13 will be from March 1-March 31, 2011. Submissions of poems, dramas, fictions, whatnots, creative nonfiction, wit & whimsies, and other categories detailed in our submission guidelines must be sent via our new online submissions form. All submissions, other than those detailed in our guidelines, will be deleted, unread. We are always looking for visual artists, experienced reviewers, and musicians. We do NOT respond to social networking invitations."

HOW TO CONTACT Accepts submissions by e-mail only. Include estimated word count, brief bio. Now has a submission form for most issues. Responds to queries in 1 week. Responds to mss in 1-6 weeks. Considers simultaneous submissions. Guidelines available on website. **Payment/Terms** Acquires first rights. Sends galleys to author. "We offer contests in most issues."

TIPS "Imagination, skill with and appreciation of language, inventiveness, rhythm, sense of humor/irony/satire and compelling style make a manuscript stand out. Read the magazine. Don't necessarily follow the rules you've been taught in the usual MFA program or workshop."

O MCCROSKEY MEMORIAL INTERNET PLAYHOUSE

MMIP, 416 101st Ave SE #308, Bellevue WA 98004. (206)417-5965. E-mail: administrator@theinternetplayhouse.com; submissions@theinternetplayhouse.com. Website: www.theinternetplayhouse.com. **Contact:** Jim Snowden, artistic director. Quarterly. Circ. 500. Publisher of short story collections, novellas, and novels. "We publish two short fiction collections per year, based on a theme posted on our website. We also take novels and novella length fiction. Query first. In addition, short stories selected for the anthology will be assigned to actors in the Seattle area and read for our podcast and in our live performance venue in Seattle." Payment: royalties. See guidelines for specifics. Publication is copyrighted. Acquires first English Anthology Rights (including e-book rights), onetime podcast performance rights.

NEEDS erotica, ethnic/multicultural (general), experimental, feminist, gay, historical (general), humor/satire, lesbian, literary, science fiction (other), translations. Does not want religious, romance, or fanfic. For upcoming themes, check the website. Accepts 6 mss/issue; 24 mss/year. Manuscript published 2 months after acceptance. Length: 2,000 words (min)-8,000 words (max). Also publishes poetry. Rarely comments on/critiques rejected manuscripts.

HOW TO CONTACT Please e-mail all submissions. Use .rtf, .doc, or Pages format for all manuscripts. Cover letters aren't required, but are welcome. Include brief bio, list of publications. Responds to mss in 3 months. Considers simultaneous submissions, previously published submissions, multiple submissions. Guidelines available on website.

PAYMENT/TERMS Writers receive 3 contributor's copies in the form of CD. Pays on publication. Acquires electronic rights. Sends galleys to author. Publication is not copyrighted.

TIPS "We're looking for a strong and original voice, a willingness to tackle uncomfortable subject matter, suitability for the all-audio format. Read the guidelines, read your work out loud, read everything you can, and send your best."

MCSWEENEY'S

849 Valencia St., San Francisco CA 94110. E-mail: printsubmissions@mcsweeneys.net; websubmissions@mcsweeneys.net. Website: www.mcsweeneys.net. Online literary journal. "Timothy McSweeney's *Internet Tendency* is an offshoot of Timothy McSweeney's *Quarterly Concern*, a journal created by nervous people in relative obscurity, and published four times a year." Daily.

NEEDS literate humor. Sometimes comments on rejected mss.

HOW TO CONTACT Accepts submissions by e-mail. "For submissions to the website, paste the entire piece into the body of an e-mail. Absolute length limit of 1,500 words, with a preference for pieces significantly shorter (700-1,000 words)." Sample copy online. Writer's guidelines online.

TIPS "Please read the writer's guidelines before submitting and send your submissions to the appropriate address." "Do not submit your work to both the print submissions address and the Web submissions address, as seemingly hundreds of writers have been doing lately. If you submit a piece of writing intended for the magazine to the Web submissions address, you will confuse us, and if you confuse us, we will accidentally delete your work without reading it."

◐ MICROHORROR: SHORT STORIES. ENDLESS NIGHTMARES

P.O. Box 32259, Pikesville MD 21282-2259. (443) 670-6133. E-mail: microhorror@gmail.com. Website: www.microhorror.com. **Contact:** Nathan Rosen, editor. Estab. 2006. Online magazine. "*MicroHorror* is not a magazine in the traditional sense. Instead, it is a free online archive for short-short horror fiction. With a strict limit of 666 words, *MicroHorror* showcases the power of the short-short horror to convey great emotional impact in only a few brief paragraphs." Estab. 2006.

Golden Horror Award from Horrorfind.com in 2007.

NEEDS horror (dark fantasy, futuristic, psychological, supernatural), young adult/teen (horror). Receives 25 mss/month. Accepts 300 mss/year. Ms published 1-3 days after acceptance. **Publishes 50 new writers/year.** Published Chris Allinotte, Kevin G. Bufton, Santiago Eximeno, Oonah V Joslin, Brian Laing, Caroline Robinson, and Chris Yodice. Length: 666 words (max). Publishes short shorts. Average length of short shorts: 500 words. Often comments on/critiques rejected mss.

HOW TO CONTACT Send complete ms with cover letter. Accepts submissions by e-mail. Include estimated word count, brief bio. Responds to queries in 1 week. Responds to mss in 1 week. Send either SASE (or IRC) for return of ms or disposable copy of ms and #10 SASE for reply only. Considers simultaneous submissions, previously published submissions, multiple submissions. Guidelines available on website.

PAYMENT/TERMS Acquires onetime rights. Publication is copyrighted.

TIPS "This is horror. Scare me. Make shivers run down my spine. Make me afraid to look behind the shower curtain. Pack the biggest punch you can into a few well chosen sentences. Read all the horror you can, and figure out what makes it scary. Trim away all the excess trappngs until you get right to the core, and use what you find."

◐ MIDWAY JOURNAL

P.O. Box 14499, St. Paul MN 55114. (612) 825-4811. E-mail: editors@midwayjournal.com. Website: www.midwayjournal.com. **Contact:** Ralph Pennel, fiction editor. Estab. 2006. Online magazine. "*Midway Journal* accepts submissions of aesthetically ambitious work that occupies the realms between the experimental and transitional. *Midway*, or its position is midway, is a place of boundary crossing, where work complicates and even questions the boundaries between forms, binaries and genres." Bimonthly. Member CLMP.

NEEDS comics/graphic novels, ethnic/multicultural (general), experimental, feminist, gay, historical (general), humor/satire, lesbian, literary, science fiction (soft/sociological), translations. Does not want new age, young adult/teen, children/juvenile or erotica. "Writers should visit current and back issues to see what we have or have not published in the past." Receives 30 mss/month. Accepts 3-4 mss/issue; 18-24 mss/year. Does not read June 1-Nov 30. Ms published 4-12 months after acceptance. Agented fiction 1%. **Publishes 2-5 new writers/year.** Published Steve Almond, Alden Jones, Scott T. Hutchinson, and Marjorie Maddox. Length: 250-25,000 words. Average length: 3,000 words. Publishes short shorts. Average length of short shorts: 600 words. Also publishes literary essays, poetry, and drama. Sometimes comments on/critiques rejected mss.

HOW TO CONTACT Send complete ms with cover letter. Accepts international submissions by e-mail. Include estimated word count, brief bio, list of publications. Responds to queries in 1-2 weeks. Please see website for submission guidelines. Send either SASE (or IRC) for return of ms or disposable copy of ms and #10 SASE for reply only. Considers simultaneous submissions, previously published submissions. Guidelines available on website.

PAYMENT/TERMS Acquires onetime rights. Publication is copyrighted.

TIPS "An interesting story with engaging writing, both in terms of style and voice, make a manuscript stand out. Round characters are a must. Writers who take chances either with content or with form grab an editor's immediate attention. Spend time with the words on the page. Spend time with the language. The language and voice are not vehicles, they, too, are tools."

NECROLOGY SHORTS: TALES OF MACABRE AND HORROR

Isis International, P.O. Box 510232, Saint Louis MO 63151. E-mail: editor@necrologyshorts.com; submit@necrologyshorts.com. Website: www.necrologyshorts.com. **Contact:** John Ferguson, editor. Estab. 2009. Consumer publication published online daily and through Amazon Kindle. "We will also be publishing an annual collection for each year in print, e-book reader, and Adobe PDF format. Our main genre is suspense horror similar to H.P. Lovecraft and/or Robert E. Howard. We also publish science fiction and fantasy. We would love to see work continuing the Cthulhu Mythos, but we accept all horror."

NEEDS "*Necrology Shorts* is an online publication which publishes fiction, articles, cartoons, artwork, and poetry daily. Embracing the Internet, e-book readers, and new technology, we aim to go beyond the long time standard of a regular publication to bringing our readers a daily flow of entertainment."

HOW TO CONTACT Submit complete ms. by e-mail to submit@necrologyshorts.com. Buys 1,000 mss/year. Responds in 1 month. Guidelines on website. We review submissions in the order we receive them. Please allow 1-2 weeks for us to review your work. If your submission passes review, it will be added to *Necrology Shorts* within 72 hours. You will be notified when your submission is posted. If your submission does not pass review, we will notify you of any problems and reasons. Submission can be resubmitted once it is corrected.

TIPS "*Necrology Shorts* is looking to break out of the traditional publication types to use the Internet, e-book readers, and other technology. We not only publish works of authors and artists, we let them use their published works to brand themselves and further their profits of their hard work. We love to see traditional short fiction and artwork, but we also look forward to those that go beyond that to create multimedia works. The best way to get to us is to let your creative side run wild and not send us the typical fare. Don't forget that we publish horror, sci-fi, and fantasy. We expect deranged, warped, twisted, strange, sadistic, and things that question sanity and reality."

NUVEIN ONLINE

(626)401-3466. E-mail: editor@nuvein.com. Website: http://nuvein.net; www.nuvein.org. Online magazine published by the Nuvein Foundation for Literature and the Arts. "We are open to short fiction, poetry and essays that explore topics divergent from the mainstream. Our vision is to provide a forum for new and experienced voices rarely heard in our global community."

Nuvein Online has received the Visionary Media Award.

NEEDS fiction, poetry, plays, movie/theatre reviews/articles and art. Wants more "experimental fiction, ethnic works, and pieces dealing with the exploration of gender and sexuality, as well as works dealing with the clash of cultures." **Publishes 20 new writers/year.** Recently published work by J. Knight, Paul A. Toth, Rick Austin, Robert Levin and Scott Essman, as well as interviews with film directors Guillermo Del Toro, Alejandro Gonzalez Iñarritu and Frank Darabont.

HOW TO CONTACT Query. Accepts submissions by e-mail. Send work as attachment. Sample copy online.

TIPS "Read over each submission before sending it, and if you, as the writer, find the piece irresistable, e-mail it to us immediately!"

ON THE PREMISES: A GOOD PLACE TO START

On the Premises, LLC, 4323 Gingham Court, Alexandria, VA 22310. (202)262-2168. E-mail: questions@onthepremises.com; tarlrk@coxnet. Website: www.OnThePremises.com. **Contact:** Tarl Roger Kudrick or Bethany Granger, Co-Publishers. E-zine. "Stories published in *On the Premises* are winning entries in contests that are held every four months. Each contest challenges writers to produce a great story based on a broad premise that our editors supply as part of the contest. *On the Premises* aims to promote newer and/or relatively unknown writers who can write what we feel are creative, compelling stories told in effective, uncluttered and evocative prose. Entrants pay no fees, and winners receive cash prizes in addition to publication." Triannual. Estab. 2006. Member Small Press Promotions.

NEEDS adventure, ethnic/multicultural (general), experimental, family saga, fantasy, feminist, historical (general), horror, humor/satire, literary, mainstream, military/war, mystery, new age, psychic/supernatural/occult, romance, science fiction, thriller/

espionage, western. Does not want young adult fiction, children's fiction, X-rated fiction. "In general, we don't like stories that were written solely to make a social or political point, especially if the story seems to assume that no intelligent person could possibly disagree with the author. Save the ideology for editorial and opinion pieces, please. But above all, we NEVER EVER want to see stories that do not use the contest premise! Use the premise, and make it 'clear' and 'obvious' that you are using the premise." Themes are announced the day each contest is launched. List of past and current premises available on website. Receives 20-100 mss/month. Accepts 3-6 mss/issue; 9-18 mss/year. Does not read February, June, and October. Ms published a month or less after acceptance. **Publishes 3-6 new writers/year.** Published A'llyn Ettien, Cory Cramer, Mark Tullius, Michael Van Ornum, Ken Liu and K. Stodard Hayes. Length: 1,000 words (min)-5,000 words (max). Average length: 3,500 words. Sometimes comments on/critiques rejected mss.

HOW TO CONTACT Send complete ms with cover letter. "We are a contest-based magazine and we strive to judge all entries 'blindly.' We request that an author's name and contact information be in the body of the email." Accepts submissions by e-mail only. Responds to mss in 2 weeks after contest deadline. Guidelines available on website.

PAYMENT/TERMS Writers receive $40-180. Pays on acceptance. Acquires electronic rights. Sends galleys to author. Publication is copyrighted.

TIPS "Make sure you use the premise, not just interpret it. If the premise is 'must contain a real live dog,' then think of a creative, compelling way to use a real dog. Revise you draft, then revise again and again. Remember, we judge blindly, so craftmanship and creativity matter, not how well known you are."

OPEN WIDE MAGAZINE

40 Wingfield Road, Lakenheath, Brandon SK Ip27 9HR UK. E-mail: contact@openwidemagazine.co.uk. Website: www.openwidemagazine.co.uk. **Contact:** Liz Roberts. Estab. 2001. Online literary magazine/journal: Quarterly.

NEEDS short fiction and poetry journal enjoys adventure, ethnic/multicultural, experimental, feminist, humor/satire, mainstream, mystery/suspense, principle beat. Receives 100 mss/month. Accepts 25 mss/issue. Manuscript published 3 months after acceptance. Publishes 30 new writers/year. Length: 500-4,000. Average length: 2,500. Publishes short shorts. Also publishes poetry, reviews (music, film, art) and interviews. Rarely comments on/critiques rejected mss.

HOW TO CONTACT Accepts submissions by e-mail and online. Include estimated word count, brief bio. Send either SASE (or IRC) for return of ms or disposable copy of ms and #10 SASE for reply only. The magazine costs just £1.00 for a PDF copy that is mailed to you at the e-mail address you provide us with via your Paypal account, unless you specify otherwise.

PAYMENT/TERMS Acquires onetime rights. Publication is copyrighted.

THE ORACULAR TREE

The Oracular Tree, 29 Hillyard St., Chatham ON N7L 3E1 Canada. E-mail: editor@oraculartree.com. Website: www.oraculartree.com. **Contact:** Jeff Beardwood, editor. E-zine specializing in practical ideas for transforming our lives. "The stories we tell ourselves and each other predict the outcome of our lives. We can affect gradual social change by transforming our deeply rooted cultural stories. The genre is not as important as the message and the high quality of the writing. We accept stories, poems, articles and essays which will reach well-educated, open-minded readers around the world. We offer a forum for those who see a need for change, who want to add their voices to a growing search for positive alternatives." Monthly. Estab. 1997. Circ. 250,000 hits/month.

NEEDS Serial fiction, poetry, essays, novels and novel excerpts, visual art, short fiction, news. "We'll look at any genre that is well written and can examine a new cultural paradigm. No tired dogma, no greeting card poetry, please." Receives 20-30 unsolicited mss/month. Accepts 80-100 mss/year. Publishes ms 3 months after acceptance. **Publishes 20-30 new writers/year.** Recently published work by Elisha Porat, Lyn Lyfshin, Rattan Mann, and Dr. Elaine Hatfield. Publishes short shorts. Also publishes literary essays, poetry. Often comments on rejected mss.

HOW TO CONTACT Send complete ms. Accepts submissions by e-mail. Responds in 2 weeks to queries; 2 months to mss. Accepts simultaneous, multiple submissions and reprints. Sample copy online. Writer's guidelines online.

PAYMENT/TERMS Author retains copyright; onetime archive posting.

TIPS "The underlying idea must be clearly expressed. The language should be appropriate to the tale, using creative license and an awareness of rhythm. We look for a juxtaposition of ideas that creates resonance in the mind and heart of the reader. Write from your honest voice. Trust your writing to unfold."

OUTER ART

The University of New Mexico, 200 College Road, Gallup NM 87301. (505) 863-7647. Fax: (505) 863-7532. E-mail: smarand@unm.edu. Website: www.gallup.unm.edu/~smarandache/a/outer-art.htm. **Contact:** Florentin Smarandache, editor. E-zine. Annual. Estab. 2000.

NEEDS experimental, literary, outer-art. Publishes ms 1 month after acceptance. Publishes short shorts. Also publishes literary essays, literary criticism.

HOW TO CONTACT Accepts submissions by e-mail. Send SASE (or IRC) for return of the ms. Responds in 1 month to mss. Accepts simultaneous submissions and reprints. Writer's guidelines online.

OXFORD MAGAZINE

365 Bachelor Hall, Miami University, Oxford OH 45056. (513) 529-1279. E-mail: oxmagfictioneditor@muohio.edu. Website: www.oxfordmagazine.org. **Contact:** Fiction editor. Estab. 1984. Annual. Circ. 1,000.

National literary magazine edited by students in the graduate program in the English department. Historically, these students have largely been MA students in creative writing. The magazine has featured both celebrated and new writers working in fiction, poetry, and creative nonfiction. Interviews, photography, and other visual art have also occasionally appeared in the journal, and the possibility of including literary criticism and reviews is currently on the table. *Oxford* has been awarded two Pushcart Prizes.

NEEDS Wants quality fiction and prose; genre is not an issue, but nothing sentimental. Receives 150 unsolicited mss/month. **Publishes some new writers/year.** Recently published work by Stephen Dixon, Andre Dubus and Stuart Dybek. Publishes short shorts. Also publishes poetry.

HOW TO CONTACT Responds in 2 months, depending upon time of submissions; mss received after December 31 will be returned. Accepts simultaneous submissions if notified. Sample copy for $5.

PAYMENT/TERMS Acquires one-time rights.

TIPS "*Oxford Magazine* accepts fiction, poetry, and essays (this last genre is a catch-all, much like the space under your couch cushions, and includes creative nonfiction, critical work exploring writing, and the like). Appearing once a year, *OxMag* is a Web-based journal that acquires first North American serial rights, one-time anthology rights and online serial rights. Simultaneous submissions are okay if you would kindly let us know if and when someone beats us to the punch."

PAPERPLATES

19 Kenwood Ave., Toronto ON M6C 2R8 Canada. (416)651-2551. E-mail: magazine@paperplates.org. Website: www.paperplates.org. **Contact:** Karl Buchner, fiction editor. Estab. 1990. Electronic magazine. Quarterly. Estab. 1990.

NEEDS condensed novels, ethnic/multicultural, feminist, gay, lesbian, literary, mainstream, translations. "No science fiction, fantasy or horror." Receives 12 unsolicited mss/month. Accepts 2-3 mss/issue; 6-9 mss/year. Publishes ms 6-8 months after acceptance. Recently published work by Lyn Fox, David Bezmozgis, Fraser Sutherland, and Tim Conley. Length: 1,500-3,500 words; average length: 3,000 words. Publishes short shorts. Also publishes literary essays, literary criticism, poetry.

HOW TO CONTACT Accepts submissions by e-mail and land mail. Responds in 6 weeks to queries; 6 months to mss. Accepts simultaneous submissions. Sample copy online. Writer's guidelines online.

PAYMENT/TERMS No payment. Acquires first North American serial rights.

THE PAUMANOK REVIEW

E-mail: submissions@paumanokreview.com. Website: www.paumanokreview.com. **Contact:** Katherine Arline, editor. Online literary magazine. "TPR is dedicated to publishing and promoting the best in world art and literature." Quarterly. Estab. 2000.

J.P. Maney's *Western Exposures* was selected for inclusion in the *E2INK Best of the Web Anthology*.

NEEDS mainstream, narrative, experimental, historical, mystery, horror, western, science fiction, slice-of-life vignette, serial, novel excerpt. Receives 100 unsolicited mss/month. Accepts 6-8 mss/issue; 24-32 mss/year. Publishes ms 6 weeks after acceptance. **Publishes 4 new writers/year.** Recently published work by Patty Friedman, Elisha Porat, Barry Spacks and Walt McDonald. Length: 1,000-6,000 words; average length: 3,000 words. Publishes short shorts. Also publishes literary essays, poetry. Usually comments on rejected mss.

HOW TO CONTACT Send complete ms as attachment (Word, RTF, HTML, TXT) or pasted in body of e-mail. Include estimated word count, brief bio, two ways to contact you, list of publications, and how you discovered *TPR*. Responds in 1 week to queries; 1 month to mss. Accepts simultaneous submissions and reprints. No multiple submissions. Sample copy online. Writer's guidelines online.

PAYMENT/TERMS Acquires onetime, anthology rights. Galleys offered in HTML or PDF format.

TIPS "Though this is an English-language publication, it is not US-or UK-centric. Please submit accordingly. *TPR* is a publication of Wind River Press, which also publishes *Critique* magazine and select print and electronic books."

PBW

513 N. Central Ave., Fairborn OH 45324. (937)878-5184. E-mail: rianca@aol.com. Estab. 1988. Electronic disk zine; 700 pages, specializing in avant-garde fiction and poetry. "*PBW* is an experimental floppy disk (CD-Rom) that prints strange and 'unpublishable' in an above-ground-sense writing." Twice per year.

HOW TO CONTACT "Manuscripts are only taken if they are submitted on disk or by e-mail." Send SASE for reply, return of ms. Sample copy not available.

PAYMENT/TERMS All rights revert back to author. Not copyrighted.

THE PEDESTAL MAGAZINE

6815 Honors Court, Charlotte NC 28210. (704)643-0244. E-mail: pedmagazine@carolina.rr.com. Website: www.thepedestalmagazine.com. **Contact:** Nathan Leslie, fiction editor; John Amen, editor-in-chief. Estab. 2000. Online literary magazine/journal. "We publish poetry, fiction, reviews and interviews. We are committed to the individual voice and publish an eclectic mix of high-quality work." Bimonthly. Member CLMP.

Pedestal 56 is now online.

NEEDS adventure, ethnic/multicultural, experimental, family saga, fantasy, feminist, gay, glitz, historical, horror, humor/satire, lesbian, literary, mainstream, military/war, mystery, new age, psychic/supernatural/occult, romance, science fiction, thriller/espionage. Receives 100-150 mss/month. Accepts 3-5 mss/issue; 18-24 mss/year. Closed to submissions at the following times: January, March, May, July, September, November: from the 12th-19th; February, April, June, August, October, December: from the 14th-28th. Ms published 1-3 weeks after acceptance. **Publishes 1-2 new writers/year.** Published Grant Tracy, Mary Grabar, Karen Heuler, James Scott Iredell, Don Shea, Mary Carroll-Hackett, R.T. Smith, and Richard Peabody. Publishes short shorts. Also publishes book reviews, poetry. Send review query to pedmagazine@carolina.rr.com. Rarely comments on/critiques rejected mss.

HOW TO CONTACT Submit via the online form provided on the website. Include brief bio, list of publications. Responds to queries in 2-3 days. Responds to mss in 4-6 weeks. Considers simultaneous submissions, multiple submissions. Guidelines available on website.

PAYMENT/TERMS Writers receive 8¢/word. Pays on publication. Acquires first rights. Sends galleys to author. Publication is copyrighted.

TIPS "If you send us your work, please wait for a response to your first submission before you submit again."

PERSIMMON TREE: MAGAZINE OF THE ARTS BY WOMEN OVER SIXTY

1534 Campus Drive, Berkeley CA 94708. E-mail: editor@persimmontree.org; Submissions@persimmontree.org. Website: www.persimmontree.org. **Contact:** Nan Gefen, editor. Online magazine. "*Persimmon Tree* is a showcase for the talent and creativity of women over sixty, but the magazine appeals to readers of all ages." Quarterly. Estab. 2007. Member Council of Literary Magazines.

NEEDS ethnic/multicultural (general), experimental, family saga, feminist, gay, historical (general), humor/satire, lesbian, literary, mainstream. Receives 80-100 mss/month. Accepts 2-3 mss/issue; 8-12 mss/year. Ms published 3-6 months after acceptance. **Publishes 2-3 new writers/year.** Published Grace Paley, Paula Gunn Allen, Daphne Muse, Carole Rosenthal and Sandy Boucher. Length: 1,200 words (min)-3,000 words (max). Average length: 2,000 words. Publishes short shorts. Also publishes literary essays, literary criticism, book reviews, poetry.

HOW TO CONTACT Send complete ms with cover letter. Accepts submissions by e-mail only at Submissions@persimmontree.org. Include estimated word count, brief bio, list of publications. Responds to mss in 3-6 months. Considers simultaneous submissions, multiple submissions. Guidelines available on website.

PAYMENT/TERMS Acquires onetime rights. Sends galleys to author. Publication is copyrighted.

TIPS "High quality of writing, an interesting or unique point of view, make a manuscript stand out. Make it clear that you're familiar with the magazine. Tell us why the piece would work for our audience."

THE PINK CHAMELEON

E-mail: dpfreda@juno.com. Website: www.thepinkchameleon.com. **Contact:** Mrs. Dorothy Paula Freda, editor/publisher. Estab. 2000. Reading period from January-April 30 and September-October 31.

NEEDS fiction and nonfiction short stories, adventure, family saga, fantasy, humor/satire, literary, mainstream, mystery/suspense, religious/inspirational, romance, science fiction, western, young adult/teen, psychic/supernatural. "No violence for the sake of violence." Receives 20 unsolicited mss/month. Publishes ms within 1 year after acceptance. **Publishes 50% new writers/year.** Recently published work by Deanne F. Purcell, Martin Green, Albert J. Manachino, James W. Collins, Ron Arnold, Sally Kosmalski, Susan Marie Davniero and Glen D. Hayes. Publishes short shorts. No novels or novel excerpts. Also publishes essays, poetry. Sometimes comments on rejected mss. Length: 500-2,500 words; average length: 2,000 words.

HOW TO CONTACT Send complete ms in the body of the e-mail. No attachments. Responds in 1 month to mss. Accepts reprints. No simultaneous submissions. Sample copy online. Writer's guidelines online.

PAYMENT/TERMS "Non-profit. Acquires onetime rights for one year but will return rights earlier on request."

TIPS "Simple, honest, evocative emotion, upbeat fiction and nonfiction submissions that give hope for the future; well-paced plots; stories, poetry, articles, essays that speak from the heart. Read guidelines carefully. Use a good, but not ostentatious, opening hook. Stories should have a beginning, middle and end that make the reader feel the story was worth his or her time. This also applies to articles and essays. In the latter two, wrap your comments and conclusions in a neatly packaged final paragraph. Turnoffs include violence, bad language. Simple, genuine and sensitive work does not need to shock with vulgarity to be interesting and enjoyable."

PREMONITIONS

Pigasus Press, 13 Hazely Combe, Arreton Isle of Wight PO30 3AJ United Kingdom. Website: www.pigasuspress.co.uk. E-mail: mail@pigasuspress.co.uk. **Contact:** Tony Lee, editor. "A magazine of science fiction, horror stories, genre poetry and fantastic artwork." Biannual.

NEEDS science fiction (hard, contemporary science fiction/fantasy). "No sword and sorcery, supernatural horror." Accepts 12 mss/issue.

HOW TO CONTACT "Unsolicited submissions are always welcome, but writers must enclose SAE/IRC for reply, plus adequate postage to return ms if unsuitable. No fiction or poetry submissions accepted via e-mail." Sample copy online.

TIPS "Potential contributors are advised to study recent issues of the magazine."

PSEUDOPOD

Escape Artists, Inc., P.O. Box 965609, Marietta GA 30066. Fax: (866)373-8739. E-mail: editor@pseudopod.org. E-mail: submit@pseudopod.org. Website: pseudopod.org. **Contact:** Shawn M. Garrett, editor. Online audio magazine. 25-40 min weekly episode, 5-10 min for sporadic specials like flash fiction or movie/book reviews. "*Pseudopod* is a genre magazine in audio form. We're looking for horror: dark, weird fiction. We run the spectrum from grim realism or magic-realism to blatantly supernatural dark fantasy. We publish highly literary stories reminiscent of Poe or Lovecraft, as well as vulgar, innovative, and/or shock-value-focused pulp fiction. We don't split hairs about genre definitions, and we don't have any hard and fast taboos about what kind of content can appear in our stories. Originality demands that you're better off avoiding vampires, zombies, and other recognizable horror tropes unless you have put a very original spin on them. (Ghosts are currently somewhat more smiled upon, mainly because they haven't settled into such predictably canonical treatment; you don't know what a ghost can do until the author establishes it, so fear of the unknown is intact—which is the real lesson here.) What matters most is just that the stories are dark and entertaining." Weekly.

NEEDS Horror (dark fantasy, futuristic, psychological, supernatural, sentimental, literary, erotic, splatterpunk, romantic, humorous). Does not want archetypical vampire, zombie, or werewolf fiction. Receives 100 mss/month. Accepts 1 mss/issue; 70 mss/year. Manuscript published 1 month after acceptance. **Publishes 20 new writers/year.** Published Joel Arnold, Kevin J. Anderson, Richard Dansky, Scott Sigler, Paul Jessup, Nicholas Ozment, and Stephen Gaskell. Length: 2,000-6,000 words. Average length: 3,000 words. Publishes short shorts. Average length of short shorts: 800 words. Often comments on/critiques rejected manuscripts.

HOW TO CONTACT Send complete ms with cover letter. Accepts submissions by e-mail. Include estimated word count, brief bio, brief list of publications. Responds to queries in 2 weeks. Responds to mss in 2 months. Considers simultaneous submissions, previously published submissions. Sample copy, guidelines available on website.

PAYMENT/TERMS Writers receive $20 over 2,000 words, $100 over 2,000 words. Pays on acceptance.

TIPS "Let the writing be guided by a strong sense of who the (hopefully somewhat interesting) protagonist is, even if zero time is spent developing any other characters. Preferably, tell the story using standard past tense, third person, active voice."

RAVING DOVE

P.O. Box 28, West Linn OR 97068. E-mail: editor@ravingdove.org; ravingdog@gmail.com. Website: www.ravingdove.org/. **Contact:** Jo-Ann Moss, editor. Estab. 2004. Online literary magazine. "Raving Dove publishes writing, poetry, and art with universal, anti-violence, anti-hate, human rights, and social justice themes. We share sentiments that oppose physical and psychological violence in all its forms, including war, discrimination against sexual orientation, and every shade of bigotry." Quarterly.

NEEDS literary, mainstream. "*Raving Dove* is not a political publication. Material for or against one specific person or entity will not be considered, fictitious or otherwise." Ms published up to 3 months after acceptance. Length: 2,000 words (max). Also publishes poetry.

HOW TO CONTACT Accepts submissions by e-mail only. Include brief bio, submission genre, i.e., fiction, nonfiction, poetry, etc., in the e-mail subject line. Responds to mss in 3 months. Considers simultaneous submissions. Guidelines available on website.

PAYMENT/TERMS Not currently a paying market. (Check website for current information.) Acquires onetime North American and Internet serial rights, exclusive for the duration of the edition in which the work appears (3 months).

RESIDENTIAL ALIENS

ResAliens Press, 7412 E Brookview Cir., Wichita KS 67226. E-mail: resaliens@gmail.com. Website: www.resaliens.com; residentialaliens.blogspot.com. **Contact:** Lyn Perry, founding editor. Estab. 2007. Online magazine/E-zine. "Because reading and writing speculative fiction is a strong interest of mine, I thought I'd contribute to the genre of faith-informed speculative fiction by offering other writers and readers of science fiction, fantasy, spiritual and supernatural thrillers a quality venue in which to share their passion. You could say *ResAliens* is speculative fiction with a spiritual thread." Monthly.

NEEDS fantasy (space fantasy, sword and sorcery), horror (supernatural), science fiction (soft/sociological), thriller. Does not want straight horror, gore, erotica. Will publish another sci-fi/fantasy anthology. List of upcoming themes available for SASE, on website. Receives 50 mss/month. Accepts 5-6 mss/issue; 65-75 mss/year. Ms published 1-2 months after acceptance. **Publishes 25 new writers/year.** Published George L. Duncan (author of novel *A Cold and Distant Memory*), Patrick G. Cox (author of novel *Out of Time*), Merrie Destefano (editor of *Victorian Homes Magazine*), Brandon Barr and Mike Lynch (authors of the science fiction novel *When the Sky Fell*; Ben Loory, *Stories for Nighttime and Some for the Day (*Penguin Press*)*. Length of short stories: 500-5,000 words. Average length: 3,500 words. Publishes short shorts. Average length of short shorts: 900 words. Will take serial novellas of 2-5 installments (up to 20,000 words). Also publishes book reviews. Send review copies to resaliens@gmail.com. Often comments on/critiques rejected mss.

HOW TO CONTACT Send complete ms with cover letter via e-mail. Include estimated word count, brief bio. Responds to queries in 2-5 days; to mss in 1-2 weeks. Considers simultaneous submissions, previously published submissions, multiple submissions. Sample copy and guidelines available on website.

PAYMENT/TERMS Writers receive PDF file as their contributor's copy. Acquires onetime rights, electronic rights, 6-month archive rights. Sends galleys to author. Publication is copyrighted. "Occasionally sponsors contests."

TIPS "We want stories that read well and move quickly. We enjoy all sorts of speculative fiction, and 'tried and true' forms and themes are fine as long as the author has a slightly different take or a fresh perspective on a topic. For example, time machine stories are great—how is yours unique or interesting?"

R-KV-R-Y, A QUARTERLY LITERARY JOURNAL

90 Meetings in 90 Days Press, 499 North Canon Dr., Suite 400, Beverly Hills CA 90210. E-mail: r.kv.r.y.editor@gmail.com. Website: www.rkvry.com. **Contact:** Mary Akers, editor-in-chief. Online magazine. 100 Web pages. Contains illustrations. Includes photographs. "*r.kv.r.y.* publishes three short stories of high literary quality every quarter. We publish fiction that varies widely in style. We prefer stories of character development, psychological penetration, and lyricism, without sentimentality or purple prose. We ask that all submissions address issues related to recovery from any type of physical, psychological, or cultural loss, dislocation or oppression. We include but do not limit ourselves to issues of substance abuse. We do not publish the standard 'what it was like, what happened and what it is like now' recovery narrative. Works published by *r.kv.r.y.* embrace almost every area of adult interest related to recovery: literary affairs, history, folklore, fiction, poetry, literary criticism, art, music, and the theatre. Material should be presented in a fashion suited to a quarterly that is neither journalistic nor academic. We welcome academic articles from varying fields. We encourage our academic contributors to free themselves from the contraints imposed by academic journals, letting their knowledge, wisdom, and experience rock and roll on these pages. Our intended audience is people of discriminating taste, original ideas, heart, and love of narrative and language." Quarterly. Estab. 2004. Circ. 15,000 quarterly readers.

NEEDS literary. List of upcoming themes available on website. Receives 30 stories/month. Accepts 3 stories/issue; 12 stories/year. Manuscript published 2-3 months after acceptance. Agented fiction 10%. **Publishes 5-6 new writers/year.** Published TJ Forrester, Kim Chinquee, Alicia Gifford, Andrew Tibbets, Jason Schneiderman. Length: 3,000 words (max). Average length: 2,000 words. Publishes short shorts. Average length of short shorts: 1,000 words. Also publishes literary essays, book reviews, poetry. Sometimes comments on/critiques rejected manuscripts.

HOW TO CONTACT Submit complete manuscript with cover letter through our on-line submission system. Responds to mss in 1-3 months. Considers simultaneous submissions, previously published submissions. Guidelines available on website.

PAYMENT/TERMS Acquires electronic rights. Posts proof pages on site. Publication is copyrighted.

TIPS "Wants strong focus on character development and lively writing style with strong voice. Read our present and former issues (archived online) as well as fiction found in such journals and magazines as *Granta, The New Yorker, Tri-Quarterly, The Atlantic, Harper's, Story* and similar sources of the highest quality fiction."

ROSE & THORN JOURNAL

Website: www.roseandthornjournal.com. **Contact:** Barbara Quinn. E-mail: editor@roseandthornjournal.com. Online journal specializing in literary works of fiction, nonfiction, poetry, and essays. "We created this publication for readers and writers alike. We provide a forum for emerging and established voices. We blend contemporary writing with traditional prose and poetry in an effort to promote the literary arts." Quarterly. Circ. 120,000.

NEEDS adventure, ethnic/multicultural, experimental, fantasy, historical, horror (dark fantasy, futuristic, psychological, supernatural), humor/satire, literary, mainstream, mystery/suspense, New Age, regional, religious/inspirational, romance (contemporary, futuristic/time travel, gothic, historical, regency, romantic suspense), science fiction, thriller/espionage, western. Receives "several hundred" unsolicited mss/month. Accepts 8-10 mss/issue; 40-50 mss/year. **Publishes many new writers/year.** Publishes short shorts. Also publishes literary essays, poetry. Sometimes comments on rejected mss.

HOW TO CONTACT Query with or without published clips or send complete ms. Accepts submissions by e-mail. Include estimated word count, 150-word bio, list of publications and author's byline. Responds in 1 week to queries; 1 month to mss. Accepts simultaneous submissions and reprints. Sample copy free. Writer's guidelines online. Length: 3,000 word limit.

PAYMENT/TERMS Writer retains all rights. Sends galleys to author. Pays $5 for each piece published.

TIPS "Clarity, control of the language, evocative stories that tug at the heart and make their mark on the reader long after it's been read. We look for uniqueness in voice, style and characterization. New twists on old themes are always welcome. Use all aspects of good writing in your stories, including dynamic characters, strong narrative voice and a riveting original plot. We have eclectic tastes, so go ahead and give us a shot. Read the publication and other quality literary journals so you'll see what we look for. Always check your spelling and grammar before submitting. Reread your submission with a critical eye and ask yourself, 'Does it evoke an emotional response? Have I completely captured my reader?' Check your submission for 'it' and 'was' and see if you can come up with a better way to express yourself. Be unique."

SHORT STORY AMERICA

Short Story America, LLC, 66 Thomas Sumter St., Beaufort SC 29907. (843)597-3220. E-mail: tim@shortstoryamerica.com; sarah@shortstoryamerica.com. Website: www.shortstoryamerica.com. **Contact:** Tim Johnston or Sarah Turocy, Acquisitions. Estab. 2010.

PAYMENT/TERMS "Pays $100 per story ($50 for flash), new or reprint, and authors also share in anthology and audio royalties as well."

TIPS "We want stories which readers will remember and want to read again. If your story entertains from the first page forward, and the pacing and conflict engages the reader's interest from plot, character and thematic standpoints, then please submit your story today! If the reader genuinely wants to know what eventually happens in your story, and is still thinking about it 10 minutes after finishing, then your story works."

SLOW TRAINS LITERARY JOURNAL

P.O. 4741, Denver CO 80155. E-mail: editor@slowtrains.com. Website: www.slowtrains.com. Estab. 2000.

NEEDS literary. No romance, sci-fi, or other specific genre-writing. Receives 100+ unsolicited mss/month. Accepts 10-15 mss/issue; 40-50 mss/year. Publishes ms 3 months after acceptance. **Publishes 20- 40 new writers/year.** Length: 1,000-5,000 words; average length: 3,500 words. Publishes short shorts. Also publishes literary essays, poetry. Rarely comments on rejected mss.

HOW TO CONTACT Accepts submissions by e-mail pasted into the body of the text. Responds in 2 months. Accepts simultaneous and reprints submissions. Sample copy online. Writer's guidelines online.

PAYMENT/TERMS Pays 2 contributor's copies. Acquires one-time, electronic rights with optional archiving.

TIPS "The first page must be able to pull the reader in immediately. Use your own fresh, poetic, compelling voice. Center your story around some emotional truth, and be sure of what you're trying to say."

SNREVIEW

197 Fairchild Ave., Fairfield CT 06825-4856. (203)366-5991. E-mail: editor@snreview.org. Website: www.snreview.org. **Contact:** Joseph Conlin, editor. Estab. 1999. E-zine, Kindle and print edition specializing in literary short stories, essays and poetry. "We search for material that not only has strong characters and plot but also a devotion to imagery." Now available in a print edition. Quarterly.

NEEDS literary, mainstream. Receives 300 unsolicited mss/month. Accepts 40+ mss/issue; 150 mss/year. Publishes ms 3 months after acceptance. **Publishes 75 new writers/year.** Recently published work by Frank X. Walker, Adrian Louis, Barbara Burkhardt, E. Lindsey Balkan, Marie Griffin and Jonathan Lerner. Length: 1,000-7,000 words; average length: 4,000 words. Also publishes literary essays, literary criticism, poetry.

HOW TO CONTACT Accepts submissions by e-mail only. Copy and paste work into the body of the e-mail. Don't send attachments. Include 100 word bio and list of publications. Responds in 7 months to mss. Accepts simultaneous submissions. Sample copy online. Writer's guidelines online. A print edition and a Kindle edition of *SNReview* is now available from an on-demand printer.

PAYMENT/TERMS Acquires first electronic and print rights.

SPACEWESTERNS: THE E-ZINE OF THE SPACE WESTERN SUB-GENRE

P.O. Box 93, Parker Ford PA 19457. Website: www.spacewesterns.com. E-mail: submissions2018@spacewesterns.com. **Contact:** N.E. Lilly, editor-in-chief. E-zine. "Aside from strictly short stories we also like to see stage plays, screen plays, comics, audio files of stories, short form videos and animation." Weekly. Estab. 2007.

NEEDS adventure, comics/graphic novels, ethnic/multicultural, fantasy (space fantasy), horror (dark fantasy, futuristic, psychological, supernatural), humor/satire, mystery, science fiction (hard science/technological, soft/sociological), western (frontier saga, traditional), but it *must be space western*, science fiction western. List of upcoming themes available on website. Receives 12 mss/month. Accepts 52 mss/year. Ms published within 6 months after acceptance. **Publishes 12 new writers/year.** Published Camille Alexa, Vonnie Winslow Crist, Jens Rushing, Amanda Spikol, Donald Jacob Uitvlugt, John M. Whalen, A.R. Yngve, Filamena Young. Length: 2,500-7,500 words. Average length: 4,000-5,000 words. Also publishes literary essays, literary criticism, book reviews, poetry. Send review copies to N. E. Lilly. Often comments on/critiques rejected mss.

HOW TO CONTACT Send complete ms with cover letter. Accepts submissions by e-mail only. Include estimated word count. Responds to queries immediately. Responds to mss in 6 weeks. Considers previously published submissions, multiple submissions. Guidelines available on website.

PAYMENT/TERMS Writers receive 1¢ per word, $50 max. Pays on publication. Publication is copyrighted.

TIPS "First of all, have a well-crafted manuscript (no spelling or grammar errors). Secondly, a good idea—many errors will be forgiven for a solid concept and fresh idea. Be yourself. Write what you love. Familiarize yourself with the scope of the Universe and astronomical concepts."

◐ STILL CRAZY

OH (614)746-0859. E-mail: editor@crazylitmag.com. Website: crazylitmag.com. **Contact:** Barbara Kussow, editor. "*Still Crazy* publishes writing by people over age 50 and writing by people of any age if the topic is about people over 50. The editor is particularly interested in material that challenges the stereotypes of older people and that portrays older people's inner lives as rich and rewarding." Semiannual.

Accepts 3-4 mss/issue; 6-8/year.

NEEDS feminist. Special interests: seniors (over 50). "Does not want material that is too sentimental or inspirational, 'Geezer' humor, or anything too grim." Accepts 3-4 mss/issue; 6-8 mss/year. Manuscript published 6-12 months after acceptance. Length: 3,500 words (max) under 2,500 words more likely to be published. Publishes short shorts. Sometimes features a "First Story," a story by an author who has not been published before. Also publishes poetry and short nonfiction 1,500 words or less. Sometimes comments on/critiques rejected mss. Paper copies $10; subscriptions $18 (2 issues per year); downloads $4.

HOW TO CONTACT Upload submissions via submissions manager on website. Attach MS Word doc or cut and paste into text of e-mail. Include estimated word count, brief bio, age of writer or "Over 50." Responds to mss in 3-5 months. Considers simultaneous submissions, previously published submissions (please indicate when and where), multiple submissions. Guidelines available on website.

PAYMENT/TERMS Acquires onetime rights. Publication is not copyrighted. Pays one contributor copy.

TIPS Looking for "interesting characters and interesting situations that might interest readers of all ages. Humor and Lightness welcome."

◐ STIRRING: A LITERARY COLLECTION

Stirring: A Literary Collection, c/o Erin Elizabeth Smith, Department of English, 301 McClung Tower, University of Tennessee, Knoxville TN 37996-0430. E-mail: eesmith81@gmail.com. Website: www.sundresspublications.com/stirring/. **Contact:** Erin Elizabeth Smith, managing editor. Estab. 1999.

"*Stirring* is one of the oldest continually-published literary journals on the web. *Stirring* is a monthly literary magazine that publishes poetry, short fiction, creative nonfiction, and photography by established and emerging writers."

HOW TO CONTACT For fiction and creative nonfiction, please send your submission as a Word or RTF document to Josh Webster at stirring.fiction@gmail.com. For all submissions, please include a brief biography in the body of the email.

◐ STORY BYTES

Website: www.storybytes.com. E-mail: editor@storybytes.com. Website: www.storybytes.com. **Contact:** M. Stanley Bubien, editor. Electronic zine. "We are strictly an electronic publication, appearing on the Internet in three forms. First, the stories are sent to an electronic mailing list of readers. They also get placed on our website, both in PDF and HTML format."

NEEDS "Stories must be very short—having a length that is the power of 2, specifically: 2, 4, 8, 16, 32, etc." No sexually explicit material. "Would like to see more material dealing with religion—not necessarily 'inspirational' stories, but those that show the struggles of living a life of faith in a realistic manner." **Publishes 33% new writers/year.** Recently published work by Richard K. Weems, Joseph Lerner, Lisa Cote, and Thomas Sennet.

HOW TO CONTACT Please query first. Query with or without published clips or send complete ms. Accepts submissions by e-mail. "I prefer plain text with story title, authorship and word count. Only accepts electronic submissions. See website for complete guidelines." Sample copy online. Writer's guidelines online.

TIPS "In *Story Bytes* the very short stories themselves range in topic. Many explore a brief event—a vignette of something unusual, unique and at times something even commonplace. Some stories can be bizarre, while others quite lucid. Some are based on actual events, while others are entirely fictional. Try to develop conflict early on (in the first sentence if possible!), and illustrate or resolve this conflict through action rather than description. I believe we'll find an audience for electronic published works primarily in the short story realm."

◐ STORYSOUTH

5603B W. Friendly Ave., Suite 282, Greensboro NC 27410. E-mail: terry@storysouth.com. Website: www.storysouth.com. **Contact:** Terry Kennedy, editor. Estab. 2001. "*storySouth* is interested in fiction, creative nonfiction, and poetry by writers from the New South. The exact definition of New South varies from person to person and we leave it up to the writer to define their own connection to the southern United States." Quarterly.

NEEDS experimental, literary, regional (South), translations. Receives 70 unsolicited mss/month. Accepts 5 mss/issue; 20 mss/year. Publishes ms 1 month after acceptance. **Publishes 5-10 new writers/year.** Average length: 4,000 words. Publishes short shorts. Also publishes literary essays, literary criticism, poetry. Often comments on rejected mss.

HOW TO CONTACT Send complete ms. Accepts online submissions only. Responds in 4 months to mss. Accepts simultaneous submissions. Writer's guidelines online.

PAYMENT/TERMS Acquires onetime rights.

TIPS "What really makes a story stand out is a strong voice and a sense of urgency—a need for the reader to keep reading the story and not put it down until it is finished."

○$ STRANGE HORIZONS

Strange Horizons, Inc., P.O. Box 1693, Dubuque IA 52004-1693. Website: http://strangehorizons.com. E-mail: fiction@strangehorizons.com. Online magazine. "We're a science fiction magazine dedicated to showcasing new voices in the genre." Weekly. Estab. 2000.

NEEDS fantasy (space fantasy, sword and sorcery), feminist, science fiction (hard science/technological, soft/sociological). Does not want horror; see website. Receives 300 mss/month. Accepts 48 or 50 mss/year. Does not read December. Ms published 2-4 months after acceptance. **Publishes 5-10 new writers/year.** Published Liz Williams, Charlie Anders, Elizabeth Bear, Carrie Vaughn, Benjamin Rosenbaum and Ruth Nestvold. Length: 2,000-8,000 words. Average length: 3,600 words. Publishes short shorts rarely. Also publishes literary essays, literary criticism, book reviews, poetry. Send review queries to reviews@strangehorizons.com. Rarely comments on/critiques rejected mss.

HOW TO CONTACT Accepts submissions by submission form online. Responds to queries in 1 week. Responds to mss in 3 months. Guidelines available on website.

PAYMENT/TERMS Writers receive 5¢ per word. Pays on acceptance. Acquires first rights,.

◐$ THE SUMMERSET REVIEW

25 Summerset Dr., Smithtown NY 11787. E-mail: editor@summersetreview.org. Website: www.summersetreview.org. **Contact:** Joseph Levens, editor. Estab. 2002. Magazine: illustrations and photographs. "Our goal is simply to publish the highest quality literary fiction and essays intended for a general audience. This is a simple online literary journal of high quality material, so simple you can call it unique." Periodically releases print issues. Quarterly.

NEEDS literary. No sci-fi, horror, or graphic erotica. Receives 150 unsolicited mss/month. Accepts 4 mss/issue; 18 mss/year. Publishes ms 2-3 months after acceptance. **Publishes 5-10 new writers/year.** Length: 8,000 words; average length: 3,000 words. Publishes short shorts. Also publishes literary essays. Usually critiques on mss that were almost accepted.

HOW TO CONTACT Send complete ms. Accepts submissions by e-mail. Responds in 1-2 weeks to queries; 4-12 weeks to mss. Accepts simultaneous and reprints submissions. Writer's guidelines online.

PAYMENT/TERMS Complimentary copy of back issue in print. Acquires no rights other than onetime publishing, although we request credit if first published in the *Summerset Review*. Sends galleys to author.

TIPS "Style counts. We prefer innovative or at least very smooth, convincing voices. Even the dullest of premises or the complete lack of conflict make for an interesting story if it is told in the right voice and style. We like to find little, interesting facts and/or connections subtly sprinkled throughout the piece. Harsh language should be used only if/when necessary. If we are choosing between light and dark subjects, the light will usually win."

TERRAIN.ORG: A JOURNAL OF THE BUILT & NATURAL ENVIRONMENTS

Terrain.org, P.O. Box 19161, Tucson AZ 19161. 520-241-7390. Website: www.terrain.org. **Contact:** Simmons Buntin, editor-in-chief. "Terrain.org is based on and thus welcomes quality submissions from new and experienced authors and artists alike. Our online journal accepts only the finest poetry, essays, fiction, articles, artwork, and other contributions' material that reaches deep into the earth's fiery core, or humanity's incalculable core, and brings forth new insights and wisdom. Sponsors *Terrain.org 2nd Annual Contest in Poetry, Fiction, and Nonfiction!* Submissions due by August 1. How to Submit: Go to Submission Manager Online Tool." "Terrain.org is searching for that interface—the integration—among the built and natural environments, that might be called the soul of place. The works contained within Terrain.org ultimately examine the physical realm around us, and how those environments influence us and each other physically, mentally, emotionally and spiritually." Semiannual.

Awards: PLANetizen Top 50 Website 2002 & 2003.

NEEDS adventure, ethnic/multicultural, experimental, family saga, fantasy, feminist, historical, horror, humor/satire, literary, mainstream, military/war, mystery, psychic/supernatural/occult, science fiction, thriller/espionage, translations, western. Special interests: environmental. Does not want erotica. All issues are theme-based. List of upcoming themes available on website. Receives 25 mss/month. Accepts 3-5 mss/issue; 6-10 mss/year. Does not read August 1-September 30 and February 1-March 30. Manuscript published five weeks to 18 months after acceptance. Agented fiction 5%. **Publishes 1-3 new writers/year.** Published Al Sim, Jacob MacAurthur Mooney, T.R. Healy, Deborah Fries, Andrew Wingfield, Braden Hepner, Chavawn Kelly, Tamara Kaye Sellman. Length: 1,000-8,000 words. Average length: 5,000 words. Publishes short shorts. Average length of short shorts: 750 words. Also publishes literary essays, literary criticism, book reviews, poetry, articles, and artwork. Send review copies to Simmon Buntin. Sometimes comments on/critiques rejected mss.

HOW TO CONTACT Send complete ms with cover letter. Accepts submissions online@ http://sub.terrain.org. Include brief bio. Responds to queries in 2 weeks. Responds to mss in 8-12 weeks. Considers simultaneous submissions, previously published submissions. Guidelines available on website.

PAYMENT/TERMS Acquires onetime rights. Sends galleys to author. Publication is copyrighted.

TIPS "We have three primary criteria in reviewing fiction: 1) The story is compelling and well-crafted. 2) The story provides some element of surprise; i.e., whether in content, form or delivery we are unexpectedly delighted in what we've read. 3) The story meets an upcoming theme, even if only peripherally. Read fiction in the current issue and perhaps some archived work, and if you like what you read—and our overall enviromental slant—then send us your best work. Make sure you follow our submission guidelines (including cover note with bio), and that your manuscript is as error-free as possible."

TOAD SUCK REVIEW

Univ. of Central Arkansas, Dept. of Writing, Conway AR 72035. E-mail: toadsuckreview@gmail.com. Website: http://toadsuckreview.org. **Contact:** Mark Spitzer, Editor. Estab. 2011. 6 x 11 magazine, 150 pages, 70 lb. white. Illustrations and photographs. Accepts outstanding work by beginning and established writers. Born from the legendary *Exquisite Corpse Annual*, the innovative *Toad Suck Review* is a cutting-edge mixture of poetry, fiction, creative nonfiction, translations, reviews, and artwork with a provocative sense of humor and an interest in diverse cultures and politics. Publishes short shorts; average length: 500 words. No themes planned for 2012 issues. Reads mss in the fall. Published Kevin Brockmeie, Teresa Bergen, Daniel Grandbois, William Lychack. Publishes 5 unpublished writers each year. Rarely comments on rejected mss. Responds to ms in 1 week to 9 months. Acquires onetime rights.

No themes planned for 2012 issues. No agented submissions. Does not send prepublication galleys to author. Publication is copyrighted. Annual. 6 x 11. All forms and styles are welcome, especially those that take risks and shoot for something new.Has published poetry by Lawrence Ferlinghetti, Antler, Jack Hirschman, Jack Collom, Lyn Lifshin, Jacques Prevert. Professionally printed with perfect bound flat spine; full cover cardstock cover. Does not include ads. Press run is 1,000-2,000; goes to 10 libraries, 3 shelf sales; 333 distributed free to select reviewers. Single copy: $15 subscription (lifetime) $100. Make checks payable to UCA. Submit 1-10 poems at a time. Lines/poem: 1-111. Accepts e-mail submissions as attached document. Cover letter is required. Please send SASE with postal submissions. Reads in the fall. Does not charge reading fees. Sometimes publishes theme issues. Sometimes comments on rejected poems. Never sends prepublication galleys. Sometimes comments on rejected poems. Does not charge criticism fees. Reviews books of poetry, chapbooks of poetry, and other magazines/journals.

HOW TO CONTACT Send cover letter with complete disposable copy of ms, brief bio, and list of publications.

PAYMENT/TERMS Pays contributor's copies.

TIPS "See a recent issue or a back issue of the *Exquisite Corpse Annual* for an idea of our aesthetics." "Our guidelines are very open and ambiguous. Don't send us too much and don't make it too long. If you submit in an email, use rtf. We're easy. If it works, we'll be in touch." "It's a brutal world—wear your helmet."

O TOASTED CHEESE

E-mail: editors@toasted-cheese.com; submit@toasted-cheese.com. Website: www.toasted-cheese.com. Estab. 2001. E-zine specializing in fiction, creative nonfiction, poetry and flash fiction. "*Toasted Cheese* accepts submissions of previously unpublished fiction, flash fiction, creative nonfiction and poetry. Our focus is on quality of work, not quantity. Some issues will therefore contain fewer/more pieces than previous issues. We don't restrict publication based on subject matter. We encourage submissions from innovative writers in all genres." Quarterly.

NEEDS adventure, children's/juvenile, ethnic/multicultural, fantasy, feminist, gay, historical, horror, humor/satire, lesbian, literary, mainstream, mystery/suspense, New Age, psychic/supernatural/occult, romance, science fiction, thriller/espionage, western. "No fan fiction. No chapters or excerpts unless they read as a stand-alone story. No first drafts." Receives 150 unsolicited mss/month. Accepts 1-10 mss/issue; 5-30 mss/year. **Publishes 15 new writers/year.** Publishes short shorts. Also publishes poetry.

HOW TO CONTACT Send complete ms in body of e-mail; no attachments. Accepts submissions by e-mail. Responds in 4 months to mss. No simultaneous submissions. Sample copy online. Follow online submission guidelines.

PAYMENT/TERMS Acquires electronic rights. Sponsors awards/contests.

TIPS "We are looking for clean, professional writing from writers of any level. Accepted stories will be concise and compelling. We are looking for writers who are serious about the craft: tomorrow's literary stars before they're famous. Take your submission seriously, yet remember that levity is appreciated. You are submitting not to traditional 'editors' but to fellow writers who appreciate the efforts of those in the trenches." "Follow online submission guidelines."

TOWER OF LIGHT FANTASY FREE ONLINE

9701 Harford Road, Carney MD 21234. E-mail: msouth847@yahoo.com. Website: www.tolfantasy.net. **Contact:** Michael Southard, editor. Online magazine. "To publish great fantasy stories, especially the genre-blending kind such as dark fantasy, urban, science, and superhero fantasy. Romantic fantasy (not erotic, however) is also acceptable. And *Tower of Light* would very much like to showcase new work by beginning writers." Biannual. Estab. 2007.

NEEDS fantasy (space fantasy, sword and sorcery), horror (dark fantasy, futuristic, supernatural), psychic/supernatural/occult, religious (fantasy), romance (fantasy). Does not want erotic fantasy, or anything that does not have a mystical or supernatural element. List of upcoming themes available on website. Receives 15-30 mss/month. Accepts 6 mss/issue; 12 mss/year. Reading period: Jan 1-Mar 31; July 1-Aug 31. Ms published 6-12 months after acceptance. Published Ian Whates, Christopher Heath, Tom Williams, Daniel Henderson, Alice M. Roelke, Matthew Baron,

Eric S. Brown, Ryder Patzuk-Russell, and Mischell Lyne. Length: 500-4,000 words. Average length: 3,500 words. Publishes short shorts. Also publishes book reviews. Send review copies to Michael Southard. Sometimes comments on/critiques rejected mss.

HOW TO CONTACT Send ms in the body of e-mail. Unfortunately, artwork must be sent as an attachment. Responds to mss in 6-12 weeks. Considers previously published submissions, multiple submissions. Guidelines, sample copy available on website.

PAYMENT/TERMS Writers and artists receive $5. Pays on publication. Acquires onetime rights, electronic rights. Occasionally sends galleys to author. Publication is not copyrighted.

TIPS "Strong, well-developed characters that really elicit an emotional response, good writing, original plots and world-building catch my attention. Send me a good story, and make sure to check your spelling and grammar. I don't mind a couple of errors, but when there's more than half a dozen, it gets really irritating. Make sure to study the guidelines thoroughly; I'm looking for character-driven stories, preferably in third person limited point-of-view."

VERBSAP.COM, CONCISE PROSE. ENOUGH SAID.

AL Website: www.verbsap.com. E-mail: editor@verbsap.com. **Contact:** Laurie Seider, editor. Online magazine. "Verbsap showcases an eclectic selection of the finest in concise prose by established and emerging writers." Published quarterly. Estab. 2005.

NEEDS literary, mainstream. Does not want violent, racist or pornographic content. Accepts 200 mss/year. Ms published 2-4 weeks after acceptance. Length: 3,000 words (max). Average length: 2,000 words. Publishes short shorts. Average length of short shorts: 900 words. Also publishes literary essays, author and artist interviews, and book reviews. Always comments on/critiques rejected mss.

HOW TO CONTACT Follow online guidelines. Accepts submissions by e-mail. Responds to mss in 1-3 weeks. Considers simultaneous submissions. Guidelines available on website.

PAYMENT/TERMS Sends galleys to author. Publication is copyrighted.

TIPS "We're looking for stark, elegant prose. Make us weep or make us laugh, but move us. You might find our 'Editor's Notebook' essays helpful."

WEB DEL SOL

Wed del Sol Association, 2020 Pennsylvania Ave. NW, Suite 443, Washington D.C. 20006. E-mail: editor@webdelsol.com. Website: www.webdelsol.com. **Contact:** Michael Neff, editor-in-chief. Estab. 1994. Electronic magazine. "The goal of *Web Del Sol* is to use the medium of the Internet to bring the finest in contemporary literary arts to a larger audience. To that end, *WDS* not only web-publishes collections of work by accomplished writers and poets, but hosts over 25 literary arts publications on the WWW such as *Del Sol Review, North American Review, Global City Review, The Literary Review* and *The Prose Poem*." Estab. 1994.

NEEDS Literary. "*WDS* publishes work considered to be literary in nature, i.e. non-genre fiction. *WDS* also publishes poetry, prose poetry, essays and experimental types of writing." **Publishes 100-200 new writers/year.**

HOW TO CONTACT "Submissions by e-mail from September through November and from January through March only. Submissions must contain some brief bio, list of prior publications (if any), and a short work or portion of that work, neither to exceed 1,000 words. Editors will contact if the balance of work is required." Sample copy online.

TIPS "*WDS* wants fiction that is absolutely cutting edge, unique and/or at a minimum, accomplished with a crisp style and concerning subjects not usually considered the objects of literary scrutiny. Read works in such publications as *Conjunctions* (www.conjunctions.com) and *North American Review* (webdelsol.com/NorthAmReview/NAR) to get an idea of what we are looking for."

WHITE FUNGUS: AN EXPERIMENTAL ARTS MAGAZINE

P.O. Box 6173, Wellington, Aotearoa, New Zealand. (64)4 382 9113. E-mail: whitefungusmail@yahoo.com. Website: www.whitefungus.com **Contact:** Ron Hanson, Editor. Literary magazine/journal. Oversize A5, 104 pages, matte paper, matte card cover. Contains illustrations, photographs. "*White Fungus* covers a range of experimental arts including literature, poetry, visual arts, comics and music. We are interested in material that is bold, innovative and well-researched. Independence of thought and meaningful surprises are a high priority." Semiannual. Estab. 2004. Circ. 2,000.

NEEDS comics/graphic novels, ethnic/multicultural, experimental, feminist, gay, historical (general), humor/satire, lesbian, literary, science fiction. "*White Fungus* considers submissions on the basis of quality rather than genre." Receives 20 mss/month. Accepts 3 mss/issue; 6 mss/year. Ms published 1-12 months after acceptance. **Publishes 2 new writers/year.** Published Hamish Low, Cyril Wong, Aaron Coyes, Hamish Wyn, Tim Bollinger, Kate Montgomery, Tessa Laird, and Tobias Fischer. Average length: 1,200 words. Publishes short shorts. Average length of short shorts: 1,000 words. Also publishes literary criticism, poetry. Sometimes comments on/critiques rejected mss.

HOW TO CONTACT Query with clips of published work. Accepts submissions by e-mail, on disk. Include brief bio, list of publications. Responds to queries in 1 week. Responds to mss in 1 week. Send either SASE (or IRC) for return of ms or disposable copy of ms and #10 SASE for reply only. Considers simultaneous submissions, multiple submissions. Sample copy available for $10. Guidelines available via e-mail.

PAYMENT/TERMS Writers receive 10 contributor's copies, free subscription to the magazine. Additional copies $6. Pays on publication. Acquires first rights. Publication is copyrighted.

TIPS "We like writing that explores the world around it rather than being self-obsessed. We're not interested in personal fantasies or self-projections, just an active critical response to one's enviroment. Be direct, flexible and consider how your work might be considered in an international context. What can you contribute or shed light on?"

WHOLE LIFE TIMES

Whole Life Media, LLC, 23705 Vanowen St., #306, West Hills CA 91307. (877)807-2599. Fax: (310)933-1693. E-mail: editor@wholelifemagazine.com. Website: www.wholelifemagazine.com. Estab. 1979. Online market. "*WLT* accepts up to three longer stories (800-1,100 words) per issue, and payment ranges from $150-200 depending on topic, research required and writer experience. In addition, we have a number of regular departments that pay $75-150 depending on topic, research required and writer experience. City of Angels is our FOB section featuring short, newsy blurbs on our coverage topics, generally in the context of LA. These are generally 200-400 words and pay $25-35 depending on length and topic. This is a great section for writers who are new to us. BackWords is a 750-word personal essay that often highlights a seminal moment or event in the life of the writer and pays $100. *WLT* has editorial exchange relationships with local magazines in San Francisco and Chicago that occasionally co-assign (and increase the fee paid) or reprint at 50%. In the event that the magazine decides not to publish your assigned story, a kill fee of 50 percent of the original fee is offered. However, no kill fee is offered for unsolicited submissions or if this is your first assignment with us; you are free to publish the work elsewhere. If we do print your work, we customarily pay within 30-45 days of publication. We pay by invoice, so please be sure to submit one, and name the file with your name. We ask for one-time print rights and non-exclusive perpetual web publishing rights. Thank you for your interest in *Whole Life Times*, voice of the Los Angeles community for 33 years."

"We are a regional publication and favor material that somehow links to our area via topics, sources, similar.

HOW TO CONTACT We accept articles at any time by e-mail. If you would like your article to be considered for a specific issue, we should have it in hand 2-4 months before the issue of publication. Original photos and illustrations are welcome and may be submitted along with your article for consideration. If you are sending very large images, graphs, or other original art, please e-mail us for ftp submission guidelines. Please include a one-sentence credit line to accompany your story. If you do not include it, the story will run with your byline only.

TIPS "Send complete ms. Submissions are accepted via email. Artwork should also be sent via email as hard copies will not be returned. "Queries should be professionally written and show an awareness of current topics of interest in our subject area. We welcome investigative reporting and are happy to see queries that address topics in a political context. We are especially looking for articles on health and nutrition. No regular columns sought." Submissions should be double-spaced in AP style as an attached unformatted MS Word file (.doc). If you do not have Microsoft Word and must email in another program, please also copy and paste your story in the message section of your email."

WILD VIOLET

P.O. Box 39706, Philadelphia PA 19106-9706. E-mail: wildvioletmagazine@yahoo.com. Website: www.wild-violet.net. **Contact:** Alyce Wilson, editor. Estab. 2001. Online magazine: illustrations, photos. "Our goal is to make a place for the arts: to make the arts more accessible and to serve as a creative forum for writers and artists. Our audience includes English-speaking readers from all over the world, who are interested in both 'high art' and pop culture." Quarterly.

NEEDS comics/graphic novels, ethnic/multicultural, experimental, fantasy (space fantasy, sword and sorcery), feminist, gay, horror (dark fantasy, futuristic, psychological, supernatural), humor/satire, lesbian, literary, New Age, psychic/supernatural/occult, science fiction. "No stories where sexual or violent content is just used to shock the reader. No racist writings." Receives 30 unsolicited mss/month. Accepts 5 mss/issue; 20 mss/year. **Publishes 30 new writers/year.** Recently published work by Rik Hunik, Wayne Scheer, Jane McDonald, Mark Joseph Kiewlak, T. Richard Williams, and Susan Snowden. Length: 500-6,000 words; average length: 3,000 words. Also publishes literary essays, literary criticism, poetry. Sometimes comments on rejected mss.

HOW TO CONTACT Send complete ms. Accepts submissions by e-mail. Include estimated word count and brief bio. Send SASE for return of ms or send a disposable copy of ms and #10 SASE for reply only. Responds in 1 week to queries; 3-6 months to mss. Accepts simultaneous, multiple submissions. Sample copy online. Writer's guidelines by e-mail.

PAYMENT/TERMS Writers receive bio and links on contributor's page. Request limited electronic rights, for online publication and archival only. Sponsors awards/contests.

TIPS "We look for stories that are well-paced and show character and plot development. Even short shorts should do more than simply paint a picture. Manuscripts stand out when the author's voice is fresh and engaging. Avoid muddying your story with too many characters and don't attempt to shock the reader with an ending you have not earned. Experiment with styles and structures, but don't resort to experimentation for its own sake."

WORD RIOT

P.O. Box 414, Middletown NJ 07748-3143. (732)706-1272. Fax: (732)706-5856. E-mail: wr.submissions@gmail.com. Website: www.wordriot.org. **Contact:** Jackie Corley, publisher. Estab. 2002. Online magazine. Monthly. Member, CLMP.

NEEDS humor/satire, literary, mainstream. "No fantasy, science fiction, romance." Accepts 20-25 mss/issue; 240-300 mss/year. Publishes ms 1-2 months after acceptance. Agented fiction 5%. Publishes 8-10 new writers/year. Length: 300-6,000 words; average length: 2,700 words. Publishes flash fiction, short stories, creative nonfiction and poetry. Also publishes literary essays, poetry. Often comments on rejected mss.

HOW TO CONTACT Accepts submissions by e-mail; also by online submission form at wordriot.submishmash.com/Submit. Do not send submissions by mail. Include estimated word count and brief bio. Responds in 4-6 weeks to mss. Accepts multiple submissions. Sample copy online. Writer's guidelines online.

PAYMENT/TERMS Acquires electronic rights. Not copyrighted. Sponsors awards/contests.

TIPS "We're always looking for something edgy or quirky. We like writers who take risks."

THE WRITE PLACE AT THE WRITE TIME

E-mail: submissions@thewriteplaceatthewritetime.org. Website: www.thewriteplaceatthewritetime.org. **Contact:** Nicole M. Bouchard, Editor-in-Chief. Estab. 2008.

"We encourage new and seasoned writers to send in submissions for the next issue, benefit from resources we provide, read the current issue and enjoy themselves. It's a supportive writers' environment dedicated to artistic expression, learning and living the written word. We are a quarterly publication and our writers range from previously unpublished to having written for *The New York Times, Newsweek*, HBO, and *Business Week* and they come from all over the US and Europe." Frequently comments on rejected mss.

HOW TO CONTACT Send complete ms with cover letter by e-mail. Include est. word count, brief bio. Accepts multiple submissions, up to 3 fiction/nonfiction stories or 5 poems at a time.

PAYMENT/TERMS We are not currently offering monetary compensation.

TIPS "We sponsor writer's contests—visit the website for details." Our publication is copyrighted. Sends prepublication galleys to author depending on whether the story underwent significant edits. We like to work closely with our writers. If the material is only slightly edited, then we don't.

CONSUMER MAGAZINES

In this section of *Novel & Short Story Writer's Market* are consumer magazines with circulations of more than 10,000. Many have circulations in the hundreds of thousands or millions. And among the oldest magazines listed here are ones not only familiar to us, but also to our parents, grandparents, and even great-grandparents: *Atlantic Monthly* (1857); *Esquire* (1933); and *Ellery Queen's Mystery Magazine* (1941).

Consumer periodicals make excellent markets for fiction in terms of exposure, prestige and payment. Because these magazines are well-known, however, competition is great. Even the largest consumer publications buy only one or two stories an issue, yet thousands of writers submit to these popular magazines.

Despite the odds, it is possible for talented new writers to break into print in the magazines listed here. Your keys to breaking into these markets are careful research, professional presentation and, of course, top-quality fiction.

TYPES OF CONSUMER MAGAZINES

In this section you will find a number of popular publications, some for a broad-based, general-interest readership and others for large but select groups of readers—children, teenagers, women, men and seniors. There are also religious and church-affiliated magazines, publications devoted to the interests of particular cultures and outlooks, and top markets for genre fiction.

SELECTING THE RIGHT MARKET

Unlike smaller journals and publications, most of the magazines listed here are available at newsstands and bookstores. Many can also be found in the library, and guidelines and sample copies are almost always available by mail or online. Start your search by reviewing the listings; then familiarize yourself with the fiction included in the magazines that interest you.

Don't make the mistake of thinking that just because you are familiar with a magazine, their fiction is the same today as when you first saw it. Nothing could be further from the truth. Consumer magazines, no matter how well established, are constantly revising their fiction needs as they strive to expand their audience base.

In a magazine that uses only one or two stories an issue, take a look at the nonfiction articles and features as well. These can give you a better idea of the audience for the publication and clues to the type of fiction that might appeal to them.

FURTHERING YOUR SEARCH

See You've Got a Story (page 2) for information about the material common to all listings in this book. In this section in particular, pay close attention to the number of submissions a magazine receives in a given period and how many they publish in the same period. This will give you a clear picture of how stiff your competition can be.

While many of the magazines listed here publish one or two pieces of fiction in each issue, some also publish special fiction issues once or twice a year. When possible, we have indicated this in the listing information. We also note if the magazine is open to novel excerpts as well as short fiction, and we advise novelists to query first before submitting long work.

The Business of Fiction Writing, beginning on page 65, covers the basics of submitting your work. Professional presentation is a must for all markets listed. Editors at consumer magazines are especially busy, and anything you can do to make your manuscript easy to read and accessible will help your chances of being published. Most magazines want to see complete manuscripts, but watch for publications in this section that require a query first.

As in the previous section, we've included our own comments in many of the listings, set off by a bullet ○. Whenever possible, we list the publication's recent awards and honors. We've also included any special information we feel will help you in determining whether a particular publication interests you.

The maple leaf symbol ○ identifies our Canadian listings. You will also find some English-speaking markets from around the world. These foreign magazines are denoted with ● at the beginning of the listings. Remember to use International Reply Coupons rather than stamps when you want a reply from a country other than your own.

ADORNMENT

Association for the Study of Jewelry & Related Arts, 246 N. Regent St., Port Chester NY 10573. E-mail: ekarlin@usa.net. Website: www.jewelryandrelatedarts.com; www.asjra.net. Estab. 2002.

"My readers are collectors, appraisers, antique jewelry dealers, gemologists, jewelry artists, museum curators—anyone with an interest in jewelry."

TIPS "Know your subject and provide applicable credentials."

ADVOCATE, PKA'S PUBLICATION

1881 Little Westkill Rd., Prattsville NY 12468. (518)299-3103. E-mail: advoad@localnet.com. Website: http://Advocatepka.weebly.com or www.facebook.com/pages/Advocate-PKAs-Publication/111826035499969. **Contact:** Patricia Keller, publisher. Estab. 1987. Tabloid: 9 3/8×12¼; 20-24 pages; newsprint paper; line drawings; color and b&w photographs. "Eclectic for a general audience." Bimonthly. Estab. 1987. Circ. 10,000. *The Gaited Horse Newsletter* is currently published within the pages of PKA's *Advocate*." Receives 60 unsolicited mss/month. Accepts 6-8 mss/issue; 34-48 mss/year. Publishes ms 4 months to 1 year after acceptance. Also publishes poetry. Sometimes comments on rejected mss.

Gaited Horse Association newsletter is included in this publication. Horse-oriented stories, poetry, art and photos are currently needed.

NEEDS adventure, children's/juvenile (5-9 years), ethnic/multicultural, experimental, fantasy, feminist, historical, humor/satire, literary, mainstream, mystery/suspense, regional, romance, science fiction, western, young adult/teen (10-18 years), contemporary, prose poem, senior citizen/retirement, sports. "Nothing religious, pornographic, violent, erotic, pro-drug or anti-enviroment. Currently looking for equine (horses) stories, poetry, art, photos and cartoons."

HOW TO CONTACT Send a complete ms with cover letter. Responds in 2 months to mss. Sample copy for $5 (US currency for inside US; $6.50 US currency for Canada). Writer's Guidelines with purchase of sample copy.

PAYMENT/TERMS Pays contributor copies. Acquires first rights.

TIPS "Please, no simultaneous submissions, work that has appeared on the Internet, pornography, overt religiousity, anti-environmentalism or gratuitous violence. Artists and photographers should keep in mind that we are a b&w paper. Please do not send postcards. Use envelope with SASE."

AFRICAN AMERICAN REVIEW

St. Louis University, 317 Adorjan Hall, 3800 Lindell Blvd., St. Louis MO 63108. (314)977-3688. Fax: (314)977-1514. E-mail: keenanam@slu.edu. Website: aar.slu.edu. Estab. 1967. Magazine: 7X10; 200 pages; 55 lb., acid-free paper; 100 lb. skid stock cover; illustrations; photos. "Essays on African-American literature, theater, film, art and culture generally; interviews; poetry and fiction; book reviews." Quarterly. Circ. 2,000.

African American Review is the official publication of the Division of Black American Literature and Culture of the Modern Language Association. The magazine received American Literary Magazine Awards in 1994 and 1995.

NEEDS ethnic/multicultural, experimental, feminist, literary, mainstream. "No children's/juvenile/young adult/teen." Receives 35 unsolicited mss/month. Accepts 10 mss/year. Publishes ms 1 year after acceptance. Agented fiction 0%. Recently published work by Solon Timothy Woodward, Eugenia Collier, Jeffery Renard Allen, Patrick Lohier, Raki Jones, Olympia Vernon. Length: 2,500-5,000 words; average length: 3,000 words. Also publishes literary essays, literary criticism, poetry. Sometimes comments on rejected mss.

HOW TO CONTACT Submit complete ms only via online manuscript fasttrack at http://aar.expressacademic.org. Responds in 1 week to queries; 3 months to mss. Sample copy for $12. Writer's guidelines online. Reviews fiction.

PAYMENT/TERMS Pays 1 contributor's copy and 5 offprints. Provides first North American serial rights. Sends galleys to author.

AGNI

Creative Writing Program, Boston University, 236 Bay State Rd., Boston MA 02215. (617)353-7135. Fax: (617)353-7134. E-mail: agni@bu.edu. Website: www.agnimagazine.org. **Contact:** Sven Birkerts, editor. Estab. 1972. "Eclectic literary magazine publishing first-rate poems, essays, translations, and stories. Biannual." 3,000 in print, plus more than 60,000 distinct readers online per year. Buys serial rights. Rights to reprint in *AGNI* anthology (with author's consent). Pays on publication. Byline given. Publishes ms an average of 6 months after acceptance. Responds in 2 weeks to queries. Responds in 4 months to mss. Editorial lead time 1 year. Sample copy for $10 or online. Guidelines available online.

Reading period September 1-May 31 only. "Online magazine carries original content not found in print edition. All submissions are considered for both." Founding editor Askold Melnyczuk won the 2001 Nora Magid Award for Magazine Editing. Work from *AGNI* has been included and cited regularly in the *Pushcart Prize* and *Best American* anthologies.

NEEDS poetry, fiction, and essays by both emerging and established writers.

HOW TO CONTACT Query by mail.

PAYMENT/TERMS Pays $10/page up to $150, a one-year subscription, and for print publication: 2 contributor's copies and 4 gift copies.

TIPS "We're also looking for extraordinary translations from little-translated languages. It is important to read work published in *AGNI* before submitting, to see if your own might be compatible."

ALASKA QUARTERLY REVIEW

ESB 208, University of Alaska-Anchorage, 3211 Providence Dr., Anchorage AK 99508. (907)786-6916. E-mail: aqr@uaa.alaska.edu. Website: www.uaa.alaska.edu/aqr. **Contact:** Ronald Spatz. Estab. 1982. Magazine: 6×9; 232-300 pages; 60 lb. Glatfelter paper; 12 pt. C15 black ink or 4-color; varnish cover stock; photos on cover and photo essays. AQR "publishes fiction, poetry, literary nonfiction and short plays in traditional and experimental styles." Semiannual. Circ. 2,700.

Alaska Quarterly reports they are always looking for freelance material and new writers.

NEEDS experimental, literary, translations, contemporary, prose poem. "If the works in *Alaska Quarterly Review* have certain characteristics, they are these: freshness, honesty and a compelling subject. We look for the demonstration of craft, making the situation palpable and putting it in a form where it becomes emotionally and intellectually complex. Many of the pieces published in the *Alaska Quarterly Review* concern everyday life. We're not asking our writers to go outside themselves and their experiences to the absolute exotic to catch our interest. We look for the experiential and revelatory qualities of the work. We will, without hesitation, champion a piece that may be less polished or stylistically sophisticated, if it engages, surprises, and resonates. The joy in reading such a work is in discovering something true. Moreover, in keeping with our mission to publish new writers, we are looking for voices our readers do not know, and that, in all instances, have something important to convey." Receives 500 unsolicited mss/month. Accepts 7-18 mss/issue; 15-30 mss/year. Does not read mss May 10-August 25. Publishes ms 6 months after acceptance. **Publishes 6 new writers/year.** Recently published work by Linda LeGarde Grover, Don Lago, Mark Wisniewski, Bojan Louis, Kirstin Allio, Aurelie Sheehan, Victoria Patterson, Amy Hempel, Lily Tuck, Christopher Kennedy, Julia Salvin, Bernard Cooper, Edith Pearlman. Publishes short shorts. Responds in 4 months to queries; responds in 4 months to mss. Simultaneous submissions "undesirable, but will accept if indicated." Sample copy for $6. Writer's guidelines online.

PAYMENT/TERMS Pays $50-200 subject to funding; pays in contributor's copies and subscriptions when funding is limited. Honorariums on publication when funding permits. Acquires first North American serial rights. Upon request, rights will be transferred back to author after publication.

TIPS "All sections are open to freelancers. We rely almost exclusively on unsolicited manuscripts. *AQR* is a nonprofit literary magazine and does not always have funds to pay authors."

ALIMENTUM, THE LITERATURE OF FOOD

P.O. Box 210028, Nashville TN 37221, Nashville TN 37221. E-mail: submissions@alimentumjournal.com. Website: www.alimentumjournal.com. **Contact:** Cortney Davis, Poetry Editor. Estab. 2005. Literary magazine/journal: 6×7.5, 128 pages, matte cover. Contains illustrations. "All of our stories, poems and essays have food or drink as a theme." Semiannual.

NEEDS Literary. Special interests: food related. Receives 100 mss/month. Accepts 20-24 mss/issue. Manuscript published one to two years after acceptance. **Publishes average of 2 new writers/year.** Published Mark Kurlansky, Oliver Sacks, Dick Allen, Ann Hood, Carly Sachs. Length: 3,000 words (max). Average length: 1,000-2,000 words. Publishes short shorts. Also publishes literary essays, poetry, spot illustrations. Rarely comments on/critiques rejected mss.

HOW TO CONTACT Send complete ms with cover letter. Snail mail only. No previously published work. 5-poem limit per submission. Simultaneous submissions okay. Responds to queries and mss in 1-3 months. Send either SASE (or IRC) for return of ms or disposable copy of ms and #10 SASE for reply only. Sample copy available for $10. Guidelines available on website. Check for submission reading periods as they vary from year to year.

PAYMENT/TERMS Writers receive 1 contributor's copy. Additional contributor's copies $8. Pays on publication. Acquires first North American serial rights. Publication is copyrighted.

TIPS "No email submissions, only snail mail. Mark outside envelope to the attention of Poetry, Fiction, or Nonfiction Editor."

ALIVE NOW

1908 Grand Ave., P.O. Box 340004, Nashville TN 37203-0004. E-mail: alivenow@upperroom.org. Website: www.alivenow.org; www.upperroom.org. **Contact:** Beth A. Richardson, Editor.

ANN ARBOR OBSERVER

Ann Arbor Observer Co., 201 E. Catherine, Ann Arbor MI 48104. Fax: (734)769-3375. E-mail: hilton@aaobserver.com. Website: www.arborweb.com. Estab. 1976.

TIPS "If you have an idea for a story, write a 100-200-word description telling us why the story is interesting. We are open most to intelligent, insightful features about interesting aspects of life in Ann Arbor."

THE ANTIGONISH REVIEW

St. Francis Xavier University, P.O. Box 5000, Antigonish NS B2G 2W5 Canada. (902)867-3962. Fax: (902)867-5563. E-mail: tar@stfx.ca. Website: www.antigonishreview.com. **Contact:** Bonnie McIsaac, office manager. Estab. 1970. Literary magazine for educated and creative readers. Quarterly. Estab. 1970. Circ. 1,000. The *Antigonish Review* has decided to stop reading fiction submissions between June 1 and September 30.

NEEDS literary, translations, contemporary, prose poem. No erotica. Receives 50 unsolicited mss/month. Accepts 6 mss/issue. Publishes ms 4 months after acceptance. **Publishes some new writers/year.** Recently published work by Calvin Wharton, Stephen Morison jr., Rebecca Rosenblum. Sometimes comments on rejected mss.

HOW TO CONTACT Send complete ms. Accepts submissions by fax. Accepts electronic (disk compatible with WordPerfect/IBM and Windows) submissions. Prefers hard copy. Responds in 1 month to queries; 6 months to mss. No simultaneous submissions. Sample copy for $7 or online. Writer's guidelines for #10 SASE or online.

PAYMENT/TERMS Pays $100 per accepted story. Pays on publication. Rights retained by author.

TIPS "Send for guidelines and/or sample copy. Send ms with cover letter and SASE with submission."

ANTIOCH REVIEW

P.O. Box 148, Yellow Springs OH 45387-0148. E-mail: mkeyes@antiochreview.org. Website: http://antiochcollege.org/antioch_review/. **Contact:** Muriel Keyes. Estab. 1941. Magazine: 6×9; 200 pages; 50 lb. book offset paper; coated cover stock; illustrations "seldom." "Literary and cultural review of contemporary issues, and literature for general readership." Quarterly. Circ. 3,000. Receives 275 unsolicited mss/month. Accepts 5-6 mss/issue; 20-24 mss/year. No mss accepted June 1-September 1. Publishes ms 10 months after acceptance. Agented fiction 1-2%. **Publishes 1-2 new writers/year.** Recently published work by Edith Pearlman, Peter LaSalle, Rosellen Brown, Nathan Oates, Stephen O'Connor, and Susan Miller.

Work published in the *Antioch Review* has been included frequently in *The Best American Poetry*, *The Best New Poets* and *The Pushcart Prize*.

NEEDS Literary, experimental, contemporary, translations. No science fiction, fantasy or confessions.

HOW TO CONTACT Send complete ms with SASE, preferably mailed flat. Responds in 4-6 months to mss. Sample copy for $7. Writer's guidelines online.

PAYMENT/TERMS Pays $15/printed page. Pays on publication.

AOIFE'S KISS

The Speculative Fiction Foundation, P.O. Box 782, Cedar Rapids IA 52406-0782. E-mail: aoifeskiss@yahoo.com. Website: www.samsdotpublishing.com. **Contact:** Tyree Campbell, Managing Editor. Estab. 2002. *Aoife's Kiss* (print version) is 54 pages, magazine-sized, offset-printed, saddle-stapled, perfect-bound, with color paper cover, includes ads. Receives about 300 poems/year, accepts about 50 (17%). Press run is 150; 5 distributed free to reviewers. Single copy: $7;

subscription: $22/year, $40 for 2 years. Make checks payable to Sam's Dot Publishing.

HOW TO CONTACT Accepts e-mail submissions (pasted into body of message); no disk submissions. "Submission should include snail mail address and a short (1-2 lines) bio." Reads submissions year-round.

APEX MAGAZINE

Apex Publications, LLC, P.O. Box 24323, Lexington KY 40524. (859)312-3974. E-mail: jason@apexbookcompany.com. Website: www.apexbookcompany.com. **Contact:** Catherynne M. Valente, subm. editor. Estab. 2004. Magazine: 5½ × 8½, 128 pages, 70 lb. white offset paper, glossy #120 cover. Contains illustrations. "We publish dark speculative fiction with horror elements. Our readers are those that enjoy speculative fiction with dark themes." Monthly. Estab. 2005. Circ. 3,000. "We're not fans of 'monster' fiction." Receives 200-250 mss/month. Accepts 2 mss/issue; 24 mss/year. Manuscript published 3 months after acceptance. **Publishes 10 new writers/year.** Published Brian Keene, Cherie Priest, Ben Bova, William F. Nolan, Tom Piccirilli, M.M. Buckner, JA Rourath, and James P. Hogan. Length: 200 words (min)-7,500 words (max). Average length: 4,000 words. Publishes short shorts. Average length of short shorts: 500 words. Often comments on/critiques rejected manuscripts. Responds to queries in 3-4 weeks. Responds to mss in 3-4 weeks. E-mail submissions only.

"We want science fiction, fantasy, horror, and mash-ups of all three of the dark, weird stuff down at the bottom of your little literary heart." Monthly e-zine publishing dark speculative fiction. Circ. 10,000 unique visits per month. Nonfiction Pays writer expenses: No. Buys 24 mss/year. Send complete ms. Length: 100-7,500 words. Pays $0.05/word.

NEEDS Needs dark science fiction.

HOW TO CONTACT Send complete ms with cover letter. Include estimated word count, brief bio.

PAYMENT/TERMS Writers receive 5¢/word. Pays on publication. Acquires first World English Language rights and non-exclusive anthology rights. Publication is copyrighted.

TIPS "See submissions guidelines at submissions@apexdigest.com."

A PUBLIC SPACE

323 Dean St., Brooklyn NY 11217. (718)858-8067. E-mail: general@apublicspace.org. Website: www.apublicspace.org. **Contact:** Brigid Hughes, editor.

A Public Space, published quarterly, "is an independent magazine of literature and culture. In an era that has relegated literature to the margins, we plan to make fiction and poetry the stars of a new conversation. We believe that stories are how we make sense of our lives and how we learn about other lives. We believe that stories matter." Single copy: $15; subscription: $36/year or $60/2 years.

HOW TO CONTACT Submit one piece of fiction at a time via online submission form. Does not accept previously published ms. Accepts simultaneous submissions.

ARKANSAS REVIEW

A Journal of Delta Studies, Department of English and Philosophy, P.O. Box 1890, Office: Wilson Hall, State University AR 72467-1890. (870) 972-3043; (870)972-3674. Fax: (870)972-3045. E-mail: arkansasreview@astate.edu; jcollins@astate.edu; arkansasreview@astate.edu. Website: http://altweb.astate.edu/arkreview/. **Contact:** Dr. Janelle Collins, general editor/associate professor of English. Estab. 1998. Triannual magazine: 8¼×11; 64-100 pages; coated, matte paper; matte, 4-color cover stock; illustrations; photos. Publishes articles, fiction, poetry, essays, interviews, reviews, visual art evocative of or responsive to the Mississippi River Delta. Circ. 700. Accepts submissions by e-mail, fax. Send SASE for reply, return of ms or send a disposable copy of ms. Responds in 1 week to queries; 4 months to mss. Sample copy for $7.50. Writer's guidelines for #10 SASE.Pays 3 contributor's copies; additional copies for $5. Acquires first North American serial rights.

NEEDS literary (essays and criticism), regional (short stories). "No genre fiction. Must have a Delta focus." Receives 30-50 unsolicited mss/month. Accepts 2-3 mss/issue; 5-7 mss/year. Publishes ms 6-12 months after acceptance. Agented fiction 1%. **Publishes 3-4 new writers/year.** Recently published work by Susan Henderson, George Singleton, Scott Ely and Pia Erhart. Also publishes literary essays, poetry. Sometimes comments on rejected mss.

TIPS Submit via mail. E-mails are more likely to be overlooked or lost. Submit a cover letter, but don't try to impress us with credentials or explanations of the submission. Immerse yourself in the literature of the Delta, but provide us with a fresh and original take on its land, its people, its culture. Surprise us. Amuse us. Recognize what makes this region particular as well as universal, and take risks. Help us shape a new Delta literature.

ART TIMES

A Literary Journal and Resource for All the Arts, P.O. Box 730, Mount Marion NY 12456-0730. (845)246-6944. Fax: (845)246-6944. E-mail: info@ArtTimesJournal.com. Website: www.arttimesjournal.com. **Contact:** Raymond J. Steiner. Estab. 1984. Magazine: 12×15; 24 pages; Jet paper and cover; illustrations; photos. "*Art Times* covers the art fields and is distributed in locations most frequented by those enjoying the arts. Our copies are distributed throughout the Northeast region as well as in most of the galleries of Soho, 57th Street and Madison Avenue in the metropolitan area; locations include theaters, galleries, museums, cultural centers and the like. Our readers are mostly over 40, affluent, art-conscious and sophisticated. Subscribers are located across U.S. and abroad (Italy, France, Germany, Greece, Russia, etc.)." Monthly. Circ. 28,000. Receives 30-50 unsolicited mss/month. Accepts 1 mss/issue; 10 mss/year. Publishes ms 3 years after acceptance. **Publishes 6 new writers/year.** Publishes short shorts.

NEEDS adventure, ethnic/multicultural, fantasy, feminist, gay, historical, humor/satire, lesbian, literary, mainstream, science fiction, contemporary. "We seek literary pieces, nothing violent, sexist, erotic, juvenile, racist, romantic, political, etc."

HOW TO CONTACT Send complete ms with SASE. Responds in 6 months to mss. Accepts simultaneous, multiple submissions. Sample copy for 9×12 SAE and 6 first-class stamps. Writer's guidelines for #10 SASE or on website.

PAYMENT/TERMS Pays $25 maximum (honorarium) and 1 year's free subscription. Pays on publication for first North American serial, first rights.

TIPS "Competition is greater (more submissions received), but keep trying. We print new as well as published writers." "Be advised that we are presently on an approximate 3-year lead for short stories, 2-year lead for poetry. We are now receiving 300-400 poems and 40-50 short stories per month. Be familiar with *Art Times* and its special audience."

ASIMOV'S SCIENCE FICTION

Dell Magazine Fiction Group, 267 Broadway, 4th Floor, New York NY 10007. (212)686-7188. Fax: (212)686-7414. E-mail: asimovssf@dellmagazines.com. Website: www.asimovs.com. **Contact:** Brian Bieniowski, managing editor. Estab. 1977. Magazine: 5' 7/8 x 8' 5/8 (trim size); 112 pages; 30 lb. newspaper; 70 lb. to 8 pt. C1S cover stock; illustrations; rarely photos. Magazine consists of science fiction and fantasy stories for adults and young adults. Publishes "the best short science fiction available." Receives approximately 800 unsolicited mss/month. Accepts 10 mss/issue. Publishes ms 6-12 months after acceptance. Agented fiction 10%. **Publishes 10 new writers/year.** Recently published work by Robert Silverberg and Larry Niven. Publishes short shorts. Sometimes comments on rejected mss. Reviews fiction.

Named for a science fiction "legend," *Asimov's* regularly receives Hugo and Nebula Awards. Editor Gardner Dozois has received several awards for editing including Hugos and those from *Locus* magazine.

NEEDS fantasy, science fiction (hard science, soft sociological). No horror or psychic/supernatural. Would like to see more hard science fiction.

HOW TO CONTACT Send complete ms with SASE. Responds in 2 months to queries; 3 months to mss. No simultaneous or reprint submissions. Sample copy for $5. Writer's guidelines for #10 SASE or online.

PAYMENT/TERMS Pays 5-8¢/word. Pays on acceptance. Buys first North American serial, nonexclusive foreign serial rights; reprint rights occasionally. Sends galleys to author.

TIPS "In general, we're looking for 'character-oriented' stories, those in which the characters, rather than the science, provide the main focus for the reader's interest. Serious, thoughtful, yet accessible fiction will constitute the majority of our purchases, but there's always room for the humorous as well. Borderline fantasy is fine, but no Sword & Sorcery, please. A good overview would be to consider that all fiction is written to examine or illuminate some aspect of human existence, but that in science fiction the backdrop you work against is the size of the universe. Please do not send us submissions on disk or via e-mail. We've bought some of our best stories from people who have never sold a story before."

ATLANTIC PACIFIC PRESS

The Wale Inn Publishing House, P.O. Box 4394, Danbury CT 06813. (508)994-7869. Fax: (774) 263 2839. E-mail: lyric_songs@yahoo.com. Website: atlanticpacificpress.com. **Contact:** Christine Walen, editor. Estab. 2008. Quarterly literary magazine/journal. 8½×5½, 75 pages pages. Contains illustrations. "*Atlantic Pacific Press* publishes plays and drama screenplays 10-120 pages, as well as fiction, sci-fi, fantasy, drama, poetry, lyrics, cartoons, children's stories, art and photography. Our journal is published Winter, Spring, Summer and Fall."

NEEDS adventure, children's/juvenile, comics/graphic novels, ethnic/multicultural, experimental, family, fantasy, feminist, glitz, historical, horror (supernatural, futuristic), humor, literary, mainstream, military/war, mystery/suspense, new age, psychic/supernatural/occult, regional, religious, romance, science fiction, thriller/espionage, translations, western, YA, adventure, drama. Does not want "porn." Receives 20 fiction mss each year, accepts 16. Time between acceptance and publication is 1-3 months.

HOW TO CONTACT Send for guidelines with a SASE (self addressed stamped envelope). Submit complete mss with a cover letter, SASE, and 50-word count bio. Send copy via email after acceptance. Include estimated word count. Responds to queries in 1-6 weeks; to mss in 1-3 months. Please indicate whether you wish to have mss destroyed or returned. Will consider previously published submissions; no simultaneous submissions. Publication is copyrighted. Sample copy: $10. Pays contributor copy to author accepted for publication. Acquires onetime rights, first North American serial rights. First rights. Rights return to author upon publication.

TIPS "Consider taking a writing class or workshop. Read your mss to someone before sending."

AUTOWEEK

Crain Communications, Inc., 1155 Gratiot Ave., Detroit MI 48207. (313)446-6000. Fax: (313)446-1027. Website: www.autoweek.com. **Contact:** Roger Hart, Executive Editor. Estab. 1958.

AVIATION HISTORY

Weider History Group, 19300 Promenade Dr., Leesburg VA 20176. E-mail: aviationhistory@weiderhistorygroup.com. Website: www.thehistorynet.com. Estab. 1990.

TIPS "Choose stories with strong art possibilities. Include a hard copy as well as an IBM- or Macintosh-compatible CD. Write an entertaining, informative, and unusual story that grabs the reader's attention and holds it. All stories must be true. We do not publish fiction or poetry."

BABYBUG

Carus Publishing, 70 East Lake St., Chicago IL 60601. E-mail: babybug@caruspub.com. Website: http://www.cricketmag.com. **Contact:** Marianne Carus, editor-in-chief. Estab. 1994. "*Babybug* is 'the listening and looking board-book magazine for infants and toddlers,' intended to be read aloud by a loving adult to foster a love of books and reading in young children ages 6 months-2 years."

NEEDS Very simple stories for infants and toddlers. "Study back issues before submitting."

HOW TO CONTACT Send complete ms. Accepts simultaneous submissions. Sample copy for $5. Writer's guidelines online.

PAYMENT/TERMS Pays $25 and up. Pays on publication for variable rights.

TIPS "*Babybug* would like to reach as many children's authors and artists as possible for original contributions, but our standards are very high, and we will accept only top-quality material. Before attempting to write for *Babybug*, be sure to familiarize yourself with this age child." "Imagine having to read your story or poem—out loud—50 times or more! That's what parents will have to do. Babies and toddlers demand, 'Read it again!' Your material must hold up under repetition. And humor is much appreciated by all."

BACKHOME

Wordsworth Communications, Inc., P.O. Box 70, Hendersonville NC 28793. (828)696-3838. Fax: (828)696-0700. E-mail: backhome@ioa.com. Website: www.backhomemagazine.com. Estab. 1990.

The editor reports an interest in seeing more renewable energy experiences, *good* small houses, workshop projects (for handy persons, not experts), and community action others can copy.

TIPS Very specific in relating personal experiences in the areas of gardening, energy, and homebuilding how-to. Third-person approaches to others' experiences are also acceptable but somewhat less desirable. Clear color photo prints, especially those in which people are prominent, help immensely when deciding upon what is accepted.

THE BALTIMORE REVIEW

P.O. Box 36418, Towson MD 21286. Website: www.baltimorereview.org. **Contact:** Susan Muaddi Darraj, managing editor. Estab. 1996. Semiannual magazine: 6×9; 150 pages; 60 lb. paper; 10 pt. CS1 gloss film cover. Showcase for the best short stories, creative nonfiction and poetry by writers in the Baltimore area and beyond. Accepts 20 mss/issue; approx. 40 mss/year. Publishes ms 1-9 months after acceptance. **Publishes "at least a few" new writers/year.** Average length: 3,000 words. Publishes short shorts. Also publishes poetry. Sample copy: $10, which included postage/handling.

"We publish work of high literary quality from established and new writers. No specific preferences regarding theme or style, and all are considered."

NEEDS ethnic/multicultural, literary, mainstream. "No science fiction, westerns, children's, romance, etc."

HOW TO CONTACT Accepts submissions via online system only. Please visit website. Responds in 4-6 months to mss.

PAYMENT/TERMS Pays 2 contributor's copies. Acquires first North American serial rights.

TIPS "Please read what is being published in other literary journals, including our own. As in any other profession, writers must know what the trends and the major issues are in the field." "We look for compelling stories and a masterful use of the English language. We want to feel that we have never heard this story, or this voice, before. Read the kinds of publications you want your work to appear in. Make your reader believe and care."

THE BEAR DELUXE MAGAZINE

Orlo, 810 SE Belmont #5, Portland OR 97214. (503)242-1047. E-mail: bear@orlo.org. Website: www.orlo.org. **Contact:** Tom Webb, editor-in-chief. Estab. 1993. Magazine: 9×12; 48 pages; newsprint paper; Kraft paper cover illustrations; photos. "The *Bear Deluxe Magazine* provides a fresh voice amid often strident and polarized environmental discourse. Street level, solution-oriented, and nondogmatic, the *Bear Deluxe* presents lively creative discussion to a diverse readership." Semiannual.

"The magazine is moving away from using the term *environmental writing*. Quality writing which furthers the magazine's goal of engaging new and divergent readers will garner the most attention." The Orlo Office is open by appointment only.

NEEDS adventure, condensed novels, historical, horror, humor/satire, mystery/suspense, novel excerpts, western. "No detective, children's or horror." Environmentally focused: humor/satire, literary, science fiction. "We would like to see more nontraditional forms." List of upcoming themes available for SASE. Receives 20-30 unsolicited mss/month. Accepts 2-3 mss/issue; 8-12 mss/year. Publishes ms 3 months after acceptance. Publishes 5-6 new writers/year. Recently published work by Peter Houlahan, John Reed and Karen Hueler. Length: 750-4,500 words; average length: 2,500 words. Publishes short shorts. Also publishes literary essays, literary criticism, poetry. Sometimes comments on rejected mss.

HOW TO CONTACT Query with or without published clips or send complete ms. Send disposable copy of mss. Responds in 3 months to queries; 6 months to mss. Accepts simultaneous submissions and reprints. Sample copy for $5. Writer's guidelines for #10 SASE or on website. Reviews fiction. Also send SASE for guides to new Doug Fir Fiction Award ($1,000 top prize).

PAYMENT/TERMS Pays free subscription to the magazine, contributor's copies and 5¢/word; additional copies for postage. Pays on publication for first, onetime rights.

TIPS "Offer to be a stringer for future ideas. Get a copy of the magazine and guidelines, and query us with specific nonfiction ideas and clips. We're looking for original, magazine-style stories, not fluff or PR. Fiction, essay, and poetry writers should know we have an open and blind review policy and should keep sending their best work even if rejected once. Be as specific as possible in queries."

BELLINGHAM REVIEW

Mail Stop 9053, Western Washington University, Bellingham WA 98225. (360)650-4863. E-mail: bhreview@wwu.edu. Website: www.wwu.edu/bhreview. **Contact:** Christopher Carlson, managing editor. Estab. 1977. Magazine: 6×8¼; 150 pages; 60 lb. white paper; four-color cover. *Bellingham Review* seeks literature of palpable quality; stories, essays and poems that nudge the limits of form or execute traditional forms exquisitely. Annual. Accepts 3-4 mss/issue. Does not read ms February 2-September 14. Publishes ms 6 months after acceptance. Agented fiction 10%. Publishes 10 new writers/year. Recently published work by Patricia Vigderman, Joshua Rolnick, and A.G. Harmon. Publishes short shorts. Also publishes poetry. Two-year subscription is $20. Writer's guidelines online.

The editors are actively seeking submissions of creative nonfiction, as well as stories that push the boundaries of the form. The Tobias Wolff Award in Fiction Contest runs December 1-March 15; see website for guidelines or send SASE.

NEEDS Experimental, humor/satire, literary, regional (Northwest). Does not want anything nonliterary.

HOW TO CONTACT Send complete ms. Responds in 1-6 months to mss. Accepts simultaneous submissions. Sample copy for $12.

PAYMENT/TERMS Pays on publication when funding allows. Acquires first North American serial rights.

TIPS "Open submission period is from Sept. 15-Dec. 15. Manuscripts arriving between December 16 and September 14 will be returned unread. The *Bellingham Review* holds 3 annual contests: the 49th Parallel Poetry Award, the Annie Dillard Award in Nonfiction, and the Tobias Wolff Award in Fiction. Submissions: December 1-March 15. See the individual listings for these contests under Contests & Awards for full details."

THE BINNACLE

University of Maine at Machias, 116 O'Brien Ave., Machias ME 04654. E-mail: ummbinnacle@maine.edu. Website: www.umm.maine.edu/binnacle. Estab. 1957. "We are interested in fresh voices, not Raymond Carver's, and not the Iowa Workshop's. We want the peculiar, and the idiosyncratic. We want playful and experimental, but understandable. Please see our website (www.umm.maine.edu/binnacle) for details on our Annual Ultra-Short Competition." Semiannual, plus annual Ultra-Short Competition editon. Publishes ms 3 months after acceptance. Sample copy for $7. Writer's guidelines online at website or by e-mail. Acquires onetime rights.

NEEDS ethnic/multicultural, experimental, humor/satire, mainstream, slice-of-life vignettes. No extreme erotica, fantasy, horror, or religious, but any genre attuned to a general audience can work.

HOW TO CONTACT Submissions by e-mail only. Responds in 1 month to queries; 3 months to mss. Accepts simultaneous submissions.

PAYMENT/TERMS $300 in prizes for Ultra-Short. $50 per issue for one work of editor's choice.

TIPS "We want fiction, poetry, and images that speak to real people, people who have lives, people who have troubles, people who laugh, too."

BOMB MAGAZINE

New Arts Publications, 80 Hanson Place, Suite 703, Brooklyn NY 11217. (718)636-9100. Fax: (718)636-9200. E-mail: firstproof@bombsite.com; generalinquiries@bombsite.com. Website: www.bombsite.com. **Contact:** Monica de la Torre. Estab. 1981. Magazine: 9 x 11.5; 104 pages; 70 lb. glossy cover; illustrations; photos. Receives 200 unsolicited mss/month. Accepts 6 mss/issue; 24 mss/year. Publishes ms 3-6 months after acceptance. Agented fiction 70%. Publishes 2-3 new writers/year. Recently published work by Lynne Tillman, Dennis Cooper, Susan Wheeler, and Laurie Sheck. Annual Fiction Contest—Deadline April 16 (Postmarked by April 16th). The winner of our 2011 contest will receive a $500 prize and publication in *BOMB Magazine*'s literary supplement, First Proof. Reading Fee: $20; includes a free one-year subscription to *BOMB* (for Canadian addresses add $6, for addresses outside US and Canada, add $12); make all checks and money orders payable to *BOMB Magazine*.

NEEDS Experimental, novel excerpts, contemporary. No genre: romance, science fiction, horror, western.

HOW TO CONTACT Send completed ms with SASE.

TIPS "Mss should be typed, double-spaced, proofread and should be final drafts. Purchase a sample issue before submitting work."

BOSTON REVIEW

PO Box 425786, Cambridge MA 02142. (617)324-1360. Fax: (617)452-3356. E-mail: review@bostonreview.net. Website: www.bostonreview.net. **Contact:** Dept. Editor. Estab. 1975. Magazine: $10^3{}_4 \times 14^3{}_4$; 60 pages; newsprint. "The editors are committed to a society and culture that foster human diversity and a democracy in which we seek common grounds of principle amidst our many differences. In the hope of advancing these ideals, the *Review* acts as a forum that seeks to enrich the language of public debate." Bimonthly. Receives 150 unsolicited mss/month. Accepts 4-6 mss/year. Publishes ms 4 months after acceptance. Recently published work by Dagberto Gilb, Charles Johnson,

Deb Olin Unferth, T.E. Holt, and Yvonne Woon. Occasionally comments on rejected mss. Sample copy for $5 or online. Writer's guidelines online. Reviews fiction. *Boston Review* reads fiction submissions between September 15 and June 15 each year. Acquires first North American serial, first rights.

Boston Review is a recipient of the Pushcart Prize in Poetry.

NEEDS Ethnic/multicultural, experimental, literary, regional, translations, contemporary, prose poem. "The editors are looking for fiction in which a heart struggles against itself, in which the messy unmanageable complexity of the world is revealed. Sentences that are so sharp they cut the eye."

HOW TO CONTACT Send complete ms with SASE or submit through online submissions manager. Responds in 4 months to queries. Accepts simultaneous submissions if noted.

PAYMENT/TERMS Papys $300, and 3 contributor's copies.

TIPS The best way to get a sense of the kind of material *Boston Review* is looking for is to read the magazine. (Sample copies are available for $6.95 plus shipping.) We do not consider previously published material. Simultaneous submissions are fine as long as we are notified of the fact. We accept submissions through our **online submissions system**. We strongly encourage online submission, however, if you must use postal mail, our address is *Boston Review*, PO Box 425786, Cambridge, MA 02142. We do not accept faxed or e-mailed submissions. Payment varies. Response time is generally 2-4 months. A SASE must accompany all postal submissions.

BOULEVARD

Opojaz, Inc., 6614 Clayton Rd., Box 325, Richmond Heights MO 63117. (314)862-2643. Fax: (314)862-2982. E-mail: kellyleavitt@boulevardmagazine.org; richardburgin@att.net; richardburgin@netzero.net. E-mail: http://boulevard.submishmash.com/submit. Website: www.boulevardmagazine.org. **Contact:** Richard Burgin, editor. Estab. 1985. Magazine: $5\frac{1}{2}\times8\frac{1}{2}$; 150-250 pages; excellent paper; high-quality cover stock; illustrations; photos. "*Boulevard* is a diverse literary magazine presenting original creative work by well-known authors, as well as by writers of exciting promise." Triannual. Receives over 600 unsolicited mss/month. Accepts about 10 mss/issue. Does not accept manuscripts between May 1 and October 1. Publishes ms 9 months after acceptance. **Publishes 10 new writers/year.** Recently published work by Joyce Carol Oates, Floyd Skloot, Alice Hoffman, Stephen Dixon, and Frederick Busch. Length: 9,000 words maximum; average length: 5,000 words. Publishes short shorts. Also publishes literary essays, literary criticism, poetry. Sometimes comments on rejected mss. Send complete ms. Accepts submissions on disk. SASE for reply. Responds in 2 weeks to queries; 3-4 months to mss. Accepts multiple submissions. No simultaneous submissions. Sample copy for $9. Writer's guidelines online.

"*Boulevard* has been called 'one of the half-dozen best literary journals' by Poet Laureate Daniel Hoffman in *The Philadelphia Inquirer*. We strive to publish the finest in poetry, fiction and non-fiction."

NEEDS confessions, experimental, literary, mainstream, novel excerpts. "We do not want erotica, science fiction, romance, western or children's stories."

PAYMENT/TERMS Pays $50-500. Pays on publication for first North American serial rights.

TIPS "Read the magazine first. The work *Boulevard* publishes is generally recognized as among the finest in the country. We continue to seek more good literary or cultural essays. Send only your best work."

BOYS' LIFE

Boy Scouts of America, P.O. Box 152079, 1325 West Walnut Hills Lane, Irving TX 75015-2079. (972)580-2366. Fax: (972)580-2079. Website: www.boyslife.org. Estab. 1911.

TIPS "We strongly recommend reading at least 12 issues of the magazine before submitting queries. We are a good market for any writer willing to do the necessary homework. Write for a boy you know who is 12. Our readers demand punchy writing in relatively short, straightforward sentences. The editors demand well-reported articles that demonstrate high standards of journalism. We follow the *Associated Press* manual of style and usage. Learn and read our publications before submitting anything."

BROKEN PENCIL

P.O. Box 203, Station P, Toronto ON M5S 2S7 Canada. E-mail: editor@brokenpencil.com; fiction@brokenpencil.com. Website: www.brokenpencil.com. Estab. 1995. Magazine. "Founded in 1995 and based in Toronto, Canada, *Broken Pencil* is a website and print magazine published four times a year. It is one of the few magazines in the world devoted to underground culture and the independent arts. We are a great resource and a lively read. A cross between the *Utne Reader*, an underground *Reader's Digest*, and the now defunct *Factsheet15*, *Broken Pencil* reviews the best zines, books, Web sites, videos, and artworks from the underground and reprints the best articles from the alternative press. Also, ground-breaking interviews, original fiction, and commentary on all aspects of the independent arts. From the hilarious to the perverse, *Broken Pencil* challenges conformity and demands attention." Quarterly. Accepts 8 mss/year. Manuscript published 2-3 months after acceptance. Acquires first rights.

NEEDS Adventure, erotica, ethnic/multicultural, experimental, fantasy, historical, horror, humor/satire, amateur sleuth, romance, science fiction.

HOW TO CONTACT Accepts submissions by e-mail. The thing to do is to pitch us with specific ideas, and maybe include a few of your previous articles. Also a little background info about you would be nice. It will take us a while to get back to you, so be patient.

PAYMENT/TERMS Our payments range from $30 to $300 depending on what kind of article you are writing.

TIPS Write in to receive a list of upcoming themes and then pitch us stories based around those themes. If you keep your ear to the ground in the alternative and underground arts communities, you will be able to find content appropriate for *Broken Pencil*.

BUTTON

P.O. Box 77, Westminster MA 01473. E-mail: sally@moonsigns.net. Website: www.moonsigns.net. Magazine: 4×5; 34 pages; bond paper; color cardstock cover; illustrations; photos. "*Button* is New England's tiniest magazine of poetry, fiction and gracious living, published once a year. I started *Button* so that a century from now, when people read it in landfills or, preferably, libraries, they'll say, 'Gee, what a great time to have lived. I wish I lived back then.'" Annual. Estab. 1993. Circ. 1,500. Literary. Receives 20-40 unsolicited mss/month. Accepts 1-2 mss/issue; 3-5 mss/year. Publishes ms 3-9 months after acceptance. Recently published work by Ralph Lombreglia, John Hanson Mitchell, They Might Be Giants and Lawrence Millman. Also publishes literary essays, poetry. Sometimes comments on rejected mss. "Only reads between April 1 and September 30. We will send samples but will discard mss not sent during those periods."

NEEDS "As 'gracious living' is on the cover, we like wit, brevity, cleverly conceived essay/recipe, poetry that isn't sentimental or song lyrics." "No genre fiction, science fiction, techno-thriller." Wants more of "anything Herman Melville, Henry James or Betty MacDonald would like to read."

HOW TO CONTACT Send complete ms with bio, list of publications and explain how you found magazine. Include SASE. Responds in 1 month to queries; 2 months to mss. Sample copy for $2.50 and 1 first-class stamp. Writer's guidelines for #10 SASE. Reviews fiction.

PAYMENT/TERMS Honorium, subscription and copies. Pays on publication for first North American serial rights.

TIPS "*Button* writers have been widely published elsewhere, in virtually all the major national magazines. They include Ralph Lombreglia, Lawrence Millman, They Might Be Giants, Combustible Edison, Sven Birkerts, Stephen McCauley, Amanda Powell, Wayne Wilson, David Barber, Romayne Dawnay, Brendan Galvin, and Diana DerHovanessian. It's $2.50 for a sample, which seems reasonable. Follow the guidelines, make sure you read your work aloud, and don't inflate or deflate your publications and experience. We've published plenty of new folks, but on the merits of the work."

CADET QUEST MAGAZINE

P.O. Box 7259, Grand Rapids MI 49510-7259. (616)241-5616. Fax: (616)241-5558. E-mail: submissions@calvinistcadets.org. Website: www.calvinistcadets.org. **Contact:** G. Richard Broene, editor. Estab. 1958. Magazine: $8\frac{1}{2}$×11; 24 pages; illustrations; photos. "*Cadet Quest Magazine* shows boys 9-14 how God is at work in their lives and in the world around them." Circ. 7,500. "Avoid long dialogue and little action." No fantasy, science fiction, fashion, horror, or erotica. List of upcoming themes available for SASE or on website in February. Receives 60 unsolicited mss/month. Accepts 3 mss/issue; 18 mss/year. Publishes ms 4-11 months after acceptance. **Publishes 0-3 new writers/year.** Length: 900-1,500 words; average length: 1,200 words. Publishes short shorts. Writer's guidelines for #10 SASE.

Accepts submissions by mail, or by e-mail (must include ms in text of e-mail). Will not open attachments.

NEEDS spiritual, sports, material based on Christian perspective and articles on Christian role models.

HOW TO CONTACT Send complete ms by mail or send submissions in the body of the e-mail. Will not open an attachment. Responds in 2 months. No queries. Accepts simultaneous, multiple submissions and reprints. Sample copy for 9×12 SASE.

PAYMENT/TERMS Pays 4-6¢/word, and 1 contributor's copy. Pays on acceptance for first North American serial, onetime, second serial (reprint), simultaneous rights. Rights purchased vary with author and material.

TIPS "Best time to submit stories/articles is early in the year (February-April). Also remember readers are boys ages 9-14. Stories must reflect or add to the theme of the issue and be from a Christian perspective."

CALLIOPE

Cobblestone Publishing Co., 30 Grove St., Suite C, Peterborough NH 03458-1454. (603)924-7209. Fax: (603)924-7380. E-mail: cfbakeriii@meganet.net. Website: www.cobblestonepub.com. **Contact:** Rosalie Baker and Charles Baker, co-editors. Estab. 1990. Magazine published 9 times/year. "*Calliope* covers world history (East/West), and lively, original approaches to the subject are the primary concerns of the editors in choosing material." Buys all rights for mss and artwork. Sample copy for $5.95 and SASE with $2 postage. Writer's guidelines with SASE.

For themes and queries deadlines, visit the *Calliope* website at: www.cobblestonepub.com/magazine/CAL. 2010 themes included: Isabella of Spain-Queen of a New World; Michelangelo; Dutch East India Company; Exploring Africa with Stanley & Livingstone; Meaning of Numbers; Shades of Indigo; The Nile river, and the Zodiac.

NEEDS Middle readers and young adults: adventure, folktales, plays, history, biographical fiction. Material must relate to forthcoming themes.

HOW TO CONTACT A query must consist of the following to be considered (please use nonerasable paper): a brief cover letter stating subject and word length of the proposed article; a detailed one-page outline explaining the information to be presented in the article; an bibliography of materials the author intends to use in preparing the article; a SASE. Writers new to *Calliope* should send a writing sample with query. In all correspondence, please include your complete address as well as a telephone number where you can be reached. A writer may send as many queries for one issue as he or she wishes, but each query must have a separate cover letter, outline and bibliography as well as a SASE. Telephone and e-mail queries are not accepted. Handwritten queries will not be considered. Queries may be submitted at any time, but queries sent well in advance of deadline may not be answered for several months. Go-aheads requesting material proposed in queries are usually sent 10 months prior to publication date. Unused queries will be returned approximately three to four months prior to publication date.

PAYMENT/TERMS Pays 20-25¢/word for stories/articles. Pays on an individual basis for poetry, activities, games/puzzles.

TIPS "Authors are urged to use primary resources and up-to-date scholarly resources in their bibliography. In all correspondence, please include your complete address and a telephone number where you can be reached."

CALYX

Calyx, Inc., P.O. Box B, Corvallis OR 97339. (541)753-9384. Fax: (541)753-0515. E-mail: editor@calyxpress.org. Website: www.calyxpress.org. **Contact:** The Editor. Estab. 1976. Magazine: 6×8; 128 pages per single issue; 60 lb. coated matte stock paper; 10 pt. chrome coat cover; original art. "*Calyx* exists to publish fine literature and art by women and is committed to publishing the work of all women, including women of color, older women, working class women and other voices that need to be heard. We are committed to discovering and nurturing beginning writers." Biannual. Receives approximately 1,000 unsolicited prose and poetry mss when open. Accepts 4-8 prose mss/issue; 9-15 mss/year. Publishes ms 4-12 months after acceptance. **Publishes 10-20 new writers/year.** Recently published work by M. Evelina Galang, Chitrita Banerji, Diana Ma, Catherine Brady. Responds in 4-12 months to mss. Accepts simultaneous submissions.

"Annual open submission period is October 1-December 31. Mss received when not open will be returned. Electronic submissions are accepted only from overseas. E-mail for guidelines only."

NEEDS prose, poetry, visual art, short fiction, literary essays and literary criticism, interviews and review articles.

HOW TO CONTACT Reads mss October 1-December 31; submit only during this period. Include SASE. Mss received when not reading will be returned.

PAYMENT/TERMS Sample copy for $10 plus $4 postage. "Combination of free issues and 1 volume subscription."

TIPS "Most mss are rejected because the writers are not familiar with *Calyx*—writers should read *Calyx* and be familar with the publication. We look for good writing, imagination and important/interesting subject matter."

CANADIAN WRITER'S JOURNAL

P.O. Box 1178, New Liskeard ON P0J 1P0 Canada. (705)647-5424. E-mail: editor@cwj.ca; cwj@cwj.ca. Website: www.cwj.ca. Estab. 1984. Accepts well-written articles by all writers. Annual. Estab. 1984.

NEEDS Requirements being met by annual contest. Send SASE for rules, or see guidelines on website. "Does not want gratuitous violence, sex subject matter." Publishes ms 9 months after acceptance. **Publishes 40 new writers/year.** Also publishes poetry. Rarely comments on rejected mss.

HOW TO CONTACT Accepts submissions by e-mail. Responds in 2 months to queries. Writer's guidelines online.

PAYMENT/TERMS Pays on publication for one-time rights.

THE CAPILANO REVIEW

2055 Purcell Way, North Vancouver BC V7J 3H5 Canada. (604)984-1712. E-mail: contact@thecapilanoreview.ca; tcr@capilanou.ca. E-mail: tcr@capilanou.ca. Website: www.thecapilanoreview.ca. **Contact:** Tamara Lee, managing editor. Estab. 1972. Magazine: 7×9; 90-120 pages; book paper; glossy cover; perfect-bound; visual art. "Tri-annual visual and literary arts magazine that publishes experimental art and writing." Receives 100 unsolicited mss/month. Accepts 1 mss/issue; 3 mss/year. Publishes ms 4-6 months after acceptance. Publishes some new writers/year. Recently published work by Michael Turner, Lewis Buzbee, George Bowering.

NEEDS No traditional, conventional fiction. Want to see innovative, genre-blurring work. Also publishes literary essays, poetry.

HOW TO CONTACT Include 2- to 3-sentence bio and brief list of publications. Send Canadian SASE or IRCs for reply. Responds in 1 month to queries; 4 months to mss. No simultaneous submissions. Sample copy for $15 (CAD). Writer's guidelines online.

PAYMENT/TERMS Pays $50-200. Pays on publication for first North American serial rights.

CHA

Hong Kong E-mail: editors@asiancha.com; j@asiancha.com; submissions@asiancha.com. Website: www.asiancha.com. **Contact:** Eddie Tay, reviews editor. Estab. 2007. (Specialized: Asian); Tammy Ho Lai-ming and Jeff Zroback, editors. Online magazine. "Cha is the first and currently the only Hong Kong–based online literary quarterly journal dedicated to publishing creative works from and about Asia, primarily in English."

"Please read the guidelines on our website carefully before you submit work to us."

NEEDS creative works from and about Asia, primarily in English. List of upcoming themes available on website. Length: 100 words (min)-3,000 words (max). Publishes short shorts. Also publishes poetry.

HOW TO CONTACT Accepts submissions by e-mail at submissions@asiancha.com. Responds to queries in 3 months. Considers simultaneous submissions. Guidelines available on website.

PAYMENT/TERMS Cannot pay contributors.

TIPS "Do not send attachments in your e-mail. Include all writing in the body of -email. Include a brief biography (100 words)."

CHEMICAL HERITAGE

Chemical Heritage Foundation (CHF), 315 Chestnut St., Philadelphia PA 19106-2702. (215)925-2222. E-mail: editor@chemheritage.org. Website: www.chemheritage.org. Estab. 1982.

TIPS "CHF attends exhibits at many scientific trade shows and scholarly conferences. Our representatives are always happy to speak to potential authors genuinely interested in the past, present and future of chemistry. We are a good venue for scholars who want to reach a broader audience or for science writers who want to bolster their scholarly credentials."

CHRYSALIS READER

1745 Gravel Hill Rd., Dillwyn VA 23936. (434)983-3021. E-mail: editor@swedenborg.com; rlawson@sover.net; chrysalis@hovac.com. Website: www.swedenborg.com/chrysalis. **Contact:** Robert F. Lawson, editor. Estab. 1985. Book series: $7\frac{1}{2}$×10; 192 pages;

coated cover stock; illustrations; photos. "*The Chrysalis Reader* audience includes people from numerous faiths and backgrounds. Many of them work in psychology, education, religion, the arts, sciences, or one of the helping professions. The style of writing may be humorous, serious, or some combination of these approaches. Essays, poetry, and fiction that are not evangelical in tone but that are unique in addressing the *Chrysalis Reader* theme are more likely to be accepted. Our readers are interested in expanding, enriching, or challenging their intellects, hearts, and philosophies, and many also just want to enjoy a good read. For these reasons the editors attempt to publish a mix of writings. Articles and poetry must be related to the theme; however, you may have your own approach to the theme not written in our description." Query with SASE. Accepts submissions by e-mail and USPS. Responds in 1 month to queries; 4-6 months to mss. No previously published work. Sample copy for $10 and 8½×11 SAE. Writer's guidelines and themes for issues for SASE or on website.Pays $25-100. Pays at page-proof stage. Acquires first rights, makes work-for-hire assignments. Sends galleys to author.

"This journal explores contemporary questions of spirituality from a Swedenborgian multifaith perspective."

NEEDS adventure, experimental, historical, literary, mainstream, mystery/suspense, science fiction, fiction (leading to insight), contemporary, spiritual, sports. No religious works. See upcoming theme at website. Receives 50 unsolicited mss/month. Accepts 20-40 mss/year. Publishes ms 9 months after acceptance. **Publishes 10 new writers/year.** Recently published work by Robert Bly, William Kloefkorn, Raymond Moody, Virgil Suárez, Carol Lem, Alan Magee, John Hitchcock. Also publishes literary essays, literary criticism, poetry. Sometimes comments on rejected mss.

CICADA MAGAZINE

Cricket Magazine Group, 70 E. Lake St., Suite 300, Chicago IL 60601. (312)701-1720. Fax: (312)701-1728. E-mail: dvetter@caruspub.com. Website: www.cicadamag.com. **Contact:** Deborah Vetter, executive editor; John Sandford, art director. Estab. 1998. Literary magazine: 48 pages; some illustrations. "*Cicada*, for ages 14 and up, publishes original short stories, poems, artwork and first-person essays written for teens and young adults." Bimonthly. Circ. 10,000.

NEEDS adventure, fantasy, historical, humor/satire, mainstream, mystery/suspense, romance, science fiction, western, young adult/teen, sports. "Our readership is age 14-23. Submissions should be tailored for high school and college-age audience, not junior high or younger. We especially need humor, contemporary realistic fiction, and fantasy. Accepts 7 mss/issue; 42 mss/year.

HOW TO CONTACT See website for updated submissions guidelines as editorial needs fluctuate.

PAYMENT/TERMS Pays up to 25¢ a word.

TIPS "Quality writing, good literary style, genuine teen sensibility, depth, humor, good character development, avoidance of stereotypes. Read several issues to familarize yourself with our style."

CIMARRON REVIEW

English Dept., Oklahoma State Univ., 205 Morrill Hall, Stillwater OK 74078. E-mail: cimarronreview@okstate.edu. Website: http://cimarronreview.okstate.edu. **Contact:** Toni Graham, fiction editor. Estab. 1967. Magazine: 6×9; 110 pages. "Poetry and fiction on contemporary themes; personal essays on contemporary issues that cope with life in the 21st century. We are eager to receive manuscripts from both established and less experienced writers who intrigue us with their unusual perspective, language, imagery and character." Quarterly. Recently published work by Molly Giles, Gary Fincke, David Galef, Nona Caspers, Robin Beeman, Edward J. Delaney. Also publishes literary essays, literary criticism, poetry. Reviews fiction.

NEEDS Literary-quality short stories and novel excerpts. No juvenile or genre fiction. Accepts 3-5 mss/issue; 12-15 mss/year. Publishes ms 2-6 months after acceptance. **Publishes 2-4 new writers/year.**

HOW TO CONTACT Send complete ms with SASE. Responds in 2-6 months to mss. Accepts simultaneous submissions. Sample copy for $7.

PAYMENT/TERMS Pays 2 contributor's copies. Acquires first North American serial rights.

TIPS "All work must come with SASE. A cover letter is encouraged. No email submissions from authors living in North America. Query first and follow guidelines." "In order to get a feel for the kind of work we publish, please read an issue or two before submitting."

CONFRONTATION MAGAZINE

Confrontation Press, English Dept., C. W. Post Campus Long Island University, 720 Northern Blvd., Brookville NY 11548-1300. (516)299-2720. Fax:

(516)299-2735. E-mail: confrontation@liu.edu; martin.tucker@liu.edu. Website: www.liu.edu/confrontation. **Contact:** Jonna Semeiks, editor. Estab. 1968.

Confrontation has garnered a long list of awards and honors, including the Editor's Award for Distinguished Achievement from CCLP (to Martin Tucker) and NEA grants. Work from the magazine has appeared in numerous anthologies including the *Pushcart Prize*, *Best Short Stories* and *The O. Henry Prize Stories*. *Confrontation* does not read mss during June, July, or August and will be returned unread unless commissioned or requested.

TIPS Most open to fiction and poetry. Prizes are offered for the Sarah Tucker Award for fiction and the John V. Gurry Drama Award. "We look for literary merit. Keep trying."

CONNECTICUT REVIEW

Connecticut State University, 39 Woodland St., Hartford CT 06105-2337. E-mail: ctreview@southernct.edu. Website: www.ctstateu.edu/ctreview/index.html. **Contact:** Vivian Shipley, editor. Estab. 1967. Magazine: 6x9; 208 pages; white/heavy paper; glossy/heavy cover; color and b&w illustrations and photos; artwork. *Connecticut Review* presents a wide range of cultural interests that cross disciplinary lines. Annual. Circ. 2,500. Member CLMP. Literary. Receives 250 unsolicited mss/month. Accepts 40 mss/issue; 80 mss/year. Does not accept mss to read May 15-September 1. Publishes ms 1-2 years after acceptance. **Publishes 15-20 new writers/year.** Has published work by John Searles, Michael Schiavone, Norman German, Tom Williams, Paul Ruffin, Dick Allen.

Poetry published in *Connecticut Review* has been included in *The Best American Poetry* and *The Pushcart Prize* anthologies; has received special recognition for Literary Excellence from Public Radio's series *The Poet and the Poem*; and has won the Phoenix Award for Significant Editorial Achievement from the Council of Editors of Learned Journals (CELJ).

NEEDS "We're looking for the best in literary writing in a variety of genres. Some issues contain sections devoted to announced themes. The editors invite the submission of academic articles of general interest, creative essays, translations, short stories, short-shorts, plays, poems and interviews."

HOW TO CONTACT Send two disposable copies of ms and #10 SASE for reply only. Content must be under 4,000 words and suitable for circulation to libraries and high schools. Responds in 6 months to queries. Considers simultaneous submissions. Sample copy for $12. Writer's guidelines for SASE, but forms for submissions and guidelines available on website.

PAYMENT/TERMS Pays 2 contributor's copies; additional copies $10. Pays on publication for first rights. Rights revert to author on publication. Sends galleys to author.

TIPS "We read manuscripts blind—stripping off the cover letter—but the biographical information should be there. Be patient. Our editors are spread over 4 campuses and it takes a while to move the manuscripts around."

COSMOS MAGAZINE

Luna Media Pty Ltd., Level 1, 49 Shepherd St., Chippendale, Sydney NSW 2008 Australia. (61)(2)9310-8500. Fax: (61)(2)9698-4899. E-mail: submissions@cosmosmagazine.com. Website: www.cosmosmagazine.com. Estab. 2005. "An Australian brand with a global outlook, *COSMOS* is internationally respected for its literary writing, excellence in design and engaging breadth of content. Won the 2009 Magazine of the Year and twice Editor of the Year at the annual Bell Awards for Publishing Excellence; the American Institute of Physics Science Writing Award; the Reuters/IUCN Award for Excellence in Environmental Journalism; the City of Sydney Lord Mayor's Sustainability Award and an Earth Journalism Award. *COSMOS* is the brainchild of Wilson da Silva, a former ABC TV science reporter and past president of the World Federation of Science Journalists. It is backed by an Editorial Advisory Board that includes Apollo 11 astronaut Buzz Aldrin, ABC Radio's Robyn Williams, and is chaired by Dr. Alan Finkel, the neuroscientist and philanthropist who is the Chancellor of Monash University in Melbourne."

NEEDS science fiction

CRAB ORCHARD REVIEW

Southern Illinois University at Carbondale, English Department, Faner Hall, Carbondale IL 62901-4503. (618)453-6833. Fax: (618)453-8224. Website: www.siu.edu/~crborchd. Estab. 1995. Magazine: 5½×8½; 275 pages; 55 lb. recycled paper, card cover; photo on cover. "We are a general interest literary journal published twice/year. We strive to be a journal that writers admire and readers enjoy. We publish fiction, poetry, creative nonfiction, fiction translations, interviews and reviews." Circ. 2,500.

NEEDS ethnic/multicultural, literary, excerpted novel. No science fiction, romance, western, horror, gothic or children's. Wants more novel excerpts that also stand alone as pieces. List of upcoming themes available on website. Receives 900 unsolicited mss/month. Accepts 15-20 mss/issue; 20-40 mss/year. Reads February-April and August-October. Publishes ms 9-12 months after acceptance. Agented fiction 1%. **Publishes 4 new writers/year.** Recently published work by Francisco Aragón, Kerry Neville Bakken, Timothy Crandle, Amina Gautier, Jodee Stanley, Alia Yunis. Length: 1,000-6,500 words; average length: 2,500 words. Also publishes literary essays, poetry. Rarely comments on rejected mss.

HOW TO CONTACT Send SASE for reply, return of ms. Responds in 3 weeks to queries; 9 months to mss. Accepts simultaneous submissions. Sample copy for $12. Writer's guidelines for #10 SASE.

PAYMENT/TERMS Pays $100 minimum; $25/page maximum, 2 contributor's copies and a year subscription. Acquires first North American serial rights.

TIPS We publish two issues per volume—one has a theme (we read from May to November for the theme issue), the other doesn't (we read from January through April for the nonthematic issue). Consult our website for information about our upcoming themes.

CRAZYHORSE

College of Charleston, Dept. of English, 66 George St., Charleston SC 29424. (843)953-7740. E-mail: crazyhorse@cofc.edu. Website: www.crazyhorsejournal.org. Estab. 2,000. Semiannual literary magazine: $8^3{}_4$×$8^1{}_4$; 150 pages; illustrations; photos. Submit up to two manuscripts per year between August 1 and May 31. The journal's mission is to publish the entire spectrum of today's fiction, essays, and poetry—from the mainstream to the avant-garde, from the established to the undiscovered writer. The editors are especially interested in original writing that engages in the work of honest communication. *Crazyhorse* publishes writing of fine quality regardless of style, predilection, subject. Raymond Carver called *Crazyhorse* "an indispensable literary magazine of the first order."

NEEDS Receives 200 unsolicited mss/month. Accepts 8-10 mss/issue; 16-20 mss/year. Publishes ms 6-12 months after acceptance. Recently published work by Luke Blanchard, Karen Brown, E. V. Slate, Melanie Rae Thon, Lia Purpura, Carolyn Walker. Length: 25 pages; average length: 15 pages. Publishes short shorts. Pays $20-35 per page of layout, depending on annual budget and grants received.

HOW TO CONTACT No longer accepts submissions by mail. Responds in 1 week to queries; 3 months to mss. Accepts simultaneous submissions. Sample copy for $5; year subscription for $16. Writer's guidelines for SASE or by e-mail. Acquires first North American serial rights. Sends galleys to author. Click online to use our Submission Manager.

TIPS Write to explore subjects you care about. The subject should be one in which something is at stake. Before sending, ask, "What's reckoned with that's important for other people to read?"

⊕ CRICKET

Carus Publishing Co., 700 E. Lake St., Suite 300, Chicago IL 60601. (312)701-1720, ext. 10. Website: www.cricketmag.com. **Contact:** Submissions Editor. Marianne Carus, editor-in-chief. Magazine: 8×10; 64 pages; illustrations; photos. Magazine for children, ages 9-14. Monthly. Estab. 1973. Circ. 73,000.

NEEDS adventure, children's/juvenile, ethnic/multicultural, fantasy, historical, humor/satire, mystery/suspense, novel excerpts, science fiction, suspense, thriller/espionage, western, folk and fairy tales. No didactic, sex, religious, or horror stories. All issues have different "mini-themes." Receives 1,100 unsolicited mss/month. Accepts 150 mss/year. Publishes ms 6-24 months after acceptance. Agented fiction 1-2%. **Publishes some new writers/year.** Recently published work by Aaron Shepard, Arnold Adoff, and Nancy Springer.

HOW TO CONTACT Send complete ms. Responds in 3 months to mss. Accepts reprints submissions. Sample copy for $5 and 9×12 SAE. Writer's guidelines for SASE and on website.

PAYMENT/TERMS Pays 25¢/word maximum, and 6 contributor's copies; $2.50 charge for extras. Pays on publication. Rights vary. Sponsors awards/contests.

TIPS Writers: "Read copies of back issues and current issues. Adhere to specified word limits. *Please* do not query." Would currently like to see more fantasy and science fiction." Illustrators: "Send only your best work and be able to reproduce that quality in assignments. Put name and address on *all* samples.

Know a publication before you submit your style appropriate?"

CURVE MAGAZINE

P.O. Box 467, New York, NY 10034. E-mail: editor@curvemag.com. Website: www.curvemag.com. Estab. 1990.

TIPS Feature articles generally fit into 1 of the following categories: Celebrity profiles (lesbian, bisexual, or straight women who are icons for the lesbian community or actively involved in coalition-building with the lesbian community); community segment profiles—i.e., lesbian firefighters, drag kings, sports teams (multiple interviews with a variety of women in different parts of the country representing a diversity of backgrounds); noncelebrity profiles (activities of unknown or low-profile lesbian and bisexual activists/political leaders, athletes, filmmakers, dancers, writers, musicians, etc.); controversial issues (spark a dialogue about issues that divide us as a community, and the ways in which lesbians of different backgrounds fail to understand and support one another). We are not interested in inflammatory articles that incite or enrage readers without offering a channel for action, but we do look for challenging, thought-provoking work. The easiest way to get published in *Curve* is with a front-of-the-book piece for our Curvatures section, topical/fun/newsy pop culture articles that are 100-350 words.

DESCANT

P.O. Box 314, Station P, Toronto ON M5S 2S8 Canada. (416)593-2557. Fax: (416)593-9362. E-mail: info@descant.ca. Website: descant.ca. Estab. 1970. Magazine: 6×9; 120-150 pages; acid-free paper; paper cover. "*Descant* seeks high quality poems and stories in both traditional and innovative form." Annual. Circ. 500-750. Member CLMP. Literary. "No horror, romance, fantasy, erotica." Receives 20-30 unsolicited mss/month. Accepts 25-35 mss/year. Publishes ms 1 year after acceptance. **Publishes 50% new writers/year.** Recently published work by William Harrison, Annette Sanford, Miller Williams, Patricia Chao, Vonesca Stroud, and Walt McDonald. Length: 1,000-5,000 words; average length: 2,500 words. Publishes short shorts. Also publishes poetry. Pays on publication for one-time rights. Sponsors awards/contests.

Pays $100 honorarium, plus 1-year's subscription for accepted submissions of any kind.

HOW TO CONTACT Send complete ms with cover letter. Include estimated word count and brief bio. Responds in 6-8 weeks to mss. Accepts simultaneous submissions. Sample copy for $10. SASE, e-mail or fax.

PAYMENT/TERMS Pays 2 contributor's copies, additional copies $6.

TIPS Familiarize yourself with our magazine before submitting.

DIABETES SELF-MANAGEMENT

R.A. Rapaport Publishing, Inc., 150 W. 22nd St., Suite 800, New York NY 10011-2421. (212)989-0200. Fax: (212)989-4786. E-mail: editor@rapaportpublishing.com. Website: www.diabetesselfmanagement.com. **Contact:** Editor. Estab. 1983.

TIPS "The rule of thumb for any article we publish is that it must be clear, concise, useful, and instructive, and it must have immediate application to the lives of our readers. If your query is accepted, expect heavy editorial supervision."

DIAGRAM

Dept. of English, Univ. of Arizona, P.O. Box 210067, Tucson AZ 85721-0067. E-mail: editor@thediagram.com. Website: www.thediagram.com. "We specialize in work that pushes the boundaries of traditional genre or work that is in some way schematic. We do publish traditional fiction and poetry, too, but hybrid forms (short stories, prose poems, indexes, tables of contents, etc.) are particularly welcome! We also publish diagrams and schematics (original and found). Bimonthly. Circ. 300,000 + hits/month. Member CLMP.

"We sponsor yearly contests for unpublished hybrid essays and innovative fiction. Guidelines on website."

NEEDS experimental, literary. "We don't publish genre fiction, unless it's exceptional and transcends the genre boundaries." Receives 100 unsolicited mss/month. Accepts 2-3 mss/issue; 15 mss/year. **Publishes 6 new writers/year.** Average length: 250-2,000 words. Publishes short shorts. Also publishes literary essays, poetry. Often comments on rejected mss.

HOW TO CONTACT Send complete ms. Accepts submissions by Web submissions manager; no e-mail, please. If sending by post, send SASE for return of the ms, or send disposable copy of the ms and #10 SASE for reply only. Responds in 2 weeks to queries; 1-2 months to mss. Accepts simultaneous submissions. Sample copy for $12 for print version. Writer's guidelines online.

PAYMENT/TERMS Acquires first, serial, electronic rights.

TIPS "Submit interesting text, images, sound and new media. We value the insides of things, vivisection, urgency, risk, elegance, flamboyance, work that moves us, language that does something new, or does something old—well. We like iteration and reiteration. Ruins and ghosts. Mechanical, moving parts, balloons, and frenzy. We want art and writing that demonstrates/interaction; the processes of things; how functions are accomplished; how things become or expire, move or stand. We'll consider anything. We do not consider email submissions, but encourage electronic submissions via our submissions manager software. Look at the journal and submissions guidelines before submitting."

DIALOGUE

Blindskills, Inc., P.O. Box 5181, Salem OR 97304-0181. E-mail: magazine@blindskills.com. Website: www.blindskills.com. Estab. 1962.

DIRECTED BY

Visionary Media, P.O. Box 1722, Glendora CA 91740-1722. Fax: (626)608-0309. E-mail: visionarycinema@yahoo.com. Website: www.directed-by.com. Estab. 1998.

TIPS "We have been inundated with 'shelf-life' article queries and cannot publish even a small fraction of them. As such, we have restricted our interest in freelancers to writers who have direct access to a notable director of a current film which has not been significantly covered in previous issues of magazines; said director must be willing to grant an exclusive personal interview to *DIRECTED BY.* This is a tough task for a writer, but if you are a serious freelancer and have access to important filmmakers, we are interested in you."

DIVER

216 East Esplanade, North Vancouver BC V7L 1A3 Canada. (604)988-0711. Fax: (604)988-0747. E-mail: editor@divermag.com. Website: www.divermag.com.

DOWNSTATE STORY

1825 Maple Ridge, Peoria IL 61614. (309)688-1409. E-mail: ehopkins@prairienet.org. Website: www.wiu.edu/users/mfgeh/dss. Estab. 1992. Magazine: includes illustrations. "Short fiction—some connection with Illinois or the Midwest." Annually in the Fall. Circ. 250.

NEEDS adventure, ethnic/multicultural, experimental, historical, horror, humor/satire, literary, mainstream, mystery/suspense, psychic/supernatural/occult, regional, romance, science fiction, suspense, western. No porn. Accepts 10 mss/issue. Publishes ms 1 year after acceptance. Publishes short shorts. Also publishes literary essays.

HOW TO CONTACT Send complete ms with a cover letter and SASE for return of ms. Responds "ASAP" to mss. Deadline June 30th for each issue. Accepts simultaneous submissions. Sample copy for $8. Writer's guidelines online.

PAYMENT/TERMS Pays $50. Pays on acceptance for first rights.

TIPS Wants more political fiction. Publishes short shorts and literary essays.

DUCTS

P.O. Box 3203, Grand Central Station, New York NY 10163. E-mail: fiction@ducts.org; essays@ducts.org. Website: http://ducts.org. **Contact:** Jonathan Kravetz. Estab. 1999. Semi-annual. *DUCTS* is a webzine of personal stories, fiction, essays, memoirs, poetry, humor, profiles, reviews and art. "*DUCTS* was founded in 1999 with the intent of giving emerging writers a venue to regularly publish their compelling, personal stories. The site has been expanded to include art and creative works of all genres. We believe that these genres must and do overlap. *DUCTS* publishes the best, most compelling stories and we hope to attract readers who are drawn to work that rises above."

NEEDS ethnic/multicultural, humor/satire, literary, mainstream. "Please do not send us genre work, unless it is extraordinarily unique." Receives 50 unsolicited mss/month. Accepts 40 mss/issue; 80 mss/year. Publishes ms 1-6 months after acceptance. Publishes 10-12 new writers/year. Recently published work by Charles Salzberg, Mark Goldblatt, Richard Kostelanz, and Helen Zelon. Publishes short shorts. Also publishes literary essays, literary criticism, poetry. Sometimes comments on rejected mss.

HOW TO CONTACT Reading period is January 1-August 31. Send complete ms. Accepts submissions by e-mail to appropriate departments. Responds in 1-4 weeks to queries; 1-6 months to mss. Accepts simultaneous and reprints submissions. Writer's guidelines on ducts.org.

PAYMENT/TERMS $15. Acquires onetime rights.

TIPS "We prefer writing that tells a compelling story with a strong narrative drive."

EARTH ISLAND JOURNAL

Earth Island Institute, 300 Broadway, Suite 28, San Francisco CA 94133. E-mail: editor@earthisland.org. Website: www.earthislandjournal.org. Estab. 1985.

TIPS Given our audience, we are looking for stories that break new ground when it comes to environmental coverage. We are not going to publish a story "about recycling." (I have seriously gotten this pitch.) We MAY, however, be interested in a story about, say, the waste manager in Kansas City, KS, who developed an innovative technology for sorting trash, and how his/her scheme is being copied around the world; that is: we are looking for fresh angles on familiar stories, stories that so far have been overlooked by larger publications.

ECLECTICA

No public address available, E-mail: editors@eclectica.org. E-mail: submissions@eclectica.org; editors@eclectica.org. Website: www.eclectica.org. Estab. 1996. Online magazine. "*Eclectica* is a quarterly World Wide Web journal devoted to showcasing the best writing on the Web, regardless of genre. 'Literary' and 'genre' work appear side-by-side in each issue, along with pieces that blur the distinctions between such categories. Pushcart Prize, National Poetry Series, and Pulitzer Prize winners, as well as Nebula Award nominees, have shared issues with previously unpublished authors."

NEEDS High quality work in any genre. Also publishes poetry.

HOW TO CONTACT Accepts submissions by e-mail. "While we will consider simultaneous submissions, please be sure to let us know that they are simultaneous and keep us updated on their publication status." Guidelines available on website.

PAYMENT/TERMS Acquires first North American serial rights, electronic rights.

TIPS "Works which cross genres—or create new ones—are encouraged. This includes prose poems, 'heavy' opinion, works combining visual art and writing, electronic multimedia, hypertext/html, and types we have yet to imagine. No length restrictions. We will consider long stories and novel excerpts, and serialization of long pieces. Include short cover letter."

◐ ECLIPSE

Glendale College, 1500 N. Verdugo Rd., Glendale CA 91208. (818)240-1000. Fax: (818)549-9436. E-mail: eclipse@glendale.edu. Magazine: $8\frac{1}{2}\times5\frac{1}{2}$; 150-200 pages; 60 lb. paper. "Eclipse is committed to publishing outstanding fiction and poetry. We look for compelling characters and stories executed in ways that provoke our readers and allow them to understand the world in new ways." Annual. Circ. 1,800. CLMP.

NEEDS ethnic/multicultural, experimental, literary. "Does not want horror, religious, science fiction or thriller mss." Receives 50-100 unsolicited mss/month. Accepts 10 mss/year. Publishes ms 6-12 months after acceptance. **Publishes 8 new writers/year.** Recently published work by Amy Sage Webb, Ira Sukrungruang, Richard Schmitt, George Rabasa. Length: 6,000 words; average length: 4,000 words. Publishes short shorts. Also publishes poetry. Sometimes comments on rejected mss.

HOW TO CONTACT Send complete ms. Responds in 2 weeks to queries; 4-6 weeks to mss. Accepts simultaneous submissions. Sample copy for $8. Writer's guidelines for #10 SASE or by e-mail.

PAYMENT/TERMS Pays 2 contributor's copies; additional copies $7. Pays on publication for first North American serial rights.

TIPS "We look for well crafted fiction, experimental or traditional, with a clear unity of elements. A good story is important, but the writing must transcend the simple act of conveying the story."

ECOTONE

Creative Writing Dept., Univ. of No. Carolina Wilmington, 601 S. College Rd., Wilmington NC 28403. (910)962-2547. Fax: (910)962-7461. E-mail: info@ecotonejournal.com. Website: www.ecotonejournal.com.

TIPS "www.ecotonejournal.com/submissions.html."

EFCA TODAY

Evangelical Free Church of America, 418 Fourth St., NE, Charlottesville VA 22902. E-mail: dianemc@journeygroup.com. Website: www.efca.org. Estab. 1931.

TIPS "One portion of each *EFCA Today* is devoted to a topic designed to stimulate thoughtful dialog and leadership growth, and to highlight how EFCA leaders are already involved in living out that theme. Examples of themes are: new paradigms for 'doing church,' church planting and the 'emerging' church. These articles differ from those in the above sections, in that their primary focus in on the issue rather than the person; the person serves to illustrate the issue. These articles should run between 400 and 800 words. Include contacts for verification of article."

ELLERY QUEEN'S MYSTERY MAGAZINE

Dell Magazines Fiction Group, 267 Broadway, 4th Floor, New York NY 10017. (212)686-7188. Fax: (212)686-7414. E-mail: elleryqueenmm@dellmagazines.com. Website: www.themysteryplace.com/eqmm. Estab. 1941. Magazine: 5⅞×8⅝, 112 pages with special 192-page combined March/April and September/October issues. "*Ellery Queen's Mystery Magazine* welcomes submissions from both new and established writers. We publish every kind of mystery short story: the psychological suspense tale, the deductive puzzle, the private eye case, the gamut of crime and detection from the realistic (including the policeman's lot and stories of police procedure) to the more imaginative (including locked rooms and impossible crimes). *EQMM* has been in continuous publication since 1941. From the beginning, three general criteria have been employed in evaluating submissions: We look for strong writing, an original and exciting plot, and professional craftsmanship. We encourage writers whose work meets these general criteria to read an issue of *EQMM* before making a submission." Magazine for lovers of mystery fiction.

"*EQMM* uses an online submission system (http://eqmm.magazinesubmissions.com) that has been designed to streamline our process and improve communication with authors. We ask that all submissions be made electronically, using this system, rather than on paper. All stories should be in standard manuscript format and submitted in .DOC format. We cannot accept .DOCX, .RTF, or .TXT files at this time. For detailed submission instructions, see http://eqmm.magazinesubmissions.com or our writers guidelines page (http://www.themysteryplace.com/eqmm/guidelines)."

NEEDS mystery/suspense. No explicit sex or violence, no gore or horror. Seldom publishes parodies or pastiches. "We accept only mystery, crime, suspense and detective fiction." 2,500-8,000 words is the preferred range. Also publishes minute mysteries of 250 words; novellas up to 20,000 words from established authors. Publishes ms 6-12 months after acceptance. Agented fiction 50%. **Publishes 10 new writers/year.** Recently published work by Jeffery Deaver, Joyce Carol Oates, and Margaret Maron. Sometimes comments on rejected mss.

HOW TO CONTACT Send complete ms with SASE for reply. No e-mail submissions. No query necessary. Responds in 3 months to mss. Accepts simultaneous, multiple submissions. Sample copy for $5.50. Writer's guidelines for SASE or online.

PAYMENT/TERMS Pays 5-8¢/ a word, occasionally higher for established authors. Pays on acceptance for first North American serial rights.

TIPS "We have a Department of First Stories to encourage writers whose fiction has never before been in print. We publish an average of 10 first stories every year. Mark subject line Attn: Dept. of First Stories."

ENRICHMENT

The General Council of the Assemblies of God, 1445 N. Boonville Ave., Springfield MO 65802. (417)862-2781. Fax: (417)862-0416. E-mail: enrichmentjournal@ag.org. Website: www.enrichmentjournal.ag.org. **Contact:** Rick Knoth, managing editor.

EPOCH

Cornell University, 251 Goldwin Smith Hall, Cornell University, Ithaca NY 14853. (607)255-3385. Fax: (607)255-6661. Estab. 1947. Magazine: 6×9; 128 pages; good quality paper; good cover stock. "Well-written literary fiction, poetry, personal essays. Newcomers always welcome. Open to mainstream and avant-garde writing." Circ. 1,000.

NEEDS ethnic/multicultural, experimental, literary, mainstream, novel excerpts, literary short stories. "No genre fiction. Would like to see more Southern fiction (Southern US)." Receives 500 unsolicited mss/month. Accepts 15-20 mss/issue. Does not read in summer (April 15-September 15). Publishes ms an average of 6 months after acceptance. **Publishes 3-4 new writers/year.** Recently published work by Antonya Nelson, Doris Betts, Heidi Jon Schmidt. Also publishes poetry. Sometimes comments on rejected mss.

HOW TO CONTACT Send complete ms. Responds in 2 weeks to queries; 6 weeks to mss. No simultaneous submissions. Sample copy for $5. Writer's guidelines for #10 SASE.

PAYMENT/TERMS Pays $5 and up/printed page. Pays on publication for first North American serial rights.

TIPS "Tell your story, speak your poem, straight from the heart. We are attracted to language and to good writing, but we are most interested in what the good writing leads us to, or where."

EXOTIC MAGAZINE

X Publishing Inc., 818 SW 3rd Ave., Suite 324, Portland OR 97204. Fax: (503)241-7239. E-mail: webmaster@xmag.com; exoticunderground2004@yahoo.com. Website: www.xmag.com. Estab. 1993.

TIPS "Read adult publications, spend time in the clubs doing more than just tipping and drinking. Look for new insights in adult topics. For the industry to continue to improve, those who cover it must also be educated consumers and affiliates. Please type, spell-check and be realistic about how much time the editor can take 'fixing' your manuscript."

FASHION FORUM

Business Journals, Inc., 1384 Broadway, 11th Floor, New York NY 10018. (212)710-7442. E-mail: jillians@busjour.com. Website: www.busjour.com. **Contact:** Jillian Sprague, managing editor.

TIPS "Be prepared to write like you know the upscale lifestyle. Even if you only own one jacket, or stay in hostels, remember our readers, for the most part, don't even know about hostels! Experience in a specific category, or direct access to designers for profiles is a huge in!"

FAULTLINE

Dept. of English and Comparative Literature, University of California at Irvine, Irvine CA 92697-2650. (949) 824-1573. E-mail: faultline@uci.edu. Website: www.humanities.uci.edu/faultline. **Contact:** Editors change in September each year. Literary magazine: 6×9; 200 pages; illustrations; photos. "We publish the very best of what we receive. Our interest is quality and literary merit." Annual. Estab. 1992.

Reading period is September 15-February 15. Submissions sent at any other time will not be read.

NEEDS translations, literary fiction, nonfiction up to 20 pages. Receives 150 unsolicited mss/month. Accepts 6-9 mss/year. Does not read mss April-September. Publishes ms 9 months after acceptance. Agented fiction 10-20%. **Publishes 30-40% new writers/year.** Recently published work by Maile Meloy, Aimee Bender, David Benioff, Steve Almond, Helen Maria Viramontes, Thomas Keneally. Publishes short shorts. Also publishes literary essays, poetry.

HOW TO CONTACT Send SASE for reply, return of ms or send a disposable copy of ms. Responds in 2 weeks to queries; 4 months to mss. Accepts simultaneous submissions. Sample copy for $5. Writer's guidelines for business-size envelope.

PAYMENT/TERMS Pays 2 contributor's copies. Pays on publication for onetime rights.

TIPS "Our commitment is to publish the best work possible from well-known and emerging authors with vivid and varied voices."

FICTION

c/o Dept. of English, City College, 138th St. & Covenant Ave., New York NY 10031. Website: www.fictioninc.com. Estab. 1972. Magazine: 6×9; 150-250 pages; illustrations; occasionally photos. "As the name implies, we publish only fiction; we are looking for the best new writing available, leaning toward the unconventional. *Fiction* has traditionally attempted to make accessible the unaccessible, to bring the experimental to a broader audience." Semiannual. Estab. 1972.

Reading period for unsolicited mss is September 15-May 15.

NEEDS experimental, humor/satire (satire), literary, translations, contemporary. No romance, science fiction, etc. Receives 250 unsolicited mss/month. Accepts 12-20 mss/issue; 24-40 mss/year. Reads mss September 15-April 15. Publishes ms 1 year after acceptance. Agented fiction 10-20%. Recently published work by Joyce Carol Oates, John Barth, Robert Musil, Romulus Linney. Publishes short shorts. Sometimes comments on rejected mss.

HOW TO CONTACT To submit, please send a complete manuscript with cover letter and SASE. No e-mail submissions. Responds in 3 months to mss. Accepts simultaneous submissions. Sample copy for $5. Writer's guidelines online.

PAYMENT/TERMS Pays $75 plus subscription. Acquires first rights.

TIPS "The guiding principle of *Fiction* has always been to go to terra incognita in the writing of the imagination and to ask that modern fiction set itself serious questions, if often in absurd and comedic voices, interrogating the nature of the real and the fantastic. It represents no particular school of fiction, except the innovative. Its pages have often been a harbor for writers at odds with each other. As a result of its willingness to publish the difficult, experimental, and unusual, while not excluding the well known, *Fiction* has a unique reputation in the US and abroad as a journal of future directions."

FINE GARDENING

Taunton Press, 63 S. Main St., P.O. Box 5506, Newtown CT 06470-5506. (203)426-8171. Fax: (203)426-3434. E-mail: fg@taunton.com. Website: www.finegardening.com. Estab. 1988.

TIPS It's most important to have solid firsthand experience as a gardener. Tell us what you've done with your own landscape and plants.

FIVE POINTS

Georgia State University, P.O. Box 3999, Atlanta GA 30302-3999. E-mail: info@langate.gsu.edu. Website: www.webdelsol.com/Five_Points. Estab. 1996. Magazine: 6×9; 200 pages; cotton paper; glossy cover; photos. *Five Points* is "committed to publishing work that compels the imagination through the use of fresh and convincing language." Triannual. Circ. 2,000.

NEEDS List of upcoming themes available for SASE. Receives 250 unsolicited mss/month. Accepts 4 mss/issue; 15-20 mss/year. Does not read mss April 30-September 1. Publishes ms 6 months after acceptance. **Publishes 1 new writer/year.** Recently published work by Frederick Busch, Ursula Hegi, Melanie Rae Thon. Average length: 7,500 words. Publishes short shorts. Also publishes literary essays, poetry. Sometimes comments on rejected mss.

HOW TO CONTACT Use online submission manager. Sample copy for $7.

PAYMENT/TERMS Pays $15/page minimum ($250 maximum), free subscription to magazine and 2 contributor's copies; additional copies $4. Acquires first North American serial rights. Sends galleys to author. Sponsors awards/contests.

TIPS "We place no limitations on style or content. Our only criteria is excellence. If your writing has an original voice, substance and significance, send it to us. We will publish distinctive, intelligent writing that has something to say and says it in a way that captures and maintains our attention."

FLAUNT MAGAZINE

1422 N. Highland Ave., Los Angeles CA 90028. (323)836-1000. E-mail: info@flauntmagazine.com. Website: www.flaunt.com. **Contact:** Lee Corbin, art director; Andrew Pogany, senior editor. Magazine. "10 times a year, *Flaunt* features the bold work of emerging photographers, writers, artists, and musicians. The quality of the content is mirrored in the sophisticated, interactive format of the magazine, using advanced printing techniques, fold-out articles, beautiful papers, and inserts to create a visually stimulating, surprisingly readable, and intelligent book that pushes the magazine into the realm of art-object. *Flaunt* magazine has for the last eight years made it a point to break new ground, earning itself a reputation as an engine and outlet for the culture of the cutting edge. *Flaunt* takes pride in reinventing itself each month, while consistently representing a hybrid of all that is interesting in entertainment, fashion, music, design, film, art, and literature." Estab. 1998. Circ. 110,000.

NEEDS Experimental, urban, academic. We publish 3 fiction peices a year. Length: 500-5,000 words.

HOW TO CONTACT Guidelines available via e-mail.

PAYMENT/TERMS Acquires onetime rights and first option to reprint. Pays onetime flat rate to be determined upon correspondence.

FLORIDA SPORTSMAN

Wickstrom Communications Division of Intermedia Outdoors, 2700 S. Kanner Hwy., Stuart FL 34994. (772)219-7400. Fax: (772)219-6900. E-mail: editor@floridasportsman.com. Website: www.floridasportsman.com.

TIPS "Feature articles are sometimes open to freelancers; however there is little chance of acceptance unless contributor is an accomplished and avid outdoorsman *and* a competent writer-photographer with considerable experience in Florida."

O FOLIATE OAK LITERARY MAGAZINE

University of Arkansas-Monticello, P.O. Box 3460, Monticello AR 71656. (870)460-1247. E-mail: foliateoak@uamont.edu. Website: www.Foliateoak.Uamont.edu. **Contact:** Online Submission Manager. Estab. 1973. Magazine: 6×9; 80 pages. Monthly.

NEEDS adventure, comics/graphic novels, ethnic/multicultural, experimental, family saga, feminist, gay, historical, humor/satire, lesbian, literary, mainstream, science fiction (soft/sociological). No religious, sexist, or homophobic work. Receives 80 unsolicited mss/month. Accepts 20 mss/issue; 160 mss/year. Does not read mss May-August. Publishes ms 1 month after acceptance. Publishes 130 new writers/year. Recently published work by David Barringer, Thom Didato,

Joe Taylor, Molly Giles, Patricia Shevlin, Tony Hoagland. Length: 50-2,500 words; average length: 1,500 words. Publishes short shorts. Also publishes literary essays, literary criticism, poetry. Rarely comments on rejected mss.

HOW TO CONTACT Use our online submission manager to submit work. Postal submissions will not be read. Responds in 4 weeks. Only accepts submissions August through April. Accepts simultaneous submissions and multiple submissions. Please contact ASAP if work is accepted elsewhere. Sample copy with SASE and 6×8 envelope. Read writer's guidelines online. Reviews fiction.

PAYMENT/TERMS Pays contributor's copy if included in the annual print anthology. Acquires electronic rights. Sends galleys to author. Not copyrighted.

TIPS "We're open to honest, experimental, offbeat, realistic and surprising writing, if it has been edited. Limit poems to five per submission, and one short story or creative nonfiction (less than 2,500 words. You may send up to three flash fictions. Please put your flash fiction in one attachment. Please don't send more writing until you hear from us regarding your first submission. We are also looking for artwork sent as.jpg or.gif files."

FOLIO

10 Gate St., Lincoln's Inn Fields London WC2A-3P England. +44 0207 242 9562. Fax: +44 0207 242 1816. E-mail: info@folioart.co.uk. Website: www.folioart.co.uk.

FORWARD IN CHRIST

WELS Communication Services, 2929 N. Mayfair Rd., Milwaukee WI 53222-4398. (414)256-3210. Fax: (414)256-3210. E-mail: fic@wels.net. Website: www.wels.net. **Contact:** Julie K. Wietzke, managing editor. Estab. 1913.

TIPS "Topics should be of interest to the majority of the members of the synod—the people in the pews. Articles should have a Christian viewpoint, but we don't want sermons. We suggest you carefully read at least 5 or 6 issues with close attention to the length, content, and style of the features."

FREEFALL MAGAZINE

Freefall Literary Society of Calgary, 922 Ninth Ave. SE, Calgary AB T2G 0S4 Canada. E-mail: freefallmagazine@yahoo.com. Website: www.freefallmagazine.ca. **Contact:** Lynn S. Fraser, managing editor. Estab. 1990. Magazine: $8\frac{1}{2}\times5\frac{3}{4}$; 100 pages; bond paper; bond stock; b&w illustrations; photos. "*FreeFall* features the best of new, emerging writers and gives them the chance to get into print along with established writers. Magazine published biannually containing fiction, poetry, creative nonfiction, essays on writing, interviews, and reviews. Submit up to 5 poems at once. We are looking for exquisite writing with a strong narrative." Circ. 1,000. Buys first North American serial rights (ownership reverts to author after onetime publication). Pays on publication. 100% freelance.

NEEDS fiction

PAYMENT/TERMS Pays $25 per poem and one copy of the issue poems appear in. Wants prose of all types, up to 3,000 words; pays $10/page to a maximum of $100 per piece and one copy of issue piece appears in.

TIPS "We look for thoughtful word usage, craftmanship, strong voice and unique expression coupled with clarity and narrative structure. Professional, clean presentation of work is essential. Carefully read *FreeFall* guidelines before submitting. Do not fold manuscript, and submit 9×11 envelope. Include SASE/IRC for reply and/or return of manuscript. You may contact us by e-mail after initial hardcopy submission. For accepted pieces a request is made for disk or e-mail copy. Strong Web presence attracts submissions from writers all over the world."

FUNNY TIMES

Funny Times, Inc., P.O. Box 18530, Cleveland Heights OH 44118. (216)371-8600. Fax: (216)371-8696. E-mail: info@funnytimes.com. Website: www.funnytimes.com. Estab. 1985. Zine specializing in humor: tabloid; 24 pages; newsprint; illustrations. "*Funny Times* is a monthly review of America's funniest cartoonists and writers. We are the *Reader's Digest* of modern American humor with a progressive/peace-oriented/environmental/politically activist slant." Monthly. Circ. 70,000.

NEEDS humor/satire. "Anything funny." Receives hundreds of unsolicited mss/month. Accepts 5 mss/issue; 60 mss/year. Publishes ms 3 months after acceptance. Agented fiction 10%. **Publishes 10 new writers/year.** Publishes short shorts.

HOW TO CONTACT Query with published clips. Include list of publications. Send SASE for return of ms or disposable copy of ms. Responds in 3 months to mss. Accepts simultaneous and reprints submissions. Sample copy for $3 or 9×12 SAE with 4 first-class stamps ($1.22 postage). Writer's guidelines online.

PAYMENT/TERMS Pays $50-150. Pays on publication for one-time, second serial (reprint) rights.

TIPS "It must be funny." Send us a small packet (1-3 items) of only your very funniest stuff. If this makes us laugh, we'll be glad to ask for more. We particularly welcome previously published material that has been well received elsewhere.

FUR-FISH-GAME

2878 E. Main St., Columbus OH 43209-9947. E-mail: ffgcox@ameritech.net. Website: www.furfishgame.com. **Contact:** Mitch Cox, editor. Estab. 1900.

TIPS "We are always looking for quality how-to articles about fish, game animals, or birds that are popular with everyday outdoorsmen but often overlooked in other publications, such as catfish, bluegill, crappie, squirrel, rabbit, crows, etc. We also use articles on standard seasonal subjects such as deer and pheasant, but like to see a fresh approach or new technique. Instructional trapping articles are useful all year. Articles on gun dogs, ginseng, and do-it-yourself projects are also popular with our readers. An assortment of photos and/or sketches greatly enhances any manuscript, and sidebars, where applicable, can also help. No phone queries, please."

GARGOYLE

Paycock Press, 3819 N. 13th St., Arlington VA 22201. (703)525-9296. E-mail: hedgehog2@erols.com. Website: www.gargoylemagazine.com. **Contact:** Richard Peabody, co-editor, Lucinda Ebersole, co-editor. Estab. 1976. Literary magazine: 5½×8½; 200 pages; illustrations; photos. "*Gargoyle* Magazine has always been a scallywag magazine, a maverick magazine, a bit too academic for the underground and way too underground for the academics. We are a writer's magazine in that we are read by other writers and have never worried about reaching the masses." Annual. Circ. 2,000.

NEEDS erotica, ethnic/multicultural, experimental, gay, lesbian, literary, mainstream, translations. "No romance, horror, science fiction." Wants "edgy realism or experimental works. We run both." Wants to see more Canadian, British, Australian, and Third World fiction. Receives 50-200 unsolicited mss/month. Accepts 10-15 mss/issue. Accepts submissions during June, July, and Aug. Publishes ms 6-12 months after acceptance. Agented fiction 5%. **Publishes 2-3 new writers/year.** Recently published work by Stephanie Allen, Tom Carson, Susaan Cokal, Ramola D., Janice Eidus, James Grady, Susan Smith Nash, Zena Polin, Wena Poon, Elisabeth Sheffield, and Daniel Stola. Length: 30 pages maximum; average length: 5-10 pages. Publishes short shorts. Also publishes literary essays, literary criticism, poetry. Sometimes comments on rejected mss.

HOW TO CONTACT "We prefer electronic submissions. Please use submission engine online." For snail mail, send SASE for reply, return of ms or send a disposable copy of ms. Responds in 2 weeks to queries; 3 months to mss. Accepts simultaneous submissions. Sample copy for $12.95.

PAYMENT/TERMS Pays 10% of print run and so-so split (after/if) we break even. Acquires first North American serial, and first British rights. Sends galleys to author.

TIPS "We have to fall in love with a particular fiction."

GATEWAY (FORMERLY GATEWAY HERITAGE)

Missouri History Museum, P.O. Box 11940, St. Louis MO 63112-0040. (314)746-4558. Fax: (314)746-4548. E-mail: vwmonks@mohistory.org. Website: www.mohistory.org. Estab. 1980.

TIPS "You'll get our attention with queries reflecting new perspectives on historical and cultural topics."

THE GEORGIA REVIEW

The University of Georgia, Athens GA 30602-9009. (706)542-3481. Fax: (706)542-0047. E-mail: garev@uga.edu. Website: www.uga.edu/garev. **Contact:** Stephen Corey, editor. Estab. 1947. Journal: 7×10; 180-200 pages (average); 50 lb. woven old-style paper; 80 lb. cover stock; illustrations; photos. "Our readers are educated, inquisitive people who read a lot of work in the areas we feature, so they expect only the best in our pages. All work submitted should show evidence that the writer is at least as well educated and well read as our readers. Essays should be authoritative but accessible to a range of readers." Quarterly. Estab. 1947. Circ. 3,000.

No simultaneous or electronic submissions.

NEEDS "Ordinarily we do not publish novel excerpts or works translated into English, and we strongly discourage authors from submitting these." Receives 300 unsolicited mss/month. Accepts 3-4 mss/issue; 12-15 mss/year. Does not read unsolicited mss May 5-August 15. Publishes ms 6 months after acceptance. **Publishes some new writers/year.** Recently published work by Lee K. Abbot, Kevin Brockmeier, Ann Pancake, Janisse Ray, George Singleton. Also publishes literary essays, reviews, poetry. Occasionally comments on rejected mss.

HOW TO CONTACT Send complete ms. Responds in 2 weeks to queries; 2-4 months to mss. No simultaneous submissions or electronic submissions. Sample copy for $10. Writer's guidelines online.

PAYMENT/TERMS Pays $50/published page. Pays on publication for first North American serial rights. Sends galleys to author.

TIPS "Unsolicited manuscripts will not be considered from May 15-August 15 (annually); all such submissions received during that period will be returned unread. Check website for submission guidelines."

THE GETTYSBURG REVIEW

Gettysburg College, Gettysburg PA 17325. (717)337-6770. Fax: (717)337-6775. Website: www.gettysburgreview.com. Estab. 1988. Magazine: 6¼×10; 170 pages; acid free paper; full color illustrations. "Our concern is quality. Manuscripts submitted here should be extremely well written." Reading period September-May. Quarterly. Estab. 1988. Circ. 4,000.

NEEDS experimental, historical, humor/satire, literary, mainstream, novel excerpts, regional, serialized novels, contemporary. "We require that fiction be intelligent and esthetically written." Receives 350 unsolicited mss/month. Accepts 15-20 mss/issue; 60-80 mss/year. Publishes ms within 1 year after acceptance. **Publishes 1-5 new writers/year.** Recently published work by Nicholas Montemarano, Victoria Lancelotta, Leslie Pietrzyk, Kyle Minor, Kerry Neville-Bakken, Margot Singer. Length: 2,000-7,000 words; average length: 3,000 words. Publishes short shorts. Also publishes literary essays, literary criticism, poetry. Sometimes comments on rejected mss.

HOW TO CONTACT Send complete ms with SASE. Responds in 1 month to queries; 3-6 months to mss. Accepts simultaneous submissions. Sample copy for $10. Writer's guidelines online.

PAYMENT/TERMS Pays $30/page. Pays on publication for first North American serial rights.

GLIMMER TRAIN STORIES

Glimmer Train Press, Inc., 1211 NW Glisan St., Suite 207, Portland OR 97209. Fax: (503)221-0837. E-mail: eds@glimmertrain.org. Website: www.glimmertrain.org. Magazine: 225 pages; recycled; acid-free paper; 12 photographs. "We are interested in literary short stories published by new and established writers." Quarterly. Estab. 1991. Circ. 16,000.

NEEDS literary. Receives 4,000 unsolicited mss/month. Accepts 10 mss/issue; 40 mss/year. Publishes ms up to 18 months after acceptance. Agented fiction 5%. **Publishes 20 new writers/year.** Recently published work by Charles Baxter, Thisbe Nissen, Herman Carrillo, Andre Dubus III, William Trevor, Patricia Henley, Alberto Rios, Ann Beattie. Sometimes comments on rejected mss.

HOW TO CONTACT Submit work online at www.glimmertrain.org. Different submission categories are open each month of the year. Accepted work published in *Glimmer Train Stories*. Responds in 2 months to mss. Accepts simultaneous submissions. Sample copy for $12 on website. Writer's guidelines online.

PAYMENT/TERMS Pays $700 for standard submissions, up to $2,000 for contest winning stories. Pays on acceptance for first rights.

TIPS "We are very open to the work of new writers. Of the 100 Distinguished Short Stories listed in the current edition of Best American Short Stories, 10 first appeared in *Glimmer Train Stories*, more than in any other publication, including the *New Yorker*. Three of those 10 were the author's first publication." Make submissions using the online submission procedure on website. Saves paper, time, and allows you to track your submissions. See our contest listings in contest and awards section."

GO MAGAZINE

INK Publishing, 68 Jay St., Suite 315, Brooklyn NY 11201. (347)294-1220. Fax: (917)591-6247. E-mail: editorial@airtranmagazine.com. E-mail: trcrosby@mailaaa. Website: www.airtranmagazine.com. **Contact:** Shane Luitjens, art director. Estab. 2003.

TIPS "Review past issues online and study the guidelines to get a true sense of the types of features we are looking for."

GOOD OLD DAYS

Dynamic Resource Group, 306 E. Parr Rd., Berne IN 46711. Fax: (260)589-8093. E-mail: editor@goodolddaysonline.com. Website: www.goodolddaysonline.com. **Contact:** Ken Tate, editor.

Queries accepted, but are not necessary.

TIPS "Most of our writers are not professionals. We prefer the author's individual voice, warmth, humor, and honesty over technical ability."

GRAIN LITERARY MAGAZINE

P.O. Box 67, Saskatoon SK S7K 3K1 Canada. (306)244-2828. Fax: (306)244-0255. E-mail: grainmag@sasktel.net (inquiries only). Website: www.grainmagazine.ca. **Contact:** Mike Thompson, bus. admin. Estab. 1973. Literary magazine: 6×9; 128 pages; Chinook offset printing; chrome-coated stock; some photos. "*Grain* is an internationally acclaimed literary journal that publishes engaging, surprising, eclectic, and challenging writing and images by Canadian and international writers and artists." Quarterly. Circ. 1,500.

"Queries for submissions of work in other forms, less easy to categorize forms, cross-genre work, are welcome."

NEEDS experimental, literary, mainstream, contemporary, prose poem, poetry. "No romance, confession, science fiction, vignettes, mystery." Receives 80 unsolicited mss/month. Accepts 8-12 mss/issue; 32-48 mss/year. Publishes ms 11 months after acceptance. Recently published work by Yann Martel, Tom Wayman, Lorna Crozier. Also publishes poetry. Occasionally comments on rejected mss.

HOW TO CONTACT Send complete ms with SASE (or IRC) and brief letter. Accepts queries by e-mail, mail, fax, phone. Responds in 1 month to queries; 4 months to mss. No simultaneous submissions. Sample copy for $13 or online. Writer's guidelines for #10 SASE or online.

PAYMENT/TERMS Pays $50-225. Pays on publication for first Canadian serial rights.

TIPS "Submissions read Sept.-May only. Mss postmarked between June 1 and August 31 will not be read. Only work of the highest literary quality is accepted. Read several back issues."

GUD MAGAZINE

Greatest Uncommon Denominator Publishing, P.O. Box 1537, Laconia NH 03247. E-mail: editor@gudmagazine.com. Website: www.gudmagazine.com. Estab. 2006. Literary magazine/journal. "*GUD Magazine* transcends and encompasses the audiences of both genre and literary fiction. We're selling content, not media. If people want to buy just one story, they'll get it. If they want a PDF magazine, they'll get the whole issue. If they want a beautifully bound paper mag, they'll pay a little extra, but they'll get it. *GUD* features fiction (from flash to 15,000 word stories), art, poetry, essays, comics, reports and short drama. See website for more."

NEEDS Adventure, erotica, ethnic/multicultural, experimental, fantasy, horror, humor/satire, literary, science fiction, alternate history, mystery, why. Accepts 40 mss/year. Manuscript published 6 months after acceptance. Length: 15,000 words (max).

HOW TO CONTACT Submit via online form only. Responds to mss in up to 6 months. Considers simultaneous submissions, previously published submissions, and multiple submissions (art and poetry only). Guidelines available on website.

TIPS "We publish work in any genre, plus artwork, factual articles, and interviews. We'll publish something as short as 20 words or as long as 15,000, as long as it grabs us. Be warned: We read a lot. We've seen it all before. We are not easy to impress. Is your work original? Does it have something to say? Read it again. If you genuinely believe it to be so, send it. We do accept simultaneous submissions, as well as multiple submissions but read the guidelines first."

GUERNICA: A MAGAZINE OF ART & POLITICS

Attn: Michael Archer, 165 Bennett Ave., 4C, New York NY 10040. E-mail: editors@guernicamag.com; art@guernicamag.com (art/photography); poetry@guernicamag.com; publisher@guernicamag.com. Website: www.guernicamag.com. **Contact:** Erica Wright, poetry; Dan Eckstein, art/photography. Estab. 2005.

Received Caine Prize for African Writing, Best of the Net, cited by *Esquire* as a "great literary magazine."

NEEDS Literary, preferably with an international approach. No genre fiction.

HOW TO CONTACT Submit complete ms with cover letter, attn: Meakin Armstrong to fiction@guernicamag.com. In subject line (please follow this format exactly): "fiction submission."

TIPS "Please read the magazine first before submitting. Most stories that are rejected simply do not fit our approach. Submission guidelines available online."

GULF COAST: A JOURNAL OF LITERATURE AND FINE ARTS

University of Houston, Dept. of English, University of Houston, Houston TX 77204-3013. (713)743-3223.

E-mail: editors@gulfcoastmag.org. Website: www.gulfcoastmag.org. **Contact:** The Editors. Estab. 1986. Magazine: 7×9; approx. 300 pages; stock paper, gloss cover; illustrations; photos. "Innovative fiction for the literary-minded." Estab. 1987. Receives 300 unsolicited mss/month. Accepts 4-8 mss/issue; 12-16 mss/year. Publishes ms 6 months-1 year after acceptance. Agented fiction 5%. **Publishes 2-8 new writers/year.** Recently published work by Matt Bell, Megan Mayhew Bergman, Sarah Shun-Lien Bynum, Jenine Capot Crucet, Benjamin Percy, John Weir. Publishes short shorts. Sometimes comments on rejected mss. Back issue for $7, 7×10 SASE with 4 first-class stamps. Writer's guidelines for #10 SASE or on website. Acquires onetime rights. Please do not send multiple submissions; we will read only one submission per author at a given time, except in the case of our annual contests.

NEEDS Ethnic/multicultural, experimental, literary, regional, translations, contemporary. "No children's, genre, religious/inspirational." Wants more "cutting-edge, experimental" fiction.

PAYMENT/TERMS **Payment for accepted work** varies depending on availability of funds, but is a minimum of $30 per poem, $20 per page of prose up to $150, $50 per review, and $100 per interview.

TIPS "Submit only previously unpublished works. Include a cover letter. Online submissions are strongly preferred. Stories or essays should be typed, double-spaced, and paginated with your name, address, and phone number on the 1st page, title on subsequent pages. Poems should have your name, address, and phone number on the 1st page of each." The 2011 Gulf Coast Contests, awarding publication and $1,000 each in Poetry, Fiction, and Nonfiction, are now open. Honorable mentions in each category will receive a $250 second prize. Ilya Kaminsky will judge the contest in poetry, Frederick Reiken will judge in fiction, and John D'Agata will judge in nonfiction. Postmark/online entry deadline: March 15, 2011. Winners and Honorable Mentions will be announced in May. Entry fee: $20 (includes one-year subscription). Make checks payable to *Gulf Coast*. Guidelines available on website.

HADASSAH MAGAZINE

50 W. 58th St., New York NY 10019. (212)688-0227. Fax: (212)446-9521. E-mail: magazine@hadassah.org. Website: www.hadassah.org; www.hadassah.org/magazine. **Contact:** Rachel Fyman Schwartzberg; Zelda Shluker, managing editor. Jewish general-interest magazine: 7 7/8 ×10½; 64-80 pages; coated and uncoated paper; slick, medium weight coated cover; drawings and cartoons; photos. "*Hadassah* is a general interest Jewish feature and literary magazine. We speak to our readers on a vast array of subjects ranging from politics to parenting, to midlife crisis to Mideast crisis. Our readers want coverage on social and economic issues, Jewish women's (feminist) issues, the arts, travel and health." Monthly. Circ. 243,000.

NEEDS Ethnic/multicultural (Jewish). No personal memoirs, "schmaltzy" or shelter magazine fiction. Receives 20-25 unsolicited mss/month. Publishes some new writers/year. Recently published work by Joanne Greenberg and Jennifer Traig.

HOW TO CONTACT Must submit appropriate sized SASE. Responds in 4 months to mss. Sample copy and writer's guidelines for 9×12 SASE.

PAYMENT/TERMS Pays $700 minimum. Pays on acceptance for first North American serial, first rights.

TIPS "Stories on a Jewish theme should be neither self-hating nor schmaltzy."

HARPER'S MAGAZINE

666 Broadway, 11th Floor, New York NY 10012. (212)420-5720. Fax: (212)228-5889. E-mail: readings@harpers.org. Website: www.harpers.org. **Contact:** Stacey Clarkson, art director. Estab. 1850. Magazine: 8×10¾; 80 pages; illustrations. "*Harper's Magazine* encourages national discussion on current and significant issues in a format that offers arresting facts and intelligent opinions. By means of its several shorter journalistic forms—Harper's Index, Readings, Forum, and Annotation—as well as with its acclaimed essays, fiction, and reporting, *Harper's* continues the tradition begun with its first issue in 1850: to inform readers across the whole spectrum of political, literary, cultural, and scientific affairs." Monthly. Estab. 1850. Circ. 230,000.

Harper's Magazine will neither consider nor return unsolicited nonfiction manuscripts that have not been preceded by a written query. Harper's will consider unsolicited fiction. Unsolicited poetry will not be considered or returned. No queries or manuscripts will be considered unless they are accompanied by a SASE. All submissions and written queries (with the exception of Readings submissions) must be sent by mail to above address.

NEEDS humor/satire. Stories on contemporary life and its problems. Receives 50 unsolicited mss/month. Accepts 12 mss/year. Publishes ms 3 months after acceptance. **Publishes some new writers/year.** Recently published work by Rebecca Curtis, George Saunders, Haruki Murakami, Margaret Atwood, Allan Gurganus, Evan Connell, and Dave Bezmosgis.

HOW TO CONTACT Query by mail, except for submissions to the Readings section, which can be submitted via readings@harpers.org. Responds in 3 months to queries. Accepts reprints submissions. SASE required for all unsolicited material. Sample copy for $6.95.

PAYMENT/TERMS Generally pays 50¢-$1/word. Pays on acceptance. Vary with author and material. Sends galleys to author.

TIPS Some readers expect their magazines to clothe them with opinions in the way that Bloomingdale's dresses them for the opera. The readers of *Harper's Magazine* belong to a different crowd. They strike me as the kind of people who would rather think in their own voices and come to their own conclusions.

HARPUR PALATE

English Department, P.O. Box 6000, Binghamton University, Binghamton NY 13902-6000. Website: http://harpurpalate.blogspot.com. **Contact:** Barrett Bowlin, managing editor. Estab. 2000. Magazine: 6×9; 180-200 pages; coated or uncoated paper; 100 lb. coated cover; 4-color art portfolio insert. "We have no restrictions on subject matter or form. Quite simply, send us your highest-quality prose or poetry." Semiannual. Circ. 800.

NEEDS Adventure, ethnic/multicultural, experimental, historical, humor/satire, mainstream, mystery/suspense, novel excerpts, literary, fabulism, magical realism, metafiction, slipstream. Receives 400 unsolicited mss/month. Accepts 5-10 mss/issue; 12-20 mss/year. Publishes ms 1-2 months after acceptance. **Publishes 5 new writers/year.** Recently published work by Darryl Crawford and Tim Hedges, Jesse Goolsby, Ivan Faute, and Keith Meatto. Length: 250-8,000 words; average length: 2,000-4,000 words. Publishes short shorts. Also publishes poetry. Sometimes comments on rejected mss.

HOW TO CONTACT Send complete ms with a cover letter. Fiction and flash fiction should be 250-8,000 words. Include e-mail address on cover. Include estimated word count, brief bio, list of publications. Send a disposable copy of ms and #10 SASE for reply only. Submission periods are: July 15-November 15 for the winter issue, and December 15-April 15 for summer. Responds in 1-3 week to queries; 4- 8 months to mss. Accepts simultaneous submissions if stated in the cover letter. Sample copy for $10. Writer's guidelines online.

PAYMENT/TERMS Pays 2 copies. Pays on publication for first North American serial, electronic rights. Sponsors awards/contests.

TIPS "*Harpur Palate* now accepts submissions all year; deadline for Winter issue is November 15, for Summer issue is April 15. We also sponsor a fiction contest for the Summer issue and a poetry contest for the Winter issue. We do not accept submissions via e-mail. We are interested in high quality writing of all genres, but especially literary poetry and fiction."

HEARING HEALTH

Deafness Research Foundation, 363 Seventh Avenue, 10th Floor, New York NY 10001. E-mail: info@drf.org. Website: www.drf.org/magazine.

➒⊘ THE HELIX

Central Connecticut State University English Dept., E-mail: helixmagazine@gmail.com. Website: http://helixmagazine.org.

HIGHLIGHTS FOR CHILDREN

803 Church St., Honesdale PA 18431-1824. (570)253-1080. Fax: (570)251-7847. Website: www.Highlights.com. **Contact:** Manuscript Coordinator. Estab. 1946. Magazine: 42 pages; uncoated paper; coated cover stock; illustrations; photos. "This magazine of wholesome fun is dedicated to helping children grow in basic skills and knowledge, in creativeness, in ability to think and reason, in sensitivity to others, in high ideals and worthy ways of living—for children are the world's most important people. Publishes stories for children up to age 12; up to 500 words for beginners (ages 3-7), up to 800 words for advanced (ages 8-12)." Monthly.

NEEDS adventure, fantasy, mystery, historical, humor, mystery, animal, contemporary, retellings of folk tales, multicultural, sports. Prefers stories appealing to both girls and boys and stories with good characterization, strong emotional appeal, action, strong plot, believable setting. Receives 600-800 unsolicited mss/month. **Publishes 30 new writers/year.**

HOW TO CONTACT Send complete ms. Responds in 4 to 6 weeks. Accepts multiple submissions. Sample copy free. Writer's guidelines in "About Us" section of website.

PAYMENT/TERMS Pays $150 minimum, plus 2 contributor's copies. **Pays on acceptance.** Sends galleys to author.

TIPS "We are pleased that many authors of children's literature report that their first published work was in the pages of *Highlights*. It is not our policy to consider fiction on the strength of the reputation of the author. We judge each submission on its own merits. With factual material, however, we do prefer that writers be authorities in their field or people with first-hand experience. In this manner we can avoid the encyclopedic article that merely restates information readily available elsewhere. We don't make assignments. Query with simple letter to establish whether the nonfiction subject is likely to be of interest. A beginning writer should first become familiar with the type of material that *Highlights* publishes. Include special qualifications, if any, of author. Write for the child, not the editor. Write in a voice that children understand and relate to. Speak to today's kids, avoiding didactic, overt messages. Even though our general principles haven't changed over the years, we are contemporary in our approach to issues. Avoid worn themes."

HILTON HEAD MONTHLY

P.O. Box 5926, Hilton Head Island SC 29938. Fax: (843)842-5743. E-mail: editor@hiltonheadmonthly.com. Website: www.hiltonheadmonthly.com. **Contact:** Jeff Vrabel, Editor.

TIPS Sure, *Hilton Head* is known primarily as an affluent resort island, but there's plenty more going on than just golf and tennis; this is a lively community with a strong sense of identity and decades-long tradition of community, volunteerism and environmental preservation. We don't need any more tales of why you chose to retire here or how you fell in love with the beaches, herons or salt marshes. Seek out lively, surprising characters—there are plenty—and offer fresh (but not trendy) takes on local personalities, Southern living, and green issues.

HOBART

P.O. Box 1658, Ann Arbor MI 48103. E-mail: aaron@hobartpulp.com. Website: www.hobartpulp.com. PO Box 1658, Ann Arbor MI 48106. (206) 399-0410. E-mail: aaron@hobartpulp.com. Website: http://www.hobartpulp.com. **Contact:** Aaron Burch, Editor. Literary magazine/journal. 6×9, 200 pages. Contains illustrations. Includes photographs. "We publish non-stuffy, unpretentious, high quality fiction that never takes itself too serious and always entertains." Semiannual. Estab. 2002. Circ. 1000. Member CLMP.

Send submissions to: websubmissions@hobartpulp.com. Query first if you'd like to interview someone for Hobart.

NEEDS literary. Receives 200 mss/month. Accepts 20 mss/issue; 40 mss/year. Ms published 2-8 months after acceptance. **Publishes 2-5 new writers/year.** Published Benjamin Percy, Tod Goldberg, Chris Bachelder, Sheila Heti, Stephany Aulenback, Catherine Zeidler, and Ryan Call. Length: 1,000 words (min)-7,000 words (max). Average length: 3,000 words. Publishes short shorts. Also publishes literary essays. Sometimes comments on/critiques rejected mss.

HOW TO CONTACT Send complete ms with cover letter. Accepts submissions by e-mail. Responds to queries in 2 weeks. Responds to mss in 1-4 months. Send disposable copy of ms and #10 SASE for reply only. Considers simultaneous submissions. Sample copy available for $2. Guidelines available for SASE, via e-mail, on website.

PAYMENT/TERMS Writers receive $50-150, 2 contributor's copies, free subscription to the magazine. Additional copies $5. Pays on publication. Acquires first rights. Publication is copyrighted. **Tips** "We'd love to receive fewer run-of-the-mill relationship stories and more stories concerning truck drivers, lumberjacks, carnival workers, and gunslingers. In other words: surprise us. Show us a side of life rarely depicted in literary fiction."

TIPS The subject line must say, "print submission" and include your name, story title. Attach it as either a Word or .rtf document. For website submissions, we want stories shorter than 2,000 words, though 1,000 is better.

HORIZONS

100 Witherspoon St., Louisville KY 40202-1396. (502)569-5897. Fax: (502)569-8085. E-mail: susan.jackson-dowd@pcusa.org. Website: www.pcusa.org/horizons/. **Contact:** Susan Jackson Dowd, communications coordinator. "We include fiction and nonfiction, memoirs, essays, historical, and informational articles, all of interest to the Orthodox Jewish Woman." Quarterly. Estab. 1988.

NEEDS historical, humor/satire, mainstream, slice-of-life vignettes. Nothing not suitable to Orthodox Jewish values. Receives 4-6 unsolicited mss/month. Accepts 2-3 mss/issue; 10-12 mss/year. Publishes ms 6 months after acceptance. **Publishes 15- 20 new writers/year.** Length: 1,000-3,000 words; average length: 1,500 words. Also publishes poetry.

HOW TO CONTACT Send complete ms. Accepts submissions by e-mail, fax. Responds in 1 week to queries; 2 months to mss. Accepts simultaneous submissions. Writer's guidelines available.

PAYMENT/TERMS Pays 5¢/word. Pays 4-6 weeks after publication. Acquires one-time rights.

HUNGER MOUNTAIN

Vermont College of Fine Arts, Vermont College of Fine Arts, 36 College St., Montpelier VT 05602. (802)828-8517. E-mail: hungermtn@vermontcollege.edu. Website: www.hungermtn.org. Estab. 2002.

TIPS "We want high quality work! Submit in duplicate. Manuscripts must be typed, prose double-spaced. Poets submit at least 3 poems. No multiple genre submissions. We need more b&w photography and short shorts. Fresh viewpoints and human interest are very important, as is originality. We are committed to publishing an outstanding journal of arts & letters. Do not send entire novels, manuscripts, or short story collections. Do not send previously published work. See website for *Hunger Mountain*-sponsored literary prizes."

ILLUMEN

Sam's Dot Publishing, P.O. Box 782, Cedar Rapids IA 52406-0782. E-mail: illumensdp@yahoo.com. Website: www.samsdotpublishing.com/aoife/cover.htm. **Contact:** Karen L. Newman, ed. Estab. 2004.

TIPS "*Illumen* publishes beginning writers, as well as seasoned veterans. Be sure to read and follow the guidelines before submitting your work. The best advice for beginning writers is to send your best effort, not your first draft."

IMAGE

3307 Third Ave. W., Seattle WA 98119. (206)281-2988. Fax: (206)281-2979. E-mail: gwolfe@imagejournal.org. Website: www.imagejournal.org. **Contact:** Gregory Wolfe, publisher/editor. Estab. 1989. Magazine: 7×10; 136 pages; glossy cover stock; illustrations; photos. "*Image* is a showcase for the encounter between religious faith and world-class contemporary art. Each issue features fiction, poetry, essays, memoirs, reviews, an in-depth interview and articles about visual artists, film, music, etc. and glossy 4-color plates of contemporary visual art." Quarterly. Circ. 4,500. Member CLMP.

NEEDS literary, essays. Receives 100 unsolicited mss/month. Accepts 2 mss/issue; 8 mss/year. Publishes ms 1 year after acceptance. Agented fiction 5%. Has published work by Annie Dillard, David James Duncan, Robert Olen Butler, Bret Lott, Melanie Rae Thon. Length: 4,000-6,000 words; average length: 5,000 words.

HOW TO CONTACT Send SASE for reply, return of ms or send disposable copy of ms. Responds in 1 month to queries; 3 months to mss. Sample copy for $16. Reviews fiction.

PAYMENT/TERMS Pays $10/page and 4 contributor's copies; additional copies for $6. Pays on acceptance. Sends galleys to author.

TIPS "Fiction must grapple with religious faith, though the settings, and subjects need not be overtly religious."

INDIANA REVIEW

Ballantine Hall 465, 1020 E. Kirkwood, Indiana University, Bloomington IN 47405-7103. (812)855-3439. E-mail: inreview@indiana.edu. Website: www.indiana.edu/~inreview. Estab. 1976. Magazine: 6×9; 160 pages; 50 lb. paper; Glatfelter cover stock. "*Indiana Review*, a nonprofit organization run by IU graduate students, is a journal of previously unpublished poetry and fiction. Literary interviews and essays also considered. We publish innovative fiction and poetry. We're interested in energy, originality and careful attention to craft. While we publish many well-known writers, we also welcome new and emerging poets and fiction writers." Semiannual.

Work published in *Indiana Review* received a Pushcart Prize (2001) and was included in *Best New American Voices* (2001). *IR* also received an Indiana Arts Council Grant and a NEA grant.

NEEDS ethnic/multicultural, experimental, literary, mainstream, novel excerpts, regional, translations. No genre fiction. Receives 300 unsolicited mss/month. Accepts 7-9 mss/issue. Reads year-round, but refer to website for closed submission periods. Publishes ms an average of 3-6 months after acceptance. **Publishes 6-8 new writers/year.** Recently published work by Kim Addonizio, Stuart Dybek, Marilyn Chin,

Ray Gonzalez, Michael Martone, Melanie Rae Thon. Also publishes literary essays, poetry.

HOW TO CONTACT Send complete ms. Accepts online submissions. Cover letters should be *brief* and demonstrate specific familiarity with the content of a recent issue of *Indiana Review.* Include SASE. Responds in 4 months to mss. Accepts simultaneous submissions if notified *immediately* of other publication. Sample copy for $9. Writer's guidelines online.

PAYMENT/TERMS Pays $5/page, plus 2 contributor's copies. Pays on publication for first North American serial rights. Sponsors awards/contests.

TIPS "We're always looking for nonfiction essays that go beyond merely autobiographical revelation and utilize sophisticated organization and slightly radical narrative strategies. We want essays that are both lyrical and analytical where confession does not mean nostalgia. Read us before you submit. Often reading is slower in summer and holiday months. Only submit work to journals you would proudly subscribe to, then subscribe to a few. Take care to read the latest 2 issues and specifically mention work you identify with and why. Submit work that 'stacks up' with the work we've published. Offers annual poetry, fiction, short-short/prose-poem prizes. See website for full guidelines."

O INKWELL

Manhattanville College, 2900 Purchase St., Purchase NY 10577. (914)323-7239. Fax: (914)323-3122. E-mail: inkwell@mville.edu. Website: www.inkwelljournal.org. Estab. 1995. Literary Journal: $5\frac{1}{2} \times 7\frac{1}{2}$; 120-170 pages; 60 lb. paper; 10 pt C1S, 4/c cover; illustrations; photos. "*Inkwell* Magazine is committed to presenting top quality poetry, prose and artwork in a high quality publication. *Inkwell* is dedicated to discovering new talent and to encouraging and bringing talents of working writers and artists to a wider audience. We encourage diverse voices and have an open submission policy for both art and literature." Annual. Circ. 1,000. Member CLMP.

NEEDS experimental, humor/satire, literary. "No erotica, children's literature, romance, religious." Receives 120 unsolicited mss/month. Accepts 45 mss/issue. Does not read mss December-July. Publishes ms 2 months after acceptance. **Publishes 3-5 new writers/year.** Recently published work by Alice Quinn, Margaret Gibson, Benjamin Cheever, Paul Muldoon, Pablo Medina, Carol Muske-Dukes. Length: 5,000 words; average length: 3,000 words. Publishes short shorts. Also publishes poetry. Send a disposable copy of ms and #10 SASE for reply only. Responds in 1 month to queries; 4-6 months to mss. Sample copy for $6. Writer's guidelines for SASE.

Inkwell is produced in affiliation with the Master of Arts in Writing program at Manhattanville College, and is staffed by faculty and graduate students of the program.

PAYMENT/TERMS Pays $10/page and 2 contributor's copies; additional copies $8. Acquires first North American serial, first rights. Sponsors awards/contests.

TIPS "We cannot accept electronic submissions."

IRREANTUM

The Association for Mormon Letters, P.O. Box 1315, Salt Lake City UT 84110-1315. E-mail: editor@amlpubs.org. Website: www.irreantum.org. Estab. 1999. Magazine or Zine: $8\frac{1}{2} \times 7\frac{1}{2}$; 100-120 pages; 20 lb. paper; 20 lb. color cover; illustrations; photos. "While focused on Mormonism, *Irreantum* is a cultural, humanities-oriented magazine, not a religious magazine. Our guiding principle is that Mormonism is grounded in a sufficiently unusual, cohesive, and extended historical and cultural experience that it has become like a nation, an ethnic culture. We can speak of Mormon literature at least as surely as we can of a Jewish or Southern literature. *Irreantum* publishes stories, one-act dramas, stand-alone novel and drama excerpts, and poetry by, for, or about Mormons (as well as author interviews, essays, and reviews). The magazine's audience includes readers of any or no religious faith who are interested in literary exploration of the Mormon culture, mindset, and worldview through Mormon themes and characters. *Irreantum* is currently the only magazine devoted to Mormon literature." Biannual. Circ. 300.

Also publishes short shorts, literary essays, literary criticism, and poetry.

NEEDS "High quality work that explores the Mormon experience, directly or by implication, through literature. We acknowledge a broad range of experience with Mormonism, both as a faith and as a culture—on the part of devoted multi-generation Mormons, ethnic Mormons, new converts, and people outside the faith and culture who interact with Mormons and Mormon culture. We are committed to respectful exploration of Mormonism through literature. Receives 5 unsolicited mss/month. Accepts

CONSUMER MAGAZINES

3 mss/issue; 6 mss/year. Publishes ms 3-12 months after acceptance. **Publishes 3 or more new writers/year.** Recently published work by Orson Scott Card, Terryl Givens, Jack Harrell, Eric Samuelsen, Michael Collins, Phyllis Barber, Paul Swenson. Length: 1,000-5,000 words; average length: 5,000 words. Publishes short shorts. Also publishes literary essays, literary criticism, poetry. Sometimes comments on rejected mss. Annual fiction contest and annual personal essay contest with cash prizes.

HOW TO CONTACT Accepts submissions by e-mail in Microsoft Word or rich text files only. Accepts critical essays to criticalessaysubmissions@mormonletter.org. "The fiction and personal essay/creative nonfiction we publish is selected from the contest entries for the annual fiction contest and annual personal essay contest with offer cash prizes. There is a submission window—January 1-May 31st—for fiction and creative nonfiction submissions. All unsolicited fiction and creative nonfiction must be submitted according to contest rules which can be found on the website." Winner will receive a copy of the *Irreantum* issue in which his or her work appears. Send complete ms. with cover letter. Include a brief bio and list of publications. Responds in 2 weeks to queries, 2 months to mss. Accepts simultaneous and reprints, multiple submissions. Sample copy $15. Writer's guidelines on website. Reviews fiction.

PAYMENT/TERMS Pays $0-100. Pays on publication for one-time rights.

TIPS *Irreantum* is not interested in didactic or polemnical fiction that primarily attempts to prove or disprove Mormon doctrine, history, or corporate policy. We encourage beginning writers to focus on human elements first, with Mormon elements introduced only as natural and organic to the story. Readers can tell if you are honestly trying to explore human experience or if you are writing with a propagandistic agenda either for or against Mormonism. For conservative, orthodox Mormon writers, beware of sentimentalism, simplistic resolutions, and foregone conclusions.

JACK AND JILL

Children's Better Health Institute, P.O. Box 567, Indianapolis IN 46206-0567. (317)636-8881. E-mail: j.goodman@cbhi.org. Website: www.jackandjillmag.org. Estab. 1938.

TIPS "We are constantly looking for new writers who can tell good stories with interesting slants—stories that are not full of out-dated and time-worn expressions. We like to see stories about kids who are smart and capable, but not sarcastic or smug. Problem-solving skills, personal responsibility, and integrity are good topics for us. Obtain current issues of the magazine and study them to determine our present needs and editorial style."

THE JOURNAL

The Ohio State University, 164 W. 17th Ave., Columbus OH 43210. (614)292-4076. Fax: (614)292-7816. E-mail: thejournal@osu.edu; thejournalmag@gmail.com. Website: english.osu.edu/research/journals/thejournal/. Estab. 1972. Magazine: 6×9; 150 pages. "We're open to all forms; we tend to favor work that gives evidence of a mature and sophisticated sense of the language." Semiannual.

"We are interested in quality fiction, poetry, nonfiction, and reviews of new books of poetry. We impose no restrictions on category, type, or length of submission for Fiction, Poetry, and Nonfiction. We are happy to consider long stories and self-contained excerpts of novels. Please double-space all prose submissions. Address correspondence to the Editors. We will only respond to submissions accompanied by a SASE."

NEEDS novel excerpts, literary short stories. No romance, science fiction or religious/devotional. Receives 100 unsolicited mss/month. Accepts 2 mss/issue. Publishes ms 1 year after acceptance. Agented fiction 10%. **Publishes some new writers/year.** Recently published work by Michael Martone, Gregory Spatz, and Stephen Graham Jones. Sometimes comments on rejected mss.

HOW TO CONTACT Send complete ms with cover letter and SASE. Responds in 2 weeks to queries; 2 months to mss. Accepts simultaneous submissions. No electronic submissions. Sample copy for $7 or online. Writer's guidelines online.

PAYMENT/TERMS Pays $20. Pays on publication for first North American serial rights. Sends galleys to author.

TIPS "Manuscripts are rejected because of lack of understanding of the short story form, shallow plots, undeveloped characters. Cure: Read as much well-written fiction as possible. Our readers prefer 'psychological' fiction rather than stories with intricate plots. Take care to present a clean, well-typed submission."

JOURNAL PLUS MAGAZINE

654 Osos Street, San Luis Obispo CA 93401. (805)546-0609 or (805)544-8711. Fax: (805)546-8827. E-mail: slojournal@fix.net. **Contact:** Erin Mott.

KALEIDOSCOPE

Kaleidoscope Press, 701 S. Main St., Akron OH 44311-1019. (330)762-9755. Fax: (330)762-0912. E-mail: mshiplett@udsakron.org. Website: www.udsakron.org/kaleidoscope.htm. **Contact:** Mildred Shiplett. Estab. 1979. Magazine: 8½×11; 64 pages; non-coated paper; coated cover stock; illustrations (all media); photos. Subscribers include individuals, agencies, and organizations that assist people with disabilities and many university and public libraries. Open to new writers but appreciates work by established writers as well. Especially interested in work by writers with a disability, but features writers both with and without disabilities. "Writers without a disability must limit themselves to our focus, while those with a disability may explore any topic (although we prefer original perspectives about experiences with disability)." Semiannual.

Kaleidoscope has received awards from the American Heart Association, the Great Lakes Awards Competition and Ohio Public Images.

NEEDS "We look for well-developed plots, engaging characters and realistic dialogue. We lean toward fiction that emphasizes character and emotions rather than action-oriented narratives. No fiction that is stereotypical, patronizing, sentimental, erotic, or maudlin. No romance, religious or dogmatic fiction; no children's literature." Receives 35-40 unsolicited mss/month. Accepts 20 mss/year. Agented fiction 1%. **Publishes 2 new writer/year.** Recently published work by Carole Hall, Deshae E. Lott, and James M. Bellarosa. Also publishes poetry.

HOW TO CONTACT Accepts submissions by fax and e-mail, double-spaced with full address. Query first or send complete ms and cover letter. Include author's education and writing background and, if author has a disability, how it influenced the writing. SASE. Responds in 3 weeks to queries; 6 months to mss. Accepts simultaneous, multiple submissions and reprints. Sample copy for $6 prepaid. Writer's guidelines online.

PAYMENT/TERMS Pays $10-25, and 2 contributor's copies. Pays on publication for first rights, reprints permitted with credit given to original publication. Rights revert to author upon publication.

TIPS "Articles and personal experiences should be creative rather than journalistic and with some depth. Writers should use more than just the simple facts and chronology of an experience with disability. Inquire about future themes of upcoming issues. Sample copy very helpful. Works should not use stereotyping, patronizing, or offending language about disability. We seek fresh imagery and thought-provoking language. Please double-space work, number pages & include full name and address."

KENTUCKY MONTHLY

P.O. Box 559, Frankfort KY 40602-0559. (502)227-0053; (888)329-0053. Fax: (502)227-5009. E-mail: kymonthly@kentuckymonthly.com; steve@kentuckymonthly.com. Website: www.kentuckymonthly.com. **Contact:** Stephen Vest, editor. Estab. 1998. We publish stories about Kentucky and by Kentuckians, including stories written by those who live elsewhere."

NEEDS Adventure, historical, mainstream, novel excerpts. Publishes ms 3 months after acceptance.

HOW TO CONTACT Query with published clips. Accepts submissions by e-mail, fax. Responds in 3 weeks to queries; 1 month to mss. Accepts simultaneous submissions. Sample copy online. Writer's guidelines online.

PAYMENT/TERMS Pays $50-100. Pays within 3 months of publication. Acquires first North American serial rights.

TIPS "Please read the magazine to get the flavor of what we're publishing each month. We accept articles via e-mail, fax, and mail."

THE KENYON REVIEW

Finn House, 102 W. Wiggin, Gambier OH 43022. (740)427-5208. Fax: (740)427-5417. E-mail: kenyonreview@kenyon.edu. Website: KenyonReview.org. **Contact:** Marlene Landefeld. Estab. 1939. An international journal of literature, culture, and the arts, dedicated to an inclusive representation of the best in new writing (fiction, poetry, essays, interviews, criticism) from established and emerging writers.

NEEDS excerpts from novels, condensed novels, ethnic/multicultural, experimental, feminist, gay, historical, humor/satire, lesbian, literary, mainstream, translations, contemporary. Receives 900 unsolicited mss/month. Unsolicited mss read September 15-January 15 only. Publishes ms 1 year after acceptance. Recently published work by Alice Hoffman, Beth Ann Fennelly, Romulus Linney, John Koethe, Albert Goldbarth, Erin McGraw.

HOW TO CONTACT Only accepting mss via online submissions program. Please visit website for instructions. Do not submit via e-mail or snail mail. No simultaneous submissions. Sample copy $12 single issue, includes postage and handling. Please call or e-mail to order. Writer's guidelines online.

PAYMENT/TERMS Pays $15-40/page. Pays on publication for first rights.

TIPS "We no longer accept mailed or e-mailed submissions. Work will only be read if it is submitted through our online program on our website. Reading period is September 15-January 15. We look for strong voice, unusual perspective, and power in the writing."

THE KIT-CAT REVIEW

244 Halstead Ave., Harrison NY 10528. (914)835-4833. E-mail: kitcatreview@gmail.com. **Contact:** Claudia Fletcher, editor. Estab. 1998. Magazine: 8½×5½; 75 pages; laser paper; colored card cover stock; illustrations. "The *Kit-Cat Review* is named after the 18th Century Kit-Cat Club, whose members included Addison, Steele, Congreve, Vanbrugh and Garth. Its purpose is to promote/discover excellence and originality." The *Kit-Cat Review* is part of the collections of the University of Wisconsin (Madison) and State University of New York (Buffalo). Quarterly.

NEEDS ethnic/multicultural, experimental, literary, novel excerpts, slice-of-life vignettes. No stories with "O. Henry-type formula endings. Shorter pieces stand a better chance of publication." No science fiction, fantasy, romance, horror or new age. Receives 40 unsolicited mss/month. Accepts 6 mss/issue; 24 mss/year. Time between acceptance and publication is 6 months. **Publishes 14 new writers/year.** Recently published work by Chayym Zeldis, Michael Fedo, Louis Phillips, Elisha Porat. Length: 5,000 words maximum; average length: 2,000 words. Publishes short shorts. Also publishes literary essays, literary criticism, poetry.

HOW TO CONTACT Send complete ms. Accepts submissions by disk. Send SASE (or IRC) for return of ms, or send disposable copy of ms and #10 SASE for reply only. Responds in 1 week to queries; 2 months to mss. Accepts simultaneous, multiple submissions. Sample copy for $7 (payable to Claudia Fletcher). Writer's guidelines not available.

PAYMENT/TERMS Pays $25-200 and 2 contributor's copies; additional copies $5. Pays on publication for first rights.

TIPS "Obtaining a sample copy is strongly suggested. Include a short bio, SASE, and word count for fiction and nonfiction submissions."

LADYBUG

Carus Publishing Co., 700 E. Lake St., Suite 300, Chicago IL 60601. (312)701-1720. Website: www.cricketmag.com. **Contact:** Marianne Carus, editor-in-chief. Estab. 1990. Magazine: 8×10; 36 pages plus 4-page pullout section; illustrations. "We look for quality writing—quality literature, no matter the subject. For young children, ages 3-6." Monthly.

NEEDS "Looking for age-appropriate read-aloud stories for preschoolers."

HOW TO CONTACT Send complete ms. SASE. Responds in 6-8 months to mss. Accepts reprints submissions. Sample copy for $5 and 9×12 SAE. Writer's guidelines online.

PAYMENT/TERMS Pays 25¢/word (less for reprints). Pays on publication. Rights purchased vary. For recurring features, pays flat fee and copyright becomes property of Cricket Magazine Group.

TIPS "Reread ms before sending. Keep within specified word limits. Study back issues before submitting to learn about the types of material we're looking for. Writing style is paramount. We look for rich, evocative language and a sense of joy or wonder. Remember that you're writing for preschoolers—be age-appropriate, but not condescending or preachy. A story must hold enjoyment for both parent and child through repeated read-aloud sessions. Remember that people come in all colors, sizes, physical conditions, and have special needs. Be inclusive!"

LAKE SUPERIOR MAGAZINE

Lake Superior Port Cities, Inc., P.O. Box 16417, Duluth MN 55816-0417. (218)722-5002. Fax: (218)722-4096. E-mail: edit@lakesuperior.com. Website: www.lakesuperior.com. Estab. 1979.

NEEDS ethnic/multicultural, historical, humor/satire, mainstream, novel excerpts, slice-of-life vignettes, ghost stories. "All stories must be Lake Superior related." Receives 5 unsolicited mss/month. Accepts 1-3 mss/year. Publishes ms 10 months after acceptance. Publishes 1-6 new writers/year. Length: 300-1,500 words; average length: 1,000 words. Publishes short shorts. Also publishes, though rarely, literary essays, poetry. Often comments on rejected mss.

HOW TO CONTACT Query with published clips. Discourages submissions by e-mail. Responds in 3 months to queries. Sample copy for $4.95 and 5 first-class stamps. Writer's guidelines for #10 SASE or go online.

PAYMENT/TERMS Pays $1-125. Pays on publication for first North American serial, second serial (reprint) rights.

TIPS "Well-researched queries are attended to. We actively seek queries from writers in Lake Superior communities. We prefer manuscripts to queries. Provide enough information on why the subject is important to the region and our readers, or why and how something is unique. We want details. The writer must have a thorough knowledge of the subject and how it relates to our region. We prefer a fresh, unused approach to the subject which provides the reader with an emotional involvement. Almost all of our articles feature quality photography, color or black and white. It is a prerequisite of all nonfiction. All submissions should include a *short* biography of author/photographer; mug shot sometimes used. Blanket submissions need not apply."

LEADING EDGE

4087 JKB, Provo UT 84602. E-mail: editor@leadingedgemagazine.com. Website: www.leadingedgemagazine.com. Estab. 1980. Magazine specializing in science fiction and fantasy. *Leading Edge* is dedicated to helping new writers make their way into publishing. "We send back critiques with every story. We don't print anything with explicit language, graphic violence or sex." Semiannual.

Accepts unsolicited submissions.

NEEDS fantasy and science fiction short stories, poetry, and artwork. Receives 50 unsolicited mss/month. Accepts 6 mss/issue; 12 mss/year. Publishes ms 1-6 months after acceptance. **Publishes 9-10 new writers/year.** Have published work by Orson Scott Card, Brandon Sanderson, and Dave Wolverton. Max length: 15,000; average length: 10,000 words.

HOW TO CONTACT Send complete ms with cover letter and SASE. Include estimated word count. Send #10 SASE for reply only if disposable ms. Responds in 4-6 months to mss. Sample copy for $5.95. Writer's guidelines on website or send a SASE.

PAYMENT/TERMS 1¢/word for fiction; $10 for first 4 pages of poetry, $1.50 for each subsequent page; 2 contributor's copies; additional copies $4.95. Pays for publication for first North American serial rights. Sends galleys to author.

TIPS "Buy a sample issue to know what is currently selling in our magazine. Also, make sure to follow the writer's guidelines when submitting."

THE LEATHER CRAFTERS & SADDLERS JOURNAL

222 Blackburn St., Rhinelander WI 54501-3777. (715)362-5393. Fax: (715)362-5391. E-mail: tworjournal@newnorth.net. Estab. 1990.

TIPS "We want to work with people who understand and know leathercraft and are interested in passing on their knowledge to others. We would prefer to interview people who have achieved a high level in leathercraft skill."

LIGUORIAN

One Liguori Dr., Liguori MO 63057-9999. (636)464-2500. Fax: (636)464-8449; (636)464-2503. E-mail: liguorianeditor@liguori.org. Website: www.liguorian.org. **Contact:** Cheryl Plass, managing editor. Estab. 1913. Magazine: 40 pages; 4-color illustrations; photos. "Our purpose is to lead our readers to a fuller Christian life by helping them better understand the teachings of the gospel and the church and by illustrating how these teachings apply to life and the problems confronting them as members of families, the church, and society."

NEEDS Religious/inspirational, young adult/teen, senior citizen/retirement. "Stories submitted to *Liguorian* must have as their goal the lifting up of the reader to a higher Christian view of values and goals. We are not interested in contemporary works that lack purpose or are of questionable moral value." Receives 25 unsolicited mss/month. Accepts 10 mss/year. **Publishes 8-10 new writers/year.**

HOW TO CONTACT Send complete mss of 400-2,000 words. Accepts submissions by e-mail, fax, disk. Responds in 3 months to mss. Sample copy for 9×12 SASE with 3 first-class stamps or online. Writer's guidelines for #10 SASE and on website.

PAYMENT/TERMS Pays 12-15¢/word and 5 contributor's copies. Pays on acceptance. Buys first rights.

TIPS "First read several issues containing short stories. We look for originality and creative input in each story we read. Since most editors must wade through mounds of manuscripts each month, consideration for the editor requires that the market be studied, the manuscript be carefully presented and polished before submitting. Our publication uses only one story a month. Compare this with the 25 or more we receive over the transom each month. Also, many fiction mss are written without a specific goal or thrust, i.e., an interesting incident that goes nowhere is *not a story.* We believe fiction is a highly effective mode for transmitting the Christian message and also provides a good balance in an unusually heavy issue."

LISTEN MAGAZINE

The Health Connection, 55 W. Oak Ridge Dr., Hagerstown MD 21740. (301)393-4010; (301)393-4082. E-mail: editor@listenmagazine.org. Website: www.listenmagazine.org. **Contact:** Celeste Perrino-Walker, editor. Magazine: 16 pages; glossy paper; illustrations; photos. "*Listen* is used in many high school classes and by professionals: medical personnel, counselors, law enforcement officers, educators, youth workers, etc. *Listen* publishes true lifestories about giving teens choices about real-life situations and moral issues in a secular way." Monthly.

NEEDS Young adult/teen (hobbies, sports), anti-drug, alcohol, tobacco, positive role models, life skills. Publishes ms 6 months after acceptance. Length: 350-700; average length: 500 words.

HOW TO CONTACT Query with published clips or send complete ms. Accepts submissions by e-mail. Prefers submissions by e-mail. Considers manuscripts once a year—around October. Accepts simultaneous and multiple submissions, and reprints. Sample copy for $2 and 9×12 SASE. Writer's guidelines for SASE, by e-mail, fax or on website.

PAYMENT/TERMS Pays $50-200, and 3 contributor's copies; additional copies $2. Pays on acceptance for first rights.

TIPS "In query, briefly summarize article idea and logic of why you feel it's good. Make sure you've read the magazine to understand our approach. Yearly theme lists available on our website."

LITERARY MAMA

SC 29843. E-mail: lminfo@literarymama.com. Website: www.literarymama.com. **Contact:** Caroline Grant, Editor-in-Chief. Estab. 2003.

TIPS "We seek top-notch creative writing. We also look for quality literary criticism about mother-centric literature and profiles of mother writers. We publish writing with fresh voices, superior craft, vivid imagery. Please send submission (copied into e-mail) to appropriate departmental editors. Include a brief cover letter. We tend to like stark revelation (pathos, humor & joy), clarity, concrete details, strong narrative development; ambiguity, thoughtfulness, delicacy, irreverence, lyricism, sincerity; the elegant. We need the submissions 3 mos. before Oct.: Desiring Motherhood; May: Mother's Day Month; June: Father's Day Month."

LIVE

Gospel Publishing House, 1445 N. Boonville Ave., Springfield MO 65802-1894. (417)862-1447. Fax: (417)862-6059. E-mail: rl-live@gph.org. Website: www.gospelpublishing.com. Estab. 1928. "*LIVE* is a take-home paper distributed weekly in young adult and adult Sunday school classes. We seek to encourage Christians to live for God through fiction and true stories which apply Biblical principles to everyday problems." Weekly.

NEEDS religious/inspirational, inspirational, prose poem. No preachy fiction, fiction about Bible characters, or stories that refer to religious myths (e.g., Santa Claus, Easter Bunny, etc.). No science fiction or biblical fiction. No controversial stories about such subjects as feminism, war or capital punishment, "city, ethnic, racial settings." Accepts 2 mss/issue. Publishes ms 18 months after acceptance. **Publishes 50-70 new writers/year.** Recently published work by Tim Woodruff, Barbara Bryden, Katherine Crawford, Roy Borges.

HOW TO CONTACT Send complete ms. Accepts submissions by e-mail or regular mail. Responds in 6 weeks to mss. Accepts simultaneous submissions. Sample copy for #10 SASE. Writer's guidelines for #10 SASE or by e-mail request.

PAYMENT/TERMS Pays 7-10¢/word. Pays on acceptance for first, second serial (reprint) rights.

TIPS "Don't moralize or be preachy. Provide human interest articles with Biblical life application. Stories should consist of action, not just thought-life; interaction, not just insight. Heroes and heroines should rise above failures, take risks for God, prove that scriptural principles meet their needs. Conflict and suspense should increase to a climax! Avoid pious conclusions. Characters should be interesting, believable, and realistic. Avoid stereotypes. Characters should be active, not just pawns to move the plot along. They should confront conflict and change in believable ways. Describe the character's looks and reveal his personality through his actions to such an extent that the reader feels he has met that person. Readers should care about the character enough to finish the story. Feature racial, ethnic, and regional characters in rural and urban settings."

LULLWATER REVIEW

Emory University, P.O. Box 122036, Emory University, Atlanta GA 30322. Fax: (404)727-7367. E-mail: lullwater@lullwaterreview.com. **Contact:** Arina Korneva, editor-in-chief. Estab. 1990. Magazine: 6×9; 100 pages; 60 lb. paper; photos. "*Lullwater Review* seeks submissions that are strong and original. We require no specific genre or subject." Semiannual. Member, Council of Literary Magazines and Presses.

NEEDS Adventure, condensed novels, ethnic/multicultural, experimental, fantasy, historical, humor/satire, mainstream, mystery/suspense, novel excerpts, religious/inspirational, science fiction, slice-of-life vignettes, suspense, western. "No romance or science fiction, please." Receives 75-115 unsolicited mss/month. Accepts 3-7 mss/issue; 6-14 mss/year. Does not read mss in June, July, August. Publishes ms 1-2 months after acceptance. Publishes 25% new writers/year. Recently published work by Greg Jenkins, Thomas Juvik, Jimmy Gleacher, Carla Vissers, and Judith Sudnolt. Also publishes poetry.

HOW TO CONTACT Send complete ms. Accepts submissions by postal mail only. Responds in 1-3 months to queries; 3-6 months to mss. Accepts simultaneous submissions. Sample copy for $5. Writer's guidelines for #10 SASE.

PAYMENT/TERMS Pays 3 contributor copies. Pays on publication for first North American serial rights. Sponsors awards/contests.

TIPS "We at the *Lullwater Review* look for clear cogent writing, strong character development and an engaging approach to the story in our fiction submissions. Stories with particularly strong voices and well-developed central themes are especially encouraged. Be sure that your manuscript is ready before mailing it off to us. Revise, revise, revise! Be original, honest, and of course, keep trying."

◐ THE MADISON REVIEW

University of Wisconsin, 600 N, Park St., 6193 Helen C. White Hall, Madison WI 53706. E-mail: madisonreview@gmail.com. Website: www.english.wisc.edu/madisonreview/. Estab. 1972. Magazine: 6×9; 180 pages. "We are an independent literary journal featuring quality fiction, poetry, artwork, and interviews. Both established and emerging writers are encouraged to submit." Semiannual.

"We do not publish unsolicited interviews or genre ficion."

NEEDS "Well-crafted, compelling fiction featuring a wide range of styles and subjects." Receives 300 unsolicited mss/period. Accepts 6 mss/issue. Does not read May-September. Publishes ms 4 months after acceptance. **Publishes 4 new writers/year.** Recently published work by Lori Rader Day and Ian Williams. Average length: 4,000 words. Also publishes poetry.

HOW TO CONTACT Accepts multiple submissions. Sample copy for $4 via postal service or e-mail.

PAYMENT/TERMS Pays 2 contributor's copies; $5 charge for extras. Acquires first North American serial rights.

TIPS "Our editors have very ecclectic tastes, so don't specifically try to cater to us. Above all, we look for original, high quality work."

THE MAGAZINE OF FANTASY & SCIENCE FICTION

P.O. Box 3447, Hoboken NJ 07030. (201) 876-2551. E-mail: fandsf@aol.com. Website: www.fandsf.com. **Contact:** Gordon Van Gelder, editor. Estab. 1949. Magazine: 5×8; 240 pages; groundwood paper; card stock cover; illustrations on cover only. "For more than 60 years, we have been one of the leading publishers of fantastic fiction (which includes fantasy stories, science fiction, and some horror fiction). Our vision has changed little over six decades—we remain committed to publishing great stories without regard for whether they're classified as sf or fantasy. The *Magazine of Fantasy and Science Fiction* publishes various types of science fiction and fantasy short stories and novellas, making up about 80% of each issue. The balance of each issue is devoted to articles about science fiction, a science column, book and film reviews, cartoons, and competitions." Monthly. Circ. 30,000.

The *Magazine of Fantasy and Science Fiction* won a Nebula Award for Best Novelet for "The Merchant and the Alchemist's Gate" by Ted Chiang in in 2008. Also won the 2007 World Fantasy Award for Best Short Story for "Journey into the Kingdom" by M. Rickert. Editor

CONSUMER MAGAZINES

Van Gelder won the Hugo Award for Best Editor (short form), 2007 and 2008.

NEEDS adventure, fantasy (space fantasy, sword and sorcery), horror (dark fantasy, futuristic, psychological, supernatural), psychic/supernatural/occult, science fiction (hard science/technological, soft/sociological), young adult/teen (fantasy/science fiction, horror). "We're always looking for more science fiction." Receives 60-900 unsolicited mss/month. Accepts 5-10 mss/issue; 600-100 mss/year. Publishes ms 6-9 months after acceptance. **Publishes 3-6 new writers/year.** Agented fiction 5%. Recently published work by Peter S. Beagle, Ursula K. Le Guin, Alex Irvine, Pat Murphy, Joyce Carol Oates, Gene Wolfe, Ted Chiang, S.L. Gilbow, and Robert Silverberg. Length: Up to 25,000 words; average length: 7,500 words. Publishes short shorts. Send book review copies to Gordon Van Gelder. Sometimes comments on rejected mss.

HOW TO CONTACT Send complete ms with SASE (or IRC). Include list of publications, estimated word count. No electronic submissions. Responds in 2 months to queries, 6-8 weeks to mss. Accepts reprint submissions. Sample copy for $6. Writer's guidelines for SASE or on website. P.O. Box 3447, Hoboken NJ 07030. Phone: (201) 876-2551; Fax: (201) 876-2551. Email: fandsf@aol.com. Website: www.fandsf.com. Contact: Gordon Van Gelder, editor

PAYMENT/TERMS Pays 6-9¢/word, 2 contributor's copies; additional copies $4.20. Pays on acceptance for first North American serial rights. Sends galleys to author. Publication is copyrighted.

TIPS "Good storytelling makes a submission stand out. Regarding manuscripts, a well-prepared manuscript (i.e., one that follows the traditional format, like that describted here: http://www.sfwa.org/writing/vonda/vonda.htm) stands out more than any gimmicks. Read an issue of the magazine before submitting. New writers should keep their submissions under 15,000 words—we rarely publish novellas by new writers."

THE MALAHAT REVIEW

The University of Victoria, P.O. Box 1700, STN CSC, Victoria BC V8W 2Y2 Canada. (250)721-8524. E-mail: malahat@uvic.ca (for queries only). Website: www.malahatreview.ca. **Contact:** John Barton, editor. Estab. 1967. "We try to achieve a balance of views and styles in each issue. We strive for a mix of the best writing by both established and new writers." Quarterly.

NEEDS "General fiction, poetry, and creative nonfiction." Accepts 3-4 fiction mss/issue and 1 creative nonfiction ms/issue. Publishes ms within 6 months after acceptance. **Publishes 4-5 new writers/year.** Recently published work by Bill Gaston, Daryl Hine, Jan Zwicky, Stephen Henighan.

HOW TO CONTACT Send complete ms. "Enclose proper Canadian postage on the SASE (or send IRC)." Responds in 2 weeks to queries; approx. 3 months to mss. No simultaneous submissions. Sample copy for $16.45 (US). Writer's guidelines online.

PAYMENT/TERMS Pays $40 CAD/magazine page. Pays on acceptance for second serial (reprint), first world rights.

TIPS "Please do not send more than 1 submission at a time: 4-8 poems, 1 piece of creative non-fiction, or 1 short story (do not mix poetry and prose in the same submission). See *The Malahat Review*'s Open Season Awards for poetry and short fiction, creative non-fiction, long poem, and novella contests in the Awards section of our website."

MANOA

English Dept., University of Hawaii, Honolulu HI 96822. (808)956-3070. Fax: (808)956-3083. E-mail: mjournal-l@listserv.hawaii.edu. Website: manoajournal.hawaii.edu. **Contact:** Frank Stewart, Poetry Editor. Estab. 1989. Magazine: 7×10; 240 pages. Most of each issue devoted to new work from Pacific and Asian nations, including high quality literary fiction, poetry, essays, personal narrative. Please see website for current projects. Authors should query before sending submissions. Semiannual.

Manoa has received numerous awards, and work published in the magazine has been selected for prize anthologies. *Manoa* has received numerous awards, and work published in the magazine has been selected for prize anthologies. See website for recently published issues.

HOW TO CONTACT Please query first before sending in mss. Include SASE. Does not accept submissions by e-mail. Sample copy for $20 (U.S.). Writer's guidelines online.

PAYMENT/TERMS Pays $100-500 normally ($25/printed page). Pays on publication for first North American serial, non-exclusive, onetime print rights. Sends galleys to author.

TIPS "Not accepting unsolicited manuscripts at this time because of commitments to special projects. See website for more information."

THE MASSACHUSETTS REVIEW

South College, University of Massachusetts, Amherst MA 01003-9934. (413)545-2689. Fax: (413)577-0740. E-mail: massrev@external.umass.edu. Website: www.massreview.org. Estab. 1959. Magazine: 6×9; 172 pages; 52 lb. paper; 65 lb. vellum cover; illustrations; photos. Quarterly.

Does not respond to mss without SASE.

NEEDS short stories. Wants more prose less than 30 pages. Does not read fiction mss May 2-September 30. Publishes ms 18 months after acceptance. Agented fiction Approximately 5%. **Publishes 3-5 new writers/year.** Recently published work by Ahdaf Soueif, Elizabeth Denton, Nicholas Montemarano. Also publishes poetry. Sometimes comments on rejected mss.

HOW TO CONTACT Send complete ms electronically or by mail. **If submitting online, there is a $3 submission fee**. No returned ms without SASE. Responds in 3 months to mss. Accepts simultaneous, multiple submissions. Sample copy for $8. Writer's guidelines online.

PAYMENT/TERMS Pays $50. Pays on publication for first North American serial rights.

TIPS "No manuscripts are considered May-September. Electronic submission process on website. No fax or e-mail submissions. No simultaneous submissions. Shorter rather than longer stories preferred (up to 28-30 pages)." Looks for works that "stop us in our tracks." Manuscripts that stand out use "unexpected language, idiosyncrasy of outlook and are the opposite of ordinary."

MATURE LIVING

Lifeway Christian Resources, 1 Lifeway Plaza, Nashville TN 37234. (615)251-2000. E-mail: matureliving@lifeway.com. Website: www.lifeway.com. **Contact:** Rene Holt. Estab. 1977. Magazine: 8½×11; 52 pages; slick cover stock; full-color illustrations; photos. "Our magazine is Christian in content, and the material required is what would appeal to 55 and over age group: inspirational, informational, nostalgic, humorous. Our magazine is distributed mainly through churches (especially Southern Baptist churches) that buy the magazine in bulk and distribute it.

NEEDS humor/satire, religious/inspirational, senior citizen/retirement. No reference to liquor, dancing, drugs, gambling; no pornography, profanity, or occult. Accepts 8-10 mss/issue. Publishes ms 7-8 months after acceptance. Length: 600-1,200 words preferred; average length: 1,000 words.

HOW TO CONTACT Send complete ms. by e-mail or postal mail. "No queries please." Responds in 2 months to mss. Sample copy for 9×12 SAE with 4 first-class stamps. Writer's guidelines for #10 SASE.

PAYMENT/TERMS Pays $85-115 for feature articles; 3 contributor's copies. Pays on publication.

TIPS "Mss are rejected because they are too long or subject matter unsuitable. Our readers seem to enjoy an occasional short piece of fiction. It must be believable, however, and present senior adults in a favorable light."

MATURE YEARS

The United Methodist Publishing House, 201 Eighth Ave. S., P.O. Box 801, Nashville TN 37202-0801. (615)749-6292. Fax: (615)749-6512. E-mail: matureyears@umpublishing.org. Estab. 1954. Magazine: 8½×11; 112 pages; illustrations; photos. Magazine "helps persons in and nearing retirement to appropriate the resources of the Christian faith as they seek to face the problems and opportunities related to aging." Quarterly.

NEEDS humor/satire, religious/inspirational, slice-of-life vignettes, retirement years issues, intergenerational relationships. "We don't want anything poking fun at old age, saccharine stories or anything not for older adults. Must show older adults (age 55 plus) in a positive manner." Accepts 1 mss/issue; 4 mss/year. Publishes ms 1 year after acceptance. **Publishes some new writers/year.** Recently published work by Harriet May Savitz, Donita K. Paul, and Ann Gray.

HOW TO CONTACT Send complete ms. Responds in 2 weeks to queries; 2 months to mss. No simultaneous submissions. Sample copy for $6 and 9×12 SAE. Writer's guidelines for #10 SASE or by e-mail.

PAYMENT/TERMS Pays $60-125. Pays on acceptance for first North American serial rights.

TIPS "Practice writing dialogue! Listen to people talk; take notes; master dialogue writing! Not easy, but well worth it! Most inquiry letters are far too long. If you can't sell me an idea in a brief paragraph, you're not going to sell the reader on reading your finished article or story."

MEMOIR (AND)

Memoir Journal, **1316 67th Street, #8,** Emeryville CA 94608. (415)339-3142. E-mail: submissions@memoirjournal.com. Website: www.memoirjournal.com. Estab. 2006.

"We have two reading periods per year, with 4 prizes awarded in each: the *Memoir (and)* Prizes for Prose and Poetry ($100, $250, $500 & publication in publication in print and online, plus 3-6 copies of the journal) and the *Memoir (and)* Prize for Graphic Memoir ($100 & publication in print & online, 6 copies). Deadline: **noon Pacific time, August 16, 2011.**"

TIPS "The editors particularly invite submissions that push the traditional boundaries of form and content in the exploration of the representation of self. They also just love a well-told memoir."

MICHIGAN QUARTERLY REVIEW

0576 Rackham Bldg., 915 E. Washington, University of Michigan, Ann Arbor MI 48109-1070. (734)764-9265. E-mail: mqr@umich.edu. Website: www.umich.edu/~mqr. Estab. 1962. "An interdisciplinary journal which publishes mainly essays and reviews, with some high-quality fiction and poetry, for an intellectual, widely read audience." Quarterly.

"The Laurence Goldstein Award is a $1,000 annual award to the best poem published in the *Michigan Quarterly Review* during the previous year. The Lawrence Foundation Award is a $1,000 annual award to the best short story published in the *Michigan Quarterly Review* during the previous year."

NEEDS Literary. "No genre fiction written for a market. Would like to see more fiction about social, political, cultural matters, not just centered on a love relationship or dysfunctional family." Receives 200 unsolicited mss/month. Accepts 2 mss/issue; 8 mss/year. Publishes ms 1 year after acceptance. **Publishes 1-2 new writers/year.** Recently published work by Robert Boyers, Laura Kasischke, Herbert Gold, Alice Mattison, Joyce Carol Oates, Vu Tran. Length: 1,500-7,000 words; average length: 5,000 words. Also publishes literary essays, poetry.

HOW TO CONTACT Send complete ms. "I like to know if a writer is at the beginning, or further along, in his or her career. Don't offer plot summaries of the story, though a background comment is welcome." Include SASE. Responds in 2 months to queries; 6 weeks to mss. No simultaneous submissions. Sample copy for $4. Writer's guidelines online.

PAYMENT/TERMS Pays $10/published page. Pays on publication. Buys first serial rights. Sponsors awards/contests.

TIPS "Read the journal and assess the range of contents and the level of writing. We have no guidelines to offer or set expectations; every manuscript is judged on its unique qualities. On essays—query with a very thorough description of the argument and a copy of the first page. Watch for announcements of special issues which are usually expanded issues and draw upon a lot of freelance writing. Be aware that this is a university quarterly that publishes a limited amount of fiction and poetry and that it is directed at an educated audience, one that has done a great deal of reading in all types of literature."

MID-AMERICAN REVIEW

Bowling Green State University, Department of English, Box W, Bowling Green OH 43403. (419)372-2725. E-mail: mikeczy@bgsu.edu. Website: www.bgsu.edu/midamericanreview. **Contact:** Michael Czyzniejewski. Estab. 1981. Magazine: 6×9; 232 pages; 60 lb. bond paper; coated cover stock. "We try to put the best possible work in front of the biggest possible audience. We publish serious fiction and poetry, as well as critical studies in contemporary literature, translations and book reviews." Semiannual.

NEEDS Experimental, literary, translations, memoir, prose poem, traditional. "No genre fiction. Would like to see more short shorts." Receives 700 unsolicited mss/month. Accepts 4-8 mss/issue. Publishes ms 6 months after acceptance. Agented fiction 5%. Publishes 4-8 new writers/year. Recently published work by Matthew Eck, Becky Hagentson, and Kevin Wilson. Occasionally comments on rejected mss.

HOW TO CONTACT Send complete ms with SASE. Responds in 4 months to mss. Sample copy for $9 (current issue), $5 (back issue); rare back issues $10. Writer's guidelines online. Reviews fiction.

PAYMENT/TERMS Pays $10/page up to $50, pending funding. Pays on publication when funding is available. Acquires first North American serial, one-time rights. Sponsors awards/contests.

TIPS "We are seeking translations of contemporary authors from all languages into English; submissions must include the original and proof of permission to translate. We would also like to see more creative nonfiction."

MIDWEST OUTDOORS

MidWest Outdoors, Ltd., 111 Shore Dr., Burr Ridge IL 60527-5885. (630)887-7722. Fax: (630)887-1958. Website: www.midwestoutdoors.com. Estab. 1967.

"Submissions must be e-mailed to info@midwestoutdoors.com (Microsoft Word format preferred)."

TIPS "Break in with a great unknown fishing hole or new technique within 500 miles of Chicago. Where, how, when, and why. Know the type of publication you are sending material to."

MINDFLIGHTS

Double-Edged Publishing Inc., 9618 Misty Brook Cove, Cordova TN 38016. (901)213-3768. E-mail: editor@mindflights.com; MindFlightsEditors@gmail.com. Website: www.mindflights.com. **Contact:** Selena Thomason, managing editor. Estab. 2007. Magazine/E-zine. "Publishes science fiction, fantasy, and all genres of speculative fiction and poetry. We want work that is grounded in a Christian or Christian-friendly worldview, without being preachy. Please see our vision and guidelines page for details. *MindFlights* is the merging of two established magazines: *The Sword Review* and *Dragons, Knights, & Angels*." Monthly e-zine, annual print edition.

"No postal submissions accepted. See our portal entry and submission process online."

NEEDS Fantasy (space fantasy, sword and sorcery), science fiction (hard science/technological, soft/sociological), special interests: speculative fiction and poetry with Christian themes. Does not want to see work "that would be offensive to a Christian audience. Also, we are a family-friendly market and thus do not want to see explicit sex, illicit drug use, gratuitous violence or excessive gore." Receives 30 mss/month. Accepts 4 mss/issue; 48 mss/year. Ms published 2 months after acceptance. **Publishes 6-12 new writers/year.** Length: 500-5,000 words. Average length: 3,000 words. Publishes short shorts. Average length of short shorts: 700 words. Also publishes poetry. Always comments on/critiques rejected mss.

HOW TO CONTACT Send complete ms via online form. Include estimated word count. Responds to queries in 2 weeks. Responds to mss in 4 weeks. Considers previously published submissions, multiple submissions. Guidelines available on website.

PAYMENT/TERMS Writers receive ½¢ per word, $5 min and $25 max, 1 contributor's copy if selected for print edition. Additional copies $7.50. Pays on acceptance. Acquires first rights, first North American serial rights, onetime rights, electronic rights. Sends galleys to author. Publication is copyrighted. Occasional contests. "Details and entry process would be on our website when contest is announced."

TIPS "Only a very small portion of the works accepted for *MindFlights* will appear in our annual print edition. Most will appear online only. Although our guidelines currently indicate that upon acceptance of a work we will ask for rights for either print, the web, or both, and our contracts clearly indicate which rights we are requesting, we are concerned that authors may be assuming that all works accepted will appear in the print edition. Thank you."

MISSISSIPPI REVIEW

Univ. of Southern Mississippi, 118 College Dr., #5144, Hattiesburg MS 39406-0001. (601)266-4321. Fax: (601)266-5757. E-mail: elizabeth@mississippireview.com. Website: www.mississippireview.com. Estab. 1972.

"We do not accept unsolicited manuscripts except under the rules and guidelines of the *Mississippi Review* Prize Competition. See website for guidelines."

NEEDS Annual fiction and poetry competition. $1,000 awarded in each category plus publication of all winners and finalists. Fiction entries 5,000 words or less. Poetry entry equals 1-3 poems; page limit is 10. $15 entry fee includes copy of prize issue. No limit on number of entries. Deadline October 1. No mss returned. **Publishes 25-30 new writers/year.**

HOW TO CONTACT Sample copy for $8. Writer's guidelines online.

PAYMENT/TERMS Acquires first North American serial rights.

THE MISSOURI REVIEW

357 McReynolds Hall, University of Missouri, Columbia MO 65211. (573)882-4474. Fax: (573)884-4671. E-mail: tmr@missourireview.com. Website: www.missourireview.com. Estab. 1978. Magazine: 6¾×10; 200 pages.

"We publish contemporary fiction, poetry, interviews, personal essays, cartoons, special features—such as History as Literature series and Found Text series—for the literary and the general reader interested in a wide range of subjects."

NEEDS literary fiction on all subjects, novel excerpts. Word count is best if between 2,000 and 30,000 words; shorter or longer must be truly exceptional to be published. No genre fiction. Receives 500 unsolicited mss/month. Accepts 5-7 mss/issue; 16-20 mss/year. **Publishes 6-10 new writers/year.** Recently published work by Nat Akin, Jennifer Bryan, Bruce Ducker, William Lychack, Cynthia Morrison Phoel. Also publishes literary essays, poetry. Often comments on rejected mss.

HOW TO CONTACT Send complete ms. May include brief bio and list of publications. Send SASE for reply, return of ms or send disposable copy of ms. **Online submissions via website with a $3 charge**. Responds in 2 weeks to queries; 12 weeks to mss. Writer's guidelines online.

PAYMENT/TERMS Pays $30/printed page up to $750. Offers signed contract. Sponsors awards/contests.

TIPS "Send your best work." The *Missouri Review* holds two annual contests, the **Jeffrey E. Smith Editors' Prize** in Fiction, Essay and Poetry, and our recently instituted **Audio Competition**.

THE MOCHILA REVIEW

Missouri Western State University, 4525 Downs Dr., St. Joseph MO 64507. E-mail: church@missouriwestern.edu. Website: www.missouriwestern.edu/orgs/mochila/homepage.htm. **Contact:** Bill Church, editor. Estab. 2000. "Good readership, no theme." Annual. Estab. 2000.

NEEDS literary. Does not accept genre work, erotica. Receives 25 unsolicited mss/month. Accepts 5-10 mss/issue. Does not read mss December-July. Publishes ms 6 months after acceptance. **Publishes 2-3 new writers/year.** Length: 5,000 words (max); average length: 3,000 words. Publishes short shorts; average 500 words. Also publishes literary essays, poetry. Rarely comments on rejected mss.

HOW TO CONTACT Send complete disposable copy of ms with cover letter and #10 SASE for reply only. Include estimated word count, brief bio, and list of publications. Responds in 3-5 months to mss. Accepts simultaneous submissions. Sample copy for $7. Writer's guidelines for SASE or on website.

PAYMENT/TERMS Pays 2 contributor's copies; additional copies $5. Acquires first rights. Publication not copyrighted.

TIPS "Manuscripts with fresh language, energy, passion and intelligence stand out. Study the craft and be entertaining and engaging."

NA'AMAT WOMAN

350 Fifth Ave., Suite 4700, New York NY 10118. (212)563-5222. Fax: (212)563-5710. E-mail: naamat@naamat.org; judith@naamat.org. Website: www.naamat.org. **Contact:** Judith Sokoloff, editor. Estab. 1926. "Magazine covering a wide variety of subjects of interest to the Jewish community—including political and social issues, arts, profiles; many articles about Israel and women's issues. Fiction must have a Jewish theme. Readers are the American Jewish community." Circ. 15,000.

NEEDS Ethnic/multicultural, historical, humor/satire, literary, novel excerpts, women-oriented. Receives 10 unsolicited mss/month. Accepts 3-5 mss/year.

HOW TO CONTACT Query with published clips or send complete mss. Responds in 6 months to queries; 6 months to mss. Sample copy for 9×11½ SAE and $1.20 postage. Sample copy for $2. Writer's guidelines for #10 SASE, or by e-mail.

PAYMENT/TERMS Pays 10¢/word and 2 contributor's copies. Pays on publication for first North American serial, first, onetime, second serial (reprint) rights, makes work-for-hire assignments.

TIPS "No maudlin nostalgia or romance; no hackneyed Jewish humor."

NATURAL HISTORY

Natural History, Inc., 105 W. Highway 54, Suite 265, Durham NC 27713. (212)769-5500. E-mail: nhmag@naturalhistorymag.com. Website: www.naturalhistorymag.com.

TIPS "We expect high standards of writing and research. We do not lobby for causes, environmental, or other. Scientist should submit proposed articles either in query or by manuscript."

NECROLOGY SHORTS: TALES OF MACABRE AND HORROR

Isis International, P.O. Box 510232, St. Louis MO 63151. E-mail: editor@necrologyshorts.com; submit@necrologyshorts.com. Website: www.necrologyshorts.com. **Contact:** John Ferguson, editor. Estab. 2009. Consumer publication published online daily and through Amazon Kindle. "We will also be publishing an annual collection for each year in print, e-book reader, and Adobe PDF format. Our main genre is suspense horror similar to H.P. Lovecraft and/or Robert E. Howard. We also publish science fiction and fantasy. We would love to see work continuing the Cthulhu Mythos, but we accept all horror."

NEEDS "*Necrology Shorts* is an online publication which publishes fiction, articles, cartoons, artwork, and poetry daily. Embracing the Internet, e-book readers, and new technology, we aim to go beyond the long time standard of a regular publication to bringing our readers a daily flow of entertainment."

HOW TO CONTACT Submit complete ms. by e-mail to submit@necrologyshorts.com. Buys 1,000 mss/year. Responds in 1 month. Guidelines on website. We review submissions in the order we receive them. Please allow 1-2 weeks for us to review your work. If your submission passes review, it will be added to *Necrology Shorts* within 72 hours. You will be notified when your submission is posted. If your submission does not pass review, we will notify you of any problems and reasons. Submission can be resubmitted once it is corrected.

TIPS "*Necrology Shorts* is looking to break out of the traditional publication types to use the Internet, e-book readers, and other technology. We not only publish works of authors and artists, we let them use their published works to brand themselves and further their profits of their hard work. We love to see traditional short fiction and artwork, but we also look forward to those that go beyond that to create multimedia works. The best way to get to us is to let your creative side run wild and not send us the typical fare. Don't forget that we publish horror, sci-fi, and fantasy. We expect deranged, warped, twisted, strange, sadistic, and things that question sanity and reality."

NERVE COWBOY

Liquid Paper Press, P.O. Box 4973, Austin TX 78765. Website: www.jwhagins.com/nervecowboy.html. **Contact:** Joseph Shields or Jerry Hagins. Estab. 1996. Magazine: 7×8½; 64 pages; 20 lb. paper; card stock cover; illustrations. "*Nerve Cowboy* publishes adventurous, comical, disturbing, thought-provoking, accessible poetry and fiction. We like to see work sensitive enough to make the hardest hard-ass cry, funny enough to make the most helpless brooder laugh and disturbing enough to make us all glad we're not the author of the piece." Semiannual.

NEEDS literary. No "racist, sexist or overly offensive work. Wants more unusual stories with rich description and enough twists and turns that leave the reader thinking." Receives 40 unsolicited mss/month. Accepts 2-3 mss/issue; 4-6 mss/year. Publishes ms 6-12 months after acceptance. **Publishes 5-10 new writers/year.** Recently published work by Lori Jakiela, Michele Anne Jaquays, Tom Schmidt, David Elsey, Michael A. Flanagan. Length: 1,500 words; average length: 750-1,000 words. Publishes short shorts. Also publishes poetry.

HOW TO CONTACT Send SASE for reply, return of ms or send a disposable copy of ms. Responds in 6 weeks to queries; 3 months to mss. Accepts reprint submissions. No simultaneous submissions. Sample copy for $6. Writer's guidelines for #10 SASE or online.

PAYMENT/TERMS Pays 1 contributor's copy. Acquires onetime rights.

TIPS "We look for writing which is very direct and elicits a visceral reaction in the reader. Read magazines you submit to in order to get a feel for what the editors are looking for. Write simply and from the gut."

NEW ENGLAND REVIEW

Middlebury College, Middlebury VT 05753. (802)443-5075. E-mail: nereview@middlebury.edu. Website: go.middlebury.edu/nereview; www.nereview.com. Estab. 1978.

No e-mail submissions.

NEEDS Literary. Receives 550 unsolicited mss/month. Accepts 6 mss/issue; 24 fiction mss/year. Does not accept mss June-August. Publishes ms approx 2-6 months after acceptance. Agented fiction less than 5%. **Publishes approx. 10 new writers/year.** Recently published work by Steve Almond, Christine Sneed, Roy Kesey, Thomas Gough, Norman Lock, Brock Clarke. Publishes short shorts and translations. Sometimes comments on rejected mss.

HOW TO CONTACT "Send complete mss with cover letter, hard copy only. Will consider simultaneous submissions, but must be stated as such and you must notify us immediately if the manuscript is accepted for publication elsewhere." No poetry simultaneous submissions please. SASE. Responds in 2 weeks to queries; 3 months to mss. Sample copy for

$10, add $3 CAN or $5 for overseas. Writer's guidelines online. No electronic submissions.

PAYMENT/TERMS Pays $10/page ($20 minimum), and 2 copies. Pays on publication for first North American serial, first, second serial (reprint) rights. Sends galleys to author.

TIPS "We consider short fiction, including short-shorts, novellas, and self-contained extracts from novels in both traditional and experimental forms. In nonfiction, we consider a variety of general and literary, but not narrowly scholarly essays; we also publish long and short poems; screenplays; graphics; translations; critical reassessments; statements by artists working in various media; testimonies; and letters from abroad. We are committed to exploration of all forms of contemporary cultural expression in the US and abroad. With few exceptions, we print only work not published previously elsewhere."

NEW LETTERS

University of Missouri-Kansas City, University House, 5101 Rockhill Rd., Kansas City MO 64110-2499. (816)235-1168. Fax: (816)235-2611. E-mail: newletters@umkc.edu. Website: www.newletters.org. Estab. 1934. Magazine: 6x9, 14 lb. cream paper; illustrations. "*New Letters* is intended for the general literary reader. We publish literary fiction, nonfiction, essays, poetry. We also publish art."

Submissions are not read May 1-October 1.

NEEDS Ethnic/multicultural, experimental, humor/satire, literary, mainstream, translations, contemporary. No genre fiction. Does not read mss May 1-October 1. Publishes ms 5 months after acceptance. Recently published work by Thomas E. Kennedy, Sheila Kohler, Charlotte Holmes, Rosellen Brown, Janet Burroway. Publishes short shorts. Average length is 3,000-5,000 words.

HOW TO CONTACT Send complete ms. Do not submit by e-mail. Responds in 1 month to queries; 3 months to mss. "We discourage multiple submissions but appreciate being told if you are simultaneously submitting your work to us and other magazines; we expect to be notified immediately if the work you sent us has been accepted for publication elsewhere." Sample copy for $10 or sample articles on website. Writer's guidelines online.

PAYMENT/TERMS Pays $30-75 for fiction and $15 for single poem. Pays on publication for first North American serial rights. Sends galleys to author. $4,500 awarded annually in writing contest for short fiction, essay, and poetry. Visit www.newletters.org for contest guidelines.

TIPS "We aren't interested in essays that are footnoted, or essays usually described as scholarly or critical. Our preference is for creative nonfiction or personal essays. We prefer shorter stories and essays to longer ones (an average length is 3,500-4,000 words). We have no rigid preferences as to subject, style, or genre, although commercial efforts tend to put us off. Even so, our only fixed requirement is on good writing."

NEW MILLENNIUM WRITINGS

612 Gist Creek Rd., Sevierville TN 37876. Website: www.newmillenniumwritings.com. **Contact:** Elizabeth Petty, sub. editor.

TIPS "Include email address and/or letter-size SASE for response only. We do not return manuscripts except in hardship cases."

NEW ORLEANS REVIEW

Box 195, Loyola University, New Orleans LA 70118. (504)865-2295. E-mail: noreview@loyno.edu. Website: neworleansreview.org. **Contact:** Christopher Chambers, editor. Estab. 1968. Journal: 6×9; perfect bound; 200 pages; photos. "Publishes poetry, fiction, translations, photographs, nonfiction on literature, art and film. Readership: those interested in contemporary literature and culture." Biannual.

NEEDS "Quality fiction from conventional to experimental." **Publishes 12 new writers/year.** Recently published work by Gordon Lish, Michael Martone, Dylan Landis, Stephen Graham Jones, Carolyn Sanchez and Josh Russell.

HOW TO CONTACT Responds in 4-6 months to mss. Accepts simultaneous submissions "if we are notified immediately upon acceptance elsewhere." Sample copy for $5. Reviews fiction. Pays 2 copies.

PAYMENT/TERMS Pays $25-50 and 2 copies. Pays on publication for first North American serial rights.

TIPS "We're looking for dynamic writing that demonstrates attention to the language, and a sense of the medium, writing that engages, surprises, moves us. We're not looking for genre fiction, or academic articles. We subscribe to the belief that in order to truly write well, one must first master the rudiments: grammar and syntax, punctuation, the sentence, the paragraph, the line, the stanza. We receive about 3,000 manuscripts a year, and publish about 3% of them.

Check out a recent issue, send us your best, proofread your work, be patient, be persistent."

THE NEW QUARTERLY

St. Jerome's University, 290 Westmount Rd. N., Waterloo ON N2L 3G3 Canada. (519)884-8111, ext. 28290. E-mail: editor@tnq.ca. Website: www.tnq.ca. Estab. 1981.

NEEDS Publishes ms 4 months after acceptance. "Publishes Canadian writing only, fiction and poetry plus essays on writing. Emphasis on emerging writers and genres, but we publish more traditional work as well if the language and narrative structure are fresh."

Open to Canadian writers only.

HOW TO CONTACT Send complete ms. Does not accept submissions by e-mail. Responds in 2 weeks to queries; 3-6 months to mss. Accepts simultaneoues submissions if indicated in cover letter. Sample copy for $15 (cover price, plus mailing). Writer's guidelines for #10 SASE or online.

PAYMENT/TERMS Pays $200/story, $30/poem. Pays on publication for first Canadian rights.

TIPS "Reading us is the best way to get our measure. We don't have preconceived ideas about what we're looking for other than that it must be Canadian work (Canadian writers, not necessarily Canadian content). We want something that's fresh, something that will repay a second reading, something in which the language soars and the feeling is complexly rendered."

NEW SOUTH

Campus Box 1894, Georgia State Univ., MSC 8R0322 Unit 8, Atlanta GA 30303-3083. (404)651-4804. Fax: (404)651-1710. E-mail: new_south@langate.gsu.edu. Website: www.review.gsu.edu. Estab. 1980. Literary journal. "*New South* is a biannual literary magazine publishing poetry, fiction, creative nonfiction, and visual art. We're looking for original voices and well-written manuscripts. No subject or form biases." Biannual.

NEEDS literary fiction and creative nonfiction. Receives 200 unsolicited mss/month. Publishes and welcomes short shorts.

HOW TO CONTACT Include SASE for notification. Responds in 3-5 months. Sample copy for $5. Writer's guidelines for SASE or on website.

PAYMENT/TERMS Pays in contributor's copy. Acquires one-time rights.

THE NEW WRITER

P.O. Box 60, Cranbrook Kent TN17 2ZR United Kingdom. (44)(158)021-2626. E-mail: editor@thenewwriter.com. Website: www.thenewwriter.com. **Contact:** Sarah Jackson, poetry editor. Estab. 1996. Magazine: A4; 56 pages; illustrations; photos. Contemporary writing magazine which publishes "the best in fact, fiction and poetry." Publishes 6 issues per annum.

NEEDS "We will consider most categories apart from stories written for children. No horror, erotic or cosy fiction." Accepts 4 mss/issue; 24 mss/year. Publishes ms 1 year after acceptance. Agented fiction 5%. **Publishes 12 new writers/year.** Recently published work by Sally Zigmond, Lorna Dowell, Wes Lee, Amy Licence, Cathy Whitfield, Katy Darby, Clio Gray. Length: 2,000-5,000 words; average length: 3,500 words. Publishes short shorts. Also publishes literary essays, literary criticism, poetry. Often comments on rejected mss.

HOW TO CONTACT Query with published clips. Accepts submissions by e-mail, fax. Send SASE (or IRC) for return of ms or send a disposable copy of ms and #10 SASE for reply only. "We consider short stories from subscribers only but we may also commission guest writers." Responds in 2 months to queries; 4 months to mss. Accepts simultaneous submissions. Sample copy for SASE and A4 SAE with IRCs only. Writer's guidelines for SASE. Reviews fiction.

PAYMENT/TERMS Pays £10 per story by credit voucher; additional copies for £1.50. Pays on publication for onetime rights. Sponsors awards/contests.

TIPS "Hone it—always be prepared to improve the story. It's a competitive market."

THE NEW YORKER

4 Times Square, New York NY 10036. (212) 286-5900. E-mail: beth_lusko@newyorker.com. E-mail: toon@cartoonbank.com. Website: www.newyorker.com; www.cartoonbank.com. **Contact:** Deborah Treisman, fiction editor. Estab. 1925. A quality magazine of interesting, well-written stories, articles, essays and poems for a literate audience. Weekly.

the *New Yorker* receives approximately 4,000 submissions per month.

NEEDS Accepts 1 mss/issue.

HOW TO CONTACT Send complete ms as .pdf attachments via online e-mail manager. No more than 1 story or 6 poems should be submitted. No attachments. Responds in 3 months to mss. No simultaneous submissions. Writer's guidelines online.

PAYMENT/TERMS Payment varies. Pays on acceptance.

TIPS "Be lively, original, not overly literary. Write what you want to write, not what you think the editor would like. Send poetry to Poetry Department."

THE NORTH AMERICAN REVIEW

University of Northern Iowa, 1222 W. 27th St., Cedar Falls IA 50614-0516. (319)273-6455. Fax: (319)273-4326. E-mail: nar@uni.edu. Website: www.webdelsol.com/northamreview/nar/. Estab. 1815. "The *NAR* is the oldest literary magazine in America and one of the most respected. Though we have no prejudices about the subject matter of material sent to us, our first concern is quality." Bimonthly. Estab. 1815. Circ. under 5,000.

"This is the oldest literary magazine in the country and one of the most prestigious. Also one of the most entertaining—and a tough market for the young writer."

NEEDS Open (literary). "No flat narrative stories where the inferiority of the character is the paramount concern." Wants to see more "well-crafted literary stories that emphasize family concerns. We'd also like to see more stories engaged with environmental concerns." Reads fiction mss all year. Publishes ms an average of 1 year after acceptance. **Publishes 2 new writers/year.** Recently published work by Lee Ann Roripaugh, Dick Allen, Rita Welty Bourke.

HOW TO CONTACT Accepts submissions by USPS mail only. Send complete ms with SASE. Responds in 3 months to queries; 4 months to mss. No simultaneous submissions. Sample copy for $5. Writer's guidelines online.

PAYMENT/TERMS Pays $5/350 words; $20 minimum, $100 maximum. Pays on publication for first North American serial, first rights.

TIPS "We like stories that start quickly and have a strong narrative arc. Poems that are passionate about subject, language, and image are welcome, whether they are traditional or experimental, whether in formal or free verse (closed or open form). Nonfiction should combine art and fact with the finest writing. We do not accept simultaneous submissions; these will be returned unread. We read poetry, fiction, and nonfiction year-round."

NORTH CAROLINA LITERARY REVIEW

East Carolina University, ECU Mailstop 555 English, Greenville NC 27858-4353. (252)328-1537. Fax: (252)328-4889. E-mail: nclrsubmissions@ecu.edu; bauerm@ecu.edu. Website: www.nclr.ecu.edu. Estab. 1992. "Articles should have a North Carolina literature slant. First consideration is always for quality of work. Although we treat academic and scholarly subjects, we do not wish to see jargon-laden prose; our readers, we hope, are found as often in bookstores and libraries as in academia. We seek to combine the best elements of a magazine for serious readers with the best of a scholarly journal."

NEEDS Regional (North Carolina). Must be North Carolina related—either a North Carolina–connected writer or set in North Carolina. Publishes ms 1 year after acceptance.

HOW TO CONTACT Accepts submissions via online submissions manager. Responds in 1 month to queries; within 6 months to mss. Sample copy for $10-25. Writer's guidelines online.

PAYMENT/TERMS Pays on publication for first North American serial rights. Rights returned to writer on request.

TIPS "By far the easiest way to break in is with special issue sections. We are especially interested in reports on conferences, readings, meetings that involve North Carolina writers, and personal essays or short narratives with a strong sense of place. See back issues for other departments. Interviews are probably the other easiest place to break in; no discussions of poetics/theory, etc., except in reader-friendly (accessible) language; interviews should be personal, more like conversations, that explore connections between a writer's life and his/her work."

NOTRE DAME REVIEW

University of Notre Dame, 840 Flanner Hall, Notre Dame IN 46556. (574)631-6952. Fax: (574)631-4795. E-mail: english.ndreview.1@nd.edu. Website: www.nd.edu/~ndr/review.htm. Estab. 1995. Literary magazine: 6×9; 200 pages; 50 lb. smooth paper; illustrations; photos. "*The Notre Dame Review* is an indepenent, noncommercial magazine of contemporary American and international fiction, poetry, criticism and art. We are especially interested in work that takes on big issues by making the invisible seen, that gives voice to the voiceless. In addition to showcasing celebrated authors like Seamus Heaney and Czelaw

Milosz, the *Notre Dame Review* introduces readers to authors they may have never encountered before, but who are doing innovative and important work. In conjunction with the *Notre Dame Review*, the online companion to the printed magazine engages readers as a community centered in literary rather than commercial concerns, a community we reach out to through critique and commentary as well as aesthetic experience." Semiannual.

NEEDS No genre fiction. Upcoming theme issues planned. Receives 75 unsolicited mss/month. Accepts 4-5 mss/issue; 10 mss/year. Does not read mss November-January or April-August. Publishes ms 6 months after acceptance. **Publishes 1 new writer/year.** Recently published work by Ed Falco, Jarda Cerverka, David Green. Publishes short shorts. Also publishes literary criticism, poetry.

HOW TO CONTACT Send complete ms with cover letter. Include 4-sentence bio. Send SASE for response, return of ms, or send a disposable copy of ms. Responds in 6 months to mss. Accepts simultaneous submissions. Sample copy for $6. Writer's guidelines online. Mss sent during summer months will be returned unread.

PAYMENT/TERMS Pays $5-25. Pays on publication for first North American serial rights.

TIPS "We're looking for high quality work that takes on big issues in a literary way. Please read our back issues before submitting."

NTH DEGREE

3502 Fernmoss Ct., Charlotte NC 28269. E-mail: submissions@nthzine.com. Website: www.nthzine.com. **Contact:** Michael Pederson. Estab. 2002. 1211 Lauderdale Dr., Richmond, VA 23238. Magazine: Online downloadable ezine; illustrations; photos. "We print the best SF/Fantasy from the genre's newest writers and run artwork by the hottest new artists. Our goal is to help make it easier for new artists and writers to break into the field." Bi-monthly. Circ. 3,500.

NEEDS Fantasy (space fantasy, sword and sorcery), historical (alternate history), horror (dark fantasy, futuristic, psychological, supernatural), humor/satire, science fiction (hard science/technological), young adult/teen (fantasy/science fiction), comic strips. Receives 3 unsolicited mss/month. Accepts 4 mss/issue; 6 mss/year. Publishes ms 6 months after acceptance. **Publishes 6 new writers/year.** Recently published work by Robert E. Waters, Scott D. Coon, and Helen Lloyd Montgomery. Length: 2,000-7,000 words; average length: 3,500 words. Publishes short shorts. Also publishes poetry. Always comments on rejected mss.

HOW TO CONTACT Send complete ms. Accepts submissions by e-mail, disk. Send SASE (or IRC) for return of ms, or send disposable copy of the ms and #10 SASE for reply only. Responds in 2 weeks to queries; 2 months to mss. Accepts simultaneous, multiple submissions. Writer's guidelines online, or by e-mail.

PAYMENT/TERMS Pays 5 contributor's copies and free subscription to the magazine. Pays on publication for onetime rights.

TIPS "Don't submit anything that you may be ashamed of ten years later."

ONE-STORY

One-Story, LLC, 232 3rd St., #A111, Brooklyn NY 11215. Website: www.one-story.com. **Contact:** Maribeth Batcha, publisher. Estab. 2002. "*One Story* is a literary magazine that contains, simply, **one story**. It is a subscription-only magazine. Every 3 weeks subscribers are sent *One Story* in the mail. *One Story* is artfully designed, lightweight, easy to carry, and ready to entertain on buses, in bed, in subways, in cars, in the park, in the bath, in the waiting rooms of doctor's, on the couch, or in line at the supermarket. Subscribers also have access to a website, www.one-story.com, where they can learn more about *One Story* authors, and hear about readings and events. There is always time to read *One Story*."

"Accepts submissions via website only (.rtf files). Receives 100 submissions a week. Submit between June & Sept. Publishes each writer one time only."

NEEDS literary short stories. *One Story* only accepts short stories. Do not send excerpts. Do not send more than 1 story at a time. Publishes ms 3-6 months after acceptance. Recently published work by John Hodgman, Melanie Rae Thon, Daniel Wallace and Judy Budnitz.

HOW TO CONTACT Send complete ms. Accepts online submissions only. Responds in 2-6 months to mss. Sample copy for $5. Writer's guidelines online.

PAYMENT/TERMS Pays $100. Pays on publication for first North American serial rights. Buys the rights to publish excerpts on website and in promotional materials.

TIPS "*One-Story* is looking for stories that are strong enough to stand alone. Therefore they must be very good. We want the best you can give."

ON MISSION

North American Mission Board, SBC, 4200 North Point Pkwy., Alpharetta GA 30022-4176. E-mail: onmission@namb.net. Website: www.onmission.com. Estab. 1998.

TIPS "Readers might be intimidated if those featured appear to be 'super Christians' who seem to live on a higher spiritual plane. Try to introduce subjects as three-dimensional, real people. Include anecdotes or examples of their fears and failures, including ways they overcame obstacles. In other words, take the reader inside the heart of the missionary or on mission Christian and reveal the inevitable humanness that makes that person not only believable, but also approachable. We want the reader to feel encouraged to become on mission by identifying with people like them who are featured in the magazine."

ONSPEC

P.O. Box 4727, Station South, Edmonton AB T6E 5G6 Canada. (780)413-0215. Fax: (780)413-1538. E-mail: onspec@onspec.ca; onspecmag@gmail.com. Website: www.onspec.ca. Estab. 1989. Magazine: 5¼×8; 112-120 pages; illustrations. "We publish speculative fiction by new and established writers, with a strong preference for Canadian authored works. We are moving towards offering a digital version of our issues in addition to our print circulation." Quarterly.

Submission deadlines are February 28, May 31, August 31, and November 30.

NEEDS fantasy, horror, science fiction, magic realism. No media tie-in or shaggy-alien stories. No condensed or excerpted novels, religious/inspirational stories, fairy tales. "We would like to see more horror, fantasy, science fiction—well-developed stories with complex characters and strong plots." Receives 100 unsolicited mss/month. Accepts 10 mss/issue; 40 mss/year. "We read manuscripts during the month after each deadline: February 28/May 31/August 31/November 30." Publishes ms 6-18 months after acceptance. **Publishes 10-15 new writers/year.** Recently published work by Mark Shainblum, Hugh Spencer, Kate Riedel, and Leah Bobet. Length: 1,000-6,000 words; average length: 4,000 words. Also publishes poetry. Often comments on rejected mss.

HOW TO CONTACT Send complete ms. Accepts submissions by disk. SASE with Canadian postage for return of ms or send a disposable copy of ms plus #10 SASE for response. Include Canadian postage or IRCs. No e-mail or fax submissions. Responds in 2 weeks to queries; 4 months after deadline to mss. Accepts simultaneous submissions. Sample copy for $8. Writer's guidelines for #10 SASE or on website.

PAYMENT/TERMS Pays $50-200 for fiction. Short stories (under 1,000 words): $50 plus 1 contributor's copy. Pays on acceptance for first North American serial rights.

TIPS "We want to see stories with plausible characters, a well-constructed, consistent, and vividly described setting, a strong plot and believable emotions; characters must show us (not tell us) their emotional responses to each other and to the situation and/or challenge they face. Also: don't send us stories written for television. We don't like media tie-ins, so don't watch TV for inspiration! Read, instead! Absolutely no e-mailed or faxed submissions. Strong preference given to submissions by Canadians."

OYEZ REVIEW

Roosevelt University, Dept. of Literature & Languages, 430 S. Michigan Ave., Chicago IL 60605-1394. (312)341-3500. E-mail: oyezreview@roosevelt.edu. Website: legacy.roosevelt.edu/roosevelt.edu/oyezreview. Estab. 1965. Literary magazine/journal. "*Oyez Review* publishes fiction, creative nonfiction, poetry and art. There are no restrictions on style, theme, or subject matter."

Reading period is August 1-October 1. Responds by mid-December.

NEEDS Publishes short stories and flash fiction from established authors and newcomers. Literary excellence is our goal and our primary criterion. Send us your best work, and you will receive a thoughtful, thorough reading. Recently published J. Weintraub, Lori Rader Day, Joyce Goldenstern, Norman Lock, Peter Obourn, Jotham Burrello.

HOW TO CONTACT Accepts art and international submissions by e-mail. Sample copy available for $5. Guidelines available on website.

PAYMENT/TERMS Writers receive 2 contributors copies. Acquires first North American serial rights.

PAKN TREGER

National Yiddish Book Center, 1021 West St., Amherst MA 01002. (413)256-4900. E-mail: aatherley@bikher.org; pt@bikher.org; bwolfson@bikher.org. Website: www.yiddishbookcenter.org. **Contact:** Anne Atherley, editor's assistant. Estab. 1980. Literary magazine/journal. "*Pakn Treger* is looking for high-quality writing for a secular audience interested in Yiddish and Jewish history, literature, and culture." Biannual.

NEEDS historical, humor/satire, mystery. Accepts 2 mss/year. Manuscript published 4 months after acceptance. Length: 1,200-5,000 words.

HOW TO CONTACT Query first. Accepts submissions by e-mail. Responds to queries in 2 weeks; mss in 2 months. Sample copy available via e-mail request or viewed on website. Guidelines available via e-mail.

PAYMENT/TERMS Acquires onetime rights.

TIPS "Read the magazine and visit our website."

THE PARIS REVIEW

62 White Street, New York NY 10013. (212)343-1333. E-mail: queries@theparisreview.org. Website: www.theparisreview.org. **Contact:** Philip Gourevitch, editor. Magazine: about 192 pages; illustrations; photography portfolios (unsolicited artwork not accepted). Fiction, nonfiction and poetry of superlative quality. "Our contributors include prominent as well as previously unpublished writers. The Writers at Work interview series features important contemporary writers discussing their own work and the craft of writing." Published quarterly.

Address submissions to proper department. Do not make submissions via e-mail.

NEEDS Fiction, nonfiction, poetry. Receives 2,000 unsolicited mss/month. Recently published work by Karl Taro Greenfeld, J. Robert Lennon, and Belle Boggs.

HOW TO CONTACT Send complete ms and SASE. Responds in 2 months to fiction mss; 6 months for poetry. Accepts simultaneous, multiple submissions. Sample copy for $12. Writer's guidelines online.

PAYMENT/TERMS Payment varies depending on length. Pays on publication for first English-language rights. Sends galleys to author. Sponsors awards/contests.

PEARL

3030 E. Second St., Long Beach CA 90803. (562)434-4523. E-mail: pearlmag@aol.com. Website: www.pearlmag.com. **Contact:** Joan Jobe Smith, Marilyn Johnson, and Barbara Hauk, poetry editors. Estab. 1974. Magazine: $5^{1}/_{2}$×$8^{1}/_{2}$; 96 pages; 60 lb. recycled, acid-free paper; perfect bound; coated cover; b &w drawings and graphics. "We are primarily a poetry magazine, but we do publish some very short fiction. We are interested in lively, readable prose that speaks to real people in direct, living language; for a general literary audience." Biannual.

Submissions are accepted from Jan. - June only. Mss. received between July and Dec. will be returned unread. No e-mail submissions, except from countries outside the U.S. See guidelines.

NEEDS humor/satire, literary, mainstream, contemporary, prose poem. "We will consider short-short stories up to 1,200 words. Longer stories (up to 4,000 words) may only be submitted to our short story contest. All contest entries are considered for publication. Although we have no taboos stylistically or subject-wise, obscure, predictable, sentimental, or cliché-ridden stories are a turn-off." Publishes an all-fiction issue each year. Receives 30-40 unsolicited mss/month. Accepts 15-20 mss/issue; 12-15 mss/year. Submissions accepted January-June only. Publishes ms 6-12 months after acceptance. **Publishes 1-5 new writers/year.** Recently published work by Ruth Moon Kempher, Sharon Reitman, Erin Campbell, Michael Lee Phillips, John Stacy, Suzanne Greenberg, Gerald Locklin, Lisa Glatt. Length: 500-1,200 words; average length: 1,000 words. Also publishes poetry.

HOW TO CONTACT Include SASE. Responds in 2 months to mss. Accepts simultaneous, multiple submissions. Sample copy for $8 (postpaid). Writer's guidelines for #10 SASE.

PAYMENT/TERMS Pays 1 contributor's copy. Acquires first North American serial rights. Sends galleys to author. Sponsors awards/contests.

TIPS "We look for vivid, *dramatized* situations and characters, stories written in an original 'voice,' that make sense and follow a clear narrative line. What makes a manuscript stand out is more elusive, though—more to do with feeling and imagination than anything else."

THE PEDESTAL MAGAZINE

6815 Honors Court, Charlotte NC 28210. (704)643-0244. E-mail: pedmagazine@carolina.rr.com. Website: www.thepedestalmagazine.com. **Contact:** Nathan Leslie, fiction editor; John Amen, editor-in-chief.

Estab. 2000. Online literary magazine/journal. "We publish poetry, fiction, reviews and interviews. We are committed to the individual voice and publish an eclectic mix of high-quality work." Bimonthly. Member CLMP.

Pedestal 56 is now online.

NEEDS adventure, ethnic/multicultural, experimental, family saga, fantasy, feminist, gay, glitz, historical, horror, humor/satire, lesbian, literary, mainstream, military/war, mystery, new age, psychic/supernatural/occult, romance, science fiction, thriller/espionage. Receives 100-150 mss/month. Accepts 3-5 mss/issue; 18-24 mss/year. Closed to submissions at the following times: January, March, May, July, September, November: from the 12th-19th; February, April, June, August, October, December: from the 14th-28th. Ms published 1-3 weeks after acceptance. **Publishes 1-2 new writers/year.** Published Grant Tracy, Mary Grabar, Karen Heuler, James Scott Iredell, Don Shea, Mary Carroll-Hackett, R.T. Smith, and Richard Peabody. Publishes short shorts. Also publishes book reviews, poetry. Send review query to pedmagazine@carolina.rr.com. Rarely comments on/critiques rejected mss.

HOW TO CONTACT Submit via the online form provided on the website. Include brief bio, list of publications. Responds to queries in 2-3 days. Responds to mss in 4-6 weeks. Considers simultaneous submissions, multiple submissions. Guidelines available on website.

PAYMENT/TERMS Writers receive 8¢/word. Pays on publication. Acquires first rights. Sends galleys to author. Publication is copyrighted.

TIPS "If you send us your work, please wait for a response to your first submission before you submit again."

PEDIATRICS FOR PARENTS

Pediatrics for Parents, Inc., 35 Starknaught Heights, Gloucester MA 01930. (215)253-4543. Fax: (973)302-4543. E-mail: richsagall@pedsforparents.com. Estab. 1981.

PLANET-THE WELSH INTERNATIONALIST

P.O. Box 44, Aberystwyth Ceredigion SY23 3ZZ United Kingdom. E-mail: planet.enquiries@planetmagazine.org.uk. Website: www.planetmagazine.org.uk. **Contact:** Jasmine Donahaye, Editor. Estab. 1970. "A literary/cultural/political journal centered on Welsh affairs but also covering international issues, with a strong interest in minority cultures in Europe and elsewhere." Quarterly.

NEEDS No horror or science fiction. Recently published work by Emyr Humphreys, Anne Stevenson, and Robert Minhinnick.

HOW TO CONTACT No submissions returned unless accompanied by an SASE. Writers submitting from abroad should send at least 3 IRCs for return of typescript; 1 IRC for reply only. E-mail queries accepted. Writer's guidelines online.

PAYMENT/TERMS Pays £50/1,000 words.

TIPS "We do not look for fiction which necessarily has a 'Welsh' connection, which some writers assume from our title. We try to publish a broad range of fiction and our main criterion is quality. Try to read copies of any magazine you submit to. Don't write out of the blue to a magazine which might be completely inappropriate for your work. Recognize that you are likely to have a high rejection rate, as magazines tend to favor writers from their own countries."

PLEIADES

Pleiades Press, Department of English, University of Central Missouri, Martin 336, Warrensburg MO 64093. (660)543-4425. Fax: (660)543-8544. E-mail: pleiades@ucmo.edu. Website: www.ucmo.edu/englphil/pleiades. **Contact:** G.B. Crump, Matthew Eck and Phong Nguyen, prose editors. Estab. 1991. Magazine: 5½×8½; 250 pages; 60 lb. paper; perfect-bound; 8 pt. color cover. "We publish contemporary fiction, poetry, interviews, literary essays, special-interest personal essays, reviews for a general and literary audience." Semiannual.

"Also sponsors the Lena-Miles Wever Todd Poetry Series competition, a contest for the best book ms by an American poet. The winner receives $1,000, publication by Pleiades Press, and distribution by Louisiana State University Press. Deadline September 30. Send SASE for guidelines."

NEEDS ethnic/multicultural, experimental, feminist, gay, humor/satire, literary, mainstream, novel excerpts, regional, translations, magical realism. No science fiction, fantasy, confession, erotica. Receives 100 unsolicited mss/month. Accepts 8 mss/issue; 16 mss/year. "We're slower at reading manuscripts in the summer." Publishes ms 9 months after acceptance. **Publishes 4-5 new writers/year.** Recently published work by Sherman Alexie, Edith Pearlman, Joyce Carol Oates, James Tate. Length: 2,000-6,000 words; average length: 3,000-6,000 words. Also publishes literary essays, literary criticism, poetry. Sometimes comments on rejected mss.

HOW TO CONTACT Send complete ms. Include 75-100 word bio and list of publications. Send SASE for reply, return of ms or send a disposable copy of ms. Responds in 2 months to queries; 2 months to mss. Accepts simultaneous submissions. Sample copy for $6 (back issue), $8 (current issue). Writer's guidelines for #10 SASE.

PAYMENT/TERMS Pays 2 contributor copies. Pays on publication for first North American serial, second serial (reprint) rights. Occasionally requests rights for TV, radio reading, website.

TIPS "Submit only 1 genre at a time to appropriate editors. Show care for your material and your readers—submit quality work in a professional format. Include cover letter with brief bio and list of publications. Include SASE. Cover art is solicited directly from artists. We accept queries for book reviews. For summer submissions, the Poetry and Nonfiction Editors will no longer accept mss sent between June 1 & August 31. Any sent after May 31 will be held until the end of summer. Please do not send your only copy of anything."

PMS POEMMEMOIRSTORY

University of Alabama at Birmingham, HB 217, 1530 3rd Ave. South, Birmingham AL 35294-1260. (205)934-8578; (205)934-8583. E-mail: kmadden@uab.edu. Website: www.pms-journal.org; www.pms-journal.org/submissions-guidelines. **Contact:** Kerry Madden, Editor-in-Chief. Literary magazine/journal: 6x9; 120 pages; recycled white; matte paper; cover photos. "We print one issue a year, our cover price is $7, and our journal publishes fine creative work by women writers from across the nation (and beyond) in the three genres listed in the title." Circ. 1,500. Member Council of Literary Magazines and Presses and the Council of Editors of Learned Journals." Receives 30 mss/month. Accepts 4-6 mss/issue. As of 2009, reading period is January 1 through March 30. Ms published within 6 months after acceptance. Publishes 5 new writers/year. Published Vicki Covington, Kim Aubrey, Patricia Brieschke, Gaines Marsh. Length: 4,500 words (max). Average length: 3,500-4,000 words. Publishes short shorts. Average length of short shorts: 300-350 words. Also publishes literary essays, poetry. Rarely comments on/critiques rejected mss.

Work from PMS has been reprinted in a number of award anthologies: *New Stories from the South 2005, The Best Creative Nonfiction 200* and *2008, Best American Poetry 2003* and *2004*, and *Best American Essays 2005* and *2007.*

NEEDS comics/graphic novels, ethnic/multicultural (general), experimental, feminist, literary, translations. "We don't do erotic, mystery work, and most popular forms. We publish short stories and essays including memoirs and other brands of creative nonfiction.

HOW TO CONTACT Send complete ms with cover letter. Include list of publications. Responds to queries in 1 month. Responds to mss in 1-4 months. Send disposable copy of ms and #10 SASE for reply only. Considers simultaneous submissions, multiple submissions. Sample copy available for $7. Guidelines available for SASE, on website.

PAYMENT/TERMS Writers receive 2 contributor's copies. Additional copies $7. Pays on publication. Acquires one-time rights. Publication is copyrighted.

TIPS "We seek unpublished original work that we can recycle. Include cover letter, brief bio with SASE. All mss should be typed on 1-side of 8 x 11 white paper with author's name, address, phone no. and email address on front of each submission." Reading period runs Jan. 1-Mar. 31. Submissions received at other times of the year will be returned unread. Best way to make contact is through e-mail.

POCKETS

Upper Room, P.O. Box 340004, 1908 Grand Ave., Nashville TN 37203-0004. (800)972-0433. Fax: (615)340-7275. E-mail: pockets@upperroom.org. Website: http://pockets.upperroom.org/. Estab. 1981. Magazine: 7×11; 48 pages; some photos. "*Pockets* is a Christian, inter-denominational publication for children 8-12 years of age. Each issue reflects a specific theme."

NEEDS Adventure, ethnic/multicultural, historical (general), religious/inspirational, slice-of-life vignettes. No fantasy, science fiction, talking animals. "All submissions should address the broad theme of the magazine. Each issue is built around one theme with material which can be used by children in a variety of ways. Scripture stories, fiction, poetry, prayers, art, graphics, puzzles and activities are included. Submissions do not need to be overtly religious. They should help children experience a Christian lifestyle that is not always a neatly-wrapped moral package, but is open to the continuing revelation of God's will. Seasonal material, both secular and liturgical, is desired. No violence, horror, sexual, racial stereotyping or fiction containing heavy moralizing." Receives 200 unsolicited mss/month. Accepts 3-4 mss/issue; 33-44 mss/year. Publishes ms 1 year to 18 months after acceptance. **Publishes 15 new writers/year.** Length: 600-1,400 words; average length: 1,200 words.

HOW TO CONTACT Contributions should be typed, double-spaced, on 8½ × 11 paper, accompanied by a SASE for return. Writers who wish to save postage and are concerned about paper conservation may send a SASP for notification of unaccepted manuscripts, and we will recycle the manuscript. Please list the name of the submission(s) on the card. **We do not accept manuscripts sent by fax or e-mail.** Writer's guidelines, themes, and due dates available online. Lynn W. Gilliam, Editor.

PAYMENT/TERMS Pays 14¢/word, $25 and up for poetry, $25 and up for activities, games. Pays on acceptance for first North American serial rights. Sponsors an annual fiction-writing contest.

TIPS "Theme stories, role models, and retold scripture stories are most open to freelancers. Poetry is also open. It is very helpful if writers read our writers' guidelines and themes on our website."

POETRY INTERNATIONAL

San Diego State University, 5500 Campanile Dr., San Diego CA 92182-6020. (619)594-1522. Fax: (619)594-4998. E-mail: poetryinternational@yahoo.com. Website: http://poetryinternational.sdsu.edu. **Contact:** Fred Moramarco, Founding Editor. Estab. 1997.

Features the Poetry International Prize ($1,000) for best original poem. Submit up to 3 poems with a $10 entry fee.

TIPS "Seeks a wide range of styles and subject matter. We read unsolicited mss. only between Sept. 1st and Dec. 31st of each year. Mss. received any other time will be returned unread."

PORTLAND MAGAZINE

165 State, Portland ME 04101. (207)775-4339. E-mail: staff@portlandmonthly.com. Website: www.portlandmagazine.com. **Contact:** Colin Sargent. Estab. 1985.

THE PORTLAND REVIEW

Portland State University, P.O. Box 347, Portland OR 97207-0347. (503)725-4533. E-mail: theportlandreview@gmail.com. Website: http://portlandreview.tumblr.com. **Contact:** Jacqueline Treiber, Editor. Estab. 1956.

NEEDS unpublished poetry and prose. Fiction/nonfiction prose of up to 5,000 words or 5 poems per submission. Receives 200 unsolicited mss/week. Accepts up to 24 mss/issue.

HOW TO CONTACT Ms and SASE for submissions. Review queries via e-mail. Submission guidelines online. All ms submissions not following guidelines are immediately rejected.

PAYMENT/TERMS Pays contributor's copies. Acquires first North American serial rights.

TIPS "View website for current samples and guidelines."

THE PRAIRIE JOURNAL

Prairie Journal Trust, P.O. Box 68073, 28 Crowfoot Terrace NW, Calgary AB Y3G 3N8 Canada. E-mail: editor@prairiejournal.org (queries only); prairiejournal@yahoo.com. Website: prairiejournal.org. **Contact:** A.E. Burke, literary editor. Estab. 1983. Journal: 7×8½; 50-60 pages; white bond paper; Cadillac cover stock; cover illustrations. "The audience is literary, university, library, scholarly and creative readers/writers."

"Use our mailing address for submissions and queries with samples sor clippings."

NEEDS literary, regional. No genre (romance, horror, western—sagebrush or cowboys—erotic, science fiction, or mystery). Receives 100 unsolicited mss/month. Accepts 10-15 mss/issue; 20-30 mss/year. Suggested deadlines: April 1 for spring/summer issue; October 1 for fall/winter. Publishes ms 4-6 months after acceptance. Publishes 60 new writers/year. Recently published work by Robert Clark, Sandy Campbell, Darcie Hasack, Christopher Blais. Length: 100-3,000 words; average length: 2,500 words. Also publishes literary essays, literary criticism, poetry. Sometimes comments on rejected mss.

HOW TO CONTACT Send complete ms with SASE (IRC). Include cover letter of past credits, if any. Reply to queries for SAE with 55¢ for postage or IRC. No American stamps. Responds in 2 weeks to queries; 6 months to mss. No simultaneous submissions. No e-mail submissions. Sample copy for $6. Writer's guidelines online. Reviews fiction.

PAYMENT/TERMS Pays $10-75. Pays on publication for first North American serial rights. In Canada, author retains copyright with acknowledgement appreciated.

TIPS "We publish many, many new writers and are always open to unsolicited submissions because we are 100% freelance. Do not send US stamps, always use IRCs. We have poems and reviews online (query first)."

PRAIRIE SCHOONER

The University of Nebraska Press, Prairie Schooner, 123 Andrews Hall, University of Nebraska, Lincoln NE 68588-0334. (402)472-7211, 1-800-715-2387. E-mail: jengelhardt2@unlnotes.unl.edu. Website: http://prairieschooner.unl.edu. Estab. 1926. Magazine: 6×9; 200 pages; good stock paper; heavy cover stock. "A fine literary quarterly of stories, poems, essays and reviews for a general audience that reads for pleasure."

Submissions must be received between September 1 and May 1.

NEEDS good fiction (literary). Receives 500 unsolicited mss/month. Accepts 4-5 mss/issue. Mss are read September through May only. **Publishes 5-10 new writers/year.** Recently published work by Robert Olen Butler, Janet Burroway, Aimee Phan, Valerie Sayers, Daniel Stern. Also publishes poetry.

HOW TO CONTACT Send complete ms with SASE and cover letter listing previous publications—where, when. Responds in 4 months to mss. Sample copy for $6. Writer's guidelines and excerpts online. Reviews fiction.

PAYMENT/TERMS Pays in contributor's copies and prize money awarded. Will reassign rights upon request after publication. Sponsors awards/contests.

TIPS "Send us your best, most carefully crafted work and be persistent. Submit again and again. Constantly work on improving your writing. Read widely in literary fiction, nonfiction, and poetry. Read *Prairie Schooner* to know what we publish."

PRISM INTERNATIONAL

Department of Creative Writing, Buch E462, 1866 Main Mall, University of British Columbia, Vancouver BC V6T 1Z1 Canada. (604)822-2514. Fax: (604)822-3616. Website: www.prismmagazine.ca. Estab. 1959. Magazine: 6×9; 80 pages; Zephyr book paper; Cornwall, coated one-side cover; artwork on cover. "An international journal of contemporary writing—fiction, poetry, drama, creative nonfiction and translation." Readership: "public and university libraries, individual subscriptions, bookstores—a worldwide audience concerned with the contemporary in literature." Quarterly.

NEEDS experimental, traditional. New writing that is contemporary and literary. Short stories and self-contained novel excerpts (up to 25 double-spaced pages). Works of translation are eagerly sought and should be accompanied by a copy of the original. Would like to see more translations. "No gothic, confession, religious, romance, pornography, or sci-fi." Also looking for creative nonfiction that is literary, not journalistic, in scope and tone. Receives over 100 unsolicited mss/month. Accepts 70 mss/year. "PRISM publishes both new and established writers; our contributors have included Franz Kafka, Gabriel Garciía Maárquez, Michael Ondaatje, Margaret Laurence, Mark Anthony Jarman, Gail Anderson-Dargatz and Eden Robinson." Publishes ms 4 months after acceptance. **Publishes 7 new writers/year.** Recently published work by Ibi Kaslik, Melanie Little, Mark Anthony Jarman. Publishes short shorts. Also publishes poetry.

HOW TO CONTACT Send complete ms by mail. Department of Creative Writing, Buch E462, 1866 Main Mall, University of British Columbia, Vancouver BC V6T 1Z1 Canada. "Keep it simple. U.S. contributors take note: Do not send SASEs with U.S. stamps, they are not valid in Canada. Send International Reply Coupons instead." Responds in 4 months to queries; 3-6 months to mss. Sample copy for $11 or on website. Writer's guidelines online.

PAYMENT/TERMS Pays $20/printed page of prose, $40/printed page of poetry, and 1-year subscription. Pays on publication for first North American serial rights. Selected authors are paid an additional $10/page for digital rights. Cover art pays $300 and 4 copies of issue. Sponsors awards/contests, including annual short fiction, poetry, and nonfiction contests.

TIPS "We are looking for new and exciting fiction. Excellence is still our No. 1 criterion. As well as poetry, imaginative nonfiction and fiction, we are especially open to translations of all kinds, very short fiction pieces and drama which work well on the page. Translations must come with a copy of the original language work. We pay an additional $10/printed page to selected authors whose work we place on our online version of *Prism*."

PURPOSE

616 Walnut Ave., Scottdale PA 15683-1999. (724)887-8500. Fax: (724)887-3111. E-mail: purposeeditor@mpn.net. Website: www.mpn.net. **Contact:** Carol Duerksen, editor. Estab. 1968. Magazine: 5 3/8×8 3/8; 8 pages; illustrations; photos. Monthly.

NEEDS Historical (related to discipleship theme), humor/satire, religious/inspirational. No militaristic, narrow patriotism, or racist themes. Receives 150 unsolicited mss/month. Accepts 12 mss/issue; 140 mss/year. Publishes ms 1 year after acceptance. **Publishes 15-25 new writers/year.** Length: 600 words; average length: 400 words. Occasionally comments on rejected mss.

HOW TO CONTACT Send complete ms. Send all submissions by Word attachment via e-mail. Responds in 3 months to queries. Accepts simultaneous submissions, reprints, multiple submissions. Sample copy and writer's guidelines for $2, 6×9 SAE and 2 first-class stamps. Writer's guidelines online.

PAYMENT/TERMS Pays up to 7¢/word for stories, and 2 contributor's copies. Pays on acceptance for one-time rights.

TIPS "Many stories are situational, how to respond to dilemmas. Looking for first-person storylines. Write crisp, action moving, personal style, focused upon an individual, a group of people, or an organization. The story form is an excellent literary device to help readers explore discipleship issues. The first two paragraphs are crucial in establishing the mood/issue to be resolved in the story. Work hard on the development of these."

QUARTERLY WEST

University of Utah, 255 S. Central Campus Dr., Room 3500, Salt Lake City UT 84112. E-mail: quarterlywest@gmail.com. Website: www.utah.edu/quarterlywest. **Contact:** Matt Kirkpatrick & Cami Nelson, editors. Estab. 1976. Magazine: 7×10; 50 lb. paper; 4-color cover stock. "We publish fiction, poetry, and nonfiction in long and short formats, and will consider experimental as well as traditional works." Semiannual.

Quarterly West was awarded First Place for Editorial Content from the American Literary Magazine Awards. Work published in the magazine has been selected for inclusion in the *Pushcart Prize* anthology and *The Best American Short Stories* anthology.

NEEDS ethnic/multicultural, experimental, humor/satire, literary, mainstream, novel excerpts, slice-of-life vignettes, translations, short shorts, translations. No detective, science fiction or romance. Receives 300 unsolicited mss/month. Accepts 6-10 mss/issue; 12-20 mss/year. Reads mss between September 1 and May 1 only. "Submissions received between May 2 and August 31 will be returned unread." Publishes ms 6 months after acceptance. **Publishes 3 new writers/year.** Recently published work by Steve Almond, Linh Dinh.

HOW TO CONTACT Send complete ms. Brief cover letters welcome. Send SASE for reply or return of ms. Responds in 6 months to mss. Accepts simultaneous submissions if notified. Sample copy for $7.50. Writer's guidelines online.

PAYMENT/TERMS Pays $15-50, and 2 contributor's copies. Pays on publication for first North American serial rights.

TIPS We publish a special section of short shorts every issue, and we also sponsor a biennial novella contest. We are open to experimental work—potential contributors should read the magazine! Don't send more than 1 story/submission. Biennial novella competition guidelines available upon request with SASE. We prefer work with interesting language and detail—plot or narrative are less important. We don't do Western themes or religious work.

QUEEN'S QUARTERLY

144 Barrie St., Queen's University, Kingston ON K7L 3N6 Canada. (613)533-2667. Fax: (613)533-6822. E-mail: queens.quarterly@queensu.ca. Website: www.queensu.ca/quarterly. **Contact:** Joan Harcourt, editor. Estab. 1893. Magazine: 6×9; 800 pages/year; illustrations. "A general interest intellectual review, featuring articles on science, politics, humanities, arts and letters. Book reviews, poetry and fiction." Quarterly.

Submissions can be sent as e-mail attachment or on hard copy with a S.A.S.E. (if submitting from the US or Int'l, the S.A.S.E. must have Canadian postage or be accompanied by an International Reply Coupon in order to receive a reply and will be responded to by same). Payment will be determined at time of acceptance.

NEEDS historical, literary, mainstream, novel excerpts, short stories, women's. "Special emphasis on work by Canadian writers." Accepts 2 mss/issue; 8 mss/year. Publishes ms 6-12 months after acceptance. **Publishes 5 new writers/year.** Recently published work by Gail Anderson-Dargatz, Tim Bowling, Emma Donohue, Viktor Carr, Mark Jarman, Rick Bowers, and Dennis Bock. Also publishes literary essays, literary criticism, poetry.

HOW TO CONTACT "Send complete ms with SASE and/or IRC. No reply with insufficient postage." Responds in 2-3 months to queries. Sample copy online. Writer's guidelines online. Reviews fiction.

PAYMENT/TERMS Pays on publication for first North American serial rights. Sends galleys to author.

RADIX MAGAZINE

Radix Magazine, Inc., P.O. Box 4307, Berkeley CA 94704. (510)548-5329. E-mail: radixmag@aol.com. Website: www.radixmagazine.com. **Contact:** Sharon Gallagher, editor. Estab. 1979.

"Needs poetry and book reviews. Email submissions only."

TIPS "We accept very few unsolicited manuscripts. We do not accept fiction. All articles and poems should be based on a Christian world view. Freelancers should have some sense of the magazine's tone and purpose."

RAILROAD EVANGELIST

Railroad Evangelist Association, Inc., P.O. Box 5026, Vancouver WA 98668. (360)699-7208. E-mail: rrjoe@comcast.net. Website: www.railroadevangelist.com. Estab. 1938.

All content must be railroad related.

RATTAPALLAX

Rattapallax Press, 217 Thompson St., Suite 353, New York NY 10012. (212)560-7459. E-mail: info@rattapallax.com. Website: www.rattapallax.com. **Contact:** Alan Cheuse, fiction editor. Estab. 1999. Literary magazine: 9×12; 128 pages; bound; some illustrations; photos. "General readership. Our stories must be character driven with strong conflict. All accepted stories are edited by our staff and the writer before publication to ensure a well-crafted and written work." Semiannual.

NEEDS literary. Receives 15 unsolicited mss/month. Accepts 3 mss/issue; 6 mss/year. Publishes ms 3-6 months after acceptance. Agented fiction 15%. **Publishes 3 new writers/year.** Recently published work by Stuart Dybek, Howard Norman, Molly Giles, Rick Moody. Length: 1,000-10,000 words; average length: 5,000 words. Publishes short shorts. Also publishes poetry. Often comments on rejected mss.

HOW TO CONTACT Send SASE for return of ms. Responds in 3 months to queries; 3 months to mss. Sample copy for $7.95. Writer's guidelines for SASE or on website.

PAYMENT/TERMS Pays 2 contributor's copies; additional copies for $7.95. Pays on publication for first North American serial rights. Sends galleys to author.

REDACTIONS: POETRY & POETICS

58 So. Main St., 3rd Floor, Brockport NY 14420. E-mail: redactionspoetry@yahoo.com. Website: www.redactions.com.

TIPS "We only accept submissions by e-mail. We read submissions throughout the year. Email us and attach submission into one Word, Wordpad, Notepad, .rtf, or .txt document, or, place in the body of an e-mail. Include brief bio and your snail mail address. Query after 90 days if you haven't heard from us."

RED ROCK REVIEW

College of Southern Nevada, CSN Department of English, J2A, 3200 E. Cheyenne Ave., North Las Vegas NV 89030. (702)651-4094. Fax: (702)651-4639. E-mail: redrockreview@csn.edu. Website: sites.csn.edu/english/redrockreview/. **Contact:** Rich Logsdon, Senior Editor. Estab. 1994. Magazine: 5×8; 125 pages. "We're looking for the very best literature. Stories need to be tightly crafted, strong in character development, built around conflict. Poems need to be tightly crafted, characterised by expert use of language."

NEEDS experimental, literary, mainstream. Receives 350 unsolicited mss/month. Accepts 40-60 mss/issue; 80-120 mss/year. Does not read mss during summer. Publishes ms 3-5 after acceptance. **Publishes 5-10 new writers/year.** Recently published work by Charles Harper Webb, Mary Sojourner, Mark Irwin. Length: less than 7,500 words. Publishes short shorts. Also publishes literary essays, literary criticism, poetry. Sometimes comments on rejected mss.

HOW TO CONTACT Send SASE (or IRC) for return of ms. Responds in 2 weeks to queries; 3 months to mss. Does not accept general submissions June-August, or in December. Accepts simultaneous, multiple submissions. Sample copy for $5.50. Writer's guidelines for SASE, by e-mail or on website.

PAYMENT/TERMS Pays 2 contributor's copies. Pays on acceptance for first rights.

TIPS "Open to short fiction and poetry submissions from Sept. 1-May 31. Include SASE and include brief bio. No general submissions between June 1st and August 31st. See guidelines online."

REFORM JUDAISM

Union for Reform Judaism, 633 Third Ave., 7th Fl., New York NY 10017-6778. (212)650-4240. Fax: (212)650-4249. E-mail: rjmagazine@urj.org. Website: www.reformjudaismmag.org. Estab. 1972. Magazine: 8×10 7/8; 80-112 pages; illustrations; photos. "*Reform Judaism* is the official voice of the Union for Reform Judaism, linking the institutions and affiliates of Reform Judaism with every Reform Jew. *RJ* covers developments within the Movement while interpreting events and Jewish tradition from a Reform perspective." Quarterly.

NEEDS Humor/satire, religious/inspirational, Sophisticated, cutting-edge, superb writing. Receives 75 unsolicited mss/month. Accepts 3 mss/year. Publishes ms 3 months after acceptance. Recently published work by Published work by Frederick Fastow and Bob Sloan. Length: 600-2,500 words; average length: 1,500 words.

HOW TO CONTACT Send complete ms. SASE. "For quicker response time, send mss and stamped postcard with 'yes'; 'no'; 'maybe' options." Responds in 2 months to queries; 2 months to mss. Accepts simultaneous and reprints submissions. Sample copy for $3.50. Writer's guidelines online.

PAYMENT/TERMS Pays 30¢/word. Pays on publication for first North American serial rights.

TIPS "We prefer a stamped postcard including the following information/checklist: __Yes, we are interested in publishing; __No, unfortunately the submission doesn't meet our needs; __Maybe, we'd like to hold on to the article for now. Submissions sent this way will receive a faster response."

REVIEW FOR RELIGIOUS

3601 Lindell Blvd., St. Louis MO 63108-3393. (314)633-4610. Fax: (314)633-4611. E-mail: reviewrfr@gmail.com. Website: www.reviewforreligious.org. Estab. 1942.

TIPS "The writer must know about religious life in the Catholic Church and be familiar with prayer, vows, community life, and ministry."

RHINO

The Poetry Forum, Inc., P.O. Box 591, Evanston IL 60204. E-mail: editors@rhinopoetry.org. Website: www.rhinopoetry.org. **Contact:** Ralph Hamilton Sr., Editor; Helen Degen Cohen, Sr. Editor and Founder. *RHINO*, published annually in spring, prints poetry, short-shorts, and poetry-in-translation. Wants "work that reflects passion, originality, engagement with contemporary culture, and a love affair with language. We welcome free verse, formal poetry, innovation, and risk-taking." Has published poetry by Geoffrey Forsyth, Penelope Scambly Schott, F. Daniel Rzicznek, and Ricardo Pau-Llosa. *RHINO* is 150 pages, 7×10, printed on high-quality paper, with card cover with art. Receives 8,000-10,000 submissions/year, accepts 90-100, or 1%. Press run is 800. Single copy: $12. Sample: $5 (back issue). Submit 3-5 poems or 1-3 short-shorts once during reading period. Considers simultaneous submissions with notification; no previously published poems. Expects electronic copy upon acceptance. Reads submissions April 1-October 1. Guidelines available on website. Responds in up to 6 months. Acquires first rights only.

"Founders' Contest submission period is from July 1-October 1."

HOW TO CONTACT Submit onliine and by mail. Include SASE for USPS mail only.

PAYMENT/TERMS Pays 2 contributor's copies.

TIPS "Please visit our website for further examples that will indicate the quality of poetry we look for, plus additional submission information, including updates on the Rhino Founders' Contest."

RIVER STYX MAGAZINE

Big River Association, 3547 Olive St., Suite 107, St. Louis MO 63103. (314)533-4541. E-mail: bigriver@riverstyx.org. Website: www.riverstyx.org. **Contact:** Richard Newman, Editor. Estab. 1975. Magazine: 6×9; 100 pages; color card cover; perfect-bound; b&w visual art. "*River Styx* publishes the highest quality fiction, poetry, interviews, essays, and visual art. We are an internationally distributed multicultural literary magazine." Mss read May-November. Estab. 1975.

Work published in *River Styx* has been selected for inclusion in past volumes of *New Stories From the South, The Best American Poetry, Beacon's Best, Best New Poets* and *The Pushcart Prize Anthology*

NEEDS ethnic/multicultural, experimental, feminist, gay, lesbian, literary, mainstream, novel excerpts, translations, short stories, literary. "No genre fiction, less thinly veiled autobiography." Receives 350 unsolicited mss/month. Accepts 2-6 mss/issue; 6-12 mss/year. Reads only May through November. Publishes ms 1 year after acceptance. **Publishes 20 new writers/year.** Recently published work by George Singleton, Philip Graham, Katherine Min, Richard Burgin, Nancy Zafris, Jacob Appel, and Eric Shade. Publishes short shorts. Also publishes poetry. Sometimes comments on rejected mss.

HOW TO CONTACT Send complete ms. SASE required. Responds in 4 months to mss. Accepts simultaneous submissions "if a note is enclosed with your work and if we are notified immediately upon acceptance elsewhere." Sample copy for $8. Writer's guidelines online.

PAYMENT/TERMS Pays 2 contributor copies, plus 1-year subscription; cash payment as funds permit. Pays on publication for first North American serial, onetime rights.

RUNNING TIMES

Rodale, Inc., c/o Zephyr Media, P.O. Box 20627, Boulder CO 80308. (203)761-1113. Fax: (203)761-9933. E-mail: editor@runningtimes.com. Website: www.runningtimes.com. Estab. 1977.

TIPS "Thoroughly get to know runners and the running culture, both at the participant level and the professional, elite level."

THE SAVAGE KICK LITERARY MAGAZINE

Murder Slim Press, 129 Trafalgar Road West, Gt. Yarmouth Norfolk NR31 8AD United Kingdom. E-mail: moonshine@murderslim.com. Website: www.murderslim.com/savagekick.html. Estab. 2005.

THE SEATTLE REVIEW

Box 354330, University of Washington, Seattle WA 98195. (206)543-2302. E-mail: seaview@u.washington.edu. Website: www.seattlereview.org. Estab. 1978. **Contact:** Andrew Feld, editor-in-chief. Magazine: 6×9; 150 pages; illustrations; photos. "Includes fiction, nonfiction, poetry and one interview per issue with an established writer." Semiannual. Estab. 1978. Circ. 1,000.

NEEDS literary. Nothing in "bad taste (porn, racist, etc.)." Receives 200 unsolicited mss/month. Accepts 2-4 mss/issue; 4-8 mss/year. Does not read mss May 31-October 1. Publishes ms 1-2½ years after acceptance. **Publishes 3-4 new writers/year.** Recently published work by Rick Bass, Lauren Whitehurst, Martha Hurwitz. Length: 4,000 words; average length: 3,000 words.

Editors accept submissions only from October 1 through May 31.

HOW TO CONTACT Mail submissions with SASE, Attention: Guest Fiction Editor. Submissions must be typed on white, 8½×11 paper. The title page must include the word count (no more than 4,000 words), as well as the author's name and address. Send complete ms. Send SASE (or IRC) for return of ms or send disposable copy of ms and #10 SASE for reply only. Responds in 4-6 months to mss. No simultaneous submissions, accepts multiple submissions. Sample copy for $8. Writer's guidelines for #10 SASE, online or by e-mail.

PAYMENT/TERMS Pays 2 contributor's copies. Acquires first North American serial rights.

TIPS "Know what we publish: no genre fiction; look at our magazine and decide if your work might be appreciated. Beginners do well in our magazine if they send clean, well-written manuscripts. We've published a lot of 'first stories' from all over the country and take pleasure in discovery."

THE SECRET PLACE

American Baptist Home Mission Societies, ABC/USA, P.O. Box 851, Valley Forge PA 19482-0851. (610)768-2240. E-mail: thesecretplace@abc-usa.org. Estab. 1937.

TIPS "Prefers submissions via e-mail."

SEEK

8805 Governor's Hill Dr., Suite 400, Cincinnati OH 45239. (513)931-4050, ext. 351. E-mail: seek@standardpub.com. Website: www.standardpub.com. Estab. 1970. Magazine: 5½×8½; 8 pages; newsprint paper; art and photo in each issue. "Inspirational stories of faith-in-action for Christian adults; a Sunday School take-home paper." Quarterly. Circ. 27,000.

NEEDS religious/inspirational, religious fiction and religiously slanted historical and humorous fiction. No poetry. List of upcoming themes available online. Accepts 150 mss/year. Publishes ms 1 year after acceptance.

HOW TO CONTACT Send complete ms. Accepts submissions by e-mail. Prefers submissions by e-mail. Writer's guidelines online.

PAYMENT/TERMS Pays 7¢/word. Pays on acceptance for first North American serial, pays 5¢ for second serial (reprint) rights.

TIPS "Write a credible story with a Christian slant—no preachments; avoid overworked themes such as joy in suffering, generation gaps, etc. Most manuscripts are rejected by us because of irrelevant topic or message, unrealistic story, or poor character and/or plot development. We use fiction stories that are believable."

THE SEWANEE REVIEW

University of the South, 735 University Ave., Sewanee TN 37383-1000. (931)598-1000. Website: www.sewanee.edu/sewanee_review. Estab. 1892. "A literary quarterly, publishing original fiction, poetry, essays on literary and related subjects, and book reviews for well-educated readers who appreciate good American and English literature." Quarterly. Estab. 1892.

Does not read mss June 1-August 31.

NEEDS Literary, contemporary. No erotica, science fiction, fantasy or excessively violent or profane material.

PAYMENT/TERMS Pays $10-12/printed page of prose; $2.50/line of poetry. 2 contributor copies. Pays on publication for first North American serial, second serial (reprint) rights.

TIPS "Please keep in mind that for each poem published in *The Sewanee Review*, approximately 250 poems are considered."

SHENANDOAH

Washington and Lee University, Mattingly House, 2 Lee Ave., Lexington VA 24450-2116. (540)458-8765. Fax: (540)458-8461. E-mail: shenandoah@wlu.edu. Website: shenandoah.wlu.edu/faq.html. **Contact:** R. T. Smith, editor. Triannual. Estab. 1950. Circ. 2,000.

NEEDS Mainstream, novel excerpts. No sloppy, hasty, slight fiction. Publishes ms 10 months after acceptance.

HOW TO CONTACT Send complete ms. Responds in 2 months to mss. Sample copy for $10. Writer's guidelines online.

PAYMENT/TERMS Pays $25/page (cap $250). Pays on publication for first North American serial, one-time rights.

SHINE BRIGHTLY

GEMS Girls' Clubs, P.O. Box 7259, Grand Rapids MI 49510. (616)241-5616. Fax: (616)241-5558. E-mail: shinebrightly@gemsgc.org. Website: www.gemsgc.org. **Contact:** Jan Boone, editor; Kelli Ponstein, managing editor. Estab. 1970. Monthly with combined summer issue. Circ. 17,000. "*SHINE brightly* is designed to help girls ages 9-14 see how God is at work in their lives and in the world around them."

NEEDS adventure, animal, contemporary, health, history, humorous, multicultural, nature/environment, problem-solving, religious, sports. Does not want "unrealistic stories and those with trite, easy endings. We are interested in manuscripts that show how girls can change the world." Buys 30 mss/year. Length: 400-1,000 words; average length: 800 words.

HOW TO CONTACT Send complete ms within body of e-mail. No attachments. Responds to mss in 1 month. Will consider simultaneous submissions. Guidelines are on website.

PAYMENT/TERMS Pays on publication for first North American serial, second serial (reprint), simultaneous rights. Original artwork not returned at job's completion.

TIPS Prefers not to see anything on the adult level, secular material, or violence. Writers frequently oversimplify the articles and often write with a Pollyanna attitude. An author should be able to see his/her writing style as exciting and appealing to girls ages 9-14. The style can be fun, but also teach a truth. Subjects should be current and important to *SHINE brightly* readers. Use our theme update as a guide. We would like to receive material with a multicultural slant.

SHOTGUN SPORTS MAGAZINE

P.O. Box 6810, Auburn CA 95604. (530)889-2220. Fax: (530)889-9106. E-mail: shotgun@shotgunsportsmagazine.com. Website: www.shotgunsportsmagazine.com. **Contact:** Linda Martin, production coordinator.

Responds within 3 weeks. Subscription: $32.95 (U.S.); $39.95 (Canada); $70 (foreign).

TIPS "Do not fax manuscript. Send good photos. Take a fresh approach. Create a professional, yet friendly article. Send diagrams, maps, and photos of unique details, if needed. For interviews, more interested in 'words of wisdom' than a list of accomplishments. Reloading articles must include source information and backup data. Check your facts and data! If you can't think of a fresh approach, don't bother. If it's not about shotguns or shotgunners, don't send it. Never say, 'You don't need to check my data; I never make mistakes.'"

SOFA INK QUARTERLY

Sofa Ink, P.O. Box 625, American Fork UT 84003. E-mail: publisher@sofaink.com; acquisitions@sofaink.com. Website: www.sofaink.com; www.sofainkquarterly.com. **Contact:** David Cowsert, publisher. Literary magazine/journal. "The magazine is distributed primarily to waiting rooms and lobbies of medical facilities. All our stories and poetry have positive endings. We like to publish a variety of genres with a focus on good storytelling and word mastery that does not include swearing, profaning deity, gore, excessive violence or gratuitous sex." Quarterly. Estab. 2005. Circ. 650.

NEEDS Adventure, ethnic/multicultural, experimental, fantasy, historical, humor/satire, mainstream, mystery/suspense, romance, science fiction, slice-of-life vignettes, western. Does not want erotic or religious. Accepts 12-20 mss/year. Manuscript published 3 months after acceptance. Length: 7,500 words (max). Also publishes poetry.

HOW TO CONTACT Send complete ms with cover letter. Accepts submissions by e-mail. Responds to queries in 1-3 months. Responds to mss in 1-3 months. Considers simultaneous submissions. Sample copy available for $6. Guidelines available for SASE, on website.

PAYMENT/TERMS Writers receive $5 flat-rate payment. **Pays on acceptance.** Acquires first North American serial rights. Publication is copyrighted.

TIPS Follow the content guidelines. Electronic submissions should be in a Word attachment rather than in the body of the message.

SOLDIER OF FORTUNE

2135 11th Street, Boulder CO 80302-4045. (303)449-3750. E-mail: editorsof@aol.com. Website: www.sofmag.com. **Contact:** Lt. Col. Robert A. Brown, editor/publisher. Estab. 1975.

TIPS Submit a professionally prepared, complete package. All artwork with cutlines, double-spaced typed manuscript with 5.25 or 3.5 IBM-compatible disk, if available, cover letter including synopsis of article, supporting documentation where applicable, etc. Manuscript must be factual; writers have to do their homework and get all their facts straight. One error means rejection. Vietnam features, if carefully researched and art heavy, will always get a careful look. Combat reports, again, with good art, are No. 1 in our book and stand the best chance of being accepted. Military unit reports from around the world are well received, as are law-enforcement articles (units, police in action). If you write for us, be complete and factual; pros read *Soldier of Fortune*, and are very quick to let us know if we (and the author) err.

SOUTHERN HUMANITIES REVIEW

Auburn University, 9088 Haley Center, Auburn University AL 36849. (334)844-9088. E-mail: shrengl@auburn.edu. E-mail: shrsubmissions@auburn.edu. Website: www.auburn.edu/english/shr/home.htm. **Contact:** Karen Beckwith. Estab. 1967. Magazine: 6×9; 100 pages; 60 lb neutral pH, natural paper; 65 lb. neutral pH medium coated cover stock; occasional illustration; photos. "We publish essays, poetry, fiction and reviews. Our fiction has ranged from very traditional in form and content to very experimental. Literate, college-educated audience. We hope they read our journal for both enlightenment and pleasure." Quarterly. Circ. 800.

NEEDS feminist, humor/satire, regional. Slower reading time in summer. Receives 25 unsolicited mss/month. Accepts 1-2 mss/issue; 4-6 mss/year. Recently published work by Chris Arthur, Andrea Deagon, Sheryl St. Germain, Patricia Foster, Janette Turner Hospital, Paula Koöhlmeier, David Wagner, Yves Bonnefoy, Neil Grimmett, and Wayne Flynt. Also publishes literary essays, literary criticism, poetry. Sometimes comments on rejected mss.

HOW TO CONTACT Send complete ms, cover letter with an explanation of the topic chosen—"special, certain book, etc., a little about the author if he/she has never submitted." No e-mail submissions. No simultaneous submissions. Responds in 3 months to mss.

PAYMENT/TERMS Pays in contributor copies. Rights revert to author on publication.

TIPS "Send us the ms with SASE. If we like it, we'll take it or we'll recommend changes. If we don't like it, we'll send it back as promptly as possible. Read the journal. Send typewritten, clean copy, carefully proofread. We also award the annual Hoepfner Prize of $100 for the best published essay or short story of the year. Let someone whose opinion you respect read your story and give you an honest appraisal. Rewrite, if necessary, to get the most from your story."

THE SOUTHERN REVIEW

Louisiana State University, Old President's House, Baton Rouge LA 70803-5001. (225)578-5108. Fax: (225)578-5098. E-mail: southernreview@lsu.edu. Website: www.lsu.edu/tsr. **Contact:** Jeanne Leiby, Editor. Estab. 1935. Magazine: 6¼×10; 240 pages; 50

lb. Glatfelter paper; 65 lb. #1 grade cover stock. Quarterly. Circ. 3,000.

NEEDS Literary. "We select fiction that conveys a unique and compelling voice and vision." Receives approximately 300 unsolicited mss/month. Accepts 4-6 mss/issue. Reading period: September-May. Publishes ms 6 months after acceptance. Agented fiction 1%. **Publishes 10-12 new writers/year.** Recently published work by Jack Driscoll, Don Lee, Peter Levine, and Debbie Urbanski. Also publishes literary essays, literary criticism, poetry, and book reviews.

HOW TO CONTACT Mail hard copy of ms with cover letter and SASE. No queries. "Prefer brief letters giving author's prefessional information, including recent or notable publcations. Biographical info not necessary." Responds within 10 weeks to mss. Sample copy for $8. Writer's guidelines online. Reviews fiction, poetry.

PAYMENT/TERMS Pays $30/page. Pays on publication for first North American serial rights. Sends page proof to author via e-mail. Sponsors awards/contests.

TIPS "Careful attention to craftsmanship and technique combined with a developed sense of the creation of story will always make us pay attention."

SPIDER

Cricket Magazine Group, 70 East Lake St., Suite 300, Chicago IL 60601. (312)701-1720. Fax: (312)701-1728. Website: www.cricketmag.com. Estab. 1994. **Contact:** Marianne Carus, editor-in-chief; May-May Sugihara, editor. Magazine: 8×10; 34 pages; illustrations; photos. "*Spider* introduces 6- to 9-year-old children to the highest quality stories, poems, illustrations, articles, and activities. It was created to foster in beginning readers a love of reading and discovery that will last a lifetime. We're looking for writers who respect children's intelligence." Monthly. Estab. 1994. Circ. 60,000.

NEEDS adventure, children's/juvenile (6-9 years), ethnic/multicultural, fantasy (children's fantasy), historical, humor/satire, mystery/suspense, science fiction, suspense, realistic fiction, folk tales, fairy tales. No romance, horror, religious. Publishes ms 2-3 years after acceptance. Agented fiction 2%. Recently published work by Polly Horvath, Andrea Cheng, and Beth Wagner Brust. Length: 300-1,000 words; average length: 775 words. Also publishes poetry. Often comments on rejected mss.

HOW TO CONTACT Send complete ms. Send SASE for return of ms. Responds in 6 months to mss. Accepts simultaneous and reprints submissions. Sample copy for $5 and 9X12 SASE. Writer's guidelines on website.

PAYMENT/TERMS Pays 25¢/word and 6 contributor's copies; additional copies $2.50. Pays on publication. Rights vary.

TIPS We'd like to see more of the following: engaging nonfiction, fillers, and "takeout page" activities; folk tales, fairy tales, science fiction, and humorous stories. Most importantly, do not write down to children.

SPORTS AFIELD

Field Sports Publishing, 15621 Chemical Lane, Ste. B, Huntington Beach CA 92649. (714)373-4910. E-mail: letters@sportsafield.com. Website: www.sportsafield.com. **Contact:** Jerry Gutierrez, art director. Estab. 1887.

STAND MAGAZINE

School of English, University of Leeds, Leeds LS2 9JT United Kingdom. (44)(113)343-4794. E-mail: stand@leeds.ac.uk. Website: www.standmagazine.org. Estab. 1952. North American Office: Department of English, VCU, Richmond VA 23284-2005. (804) 828-1331. E-mail: dlatane@vcu.edu. Website: www.standmagazine.org. "*Stand Magazine* is concerned with what happens when cultures and literatures meet, with translation in its many guises, with the mechanics of language, with the processes by which the policy receives or disables its cultural makers. Stand promotes debate of issues that are of radical concern to the intellectual community worldwide." Quarterly. Estab. 1952 in Leeds UK. Circ. 3,000 worldwide.

"U.S. submissions can be made through the Virginia office (see separate listing)."

NEEDS "No genre fiction." Publishes ms 12 months after acceptance.

HOW TO CONTACT Send complete ms. Responds in 6 weeks to queries; 3 months to mss. Sample copy for $12. Writer's guidelines for #10 SASE with sufficient number of IRCs or online.

PAYMENT/TERMS Payment varies. Pays on publication. Acquires first world rights.

ST. ANTHONY MESSENGER

28 W. Liberty St., Cincinnati OH 45202-6498. (513)241-5615. Fax: (513)241-0399. E-mail: mageditors@americancatholic.org. Website: www.americancatholic.org. **Contact:** John Feister, editor-in-chief.

Magazine: 8×10¾; 60 pages; illustrations; photos. "*St. Anthony Messenger* is a Catholic family magazine which aims to help its readers lead more fully human and Christian lives. We publish articles which report on a changing church and world, opinion pieces written from the perspective of Christian faith and values, personality profiles, and fiction which entertains and informs." Estab. 1893. Circ. 308,884.

NEEDS mainstream, religious/inspirational, senior citizen/retirement. "We do not want mawkishly sentimental or preachy fiction. Stories are most often rejected for poor plotting and characterization; bad dialogue—listen to how people talk; inadequate motivation. Many stories say nothing, are 'happenings' rather than stories." No fetal journals, no rewritten Bible stories. Receives 60-70 unsolicited mss/month. Accepts 1 mss/issue; 12 mss/year. Publishes ms 1 year after acceptance. **Publishes 3 new writers/year.** Recently published work by Geraldine Marshall Gutfreund, John Salustri, Beth Dotson, Miriam Polikatsikis and Joseph Pici. Sometimes requests revisions before acceptance.

HOW TO CONTACT Send complete ms. Accepts submissions by e-mail, fax. "For quickest response send self-addressed stamped postcard with choices: 'Yes, we're interested in publishing; Maybe, we'd like to hold for future consideration; No, we've decided to pass on the publication.'" Responds in 3 weeks to queries; 2 months to mss. No simultaneous submissions. Sample copy for 9×12 SASE with 4 first-class stamps. Writer's guidelines online. Reviews fiction.

TIPS "The freelancer should consider why his or her proposed article would be appropriate for us, rather than for *Redbook* or *Saturday Review*. We treat human problems of all kinds, but from a religious perspective. Articles should reflect Catholic theology, spirituality, and employ a Catholic terminology and vocabulary. We need more articles on prayer, scripture, Catholic worship. Get authoritative information (not merely library research); we want interviews with experts. Write in popular style; use lots of examples, stories, and personal quotes. Word length is an important consideration."

STONE SOUP

Children's Art Foundation, P.O. Box 83, Santa Cruz CA 95063-0083. (831)426-5557. Fax: (831)426-1161. E-mail: editor@stonesoup.com. Website: www.stonesoup.com. **Contact:** Ms. Gerry Mandel, editor. Estab. 1973. Magazine: 7×10; 48 pages; high quality paper; photos. Audience is children, teachers, parents, writers, artists. "We have a preference for writing and art based on real-life experiences; no formula stories or poems. We only publish writing by children ages 8 to 13. We do not publish writing by adults." Bimonthly. Circ. 15,000. "We do not like assignments or formula stories of any kind." Receives 1,000 unsolicited mss/month. Accepts 10 mss/issue. Publishes ms 4 months after acceptance. **Publishes some new writers/year.** Also publishes literary essays, poetry. Send complete ms. "We like to learn a little about our young writers, why they like to write, and how they came to write the story they are submitting." Sample copy by phone. Writer's guidelines online.

"Stories and poems from past issues are available online."

NEEDS Adventure, ethnic/multicultural, experimental, fantasy, historical, humor/satire, mystery/suspense, science fiction, slice-of-life vignettes, suspense.

HOW TO CONTACT Please do not include SASE. Do not send originals. Responds only to those submissions being considered for possible publication. "If you do not hear from us in 4 to 6 weeks it means we were not able to use your work. Don't be discouraged! Try again!" No simultaneous submissions.

PAYMENT/TERMS Pays $40 for stories. Authors also receive 2 copies, a certificate, and discounts on additional copies and on subscriptions. Pays on publication.

TIPS "All writing we publish is by young people ages 13 and under. We do not publish any writing by adults. We can't emphasize enough how important it is to read a couple of issues of the magazine. You can read stories and poems from past issues online. We have a strong preference for writing on subjects that mean a lot to the author. If you feel strongly about something that happened to you or something you observed, use that feeling as the basis for your story or poem. Stories should have good descriptions, realistic dialogue, and a point to make. In a poem, each word must be chosen carefully. Your poem should present a view of your subject, and a way of using words that are special and all your own."

THE STORYTELLER

Fossil Creek Publishing, 2441 Washington Rd., Maynard AR 72444. (870)647-2137. Fax: (870)647-2454. E-mail: storyteller1@hightowercom.com; storytellermag@@yahoo.com. Website: www.thestoryteller-magazine.com; www.freewebs.com/fossilcreek/storyteller.html. Estab. 1996. Tabloid: 8½x11; 72 pages; typing paper; glossy cover; illustrations. "This magazine is open to all new writers regardless of age. I will accept short stories in most genres and poetry in any type. Please keep in mind, this is a family publication." Quarterly.

NEEDS Adventure, historical, humor/satire, literary, mainstream, mystery/suspense, religious/inspirational, romance, western, senior citizen/retirement, sports. "I will not accept pornography, erotica, science fiction, new age, foul language, graphic horror or graphic violence." No children's stories or young adult. Wants more well-plotted mysteries. Publishes ms 3-9 months after acceptance. **Publishes 30-50 new writers/year.** Recently published work by Jodi Thomas, Jory Sherman, David Marion Wilkinson, Dusty Richards and Tony Hillerman. Publishes short shorts. Also publishes literary essays, poetry. Sometimes comments on rejected mss. Word length 2,500.

HOW TO CONTACT Send complete ms with cover letter. Include estimated word count and 5-line bio. Submission by mail only. Responds in 1-2 weeks to mss. No queries. Accepts simultaneous submissions and reprints. Sample copy for $6. Writer's guidelines for #10 SASE.

PAYMENT/TERMS Pays ¼ ¢ per word. Sponsors awards/contests.

TIPS *The Storyteller* is one of the best places you will find to submit your work, especially new writers. Our best advice, be professional. You have one chance to make a good impression. Don't blow it by being unprofessional.

O STRUGGLE: A MAGAZINE OF PROLETARIAN REVOLUTIONARY LITERATURE

P.O. Box 28536, Detroit MI 48228. (313)273-9039. E-mail: timhall11@yahoo.com. Website: www.strugglemagazine.net. **Contact:** Tim Hall, Editor. Estab. 1985. Magazine: 512×812; 36-72 pages; 20 lb. white bond paper; colored cover; illustrations; occasional photos. Publishes short shorts. Normally comments on rejected mss. Recently published work by Billie Louise Jones, Stephen Graf, Juan H. Rodriguez, Paris Smith, Gregory Alan Norton.

HOW TO CONTACT Email.

PAYMENT/TERMS Pays 1 contributor's copy. No rights acquired. Not copyrighted.

SUBTROPICS

University of Florida, P.O. Box 112075, 4008 Turlington Hall, Gainesville FL 32611-2075. E-mail: dleavitt@ufl.edu; subtropics@english.ufl.edu. Website: www.english.ufl.edu/subtropics. **Contact:** David Leavitt. Estab. 2005. Literary magazine/journal: 9x6, 160 pages. Includes photographs. "*Subtropics* —headed by fiction editor David Leavitt, poetry editor Sidney Wade, and managing editor Mark Mitchell—is committed to publishing the best new fiction, poetry, literary nonfiction, and translation by emerging and established writers. In addition to new work, Subtropics also, from time to time, republishes important and compelling stories, essays, and poems that have lapsed out of print." Triannual. Circ. 3,500. Member CLMP.

NEEDS literary. Does not want genre fiction. Receives 1,000 mss/month. Accepts 5-6 mss/issue; 15-18 mss/year. Does not read May 1-August 31. Ms published 3-6 months after acceptance. Agented fiction 33%. **Publishes 1-2 new writers/year.** Published John Barth, Ariel Dorfman, Tony D'Souza, Allan Gurganus, Frances Hwang, Kuzhali Manickavel, Eileen Pollack, Padgett Powell, Nancy Reisman, Jarret Rosenblatt, Joanna Scott, and Olga Slavnikova. Average length: 5,000 words. Publishes short shorts. Average length of short shorts: 400 words. Also publishes literary essays, poetry. Rarely comments on/critiques rejected mss.

HOW TO CONTACT Send complete ms with cover letter. Responds to mss in 2-6 weeks. Send disposable copy of ms. Replies via e-mail only. Do not include SASE. Considers simultaneous submissions. Sample copy available for $12.95. Guidelines available on website.

PAYMENT/TERMS Writers receive $500-1,000, 2 contributor's copies. Additional copies $12.95. Pays on acceptance. Acquires first North American serial rights. Publication is copyrighted.

TIPS "We publish longer works of fiction, including novellas and excerpts from forthcoming novels. Each issue will include a short-short story of about 250 words on the back cover. We are also interested in publishing works in translation for the magazine's English-speaking audience."

THE SUN

The Sun Publishing Co., 107 N. Roberson St., Chapel Hill NC 27516. (919)942-5282. Fax: (919)932-3101. Website: www.thesunmagazine.org. **Contact:** Luc Sanders, editorial associate. Estab. 1974. Magazine: 8½×11; 48 pages; offset paper; glossy cover stock; photos. "We are open to all kinds of writing, though we favor work of a personal nature." Monthly.

NEEDS Literary. Open to all fiction. Receives 800 unsolicited mss/month. Accepts 20 short stories/year. Publishes ms 6-12 months after acceptance. Recently published work by Tony Hoagland, David James Duncah, Poe Ballantine, Linda McCullough Moore, Brenda Miller. Also publishes poetry and nonfiction. No science fiction, horror, fantasy, or other genre fiction.

HOW TO CONTACT Send complete ms. Accepts reprint submissions. Sample copy for $5. Writer's guidelines online.

PAYMENT/TERMS Pays $300-1,500. Pays on publication for first, one-time rights.

TIPS "Do not send queries except for interviews. We're looking for artful and sensitive photographs that aren't overly sentimental. We're open to unusual work. Read the magazine to get a sense of what we're about. Send the best possible prints of your work. Our submission rate is extremely high. Please be patient after sending us your work. Send return postage and secure return packaging."

SUSPENSE MAGAZINE

JRSR Ventures, 26500 W. Agoura Rd., Suite 102-474, Calabasas CA 91302. Fax: (310)626-9670. E-mail: editor@suspensemagazine.com. Website: www.suspensemagazine.com. **Contact:** John Raab, editor. Estab. 2007.

TIPS "Unpublished writers are welcome and encouraged to query. Our emphasis is on horror, suspense, thriller and mystery."

SYCAMORE REVIEW

Purdue University Dept. of English, 500 Oval Dr., West Lafayette IN 47907. (765)494-3783. Fax: (765)494-3780. E-mail: sycamore@purdue.edu. Website: www.sycamorereview.com. **Contact:** Anthony Cook. Magazine: 8×8; 130-180 pages; heavy, textured, uncoated paper; heavy laminated cover. "Journal devoted to contemporary literature. We publish both traditional and experimental fiction, personal essay, poetry, interviews, drama and graphic art. Novel excerpts welcome if they stand alone as a story." Semiannual. Estab. 1989. Circ. 1,000.

Sycamore Review is Purdue University's internationally acclaimed literary journal, affiliated with Purdue's College of Liberal Arts and the Dept. of English. Art should present politics in a language that can be felt.

NEEDS experimental, humor/satire, literary, mainstream, regional, translations. "We generally avoid genre literature but maintain no formal restrictions on style or subject matter. No romance, children's." Would like to see more experimental fiction. Publishes ms 11 months after acceptance. Recently published work by Lucia Perillo, Sherman Alexie, G.C. Waldrep, June Armstrong, W.P. Osborn, William Giraldi. Also publishes poetry. Sometimes comments on rejected mss.

HOW TO CONTACT Send complete ms with SASE, cover letter with previous publications and address. Responds in 3-4 months to mss. Accepts simultaneous submissions. Sample copy for $5. Writer's guidelines for #10 SASE or online.

PAYMENT/TERMS Copies of journal/acquires one-time rights.

TIPS "We look for originality, brevity, significance, strong dialogue, and vivid detail. We sponsor the Wabash Prize for Poetry (deadline: mid-October) and Fiction (deadline: March 1). $1,000 award for each. All contest submissions will be considered for regular inclusion in the *Sycamore Review.* No e-mail submissions—no exception. Include SASE.

TALENT DRIPS EROTIC PUBLISHINGS

Cleveland OH 44102. (216)799-9775. E-mail: talent_drips_eroticpublishing@lycos.com. Website: http://ashygirlforgirls.tripod.com/talentdripseroticpublishings. **Contact:** Kimberly Steele, founder. Estab. 2007.

NEEDS Wants erotic short stories.

HOW TO CONTACT Submit short stories between 5,000 and 10,000 words by e-mail to talent_drips_eroticpublishing@lycos.com. Should be pasted into body of message. Reads submissions during publication months only. Time between acceptance and publication is 2 months. Guidelines available on website. Responds in 3 weeks. Pays $15 for each accepted short story. Acquires electronic rights only. Work archived on the site for one year.

TIPS "Does not want sci-fi/fantasy submissions; mythical creatures having pointless sex is not a turn-on; looking for more original plots than 'the beast takes the submissive maiden' stuff."

TALES OF THE TALISMAN

Hadrosaur Productions, P.O. Box 2194, Mesilla Park NM 88047-2194. E-mail: hadrosaur@zianet.com. Website: www.talesofthetalisman.com. **Contact:** David Lee Summers, editor. Estab. 1995. Zine specializing in science fiction: 8½×10½; 90 pages; 60 lb. white stock; 80 lb. cover. "*Tales of the Talisman* is a literary science fiction and fantasy magazine published 4 times a year. We publish short stories, poetry, and articles with themes related to science fiction and fantasy. Above all, we are looking for thought-provoking ideas and good writing. Speculative fiction set in the past, present, and future is welcome. Likewise, contemporary or historical fiction is welcome as long as it has a mythic or science fictional element. Our target audience includes adult fans of the science fiction and fantasy genres along with anyone else who enjoys thought-provoking and entertaining writing." Quarterly. Circ. 200.

Fiction and poetry submissions are limited to reading periods of January 1-February 15 and July 1-August 15.

NEEDS Fantasy (space fantasy, sword and sorcery), horror, science fiction (hard science/technological, soft/sociological). "We do not want to see stories with graphic violence. Do not send 'mainstream' fiction with no science fictional or fantastic elements. Do not send stories with copyrighted characters, unless you're the copyright holder." Receives 60 unsolicited mss/month. Accepts 7-10 mss/issue; 21-30 mss/year. Publishes ms 9 months after acceptance. **Publishes 8 new writers/year.** Recently published work by Tyree Campbell, Carol Hightshoe Ed Cox, Richard Harland, Janni Lee Simner, and Jill Knowles. Length: 1,000-6,000 words; average length: 4,000 words. Also publishes poetry. Often comments on rejected mss.

HOW TO CONTACT Send complete ms. Accepts submissions by e-mail (hadrosaur@zianet.com). Accepts submissions from January 1-February 15 and July 1-August 15. Include estimated word count, brief bio and list of publications. Send SASE (or IRC) for return of ms or send a disposable copy of ms and #10 SASE for reply only. Responds in 1 week to queries; 1 month to mss. Sometimes comments on rejected works. Accepts reprint submissions. No simultaneous submissions. Sample copy for $8. Writer's guidelines online.

PAYMENT/TERMS Pays $6-10. Pays on acceptance for one-time rights.

TIPS "Let your imagination soar to its greatest heights and write down the results. Above all, we are looking for thought-provoking ideas and good writing. Our emphasis is on character-oriented science fiction and fantasy. If we don't believe in the people living the story, we generally won't believe in the story itself."

TEA A MAGAZINE

Olde English Tea Company, Inc., 3 Devotion Rd., P.O. Box 348, Scotland CT 06264. (860)456-1145. Fax: (860)456-1023. E-mail: teamag@teamag.com. Website: www.teamag.com. Estab. 1994. Magazine. "An exciting quarterly magazine all about tea, both as a drink and for its cultural significance in art, music, literature, history and society." Needs fiction that is tea related.

HOW TO CONTACT Send complete ms with cover letter. Responds to mss in 6 months. Guidelines available for SASE.

PAYMENT/TERMS Pays on publication. Acquires all rights.

TIPS "Please submit full manuscripts with photos and make sure it is tea related."

TECHNICAL ANALYSIS OF STOCKS & COMMODITIES

Technical Analysis, Inc., 4757 California Ave. SW, Seattle WA 98116. (206)938-0570. E-mail: editor@traders.com. Website: www.traders.com. Estab. 1982.

"Eager to work with new/unpublished writers."

TIPS "Describe how to use technical analysis, charting, or computer work in day-to-day trading of stocks, bonds, commodities, options, mutual funds, or precious metals. A blow-by-blow account of how a trade was made, including the trader's thought processes, is the very best-received story by our subscribers. One of our primary considerations is to instruct in a manner that the layperson can comprehend. We are not hypercritical of writing style."

TELLURIDE MAGAZINE

Big Earth Publishing, Inc., P.O. Box 964, Telluride CO 81435-0964. (970)728-4245. Fax: (970)728-4302. E-mail: duffy@telluridemagazine.com. Website: www.

telluridemagazine.com. **Contact:** Mary Duffy, editor-in-chief. Estab. 1982.

TEXAS HOME & LIVING

Publications & Communications, Inc., 13581 Pond Springs Rd., Suite 450, Austin TX 78729. (512)381-0576. Fax: (512)331-3950. E-mail: bronas@pcinews.com. Website: www.texasHomeandLiving.com. Estab. 1994.

⊘ THEMA

Box 8747, Metairie LA 70011-8747. E-mail: thema@cox.net. Website: members.cox.net/thema. Estab. 1988. Magazine: 5½×8½; 150 pages; Grandee Strathmore cover stock; b&w illustrations. "Thema is designed to stimulate creative thinking by challenging writers with unusual themes, such as ' rage over a lost penny.' Appeals to writers, teachers of creative writing, and general reading audience." Circ. 350.

NEEDS adventure, ethnic/multicultural, experimental, fantasy, historical, humor/satire, literary, mainstream, mystery/suspense, novel excerpts, psychic/supernatural/occult, regional, religious/inspirational, science fiction, slice-of-life vignettes, western, contemporary, sports, prose poem. "No erotica." Themes with deadlines for submission in 2011 (publication in 2012): "Your Reality or Mine?" (March 1); "Wisecracks & Poems" (July 1); "Who Keeps Them Tidy?" (November 1). For more information, visit *THEMA*'s website. Publishes ms within 6 months after acceptance. **Publishes 9 new writers/year.** Recently published work by Michael Fontana, Sky Andrews Gerspacher, Malaika Favorite, and Mark Krieger. Publishes short shorts. Also publishes poetry. Sometimes comments on rejected mss.

HOW TO CONTACT Send complete ms with SASE, cover letter, include "name and address, brief introduction, specifying the intended target issue for the mss." SASE. Responds in 1 week to queries; 5 months to mss. Accepts simultaneous, multiple submissions and reprints. Does not accept e-mailed submissions. Sample copy for $10. Writer's guidelines for #10 SASE.

PAYMENT/TERMS Pays $10-25. Pays on acceptance for one-time rights.

TIPS "Be familiar with the themes. Don't submit unless you have an upcoming theme in mind. Specify the target theme on the first page of your manuscript or in a cover letter. Put your name on first page of manuscript only. (All submissions are judged in blind review after the deadline for a specified issue.) Most open to fiction and poetry. Don't be hasty when you consider a theme—mull it over and let it ferment in your mind. We appreciate interpretations that are carefully constructed, clever, subtle, and well thought out."

THREADS

Taunton Press, 63 S. Main St., P.O. Box 5506, Newtown CT 06470. (203)426-8171. Fax: (203)426-3434. E-mail: th@taunton.com. Website: www.threadsmagazine.com. Estab. 1985.

TIPS Article proposal recommendation: "Send us a proposal (outline) with photos of your own work (garments, samples, etc.)."

TRACES OF INDIANA AND MIDWESTERN HISTORY

Indiana Historical Society, 450 W. Ohio St., Indianapolis IN 46202-3269. (317)232-1877. Fax: (317)233-0857. E-mail: rboomhower@indianahistory.org. Website: www.indianahistory.org. **Contact:** Ray E. Boomhower, Senior editor. Estab. 1989.

TIPS "Freelancers should be aware of prerequisites for writing history for a broad audience. Writers should have some awareness of this magazine and other magazines of this type published by Midwestern historical societies. Preference is given to subjects with an Indiana connection and authors who are familiar with *Traces*. Quality of potential illustration is also important."

⊕ ULTIMATE MMA

Apprise Media, 2400 E. Katella Ave., Suite 300, Anaheim CA 92806. (714)939-9991. Fax: (714)939-9909. E-mail: djeffrey@beckett.com. Website: www.ultimatemmamg.com. Estab. 2,000.

TIPS "Know the subject material. Be creative. Be unique. Be accessible and flexible and open to input. Those who can produce on short notice are invaluable."

U.S. 1 WORKSHEETS

U.S. 1 Poets' Cooperative, U.S. 1 Worksheets, P.O. Box 127, Kingston NJ 08528. Website: www.us1poets.com. Estab. 1972.

TIPS "Mss are accepted from April 15-June 30 and are read by rotating editors from the cooperative. Send us something unusual, something we haven't seen before, but make sure it's poetry. Proofread carefully."

U.S. CATHOLIC

Claretian Publications, 205 W. Monroe St., Chicago IL 60606. (312)236-7782. Fax: (312)236-8207. E-mail: editors@uscatholic.org. E-mail: submissions@uscatholic.org. Website: www.uscatholic.org. Estab. 1935.

Please include SASE with written ms.

HOW TO CONTACT literaryeditor@uscatholic.org

VERSAL

Postbus 3865, Amsterdam 1054 EJ The Netherlands. +31 (0)63 433 8875. E-mail: Info@wordsinhere.com. Website: www.wordsinhere.com. **Contact:** Megan M. Garr, editor. Estab. 2002. Literary magazine/journal: 20 cm x 20 cm, 100 pages, offset, perfect-bound, acid-free color cover. Includes artwork. "*Versal* is the only English-language literary magazine in the Netherlands and publishes new poetry, prose and art from around the world. We publish writers with an instinct for language and line break, content and form that is urgent, involved and unexpected." Annual. Circ. 750.

NEEDS Experimental, literary. Receives 125 mss/month. Accepts 10 mss/year. Does not read mss January 16-September 14. Manuscript published 4-7 months after acceptance. Publishes 4 new writers/year.Published Derek White, Alissa Nutting, Russell Edson, Sawako Nakayasu. Length: 1,000 words (max). Publishes short shorts. Average length of short shorts: 1,500 words. Also publishes poetry. Sometimes comments on/critiques rejected mss.

HOW TO CONTACT Send complete ms with cover letter. Accepts submissions electronically only. Include brief bio. Responds to queries in 1 week. Responds to mss in 2 months. Considers simultaneous submissions. Guidelines available on website.

PAYMENT/TERMS Writers receive 1 contributor copy. Additional copies $15. Pays on publication. Acquires one-time rights. Sends galleys to author. Publication is copyrighted.

TIPS "We ask that all writers interested in submitting work first purchase a copy (available from our website) to get an idea of *Versal*'s personality. All unsolicited submissions must be submitted through our online submission system. The link to this system is live during the submission period, which is September 15–January 15 each year." "We like to see that a story is really a story, or, regardless of your definition of story, that the text has a shape. Often, we receive excellent ideas or anecdotes that have no real sense of development, evolution, or involution. Because we have a story limit of 3,000 words, the best stories have carefully considered their shape. A good shape for an 8,000 word story will rarely be successful in a two- or three thousand word story. We prefer work that has really thought through and utilized detail/imagery which is both vivid and can carry some symbolic/metaphoric weight. While we like stories that test or challenge language and syntax, we do publish plenty of amazing stories that imply traditional syntax. Even in these stories, however, it is clear that the writers pay close attention to sound and language, which allows the stories to best display their power."

VESTAL REVIEW

2609 Dartmouth Dr., Vestal NY 13850. E-mail: submissions@vestalreview.net. Website: www.vestalreview.net.

Vestal Review's stories have been reprinted in the *Mammoth Book of Miniscule Fiction, Flash Writing, E2Ink Anthologies*, and in the *WW Norton Anthology Flash Fiction Forward.*

TIPS "We like literary fiction, with a plot, that doesn't waste words. Don't send jokes masked as stories."

WATERWAYS WORLD

Waterways World Ltd, 151 Station St., Burton-on-Trent Staffordshire DE14 1BG United Kingdom. 01283 742950. E-mail: richard.fairhurst@wwonline.co.uk. Estab. 1972.

WESTERN HUMANITIES REVIEW

University of Utah, English Department, 255 S. Central Campus Dr., Room 3500, Salt Lake City UT 84112-0494. (801)581-6070. Fax: (801)585-5167. E-mail: whr@mail.hum.utah.edu. Website: www.hum.utah.edu/whr. **Contact:** Dawn Lonsinger, Managing Editor. Estab. 1947. Circ. 1,300.

Reads mss September 1-April 1. Mss sent outside these dates will be returned unread.

NEEDS "Looking for work that continues to resonate after reading is over. Especially interested in experimental and innovative fiction." Does not want genre (romance, sci-fi, etc.). Receives 100 mss/month. Accepts 5-6 mss/issue; 6-8 mss/year. Does not read April-September. Publishes ms up to 1 year after acceptance. **Publishes 3-5 new writers/year.** Recently published work by Michael Martone, Steve Almond, Craig Dworkin, Benjamin Percy, Francois Camoin, Kate Bernheimer, Lidia Yuknavitch. Publishes short shorts. Also innovative literary criticism and poetry. Rarely comments on rejected mss.

HOW TO CONTACT Send one story per reading period. No e-mail submissions or queries. Sample copy for $10. Writer's guidelines online.

PAYMENT/TERMS Pays in contributor's copies on publication.Additional Information Runs Utah Writers' Contest every fall.

TIPS "Because of changes in our editorial staff, we urge familiarity with recent issues of the magazine. We do not publish writer's guidelines because we think that the magazine itself conveys an accurate picture of our requirements. Please, no e-mail submissions."

WHISKEY ISLAND MAGAZINE

Cleveland State University, English Dept., 2121 Euclid Ave., Cleveland OH 44115-2214. (216)687-2000. E-mail: whiskeyisland@csuohio.edu. Website: www.csuohio.edu/class/english/whiskeyisland/. Editors change each year. Magazine of fiction, creative nonfiction, theater writing, poetry and art. "We provide a forum for new writers, for themes and points of view that are both traditional and experimental." Semiannual. Press run: 1,000.

NEEDS "From flash fiction to 5,000 words." Receives 100 unsolicited mss/month. Accepts 46 mss/issue. Recently published work by Carolyn Furnish, Carl Peterson, and Shannon Robinson. "Most recent issue features three writers' first publications. We nominate for *Pushcart Prize*."

HOW TO CONTACT Send complete ms. Accepts submissions by mail and e-mail. Accepts simultaneous submissions. Responds in 6 months. Sample copy for $6. Subscription $12.

PAYMENT/TERMS Pays 2 contributor copies and 1-year subscription. Acquires one-time rights. Sponsors annual fiction contest with $500 prize and publication. $10 per entry.

TIPS "See submissions page. Include SASE. Wait at least a year before submitting again."

WHOLE LIFE TIMES

Whole Life Media, LLC, 23705 Vanowen St., #306, West Hills CA 91307. (877)807-2599. Fax: (310)933-1693. E-mail: editor@wholelifemagazine.com. Website: www.wholelifemagazine.com. Estab. 1979. Online market. "*WLT* accepts up to three longer stories (800-1,100 words) per issue, and payment ranges from $150-200 depending on topic, research required and writer experience. In addition, we have a number of regular departments that pay $75-150 depending on topic, research required and writer experience. City of Angels is our FOB section featuring short, newsy blurbs on our coverage topics, generally in the context of LA. These are generally 200-400 words and pay $25-35 depending on length and topic. This is a great section for writers who are new to us. BackWords is a 750-word personal essay that often highlights a seminal moment or event in the life of the writer and pays $100. *WLT* has editorial exchange relationships with local magazines in San Francisco and Chicago that occasionally co-assign (and increase the fee paid) or reprint at 50%. In the event that the magazine decides not to publish your assigned story, a kill fee of 50 percent of the original fee is offered. However, no kill fee is offered for unsolicited submissions or if this is your first assignment with us; you are free to publish the work elsewhere. If we do print your work, we customarily pay within 30-45 days of publication. We pay by invoice, so please be sure to submit one, and name the file with your name. We ask for one-time print rights and non-exclusive perpetual web publishing rights. Thank you for your interest in *Whole Life Times*, voice of the Los Angeles community for 33 years." Email: editor@wholelifemagazine.com.

"We are a regional publication and favor material that somehow links to our area via topics, sources, similar.

HOW TO CONTACT We accept articles at any time by e-mail. If you would like your article to be considered for a specific issue, we should have it in hand 2-4 months before the issue of publication. Original photos and illustrations are welcome and may be submitted along with your article for consideration. If you are sending very large images, graphs or other original art, please e-mail us for ftp submission guidelines. Please include a one-sentence credit line to accompany your story. If you do not include it, the story will run with your byline only.

TIPS Send complete ms. Submissions are accepted via email. Artwork should also be sent via email as hard copies will not be returned. "Queries should be professionally written and show an awareness of current topics of interest in our subject area. We welcome investigative reporting and are happy to see queries that address topics in a political context. We are especially looking for articles on health and nutrition. No regular columns sought." Submissions should be double-spaced in AP style as an attached unformat-

CONSUMER MAGAZINES

ted MS Word file (.doc). If you do not have Microsoft Word and must email in another program, please also copy and paste your story in the message section of your email. Please suggest a hed and dek for your submission."

WINDSOR REVIEW

Dept. of English, University of Windsor, Windsor ON N9B 3P4 Canada. (519)253-3000; (519)253-4232, ext. 2290. Fax: (519)971-3676. E-mail: uwrevu@uwindsor.ca. Website: www.uwindsor.ca. Estab. 1965. Biannual 4-color literary magazine featuring poetry, short fiction and art. Circ. 400. Guidelines free for #10 SASE with first-class postage.

NEEDS No genre fiction (science fiction, romance), but would consider if writing is good enough.

HOW TO CONTACT Send complete ms. Length: 1,000-5,000 words

PAYMENT/TERMS Pays $25, 1 contributor's copy and a free subscription.

TIPS "Good writing, strong characters, and experimental fiction is appreciated."

WITCHES AND PAGANS

BBI Media, Inc., P.O. Box 687, Forest Grove OR 97116. (888)724-3966. E-mail: editor2@bbimedia.com. Website: www.witchesandpagans.com. Estab. 2002. Magazine. "*Witches and Pagans* is dedicated to Witches, Wiccans, Neo-Pagans, and various other earth-based, ethnic, pre/post-christian, shamanic and magical practitioners. We hope to reach not only those already involved in what we cover, but also the curious and completely new as well." Quarterly.

"Devoted exclusively to promoting and covering contemporary Pagan culture, *W&P* features exclusive interviews with the teachers, writers and activists who create and lead our traditions, visits to the sacred places and people who inspire us and in-depth discussions of our ever-evolving practices. You'll also find practical daily magic, ideas for solitary ritual and devotion, God/dess-friendly craft-projects, Pagan poetry and short fiction, reviews, and much more in every 96-page issue. *Witches&Pagans* is available in either traditional paper copy sent by postal mail or as a digital PDF-eZine download that is compatible with most computers and readers."

NEEDS contemporary Pagan-themed fiction only. Does not accept fictionalized retellings of real events. Avoid gratuitous sex and violence: in movie rating terms think PG-13. Also avoid gratuitous sentimentality and Pagan moralizing: don't beat our readers with the Rede or the Threefold Law. Accepts 3-4 mss/year. Length: 1,000 words (min)-5,000 words (max).

PAYMENT/TERMS Send complete ms with cover letter. Accepts submissions by e-mail. Responds to queries in 1-2 weeks. Responds to mss in 1 month. Sample copy available. Guidelines available on website.

TIPS "Read the magazine, do your research, write the piece, send it in. That's really the only way to get started as a writer: everything else is window dressing."

WOMAN'S WORLD

Bauer Publishing Co., 270 Sylvan Ave., Englewood Cliffs NJ 07632. (201)569-6699. Fax: (201)569-3584. E-mail: dearww@aol.com. Website: http://winit.womansworldmag.com. **Contact:** Stephanie Saible, editor-in-chief; Johnene Granger, fiction editor. Magazine: $9^1{}_2$×11; 54 pages. "We publish short romances and mini-mysteries for all woman, ages 18-68." Weekly. Estab. 1980. Circ. 1,600,000.

Woman's World is not looking for freelancers to take assigments generated by the staff, but it will assign stories to writers who have made a successful pitch.

NEEDS mystery/suspense, romance (contemporary). Not interested in science fiction, fantasy, historical romance, or foreign locales. No explicit sex, graphic language, or seamy settings. "We buy contemporary romances of 1,400 words. Stories must revolve around a compelling, true to life relationship dilemma; may feature a male or female protagonist, and may be written in either first or third person. We are *not* interested in stories of life-or-death, or fluffy, fly-away style romances. When we say romance, what we really mean is relationship, whether it's just beginning or is about to celebrate its 50th anniversary." Receives 2,500 unsolicited mss/month. Accepts 2 mss/issue; 104 mss/year. Publishes ms 4 months after acceptance. Recently published work by Linda S. Reilly, Linda Yellin, and Tim Myers. Publishes short shorts.

HOW TO CONTACT Send complete ms with SASE. *No queries.* Responds in 2 months to mss. Sample copy not available. Writer's guidelines for #10 SASE.

PAYMENT/TERMS Pays $500-1,000. Pays on acceptance. First North American Serial rights for 6 months.

TIPS The whole story should be sent when submitting fiction. Stories slanted for a particular holiday should be sent at least 6 months in advance. "Familiarize yourself totally with our format and style. Read at least a year's worth of *Woman's World* fiction. Analyze and dissect it. Regarding romances, scrutinize them not only for content but tone, mood and sensibility."

WORLD WAR II

Weider History Group, 19300 Promenade Dr., Leesburg VA 20176. E-mail: worldwar2@weiderhistorygroup.com. Website: www.historynet.com. **Contact:** Editor, World War II. Estab. 1986.

TIPS "We no longer consider full manuscripts submitted on spec. All assigned articles are based on queries and prior discussion."

THE YALOBUSHA REVIEW

University of Mississippi, P.O. Box 1848, Dept. of English, University MS 38677. (662)915-3175. E-mail: yreditor@yahoo.com. Website: www.olemiss.edu/yalobusha. Estab. 1995. Magazine: 5×10; 125 pages; illustrations; photos. Annual. "Literary journal seeking quality submissions from around the world." Circ. 500.

NEEDS experimental, historical, humorous, literary, novel excerpts, short shorts. Does not want sappy confessional or insights into parenthood. Receives 100 unsolicited mss/month. Accepts 3-6 mss/issue. Reading period: July 15-November 15. Publishes ms 4 months after acceptance. **Publishes 2-4 new writers/year.** Recently published work by John Brandon, Steve Almond, Shay Youngblood, Dan Chaon. Length: 10,000 words; average length: 4,000 words. Publishes short shorts. Also publishes nonfiction, poetry.

HOW TO CONTACT Send complete ms. Include a brief bio. and #10 SASE for reply only. Does not accept electronic submissions unless from outside the U.S. Accepts simultaneous submissions; no previously published work. Send disposable copy of ms and #10 SASE for reply only. Responds in 2-4 months to mss. Reading period is July 15-November 15. Sample copy for $10. Writer's guidelines for #10 SASE.

PAYMENT/TERMS Pays 2 contributor's copies. Pays honorarium when funding available. Acquires first North American serial rights.

YEMASSEE

University of South Carolina, Department of English, Columbia SC 29208. (803)777-2085. Fax: (803)777-9064. E-mail: editor@yemasseejournalonline.org; manager@yemasseejournalonline.org. E-mail: See applicable department editor. Website: http://yemasseejournalonline.org. **Contact:** Zack O'Neill and Bhavin Tailor, co-editors. Magazine: $5\frac{1}{2}\times8\frac{1}{2}$; 70-90 pages; 60 lb. natural paper; 65 lb. cover; cover illustration. "We are open to a variety of subjects and writing styles. We publish primarily fiction and poetry, but we are also interested in one-act plays, brief excerpts of novels, and interviews with literary figures. Our essential consideration for acceptance is the quality of the work." Semiannual. Estab. 1993. Circ. 750. Condensed novels, ethnic/multicultural, experimental, feminist, gay, historical, humor/satire, lesbian, literary, regional. "No romance, religious/inspirational, young adult/teen, children's/juvenile, erotica. Wants more experimental work." Receives 30 unsolicited mss/month. Accepts 1-3 mss/issue; 2-6 mss/year. "We read from August-May and hold ms over to the next year if they arrive in the summer." **Publishes 6 new writers/year.** Recently published work by Robert Coover, Chris Railey, Virgil Suárez, Susan Ludvigson, Kwame Dawes. Publishes short shorts. Also publishes literary essays, poetry. Send complete ms. Include estimated word count, brief bio, list of publications. Send SASE for reply, return of ms, or send disposable copy of ms. Responds in 2 weeks to queries; 4 months to mss. Accepts simultaneous submissions. William Richey Short Fiction Contest submission deadline: November 15, 2010. See separate listing.

Stories from *Yemassee* have been published in *New Stories From the South.*

HOW TO CONTACT Sample copy for $5. Writer's guidelines for #10 SASE. Acquires first rights.

PAYMENT/TERMS Pays 3 contributor's copies.

ZAHIR

Zahir Publishing, 315 South Coast Hwy. 101, Suite U8, Encinitas CA 92024. E-mail: zahirtales@gmail.com. Website: www.zahirtales.com. **Contact:** Sheryl Tempchin, editor. Estab. 2003. Online magazine. "We publish literary speculative fiction." Quarterly.

NEEDS fantasy, literary, psychic/supernatural/occult, science fiction, surrealism, magical realism. No children's stories, excessive violence or pornography. Accepts 5-8 mss/issue; 20-25 mss/year. Publishes ms 2-12 months after acceptance. **Publishes 6 new writers/year.** Sometimes comments on rejected mss.

HOW TO CONTACT Send complete ms. Send SASE (or IRC) for return of ms, or send disposable copy of the ms and #10 SASE or e-mail address for reply only. E-mail queries okay. E-mail submissions okay through online submission form on our website. Responds in 1-2 weeks to queries; 1-3 months to mss. Accepts reprints submissions. Accepts simultaneous submissions. No multiple submissions. Writer's guidelines for #10 SASE, by e-mail, or online.

PAYMENT/TERMS Pays $10 and one copy of annual print anthology. Pays on publication for electronic rights and first, second serial (reprint) rights.

TIPS "We look for great storytelling and fresh ideas. Let your imagination run wild and capture it in concise, evocative prose."

ZOETROPE: ALL-STORY

Zoetrope: All-Story, The Sentinel Bldg., 916 Kearny St., San Francisco CA 94133. (415)788-7500. Website: www.all-story.com. **Contact:** Michael Ray, editor. Magazine specializing in the best of contemporary short fiction. "*Zoetrope: All Story* presents a new generation of classic stories." Quarterly. Estab. 1997. Circ. 20,000.

Does not accept submissions September 1-December 31 (with the exception of stories entered in the annual Short Fiction Contest, which are considered for publication in the magazine).

NEEDS Literary short stories, one-act plays. Accepts 25-35 mss/year. Publishes ms 5 months after acceptance. Length: 7,000 words (max).

HOW TO CONTACT Send complete ms. Does not accept mss June 1-August 1, or via e-mail. Responds in 5 months (if SASE included) to mss. Accepts simultaneous submissions. Sample copy for $6.95. Writer's guidelines online. Send stories to: *Zoetrope: All-Story* Attn: Fiction Editor.

PAYMENT/TERMS Pays $1,000. Acquires first serial rights.

TIPS "The 2011 Short Fiction Contest opens July 1, 2011; for details, please visit the website this summer."

ZYZZYVA

466 Geary Street, Suite 401, San Francisco CA 94102. (415)440-1510. E-mail: editor@zyzzyva.org. Website: www.zyzzyva.org. **Contact:** Howard Junker. Estab. 1985. "We feature work by writers currently living on the West Coast or in Alaska and Hawaii only. We are essentially a literary magazine, but of wide-ranging interests and a strong commitment to nonfiction." Circ. 2,500.

NEEDS Ethnic/multicultural, experimental, humor/satire, mainstream. Receives 300 unsolicited mss/month. Accepts 15 mss/issue; 45 mss/year. Publishes ms 3 months after acceptance. Agented fiction 1%. **Publishes 15 new writers/year.** Recently published work by Rick Barot, Jackson Bliss, Dust Wells. Publishes short shorts. Also publishes literary essays, poetry.

HOW TO CONTACT Send complete ms. Responds in 1 week to queries; 1 month to mss. Sample copy for $7 or online. Writer's guidelines online.

PAYMENT/TERMS Pays $50. Pays on acceptance for first North American serial and one-time anthology rights.

TIPS "West Coast writers means those currently living in California, Alaska, Washington, Oregon, or Hawaii."

BOOK PUBLISHERS

In this section, you will find many of the "big name" book publishers. Many of these publishers remain tough markets for new writers or for those whose work might be considered literary or experimental. Indeed, some only accept work from established authors, and then often only through an author's agent. Although having your novel published by one of the big commercial publishers listed in this section is difficult, it is not impossible. The trade magazine *Publishers Weekly* regularly features interviews with writers whose first novels are being released by top publishers. Many editors at large publishing houses find great satisfaction in publishing a writer's first novel.

Starting on page 164, you'll find the publishing industry's "family tree," which maps out each of the large book publishing conglomerates' divisions, subsidiaries and imprints. Remember, most manuscripts are acquired by imprints, not their parent company, so avoid submitting to the conglomerates themselves. (For example, submit to Dutton or Berkley Books, not their parent, Penguin.)

Also listed here are "small presses" publishing four or more titles annually. Included among them are independent presses, university presses, and other nonprofit publishers. Introducing new writers to the reading public has become an increasingly important role of these smaller presses at a time when the large conglomerates are taking fewer chances on unknown writers. Many of the successful small presses listed in this section have built their reputations and their businesses in this way and have become known for publishing prize-winning fiction.

These smaller presses also tend to keep books in print longer than larger houses. And, since small presses publish a smaller number of books, each title is equally important to the publisher, and each is promoted in much the same way and with the same commitment. Editors also stay at small presses longer because they have more of a stake in the business—often they own the business. Many smaller book publishers are writers themselves and know firsthand the importance of a close editor-author or publisher-author relationship.

TYPES OF BOOK PUBLISHERS

Large or small, the publishers in this section publish books "for the trade." That is, unlike textbook, technical, or scholarly publishers, trade publishers publish books to be sold to the general consumer through bookstores, chain stores or other retail outlets. Within the trade book field, however, there are a number of different types of books.

The easiest way to categorize books is by their physical appearance and the way they are marketed. Hardcover books are the more expensive editions of a book, sold through bookstores and carrying a price tag of around $20 and up. Trade paperbacks are soft-bound books, also sold mostly in bookstores, but they carry a more modest price tag of usually around $10 to $20. Today a lot of fiction is published in this form because it means a lower financial risk than hardcover.

Mass market paperbacks are another animal altogether. These are the smaller "pocket-size" books available at bookstores, grocery stores, drug stores, chain retail outlets, etc. Much genre or category fiction is published in this format. This area of the publishing industry is very open to the work of talented new writers who write in specific genres, such as science fiction, romance and mystery.

At one time publishers could be easily identified and grouped by the type of books they produce. Today, however, the lines between hardcover and paperback books are blurred. Many publishers known for publishing hardcover books also publish trade paperbacks and have paperback imprints. This enables them to offer established authors (and a very few lucky newcomers) hard-soft deals in which their book comes out in both versions. Thanks to the mergers of the past decade, too, the same company may own several hardcover and paperback subsidiaries and imprints, even though their editorial focuses may remain separate.

CHOOSING A BOOK PUBLISHER

In addition to checking the bookstores and libraries for books by publishers that interest you, you may want to refer to the Category Index at the back of this book to find publishers divided by specific subject categories. The subjects listed in the index are general. Read individual listings to find which subcategories interest a publisher. For example, you will find several romance publishers listed, but read the listings to find which type of romance is considered—gothic, contemporary, regency or futuristic. See You've Got a Story on page 2 for more on how to refine your list of potential markets.

The icons appearing before the names of the publishers will also help you in selecting a publisher. These codes are especially important in this section, because many of the publishing houses listed here require writers to submit through an agent. The Ⓐ icon indicates that a publisher accepts agented submissions only. A ● icon identifies those that mostly publish established and agented authors, while a ○ points to publishers most open to new writers. See the inside front cover of this book for a complete list and explanations of symbols used in this book.

IN THE LISTINGS

As with other sections in this book, we identify new listings with a ⊕ icon. In this section, most with this symbol are not new publishers, but instead are established publishers who were unable or decided not to list last year and are therefore new to this edition.

In addition to the ⊕ icon indicating new listings, we include other symbols to help you in narrowing your search. English-speaking foreign markets are denoted by a ◐. The maple leaf icon ◯ identifies Canadian presses. If you are not a Canadian writer but are interested in a Canadian press, check the listing carefully. Many small presses in Canada receive grants and other funds from their provincial or national government and are, therefore, restricted to publishing Canadian authors.

We also include editorial comments set off by a bullet ◯ within listings. This is where we include information about any special requirements or circumstances that will help you know even more about the publisher's needs and policies. The ◉ icon signals that this market is an imprint or division of a larger publisher. The ◯ icon identifies publishers who have recently received honors or awards for their books. The ◯ denotes publishers who produce comics and graphic novels.

Each listing includes a summary of the editorial mission of the house, an overarching principle that ties together what they publish. Under the heading **Contact** we list one or more editors, often with their specific area of expertise.

Book editors asked us again this year to emphasize the importance of paying close attention to the **Needs** and **How to Contact** subheads of listings for book publishers. Unlike magazine editors who want to see complete manuscripts of short stories, most of the book publishers listed here ask that writers send a query letter with an outline and/or synopsis and several chapters of their novel.

There are no subsidy book publishers listed in *Novel & Short Story Writer's Market*. By subsidy, we mean any arrangement in which the writer is expected to pay all or part of the cost of producing, distributing, and marketing his or her book. We feel a writer should not be asked to share in any cost of turning his manuscript into a book. All the book publishers listed here told us that they *do not charge writers* for publishing their work. **If any of the publishers listed here ask you to pay any part of publishing or marketing your manuscript, please let us know.** See our Complaint Procedure on the copyright page of this book.

A NOTE ABOUT AGENTS

Some publishers are willing to look at unsolicited submissions, but most feel having an agent is in the writer's best interest. In this section more than any other, you'll find a number of publishers who prefer submissions from agents. That's why we've included a section of agents open to submissions from fiction writers (page **198**). For even more agents along with a great deal of helpful articles about approaching and working with them, refer to *Guide to Literary Agents* (Writer's Digest Books).

If you use the Internet or another resource to find an agent not listed in this book, be wary of any agents who charge large sums of money for reading a manuscript. Reading fees do not guarantee representation. Think of an agent as a potential business partner, and feel free to ask tough questions about his or her credentials, experience, and business practices.

HARRY N. ABRAMS, INC.

Subsidiary of La Martiniere Group, 115 West 18th St., 6th Floor, New York NY 10011. (212)206-7715. Fax: (212)519-1210. E-mail: abrams@abramsbooks.com. Website: www.abramsbooks.com. **Contact:** Managing editor. Estab. 1951. Publishes hardcover and "a few" paperback originals. Averages 150 total titles/year. Responds in 6 months to queries. No simultaneous submissions, electronic submissions.

Does not accept unsolicited materials.

IMPRINTS Stewart, Tabori & Chang; Abrams Books for Young Readers; Abrams Gifts & Stationery.

TERMS Pays royalty. Average advance: variable. Publishes ms 2 years after acceptance. Book catalog for $5.

TIPS "We are one of the few publishers who publish almost exclusively illustrated books. We consider ourselves the leading publishers of art books and high-quality artwork in the U.S. Once the author has signed a contract to write a book for our firm the author must finish the manuscript to agreed-upon high standards within the schedule agreed upon in the contract."

ACE SCIENCE FICTION AND FANTASY

Imprint of the Berkley Publishing Group, Penguin Group (USA), Inc., 375 Hudson St., New York NY 10014. (212)366-2000. Website: www.penguin.com. **Contact:** Susan Allison, editor-in-chief; Anne Sowards, editor. Estab. 1953. Publishes hardcover, paperback, and trade paperback originals and reprints. Averages 75 total titles, 75 fiction titles/year.

NEEDS fantasy, science fiction. No other genre accepted. No short stories. Published *Iron Sunrise*, by Charles Stross; *Neuromancer*, by William Gibson; *King Kelson's Bride*, by Katherine Kurtz. Does not accept unsolicited mss.

HOW TO CONTACT Submit 1-2 sample chapter(s), synopsis. Send SASE or IRC. Responds in 2-3 months to queries.

TERMS Accepts simultaneous submissions. Pays royalty. Offers advance. Publishes ms 1-2 years after acceptance. Ms guidelines for #10 SASE.

ACME PRESS

P.O. Box 1702, Westminster MD 21158-1702. (410)848-7577. **Contact:** (Ms.) E.G. Johnston, man. ed. Estab. 1991. "We operate on a part-time basis." Publishes hardcover and trade paperback originals. **Published some debut authors within the last year.** Averages 1-2 total titles/year.

NEEDS humor. "We accept submissions on any subject as long as the material is humorous; prefer full-length novels. No cartoons or art (text only). No pornography, poetry, short stories or children's material." Published *She-Crab Soup* by Dawn Langley Simmons (fictional memoir); *Biting the Wall*, by J.M. Johnston (mystery); *SuperFan*, by Lyn A. Sherwood (football); and *Hearts of Gold*, by James Magorian (caper).

HOW TO CONTACT Accepts unsolicited mss. Agented fiction 25%. Responds in 2 weeks to queries; 2 months to mss. Accepts simultaneous submissions. Always comments on rejected mss. Please include the following contact information in your cover letter and on your manuscript: Byline (name as you want it to appear if published), mailing address, phone number, and e-mail. Include a self-addressed stamped envelope (SASE). If a SASE is not enclosed, you will only hear from us if we are interested in your work. Include the genre (e.g., fiction, et al.) of your work in the address. **"Acme Press is** 'always looking for the great comic novel.' Send for their submission guidelines or ask how to receive a book catalogue, by writing to them at PO Box 1702, Westminster MD 21158-1702."

TERMS Pays 25 author's copies and 50% of profits. Average advance: small. Publishes ms 1 year after acceptance. Book catalog and ms guidelines for #10 SASE.

TIPS "We are always looking for the great comic novel."

AGELESS PRESS

3759 Collins St., Sarasota FL 34232. Website: www.agelesspress.com. Estab. 1992. Independent publisher. Publishes paperback originals. Books: acid-free paper; notched perfect binding; no illustrations. Averages 1 total title/year.

NEEDS experimental, fantasy, humor, literary, mainstream/contemporary, mystery, new age/mystic, science fiction, short story collections, thriller/espionage. Looking for material "based on personal computer experiences." Stories selected by editor. Published *Computer Legends, Lies & Lore*, by various (anthology); and *Computer Tales of Fact and Fantasy*, by various (anthology).

HOW TO CONTACT Does not accept unsolicited mss. Query with SASE. Accepts queries by e-mail, fax, mail. Responds in 1 week to queries; 1 week to mss. Accepts simultaneous submissions, electronic submissions, submissions on disk. Sometimes comments on rejected mss.

TERMS Average advance: negotiable. Publishes ms 6-12 months after acceptance.

TIPS "Query! Don't send work without a query!"

ALLEN A. KNOLL, PUBLISHERS

200 W. Victoria Street, Santa Barbara CA 93101. (805)564-3377. E-mail: bookinfo@knollpublishers.com. Website: www.knollpublishers.com. **Contact:** Submissions. Estab. 1990. Small independent publisher, publishes a few titles a year. Specializes in "books for intelligent people who read for fun." Publishes hardcover originals. Books: offset printing; sewn binding. Titles distributed through Ingram, Baker & Taylor.

NEEDS fiction published: *They Fall Hard*, by Alistair Boyle (mystery); Bomber Hanson series, by David Champion (mystery); *The Duchess to the Rescue*, by Alexandra Eden (children's fiction); *The Real Sleeper*, by T.R. Gardner II (a love story). Nonfiction. Published: *Lotusland: A Photographic Odyssey* (garden book); *To Die For*, by David Champion (mystery).

HOW TO CONTACT *Does not accept unsolicited mss.*

TERMS Varies.

ALLWORTH PRESS

An imprint of Skyhorse Publishing, 307 West 36th St., 11th floor, New York NY 10010-4402. (212)777-8395. Fax: (212)777-8261. E-mail: pub@allworth.com. E-mail: bporter@allworth.com. Website: www.allworth.com. **Contact:** Bob Porter, associate publisher. Estab. 1989.

TIPS We are helping creative people in the arts by giving them practical advice about business and success.

ALONDRA PRESS, LLC

4119 Wildacres Dr., Houston TX 77072. E-mail: lark@alondrapress.com. Website: www.alondrapress.com. **Contact:** Pennelope Leight, fiction editor; Solomon Tager, nonfiction editor. Estab. 2007.

TIPS "Be sure to read our guidelines before sending a submission. We will not respond to authors who do not observe our simple guidelines. Send your submissions in an email attachment only."

AMERICAN ATHEIST PRESS

P.O. Box 5733, Parsippany NJ 07054-6733. (908)276-7300. Fax: (908)276-7402. E-mail: editor@americanatheists.org; info@americanatheists.org. Website: www.atheists.org. **Contact:** Framl Zindler, editor. Estab. 1963. Publishes trade paperback originals and reprints. Publishes monthly journal, *American Atheist*, for which are needed poetry, book reviews, and articles of interest to atheists. **Published 40-50% debut authors within the last year.** Averages 12 total titles/year.

IMPRINTS Gustav Broukal Press

NEEDS humor (satire of religion or of current religious leaders), anything of particular interest to atheists. "We rarely publish any fiction. But we have occasionally released a humorous book. No mainstream. For our press to consider fiction, it would have to tie in with the general focus of our press, which is the promotion of atheism and free thought."

HOW TO CONTACT Submit outline, sample chapter(s). Responds in 4 months to queries. Accepts simultaneous submissions.

TERMS Pays 5-10% royalty on retail price. Publishes ms within 2 years after acceptance. Ms to be submitted as MS Word attachments with e-mail. Hard copy may be requested.

TIPS "We will need more how-to types of material—how to argue with creationists, how to fight for state/church separation, etc. We have an urgent need for literature for young atheists."

◐ AMIRA PRESS

Wales. (704)858-7533. E-mail: yvette@amirapress.com. Website: www.amirapress.com. **Contact:** Yvette A. Lynn, CEO (any subgenre). Estab. 2007. Phone: (704)858-7533. E-mail: yvette@amirapress.com. Website: www.amirapress.com. "We are a small press which publishes sensual and erotic romance. Our slogan is "Erotic and Sensual Romance. Immerse Yourself." Our authors and stories are diverse. Our slogan is 'Fiction That Is Coloring the World,' which means we are bringing all types of people together with our books." Publishes paperback originals, e-books. POD printing. **Published 30 new writers last year.** Averages 50 fiction titles/year. Member EPIC. Distributes/promotes titles through Amazon, Mobipocket, Fictionwise, BarnesandNoble.com, Target.com, Amirapress.com, All Romance Ebooks, and Ingrams.

NEEDS romance in the following subgenres: erotica, ethnic/multicultural, fantasy, historical, mystery/suspense, science fiction, psychic/supernatural, contemporary, futuristic/time travel, historical, regency period. Special interests: interracial, paranormal, fantasy, menage, gay. Published *Something Unexpected*, by Tressie Lockwood (interracial romance), *Scared of Spiders*, by Even Langlais (menage a trois) paranormal romance.

HOW TO CONTACT Submit complete ms with cover letter by e-mail. "No snail mail." Include estimated word count, heat level, brief bio, list of publishing credits. Accepts unsolicited mss. Considers simultaneous submissions. Sometimes critiques/comments on rejected mss. Responds to mss in 3 months.

TERMS Ms published 1-4 months after acceptance. Please read our submission guidelines found on website. Pays royalties, 8.5% of cover price (print)—30% of cover price (Ebooks).

TIPS "Please read our submission guidelines thoroughly and follow them when submitting. We do not consider a work until we have all the requested information and the work is presented in the format we outline."

ANAPHORA LITERARY PRESS

104 Banff Dr., Apt. 101, Edinboro PA 16412. (814)273-0004. E-mail: pennsylvaniajournal@gmail.com. Website: www.anaphoraliterary.wordpress.com. **Contact:** Anna Faktorovich, editor-in-chief (general interest). Estab. 2007. "We are actively seeking submissions at this time. Single and multiple-author books in fiction (poetry, novels, and short story collections). The genre is not as important as the quality of work. You should have a completed full-length ms ready to be emailed or mailed upon request."

NEEDS Short stories can be included in *Pennsylvania Literary Journal*. Two novellas might be published in a single book.

HOW TO CONTACT Query with SASE. Submit proposal package, including synopsis, 1 sample chapter, and completed ms.

TERMS Pays 10-30% royalty on retail price. "We currently publish journals, which are authored by several people. If we publish a novel or a critical book by a single author, we will share our profits with the author."

TIPS "Our audience is academics, college students and graduates, as well as anybody who loves literature. Regardless of profits, we love publishing great books and we enjoy reading submissions. So, if you are reading this book because you love writing and hope to publish as soon as possible, send a query letter or a submission to us. But, remember—proofread your work (most of our editors are English instructors)."

ANGOOR PRESS LLC

2734 Bruchez Pkwy., Unit 103, Denver CO 80234. E-mail: submissions@angoorpress.com. Website: www.angoorpress.com. **Contact:** Carolina Maine, Founder, Editor. Estab. 2010.

IMPRINTS Hardcover, Trade paperback, and electronic originals.

TIPS "Christians."

ANNICK PRESS, LTD.

15 Patricia Ave., Toronto ON M2M 1H9 Canada. (416)221-4802. Fax: (416)221-8400. E-mail: annickpress@annickpress.com. Website: www.annickpress.com. **Contact:** Rick Wilks, director; Colleen MacMillan, associate publisher.

Does not accept unsolicited mss.

NEEDS Not accepting picture books at this time. Annick publishes books for children ages six months to twelve years and for young adults. Annick Press is committed to publishing **CANADIAN** authors.

HOW TO CONTACT Query with SASE. Responds in 1 month to queries; 3 months to mss. No simultaneous submissions, electronic submissions. Sometimes comments on rejected mss. Publishes ms 2 years after acceptance. Ms guidelines online. Send printed copies of your illustrations to e-mail at: annickpress@annickpress.com.

ANTARCTIC PRESS

7272 Wurzbach, Suite 204, San Antonio TX 78240. (210)614-0396. E-mail: davidjhutchison@yahoo.com; apcog1@gmail.com; rod_espinosa@antarctic-press.com. Website: www.antarctic-press.com. **Contact:** David Hutchison. Estab. 1985. "Antarctic Press is a Texas-based company that was started in 1984. Since then, we have grown to become one of the largest publishers of comics in the United States. Over the years we have produced over 850 titles with a total circulation of over 5 million. Among our titles are some of the most respected and longest-running independent series in comics today. Since our inception, our main goal has been to establish a series of titles that are unique, entertaining, and high in both quality and profitability. The titles we currently publish exhibit all these traits, and appeal to a wide audience."

NEEDS comic books, graphic novels.

TERMS Pays royalty on net receipts; ms guidelines online.

ANVIL PRESS

P.O. Box 3008 MPO, Vancouver BC V6B 3X5 Canada. (604)876-8710. Fax: (604)879-2667. E-mail: info@anvilpress.com; christine@anvilpress.com. Website: www.anvilpress.com. **Contact:** Brian Kaufman. Estab. 1988. "Three-person operation with volunteer editorial board." Publishes trade paperback originals. Books: offset or web printing; perfect bound. **Published some debut authors within the last year.** Averages 8-10 total titles/year. Published *Stolen*, by Annette Lapointe (novel); *Suburban Pornography*, by Matthew Firth (stories); *Elysium and Other Stories*, by Pamela Stewart; *Dirtbags*, by Teresa McWhirter (novel); *Black Rabbit and Other Stories* by Salvatore DiFalco. Publishes ms 8 months after acceptance. Book catalog for 9×12 SAE with 2 first-class stamps. Ms guidelines online.

Canadian authors only.

NEEDS experimental, literary, short story collections. Contemporary, progressive, modern literature—no formulaic or genre.

HOW TO CONTACT Accepts unsolicited mss, or query with SASE. Include estimated word count, brief bio. Send SASE for return of ms or send a disposable ms and SASE for reply only. No e-mail submissions. Responds in 2 months to queries; 6 months to mss. Accepts simultaneous submissions. Submit to: Anvil Press P.O. Box 3008, Main Post Office, Vancouver, BC V6B 3X5.

TERMS Pays 15% royalty on net receipts. Average advance: $500.

TIPS "Audience is young, informed, educated, aware, with an opinion, culturally active (films, books, the performing arts). No U.S. authors. Research the appropriate publisher for your work."

ARCHAIA

1680 Vine St., Suite 912, Los Angeles CA 90028. E-mail: editorial@archaia.com; submissions@archaia.com. Website: www.archaia.com. **Contact:** Submissions Editor. "Archaia Entertainment, LLC is a multi-award-winning graphic novel publisher with more than 50 renowned publishing brands, including such domestic and international hits as *Artesia, Mouse Guard, The Killer, Gunnerkrigg Court, Awakening, Titanium Rain, Days Missing, Tumor, Syndrome, Okko, The Secret History*, and a line of Jim Henson graphic novels including *Fraggle Rock* and *The Dark Crystal*. Archaia has built an unparalleled reputation for producing meaningful content that perpetually transforms minds, building one of the industry's most visually stunning and eclectic slates of graphic novels. Archaia is the reigning 2010 Graphic Novel Publisher of the Year according to *Ain't It Cool News, Graphic Policy*, and *Comic Related*. Archaia has also successfully emerged as a prolific storyteller in all facets of the entertainment industry, extending its popular brands into film, television, gaming, and branded digital media."

NEEDS "Archaia publishes creator-owned comic books and graphic novels in the adventure, fantasy, horror, pulp noir, and science fiction genres that contain idiosyncratic and atypical writing and art. *Archaia does not generally hire freelancers or arrange for freelance work, so submissions should only be for completed book and series proposals.*"

HOW TO CONTACT Query with outline/synopsis and photocopies of completed pages. Prefers e-mail submissions with pdf attachments. Accepts queries by snail mail. Include info on estimated page count, intended formats, and other technical details.

TERMS Submissions guidelines on website.

ARIEL STARR PRODUCTIONS, LTD.

P.O. Box 17, Demarest NJ 07627. E-mail: arielstarrprod@aol.com. **Contact:** Attn: Acquisitions Editor. Estab. 1993. Publishes paperback originals.

"Just make sure you submit the query with outline first unless we ask for something else."

HOW TO CONTACT Submit outline, 1 sample chapter. Accepts queries by e-mail. Include brief bio. Send SASE or IRC. Responds in 6 weeks to queries; 4 months to mss. Sometimes comments on rejected mss.

TERMS Publishes ms one year after acceptance.

TIPS "We want books that stimulate the brain and inspire the mind. Be honest and decent in your queries."

ARSENAL PULP PRESS

#101-211 East Georgia St., Vancouver BC V6A 1Z6 Canada. (604)687-4233. Fax: (604)687-4283. E-mail: info@arsenalpulp.com. Website: www.arsenalpulp.com. **Contact:** Editorial Board. Estab. 1980. Literary press. Publishes hardcover and trade paperback originals, and trade paperback reprints. **Published some debut authors within the last year.** Plans 1,500 first novels this year. Plans 2 first novels this year. Averages 20 total titles/year. Distributes titles through Whitecap Books (Canada) and Consortium (U.S.). Promotes titles through reviews, excerpts, and print advertising. Accepts unsolicited mss. Accepts 10% agented fiction. Responds in 2 months to queries; 4 months to mss. Accepts simultaneous submissions. Sometimes comments on rejected mss. Publishes ms 1 year after acceptance. Book catalog and submission guidelines on website.

"We are interested in literature that traverses uncharted territories, publishing books that challenge and stimulate and ask probing questions about the world around us. With a staff of five, located in a second-floor office in the historic Vancouver district of Gastown, we publish between 14 and 20 new titles per year, as well as an average of 12 to 15 reprints."

IMPRINTS Tillacum Library, Advance Editions

NEEDS gay/lesbian, literary fiction and nonfiction, multicultural, regional (British Columbia), cultural studies, pop culture, political/sociological issues, cookbooks

HOW TO CONTACT Submit outline, 2-3 sample chapter(s), synopsis. Include list of publishing credits. Send copy of ms and SASE (or with International Reply Coupons if sent from outside Canada) OR include e-mail address if manuscript does not need to be returned. Address: Editorial Board, Arsenal Pulp Press, #101-211 East Georgia St., Vancouver BC V6A 1Z6 Canada. No e-mail or fax submissions.

ARTEMIS PRESS

236 W. Portal Avenue #525, San Francisco CA 94127. (866)216-7333. E-mail: artemispressdigital-info@yahoo.com; submissions@artemispress.com. Website: www.artemispress.com. **Contact:** Susan R. Skolnick, publisher and editor-in-chief. Estab. 2000. "Publisher of short fiction of interest to the worldwide women's community. We specialize in lesbian-related titles but are interested in all women-centered titles. We are open to working with new authors." Publishes electronic editions of original, previously published material. **Published no debut authors within the last year.** Titles distributed and promoted online to target market.

NEEDS "Artemis Press is currently looking to purchase novellas, flash fiction, short fiction works of interest to women of all backgrounds, sexual orientations and ethnicities. We are especially interested in purchasing lesbian romance and erotica, lesbian and female detective fiction, as well as lesbian erotica. We will consider short fiction featuring strong, dynamic women characters in other genres. We are also looking for authors who are interested in writing short fiction to spec. Our short fiction needs are as follows: Flash Fiction—1000 to 1500 words; Short Short Fiction—1501 to 3000 words; Short Fiction—3001-15,000 words; Novellas—15,001 to 40,000 words. Send us a query email for more information. Please note: we no longer accept unsolicited manuscripts! Please query first via email." Wants: Mystery/detective, suspense, romance, erotica, paranormal/ghost stories, and science fiction. Published *The Ladies Next Door*, by Jacqui Singleton (humor/satire); *Selects Her Own*, by Claire Garden (humor/satire); *Clicking Stones*, by Nancy Tyler Glenn (New Age/mystic); *Moon Madness and Other Stories*, by Liann Snow (short story collection); *Faith in Love*, by Liann Snow (humor/satire); *Luna Ascending: Stories of Love and Magic*, by Renee Brown (short story collection); *Windrow Garden*, by Janet McClellan (romance); *Never Letting Go*, by Suzanne Hollo (humor/satire); *Minding Therapy*, by Ros Johnson (humor/satire).

HOW TO CONTACT Does not accept unsolicited mss. Agented fiction 5%. Responds in 3 months to queries. Does not accept simultaneous submissions.

TERMS Buys all rights. Publishes ms 6 months after acceptance. Ms guidelines online.

TIPS "We like to see clean manuscripts and an indication that the author has proofed and self-edited before submitting. Query via e-mail only to artemispress-digital-editor@yahoo.com."

ARTE PUBLICO PRESS

University of Houston, 452 Cullen Performance Hall, Houston TX 77204-2004. Fax: (713)743-3080. E-mail: submapp@mail.uh.edu. Website: www.artepublicopress.com. **Contact:** Nicolas Kanellos, editor. Estab. 1979. "Small press devoted to the publication of contemporary U.S.-Hispanic literature." Publishes hardcover originals, trade paperback originals and reprints. Averages 36 total titles/year.

Arte Publico Press is the oldest and largest publisher of Hispanic literature for children and adults in the United States. "We are a showcase for **Hispanic** literary creativity, arts and culture. Our endeavor is to provide a national forum for U.S.-Hispanic literature."

IMPRINTS Piñata Books.

NEEDS ethnic, literary, mainstream/contemporary, written by U.S.-Hispanic authors. Recent publications include *Women Who Live in Coffee Shops and Other Stories*, by Stella Pope Duarte; *The Name Partner*, by Carlos Cisneros; and *The Party for Papá Luis/La fiesta para Papá Luis*, by Diane Gonzales Bertrand.

HOW TO CONTACT Manuscripts must be submitted online at: www.artepublicopress.com. Agented fiction 1%. Responds in 2-4 months to queries; 3-6 months to mss. Accepts simultaneous submissions. Sometimes comments on rejected mss.

TERMS Pays 10% royalty on wholesale price. Provides 20 author's copies; 40% discount on subsequent copies. Average advance: $1,000-3,000. Publishes ms 2 years after acceptance. Ms guidelines online.

TIPS "Include cover letter in which you 'sell' your book—why should we publish the book, who will want to read it, why does it matter, etc." "Use our ms submission online form. Format files accepted are: Word, plain/text, rich/text files. Other formats will not be accepted. Manuscript files cannot be larger than 5MB. Once editors review your ms, you will receive an email with the decision. Revision process could take up to four (4) months."

ASPEN MOUNTAIN PRESS

18121-C East Hampden Ave., Aurora CO 80013. E-mail: submissions@aspenmountainpress.com. Website: www.AspenMountainPress.com. **Contact:** Sandra Hicks, Editor-in-Chief. Estab. 2006. "**Aspen Mountain Press is closed to queries and submissions until further notice. Currently, we are booked into winter 2011.**" "We are a small electronic press that specializes in e-books. A few outstanding stories are considered for print. We currently encourage newer, outstanding writers to take their craft to the next level. The bulk of our stories are romantic with varying degrees of sensuality/sexuality. We encourage romances between consenting adults. We encourage discussion among our authors; we frequently discuss marketing, we take author input into covers seriously, we pay every month royalties are earned." Publishes e-books. Format: POD printing; perfect bound. Average print order: 250-500. Debut novel print order: 250. **Published 30 debut writers last year in e-book**. Plans 25-30 debut novels this year. Averages 65 fiction titles/year. Member RWA, CIPA. Distributes/promotes titles through Fictionwise, AllRomance eBooks, Mobipocket, Amazon, 1Romance eBooks, Bookstrand.

IMPRINTS Aurora Regency

NEEDS erotica, fantasy (space fantasy, sword and sorcery), gay, historical (erotic regency), horror (dark fantasy, futuristic, psychological, supernatural), lesbian, mystery/suspense (amateur sleuth, cozy, police procedural, private eye/hardboiled), psychic/supernatural, romance (contemporary, futuristic/time travel, gothic, regency, romantic suspense), science fiction (hard science/technological, soft/sociological), western (frontier saga, traditional, gay). Special interests: "We want heroes the reader can identify with and science fiction romance—No first person!" Published *Cold Warriors*, by Clare Dargin (science fiction romance); *Del Fantasma: Texas Tea*, by Maura Anderson (erotic paranormal romance); and *Cover Me*, by L.B. Gregg (erotic gay thriller). "We are also opening a regency line late summer 2010. See our website for details regarding Aurora Regency.

HOW TO CONTACT Query with outline/synopsis and 4 sample chapters. Accepts queries by e-mail only; does not accept mail. Include estimated word count, brief bio, list of publishing credits, and indicate whether the ms is finished. Responds to queries in 3 months. Accepts unsolicited mss. Often critiques/comments on rejected mss. Responds to mss in 3-4 months.

TERMS Sends preproduction galleys to author. Ms published 3-12 months after acceptance. Writer's guidelines on website. Pays royalties of 8% min for print, 35-40% max for e-books, 50% of net from resellers.

TIPS "Gay romances and erotica are very popular in e-books. Well-written science fiction and fantasy are also doing well. Eliminate dialogue tags when possible. Have someone outside your family read your submission and check for continuity errors, typing mistakes, and pacing. Follow the submission guidelines. Have a website and a blog. Have some idea on how you are going to market your book and let people know about it. Think outside the box. Traditional marketing, such as book marks, does not make sense in our industry."

ATHENEUM BOOKS FOR YOUNG READERS

Imprint of Simon & Schuster, 1230 Avenue of the Americas, New York NY 10020. Website: http://imprints.simonandschuster.biz/atheneum; www.simonsayskids.com. **Contact:** Caitlyn Dlouhy, editorial director; Justin Chanda, VP/publisher; Namrata Tripathi, executive editor; Emma Dryden, vice president. Estab. 1960. Atheneum Books for Young Readers is a hardcover imprint with a focus on literary fiction and fine picture books for preschoolers through young adults. Publishes special interest, first novels and new talent. Publishes 20+ picture books/year; 20+ middle readers/year; 20+ young adult titles/year. "We do not need how-to pamphlets, ABC books, coloring books, or board books." Average print order is 10,000-15,000 for a first middle grade or young adult book; 7,500-20,000 for a first picture book.

"In recent years, Atheneum has received the Newberry Medal for *Kira-Kira* by Cynthia Kadohata and *The Higher Power of Lucky* by Susan Patron; the Caldecott Honor for international bestseller *Olivia* written and illustrated by Ian Falconer; the Siebert Honor for *Lightship* written and illustrated by Brian Floca; and National Book Award finalists *Skin Hunger* by Kathleen Duey and *The Underneath* by Kathi Appelt."

NEEDS middle grade and YA adventure, fantasy, humor, mainstream/contemporary, mystery, suspense, and picture books.

HOW TO CONTACT "*We do not accept unsolicited queries, partial, or full manuscript submissions, unless from an agent.*"

TERMS Pays royalty on hardcover retail price: 10% fiction; 5% author, 5% illustrator (picture book). Offers $5,000-$8,000 advance for new authors. Publishes ms up to 3 years after acceptance.

TIPS "Study our titles."

AUNT LUTE BOOKS

P.O. Box 410687, San Francisco CA 94141. (415)826-1300. Fax: (415)826-8300. E-mail: books@auntlute.com; submissions@auntlute.com. Website: www.auntlute.com. **Contact:** Acquisitions editor. Estab. 1982. Small feminist and women-of-color press. Publishes hardcover and paperback originals. Does not publish single-author collections of poetry. Averages 4 total titles/year.

NEEDS ethnic, feminist, lesbian. We encourage you to consult our catalog to get a sense of the areas in which we publish and the audiences we currently serve.

HOW TO CONTACT Accepts unsolicited ms queries. Please include SASE. Please do not send manuscripts by certified mail or return receipt requested. We do not accept e-mailed submissions. Alternately, submit cover letter, two sample chapters (approx 50 pages), brief synopsis, and SASE to: Aunt Lute Books, Attn. Acquisitions Editor, P.O. Box 410687, San Francisco, CA 94141. Do not staple any pages, and make sure that each page is numbered and has your name at the top. Responds in 3 months.

TERMS Pays royalty.

TIPS "We seek manuscripts, both fiction and nonfiction, by women from a variety of cultures, ethnic backgrounds and subcultures; women who are self-aware and who, in the face of all contradictory evidence, are still hopeful that the world can reserve a place of respect for each woman in it. We seek work that explores the specificities of the worlds from which we come, and which examines the intersections between the borders which we all inhabit."

AURORA PUBLISHING

Ohzora Publishing Co., 3655 Torrance Blvd., Suite 430, Torrance CA 90503. (310)540-2800. Fax: (310)540-2877. E-mail: info@aurora-publishing.com. Website: www.aurora-publishing.com. Estab. 2006. It is Aurora's mission to introduce the highest quality manga titles to the wider population of North America and to the rest of the world, and to develop the manga market for a more mature audience.

AUTUMN HOUSE PRESS

87½ Westwood St., Pittsburgh PA 15211. (412)381-261. E-mail: info@autumnhouse.org. Website: www.autumnhouse.org. **Contact:** Michael Simms, editor-in-chief (fiction). Estab. 1998. Holds competition/award for short stories, novels, story collections, translations. *We ask that all submissions from authors new to Autumn House come through one of our annual contests.* "To identify and publish the best fiction manuscripts we can find." Annual. Prize: $2,500 and book publication. Only one category: all genres of fiction (short stories, short-shorts, novellas, and novels, or any combination of genres) are eligible. Entries should be unpublished. Open to all writers over the age of 18. Length: approx 200-300 pages. Cover letter should include name, address, phone, e-mail, novel/story title. The mss are judged blind, so please include two cover pages, one with contact information and one without. "The competition is tough, so submit only your best work!" Results announced September. Winners notified by mail, by phone, by e-mail. Results made available to entrants with SASE, by fax, by e-mail, on website. Published *New World Order*, by Derek Green (collection of stories); and *Drift and Swerve*, by Samuel Ligon (collection of stories). All submissions come through our annual contests; deadline June 30 each year. See website for official guidelines. Responds to queries in 2 days. Accepts mss only through contest. Never critiques/comments on rejected mss. Responds to mss by August. Questions answered through e-mail at: info@autumnhouse.org.

"Extraordinary poetry and fiction."

NEEDS well-crafted prose fiction

HOW TO CONTACT Entry fee: $25. Make checks payable to Autumn House Press. Send manuscript and $25.00 fee to: Autumn House Press, PO Box 60100, Pittsburgh, PA 15211. Accepts inquiries by e-mail, phone. **Entry deadline is June 30.** Fiction submissions should be 200-300 pages long. Sends preproduction galleys to author. Ms published 9-12 months after acceptance. Submission guidelines on website at www.autumnhouse.org.

TERMS Prize winners will receive book publication, $1,000 advance against royalties, and $1,500 travel grant to participate in the 2011 Autumn House Master Authors Series in Pittsburgh. Pays royalties 7%, advance average of $2,500. Book catalogs free upon request, on website.

TIPS "The competition to publish with Autumn House is very tough. Submit only your best work."

AVALON BOOKS

Thomas Bouregy & Sons, Inc., 160 Madison Ave., 5th Floor, New York NY 10016. (212)598-0222. Fax: (212)979-1862. E-mail: editorial@avalonbooks.com; avalon@avalonbooks.com; lbrown@avalonbooks.com. Website: www.avalonbooks.com. **Contact:** Lia Brown, editor. Estab. 1950. Publishes hardcover originals. **Published some debut authors within the last year.** Under its **AVALON BOOKS** imprint, Thomas Bouregy & Co., Inc., is a publisher of hardcover romances, mysteries, and westerns focusing primarily on the library market. There is no explicit sexual content or profanity in any of our novels. It is the author's responsibility to heighten the romantic atmosphere by developing love scenes with tenderness, emotion, and perception. We publish 60 books a year in bimonthly cycles of ten. A cycle consists of four contemporary romances, two historical romances, two mysteries, and two westerns. Books range in length from a minimum of 50,000 words to a maximum of 70,000 words. However, if the manuscript is exceptional, we will accept somewhat longer books. Please address any inquiries regarding manuscript submissions to: **editorial@avalonbooks.com.** Distributes titles through Baker & Taylor, libraries, Barnes&Noble.com, and Amazon.com. Promotes titles through Library Journal, Booklist, Publishers Weekly, and local papers.

HOW TO CONTACT *We do accept unagented material.* We accept queries by e-mail but not partials. Query with SASE or IRC. Responds in 1 month to queries; 6-8 months to mss.

TERMS Average advance: $1,000. Publishes ms 12-18 months after acceptance. Ms guidelines online.

TIPS "Avalon Books are geared and marketed for librarians to purchase and distribute."

AVATAR PRESS

515 N. Century Blvd, Rantoul IL 61866. Fax: (217)893-9671. E-mail: submissions@avatarpress.net. Website: www.avatarpress.com.

NEEDS comic books, both freelance artists working within company-owned storylines, or creator-owned comics. Published Warren Ellis's *Anna Mercury*, George A. Romero's *Night of the Living Dead*, Frank Miller's *Robocop*, Alan Moore's *The Courtyard*, and more.

HOW TO CONTACT *Not currently seeking script-only submissions at this time.* "Send us an 8-12 page story with panel to panel descriptions and in full script format. The story should feature an adventure by any Avatar Press company-owned character. Do not send us stories featuring characters owned by other comic companies or any creator-owned characters (even if the creator who owns the character is you - if you want to submit a creator-owned project see our listed guidelines for that). E-mail submissions are OK. If you have been previously published you may send copies of those comics. Don't forget to include your name, address, e-mail address and/or a phone number at which you can be contacted."

TERMS Writer's guidelines on website.

AVON BOOKS

Harper Collins Publishers, 10 E. 53 Street, New York NY 10022. Website: www.harpercollins.com. **Contact:** Michael Morrison, publisher. Estab. 1941. Estab. 1941. "Avon has been publishing award-winning books since 1941. It is recognized for having pioneered the historical romance category and continues to bring the best of commercial literature to the broadest possible audience." Publishes hardcover and paperback originals and reprints. Averages 400 total titles/year.

NEEDS historical, literary, mystery, romance, science fiction, young adult, health, pop culture.

HOW TO CONTACT *Does not accept unsolicited mss.* Query with SASE. Send SASE or IRC. www.harpercollins.com.

TERMS Varies.

B & H PUBLISHING

127 Ninth Ave. N., Nashville TN 37234. Website: www.bhpublishinggroup.com. Estab. 1934. Publishes hardcover and paperback originals. B & H is the book division of LifeWay, the world's largest publisher of Christian materials. Averages 90 total titles, 20 fiction titles/year. Member: ECPA.

NEEDS religious/inspirational (contemporary women's fiction, suspense, romance, thriller, historical romance). Engaging stories told from a Christian worldview. Published *Elvis Takes a Back Seat*, by Leanna Ellis (contemporary); *Snow Angel*, by Jamie Carie (romance); *The Moon in the Mango Tree*, by Pamela Binnings Ewin (historical); *Shade*, by John B. Olson (thriller); and *Forsaken*, by James David Jordan (suspense).

HOW TO CONTACT *At this time B&H only accepts manuscripts from literary agents.* For additional information, the agent may call us at 615-251-2438. Writer's Guidelines are available by sending a self-addressed stamped envelope to: Pat Carter: Writer's Guidelines, B&H Publishing Group, 127 9th Avenue North, MSN 115. Accepts simultaneous submissions.

TERMS Pays negotiable royalty. Publishes ms 10-12 months after acceptance. Ms guidelines for #10 SASE.

BAEN PUBLISHING ENTERPRISES

P.O. Box 1403, Riverdale NY 10471-0671. (718) 548-3100. E-mail: info@baen.com. Website: www.baen.com. **Contact:** Toni Weisskopf, publisher. Estab. 1983. "We publish books at the heart of science fiction and fantasy." Publishes hardcover, trade paperback, and mass market paperback originals and reprints. **Published some debut authors within the last year.** Plans 2-3 first novels this year. Averages 120 total titles, 120 fiction titles/year. Distributes titles through Simon & Schuster.

NEEDS fantasy, science fiction. Interested in science fiction novels (based on real science) and fantasy novels "that at least strive for originality." Length: 110,000-150,000 words. Published *In Fury Born*, by David Weber; *Music to My Sorrow*, by Mercedes Lackey and Rosemary Edghill; *Ghost*, by John Ringo.

HOW TO CONTACT Submit synopsis and complete ms. "Electronic submissions are strongly preferred. Attach manuscript as a Rich Text Format (.rtf) file. Any other format will not be considered." Additional submission guidelines online. Include estimated word count, brief bio. Send SASE or IRC. Responds in 9-12 months. No simultaneous submissions. Sometimes comments on rejected mss.

TERMS Pays royalty on retail price. Offers advance. Ms guidelines online.

TIPS "Keep an eye and a firm hand on the overall story you are telling. Style is important but less important than plot. Good style, like good breeding, never calls attention to itself. Read *Writing to the Point*, by Algis Budrys. We like to maintain long-term relationships with authors."

BAKER BOOKS

6030 East Fulton Rd., Ada MI 49301. Website: www.bakerbooks.com. Baker Book House Company, P.O. Box 6287, Grand Rapids MI 49516-6287. (616)676-9185. Fax: (616)676-2315. **Contact:** Jeanette Thomason, special projects editor (mystery, literary, women's fiction); Lonnie Hull DuPont, editoral director (all genres); Vicki Crumpton, acquisitions editor (all genres). Estab. 1939. "Midsize publisher of work that interests Christians." Publishes hardcover and trade paperback originals and trade paperback reprints. Books: web offset print. Plans 5 first novels this year. Averages 200 total titles/year. Distributes titles through Ingram and Spring Arbor into both CBA and ABA markets worldwide.

"Baker Books publishes popular religious nonfiction reference books and professional books for church leaders. Most of our authors and readers are evangelical Christians, and our books are purchased from Christian bookstores, mail-order retailers, and school bookstores. Does not accept unsolicited queries."

NEEDS literary, mainstream/contemporary, mystery, picture books, religious. "We are mainly seeking fiction of two genres: contemporary women's fiction and mystery." Published *Praise Jerusalem!* and *Resting in the Bosom of the Lamb*, by Augusta Trobaugh (contemporary women's fiction); *Touches the Sky*, by James Schaap (western, literary); and *Face to Face*, by Linda

Dorrell (mystery); *Flabbergasted*, by Ray Blackston; *The Fisherman*, by Larry Huntsberger.

HOW TO CONTACT Does not accept unsolicited mss. We will consider unsolicited work only through one of the following avenues. Materials sent to our editorial staff through a professional literary agent will be considered. In addition, our staff attends various writers' conferences at which prospective authors can develop relationships with those in the publishing industry. You may also submit your work to one or more of the following manuscript submission services, which serve as a liaison between publishers and prospective authors: Authonomy.com, The Writer's Edge, and Christian Manuscript Submissions, an online service of the Evangelical Christian Publishers' Association.

TERMS Pays 14% royalty on net receipts. Offers advance. Publishes ms within 1 year after acceptance. Ms guidelines for #10 SASE.

TIPS "We are not interested in historical fiction, romances, science fiction, biblical narratives or spiritual warfare novels. Do not call to 'pass by' your idea."

Ⓐ BALLANTINE BOOKS

1745 Broadway, New York NY 10019. (212)782-9000. Website: www.randomhouse.com/BB. Estab. 1952. "Ballantine's list encompasses a large, diverse offering in a variety of formats." Publishes hardcover, trade paperback, mass market paperback originals.

NEEDS confession, ethnic, fantasy, feminist, gay/lesbian, historical, humor, literary, mainstream/contemporary (women's), military/war, multicultural, mystery, romance, short story collections, spiritual, suspense, general fiction.

HOW TO CONTACT *Agented submissions only.*

TERMS Pays 8-15% royalty. Average advance: variable. Ms guidelines online.

BANCROFT PRESS

P.O. Box 65360, Baltimore MD 21209-9945. (410)358-0658. Fax: (410)764-1967. E-mail: bruceb@bancroftpress.com; HDemchick@bancroftpress.com (if bancrof account is down). Website: www.bancroftpress.com. **Contact:** Bruce Bortz, editor/publisher (health, investments, politics, history, humor, literary novels, mystery/thrillers, chick lit, young adult). "Small independent press publishing literary and commercial fiction." Publishes hardcover and trade paperback originals. Also packages books for other publishers (no fee to authors). **Published 5 debut authors within the last two years.** Averages 4-6 fiction titles/year. Published *The Re-Appearance of Sam Webber*, by Scott Fugua (literary); *Hume's Fork*, by Ron Cooper (literary); *The Case against My Brother*, by Libby Sternberg (historical/young adult); *Finn* by Matthew Olshan (young adult); and *The Sinful Life of Lucy Burns* by Elizabeth Leikness (fantasy/women's). Accepts unsolicited mss. Agented fiction 100%. Responds in 6-12 months to mss. Accepts simultaneous submissions. Sometimes comments on rejected mss. Ms guidelines online.

The Re-Appearance of Sam Webber, by Jonathon Scott Fugua, is an ALEX Award winner; *Uncovering Sadie's Secrets*, by Libby Sternberg, is an Edgar Award finalist.

NEEDS PET, PFS, PFE, PGA, PGL, PHI, PHS, PLE, PLI, PMS, PMW, PMY, PNA, PRE, PSF, PYA

HOW TO CONTACT Query with SASE or submit outline, 2 sample chapter(s), synopsis, by mail or e-mail or submit complete ms. Accepts queries by e-mail, fax. Include brief bio, list of publishing credits. Send SASE for return of ms or send a disposable ms and SASE for reply only.

TERMS Pays various royalties on retail price. Average advance: $1500. Publishes ms up to 3 years after acceptance.

TIPS "We advise writers to visit our website and to be familiar with our previous work. Patience is the number one attribute contributors must have. It takes us a very long time to get through submitted material, because we are such a small company. Also, we only publish 4-6 books per year, so it may take a long time for your optioned book to be published. We like to be able to market our books to be used in schools and in libraries. We prefer fiction that bucks trends and moves in a new direction. We are especially interested in mysteries and humor (especially humorous mysteries)."

Ⓐ BANTAM DELL PUBLISHING GROUP

1745 Broadway, New York NY 10019. E-mail: bdpublicity@randomhouse.com. Website: www.bantamdell.com. Estab. 1945. "In addition to being the nation's largest mass market paperback publisher, Bantam publishes a select yet diverse hardcover list." Publishes hardcover, trade paperback, and mass market paperback originals; mass market paperback reprints. Averages 350 total titles/year.

NEEDS adventure, fantasy, horror.

HOW TO CONTACT *Agented submissions only.*

TERMS Offers advance. Publishes ms 1 year after acceptance.

BANTAM DOUBLEDAY DELL BOOKS FOR YOUNG READERS

Random House Children's Publishing, 1745 Broadway, New York NY 10019. (212)782-9000. Fax: (212)782-8234. Website: www.randomhouse.com/kids. **Contact:** Michelle Poplof, editorial director. Publishes hardcover, trade paperback, and mass market paperback series originals, trade paperback reprints. Averages 300 total titles/year.

Bud, Not Buddy, by Christopher Paul Curtis won the Newberry Medal and the Coretta Scott King Award.

NEEDS adventure, fantasy, historical, humor, juvenile, mainstream/contemporary, mystery, picture books, suspense, chapter books, middle-grade. Published *Bud, Not Buddy*, by Christopher Paul Curtis; *The Sisterhood of the Traveling Pants*, by Ann Brashares.

HOW TO CONTACT Does not accept unsolicited mss. *Agented submissions only.*

TERMS Pays royalty. Average advance: varied. Publishes ms 2 years after acceptance. Book catalog for 9×12 SASE.

BARBOUR PUBLISHING, INC.

1800 Barbour Dr., PO Box 719, Urichsville OH 44683. (740)922-6045. E-mail: editors@barbourbooks.com; aschrock@barbourbooks.com; fictionsubmit@barbourbooks.com. Website: www.barbourbooks.com. **Contact:** Ashley Schrock, creative director. Estab. 1981. Publishes hardcover, trade paperback and mass market paperback originals and reprints. Published 40% debut authors within the last year. Averages 250 total titles/year. "Heartsong romance is 'sweet'—no sex, no bad language. All stories must have Christian faith as an underlying basis. Common writer's mistakes are a sketchy proposal, an unbelieveable story, and a story that doesn't fit our guidelines for inspirational romances." Published *A Sister's Secret*, by Wanda E. Brunstetter (fiction). From time to time, we do look for specific types of manuscripts. These are usually announced through various writers' organizations including the American Christian Writers'. You can follow a link for a submission form and e-mail address that you can send your questions to. Responds in 6 months to mss. Accepts simultaneous submissions. Book catalog online or for 9×12 SAE with 2 first-class stamps; ms guidelines for #10 SASE or online.

"Please note that Barbour Publishing now only accepts book proposals via e-mail; paper proposals will not be reviewed by our editors and will ultimately be destroyed. Download the guidelines to ensure that your materials meet our specifications and will receive the proper attention from our editorial staff."

IMPRINTS Heartsong Presents (contact Joanne Simmons, managing editor).

NEEDS historical, contemporary, religious, romance, western, mystery. All submissions must be Christian mss.

HOW TO CONTACT Submit 3 sample chapter(s), synopsis by e-mail only. For submission of your manuscripts, please follow the link online to download the appropriate guidelines.

TERMS Pays 8-16% royalty on net price. Average advance: $1,000-8,000. Publishes ms 1-2 years after acceptance.

TIPS "Audience is evangelical/Christian conservative, nondenominational, young and old. We're looking for great concepts, not necessarily a big name author or agent. We want to publish books that will consistently sell large numbers, not just 'flash in the pan' releases. Send us your ideas!"

BARRON'S EDUCATIONAL SERIES, INC.

250 Wireless Blvd., Hauppauge NY 11788. Website: barronseduc.com. Estab. 1941. waynebarr@barronseduc.com. **Contact:** Wayne Barr, Acquisitions. Publishes hardcover, paperback, and mass market originals and software. Published 10% debut authors within the last year. Averages 400 total titles/year. Estab. 1941.

NEEDS middle grade, YA.

HOW TO CONTACT Accepts simultaneous submissions. E-mail queries only, no attachments.

TERMS Pays 12-13% royalty on net receipts. Average advance: $3-4,000. Publishes ms 18 months after acceptance. Ms queries via e-mail, but no attached proposals.

TIPS "The writer has the best chance of selling us a book that will fit into one of our series. Children's books have less chance for acceptance because of the glut of submissions. SASE must be included for the return of all materials. Please be patient for replies."

BAYLOR UNIVERSITY PRESS

One Bear Place 97363, Waco TX 76798. (254)710-3164; 3522. Fax: (254)710-3440. E-mail: carey_newman@baylor.edu. Website: www.baylorpress.com. **Contact:** Dr. Carey C. Newman, Director.

FREDERIC C. BEIL, PUBLISHER, INC.

609 Whitaker St., Savannah GA 31401. (912)233-2446. Fax: (912)233-6456. E-mail: books@beil.com. Website: www.beil.com. **Contact:** Mary Ann Bowman, editor. Estab. 1982. "Our objectives are (1) to offer to the reading public carefully selected texts of lasting value; (2) to adhere to high standards in the choice of materials and bookmaking craftsmanship; (3) to produce books that exemplify good taste in format and design; and (4) to maintain the lowest cost consistent with quality." Publishes hardcover originals and reprints. Books: acid-free paper; offset printing; Smyth-sewn, hardcover binding; illustrations. Plans 3 first novels this year. Averages 10 total titles, 4 fiction titles/year.

IMPRINTS The Sandstone Press; Hypermedia, Inc.

NEEDS history, biography, fiction. Published *Dancing by the River*, by Marlin Barton; *Joseph Jefferson*, by Arthur Bloom (biography); *The Invisible Country*, by H.E. Francis (fiction).

HOW TO CONTACT *Does not accept unsolicited mss.* We prefer postal mail queries. Query with SASE. Responds in 3 days to queries. Accepts simultaneous submissions.

TERMS Pays 7.5% royalty on retail price. Publishes ms 20 months after acceptance.

TIPS Our objectives are (1) to offer to the reading public carefully selected texts of lasting value; (2) to adhere to high standards in the choice of materials and in bookmaking craftsmanship; (3) to produce books that exemplify good taste in format and design; and (4) to maintain the lowest cost consistent with quality.

BELLEVUE LITERARY PRESS

New York University School of Medicine, Dept. of Medicine, NYU School of Medicine, 550 First Avenue, OBV 612, New York NY 10016. (212) 263-7802. E-mail: BLPsubmissions@gmail.com. Website: http://blpress.org. Dept. of Medicine, NYU School of Medicine, 550 First Ave., OBV A-640, New York NY 10016. (212) 263-7802. Fax: (212) 263-7803. E-mail: egoldman@blreview.org. **Contact:** Erika Goldman, editorial director (literary fiction); Leslie Hodgkins, editor (literary fiction). Estab. 2005. "We're a small literary press that publishes nonfiction and fiction that ranges the intersection of the sciences (or medicine) and the arts." Publishes hardcover originals, paperback originals. Debut novel print order: 3000. Plans 2 debut novels this year. Averages 8 total titles/year; 2 fiction titles/year. Member CLMP. Distributes/promotes titles through Consortium.

NEEDS literary. Published *The Cure*, by Varley O'Connor; *The Leper Compound*, by Paula Nangle (literary); *A Proper Knowledge*, by Michelle Latiolais; and *Tinkers*, by Paul Harding.

HOW TO CONTACT Send query letter or query with outline/synopsis and 3 sample chapters. Accepts queries by snail mail, e-mail. Include estimated word count, brief bio, list of publishing credits. Send disposable copy of ms and SASE for reply only. Agented fiction: 75%. Responds to queries in 2 weeks. Accepts unsolicited mss. Considers simultaneous submissions. Rarely critiques/comments on rejected mss. Responds to mss in 6 weeks.

TERMS Sends preproduction galleys to author. Manuscript published 8-12 months after acceptance. Writer's guidelines not available. Pays royalties 6-15%, advance $1,000. Book catalogs on website.

TIPS "We are a project of New York University's School of Medicine and while our standards reflect NYU's excellence in scholarship, humanistic medicine, and science, our authors need not be affiliated with NYU. We are not a university press and do not receive any funding from NYU. Our publishing operations are financed exclusively by foundation grants, private donors, and book sales revenue."

THE BERKLEY PUBLISHING GROUP

Penguin Putnam, Inc., 375 Hudson St., New York NY 10014. (212)366-2000. Website: www.penguinputnam.com. Estab. 1954. Accepts agented submissions. "Berkley is proud to publish in paperback some of the country's most significant best-selling authors." Publishes paperback and mass market originals and reprints. Averages approximately 800 total titles/year.

NEEDS adventure, historical, literary, mystery, romance, spiritual, suspense, western, young adult.

HOW TO CONTACT Does not accept unsolicited mss.

TERMS Pays 4-15% royalty on retail price. Offers advance. Publishes ms 2 years after acceptance.

BILINGUAL REVIEW PRESS

Hispanic Research Center, Arizona State University, P.O. Box 875303, Tempe AZ 85287-5303. (480)965-3867. Fax: (480)965-0315. E-mail: brp@asu.edu. Website: www.asu.edu/brp. **Contact:** Gary Keller, publisher. Estab. 1973. "University affiliated." Publishes hardcover and paperback originals and reprints. Books: 60 lb. acid-free paper; single sheet or web press printing; perfect-bound.

NEEDS ethnic, literary, short story collections. Always seeking Chicano, Puerto Rican, Cuban-American, or other U.S. Hispanic themes with strong and serious literary qualities and distinctive and intellectually important themes. Does *not* publish children's literature or trade genres such as travelogues and adventure fiction. Novels set in a pre-Columbian past are not likely to be published. Published *Moving Target: A Memoir of Pursuit*, by Ron Arias; *Contemporary Chicano and Chicana Art: Artists, Works, Culture, and Education*, Gary Keller, et al; *Triumph of Our Communities: Four Decades of Mexican American Art*, Gary Keller et al; *Assumption and Other Stories*, by Daniel A. Olivas; *Renaming Ecstasy: Latino Writings on the Sacred*, edited by Orlando Ricardo Menes.

HOW TO CONTACT Accepts unsolicited mss. Query with SASE or submit 2-3 sample chapter(s). Accepts queries by e-mail, mail. Include brief bio, list of publishing credits. Send SASE or IRC. Responds in 3-4 weeks to queries; 3-4 months to mss. Address: Gary Francisco Keller, Publisher Bilingual Review/Press, Hispanic Research Center, Arizona State University, PO Box 875303, Tempe, AZ 85287-5303.

TERMS Pays 10% royalty. Average advance: $500-1,000. Publishes ms 2 years after acceptance. Ms guidelines by e-mail.

TIPS "Writers should take the utmost care in assuring that their manuscripts are clean, grammatically impeccable, and have perfect spelling. This is true not only of the English but the Spanish as well. All accent marks need to be in place as well as other diacritical marks. When these are missing it's an immediate first indication that the author does not really know Hispanic culture and is not equipped to write about it. We are interested in publishing creative literature that treats the U.S Hispanic experience in a distinctive, creative, revealing way. The kind of books that we publish we keep in print for a very long time irrespective of sales. We are busy establishing and preserving a U.S. Hispanic canon of creative literature."

BIRCH BROOK PRESS

P.O. Box 81, Delhi NY 13753. Fax: (607)746-7453. E-mail: birchbrook@copper.net. Website: www.birchbrookpress.info. **Contact:** Tom Tolnay, editor/publisher; Barbara dela Cuesta, assoc. editor. Estab. 1982. Small publisher of popular culture and literary titles in mostly handcrafted letterpress editions. Specializes in fiction anthologies with specific theme, and an occasional novella. "Not a good market for full-length novels." Occasionally publishes hardcover and trade paperback originals. Books: 70 lb. vellum paper; letterpress printing; wood engraving illustrations. Averages 4 total titles, 2 fiction, 2 poetry titles/year. Member, Small Press Center, Publishers Marketing Association, Academy of American Poets. Distributes titles through Barnes&Noble.com, Amazon.com, Gazelle Book Services in Europe, Multicultural Books in Canada. Abe Books, and Alibris Books online. Promotes titles through website, catalogs, direct mail and group ads, book fairs. "Mostly we do anthologies around a particular theme generated in-house. Currently seeking short fiction and non-fiction on the theme of Christmas in the Wilderness. We make specific calls for fiction when we are doing an anthology." Published *The Bells of Moses Henry*, by Peter Skinner; *Birthright*, by Gwendolyn Jensen; *Tony's World*, by Barry Wallenstein; *Seasons of Defiance*, by Lance Lee; *And This Is What Happens Next*, by Marcus Rome; *Magic and Madness in the Library* (fiction collection); *Life & Death of a Book*, by William MacAdams; *Kilimanjaro Burning*, by John B. Robinson; *The Suspense of Loneliness* (anthology); *Tales for the Trail* (anthology); *Sexy Sixties*, by Harry Smith; *The Alchemy of Words*, by Edward Francisco; *Where Things Are When You Lose Them*, by Martin Golan; *The Sea-Crossing of St. Brendan*, by Matthew Brennan; *Baseball & the Game of Life* (anthology). Ms guidelines for #10 SASE.

"No manuscripts, inquiries only."

IMPRINTS Birch Brook Press; Birch Brook Impressions. "Letterpress editions are printed in our own shop."

NEEDS literary, regional (Adirondacks), popular culture, special interest (flyfishing, baseball, books about books, outdoors)

BOOK PUBLISHERS

HOW TO CONTACT Query with SASE or submit sample chapter(s), synopsis. Responds in 2 months to queries. Accepts simultaneous submissions. Sometimes comments on rejected mss.

TERMS Modest flat fee on anthologies. Usually publishes ms 10-18 months after acceptance.

TIPS "Write well on subjects of interest to BBP, such as outdoors, flyfishing, baseball, music, literary stories and occasional novellas, books about books."

BKMK PRESS

University of Missouri–Kansas City, 5101 Rockhill Rd., Kansas City MO 64110-2499. (816)235-2558. Fax: (816)235-2611. E-mail: bkmk@umkc.edu. Website: www.umkc.edu/bkmk. **Contact:** Ben Furnish, managing editor. Estab. 1971. Ms guidelines online.

NEEDS literary, short story collections. Not currently acquiring novels.

HOW TO CONTACT Query with SASE or submit 2-3 sample stories between January 1 and June 30. Responds in 8 months to mss. Accepts simultaneous submissions.

TERMS Pays 10% royalty on wholesale price. Publishes ms 1 year after acceptance.

TIPS "We skew toward readers of literature, particularly contemporary writing. Because of our limited number of titles published per year, we discourage apprentice writers or `scattershot' submissions."

O BLACK LYON PUBLISHING, LLC

P.O. Box 567, Baker City OR 97814. E-mail: info@blacklyonpublishing.com; queries@blacklyonpublishing.com. Website: www.blacklyonpublishing.com. **Contact:** The Editors (romance & general fiction love stories). Estab. 2007. "Black Lyon Publishing is a small, independent publisher. We produce 1-2 romance or general fiction novels each month in both 5x8 trade paperback and PDF e-books formats. We are very focused on giving new novelists a launching pad into the industry." Publishes paperback originals, e-books. **Published 4 new writers last year.** Plans 12 debut novels this year. Averages 15-20 fiction titles/year. Distributes/promotes titles through website, Ingram and Baker & Taylor, bookstores, and major online retailers. "Our novellas follow the guidelines of the full-length novels—only shorter! We are currently accepting contemporary and paranormal romances, as well as inspirational romances. (Note: We are especially interested in novellas with holiday settings and themes, i.e., Christmas, Halloween, Independence Day.) *20,000-40,000 words.*

"We are now seeking novella submissions for our upcoming Lyonettes imprint. Please see information online."

NEEDS romance (contemporary, futuristic/time travel, gothic, historical, regency period, romantic suspense). Special interests: ancient times. Published *Cast in Stone*, by Kerry A. Jones (paranormal romance); *The Medallion of Solaus*, by Kimberly Adkins (paranormal romance); *Maya's Gold*, by Mary Vine (contemporary romance).

HOW TO CONTACT We prefer e-mail, but will accept snail mail queries. No unrequested manuscripts or file attachments please. We delete them. And please, no multiple submissions. Send query letter. Query with outline/synopsis and sample chapters. Include estimated word count, brief bio, list of publishing credits. Send SASE or IRC for return of ms or disposable copy of ms and SASE/IRC for reply only. Responds to queries in 8-12 weeks. No unsolicited mss. Considers simultaneous submissions, submissions on CD or disk. Often critiques/comments on rejected mss. Responds to mss in 1 week.

TERMS Sends preproduction galleys to author. Ms published within 6 months after acceptance. Writer's guidelines on website. Pays royalties and author's copies. Book catalogs on website.

TIPS "Write a good, solid romance with a setting, premise, character or voice just a little 'different' than what you might usually find on the market. We like unique books—but they still need to be romances."

BLACK ROSE WRITING

P.O. Box 1540, Castroville TX 78009. E-mail: creator@blackrosewriting.com. Website: www.blackrosewriting.com. **Contact:** Reagan Rothe. "Black Rose Writing is an independent publishing house that believes in developing a personal relationship with our authors." "We publish only one genre . . . our genre. Publishes nonfiction books, novels, short story collections, novellas, juvenile. Actively seeking fiction, novels and short story collections. We are seeking growth in an array of different genres and searching for new publicity venues for our authors everyday. Black Rose Writing doesn't promise our authors the world, leading them to become overwhelmed by the competitive and difficult venture. We are honest with our authors, and we give them the insight to generate solid leads without wasting their time. Black Rose Writing is able to promote, showcase, and produce your dedicated stories through the company itself and with our publishing/printing connections. We want to make your writing successes possible and eliminate the fear of a toilsome and lengthy experience."

TIPS "Please query first with synopsis and author information. Allow 3-4 weeks for response. Always check spelling and do not forward your initial contact emails."

BLACK VELVET SEDUCTIONS PUBLISHING

1350-C W. Southport, Box 249, Indianapolis IN 46217. (888)556-2750. E-mail: lauriesanders@blackvelvetseductions.com. Website: www.blackvelvetseductions.com. **Contact:** Laurie Sanders, acquisitions editor. Estab. 2005. "We publish two types of material: 1) romance novels and short stories and 2) romantic stories involving spanking between consenting adults. We look for well-crafted stories with a high degree of emotional impact. No first person point of view. All material must be in third person point of view." Publishes trade paperback and electronic originals. "We have a high interest in republishing backlist titles in electronic and trade paperback formats once rights have reverted to the author." Catalog free or online. Guidelines online or by e-mail (guidelines@blackvelvetseductions.com). Query with SASE. Submit complete ms. Only accepts electronic submissions. Recent Titles: *Her Cowboy's Way*, by Starla Kaye; *Spanked!* by Cara Bristol, Starla Kaye, and Richard Savage; *Night Angel*, by Renee Reeves; *Toy's Story: Acquisition of a Sex Toy*, by Robert Cloud; *His Perfect Submissive*, by Alyssa Aaron.

IMPRINTS Forbidden Experiences (erotic romance of all types); Tender Destinations (sweet romance of all types); Sensuous Journeys (sensuous romance of all types); Amorous Adventures (romantic suspense); erotic relationship stories (erotic short stories) usually including spanking, with a romantic relationship at their core).

NEEDS erotic romance, historical romance, multicultural romance, romance, short story collections, romantic stories, romantic suspense, western romance.

HOW TO CONTACT Contact us electronically.

TERMS Pays 10% royalty for paperbacks; 50% royalty for electronic books. Reports in 6-12 months. Accepts simultaneous submissions: Yes. SASE returns. Responds in 6 months to queries. Accepts only complete mss. Only accepts electronic submissions.

TIPS "We publish romance and erotic romance. We look for books written in very deep point of view."

BLIND EYE BOOKS

1141 Grant Street, Bellingham WA 98225. E-mail: editor@blindeyebooks.com. Website: www.blindeyebooks.com. **Contact:** Nicole Kimberling, editor. Estab. 2007. "Blind Eye Books publishes science fiction, fantasy and paranormal romance novels featuring gay or lesbian protagonists. We do not publish short story collections, poetry, erotica, horror or non-fiction. We would hesitate to publish any manuscript that is less than 70,000 or over 150,000 words."

NEEDS science fiction, fantasy, and paranormal romance novels featuring gay or lesbian protagonists. Published *The Archer's Heart* by Astrid Amara, *Tangle* (anthology), and *Wicked Gentlemen* by Ginn Hale.

HOW TO CONTACT Submit complete ms with cover letter. Accepts queries by snail mail. Send disposable copy of ms and SASE for reply only. Does not return rejected mss. Authors living outside the U.S. can e-mail the editor for submission guidelines.

TERMS Writer's guidelines on website.

BLOODFIRE STUDIOS

P.O. Box 710451, San Diego CA 92171. E-mail: likewecare@bloodfire.com. Website: www.bloodfire.com. **Contact:** Dennis Greenhil, VP of Publishing. Estab. 1997. "Midsize Independent Publisher working mostly in Sci/Fi, Horror, and Manga. We pride ourselves on maintaining a high level of quality comparable to the big publishers. Art, Story, paper, etc meet or exceed Marvel and DC standards." Publishes paperback originals, paperpack reprints. Format: 60-80 lb gloss paper; saddle stitch, perfect bound binding; illustrations. **Publishes 4 debut writers/year.** Publishes 6-10 titles/year. Various distributors including Diamond Comics, direct sales, conventions, etc. Advertising and self-promotion through various channels;

"No longer able to accept unsolicited submissions."

HOW TO CONTACT Prefers submissions from writers, artists, writer-artists, creative teams. BloodFire Studios is not actively looking for new stories or character ideas. Writing submissions should be submitted in a script format like a play or movie (novel and short story formats are usually passed over). Presentation is important, so make sure it's easy to read. A 12 point font and double spaced lines are recommended. It also helps to make sure it's clean. Submission can be sent via e-mail but ONLY AS HYPERLINKS. Use the "Click here to email us" button online and enter "Writing submission" in the subject line. It will be forwarded to the appropriate editor. Follow guidelines posted on website closely or submissions will be trashed. "We attend major industry shows such as San Diego Comic Con, Wizard World LA and Wizard World Chicago." Responds to mss/art packets in a few weeks. Considers simultaneous submissions. Often comments on rejected mss.

TERMS Payment and rights varies on contract terms for each book. Ms published about a year after acceptance. Writer's and artist's guidelines, book catalog on website.

TIPS "Make sure you follow the guidelines to the letter. Make sure the art, writing, etc fits within the genres published."

BOBO STRATEGY

2506 N. Clark, #301, Chicago IL 60614. E-mail: info@bobostrategy.com; submissions@bobostrategy.com. Website: www.bobostrategy.com. **Contact:** Chris Cunliffe, editor-in-chief. Estab. 2008. "We seek writing that brings clarity and simplicity to the complex. If your idea is good, we may be willing to take a chance on you." Publishes trade paperback originals. Accepts simultaneous submissions.

NEEDS fiction: Accepts poetry, regional, short story collections. Nonfiction: accepts architecture, art, chess, creative nonfiction, government, humanities, memoirs, politics, regional, travel, world affairs, general nonfiction, how-to, humor, technical, textbook.

HOW TO CONTACT Query with SASE; submit proposal package, including: outline, 1 sample chapter. E-mail preferred.

TERMS Pays 0-10% royalty on retail price; outright purchase up to $2,500. Responds in 1 month on queries and proposals; responds in 2 months on mss. Catalog online at website. Guidelines available by e-mail. Reviews artwork; send photocopies. E-mail preferred.

BOOKS FOR ALL TIMES, INC.

Box 202, Warrenton VA 20188. (540)428-3175. E-mail: staff@bfat.com. Website: www.bfat.com. **Contact:** Joe David, publisher & editor. Estab. 1981. One-man operation. Publishes paperback originals.

NEEDS literary, mainstream/contemporary, short story collections. "No novels at the moment; hopeful, though, of publishing a collection of quality short stories. No popular fiction or material easily published by the major or minor houses specializing in mindless entertainment. Only interested in stories of the Victor Hugo or Sinclair Lewis quality."

HOW TO CONTACT Query with SASE. Responds in 1 month to queries. Sometimes comments on rejected mss. Joe David, publisher.

TERMS Pays negotiable advance. "Publishing/payment arrangement will depend on plans for the book."

TIPS Interested in "controversial, honest stories which satisfy the reader's curiosity to know. Read Victor Hugo, Fyodor Dostoyevsky and Sinclair Lewis for example."

BRANDEN PUBLISHING CO., INC.

P.O. Box 812094, Wellesley MA 02482. (781)235-3634. Fax: (781)235-3634. E-mail: branden@brandenbooks.com. Website: www.brandenbooks.com. **Contact:** Adolph Caso, editor. Estab. 1909. Publishes hardcover and trade paperback, plus Kindle and Nook editions. Reprints and software. Books: 55-60 lb. acid-free paper; case—or perfect-bound; illustrations. Averages 15 total titles, 5 fiction titles/year.

NEEDS ethnic (histories, integration), historical, literary, military/war, religious (historical-reconstructive), short story collections. Looking for "contemporary, fast pace, modern society." Published *I, Morgain*, by Harry Robin; *The Bell Keeper*, by Marilyn Seguin; *The Straw Obelisk*, by Adolph Caso; *Priest to Mafia Don* by Father Bascio; *Erebus—Nightmare of a Social Worker*, by Sam Saladino.

HOW TO CONTACT Does not accept unsolicited mss. Query with SASE. Responds in 1 month to queries.

TERMS Pays 5-10% royalty on net receipts. 10 author's copies. Average advance: $1,000 maximum. Publishes ms 10 months after acceptance.

BRIDGE WORKS PUBLISHING CO.

Box 1798, 221 Bridge Lane, Bridgehampton NY 11932. (631)537-3418. Fax: (631)537-5092. Website: www.bridgeworksbooks.com. **Contact:** Barbara Phillips, editorial director. Estab. 1992. "Bridge Works is very small, publishing only 1-6 titles a year." **Publishing some debut authors.** Distributes titles through National Book Network. "Our books are routinely reviewed in major publications, and we work closely with authors in both the editorial and marketing processes."

NEEDS Publishes mainstream quality fiction and nonfiction, also thrillers. "Query with SASE before submitting ms. Recent publications include *Mineral Spirits*, by Heather Sharfeddin; and *Chest Pains*, by Janet Nichols Lynch.

HOW TO CONTACT We now can only consider queries coming via literary agents. They may be accompanied by the first 50 pages of the manuscript. A SASE should be enclosed for reply and return of any enclosure. The query should be addressed to Barbara Phillips, Editorial Director and Co-Publisher. Write to address above, including synopsis and estimated word count, or query Barbara Phillips at: bap@hamptons.com. Responds in 1 month to query and 50 pages, 2 months to entire ms. Sometimes comments on rejected mss. Query with SASE before submitting ms. Does not read simultaneous submissions.

TERMS Pays 8% of net received from wholesalers and bookstores. Average advance: $1,000. Publishes ms 1 year after acceptance. Book catalog and ms guidelines for #10 SASE.

BROADWAY BOOKS

The Crown Publishing Group/Random House, 1745 Broadway, New York NY 10019. (212)782-9000. Fax: (212)782-9411. Website: www.broadwaybooks.com. **Contact:** William Thomas, editor-in-chief. Estab. 1995. Broadway publishes general interest nonfiction and fiction for adults. Publishes hardcover and trade paperback originals and reprints.

"Broadway publishes high quality general interest nonfiction and fiction for adults."

IMPRINTS Broadway Books; Broadway Business; Doubleday; Doubleday Image; Doubleday Religious Publishing; Main Street Books; Nan A. Talese.

NEEDS Broadway Books publishes a variety of nonfiction books across several categories, including memoir, health & fitness, inspiration & spirituality, history, current affairs & politics, marriage & relationships, animals, travel & adventure narrative, pop culture, humor, and personal finance. Publishes a limited list of commercial literary fiction. Published *Freedomland*, by Richard Price.

HOW TO CONTACT *Agented submissions only.*

BROKEN JAW PRESS

Box 596, STN A, Fredericton NB E3B 5A6 Canada. (506)454-5127. E-mail: editors@brokenjaw.com. Website: www.brokenjaw.com. **Contact:** Editorial Board.

IMPRINTS Book Rat; Broken Jaw Press; SpareTime Editions; Dead Sea Physh Products; Maritimes Arts Projects Productions.

TIPS "Unsolicited queries and manuscripts are not welcome at this time."

CALAMARI PRESS

Via Titta Scarpetta #28, Rome 00153 Italy. E-mail: derek@calamaripress.net. Website: www.calamaripress.com. "Calamari Press publishes book objects of literary text and art and experimental fiction." Publishes paperback originals. Format: 60 lb. natural finch opaque paper; digital printing; perfect or saddle-stitched bound. Average print order: 500-1,000. Debut novel print order: 300. Averages 2-3 total titles/year; 2 fiction titles/year. Published *Land of the Snow Men*, by George Belden (Norman Lock) (fictional literary canard with illustrations); *The Singing Fish*, by Peter Markus (prose poem/short fiction collection); *The Night I Dropped Shakespeare on the Cat*, by John Olson; *The Revisionist*, by Miranda Mellis; *Part of the World*, by Robert Lopez; *Ever*, by Blake Butler; reissued *Motorman*, by David Ohle; and *Stories in the Worst Way*, by Gary Lutz. Responds to queries in 2 weeks. Accepts unsolicited mss. Considers e-mail submissions only. Sometimes critiques/comments on rejected mss. Responds to mss in 2 weeks. Sends preproduction galleys to author. Manuscript published 2-6 months after acceptance. Writer's guidelines on website.

NEEDS Adventure, comics/graphic novels, ethnic/multicultural, experimental, literary, short story collections.

HOW TO CONTACT Query with outline/synopsis and 3 sample chapters. Accepts queries by e-mail only. Include brief bio. Send SASE or IRC for return of ms.

TERMS Pays in author's copies.

CANDLEWICK PRESS

99 Dover St., Somerville MA 02144. (617)661-3330. Fax: (617)661-0565. E-mail: bigbear@candlewick.com. Website: www.candlewick.com. **Contact:** Deb Wayshak, executive editor (fiction); Joan Powers, editor-at-large (picture books); Liz Bicknell, editorial director/associate publisher (poetry, picture books,

fiction); Mary Lee Donovan, executive editor (picture books, nonfiction/fiction); Hilary Van Dusen, senior editor (nonfiction/fiction); Sarah Ketchersid, senior editor (board, toddler). Estab. 1991. "We are a truly child-centered publisher." Publishes hardcover originals, trade paperback originals, and reprints. Averages 200 total titles/year. Published *The Tale of Despereaux*, by Kate DiCamillo; the Judy Moody series, by Megan McDonald, illustrated by Peter Reynolds; *Feed* by M.T. Anderson; *Fairieality*, by David Ellwand. Does not accept unsolicited mss.

Candlewick Press is not accepting queries and unsolicited mss at this time. Candlewick title *Good Masters! Sweet Ladies! Voices from a Medieval Village* by Amy Schlitz won the John Newbery Medal in 2008. Their title *Twelve Rounds to Glory: The Strong of Muhammad Ali* by Charles R. Smith Jr., illustrated by Bryan Collier, won a Coretta Scott King Author Honor Award in 2008. Their title *The Astonishing Life of Octavian Nothing*, by M.T. Anderson, won the Boston Globe-Hornbook Award for Fiction and Poetry in 2007.

NEEDS Juvenile, picture books, young adult

TIPS "*We no longer accept unsolicited mss.* See our website for further information about us."

CAROLINA WREN PRESS

120 Morris St., Durham NC 27701. (919)560-2738. E-mail: carolinawrenpress@earthlink.net. Website: www.carolinawrenpress.org. **Contact:** Andrea Selch, president. Estab. 1976. Books: 6×9 paper; typeset; various bindings; illustrations. **Published 2 debut authors within the last year.** Distributes titles through Amazon.com, Barnes & Noble, Borders, Ingram, and Baker & Taylor, and on their website. "Though we accept unsolicited manuscripts of nonfiction September-December, we very rarely accept any. We suggest you submit to our Doris Bakwin Award for Writing by a Woman; contest is held in fall of odd-numbered years." Published *Downriver* by Jeanne Leiby in 2007. Guidelines on our website in summer." Publishes ms 2 year after acceptance. Ms guidelines online.

"We are no longer accepting general submissions of poetry and fiction. We welcome submissions to our two contests, which run in alternate years." Reads unsolicited mss of fiction and nonfiction from September 1 to December 1 and poetry and children's lit from February 1 to June 1, but prefers writers to wait and enter their contests—poetry contest in Fall 2012 and 2014; Doris Bawkin Award for Writing by a Woman—prose fiction (a collection of short stories or a novel) or memoir. Submissions are accepted in odd-numbered autumns, with a final deadline of December 1st, 2011, 2013, 2015, etc. There is a $20 reading fee for this contest. Full guidelines should be followed—check the website in late summer to see the current guidelines. See below for poetry contest.

NEEDS poetry, fiction, nonfiction, biography, autobiography, literary nonfiction work by and/or about people of color, women, gay/lesbian issues, health and mental health topics in children's literature. Does not publish genre fiction or religious texts or self-help books.

HOW TO CONTACT Reads unsolicited mss in September only. Accepts queries by e-mail, mail. Include brief bio. Send SASE or IRC. Responds in 3 months to queries; 6 months to mss. "Please query before you send or else plan to enter one of our contests; entry fee is required."

TIPS Manuscripts are read year-round, but reply time is long unless submitting for a contest.

CAVE HOLLOW PRESS

P.O. Drawer J, Warrensburg MO 64093. E-mail: gbcrump@cavehollowpress.com. Website: www.cavehollowpress.com. **Contact:** G.B. Crump, editor. Estab. 2001. "Our website is updated frequently to reflect the current type of fiction Cave Hollow Press is seeking."

TIPS "Our audience varies based on the type of book we are publishing. We specialize in Missouri and Midwest regional fiction. We are interested in talented writers from Missouri and the surrounding Midwest. Check our submission guidelines on the website for what type of fiction we are interested in currently."

CHAMPAGNE ROSE PRESS

The Wild Rose Press, P.O. Box 708, Adam's Basin NY 14410. E-mail: queryus@thewildrosepress.com. Website: www.thewildrosepress.com. **Contact:** Roseann Armstrong, editor. Estab. 2006. "The Champagne Rose line is the contemporary romance line of the Wild Rose Press. Our contemporary stories are filled with sexual tension and passionate chemistry. The setting can take place anywhere in the world today. Champagne Rose couples explore their relationship both emotionally and physically. In each full-length novel, there must be one fully consummated love scene. In the case of short stories, if this isn't realistic for the plot of the story, then the physical encounters must be ripe with tension. The characters should leave us remembering them long after we turn the last page. We should feel their feelings, share their joys and their heartaches. And, as with all romances, we should close the book completely satisfied by the happy-ever-after ending." Publishes paperback originals, reprints, and e-books in a POD format. **Published 25 debut authors last year.** Publishes approximately 60 fiction titles/year. Member: EPIC, Romance Writers of America. Distributes/promotes titles through major distribution chains, including Ingram, Baker & Taylor, Sony, Amazon.com, Kindle, as well as smaller and online distributors.

NEEDS contemporary, futuristic/time travel, gothic, historical, regency, romantic suspense, erotic, and paranormal romances. Plans several anthologies "in several lines of the company in the next year, including Cactus Rose, Yellow Rose, American Rose, Black Rose, and Scarlet Rose." Has published *Calendar of Love*, by Susan Lyons; *Seduction's Stakes*, by Claire Ashgrove; and *A Perfect Fit*, by Sheridon Smythe.

HOW TO CONTACT *Does not accept unsolicited mss.* Send query letter with outline and synopsis of up to 5 pages. Prefers queries by e-mail; accepts by mail. Include estimated word count, brief bio, and list of publishing credits. Send SASE or IRC for return of ms. Agented fiction less than 1%. Responds to queries in 4 weeks; to mss in 12 weeks. Does not consider simultaneous submissions. Always comments on rejected mss.

TERMS Pays royalty of 7% minimum; 35% maximum. Sends prepublication galleys to author. Time between acceptance and publication is approximately 1 year. Writer's guidelines available on website.

TIPS "Polish your manuscript, make it as error free as possible, and follow our submission guidelines."

CHANGELING PRESS LLC

P.O. Box 1046, Martinsburg WV 25402. E-mail: Submissions@changelingpress.com. Website: www.changelingpress.com. **Contact:** Sheri Ross Fogarty, editor-in-chief. Publishes print and e-books.

NEEDS Special interests: "We publish Sci-Fi, Futuristic, Paranormal, Fantasy, Suspense, Horror, and Humor, BDSM, and Fetish Love Stories. We publish Interludes and Novellas only, from 8,000 to 25,000 words total length—NO 100,000 word sagas, please! (Series and Serials welcome)."

HOW TO CONTACT Submit complete ms with cover letter via e-mail only. Responds to queries in 2 months. Accepts unsolicited mss. Considers e-mail submissions.

TERMS Pays royalties of 35% gross paid monthly.

TIPS 'ePublishing' does not mean 'no editing.' 'Good enough' is never good enough. From editors to proofreaders to artists and marketing staff, our team of dedicated professionals is here for your support."

CHANNEL LAKE, INC.

P.O. Box 1771, New York NY 10156-1771. (800)592-1566. Fax: (866)794-5507. E-mail: info@channellake.com; submissions@channellake.com. Website: www.touristtown.com; www.channellake.com. **Contact:** Dirk Vanderwilt, publisher (travel guide books). Estab. 2005.

IMPRINTS Tourist Town Guides, Dirk Vanderwilt, Publisher

TIPS "Our books are 'local interest' and 'travel books' that are marketed and sold near or in the destination city. Our audience is primarily tourists and vacationers to the destination city. Query first for ms guidelines. The query should include the destination city (U.S. only) that you are interested in writing about."

CHARLESBRIDGE PUBLISHING

85 Main St., Watertown MA 02472. (617)926-0329. Fax: (617)926-5720. E-mail: tradeart@charlesbridge.com. Website: www.charlesbridge.com. **Contact:** Submissions Editors. Estab. 1980. Publishes hardcover and paperback nonfiction and fiction children's picture books, early readers, and middle-grade chapter books. Averages 36 total titles/year. Multicultural, nature, science, social studies, bedtime, math, etc.

"We're always interested in innovative approaches to a difficult genre, the nonfiction picture book."

IMPRINTS Charlesbridge, Imagine Publishing

HOW TO CONTACT Submit complete ms as exclusive submission for three months. Please send your work to the attention of: Submissions Editor, Trade Division, etc. Responds only to ms of interest. Please do not include SASE.

TERMS Royalty and advance vary. Publishes ms 2 years after acceptance. Ms guidelines online.

TIPS "To become acquainted with our publishing program, we encourage you to review our books and visit our website (www.charlesbridge.com), where you will find our catalog. To request a printed catalog, please send a 9" x 12" SASE with $2.50 in postage."

CHRISTIAN BOOKS TODAY LTD

136 Main St., Buckshaw Village Chorley, Lancashire PR7 7BZ UK. E-mail: submissions@christianbookstoday.com. Website: www.christianbookstoday.com. **Contact:** Jason Richardson, MD (nonfiction); Lynda McIntosh, Editor (fiction). Estab. 2009.

TIPS "We appeal to an audience of practicing Christians, Catholics in particular. We are not interested in Hallmark-ish work but writing by Catholics, rather Catholic writing. If you want to take a risk in subject, you are particularly encouraged to submit. Catholic or general Christian life is real life to us."

CHRONICLE BOOKS FOR CHILDREN

Chronicle Books; Submissions Editor, 680 Second St., 6th Floor, San Francisco CA 94105. E-mail: kided@chroniclebooks.com; submissions@chroniclebooks.com. Website: www.chroniclekids.com. **Contact:** Victoria Rock, founding publisher and editor-at-large. Publishes hardcover and trade paperback originals. **Published 5% debut authors within the last year.** Averages 90 total titles/year.

NEEDS mainstream/contemporary, multicultural, young adult, picture books, middle grade fiction, young adult projects. Published *Wave*, by Suzy Lee (all ages, picture book); Ivy and Bean series, by Annie Barrows, illustrated by Sophie Blackwell (ages 6-11, chapter book); *Delicious: The Art and Life of Wayne Theibaud*, by Susan Goldman Rubin (ages 9-14, chapter book).

HOW TO CONTACT Submit complete ms (picture books); submit outline synopsis and 3 sample chapters (for older readers). Prefers mail submissions. Responds to queries in 6 months; will not respond to submissions unless interested. Do not send SASE; send SASP to confirm receipt.

TERMS Royalty varies. Average advance: variable. Publishes ms 18-24 months after acceptance. Ms guidelines online.

TIPS "We are interested in projects that have a unique bent to them—be it in subject matter, writing style or illustrative technique. As a small list, we are looking for books that will lend our list a distinctive flavor. Primarily, we are interested in fiction and nonfiction picture books for children ages up to 8 years, and nonfiction books for children ages up to 12 years. We publish board, pop-up and other novelty formats as well as picture books. We are also interested in early chapter books, middle grade fiction and young adult projects."

CITY LIGHTS BOOKS

261 Columbus Ave., San Francisco CA 94133. (415)362-1901. Fax: (415)362-4921. E-mail: staff@citylights.com. Website: www.citylights.com. **Contact:** Editorial staff. Estab. 1953. Publishes paperback originals. Plans 1-2 first novels this year. Averages 12 total titles, 4-5 fiction titles/year.

NEEDS Fiction, essays, memoirs, translations, poetry and books on social and political issues.

HOW TO CONTACT Submit one-page description of the book and a sample chapter or two with SASE. Does not accept unsolicited mss. Does not accept queries by e-mail. See website for guidelines.

CLARION BOOKS

Houghton Mifflin Co., 215 Park Ave. S., New York NY 10003. Website: www.houghtonmifflinbooks.com; www.hmco.com. **Contact:** Dinah Stevenson, vice president and publisher; Jennifer B. Greene, senior editor (contemporary fiction, picture books for all ages, nonfiction); Jennifer Wingertzahn, editor (fiction, picture books); Lynne Polvino, editor (fiction, nonfiction, picture books). Estab. 1965. "Clarion is a strong presence in the fiction market for young readers. We are highly selective in the areas of historical and contemporary fiction. We publish chapter books for children ages 7-10 and middle-grade novels for ages 9-12, as well as picture books and nonfiction." Publishes hardcover originals for children. Averages 50 total titles/year. Mss are not responded to unless there is an interest in publishing. Published *A Taste for Red*, by Lewis Harris (contemporary, middle-grade); *The Wednesday Wars*, by Gary D. Schmidt (historical fiction); *Keeping Score*, by Linda Sue Park (middle-grade historical fiction).

"We are no longer responding to your unsolicited submission unless we are interested in publishing it. Please do not include a SASE. Submissions will be recycled, and you will not hear from us regarding the status of your submission unless we are interested. We regret that we cannot respond personally to each submission, but we do consider each and every submission we receive."

NEEDS adventure, historical, humor, mystery, suspense, strong character studies. Clarion is highly selective in the areas of historical fiction, fantasy, and science fiction. A novel must be superlatively written in order to find a place on the list. Accepts fiction translations.

HOW TO CONTACT Submit complete ms. Responds in 2 months to queries. Prefers no multiple submissions of mss.

TERMS Pays 5-10% royalty on retail price. Average advance: start at $6,000. Publishes ms 2 years after acceptance. Ms guidelines available at website.

TIPS "Looks for freshness, enthusiasm—in short, life."

CLEIS PRESS

Cleis Press & Viva Editions, 2246 Sixth St., Berkeley CA 94710. (510)845-8000 or (800)780-2279. Fax: (510)845-8001. E-mail: cleis@cleispress.com; bknight@cleispress.com. Website: www.cleispress.com and www.vivaeditions.com. **Contact:** Brenda Knight, associate publisher. Estab. 1980. "Cleis Press publishes provocative works by women and men in the areas of gay and lesbian studies, sexual politics, fiction, feminism, self-help, erotica, gender studies, and human rights." Publishes trade paperback originals and reprints. **Published some debut authors within the last year.** Averages 50 total titles, 30 fiction titles/year. Forthcoming for 2011: *Better Than Great: A Plenitudinous Compendium of Wallopingly Fresh Superlatives*, by Arthur Plotnik (Nonfiction, Viva Editions); *The Unreal Life of Sergey Nabokov: A Novel*, by Paul Russell (Fiction, Cleis Press); *Pride & Prejudice: Hidden Lusts*, by Mitzi Szereto (Fiction, Cleis Press); *The Ultimate Guide to Orgasm for Women*, by Mikaya Heart (Nonfiction, Cleis Press); *The Power of Wow: A 9 Week Program to Unleash the Confident, Sexy You*, by Lori Bryant-Woolridge (Nonfiction, Viva Editions). Accepts unsolicited mss.

IMPRINTS Viva Edition

NEEDS feminist, gay/lesbian, literary

HOW TO CONTACT Submit complete ms. Accepts queries by e-mail. Include brief bio, list of publishing credits. Send SASE for return of ms or send a disposable ms and SASE for reply only. Agented fiction 10%. Responds in 1 month to queries.

TERMS Pays royalty on retail price. Publishes ms 1 year after acceptance.

TIPS "Be familiar with publishers' catalogs; be absolutely aware of your audience; research potential markets; present fresh new ways of looking at your topic; avoid `PR' language and include publishing history in query letter."

COACH HOUSE BOOKS

401 Huron St. on bpNichol Lane, 80 bpNichol Lane, Toronto ON M5S 3J4 Canada. (416)979-2217. Fax: (416)977-1158. E-mail: editor@chbooks.com. Website: www.chbooks.com. **Contact:** Alana Wilcox, editor.

NEEDS "Coach House publishes innovative poetry, literary fiction, drama and books about Toronto. We do NOT publish children's books, memoirs, cookbooks, historical romances, mysteries or science-fiction."

HOW TO CONTACT Submit ms to **80 bpNichol Lane, Toronto, Ontario, M5S 3J4** with SASE. Please do **not** send it by ExpressPost or Canada Post courier—regular Canada Post mail is much more likely to arrive here. Include an introductory letter that describes your work and compares it to at least two current Coach House titles, explaining how your book would fit our list and literary CV. Electronic submissions of fiction and drama are welcome. Please send hard copies of all poetry manuscripts. If submitting electronically, please email a Word file—no PDFs please —to editor@chbooks.com. You can include the cover letter and CV as a separate file or as a part of the MS. **If you are submitting electronically, please send your manuscript only once. Revised and updated versions will not be read, so make sure you're happy with your text before sending.**

TIPS "We are not a general publisher, and publish only Canadian poetry, fiction, artist books and drama. We are interested primarily in innovative or experimental writing."

CONCORDIA PUBLISHING HOUSE

3558 S. Jefferson Ave., St. Louis MO 63118. E-mail: publicity@cph.org;rosemary.parkinson@cph.org. Website: www.cph.org. **Contact:** Peggy Kuethe, senior editor (children's product, adult devotional, women's resources); Dawn Weinstock, managing production editor (adult nonfiction on Christian spirituality and culture, academic works of interest in Lutheran markets). Estab. 1869.

TIPS "Do not send finished artwork with the manuscript. If sketches will help in the presentation of the manuscript, they may be sent. If stories are taken from the Bible, they should follow the Biblical account closely. Liberties should not be taken in fantasizing Biblical stories."

CONSTABLE & ROBINSON, LTD.

3 The Lanchesters, 162 Fulham Palace Rd., London En WG 9ER United Kingdom. 0208-741-3663. Fax: 0208-748-7562. E-mail: enquiries@constablerobinson.com. Website: http://constablerobinson.co.uk/. **Contact:** Krystyna Green, editorial director (crime fiction). Constable & Robinson continues into the 21st century as a truly independent company. We publish a nonfiction list of current affairs, history and biography, military history, psychology and health, as well as literary novels and a constantly growing list of genre fiction in both hardback and paperback. Among our commercially successful series are the well-known Mammoth paperback anthologies, the best-selling and widely respected Overcoming list of CBT self-help titles, and the Brief History and Guide series. Our new fiction imprint, Corsair, launched in April 2010. Averages 160 total titles/year.

IMPRINTS Corsair, Constable Hardback; Robinson Paperback.

NEEDS Publishes "crime fiction (mysteries) and historical crime fiction." Length 80,000 words minimum; 130,000 words maximum. Recently published *Roma* and *The Judgement of Caesar*, by Steven Saylor; *The Yeane's Midnight*, by Ed O'Connor; *The More Deceived*, by David Roberts.

HOW TO CONTACT *Agented submissions only.* No e-mail submissions. Submit by post 3 sample chapter(s), synopsis, and cover letter. Responds in 1 month to queries; 3 months to mss. Accepts simultaneous submissions.

TERMS Pays royalty. Offers advance. Publishes ms 1 year after acceptance.

TIPS Constable & Robinson Ltd. is looking for "crime novels with good, strong identities. Think about what it is that makes your book(s) stand out from the others. We do not publish thrillers."

CORNELL MARITIME PRESS / TIDEWATER PUBLISHERS

Schiffer Publishing, Ltd., P.O. Box 456, Centreville MD 21617-0456. Website: www.cmptp.com. Estab. 1938. Cornell Maritime Press, Inc., P.O. Box 456, Centreville MD 21617-0456. (410)758-1075. Fax: (410)758-6849. E-mail: cornell@crosslink.net. Website: www.tidewaterpublishers.com. **Contact:** Charlotte Kurst, managing editor. Estab. 1938. "Tidewater Publishers issues adult nonfiction works related to the Chesapeake Bay area, Delmarva or Maryland in general. The only fiction we handle is juvenile and must have a regional focus." Publishes hardcover and paperback originals. **Published some debut authors within the last year.** Averages 7-9 total titles/year.

NEEDS regional juvenile fiction only. Published *Majesty from Assateague*, by Harvey Hagman and illustrated by David Aiken; *Chesapeake Bay Buyboats*, by Larry S. Chowning; and *Annapolis, A Walk Through History*, by Elizabeth B. Anderson; photograpy by M.E. Warren.

HOW TO CONTACT Query with SASE or submit outline, sample chapter(s), synopsis. Responds in 2 months to queries. No simultaneous submissions.

TERMS Pays 7½-15% royalty on retail price. Publishes ms 1 year after acceptance.

TIPS "Our audience is made up of readers interested in works that are specific to the Chesapeake Bay and Delmarva Peninsula area."

COTEAU BOOKS

Thunder Creek Publishing Co-operative Ltd., 2517 Victoria Ave., Regina SK S4P 0T2 Canada. (306)777-0170. Fax: (306)522-5152. E-mail: coteau@coteaubooks.com. Website: www.coteaubooks.com. **Contact:** Geoffrey Ursell, publisher. Estab. 1975. AKA Thunder Creek Publishing Co-operative Ltd. "Coteau Books publishes the finest Canadian fiction, poetry, drama and children's literature, with an emphasis on western writers." Publishes trade paperback originals and reprints. Books: offset printing; perfect bound; 4-color illustrations. Averages 16 total titles, 4-6 fiction titles/year. Distributes titles through Fitzhenry & Whiteside.

NEEDS ethnic, fantasy, feminist, gay/lesbian, historical, humor, juvenile, literary, mainstream/contemporary, multicultural, multimedia, mystery, regional, short story collections, spiritual, sports, young adult. Canadian authors *only*. Published *The Knife Sharpener's Bell*, by Rhea Tregebov (novel); *Passchendaele: Canada's Triumph and Tragedy on the Fields of Flanders*, by Norman Leach (adult nonfiction); *We Want You to Know*, by Deborah Ellis (juvenile nonfiction); *Summer of Fire*, by Karen Bass (teen novel).

HOW TO CONTACT Accepts unsolicited mss. Fiction accepted January 1-April 30; children's/teen novels May 1-August 31; poetry September 1-December 31; nonfiction accepted year-round. Submit complete manuscript, or 3-4 sample chapter(s), author bio. Responds in 2-3 months to queries; 6 months to mss. No simultaneous submissions. Sometimes comments on rejected mss.

TERMS Pays 10% royalty on retail price. "We're a co-operative and receive subsidies from the Canadian, provincial and local governments. We do not accept payments from authors to publish their works." Publishes ms 1-2 years after acceptance. Ms guidelines online.

TIPS "Look at past publications to get an idea of our editorial program. We do not publish romance, horror, or picture books but are interested in juvenile and teen fiction from Canadian authors. Submissions, even queries, must be made in hard copy only. We do not accept simultaneous/multiple submissions. Check our website for new submission timing guidelines."

COVENANT COMMUNICATIONS, INC.

920 E. State Rd., American Fork UT 84003. (801)756-9966. Fax: (801)756-1049. E-mail: info@covenant-lds; submissions@covenant-lds.com. Website: www.covenant-lds.com. **Contact:** Kathryn Jenkins, managing editor. Estab. 1958. Averages 80+ total titles/year.

NEEDS historical fiction, suspense, mystery, romance, children's; all submissions must have strong LDS (Church of Jesus Christ of Latter-day Saints, or "Mormons") content.

HOW TO CONTACT E-mail your manuscript, along with a 1-page cover letter, a 1- to 2-page plot summary, and the Author Questionnaire. We request that all submissions be submitted via e-mail as Microsoft Word attachments. If you cannot e-mail your submission, please burn the Word document onto a CD and mail it. Follow submission guidelines on website. Requires electronic submission. Responds in 4 months to mss.

TERMS Pays 6½-15% royalty on retail price. Generally publishes ms 6-12 months after acceptance. Ms guidelines online.

TIPS "Our audience is exclusively LDS (Latter-Day Saints, 'Mormon')." We do not accept manuscripts that do not have a strong LDS theme or feature strong LDS characters.

CRESCENT MOON PUBLISHING

P.O. Box 393, Maidstone Kent ME14 5XU UK. (44)(162)272-9593. E-mail: cresmopub@yahoo.co.uk. Website: www.crescentmoon.org.uk. **Contact:** Jeremy Robinson, director (arts, media, cinema, literature); Cassidy Hushes (visual arts). Estab. 1988. Small, independent publisher. Publishes hardcover and trade paperback originals. **Published some debut authors within the last year.** Plans 1-2 first novels this year. Averages 25 total titles, 1-2 fiction titles/year.

IMPRINTS *Joe's Press, Pagan America Magazine, Passion Magazine.*

NEEDS Erotica, experimental, feminist, gay/lesbian, literary, new age/mystic, short story collections. "We do not publish much fiction at present, but will consider high quality new work." Plans anthology. Send short stories to editor.

HOW TO CONTACT Does not accept whole unsolicited mss. Submit outline, 2 sample chapter(s), synopsis. Include estimated word count, list of publishing credits. Send SASE for return of ms or send a disposable ms and SASE for reply only. Agented fiction 10%. Responds in 2 months to queries; 4 months to mss. Accepts simultaneous submissions. Sometimes comments on rejected mss.

TERMS Pays royalty. Average advance: negotiable. Publishes ms 18 months after acceptance.

TIPS "Our audience is interested in new contemporary writing."

CRICKET BOOKS

Imprint of Carus Publishing, 70 E. Lake St., Suite 300, Chicago IL 60601. (603)924-7209. Fax: (603)924-7380. E-mail: cricketbooks@caruspub.net. Website: www.cricketmag.com. **Contact:** Submissions Editor. Estab. 1999. "Small, independent publisher able to integrate publishing with related Cricket and Cobblestone magazine groups. We publish children's fiction and nonfiction, from picture books to high young adult." Publishes hardcover and paperback originals. Distributes titles through PGW. Promotes titles through in-house marketing.

Currently not accepting queries or ms. Check website for submissions details and updates.

NEEDS children's/juvenile (adventure, animal, easy-to-read, fantasy, historical, mystery, preschool/picture book, sports), juvenile, young adult (adventure, easy-to-read, fantasy/science fiction, historical, horror, mystery/suspense, problem novels, romance, sports, western), early chapter books, and middle grade fiction. Plans anthologies for Christmas, dragons, poetry, and *Cricket* magazine's anniversary edition. Editors select stories. Published *Seek*, by Paul Fleischman (YA fiction); *Robert and the Weird and Wacky Facts*, by Barbara Seuling (chapter book); and *Scorpio's Child*, by Kezi Matthews (fiction, ages 11-14).

HOW TO CONTACT Currently only accepting submissions by authors previously published in *Cricket* magazine. Does not accept unsolicited mss. Submit complete ms. Include estimated word count, list of publishing credits. Send SASE for return of ms or send a disposable ms and SASE for reply only. Agented fiction 20%. Responds in 4 months to queries; 6 months to mss. Accepts simultaneous submissions. No electronic submissions, submissions on disk. Sometimes comments on rejected mss.

TERMS Pays 10% royalty on net receipts. Open to first-time and unagented authors. Pays up to 10% royalty on retail price. Average advance: $1,500 and up. Publishes ms 18 months after acceptance. Ms guidelines online.

TIPS "Take a look at the recent titles to see what sort of materials we're interested in, especially for nonfiction. Please note that we aren't doing the sort of strictly educational nonfiction that other publishers specialize in."

⊘ CROSSQUARTER PUBLISHING GROUP

PO BOX 23749, Santa Fe NM 87502. E-mail: info@crossquarter.com. Website: www.crossquarter.com. **Contact:** Anthony Ravenscroft, Acquisitions. "We emphasize personal sovereignty, self responsibility and growth with pagan or pagan-friendly emphasis for young adults and adults." Query letters are required. *No unsolicited mss.* Publishes trade paperback originals and reprints. 5-10 titles published/year. 1,200 queries received/year. Publishes 90% first-time authors. Pays 8-10% royalty on wholesale or retail price. Publishes work 1-2 years after acceptance. Responds in 3 months to queries. Book catalog for $1.75. Guidelines available online.

Query letters are required. *No unsolicited mss.*

TIPS "Our audience is earth-conscious people looking to grow into balance of body, mind, heart and spirit."

⊘ CROSSTIME

Crossquarter Publishing Group, P.O. Box 23749, Santa Fe, NM 87502. (505)690-3923. Fax: (214)975-9715. E-mail: info@crossquarter.com. Website: www.crossquarter.com. **Contact:** Anthony Ravenscroft. Estab. 1985. Small publisher. Publishes paperback originals. Books: recycled paper; docutech or offset printing; perfect bound. **Published 2 debut authors within the last year.** Plans 2 first novels this year. Member SPAN, PMA.

NEEDS mystery (occult), new age/mystic, psychic/supernatural, romance (occult), science fiction, young adult (fantasy/science fiction). Sponsors Short Science Fiction contest. Guidelines on website. Recently published *Many Voices, One Song*, by Barbara Percival; *When Dharma Fails Its King*, by Spencer Johnson; *Swamp Poet*, by Ben Goodridge; *CrossTIME Science Fiction Anthology Vol IX.*

TERMS Pays 6-10% royalty. Publishes ms 1-2 years after acceptance. Ms guidelines online.

CROSSWAY BOOKS

A division of Good News Publishers, 1300 Crescent St., Wheaton IL 60187-5800. (630)682-4300. Fax: (630)682-4785. E-mail: info@crossway.org; submissions@crossway.org. Website: www.crossway.com; www.crosswaybooks.org. **Contact:** Jill Carter. Email: submissions@crossway.org. If you submit a proposal in hard-copy form, however, please include a SASE so that, if we're unable to accept the project for publication, we can return the proposal to you. "'Making a difference in people's lives for Christ' as its maxim, Crossway Books lists titles written from an evangelical Christian perspective." Midsize evangelical Christian publisher. Publishes hardcover and trade paperback originals. Averages 85 total titles, 1 fiction titles/year. Member ECPA. Distributes titles through Christian bookstores and catalogs. Promotes titles through magazine ads, catalogs.

NEEDS *Currently not accepting fiction manuscripts.*

HOW TO CONTACT Send us an e-mail query and, if your idea fits within our acquisitions guidelines, we'll invite a proposal. Does not accept unsolicited mss. Agented fiction 5%.

TERMS Allow 3-6 months for a response. Pays negotiable royalty. Average advance: negotiable. Publishes ms 18 months after acceptance. Ms guidelines online.

CROWN BOOKS FOR YOUNG READERS

1540 Broadway, New York NY 10171. (212)572-2600 or (800)200-3552. Website: www.randomhouse.com/kids. See listing for Bantam, Doubleday, Dell/Delacorte, Knopf and Crown Books for Young Readers.

Random House Children's Publishing only accepts submissions through agents.

CROWN PUBLISHING GROUP

Imprint of Random House, Inc., 1745 Broadway, New York NY 10019. (212)782-9000. E-mail: CrownBiz@randomhouse.com. Website: www.randomhouse.com/crown. Estab. 1933. "The group publishes a selection of popular fiction and nonfiction by both established and rising authors."

Agented submissions only. See website for more details.

IMPRINTS Bell Tower; Broadway Business; Clarkson Potter; Crown Business; Crown Forum; Harmony Books; Shaye Arehart Books; Three Rivers Press.
HOW TO CONTACT *Agented submissions only.*

JOHN DANIEL AND CO.

P.O. Box 2790, McKinleyville CA 95519. (707)839-3495. Fax: (707)839-3242. E-mail: dandd@danielpublishing.com. Website: www.danielpublishing.com. **Contact:** John Daniel, publisher. Estab. 1980. "We publish small books, usually in small editions, but we do so with pride." Publishes hardcover originals and trade paperback originals. Publishes poetry, fiction, essay, and memoir. Averages 4 total titles/year. Distributes through SCB Distributors. Promotes through direct mail, reviews.
NEEDS Literary, short story collections. Publishes poetry, fiction and nonfiction; specializes in belles lettres, literary memoir. Published *Murder in Los Lobos*, by Sue McGinty (mystery novel); *Wolf Tones*, by Irving Weinman (novel).
HOW TO CONTACT *Currently closed to fiction submissions.*
TERMS Pays 10% royalty on wholesale price. Average advance: $0-500. Publishes ms 1 year after acceptance. Ms guidelines online.
TIPS "Having downsized from small to tiny, we can't publish as many books as before, and must be very selective. So it's a long shot. Never the less, we do consider all submissions."

DANTE UNIVERSITY OF AMERICA PRESS, INC.

P.O. Box 812158, Wellesley MA 02482. Fax: (781)790-1056. E-mail: danteu@danteuniversity.org. Website: www.danteuniversity.org/dpress.html. **Contact:** Josephine Tanner, president. Estab. 1975.

DARK HORSE COMICS, INC.

10956 SE Main St., Milwaukie OR 97222. (503)652-8815. Fax: (503) 654-9440. E-mail: dhcomics@darkhorse.com. Website: www.darkhorse.com. **Contact:** Submissions Editor. "In addition to publishing comics from top talent like Frank Miller, Mike Mignola, Stan Sakai and internationally-renowned humorist Sergio Aragonés, Dark Horse is recognized as the world's leading publisher of licensed comics."
NEEDS Comic books, graphic novels. Published *Astro Boy Volume 10 TPB*, by Osamu Tezuka and Reid Fleming; *Flaming Carrot Crossover #1* by Bob Burden and David Boswell.
HOW TO CONTACT Submit synopsis to dhcomics@darkhorse.com. See website (www.darkhorse.com) for detailed submission guidelines and submission agreement, which must be signed. Include a full script for any short story or single-issue submission, or the first eight pages of the first issue of any series. Submissions can no longer be mailed back to the sender.
TIPS "If you're looking for constructive criticism, show your work to industry professionals at conventions."

DAW BOOKS, INC.

Distributed by Penguin Group (USA), 375 Hudson St., New York NY 10014-3658. (212)366-2096. Fax: (212)366-2090. Website: www.dawbooks.com. **Contact:** Peter Stampfel, submissions editor. Estab. 1971. Publishes hardcover and paperback originals and reprints. Averages 60 total titles/year.

Simultaneous submissions not accepted, unless prior arrangements are made by agent.

NEEDS Fantasy, science fiction. "We are interested in science fiction and fantasy novels. We are also interested in paranormal romantic fantasy. We like character-driven books. We accept both agented and unagented manuscripts. Long books are not a problem. We are not seeking short stories, poetry, or ideas for anthologies. We do not want any nonfiction manuscripts."
HOW TO CONTACT Submit complete ms with SASE. Do not submit your only copy of anything. Responds within 3 months to mss. The average length of the novels we publish varies but is almost never less than 80,000 words. Send us the entire manuscript with a cover letter. We do not accept electronic submissions of any kind.
TERMS Pays in royalties with an advance negotiable on a book-by-book basis. Ms guidelines online.

DELACORTE PRESS BOOKS FOR YOUNG READERS

Imprint of Random House Children's Books/Random House, Inc., 1745 Broadway, New York NY 10019. (212)782-9000. Website: www.randomhouse.com/kids; www.randomhouse.com/teens. Random House Children's Books, 1540 Broadway, New York NY 10036. (212)782-900. Website: www.randomhouse.com/kids; www.randomhouse.com/teens. Distinguished literary fiction and commercial fiction for the middle grade and young adult categories.

Although not currently accepting unsolicited mss, mss are being sought for 2 contests: Delacorte Dell Yearling Contest for a First Middle-Grade Novel and Delacorte Press Contest for a First Young Adult Novel. Submission guidelines can be found online at www.randomhouse.com/kids/writingcontests.

NEEDS Although not currently accepting unsolicited mss, mss are being sought for 2 contests: Delacorte Dell Yearling Contest for a first middle-grade novel and Delacorte Press Contest for a first young adult novel. Submission guidelines can be found online at www.randomhouse.com/kids/writingcontests.

DEL REY BOOKS

Imprint of Random House Publishing Group, 1745 Broadway, 18th Floor, New York NY 10019. (212)782-9000. E-mail: delrey@randomhouse.com. Website: www.randomhouse.com. Estab. 1977. "We are a long-established imprint with an eclectic frontlist. We're seeking interesting new voices to add to our best-selling backlist. Publishes hardcover, trade paperback, and mass market originals and mass market paperback reprints. Averages 120 total titles, 80 fiction titles/year.

NEEDS fantasy (should have the practice of magic as an essential element of the plot), science fiction (well-plotted novels with good characterizations and interesting extrapolations), alternate history. Published *Gentlemen of the Road*, by Michael Chabon; *Kraken*, by China Mieville; *His Majesty's Dragon*, by Naomi Novik; *The Man with the Iron Heart*, by Harry Turtledove; and *Star Wars: Order 66*, by Karen Traviss.

HOW TO CONTACT Does not accept unsolicited mss. *Agented submissions only.*

TERMS Pays royalty on retail price. Average advance: competitive. Publishes ms 1 year after acceptance. Ms guidelines online.

TIPS "Del Rey is a reader's house. Pay particular attention to plotting, strong characters, and dramatic, satisfactory conclusions. It must be/feel believable. That's what the readers like. In terms of mass market, we basically created the field of fantasy bestsellers. Not that it didn't exist before, but we put the mass into mass market."

DIAL BOOKS FOR YOUNG READERS

Imprint of Penguin Group USA, 345 Hudson St., New York NY 10014. (212)366-2000. Website: www.penguin.com/youngreaders. **Contact:** Submissions Editor. Estab. 1961. Trade children's book publisher. Publishes hardcover originals. Averages 50 total titles/year.

NEEDS adventure, fantasy, juvenile, picture books, young adult. Especially looking for "lively and well-written novels for middle grade and young adult children involving a convincing plot and believable characters. The subject matter or theme should not already be overworked in previously published books. The approach must not be demeaning to any minority group, nor should the roles of female characters (or others) be stereotyped, though we don't think books should be didactic, or in any way message-y. No topics inappropriate for the juvenile, young adult and middle grade audiences. No plays." Published *A Year Down Yonder*, by Richard Peck; *The Missing Mitten Mystery*, by Steven Kellog.

HOW TO CONTACT Accepts unsolicited mss. "Submit entire picture book mss or the first three chapters of longer works. A maximum of 10 pages for longer works (novels, easy-to-reads) from the opening chapter(s) of the ms. Please include a cover letter with brief bio and publication credits. Please note that, unless interested in publishing your book, Dial will not respond to unsolicited submissions. Please do NOT include a SASE. If Dial is interested, expect a reply from us within four months."

TERMS Pays royalty. Average advance: varies.

TIPS "Our readers are anywhere from preschool age to teenage. Picture books must have strong plots, lots of action, unusual premises, or universal themes treated with freshness and originality. Humor works well in these books. A very well-thought-out and intelligently presented book has the best chance of being taken on. Genre isn't as much of a factor as presentation."

Ⓐ DIAL PRESS

Bantam Dell Publishing Group, Random House, Inc., 1745 Broadway, New York NY 10019. (212)782-9000. Fax: (212)782-9523. Website: www.randomhouse.com/bantamdell/. **Contact:** Susan Kamil, vice president, editorial director. Estab. 1924. Averages 6-12 total titles/year.

NEEDS Literary (general). Published *Mary and O'Neil* (short story collection); *Niagara Falls over Again*, by Elizabeth Mccracken (fiction).

HOW TO CONTACT *Agented submissions only.* Accepts simultaneous submissions.

TERMS Pays royalty on retail price. Offers advance. Publishes ms 18 months after acceptance.

DIGITAL MANGA PUBLISHING

1487 West 178th St., Suite 300, Gardenia CA 90248. Website: www.emanga.com; http://www.dmpbooks.com. "We are currently accepting open submissions of completed works for inclusion on our Emanga.com storefront. Submissions must be original and not infringe on copyrighted works by other creators. Please note that we are a manga publisher; we do not distribute Western style comics or literary novels. Completed works must contain a minimum of 90 pages of content. Submissions may be in black and white or full color. Submissions must be mailed in to DIGITAL MANGA PUBLISHING, ATTN: SUBMISSIONS, 1487 West 178th St., Suite 300, Gardenia CA 90248. We accept submissions for all genres of manga which comply to US law and we only accept submissions from persons aged 18 and over. Please do not send your original copies as we cannot return them to you. If your work is published online elsewhere, please feel free to include a link for us to further view your portfolio." Phone: (310)817-8010. Fax: (310)817-8018. E-mail: dmp@emanga.com; contact@emanga.com.

⊘ DISKUS PUBLISHING

P.O. Box 43, Albany IN 47320. E-mail: editor@diskuspublishing.com. Website: www.diskuspublishing.com; submissions@diskpublishing.com. **Contact:** Marilyn Nesbitt, editor-in-chief; Joyce McLaughlin, inspirational and children's editor; Holly Janey, submissions editor. Estab. 1997. Publishes paperback originals and e-books. **Published 10 debut authors within the last year.** Averages 100 total titles, 80 fiction titles/year. Member AEP, PMA, EPIC.

At this time DiskUs Publishing is closed for submissions. We will reopen for submissions in the near future. We get thousands of submissions each month, and our editors need time to get through the current ones. Keep checking our website for updates on the status of our submissions reopen date.

NEEDS adventure, children's/juvenile, ethnic (general), family saga, fantasy (space fantasy), historical, horror, humor, juvenile, literary, mainstream/contemporary, military/war, multicultural (general), mystery, psychic/supernatural, religious, romance, science fiction, short story collections, suspense, thriller/espionage, western, young adult. "We are actively seeking confessions for our Diskus Confessions line. As well as short stories for our Quick Pick line. We only accept e-mailed submissions for these lines." *The Quest for the White Jewel*, by Janet Lane Walters; *Brazen*, by Lori Foster (adventure/romance); *A Change of Destiny*, by Marilynn Mansfield (science fiction/futuristic)

HOW TO CONTACT Accepts unsolicited mss. Submit publishing history, author bio, estimated word count, genre, and complete ms. Send SASE for return of ms or send a disposable ms and SASE for reply only. Prefers submissions by e-mail. Agented fiction 5%. Accepts simultaneous submissions. Sometimes comments on rejected mss.

TERMS Pays 40% royalty. Publishes ms usually within the year after acceptance. Ms guidelines online.

⊕ DIVERTIR

P.O. Box 232, North Salem NH 03073. E-mail: info@divertirpublishing.com; query@divertirpublishing.com. Website: http://divertirpublishing.com/. **Contact:** Dr. Kenneth Tupper, Publisher (nonfiction); Estab. 2009. Elizabeth Harvey, Acquisitions Editor (fiction). Format publishes in trade paperback and electronic originals. Publishes 6-12 title/year. 100% new/unagented authors. Pays 10-15% royalty on wholesale price (for novels and nonfiction); outright purchase: $10-50 (for short stories) with additional bonus payments to authors when certain sales milestones are met. 6-9 months from acceptance to publication. SASE returns. Responds in 1-2 months on queries; 3-4 months on proposals and mss. Catalog available online at http://divertirpublishing.com/bookstore.aspx. Guidelines online at website: http://divertirpublishing.com/authorinfo.aspx. Reviews artwork/photos as part of the ms package. Submit electronically. "We are particularly interested in the following: science fiction, fantasy, historical, alternate history, contemporary mythology, mystery and suspense, paranormal, and urban fantasy. Recent titles: *When Nightmares Fall*, by Elizabeth Harvey (short story collection/trade paperback); *Under the Stairs*, by Lisa D. Keele (short story collection/trade paperback); *Shades of Shadow*, by KJ Shadow Rose (single-author poetry collection/trade paperback).

NEEDS adventure, contemporary, fantasy, gothic, historical, horror, humor, literary, mainstream, mystery, occult, poetry, religious, romance, science fiction, short story collections, spiritual, translation, young adult.

HOW TO CONTACT Electronically submit proposal package, including synopsis and query letter with author's bio. Poetry: Query.

TIPS "We are currently accepting submissions in the following areas: Fictional Satire (submissions deadline 3/15), Noir (submissions deadline 5/15), Poetry (submissions deadline 3/15). Please see our Author Info page (online) for more information."

DOUBLEDAY

Knopf Doubleday Broadway Publishing Group, Random House, Inc. 1745 Broadway, New York NY 10019. E-mail: ddaypub@randomhouse.com. Website: www.randomhouse.biz. Estab. 1897. Publishes hardcover originals. Averages 70 total titles/year.

NEEDS adventure, confession, ethnic, experimental, feminist, gay/lesbian, historical, humor, literary, mainstream/contemporary, religious, short story collections.

HOW TO CONTACT *Agented submissions only.* Does not accept unsolicited mss by e-mail. No simultaneous submissions.

TERMS Pays royalty on retail price. Offers advance. Publishes ms 1 year after acceptance.

DOUBLEDAY BOOKS FOR YOUNG READERS

1540 Broadway, New York NY 10036. (212)782-9000. Website: www.randomhouse.com/kids.

Only accepts manuscripts submitted by an agent. Trade picture book list, from preschool to age 8.

DOWN THERE PRESS

Subsidiary of Open Enterprises Cooperative, Inc., 938 Howard Street #101, San Francisco CA 94103-4100. E-mail: customerservice@goodvibes.com. Website: www.goodvibes.com/dtp/dtp.html. **Contact:** Leigh Davidson, managing editor. Estab. 1975. Small, independent press with part-time staff; part of a large worker-owned cooperative. "Devoted exclusively to the publication of sexual health books for children and adults. We publish books that are innovative, lively and practical, providing realistic physiological information with nonjudgmental techniques for strengthing sexual communication." Publishes paperback originals. Books: Web offset printing; perfect binding; some illustrations. Average print order: 5,000. First novel print order: 3,000-5,000. Averages 1-2 total titles, 1 fiction titles/year. Member, Publishers Marketing Association and Northern California Book Publicity and Marketing Association.

NEEDS erotica, feminist, sex education/sex-positive nonfiction. Published *Herotica 6*, edited by Marcy Sheiner (anthology); *Sex Spoken Here: Erotic Reading Circle Stories*, edited by Carol Queen and Jack Davis (anthology); *Any 2 People Kissing*, by Kate Dominic (short stories, erotic); and *Sex Toy Tales*, edited by A. Semans and Cathy Weeks.

HOW TO CONTACT Publishes exclusively sexual self-help books for adults and children. Accepts unsolicited manuscripts; send query letter with table of contents and sample chapters first. Reaches market through direct mail, wholesalers, and distributors. Accepts queries by mail. Include estimated word count. Send SASE for return of ms or send a disposable ms and SASE for reply only. Responds in 9 months to mss. Accepts simultaneous submissions. No electronic submissions. Sometimes comments on rejected mss. Website: www.goodvibes.com.

TERMS Pays royalty. Publishes ms 18 months after acceptance. Ms guidelines for #10 SASE.

DOWN THE SHORE PUBLISHING

Box 100, West Creek NJ 08092. Fax: (609)597-0422. E-mail: dtsbooks@comcast.net. Website: www.down-the-shore.com.

TIPS "Carefully consider whether your proposal is a good fit for our established market."

DRAGON MOON PRESS

3521 43A Ave., Red Deer AB T4N 3E9 Canada. E-mail: dmpsubmissions@gmail.com. Website: www.dragonmoonpress.com. **Contact:** Gwen Gaddes, publisher. Estab. 1994. "Dragon Moon Press is dedicated to new and exciting voices in science fiction and fantasy." Publishes trade paperback and electronic originals. Books: 60 lb. offset paper; short run printing and offset printing. Average print order: 250-3,000. **Published several debut authors within the last year.** Plans 5 first novels this year. Averages 4-6 total titles, 4-5 fiction titles/year. Distributed through Baker & Taylor. Promoted locally through authors and online at leading retail bookstores like Amazon, Barnes & Noble, Chapters, etc.

NEEDS "At present, we are only accepting solicited manuscripts via referral from our authors and partners. All manuscripts already under review will still be considered by our readers, and we will notify you of our decision." For solicited submissions: Market: "We prefer manuscripts targeted to the adult market or the upper border of YA. No middle grade or children's literature, please. Fantasy, science fiction (soft/sociological). No horror or children's fiction, short stories or poetry."

HOW TO CONTACT Please visit our website at www.dragonmoonpress.com for submission guidelines. Accepts simultaneous submissions. No submissions on disk. "All submissions are requested electronically—do not mail submissions, as we will not respond. All mailed submissions are shredded and recycled. All queries should be emailed to dmpsubmissions@gmail.com with the words BOOK SUBMISSION: and your book title in the subject line."

TERMS Pays 8-15% royalty on retail price. Publishes ms 2 years after acceptance.

TIPS "First, be patient. Read our guidelines. Not following our submission guidelines can be grounds for automatic rejection. Second, be patient, we are small and sometimes very slow as a result, especially during book launch season. Third, we view publishing as a family affair. Be ready to participate in the process and show some enthusiasm and understanding in what we do. Remember also, this is a business and not about egos, so keep yours on a leash! Show us a great story with well-developed characters and plot lines, show us that you are interested in participating in marketing and developing as an author, and show us your desire to create a great book and you may just find yourself published by Dragon Moon Press."

DREAMCATCHER BOOKS & PUBLISHING

55 Canterbury St. #8 & 9, Saint John NB E2L 2C6 Canada. (506)632-4008. Fax: (506)632-4009. E-mail: dreamcatcherpub@nb.aibn.com. Website: www.dreamcatcherpublishing.ca. **Contact:** Elizabeth Margaris, publisher. Estab. 1998. Publishes mainstream fiction, with first consideration to Atlantic Canadian writers. "Especially interested in green themes, hope & inspiration (including autobiographies) with a humourous twist." Imprints: Magi Press (vanity press). "DreamCatcher Publishing, Inc. is an independent book publisher located in downtown Saint John, New Brunswick that produces original high-quality Canadian fiction and non-fiction of general interest for adults and children. Our aim is to introduce the public to some of its best hidden talent, nurturing Canadian authors who deserve to be published in distinguished works of the highest literary and design standards. We wish to publish books that provoke and inform, as well as educate and entertain readers of all ages and walks of life."

HOW TO CONTACT E-mail: dreamcatcherpub@nb.aibn.com. Website: www.dreamcatcherpublishing.ca. Publisher: Elizabeth L. Margaris. Submission Guidelines: (a) A query letter introducing your manuscript; (b) a 1-page synopsis; (c) a short author bio. A reply takes 6 to 8 weeks.

DUFOUR EDITIONS

P.O. Box 7, 124 Byers Road, Chester Springs PA 19425. (610)458-5005 or (800)869-5677. Fax: (610)458-7103. E-mail: orders@dufoureditions.com. Website: www.dufoureditions.com. **Contact:** Thomas Lavoie, associate publisher. Estab. 1948. Small, independent publisher, tending toward literary fiction. Publishes hardcover originals, trade paperback originals, and reprints. Averages 3-4 total titles, 1-2 fiction titles/year. Promotes titles through catalogs, reviews, direct mail, sales reps, Book Expo, and wholesalers.

NEEDS literary, short story collections. "We like books that are slightly off-beat, different and well-written." Published *Tideland*, by Mitch Cullin; *The Case of the Pederast's Wife*, by Clare Elfman; *Last Love in Constantinople*, by Milorad Pavic; *Night Sounds and Other Stories*, by Karen Shoemaker; *From the Place in the Valley Deep in the Forest*, by Mitch Cullen (short stories); and *Beyond Faith and Other Stories*, by Tom Noyes.

HOW TO CONTACT Query with SASE. Accepts queries by e-mail, fax. Include estimated word count, brief bio, list of publishing credits. Responds in 3 months to queries; 6 months to mss. Accepts simultaneous submissions.

TERMS Pays 6-10% royalty on net receipts. Average advance: $100-500. Publishes ms 18 months after acceptance.

TIPS Audience is sophisticated, literate readers especially interested in foreign literature and translations, and a strong Irish-Celtic focus, as well as work from U.S. writers. Check to see if the publisher is really a good match for your subject matter.

DUTTON (ADULT TRADE)

Penguin Group, Inc., 375 Hudson St., New York NY 10014. (212)366-2000. Website: us.penguingroup.com. **Contact:** Brian Tart, Publisher. Estab. 1852. Publishes hardcover originals. Averages 40 total titles/year.

"Query letters **only** (must include SASE). A query letter should be typed and, ideally, fit on one page. Please include a brief synopsis of your manuscript and your publishing credits, if any."

NEEDS adventure, historical, literary, mainstream/contemporary, mystery, short story collections, suspense. Published *The Darwin Awards II*, by Wendy Northcutt (humor); *Falling Angels*, by Tracy Chevalier (fiction); *The Oath*, by John Lescroart (fiction).

HOW TO CONTACT *Agented submissions only.* Responds in 6 months to queries. Accepts simultaneous submissions.

TERMS Pays royalty. Average advance: negotiable. Publishes ms 12-18 months after acceptance.

TIPS "Write the complete manuscript and submit it to an agent or agents. They will know exactly which editor will be interested in a project."

DUTTON CHILDREN'S BOOKS

Imprint of Penguin Group (USA), Inc., 375 Hudson St., New York NY 10014. E-mail: duttonpublicity@us.penguingroup.com. Website: www.penguin.com. **Contact:** Acquisitions Editor. Estab. 1852. Dutton Children's Books publishes fiction and nonfiction for readers ranging from preschoolers to young adults on a variety of subjects. Publishes hardcover originals as well as novelty formats. Averages 50 titles/year. 10% of books form first-time authors.

"Cultivating the creative talents of authors and illustrators and publishing books with purpose and heart continue to be the mission and joy at Dutton."

NEEDS Dutton Children's Books has a diverse, general-interest list that includes picture books and fiction for all ages, from middle grade to young adult novels. Published *Big Chickens Fly the Coop*, by Leslie Helakoski, illustrated by Henry Cole (picture book); *Antsy Does Time*, by Neal Shusterman (middle-grade novel); *Paper Towns*, by John Green (young adult novel).

HOW TO CONTACT Query letter only; include SASE

TERMS Pays royalty on retail price. Offers advance

DZANC BOOKS

Dzanc Books, Inc., 2702 Lillian, Ann Arbor MI 48104. E-mail: info@dzancbooks.org; wickettd@yahoo.com; dan@dzancbooks.org. Website: http://www.dzancbooks.org. **Contact:** Steve Gillis, editor (literary fiction); Dan Wickett, editor (literary fiction); Keith Taylor, editor (literary fiction). "We're an independent non-profit publishing literary fiction. We also set up writer-in-residence programs and help literary journals develop their subscription bases." Publishes paperback originals. **Published some debut authors within the last year.** Averages 6 fiction titles/year, 20 titles/year when imprints are included. (1) If submitting a novel *(please, no young adult fiction)* or literary nonfiction, please submit the first one or two chapters (no more than 35 pages) using our submission manager. (2) If submitting a story collection, please see the Short Story Collection contest guidelines below. (3) Please note that due to an increased number of incoming manuscripts, it might take up to 5 or 6 months to respond. "Dzanc is currently holding its fourth annual contest for all authors wishing to submit a short story collection to Dzanc Books. The winning author will be published by Dzanc in late 2014, and will receive a $1000 advance. Entry to the Dzanc Short Story Collection Contest requires a $20 reading fee and a full manuscript, both submitted through our submission manager. The contest deadline is December 31, 2011."

NEEDS literary. Plans anthology *The Best of the Web*, in which online journal editors nominate stories and poems—series and press editors select from that list and selected reading. Published Roy Kesey, Yannick Murphy, Peter Markus, Hesh Kestin, Kyle Minor.

HOW TO CONTACT Query with outline/synopsis and 35 sample pages. Accepts queries by e-mail. Include brief bio. Agented fiction: 3%. Accepts unsolicited mss. Considers simultaneous submissions, submissions on CD or disk. Rarely critiques/comments on rejected mss. Responds to mss in 5 months.

TERMS Sends preproduction galleys to author. Manuscript published 12-36 months after acceptance. Writer's guidelines on website.

TIPS "Every word counts—it's amazing how many submissions have poor first sentences or paragraphs and that first impression is hard to shake when it's a bad one."

THE ECCO PRESS

HarperCollins, 10 E. 53rd St., New York NY 10022. (212)207-7000. Fax: (212)702-2460. Website: www.harpercollins.com. **Contact:** Daniel Halpern, editor-in-chief. Estab. 1970. Publishes hardcover and trade paperback originals and reprints. Books: acid-free paper; offset printing; Smythe-sewn binding; occasional illustrations. First novel print order: 3,000 copies Averages 60 total titles, 20 fiction titles/year.

NEEDS literary, short story collections. "We can publish possibly one or two original novels a year." Published *Blonde*, by Joyce Carrol Oates; *Pitching around Fidel*, by S.L. Price.

HOW TO CONTACT Does not accept unsolicited mss. Query with SASE.

TERMS Pays royalty. Average advance: negotiable. Publishes ms 1 year after acceptance.

TIPS "We are always interested in first novels and feel it's important that they be brought to the attention of the reading public."

EDGE SCIENCE FICTION AND FANTASY PUBLISHING/TESSERACT BOOKS

Hades Publications, Box 1714, Calgary AB T2P 2L7 Canada. (403)254-0160. Fax: (403)254-0456. E-mail: publisher@hadespublications.com. Website: www.edgewebsite.com. **Contact:** Editorial Manager. Estab. 1996. "We are an independent publisher of science fiction and fantasy novels in hard cover or trade paperback format. We produce high-quality books with lots of attention to detail and lots of marketing effort. We want to encourage, produce and promote thought-provoking and fun-to-read science fiction and fantasy literature by 'bringing the magic alive: one world at a time' (as our motto says) with each new book released." Publishes hardcover and trade paperback originals. Books: natural offset paper; offset/web printing; HC/perfect binding; b&w illustration only. Average print order: 2,000-3,000. Plans 20 first novels this year. Averages 16-20 total titles/year. Member of Book Publishers Association of Alberta (BPAA), Independent Publishers Association of Canada (IPAC), Publisher's Marketing Association (PMA), Small Press Center.

NEEDS fantasy (space fantasy, sword and sorcery), science fiction (hard science/technological, soft/sociological). "We are looking for all types of fantasy and science fiction, horror except juvenile/young adult, erotica, religious fiction, short stories, dark/gruesome fantasy, or poetry." Length: 75,000-100,000/words. Published *Stealing Magic*, by Tanya Huff; *Forbidden Cargo*, by Rebecca K. Rowe, *The Hounds of Ash and Other Tales of Fool Wolf* by Greg Keyes.

HOW TO CONTACT Accepts unsolicited mss. Submit first 3 chapters and synopsis, Check website for guidelines or send SAE & IRCs for same. Include estimated word count. Responds in 4-5 months to mss. No simultaneous submissions, electronic submissions. Rarely comments on rejected mss.

TERMS Pays 10% royalty on wholesale price. Average advance: negotiable. Publishes ms 18-20 months after acceptance. Ms guidelines online.

TIPS "Send us your best, polished, completed manuscript. Use proper manuscript format. Take the time before you submit to get a critique from people who can offer you useful advice. When in doubt, visit our website for helpful resources, FAQs and other tips."

WILLIAM B. EERDMANS PUBLISHING CO.

2140 Oak Industrial Dr. NE, Grand Rapids MI 49505. (616)459-4591. Fax: (616)459-6540. E-mail: info@eerdmans.com. Website: www.eerdmans.com. **Contact:** Jon Pott, editor-in-chief. Estab. 1911.

Will not respond to or accept mss, proposals, or queries sent by e-mail or fax.

IMPRINTS Eerdmans Books for Young Readers.

ELIXIRIST

P.O. Box 17132, Sugar Land TX 77496. E-mail: support@elixirist.com; submissions@elixirist.com. Website: www.elixirist.com. **Contact:** Juanita Samborski, Acquisitions Editor (romance, comedy, chicklit, urban fantasy); Sean Samborski, Publisher (speculative, comedy, horror, literary). Estab. 2010. Small, commercial publisher dealing primarily in the print market in multiple genre formats.

NEEDS adventure, comic books, contemporary, experimental, fantasy, gothic, historical, horror, humor, juvenile, literary, mainstream, mystery, occult, religious, romance, science fiction, sports, suspense, western, young adult, speculative subgenres

HOW TO CONTACT Query with SASE; submit synopsis and 3 sample chapters.

TIPS "We publish novels in genres ranging from young adult to literary, multi-genres appealing to both male and female readers."

ELOHI GADUGI / THE HABIT OF RAINY NIGHTS PRESS

2727 NE 13th Ave., #2, Portland OR 97212-3221. E-mail: editors@elohigadugi.org. Website: http://rainynightspress.org. **Contact:** Patricia McLean, Nonfiction Editor (Narrative Nonfiction). Estab. 2003.

IMPRINTS The Habit of Rainy Nights Press (Patricia McLean or Duane Poncy, Editors); Elohi Gadugi Books / Elohi Gadugi Digital (Duane Poncy, Editor).

TIPS "Respect your work. Make sure it is ready for publication. Polish, polish, polish. We cannot consider books that need a lot of basic cleaning up. Have something to say—we are not interested in using up vital resources to publish fluff."

ENGLISH TEA ROSE PRESS

The Wild Rose Press, P.O. Box 708, Adams Basin NY 14410-0708. (585)752-8770. E-mail: queryus@thewildrosepress.com. Website: www.thewildrosepress.com. **Contact:** Nicole D'Arienzo, editor. Estab. 2006. "In the English Tea Rose line we have conquering heroes, high seas adventure, and scandalous gossip. The love stories that will take you back in time. From the windswept moors of Scotland, to the Emerald Isle, to the elegant ballrooms of Regency England, the men and women of this time are larger than life and willing to risk it all for the love of a lifetime. English Tea Rose stories encompass historical romances set before 1900 which are not set on American soil. Send us your medieval knights, Vikings, Scottish highlanders, marauding pirates, and ladies and gentlemen of the Ton. English Tea Rose romances should have strong conflict and be emotionally driven; and, whether the story is medieval, Regency, set during the renaissance, or any other pre-1900 time, they must stay true to their period in historical accuracy and flavor. English Tea Roses can range from sweet to spicy, but should not contain overly explicit language."Publishes paperback originals, reprints, and e-books in a POD format. Published 5 debut authors last year. Publishes approximately 10 fiction titles/year. Member: EPIC, Romance Writers of America. Distributes/promotes titles through major distribution chains, including Ingrams, Baker & Taylor, Sony, Amazon.com, Kindle, as well as smaller and online distributors.

Does not accept unsolicited mss. Agented fiction less than 1%. Always comments on rejected mss. Sends prepublication galleys to author.

NEEDS contemporary, futuristic/time travel, gothic, historical, regency, romantic suspense, erotic, and paranormal romances. Plans several anthologies "in several lines of the company in the next year, including Cactus Rose, Yellow Rose, American Rose, Black Rose, and Scarlet Rose." Has published *Nothing to Commend Her*, by Jo Barrett; *The Dragon & The Rose*, by Gini Rifkin; and *Wish for the Moon*, by Sandra Jones.

HOW TO CONTACT *Does not accept unsolicited mss.* Send query letter with outline and a list of publishing credits. Include estimated word count, brief bio, and list of publishing credits. Agented fiction less than 1%. Responds to queries in 4 weeks; to mss in 12 weeks. Does not consider simultaneous submissions. Always comments on rejected mss.

TERMS Pays royalty of 7% minimum; 35% maximum. Sends prepublication galleys to author. Time between acceptance and publication is approximately 1 year. Writer's guidelines available on website. **Advice** "Polish your manuscript, make it as error free as possible, and follow our submission guidelines."

TIPS "Polish your manuscript, make it as error free as possible, and follow our submission guidelines."

EOS

Imprint of HarperCollins General Books Group, 10 E. 53rd St., New York NY 10022. (212)207-7000. Website: www.eosbooks.com. HarperCollins, 10 E. 53rd St., New York NY 10022. (212)207-7000. E-mail: eossubs@harpercollins.com. **Contact:** Diana Gill, senior editor. Estab. 1998. Publishes hardcover originals, trade and mass market paperback originals, and reprints. Averages 40-46 total titles, 40 fiction titles/year.

NEEDS Fantasy, science fiction. Published *The Isle of Battle*, by Sean Russell (fantasy); *Trapped*, by James Alan Gardner.

HOW TO CONTACT *Agented submissions only.* Include list of publishing credits, brief synopsis. Agented fiction 99%. Responds in 6 months to queries. Never comments on rejected mss.

TERMS Pays royalty on retail price. Average advance: variable. Publishes ms 18-24 months after acceptance. Ms guidelines for #10 SASE.

TIPS "Query via e-mail. Your query should be brief—no more than a 2-page description of your book. Do not send chapters or full synopsis at this time. You will receive a response—either a decline or a request for more material—in approximately 1-2 months."

ETERNAL PRESS

Canada. E-mail: submissionseternalpress@gmail.com. Website: www.eternalpress.biz. **Contact:** Ally Robertson. Estab. 2007. Publishes ebooks. "Although we will always primarily function as an eBook publisher, we also offer many of our titles in print." Eternal Press clearly distinguishes between romance, erotic romance, and erotica. GLBT romance may be any flame level depending on language, theme, the development of the romantic relationship, and sexual frequency and intensity.

NEEDS "We are currently accepting: Novellas, and full-length manuscripts from 20,000-140,000 words. Genres: Romance, Erotica, GBLT and BDSM, Paranormal, Fantasy, Mystery, Sci-Fi, Suspense, Thriller, Historical, Young Adult. **We are particularly interested in:** Erotica Paranormal (vampire/shapeshifter/witch) GBLT Romance BDSMYoung Adult Longer length novellas and novels. **We are currently NOT seeking:** Short Stories, Short story collections or anthologies, Poetry, Nonfiction, Religious genre fiction. Thematic elements of spiritual beliefs are welcome, but we are not currently publishing stories that fall into the religious category."

HOW TO CONTACT Query with cover letter in the body of the email (submissionseternalpress@gmail.com) that contains the outline/synopsis, bio, word count, genre; with a subject line: SUBMISSIONS_your name_book title. Address: Eternal Press, PO Box 3931, Santa Rosa, CA 95402-9998. Website: www.eternalpress.biz.

TERMS Writer's guidelines on website. Eternal Press pays 40% royalties on net revenue to the author for eBooks and 25% net on revenue for print. We hold all rights for five (5) years from date of publication. Open to new writers but please follow our guidelines. "If we accept your manuscript for publication, we will supply you with specific formatting guidelines. You must be able to do edits in MS Word's track changes."

FAERY ROSE

The Wild Rose Press, P.O. Box 708, Adams Basin NY 14410-0708. (585)752-8770. E-mail: queryus@thewildrosepress.com. Website: www.thewildrosepress.com. **Contact:** Amanda Barnett, editor. Estab. 2006. "Our Fairy Tales are not for children. The Faery line is a fantasy world where you can allow your imagination free rein, a place to enjoy romance with mystical or mythical characters. We are looking for a sensual hero who knows what he wants and who goes after his leading lady. The heroine should always be a female we can identify with, 'someone we want to see achieve her dreams with strength she draws from inside.' Dragons don't just frolic in the mist but turn into mortal men and women with love and lust on their minds. Elves have minds and hearts, looking for love with a bit of mischief thrown in. Ghosts who come back to life for the love of their life and wizards, warlocks, and witches who crank up the romance like they spit out a spell. Futuristic worlds, filled with science fiction warriors who can wield a sword as well as a laser and not afraid, be they woman or man, to go after what their heart desires. Time travels moving through centuries with the hero and heroine seeking not the secrets of the ages but love." Publishes paperback originals, reprints, and e-books in a POD format. Published 25 debut authors last year. Publishes approximately 60 fiction titles/year. Member: EPIC, Romance Writers of America. Distributes/promotes titles through major distribution chains, including Ingrams, Baker & Taylor, Sony, Amazon.com, Kindle, as well as smaller and online distributors.

Has published *It Takes Two*, by Sheridon Smythe; *Ties That Bind*, by Keena Kincaid; and *Human Touch*, by J.L. Wilson.

NEEDS contemporary, futuristic/time travel, gothic, historical, regency, romantic suspense, erotic, and paranormal romances. Plans several anthologies "in several lines of the company in the next year, including Cactus Rose, Yellow Rose, American Rose, Black Rose, and Scarlet Rose." *Does not accept unsolicited mss.*

TIPS "Polish your manuscript, make it as error free as possible, and follow our submission guidelines."

FARRAR, STRAUS & GIROUX/ BOOKS FOR YOUNG READERS

Books for Young Readers, 175 Fifth Ave., New York NY 10010. (646)307-5151. Website: www.fsgkids-

BOOK PUBLISHERS

books.com. **Contact:** Children's Editorial Department. Estab. 1946. "We publish original and well-written materials for all ages." Publishes hardcover originals and trade paperback reprints. **Published some debut authors within the last year.** Averages 75 total titles/year.

IMPRINTS Frances Foster Books.

NEEDS children's/juvenile, picture books, middle grade, young adult, narrative nonfiction. "Do not query picture books; just send manuscript. Do not fax queries or manuscripts." Published *Adele and Simon*, by Barbara McClintock; *The Cabinet of Wonders*, by Marie Rutkoski.

HOW TO CONTACT For novels and other longer mss, query with SASE and three sample chapters. Do not query picture books; just send ms with cover letter. Include brief bio, list of publishing credits. Agented fiction 50%. Responds in 2 months to queries; 4 months to mss. Accepts simultaneous submissions. No electronic submissions or submissions on disk.

TERMS Pays 2-6% royalty on retail price for paperbacks, 3-10% for hardcovers. Average advance: $3,000-25,000. Publishes ms 18 months after acceptance. Book catalog for 9×12 SAE with $2.00 postage. Ms guidelines for #10 SASE.

TIPS "Study our list to avoid sending something inappropriate. Send query letters for long manuscripts; don't ask for editorial advice (just not possible, unfortunately); and send SASEs!" Audience is full age range, preschool to young adult. Specializes in literary fiction.

Ⓐ FARRAR, STRAUS & GIROUX PAPERBACKS

18 West 18th St., New York NY 10011. (212)741-6900. E-mail: fsg.publicity@fsgbooks.com; fsg.editorial@fsgbooks.com. Website: http://www.fsgbooks.com/. FSG Paperbacks emphasizes literary nonfiction and fiction, as well as poetry. Publishes hardcover and trade paperback originals and reprints. Averages 180 total titles/year.

NEEDS Literary. Published *The Corrections*, by Jonathan Franzen; *The Haunting of L.*, by Howard Norman.

HOW TO CONTACT Unsolicited submissions are accepted at Farrar, Straus & Giroux. All submissions must be submitted through the mail—we do not accept electronic submissions, or submissions delivered in person. Please include a cover letter describing your submission, along with the first 50 pages of the manuscript. If you are submitting poems, please include 3-4 poems. Address: Farrar, Straus and Giroux, 18 West 18th St., New York NY 10011

FC2

Center for Publications, School of Arts and Sciences-UHV, 3007 N. Ben Wilson, Victoria TX 77901. E-mail: fc2@uhv.edu. Website: http://fc2.org. **Contact:** Carmen Edington, managing editor. Estab. 1974. Publisher of innovative fiction. Publishes hardcover and paperback originals. Books: perfect/Smyth binding; illustrations. Average print order: 2,200. **Published some debut authors within the last year.** Plans 2 first novels this year. Averages 6 total titles, 6 fiction titles/year. Titles distributed through Univ. of Alabama Press. No open submissions except through Ronald Sukenick Innovative Fiction Prize.

NEEDS experimental, feminist, gay/lesbian, innovative; modernist/postmodern; avant-garde; anarchist; minority; cyberpunk. Published *Book of Lazarus*, by Richard Grossman; *Is It Sexual Harassment Yet?* by Cris Mazza; *Liberty's Excess*, by Lidia Yuknavitch; *The Wavering Knife*, by Brian Evenson.

HOW TO CONTACT Does not accept unsolicited mss. See website for contest info. Agented fiction 5%. Responds in 3 weeks to queries; 9-6 months to mss. Accepts simultaneous submissions.

TERMS Pays 10% royalty. Publishes ms 1-3 years after acceptance. Ms guidelines online.

TIPS "Be familiar with our list."

FENCE BOOKS

Science Library 320, Univ. of Albany, 1400 Washington Ave., Albany NY 12222. (518)591-8162. E-mail: fence.fencebooks@gmail.com; robfence@gmail.com. Website: www.fenceportal.org. **Contact:** Rob Arnold, Submissions Manager. "*Fence is closed to submissions right now.* We'll have another reading period in the Spring. Fence Books offers 2 book contests (in addition to the National Poetry Series) with 2 sets of guidelines and entry forms on our website."

TIPS "At present Fence Books is a self-selecting publisher; mss come to our attention through our contests and through editors' investigations. We hope to become open to submissions of poetry and fiction mss in the near future."

FLORIDA ACADEMIC PRESS

P.O. Box 540, Gainesville FL 32602. (352)332-5104. Fax: (352)331-6003. E-mail: fapress@gmail.com. Website: www.floridaacademicpress.com. Estab. 1997. Publishes hardcover and trade paperback originals. **Published 90% debut authors within the last year.** Averages 10 total titles/year.

NEEDS Serious fiction and scholarly social science manuscripts. Does not want "children's books, poetry, science fiction, religious tracts, anthologies, or booklets."

HOW TO CONTACT Submit complete ms. by hard copy only. Responds in 4-12 weeks to mss.

TERMS Pays 5-8% royalty on retail price, depending if paperback or hardcover. Publishes ms 3-5 months after acceptance.

TIPS Considers complete mss only. "Manuscripts we decide to publish must be re-submitted by the author in ready-to-print PDF files. Match our needs—do not send blindly. Books we accept for publication must be submitted in camera-ready format. The Press covers all publication/promotional expenditures."

FORGE AND TOR BOOKS

175 Fifth Ave. 14th Floor, New York NY 10010. Website: www.tor.com; us.macmillan.com/TorForge.aspx. Estab. 1980. "Tor Books are science fiction, fantasy and horror, and occasionally, related nonfiction. Forge books are everything else—general fiction, historical fiction, mysteries and suspense, women's fiction and nonfiction. Orb titles are trade paperback reprint editions of science fiction, fantasy and horror books." Publishes hardcover, trade paperback and mass market paperback originals, trade and mass market paperback reprints. **Published some debut authors within the last year.**

Tor was named Best Publisher at the Locus Awards for the sixteenth consecutive year.

NEEDS historical, horror, mainstream/contemporary, mystery (amateur sleuth, police procedural, private eye/hard-boiled), science fiction, suspense, thriller/espionage, western (frontier saga, traditional), thriller; general fiction and fantasy.

HOW TO CONTACT Accepts unsolicited mss. Do not query; "submit only the first 3 chapters of your book and a synopsis of the entire book. Your cover letter should state the genre of the submission and previous sales or publications if relevant." Include estimated word count, brief bio, list of publishing credits. Agented fiction 95%. Sometimes comments on rejected mss. Responds in 6-8 months. No simultaneous submissions. Additional guidelines on website. Tor.com welcomes original speculative fiction short stories and poetry. We define speculative fiction broadly, including SF, fantasy, horror, alternate history, and related genres. We're particularly interested in stories under 12,000 words, and may even be slightly more likely to take a chance on shorter stories from new writers. We will consider stories that are slightly longer than 12k—we will not read anything over 17,500 words. You can send your novel to our corporate cousins at Tor Books, as long as you follow their submissions guidelines. E-mail: tor.comsubs@gmail.com.

TERMS "We pay 25 cents a word for the first 5,000 words, 15 cents a word for the next 5,000, and 10 cents a word after that." Paperback: Pays 6-8% royalty for first-time authors, 8-10% royalty for established authors. Hardcover: Pays 10% first 5,000; 12½% second 5,000; 15% thereafter. Offers advance. Publishes ms 12-18 months after acceptance.

TIPS "The writing must be outstanding for a new author to break into today's market."

FORT ROSS INC. INTERNATIONAL RIGHTS

26 Arthur Place, Yonkers NY 10701. (914)375-6448. E-mail: fortross@optonline.net. Website: www.fortrossinc.com. **Contact:** Dr. Vladimir P. Kartsev, executive director. Estab. 1992. "We welcome Russia-related manuscripts as well as books from well-established fantasy and romance novel writers who would like to have their novels translated in Russia by our publishing house in cooperation with the local publishers." Publishes hardcover and paperback originals. Published 2 debut authors within the last year. Averages 20 total titles/year.

HOW TO CONTACT Does not accept unsolicited mss. Query with SASE. Include estimated word count, brief bio, list of publishing credits. Send SASE for return of ms or send a disposable ms and SASE for reply only. Responds in 1 month to queries; 3 months to mss. Accepts simultaneous submissions. Pays 5-10% royalty on wholesale price or makes outright purchase of $500-1,500. Average advance: $500-1,000; negotiable.

FOUR WAY BOOKS

Box 535, Village Station, New York NY 10014. E-mail: fourwayeditors@fourwaybooks.com; editors@fourwaybooks.com. Website: www.fourwaybooks.com. Estab. 1993. June 1-30, 2011. Open Reading Period. Four Way Books editors make selections. Open to all poets and fiction writers. Book-length poetry collections, story collections, and novellas. We do not publish novels, translations, or nonfiction. Submission guidelines will be posted on our website at the end of May.

NEEDS short stories.

FREYA'S BOWER

Wild Child Publishing, P.O. Box 4897, Culver City CA 90231-4897. E-mail: mbaun@freyasbower.com. Website: http://www.freyasbower.com. **Contact:** Marci Baun, publisher. Estab. 2006. Closed to submissions from authors not already signed with either Freya's Bower or Wild Child Publishing from March 15, 2011 to September 15, 2011. "Freya's Bower is a small, independent press that started out in March 2006. We are known for working with newer/unpublished authors and editing to the standards of NYC publishers. We respond promptly to submissions." Publishes paperback originals, e-books. Average print order: 50-200. Debut novel print order: 50. **Published over 30 new writers last year.** Plans 10-15 debut novels this year. Averages 75 total titles/year; 75 fiction titles/year. Member EPIC. Distributes/promotes titles through Ingram, All Romance eBooks, Fictionwise, Mobipocket, Amazon, Omnilit, and website.

NEEDS erotica and romance of all genres. Has published *Love Bites Back*, by Christopher C. Newman (vampire/paranormal novella); *Dark Succession*, by Teresa D'Amario (a shapeshifter/paranormal novel); *The Art of Losing*, by Lisa Troy (a contemporary erotica novel); *Two Hearts and a Crow*, by Jane Toombs (a contemporary romance novella).

HOW TO CONTACT Query with outline/synopsis and one sample chapter. Accepts queries by e-mail only. Include estimated word count, brief bio. Writers submit material per submissions guidelines. See website for details. Responds to queries in 2-4 weeks. Accepts unsolicited mss. Often critiques/comments on rejected mss. Responds to mss in 6-8 weeks. Does not accept simultaneous submissions. To contact us: Click on the contact link that appears at the bottom of every page on the website and complete the form.

TERMS Sends preproduction galleys to author. Ms published 2-5 months after acceptance. Writer's guidelines on website. Pays royalties 10-40%. Book catalogs on website.

TIPS "We look for good stories. While we accept material that is popular, we are more focused on quality. Do your homework. Read our submission guidelines thoroughly. Read a few of our books. Study your craft. While we are willing to work with newer authors, we expect them to be willing to revise and eager to learn. A good attitude goes a long way . . . on both sides."

FRONT STREET

Boyds Mills Press, 815 Church St., Honesdale PA 18431. Website: www.frontstreetbooks.com. **Contact:** Acquisitions Editor. Estab. 1994.

NEEDS adventure, ethnic, historical, humor, juvenile, literary, picture books, young adult (adventure, fantasy/science fiction, historical, mystery/suspense, problem novels, sports). "We look for fresh voices for children and young adults. Titles on our list entertain, challenge, or enlighten, always employing novel characters whose considered voices resonate." Published *The Bear Makers* by Andrea Cheng; *Drive* by Nathan Clement; *The Adventurous Deeds of Deadwood Jones* by Helen Hemphill.

HOW TO CONTACT Accepts unsolicited and international mss. Query with outline/synopsis, first 3 chapters, and SASE and label the package "Manuscript Submission." Agented fiction 30%. Responds in 3 months to mss. Accepts simultaneous submissions.

TIPS "Read through our recently published titles and review our website. Check to see what's on the market and in our catalog before submitting your story. Feel free to query us if you're not sure."

GASLIGHT PUBLICATIONS

Empire Publishing Services, P.O. Box 1344, Studio City CA 91614. (818)784-8918. Website: http://playerspress.home.att.net/gaslight_catalogue.htm. **Contact**: Simon Waters, fiction editor (Sherlock Holmes only). Estab. 1960. Publishes hardcover and paperback originals and reprints. Books: paper varies; offset printing; binding varies; illustrations. Average print order: 5,000. **Published 1 debut author within the last year.** Averages 4-12 total titles, 2-4 fiction titles/year. Promotes titles through sales reps, trade, library, etc.

NEEDS Sherlock Holmes only. Recently published *Sherlock Holmes, The Complete Bagel Street Saga*, by

Robert L. Fish; *Subcutaneously: My Dear Watson*, by Jack Tracy (all Sherlock Holmes).

HOW TO CONTACT Accepts unsolicited mss. Query with SASE. Include estimated word count, brief bio, list of publishing credits. Send SASE for return of ms or send a disposable ms and SASE for reply only. Agented fiction 10%. Responds in 2 weeks to queries; 1 year to mss.

TERMS Pays 8-10% royalty. Royalty and advance dependent on the material. Publishes ms 1-6 months after acceptance.

TIPS "Please send only Sherlock Holmes material. Other stuff just wastes time and money."

GAUTHIER PUBLICATIONS, INC.

Frog Legs Ink, P.O. Box 806241, Saint Clair Shores MI 48080. Fax: (586)279-1515. E-mail: info@gauthierpublications.com; submissions@gauthierpublications.com. Website: www.eatabook.com. **Contact:** Elizabeth Gauthier, Creative Director (Children's/Fiction).

Frog Legs Ink (imprint) is always looking for new writers and illustrators. We are currently looking for Horror/Thriller short stories for an upcoming collection.

IMPRINTS Frog Legs Ink, Hungry Goat Press, Dragon-Fish Comics

GEMSTONE PUBLISHING

Diamond Comic Distributors, 3679 Concord Road, P.O. Box 12001, York PA 17402. (888) 375-9800 ext. 1617. Fax: (717) 434-1690. E-mail: wheather@gemstonepub.com. Website: www.gemstonepub.com. **Contact:** Heather Winter. "Best known as the home of *The Overstreet Comic Book Price Guide*, Gemstone Publishing, a division of Geppi's Entertainment Publishing & Auctions, was formed by Diamond Comic Distributors President and Chief Executive Officer Stephen A. Geppi as a conduit for his efforts in preserving and promoting the history of the comics medium."

GENESIS PRESS, INC.

P.O. Box 101, Columbus MS 39701. (888)463-4461. Fax: (662)329-9399. E-mail: customerservice@genesis-press.com. Website: www.genesis-press.com. Estab. 1993. Publishes hardcover and trade paperback originals and reprints. **Published 50% debut authors within the last year.**

IMPRINTS Indigo (romance); Black Coral (fiction); Indigo Love Spectrum (interracial romance); Indigo after Dark (erotica); Obsidian (thriller/myster); Indigo Glitz (love stories for young adults); Indigo Vibe (for stylish audience under 35 years old); Mount Blue (Christian); Inca Books (teens); Sage (self-help/inspirational).

NEEDS Averages 30 total titles/year. Erotica, ethnic, literary, multicultural, romance, women's. Published *Cherish the Flame*, by Beverly Clark; *No Apologies*, by Seressia Glass.

HOW TO CONTACT Query with SASE or submit 3 sample chapter(s), synopsis. Responds in 2 months to queries; 4 months to mss.

TERMS Pays 6-12% royalty on invoice price. Average advance: $750-5,000. Publishes ms 1 year after acceptance. Ms guidelines online.

TIPS Be professional. Always include a cover letter and SASE. Follow the submission guidelines posted on our website or send SASE for a copy.

GERTRUDE PRESS

P.O. Box 83948, Portland OR 97283. (503)515-8252. E-mail: edelehoy@fc.edu. Website: www.gertrudepress.org. **Contact:** Justus Ballard (all fiction). Estab. 2005. "Gertrude Press is a nonprofit organization developing and showcasing the creative talents of lesbian, gay, bisexual, trans, queer-identified and allied individuals. We publish limited-edition fiction and poetry chapbooks plus the biannual literary journal, *Gertrude*." Format: 60 lb. paper; high-quality digital printing; perfect (lit mag) or saddle-stitch (chapbook) bound. Average print order: 350. Published 5-10 new writers last year. Averages 4 total titles/year; 1 fiction title/year. *Gertrude* accepts manuscripts from new and established writers and artists. We accept simultaneous submissions with notification. We do not accept previously published work. Please note that we do not publish novels. We read chapbook manuscripts ONLY through our annual competition. *Gertrude* accepts electronic submissions submitted through our online submission form. We highly prefer online submissions. If submitting by snail mail, please provide us with an e-mail address for notification. Do not place your name directly on manuscripts. Submissions that do not include an SASE will be discarded. For electronic submissions, please use our online submission form only. **Fiction/Novel Excerpts*/Creative Nonfiction:** Submit 1-2 pieces, double-spaced, up to 3,000 words, of any subject matter. Include a word count for each piece in your cover letter. **Interviews:** Please query the editor by e-mail with your proposal. **Art:** *Gertrude* showcases one visual artist per issue, including full-color cover and 6-8 black and white images inside the journal. To submit artwork for future issues, please send slides, prints (do not send originals), or a website URL to the attention of the art editor. **Send all manuscripts and artwork to:** Gertrude Press PO Box 83948 Portland OR 97283. Response time is 9-12 months and varies based on when the submission was received. *Gertrude Press does not publish novels at this time.

NEEDS ethnic/multicultural, experimental, feminist, gay, humor/satire, lesbian, literary, mainstream, short story collections.

HOW TO CONTACT Submit complete ms with cover letter. Submissions accepted year-round. Accepts queries by snail mail, e-mail. Include estimated word count, brief bio, list of publishing credits. Send disposable copy of ms and SASE for reply only. Responds to queries in 3-4 weeks; mss in 3-6 months. Accepts unsolicited mss. Considers simultaneous submissions, e-mail submissions. Sometimes critiques/comments on rejected mss.

TERMS Manuscript published 3 months after acceptance. Writer's guidelines on website. Pays in author's copies (1 for lit mag, 50 for chapbook). Book catalogs not available.

TIPS Sponsors poetry and fiction chapbook contest. Prize is $50 and 50 contributor's copies. Submission guidelines and fee information on website. "Read the journal and sample published work. We are not impressed by pages of publications; your work should speak for itself."

⊕ GHOST ROAD PRESS

820 S. Monaco Pkwy #288, Denver CO 80224. (303)758-7623. E-mail: info@ghostroadpress.com; matt@ghostroadpress.com; evan@ghostroadpress.com. Website: ghostroadpress.com.

NEEDS "Genre-based mss in literary, science fiction, young adult, fantasy, mystery, and crime fiction."

HOW TO CONTACT *Not currently accepting submissions.* "Send an attachment (word or.rtf only) that includes a complete synopsis, a description of your marketing plan and platform, and the first three chapters. To view a complete list of our titles and changing submission guidelines, please visit website." Responds in 2-3 months. Accepts simultaneous submissions.

GIVAL PRESS

Gival Press, LLC, P.O. Box 3812, Arlington VA 22203. (703)351-0079. E-mail: givalpress@yahoo.com. Website: www.givalpress.com. **Contact:** Robert L. Giron, editor-in-chief (area of interest: literary). Estab. 1998. A small, award-winning independent publisher that publishes quality works by a variety of authors from an array of walks of life. Works are in English, Spanish, and French and have a philosophical or social message. Publishes paperback originals and reprints and e-books. Books: perfect-bound. Average print order: 500. **Publishes established and debut authors.** Publishes 2 novels/year. Member AAP, PMA, Literary Council of Small Presses and Magazines. Distributes books through Ingram and BookMasters, Inc.

IMPRINTS Gival Press

NEEDS literary, multicultural, GLBT. "Looking for French books with English translation." The Annual Gival Press Novel Award contest deadline is May 30. The Annual Gival Press Short Story Award contest deadline is August. Guidelines on website. Recently published *That Demon Life*, by Lowell Mick White; *Twelve Rivers of the Body*, by Elizabeth Oness; and *A Tomb of the Periphery*, by John Domini.

HOW TO CONTACT Does not accept unsolicited mss. Query by e-mail first. Include description of project, estimated word count, brief bio, list of publishing credits. Agented fiction 5%. Responds by e-mail within 2-3 weeks. Rarely comments on rejected mss.

TERMS Pays 20 contributor's copies. Offers advance. Publishes ms 1 year after acceptance. For book catalog send SASE and on website. Ms guidelines by SASE or on website.

TIPS "Our audience is those who read literary works with depth to the work. Visit our website—there is much to be read/learned from the numerous pages."

O THE GLENCANNON PRESS

P.O. Box 1428, El Cerrito CA 94530. (510)528-4216. Fax: (510)528-3194. E-mail: merships@yahoo.com. Website: www.glencannon.com. **Contact:** Bill Harris (maritime, maritime children's). Estab. 1993. "We publish quality books about ships and the sea." Publishes hardcover and paperback originals and hardcover reprints. Books: Smyth: perfect binding; illustrations. Average print order: 1,000. First novel print order: 750. Averages 4-5 total titles, 1 fiction titles/year. Member PMA, BAIPA. Distributes titles through Baker & Taylor. Promotes titles through direct mail, magazine advertising and word of mouth.

IMPRINTS Smyth: perfect binding; illustrations.

NEEDS adventure, children's/juvenile (adventure, fantasy, historical, mystery, preschool/picture book), ethnic (general), historical (maritime), humor, mainstream/contemporary, military/war, mystery, thriller/espionage, western (frontier saga, traditional maritime), young adult (adventure, historical, mystery/suspense, western). Currently emphasizing children's maritime, any age. Recently published *Good Shipmates*, by Ernest F. Imhoff (anthology, merchant marine); *Fort Ross*, by Mark West (Palo Alto Books, western).

HOW TO CONTACT Accepts unsolicited mss. Submit complete ms. Include brief bio, list of publishing credits. Send SASE for return of ms or send a disposable ms and SASE for reply only. Responds in 1 month to queries; 2 months to mss. Accepts simultaneous submissions. Often comments on rejected mss.

TERMS Pays 10-20% royalty. Publishes ms 6-24 months after acceptance.

TIPS "Write a good story in a compelling style."

GO! COMI

Go! Media Entertainment, LLC, 5737 Kanan Rd. #591, Agoura Hills CA 91301. E-mail: info@gomedia-ent.com. Website: http://www.gocomi.com/index.php.

NEEDS *Go! Comi is closed to unsolicited submissions for original material.* See the jobs section on website for information about possible freelance opportunities on existing manga.

TIPS "Go! Comi is not accepting submissions for original ideas or material at this time. Submissions will not be looked at and will automatically be deleted. If you ignore this policy and send us scripts, stories, artwork, ideas, or any material, either through email or regular mail, your submissions become the property of Go! Media Entertainment LLC, and we will not be responsible for any use or disclosure of your material. Furthermore, by sending us unsolicited submissions without a release, you agree not to hold us liable for any similarities between your work and any work subsequently published by us."

DAVID R. GODINE, PUBLISHER, INC.

9 Hamilton Place, Boston MA 02108. (617) 451-9600. Fax: (617) 350-0250. E-mail: info@godine.com. Website: www.godine.com. **Contact:** David R. Godine, president. Estab. 1970. Small, independent publisher (5-person staff). Publishes hardcover and trade paperback originals and reprints. Averages 35 total titles/year.

NEEDS children's/juvenile, historical, literary. *No unsolicited mss.*

HOW TO CONTACT Does not accept unsolicited mss. Query with SASE.

TERMS Pays royalty on retail price. Publishes ms 3 years after acceptance.

TIPS "Have your agent contact us. Please visit our website for more information about our books and detailed submission policy. No phone calls, please."

GOOSE LANE EDITIONS

500 Beaverbrook Ct., Suite 330, Fredericton, New Brunswick E3B 5X4 Canada. (506)450-4251. Fax: (506)459-4991. Website: www.gooselane.com/submissions.php. **Contact:** Angela Williams, publishing assistant. Estab. 1954. Publishes hardcover and paperback originals and occasional reprints. Books: some illustrations. Average print order: 3,000. First novel print order: 1,500. Averages 16-18 total titles, 6-8 fiction titles/year. Distributes titles through University of Toronto Press (UTP).

NEEDS Literary (novels), mainstream/contemporary, short story collections. "Our needs in fiction never change: substantial, character-centered literary fiction." Published *Reading by Lightning* by Joan Thomas.

HOW TO CONTACT Accepts unsolicited mss. Query with SASE. Responds in 6-8 months to mss. No simultaneous submissions. **Send submissions to:** Managing Editor, Goose Lane Editions, Suite 300, 500 Beaverbrook Court, Fredericton, NB E3B 5×4 CA.

TERMS Pays 8-10% royalty on retail price. Average advance: $200-1,000, negotiable. Ms guidelines online. **TIPS** "Specializes in high quality Canadian literary fiction, poetry, and nonfiction. We consider submissions from outside Canada only when the author is Canadian and the book is of extraordinary interest to Canadian readers. We do not publish books for children or for the young adult market. Writers should send us outlines and samples of books that show a very well-read author with highly developed literary skills. Our books are almost all by Canadians living in Canada; we seldom consider submissions from outside Canada. If I were a writer trying to market a book today, I would contact the targeted publisher with a query letter and synopsis, and request manuscript guidelines. Purchase a recent book from the publisher in a relevant area, if possible. Always send an SASE with IRCs or suffient return postage in Canadian stamps for reply to your query and for any material you'd like returned should it not suit our needs."

GOTHIC CHAPBOOK SERIES

2272 Quail Oak, Baton Rouge LA 70808. E-mail: gothicpt12@aol.com. Website: www.gwcgothicpress.com. Estab. 1979. "One person operation on a part-time basis." Publishes paperback originals. Books: printing or photocopying. Average print order: 150-200. Distributes titles through direct mail and book dealers.

NEEDS horror (dark fantasy, psychological, supernatural). Need novellas and short stories.

HOW TO CONTACT *Submissions are sought by invitation only.* Include estimated word count, brief bio, list of publishing credits. Send SASE for return of ms or send a disposable ms and SASE for reply only. Responds in 2 weeks to queries; 2 months to mss. Sometimes comments on rejected mss.

TERMS Pays 10% royalty. Ms guidelines for #10 SASE.

TIPS "Know gothic and horror literature well."

GRAYWOLF PRESS

250 Third Avenue North, Suite 600, Minneapolis MN 55401. E-mail: wolves@graywolfpress.org. Website: www.graywolfpress.org. **Contact:** Katie Dublinski, editorial manager (nonfiction, fiction). Estab. 1974. Growing independent literary press, nonprofit corporation. Publishes trade cloth and paperback originals. Books: acid-free quality paper; offset printing; hardcover and soft binding. Average print order: 3,000-10,000. First novel print order: 3,000-7,500. Averages 27 total titles, 8-10 fiction titles/year. Distributes titles nationally through Farrar, Straus and Giroux.

NEEDS literary novels, short story collections. "Familiarize yourself with our list before submitting your work." Published *The Adderall Diaries*, by Stephen Elliot; *Castle*, by J. Robert Lennon; *The Heyday of the Insensitive Bastards*, by Robert Boswell; *I Am Not Sidney Poitier*, by Percival Everett.

HOW TO CONTACT Send full ms during open submission period including SASE/IRC, estimated word count, brief bio, list of publishing credits. Agented fiction 90%. Does not accept unsolicited queries, book proposals, or sample chapters. Responds in 3-6 months to submissions. Accepts simultaneous submissions.

TERMS Pays royalty on retail price, author's copies. Average advance: $2,500-15,000. Publishes ms 18-24 months after acceptance. Ms guidelines online.

GREENE BARK PRESS

P.O. Box 1108, Bridgeport CT 06601. (610)434-2802. Fax: (610)434-2803. E-mail: service@greenebarkpress.com. Website: www.greenebarkpress.com. **Contact: Thomas J. Greene, publisher;** Tara Maroney, associate publisher. Estab. 1991. "We only publish children's fiction—all subjects, but usually reading picture book format appealing to ages 3-9 or all ages." Publishes hardcover originals. **Published some debut authors within the last year.** Averages 1-6 total titles/year. Distributes titles through Baker & Taylor and Quality Books. Promotes titles through ads, trade shows (national and regional), direct mail campaigns.

NEEDS juvenile. Published *Edith Ellen Eddy*, by Julee Granger.

HOW TO CONTACT Submit complete ms. Responds in 3 months to queries; 6 months to mss. Accepts simultaneous submissions. No electronic submissions.

TERMS Pays 10-15% royalty on wholesale price. Publishes ms 1 year after acceptance. Ms guidelines for SASE or e-mail request.

TIPS "Audience is children who read to themselves and others. Mothers, fathers, grandparents, godparents who read to their respective children, grandchildren. Include SASE, be prepared to wait, do not inquire by telephone."

GROUNDWOOD BOOKS

Groundwood Books, 110 Spadina, Suite 801, Toronto ON M5V 2K4 Canada. Contact Acquisitions editor. Email: nfroman@groundwoodbooks.com. (416)363-4343. Fax: (416)363-1017. Website: www.groundwoodbooks.com. Publishes 10 picture books/year; 3 young readers/year; 5 middle readers/year; 5 young adult titles/year, approximately 2 nonfiction titles/year. 10% of books by first-time authors.

TIPS "Try to familiarize yourself with our list before submitting to judge whether or not your work is appropriate for Groundwood. Visit our website for guidelines (http://www.groundwoodbooks.com/gw_guidelines.cgm)."

GUERNICA EDITIONS

Box 117, Station P, Toronto ON M5S 2S6 Canada. (416)658-9888. Fax: (416)657-8885. E-mail: antoniodalfonso@sympatico.ca. Website: www.guernicaeditions.com. **Contact:** Antonio D'Alfonso, editor/publisher (poetry, nonfiction, novels). Estab. 1978. "Guernica Editions is a small press that produces works of fiction and nonfiction on the viability of pluriculturalism." Publishes trade paperback originals, reprints, and software. Books: various paper; offset printing; perfect binding. Average print order: 1,000. **Published 4 debut authors within the last year.** Averages 25 total titles, 18-20 fiction titles/year. Distributes titles through professional distributors.

NEEDS literary, multicultural. "We wish to open up into the fiction world and focus less on poetry. We specialize in European, especially Italian, translations." Publishes anthology of Arab women/Italian women writers. Published *At the Copa*, by Marisa Labozzetta; *In the Claws of the Cat*, by Claude Forand; *Unholy Stories*, by Carole David; *Girls Closed In*, by France Theoret.

HOW TO CONTACT Accepts unsolicited mss. Query with SASE. Must have Canadian postage. Include estimated word count, brief bio, list of publishing credits. Responds in 1 month to queries; 1 year to mss. No simultaneous submissions. Guernica prefers to receive manuscript queries by e-mail. However, we also accept such queries by snail mail at our postal address. Before inquiring, however, please check our website to determine the type of material that best fits our publishing house. Address: Guernica Editions, Attn: Editor, ___ Series, 489 Strathmore Blvd., Toronto, Ontario, Canada M4C 1N8.

TERMS Pays 8-10% royalty on retail price. Or makes outright purchase of $200-5,000. Average advance: $200-2,000. Publishes ms 15 months after acceptance.

HADLEY RILLE BOOKS

P.O. Box 25466, Overland Park KS 66225. E-mail: contact@hadleyrillebooks.com. Website: http://www.hadleyrillebooks.com. **Contact:** Eric T. Reynolds, Editor (science fiction, fantasy). Estab. 2005. "Small publisher, one to two person operation. The first 9 titles are anthologies, mostly science fiction, with a little fantasy (in two titles). We've published new works by well-known authors (for example, new works by Sir Arthur C. Clarke, Mike Resnick, Stephen Baxter, Jay Lake, G. David Nordley, Robert Sheckley, Terry Bisson) as well as up-and-coming and new authors. At present time, about half of our anthologies are by invitation only, the other half are open to unsolicited submissions. We publish the kind of innovative anthologies that are generally not considered by larger publishers (somewhat common in the SF genre). Some of our anthologies are experimental, for example, the first title (*Golden Age SF*) had well-known authors write 'Golden Age' SF stories as if they were living during that time. The second title, *Visual Journeys*, asked each contributing author to choose a work of space art and write a story based on it. We included color plates of the art with each story. We're currently in the middle of a Ruins anthology series with stories that are set in or are about ruins. An anthology in 2009 will feature stories that deal with the consequences of global warming. Well-known futurists and SF writers are writing for this." Publishes hardcover originals, paperback originals. Format: Offset and POD printing. Published 50 new writers last year. Averages 6 fiction titles/year. Distributes/promotes titles via distrubtors, promotes at conventions, online advertising and by reviews.

One story from *Golden Age SF: Tales of a Bygone Future* (2006) selected for David Hartwell and Kathryn Cramer's *Year's Best SF* #12, another selected for Rich Horton's *Space Opera 2007*. Two stories reprinted in Gardner Dozois' *The Year's Best Science Fiction #2* and ten stories received honorable mentions.

NEEDS science fiction, fantasy, short story collections. Check website for current needs. Some anthologies are and will be open to unsolicited submissions, and will be announced on website. Published *Golden Age SF: Tales of a Bygone Future* (science fiction), *Visual Journeys: A Tribute to Space* (science fiction), *Ruins Terra* (SF/fantasy/horror).

HOW TO CONTACT Send query letter. Accepts queries by e-mail. Include estimated word count, brief bio. Agented fiction: less than 5%. Accepts unsolicited mss. Often critiques/comments on rejected mss.

TERMS Sends preproduction galleys to author. Ms published generally 6 months after acceptance. Writer's guidelines on website. Pays royalties of ½ of the ratio of 1 to the number of stories in the book, advance of $30 for unsolicated work. Book catalogs on website.

TIPS "We aim to produce books that are aligned with current interest in the genres. Anthology markets are somewhat rare in SF these days, we feel there aren't enough good anthologies being published each year and part of our goal is to present the best that we can. We like stories that fit well within the guidelines of the particular anthology for which we are soliciting manuscripts. Aside from that, we want stories with strong characters (not necessarily characters with strong personalities, flawed characters are welcome). We want a sense of wonder and awe. We want to feel the world around the character and so scene description is important (however, this doesn't always require a lot of text, just set the scene well so we don't wonder where the character is). We strongly recommend workshopping the story or having it critiqued in some way by readers familiar with the genre. We prefer clichés be kept to a bare minimum in the prose and avoid re-working old story lines."

HAMPTON ROADS PUBLISHING CO., INC.

665 Third Street, Suite 400, San Francisco CA 94107. E-mail: submissions@hrpub.com; submissions@redwheelweiser.com. Website: www.hrpub.com. **Contact:** Ms. Pat Bryce, Acquisitions Editor. Estab. 1989. 1125 Stoney Ridge Rd., Charlottesville VA 22902. (434)296-2772. Fax: (434)296-5096. E-mail: editorial@hrpub.com. Website: www.hamptonroadspub.com **Contact:** Frank Demarco, chief editor. Estab. 1989. "We work as a team to produce the best books we are capable of producing which will impact, uplift and contribute to positive change in the world. We publish what defies or doesn't quite fit the usual genres. We are noted for visionary fiction." Publishes and distributes hardcover and trade paperback originals on subjects including metaphysics, health, complementary medicine, visionary fiction, and other related topics. Average print order: 3,000-5,000. **Published 6 debut authors within the last year.** Averages 24-30 total titles, 4 fiction titles/year. Distributes titles through distributors. Promotes titles through advertising, representatives, author signings, and radio-TV interviews with authors.

"Please know that we only publish a handful of books every year, and that we pass on many well written, important works, simply because we cannot publish them all. We review each and every proposal very carefully. However, due to the volume of inquiries, we cannot respond to them all individually. Please give us 30 days to review your proposal. If you do not hear back from us within that time, this means we have decided to pursue other book ideas that we feel fit better within our plan."

NEEDS literary, new age/mystic, psychic/supernatural, spiritual, visionary fiction, past-life fiction, based on actual memories. "Fiction should have one or more of the following themes: spiritual, inspirational, metaphysical, i.e., past life recall, out-of-body experiences, near death experience, paranormal." Published *Rogue Messiahs*, by Colin Wilson; *Spirit Matters*, by Michael Lerner; and *The Authenticator*, by William M. Valtos.

HOW TO CONTACT Accepts unsolicited mss. Submit outline, 2 sample chapter(s), synopsis. Accepts queries by e-mail, fax. Send SASE for return of ms or send a disposable ms and SASE for reply only. Agented fiction 5%. Responds in 1-2 months to queries; 1-6 months to mss. Accepts simultaneous submissions.

TERMS Pays royalty. Average advance: less than $10,000. Publishes ms 1 year after acceptance. Ms guidelines online.

HARLEQUIN AMERICAN ROMANCE

A Harlequin book line, 233 Broadway, Suite 1001, New York NY 10279. (212)553-4200. Website: www.eharlequin.com. **Contact:** Melissa Jeglinski, associate senior editor. "Upbeat and lively, fast paced and well plotted, American Romance celebrates the pursuit of love in the backyards, big cities and wide-open spaces of America." Publishes paperback originals and reprints. Books: newspaper print paper; web printing; perfect bound. Length: 55,000-60,000 words. Senior Editor: Kathleen Scheibling; Editor: Johanna Raisanen; Assistant Editor: Laura Barth. Editorial Office: Toronto, Canada. "American Romance features heartwarming romances with strong family elements. These are stories about the pursuit of love, marriage and family in America today."

NEEDS romance (contemporary, American). Needs "all-American stories with a range of emotional and sensual content that are supported by a sense of community within the plot's framework. In the confident and caring heroine, the tough but tender hero, and their dynamic relationship that is at the center of this series, real-life love is showcased as the best fantasy of all!"

HOW TO CONTACT Query with SASE. No simultaneous submissions, electronic submissions, or submissions on disk.

TERMS Pays royalty. Offers advance. Ms guidelines online.

HARLEQUIN BLAZE

225 Duncan Mill Road, Don Mills ON M3B 3K9 Canada. (416)445-5860. Website: www.eharlequin.com. **Contact:** Brenda Chin, associate editor. "Harlequin Blaze is a red-hot series. It is a vehicle to build and promote new authors who have a strong sexual edge to their stories. It is also the place to be for seasoned authors who want to create a sexy, sizzling, longer contemporary story." Publishes paperback originals. Books: newspaper print; web printing; perfect bound. **Published some debut authors within the last year.**

NEEDS romance (contemporary). "Sensuous, highly romantic, innovative plots that are sexy in premise and execution. The tone of the books can run from fun and flirtatious to dark and sensual. Submissions should have a very contemporary feel—what it's like to be young and single today. We are looking for heroes and heroines in their early 20s and up. There should be a a strong emphasis on the physical relationship between the couples. Fully described love scenes along with a high level of fantasy and playfulness." Length: 55,000-60,000 words.

HOW TO CONTACT No simultaneous submissions, electronic submissions, submissions on disk. Kathryn Lye, editor. Toronto, Canada. http://www.eharlequin.com/articlepage.html?articleId=544&chapter=0.

TERMS Pays royalty. Offers advance. Ms guidelines online.

TIPS "Are you a *Cosmo* girl at heart? A fan of *Sex and the City*? Or maybe you have a sexually adventurous spirit. If so, then Blaze is the series for you!"

HARLEQUIN DESIRE

233 Broadway, Suite 1001, New York NY 10279. (212)553-4200. Website: www.eharlequin.com. **Contact:** Krista Stroever. Always powerful, passionate, and provocative. Starting with April titles, Silhouette Desire books will be published as Harlequin Desire. "Desire novels are sensual reads and a love scene or scenes are still needed. But there is no set number of pages that needs to be fulfilled. Rather, the level of sensuality must be appropriate to the storyline. Above all, every Silhouette Desire novel must fulfill the promise of a powerful, passionate and provocative read." Publishes paperback originals and reprints. Books: newspaper print; web printing; perfect bound. **Published some debut authors within the last year.**

NEEDS romance. Looking for novels in which "the conflict is an emotional one, springing naturally from the unique characters you've chosen. The focus is on the developing relationship, set in a believable plot. Sensuality is key, but lovemaking is never taken lightly. Secondary characters and subplots need to blend with the core story. Innovative new directions in storytelling and fresh approaches to classic romantic plots are welcome." Manuscripts must be 50,000-55,000 words.

HOW TO CONTACT Does not accept unsolicited mss. Query with word count, brief bio, publishing history, synopsis (no more than 2 single-spaced pages), SASE/IRC. No simultaneous submissions. www.eharlequin.com.

TERMS Pays royalty. Offers advance. Detailed ms guidelines for SASE or on website.

HARLEQUIN HISTORICALS

Eton House, 18-24 Paradise Road, Richmond Surrey TW9 1SR United Kingdom. Website: www.eharlequin.com. **Contact:** Linda Fildew, senior editor. "The primary element of a Harlequin Historical novel is romance. The story should focus on the heroine and how her love for one man changes her life forever. For this reason, it is very important that you have an appealing hero and heroine, and that their relationship is a compelling one. The conflicts they must overcome—and the situations they face—can be as varied as the setting you have chosen, but there must be romantic tension, some spark between your hero and heroine that keeps your reader interested." Publishes paperback originals and reprints. Books: newsprint paper; perfect bound. **Published some debut authors within the last year.**

NEEDS romance (historical). "We will not accept books set after 1900. We're looking primarily for books set in North America, England or France between 1100 and 1900 A.D. We do not buy many novels set during the American Civil War. We are, however, flexible and will consider most periods and settings. We are not looking for gothics or family sagas, nor are we interested in the kind of comedy of manners typified by straight Regencies. Historical romances set during the Regency period, however, will definitely be considered." Length: 70,000-75,000/words.

HOW TO CONTACT Submit the first three chapters along with a 1-2 page synopsis of your novel.

TERMS Pays royalty. Offers advance. Ms guidelines online.

HARLEQUIN SUPERROMANCE

225 Duncan Mill Road, Don Mills ON M3B 3K9 Canada. Website: www.eharlequin.com. **Contact:** Victoria Curran, editor. "The Harlequin Superromance line focuses on believable characters triumphing over true-to-life drama and conflict. At the heart of these contemporary stories should be a compelling romance that brings the reader along with the hero and heroine on their journey of overcoming the obstacles in their way and falling in love. Because of the longer length relevant subplots and secondary characters are welcome but not required. This series publishes a variety of story types—family sagas, romantic suspense, Westerns, to name a few—and tones from light to dramatic, emotional to suspenseful. Settings also vary from vibrant urban neighborhoods to charming small towns. The unifying element of Harlequin Superromance stories is the realistic treatment of character and plot. The characters should seem familiar to readers—similar to people they know in their own lives—and the circumstances within the realm of possibility. The stories should be layered and complex in that the conflicts should not be easily resolved. The best way to get an idea of we're looking for is to read what we're currently publishing." "The aim of Superromance novels is to produce a contemporary, involving read with a mainstream tone in its situations and characters, using romance as the major theme. To achieve this, emphasis should be placed on individual writing styles and unique and topical ideas." Publishes paperback originals. Books: newspaper print; perfect bound.

NEEDS Romance (contemporary)."The criteria for Superromance books are flexible. Aside from length (70,000-75,000 words), the determining factor for publication will always be quality. Authors should strive to break free of stereotypes, clichés and worn-out plot devices to create strong, believable stories with depth and emotional intensity. Superromance novels are intended to appeal to a wide range of romance readers."

HOW TO CONTACT Accepts unsolicited submissions. Submit 3 sample chapter(s) and synopsis. Send SASE for return of ms or send a disposable ms and SASE for reply only. No simultaneous submissions, electronic submissions, submissions on disk. Victoria Curran, editor.

TERMS Pays royalty. Offers advance. Ms guidelines online.

TIPS "A general familiarity with current Superromance books is advisable to keep abreast of ever-changing trends and overall scope, but we don't want imitations. We look for sincere, heartfelt writing based on true-to-life experiences the reader can identify with. We are interested in innovation."

HARPERCOLLINS CHILDREN'S BOOKS / HARPERCOLLINS PUBLISHERS

10 East 53rd, New York NY 10022. (212)207-6901. E-mail: Dana.fritts@Harpercollins.com; Mischa.Rosenberg@Harpercollins.com. Website: www.Harpercollins.com. **Contact:** Mischa Rosenberg, assistant designer; Dana Fritts, designer. Imprints: HarperTrophy, HarperTeen, EOS, HarperFestival, Greenwillow Books, Joanna Cotler Books, Laura Geringer Books, Katherine Tegen Books.; Art samples may be sent to Martha Rago or Stephanie Bart-Horvath. *Please do not send original art.* Works with over 100 illustrators/year. Responds only if interested. Samples returned with SASE; samples filed only if interested.

IMPRINTS **HarperCollins Australia/New Zealand:** Angus & Robertson, Fourth Estate, HarperBusiness, HarperCollins, HarperPerenniel, HarperReligious, HarperSports, Voyager; **HarperCollins Canada**: HarperFlamingoCanada, PerennialCanada; **HarperCollins Children's Books Group:** Amistad, Julie Andrews Collection, Avon, Joanna Cotler Books, Eos, Laura Geringer Books, Greenwillow Books, HarperAudio, HarperCollins Children's Books, HarperFestival, HarperTempest, HarperTrophy, Rayo, Katherine Tegen Books; **HarperCollins General Books Group:** Access, Amistad, Avon, Caedmon, Ecco, Eos, Fourth Estate, HarperAudio, HarperBusiness, HarperCollins, HarperEntertainment, HarperLargePrint, HarperResource, HarperSanFrancisco, HarperTorch, Harper Design International, Perennial, PerfectBound, Quill, Rayo, ReganBooks, William Morrow, William Morrow Cookbooks; **HarperCollins UK:** Collins Bartholomew, Collins, HarperCollins Crime & Thrillers, Collins Freedom to Teach, HarperCollins Children's Books, Thorsons/Element, Voyager Books; **Zondervan:** Inspirio, Vida, Zonderkidz, Zondervan.

HOW TO CONTACT Only accepts agented mss.
TERMS Art guidelines available with SASE.
TIPS "We do not accept any unsolicited material."

HAWK PUBLISHING GROUP

7107 S. Yale Ave., #345, Tulsa OK 74136. (918)492-3677. Fax: (918)492-3677. Website: www.hawkpub.com. Estab. 1999. Independent publisher of general trade/commercial books, fiction and nonfiction. Publishes hardcover and trade paperback originals. **Published 4 debut authors within the last year.** Plans 2 first novels this year. Averages 6-8 total titles, 3 fiction titles/year. Member PMA. Titles are distributed by NBN/Biblio Distribution.

"Hawk Publishing is a royalty paying small press publisher of non-fiction instructional pamphlets, guides, cards, books and fine art photographic posters by some of today's most critically acclaimed artists, craftsmen, experts and hobbyists. We'll have three main imprints to start." "We will print various lengths from pamphlet or booklet form to actual books. We may also offer some manuscripts in ebook formats, where appropriate. Currently, manuscripts with a large number of graphics do not readily lend themselves to ebook formats, so we will make decisions on ebook offerings on a case by case basis."

IMPRINTS Art Works, Earth Works, Paper Works
NEEDS Looking for good books of all kinds. Not interested in juvenile, poetry, or short story collections. Published *I Survived Cancer*, by Jim Chastain; *Everlasting*, by Carol Johnson; *Ghost Band*, by John Wooley.
HOW TO CONTACT Accepts unsolicited mss. Submit first 20 pages of your book, synopsis, author bio. Include list of publishing credits. Accepts simultaneous submissions.
TERMS Pays royalty. Publishes ms 1-2 years after acceptance. Ms guidelines online.
TIPS "Prepare a professional submission and follow the guidelines. The simple things really do count; use 12 pt. pitch with 1-inch margins and only send what is requested."

HELICON NINE EDITIONS

Subsidiary of Midwest Center for the Literary Arts, Inc., P.O. Box 22412, Kansas City MO 64113. (816) 753-1016. E-mail: helicon9@aol.com. Website: www.heliconnine.com. **Contact:** Gloria Vando Hickok. Estab. 1990. Small, not-for-profit press publishing poetry, fiction, creative nonfiction, and anthologies. Publishes paperback originals. Also publishes one-story chapbooks called *feuillets*, which come with envelope, 250 print run. Books: 60 lb. paper; offset printing; perfect bound; 4-color cover. Average print order: 1,000-5,000. **Published 1 debut author within the last year.** Distributes titles through Baker & Taylor, Brodart, Ingrams, Follet (library acquisitions), and booksellers. Promotes titles through reviews, readings, radio, and television interviews.

HOW TO CONTACT Does not accept unsolicited mss.
TERMS Pays royalty. Author's copies. Offers advance. Publishes ms 12-18 months after acceptance.
TIPS "We accept short story collections, welcome new writers and first books. Submit a clean, readable copy in a folder or box—paginated with title and name on each page. Also, do not pre-design book, i.e., no illustrations, unless they are an integral part of the book. We'd like to see books that will be read 50-100 years from now."

HENDRICK-LONG PUBLISHING CO., INC.

10635 Tower Oaks, Suite D, Houston TX 77070. 832-912-READ. Fax: (832)912-7353. E-mail: hendrick-long@att.net. Website: hendricklongpublishing.com. **Contact:** Vilma Long. Estab. 1969. Only considers manuscripts with Texas theme. Publishes hardcover and trade paperback originals and hardcover reprints. Averages 4 total titles/year.

NEEDS Juvenile, young adult.
HOW TO CONTACT Submit outline, 2 sample chapter(s), synopsis. Responds in 3 months to queries. No simultaneous submissions. Please, no e-mail submissions.
TERMS Pays royalty on selling price. Offers advance. Publishes ms 18 months after acceptance. Book catalog for 8½×11 or 9×12 SASE with 4 first-class stamps. Ms guidelines online.

HENRY HOLT

Henry Holt and Company, 175 Fifth Avenue, New York NY 10011. (646)307-5095. Website: www.henryholt.com. Publishes hardcover and paperback originals and reprints.

HOW TO CONTACT Closed to submissions. *Agented submissions only.*

BOOK PUBLISHERS

HESPERUS PRESS

19 Bulstrode St., London W1U 2JN UK. +44 (0) 20 7486 5005. E-mail: info@hesperuspress.com. Website: www.hesperuspress.com. Estab. 2001. Hesperus is a small, independent publisher mainly of classic literary fiction translated fiction, and biographies of literary figures. Publishes paperback originals. Books: munken paper; traditional printing; sewn binding. Average print order: 2,000. Distributes titles through Trafalgar Square in the US, Grantham Book Services in the UK. 19 Bulstrode St., London W1U 2JN, UK. Phone: +44 (0) 20 7486 5005.

Does not accept unsolicited mss. *Agented submissions only.* Query with SASE. Accepts queries by mail. Include estimated word count, brief bio, list of publishing credits. Agented fiction 100%. No submissions on disk.

NEEDS literary. Published *Carlyle's House*, by Virginia Woolf (rediscovered modern classic); *No Man's Land*, by Graham Greene (rediscovered modern classic); *The Princess of Mantua*, by Marie Ferranti (award-winning fiction in translation); *The Maytrees*, by Annie Dillard (new fiction).

HOW TO CONTACT Does not accept unsolicited mss. *Agented submissions only.* Query with SASE. Accepts queries by mail. Include estimated word count, brief bio, list of publishing credits. Agented fiction 100%. Responds in 8-10 weeks to queries; 8-10 weeks to mss. Accepts simultaneous submissions. No submissions on disk.

TIPS Find an agent to represent you.

HIGHLAND PRESS PUBLISHING

P.O. Box 2292, High Springs FL 32655. (386) 454-3927. Fax: (386) 454-3927. E-mail: The.Highland.Press@gmail.com; submissions.hp@gmail.com. Website: www.highlandpress.org. **Contact:** Leanne Burroughs, CEO (fiction); she will forward all mss to appropriate editor. Estab. 2005. "With our focus on historical romances, Highland Press Publishing is known as your 'Passport to Romance.' We focus on historical romances and our award-winning anthologies. Many people have told us they can once again delight in reading with the anthologies, since they do not have to feel guilty about reading and then putting a book down before it is finished. With the short stories/novellas, they can read a heart warming story, yet still get back to the demands of today's busy lives. As for our historicals, we publish historical novels like many of us grew up with and loved. History is a big part of the story and is tactfully woven throughout the romance." Publishes paperback originals, paperback reprints. Format: off set printing; perfect bound. Average print order: 1,000. Debut novel print order: 1,000. **Published 15 new writers last year.** Plans 25 debut authors this year. Averages 30 total titles/year; 30 fiction titles/year. Distributes/promotes titles through Ingrams, Baker & Taylor, Nielsen, Powells.

Highland Wishes was a 2006 Winner, Reviewers International Award of Excellence. *Blue Moon Enchantment* won the 2007 P.E.A.R.L. Award (two separate stories). *Christmas Wishes* received the 2007 Linda Howard Award of Excellence. *Her Highland Rogue* received the 2006 Reviewer's International Award, the 2006 National Readers Choice Award and was a 2007 finalist for Readers and Booksellers Best. *Cat O'Nine Tales* had several stories as finalists or won the 2007 P.E.A.R.L. Award, 2007 Linda Howard Award of Excellence, and the 2007 Reviewers International Organization Award of Excellence. *Highland Wishes* was a Finalist, 2005 Readers and Booksellers Best and 2006 Winner, Reviewers International Award of Excellence. *Faery Special Romances* was a nominee for 2007 Night Owl Romances. *Christmas Wishes* had several stories nominated for the 2007 P.E.A.R.L. Award and received the 2007 Linda Howard Award of Excellence.

NEEDS children's/juvenile (adventure, animal, easy-to-read, fantasy, historical, mystery, preschool/picture book, series), comedy (romance/suspense), contemporary (romance/mystery/suspense); family saga, fantasy (space fantasy), historical, horror (dark fantasy, futuristic, supernatural), mainstream, military/war, mystery/suspense (amateur/sleuth, cozy, police, private eye/hardboiled), religious (children's, general, family, inspirational, fantasy, mystery/suspense, thriller, romance), romance (contemporary, futuristic/time travel, gothic, historical, regency period, suspense), short story collections, thriller/espionage, western (frontier saga, traditional), young adult/teen (adventure, paranormal, fantasy/science fiction, historical, horror, mystery/suspense, romance, series, western, chapter books).

HOW TO CONTACT Send query letter. Query with outline/synopsis and sample chapters. Accepts queries by snail mail, e-mail. Include estimated word count, target market. Send disposable copy of ms and SASE for reply only. Agented fiction: 10%. Responds to queries in 8 weeks. Accepts unsolicited mss. Considers simultaneous submissions, e-mail submissions. Sometimes critiques/comments on rejected mss. Responds to mss in 3-12 months.

TERMS Sends preproduction galleys to author. Ms published within 12 months after acceptance. Writer's guidelines on Website. Pays royalties 7.5-8%. Book catalogs on Website.

TIPS Special interests: Children's ms must come with illustrator. "We will always be looking for good historical manuscripts. In addition, we are actively seeking inspirational romances and Regency period romances." Numerous romance anthologies are planned. Topics and word count are posted on the Website. Writers should query with their proposal. After the submission deadline has passed, editors select the stories. "I don't publish based on industry trends. We buy what we like and what we believe readers are looking for. However, often this proves to be the genres and time-periods larger publishers are not currently interested in. Be professional at all times. Present your manuscript in the best possible light. Be sure you have run spell check and that the manuscript has been vetted by at least one critique partner, preferably more. Many times we receive manuscripts that have wonderful stories involved, but would take far too much time to edit to make it marketable."

HOLIDAY HOUSE, INC.

425 Madison Ave., New York NY 10017. (212)688-0085. Fax: (212)421-6134. E-mail: info@holidayhouse.com. Website: holidayhouse.com. **Contact:** Mary Cash, editor-in-chief. Estab. 1935. Publishes 35 picture books/year; 3 young readers/year; 15 middle readers/year; 8 young adult titles/year. 20% of books by first-time authors; 10% from agented writers. Mission Statement: "To publish high-quality books for children."

"Holiday House is an independent publisher of children's books only. We specialize in quality hardcovers, from picture books to young adult, both fiction and nonfiction. We publish children's books for ages four and up. We do not publish mass-market books, including, but not limited to, pop-ups, activity books, sticker books, coloring books, or licensed books."

NEEDS all levels of young readers: adventure, contemporary, fantasy, folktales, ghost, historical, humor, literary, multicultural, school, suspense/mystery, sports. Recently published *Anansi's Party Time*, by Eric Kimmel, illustrated by Janet Stevens; *The Blossom Family* series, by Betsy Byars; *Washington at Valley Forge*, by Russell Freedman.

HOW TO CONTACT Send queries only to editor. Responds to queries in 3 months; mss in 4 months. "If we find your book idea suits our present needs, we will notify you by mail." Once a ms has been requested, the writers should send in the exclusive submission. Please send the entire manuscript, whether submitting a picture book or novel. All submissions should be directed to the Editorial Department, Holiday House, 425 Madison Ave., New York, NY 10017. Send your manuscript via U.S. Mail. We do not accept certified or registered mail. There is no need to include a SASE. We do not consider submissions by e-mail or fax. Please note that you do not have to supply illustrations. However, if you have illustrations you would like to include with your submission, you may send detailed sketches or photocopies of the original art. Do not send original art.

TERMS Pays authors and illustrators an advance against royalties. Originals returned at job's completion. Book catalog, ms guidelines available for a SASE.

TIPS "We need manuscripts with strong stories and writing."

HOMA & SEKEY BOOKS

P.O. Box 103, Dumont NJ 07628. Fax: (201)384-6055. E-mail: info@homabooks.com. E-mail: submission@homabooks.com. Website: www.homabooks.com. **Contact:** Shawn Ye, editor (fiction and nonfiction). Estab. 1997. Homa & Sekey Books, 3rd Floor, North Tower, Mack-Cali Center III, 140 East Ridgewood Ave, Paramus NJ 07652. (201)261-8810. Fax: (201)261-8890. E-mail: submission@homabooks.com. Website: www.homabooks.com. "We focus on publishing East Asia-related titles. Both translations and original English manuscripts are welcome." Publishes hardcover and paperback originals. Books: natural paper; web press; perfect bound; illustrations. **Published 3 debut authors within the last year.** Averages 7 total titles, 3 fiction titles/year. Member PMA. Distributes titles through Ingram, Baker & Taylor, etc.

NEEDS ethnic (Asian), literary, mystery, young adult (adventure, historical, mystery/suspense, romance).

Wants China-related titles. Published *Willow Leaf, Maple Leaf: A Novel of Immigration Blue*, by David Ke; *The Curse of Kim's Daughter*, by Park Kyong-Ni (translation); *A Floating City on The Water* (translation).

HOW TO CONTACT Accepts unsolicited mss. Query with SASE or submit outline, 2 sample chapter(s). Accepts queries by e-mail (as attachments), mail (Address: Acquisitions Editor, Homa & Sekey Books, P. O. Box 103, Dumont, NJ 07628. Include estimated word count, brief bio, list of publishing credits and marketing analysis. Send SASE for return of ms or send a disposable ms and SASE for reply only. Responds in 8 weeks to queries; 8-10 weeks to proposals; 20 weeks to mss. Accepts simultaneous submissions, electronic submissions. Sometimes comments on rejected mss.

TERMS Pays 5-10% royalty. Publishes ms 1 year after acceptance. Book catalog for 9×12 SASE. Ms guidelines online.

HOPEWELL PUBLICATIONS

P.O. Box 11, Titusville NJ 08560. Website: www.hopepubs.com. **Contact:** E. Martin, publisher. Estab. 2002. "Hopewell Publications specializes in classic reprints—books with proven sales records that have gone out of print—and the occasional new title of interest. Our catalog spans from one to sixty years of publication history. We print fiction and nonfiction, and we accept agented and unagented materials. Books are only accepted after a formal email query. Please follow our online query guidelines. While it may take months for us to respond, your query will be read, and if we are interested, we will contact you." Imprints: Egress Books, Legacy Classics. Format publishes in hardcover, trade paperback, & electronic originals; trade paperback & electronic reprints. Publishes 20-30 titles/year. Accepts unagented work. Receives 2,000 queries/year; 500 mss/year. Time from acceptance to publication is 6-12 months. SASE returns. Responds in 3 months on queries; 6 months on proposals; 9 months on mss. Catalog online at website. Guidelines online at website (e-mail query guidelines) www.hopepubs.com.

IMPRINTS Egress Books, Legacy Classics.

NEEDS adventure, contemporary, experimental, fantasy, gay, historical, humor, juvenile, literary, mainstream, mystery, plays, short story collections, spiritual, suspense, young adult. All fiction subjects.

TERMS Pays royalty on retail price.

HOUGHTON MIFFLIN HARCOURT CHILDREN'S BOOKS

215 Park Ave. S., New York NY 10003. Website: www.hmhbooks.com. Estab. 1919. The Children's Book Division will read unsolicited manuscripts. Please send them to us by conventional mail only. We do not accept e-mailed or faxed manuscripts. Because confirmation postcards are easily separated from the manuscript or hidden, we do not encourage you to include them with your submission. We prefer a typed (letter-quality), double-spaced manuscript on unfolded plain white paper in a 9 x 12 envelope. We do not accept manuscripts that are handwritten or submitted on computer disk. You do not have to furnish illustrations, but if you wish, copies of a few comprehensive sketches or duplicate copies of original art will suffice. For fiction we prefer to see the entire manuscript, and for nonfiction a synopsis and sample chapters. 20% of books by first-time authors; 75% of books from agented writers. "Harcourt Children's Books publishes hardcover picture books and fiction only."

HOW TO CONTACT Submission, Houghton Mifflin Harcourt Children's Books, 222 Berkeley St., Boston, MA 02116-3764.

TERMS Pays authors royalty based on retail price. Sends preproduction galleys to authors.

HOUGHTON MIFFLIN HARCOURT CO.

222 Berkeley St., Boston MA 02116. (617)351-5000. Website: www.hmhco.com; www.hmhbooks.com. Estab. 1832. Publishes hardcover originals and trade paperback originals and reprints. **Published 5 debut authors within the last year.** Averages 250 total titles/year.

> "Houghton Mifflin Harcourt gives shape to ideas that educate, inform and delight. In a new era of publishing, our legacy of quality thrives as we combine imagination with technology, bringing you new ways to know."

IMPRINTS American Heritage Dictionaries; Clarion Books; Great Source Education Group; Houghton Mifflin; Houghton Mifflin Books for Children; Houghton Mifflin Paperbacks; Mariner Books; McDougal Littell; Peterson Field Guides; Riverside Publishing; Sunburst Technology; Taylor's Gardening Guides; Edusoft; Promissor; Walter Lorraine Books; Kingfisher.

NEEDS literary. "We are not a mass market publisher. Study the current list." Published *Extremely Loud and Incredibly Close*, by Jonathan Safran Foer; *The Plot against America*, by Philip Roth; *Heir to the Glimmering World*, by Cynthia Ozick.

HOW TO CONTACT Does not accept unsolicited mss. *Agented submissions only.* Accepts simultaneous submissions.

TERMS Hardcover: pays 10-15% royalty on retail price, sliding scale, or flat rate based on sales; paperback: 7½% flat rate, but negotiable. Average advance: variable. Publishes ms 3 years after acceptance.

ILIUM PRESS

2407 S. Sonora Dr., Spokane WA 99037-9011. (509)928-7950. E-mail: contact@iliumpress.com; submissions@iliumpress.com. Website: www.iliumpress.com. **Contact:** John Lemon, Owner/editor (literature, epic poetry, how-to). Estab. 2010.

TIPS "Read submission guidelines on my website."

IMAGE COMICS

Submissions, c/o Image Comics, 2134 Allston Way, 2nd Floor, Berkeley CA 94704. E-mail: submissions@imagecomics.com. Website: www.imagecomics.com. **Contact:** Eric Stephenson, publisher. Estab. 1992. "We are looking for good, well-told stories and exceptional artwork that run the gamut in terms of both style and genre. Image is a comics and graphic novels publisher formed by seven of Marvel Comics' best-selling artists: Erik Larsen, Jim Lee, Rob Liefeld, Todd McFarlane, Whilce Portacio, Marc Silvestri, and Jim Valentino. Since that time, Image has gone on to become the third largest comics publisher in the United States."

NEEDS "We are not looking for any specific genre or type of comic book. We are looking for comics that are well written and well drawn, by people who are dedicated and can meet deadlines."

HOW TO CONTACT Query with 1 page synopsis and 5 pages or more of samples. "We do not accept writing (that is plots, scripts, whatever) samples! If you're an established pro, we might be able to find somebody willing to work with you but it would be nearly impossible for us to read through every script that might find its way our direction. Do not send your script or your plot unaccompanied by art—it will be discarded, unread." Accepts queries by snail mail, e-mail. Sometimes critiques/comments on rejected mss.

TERMS Writer's guidelines on website.

IMAJINN BOOKS

P.O. Box 74274, Phoenix AZ 85087-4274. (623)236-3361. E-mail: editors@imajinnbooks.com. Website: www.imajinnbooks.com. **Contact:** Linda J. Kichline, editor. Estab. 1998. "ImaJinn Books, Inc. is a small independent print-on-demand publishing house that specializes in Regency Romance, Urban Fantasy, and paranormal romances with story lines involving psychics or psychic phenomena, witches, vampires, werewolves, space travel, the future." Publishes trade paperback originals. Books: print-on-demand; perfect binding; no illustrations. **Published 3-4 debut authors per year.** Distributes titles through Ingram Books and imajinnbooks.com. Promotes titles through advertising and review magazines.

NEEDS fantasy (romance), horror (romance), psychic/supernatural (romance), all Urban Fantasy story lines, and all Regency romance story lines. "We look for specific story lines based on what the readers are asking for and what story lines in which we're short. We post our current needs on our website." Published *Half Past Hell*, by Jaye Roycraft (horror romance); *Grave Illusions*, by Lina Gardiner (urban fantasy), and *The Hermitage*, by Sharon Sobel (Regency romance).

HOW TO CONTACT Query by e-mail only. Include estimated word count, brief bio, list of publishing credits. Agented fiction 20%. Responds in 3 months to queries; 9-12 months to mss. Often comments on rejected mss.

TERMS Pays 6-10% royalty on retail price. Average advance: 100-200. Publishes ms 1-3 years after acceptance. Book catalog and ms guidelines online.

TIPS "Carefully read the author guidelines, and read books published by ImaJinn Books. Do not submit manuscript without querying first."

INGALLS PUBLISHING GROUP, INC

P.O. Box 2500, Banner Elk NC 28604. E-mail: editor@ingallspublishinggroup.com; sales@ingallspublishinggroup.com. (828)297-6884. Fax: (828)297-1057. Website: www.ingallspublishinggroup.com. **Contact:** Rebecca Owen, Operations and Sales Manager. Estab. 2001. "We are a small regional house focusing on popular fiction and memoir. At present, we are most interested in regional fiction, historical fiction and mystery fiction." Publishes hardcover originals, paperback originals and paperback reprints. Exploring digital technologies for printing and e-books. Member IBPA, MWA, SIBA.

NEEDS regional (southeast US), mystery (amateur sleuth, cozy, police procedural, private eye/hard-boiled), regional (southern Appalachian), romance (contemporary, historical, romantic suspense adventure). Upcoming list for 2011 includes: *Corpus Conundrum: A Third Case from the Notebooks of Pliny the Younger*, by Albert A. Bell Jr.; *The Chamomile*, by Susan F. Craft; *The Ninth Man*, by Brad Crowther; *One Shot Too Many*, by Maggie Bishop; *The Ocean Forest*, by Troy Nooe; *Naked and Hungry*, by Ashley Memory and *Getorix: Games of the Underworld*, by Judith Geary.

HOW TO CONTACT Accepts unsolicited mss. Query first. Will specifically request if interested in reading synopsis and 3 sample chapters. Accepts queries by e-mail. Include estimated word count, brief bio, list of publishing credits. Agented fiction 10%. Responds in 6 weeks to queries or mss. Accepts simultaneous submissions, electronic submissions. No submissions on disk. Often comments on rejected mss.

TERMS Pays 10% royalty. Publishes ms 6 months-2 years after acceptance. Ms guidelines online.

INSOMNIAC PRESS

520 Princess Ave., London ON N6B 2B8 Canada. (416)504-6270. E-mail: mike@insomniacpress.com. Website: www.insomniacpress.com. **Contact:** Mike O'Connor, publisher. Estab. 1992. "Midsize independent publisher with a mandate to produce edgy experimental fiction." Publishes trade paperback originals and reprints, mass market paperback originals, and electronic originals and reprints. First novel print order: 3,000. **Published 15 debut authors within the last year.** Plans 4 first novels this year. Averages 20 total titles, 5 fiction titles/year. We publish a mix of commercial (mysteries) and literary fiction. Published *Pray for Us Sinners*, by Patrick Taylor (novel). Agented fiction 5%. Responds in 1 week to queries; 2 months to mss. Accepts simultaneous submissions. Sometimes comments on rejected mss. Ms guidelines online.

NEEDS Comic books, ethnic, experimental, gay/lesbian, humor, literary, mainstream/contemporary, multicultural, mystery, suspense.

HOW TO CONTACT Accepts unsolicited mss. Accepts queries by e-mail. Include estimated word count, brief bio, list of publishing credits. Send SASE for return of ms or send a disposable ms and SASE for reply only.

TERMS Pays 10-15% royalty on retail price. Average advance: $500-1,000. Publishes ms 6 months after acceptance.

TIPS "We envision a mixed readership that appreciates up-and-coming literary fiction and poetry as well as solidly researched and provocative nonfiction. Peruse our website and familiarize yourself with what we've published in the past."

INTERLINK PUBLISHING GROUP, INC.

46 Crosby St., Northampton MA 01060. (413)582-7054. Fax: (413)582-7057. E-mail: info@interlinkbooks.com; editor@interlinkbooks.com. Website: www.interlinkbooks.com. **Contact:** Michel Moushabeck, publisher; Pam Thompson, editor. Estab. 1987. "Midsize independent publisher specializing in world travel, world literature, world history and politics." Publishes hardcover and trade paperback originals. Books: 55 lb. Warren Sebago Cream white paper; web offset printing; perfect binding. Average print order: 5,000. Published new writers within the last year. Averages 50 total titles, 2-4 fiction titles/year. Distributes titles through Baker & Taylor. Promotes titles through book mailings to extensive, specialized lists of editors and reviews; authors read at bookstores and special events across the country.

IMPRINTS Crocodile Books, USA; Codagan Guides, USA; Interlink Books; Olive Branch Press; Clockroot Books.

NEEDS ethnic, international. "Adult—We are looking for translated works relating to the Middle East, Africa or Latin America." Recently published *Everything Good Will Come*, by Sefi Atta (first novel); *The Gardens of Light*, by Amin Maalouf (novel translated from French); *War in the Land of Egypt*, by Yusef Al-Qaid (novel translated from Arabic).

HOW TO CONTACT "Become familiar with the kinds of books we publish. Request a catalog or read them at your local library, If you believe your ms might fit our list, please send a query letter to the attention of Pam Thompson. The query letter may (but doesn't have to) include any of the following: a writing sample (preferably the opening of the book) of no more than 10 pages, a brief synopsis and bio. Send an SASE as well. The only fiction we publish falls into our 'Interlink WorldFiction' series. Most of these books, as you can see in our catalog, are translated fiction from around the world. The idea behind the series is to bring fiction from other countries to a North American audience. So unless you were born outside the United States, your novel will not fit into the series. All of our children's books are picture books designed for ages 3-8. We publish very few of them, and most are co-published with overseas publishing houses. We do not consider unsolicited manuscripts of children's books." Query with SASE and a brief sample. Responds in 3 months to queries. Accepts simultaneous submissions. No electronic submissions. Interlink Publishing Group, Inc., 46 Crosby St., Northampton MA 01060.

TERMS Pays 6-8% royalty on retail price. Average advance: small. Publishes ms 18 months after acceptance. Ms guidelines online.

TIPS "Any submissions that fit well in our publishing program will receive careful attention. A visit to our website, your local bookstore, or library to look at some of our books before you send in your submission is recommended."

INVERTED-A

P.O. Box 267, Licking MO 65542. E-mail: amnfn@well.com. **Contact:** Aya Katz, chief editor (poetry, novels, political); Nets Katz, science editor (scientific, academic). Estab. 1985. Publishes paperback originals. Books: offset printing. Average print order: 1,000. Average first novel print order: 500. Distributes through Baker & Taylor, Amazon, Bowker.

NEEDS Utopian, political. Needs poetry submission for our newsletter, *Inverted-A Horn*.

HOW TO CONTACT Does not accept unsolicited mss. Query with SASE. Reading period open from January 2 to March 15. Accepts queries by e-mail. Include estimated word count. Responds in 1 month to queries; 3 months to mss. Accepts simultaneous submissions. Sometimes comments on rejected mss.

TERMS Pays in 10 author's copies. Publishes ms 1 year after acceptance. Ms guidelines for SASE.

TIPS "Read our books. Read the *Inverted-A Horn*. We are different. We do not follow industry trends."

ION IMAGINATION PUBLISHING

A division of Ion Imagination Entertainment, Inc., P.O. Box 210943, Nashville TN 37221-0943. Fax: (615)646-6276. E-mail: ionimagin@aol.com. Website: www.flumpa.com. **Contact:** Keith Frickey, editor. Estab. 1994. Small, independent publisher of science-related children's fiction, multimedia and audio products. Publishes hardcover and paperback originals. Average first novel print order: 10,000. Member SPAN and PMA.

Received the Parents' Choice, National Parenting Centers Seal of Approval, Dr. Toy, Parent Council.

NEEDS children's/juvenile (adventure, animal, preschool/picture book, science).

HOW TO CONTACT Does not accept unsolicited mss. Query with SASE. Include brief bio, list of publishing credits. Responds in 1 month to queries. Accepts simultaneous submissions. Sometimes comments on rejected queries.

TERMS Pays royalty.

ITALICA PRESS

595 Main St., Suite 605, New York NY 10044-0047. (212)935-4230. Fax: (212)838-7812. E-mail: inquiries@italicapress.com. Website: www.italicapress.com. **Contact:** Ronald G. Musto and Eileen Gardiner, publishers. Estab. 1985. Small, independent publisher of Italian fiction in translation. "First-time translators published. We would like to see translations of Italian writers who are well-known in Italy who are not yet translated for an American audience." Publishes trade paperback originals. Books: 50-60 lb. natural paper; offset printing; illustrations. Average print order: 1,500. Averages 6 total titles, 2 fiction titles/year. Distributes/promotes titles through website.

NEEDS Translations of 20th-century Italian fiction. Published *Game Plan for a Novel*, by Gianna Manzini; *The Great Bear*, by Ginevra Bompianai; *Sparrow*, by Giovanni Verga.

HOW TO CONTACT Accepts unsolicited mss. Query with SASE. Accepts queries by e-mail, fax. Responds in 1 month to queries; 2 months to mss. Accepts simultaneous submissions, electronic submissions, submissions on disk. **Mail:** Italica Press, 595 Main Street, Suite 605, New York, NY 10044, **Fax:** 212-838-7812. **E-mail:** inquiries@italicapress.com.

TERMS Pays 7-15% royalty on wholesale price. Pays author's copies. Publishes ms 1 year after acceptance. Ms guidelines online.

TIPS "We are interested in considering a wide variety of medieval and Renaissance topics (not historical fiction), and for modern works we are only interested in translations from Italian fiction by well-known Italian authors." *Only* fiction that has been previously published in Italian. A *brief* call saves a lot of postage. 90% of proposals we receive are completely off base—but we are very interested in things that are right on target. Please send return postage if you want your *only* fiction that has been previously published in Italian.

◐ JOHN F. BLAIR, PUBLISHER

1406 Plaza Dr., Winston-Salem NC 27103-1470. (336)768-1374. Fax: (336)768-9194. Website: www.blairpub.com. **Contact:** Carolyn Sakowski, president. Estab. 1954. Small, independent publisher. Publishes hardcover originals and trade paperbacks. Books: Acid-free paper; offset printing; illustrations. Averages 20 total titles/year.

NEEDS We specialize in regional books, with an emphasis on nonfiction categories such as history, travel, folklore, and biography. We publish only one or two works of fiction each year. Fiction submitted to us should have some connection with the Southeast. We do not publish children's books, poetry, or category fiction such as romances, science fiction, or spy thrillers. We do not publish collections of short stories, essays, or newspaper columns. Published *The Minotaur Takes a Cigarette Break*, by Steven Sherrill; *Rocks That Float*, by Kathy Steele.

HOW TO CONTACT Accepts unsolicited mss. Any fiction submitted should have some connection with the Southeast, either through setting or author's background. Send a cover letter, giving a synopsis of the book. Include the first two chapters (at least 50 pages) of the manuscript. You may send the entire manuscript if you wish. If you choose to send only samples, please include the projected word length of your book and estimated completion date in your cover letter. Send a biography of the author, including publishing credits and credentials. Responds in 3 months to queries. Accepts simultaneous submissions. Do NOT submit original artwork or photography, and please make a copy of your ms. Please note that materials unaccompanied by a SASE will not be returned. We do not accept proposals on disks, over the Internet, or by fax. Mail all submissions to: Acquisitions Committee, John F. Blair, Publisher, 1406 Plaza Drive, Winston-Salem, NC 27103.

TERMS Royalty negotiable. Offers advance. Publishes ms 18 months after acceptance. Book catalog online.

TIPS "We are primarily interested in nonfiction titles. Most of our titles have a tie-in with North Carolina or the southeastern United States, we do not accept short-story collections. Please enclose a cover letter and outline with the manuscript. We prefer to review queries before we are sent complete manuscripts. Queries should include an approximate word count."

JOURNEYFORTH

Imprint of BJU Press, 1700 Wade Hampton Blvd., Greenville SC 29614. (864)242-5100, ext. 4350. Fax: (864)298-0268. E-mail: jb@bju.edu. Website: www.journeyforth.com. **Contact:** Nancy Lohr. Estab. 1974. "Small independent publisher of excellent, trustworthy novels for readers pre-school through high school. We desire to develop in our children a love for and understanding of the written word, ultimately helping them love and understand God's word." Publishes paperback originals. Average print order varies. Published some debut authors within the last year. Averages 20-24 total titles. Distributes titles through Genesis/Spring Arbor and Appalachian.

NEEDS adventure (children's/juvenile, young adult), historical (children's/juvenile, young adult), juvenile (animal, easy-to-read, series), mystery (children's/juvenile, young adult), sports (children's/juvenile, young adult), suspense (young adult), western (young adult), young adult (series). "Our fiction is all based on a moral and Christian worldview." Published *Susannah and the Secret Coins*, by Elaine Schulte (historical children's fiction); *Arby Jenkins Meets His Match*, by Sharon Hambrick (contemporary children's fiction); *Over the Divide*, by Catherine Farnes (young adult fiction); *Beyond the Smoke*, by Terry Burns (young adult western); *What about Cimmaron?* by Laurain Snelling (youth fiction).

HOW TO CONTACT Accepts unsolicited mss. Query with SASE or submit outline, 5 sample chapters or submit complete ms. Include estimated word count, brief bio, list of publishing credits. Send SASE for return of ms or send a disposable ms and SASE for reply only. Responds 3 months to mss.

TERMS Pays royalty. Publishes ms 12-18 months after acceptance. Ms guidelines online. Guidelines at http://www.bjupress.com/books/freelance.php.

TIPS "Study the publisher's guidelines. No picture books and no submissions by e-mail."

JUPITER GARDENS PRESS

Jupiter Gardens, LLC, PO Box 191, Grimes IA 50111-0191. E-mail: submissions@jupitergardens.com. Website: www.jupitergardens.com. **Contact:** Mary Wilson, publisher (romance, sf/f, new age). Estab. 2007. "We only publish romance (all sub-genres), science fiction & fantasy & metaphysical fiction. Our science fiction and fantasy covers a wide variety of topics, such as feminist fantasy, or more hard science fiction and fantasy which looks at the human condition. Our young adult imprint, Jupiter Storm, with thought provoking reads that explore the full range of speculative fiction, includes science fiction or fantasy and metaphysical fiction. These readers would enjoy edgy contemporary works. Our romance readers love seeing a couple, no matter the gender, overcome obstacles and grow in order to find true love. Like our readers, we believe that love can come in many forms."

IMPRINTS Pink Petal Books, Mary Wilson, publisher; Jupiter Storm, Sasha Vivelo, senior editor.

HOW TO CONTACT "To submit your work for consideration, please email submissions@jupitergardens.com with a cover letter detailing your writing experience (if any, we do welcome new authors), and attach in DOC or RTF format, a 2-4 page synopsis, and the first 3 chapters. Our current response time is 2-4 weeks. We accept simultaneous submissions, but ask that you be prepared to allow us our regular response times."

TIPS "No matter which line you're submitting to, know your genre and your readership. We publish a diverse catalog, and we're passionate about our main focus. We want romance that takes your breath away and leaves you with that warm feeling that love does conquer all. Our science fiction takes place in wild and alien worlds, and our fantasy transports readers to mythical realms and finds strange worlds within our own. And our metaphysical non-fiction will help readers gain new skills and awareness for the coming age. We want authors who engage with their readers and who aren't afraid to use social media to connect. Read and follow our submission guidelines."

JUST US BOOKS, INC.

356 Glenwood Ave, Third Floor, East Orange NJ 07017. (973)672-7701. Fax: (973)677-7570. E-mail: katura_hudson@justusbooks.com; cheryl_hudson@justusbooks.com. Website: www.facebook.com/JustUsBooks. **Contact:** Wade and Cheryl Hudson. Estab. 1988. Small, independent publisher of children's books that focus on black history, culture, and experiences (fiction and nonfiction). Publishes hardcover originals, paperback originals, hardcover reprints, and paperback reprints (under its Sankofa Books imprint for previously published titles). Averages 4-8 total titles, 2-4 fiction titles/year. Member, Small Press Association; Children Book Council.

NEEDS ethnic (African American), young adult (adventure, easy-to-read, historical, mystery/suspense, problem novels, series, sports). Published *Path to My African Eyes*, by Ermila Moodley; *12 Brown Boys*, by Omar Tyree.

HOW TO CONTACT Currently accepting queries for young adult titles only. We are not considering picture books, poetry, activity books, or any other manuscripts at this time. Query with SASE, ms synopsis, and pitch letter by mail only. Include brief bio, list of publishing credits. Send SASE for reply. Responds to queries in 10-12 weeks. Accepts simultaneous submissions.

TERMS Pays royalty. Ms guidelines for SASE or on website.

TIPS "We are looking for realistic, contemporary characters; stories and interesting plots that introduce both conflict and resolution. We will consider various themes and story-lines, but before an author submits a query we urge them to become familiar with our books."

KAEDEN BOOKS

P.O. Box 16190, Rocky River OH 44116. E-mail: lstenger@kaeden.com. Website: www.kaeden.com. **Contact:** Lisa Stenger, editor. Estab. 1986. Kaeden Books produces high-quality children's books for the educational market. At this time, we have a particular need for beginning chapter books and unique non-fiction manuscripts. **Fiction:** We are looking for stories with humor, surprise endings, and interesting characters that will appeal to children in pre-kindergarten through second grade. **Nonfiction:** Manuscripts should have interesting topics and information presented in language comprehensible to young students. Content should be supported with details and accurate facts. **Length:** Can be as minimal as 25 words for the earliest reader or as much as 2,000 words for the fluent reader. Beginning chapter books are welcome. **Text:** Our readers are in grades prekindergarten to second grade, so vocabulary and sentence structure must be appropriate for young readers. Make sure that all language used in the story is of an appropriate level for the students to read independently. Sentences should be complete and grammatically correct. No sentence fragments. Please do not submit: queries, manuscript summaries, or résumés, manuscripts that stereotype or demean individuals or groups, manuscripts that present violence as acceptable behavior.

NEEDS stories with humor suitable for the education market. "Must have well-developed plots with clear beginnings, middles and endings. No adult or religious themes." Word count range: 25-2,000.

HOW TO CONTACT Submissions should be sent to: Editorial Department, Kaeden Books, P.O. Box 16190, Rocky River, OH 44116. Submit complete ms; include SASE. Do not send originals. Respond within 1 year. For complete guidelines see www.kaeden.com. No phone calls, please.

TERMS Work purchased outright from authors. Pays royalties to previous authors.

TIPS "Our audience ranges from Kindergarten-2nd grade school children. We are an educational publisher. We are particularly interested in humorous stories with surprise endings and beginning chapter books."

KEARNEY STREET BOOKS

P.O. Box 2021, Bellingham WA 98227. (360)738-1355. E-mail: garyrmc@mac.com. Website: http://kearneystreetbooks.com.

NEEDS Only publishes books about music or musicians. Published *Such a Killing Crime*, Robert Lopresti (mystery); *Tribute to Orpheus* (short story collection).

HOW TO CONTACT Send query letter first. Accepts queries by e-mail. Send disposable copy of ms and SASE for reply only. Responds to queries in 1 week. Accepts unsolicited mss. Responds to mss in 6-10 months. Considers simultaneous submissions, submissions on CD or disk. Never critiques/comments on rejected mss. Does not return rejected mss. Phone: (360)738-1355. Email: garyrmc@mac.com. Website: http://kearneystreetbooks.com. Address: P.O. Box 2021, Bellingham, WA 98227.

TERMS Sends preproduction galleys to author. Manuscript published 18 months after acceptance. Pays "after expenses, profits split 50/50."

TIPS "We publish very few titles. Nobody makes any money. This is all about the love of good fiction shunned by the corporations."

Ⓐ KENSINGTON PUBLISHING CORP.

119 West 40th St., New York NY 10018. (800)221-2647; (212)407-1500. E-mail: kensingtonmarketing@kensingtonbooks.com; jscognamiglio@kensingtonbooks.com. Website: www.kensingtonbooks.com. **Contact:** John Scognamiglio, editor-in-chief. Estab. 1975. Full-service trade commercial publisher, all formats. Publishes hardcover and trade paperback originals, mass market paperback originals and reprints. Averages over 500 total titles/year.

NEEDS Book-length fiction and nonfiction for popular audiences. Adult and YA.

HOW TO CONTACT Accepts unsolicited and unagented mss. You may **QUERY ONLY** by e-mail. Do not attach manuscripts or proposals to e-mail queries. An editor will respond if he or she is interested in seeing your material based on your query. Submit to one editor only. Responds in 1 month to queries; 4 months to mss. Accepts simultaneous submissions. John Scognamiglio, Editor-in-Chief of Kensington, Fiction (historical romance, women's contemporary fiction, historical fiction, paranormal romance, urban fantasy, gay fiction and non-fiction, mysteries, suspense, mainstream fiction, young adult fiction, memoirs, erotica); jscognamiglio@kensingtonbooks.com. Michaela Hamilton, Editor-in-Chief of Citadel, Executive Editor of Kensington (nonfiction including popular culture, current events, narrative nonfiction, true crime, business, biography, memoir, law enforcement, military; selected fiction including thrillers, mainstream novels); mhamilton@kensingtonbooks.com. Alicia Condon, Editorial Director of Brava (paranormal and fantasy romance, romantic suspense, historical and contemporary romance, young adult paranormal romance of 80,000- 100,000 words); acondon@kensingtonbooks.com. Selena James, executive editor (African American fiction, Dafina Books); Audrey LaFehr, editorial director (women's fiction); Michaela Hamilton, executive editor. See more online at website. See all the editors' and e-mails online at website.

TERMS Advance against royalties based on net sales. Publishes ms 12-24 months after acceptance.

KINDRED PRODUCTIONS

1310 Taylor Ave., Winnipeg MB R3M 3Z6 Canada. (204)669-6575. Fax: (204)654-1865. E-mail: kindred@

mbconf.ca. Website: www.kindredproductions.com. **Contact:** Renita Kornelsen, Acquisitions.

TIPS "Most of our books are sold to churches, religious bookstores, and schools. We are concentrating on books with a Mennonite Brethren perspective. We do not accept children's manuscripts."

ALFRED A. KNOPF

1745 Broadway, 21st Floor, New York NY 10019. Website: knopf.knopfdoubleday.com. **Contact:** Senior editor. Estab. 1915. Publishes hardcover and paperback originals. **Published some debut authors within the last year.** Averages 200 total titles/year.

NEEDS Publishes book-length fiction of literary merit by known or unknown writers. Length: 40,000-150,000 words. Published *Gertrude and Claudius*, by John Updike; *The Emperor of Ocean Park*, by Stephen Carter; *Balzac and the Little Chinese Seamstress*, by Dai Sijie.

HOW TO CONTACT *Agented submissions only.* Query with SASE or submit sample chapter(s). Responds in 2-6 months to queries. Accepts simultaneous submissions.

TERMS Pays 10-15% royalty. Royalty and advance vary. Offers advance. Must return advance if book is not completed or is unacceptable. Publishes ms 1 year after acceptance. Book catalog for 7½×10½ SAE with 5 first-class stamps.

KNOPF PUBLISHING GROUP

Imprint of Random House, 1745 Broadway, New York NY 10019. (212)751-2600. Website: www.randomhouse.com/knopf. **Contact:** Senior Editor. Estab. 1915. Division of Random House, Inc. "Throughout history, Knopf has been dedicated to publishing distinguished fiction and nonfiction." Publishes hardcover and paperback originals. "We usually only accept work through an agent, but you may still send a query to our slush pile."

Knopf is a general publisher of quality nonfiction and fiction.

IMPRINTS Alfred A. Knopf; Everyman's Library; Pantheon Books; Schocken Books; Vintage Anchor Publishing (Vintage Books, Anchor Books).

NEEDS Publishes book-length fiction of literary merit by known or unknown writers. Length: 40,000-150,000 words.

HOW TO CONTACT Submit query, 25-page sample, SASE.

KRAUSE PUBLICATIONS

A Division of F+W Media, Inc., 700 E. State St., Iola WI 54990. (715)445-2214. Fax: (715)445-4087. Website: www.krausebooks.com. **Contact:** Paul Kennedy (antiques and collectibles, music, sports, militaria); Corrina Peterson (firearms); Brian Lovett (outdoors); Candy Wiza (Simple Living); Debbie Bradley (Numismatics).

TIPS Audience consists of serious hobbyists. "Your work should provide a unique contribution to the special interest."

L&L DREAMSPELL

P.O. Box 1984, Friendswood TX 77546. Website: www.lldreamspell.com. ALL SUBMISSIONS of unsolicited novels and novellas are now CLOSED through January 1, 2012. We only want to see short story submissions for our ebook anthology line, and manuscripts from our current author team, and those referred to us through our signed authors. E-mail: Administrator@lldreamspell.com. Website: www.lldreamspell.com. Contact: Lisa René Smith, editor (fiction). "L&L Dreamspell is a micro publishing company based in the Houston, Texas area, publishing both fiction and nonfiction. Run by two gusty women, Linda Houle and Lisa René Smith, we believe in making new author's dreams come true! We are a standard royalty paying publisher, and accept submissions for consideration through our website. We want to read outstanding mysteries, romance novels, and anything paranormal. New genres include thriller, horror, and young adult. Check our website for more information. We're still a young company—our nonfiction line was added in 2008. Linda and Lisa encourage all authors to follow their dreams." Publishes paperback originals, e-books. Debut novel print order: 150. **Published 12 new writers last year.** Plans 36 or more books this year. Averages at least 24- to 36 books per year. Member PMA, SPAN. Distributes/promotes titles via Lightningsource, in addition to using a local printer (we also distribute our titles).

NEEDS adventure, erotica, fantasy, horror, mainstream, mystery/suspense, new age/mystic, romance. "We still have anthologies open for submission. Writers may submit stories per our website's guidelines." Published *The Key*, by Pauline Baird Jones (mainstream romance/sci fi); *Cold Tears*, by John Foxjohn (mystery), voted best mystery in 2007 by preditors and editors readers poll; *Dance on His Grave*, by Sylvia Dickey Smith (mystery); *Murder New York*–style mystery anthology featuring an Agatha Award winning story by Elizabeth Zelvin.

HOW TO CONTACT Query with outline/synopsis and 1 sample chapter. Accepts queries, submissions by e-mail only. Include estimated word count, list of publishing credits. Responds to queries in 2 weeks. Accepts unsolicited mss. Considers simultaneous submissions. Often critiques/comments on rejected mss. Responds to mss in 3 months. Address: L&L Dreamspell 376 West Quarry Road, London, Texas 76854.

TERMS Sends preproduction galleys to author. Ms published 1 year after acceptance. Writer's guidelines on website. Pays royalties min 15%. Book catalogs not available.

TIPS "We do pay attention to trends, but a great manuscript will always find an audience. Please follow our website submission guidelines if you want us to read your work."

LAUREL-LEAF

Imprint of Random House Children's Books/Random House, Inc., 1745 Broadway, New York NY 10019. (212)782-9000. Website: www.randomhouse.com/teens.

Quality reprint paperback imprint for young adult paperback books. *Does not accept unsolicited mss.*

LEAPFROG PRESS

Box 2110, Teaticket MA 02536. (508)349-1925. Fax: (508)349-1180. E-mail: leapfrog@leapfrogpress.com; acquisitions@leapfrogpress.com. Website: www.leapfrogpress.com. **Contact:** Tasha Enseki, acquisitions editor. Estab. 1996. "We search for beautifully written literary titles and market them aggressively to national trade and library accounts. We also sell film, translation, foreign, and book club rights." Publishes paperback originals. Books: acid-free paper; sewn binding. Average print order: 3,000. First novel print order: 2,000 (average). Member, Publishers Marketing Association, PEN. Distributes titles through Consortium Book Sales and Distribution, St. Paul, MN. Promotes titles through all national review media, bookstore readings, author tours, website, radio shows, chain store promotions, advertisements, book fairs.

The Devil and Daniel Silverman by Theodore Rosak was nominated for the American Library Association Stonewall Award and was a San Francisco Chronicle best seller. *The German Money* by Lev Raphael was a Booksense 76 pick.

NEEDS "Genres often blur; look for good writing. We are most interested in works that are quirky, that fall outside of any known genre,and of course well written and finely crafted. We are most interested in literary fiction." Published *The War at Home*, by Nora Eisenberg; *Junebug*, by Maureen McCoy; *Paradise Dance*, by Michael Lee; *The Ghost Trap*, by K. Stephens; and *Billie Girl*, by Vickie Weaver. See website for more recent titles.

HOW TO CONTACT Query by e-mail only. Send letter and first 5 to 10 ms pages within e-mail message. No attachments. Responds in 2-3 weeks to queries by e-mail; 6 months to mss. May consider simultaneous submissions.

TERMS Pays 4-8% royalty on net receipts. Average advance: negotiable. Publishes ms 1-2 years after acceptance.

TIPS "We like anything that is superbly written and genuinely original. We like the idiosyncratic and the peculiar. We rarely publish nonfiction. Send only your best work, and send only completed work that is ready. That means the completed ms has already been through extensive editing and is ready to be judged. We consider submissions from both previously published and unpublished writers. We are uninterested in an impressive author bio if the work is poor; if the work is excellent, the author bio is equally unimportant."

LEAPING DOG PRESS AND ASYLUM ARTS PUBLISHING

P.O. Box 90473, Raleigh NC 27675-0473. (877)570-6873. Fax: (877)570-6873. E-mail: editor@leapingdogpress.com. Website: www.leapingdogpress.com. **Contact:** Jordan Jones, editor & publisher. Member: CLMP, SPAN, and PMA. "Leaping Dog Press and Asylum Arts Press publish accessible, edgy, witty, and challenging contemporary poetry, fiction, and works in translation, with Asylum Arts Press having an additional focus on surrealism and the avant garde."

NEEDS "Please bear in mind that we are a small press that publishes only 4-6 titles a year. Additionally, we are currently under contract for titles through calendar year 2011, so the soonest newly accepted titles could appear is 2012." Does not want "genre fiction, self help, dog books, etc."

HOW TO CONTACT Query by mail with a cover letter "containing your reasons for considering LPD or AA and your ideas for marketing your title; a proposed table of contents; a bio or CV and a list of publications; two chapters or 20 pages of fiction." Does not accept e-mail or electronic submissions or queries. Include SASE. Address: Editorial, Leaping Dog Press, PO Box 90473, Raleigh, NC 27675-0473, SAN 254-0126.

LEE & LOW BOOKS

95 Madison Ave., #1205, New York NY 10016. (212)779-4400. E-mail: general@leeandlow.com. Website: www.leeandlow.com. **Contact:** Louise May, editor-in-chief (multicultural children's fiction/nonfiction). Estab. 1991. Publishes 12-14 children's books/year. 25% of books by first-time authors. Lee & Low Books publishes books with diverse themes. "One of our goals is to discover new talent and produce books that reflect the diverse society in which we live.

NEEDS Picture books, young readers: anthology, contemporary, history, multicultural, poetry. "We are not considering folktales or animal stories." Picture book, middle reader: contemporary, history, multicultural, nature/environment, poetry, sports. Average word length: picture books—1,000-1,500 words. Recently published *Amazing Faces*, by Lee Bennett Hopkins, illustrated by Chris Soentpiet; *The Can Man*, by Laura E. Williams, illustrated by Craig Orback.

HOW TO CONTACT Fiction/nonfiction: Submit complete ms. No e-mail submissions. Publishes a book 1-2 years after acceptance. Will consider simultaneous submissions. Guidelines on website. No SASE. Writer will be notified within 6 months if we have interest in the work. Manuscripts will not be returned.

TERMS Pays authors advances against royalty. Pays illustrators advance against royalty. Photographers paid advance against royalty. Book catalog available for 9×12 SAE and $1.65 postage; ms and art guidelines available via website or with SASE.

TIPS "Check our website to see the kinds of books we publish. Do not send mss that don't fit our mission."

LERNER PUBLISHING GROUP

Editorial Office, 11430 Strand Dr., #2, Rockville MD 20852-4371. (301)984-8733. Fax: (301)881-9195. E-mail: editorial@karben.com. Website: www.karben.com. Estab. 1959. Primarily publishes books for children ages Pre-K-18. List includes titles in geography, natural and physical science, current events, ancient and modern history, high interest, sports, world cultures, and numerous biography series. Kar-Ben publishes 10-12 new titles each year. All are books on Jewish themes for children and families. "We are happy to review unsolicited manuscripts and artists' samples. If you wish a response, you MUST include a SASE. Please allow 3-5 weeks for a reply. ILLUSTRATORS: Please submit samples that show skill in children's book illustration. Color photocopies and tear sheets are preferred. Please DO NOT send original art. WRITERS: We consider fiction and non-fiction for preschool through high school, including holiday books, life-cycle stories, Bible tales, folktales, board books, and activity books. In particular, we are looking for stories that reflect the ethnic and cultural diversity of today's Jewish family. We DO NOT publish games, textbooks, or books in Hebrew. Your story should be concise, have interesting, believable characters, and action that holds the readers' attention. Good prose is far better than tortured verse."

Starting in 2007, Lerner Publishing Group no longer accepts submission in any of their imprints except for Kar-Ben Publishing.

HOW TO CONTACT "We will continue to seek targeted solicitations at specific reading levels and in specific subject areas. The company will list these targeted solicitations on our website and in national newsletters, such as the SCBWI *Bulletin*."

LETHE PRESS

118 Heritage Ave., Maple Shade NJ 08052. (609)410-7391. E-mail: editor@lethepressbooks.com. Website: www.lethepressbooks.com. **Contact:** Steve Berman, publisher. Estab. 2001. "Named after the Greek river of memory and forgetfulness (and pronounced Lee-Thee), Lethe Press is a small press devoted to ideas that are often neglected or forgotten by mainstream, profit-oriented publishers." Distributes/promotes titles. Lethe Books are distributed by Ingram Publications and Bookazine, and are available at all major bookstores, as well as the major online retailers.

NEEDS *Rarely accepts unsolicited mss.* Primarily interested in gay fiction, poetry, and nonfiction titles. Has imprint for gay spirituality titles. Also releases work of occult and supernatural, sci-fi, and East Asian interests.

HOW TO CONTACT Send query letter. Accepts queries by e-mail.

ARTHUR A. LEVINE BOOKS

Scholastic, Inc., 557 Broadway, New York NY 10012. Website: www.arthuralevinebooks.com. Estab. 1996. "Arthur A. Levine is looking for distinctive literature, for children and young adults, for whatever's extraordinary." Averages 18-20 total titles/year.

NEEDS juvenile, picture books, young adult, middle grade novels. Published *Peaceful Heroes*, by Jonah Winter, illustrated by Sean Addy; *Blue Mountain Trouble*, by Martin Mordecai; *Marcelo in the Real World*, by Francisco X Stork; *Lips Touch*, by Laini Taylor, illustrations by Jim Di Bartolo.

HOW TO CONTACT Query with SASE.

TERMS Pays variable royalty on retail price. Average advance: variable. Book catalog for 9x12 SASE.

LIQUID SILVER BOOKS

Wales. E-mail: tracey@liquidsilverbooks.com. Website: www.liquidsilverbooks.com. **Contact:** Tracey West, acquisitions editor. "Romance is the key to our stories. The stories must hold on their own if the sex scenes are omitted. Stories must have well developed characters, with depth and explosive chemistry that entice the reader to like and/or identify with them. Mix in an imaginative and fully realized plot, vivid settings, and clear dialog and you've got the ingredients for a story we'd be interested in publishing." Publishes paperback originals and e-books.

NEEDS contemporary, gay and lesbian, paranormal, supernatural, sci-fi, fantasy, historical, suspense, and western romances. We do not accept literary Erotica submissions.

HOW TO CONTACT Query with outline/synopsis and three sample chapters in rtf form, Arial 12 pt font only. Accepts queries by e-mail. E-mail submissions to submissions@liquidsilverbooks.com. You will receive a personal reply within one week of receipt. Our current read time is 4 to 6 weeks. If you have not heard from us after those time frames, please query Acquisitions Director, Tracey West, at Tracey@liquidsilverbooks.com. Include estimated word count, author bio, thoughts on e-publishing, and a snapshot synopsis of book including title and series title, if applicable, in body of e-mail. Mss must include pen name, real name, snail mail, and e-mail contact information on first page top left corner. No headers, footers, or page numbers.

TERMS Manuscript published 4 months after acceptance. Writer's guidelines on website. We pay 35% royalties on eBook retail sales from those sales originating from the Liquid Silver Books website. For other retail distributors, we pay 35% royalties on minus the distribution costs. Our contract is for electronic rights for one year. If your book is chosen for print, the contract will be amended to reflect the print terms.

LITTLE, BROWN AND CO. ADULT TRADE BOOKS

237 Park Ave., New York NY 10017. E-mail: publicity@littlebrown.com. Website: www.hachettebookgroup.com. **Contact:** Michael Pietsch, publisher. Estab. 1837. "The general editorial philosophy for all divisions continues to be broad and flexible, with high quality and the promise of commercial success as always the first considerations." Publishes hardcover originals and paperback originals and reprints. Averages 100 total titles/year.

NEEDS Literary, mainstream/contemporary. Published *Cross Country*, by James Patterson; *Outliers*, by Malcolm Gladwell; *The Historian*, by Elizabeth Kostova; *When You Are Engulfed in Flames*, by David Sedaris.

HOW TO CONTACT *Agented submissions only.*

TERMS Pays royalty. Offers advance. Ms guidelines online.

LITTLE, BROWN AND CO. BOOKS FOR YOUNG READERS

Hachette Book Group USA, 237 Park Ave., New York NY 10017. (212)364-1100. Fax: (212)364-0925. Website: www.lb-kids.com; www.lb-teens.com. Estab. 1837. "We are looking for strong writing and presentation but no predetermined topics." Publishes hardcover originals, trade paperback reprints. Averages 100-150 total titles/year.

IMPRINTS Editorial Director, Poppy (young women's commercial fiction imprint): Cynthia Eagan; Editorial Director, LB Kids (novelty and licensed books imprint): Liza Baker.

NEEDS adventure, ethnic, fantasy, historical, humor, juvenile, mystery, novelty, picture books, science fiction, suspense, young adult. "We are looking for strong fiction for children of all ages in any area, including multicultural. We always prefer full manuscripts for fiction."

HOW TO CONTACT *Agented submissions only.*

TERMS Pays royalty on retail price. Average advance: negotiable. Publishes ms 2 years after acceptance. Ms guidelines online.

TIPS "In order to break into the field, authors and illustrators should research their competition and try to come up with something outstandingly different."

⊘ LIVINGSTON PRESS

University of West Alabama, Station 22, Livingston AL 35470. E-mail: jwt@uwa.edu. Website: www.livingstonpress.uwa.edu. **Contact:** Joe Taylor, director. Estab. 1974. "Small university press specializing in offbeat and/or Southern literature." Publishes hardcover and trade paperback originals. Books: acid free; offset; some illustrations. Average print order: 2,500. First novel print order: 2,500. Plans 5 first novels this year. Averages 10 fiction titles/year.

Reads mss in March only.

IMPRINTS Swallow's Tale Press.

NEEDS Experimental, literary, short story collections, off-beat or Southern. "We are interested in form and, of course style." Published *The Gin Girl*, by River Jordan (novel); *Pulpwood*, by Scott Ely (stories); *Live Cargo*, by Paul Toutonghi (stories).

HOW TO CONTACT Query with SASE. Include estimated word count, brief bio, list of publishing credits. Send SASE for return of ms or send a disposable ms and SASE for reply only. Responds in 1 month to queries; 1 year to mss. Accepts simultaneous submissions. Send only in June and July. We are especially interested in novels and story collections that intertwine in one way or another. Contact the Livingston Press at jwt@uwa.edu or write us at: University of West Alabama Station 22, Livingston, Alabama 35470. Website: www.livingstonpress.uwa.edu.

TERMS Pays 10% of 1,500 print run, 150 copies; thereafter pays a mix of royalties and books. Publishes ms 18 months after acceptance. Book catalog for SASE. Ms guidelines online.

TIPS "Our readers are interested in literature, often quirky literature that emphasizes form and style. Please visit our website for current needs."

LOOSE ID

P.O. Box 425690, San Francisco CA 94142-5960. E-mail: submissions@loose-id.com. Website: www.loose-id.com. **Contact:** Treva Harte, editor-in-chief. Estab. 2004. "*Loose Id* is love unleashed. We're taking romance to the edge." Publishes e-books. Distributes/promotes titles. "The company promotes itself through web and print advertising wherever readers of erotic romance may be found, creating a recognizable brand identity as the place to let your id run free and the people who unleash your fantasies. It is currently pursuing licensing agreements for foreign translations, and has a print program of 2 to 5 titles per month."

NEEDS Wants nontraditional erotic romance stories, including gay, lesbian, heroes and heroines, multiculturalism, cross-genre, fantasy, and science fiction, straight contemporary or historical romances.

HOW TO CONTACT Query with outline/synopsis and three sample chapters. Accepts queries by e-mail. Include estimated word count, list of publishing credits, and why your submission is "Love Unleashed." Responds to queries in 1 months. Considers e-mail submissions. "Loose Id is actively acquiring stories from both aspiring and established authors. Before submitting a query or proposal, please read the guidelines on our website. Please don't hesitate to contact us at submissions@ loose-id.com for any information you don't see there."

TERMS Manuscript published within 1 year after acceptance. Writer's guidelines on website. Pays e-book royalties 35%.

◐ LOST HORSE PRESS

105 Lost Horse Lane, Sandpoint ID 83864. (208)255-4410. Fax: (208)255-1560. E-mail: losthorsepress@mindspring.com. Website: www.losthorsepress.org. **Contact:** Christine Holbert, editor. Estab. 1998. Publishes hardcover and paperback originals. Books: 60-70 lb. natural paper; offset printing; b&w illustration. Average print order: 500-2,500. First novel print order: 500. **Published 2 debut authors within the last year.** Averages 4 total titles/year. Distributed by Eastern Washington University Press.

"*Does not accept unsolicited mss.* However, we welcome submissions for The Idaho Prize for Poetry, a national competition offering $1000 prize money plus publication for a book-length manuscript. Please check the submission guidelines for The Idaho Prize for Poetry online."

NEEDS literary, regional (Pacific NW), short story collections, poetry. Published *Tales of a Dalai Lama*, by Pierre Delattre (literary fiction); *Love*by Valerie Martin (short stories); *The Baseball Field at Night Po-*

ems, by Patricia Goedicke; *Thistle*, by Melissa Kwasny; *Willing to Choose* and *Composing Voices*, by Robert Pack.

HOW TO CONTACT "Regrettably, Lost Horse Press is *no longer accepting unsolicited manuscripts for review.* However, we welcome submissions for The Idaho Prize for Poetry, a national competition offering $1,000 prize money plus publication for a book-length manuscript. Please check The Idaho Prize for Poetry submission guidelines for more information."

TERMS Publishes ms 6 months-1 year after acceptance. Please check submission guidelines on website before submitting ms.

LOVE SPELL

Dorchester Publishing, 200 Madison Ave., Suite 2000, New York NY 10016. (212)725-8811. Fax: (212)532-1054. E-mail: adavis@dorchesterpub.com; submissions@dorchesterpub.com. **We are currently acquiring only the following: romance, horror, Westerns, and thrillers.** Authors should attach their full manuscript in a Word or .rtf document, along with a 3- to 7-page synopsis. Website: www.dorchesterpub.com. **Contact:** Alissa Davis, editorial assistant. Dorchester Publishing is not currently accepting unsolicited manuscripts. Due to the current volume of submissions awaiting review, our usual review period of 6 months has been extended to 8 months, and in an effort to reduce that time frame once again to 6 months, we have temporarily closed submissions. If you submitted your manuscript on or before Friday March 4, 2011, your work will continue to go through the review process. We expect submissions to reopen in June. Love Spell publishes the quirky sub-genres of romance: time-travel, paranormal, futuristic. "Despite the exotic settings, we are still interested in character-driven plots." Publishes mass market paperback originals. Books: newsprint paper; offset printing; perfect bound. Average print order: varies. First novel print order: varies. Averages 48 total titles/year.

Love Spell publishes the many sub-genres of romance: time-travel, paranormal, fantasy, futuristic, romantic suspense, and African-American. Despite the exotic settings, we are still interested in character-driven plots."

NEEDS romance (futuristic, time travel, paranormal, historical), whimsical contemporaries. "Books industry-wide are getting shorter; we're interested in 90,000 words." Published *Deep Magic*, by Joy Nash (historical romance); *Immortals: The Calling*, by Jennifer Ashley (paranormal romance).

HOW TO CONTACT Accepts unsolicited mss. Submis by e-mail to: submissions@dorchesterpub.com. For those of you who prefer to send a hard copy of your material, please query or submit synopsis and first three chapters only—**no complete manuscripts unless specifically requested.** Query with SASE or IRC or submit 3 sample chapter(s), synopsis. Agented fiction 70%. Responds in 6-8 months to mss. No simultaneous submissions.

TERMS Pays royalty on retail price. Average advance: varies. Publishes ms 1 year after acceptance. Book catalog for free (800)481-9191. Ms guidelines online.

TIPS "The best way to learn to write a Love Spell Romance is by reading several of our recent releases. The best-written stories are usually ones writers feel passionate about—so write from your heart! Also, the market is very tight these days so more than ever we are looking for refreshing, standout original fiction."

MARGARET K. MCELDERRY BOOKS

Simon & Schuster Children's Publishing Division, Simon & Schuster, 1230 Sixth Ave., New York NY 10020. (212)698-7605. Fax: (212)698-2797. Website: www.simonsayskids.com. **Contact:** Emma D. Dryden, vice president/publisher. Estab. 1971. Publishes quality material for preschoolers to 18-year-olds. Publishes hardcover and paperback originals. Books: high quality paper; offset printing; three piece and POB bindings; illustrations. Average print order: 15,000. First novel print order: 10,000. **Published some debut authors within the last year.** Averages 35 total titles/year.

Books published by Margaret K. McElderry Books have received numerous awards, including the Newbery and Caldecott Medals.

NEEDS adventure, fantasy, historical, mainstream/contemporary, mystery, picture books, young adult (or middle grade). All categories (fiction and nonfiction) for juvenile and young adult. "We will consider any category. Results depend on the quality of the imagination, the artwork and the writing." Published *Dr. Ted*, by Andrea Beaty; illustrated by Pascal LeMaitre; and *Bear Feels Sick*, by Karma Wilson; illustrated by Jane Cahpeman (picture books); *Sight*, by Adrienne Maria Vrettos (middle-grade fiction); *City* *of Bones* and *City of Ashes,* by Cassandra Clare (teen fiction); *OOPS!* by Alan Kaatz; illustrated by Edward Koren (poetry).

TERMS *"We do not accept unsolicited queries or submissions. Submissions must be sent through an agent."* Average print order is 10,000-15,000 for a first middle grade or young adult book; 7,500-20,000 for a first picture book. Pays royalty on hardcover retail price: 10% fiction; 5% author, 5% illustrator (picture book). Offers $5,000-8,000 advance for new authors. Publishes ms up to 3 years after acceptance. Ms guidelines for #10 SASE.

TIPS "Imaginative writing of high quality is always in demand; also picture books that are original and unusual. Keep in mind that McElderry is a very small imprint, so we are very selective about the books we will undertake for publication. We try not to publish any 'trend' books. Be familiar with our list and with what is being published this year by all publishing houses."

MARINE TECHNIQUES PUBLISHING

126 Western Ave., Suite 266, Augusta ME 04330-7249. (207)622-7984. Fax: (207)621-0821. E-mail: info@marinetechpublishing.com. Website: www.marinetechpublishing.com. **Contact:** James L. Pelletier, president/owner(commercial maritime); Maritime Associates Globally (commercial maritime). Estab. 1983.

TIPS "Audience consists of commercial marine/maritime firms, persons employed in all aspects of the marine/maritime commercial water-transportation-related industries and recreational fresh and salt water fields, persons interested in seeking employment in the commercial marine industry; firms seeking to sell their products and services to vessel owners, operators, and managers; shipyards, vessel repair yards, recreational and yacht boat building and national and international ports and terminals involved with the commercial marine industry globally worldwide, etc."

MARTIN SISTERS PUBLISHING, LLC

P.O. Box 1749, Barbourville KY 40906-1499. E-mail: publisher@martinsisterspublishing.com. Website: http://www.martinsisterspublishing.com. **Contact:** Denise Melton, Publisher/Editor (Fiction/Non-Fiction); Melissa Newman, Publisher/Editor (Fiction/Non-Fiction). Estab. 2011. Firm/imprint publishes trade and mass market paperback originals; electronic originals.

IMPRINTS Ivy House Books—Literary/mainstream fiction; Rainshower Books—Christian fiction and nonfiction; Skyvine Books—science fiction/fantasy/paranormal; romance; Martin Sisters Books—nonfiction/short story collections/coffee table books/cookbooks; Barefoot Books—young adult. Query Ms. Newman or Ms. Melton for all imprints listed at submissions@martinsisterspublishing.com.

NEEDS adventure, confession, fantasy, historical, humor, juvenile, literary, mainstream, military, mystery, poetry in translation, regional, religious, romance, science fiction, short story collections, spiritual, sports, suspense, war, western, young adult

HOW TO CONTACT Send query letter only to submissions@martinsisterspublishing.com; publisher@martinsisterspublishing.com

TERMS Pays 7.5% royalty/max on retail price. No advance offered. Time between acceptance of ms and publication is 6 months. Accepts simultaneous submissions. No SASE returns. Responds in 1 month on queries, 2 months on proposals, 3-6 months on mss. Catalog and guidelines available online.

MARVEL COMICS

417 5th Ave., New York NY 10016. (212)576-4000. Fax: (212)576-8547. Website: marvel.com. Publishes hardcover originals and reprints, trade paperback reprints, mass market comic book originals, electronic reprints. Averages 650 total titles/year.

NEEDS adventure, comic books, fantasy, horror, humor, science fiction, young adult. "Our shared universe needs new heroes and villains; books for younger readers and teens needed."

HOW TO CONTACT "If you are an aspiring comic book artist or writer, we suggest you publish or publicly post your material, continue to create, and if you have the right stuff . . . we'll find you." Please note: Unsolicited writing samples will not be read. *Any unsolicited or solicited writing sample received without a signed Marvel Idea Submission Form will be destroyed unread."* (Download Marvel Idea Submission Form from website.) Responds only if interested in 3-5 weeks.

TERMS Pays on a per-page work-for-hire basis, which is contracted. Ms guidelines online.

MAVERICK MUSICALS AND PLAYS

89 Bergann Rd., Maleny QLD 4552 Australia. Phone/Fax: (61)(7)5494-4007. E-mail: helen@mavmuse.com.

Website: www.mavmuse.com. **Contact:** The Editor. Estab. 1978.

MAY DAVENPORT, PUBLISHERS

26313 Purissima Rd., Los Altos Hills CA 94022. (650)947-1275. Fax: (650)947-1373. E-mail: mdbooks@earthlink.net. Website: www.maydavenportpublishers.com. **Contact:** May Davenport, editor/publisher. Estab. 1976. "We prefer books which can be used in high schools as supplementary readings in English or creative writing courses. Reading skills have to be taught, and novels by humourous authors can be more pleasant to read than Hawthorne's or Melville's novels, war novels, or novels about past generations. Humor has a place in literature." Publishes hardcover and paperback originals. Averages 4 total titles/year. Distributes titles through direct mail order.

IMPRINTS md Books (nonfiction and fiction).

NEEDS Humor, literary. "We want to focus on novels junior and senior high school teachers can share with the reluctant readers in their classrooms." Published *Charlie and Champ*, by Allyson Wagoner; *Senioritis*, by Tate Thompson; *A Life on the Line*, by Michael Horton; *Matthew Livingston & The Prison of Soul*, by Marco Conelli; *Summer of Suspense*, by Frances Drummond Waines.

HOW TO CONTACT Query with SASE. Responds in 1 month to queries.

TERMS Pays 15% royalty on retail price. Publishes ms 1 year after acceptance. Ms guidelines for #10 SASE.

TIPS "Just write your fictional novel humorously. If you can't write that way, create youthful characters so teachers, as well as 15-18-year-old high school readers, will laugh at your descriptive passages and contemporary dialogue. Avoid 1-sentence paragraphs. The audience we want to reach is today's high-tech teens who are talented with digital cameras hooked up to computers. Show them what you can do 'in print' for them and their equipment."

⊘ MCBOOKS PRESS

ID Booth Building, 520 N. Meadow St., Ithaca NY 14850. (607)272-2114. Fax: (607)273-6068. E-mail: jackie@mcbooks.com. Website: www.mcbooks.com. **Contact:** Jackie Swift, editorial director. Estab. 1979. Small, independent publisher. Publishes Julian Stockwin, John Biggins, Colin Sargent, and Douglas W. Jacobson. Publishes trade paperback and hardcover originals and reprints. Averages 8 fiction titles/year. Distributes titles through Independent Publishers Group.

NEEDS "We are looking for a few good novels and are open to almost any genre or style, except romance, inspirational, science fiction, fantasy, and children's. Our main criteria is an exceptionally strong story combined with an author who can show he/she has a good grasp on self-promotion through networking, personal appearances, and tireless internet presence."

HOW TO CONTACT Does not accept unsolicited mss. Submission guidelines available on website. Query with SASE or via e-mail. Include list of publishing credits and a well thought-out marketing plan. Responds in 3 months to queries. Accepts simultaneous submissions.

TERMS Pays 5-10% royalty on retail price. Average advance: $1,000-5,000.

TIPS "In the current tough book market, the author's ability to use the internet for self promotion is almost as important as his/her ability to tell a great story really well. Unfortunately, writing ability alone is not enough. Show that you're savvy with personal web sites, blogs, and social networking. And show you nkow who your audience is and how to generate word-of-mouth."

⊕ MC PRESS

PO Box 4886, Ketchum ID 83340. Fax: (208)639-1231. E-mail: duptmor@mcpressonline.com. Website: www.mcpressonline.com. **Contact:** David Uptmor, publisher. Estab. 2001.

IMPRINTS MC Press, IBM Press.

◐ MEDALLION PRESS, INC.

1020 N. Cedar Ave., #216, St. Charles IL 60174. 630-513-8316. E-mail: submissions@medallionpress.com. Website: www.medallionpress.com. **Contact:** Emily Steele, editorial director, emily@medallionpress.com. Estab. 2003. "We are an independent publisher looking for books that are outside of the box. " Publishes trade paperback, hardcover, and e-book originals. Average print order: 5,000. **Published 5 debut authors within the last year.**

NEEDS nonfiction, mainstream fiction, historical fiction, mystery, thriller, suspense, romance (historical, time travel, paranormal, hard-boiled mystery), horror (paranormal, survival, serial killer, sci-fi, general), science fiction, fantasy (steampunk, contemporary, epic, historical, paranormal, urban life), literary fiction, young adult fiction, Christian, young adults writing for young adults. Published *Motiv8n' U*, by Staci Boyer (nonfiction, self-help); *The Clockwork Man*, by

William Jablonsky (steampunk); *Plum Blossoms in Paris*, by Sarah Hina (mainstream fiction); *The Frenzy Way*, by Greg Lamberson (horror)

HOW TO CONTACT "Minimum word count 80K for adult fiction, 60K for YA, no exceptions." No poetry, anthologies, erotica. Submit first 3 consecutive chapters and a synopsis. " Accepts queries only by e-mail to submissions@medallionpress.com. Include estimated word count, brief bio, list of publishing credits. Responds in 4-6 months to mss. Accepts simultaneous submissions. Sometimes comments on rejected mss.

TERMS Offers advance. Publishes ms 1-2 years after acceptance. Ms guidelines online.

TIPS "We are not affected by trends. We are simply looking for well crafted, original, grammatically correct works of fiction. Please visit our website at http://medallionpress.com/guidlines/index.html for the most current guidelines prior to submitting anything to us."

MERIWETHER PUBLISHING, LTD.

P.O. Box 7710, Colorado Springs CO 80903. (719)594-4422. Fax: (719)594-9916. E-mail: ahammelev@meriwether.com. Website: www.meriwetherpublishing.com; www.contemporarydrama.com. **Contact:** Theodore Zape, assoc. editor. Estab. 1969. "Mid-size, independent publisher of plays. We publish plays for teens, mostly one-act comedies, holiday plays for churches and musical comedies. Our books are on the theatrical arts." Publishes paperback originals and reprints. Books: quality paper; printing house specialist; paperback binding. Average print order: 5,000-10,000. **Published 25-35 debut authors within the last year.**

NEEDS Mainstream/contemporary, comedy, religious (children's plays and religious Christmas and Easter plays), suspense—all in playscript format. Published *Pirates and Petticoats*, by Pat Cook (a two-act pirate comedy); *Let Him Sleep Until It's Time for His Funeral*, by Peg Kehret (two-act play).

HOW TO CONTACT Accepts unsolicited mss. Query with SASE. Accepts queries by e-mail. Include list of publishing credits. Send SASE for return of ms or send a disposable ms and SASE for reply only. Responds in 3 weeks to queries; 2 months to mss. Accepts simultaneous submissions. Sometimes comments on rejected mss.

TERMS Pays 10% royalty on retail price or makes outright purchase. Publishes ms 6-12 months after acceptance. Book catalog and ms guidelines for $2 postage.

TIPS "Contemporary Drama Service is looking for creative books on comedy, monologs, staging amateur theatricals, and Christian youth activities. Our writers are usually highly experienced in theatre as teachers or performers. We welcome books that reflect their experience and special knowledge. Any good comedy writer of monologs and short scenes will find a home with us."

◐ MILKWEED EDITIONS

1011 Washington Ave. S., Suite 300, Minneapolis MN 55415. (612)332-3192. E-mail: submissions@milkweed.org. Website: www.milkweed.org. Estab. 1979. Nonprofit publisher. Publishes hardcover originals, paperback originals, and reprints. Books: book text quality—acid-free paper; offset printing; perfect or hardcover binding. Average print order: 4,000. First novel print order depends on book. **Published some debut authors within the last year.** Averages 15 total titles/year. Distributes through Publisher's Group West. Each book has its own marketing plan involving print ads, tours, conferences, etc.

Please consider our previous publications when considering submissions.

NEEDS literary. Novels for adults and for readers 8-13. High literary quality. For adult readers: literary fiction, nonfiction, poetry, essays; for children (ages 8-13): literary novels. Translations welcome for both audiences. Published *The Blue Sky*, by Galsan Tschinag (translation); *Driftless*, by David Rhodes; *The Farther Shore*, by Matthew Eck.

HOW TO CONTACT Submit complete ms via submission manager. Responds in 2 months to queries; 6 months to mss. Accepts simultaneous submissions.

TERMS Variable royalty on retail price. Average advance: varied. Publishes ms 1-2 years after acceptance. Book catalog for $1.50 postage. Ms guidelines online.

TIPS "We are looking for excellent writing with the intent of making a humane impact on society. Please read submission guidelines before submitting and acquaint yourself with our books in terms of style and quality before submitting. Many factors influence our selection process, so don't get discouraged. Nonfiction is focused on literary writing about the natural world, including living well in urban environments."

MILKWEED FOR YOUNG READERS

1011 Washington Ave. South, Open Book, Suite 300, Minneapolis MN 55415. Website: www.milkweed.org. **Contact:** Daniel Slager, Publisher; Children's reader. Estab. 1984. Estab. 1984. "Milkweed for Young Readers are works that embody humane values and contribute to cultural understanding." Publishes hardcover and trade paperback originals. Averages 1-2 total titles/year. Distributes titles through Publishers Group West. Promotes titles individually through print advertising, website and author tours.

Perfect, by Natasha Friend, was chosen as a Book Sense 76 Children's Book selection.

NEEDS adventure, historical, humor, mainstream/contemporary, animal, environmental. For ages 8-13. Published *The Cat*, By Jutta Richter, and *The Linden Tree* by Ellie Mathews. Query with SASE. Agented fiction 30%. Responds in 2 months to queries. Accepts simultaneous submissions. Pays 6% royalty on retail price. Average advance: variable. Publishes ms 1 year after acceptance. Book catalog for $1.50. Ms guidelines for #10 SASE or on the website. "Familiarize yourself with our books before submitting. You need not have a long list of credentials—excellent work speaks for itself."

HOW TO CONTACT Authors can now submit and manage their submissions through Milkweed's Submission Manager. If you have any problems, contact us through e-mail. If you send by postal mail, please address submissions to: Fiction Reader (or Nonfiction, Poetry, Children's, as appropriate), (or Nonfiction, Poetry, Young Readers, as appropriate), Milkweed Editions, 1011 Washington Avenue South, Open Book, Suite 300, Minneapolis, MN 55415 . See guidelines online.

MONDIAL

203 W. 107th St., Suite 6C, New York NY 10025. (212)851-3252. Fax: (208)361-2863. E-mail: contact@mondialbooks.com. Website: www.mondialbooks.com; www.librejo.com. **Contact:** Andrew Moore, editor. Estab. 1996.

NEEDS adventure, erotica, ethnic, gay, historical, literary, mainstream, multicultural, mystery, poetry, romance, short, translation. Published *Two People*, by David Windham; *Bitterness*, by Malama Katulwende; *Winter Ridge: A Love Story*, by Bruce Kellner.

HOW TO CONTACT Query through online submission form. Responds to queries in 3 months.

TERMS Pays 10% royalty of the selling price of each book copy sold.

MONSOON BOOKS

52 Telok Blangah Road, 098829, 139527 Singapore. E-mail: submissions@monsoonbooks.com.sg. Website: www.monsoonbooks.com.sg. **Contact:** Philip Tathum, publisher (fiction). Estab. 2002. "Monsoon Books is an independent publisher of fiction and nonfiction with Asian themes, based in Singapore with worldwide distribution." Unsolicited manuscripts are welcomed from published and unpublished authors alike. Publishes paperback originals, paperback reprints. Books: Mungken 80 gram paper; offset printing; threadsewn binding. Average print order: 3,000. First novel print order: 3,000. **Published 7 new writers last year**. Plans 10 first novels this year. Averages 20 total titles/year; 12 fiction titles/year. Distributes titles through Worldwide Distribution and promotes through Freelance Publicists for USA and Asia.

NEEDS erotica, ethnic/multicultural, family saga, gay, historical, horror (supernatural), humor satire, literary, mainstream, military/war, mystery/suspense (police procedural, private eye/hard-boiled), regional (Asia), thriller/espionage, translations, young adult (romance). Special interests: Southeast Asia. Published *Rouge Raider*, by Nigel Barley (historical fiction); *Straights and Narrow*, by Grace McClurg (thriller); *Private Dancer*, by Stephen Leather (general fiction/international relationships). Not accepting any poetry.

HOW TO CONTACT Query with outline/synopsis and submit complete ms with cover letter. Accepts queries by snail mail, fax, and e-mail (submissions@monsoonbooks.com.sg. Please include estimated word count, brief bio, list of publishing credits, and list of three comparative titles. Send hard copy submissions to: Monsoon Books Pte Ltd, 71 Ayer Rajah Crescent #01-01, Mediapolis Phase, Singapore 139951. We are not able to return hard copy manuscripts. We do not encourage hand deliveries. Agented fiction 20%. Responds in 8 weeks to your submissions. If you do not hear from us by then, e-mail us. Accepts simultaneous submissions, submissions on CD or disk. Rarely comments on rejected manuscripts. Monsoon Books regularly works with literary agents from the UK and Australia (such as David Higham Associates in London and Cameron's Management in Sydney) and we are particularly keen to hear from agents with manuscripts set in

Southeast or North Asia as well as manuscripts written by authors from this region.

TERMS Pays 7-10% royalty. Advance is negotiable. Publishes ms 6-12 months after acceptance. Guidelines online.

TIPS "Due to the difficulty of getting published in New York and London, Monsoon represents a more viable option and is attracting new writers from USA, UK and Australia."

MOODY PUBLISHERS

820 N. LaSalle Blvd., Chicago IL 60610. E-mail: pressinfo@moody.edu; acquisitions@moody.edu. Website: www.moodypublishers.org. **Contact:** Acquisitions Coordinator. Estab. 1894. Small, evangelical Christian publisher. "We publish fiction that reflects and supports our evangelical worldview and mission." Publishes hardcover, trade, and mass market paperback originals. Averages 70 total titles, 10-12 fiction titles/year. Member, CBA. Distributes and promotes titles through sales reps, print advertising, promotional events, Internet, etc.

Moody Publishers does not accept unsolicited manuscripts in any category unless submitted via:— a professional literary agent— an author who has published with us— an associate from a Moody Bible Institute ministry— personal contact at a writers conference.

NEEDS Contemporary, historical, literary, mystery, suspense, science fiction. Recently published *My Hands Came Away Red*, by Lisa McKay (suspense novel); *Feeling for Bones*, by Bethany Pierce (contemporary/literary).

HOW TO CONTACT Moody Publishers reviews unsolicited fiction manuscripts but does not accept unsolicited nonfiction manuscripts. Moody Publishers will review only those nonfiction manuscripts submitted by professional literary agents, Moody Publishers authors, authors known to us from other publishers, other people in the publishing industry, or Moody Bible Institute ministries. We return manuscripts to their authors with SASE. Accepts unsolicited fiction mss. proposal with SASE and 2 chapters. Accepts queries by mail only (no electronic submissions). Include estimated word count, brief bio, list of publishing credits. Send SASE for return of ms or send a disposable ms and SASE for reply only. Agented fiction 75%. Responds in 4-5 months to queries. See Submitting Manuscripts online at website. Address: 820 N. LaSalle Blvd., Chicago, IL 60610.

TERMS Royalty varies. Average advance: $1,000-10,000. Publishes ms 9-12 months after acceptance. Ms guidelines for SASE and on website.

TIPS "Get to know Moody Publishers and understand what kinds of books we publish. We will decline all submissions that do not support our evangelical Christian beliefs and mission."

MOON SHADOW PRESS

Wakestone Press, 200 Brook Hollow Rd., Nashville TN 37205. (615)739-6428. Website: http://www.wakestonepress.com. **Contact:** Frank Daniels III, Editor (Youth Fiction). Estab. 2010. Traditional printer and ebooks; perfect bound or hardcover. Illustrations. Average print order is 5,000; average first novel print order is 2,500. Published 2 previously unpublished writers last year. Plans to publish 3 debut authors this year. Publishes 6-8 titles/year; 1-3 fiction titles. Accepts unsolicited mss. No returns. Sends prepublication galleys to the author. Does not subsidy publish.

IMPRINTS Moon Shadow Press, Frank Daniels III, editor, Youth Fiction

NEEDS series

HOW TO CONTACT Accepts queries by e-mail, postal mail. Send query with outline/synopsis and 2 sample chapters. Include estimated word count, brief bio, list of publishing credits. Considers simultaneous submissions, e-mail, and submissions on disk. Send disposable copy of the ms and SASE for reply only.

TERMS Pays 7.5-15% royalties; pays negotiable advance of $2,000. Publishes mss 18-30 months after acceptance.

TIPS "Be honest, be creative, be interesting."

MOUNTAINLAND PUBLISHING, INC.

P.O. Box 150891, Ogden UT 84415. E-mail: editor@mountainlandpublishing.com. Website: www.mountainlandpublishing.com. **Contact:** Michael Combe, managing editor (Fiction, Non-Fiction). Estab. 2001. Publishes paperback originals, e-books. Published 50% new writers last year. Averages 6-10 total titles/year.

We are no longer accepting unsolicited submissions either via mail or e-mail.

NEEDS adventure, fantasy, historical, horror, humor, juvenile, literary, mainstream, military/war, multicultural, mystery, regional, religious, romance, science fiction, short story collections, suspense, western, young adult.

HOW TO CONTACT *Not accepting unsolicited submissions by either e-mail or mail.* Online submissions only. No simultaneous submissions.

TERMS Ms published 3 months after acceptance. Pays royalties.

TIPS "Our audience is a new generation of readers who enjoy well told stories and who want to be entertained. They want characters they can feel close to and/or love to hate. Make sure your ms is ready for print. Publishing companies will not wait for you to finish editing your story. Be confident that the work you are submitting is your best work. Please submit all ms electronically. Submissions received by mail will be returned unopened."

NAN A. TALESE

Imprint of Doubleday, Random House, Inc., 1745 Broadway, New York NY 10019. (212)782-8918. Fax: (212)782-8448. Website: www.nanatalese.com. **Contact:** Nan A. Talese, publisher and editorial director; Ronit Feldman, assistant editor. "Nan A. Talese publishes nonfiction with a powerful guiding narrative and relevance to larger cultural trends and interests, and literary fiction of the highest quality." Publishes hardcover originals. Averages 15 total titles/year.

NEEDS Literary. "We want well-written narratives with a compelling story line, good characterization and use of language. We like stories with an edge." *Agented submissions only.* Published *The Blind Assassin*, by Margaret Atwood; *Atonement*, by Ian McEwan; *Great Shame*, Thomas Keneally.

HOW TO CONTACT Responds in 1 week to queries; 2 weeks to mss. Accepts simultaneous submissions.

TERMS Pays variable royalty on retail price. Average advance: varying. Publishes ms 1 year after acceptance. Agented submissions only.

TIPS "Audience is highly literate people interested in story, information and insight. We want well-written material submitted by agents only. See our website."

NBM PUBLISHING

40 Exchange Pl., Ste. 1308, New York NY 10005. E-mail: nbmgn@nbmpub.com. Website: nbmpub.com. **Contact:** Terry Nantier, editor/art director. Estab. 1976. "One of the best regarded quality graphic novel publishers. Our catalog is determined by what will appeal to a wide audience of readers." Publishes hardcover originals, paperback originals. Format: offset printing; perfect binding. Average print order: 3,000-4,000; average debut writer's print order: 2,000. Publishes 1-2 debut writers/year. Publishes 30 titles/year. Member: PMA, CBC. Distributed/promoted "ourselves." Imprints: ComicsLit (literary comics), Eurotica (erotic comics).

NEEDS literary fiction mostly, children's/juvenile (especially fairy tales, classics), creative nonfiction (especially true crime), erotica, ethnic/multicultural, humor (satire), manga, mystery/suspense, translations, young adult/teen. Does not want superhero or overly violent comics.

HOW TO CONTACT Prefers submissions from writer-artists, creative teams. Send a 1-page synopsis of story along with a few pages of comics (copies, NOT originals) and a SASE. Attends San Diego Comicon. Agented submissions: 2%. Responds to queries in 1 week; to ms/art packages in 3-4 weeks. Sometimes comments on rejected manuscripts.

TERMS Royalties and advance negotiable. Publishes ms 6 months to 1 year after acceptance. Writer's guidelines on website. Artist's guidelines on website. Book catalog free upon request.

NEW ISSUES POETRY & PROSE

Western Michigan University, 1903 W. Michigan Ave., Kalamazoo MI 49008-5463. (269)387-8185. Fax: (269)387-2562. E-mail: new-issues@wmich.edu. Website: wmich.edu/newissues. **Contact:** Managing Editor. Estab. 1996. Publishes hardcover originals and trade paperback originals. Averages 8 titles/year. Has recently published *Vivisect*, by Lisa Lewis; *Pima Road Notebook*, by Keith Ekiss; and *Tocqueville*, by Khaled Mattawa.

NEEDS literary, poetry, translations.

HOW TO CONTACT Query first. All unsolicited mss returned unopened. 50% of books published are by first time authors. Agented submissions: less than 5%. Responds to mss in 6 months.

TERMS Manuscript published 18 months after acceptance. Accepts simultaneous submissions. Writer's guidelines by SASE, e-mail, or online.

NEW LIBRI PRESS

4230 95th Ave. SE, Mercer Island WA 98040. E-mail: stasa@newlibri.com; query@newlibri.com. Website:

http://www.newlibri.com. **Contact:** Michael Muller, Editor (Non-fiction and foreign writers). Estab. 2011.

TIPS "Our audience is someone who is comfortable reading an ebook, or someone who is tired of the recycled authors of mainstream publishing, but still wants a good, relatively fast, reading experience. The industry is changing, while we accept for the traditional model, we are searching for writings who are interested in sharing the risk and controlling their own destiny. We embrace writers with no agent."

NEW VICTORIA PUBLISHERS

P.O. Box 13173, Chicago IL 60613-0173. (773)793-2244. E-mail: newvictoriapub@att.net; queries@newvictoria.com. Website: www.newvictoria.com. **Contact:** Patricia Feuerhaken, president. Estab. 1976. "Publishes mostly lesbian fiction—strong female protagonists. Most well known for Stoner McTavish mystery series." Publishes trade paperback originals. Averages 2-3 total titles/year. Distributes titles through Amazon Books, Bella books, Bulldog Books (Sydney, Australia), and Women and Children First Books (Chicago). Promotes titles "mostly through lesbian feminist media."

Mommy Deadest, by Jean Marcy, won the Lambda Literary Award for Mystery.

NEEDS lesbian, feminist fiction including adventure, erotica, fantasy, historical, humor, mystery (amateur sleuth), or science fiction. "Looking for strong feminist, well drawn characters, with a strong plot and action. We will consider any original, well written piece that appeals to the lesbian/feminist audience." Publishes anthologies or special editions. We advise you to look through our catalog or visit our website to see our past editorial decisions as well as what we are currently marketing. Our books average 80-100,000 words, or 200-220 single-spaced pages. Published *Sparkling Rain*, by Barbara Summerhawk and Kimberly Hughes (2008); *Killing at the Cat*, by Carlene Miller (mystery); *Queer Japan*, by Barbara Summerhawk (anthology); *Skin to Skin*, by Martha Miller (erotic short fiction); *Talk Show*, by Melissa Hartman (novel); *Flight from Chador*, by Sigrid Brunel (adventure); *Owl of the Desert*, by Ida Swearingen (novel).

HOW TO CONTACT Accepts unsolicited mss, but prefers query first. Submit outline, synopsis, and sample chapters (50 pages). No queries by e-mail or fax; please send SASE or IRC. No simultaneous submissions.

TERMS Pays 10% royalty. Publishes ms 1 year after acceptance. Ms guidelines for SASE.

TIPS "We are especially interested in lesbian or feminist novels, ideally with a character or characters who can evolve through a series of books. Stories should involve a complex plot, accurate details, and protagonists with full emotional lives. Pay attention to plot and character development. Read guidelines carefully." "We advise you to look through our catalog or visit our website to see our past editorial decisions as well as what we are currently marketing. Our books average 80-100,000 words, or 200-220 single-spaced pages."

NEXT DECADE, INC.

39 Old Farmstead Rd., Chester NJ 07930. (908)879-6625. Fax: (908)879-2920. E-mail: barbara@nextdecade.com. Website: www.nextdecade.com. **Contact:** Barbara Kimmel, president (reference); Carol Rose, editor.

TIPS "We publish books that simplify complex subjects. We are a small, award-winning press that successfully publishes a handful of books each year."

NORTIA PRESS

27525 Puerta Real, Ste. 100-467, Mission Viejo CA 92701. E-mail: acquisitions@nortiapress.com. Website: www.NortiaPress.com. Estab. 2009. "We focus mainly on literary and historical fiction, but are open to other genres. No vampire stories, science fiction, or erotica, please."

HOW TO CONTACT "Submit a brief, e-mail query for both fiction and nonfiction. Please include a short bio, approximate word count of book, and expected date of completion for nonfiction titles (fiction titles should be completed before sending a query). All unsolicited snail mail will be discarded without review."

TERMS Pays negotiable royalties on wholesale price.

TIPS "We specialize in working with experienced authors who seek a more collaborative and fulfilling relationship with their publisher. As such, we are less likely to accept pitches from first-time authors, no matter how good the idea. As with any pitch, please make your e-mail very brief and to the point, so the reader is not forced to skim it. Always include some biographic information. Your life is interesting."

W.W. NORTON CO., INC.

500 Fifth Ave., New York NY 10110. Fax: (212)869-0856. E-mail: manuscripts@wwnorton.com. Website: www.wwnorton.com. **Contact:** Acquisitions editor. Estab. 1923. Midsize independent publisher of trade books and college textbooks. Publishes literary fiction. Publishes hardcover and paperback originals and reprints. Averages 300 total titles/year.

NEEDS Literary, poetry, poetry in translation, religious. High-qulity literary fiction. Published *Ship Fever*, by Andrea Barrett; *Oyster*, by Jannette Turner Hospital; *Power*, by Linda Hogan.

HOW TO CONTACT *Does not accept unagented submissions or unsolicited mss.* If you would like to submit your proposal (6 pages or less) by e-mail, paste the text of your query letter and/or sample chapter into the body of the e-mail message. Do not send attachments. Responds in 2 months to queries. No simultaneous submissions.

TERMS Pays royalty. Offers advance. Ms guidelines online.

OAK TREE PRESS

140 E. Palmer, Taylorville IL 62568. (217)824-6500. E-mail: oaktreepub@aol.com; queryotp@aol.com. Website: www.oaktreebooks.com. **Contact:** Acquisitions Editor (prefers e-mail contact). Estab. 1998. "Small independent publisher with a philosophy of author advocacy. Welcomes first-time authors, and sponsors annual contests in which the winning entries are published." Publishes hardcover, trade paperback and mass market paperback originals, and reprints. Books: acid-free paper; perfect binding. First novel print order: 1,000. **Published 5 debut authors within the last year.** Plans 8 first novels this year. Averages 12 total titles, 8 fiction titles/year. Member: SPAN, SPAWN. Distributes through Ingram, Baker & Taylor, and Amazon.com. Promotes through website, conferences, PR, author tours.

"I am always on the lookout for good mysteries, ones that engage quickly. I definitely want to add to our Timeless Love list. I am also looking at a lot of nonfiction, especially in the 'how-to' category. We are one of a few publishers who will consider memoirs, especially memoirs of folks who are not famous, and this is because I enjoy reading them myself. In addition, plans are in progress to launch a political/current affairs imprint, and I am actively looking for titles to build this list. Then, of course, there is always that 'special something' book that you can't quite describe, but you know it when you see it. "

NEEDS adventure, confession, ethnic, fantasy (romance), feminist, humor, mainstream/contemporary, mystery (amateur sleuth, cozy, police procedural, private eye/hard-boiled), new age/mystic, picture books, romance (contemporary, futuristic/time travel, romantic suspense), suspense, thriller/espionage, young adult (adventure, mystery/suspense, romance). Emphasis on mystery and romance novels. Recently published *The Poetry of Murder*, by Bernadette Steele (mystery); *Media Blitz*by Joe Nowlan (mystery); *Lake Meade*, by Heather Mosko (romance); *Secrets by the Sea*, by Mary Montague Sikes (paranormal romance); *Easy Money*, by Norm Maher (memoir-police officer), and *The Last Stop: Lincoln and the Mud Circuit*, by Alan Bower (history).

HOW TO CONTACT Does not accept or return unsolicited mss. Query with SASE. Accepts queries by e-mail. Include estimated word count, brief bio, list of publishing credits, brief description of ms. Send SASE for return of ms or send a disposable ms and SASE for reply only. Agented fiction 5%. Responds in 4-6 weeks to queries; 2 months to proposals; 3-6 months to mss. Accepts simultaneous submissions, electronic submissions. No submissions on disk. Rarely comments on rejected mss.

TERMS Pays 10-20% royalty on wholesale price. Average advance: negotiable. Publishes ms 9-18 months after acceptance. Book catalog for SASE or on website www.oaktreebooks.com. Ms guidelines for SASE or on website.

TIPS "Perhaps my most extreme pet peeve is receiving queries on projects which we've clearly advertised we don't want: science fiction, fantasy, epic tomes, bigoted diatribes and so on. Second to that is a practice I call 'over-taping,' or the use of yards and yards of tape, or worse yet, the filament tape so that it takes forever to open the package. Finding story pitches on my voice mail is also annoying."

OBRAKE BOOKS

Obrake Canada, Inc., 3401 Dufferin Street, P.O. Box 27538, Toronto, ON M6A3B8. Fax: (416) 907-5734. E-mail: editors@obrake.com. Website: www.obrake.com. **Contact:** Echez Godoy, acquisitions editor (fiction-suspense, thriller, multicultural, science fiction, literary, romance, short story collection, mystery, ethnic, African based novels, African American characters and interest). Estab. 2006. "We're a small independent publisher of hardcover and trade-paper fiction and nonfiction books. We publish mainly thriller, suspense, romance, mystery, multicutural, and ethnic novels and short story collections." Publishes hardcover originals, paperback originals, paperback reprints. Average print order: 1,500. Debut novel print order: 1,500. **Published 1 new writer(s) last year.** Plans 3 debut novels this year. Averages 10 total titles/year; 7 fiction titles/year. Member Independent Publishers Association PMA (USA), Canadian Booksellers Association (CBA), Book Promoters Association of Canada (BPAC). Distributes/promotes titles through national distributors in USA and Canada, library suppliers/buyers, chain bookstores (e.g. Barnes and Nobles USA, Chapters/Indigo Bookstore Canada), Indigo Books & Music, Online (Amazon), worldwide distribution.

NEEDS adventure, children's/juvenile (adventure, fantasy, historical, mystery), comics/graphic novels, erotica, ethnic/multicultural, feminist, gay, historical (general), horror (psychological, supernatural), lesbian, literary, mainstream, mystery/suspense, psychic/supernatural, regional, religious (mystery/suspense, thriller, romance), romance (contemporary, historical, romantic suspense), short story collections, thriller/espionage, young adult/teen (adventure, fantasy/science fiction, historical, horror, romance).

HOW TO CONTACT Send query letter. Query with outline/synopsis and 3 sample chapters, 50 pages max. Accepts queries by snail mail, e-mail. Include estimated word count, brief bio. Send SASE or IRC for return of ms or disposable copy of ms and SASE/IRC for reply only. Agented fiction: 5%. Responds to queries in 3-6 weeks. Accepts unsolicited mss. Considers simultaneous submissions, submissions on CD or disk. Rarely critiques/comments on rejected mss. Responds to mss in 3-6 months.

TERMS Sends preproduction galleys to author. Ms published 10-18 months after acceptance. Writer's guidelines available for SASE, online at website. Pays royalties 8-15%, advance $350 average. Book catalogs free upon request.

TIPS "Visit our website and follow our submission guidelines."

OCEANVIEW PUBLISHING

595 Bay Isles Rd., Suite 120-G, Longboat Key FL 34228. E-mail: submissions@oceanviewpub.com. Website: www.oceanviewpub.com. **Contact:** Robert Gussin, CEO. Estab. 2006.

ONSTAGE PUBLISHING

190 Lime Quarry Rd., Suite 106-J, Madison AL 35758-8962. (256)308-2300, (888)420-8879. E-mail: onstage123@knology.net. Website: www.onstagepublishing.com. **Contact:** Dianne Hamilton, senior editor. Estab. 1999.

To everyone who has submitted a ms, we are currently about 18 months behind. We should get back on track eventually. Please feel free to submit your ms to other houses. OnStage Publishing understands that authors work very hard to produce the finished ms and we do not have to have exclusive submission rights. Please let us know if you sell your ms. Meanwhile, keep writing and we'll keep reading for our next acquisitions.

TIPS "Study our titles and get a sense of the kind of books we publish, so that you know whether your project is likely to be right for us."

ORCA BOOK PUBLISHERS

P.O. Box 5626, Stn. B, Victoria BC V8R 6S4 Canada. Fax: (877)408-1551. E-mail: orca@orcabook.com. Website: www.orcabook.com. **Contact:** Christi Howes, editor (picture books); Sarah Harvey, editor (young readers); Andrew Wooldridge, editor (juvenile and teen fiction); Bob Tyrrell, publisher (YA, teen). Estab. 1984. Only publishes Canadian authors. Publishes hardcover and trade paperback originals, and mass market paperback originals and reprints. Books: quality 60 lb. book stock paper; illustrations. Average print order: 3,000-5,000. First novel print order: 3,000-5,000. Averages 30 total titles/year. "If you are considering submitting to Orca, it's a good idea to spend some time in a bookstore or library looking at the kind of books we publish. A quick read of 3 or 4 of our picturebooks or the back-cover copy of 3 or 4 novels will give you a good idea whether your manuscript will be a good fit with our list."

Only publishes Canadian authors.

NEEDS hi-lo, juvenile (5-9 years), literary, mainstream/contemporary, young adult (10-18 years). "Ask for guidelines, find out what we publish." Looking for "children's fiction."

HOW TO CONTACT Query with SASE or submit proposal package including outline, 2-5 sample chapter(s), synopsis, SASE. Agented fiction 20%. Responds in 1 month to queries; 1-2 months to mss. No simultaneous submissions. Sometimes comments on rejected mss. **Manuscripts can be mailed to:** Orca Book Publishers, PO Box 5626, Station B, Victoria, BC V8R 6S4.

TERMS Pays 10% royalty. Publishes ms 12-18 months after acceptance. Book catalog for 8½x11 SASE. Ms guidelines online.

TIPS "Our audience is for students in grades K-12. Know our books, and know the market."

◐ OUTRIDER PRESS, INC.

2036 North Winds Dr., Dyer IN 46311. (219)322-7270. Fax: (219)322-7085. E-mail: outriderpress@sbcglobal.net. Website: www.outriderpress.com. **Contact:** Whitney Scott, editor. Estab. 1988. Small literary press and hand bindery; publishes many first-time authors. Publishes paperback originals. Books: 70 lb. paper; offset printing; perfect bound. Average print order: 2,000. **Published 25-30 debut authors within the last year.** Distributes titles through Baker & Taylor.

NEEDS ethnic, experimental, family saga, fantasy (space fantasy, sword and sorcery), feminist, gay/lesbian, historical, horror (psychological, supernatural), humor, lesbian, literary, mainstream/contemporary, mystery (amateur sleuth, cozy, police procedural, private eye/hard-boiled), new age/mystic, psychic/supernatural, romance (contemporary, futuristic/time travel, gothic, historical, regency period, romantic suspense), science fiction (soft/sociological), short story collections, thriller/espionage, western (frontier saga, traditional). Published *Telling Time*, by Cherie Caswell Dost; *If Ever I Cease to Love*, by Robert Klein Engler; *62000 Reasons*, by Paul Miller; *Aquarium Octopus*, by Claudia Van Gerven; and *Heat*, by Deborah Thompson.

HOW TO CONTACT Accepts unsolicited mss. Query with SASE. Accepts queries by mail. Include estimated word count, brief bio, list of publishing credits. Agented fiction 10%. Responds in 6 weeks to queries; 4 months to mss. Accepts simultaneous submissions, electronic submissions, submissions on disk. Sometimes comments on rejected mss. In affiliation with Tallgrass Writers Guild, publishes an annual anthology with cash prizes. Anthology theme for 2012 is: "'Deep waters: rivers, lakes and seas.' As always, broadly interpreted with a variety of historic/geographic/psychological settings welcomed." Postmark deadline is Feb. 27, 2012. For complete guidelines, e-mail outriderpress@sbcglobal.net.

TERMS Pays honorarium. Publishes ms 6 months after acceptance. Ms guidelines for SASE or e-mail.

TIPS "It's always best to familiarize yourself with our publications. We're especially fond of humor/irony."

◐ RICHARD C. OWEN PUBLISHERS, INC.

P.O. Box 585, Katonah NY 10536. (914)232-3903; (800)262-0787. E-mail: richardowen@rcowen.com. Website: www.rcowen.com. **Contact:** Richard Owen, publisher. Estab. 1982. "We believe children become enthusiastic, independent, life-long readers when supported and guided by skillful teachers who choose books with real and lasting value. The professional development work we do and the books we publish support these beliefs." Publishes hardcover and paperback originals. Published 15 debut authors within the last year. Averages 23 total titles/year. Distributes titles to schools via mail order. Promotes titles through website, database mailing, reputation, catalog, brochures and appropriate publications—magazines, etc.

NEEDS picture books. "Brief, strong story line, believable characters, natural language, exciting—child-appealing stories with a twist. No lists books, alphabet or counting books." Seeking short, snappy stories and articles for 7-8-year-old children (2nd grade). Subjects include humor, careers, mysteries, science fiction, folk tales, women, fashion trends, sports, music, mysteries, myths, journalism, history, inventions, planets, architecture, plays, adventure, technology, vehicles. Published *Mama Cut My Hair*, by Lisa Wilkinson (fiction, debut author); *Cool*, by Steven Morse (fiction, debut author); and *Author on My Street*, by Lisa Brodie Cook (fiction).

HOW TO CONTACT Responds in 1 month to queries; 5 months to mss. Accepts simultaneous submissions.

TERMS Pays 5% royalty on wholesale price. Books for Young Learners Anthologies: flat fee for all rights. Publishes ms 2-5 years after acceptance. Ms guidelines online.

TIPS "We don't respond to queries or e-mails. Please do not fax or e-mail us. Because our books are so brief, it is better to send an entire manuscript. We publish story books with inherent educational value for young readers—books they can read with enjoyment and success."

PACIFIC PRESS PUBLISHING ASSOCIATION

Trade Book Division, P.O. Box 5353, Nampa ID 83653-5353. (208)465-2500. Fax: (208)465-2531. E-mail: booksubmissions@pacificpress.com. Website: www.pacificpress.com. **Contact:** Scott Cady, acquisitions editor (children's stories, biography, Christian living, spiritual growth); David Jarnes, book editor (theology, doctrine, inspiration). Estab. 1874.

TIPS "Our primary audience is members of the Seventh-day Adventist denomination. Almost all are written by Seventh-day Adventists. Books that do well for us relate the Biblical message to practical human concerns and focus more on the experiential rather than theoretical aspects of Christianity. We are assigning more titles, using less unsolicited material—although we still publish manuscripts from freelance submissions and proposals."

PANTHEON BOOKS

Random House, Inc., 1745 Broadway, 3rd Floor, New York NY 10019. E-mail: pantheonpublicity@randomhouse.com. Website: www.pantheonbooks.com. Estab. 1942. "Small but well-established imprint of well-known larger house." Publishes hardcover and trade paperback originals and trade paperback reprints.

> Pantheon Books publishes both Western and non-Western authors of literary fiction and important nonfiction. "We only accept mss submitted by an agent. You may still send a 20-50 page sample and a SASE to our slushpile. Allow 2-6 months for a response."

NEEDS Quality fiction and nonfiction. Published *Crooked Little Heart*, by Anne Lamott.

HOW TO CONTACT *Does not accept unsolicited mss.* Send SASE or IRC. No simultaneous submissions.

TERMS Pays royalty. Offers advance.

PAYCOCK PRESS

3819 No. 13th St., Arlington VA 22201. (703)525-9296. E-mail: hedgehog2@erols.com. Website: www.gargoylemagazine.com. **Contact:** Lucinda Ebersole and Richard Peabody. Estab. 1976. "Too academic for underground, too outlaw for the academic world. We tend to be edgy and look for ultra-literary work." Publishes paperback originals. Books: POD printing. Average print order: 500. Averages 1 total title/year. Member CLMP. Distributes through Amazon and website.

NEEDS experimental, literary, short story collections.

HOW TO CONTACT Accepts unsolicited mss. Accepts queries by e-mail. Include brief bio. Send SASE for return of ms or send a disposable ms and SASE for reply only. Agented fiction 5%. Responds in 1 month to queries; 4 months to mss. Accepts simultaneous submissions, electronic submissions. Rarely comments on rejected mss.

TERMS Publishes ms 12 months after acceptance.

TIPS "Check out our website. Two of our favorite writers are Paul Bowles and Jeanette Winterson."

PEACHTREE CHILDREN'S BOOKS

Peachtree Publishers, Ltd., 1700 Chattahoochee Ave., Atlanta GA 30318-2112. (404)876-8761. Fax: (404)875-2578. E-mail: hello@peachtree-online.com. Website: www.peachtree-online.com. **Contact:** Helen Harriss, submissions editor. "We publish a broad range of subjects and perspectives, with emphasis on innovative plots and strong writing." Publishes hardcover and trade paperback originals. Averages 30 total titles, 20-25 fiction titles/year.

IMPRINTS Freestone; Peachtree Jr.

NEEDS juvenile, picture books, young adult. Looking for very well-written middle grade and young adult novels. No adult fiction. No short stories. Published *Martina the Beautiful Cockroach, Night of the Spadefoot Toads, The Boy Who Was Raised by Librarians.*

HOW TO CONTACT Submit 3 sample chapter(s) or submit complete ms. Responds in 6 months to queries; 6 months to mss. Accepts simultaneous submissions.

TERMS Pays royalty on retail price; advance varies. Publishes ms 1 year or more after acceptance. Book catalog for 6 first-class stamps. Ms guidelines online.

PEACHTREE PUBLISHERS, LTD.

1700 Chattahoochee Ave., Atlanta GA 30318-2112. E-mail: jackson@peachtree-online.com; hello@peachtree-online.com. Website: www.peachtree-online.com. **Contact:** Helen Harriss, acquisitions. Estab. 1978. Publishes 30-35 titles/year. Peachtree currently publishes the following categories: children's fiction and nonfiction picture books, chapter books, middle readers, young adult books; Education, parenting, self-help, and health books of interest to the general trade.

NEEDS picture books, young readers: adventure, animal, concept, history, nature/environment. Middle readers: adventure, animal, history, nature/environment, sports. Young adults: fiction, mystery, adventure. Peachtree does **not** publish historical novels (except children's/young adult), science fiction, fantasy, romance, westerns, horror, poetry, short stories, plays, business, scientific or technical reference, or books intended specifically as textbooks.

HOW TO CONTACT Submit complete ms (picture books) or 3 sample chapters (chapter books), bio by postal mail only. Responds to queries/mss in 6-9 months. Publishes a book 1-2 years after acceptance. Will consider simultaneous submissions. All manuscripts must be sent by US Mail. We will not review any manuscript sent on CD or diskette. Submissions should be addressed to: Helen Harriss, Acquisitions Editor, Peachtree Publishers, 1700 Chattahoochee Ave., Atlanta, GA 30318.

TERMS "Manuscript guidelines for SASE, visit website or call for a recorded message. No fax or e-mail submittals or queries please."

PEDLAR PRESS

P.O. Box 26, Station P, Toronto ON M5S 2S6 Canada. (416)534-2011. E-mail: feralgrl@interlog.com. Website: www.pedlarpress.com. **Contact:** Beth Follett, owner/editor. Publishes hardcover and trade paperback originals. **Published 50% debut authors within the last year.** Averages 7 total titles/year. Distributes in Canada through LitDistCo.; in the US distributes directly through publisher.

NEEDS Experimental, feminist, gay/lesbian, literary, picture books, short story collections. Canadian writers only. Published *Black Stars in a White Night Sky*, by Jonarno Lawson, illustrated by Sherwin Tjia.

HOW TO CONTACT Query with SASE, sample chapter(s), synopsis.

TERMS Pays 10% royalty on retail price. Average advance: $200-400. Publishes 1 year after acceptance of final revised ms.

TIPS "I select manuscripts according to my taste, which fluctuates. Be familiar with some if not most of Pedlar's recent titles."

PELICAN PUBLISHING COMPANY

1000 Burmaster St., Gretna LA 70053. (504)368-1175. Fax: (504)368-1195. E-mail: editorial@pelicanpub.com. Website: www.pelicanpub.com. **Contact:** Nina Kooij, editor-in-chief. Estab. 1926. "We seek writers on the cutting edge of ideas. We believe ideas have consequences. One of the consequences is that they lead to a best-selling book." Publishes hardcover, trade paperback and mass market paperback originals and reprints. Books: hardcover and paperback binding; illustrations sometimes. Buys juvenile mss with illustrations. Averages 65 total titles/year. Distributes titles internationally through distributors, bookstores, libraries. Promotes titles at reading and book conventions, in trade magazines, in radio interviews, print reviews and TV interviews.

NEEDS Considers picture books for young readers or Louisiana historical middle-grade novels. All writers should send us a query letter and SASE, describing the project briefly and concisely. Multiple (or "simultaneous") or e-mail queries are not considered.

HOW TO CONTACT Does not accept unsolicited mss except for picture books (1,100 words). For Louisiana historical middle-grade novels, submit outline, 2 sample chapters. Responds in 1 month to queries; 3 months to mss. No simultaneous or multiple submissions. Rarely comments on rejected mss.

TERMS Pays royalty on actual receipts. Average advance: considered. Publishes ms 9-18 months after acceptance. Book catalog for SASE or on website. Writer's guidelines on website.

TIPS "We do extremely well with cookbooks, popular histories, and business. We will continue to build in these areas. The writer must have a clear sense of the market and knowledge of the competition. A query letter should describe the project briefly, give the author's writing and professional credentials, and promotional ideas."

PEMMICAN PUBLICATIONS

150 Henry Ave., Main Floor RM 12, Winnipeg MB R3B 0J7 Canada. (204)589-6346. Fax: (204)589-2063. E-mail: mcilroy@pemmican.mb.ca. Website: www.pemmican.mb.ca. **Contact:** Randal McIlroy, managing editor. Estab. 1980. Metis adult and children's books. Publishes paperback originals. Books: stapled-bound smaller books and perfect-bound larger ones; 4-color illustrations, where applicable. Average print order: 1,500. First novel print order: 1,000. **Published some debut authors within the last year.** Averages 6 total titles/year. Distributes titles through press releases, website, fax, catalogues, and book displays.

NEEDS stories by and about the Canadian Metis experience, especially from a modern adult or young-adult perspective. Recently published *Flight of the Wild Geese* (YA fiction), by T.D. Thompson; *River of Tears* (adult fiction), by Linda Ducharme; and *Kawlija's Blueberry Promise* (children's fiction), by Audrey Guiboche.

HOW TO CONTACT Accepts unsolicited mss by conventional mail only. Submit samples and synopsis. Send SASE for return of ms or send a disposable ms and SASE for reply only. Return postage for outside of Canada must be provided in IRCs. Accepts simultaneous submissions.

TERMS Pays 10% royalty. Provides 10 author's copies. Average advance: $350.

PENGUIN GROUP USA

375 Hudson St., New York NY 10014. (212)366-2000. Website: www.penguin.com. **Contact:** Peter Stampfel, Submission Editor, DAW Books. "The company possesses perhaps the world's most prestigious list of best-selling authors and a backlist of unparalleled breadth, depth and quality." General-interest publisher of both fiction and nonfiction.

"Penguin Young Readers Group: Never send submissions by e-mail or fax. Never send cassettes, CDs, marketing plans, or original artwork. Please mail only one ms at a time and please be sure to retain a copy of your submission. Because confirmation postcards are easily separated from or hidden within the ms, please do not include them with your submission. Please refrain from calling, faxing, or e-mailing to inquire after the status of an unsolicited submission, as we will be unable to assist you. If you have not received a reply from us after 4 months, you can safely assume that we are not interested in publishing your work."

IMPRINTS *No unsolicited mss.* Submit work through a literary agent. Exceptions are DAW Books and G.P. Putnam's Sons Books for Young Readers, which are accepting submissions. See individual listings for more information. **Penguin Adult Division**: Ace Books, Alpha Books, Avery, Berkley Books, Dutton, Gotham Books, HPBooks, Hudson Street Press, Jove, New American Library, Penguin, The Penguin Press, Perigee, Plume, Portfolio, G.P. Putnam's Sons, Riverhead, Sentinel, Jeremy P. Tarcher, Viking; **Penguin Children's Division:** Dial Books for Young Readers, Dutton Children's Books, Firebird, Grosset & Dunlap, Philomel, Price Stern Sloan, Puffin Books, G.P. Putnam's Sons, Speak, Viking Children's Books, Frederick Warne.

NEEDS science fiction/fantasy genre

HOW TO CONTACT "Due to the high volume of mss we receive, Penguin Group (USA) Inc. imprints do not normally accept unsolicited mss. On rare occasion, however, a particular imprint may be open to reading such. The Penguin Group (USA) web site features a listing of which imprints (if any) are currently accepting unsolicited manuscripts." Continue to check website for updates to the list.

TERMS Pays advance and royalties, depending on imprint.

TIPS DAW Books is currently accepting manuscripts in the science fiction/fantasy genre. Refer to DAW's Submission Guidelines. For Penguin Young Readers Group submissions, see guidelines at: http://us.penguingroup.com/static/html/aboutus/pyrg-subguides.html.

THE PERMANENT PRESS

Attn: Judith Shepard, 4170 Noyac Rd., Sag Harbor NY 11963. (631)725-1101. E-mail: judith@thepermanentpress.com; shepard@thepermanentpress.com. Website: www.thepermanentpress.com. **Contact:** Judith and Martin Shepard, acquisitions/publishers. Estab. 1978. Mid-size, independent publisher of literary fiction. "We keep titles in print and are active in selling subsidiary rights." Publishes hardcover originals. Average print order: 1,500. Averages 14 total titles. Promotes titles through reviews. Acquisitions: Judith and Martin Shepard, publishers. Estab. 1978.

NEEDS literary, mainstream/contemporary, mystery. Especially looking for high-line literary fiction, "artful, original and arresting." Accepts any fiction category as long as it is a "well-written, original full-length novel." Published *Black Swan* and five other thrillers by Chris Knopf; *All Cry Chaos* by Leonard Rosen; *The Double Life of Alfred Buber* by Davis Schmahmann; *The Singular Exploits of Wonder Mom & Party Girl* by Marc Schuster; *The Ringer* by Jenny Shank; and multiple novels by Michael Stein, Larry Duberstein, Howard Owen, Berry Fleming, and K.C. Frederick.

HOW TO CONTACT Accepts unsolicited mss. Send SASE for return of ms or send a disposable ms and SASE for reply only. Responds in weeks or months to queries and submissions. We don't accept simultaneous submissions.

TERMS Pays 10-15% royalty on wholesale price. Offers $1,000 advance. Publishes ms within 18 months after acceptance.

TIPS "We are looking for good books; be they 10th novels or first ones, it makes little difference. The fiction is more important than the track record. Send us the first 25 pages, it's impossible to judge something that begins on page 302. Also, no outlines—let the writing present itself."

PIATKUS BOOKS

Little, Brown Book Group, 100 Victoria Embankment, London WA EC4Y 0DY United Kingdom. 0207 911 8000. Fax: 0207 911 8100. E-mail: info@littlebrown.co.uk. Website: piatkus.co.uk. **Contact:** Emma Beswetherick, senior editor. Estab. 1979. "Until 2007, Piatkus operated as an independent publishing house. Now it exists as a commercial imprint of Hachette-owned Little, Brown Book Group. Publishes hardcover originals, paperback originals, and paperback reprints."

Piatkus no longer accepts fiction proposals.

NEEDS quality family saga, historical, literary. Bestselling authors include: Nora Roberts, JD Robb, Christina Jones, Julia Quinn, Nick Brownlee.

HOW TO CONTACT To submit a nonfiction proposal to Piatkus, please send a letter of enquiry outlining the work and 3 sample chapters. We do not accept e-mailed book proposals. Accepts unsolicited mss. Query with SASE or submit first 3 sample chapter(s), synopsis. Accepts queries by mail. Include estimated word count, brief bio, list of publishing credits. Send SASE for return of ms or send a disposable ms and SASE for reply only. Agented fiction 90%. Hopes to respond in 12 weeks to mss. Accepts simultaneous submissions. No submissions on disk or via e-mail. Rarely comments on rejected mss.

TERMS Pays royalty. Average advance: negotiable. Publishes ms 1 year after acceptance. Ms guidelines for SASE.

TIPS "Study our list before submitting your work."

PICADOR USA

MacMillan, 175 Fifth Ave., New York NY 10010. (212)674-5151. E-mail: david.saint@picadorusa.com; pressinquiries@macmillanusa.com. Website: www.picadorusa.com. **Contact:** Frances Coady, publisher (literary fiction). Estab. 1994. Picador publishes high-quality literary fiction and nonfiction. "We are open to a broad range of subjects, well written by authoritative authors." Publishes hardcover and trade paperback originals and reprints. Averages 70-80 total titles/year. Titles distributed through Von Holtzbrinck Publishers. Titles promoted through national print advertising and bookstore co-op.

The Amazing Adventures of Kavalier & Clay, by Michael Chabon, won the Pulitzer Prize for fiction; *In America*, by Susan Sontag, won National Book Award; Jame Crace's *Being Dead* won the National Book Critics Circle Award.

NEEDS literary. Published *No One Thinks of Greenland*, by John Griesmer (first novel, literary); *Summerland*, by Malcolm Knox (first novel, literary fiction); *Half a Heart*, by Rosellen Brown (literary fiction).

HOW TO CONTACT Does not accept unsolicited mss. *Agented submissions only.* Accepts queries by e-mail, fax, mail. Responds in 2 months to queries. Accepts simultaneous submissions.

TERMS Pays 7½-15% royalty on retail price. Average advance: varies. Publishes ms 18 months after acceptance. Book catalog for 9×12 SASE and $2.60 postage; ms guidelines for #10 SASE or online.

PINEAPPLE PRESS, INC.

P.O. Box 3889, Sarasota FL 34230. (941)739-2219. E-mail: info@pineapplepress.com. Website: www.pineapplepress.com. **Contact:** June Cussen, exec. editor. Estab. 1982. Small, independent trade publisher. Publishes hardcover and trade paperback originals. Books: quality paper; offset printing; Smyth-sewn or perfect bound; illustrations occasionally. Averages 25 total titles/year. Distributes titles through Pineapple, Ingram, and Baker & Taylor. Promotes titles through reviews, advertising in print media, direct mail, author signings, and the World Wide Web.

NEEDS Will only consider fiction set in Florida.

HOW TO CONTACT Does not accept unsolicited mss. Query with sample, SASE. Responds in 2 months to queries. Accepts simultaneous submissions.

TERMS Pays 6½-15% royalty on net receipts. Average advance: rare. Publishes ms 18 months after acceptance. Book catalog for 9×12 SAE with $1.34 postage.

TIPS "Quality first novels will be published, though we usually only do one or two novels per year and they must be set in Florida. We regard the author/editor relationship as a trusting relationship with communication open both ways. Learn all you can about the publishing process and about how to promote your book once it is published. A query on a novel without a brief sample seems useless."

PIPERS' ASH, LTD.

Pipers' Ash, Church Road, Christian Malford, Chippenham, Wiltshire SN15 4BW United Kingdom. (44)(124)972-0563. Fax: (44)(870)056-8916. E-mail: pipersash@supamasu.com. Website: www.supamasu.com. **Contact:** Manuscript Evaluation Desk. Estab. 1976. "Small press publisher. Considers all submitted manuscripts fairly—without bias or favor. This company is run by book lovers, not by accountants." Publishes hardcover and electronic originals. **Published 18 debut authors within the last year.** Averages 18 total titles, 18 fiction titles/year. Distributes and promotes titles through press releases, catalogs, website shopping basket, direct mail, and the Internet.

IMPRINTS Salisbury; Ely; Canterbury; Lincoln; Gloucester; Durham.

NEEDS adventure, children's/juvenile (adventure), confession, feminist, historical, literary, mainstream/contemporary, military/war, regional, religious, romance (contemporary, romantic suspense), science fiction (hard science/technological, soft/sociological), short story collections, sports, suspense, young adult (adventure,science fiction). "We publish 30,000-word novellas and short story collections. Visit our website for submission guidelines and tips. Authors are invited to submit collections of short stories and poetry for consideration for our ongoing programs." Published *Belly-Button Tales and Other Things*, by Sandra McTavish; *Cosmic Women*, by Margaret Karamazin; *A Sailor's Song*, by Leslie Wilkie.

HOW TO CONTACT Accepts unsolicited mss. Query with SASE or IRC or submit sample chapter(s), 25-word synopsis (that sorts out the writers from the wafflers). Accepts queries by e-mail, fax, phone. Include estimated word count. Send SASE or IRC for return of ms, or send a disposable ms and SASE or IRC for reply only. Responds in 1 month to queries; 3 months to mss. Accepts electronic submissions, submissions on disk. No simultaneous submissions. Always comments on rejected mss.

TERMS Pays 10% royalty on wholesale price. Also gives 5 author's copies. Publishes ms 6 months after acceptance. Ms guidelines online, www.supumasu.com.

TIPS "Study the market! Check your selected publisher's catalogue and website."

PLAN B PRESS

P.O. Box 4067, Alexandria VA 22303. (215)732-2663. E-mail: planbpress@gmail.com. Website: www.planbpress.com. **Contact:** Steven Allen May, president. Estab. 1999. Plan B Press is a "small publishing company with an international feel. Our intention is to have Plan B Press be part of the conversation about the direction and depth of literary movements and genres. Plan B Press's new direction is to seek out authors rarely-to-never published, sharing new voices that might not otherwise be heard. Plan B Press is determined to merge text with image, writing with art." Publishes poetry and short fiction. Wants "experimental poetry, concrete/visual work." Does not want "sonnets, political or religious poems, work in the style of Ogden Nash." Has published poetry by Lamont B. Steptoe, Michele Belluomini, Jim Mancinelli, Lyn Lifshin, Robert Miltner, and Steven Allen May. Publishes 1 poetry book/year and 5-10 chapbooks/year. Manuscripts are selected through open submission and through competition (see below). Books/chapbooks are 24-48 pages, with covers with art/graphics.

PLEXUS PUBLISHING, INC.

143 Old Marlton Pike, Medford NJ 08055-8750. (609)654-6500. Fax: (609)654-4309. E-mail: jbryans@plexuspublishing.com. Website: www.plexuspublishing.com. **Contact:** John B. Bryans, editor-in-chief/publisher. Estab. 1977. Small, regional publisher focusing on titles for New Jersey residents and visitors. Publishes hardcover and paperback originals. Query with SASE. Responds in 3 months to proposals. Average advance: $500-1,000. Book catalog and ms guidelines for 10×13 SASE.

NEEDS mysteries and literary novels with a strong regional (southern NJ) angle.

HOW TO CONTACT Query with SASE. Accepts simultaneous submissions.

POCOL PRESS

Box 411, Clifton VA 20124. (703)830-5862. Website: www.pocolpress.com. **Contact:** J. Thomas Hetrick, editor. Estab. 1999. Pocol Press publishes first-time, unagented authors. Our fiction deals mainly with single, author short story collections from outstanding niche writers. Publishes paperback originals. Books: 50 lb. paper; offset printing; perfect binding. Average print order: 500. **Published 2 debut authors within the last year.** Averages 4-6 total titles, 3 fiction titles/

year. Member: Small Press Publishers Association. Distributes titles through website, authors, e-mail, word-of-mouth and readings.

"Our authors are comprised of veteran writers and emerging talents."

NEEDS horror (psychological, supernatural), literary, mainstream/contemporary, short story collections, baseball. Published *Gulf*, by Brock Adams (short fiction); *The Last of One* by Stephan Solberg (novel); *A Good Death* by David E. Lawrence.

HOW TO CONTACT Does not accept or return unsolicited mss. Query with SASE or submit 1 sample chapter(s). Accepts queries by mail only. Include estimated word count, brief bio, list of publishing credits. Responds in 2 weeks to queries; 2 months to mss. No simultaneous submissions, submissions on disk. Sometimes comments on rejected mss.

TERMS Pays 10-12% royalty. Publishes ms 1 year or less after acceptance. Book catalog for SASE or on website. Ms guidelines for SASE or on website.

TIPS "Our audience is aged 18 and over. Pocol Press is unique; we publish good writing and great storytelling. Write the best stories you can. Read them to your friends/peers. Note their reaction. Publishes some of the finest fiction by a small press."

POISONED PEN PRESS

6962 E. 1st Ave., #103, Scottsdale AZ 85251. (480)945-3375. Fax: (480)949-1707. E-mail: editor@poisonedpenpress.com; info@poisonedpenpress.com; submissions@poisonedpenpress.com. Website: www.poisonedpenpress.com. **Contact:** Jessica Tribble. Estab. 1996. Publishes hardcover originals and paperback reprints. Books: 60 lb. paper; offset printing; hardcover binding. Average print order: 3,500. First novel print order: 3,000. **Published 4 debut authors within the last year.** Plans 5 first novels this year. Member Publishers Marketing Associations, Arizona Book Publishers Associations, Publishers Association of West. Distributes through Ingram, Baker & Taylor, Brodart.

NEEDS mystery (amateur sleuth, cozy, police procedural, private eye/hard-boiled, historical). Published *Sweeping Up Glass*, by Carolyn D. Wall (mystery/fiction); *Impulse*, by Frederick Ramsay (mystery/fiction); *Murder in the Dark*, by Kerry Greenwood(mystery/fiction); *Drive*, by James Sallis (mystery/fiction).

HOW TO CONTACT Accepts unsolicited mss. Electronic queries only. Accepts queries by e-mail to editor@poisonedpenpress.com. Responds in 1-3 weeks to queries; 9-12 months to mss. Only accepts electronic submissions. No simultaneous submissions. Often comments on rejected mss.

TERMS Pays 9-15% royalty. Average advance: $1,000. Publishes ms 12-15 months after acceptance. Ms guidelines online.

TIPS "Audience is adult readers of mystery fiction."

PRAIRIE JOURNAL PRESS

P.O. Box 68073, Calgary AB T3G 3N8 Canada. E-mail: prairiejournal@yahoo.com. Website: www.geocities.com/prairiejournal/. **Contact:** Anne Burke, literary editor. Estab. 1983. Estab. 1983. Small-press, noncommercial literary publisher. Publishes paperback originals. Books: bond paper; offset printing; stapled binding; b&w line drawings. **Published some debut authors within the last year.** Distributes titles by mail and in bookstores and libraries (public and university). Promotes titles through direct mail, reviews and in journals.

Prairie Journal Press authors have been nominees for The Journey Prize in fiction and finalists and honorable mention for the National Magazine awards. Prairie Journal Press authors have been nominees for The Journey Prize in fiction and finalists and honorable mention for the National Magazine awards.

NEEDS literary, short story collections. Published *Prairie Journal Fiction, Prairie Journal Fiction II* (anthologies of short stories); *Solstice* (short fiction on the theme of aging); and *Prairie Journal Prose*.

HOW TO CONTACT Accepts unsolicited mss. Sometimes comments on rejected mss.

TERMS Pays 1 author's copy; honorarium depends on grant/award provided by the government or private/corporate donations. SAE with IRC for individuals. No U.S. stamps please.

TIPS "We wish we had the means to promote more new writers. We look for something different each time and try not to repeat types of stories if possible. We receive fiction of very high quality. Short fiction is preferable although excerpts from novels are considered if they stand alone on their own merit."

PS BOOKS

Philadelphia Stories, Inc., 2021 S. 11th St., Philadelphia PA 19148. (215)551-5889. Fax: (215)635-0195. E-mail: info@psbookspublishing.org; marc@psbookspublishing.org. Website: www.psbookspublishing.org. **Contact:** Marc Schuster, acquisitions editor. Estab. 2008. Due to an overwhelming number of submissions, **PS Books is no longer accepting unsolicited manuscripts**. If, in the future, we return to reading unsolicited manuscripts, the following guidelines will apply. "In 2008, the publishers of *Philadelphia Stories* magazine launched a books division called PS Books. The needs of PS Books closely mirror those of the magazine; we are looking for novel-length fiction and narrative nonfiction manuscripts featuring polished prose, a controlled voice, strong characters, and interesting subjects. Please read our current titles to get a sense of what we publish. For information on submitting a query package, please visit our website." Publishes paperback originals. Format: cougar smooth paper; offset commercial printing; perfect-bound. Average print order: 500-1,000. Debut novel print order: 500-1,000. Plans 1 debut novel this year. Averages 2 total titles/year; 1-2 fiction titles/year. Member CLMP. Distributes/promotes titles Baker & Taylor, direct marketing.

NEEDS humor, literary, mainstream, regional (Delaware valley, greater Philadelphia). Anthologies planned include *The Best of Philadelphia Stories*, vol. 2; *By Any Other Name*. Published *Broad Street*, by Christine Weiser (upmarket commercial fiction); *The Singular Exploits of Wonder Mom and Party Girl*, by Marc Schuster (literary fiction).

HOW TO CONTACT Query with outline/synopsis and first 20 pages. Accepts queries by e-mail only. Include estimated word count, brief bio, list of publishing credits. Send disposable copy of ms and SASE for reply only. Responds to queries in 2 months. Considers simultaneous submissions, e-mail submissions. Rarely critiques/comments on rejected mss. Responds to mss in 3 months.

TERMS Manuscript published within 1 year after acceptance.

TIPS "We are looking for well written literary or upmarket commercial fiction and non-fiction. We prefer novels to be under 300 pages (100,000 words) and expect authors to submit a marketing plan. Only send us polished work that fits our guidelines. We encourage authors to read our current titles and to read work published on the *Philadelphia Stories* website."

PUCKERBRUSH PRESS

413 Neville Hall, Orono ME 04469. (207)581-3832. Website: http://puckerbrushreview.com. **Contact:** Sanford Phippen, editor. Estab. 1971. "Small independent trade publisher, unique because of editorial independent stance." Publishes trade paperback originals and reprints of literary fiction and poetry. Books: perfect bound, illustrations. Average print order: 500. **Published 3 debut authors within the last year.** Averages 3-4 total titles, 1-2 fiction titles/year. Titles distributed through Amazon.com, Baker & Taylor, Barnes & Noble.

NEEDS literary, short story collections. Published *Cora's Seduction*, by Mary Gray Hughes (short stories); *When Soft Was the Sun*, by Merle Hillman (fiction); *The Crow on the Spruce*, by C. Hall (Maine fiction); *Night-Sea Journey*, by M. Alpert (poetry).

HOW TO CONTACT Accepts unsolicited mss. Submit complete ms. Accepts queries by phone. Include brief bio, list of publishing credits. Responds in 1 month to queries; 3 months to mss. No simultaneous submissions. Often comments on rejected mss.

TERMS Pays 10-15% royalty on wholesale price. Book catalog for large SASE and 34¢. Ms guidelines for SASE.

TIPS "Be true to your vision, not to fashion." "For sophisticated readers who retain love of literature. Maine writers continue to be featured."

PUFFIN BOOKS

Imprint of Penguin Group (USA), Inc., 345 Hudson St., New York NY 10014. (212)366-2000. Website: www.penguinputnam.com. **Contact:** Kristin Gilson, editorial director. Puffin Books publishes high-end trade paperbacks and paperback reprints for preschool children, beginning and middle readers, and young adults. Publishes trade paperback originals and reprints. Averages 175-225 total titles/year.

NEEDS young adult, middle grade; easy-to-read grades 1-3. "We publish paperback reprints and original titles. We do not publish original picture books." Noted Puffin picture book authors and illustrators include Jan Brett, Eric Carle, Graeme Base, Tomie de Paola, Ezra Jack Keats, Rosemary Wells, Paul Zelinsky, E. B. Lewis, Jon Scieszka, Lane Smith, David Catrow, Patricia Polacco. Published *Three Cups of Tea, Young Readers Edition*by Greg Mortenson and David Oliver Relin, adapted for young readers by Sarah Thomson.

HOW TO CONTACT Does not accept unsolicited mss. Send SASE or IRC. Responds in 3 months to mss. No simultaneous submissions.

TERMS Royalty varies. Average advance: varies. Publishes ms 1 year after acceptance. Book catalog for 9×12 SAE with 7 first-class stamps; send request to Marketing Department.

TIPS "Our audience ranges from little children 'first books' to young adult (ages 14-16). An original idea has the best luck."

PUREPLAY PRESS

350 Judah St., Suite 302, San Francisco CA 94122. E-mail: info@pureplaypress.com; editor@pureplaypress.com. Website: www.pureplaypress.com. **Contact:** David Landau, editor & publisher. "We are a small, niche publisher devoted to Cuba's history and culture. The e-book is becoming the focus of our business." Books are in English, Spanish, and bilingual formats. Guidelines online.

NEEDS "Founded in 2001 by writers and editors who felt the need to publish works about Cuba's history and culture. At present we have 12 books in print, all with Cuban themes, and we are beginning to publish on other subjects. Our byword is *freedom* from the status quo. The qualities we prize in the written word are sincerity, simplicity, elegance and clarity of expression. We are convinced that culture is infinite, and creativity general. We strive to be considerate to readers and encouraging to writers. Our books are closely edited, carefully designed, printed with high-quality materials and then marketed by all plausible means, including the World Wide Web. We are interested in fiction, history, poetry, politics and culture."

HOW TO CONTACT "While we cannot receive unsolicited manuscripts, we will consider proposals of up to 250 words in length. The most effective proposal is a statement about the work that might serve as copy for a book-jacket or a back cover."

G.P. PUTNAM'S SONS

Penguin Putnam, Inc., 345 Hudson St., New York NY 10014. (212)414-3610. Fax: (212)366-2664. E-mail: susan.kochan@us.penguingroup.com. Website: www.penguinputnam.com; www.us.penguingroup.com. **Contact:** Susan Kochan, associate editorial director. Penguin Putnam Books For Young Readers, 345 Hudson St., New York NY 10014. (212)414-3610. Website: www.us.penguingroup.com. **Manuscript Acquisitions:** Publishes 25 picture books/year; 15 middle readers/year; 5 young adult titles/year. 5% of books by first-time authors; 50% of books from agented authors.

G. Putnam's Sons 2007 titles *Slam*, by Nick Hornby, and *The Three Snow Bears*, by Jan Brett, were #1 on the *New York Times* Bestseller List.

NEEDS juvenile picture books: animal, concept, contemporary, humor, multicultural. Young readers: adventure, contemporary, history, humor, multicultural, special needs, suspense/mystery. Middle readers: adventure, contemporary, history, humor, fantasy, multicultural, problem novels, sports, suspense/mystery. Young adults: contemporary, history, fantasy, problem novels, special needs. Does not want to see series. Average word length: picture books—200-1,000; middle readers—10,000-30,000; young adults—40,000-50,000. Recently published *Good Night, Goon: A Parody* by Michael Rex (ages 4-8); *Geek Magnet*, by Kieran Scott (ages 12 and up).

HOW TO CONTACT Accepts unsolicited mss. No SASE required, as will only respond if interested. Picture books: send full mss. Fiction: Query with outline/synopsis and 10 manuscript pages. When submitting a portion of a longer work, please provide an accompanying cover letter that briefly describes your manuscript's plot, genre, the intended age group, and your publishing credits, if any. Do not send art unless requested. Responds to mss within 4 months if interested. Will consider simultaneous submissions.

TERMS Pays authors royalty based on retail price. Sends prepublication galleys to authors.

TIPS "Study our catalogs and get a sense of the kind of books we publish, so that you know whether your project is likely to be right for us."

QUIXOTE PRESS

3544 Blakslee St., Wever IA 52658. (800)571-2665. Fax: (319)372-7485. Website: www.heartsntummies.com. **Contact:** Bruce Carlson. Quixote Press specializes in humorous and/or regional folklore and special-interest cookbooks. Publishes trade paperback originals and reprints. **Published many debut authors within the last year.**

NEEDS humor, short story collections. Published *Eating Ohio*, by Rus Pishnery (short stories about Ohio); *Lil' Red Book of Fishing Tips*, by Tom Whitecloud (fishing tales); *How to Talk Hoosier*, by Netha Bell (humor);

Cow Whisperer, by Skip Holmes (humor); *Flour Sack Bloomers*, by Lucy Fetterhoff (history).

HOW TO CONTACT Query with SASE. Accepts simultaneous submissions.

TERMS Pays 10% royalty on wholesale price. Publishes ms 1 year after acceptance.

TIPS "Carefully consider marketing considerations. Audience is women in gift shops, on farm sites, direct retail outlets, wineries, outdoor sport shops, etc. Contact us at *your idea* stage, not complete ms stage. Be receptive to design input by us."

RANDOM HOUSE, INC.

1745 Broadway, New York NY 10013. Website: www.randomhouse.com. Estab. 1925. "Random House has long been committed to publishing the best literature by writers both in the United States and abroad."

HOW TO CONTACT *Agented submissions only.*

TERMS Pays royalty. Offers advance. Ms guidelines online.

RANSOM PUBLISHING

Radley House, 8 St. Cross Road, Winchester Hampshire SO23 9HXUK United Kingdom. +44 (0) 01962 862307. Fax: +44 (0) 05601 148881. E-mail: ransom@ransom.co.uk. Website: www.ransom.co.uk. **Contact:** Jenny Ertle, editor. Estab. 1995. Independent UK publisher with distribution in English-speaking markets throughout the world. Specializes in books for reluctant and struggling readers. Our high-quality, visually stimulating, age appropriate material has achieved wide acclaim for its ability to engage and motivate those who either can't or won't read. One of the few English-language publishers to publish books with very high interest age and very low reading age. Has a developing list of children's books for home and school use. Specializes in phonics and general reading programs. Publishes paperback originals. **Published 5 debut authors within the last year.** Member BESA (UK), IPG (UK).

NEEDS easy reading for young adults. Books for reluctant and struggling readers.

HOW TO CONTACT Accepts unsolicited mss. Query with SASE or submit outline/proposal. Prefers queries by e-mail. Include estimated word count, brief bio, list of publishing credits. Responds in 3-4 weeks to queries. Accepts simultaneous submissions, electronic submissions, submissions on disk. Never comments on rejected mss.

TERMS Pays 10% royalty on net receipts. Ms guidelines by e-mail.

RED DEER PRESS

195 Allstate Pkwy., Markham ON L3R 4TB Canada. (905)477-9700. Fax: (905)477-9179. E-mail: rdp@reddeerpress.com; dionne@reddeerpress.com; val@reddeerpress.com. Website: www.reddeerpress.com. **Contact:** Richard Dionne, publisher. Estab. 1975. Publishes young adult, adult nonfiction, science fiction, fantasy, and paperback originals "focusing on books by, about, or of interest to Canadians." Books: offset paper; offset printing; hardcover/perfect-bound. Average print order: 5,000. First novel print order: 2,500. Distributes titles in Canada and the US, the UK, Australia, and New Zealand.

Red Deer Press has received numerous honors and awards from the Book Publishers Association of Alberta, Canadian Children's Book Centre, the Governor General of Canada and the Writers Guild of Alberta.

NEEDS young adult (juvenile and early reader), contemporary. No romance or horror. Published *A Fine Daughter*, by Catherine Simmons Niven (novel); *The Kappa Child*, by Hiromi Goto (novel); *The Dollinage*, by Martine Leavitt; and *The Game*, by Teresa Toten (nominated for the Governor General's Award); *The Drum Calls Softly*, by David Bouchard (Aboriginal Picture Book); *Greener Grass*, by Caroline Pignat (Winner of the Governor General's Award); *Big Big Sky*, by Kristyn Dunnion (novel).

HOW TO CONTACT Accepts unsolicited mss. Query with SASE. Responds in 6 months to mss. Accepts simultaneous submissions. No submissions on disk.

TERMS Pays 8-10% royalty. Advance is negotiable. Publishes ms 1 year after acceptance. Book catalog for 9×12 SASE.

TIPS "We're very interested in young adult and children's fiction from Canadian writers with a proven track record (either published books or widely published in established magazines or journals) and for manuscripts with regional themes and/or a distinctive voice. We publish Canadian authors exclusively."

RED HEN PRESS

P.O. Box 3537, Granada Hills CA 91394. (818)831-0649. Fax: (818)831-6659. E-mail: redhenpressbooks.com. Website: www.redhen.org. **Contact:** Mark E. Cull, publisher/editor (fiction). Estab. 1993. Publishes trade paperback originals. **Published 10% of books from debut authors within the last year.** Averages 22 total titles, 10 fiction titles/year.

The mission of Red Hen Press is to discover, publish, and promote works of literary excellence that have been overlooked by mainstream presses, and to build audiences for literature in two ways: by fostering the literacy of youth and by bringing distinguished and emerging writers to the public stage.

NEEDS ethnic, experimental, feminist, gay/lesbian, historical, literary, mainstream/contemporary, short story collections. "We prefer high-quality literary fiction." Published *The Misread City: New Literary Los Angeles*, edited by Dana Gioia and Scott Timberg; *Rebel*, by Tom Hayden.

HOW TO CONTACT Query with SASE. Agented fiction 10%. Accepts simultaneous submissions

TERMS Publishes book 1 year after acceptance of ms. Publishes ms 1 year after acceptance. Book catalog and ms guidelines available via website or free.

TIPS "Audience reads poetry, literary fiction, intelligent nonfiction. If you have an agent, we may be too small since we don't pay advances. Write well. Send queries first. Be willing to help promote your own book."

RED SAGE PUBLISHING, INC.

P.O. Box 4844, Seminole FL 33775. (727)391-3847. E-mail: submissions@eredsage.com. Website: www.eredsage.com. **Contact:** Alexandria Kendall, publisher; Theresa Stevens, managing editor. Estab. 1995.

RED TUQUE BOOKS, INC.

477 Martin St., Unit #6, Penticton BC V2A 5L2 Canada. (778)476-5750. Fax: (778)476-5651. Website: www.redtuquebooks.ca. **Contact:** David Korinetz, executive editor. "Red Tuque Books is a new small publisher/distributor specializing in new and established Canadian authors." Publishes paperback originals, reprints. Average first novel print order 1,200-2,000. Publishes up to 4 debut authors each year. Publishes 4 fiction titles each year.

NEEDS adventure, short story collections, young adult and teen (specifically adventure and science fiction), graphic novels, and fantasy (space fantasy, sword and sorcery).

HOW TO CONTACT Submit a query letter and first 5 pages. Include total word count. A 1-page synopsis is optional. Accepts queries by e-mail and mail. SASE for reply only. Responds in 3 weeks. Does not consider simultaneous submissions. Sometimes comments on rejected mss. $250 advance, royalties are 5-7% on net sales. Time between acceptance and publication is one year. Writer's guidelines and book catalogs on website.

TIPS "Well-plotted, character-driven stories, preferably with happy endings, will have the best chance of being accepted. Keep in mind that authors who like to begin sentences with "and, or, and but" are less likely to be considered. Don't send anything gruesome or overly explicit; tell us a good story, but think PG."

RENAISSANCE HOUSE

465 Westview Ave, Englewood NJ 07631. (800)547-5113. E-mail: raquel@renaissancehouse.net. Website: www.renaissancehouse.net. Publishes hardcover and trade paperback originals. **Published 25-30% debut authors within the last year.** Averages 30 total titles/year.

NEEDS fantasy, juvenile, multicultural, picture books, legends, fables. Recently published: *Yes, You Can Too. The Life of Barack Obama*: First Place, Young Adult Non-Fiction, Bilingual, International Latino Book Awards, 2010; *Go, Milka, Go*: First Place,Young Adult Sports/Recreation, Bilingual, International Latino Book Awards, 2009.

HOW TO CONTACT Query with SASE. Agented fiction 25%. Responds in 2 months to queries; 2 months to mss. Accepts simultaneous submissions.

TERMS Pays 5-10% royalty on net receipts. Ms guidelines online.

REPUBLIC OF TEXAS PRESS

Imprint of Taylor Trade Publishing, and part of Rowman and Littlefield Publishing Group, 5360 Manhattan Circle, #101, Boulder CO 80303. (303)543-7835, ext. 318. E-mail: tradeeditorial@rowman.com. Website: www.rlpgtrade.com. **Contact:** Acquisitions Director.

TIPS "Do not submit any original materials, as they will not be returned. Our market is adult."

RIVER CITY PUBLISHING

1719 Mulberry St., Montgomery AL 36106. E-mail: jgilbert@rivercitypublishing.com. Website: www.rivercitypublishing.com. **Contact:** Jim Gilbert, editor. Estab. 1989. Midsize independent publisher (8-10 books per year). River City primarily publishes narrative nonfiction that reflects the South. We are looking for mainly for narrative histories, sociological accounts, and travel. Only biographies and memoirs from noted persons will be considered; we are closed to all personal memoir submissions. Include a cover page detailing the project and your experience that makes you an expert in the subject, along with 3-5 sample chapters. *We do not publish self-help, how-to, business, medicine, religion, education, or psychology. Publishes hardcover and trade paperback originals. Averages 6 total titles, 2 fiction titles/year.

NEEDS literary fiction, narrative nonfiction, regional (Southern), short story collections. No poetry, memoir, or children's books. Published *Murder Creek*, by Joe Formichella (true crime); *Breathing Out the Ghost*, by Kirk Curnutt (novel); *The Bear Bryant Funeral Train*, by Brad Vice (short story collection).

HOW TO CONTACT Accepts unsolicited submissions and submissions from unagented authors, as well as those from established and agented writers. Submit 5 consecutive sample chapters or entire manuscript for review. "Please include a short biography that highlights any previous writing and publishing experience, sales opportunities the author could provide, ideas for marketing the book, and why you think the work would be appropriate for River City." **Mail submissions to:** Acquisitions Editor, River City Publishing, 1719 Mulberry Street, Montgomery, AL 36106. Send appropriate-sized SASE or IRC, "otherwise, the material will be recycled." Also accepts queries by e-mail at: jgilbert@rivercitypublishing.com. "Please include your electronic query letter as inline text and not an as attachment; we do not open unsolicited attachments of any kind. Please do not include sample chapters or your entire manuscript as inline text. We do not field or accept queries by telephone." Agented fiction 25%. Responds in 3-9 months; "please wait at least 3 months before contacting us about your submission." Accepts simultaneous submissions. No multiple submissions. Rarely comments on rejected mss.

TERMS Pays 10-15% royalty on retail price. Average advance: $500-5,000. Publishes ms 1 year after acceptance.

TIPS "Only send your best work after you have received outside opinions. From approximately 1,000 submissions each year, we publish no more than 8 books and few of those come from unsolicited material. Competition is fierce, so follow the guidelines exactly. All first-time novelists should submit their work to the Fred Bonnie Award contest."

RIVERHEAD BOOKS

Penguin Putnam, 375 Hudson Street, Office #4079, New York NY 10014. E-mail: ecommerce@us.penguingroup.com; riverhead.web@us.penguingroup.com. Website: www.riverheadbooks.com. **Contact:** Megan Lynch, senior editor.

NEEDS literary, mainstream, contemporary. Among the award-winning writers whose careers Riverhead has launched so far are Pearl Abraham (*The Romance Reader*; *Giving Up America*), Jennifer Belle (*Going Down*; *High Maintenance*), Adam Davies (*The Frog King*), Junot Diiaz (*Drown*), Alex Garland (*The Beach*; *The Tesseract*), Nick Hornby (*High Fidelity*; *About a Boy*; *How to Be Good*), Khaled Hosseini (*The Kite Runner*), ZZ Packer (*Drinking Coffee Elsewhere*), Iain Pears (*The Dream of Scipio*; *Instance of the Fingerpost*), Danzy Senna (*Caucasia*), Gary Shteyngart (*The Russian Debutante's Handbook*), Aryeh Lev Stollman (*The Far Euphrates*; *The Illuminated Soul*; *The Dialogues of Time and Entropy*), Sarah Waters (*Tipping the Velvet*; *Affinity*; *Fingersmith*).

HOW TO CONTACT Submit through agent only. No unsolicited mss.

ROCKY MOUNTAIN BOOKS

406-13th Ave. NE, Calgary AB T2E 1C2 Canada. (403)249-9490. Fax: (403)249-2968. E-mail: rmb@heritagehouse.ca. Website: www.rmbooks.com. **Contact:** Fraser Seely, publisher.

RONSDALE PRESS

3350 W. 21st Ave., Vancouver BC V6S 1G7 Canada. (604)738-4688. Fax: (604)731-4548. E-mail: ronsdale@shaw.ca. Website: http://ronsdalepress.com. **Contact:** Ronald B. Hatch, director (fiction, poetry, social commentary); Veronica Hatch, managing director (children's literature). Estab. 1988. Ronsdale Press is "dedicated to publishing books that give Canadians new insights into themselves and their country." Publishes trade paperback originals. Books: 60 lb. paper; photo offset printing; perfect binding. Average print order: 1,500. **Published some debut authors within the last year.** Averages 11 total titles, 3 fiction titles/year. Sales representation: Literary Press Group. Distribution: LitDistco. Promotes titles through ads in BC Bookworld and Globe & Mail and interviews on radio.

NEEDS literary, short story collections, novels. Canadian authors *only*. Published *The City in the Egg*by Michel Tremblay (novel); *River of Gold*, by Susan Dobbie (novel); and *What Belongs*, by F.B. Andreé (short story collection).

HOW TO CONTACT Accepts unsolicited mss. Accepts short queries by e-mail. Send SASE or IRC. Address: Ronsdale Press 3350 West 21st Avenue, Vancouver, B.C., Canada V6S 1G7. Phone: (604)738-4688; Fax: (604)731-4548. Email: ronsdale@shaw.ca. Responds in 2 weeks to queries; 2-3 months to mss. Accepts simultaneous submissions. Sometimes comments on rejected mss.

TERMS Pays 10% royalty on retail price. Publishes ms 1 year after acceptance. Ms guidelines online.

TIPS "Ronsdale Press is a literary publishing house, based in Vancouver, and dedicated to publishing books from across Canada, books that give Canadians new insights into themselves and their country. We aim to publish the best Canadian writers."

SAINT MARY'S PRESS

702 Terrace Heights, Winona MN 55987-1318. (800)533-8095. Fax: (800)344-9225. E-mail: submissions@smp.org. Website: www.smp.org. **Contact:** Submissions Editor.

TIPS "Request product catalog and/or do research online of Saint Mary Press book lists before submitting proposal."

SALVO PRESS

E-mail: schmidt@salvopress.com; query@salvopress.com. Website: www.salvopress.com. **Contact:** Scott Schmidt, publisher. Estab. 1998. "We are a small press specializing in mystery, suspense, espionage and thriller fiction. Our press publishes in trade paperback and most e-book formats." Publishes hardcover, trade paperback originals, and e-books in most formats. Books: 5½×8½; or 6×9 printing; perfect binding. **Published 6 debut authors within the last year.** Averages 6-12 fiction total titles/year, mostly fiction.

NEEDS adventure, literary, mystery (amateur sleuth, police procedural, private/hard-boiled), science fiction (hard science/technological), suspense, thriller/espionage. "Our needs change. Check our website." Published *Crown of Thorns*, by Hank Luce (religious thriller); *Terralus 4*, by Lee Gimenez (sci-fi), *Memory Leak*, by Trevor Schmidt (sci-fi), and *Gift of the Bouda*, by Richard Farnsworth (horror).

HOW TO CONTACT Query by e-mail only at query@salvopress.com. Please place the word "Query" as the subject. Include estimated word count, brief bio, list of publishing credits, "and something to intrigue me so I ask for more." Agented fiction 15%. Responds in 5 minutes to 1 month to queries; 2 months to mss. No simultaneous submissions.

TERMS Pays 10% royalty. Publishes ms 9-12 months after acceptance. Book catalog and ms guidelines online.

SAMHAIN PUBLISHING, LTD

577 Mulberry Street, Ste. 1520, Macon GA 31201. (478)314-5144. Fax: (478)314-5148. E-mail: editor@samhainpublishing.com. Website: samhainpublishing.com. **Contact:** Laurie M. Rauch, executive editor. Estab. 2005. "A small, independent publisher, Samhain's motto is 'It's all about the story.' We look for fresh, unique voices who have a story to share with the world. We encourage our authors to let their muse have its way and to create tales that don't always adhere to current trends. One never knows what the next hot genre will be or when it will start, so write what's in your soul. These are the books that, whether the story is based on formula or is an original, when written from the heart will earn you a life-time readership." Publishes e-books and paperback originals. Format: POD/offset printing; line illustrations. **Published 20-30 new writers last year.** Plans 20 or more debut novels this year. Averages 300 fiction titles/year. Distributes/promotes titles through Ingrams Publisher Services and through a variety of media outlets both online and offline.

Preditor and Editors Best Publisher 2006

NEEDS erotica and all genres and all heat levels of romance (contemporary, futuristic/time travel, gothic, historical, paranormal, regency period, romantic suspense, fantasy, action/adventure, etc.), as well as fantasy, urban fantasy, or science fiction with strong romantic elements, with word counts between 12,000 and 120,000 words. Anthologies planned include *Springtime Just Romance Anthology*, *Cyberpunk Romance Anthology*, *End of Days Post-Apocalyptic Romance Anthology*. Open calls for submissions are available on the website. Full manuscript is required for special anthologies, and the editor in charge of anthology selects final stories. Published *Here Kitty, Kitty*, by Shelly Laurenston (paranormal); *Unbroken*, by Maya Banks (contemporary erotic romance); *Silent Blade*, by Ilona Andrews (sci-fi/futuristic).

HOW TO CONTACT Query with outline/synopsis and either 3 sample chapters or the full manuscript. Accepts queries by e-mail only. Include estimated word count, brief bio, list of publishing credits, and "how the author is working to improve craft: association, critique groups, etc." Responds to queries and mss within 10-16 weeks. Accepts unsolicited mss. Sometimes critiques/comments on rejected mss. Guidelines on website.

TERMS Sends preproduction galleys to author. Ms published 6-18 months after acceptance. Writers' guidelines on website. Pays royalties 30-40% for e-books, average of 8% for trade paper, and author's copies (quantity varies). Book catalogs on website.

TIPS "Because we are an e-publisher first, we do not have to be as concerned with industry trends and can publish less popular genres of fiction if we believe the story and voice are good and will appeal to our customers. Please follow submission guidelines located on our website, include all requested information and proof your query/manuscript for errors prior to submission."

SARABANDE BOOKS, INC.

2234 Dundee Rd., Suite 200, Louisville KY 40205. (502)458-4028. Fax: (502)458-4065. E-mail: info@sarabandebooks.org. Website: www.sarabandebooks.org. **Contact:** Sarah Gorham, editor-in-chief. Estab. 1994. "Small literary press publishing poetry, short fiction and literary nonfiction." Publishes trade paperback originals. **Published some debut authors within the last year.** Averages 12 total titles, 3-4 prose titles/year. Distributes titles through Consortium Book Sales & Distribution. Promotes titles through advertising in national magazines, sales reps, brochures, newsletters, postcards, catalogs, press release mailings, sales conferences, book fairs, author tours and reviews.

Charges $10 handling fee with alternative option of purchase of book from website (e-mail confirmation of sale must be included with submission).

NEEDS literary, novellas, short novels, 250 pages maximum, 150 pages minimum. We consider novels and nonfiction in a wide variety of genres and subject matters with a special emphasis on mysteries and crime fiction. We do not consider science fiction, fantasy, or horror. Our target length is 70-90,000 words. Queries can be sent via e-mail, fax or regular post. Submissions to Mary McCarthy Prize in Short Fiction accepted January-February. Published *Other Electricities*, by Ander Monson; *More Like Not Running Away*, by Paul Shepherd, and *Water: Nine Stories*, by Alyce Miller.

HOW TO CONTACT See website for McCarthy Contest entry form. Accepts simultaneous submissions. **Charges $10 handling fee** with alternative option of purchase of book from website (e-mail confirmation of sale must be included with submission).

TERMS Pays royalty of 10% on actual income received. Publishes ms 18 months after acceptance. Ms guidelines for #10 SASE.

TIPS "Make sure you're not writing in a vacuum, that you've read and are conscious of contemporary literature. Have someone read your manuscript, checking it for ordering, coherence. Better a lean, consistently strong manuscript than one that is long and uneven. We like a story to have good narrative, and we like to be engaged by language. Sarabande publishes for a general literary audience. Know your market. Read and buy books of literature. Sponsors contests for poetry and fiction."

SCHOLASTIC PRESS

Imprint of Scholastic, Inc., 557 Broadway, New York NY 10012. (212)343-6100. Fax: (212)343-4713. Website: www.scholastic.com. **Contact:** David Saylor, editorial director (picture books) David Levithan, editorial director, middle grade, young adult; Dianne Hess, executive editor (picture books, early chapter books, middle grade, YA); Tracy Mack, executive editor (picture books, middle grade, young adult); Kara LaReau, executive editor; Anamika Bhatnager, senior editor (picture books, early chapter books, middle grade). Publishes hardcover originals. **Published some debut authors within the last year.** Averages 30 total titles/year. Promotes titles through trade and library channels.

NEEDS Juvenile, picture books, novels. Wants "fresh, exciting picture books and novels—inspiring, new talent." Published *Chasing Vermeer*, by Blue Balliet; *Here Today*, by Ann M. Martin; *Detective LaRue*, by Mark Teague.

HOW TO CONTACT Does not accept unsolicited mss. *Agented submissions and submissons by published authors only.* No simultaneous submissions.

TERMS Pays royalty on retail price. Average advance: variable. Publishes ms 18-24 months after acceptance.

TIPS "Be a big reader of juvenile literature before you write and submit!"

SCIENCE & HUMANITIES PRESS

P.O. Box 7151, Chesterfield MO 63006-7151. (636)394-4950. E-mail: banis@sciencehumanitiespress.com; publisher@sciencehumanitiespress.com. Website: www.sciencehumanitiespress.com. **Contact:** Dr. Bud Banis, publisher. Publishes trade paperback originals and reprints, and electronic originals and reprints. **Published 25% of books from debut authors within the last year.** Averages 20-30 total titles/year.

IMPRINTS Science & Humanities Press, BeachHouse Books, MacroPrintBooks (large print editions), Heuristic Books, Early Editions Books.

NEEDS adventure, historical, humor, literary, mainstream/contemporary, military/war, mystery, regional, romance, science fiction, short story collections, spiritual, sports, suspense, western, young adult. "We prefer books with a theme that gives a market focus. Brief description by e-mail."

HOW TO CONTACT Responds in 3 months to queries; 3 months to solicited mss. Do not send unsolicited mss. Accepts simultaneous submissions.

TERMS Pays 8% royalty on retail price. Publishes ms 6-12 months after acceptance. Ms guidelines online.

TIPS "Our expertise is electronic publishing for continuous short-run-in-house production."

SEAL PRESS

1700 4th St., Berkeley CA 94710. (510)595-3664. E-mail: Seal.Press@perseusbooks.com; sealacquisitions@avalonpub.com. Website: www.sealpress.com. **Contact:** Acquisitions Editor. Estab. 1976. "Midsize independent feminist book publisher interested in original, lively, radical, empowering and culturally diverse books by women." Publishes mainly trade paperback originals. Books: 55 lb. natural paper; Cameron Belt, Web or offset printing; perfect binding; illustrations occasionally. Averages 22 total titles/year. Titles distributed by Publishers Group West.

NEEDS ethnic, feminist, gay/lesbian, literary, multicultural. "We are interested in alternative voices." Published *Valencia*, by Michelle Tea (fiction); *Navigating the Darwin Straits*, by Edith Forbes (fiction); and *Bruised Hibiscus*, by Elizabeth Nunez (fiction).

HOW TO CONTACT Does not accept fiction at present. Query with SASE or submit outline, 2 sample chapter(s), synopsis. See guidelines online. Responds in 2 months to queries. Accepts simultaneous submissions.

TERMS Pays 7-10% royalty on retail price. Pays variable advance. Publishes ms 18 months after acceptance. Book catalog and ms guidelines for SASE or online. Ms guidelines online.

TIPS "Our audience is generally composed of women interested in reading about women's issues addressed from a feminist perspective."

SECOND STORY PRESS

20 Maud St., Suite 401, Toronto ON M5V 2M5 Canada. Phone: (416)537-7850. Fax: (416)537-0588. E-mail: info@secondstorypress.ca. Website: www.secondstorypress.ca. Accepts appropriate material from residents of Canada only. Fiction and nonfiction: Submit complete ms or submit outline and sample chapters by postal mail only. No electronic submissions or queries.

NEEDS Considers nonsexist, non-racist, and non-violent stories, as well as historical fiction, chapter books.

HOW TO CONTACT Fiction and nonfiction: Submit complete ms or submit outline and sample chapters by postal mail only. No electronic submissions or queries.

SEVEN STORIES PRESS

140 Watts St., New York NY 10013. (212)226-8760. Fax: (212)226-1411. E-mail: anna@sevenstories.com; info@sevenstories.com. Website: www.sevenstories.com. **Contact:** Daniel Simon; Anna Lui. Estab. 1995. "Publishers of a distinguished list of authors in fine literature, journalism and contemporary culture." Publishes hardcover and trade paperback originals. Average print order: 5,000. **Published some debut authors within the last year.** Averages 40-50 total titles, 10 fiction titles/year. Distributes through Consortium Book Sales and Distribution.

NEEDS literary. Plans anthologies. Ongoing series of short story collections for other cultures (e.g., contemporary fiction from Central America; from Vietnam, etc.). *A Place to Live and Other Selected Essays of Natalia Ginzburg*, edited by Lynne Sharon Schwartz; *American Falls*, by Barry Gifford; *The Incantation of Frida K.*, by Kate Braverman.

HOW TO CONTACT Currently not accepting submissions. Please check website for updates.

TERMS Pays 7-15% royalty on retail price. Offers advance. Publishes ms 1-3 years after acceptance. Book catalog and ms guidelines free.

SEVERN HOUSE PUBLISHERS

9-15 High St., Sutton Surrey SM1 1DF United Kingdom. (0208)770-3930. Fax: (0208)770-3850. Website: www.severnhouse.com. **Contact:** Amanda Stewart, editorial director. Publishes hardcover and trade paperback originals and reprints Averages 150 total titles/year.

IMPRINTS Creme de la Crime

NEEDS adventure, fantasy, historical, horror, mainstream/contemporary, mystery, romance, short story collections, suspense. Recently published *Future Scrolls*, by Fern Michaels (historical romance); *Weekend Warriors*, by Fern Michaels; *The Hampton Passion*, by Julie Ellis (romance); *Looking Glass Justice*, by Jeffrey Ashford (crime and mystery); and *Cold Tactics*, by Ted Allbeury (thriller).

HOW TO CONTACT *Agented submissions only.* Accepts simultaneous submissions.

TERMS Pays 7½-15% royalty on retail price. Average advance: $750-5,000.

SILVER LEAF BOOKS, LLC

P.O. Box 6460, Holliston MA 01746. E-mail: editor@silverleafbooks.com. Website: www.silverleafbooks.com. **Contact:** Brett Fried, editor. "Silver Leaf Books is a small press featuring primarily new and upcoming talent in the fantasy, science fiction, mystery, thrillers, suspense, and horror genres. Our editors work closely with our authors to establish a lasting and mutually beneficial relationship, helping both the authors and company continue to grow and thrive." Publishes hardcover originals, trade paperback originals, paperback originals, electronic/digital books. Average print order: 3,000. Debut novel print order: 3,000. **Published 1 new writer last year.** Plans 4 debut novels this year. Averages 6 total titles/year; 6 fiction titles/year. Distributes/promotes titles through Baker & Taylor Books and Ingram.

NEEDS fantasy (space fantasy, sword and sorcery), horror (dark fantasy, futuristic, psychological, supernatural), mystery/suspense (amateur sleuth, cozy, police procedural, private eye/hard-boiled), science fiction (hard science/technological, soft/sociological), young adult (adventure, fantasy/science fiction, horror, mystery/suspense). Published *The Apprentice of Zoldex* and *The Darkness Within*, by Clifford B. Bowyer, and *When the Sky Fell* by Mike Lynch and Brandon Barr.

HOW TO CONTACT Query with outline/synopsis and 3 sample chapters. Accepts queries by snail mail. Include estimated word count, brief bio, and marketing plan. Send SASE or IRC for return of ms or disposable copy of ms and SASE/IRC for reply only. Agented fiction: 25%. Responds to queries in 6 months. Responds to mss in 4 months. Accepts unsolicited mss. Sometimes critiques/comments on rejected mss.

TERMS Manuscript published 12-24 months after acceptance. Writer's guidelines on website. Pays royalties, and provides author's copies.

TIPS "Follow the online guidelines, be thorough and professional."

SIMON & SCHUSTER ADULT PUBLISHING GROUP

1230 Avenue of the Americas, New York NY 10020. E-mail: ssonline@simonsays.com; Lydia.Frost@simonandschuster.com. Website: www.simonsays.com. Estab. 1924 (formerly Simon & Schuster Trade Division, Division of Simon & Schuster). The Simon & Schuster Adult Publishing Group includes a number of publishing units that offer books in several formats. Each unit has its own publisher, editorial group, and publicity department. Common sales and business departments support all the units. The managing editorial, art, production, marketing, and subsidiary rights departments have staff members dedicated to the individual imprints.

HOW TO CONTACT *Agented submissions only.*

SMALL BEER PRESS

150 Pleasant St., #306, Easthampton MA 01027. (413) 203-1636. Fax: (413) 203-1636. E-mail: info@smallbeerpress.com. Website: www.smallbeerpress.com. **Contact:** Gavin J. Grant, Acquisitions. Estab. 2000. Averages 8-10 fiction titles/year.

Small Beer Press also publishes the zine *Lady Churchill's Rosebud Wristlet*. "SBP's books have recently received the Tiptree and Crawford Awards and have been Indiebound."

NEEDS literary, experimental, speculative, story collections. Recently published *The Monkey's Wedding and Other Stories*, by Joan Aiken; *Meeks*, by Julia Holmes; *What I Didn't See and Other Stories*, by Karen Joy Fowler.

HOW TO CONTACT "We do not accept unsolicited novel or short story collection manuscripts. Queries are welcome. Please send queries with an SASE by mail."

TIPS "Please be familiar with our books first to avoid wasting your time and ours, thank you."

SOFT SKULL PRESS INC.

Counterpoint, 1919 Fifth St., Berkeley CA 94710. (510)704-0230. Fax: (510)704-0268. E-mail: info@softskull.com. Website: www.softskull.com. **Contact:** Fiction or nonfiction editor (whichever is appropriate). Publishes hardcover and trade paperback originals. Averages 40 titles/year.

NEEDS confession, experimental, pop culture, gay/lesbian, erotica, graphic novels and comics, literary, mainstream/contemporary, multicultural, short story collections. Agented submissions encouraged.

HOW TO CONTACT Soft Skull Press accepts unsolicited submissions. Email with a subject heading of "SUBMISSION OF Fiction/Nonfiction/Graphic Novel" (whichever is appropriate). Include contact information on your attachment/s, be that a sample chapter or the whole manuscript. Attachments should be no bigger than 2 megabytes. For graphic novels, send a minimum of five fully inked pages of art, along with a synopsis of your storyline. Responds in 2 months to proposals; 3 months to mss. No simultaneous submissions.

TERMS Pays 7-10% royalty. Average advance: $100-15,000. Publishes ms 6 months after acceptance. Book catalog free or on website. Ms guidelines online.

TIPS "See our website for updated submission guidelines. Submit electronically."

SOHO PRESS, INC.

853 Broadway, New York NY 10003. E-mail: soho@sohopress.com. Website: www.sohopress.com. **Contact:** Bronwen Hruska, Publisher; Katie Herman, editor. Estab. 1986. "Independent publisher known for sophisticated fiction, mysteries set abroad, women's interest (no genre) novels and multicultural novels." Publishes hardcover and trade paperback originals and reprint editions. Books: perfect binding; halftone illustrations. First novel print order varies. **Published 7 debut authors within the last year.** Averages 70 total titles, 65 fiction titles/year. Distributes titles through Consortium Book Sales & Distribution in the US and Canada, Turnaround in England.

NEEDS adventure, ethnic, feminist, historical, literary, mainstream/contemporary, mystery (police procedural), suspense, multicultural. Published *Thirty-Three Teeth*, by Colin Cotterill; *When Red Is Black*, by Qiu Xiaolong; *Murder on the Ile Saint-Louis*, by Cara Black; *The Farming of Bones*, by Edwidge Danticat; *The Darkest Child*, by Delores Phillips; *The First Wave*, by James R. Benn.

HOW TO CONTACT Send first three chapters. Include estimated word count, brief bio, list of publishing credits. Send SASE for return of ms or send a disposable ms and SASE for reply only. Agented fiction 85%. Responds in 3 months to queries; 3 months to mss. Accepts simultaneous submissions. No electronic submissions. Sometimes comments on rejected mss.

TERMS Pays 10-15% royalty on retail price for hardcovers, 7.5% on trade paperbacks. Offers advance. Publishes ms 18-24 months after acceptance. Ms guidelines online.

TIPS "Soho Press publishes discerning authors for discriminating readers, finding the strongest possible writers and publishing them. Before submitting, look at our website for an idea of the types of books we publish, and read our submission guidelines."

Ⓐ SOURCEBOOKS LANDMARK

Sourcebooks, Inc., P.O. Box 4410, Naperville IL 60567-4410. E-mail: info@sourcebooks.com; romance@sourcebooks.com. Website: www.sourcebooks.com. **Contact:** Leah Hultenschmidt. "Our fiction imprint, Sourcebooks Landmark, publishes a variety of commercial fiction, including specialties in historical fiction and Austenalia. We are interested first and foremost in books that have a story to tell."

> We publish a variety of titles. We are currently only reviewing agented fiction manuscripts with the exception of Romance fiction. Find out more information about our Romance fiction submission guidelines online at our website.

NEEDS "We are actively acquiring single-title and single-title series Romance fiction (90,000 to 120,000 actual digital words) for our Casablanca imprint. We are looking for strong writers who are excited about marketing their books and building their community of readers, and whose books have something fresh to offer in the genre of Romance." Receipt of e-mail submissions will be acknowledged within 21 days via e-mail.

HOW TO CONTACT Responds to queries in 6-8 weeks. E-mail: romance@sourcebooks.com. Or mail hard copy to: Leah Hulltenschmidt, Sourcebooks, Inc., 390 Fifth Ave., Suite 907, New York, NY 10018. If you have any questions about our guidelines, please don't hesitate to e-mail deb.werksman@sourcebooks.com. Please allow 21 days for response.

SOUTHERN METHODIST UNIVERSITY PRESS

P.O. Box 750415, Dallas TX 75275-0415. (214)768-1436. Fax: (214)768-1428. E-mail: d-vance@tamu.edu. Website: www.tamupress.com. **Contact:** Diana Vance. Estab. 1937. "Small university press publishing in areas of Southwest life and letters, medical humanities, sports (with emphasis on baseball), creative nonfiction and contemporary fiction." Publishes hardcover and trade paperback originals and reprints. Books: acid-free paper; perfect bound; some illustrations. Average print order: 1,500. **Published 2 debut authors within the last year.** Averages 8 total titles, 3-4 fiction titles/year. Distributes titles through Texas A&M University Press Consortium. Promotes titles through writers' publications.

NEEDS literary, short story collections, novels. "We are willing to look at 'serious' or 'literary' fiction." No "mass market, science fiction, formula, thriller, romance." Published *Mrs. Somebody Somebody: A Linked Story Collection*, by Tracy Winn; and *God's Dogs: A Novel in Stories*, by Mitch Wieland.

HOW TO CONTACT Accepts unsolicited mss. Query with SASE. Responds in 2 weeks to queries; up to 1 year to mss. No simultaneous submissions. Sometimes comments on rejected mss. Proposals may be submitted in hard copy or as attachments to e-mails addressed to the appropriate acquisitions editor. To determine who that is, send a brief description of your manuscript to the acquisitions assistant, Diana Vance, at d-vance@tamu.edu. If one of our editors has invited your manuscript, please use this downloadable proposal form. Because of the volume of proposals received, the Press cannot normally return material to authors. Please do not send original art or other irreplaceable materials. Address: John H. Lindsey Building, Lewis St., 4354 TAMU, College Station, Texas 77843-4354. Main Press Phone: 979-845-1436; Main Press Fax: 979-847-8752.

TERMS Pays 10% royalty on wholesale price, 10 author's copies. Average advance: $500. Publishes ms 1 year after acceptance. Ms guidelines online.

⊕○ SPEAK UP PRESS

P.O. Box 100506, Denver CO 80250. (303)715-0837. Fax: (303)715-0793. E-mail: info@speakuppress.org. Website: www.speakuppress.org. Estab. 1999. "Speak Up Press is a small, nonprofit publisher of young adult nonfiction." Publishes paperback originals. Plans 2 debuts this year. Averages 2 nonfiction titles/year.

NEEDS Nonfiction: Young adult nonfiction, with an emphasis on stories about overcoming adversity and finding a voice.

HOW TO CONTACT Query only. Accepts queries by e-mail only. Responds to queries in 6 weeks. Considers simultaneous submissions, e-mail submissions. Never critiques/comments on rejected mss.

TERMS Writer's guidelines on website. Payment is determined "per individual author depending on book."

TIPS "Follow submission guidelines."

● SPIRE PRESS

217 Thompson St., Suite 298, New York NY 10012. E-mail: editor@spirepress.org. Website: www.spirepress.org. **Contact:** Shelly Reed. Publishes 5-6 books/year. **Publishes 1-2 new writers/year.**

NEEDS literary story collections. Also publishes memoir, poetry. No novels. No horror, romance, or religious work. Length: 30,000+ words. Recently published work by Damiam Dressick and Christiana Olson. Acquisitions: Shelly Reed.

HOW TO CONTACT Send first 15 pages and synopsis in August only. Send disposable copy and #10 SASE for reply only. Responds in 3 months. Accepts simultaneous submissions. Rarely comments on rejected queries. Writer's guidelines online.

TERMS Pays in advance copies and 15% royalty.

TIPS "You should have published short stories and/or essays in established literary journals before querying us."

◐ SPOUT PRESS

P.O. Box 581067, Minneapolis MN 55458. (612) 782-9629. E-mail: editors@spoutpress.org; spoutpress@hotmail.com. Website: www.spoutpress.org. **Contact:** Carrie Eidem, fiction editor. Estab. 1989. "Small independent publisher with a permanent staff of five—interested in experimental fiction for our magazine and books." Publishes paperback originals. Books: perfect bound; illustrations. Average print order: 1,000. **Published 1 debut author within the last year.** Distibutes and promotes books through the website, events and large Web-based stores such as Amazon.com.

NEEDS ethnic, experimental, literary, short story collections. Published *Northern Oracle,* by Kirsten Dierking, *Hotel Sterno,* by Jeffrey Little, and other single- author collections. Runs annual. Accepts submissions all year around fall through spring. See website for specific dates and details.

HOW TO CONTACT Does not accept unsolicited mss. Query with SASE. Accepts queries by mail. Include estimated word count, brief bio, list of publishing credits. Send SASE for return of ms or send a disposable ms and SASE for reply only. Responds in 1 month to queries; 3-5 months to mss. Accepts simultaneous submissions. Rarely comments on rejected mss.

TERMS Individual arrangement with author depending on the book. Publishes ms 12-15 months after acceptance. Ms guidelines for SASE or on website.

TIPS "We tend to publish writers after we know their work via publication in our journal, *Spout Magazine.*"

STARCHERONE BOOKS

Dzanc Books, P.O. Box 303, Buffalo NY 14201-0303. (716)885-2726. E-mail: starcherone@gmail.com; publisher@starcherone.com. Website: www.starcherone.com. **Contact:** Ted Pelton, publisher. Estab. 2000. Non-profit publisher of literary and experimental fiction. Publishes paperback originals and reprints. Books: acid-free paper; perfect bound; occasional illustrations. Average print order: 1,000. Average first novel print order: 1,000. **Published 2 debut authors within the last year.** Member CLMP. Titles distributed through website, Small Press Distribution, Amazon, independent bookstores.

NEEDS experimental, literary. Published *Quinnehtukqut,* by Joshua Harmon (debut author, novel); *Hangings,* by Nina Shope (debut author, short stories); *My Body in Nine Parts,* by Raymond Federman (experimental).

HOW TO CONTACT Accepts queries by mail or e-mail during August and September of each year. WE WILL NOT BE ACCEPTING ANY MANUSCRIPTS OR QUERIES OUTSIDE OF OUR CONTEST UNTIL ANNUAL CONTEST IS CONCLUDED. Submissions of unsolicited manuscripts will risk being returned or discarded, unread. Include brief bio, list of publishing credits. Always query before sending ms. Responds in 2 months to queries; 6-10 months to mss. Accepts simultaneous submissions if noted in cover letter. Contact: Acquisitions Editor: Carra Stratton. E-mail: starcherone@gmail.com. snail mail: Starcherone Books, P.O. Box 303, Buffalo, NY 14201-0303.

TERMS Pays 10-12.5% royalty. Publishes ms 9-18 months after acceptance. Guidelines and catalog available on website.

TIPS During the late summer/early fall each year, after our contest has concluded, we have an OPEN CONSIDERATION PERIOD of approximately six weeks. During this time, we read queries from authors who already have established their credentials in some way, generally through prior publication, awards, and the like. We ask for queries from writers describing their projects and their writing credentials. From these, we invite submissions. Our next period for receiving queries will be in the late summer/early fall. In October of each year, we begin our ANNUAL CONTEST. "Become familiar with our interests in fiction. We are interested in new strategies for creating stories and fictive texts. Do not send genre fiction unless it is unconventional in approach."

STEEPLE HILL BOOKS

Imprint of Harlequin Enterprises, 233 Broadway, Suite 1001, New York NY 10279. (212)553-4200. Fax: (212)227-8969. Website: www.eharlequin.com. **Contact:** Joan Marlow Golan, executive editor; Melissa Endlich, senior editor (inspirational contemp. romance, historical romance, romantic suspense); Tina Colombo, senior editor (inspirational romantic suspense and historical romance); Emily Rodmell, assistant editor. Estab. 1997. Publishes mass market paperback originals.

IMPRINTS Love Inspired; Love Inspired Suspense; Love Inspired Historical.

NEEDS romance (Christian, 70,000-75,000 words). Wants all genres of inspirational woman's fiction including contemporary and historical romance, chick/mom-lit, relationship novels, romantic suspense, mysteries, family sagas, and thrillers. Published *A Mother at Heart,* by Carolyne Aarsen.

HOW TO CONTACT No unsolicited mss. Query with SASE, synopsis. No simultaneous submissions.

TERMS Pays royalty. Offers advance. Detailed ms guidelines online.

TIPS "Drama, humor, and even a touch of mystery all have a place in Steeple Hill. Subplots are welcome and should further the story's main focus or intertwine in a meaningful way. Secondary characters (children, family, friends, neighbors, fellow church members, etc.) may all contribute to a substantial and satisfying story. These wholesome tales include strong family values and high moral standards. While there is no premarital sex between characters, in the case of romance, a vivid, exciting tone presented with a mature perspective is essential. Although the element of faith must clearly be present, it should be well integrated into the characterizations and plot. The conflict between the main characters should be an emotional one, arising naturally from the well-developed personalities you've created. Suitable stories should also impart an important lesson about the powers of trust and faith."

STONE BRIDGE PRESS

P.O. Box 8208, Berkeley CA 94707. (510)524-8732. Fax: (510)524-8711. Website: www.stonebridge.com. **Contact:** Peter Goodman, publisher. Estab. 1989. "Independent press focusing on books about Japan and Asia in English (business, language, culture, literature, animation)." Publishes hardcover and trade paperback originals. Books: 60-70 lb. offset paper; web and sheet paper; perfect bound; some illustrations. Averages 12 total titles/year. Distributes titles through Consortium. Promotes titles through Internet announcements, special-interest magazines, and niche tie-ins to associations.

Stone Bridge Press received a Japan-U.S. Friendship Prize for *Life in the Cul-de-Sac*, by Senji Kuroi.

NEEDS experimental, gay/lesbian, literary, Japan-themed. "Primarily looking at material relating to Japan. Translations only."

HOW TO CONTACT Does not accept unsolicited mss. Query with SASE. Accepts queries by e -mail, fax. Agented fiction 25%. Responds in 4 months to queries; 8 months to mss. Accepts simultaneous submissions. Sometimes comments on rejected mss. If you need to send hard copy or other materials, send it to P.O. Box 8208, Berkeley, CA 94707. **Use media mail or priority mail ONLY**. IMPORTANT: If you require a certificate of delivery or are using Express Mail or a delivery service like UPS, **DO NOT USE THE POST OFFICE BOX ADDRESS AND MAKE THE EDITOR STAND IN LINE**; instead use our street address: 1393 Solano Avenue, Suite C, Albany, CA 94706. We will be **VERY** unhappy if you don't do this. Please note that we are primarily interested in books with a Japan/Asia connection (however tenuous). No materials can be returned to you unless you provide us with sufficient return postage. **We prefer to reply by e-mail.**

TERMS Pays royalty on wholesale price. Average advance: variable. Publishes ms 2 years after acceptance. Book catalog for 2 first-class stamps and SASE. Ms guidelines online.

TIPS "Fiction translations only for the time being. No poetry."

SUNBURY PRESS, INC.

100 South Front St., Lemoyne PA 17043. E-mail: info@sunburypress.com; proposals@sunburypress.com. Website: www.sunburypress.com. Estab. 2004.

Submit proposal package, including synopsis and 4 sample chapters.

TIPS "Our books appeal to very diverse audiences. We are building our list in many categories, focusing on many demographics. We are not like traditional publishers—we are digitally adept and very creative. Don't be surprised if we move quicker than you are accustomed to!"

TANGLEWOOD BOOKS

P.O. Box 3009, Terre Haute IN 47803. E-mail: ptierney@tanglewoodbooks.com. Website: www.tanglewoodbooks.com. **Contact:** Kairi Hamlin, Acquisitions Editor. Estab. 2003.

TIPS "Please see lengthy 'Submissions' page on our website."

TAYLOR TRADE PUBLISHING

5360 Manhattan Circle, #101, Boulder CO 80303. (303)543-7835. E-mail: rrinehart@rowman.com. E-mail: tradeeditorial@rowman.com. Website: www.rlpgtrade.com. **Contact:** Acquisitions Editor.

THIRD WORLD PRESS

P.O. Box 19730, Chicago IL 60619. (773)651-0700. Fax: (773)651-7286. E-mail: twpress3@aol.com; GWENMTWP@aol.com. Website: www.thirdworldpressinc.com. **Contact:** Bennett J. Johnson. Estab. 1967. "Black-owned and operated independent publisher of fiction and nonfiction books about the black experience throughout the Diaspora." Publishes hardcover and trade paperback originals and reprints. Averages 20 total titles/year. Distibutes titles through Independent Publisher Group. "We publish nonfiction, primarily, but will consider fiction." Published *The Covenant with Black America*, with an introduction by Tavis Smiley; 1996, by Gloria Naylor.

Third World Press is open to submissions in July only.

NEEDS material for literary, ethnic, contemporary, juvenile and children's books.

HOW TO CONTACT Accepts unsolicited mss. Submit outline, 5 sample chapter(s), synopsis. Responds in 8 weeks to queries; 5 months to mss. Accepts simultaneous submissions.

TERMS Pays royalty on net revenues. Individual arrangement with author depending on the book, etc. Publishes ms 18 months after acceptance. Ms guidelines for #10 SASE.

TIGHTROPE BOOKS

602 Markham St., Toronto ON M6G 2L8 Canada. (647)348-4460. E-mail: shirarose@tightropebooks.com. Website: www.tightropebooks.com. **Contact:** Shirarose Wilensky, editor. Estab. 2005.

IMPRINTS Zurita, Latino-Canadian imprint, Halli Villegas, Publisher.

TIPS "Audience is young, urban, literary, educated, unconventional."

TIN HOUSE BOOKS

2617 NW Thurman St., Portland OR 97210. (503)473-8663. Fax: (503)473-8957. E-mail: meg@tinhouse.com. Website: www.tinhouse.com. **Contact:** Lee Montgomery, editorial director; Meg Storey, editor; Tony Perez, associate editor. "We are a small independent publisher dedicated to nurturing new, promising talent as well as showcasing the work of established writers. Our Tin House New Voice series features work by authors who have not previously published a book." Publishes hardcover originals, paperback originals, paperback reprints. **Plans 3 debut novels/year.** Averages 8-10 total titles/year; 4-6 fiction titles/year. Distributes/promotes titles through Publishers Group West.

NEEDS literary, novels, short story collections, poetry, translations. Publishes A New Voice series.

HOW TO CONTACT Agented mss only. We no longer read unsolicited submissions by authors with no representation. We will continue to accept submissions from agents. Please send fiction, memoir, and/or nonfiction manuscripts to: **Tin House Books**, 2617 NW Thurman St., Portland, OR 97210. Phone: 503-473-8663. **Attention:** Lee Montgomery, Editorial Director/Associate Publisher; Meg Storey, Editor; Tony Perez, Associate Editor. Accepts queries by snail mail, e-mail, phone. Include brief bio, list of publishing credits. Send SASE or IRC for return of ms or disposable copy of ms and SASE/IRC for reply only. Agented fiction 80%. Responds to queries in 2-3 weeks. Responds to mss in 2-3 months. Considers simultaneous submissions. Sometimes critiques/comments on rejected mss.

TERMS Sends preproduction galleys to author. Manuscript published approximately 1 year after acceptance. Writer's guidelines on website. Advance is negotiable. Book catalogs not available.

TITAN PRESS

PMB 17897, Encino CA 91416. E-mail: titan91416@yahoo.com. Website: www.calwriterssfv.com. **Contact:** Stefanya Wilson, editor. Estab. 1981. Publishes hardcover originals and paperback originals. Books: recycled paper; offset printing; perfect bound. Average print order: 2,000. Average first novel print order: 1,000. **Published 3 debut authors within the last year.** Averages 12 total titles, 6 fiction titles/year. Distributed at book fairs and through the Internet and at Barnes & Noble.

NEEDS literary, mainstream/contemporary, short story collections. Published *Orange Messiahs*, by Scott Alixander Sonders (fiction).

HOW TO CONTACT Does not accept unsolicited mss. Query with SASE. Include brief bio, social security number, list of publishing credits. Agented fiction 50%. Responds in 3 months to mss. Accepts simultaneous submissions. Sometimes comments on rejected mss.

TERMS Pays 20-40% royalty. Publishes ms 1 year after acceptance. Ms guidelines for #10 SASE.

TIPS "Look, act, sound and *be* professional."

TO BE READ ALOUD PUBLISHING, INC.

PO Box 632426, Nacogdoches TX 75963. E-mail: michael@tobereadaloud.org; submissions@tobereadaloud.org. Website: www.tobereadaloud.org. **Contact:** Michael Powell, President (short stories); Stephen Powell, Editor (poetry). Estab. 2006. Aims to be a resource for oral interpretation coaches and their students. All submissions should be written by authors born in one of the following states: Alabama, Arkansas, Florida, Georgia, Louisiana, Kentucky, Mississippi, North Carolina, South Carolina, Tennessee, Virginia, or West Virginia.

TIPS "Our audience is high school drama students. Read your selection aloud before submitting." "We service the UIL of Texas mostly; check their annual categories and write accordingly to match them."

TOP COW PRODUCTIONS

10390 Santa Monica Blvd., Suite 340, Los Angeles CA 90025. E-mail: editorial@topcowent.com. Website: http://www.topcow.com/Site/.

HOW TO CONTACT *No unsolicited submissions.* Prefers submissions from artists. See website for details and advice on how to break into the market.

TOP PUBLICATIONS, LTD.

3100 Independence Pkwy., Suite 311-349, Plano TX 75075. (972)490-9686. Fax: (972)233-0713. E-mail: info@toppub.com; submissions@toppub.com. Website: www.toppub.com. **Contact:** Sara Mendoza, Editor. Estab. 1999. Primarily a mainstream fiction publisher. "It is imperative that our authors realize they will be required to promote their book extensively for it to be a success. Unless they are willing to make this commitment, they shouldn't submit to TOP." Publishes 2-3 titles/year.

"Top strives to be an author friendly publisher."

HOW TO CONTACT Guidelines available online. SASE returns.

TERMS Pays 15-20% royalty on wholesale price. Pays $250-2,500 advance. Acceptance to publishing time is 8 months. Acknowledges receipt of queries but only responds if interested in seeing ms. Responds in 6 months to mss.

TIPS "We recommend that our authors write books that appeal to a large mainstream audience to make marketing easier and increase the chances of success. We only publish a few titles a year so the odds at getting published at TOP are slim. If we reject your work, it probably doesn't have any reflection on your work. We have to pass on a lot of good material each year simply by the limitations of our time and budget."

TORQUERE PRESS

P.O. Box 2545, Round Rock TX 78680. (512)586-3553. Fax: (866)287-2968. E-mail: editor@torquerepress.com; submissions@torquerepress.com. Website: www.torquerepress.com. **Contact:** Shawn Clements, submissions editor (homoerotica, suspense, gay/lesbian); Lorna Hinson, senior editor (gay/lesbian romance, historicals). Estab. 2003. "We are a gay and lesbian press focusing on romance. We particularly like paranormal and western romance." Publishes paperback originals. Averages 140 total titles/year.

IMPRINTS Top Shelf (Shawn Clements, editor); Single Shots (Kil Kenny, editor); Screwdrivers (M. Rode, editor); High Balls (Vincent Diamond, editor).

NEEDS All categories gay and lesbian themed. Adventure, erotica, historical, horror, mainstream, multicultural, mystery, occult, romance, science fiction, short story collections, suspense, western. Published *Broken Road*, by Sean Michael (romance); *Soul Mates: Bound by Blood*, by Jourdan Lane (paranormal romance). Imprints accepting submissions.

HOW TO CONTACT Query with outline/synopsis and 3 sample chapters. Responds to queries in 2 months; mss in 3-4 months. Electronic submissions preferred. Send query to submissions@torquerepress.com. No simultaneous submissions.

TERMS Manuscript published 6 months after acceptance. Pays royalties. Book catalogs on website.

TIPS "Our audience is primarily people looking for a familiar romance setting featuring gay or lesbian protagonists. Please read guidelines carefully and familiarize yourself with our lines."

TORREY HOUSE PRESS, LLC

P.O. Box 750196, Torrey UT 84775. (801)810-9THP. E-mail: mark@torreyhouse.com. Website: http://torreyhouse.com. **Contact:** Kirsten Allen, editor: (areas of interest: literary fiction, creative nonfiction). Estab. 2010. "Torrey House Press (THP) publishes literary fiction and creative nonfiction about the issues, people, history, cultures, and landscape of the Colorado Plateau and the American West. Located in the heart of the Plateau in Torrey, Utah, THP sponsors 4 writing contests each year and accepts unsolicited manuscripts. See the website at www.torreyhouse.com for guidelines about submitting your work; peruse the columns and book reviews and read some of THP's favorite fiction and nonfiction excerpts to get a sense of the writing that the company seeks. Follow us at Torrey House Press on Facebook and on our website for contest updates, and please contact us any time with questions at mark@torreyhouse.com. Spring 2011: Creative Literary Nonfiction (2,000 to 10,000 words). Deadline: May 31, 2011. Fall 2011: Short Fiction and Creative Nonfiction (2,000 to 10,000 words).

Deadline: September 30, 2011. Contest submissions must be original and not previously published. Please, no stories written for children for contest entries. Torrey House Press writing contest: Fiction and Short Fiction. See website for 2012 deadline."

Envisions reading audience of the American West literary fiction and creative nonfiction.

IMPRINTS Mark Bailey, publisher

HOW TO CONTACT Query with SASE; submit proposal package, including: outline, sample chapter, about the author. Responds in 2 months.

TIPS "Include writing experience (none okay) and something about your passion for the land." Sponsors *Torrey House Press writing contest: Fiction and Short Fiction*. **Deadline: check website**—$1000 First Place; $250 Second Place; $100 Third Place.

TOTAL-E-BOUND PUBLISHING

Total-e-Ntwined Limited, 1 Faldingworth Road, Spridlington, Market Rasen, Lincolnshire, UK LN8 2DE. E-mail: info@total-e-bound.com. Website: www.total-e-bound.com; www.forum.totalebound.com. **Contact:** Claire Siemaszkiewicz, editor; Michele Paulin, editor; Janice Bennett, editor. Estab. 2006. "The team at Total-e-bound came together to provide a unique service to our authors and readers. We are a royalty paying, full-service e-publisher. This means that there are no fees to the author to become published with us. Brought together by a mutual love of outstanding erotic fiction, we offer a mass of business experience in the form of editors, artists, marketeers, IT technicians and support staff to meet all of your needs. We love what we do and are totally dedicated, committed and loyal to providing the best service that we can to our authors and our readers. TEB publishes, markets and promotes top quality erotic romance e-books and paperback books. Publishes paperback originals, e-books. Averages 100 fiction titles/year. Distributes/promotes titles through the Total-e-bound shop and through channel partners/distributors."

NEEDS "We are currently accepting manuscripts between 10,000 and 100,000+ words in the following genres: Action/Adventure, Bondage/BDSM, Comedy/Humour, Contemporary, Cowboy/Western, Fantasy/Fairytale, Futuristic/Sci-fi, Gay/Lesbian, Historical/Rubenesque, Mènage-á-trois/Multiple Partners, Multicultural, Older Woman/Younger Man, Paranormal/Timetravel, Thriller/Crime, Shapeshifters/Morphers, Vampire/Werewolf." Throughout the year we do special-themed short stories. General guidelines: 10K–15K word count. Any genre (see below for specific themes). Anthologies are released every quarter—each with a distinctive theme. "We produce a series of four anthologies per year, six short stories in each. Published Campus Cravings Series, by Carol Lynne (gay/contemporary); *Sink or Swim*, by Alexis Fleming (paranormal); and *Wild in the Country*, by Portia Da Costa (contemporary/erotica). Current and planned series include Campus Cravings (M/M), Good-time Boys (M/M), Cattle Valley (M/M), Horsemen of Apocalypse Island (fantasy), Wives R Us (contemporary), The Goddess Grind (contemporary/paranormal), Sons of Olympus (paranormal), Psychic Detective (paranormal), and The Watchers (paranormal/fantasy).

HOW TO CONTACT Query with outline/synopsis and first 3 and last chapters. Accepts queries by online submission e-mail. Include estimated word count, brief bio, list of publishing credits. Agented fiction: 10%. Responds to queries in 1-2 weeks. Accepts unsolicited mss. Often critiques/comments on rejected mss. Responds to mss in 2-8 weeks.

TERMS Ms published 2-6 months after acceptance. Pays royalties 40% e-book, 10% print. Book catalogs on website.

TIPS "First impressions are important. Send in a good intro letter with your synopsis and manuscript, giving details of what you will do yourself to promote your work. Always read and follow the submission guidelines."

TRADEWIND BOOKS

202-1807 Maritime Mews, Granville Island, Vancouver BC V6H 3W7 Canada. (604)662-4405. E-mail: tradewindbooks@mail.lycos.com. Website: www.tradewindbooks.com. **Contact:** Michael Katz, publisher; Carol Frank, art director. Publishes 2 picture books; 2 chapter books, 3 young adult titles/year; 1 book of poetry. 15% of books by first-time authors. Tradewind Books is a publisher of books for children and young adults. Please review our online catalog to see the types of books that we publish before you submit your work.

SUBMISSIONS POLICY AT TRADEWIND BOOKS We accept unsolicited submissions from both writers and illustrators. **We ask that writers show that they have read at least 3 of our titles before submitting a manuscript. All submissions**

must include a SASE. We try to respond within 3 months. Do not submit more than one manuscript at a time.

TYPES OF SUBMISSION Picture Books: We accept submissions from both writers and illustrators. Writers should submit the entire manuscript of their picture book. If you are a professional illustrator submitting a picture book, please include the manuscript, a dummy, and a sample reproduction of the final artwork. Do not send original artwork. **Chapter Books:** Please submit the first 3 chapters, a chapter outline, and a plot summary. We do accept chapter book submissions from non-Canadians for books that will be illustrated. **Young Adult Fiction:** We accept YA fiction only from Canadian authors. See guidelines for chapter books above. **Poetry:** Please send a book-length collection of your own poems. **Non-fiction:** We do not publish information books. Illustrators: We accept picture book projects and sample illustrations. To submit a picture book, please see guidelines for picture books above. To submit samples, please send them in the form best suited to the art.

NEEDS juvenile picture books: adventure, multicultural, folktales. Average word length: 900 words. Recently published *City Kids*, by X.J. Kennedy; *Roxy*, by P.J. Reece; *Viva Zapata* by Emelie Smith.

HOW TO CONTACT Picture books: submit complete ms. YA novels by Canadian authors only. Chapter books by US authors considered. Will consider simultaneous submissions. Do not send query letter. Responds to mss in 12 weeks. Unsolicited submissions accepted only if authors have read a selection of books published by Tradewind Books. Submissions must include a reference to these books.

TERMS Royalties negotiable. Offers advances against royalties. Catalog available on website.

TURNSTONE PRESS

206-100 Arthur St., Winnipeg MB R3B 1H3 Canada. (204)947-1555. Fax: (204)942-1555. E-mail: info@turnstonepress.com; editor@turnstonepress.com. Website: www.ravenstonebooks.com. **Contact:** Jamis Paulson, Associate Publisher. Estab. 1976. "Turnstone Press is a literary press that publishes Canadian writers with an emphasis on writers from, and writing on, the Canadian west." Focuses on eclectic new writing, prairie writers, travel writing and regional mysteries. Publishes trade paperback originals. Books: offset paper; perfect-bound. First novel print order: 1,500. **Published 5 debut authors within the last year.** Averages 8-12 total titles/year. Distributes titles through Lit DistCo (Canada and US). Promotes titles through Canadian national and local print media and select US print advertising.

Turnstone Press was a 2004 Nominee for Small Press Publisher of the Year. *Tatsea* won the McNally Robinson book of the Year and the Margaret Laurence Award for Fiction. *Kilter: 55 Fictions* was a finalist for the Giller Prize and the winner of the Mary Scorer Award. Turnstone Press is a past nominee for Small Press Publisher of the Year. In addition to winning a Governor General's award, Turnstone Press has been shortlisted for numerous national and regional writing awards including the Giller Prize, the Leacock Award, the Arthur Ellis awards, and the ReLit Awards.

NEEDS contemporary literary novels, short story collections, cultural nonfiction, and poetry. Canadian authors only. Published *An Unexpected Break in the Weather* (novels), *mama dada* (poetry) and *The Finger's Twist* (Ravenstone, action/thriller).

HOW TO CONTACT Accepts unsolicited mss. Include list of publishing credits. Send SASE or IRC. Responds in 4 months to queries. No simultaneous submissions. "Although we do review unsolicited manuscripts, we prefer a query first, accompanied by a sample. Samples should be 20 to 40 pages, typed/printed in a minimum 10-12 pt. font, double-spaced on 8.5 x 11 white paper, with all pages numbered, name and address on all pages, and without binding or stapling. For fiction and nonfiction, also provide a 1-page synopsis of the work. We regret to inform that, due to time constraints, we are unable to provide feedback on all the manuscripts we receive. Only submissions including a SASE will be responded to and/or returned. Please make sure the SASE is of sufficient size, with sufficient postage, for your manuscript if you wish it sent back. For Canadian citizens submitting from a foreign country, please include an international reply coupon. Manuscripts arriving without a SASE will be recycled. We consider only exclusive queries/submissions. We do not accept submissions/queries sent on computer disk/CD, by e-mail or by fax — these are discarded."

TERMS Pays 10% royalty on retail price and 10 author's copies. Offers advance. Publishes ms 1 year after acceptance. Ms guidelines online.

TIPS "As a Canadian literary press, we have a mandate to publish Canadian writers only. Do some homework before submitting works to make sure your subject matter/genre/writing style falls within the publishers area of interest."

◐ TWILIGHT TIMES BOOKS

P.O. Box 3340, Kingsport TN 37664. (423)323-0183. Fax: (423)323-0183. E-mail: publisher@twilighttimesbooks.com. Website: www.twilighttimesbooks.com. **Contact:** Ardy M. Scott, managing editor. Estab. 1999. "We publish compelling literary fiction by authors with a distinctive voice." Publishes hardcover and paperback originals and e-books. Book: 60 lb. paper; offset and digital printing; perfect bound. Average print order: 1500. **Published 3 debut authors within the last year.** Averages 50 total titles, 12 fiction titles/year. Member: AAP, PAS, SPAN, SLF. Nationally distributed by Twilight Trade Books.

NEEDS historical, literary, mystery, nonfiction, science fiction, and young adult. Published *Burnout*, by Stephanie Osborn; *Human by Choice*, by Travis S. Taylor and Darrell Bain; *Murder in the Pit*, by Erica Miner.

HOW TO CONTACT Accepts unsolicited mss. Do not send complete mss. Queries via e-mail only. Include estimated word count, brief bio, list of publishing credits, marketing plan. Agented fiction 10%. Responds in 4 weeks to queries; 2 months to mss. Accepts electronic submissions, submissions on disk. Rarely comments on rejected mss.

TERMS Pays 8-15% royalty. Ms guidelines online.

TIPS "The only requirement for consideration at Twilight Times Books is that your novel must be entertaining and professionally written."

O UNBRIDLED BOOKS

200 North 9th Street, Suite A, Columbia MO 65201. 573-256-4106. Fax: 573-256-5207. Website: www.unbridledbooks.com. **Contact**: Greg Michalson and Fred Ramey, editors. Estab. 2004. "Unbridled Books is a premier publisher of works of rich literary quality that appeal to a broad audience." Publishes fiction, memoir, micro-history, and creative nonfiction. Hardcover and trade paperback originals. **Published 4 debut authors within the last year.** Averages 10 total titles, 6 fiction titles/year.

NEEDS Literary, nonfiction, memoir. *Last Night in Montreal*, by Emily St. John Mandel; *31 Hours*, by Masha Hamilton; *Fear Itself*, by Candida Lawrence; *Saint John of the Five Boroughs*, by Edward Falco; *An Unfinished Score*, by Elise Blackwell.

HOW TO CONTACT Accepts electronic queries by mail. No electronic submissions.

TIPS "We try to read each ms that arrives, so please be patient."

UNITY HOUSE

Unity, 1901 NW Blue Parkway, Unity Village MO 64065-0001. (816)524-3559 ext. 3190. Fax: (816)251-3559. E-mail: unity@unityonline.org; sartinson@unityonline.org. Website: www.unityonline.org. **Contact:** Sharon Sartin, exec. asst. Estab. 1889. "We are a bridge between traditional Christianity and New Age spirituality. Unity is based on metaphysical Christian principles, spiritual values and the healing power of prayer as a resource for daily living." Publishes hardcover and trade paperback originals and reprints.

IMPRINTS Unity House

NEEDS Spiritual, visionary fiction, inspirational, metaphysical.

HOW TO CONTACT Send complete mss (3 copies). Responds in 6-8 months. No simultaneous submissions.

TERMS Pays 10-15% royalty on net receipts. Offers advance. Publishes ms 13 months after acceptance. Ms guidelines online.

TIPS "We target an audience of spiritual seekers."

UNIVERSITY OF GEORGIA PRESS

330 Research Dr., Athens GA 30602-4901. (706)369-6130. Fax: (706)369-6131. E-mail: books@ugapress.uga.edu. Website: www.ugapress.org. Estab. 1938. University of Georgia Press is a midsized press that publishes fiction only through the Flannery O'Connor Award for Short Fiction competition. Publishes hardcover originals, trade paperback originals, and reprints. Averages 75 total titles/year.

NEEDS short story collections published in Flannery O'Connor Award Competition. Most recent titles include *Copy Cats*, by David Crouse; *Sorry I Worried You*, by Gary Finke; *The Send-Away Girl*, by Barbara Sutton.

HOW TO CONTACT Manuscripts for Flannery O'Connor Award for Short Fiction accepted in April and May. Please see submissions guidelines on website for full details. Responds in 2 months to queries. No simultaneous submissions.

TERMS Pays 7-10% royalty on net receipts. Average advance: rare, varying. Publishes ms 1 year after acceptance. Book catalog and ms guidelines for #10 SASE. Ms guidelines online.

TIPS "Please visit our website to view our book catalogs and for all manuscript submission guidelines."

UNIVERSITY OF IOWA PRESS

100 Kuhl House, 119 W. Park Road, Iowa City IA 52242-1000. (319)335-2000. Fax: (319)335-2055. E-mail: uipress@uiowa.edu. Website: www.uiowapress.org. **Contact:** Holly Carver, director; Joseph Parsons, acquisitions editor. Estab. 1969. Publishes paperback originals. Average print run for a first book is 1,000-1,500. Averages 40 total titles/year.

NEEDS Currently publishes the Iowa Short Fiction Award selections.

HOW TO CONTACT See website for details.

TERMS Pays 7-10% royalty on net receipts. Publishes ms 1 year after acceptance. Ms guidelines online.

UNIVERSITY OF NEBRASKA PRESS

1111 Lincoln Mall, Lincoln NE 68588-0630. (800)755-1105. Fax: (402)472-6214. E-mail: pressmail@unl.edu. Website: nebraskapress.unl.edu. **Contact:** Heather Lundine, editor-in-chief.

IMPRINTS Bison Books (paperback reprints of classic books).

UNIVERSITY OF NEVADA PRESS

Morrill Hall, Mail Stop 0166, Reno NV 89557. (775)784-6573. Fax: (775)784-6200. Website: www.unpress.nevada.edu. **Contact:** Joanne O'Hare, director. Estab. 1961. "Small university press. Publishes fiction that primarily focuses on the American West." Publishes hardcover and paperback originals. Averages 25 total titles, 2 fiction titles/year. Member: AAUP

NEEDS "We publish in Basque Studies, Gambling Studies, Western literature, Western history, Natural science, Environmental Studies, Travel and Outdoor books, Archeology, Anthropology, and Political Studies, all focusing on the West." The Press also publishes creative nonfiction and books on regional topics for a general audience. Has published *The Mechanics of Falling and Other Stories*, by Catherine Brady; *Little Lost River*, by Pamela Johnston; *Moon Lily*, by Susan Lang.

HOW TO CONTACT Submit outline, 2-4 sample chapter(s), synopsis. Include estimated word count, brief bio, list of publishing credits. Send SASE or IRC. Responds in 2 months to queries. No simultaneous submissions. No e-mail submissions.

TERMS Publishes ms 18 months after acceptance. Book catalog and ms guidelines free Ms guidelines online.

UNIVERSITY OF NEW MEXICO PRESS

1 University of New Mexico, MSC05 3185, Albuquerque NM 87131-0001. (505)277-3324 or (800)249-7737. Fax: (505)277-3343. E-mail: clark@unm.edu; wcwhiteh@unm.edu. Website: www.unmpress.com. **Contact:** W. Clark Whitehorn, Editor-in-Chief. Estab. 1929. "The Press is well known as a publisher in the fields of anthropology, archeology, Latin American studies, art and photography, architecture and the history and culture of the American West, fiction, some poetry, Chicano/a studies and works by and about American Indians. We focus on American West, Southwest and Latin American regions." Publishes hardcover originals and trade paperback originals and reprints.

TERMS Pays variable royalty.

UNIVERSITY OF WISCONSIN PRESS

1930 Monroe Street, 3rd Floor, Madison WI 53711. (608)263-1110. Fax: (608)263-1132. E-mail: uwiscpress@uwpress.wisc.edu; kadushin@wisc.edu. Website: www.wisc.edu/wisconsinpress. **Contact:** Raphael Kadushin, senior acquisitions editor. Estab. 1937. Publishes hardcover originals, paperback originals, and paperback reprints. **Published 5-8 debut authors within the last year.** Averages 98 total titles, 15 fiction titles/year. Member, AAUP Distributes titles through ads, reviews, catalog, sales reps, etc.

NEEDS gay/lesbian, historical, lesbian, mystery, regional (Wisconsin), short story collections. Recently published *A Friend of Kissinger*, by David Milofsky; *Beijing*, by Philip Gambone; *Latin Moon in Manhattan*, by Jaime Manrique.

HOW TO CONTACT Does not accept unsolicited mss. Query with SASE or submit outline, 1-2 sample chapter(s), synopsis. Accepts queries by e-mail, mail, fax. Include estimated word count, brief bio. Send copy of ms and SASE. Direct your inquiries in the areas of autobiography/memoir, biography, classical studies, dance and performance studies, film, food, gender studies, GLBT studies, Jewish studies, Latino/a memoirs, and travel to Raphael Kadushin, kadushin@wisc.edu. Agented fiction 40%. Direct nonfiction inquiries in the areas of African studies, anthropology, environmental studies, human rights, Irish studies, Latin American studies, Slavic studies, Southeast Asian studies, and U.S. History to: Gwen Walker, gcwalker@uwpress.wisc.edu. See website for more contact info. Responds in 2 weeks to queries; 8 weeks to mss. Rarely comments on rejected mss.

TERMS Pays royalty. Publishes ms 9-18 months after acceptance. Ms guidelines online.

TIPS "Make sure the query letter and sample text are well-written, and read guidelines carefully to make sure we accept the genre you are submitting."

⊕ UNTREED READS PUBLISHING

506 Kansas St., San Francisco CA 94107. (415)621-0465. Fax: (415)621-0465. E-mail: general@untreedreads.com; submissions@untreedreads.com. Website: www.untreedreads.com. **Contact:** Jay A. Hartman, editor-in-chief (fiction—all genres). Estab. 2009. "We welcome short story collections. Also, we look forward to publishing children's books, cookbooks, and other works that have been known for illustrations in print as the technology in the multiple ereaders improves. We hope to be a large platform for diverse content and authors. We seek mainstream content, but if you're an author or have content that doesn't seem to always 'fit' into traditional market we'd like to hear from you." No erotica, picture books, poetry, poetry in translation, or romance. Submit proposal package with 3 sample chapters. Submit completed ms.

IMPRINTS Untreed Reads, Jay Hartman, editor-in-chief.

TIPS "For our fiction titles we lean toward a literary audience. For nonfiction titles, we want to be a platform for business people, entrepreneurs, and speakers to become well known in their fields of expertise. However, for both fiction and nonfiction we want to appeal to many audiences."

UPPER ACCESS, INC.

87 Upper Access Rd., Hinesburg VT 05461. (802)482-2988. Fax: (802)304-1005. E-mail: info@upperaccess.com. Website: www.upperaccess.com. **Contact:** Steve Carlson, Publisher. Estab. 1986.

TIPS "We target intelligent adults willing to challenge the status quo, who are interested in more self-sufficiency with respect for the environment. Most of our books are either unique subjects or unique or different ways of looking at major issues or basic education on subjects that are not well understood by most of the general public. We make a long-term commitment to each book that we publish, trying to find its market as long as possible."

VANDAMERE PRESS

P.O. Box 149, St. Petersburg FL 33731. Fax: (727)556-2560. E-mail: webmaster@vandamere.com. Website: www.vandamere.com **Contact:** Jerry Frank, senior acquistions editor. Estab. 1984. Publishes hardcover and trade paperback originals and reprints. **Published 25% debut authors within the last year.** Averages 6-12 total titles/year.

NEEDS adventure, mystery, suspense. Recently published *Classified Waste*, by Alexander M. Grace (fiction).

HOW TO CONTACT Submit 5-10 sample chapter(s), synopsis. Responds in 6 months to queries. Accepts simultaneous submissions.

TERMS Pays royalty on revenues generated. Offers advance. Publishes ms 1-3 years after acceptance.

TIPS "Authors who can provide endorsements from significant published writers, celebrities, etc., will always be given serious consideration. Clean, easy-to-read, dark copy is essential. Patience in waiting for replies is essential. All unsolicited work is looked at, but at certain times of the year our review schedule will stop. No response without SASE. No electronic submissions or queries!"

⊕ VANHOOK HOUSE

925 Orchard St., Charleston WV 25302. E-mail: editor@vanhookhouse.com. E-mail: acquisitions@vanhookhouse.com. Website: www.vanhookhouse.com. **Contact:** Jim Whyte, acquisitions, all fiction/true crime/military/war. Estab. 2009.

"We employ the expertise of individuals qualified to review works falling within their field of study. Be sure of all sources and facts, as VanHook House *will* confirm any and all information. All editing is done in a way to ensure the author's voice remains unchanged."

TIPS "Visit our website."

VÉHICULE PRESS

Box 125, Place du Parc Station, Montreal QC H2X 4A3 Canada. (514)844-6073. Fax: (514)844-7543. E-mail: vp@vehiculepress.com. Website: www.vehiculepress.com. **Contact:** Simon Dardick, president/publisher. Estab. 1973. Small publisher of scholarly, literary, and cultural books. Publishes trade paperback originals by Canadian authors only. Books: good quality paper; offset printing; perfect and cloth binding; illustrations. Average print order: 1,000-3,000. Averages 15 total titles/year.

Mostly Canadian authors.

IMPRINTS Signal Editions (poetry); Dossier Quebec (history, memoirs); Esplanade Editions (fiction).

NEEDS literary, regional, short story collections. Published *Optique*, by Clayton Bailey; *Seventeen Tomatoes: Tales from Kashmir*, by Jaspreet Singh; *A Short Journey by Car*, by Liam Durcan.

HOW TO CONTACT Query first with SASE. We mostly publish Canadian authors. Responds in 4 months to queries.

TERMS Pays 10-15% royalty on retail price. Average advance: $200-500. "Depends on press run and sales. Translators of fiction can receive Canada Council funding, which publisher applies for." Publishes ms 1 year after acceptance. Book catalog for 9×12 SAE with IRCs.

TIPS "Quality in almost any style is acceptable. We believe in the editing process."

VERTIGO

DC Universe, Vertigo-DC Comics, 1700 Broadway, New York NY 10019. Website: www.dccomics.com.

NEEDS "We're seeking artists for all our imprints, including the DC Universe, Vertigo, WildStorm, Mad magazine, Minx, kids comics and more!"

HOW TO CONTACT "The DC TALENT SEARCH program is designed to offer aspiring artists the chance to present artwork samples directly to the DC Editors and Art Directors. The process is simple: during your convention visit, drop off photocopied samples of your work and enjoy the show! No lines, no waiting. If the DC folks like what they see, a time is scheduled for you the following day to meet a DC representative personally and discuss your artistic interests and portfolio.: At this time, DC Comics does not accept unsolicited writing submissions by mail. See submission guidelines online.

VIKING

Imprint of Penguin Group (USA), Inc., Penguin Putnam Inc., 375 Hudson St., New York NY 10014. (212)366-2000. Website: us.penguingroup.com/static/pages/publishers/adult/viking.html. **Contact:** Acquisitions Editor. Publishes a mix of literary and popular fiction and nonfiction. Publishes hardcover and originals.

NEEDS literary, mainstream/contemporary, mystery, suspense. Published *Lake Wobegon Summer 1956*, by Garrison Keillor; *A Day Late and a Dollar Short*, by Terry McMillian; *A Common Life*, by Jan Karon; *In the Heart of the Sea*, by Nathaniel Philbrick.

HOW TO CONTACT *Agented submissions only.* Responds in 6 months to queries. Accepts simultaneous submissions.

TERMS Pays 10-15% royalty on retail price. Average advance: negotiable. Publishes ms 12-18 months after acceptance.

VIKING CHILDREN'S BOOKS

345 Hudson St., New York NY 10014. E-mail: averystudiopublicity@us.penguingroup.com. Website: www.penguingroup.com. **Contact:** Catherine Frank, exec. editor. A division of Penguin Young Readers Group, "Viking Children's books publishes high quality trade hardcover books for children through young adults. These include fiction and nonfiction." Publishes hardcover originals. **Published some debut authors within the last year.** Averages 70 total titles/year. Promotes titles through press kits, institutional ads.

Does not accept unsolicited submissions. Viking Children's Books publishes high-quality trade books for children including fiction, nonfiction and picture books for preschoolers through young adults.

NEEDS juvenile, picture books, young adult. Published *Just Listen*, by Sarah Dessen (novel); *Llama, Llama Red Pajama*, by Anna Dewdney (picture book).

HOW TO CONTACT Only accepts solicited mss. Submit complete ms. Send SASE. Responds in 12 months to queries.

TERMS Pays 5-10% royalty on retail price. Average advance: negotiable. Publishes ms 1 year after acceptance.

TIPS No "cartoony" or mass-market submissions for picture books.

VILLARD BOOKS

Imprint of Random House Publishing Group, 1745 Broadway 18th Fl., New York NY 10019. (212)572-2600. Website: www.atrandom.com. Estab. 1983. Publishes hardcover and trade paperback originals. Averages 40-50 total titles/year.

NEEDS commercial fiction.

HOW TO CONTACT *Agented submissions only.* Agented fiction 95%. Accepts simultaneous submissions.

TERMS Pays negotiable royalty. Average advance: negotiable.

VINTAGE ANCHOR PUBLISHING

1745 Broadway, New York NY 10019. E-mail: vintageanchorpublicity@randomhouse.com. Website: www.randomhouse.com. **Contact:** Furaha Norton, editor. The Knopf Publishing Group, a Division of Random House, Inc., publishes trade paperback originals and reprints.

NEEDS literary, mainstream/contemporary, short story collections. Published *Snow Falling on Cedars*, by Guterson (contemporary); *Martin Dressler*, by Millhauser (literary).

HOW TO CONTACT *Agented submissions only.* Accepts simultaneous submissions. No electronic submissions.

TERMS Pays 4-8% royalty on retail price. Average advance: $2,500 and up. Publishes ms 1 year after acceptance.

VIZ MEDIA LLC

P.O. Box 77010, 295 Bay Street, San Francisco CA 94133. (415)546-7073. E-mail: evelyn.dubocq@viz.com. Website: www.viz.com. "VIZ Media, LLC is one of the most comprehensive and innovative companies in the field of manga (graphic novel) publishing, animation and entertainment licensing of Japanese content. Owned by three of Japan's largest creators and licensors of manga and animation, Shueisha Inc., Shogakukan Inc., and Shogakukan-Shueisha Productions, Co., Ltd., VIZ Media is a leader in the publishing and distribution of Japanese manga for English speaking audiences in North America, the United Kingdom, Ireland, and South Africa and is a global ex-Asia licensor of Japanese manga and animation. The company offers an integrated product line including magazines such as *SHONEN JUMP* and *SHOJO BEAT*, graphic novels, and DVDs, and develops, markets, licenses, and distributes animated entertainment for audiences and consumers of all ages."

NEEDS VIZ Media is currently accepting submissions and pitches for original comics. Keep in mind that all submissions must be accompanied by a signed release form.

HOW TO CONTACT Accepts queries by snail mail. VIZ Media, LLC, P.O. BOX 77010, San Francisco, CA 94107. Website: www.viz.com.

WAKESTONE PRESS

200 Brook Hollow Rd., Nashville TN 37205-3504. (615)739-6428. E-mail: submissions@wakestonepress.com. Website: www.wakestonepress.com. **Contact:** Frank Daniels III, Editor; interested in nonfiction. Estab. 2010.

IMPRINTS Wakestone Press LLC; Moonshadow Press (subsidiary): Fiction imprint targeting young adults (10 - up).

WALKER AND CO.

Walker Publishing Co., 175 Fifth Ave., 7th Floor, New York NY 10010. (212)727-8300. Fax: (212)727-0984. E-mail: rebecca.mancini@bloomsburyusa.com. Website: www.walkeryoungreaders.com. Submissions to Adult Nonfiction Editor limited to agents, published authors, and writers wtih professional credentials in their field of expertise. Children's books to Submissions Editor-Juvenile. Estab. 1959. Walker Publishing Co., 175 Fifth Ave., 8th Floor, New York NY 10010. Website: www.walkeryoungreaders.com. **Contact:** Emily Easton, publisher (picture books, middle grade & young adult novels); Stacy Cantor, Associate editor (picture books, middle grade, and young adult novels); Mary Kate Castellani, assistant editor (picture books, middle grade, and young adult novels). Midsize publisher. Publishes hardcover trade originals. Average first novel print order: 5,000-7,500. Averages 25 total titles/year.

NEEDS juvenile (fiction, nonfiction), picture books (juvenile). Published *Stolen Car*, by Patrick Jones; *Skinny*, by Ibi Kaslik, *Violent Raines Almost Got Struck by Lightning*, by Danette Haworth, *Gimme Cracked Corn and I Will Share*, by Kevin O'Malley.

HOW TO CONTACT Accepts unsolicited mss. Query with SASE. Include "a concise description of the story line, including its outcome, word length of story, writing experience, publishing credits, particular expertise on this subject and in this genre. Common mistake: not researching our publishing program and forgetting SASE." Agented fiction 75%. Sometimes comments on rejected mss. Send SASE for our reponse to your submission. We do not return manuscripts and proposals.

TERMS Pays 5%-10% royalty. Average advance: competitive. Generally publishes ms 1 year after acceptance.

WATERBROOK MULTNOMAH PUBLISHING GROUP

Subsidiary of Random House, 12265 Oracle Blvd., Suite 200, Colorado Springs CO 80921. (719)590-4999. Fax: (719)590-8977. E-mail: info@waterbrookmultnomah.com. Website: www.waterbrookmultnomah.com; www.waterbrookpress.com. The evangelical division of Random House Books. Dudley Delffs, editor-in-chief. Estab. 1996. Publishes hardcover and trade paperback originals. Averages 70 total titles/year. Website: http://waterbrookmultnomah.com.

Multnomah Books has received several Gold Medallion Book Awards from the Evangelical Christian Publishers Association.

NEEDS Adventure, historical, literary, mainstream/contemporary, mystery, religious (inspirational, religious mystery/suspense, religious thriller, religious romance), romance (contemporary, historical), science fiction, spiritual, suspense. Published *A Name of Her Own*, by Jane Kirkpatrick (historical); *Women's Intuition*, by Lisa Samson (contemporary); *Thorn in My Heart*, by Liz Curtis Higgs (historical).

HOW TO CONTACT Does not accept unsolicited mss. *Agented submissions only.* Responds in 1-2 months to queries; 1-2 months to mss. Accepts simultaneous submissions, electronic submissions.

TERMS Pays royalty. Publishes ms 11 months after acceptance.

TIPS "Looking for moral, uplifting fiction. We're particularly interested in contemporary women's fiction, historical fiction, superior romance and mystery/suspense."

WHITE MANE KIDS

P.O. Box 708, Shippensburg PA 17257. (717)532-2237. Fax: (717)532-6110. E-mail: marketing@whitemane.com. Website: www.whitemane.com. **Contact:** Editor. White Mane Kids publishes historical based children's fiction for middle grade and young adult readers. Each book contains accurate historical information while captivating the readers with fascinating stories. White Mane Kids does not, however, publish picture books at this time. Publishes hardcover originals and paperback originals.

NEEDS Children's/juvenile (historical), young adult (historical). Published *Anybody's Hero: Battle of Old Men & Young Boys*, by Phyllis Haslip; *Crossroads at Gettysburg*, by Alan Kay.

HOW TO CONTACT Accepts unsolicited mss. Query with SASE. Accepts queries by fax, mail. Include estimated word count, brief bio, summary of work and marketing ideas. Send SASE for return of ms or send a disposable ms and SASE for reply only. Responds in 1 month to queries; 3-4 months to mss. Accepts simultaneous submissions. Rarely comments on rejected mss. Please mail the completed Proposal Guidelines form found on our website and your materials to: Attn: Acquisitions Department, White Mane Publishing Co., Inc., 73 W. Burd St., P.O. Box 708, Shippensburg, PA 17257.

TERMS Pays royalty. Publishes ms 12-18 months after acceptance. Ms guidelines for #10 SASE.

TIPS "Make your work historically accurate." "We are interested in historically accurate fiction for middle and young adult readers. We do *not* publish picture books. Our primary focus is the American Civil War and some America Revolution topics."

WILD CHILD PUBLISHING

PO Box 4897, Culver City CA 90231. (310) 721-4461. E-mail: admin@wildchildpublishing.com. Website: www.wildchildpublishing.com. **Contact:** Marci Baun, editor-in-chief (genres not covered by other editors); Faith Bicknell-Brown, managing editor (horror and romance); S.R. Howen, editor (science fiction and nonfiction). Estab. 1996. "We are closed to submissions from authors not already signed with either Wild Child Publishing or Freya's Bower from March 15, 2011 to September 15, 2011. Any submissions sent during this time will be deleted without consideration." Wild Child Publishing is a small, independent press that started out as a magazine in September 1999. We are known for working with newer/unpublished authors and editing to the standards of NYC publishers. Publishes paperback originals, e-books. Format: POD printing; perfect bound. Average print order: 50-200. Debut novel print order: 50. **Published 12 new writers last year.** Plans 10 debut novels this year. Averages 12 fiction titles/year. Member EPIC. Distributes/promotes titles through Ingrams and own website, Mobipocket Kindle, Amazon, and soon with Fictionwise. Freya's Bower already distributed with through Fictionwise.

Was named a Top 101 Writers' Web site in 2005.

NEEDS adventure, children's/juvenile, erotica for Freya's Bower only, ethnic/multicultural, experimental, fantasy, feminist, gay, historical, horror, humor/satire, lesbian, literary, mainstream, military/war, mystery/suspense, New Age/mystic, psychic/supernatural, romance, science fiction, short story collections, thriller/espionage, western, young adult/teen (fantasy/science fiction). Multiple anthologies planned. Writers should submit material per our submissions guidelines. Published *Weirdly: A Collection of Strange Tales*, by Variety (horror/psychological thriller); *Quits: Book 2: Devils*, by M.E. Ellis (horror, psychological thriller, paranormal).

HOW TO CONTACT Query with outline/synopsis and 1 sample chapter. Accepts queries by e-mail only. Include estimated word count, brief bio. Responds to queries in 2-4 weeks. Often critiques/comments on rejected mss. Responds to mss in 2-4 weeks.

TERMS Sends preproduction galleys to author. Ms published 2-4 months after acceptance. Pays royalties 10-40%. Book catalogs on website.

TIPS "Read our submission guidelines thoroughly. Send in entertaining, well-written stories. Be easy to work with and upbeat."

WILDE PUBLISHING

P.O. Box 4581, Albuquerque NM 87196. Fax: (419)715-1430. E-mail: wilde@unm.edu. **Contact:** Josiah Simon, Dusty McGowan, and David Wilde. Estab. 1989. Publishes hardcover and paperback originals. **Published 6 debut authors within the last year.** Twelve months to publication.

NEEDS children's/juvenile, fantasy (sword and sorcery), historical, literary, military/war, mystery, psychic/supernatural, romance, short story collections, thriller/espionage, western, young adult. Published *Scuttlebut*, by David Wilde (military) and *Harry the Magician*, by Dusty McGowan (children).

HOW TO CONTACT Does not accept unsolicited mss. Query with SASE. Accepts queries by e-mail, fax, mail. Include cover letter, brief bio, list of publishing credits. Send SASE for return of ms or send a disposable ms and SASE for reply only. Accepts submissions on disk. No simultaneous submissions.

TERMS Pay depends on grants/awards. Publishes ms 12 after acceptance. Ms guidelines for #10 SASE.

TIPS "Check spelling, write frequently, avoid excuses!"

THE WILD ROSE PRESS

P.O. Box 708, Adams Basin NY 14410. (585) 752-8770. E-mail: queryus@thewildrosepress.com; rpenders@thewildrosepress.com. Website: http://www.thewildrosepress.com. **Contact:** Nicole D'Arienzo, editor. Estab. 2006. "The American Rose line publishes stories about the French and Indian wars; Colonial America; the Revolutionary War; the war of 1812; the War Between the States; the Reconstruction era; the dawn of the new century. These are the struggles at the heart of the American Rose story. The central romantic relationship is the key driving force, set against historically accurate backdrop. These stories are for those who long for the courageous heroes and heroines who fought for their freedom and settled the new world; for gentle southern belles with spines of steel and the gallant gentlemen who sweep them away. This line is wide open for writers with a love of American history." Publishes paperback originals, reprints, and e-books in a POD format. Published 5 debut authors last year. Publishes approximately 10 fiction titles/year. Member: EPIC, Romance Writers of America. Distributes/promotes titles through major distribution chains, including Ingrams, Baker & Taylor, Sony, Kindle, Amazon.com, as well as smaller and online distributors.

Published 5 debut authors last year. Has received two Eppie Awards (2007) for First Place, and the New Jersey Golden Leaf Award for 2006 and 2007.

NEEDS contemporary, futuristic/time travel, gothic, historical, regency, romantic suspense, erotic and paranormal. Plans several anthologies "in several lines of the company in the next year, including Cactus Rose, Yellow Rose, American Rose, Black Rose, and Scarlet Rose." Has published *Enemy of the King*, by Beth Trissel; *An April to Remember*, by Lauri Robinson; and *Hero For Hire*, by Sheridon Smythe.

HOW TO CONTACT *Does not accept unsolicited mss.* Send query letter with outline and synopsis of up to 5 pages. Accepts all queries by e-mail. Include estimated word count, brief bio, and list of publishing credits. Agented fiction less than 1%. Responds to queries in 4 weeks; to mss in 12 weeks. Does not consider simultaneous submissions. Always comments on rejected mss.

TERMS Pays royalty of 7% minimum; 35% maximum. Sends prepublication galleys to author. Time between acceptance and publication is approximately 1 year. Writer's guidelines available on website.

TIPS "Polish your manuscript, make it as error free as possible, and follow our submission guidelines."

WILDSTORM

DC Universe, 1700 Broadway, New York NY 10019. (212)636-5400. Website: http://www.dccomics.com/wildstorm/. Wildstorm is part of the DC Universe.

HOW TO CONTACT "At this time, DC Comics does not accept unsolicited artwork or writing submissions."

WILLIAM MORROW

HarperCollins, 10 E. 53rd St., New York NY 10022. (212)207-7000. Fax: (212)207-7145. Website: www.harpercollins.com. **Contact:** Acquisitions Editor. Estab. 1926. Approximately half of the books published are fiction. Averages 160 total titles/year.

NEEDS Publishes adult fiction. "Morrow accepts only the highest quality submissions" in adult fiction.

HOW TO CONTACT *Agented submissions only.*

TERMS Pays standard royalty on retail price. Average advance: varying. Publishes ms 2 years after acceptance.

WILSHIRE BOOK COMPANY

9731 Variel Ave., Chatsworth CA 91311-4315. (818)700-1522. Fax: (818)700-1527. E-mail: mpowers@mpowers.com. Website: www.mpowers.com. **Contact:** Rights Department. Estab. 1947. "You are not only what you are today, but also what you choose to become tomorrow." Looking for adult fables that teach principles of psychological growth. Publishes trade paperback originals and reprints. Published 7 debut authors within the last year. Averages 25 total titles/year. Distributes titles through wholesalers, bookstores, and mail order. Promotes titles through author interviews on radio and television.

NEEDS adult allegories that teach principles of psychological growth or offer guidance in living. Minimum 25,000 words. Published *The Princess Who Believed in Fairy Tales*, by Marcia Grad; *The Knight in Rusty Armor*, by Robert Fisher; *The Dragon Slayer with a Heavy Heart*, by Marcia Powers.

HOW TO CONTACT Accepts unsolicited mss. Query with SASE or submit 3 sample chapter(s), synopsis or submit complete ms. Accepts queries by e-mail. Responds in 2 months to queries. Accepts simultaneous submissions.

TERMS Pays standard royalty. Offers advance. Publishes ms 6 months after acceptance. Ms guidelines online.

TIPS "We are vitally interested in all new material we receive. Just as you are hopeful when submitting your manuscript for publication, we are hopeful as we read each one submitted, searching for those we believe could be successful in the marketplace. Writing and publishing must be a team effort. We need you to write what we can sell. We suggest you read the successful books similar to the one you want to write. Analyze them to discover what elements make them winners. Duplicate those elements in your own style, using a creative new approach and fresh material, and you will have written a book we can catapult onto the bestseller list. You are welcome to telephone or e-mail us for immediate feedback on any book concept you may have. To learn more about us and what we publish, and for complete manuscript guidelines, visit our website."

WINDRIVER PUBLISHING, INC.

72 N. WindRiver Rd., Silverton ID 83867-0446. (208)752-1836. Fax: (208)752-1876. E-mail: info@windriverpublishing.com. Website: www.windriverpublishing.com. **Contact:** E. Keith Howick, Jr., president; Gail Howick, vice president/editor-in-chief. Estab. 2003. Publishes hardcover originals and reprints, trade paperback originals, mass market originals. Averages 8 total titles/year.

NEEDS Adventure, fantasy, historical, humor, juvenile, literary, military/war, mystery, religious, science fiction, spiritual, suspense, young adult.

HOW TO CONTACT WindRiver Publishing does not accept manuscript submissions via e-mail. Authors interested in publishing with us should review our Publishing Guidelines page. Responds in 2 months to queries; 4-6 months to mss. Accepts simultaneous submissions. Website is used to accept manuscripts for all four imprints of WindRiver Publishing, Inc.: Silverton House Publishing, Mapletree Publishing Company, WindRiver Publishing, Trumpet Media. These four imprints each deal with non-overlapping genres. Whether you submit online or as hard copy, the imprint will be determined based on the genre you assign for your project. Send hard copy to: WindRiver Publishing, Manuscript Submissions, 72 N. WindRiver Rd., Silverton ID 83867-0446. Submit a cover letter that includes all of the required information shown on our online form. If you choose, you can fill out the form, then click "Format for Printing" and print the resulting web page. Include SASE.

TERMS Pays 8-15% royalty on wholesale price. Publishes ms 12-18 months after acceptance. Ms guidelines online.

TIPS "We do not accept manuscripts containing graphic or gratuitous profanity, sex, or violence. See online instructions for details."

WIZARDS OF THE COAST BOOKS FOR YOUNG READERS

P.O. Box 707, Renton WA 98057. (425)254-2287. E-mail: nina.hess@wizards.com. Website: www.wizards.com. **Contact:** Nina Hess; Novel Submissions. (425)226-6500. Estab. 2003. "We publish shared-world fiction set in the worlds of Forgotten Realms, Dragonlance, Eberron, Ravenloft, and Magic: The Gathering. We also publish young reader fiction, in such series as Knights of the Silver Dragon, and select original speculative fiction." Publishes hardcover, mass market and trade paperback originals and mass market, and trade paperback reprints. Wizards of the Coast publishes games as well, including the Dungeons & Dragons role-playing game. Books: standard paperbacks; offset printing; perfect binding; b&w (usually) illustrations. Averages 70-90 total titles/year. Distributes titles through Random House. See for current guidelines. Currently not accepting manuscripts or proposals for any of our shared world lines. Open to original speculative fiction novel proposals from September 1 to January 1 of each year. Recently published *A Practical Guide to Dragon-Riding,* by Lisa Trumbauer; *Empire of Blood*, by Richard A. Knaak; *Promise of the Witch-King*, by R.A. Salvatore (fantasy); *Resurrection*, by Paul S. Kemp.

TERMS Agented fiction 65%. Responds in 4-8 months to queries. Accepts simultaneous submissions. Pays royalty on retail price with advance. Publishes ms 1-3 years after acceptance. Ms guidelines for #10 SASE.

TIPS Editorial staff attended or plans to attend ALA conference.

WOODLEY MEMORIAL PRESS

English Dept., Washburn University, Topeka KS 66621. E-mail: karen.barron@washburn.edu. Website: www.washburn.edu/reference/woodley-press. **Contact:** Kevin Rabas, acquisitions editor at Dept. of English, Box 4019, Emporia State University, 1200 Commercial St., Emporia KS 66801. Estab. 1980. "Woodley Memorial Press is a small, nonprofit press which publishes novels and fiction collections by Kansas writers only; by 'Kansas writers' we mean writers who reside in Kansas or have a Kansas connection." Publishes paperback originals.

NEEDS literary, mainstream/contemporary, short story collections. Published KS Notable Book winner *Great Blues*, by Steve Semken; *The Trouble with Campus Security*, by G.W. Clift; and *Loading the Stone*, by Harley Elliot.

HOW TO CONTACT Accepts unsolicited mss. Accepts queries by e-mail. Responds in 2 weeks to queries; 6 months to mss. Often comments on rejected mss.

TERMS Publishes ms 1 year after acceptance. "We prefer to work with authors of first books, for whom the book is an important step in a writing career. We rely heavily on the author's enthusiasm for the book, because almost all sales are generated by the author's promotion of the book through mailings (we'll pay), readings and book signings." Ms guidelines online.

TIPS "We only publish one to three works of fiction a year, on average, and those will definitely have a Kansas connection. We seek authors who are dedicated to promoting their works."

◐ WRITERS DIRECT

4330 Kauai Beach Dr., Suite G21, Lihue HI 96766. (808)822-7449. Fax: (808)822-2312. E-mail: sales@hshawaii.com. Website: www.bestplacesonearth.com. **Contact:** Rob Sanford, editor. Estab. 1985. "Small independent publishing house founded and run by published authors." Publishes hardcover and paperback orginals and reprints. Books: recycled paper; digital printing; perfect binding; illustrations.

NEEDS adventure, humor, literary, mainstream/contemporary, new age/mystic, regional (Hawaii), inspirational, religious mystery/suspense, religious thriller, thriller/espionage.

HOW TO CONTACT Send 1st chapter and synopsis. Include estimated word count, why author wrote book, and marketing plan. Send SASE for return of ms or send a disposable ms and SASE for reply only. Responds in 1 month to queries; 3 months to mss. Accepts simultaneous submissions. Sometimes comments on rejected mss.

TERMS Pays 15-35% royalty.

TIPS "Do what you do best and enjoy most. Your writing is an outcome of the above."

YELLOW SHOE FICTION SERIES

P.O. Box 25053, Baton Rouge LA 70894-5053. Website: www.lsu.edu/lsupress. **Contact:** Michael Griffith, Editor. Estab. 2004. Literary fiction series. Averages 2 titles/year.

NEEDS literary. "Looking first and foremost for literary excellence, especially good manuscripts that have fallen through the cracks at the big commercial presses. I'll cast a wide net." Published *Stations West*, by Allison Amend; *My Bright Midnight*, by Josh Russell; new and upcoming titles from Chris Bachelder, Lori Baker.

HOW TO CONTACT Does not accept unsolicited mss. Accepts queries by mail, attn: Rand Dotson. No electronic submissions.

TERMS Pays royalty. Offers advance. Ms guidelines online.

ZEBRA BOOKS

Kensington, 850 Third Ave., 16th Floor, New York NY 10022. (877)422-3665; (212)407-1500. E-mail: mrecords@kensingtonbooks.com. Website: www.kensingtonbooks.com. Contact: Megan Records, Associate Editor (mrecords@kensingtonbooks.com) (romance for Zebra and Brava, urban fantasy, young adult, select women's fiction); Michaela Hamilton, editor-in-chief; Ann La Farge, executive editor; Kate Duffy, editorial director (romance); John Scognamiglio, editorial director; Karen Thomas, editorial director (Dafina); Bruce Bender, managing director (Citadel); Margaret Wolf, editor; Richard Ember, editor; Bob Shuman, senior editor; Jeremie Ruby-Strauss, senior editor; Miles Lott, editor. Publishes hardcover originals, trade paperback and mass market paperback originals and reprints. Averages 600 total titles/year.

NEEDS Zebra books is dedicated to women's fiction, which includes but is not limited to romance.

HOW TO CONTACT Accepts simultaneous submissions. You may QUERY ONLY by e-mail. Do not attach manuscripts or proposals to e-mail queries. An editor will respond if he or she is interested in seeing your material based on your query. SUBMIT TO ONE EDITOR ONLY. For fiction, send cover letter, first 3 chapters, and synopsis (no more than 5 pages). Note that we do not publish science fiction or fantasy. We do not publish poetry. For nonfiction, send cover letter/query, including the author's qualifications and connections relevant to the book's content and marketing, and summary or outline of book's content. All submissions should be double-spaced, paginated, cleanly printed and readable. Do not bind pages together.

TERMS Publishes ms 12-18 months after acceptance. Please, no queries. Send synopsis and sample chapters with SASE.

ZONDERVAN, A HARPERCOLLINS COMPANY

Division of HarperCollins Publishers, 5300 Patterson Ave. SE, Grand Rapids MI 49530-0002. (616)698-6900. Fax: (616)698-3454. E-mail: submissions@zondervan.com. E-mail: christianmanuscriptsubmissions.com. Website: www.zondervan.com. **Contact:** Manuscript Review Editor. Manuscript submission line (616) 698-3447. Submissions accepted only by e-mail and only for certain types of manuscripts. See website for current submission guidelines and e-mail address: www.zondervan.com. **Background**: Zondervan Corporation estab. 1931. "Our mission is to be the leading Christian communications company meeting the needs of people with resources that glorify Jesus Christ and promote biblical principles." Large evangelical Christian publishing house. Published some debut authors within the last year. Averages 120 trade books per year.

We're currently accepting unsolicited book proposals only for the following categories: academic (only college and seminary textbooks in the areas of theology, biblical studies, church history, etc.); reference (commentaries, handbooks, encyclopedias, etc.); ministry resources (books and resources for pastors and ministry professionals). A proposal for one of these categories should be saved as a Microsoft Word document (unless it contains Hebrew, Greek, or language other than English, in which case it should be saved as an Adobe PDF document) and sent electronically as an attachment to submissions@zondervan.com, putting the appropriate category in the subject line. Your proposal should include the book title, a table of contents, including a 2 or 3-sentence description of each chapter, a brief description of the proposed book, including the unique contribution of the book and why you feel it must be published, your intended reader and your vita, including your qualifications to write the book. The proposal should be no more than 5 pages. If we're interested in reviewing more material from you, we'll respond within 6 weeks. All unsolicited proposals or manuscripts received outside of the above instructions, either hard copy or electronically, will be discarded. No longer accepts unsolicited mailed submissions. Instead, submissions may be submitted electronically to ChristianManuscriptSubmissions.com.

IMPRINTS Zondervan, Zonderkidz, Youth Specialties, Editorial Vida.

NEEDS Zondervan is currently accepting unsolicited book proposals for the following categories: academic (only college and seminary textbooks in the areas of theology, biblical studies, church history, etc.); reference (commentaries, handbooks, encyclopedias, etc.); ministry resources (books and resources for pastors and ministry professionals). If your manuscript fits within one of the above categories, please carefully follow the online submission guidelines. We are not currently accepting manuscripts for Christian living, devotionals, Bibles, or small group/Bible study materials. See website. www.zondervan.com. **Format in which to submit**: Include a vita, tentative title of the book, description of the book with strong case for why the book must be written and published (2-4 pages), plot outline or table of contents, and one or two sample chapters. DO NOT SEND ENTIRE MANUSCRIPT. Manuscripts should be typed in Microsoft Word in 8½"× 11"portrait format, double-spaced with one-inch margins on all sides. Number pages consecutively through the entire manuscript. Do not have separate pagination for each chapter. Place your "footnotes" after each chapter as endnotes. Book proposals should be single-spaced with 1-inch margins on all sides.

TERMS Normally pays royalties based on net amount received from sales. Advice: Almost no unsolicited manuscripts are published.

CONTESTS & AWARDS

In addition to honors and, quite often, cash prizes, contests and awards programs offer writers the opportunity to be judged on the basis of quality alone without the outside factors that sometimes influence publishing decisions. New writers who win contests may be published for the first time, while more experienced writers may gain public recognition of an entire body of work.

Listed here are contests for almost every type of fiction writing. Some focus on form, such as short stories, novels, or novellas, while others feature writing on particular themes or topics. Still others are prestigious prizes or awards for work that must be nominated, such as the Pulitzer Prize in Fiction. Chances are, no matter what type of fiction you write, there is a contest or award program that may interest you.

SELECTING & SUBMITTING TO A CONTEST

Use the same care in submitting to contests as you would sending your manuscript to a publication or book publisher. Deadlines are very important, and where possible, we've included this information. At times contest deadlines were only approximate at our press deadline, so be sure to write, call, or look online for complete information.

Follow the rules to the letter. If, for instance, contest rules require your name on a cover sheet only, you will be disqualified if you ignore this and put your name on every page. Find out how many copies to send. If you don't send the correct amount, by the time you are contacted to send more, it may be past the submission deadline. An increasing number of contests invite writers to query by e-mail, and many post contest information on their websites. Check listings for e-mail and website addresses.

One note of caution: Beware of contests that charge entry fees that are disproportionate to the amount of the prize. Contests offering a $10 prize, but charging $7 in entry fees, are a waste of your time and money.

If you are interested in a contest or award that requires your publisher to nominate your work, it's acceptable to make your interest known. Be sure to leave the publisher plenty of time, however, to make the nomination deadline.

AESTHETICA CREATIVE WORKS COMPETITION

P.O. Box 371, York YO23 1WL UK. E-mail: pauline@aestheticamagazine.com. E-mail: submissions@aestheticamagazine.com. Website: www.aestheticamagazine.com. The Aesthetica Creative Works Competition represents the scope of creative activity today, and provides an opportunity for both new and established artists to nurture their reputations on an international scale. There are three categories: Artwork & Photography, Fiction, and Poetry. See guidelines online.

AHWA FLASH & SHORT STORY COMPETITION

AHWA (Australian Horror Writers Association), E-mail: competitions@australianhorror.com. Website: australianhorror.com. **Contact:** David Carroll, competitions officer. "To showcase the diversity and talent of writers of horror fiction." Annual. Competition/award for short stories and flash fiction. The writers of the winning story in each category will receive paid publication in *Midnight Echo*, the magazine of the Australian Horror Writers Association, and an engraved plaque. "We're after horror stories, tales that frighten, yarns that unsettle us in our comfortable homes. All themes in this genre will be accepted, from the well-used (zombies, vampires, ghosts etc) to the highly original, so long as the story is professional and well written. No previously published entries will be accepted—all tales must be an original work by the author. Stories can be as violent or as bloody as the storyline dictates, but those containing gratuitous sex or violence will not be considered. Please check your entries for spelling and grammar mistakes and follow standard submission guidelines (eg, 12 point font, Arial, Times New Roman, or Courier New, one and a half spacing between lines, with title and page number on each page)." There are 2 categories: short stories (1,001 to 8,000 words) and flash fiction (less than 1,000 words). Writers may submit to one or both categories, but entry is limited to 1 story per author per category. Please send your submission as an attached rtf or doc to competitions@australianhorror.com. Alternatively, contact us to arrange postal submissions. Entry free for AHWA members; for non-members, $5 for flash, $10 for short story. Payment can be made via our secure Paypal option using ahwa@australianhorror.com. Alternatively, contact us and we can arrange other payment methods (eg, direct debit). Cheques will not be accepted due to the cost associated with banking them. Full guidelines available from on website. Accepts inquiries by e-mail. Entry deadline each year is May 31. Results announced July/August.

AKC GAZETTE ANNUAL FICTION CONTEST

260 Madison Ave., New York NY 10016. (212)696-8333. The *Gazette* sponsors an annual fiction contest for short short stories on some subject relating to purebred or mixed breed dogs. Fiction for our magazine needs a slant toward the serious fancier with real insight into the human/dog bond. Deadline: Begins April 15, until January 31 (postmark). $500, $250, and $100 for top 3 entries. Top entry published in AKC magazines. Guidelines online or for SASE.

ALABAMA STATE COUNCIL ON THE ARTS INDIVIDUAL ARTIST FELLOWSHIP

201 Monroe St., Montgomery AL 36130-1800. (334) 242-4076, ext. 224. Fax: (334) 240-3269. E-mail: anne.kimzey@arts.alabama.gov. Website: www.arts.state.al.us. **Contact:** Anne Kimzey, literature program manager. "To recognize the achievements and potential of Alabama writers." Judged by independent peer panel. Guidelines available in January. For guidelines, fax, e-mail, visit website. Accepts inquiries by fax, e-mail and phone. "Two copies of the following should be submitted: a résumé and a list of published works with reviews, if available. A minimum of 10 pages of poetry or prose, but no more than 20 pages. Please label each page with title, artist's name and date. If published, indicate where and the date of publication." Winners announced in June and notified by mail. List of winners available for SASE, fax, e-mail or visit website. No entry fee. Deadline: March 1 and applications can be submitted by egrant. Competition receives 25 submissions annually. Two-year residency required.

AMERICAN ASSOCIATION OF UNIVERSITY WOMEN AWARD IN JUVENILE LITERATURE

4610 Mail Service Center, Raleigh NC 27699-4610. (919)733-9375. E-mail: michael.hill@ncdcr.gov. **Contact:** Michael Hill, Awards Coordinator. North Carolina Literary and Historical Association, 4610 Mail Service Center, Raleigh NC 27699-4610. (919) 807-7290. Fax: (919) 733-8807. E-mail: michael.hill@ncdcr.gov. Award's purpose is to "select the year's best work of literature for young people by a North Carolina writer." Annual award for published books. Award: cup. Competition receives 10-15 submissions per category. Judged by three-judge panel. No entry fee. **Deadline: July 15.** Entries must be previously published. Contest open to "residents of North Carolina (three-year minimum)." Guidelines available July 15. For guidelines, send SASE, fax, e-mail, or call. Accepts inquiries by fax, e-mail, phone. Winners announced October 15. Winners notified by mail. List of winners available for SASE, fax, e-mail.

Competition receives 10-15 submissions per category.

AMERICAN SCANDINAVIAN FOUNDATION TRANSLATION PRIZE

American Scandinavian Foundation, 58 Park Ave., New York NY 10016. E-mail: info@amscan.org. Website: www.amscan.org. **Contact:** Valerie Hymas. (212) 879-9779. Fax: (212)686-2115. Award to recognize excellence in fiction, poetry and drama translations of Scandinavian writers born after 1800. Prize: $2,000 grand prize; $1,000 prize. No entry fee. Cover letter should include name, address, phone, e-mail and title. Deadline: June 1. Entries must be unpublished. Length: no more than 50 pages for drama, fiction; no more than 35 pages for poetry. Open to any writer. Guidelines available in January for SASE, by fax, phone, e-mail, or on website.

AMERICAN SHORT STORY CONTEST

American Short Fiction, P.O. Box 301209, Austin TX 78703. (512)538-1305. Fax: (512)538-1306. Website: www.americanshortfiction.org. **Contact:** Jill Meyers, editor. "Contest offered annually to reward and recognize short stories under 1,000 words." Submissions accepted only via the online submission manager on website. Please see website for full guidelines. Feb. 15-May 1. 1st Place: $500 and publication; 2nd Place: $250 and publication. Costs $15 for up to three 1,000 word entries.

A MIDSUMMER TALE

E-mail: editors@toasted-cheese.com. Website: www.toasted-cheese.com. **Contact:** Theryn Fleming, editor. A Midsummer Tale is a contest open to non-genre fiction, creative nonfiction, and hybrids thereof. Theme changes each year. Ideally, stories will take place during a warm time of the year, and this element will be an integral part of the story. The word range is 1,000-5,000 words. Check website for current focus and contest address. First prize: $20 Amazon gift certificate, publication; Second prize: $15 Amazon gift certificate, publication; Third prize: $10 Amazon gift certificate, publication. Categories: non-genre fiction, creative nonfiction. Judged by two Toasted Cheese editors who blind-judge each contest. Each judge has her own criteria for selecting winners. No entry fee. Guidelines, including the e-mail address to which you should send your entry and instructions for what to include and how to format, are available April 1 on website. Accepts inquiries by e-mail. **Deadline: June 21.** Entries must be unpublished. Open to any writer. Results announced July 31 on website. Winners notified by e-mail.

ANNUAL BOOK COMPETITION

Washington Writers' Publishing House, P.O. Box 15271, Washington DC 20003. E-mail: wwphpress@gmail.com; wwph@gmail.com. Website: http://www.washingtonwriters.org; www.wwph.org. "To award literary excellence in the greater Washington DC-Baltimore area." Annual. Competition/award for fiction (novel or story collection) and poetry collection. Prize: $500, publication, and 50 copies of book. The winning poet becomes a member of the organization and should be prepared to actively participate in the work of the press, including such areas as publicity, distribution, production, and fundraising. Our tradition of poets actively working on behalf of other poets is essential to the continued vitality and success of WWPH. Contest entrants should be willing to make this commitment should their work be selected for publication. Categories: fiction (novel or collection of short stories). Receives about 40 entries per category. Judged by members of the press. Entry fee: $25. Make checks payable to WWPH. Guidelines available all year with SASE, on website. Accepts inquiries by e-mail. Deadline: Nov. 1. Entries should be unpublished. "Individual stories or excerpts may have been published in journals and anthologies." Open to fiction writers living within 60 miles of the Capitol (Baltimore area included). Length: no more than 350 pages, double or 1½ spaced. Cover letter should include name, address, phone, e-mail, novel/collection title, acknowledgments. None of this information should appear on the actual manuscript. Results announced January of each year. Winners notified by phone, by e-mail.

ARROWHEAD REGIONAL ARTS COUNCIL INDIVIDUAL ARTIST CAREER DEVELOPMENT GRANT

1301 Rice Lake Rd., Suite 120, Duluth MN 55811. Website: www.aracouncil.org. Arrowhead Regional Arts Council, 1301 Rice Lake Rd., Suite 111, Duluth MN 55811. (218) 722-0952 or (800) 569-8134. Fax: (218) 722-4459. E-mail: info@aracouncil.org. Website: www.aracouncil.org. Award to "provide financial support to regional artists wishing to take advantage of impending, concrete opportunities that will advance their work or careers." Prize: up to $1,000. Categories: novels, short stories, story collections and translations. Judged by ARAC Board. No entry fee. Guidelines available by phone, e-mail, or on website. **See website for 2009 deadlines.** Entries must be unpublished. Award is offered 3 times per year. Applicants must live in the seven-county region of northeastern Minnesota. Results announced approximately 6 weeks after deadline. Winners notified by mail. List of winners available by phone and also listed on the website.

ART AFFAIR SHORT STORY AND WESTERN SHORT STORY CONTESTS

P.O. Box 54302, Oklahoma City OK 73154. E-mail: artaffair@aol.com. Website: www.shadetreecreations.com. **Contact:** Barbara Shepherd. The annual Art Affair Writing Contests include (General) Short Story and Western Short Story categories and offer 1st Prize: $50 and certificate; 2nd Prize: $25 and certificate; and 3rd Prize: $15 and certificate in both categories. Honorable Mention certificates will be awarded at the discretion of the judges. Open to any writer. All short stories must be unpublished. Multiple entries accepted in both categories with separate entry fees for each. Submit original stories on any subject and timeframe for general Short Story category, and submit original western stories for Western Short Story word limit for all entries is 5,000 words. (Put word count in the upper right-hand corner of first page; mark "Western" on western short stories. All ms. must be double-spaced on 8.5x11 white paper. Type title of short story on first page and headers on following pages. Include cover page with writer's name, address, phone number, and ms title. Do not include SASE; mss will not be returned. Guidelines available on website. **Deadline: October 1, 2011 (postmark). Entry Fee:** $5 per story. Make check payable to Art Affair. Winners' list will be published on the Art Affair website in December.

THE ART OF MUSIC ANNUAL WRITING CONTEST

The Art of Music, Inc., P.O. Box 85, Del Mar CA 92014-0085. (619) 884-1401. Fax: (858) 755-1104. E-mail: info@theartofmusicinc.org. Website: www.theartofmusicinc.org. **Contact:** Elizabeth C. Axford. Offered annually. Categories are: essay, short story, poetry, song lyrics, and illustrations for cover art. All writings must be on music-related topics. The purpose of the contest is to promote the art of music through writing. Acquires onetime rights. All entries must be accompanied by an entry form indicating category and age; parent signature is required of all writers under age 18. Poems may be of any length and in any style; essays and short stories should not exceed 5 double-spaced, typewritten pages. All entries shall be previously unpublished (except poems and song lyrics) and the original work of the author. Prize: Cash, medal, certificate, publication in the anthology titled *The Art of Music: A Collection of Writings*, and copies of the book. Judged by a panel of published poets, authors, and songwriters. Entry fee: $20 fee. Inquiries accepted by e-mail, phone. **Deadline: June 30.** Short stories should be no longer than 5 pages typed and double spaced. Open to any writer. "Make sure all work is fresh and original. Music-related topics only." Results announced October 31. Winners notified by mail. For contest results, send SASE or visit website.

ARTIST TRUST FELLOWSHIP AWARD

Artist Trust, 1835 12th Ave, Seattle WA 98122. (209) 467-8734, ext 9. Fax: (206) 467-9633. E-mail: miguel@artisttrust.org. Website: artisttrust.org. **Contact:** Miguel Guillen, Program Manager. "Artist Trust Fellowship awards practicing professional Washington State artists of exceptional talent and demonstrated ability." Annual. Prize: $7,500. "The Fellowship awards are multidisciplinary awards. The categories for 2012 are Emerging Fields & Cross-disciplinary, Folk & Traditional, Visual and Performing Art; for 2012 are Literary, Music, Media and Craft. Accepted genres for Literary are: poetry, fiction, graphic novels, experimental works, creative non-fiction, screen plays, film scripts and teleplays." Receives about 175 entries per category. Entries are judged by work samples as specified in the guidelines. Winners are selected by a multidisciplinary panel of artists and arts professionals. No entry fee. Guidelines available around December; please check website. Accepts inquiries by e-mail, phone. Submission period is December-February. Website should be consulted for the exact date. Entries can be unpublished or previously published. Washington State residents only. Length: up to 15 pages for poetry, fiction, graphic novels, experimental works and creative nonfiction, and up to 20 pages for screen plays, film scripts and teleplays. All mss must be typed with a 12-pt font size or larger and cannot be single spaced (except for poetry). Include artist statement and résumé with name, address, phone, e-mail, and novel/story title. "The Fellowship awards are highly competitive. Please follow guidelines with care." Results announced in the spring. Winners notified by mail. Results made available to entrants on website.

THE ATHENAEUM LITERARY AWARD

219 S. Sixth St., Philadelphia PA 19106-3794. Website: www.PhilaAthenaeum.org. **Contact:** Jill LeMin Lee. Annual award to recognize and encourage outstanding literary achievement in Philadelphia and its vicinity. Prize: A certificate bearing the name of the award, the seal of the Athenaeum, the title of the book, the name of the author and the year. Categories: The Athenaeum Literary Award is granted for a work of general literature, not exclusively for fiction. Judged by a committee appointed by the Board of Directors. No entry fee. Deadline: December 31 of the year of publication. Entries must be previously published. Nominations shall be made in writing to the Literary Award Committee by the author, the publisher, or a member of the Athenaeum, accompanied by a copy of the book. Open to work by residents of Philadelphia and its vicinity. Guidelines available for SASE, by fax, by e-mail and on website. Accepts inquiries by fax, e-mail and phone. Juvenile fiction is not included. Results announced in spring. Winners notified by mail. For contest results, see website.

ATLANTIC WRITING COMPETITION FOR UNPUBLISHED MANUSCRIPTS

Writers' Federation of Nova Scotia, 1113 Marginal Rd., Halifax NS B3H 4P7. (902)423-8116. Fax: (902)422-0881. E-mail: director@writers.ns.ca; talk@writers.ns.ca. Website: www.writers.ns.ca. **Contact:** Nate Crawford, program coordinator. Estab. 1975. "Annual contest for beginners to try their hand in a number of categories: novel, short story, poetry, writing for younger children, writing for juvenile/young adult. Only 1 entry/category is allowed. Established writers are also eligible, but must work in an area that's new to them. Because our aim is to help Atlantic Canadian writers grow, judges return written comments when the competition is concluded. Anyone residing in the Atlantic Provinces for at least 6 months prior to the contest deadline is eligible to enter." $35 fee for novel ($30 for WFNS members); $25 fee for all other categories ($20 for WFNS members). Needs poetry, essays, juvenile, novels, articles, short stories.

AUTUMN HOUSE FICTION PRIZE

Autumn House Press, 87½ Westwood Street, Pittsburgh PA 15211. (412)381-4261. E-mail: info@autumnhouse.org. Website: http://autumnhouse.org. **Contact:** Michael Simms, executive editor. "To identify and publish the best fiction manuscripts we can find." Annual. Competition/award for short stories, novels, story collections, translations. Prize: $2,500 and book publication. Only one category: all genres of fiction (short stories, short-shorts, novellas, and novels, or any combination of genres) are eligible. Entries are screened by an able team of experienced, published writers. Entry fee: $25. Make checks payable to Autumn House Press. Final judge is Stewart O'Nan.

AWP AWARD SERIES

Mail Stop 1E3, George Mason Univ., Fairfax VA 22030. E-mail: awp@awpwriter.org. Website: www.awpwriter.org. **Contact:** Supriya Bhatnagar, Dir. of Publications. The AWP Award Series was established in cooperation with several university presses in order to publish and make fine fiction and nonfiction available to a wide audience. Offered annually to foster new literary talent. Guidelines for SASE and on website. Categories: novel ($2,000), Donald Hall Prize in Poetry ($5,000), Grace Paley Prize in Short Fiction ($5,000), and creative nonfiction ($2,000). Entry fee: $30 for nonmembers, $15 for members. Entries must be unpublished. "This information should appear in cover letter only." Open to any writer. Guidelines available on website in November. No phone calls, please. Manuscripts published previously in their entirety, including self-publishing, are not eligible. No mss returned. Results announced in August. Winners notified by mail or phone. For contest results send SASE, or visit website. No phone calls, please.

BEST LESBIAN EROTICA

BLE 2010, 31-64 21st St., #319, Long Island City NY 11106. E-mail: kwarnockble@gmail.com. **Contact:** Kathleen Warnock, series editor. Categories: Novel excerpts, short stories, other prose; poetry will be considered but is not encouraged. No entry fee. Include cover page with author's name, title of submission(s), address, phone, fax, e-mail. All submissions must be typed and double-spaced. You may submit double-sided copies. Length: 5,000 words. You may submit 2 different pieces of work. Submit 2 hard copies of each submission. Will only accept e-mail copies if the following conditions apply: You live outside of North America or Europe, the cost of postage would be prohibitive from your home country, the post office system in your country is dreadful (U.S. does not count); the content of your submission may be illegal to send via postal mail in your home country. Accepts both previously published and unpublished material, but does not accept simultaneous submissions to another annual erotica anthology. Open to any writer. All submissions must include SASE or an e-mail address for response. If no e-mail address, then please include SASP. No mss will be returned.

● BINGHAMTON UNIVERSITY JOHN GARDNER FICTION BOOK AWARD

P.O. Box 6000, Binghamton NY 13902. (607)777-2713. Fax: (607)777-2408. E-mail: cwpro@binghamton.edu. Website: english.binghamton.edu/cwpro. **Contact:** Maria Mazziotti Gillan, director. Estab. 2001. Award's purpose is "to serve the literary community by calling attention to outstanding books of fiction." Prize: $1,000. Categories: novels and short story collections. Judged by "rotating outside judges." No entry fee. Entries must have appeared in print in book form between January 1 and December 31 of the year preceding the award. Print on demand will be acceptable, but no self-published or vanity press books will be considered. Each book submitted must be accompanied by an application form, available online, or send SASE to above address. Submit 3 copies of the book; copies will not be returned. Publishers may submit more than 1 book for prize consideration. Deadline: March 1. Books must be written in English by an American author. Results announced in summer. Winners notified by e-mail or phone. For contest results, send SASE or visit website.

●● JAMES TAIT BLACK MEMORIAL PRIZES

University of Edinburgh, Department of English Literature, David Hume Tower, George, Edinburgh, Scotland EH8 9JX UK. (44-13)1650-3619. Fax: (44-13)1650-6898. E-mail: s.strathdee@ed.ac.uk. Website: www.englit.ed.ac.uk/jtbinf.htm. **Contact:** Sheila Strathdee, Department of English Literature. "Two prizes each of £10,000 are awarded: one for the best work of fiction, one for the best biography or work of that nature, published during the calendar year January 1 to December 31." Judged by professors of English Literature with the assistance of teams of postgraduate readers. No entry fee. Accepts inquiries by fax, e-mail, phone. **Deadline: December 1.** Entries must be previously published. "Eligible works are those written in English and first published or co-published in Britain in the year of the award. Works should be submitted by publishers." Open to any writer. Winners notified by phone, via publisher. Contact department of English Literature for list of winners or check website.

●● THE BOARDMAN TASKER AWARD FOR MOUNTAIN LITERATURE

The Boardman Tasker Charitable Trust, 8 Bank View Rd., Darley Abbey Derby DE22 1EJ UK. Phone/fax: UK 01332342246. E-mail: steve@people-matter.co.uk. Website: www.boardmantasker.com. **Contact:** Steve Dean. "The award is to honor Peter Boardman and Joe Tasker, who disappeared on Everest in 1982." Offered annually to reward a work of nonfiction or fiction, in English or in translation, which has made an outstanding contribution to mountain literature. Books must be published in the UK between November 1 of previous year and October 31 of year of the prize. Writers may obtain information, but entry is by publishers only (includes self-publishing). "No restriction of nationality, but work must be published or distributed in the UK." Prize: £3,000. Judged by a panel of 3 judges elected by trustees. No entry fee. "May be fiction, nonfiction, poetry or drama. Not an anthology. Subject must be concerned with a mountain environment. Previous winners have been books on expeditions, climbing experiences, a biography of a mountaineer, novels." Guidelines available in January by e-mail or on website. Deadline: Midnight of August 17. Entries must be previously published. Publisher's entry only. Open to any writer. Results announced in November. Winners notified by phone or e-mail. For contest results, send e-mail or visit website. "The winning book needs to be well written to reflect a knowledge of and a respect and appreciation for the mountain environment."

BOSTON GLOBE-HORN BOOK AWARDS

The Boston Globe, Horn Book, Inc., 56 Roland St., Suite 200, Boston MA 02129. (617)628-0225. Fax: (617)628-0882. E-mail: info@hbook.com; khedeen@hbook.com. Website: http://hbook.com/bghb/. **Contact:** Katrina Hedeen. Estab. 1967. The Boston Globe's Horn Book Awards are among the most prestigious honors in the field of children's and young adult literature. Winners are selected in three categories: Picture Book, Fiction and Poetry, and Nonfiction. Two Honor Books may be named in each category. On occasion, a book will receive a special citation for its high quality and overall creative excellence. The winning titles must be published in the United States, but they may be written or illustrated by citizens of any country. The awards are chosen by an independent panel of three judges who are annually appointed by the Editor of the Horn Book.

THE BRIAR CLIFF REVIEW FICTION, POETRY, AND CREATIVE NONFICTION COMPETITION

The Briar Cliff Review, Briar Cliff University, 3303 Rebecca St., Sioux City IA 51104-0100. (712)279-5321. Fax: (712)279-5410. E-mail: curranst@briarcliff.edu; jeanne.emmons@briarcliff.edu. Website: www.briarcliff.edu/bcreview. **Contact:** Tricia Currans-Sheehan, editor. Purpose of Award: "to reward good writers and showcase quality writing." Offered annually for unpublished poem, story, and essay. Prize: $ 1,000, and publication in spring issue. All entrants receive a copy of the magazine with winning entries. Judged by editors. "We guarantee a considerate reading." Entry fee: $20. Guidelines available in August for SASE. Inquiries accepted by e-mail. **Deadline: Submissions between August 1 and November 1.** No mss returned. Entries must be unpublished. Length: 6,000 words maximum. Open to any writer. Results announced in December or January. Winners notified by phone or letter around December 20. "Send us your best. We want stories with a plot."

"Send us your best work. We want stories with a plot."

THE BRIDPORT PRIZE

P.O. Box 6910, Dorset DT6 9QB United Kingdom. +44 (0)1308 428 333. E-mail: frances@bridportprize.org.uk. Website: www.bridportprize.org.uk. **Contact:** Frances Everitt, administrator. Award to "promote literary excellence, discover new talent." Prize: £5,000 sterling; £1,000 sterling; £500 sterling, plus various runners-up prizes and publication of approximately 13 best stories and 13 best poems in anthology. Categories: short stories and poetry and flash fiction. Judged by 1 judge for fiction (in 2011, Al Kennedy) and 1 judge for poetry (in 2011, Carol Ann Duffy). 2010 introduced a new category for flash fiction. £1,000 sterling first prize for the best short, short story of under 250 words. Entry fee: £6 sterling for poems, £7 for fiction, and £5 for flash fiction. **Deadline: June 30.** Entries must be unpublished. Length: 5,000 maximum for short stories; 42 lines for poetry, and 250 words for flash fiction.

BRITISH CZECH AND SLOVAK ASSOCIATION WRITING COMPETITION

24 Ferndale, Tunbridge Wells Kent TN2 3NS England. E-mail: prize@bcsa.co.uk. Website: www.bcsa.co.uk. **Contact:** Prize Administrator. Estab. 2002.

BURNABY WRITERS' SOCIETY CONTEST

E-mail: info@bws.bc.ca. Website: www.bws.bc.ca; http:burnabywritersnews.blogspot.com. **Contact:** Eileen Kernaghan. Offered annually for unpublished work. Open to all residents of British Columbia. Categories vary from year to year. Send SASE for current rules. Purpose is to encourage talented writers in all genres. Prize: 1st Place: $200; 2nd Place: $100; 3rd Place: $50; and public reading. Entry fee: $5. For complete guidelines, see website or burnabywritersnews.blogspot.com.

THE CAINE PRIZE FOR AFRICAN WRITING

51a Southwark St., London SE1 1RU United Kingdom. E-mail: info@caineprize.com. Website: www.caineprize.com. **Contact:** Nick Elam, administrator. Annual award for a short story (3,000-10,000 words) by an African writer. "An 'African writer' is normally taken to mean someone who was born in Africa, who is a national of an African country, or whose parents are African, and whose work has reflected African sensibilities." Entries must have appeared for the first time in the 5 years prior to the closing date for submissions, which is January 31 each year. Publishers should submit 6 copies of the published original with a brief cover note (no pro forma application). "Please indicate nationality or passport held." Prize: £10,000. Judged by a panel of judges appointed each year. No entry fee. Cover letter should include name, address, phone, e-mail, title, and publication where story was previously published. Deadline: January 31. Entries must be previously published. Word length: 3,000-10,000 words. Manuscripts not accepted. Entries must be submitted by publishers, not authors. Results announced in mid-July. Winners notified at event/banquet. For contest results, send fax, e-mail or visit our website.

JAMIE CAT CALLAN HUMOR PRIZE

National League of American Pen Women, The Webhallow House, 1544 Sweetwood Dr., Broadmoor Village CA 94015-2029. E-mail: pennobhill@aol.com. Website: www.soulmakingcontest.us. **Contact:** Eileen Malone.

KAY CATTARULLA AWARD FOR BEST SHORT STORY

Texas Institute of Letters, P.O. Box 609, Round Rock TX 78680. (512) 238-1871. E-mail: tilsecretary@yahoo.com. Website: http://texasinstituteofletters.org/. **Contact:** W.K. (Kip) Stratton, acquisitions. Offered annually for work published January 1-December 31 of previous year to recognize the best short story. The story submitted must have appeared in print for the first time to be eligible. Writers must have been born in Texas, must have lived in Texas for at least 2 consecutive years, or the subject matter of the work must be associated with Texas. See website for guidelines. Deadline: Jan. 1. Prize: $1,000.

⊕$ *THE CHARITON REVIEW* SHORT FICTION PRIZE

Truman State University Press, 100 East Normal Ave., Kirksville MO 63501-4221. Website: tsup.truman.edu. **Contact:** Nancy Rediger. An annual award for the best unpublished short fiction on any theme up to 5,000 words in English. Include a nonrefundable reading fee of $20 for each ms submitted. Check payable to: Truman State University Press. If you prefer to pay by Visa, MasterCard, or Discover, include your credit card number, expiration date, cardholder name, and signature. $1,000 prize and publication in the *Chariton Review*. All U.S. entrants receive a 1-year subscription (2 issues) to the *Chariton Review*. Entrants outside the U.S. receive the prizewinning issue only. The final judge will be announced after the finalists have been selected in January. The winning entries will be published in the Spring issue. All U.S. entrants will receive a complimentary copy of the Spring prize issue.

N$ CHIZINE SHORT STORY CONTEST

Dorchester Publications, 200 Madison Ave, Suite 2000, New York NY 10016. Website: http://chizine.com. **Contact:** Brett Alexander Savory, editor-in-chief. Held annually "to find the top three dark fiction stories." Competition/award for short stories. Prize: 7¢/word, up to 4,000 words. Judged by a revolving panel of writers and editors of dark fiction selected by the editor-in-chief of Chizine. No entry fee. Guidelines available in May. Accepts inquiries by e-mail. **Submissions accepted June 1 through 30.** Entries should be unpublished. Contest open to anyone. Cover letter and ms should include name, address, e-mail, word count, short story title. Writers may submit own work. Results announced end of July. Winners and honorable mentions notified by e-mail. Results made available to entrants on website.

COLORADO BOOK AWARDS

Colorado Center for the Book, 1490 Lafayette St., Suite 101, Denver CO 80218. (303)894-7951, ext. 21. Fax: (303)864-9361. E-mail: long@coloradohumanities.org. Website: www.coloradocenterforthebook.org. **Contact:** Margaret Coval, Exec. Director, or Jennifer Long, Prog. Adjudicator. Offered annually for work published by December of previous year. "The purpose is to champion all Colorado authors, editors, illustrators, and photographers, and in particular, to honor the award winners raising the profiles of both their work and Colorado as a state whose people promote and support reading, writing, and literacy through books. The categories are generally: children's literature, young adult and juvenile literature, fiction, genre fiction (romance, mystery/thriller, science fiction/fantasy, historical), biography, history, anthology, poetry, pictorial, graphic novel/comic, creative nonfiction, and general nonfiction, as well as other categories as determined each year. Open to authors who reside or have resided in Colorado." Cost: $53 fee. Needs fiction, nonfiction, poetry, juvenile, novels. Deadline: January 16, 2012.

COMMONWEALTH CLUB OF CALIFORNIA BOOK AWARDS

Commonwealth Club of California, 595 Market St., San Francisco CA 94105. (415)597-6724. Fax: (415)597-6729. E-mail: gdobbins@commonwealthclub.org. Website: www.commonwealthclub.org/bookawards. **Contact:** Wendy Wanderman, Associate Program Director. Estab. 1931. E-mail: bookawards@commonwealthclub.org. Website: www.commonwealthclub.org/features/caBookAwards/. Award to honor excellence in literature written by California residents. Prize: $2,000, gold medal; $300, silver medal. Categories: fiction, first work of fiction, nonfiction, juvenile, young adult, poetry, Californiana, contribution to publishing. Judged by jury. No entry fee. Entries must be previously published. California residents only. Writer or publisher may nominate work. Guidelines available in January on website. Results announced in Spring. Winners notified by phone. For contest results, send e-mail.

⊕ COPTALES CONTEST

Sponsored by Oak Tree Press, 140 E. Palmer St., Taylorville IL 62568. E-mail: oaktreepub@aol.com. Website: www.oaktreebooks.com. **Contact:** Billie Johnson, award director. "The goal of the CopTales Contest is to discover and publish new authors, or authors shifting to a new genre. This annual contest is open to writers who have not published in the crime fiction, nonfiction, and true crime genre in the past three years, as well as completely unpublished authors. Deadline: July 31. The prize consists of a Publishing Agreement, and launch of the title. Winners or runners up who are offered publishing agreements are asked to transfer rights. Publishing industry professionals prescreen the entries; publisher makes final selection." $25 entry fee.

O CRAZYHORSE FICTION PRIZE

College of Charleston, Dept. of English, 66 George St., Charleston SC 29424. (843)953-7740. Fax: (843)953-7740. E-mail: crazyhorse@cofc.edu. Website: www.crazyhorsejournal.org. **Contact:** Editors. The journal's mission is to publish the entire spectrum of today's fiction, essays, and poetry—from the mainstream to the avant-garde, from the established to the undiscovered writer. The editors are especially interested in original writing that engages in the work of honest communication. *Crazyhorse* publishes writing of fine quality regardless of style, predilection, subject. Contest open to any writer. Entry fee: $16 (covers 1-yr subscription to *Crazyhorse*; make checks payable to Crazyhorse). To enter, please send up to 25 pages of prose. **Deadline: January 15 of each year**; see website. Prize: $2,000 and publication in *Crazyhorse*. Judged by anonymous writer whose identity is disclosed when the winners are announced in April.

O CROSSTIME SHORT SCIENCE FICTION CONTEST

Crossquarter Publishing Group, P.O. Box 23749, Santa Fe NM 87502. Website: www.crossquarter.com. E-mail: contest@crossquarter.com. Phone: (505)690-3923. Fax: (214)975-9715. Acquisitions: Anthony Ravenscroft. Annual contest for short science fiction (up to 7,500 words) showcasing the best of the human spirit. No horror or dystopia. Deadline: March 15. Prizes: 1st place: $250; 2nd place: $125; 3rd place: $75; 4th place: $50; Winners are also combined into an anthology. Costs $15; $10 for each additional submission. Guidelines and entry form available online.

DANA AWARDS IN THE NOVEL, SHORT FICTION, ESSAY AND POETRY

200 Fosseway Dr., Greensboro NC 27445. (336)644-8028. E-mail: danaawards@pipeline.com; danaawards@gmail.com. Website: www.danaawards.com. **Contact:** Mary Elizabeth Parker, chair.

DARK OAK MYSTERY CONTEST

Oak Tree Press, 140 E. Palmer St., Taylorville IL 62568. (217)824-6500. E-mail: oaktreepub@aol.com. Website: www.oaktreebooks.com. **Contact:** Editor (prefers e-mail contact). Offered annually for an unpublished mystery manuscript (up to 85,000 words) of any sort from police procedurals to amateur sleuth novels. Acquires first North American, audio and film rights to winning entry. Open to authors not published in the past 3 years. Entry fee: $35/mss.

O DEAD OF WINTER

E-mail: editors@toasted-cheese.com. Website: www.toasted-cheese.com. **Contact:** Stephanie Lenz, editor. The contest is a winter-themed horror fiction contest with a new topic each year. Topic and word limit announced Nov. 1. The topic is usually geared toward a supernatural theme. Prize: Amazon gift certificates in the amount of $20, $15 and $10; publication in *Toasted Cheese*. Also offers honorable mention. Categories: short stories. Judged by two *Toasted Cheese* editors who blind judge each contest. Each judge uses her own criteria to rate entries. No entry fee. Cover letter should include name, address, e-mail, word count, and title. **Deadline: December 21.** Entries must be unpublished. Word limit varies each year. Open to any writer. Guidelines available in November on website. Accepts inquiries by e-mail. "Follow guidelines. Write a smart, original story. We have further guidelines on the website." Results announced January 31. Winners notified by e-mail. List of winners on website.

DELAWARE DIVISION OF THE ARTS

820 N. French St., Wilmington DE 19801. (302)577-8278. Fax: (302)577-6561. E-mail: kristin.pleasanton@state.de.us. Website: www.artsdel.org. **Contact:** Kristin Pleasanton, coordinator. Award "to help further careers of emerging and established professional artists." For Delaware residents only. Prize: $10,000 for masters; $6,000 for established professionals; $3,000 for emerging professionals. Judged by out-of-state, nationally recognized professionals in each artistic discipline. No entry fee. Guidelines available after May 1 on website. Accepts inquiries by e-mail, phone. Expects to receive 25 fiction entries. Deadline: August 1. Open to any Delaware writer. Results announced in December. Winners notified by mail. Results available on website. "Follow all instructions and choose your best work sample."

RICK DEMARINIS SHORT FICTION PRIZE

Cuthroat, A Journal of the Arts, P.O. Box 2414, Durango CO 81302. (970) 903-7914. E-mail: cutthroatmag@gmail.com. Website: http://www.cutthroatmag.com. **Contact:** Pamela Uschuk, editor-In-chief. "To recognize a fine piece of fiction by giving the author an honorarium and a venue for publication." Annual. Competition/award for short stories. $1,250 plus publication for First Prize; $250 plus publication for Second Prize. Receives about 250 plus entries. Magazine staff chooses 20-25 finalists, and a different nationally known fiction writer is selected each year as the final judge. Entry fee: $15. Make checks payable to Raven's Word Writers Center. Guidelines available in January. **Entries postmark deadline is October 11, 2011.** Entries should be unpublished. Anyone writing anywhere in English may enter contest. Length: 5,000 word limit. Cover letter should include name, address, phone, e-mail, novel/story title. No identifying information may appear anywhere on the ms. "Our criteria is excellence." Results announced December. Winners notified by phone. Results made available to entrants with SASE. SASE is mandatory. Those entries sent without an SASE will go unread.

DOBIE PAISANO FELLOWSHIPS

University Station (G0400), Austin TX 78712-0531. (512)471-7620. E-mail: adameve@mail.utexas.edu. Website: www.utexas.edu/ogs/Paisano. The annual Dobie Paisano fellowships provide an opportunity for creative or nonfiction writers to live and write for an extended period in an environment that offers isolation and tranquility. At the time of application, the applicant must: be a native Texan, have lived in Texas at some time for at least three years, or have published significant work with a Texas subject. The Ralph A. Johnston Memorial Fellowship, aimed at writers who have demonstrated some publishing and critical success, offers a $20,000 stipend over four months. The Jesse H. Jones Writing Fellowship offers an $18,000 stipend over five and a half months. Criteria for making the awards include quality of work, character of the proposed project, and suitability of the applicant for life at Paisano, the late J. Frank Dobie's ranch near Austin, TX. Annual deadline in January; awards announced in May. Application fee: $20/one fellowship, $30 both fellowships. Applications and detailed information are available on the website.

DOBIE PAISANO PROJECT

The Graduate School, The Univ. of Texas at Austin, 1 University Ave., Mail Stop G0400, Austin TX 78712. Fax: (512)471-7620. E-mail: adameve@mail.utexas.edu. Website: www.utexas.edu/ogs/Paisano. **Contact:** Dr. Michael Adams.

DZANC PRIZE

Dzanc Books, 2702 Lillian, Ann Arbor MI 48104. Website: www.dzancbooks.org. E-mail: prize@dzancbooks.org. **Contact:** Dan Wickett, executive director. "Our goal is to help authors find means of producing their work and doing community service." Annual. Prize: $5,000. Single category of a combination of work in progress and literary community service. Entries are judged by Dzanc editors (Steve Gillis, and Dan Wickett). No entry fee. Accepts inquiries by e-mail (prize@dzancbooks.org). Entry deadline is Nov. 1, 2011. Entries should be unpublished. Any author with a work of literary fiction in progress, and literary community service that is based in the United States, may enter contest. Writers may submit own work. "Have a good idea of what we're looking for in terms of literary community service (see website)." Results announced in January. Winners notified by e-mail. Results made available to entrants via e-mail, and on website.

EATON LITERARY AGENCY'S ANNUAL AWARDS PROGRAM

Eaton Literary Agency, P.O. Box 49795, Sarasota FL 34230. (941)366-6589. Fax: (941)365-4679. E-mail: eatonlit@aol.com. Website: www.eatonliterary.com. **Contact:** Richard Lawrence, V.P. Offered biannually for unpublished mss. Prize: $2,500 (over 10,000 words); $500 (under 10,000 words). Judged by an independent agency in conjunction with some members of Eaton's staff. No entry fee. Guidelines available for SASE, by fax, e-mail, or on website. Accepts inquiries by fax, phone and e-mail. Deadline: **March 31** (mss under 10,000 words); **August 31** (mss over 10,000 words). Entries must be unpublished. Open to any writer. Results announced in April and September. Winners notified by mail. For contest results, send SASE, fax, e-mail or visit website.

THE VIRGINIA FAULKNER AWARD FOR EXCELLENCE IN WRITING

Prairie Schooner, 123 Andrews Hall, P.O. Box 880334, Lincoln NE 68588-0334. (402)472-0911. Fax: (402)472-9771. E-mail: jengelhardt2@unl.edu. Website: www.prairieschooner.unl.edu. **Contact:** Kwame Dawes. Offered annually for work published in *Prairie Schooner* in the previous year. Prize: $1,000. Categories: short stories, essays, novel excerpts and translations. Judged by Editorial Board. No entry fee. Guidelines for SASE or on website. Accepts inquiries by fax and e-mail. "We only read mss from September 1 through May 1." Winning entry must have been published in *Prairie Schooner* in the year preceeding the award. Results announced in the Spring issue. Winners notified by mail in February or March.

FISH ONE-PAGE PRIZE (FLASH FICTION)

Fish Publishing, Durrus, Bantry, Co. Cork, Ireland. E-mail: info@fishpublishing.com. Website: www.fishpublishing.com. Guidelines on website or by e-mail. Flash fiction of up to 300 words. Entries must not have been published before. The ten best stories will be published in the *Annual Fish Anthology*. Recent Judge: Brian Turner. Chris Stewart will judge the 2011 prize. Entry €14 online or €16 by post. First Prize €1,000. Deadline 20 March. Results 30 April. Read full details on website or by email.

FISH SHORT STORY PRIZE

Durrus, Bantry Co. Cork Ireland. E-mail: info@fishpublishing.com. Website: www.fishpublishing.com. Fish Publishing, e-mail: info@fishpublishing.com. Website: www.fishpublishing.com. Prize: First prize of 3,000 euro and the best 10 stories published in the *Fish Anthology*. Overall prize fund 5,000 Euro. Second Prize is one week at Anam Cara Writers Retreat in West Cork plus 300 euro. Third Prize 300 euro. Closing date November 30. Winners announced March 17. Online entry fee 20 Euro story. Postal entry €25. The best 10 will be published in the 2011 *Fish Anthology*, launched in July at the West Cork Literary Festival. Entries must not have been published before. Entry online or by post. Geographical area covered: Worldwide. See our website for full details of competitions, and information on the Fish Editorial and Critique Services, and the Fish Online Writing Courses. Established in 1994, Hon. Patrons Roddy Doyle, Colum McCann, Frank McCourt, Dermot Healy.

THE FRENCH-AMERICAN AND THE FLORENCE GOULD FOUNDATIONS TRANSLATION PRIZES

28 W. 44th St., Suite 1420, New York NY 10036. **(646)588-6780**. E-mail: sschaller@frenchamerican.org. Website: www.frenchamerican.org. **Contact:** Sierra Schaller. French-American Foundation, 28 W. 44th St., Suite 1420, New York NY 10036. (212)829-8800. Fax: (212)829-8810. E-mail: earcher@frenchamerican.org. **Contact:** Emma Archer. Annual contest to "promote French literature in the United States, to give translators and their craft more visibility, and encouraging the American publishers who bring significant French texts to the English reading audience." Entries must have been published the year before the prizes are awarded. **Deadline:** December 31. Judged by a jury committee made up of translators, writers, and scholars in French literature and culture.

GEORGETOWN REVIEW

Georgetown Review, 400 East College St., Box 227, Georgetown KY 40324. (502) 863-8308. Fax: (502) 863-8888. E-mail: gtownreview@georgetowncollege.edu. Website: http://georgetownreview.georgetowncollege.edu. **Contact:** Steve Carter, editor. Annual. Publishes short stories, poetry, and creative nonfiction. Reading period: September 1-December 31. Also sponsors yearly writing contest for short stories, poetry, and creative nonfiction. Prize: $1,000 and publication; runners-up receive publication. Receives about 300 entries for each category. Entries are judged by the editors. Entry fee: $10 for first entry, $5 for each one thereafter. Make checks payable to Georgetown College. Guidelines available in July. Accepts inquiries by e-mail. **Entry deadline is Oct. 15, 2011.** Entries should be unpublished. Contest open to anyone except family, friends of the editors. "We're just looking to publish quality work. Sometimes our contests are themed, so check the website for details." Results announced Feb. or March. Winners notified by e-mail. Results made available to entrants with SASE.

O GIVAL PRESS NOVEL AWARD

Gival Press, P.O. Box 3812, Arlington VA 22203. (703)351-0079. E-mail: givalpress@yahoo.com. Website: www.givalpress.com. **Contact:** Robert L. Giron, Publisher. "To award the best literary novel." Annual. Prize: $3,000 (USD), publication and author's copies. Categories: literary novel. Receives about 100-120 entries per category. Final judge is announced after winner is chosen. Entries read anonymously. Entry fee: $50 (USD). Make checks payable to Gival Press, LLC. Guidelines with SASE, by phone, by e-mail, on website, in journals. Accepts inquiries by e-mail. **Deadline: May 30 of each year.** Entries should be unpublished. Open to any author who writes original work in English. Length: 30,000-100,000 words. Cover letter should include name, address, phone, e-mail, word count, novel title. Only the title and word count should appear on the actual ms. Writers may submit own work. "Review the types of mss Gival Press has published. We stress literary works." Results announced late fall of same year. Winners notified by phone. Results made available to entrants with SASE, by e-mail, on website.

O GIVAL PRESS SHORT STORY AWARD

Gival Press, P.O. Box 3812, Arlington VA 22203. (703)351-0079. E-mail: givalpress@yahoo.com. Website: www.givalpress.com. **Contact:** Robert L. Giron, Publisher. "To award the best literary short story." Annual. Prize: $1,000 and publication on website. Category: literary short story. Receives about 100-150 entries per category. Entries are judged anonymously. Entry fee: $25. Make checks payable to Gival Press, LLC. Guidelines available online, via e-mail, or by mail. Deadline: Aug. 8 of every year. Entries must be unpublished. Open to anyone who writes original short stories in English. Length: 5,000-15,000 words. Include name, address, phone, e-mail, word count, title on cover letter. Only the title and word count should be found on ms. Writers may submit their own fiction. "We publish literary works." Results announced in the fall of the same year. Winners notified by phone. Results available with SASE, by e-mail, on website.

GLIMMER TRAIN'S FICTION OPEN

Glimmer Train, Inc., Glimmer Train Press, Inc., 1211 NW Glisan St., Suite 207, Portland OR 97209. (503)221-0836. Fax: (503)221-0837. E-mail: eds@glimmertrain.org. Website: www.glimmertrain.org. **Contact:** Linda Swanson-Davies. Offered quarterly for unpublished stories on any theme. Word count should not exceed 20,000. Prize: 1st place: $2,000, publication in *Glimmer Train Stories*, and 20 copies of that issue; 1st/2nd runners-up: $1,000/$600 respectively, and possible publication in *Glimmer Train Stories*. Entry fee: $18/story. **Contest open during the months of March, June, September and December.** Represented in recent editions of the *Pushcart Prize, O. Henry, New Stories from the South, New Stories from the Midwest*, and *Best American Short Stories* Anthologies.

GLIMMER TRAIN'S SHORT-STORY AWARD FOR NEW WRITERS

Glimmer Train Press, Inc., 1211 NW Glisan St., Suite 207, Portland OR 97209. (503)221-0836. Fax: (503)221-0837. E-mail: eds@glimmertrain.org. Website: www.glimmertrain.org. **Contact:** Linda Swanson-Davies. Offered quarterly for any writer whose fiction hasn't appeared in a nationally distributed publication with a circulation over 5,000. Word count should not exceed 12,000 words. Stories must be previously unpublished. **Entry fee:** $15/story. **Contest open in the months of February, May, August, and November.** Make your submissions online at www.glimmertrain.org. Prize: First place: receives $1,200, publication in *Glimmer Train Stories*, and 20 copies of that issue. First/second runners-up receive $500/$300, respectively, and possible publication in *Glimmer Train Stories*. Winners will be called and results announced two months after the close of each contest. "We are very open to the work of new writers. Of the 100 distinguished short stories listed in a recent edition of the *Best American Short Stories*, 10 first appeared in *Glimmer Train Stories*, more than in any other publication, including the *New Yorker*. 3 of those 10 were the author's first publication."

GLIMMER TRAIN'S VERY SHORT FICTION AWARD (JANUARY)

Glimmer Train Press, Inc., 1211 NW Glisan St., #207, Portland OR 97209. (503)221-0836. Fax: (503)221-0837. E-mail: eds@glimmertrain.org. Website: www.glimmertrain.org. **Contact:** Linda Swanson-Davies. eds@glimmertrain.org; www.glimmertrain.org. Award to encourage the art of the very short story. "We want to read your original, unpublished, very short story—word count not to exceed 3,000 words." Prize: $1,200 and publication in *Glimmer Train Stories* and 20 author's copies (1st place); first/second runners-up: $500/$300 respectively and possible publication. Entry fee: $15/story. **Contest open in the months of January and July.** Open to all writers. Make your submissions online at www.glimmertrain.org. Winners will be called and results announced two months after the close of each contest.

● GRANTS FOR ARTIST'S PROJECTS

Artist Trust, 1835 12th Ave, Seattle WA 98122. (206) 467-8734, ext. 11. Fax: (206) 467-9633. E-mail: miguel@artisttrust.org. Website: www.artisttrust.org. **Contact:** Monica Miller, Director of Programs. "The GAP Program provides support for artist-generated projects, which can include (but are not limited to) the development, completion or presentation of new work." Annual. Prize: maximum of $1,500 for projects. Accepted are poetry, fiction, graphic novels, experimental works, creative nonfiction, screenplays, film scripts, and teleplays. Entries are judged by work sample as specified in the guidelines. Winners are selected by a discipline-specific panel of artists and artist professionals. No entry fee. Guidelines available in March. Accepts inquiries by mail, phone. Submission period is March-May. **Deadline is May 10.** Website should be consulted for exact date. Entries can be unpublished or previously published. Washington state residents only. Length: 8 pages max for poetry, fiction, graphic novels, experimental work, and creative nonfiction; up to 12 pages for screen plays, film scripts and teleplays. All mss must be typed with a 12-point font size or larger and cannot be single-spaced (except for poetry). Include application with project proposal and budget, as well as résumé with name, address, phone, e-mail, and novel/story title. "GAP awards are highly competitive. Please follow guidelines with care." Results announced in the fall. Winners notified by e-mail. Results made available to entrants by e-mail and on website.

HAMMETT PRIZE

Internatonal Association of Crime Writers/North American Branch, P.O. Box 8674, New York NY 10116-8674. Fax: (815) 361-1477. E-mail: mfrisque@igc.org. Website: www.crimewritersna.org. **Contact:** Mary A. Frisque, executive director, North American Branch. Award established "to honor a work of literary excellence in the field of crime writing by a U.S. or Canadian author." Award for novels, story collections, nonfiction by one author. Prize: trophy. Judged by committee. "Our reading committee seeks suggestions from publishers and they also ask the membership for recommendations. Eligible books are read by a committee of members of the organization. The committee chooses five nominated books, which are then sent to three outside judges for a final selection. Judges are outside the crime writing field." No entry fee. For guidelines, send SASE or e-mail. Accepts inquiries by e-mail. **Deadline: December 1.** Entries must be previously published. To be eligible "the book must have been published in the U.S. or Canada during the calendar year." The author must be a U.S. or Canadian citizen or permanent resident. Nominations announced in January; winners announced in fall. Winners notified by mail, phone, and recognized at awards ceremony. For contest results, send SASE or e-mail.

THE HILLERMAN MYSTERY NOVEL COMPETITION

Wordharvest & St. Martins Press, 304 Calle Oso, Santa Fe NM 87501. E-mail: wordharvest@wordharvest.com. Website: www.hillermanconference.com. Sponsored by Wordharvest & St. Martin's Press, (505) 471-1565. Website: www.wordharvest.com. **Contact:** Anne Hillerman, Co-organizer; Jean Schaumberg, Co-organizer. "To honor the contributions made by Tony Hillerman to the art and craft of the mystery." Annual competition/award for novels. Prize: $10,000 advance and publication by Thomas Dunne Books/St. Martin's Minotaur imprint. Categories: unpublished mystery novels set in the Southwest, written by a first-time author in the mystery genre. One entry per author. Nominees will be selected by judges chosen by the editorial staff of St. Martin's Press, with the assistance of independent judges selected by organizers of the Tony Hillerman Writers Conference (Wordharvest), and the winner will be chosen by St. Martin's editors. No entry fee. Accepts inquiries by e-mail, phone. **Entry deadline is June 1.** Entries should be unpublished; self-published work is generally accepted. All first-time writers of an unpublished mystery set in the American Southwest may enter contest. Length: no less than 220 typewritten pages or approx. 60,000 words. Cover letter should include name, address, phone, e-mail, list of publishing credits. Please include SASE for response. Writers may submit their own work. "Make sure murder or another serious crime or crimes is at the heart of the story, and emphasis is on the solution rather than the details of the crime. The story's primary setting should be the southwest US, which includes CA, AZ, CO, NV, NM, OK, TX, and UT." Results announced at the Tony Hillerman Writers Conference. St. Martin's Press notifies the winner by phone or by e-mail 2-3 weeks prior to the conference. Results made available to entrants on website

THE HODDER FELLOWSHIP

Lewis Center for the Arts, Princeton University, 6 New South, Princeton NJ 08544. (609)258-4096. E-mail: jbraude@princeton.edu. Website: www.princeton.edu/arts/lewis_center/society_of_fellows. **Contact:** Janine Braude, program assistant—Creative Writing. "The Hodder Fellowship will be given to writers of exceptional promise to pursue independent projects at Princeton University during the 2011-2012 academic year. Typically the fellows are poets, playwrights, novelists, creative nonfiction writers and translators who have published one highly acclaimed work and are undertaking a significant new project that might not be possible without the 'studious leisure' afforded by the fellowship. Preference is given to applicants outside academia. Candidates for the Ph.D. are not eligible. Submit a résumé, sample of previous work (10 pages maximum, not returnable), and a project proposal of 2-3 pages. Guidelines available on website. Princeton University is an equal opportunity employer and complies with applicable EEO and affirmative action regulations. Apply online at http://jobs.princeton.edu or for general application information and how to self-identify, see http://www.princeton.edu/dof/ApplicantsInfo.htm. Deadline: November 1, 2010 (postmarked). We strongly recommend, however, that all interested candidates use the online application process. Stipend: $63,900." The current deadline has passed.

THE JULIA WARD HOWE/BOSTON AUTHORS AWARD

The Boston Authors Club, 33 Brayton Rd., Brighton MA 02135. (617)783-1357. E-mail: bostonauthors@aol.com; lawson@bc.edu. Website: www.bostonauthorsclub.org. **Contact:** Alan Lawson. Estab. 1900. This annual award honors Julia Ward Howe and her literary friends who founded the Boston Authors Club in 1900. It also honors the membership over 110 years, consisting of novelists, biographers, historians, governors, senators, philosophers, poets, playwrights, and other luminaries. There are 2 categories: trade books and books for young readers (beginning with chapter books through young adult books). Works of fiction, nonfiction, memoir, poetry, and biography published in 2010 are eligible. Authors must live or have lived (college counts) within a 100-mile radius of Boston within the last 5 years. Subsidized books, cookbooks and picture books are not eligible. Fee is $25 per title. Deadline: January 15, 2011. Prize: $1,000 in each category.

L. RON HUBBARD'S WRITERS OF THE FUTURE CONTEST

Author Services Inc., P.O. Box 1630, Los Angeles CA 90078. (323) 466-3310. Fax: (323) 466-6474. E-mail: contests@authorservicesinc.com. Website: www.writersofthefuture.com. **Contact:** Joni, contest director. Estab. 1983. Foremost competition for new and amateur writers of unpublished science fiction or fantasy short stories or novelettes. Offered "to find, reward and publicize new speculative fiction writers so they may more easily attain professional writing careers." Open to new and amateur writers who have not professionally published a novel or short novel, more than 1 novelette, or more than 3 short stories. Eligible entries are previously unpublished short stories or novelettes (under 17,000 words) of science fiction or fantasy. Guidelines for SASE or on website. Accepts inquiries by fax, e-mail, phone. Prize: awards quarterly: 1st place: $1,000; 2nd place: $750; and 3rd place: $500. Annual grand prize: $5,000. "Contest has four quarters. There shall be 3 cash prizes in each quarter. In addition, at the end of the year, the 4 first-place, quarterly winners will have their entries re-judged, and a grand prize winner shall be determined."

Judged by K.D. Wentworth (initial judge), then by a panel of 4 professional authors. **Deadline: December 31, March 31, June 30, September 30.** Entries must be unpublished. Limit one entry per quarter. No entry fee; entrants retain all rights to their stories. Open to any writer. Manuscripts: white paper, black ink; double-spaced; typed; each page appropriately numbered with title, no author name. Include cover page with author's name, address, phone number, e-mail address (if available), as well as estimated word count and the title of the work. Results announced quarterly in e-newsletter. Winners notified by phone.

THE HUGH J. LUKE AWARD

Prairie Schooner, 123 Andrews Hall, P.O. Box 880334, Lincoln NE 68588-0334. (402)472-0911. Fax: (402)472-9771. E-mail: jengelhardt2@unl.edu. Website: www.prairieschooner.unl.edu. **Contact:** Kwame Dawes. Offered annually for work published in *Prairie Schooner* in the previous year. Prize: $250. Judged by editorial staff of Prairie Schooner. No entry fee. Work is nominated by the editorial staff. Guidelines for SASE or on website. Results announced in the Spring issue. Winners notified by mail in February or March.

INDEPENDENT PUBLISHER BOOK AWARDS

Jenkins Group/Independent Publisher Online, 1129 Woodmere Ave., Ste. B, Traverse City MI 49686. (231)933-4954, ext. 1011. Fax: (231)933-0448. E-mail: jimb@bookpublishing.com. Website: www.independentpublisher.com. **Contact:** Jim Barnes. "The Independent Publisher Book Awards were conceived as a broad-based, unaffiliated awards program open to all members of the independent publishing industry. The staff at *Independent Publisher* magazine saw the need to bring increased recognition to the thousands of exemplary independent, university, and self-published titles produced each year. The IPPY Awards reward those who exhibit the courage, innovation, and creativity to bring about change in the world of publishing. Independent spirit and expertise comes from publishers of all areas and budgets, and we judge books with that in mind. Entries will be accepted in 67 categories. Open to any published writer." Costs: $75-95. Needs: fiction, nonfiction, poetry, novels, translations. Offered annually for books published between January 1 and December 31. Deadline: March 20. Prizes: Gold, silver and bronze medals for each category; foil seals available to all. Judged by a panel of experts representing the fields of design, writing, bookselling, library, and reviewing.

INDIANA REVIEW (SHORT-SHORT/ PROSE-POEM) CONTEST

BH 465/Indiana University, 1020 E. Kirkwood Ave., Bloomington IN 47405-7103. (812)855-3439. Fax: (812)855-4253. E-mail: inreview@indiana.edu. Website: www.indianareview.edu. **Contact:** Alessandra Simmons, editor. Competition for fiction and prose poems no longer than 500 words. Prize: $1,000 plus publication, contributor's copies and a year's subscription. All entries considered for publication. Judged by guest judges; 2010 prize judged by Alberto Rios. Entry fee: $15 fee for no more than 3 pieces (includes a year's subscription, two issues). Make checks payable to Indiana Review. **Deadline: June.** Entries must be unpublished. Guidelines available in March for SASE, by phone, e-mail, on website, or in publication. Length: 500 words, 3 mss per entry. Open to any writer. Cover letter should include name, address, phone, e-mail, word count, and title. No identifying information on ms. "We look for command of language and form." Results announced in August. Winners notified by mail. For contest results, send SASE or visit website. See website for detailed guidelines.

O INDIANA REVIEW FICTION CONTEST

BH 465/Indiana University, 1020 E. Kirkwood Ave., Bloomington IN 47405-7103. (812)855-3439. Fax: (812)855-4253. E-mail: inreview@indiana.edu. Website: www.indianareview.org. **Contact:** Alessandra Simmons, Editor. Contest for fiction in any style and on any subject. Prize: $1,000, publication in the Indiana Review and contributor's copies. Judged by guest judges. 2010 prize judged by Dan Chaon. Entry fee: $15 fee (includes a year's subscription). Deadline: Mid-October. Entries must be unpublished. Mss will not be returned. No previously published work, or works forthcoming elsewhere, are eligible. Simultaneous submissions accepted, but in the event of entrant withdrawal, contest fee will not be refunded. Length: 35 pages maximum, double spaced. Open to any writer. Cover letter must include name, address, phone number, and title of story. Entrant's name should appear only in the cover letter, as all entries will be considered anonymously. Results announced January. Winners notified by mail. For contest results, send SASE. "We look for a command of language and structure, as well as a facility with compelling and unusual subject matter. It's a good idea to obtain copies of issues featuring past winners to get a more concrete idea of what we are looking for." See website for updates to guidelines.

INKWELL SHORT FICTION CONTEST

Inkwell Literary Magazine, Manhattanville College, 2900 Purchase Street, Purchase NY 10577. (914) 323-7239. Fax: (914) 323-3122. E-mail: inkwell@mville.edu. Website: http://www.inkwelljournal.org. **Contact:** Competition fiction editor. Annual. Competition/award for short stories. Prize: $1,500. Entries are judged by by editorial staff. Finalists are picked by a celebrity judge. Entry fee: $15. Make checks payable to Inkwell-Manhattanville College. Guidelines available in June. Accepts inquiries by fax, e-mail, phone. **Entry deadline is October 30.** Entries must be unpublished. Anyone may enter contest. Length: 5,000 words max. Cover letter should include name, address, phone, e-mail, word count, novel/story title. Only title on ms. Writers may submit own work. "Follow the guidelines. Proofread your work. Don't write for editors, teachers, or critics; write for you, and for your readers." Winners notified by phone, by e-mail. Results made available to entrants with SASE, by e-mail.

THE IOWA SHORT FICTION AWARD

Iowa Writers' Workshop, 102 Dey House, 507 N. Clinton St., Iowa City IA 52242-1000. (319)335-2000. Fax: (319)335-2055. Website: www.uiowapress.org. **Contact:** Jim McCoy, director. Award "to give exposure to promising writers who have not yet published a book of prose." Prize: publication by University of Iowa Press. Judged by Senior Iowa Writers' Workshop members who screen manuscripts; published fiction author of note makes final selections. No entry fee. Submission period: Aug. 1-Sept. 30. Entries must be unpublished, but stories previously published in periodicals are eligible for inclusion. "The manuscript must be a collection of short stories of at least 150 word-processed, double-spaced pages." Open to any writer. No application forms are necessary. Announcement of winners made early in year following competition. Winners notified by phone.

$ JACK DYER FICTION PRIZE

Crab Orchard Review, Dept. of English, Faner Hall, Southern Illinois Univ., Carbondale, Carbondale IL 62901-4503. E-mail: jtribble@siu.edu. Website: www.craborchardreview.siuc.edu; www.siu.edu/~crborchd. **Contact:** Jon Tribble, managing editor. Offered annually for unpublished short fiction. *Crab Orchard Review* acquires first North American serial rights to all submitted work. Open to any writer. Prize: $1,500 and publication. Judged by editorial staff (prescreening); winner chosen by genre editor. Entry fee: $15/ entry (can enter up to 3 stories, each story submitted requires a separate fee and can be up to 6,000 words), which includes a 1-year subscription to *Crab Orchard Review*. Guidelines available after January for SASE or on website. Deadline: Reading period for entries is February 1 through April 1. Entries must be unpublished. Length: 6,000 words maximum. U.S. citizens only. "Please note that no stories will be returned." Results announced by end of October. Winners notified by mail. Contest results on website or send SASE. "Carefully read directions for entering and follow them exactly. Send us your best work. Note that simultaneous submissions are accepted for this prize, but the winning entry must NOT be accepted elsewhere. No electronic submissions."

JAMES JONES FIRST NOVEL FELLOWSHIP

Wilkes University, Creative Writing Department, 245 S. River St., Wilkes-Barre PA 18766. (570)408-4534. Fax: (570)408-3333. E-mail: Jamesjonesfirstnovel@wilkes.edu. Website: www.wilkes.edu/pages/1159.asp.

JERRY JAZZ MUSICIAN NEW SHORT FICTION AWARD

Jerry Jazz Musician, 2207 NE Broadway, Portland OR 97232. E-mail: jm@jerryjazzmusician.com. Website: www.jerryjazz.com.

JOANNA CATHERINE SCOTT NOVEL EXCERPT PRIZE

National League of American Pen Women, Nob Hill, San Francisco Bay Area Branch, The Webhallow House, 1544 Sweetwood Dr., Broadmoor Village CA 94015-2029. Phone: (650)756-5279. Fax: (650)756-5279. E-mail: pennobhill@aol.com. Website: www.soulmakingcontest.us. **Contact:** Eileen Malone. Joanna Catherine Scott Novel Excerpt Prize. Open annually to any writer. $5/entry (make checks payable to NLAPW, Nob Hill Branch). Deadline: November 30. Prizes: 1st Place: $100; 2nd Place: $50; 3rd Place: $25.

JESSE JONES AWARD FOR FICTION

P.O. Box 609, Round Rock TX 78680. (214)363-7253. E-mail: dpayne@smu.edu. Website: http://texasinstituteofletters.org. **Contact:** W.K. (Kip) Stratton, acquisitions. Offered annually by Texas Institute of Letters for work published January 1-December 31 of year before award is given to recognize the writer of the best book of fiction entered in the competition. Writers must have been born in Texas, have lived in the state for at least 2 consecutive years at some time, or the subject matter of the work should be associated with the state. President changes every two years. See website for guidelines. Deadline: Jan. 1. Prize: $6,000.

JUDITH SIEGEL PEARSON AWARD

Wayne State Univ./Family of Judith Siegel Pearson, 5057 Woodward Ave., Suite 9408, Detroit MI 48202. (313)577-2450. Fax: (313)577-8618. E-mail: rhonda@wayne.edu. **Contact:** Rhonda Agnew, Contest Coordinator. Offers an annual award of up to $500 for the best creative or scholarly work on a subject concerning women. The type of work accepted rotates each year: fiction in 2011, drama in 2012, poetry in 2013 (poetry, 20 pages maximum), essays in 2014. Open to all interested writers and scholars. Submissions must be unpublished. Guidelines available for SASE or by fax or e-mail.

JUST DESSERTS SHORT-SHORT FICTION PRIZE

Passages North, NMU 1401 Presque Isle Ave, Marquette MI 49855. E-mail: passages@nmu.edu. Website: www.nmu.edu/passagesnorth. Offered every other year—check website for details. Prize: $1,000 First Prize and 2 honorable mentions. Entry fee: $10 for up to 2 stories; includes contest issue. Make checks payable to Northern Michigan University. **Submission period is Oct 15th-Feb 15th.** Entries should be unpublished. Anyone may enter contest. Length: max of 1,000 words. Cover letter should include name, address, phone, e-mail. Writers may submit own work. Winners notified by e-mail. Results made available to entrants with SASE.

KENNETH PATCHEN AWARD FOR THE INNOVATIVE NOVEL

Eckhard Gerdes Publishing, Civil Coping Mechanisms, 12 Simpson Street, Apt. D, Geneva IL 60134. Website: www.experimentalfiction.com; www.copingmechanisms.net. **Contact:** Eckhard Gerdes. This award will honor the most innovative novel submitted during the previous calendar year. Kenneth Patchen is celebrated for being among the greatest innovators of American fiction, incorporating strategies of concretism, asemic writing, digression, and verbal juxtaposition into his writing long before such strategies were popularized during the height of American postmodernist experimentation in the 1970s. His 3 great innovative novels, *Sleepers Awake, The Memoirs of a Shy Pornographer*, and *The Journal of Albion Moonlight*, have long been a benchmark for beats, postmodernists, and innovators of all ilks, inspiring younger writers on to greater significance and innovation in their own work. Preliminary selection of manuscripts will be done by JEF and CCM editors, who will select the 10 finalists, which will then be sent on for selection by the judge, famous novelist Yuriy Tarnawsky, himself an admirer of Patchen's fiction. The winner receives $1,000 and publication by JEF/CCM as well as 20 complimentary copies of the book. Deadline for entry: All submissions must be postmarked between January 1 and July 31, 2011. Winner will be announced in September. *Journal of Experimental Fiction CCM* is the new home of the *Journal of Experimental Fiction*, edited by Eckhard Gerdes. Together, we'll be releasing a series of 4 innovative novels per year, including the Patchen Award winner, as well as one traditional JEF anthology selected and edited by Eckhard himself. Fans of JEF can continue to expect the highest quality in innovative and experimental fiction.

THE LAWRENCE FOUNDATION AWARD

123 Andrews Hall, P.O. Box 880334, Lincoln NE 68588-0334. Website: www.unl.edu/schooner/psmain.htm. **Contact:** Editor in Chief. Offered annually for the best short story published in *Prairie Schooner* in the previous year. Prize: $1,000. Judged by editorial staff of *Prairie Schooner*. No entry fee. Only work published in *Prairie Schooner* in the previous year is considered. Work is nominated by editorial staff. Results announced in the Spring issue. Winners notified by mail in February or March.

LITERAL LATTÉ FICTION AWARD

Literal Latté, 200 East 10th Street Suite 240, New York NY 10003. (212)260-5532. E-mail: litlatte@aol.com. Website: www.literal-latte.com. **Contact:** Edward Estlin, contributing editor. Award "to provide talented writers with three essential tools for continued success: money, publication and recognition." Offered annually for unpublished fiction. Guidelines online. Open to any writer. Prize: $1,000 and publication in

Literal Latté (first prize), $300 (second prize), $200 (third prize), up to 7 honorable mentions. Judged by the editors. Entry fee: $10/story. Guidelines online. Accepts inquiries by e-mail. Deadline: January 15. Entries must be unpublished. Length: 10,000 words maximum. Guidelines available by e-mail or on website. Accepts inquiries by e-mail or on website. "Celebrating fifteen years of supporting great, new writers." Winners announced in April. All winners published in in Literal Latté.

LITERAL LATTÉ SHORT SHORTS CONTEST

Literal Latté, 200 E. 10th St., Suite 240, New York NY 10003. (212)260-5532. E-mail: litlatte@aol.com. Website: www.literal-latte.com. **Contact:** Jenine Gordon Bockman, editor. Estab. Annual contest. Send unpublished shorts. 2,000 words max. All styles welcome. Postmark by June 30. Name, address, phone number, e-mail address (optional) on cover page only. Include SASE or e-mail address for reply. All entries considered for publication.

THE LONG STORY CONTEST, INTERNATIONAL

A. E. Coppard Prize for Fiction, White Eagle Coffee Store Press, P.O. Box 383, Fox River Grove IL 60021. (847)639-9200. E-mail: wecspress@aol.com. Website: whiteeaglecoffeestorepress.com. **Contact:** Frank E. Smith, publisher. Estab. 1993. Offered annually since 1993 for unpublished work to recognize and promote long short stories of 8,000-14,000 words (about 30-50 pages). Sample of previous winner: $6.95, including postage. Open to any writer, no restrictions on materials. Prize: (A.E. Coppard Prize) $1,000 and publication, plus 25 copies of chapbook and 10 press kits. Categories: No limits on style or subject matter. Entry fee: $15 fee, $10 for second story in same envelope. Guidelines available in April by SASE, e-mail, or on website. Accepts inquiries by e-mail. Length: 8,000-14,000 words (30-50 pages double-spaced) single story; may have multiparts or be a self-contained novel segment. **Deadline: December 15.** Accepts previously unpublished submissions, but previous publication of small parts with acknowledgment is okay. Simultaneous submissions okay. Send cover with name, address, phone; second title page with title only. Submissions are not returned; they are recycled. "SASE for most current information." Results announced in late spring. Winners notified by phone. For contest results, send SASE or visit website in late spring. "Write with richness and depth. This has become the premiere competition in the world for long stories, giving many winners and finalists the opportunity to move to the next level of publishing success."

"This contest is designed to promote and reward the writing of long stories, especially by writers early in their careers. There are very few opportunities to publish stories of this length, but this is a perfect length for a stand-alone fiction chapbook. The story must be between 8,000 and 14,000 words (30-50 printed, double-spaced pages). It must be a single, unpublished story, though it can contain multiple parts or be a self-contained segment of an unpublished novel." Open to anyone, internationally. The story must be written in English.

LUMINA

Sarah Lawrence College, Slonim House, 1 Mead Way, Bronxville NY 10708. Website: http://pages.slc.edu/~lumina/contest.html. Sarah Lawrence College's graduate literary journal of poetry, fiction, and nonfiction accepts submissions every year from September 1-November 15. We also feature an annual contest. For more information, visit our website or e-mail us at lumina@gm.slc.edu.

THE MARY MACKEY SHORT STORY PRIZE

Soul-Making Literary Competition, National League of American Pen Women, Nob Hill, San Francisco Bay Area, The Webhallow House, 1544 Sweetwood Dr., Broadmoor Village CA 94015-2029. E-mail: pennobhill@aol.com. Website: www.soulmakingcontest.us. **Contact:** Eileen Malone. The Mary Mackey Short Story Prize. "One story/entry, up to 5,000 words. All prose works must be typed, page numbered, and double-spaced. Identify only with 3x5 card. Open annually to any writer." $5/entry (make checks payable to NLAPW, Nob Hill Branch). Needs fiction, short stories. Deadline: November 30. Prizes: 1st Place: $100; 2nd Place: $50; 3rd Place: $25.

THE MALAHAT REVIEW NOVELLA PRIZE

The Malahat Review, University of Victoria, P.O. Box 1700 STN CSC, Victoria BC V8W 2Y2 Canada. (250)721-8524. E-mail: malahat@uvic.ca. Website: malahatreview.ca. **Contact:** John Barton, Editor.

MARSH AWARD FOR CHILDREN'S LITERATURE IN TRANSLATION

Dartmouth House, 37 Charles Street, London En W1J 5ED UK. E-mail: education@esu.org; hanc@esu.org. Website: www.esu.org. **Contact:** Kate McCulloch. Award "to promote the publication of translated children's books in the UK." Biennial award for children's book translations. Judged by past winner, Colin Niven, Wendy Cooling, Elizabeth Hammill. No entry fee. Entries must be previously published. Entries should be translations into English first published in the UK. Entries must be nominated by publishers. Open to any writer. Guidelines available for SASE. Cover letter should include name, address, phone, e-mail, and title. Accepts inquiries by e-mail: Results announced in January. Winners notified by mail and at presentation event.

MARY KENNEDY EASTHAM FLASH FICTION PRIZE

National League of American Pen Women, Nob Hill, San Francisco Branch, The Webhallow House, 1544 Sweetwood Dr., Broadmoor Village CA 94015-2029. E-mail: pennobhill@aol.com. Website: www.soulmakingcontest.us. **Contact:** Eileen Malone.

DAVID NATHAN MEYERSON PRIZE FOR FICTION

Southwest Review, P.O. Box 750374, Dallas TX 75275-0374. (214) 768-1037. Fax: (214) 768-1408. E-mail: swr@smu.edu. Website: www.smu.edu/southwestreview. **Contact:** Jennifer Cranfill, senior editor. Prize will consist of $1,000 and publication in the *Southwest Review.* Open to writers who have not yet published a book of fiction, either a novel or collection of stories. Submissions must be no longer than 8,000 words. $25 entry reading fee must accompany each submission. Work should be printed without the author's name. Name and address should appear only on the cover letter. Submissions will not be returned. For notification of the winning submission, include a SASE. Postmarked deadline for entry is May 1, 2011. Winner announced in August.

MICRO AWARD

c/o Alan Presley, PSC 817 Box 23, FPO AE 09622-0023. E-mail: admin@microaward.org. Website: www.microaward.org. **Contact:** Alan Presley. The Micro Award (4th annual) was established to recognize outstanding flash fiction from both print and electronic media. It is open to all genres. Senior editors may submit two stories; authors may submit one. Guidelines and entry forms are available for a SASE or see website. No entry fee. Submissions required to be previously published that have appeared in print between Jan. 1 and Dec. 31. It is open to anyone who has a story not exceeding 1,000 words in length available for public display. No rights are acquired or purchased when writers enter work for this award. It is judged by a panel of 3 judges. The author of the winning story will receive $500 (US).

MIDLAND AUTHORS AWARD

Society of Midland Authors, P.O. Box 10419, Chicago IL 60610-0419. E-mail: writercc@aol.com. Website: www.midlandauthors.com. **Contact:** Carol Jean Carlson. "Established in 1915, the Society of Midland Authors Award (SMA) is presented to one title in each of six categories 'to stimulate creative effort,' one of SMA's goals, to be honored at the group's annual awards banquet in May." Annual. Competition/award for novels, story collections (by single author). Prize: cash prize of at least $300 and a plaque that is awarded at the SMA banquet. Categories: children's nonfiction and fiction, adult nonfiction and fiction, adult biography, and poetry. Judging is done by a panel of three judges for each category that includes a mix of experienced authors, reviewers, book sellers, university faculty and librarians. No entry fee. Guidelines available in September-November with SASE, on website, in publication. Accepts inquiries by e-mail, phone. **Deadline: Feb. 1.** Entries must be published in the prior calendar year, e.g., 2007 for 2008 award. "The contest is open to any title with a recognized publisher that has been published within the year prior to the contest year." Open to authors or poets who reside in, were born in, or have strong ties to a Midland state, which includes Illinois, Indiana, Iowa, Kansas, Michigan, Minnesota, Missouri, Nebraska, North Dakota, South Dakota, Ohio, and Wisconsin. SMA only accepts published work accompanied by a completed award form. Writers may submit own work. Entries can also be submitted by the publisher's rep. "Write a great story and be sure to follow contest rules by sending a copy of the book to each of the three judges for the given category who are listed on SMA's website." Results announced at the SMA Awards Banquet each May. Other announcements follow in the media. Winners notified by mail, by phone. Results made available to entrants on website, in our monthly membership newsletter. Results will also go to local media in the form of press releases.

THE MILTON CENTER POSTGRADUATE FELLOWSHIP

3307 Third Ave. West, Seattle WA 98119. Website: www.imagejournal.org/milton. **Contact:** Anna Johnson, program director. Award "to bring emerging writers of Christian commitment to the Center, where their primary goal is to complete their first book-length manuscript in fiction, poetry or creative nonfiction." A $16,000 stipend is offered. $25 application fee. Guidelines on website. **Deadline: March 15.** Open to any writer.

MONTANA PRIZE IN FICTION

Cutbank Literary Magazine, English Dept., LA 133, UMT, Missoula MT 59812. Fax: (406) 243-6156. E-mail: cutbank@umontana.edu. Website: www.cutbankonline.org. **Contact:** fiction editor. "Since CutBank was founded in 1973, we have watched as the landscape for literary and small magazines has broadened considerably, resulting in more quality short stories, essays, and poems finding their way to an audience each year. Occasionally, we come across a submission that seems to stand above the already impressive work being published in its genre, the sort of piece that serves to credit the wide field of literary publications generally. The goal of CutBank 's annual contests it to provoke, identify, and reward work of that caliber." Annual. Competition/award for short stories. Prize: $500 and publication in the summer issue of CutBank. Entries are narrowed down to a pool of five to ten submissions which are then submitted to a guest judge for selection of the winner. The judge of the 2010-2011 Montana Prize in Fiction is Eileen Myles. Entry fee: $18 (includes a 1-year, 2-issue subscription to CutBank). Limit of one work of fiction per submitter (though writers may also submit work to our contests in other genres). Make checks payable to Cutbank Literary Magazine. Entries are accepted online only. Guidelines available in November. Accepts inquiries by e-mail. **Submission period is December 1, 2010-February 28, 2011.** Entries should be unpublished. Anyone may enter contest. Please submit no more than 40 double-spaced pages. Cover letter should include name, address, phone, e-mail, novel/story title. Only name and title on ms. Writers may submit own work. "Read the magazine and get a sense of our style. We are seeking work that showcases an authentic voice, a boldness of form, and a rejection of functional fixedness." Results announced June. Winners notified by e-mail. Results made available to entrants on website.

NATIONAL READERS' CHOICE AWARDS

E-mail: nrca@okrwa.com. Website: www.okrwa.com. **Contact:** Penny James, Contest Chair. Contest "to provide writers of romance fiction with a competition where their published novels are judged by readers." Prize: "There is no monetary award; plaques and finalist certificates awarded at the awards banquet hosted at the Annual National Romance Writers Convention." Categories: See the website for categories and descriptions. Additional award for best first book. Entry fee: $25; PayPal accepted or make checks payable to OKRWA Treasurer. See website for entry address and contact information. All entries must have an original copyright date during the current contest year. (See website for details.) Entries will be accepted from authors, editors, publishers, agents, readers, whoever wants to fill out the entry form, pay the fee and supply the books. **Deadline**: December 1; book deadline: 15 January. (See website for exact dates.) No limit to the number of entries, but each title may be entered only in one category. Open to any writer published by an RWA-approved non-vanity/non-subsidy press. For guidelines, send e-mail or visit website. Entry form required—available on website. Deadline for entry forms is 1 December. Five copies of each entry must be mailed to the category coordinator; contact information for coordinator will be provided by December 15. Finalists announced in April. Winners notified by phone, if not at the awards ceremony, in July. Winners listed in RWA's *Romance Writers Report*. List of winners will be mailed; also available by e-mail in August.

O NATIONAL WRITERS ASSOCIATION NOVEL WRITING CONTEST

The National Writers Association, 10940 S. Parker Rd. #508, Parker CO 80134. (303)841-0246. Fax: (303)841-2607. E-mail: natlwritersassn@hotmail.com. Website: www.nationalwriters.com. **Contact:** Sandy Whelchel, director. Annual contest "to help develop creative skills, to recognize and reward outstanding ability, and to increase the opportunity for the marketing and subsequent publication of novel manuscripts." Prize: 1st place: $500; 2nd place: $300; 3rd place: $200.

Judges' evaluation sheets sent to each entry with SASE. Categories: Open to any genre or category. Judged by editors and agents. Entry fee: $35. Opens December 1. **Deadline: April 1.** Entries must be unpublished. Length: 20,000-100,000 words. Open to any writer. Contest forms are available on the NWA website or an attachment will be sent if you request one through e-mail or with an SASE. Address: 10940 S. Parker Rd. #508, Parker CO 80134.

Deadline for the 2010/11 Novel Contest is April 1, 2011. Contest forms are available on the NWA website or an attachment will be sent if you request one through e-mail or with an SASE.

THE NELLIGAN PRIZE FOR SHORT FICTION

Colorado Review/Center for Literary Publishing, 9105 Campus Delivery, Dept. of English, Colorado State University, Ft. Collins CO 80523-9105. (970)491-5449. E-mail: creview@colostate.edu. Website: http://nelliganprize.colostate.edu. **Contact:** Stephanie G'Schwind, editor. "The Nelligan Prize for Short Fiction was established in memory of Liza Nelligan, a writer, editor, and friend of many in Colorado State University's English Department, where she received her master's degree in literature in 1992. By giving an award to the author of an outstanding short story each year, we hope to honor Liza Nelligan's life, her passion for writing, and her love of fiction." Annual. Competition/award for short stories. Prize: $1,500 plus publication in *Colorado Review*. Receives approximately 900 stories. All entries are read blind by *Colorado Review*'s editorial staff. 15 entries are selected to be sent on to a final judge. Entry fee: $15. Send credit card information or make checks payable to Colorado Review. Payment also accepted via our online submission manager link from website. Guidelines available in August 2011. Accepts inquiries by e-mail, phone. **Entry deadline March 12, 2012.** Entries must be unpublished and under 50 pages. Anyone may enter contest. With the exception of Colorado State University students or friends or students of the judge of the contest. Cover letter should include name, address, phone, e-mail, and novel/story title. "Authors should provide two cover sheets: one with name, address, phone, e-mail, and title of story, and a second with only the title of the story. Manuscripts are read 'blind,' so authors'names should not appear anywhere else in the manuscript." Writers may submit own work. "Successful short story writers are those who are reading contemporary short fiction (short story collections, literary magazines, annual prize anthologies), reading about the craft, and actively engaging in the practice of writing." Results announced in July of each year. Winners notified by phone. Results made available to entrants with SASE.

THE NOMA AWARD FOR PUBLISHING IN AFRICA

Kodansha Ltd., Japan, P.O. Box 128, Witney, Oxon OX8 ORN UK. (44)(1993)775-235. Fax: (44)(1993)709-265. E-mail: maryljay@aol.com. Website: www.nomaaward.org. **Contact:** Mary Jay, Noma Award Managing Comm. secretary. Estab. 1979. Sponsored by Kodansha Ltd. Award "to encourage publication of works by African writers and scholars in Africa, instead of abroad as is still too often the case at present." Categories: scholarly or academic; books for children; literature and creative writing, including fiction, drama and poetry. Judged by a committee of African scholars and book experts and representatives of the international book community. Chairman: Walter Bgoya. No entry fee. Entries must be previously published. Guidelines and entry forms available in December by fax, e-mail or on website. Submissions are through publishers only. "Publisher must complete entry form and supply six copies of the published work." Maximum number of entries per publisher is three. Results announced in October. Winners notified through publisher. List of winners available from Secretariat or on website. "The award is for an outstanding book. Content is the overriding criterion, but standards of publication are also taken into account." Deadline: Feb. 28.

NORTH CAROLINA ARTS COUNCIL REGIONAL ARTIST PROJECT GRANTS

North Carolina Arts Council, Dept. of Cultural Resources, MSC #4632, Raleigh NC 27699-4634. (919)807-6500. Fax: (919)807-6532. E-mail: david.potorti@ncdcr.gov. Website: www.ncarts.org. **Contact:** David Potorti, Literature Director. Open to any writer living in North Carolina. See website for contact information for the local arts councils that distribute these grants. $500-3,000 awarded to writers to pursue projects that further their artistic development.

NORTH CAROLINA WRITERS' FELLOWSHIPS

North Carolina Arts Council, Dept. of Cultural Resources, Raleigh NC 27699-4632. (919)807-6500. Fax: (919)807-6532. E-mail: davidpotorti@ncdcr.gov. Website: www.ncarts.org. **Contact:** David Potorti, literature director. Acquisitions: David Potorti, literature director and arts editor. Offered every even year to support writers of fiction, poetry, literary nonfiction, literary translation, and spoken word. See website for guidelines and other eligibility requirements. Writers must be current residents of North Carolina for at least 1 year, must remain in residence in North Carolina during the grant year, and may not pursue academic or professional degrees while receiving grant. Fellowships offered to support writers in the development and creation of their work. Deadline: Next offered in fall, 2012, see website for details. $10,000 grant. Reviewed by a panel of literature professionals (writers and editors).

NORTHERN CALIFORNIA BOOK AWARDS

Northern California Book Reviewers Association, c/o Poetry Flash, 1450 Fourth St. #4, Berkeley CA 94710. (510)525-5476. Fax: (510)525-6752. E-mail: editor@poetryflash.org. Website: www.poetryflash.org. **Contact:** Joyce Jenkins, exec. director. "Offers annual awards to recognize "the best of Northern California (from Fresno north) fiction, poetry, nonfiction, and children's literature, as chosen by the Northern California Book Reviewers Association." NCBA translation award is selected by Center for the Art of Translation and the NCBR submissions must be published in the calendar year. Submit 3 copies of each book entered. The authors of the submitted books must live in Northern California. Guidelines on website. Deadline: December 1. NCBR also presents the Fred Cody Award for Lifetime Achievement for a body of work and service to the literary community. The Fred Cody Award does not accept applications. Estab. 1981.

OHIOANA BOOK AWARDS

Ohioana Library Association, 274 E. 1st Ave., Suite 300, Columbus OH 43201-3673. (614)466-3831. Fax: (614)728-6974. E-mail: ohioana@ohioana.org. Website: www.ohioana.org. **Contact:** Linda Hengst, executive director. Offered annually to bring national attention to Ohio authors and their books, published in the last 2 years. (Books can only be considered once.) Categories: fiction, nonfiction, juvenile, poetry, and books about Ohio or an Ohioan. Writers must have been born in Ohio or lived in Ohio for at least 5 years, but books about Ohio or an Ohioan need not be written by an Ohioan. Prize: certificate and glass sculpture. Judged by a jury selected by librarians, book reviewers, writers and other knowledgeable people. Each winter the jury considers all books received since the previous jury. No entry fee. **Deadline: December 31.**

OHIOANA WALTER RUMSEY MARVIN GRANT

Ohioana Library Association, 274 E. First Ave., Suite 300, Columbus OH 43201. (614)466-3831. Fax: (614)728-6974. E-mail: ohioana@ohioana.org. Website: www.ohioana.org. **Contact:** Linda Hengst. Award "to encourage young, unpublished writers 30 years of age or younger." Competition for short stories. Prize: $1,000. **No entry fee.** Up to 6 pieces of prose may be submitted; maximum 60 pages, minimum 10 pages double-spaced, 12-point type. Deadline: January 31. Entries must be unpublished. Open to unpublished authors born in Ohio or who have lived in Ohio for a minimum of five years. Must be 30 years of age or younger. Guidelines for SASE or on website. Winner notified in May or June. Award given in October.

ON THE PREMISES CONTEST

On the Premises, LLC, 4323 Gingham Court, Alexandria VA 22310. (202) 262-2168. E-mail: questions@onthepremises.com. Website: www.onthepremises.com. **Contact:** Tarl Roger Kudrick or Bethany Granger, copublishers. "*On the Premises* aims to promote newer and/or relatively unknown writers who can write what we feel are creative, compelling stories told in effective, uncluttered and evocative prose. Each contest challenges writers to produce a great story based on a broad premise that our editors supply as part of the contest." Competition/award for short stories. Prize: First prize is $180, Second prize $140, Third prize $100, and Honorable Mentions recieve $40. All prize winners are published in *On the Premises* magazine in HTML and PDF format. Entries are judged blindly by a panel of judges with professional editing and writing experience. No entry fee. Submissions are accepted by e-mail only. Contests held every four months. Check website for exact dates. Entries should be unpublished. Open to everyone. Length: min 1,000 words, max 5,000. E-mail should include name, address, e-mail, novel/story title, with ms attached. No name or contact info should be in ms. Writers may submit own work. "Write something compelling, creative and well-crafted. Above all, clearly use the contest premise. Results announced within 2 weeks of contest deadline. Winners notified via newsletter and with publication of *On the Premises*. Results made available to entrants on website, in publication.

● OREGON BOOK AWARDS

Literary Arts, 224 NW 13th Ave., Ste. 306, Portland OR 97209. (503)227-2583. E-mail: susan@literary-arts.org. Website: www.literary-arts.org. **Contact:** Susan Denning. The annual Oregon Book Awards celebrate Oregon authors in the areas of poetry, fiction, nonfiction, drama and young readers' literature published between August 1, 2010 and July 31, 2011. Prize: Finalists are invited on a statewide reading tour and are promoted in bookstores and libraries across the state. Judged by writers who are selected from outside Oregon for their expertise in a genre. Past judges include Mark Doty, Colson Whitehead and Kim Barnes. Entry fee determined by initial print run; see website for details. Deadline: last Friday in August. Entries must be previously published. Oregon residents only. Finalists announced in January. Winners announced at an awards ceremony in November. List of winners available in April.

● OREGON LITERARY FELLOWSHIPS

224 NW 13th Ave., Suite 306, Portland OR 97209. E-mail: susan@literary-arts.org. Website: www.literary-arts.org. Literary Arts, Inc., 224 NW 13th Ave., Suite 306, Portland OR 97209. (503) 227-2583. Fax: (503) 243-1167. E-mail: susan@literary-arts.org. Website: www.literary-arts.org. **Contact:** Susan Denning, Director of Programs and Events. Annual fellowships for writers of fiction, poetry, literary nonfiction, young readers and drama. Prize: $2500 minimum award, for approximately 12 writers. Judged by out-of-state writers. No entry fee. Guidelines available in February for SASE. Accepts inquiries by e-mail, phone. **Deadline: last Friday in June.** Oregon residents only. Recipients announced in January.

O PEARL SHORT STORY PRIZE

3030 E. Second St., Long Beach CA 90803-5163. (562)434-4523. E-mail: Pearlmag@aol.com. Website: www.pearlmag.com. **Contact:** Marilyn Johnson, fiction editor. Award to "provide a larger forum and help widen publishing opportunities for fiction writers in the small press and to help support the continuing publication of Pearl." Prize: $250, publication in Pearl and 10 copies of the journal. Judged by the editors of Pearl: Marilyn Johnson, Joan Jobe Smith, Barbara Hauk. Entry fee: $10/story. Include a brief bio and SASE for reply or return of mss. Accepts simultaneous submissions, but asks to be notified if story is accepted elsewhere. **Submission period: April 1-May 31 (postmark).** Entries must be unpublished. "Although we are open to all types of fiction, we look most favorably on coherent, well-crafted narratives containing interesting, believable characters in meaningful situations." Length: 4,000 words maximum. Open to any writer. Guidelines for SASE or on website. Accepts queries by e-mail or fax. Results announced in September. Winners notified by mail. For contest results, send SASE, e-mail or visit website.

PEN CENTER USA LITERARY AWARDS

PEN Center USA, P.O. Box 6037, Beverly Hills CA 90212. (424)258-1180. E-mail: awards@penusa.org. Website: www.penusa.org. **Contact:** Literary Awards Coordinator. PEN Center USA Literary Awards. PEN Center USA. Offered for work published or produced in the previous calendar year. Open to writers living west of the Mississippi River. Award categories: fiction, poetry, research nonfiction, creative nonfiction, translation, children's/young adult, drama, screenplay, teleplay, journalism. Guidelines and submission form available on website. for SASE or download from website. $35 Entry Fee. Deadline for book categories: 4 copies must be received by December 31. Deadline for non-book categories: 4 copies must be received by January 31.

PEN/FAULKNER AWARDS FOR FICTION

PEN/Faulkner Foundation, 201 E. Capitol St., Washington DC 20003. (202)675-0345. Fax: (202)675-0360. E-mail: jneely@penfaulkner.org. Website: www.penfaulkner.org. **Contact:** Jessica Neely, PEN/Faulkner Foundation Executive Director. Offered annually for best book-length work of fiction by an American citizen published in a calendar year (short story collections are eligible). Prize: $15,000 (one winner); $5,000 (4 finalists). Judged by three writers chosen by the directors of the Pen/Faulkner Foundation. No entry fee. **Deadline: October 31.** Open to US citizens only, but they need not be US residents. Writers and publishers submit four copies of eligible titles published during the current year. No juvenile or self-published books. Deadline: October 31. Prize: $15,000 (one Winner); $5,000 (4 Finalists).

PNWA LITERARY CONTEST

Pacific Northwest Writers Association, PMB 2717-1420 NW Gilman Blvd, Ste 2, Issaquah WA 98027. (425)673-2665. Fax: (206)824-4559. E-mail: staff@pnwa.org. Website: www.pnwa.org. **Contact:** Kelli Liddane.

O POCKETS FICTION-WRITING CONTEST

Upper Room Publications, P.O. Box 340004, Nashville TN 37203-0004. (615) 340-7333. Fax: (615) 340-7267. E-mail: pockets@upperroom.org;theupperroommagazine@upperroom.org. Website: www.pockets.upperroom.org; www.pockets.org. **Contact:** Lynn W. Gilliam, senior editor. *Pockets* is a devotional magazine for children between the ages of 6 and 11. Contest offered annually for unpublished work to discover new children's writers. Prize: $1,000 and publication in Pockets. Categories: short stories. Judged by *Pockets* staff and staff of other Upper Room Publications. No entry fee. Guidelines available on website or send #10 SASE. **Deadline: Must be postmarked March 1-August 15.** Entries must be unpublished. Because the purpose of the contest is to discover new writers, previous winners are not eligible. No violence, science fiction, romance, fantasy, or talking animal stories. Word length 1,000-1,600 words. Open to any writer. Winner announced November 1 and notified by U.S. mail. Contest submissions accompanied by SASE will be returned Nov. 1.

◐ EDGAR ALLAN POE AWARD

Mystery Writers of America, 1140 Broadway, Suite 1507, New York NY 10001. (212)888-8171. Fax: (212)888-8107. E-mail: mwa@mysterywriters.org. Website: www.mysterywriters.org. Annual award. Estab. 1945. Purpose of the award: to honor authors of distinguished works in the mystery field. Previously published submissions only. Submissions made by the author, author's agent; "normally by the publisher." Work must be published/produced the year of the contest. Deadline for entries: Must be received by November 30. Submission information can be found at: www.mysterywriters.org. No entry fee. Awards ceramic bust of "Edgar" for winner; scrolls for all nominees. Judging by professional members of Mystery Writers of America (writers). Nominee press release sent in mid-January. Winner announced at the Edgar® Awards Banquet, held in late April/early May.

O KATHERINE ANNE PORTER PRIZE IN SHORT FICTION

The University of North Texas Press, 1155 Union Cir., #311336, Denton TX 76203-5017. (940)565-2142. Fax: (940)565-4590. Website: web3.unt.edu/untpress. **Contact:** Laura Kopchick, Editor, Univ. of Texas at Arlington. Contest is offered annually. Prize is awarded to a collection of short fiction. "No limitations to entrants. In years when the judge is announced, we ask that students of the judge not enter to avoid a perceived conflict. All entries should contain identifying material ONLY on the one cover sheet. Entries are read anonymously. Entries may include both unpublished and previously published stories, but collection as a whole has to be previously unpublished." Entry must be postmarked between May 1 and June 30. Entry fee: $25. Prize: $1000 and publication by University of North Texas Press (standard author contract). Judged by a different eminent writer each year. Some prefer to remain anonymous until conclusion of contest.

PRAIRIE SCHOONER BOOK PRIZE

Prairie Schooner and the University of Nebraska Press, 123 Andrews Hall, University of Nebraska, Lincoln NE 68588-0334. (402)472-0911. E-mail: jengelhardt2@unlnotes.unl.edu; jengelhardt2@unl.edu. Website: prairieschooner.unl.edu. **Contact:** Kwame Dawes, editor. Annual. Competition/award for story collections. Prize: $3,000 and publication through the University of Nebraska Press for one book of short fiction and one book of poetry. Entry fee: $25. Make checks payable to Prairie Schooner. Deadline: Submissions are accepted between January 15 and March 15; check website for updates. Entries should be unpublished. Send full manuscript (the author's name should not appear anywhere on the ms). Send two cover pages: one listing only the title of the ms, and the other listing the title, author's name, address, telephone number, and e-mail address. Send SASE for notification of results. All mss will be recycled. You may also send an optional SAS postcard for confirmation of receipt of ms. Winners notified by phone, by e-mail. Results made available to entrants on website, in publication.

PURPLE DRAGONFLY BOOK AWARDS

4696 W. Tyson St., Chandler AZ 85226-2903. (480)940-8182. Fax: (480)940-8787. E-mail: info@fivestarpublications.com. Website: www.purpledragonflyawards.com; www.fivestarpublications.com; www.fivestarbookawards.com. **Contact:** Lynda Exley, Contest Coordinator. Guidelines and entry forms available by request with SASE. Entry forms are also downloadable at www.purpledragonflybookawards.com. Entry fee is $50 for one title in one category, $45 per title when multiple books are entered or $45 per category when one book is entered in multiple categories. All entry fees are per title, per category.

DAVID RAFFELOCK AWARD FOR PUBLISHING EXCELLENCE

National Writers Association, 10940 S. Parker Rd., #508, Parker CO 80134. (303)841-0246. Fax: (303)841-2607. E-mail: natlwritersassn@hotmail.com. Website: www.nationalwriters.com. **Contact:** Sandy Whelchel, executive director. E-mail: contests@nationalwriters.com. Award to "assist published authors in marketing their work and promoting them." Prize: publicity tour, including airfare, and services of a publicist (valued at $5,000). Categories: novels and short story collections. Judged by publishers and agents. Entry fee: $100. Deadline: May 1. Published works only. Open to any writer. Guidelines for SASE, by e-mail or on website. Winners announced in June at the NWAF conference and notified by mail or phone. List of winners available for SASE or visit website.

RANDOM HOUSE, INC. CREATIVE WRITING COMPETITION

One Scholarship Way, P.O. Box 297, St. Peter MN 56082. (212)782-0316. Fax: (212)940-7590. E-mail: creativewriting@randomhouse.com. Website: www.randomhouse.com/creativewriting. **Contact:** Melanie Fallon Hauska, director. Offered annually for unpublished work to NYC public high school seniors. Three categories: poetry and graphic novel, fiction & drama and personal memoir. Prize: 72 awards given in literary (3) and nonliterary (2) categories. Awards range from $500-10,000. Categories: short stories and poems. Judged by various city officials, executives, authors, editors. No entry fee. Guidelines available in October on website and in publication. **Deadline: Literature Entries—February 11 for 2011, and Graphic Novel—April 1, 2011.** Entries must be unpublished. Word length: 2,500 words or less. Applicants must be seniors (under age 21) at a New York high school. No college essays or class assignments will be accepted. Results announced mid-May. Winners notified by mail and phone. For contest results, send SASE, fax, e-mail or visit website.

ROYAL DRAGONFLY BOOK AWARDS

4696 W. Tyson St., Chandler AZ 85226-2903. (480)940-8182. Fax: (480)940-8787. E-mail: info@fivestarpublications.com. Website: www.fivestarpublications.com; www.fivestarbookawards.com; www.royaldragonflybookawards.com. **Contact:** Lynda Exley. Offered annually for any previously published work to honor authors for writing excellence of all types of literature—fiction and nonfiction—in 50 categories, appealing to a wide range of ages and comprehensive list of genres. Open to any author published in English. Guidelines and entry forms available by request with SASE. Entry forms are also downloadable at www.royaldragonflybookawards.com. Entry fee is $50 for one title in one category, $45 per title when multiple books are entered or $45 per category when one book is entered in multiple categories. All entry fees are per title, per category. The Grand Prize winner receives $300, while another entrant will be the lucky winner of a $100 drawing. All first-place winners receive foil award seals and are included in a publicity campaign announcing winners. All first- and second-place winners and honorable mentions receive certificates.

O THE SCARS EDITOR'S CHOICE AWARDS

829 Brian Ct., Gurnee IL 60031-3155. E-mail: editor@scars.tv. Website: http://scars.tv. **Contact:** Janet Kuypers, editor/publisher. Award "to showcase good writing in an annual book." Prize: publication of story/essay and 1 copy of the book. Categories: short stories. Entry fee: $18/short story. Deadline: revolves for appearing in different upcoming books as winners. Entries may be unpublished or previously published. Open to any writer. For guidelines, visit website. Accepts inquiries by e-mail. Length: "We appreciate shorter works. Shorter stories, more vivid and more real storylines in writing have a good chance." Results announced at book publication, online. Winners notified by mail when book is printed. For contest results, send SASE or e-mail or look at the contest page at website. "

THE SCENT OF AN ENDING™

White Eagle Coffee Store Press, P.O. Box 383, Fox River Grove IL 60021-0383. (847)639-9200. E-mail: scentofanending@aol.com. Website: http://thescentofanending.com, or whiteeaglecoffeestorepress.com. **Contact:** Frank Edmund Smith, publisher.

THE MONA SCHREIBER PRIZE FOR HUMOROUS FICTION & NONFICTION

15442 Vista Haven Place, Sherman Oaks CA 91403. E-mail: brad.schreiber@att.net. Website: www.brashcyber.com. **Contact:** Brad Schreiber. Estab. 2000.

SCRIPTAPALOOZA TELEVISION WRITING COMPETITION

7775 Sunset Blvd., PMB #200, Hollywood CA 90046. (323)654-5809. E-mail: info@scriptapalooza.com. Website: www.scriptapaloozatv.com. "Seeking talented writers who have an interest in American television writing." Prize: $500, $200, and $100 in each category (total $3,200), production company consideration. Categories: sitcoms, pilots, one-hour dramas and reality shows. Entry fee: $40; accepts Paypal credit card or make checks payable to Scriptapalooza. **Deadline: April 15 and October 1 of each year.** Length: standard television format whether one hour, one-half hour, or pilot. Open to any writer 18 or older. Guidelines available now for SASE or on website. Accepts inquiries by e-mail, phone. "Pilots should be fresh and new and easy to visualize. Spec scripts should stay current with the shows, up-to-date story lines, characters, etc." Winners announced February 15 and August 30. For contest results, visit website.

THE SHERWOOD ANDERSON FOUNDATION FICTION AWARD

The Sherwood Anderson Foundation, 264 Tobacco Road, Madison, NC 27025. Website: sherwoodandersonfoundation.org; Phone: (336)427-4450. **Contact:** David M. Spear, foundation co-president; e-mail: dspear003@gmail.com. Contest is to honor, preserve, and celebrate the memory and literary work of Sherwood Anderson, American realist for the first half of the 20th century. Annual award supports developing writers of short stories and novels. Entrants must have published at least one book of fiction or have had several short stories published in major literary and/or commercial publication. Self-published stories do not qualify. Send a detailed résumé that includes a bibliography of your publications. Include a cover letter that provides a history of your writing experience and your plans for writing projects. Also, submit 2 or 3 examples of what you consider to be your best work. Do not send manuscripts by e-mail. Only mss in English will be accepted. Open to any writer who meets the qualifications listed above. Accepts inquiries by e-mail. Mail your application to the above address. No mss or publications will be returned. Award: $15,000 grant. Judged by a committee established by the foundation. Entry fee: $50 application fee (payable to The Sherwood Anderson Foundation). Deadline: April 1.

SKIPPING STONES HONOR (BOOK) AWARDS

P.O. Box 3939, Eugene OR 97403-0939. Phone/fax: (541)342-4956. E-mail: editor@skippingstones.org. Website: www.skippingstones.org. **Contact:** Arun N. Toké. Estab. 1994. Annual awards since 1994 to "promote multicultural and/or nature awareness through creative writings for children and teens and their educators." Prize: honor certificates; seals; reviews; press release/publicity. Categories: short stories, novels, story collections, poetry, nonfiction and teaching resources, including DVD's. Judged by "a multicultural committee of teachers, librarians, parents, students and editors." Entry fee: $50. **Deadline: February 1** postmark/ship date each year. Entries must be previously published. Open to published books and teaching resources that appeared in print during a 2-year period prior to the deadline date. Guidelines for SASE or e-mail and on website. Accepts inquiries by e-mail, fax, phone. "We seek authentic, exceptional, child/youth friendly books that promote intercultural, international, intergenerational harmony and understanding through creative ways. Writings that come out of your own experiences and cultural understanding seem to have an edge." Results announced in May each year. Winners notified through personal notifications, press release and by publishing reviews of winning titles in the summer issue. It is often reprinted in several other educational publications and reported in others. Attractive gold honor seals available for winners. For contest results, send SASE, e-mail or visit website.

Skipping Stones received the 2007 NAME Award for outstanding contribution to multicultural education. Now in its 23rd year!

SKIPPING STONES YOUTH AWARDS

P.O. Box 3939, Eugene OR 97403-0939. Phone/fax: (541)342-4956. E-mail: editor@skippingstones.org. Website: www.skippingstones.org. **Contact:** Arun N. Toké. Annual awards to "promote creativity as well as multicultural and nature awareness in youth." Prize: publication in the Autumn issue, honor certificate, subscription to magazine, plus 5 multicultural or nature books. Categories: short stories. Entry fee: $3/entry, make checks payable to Skipping Stones. Cover letter should include name, address, phone, and e-mail. Deadline: June 20. Entries must be unpublished. Length: 1,000 words maximum. Open to any writer between 7 and 17. Guidelines available by SASE, e-mail, or on website. Accepts inquiries by e-mail or phone. "Be creative. Do not use stereotypes or excessive violent language or plots. Be sensitive to cultural diversity." Results announced in the September-October issue. Winners notified by mail. For contest results, visit website. Everyone who enters receives the issue that features the award winners.

Skipping Stones is a winner of the 2007 NAME award and now in 23rd year.

THE BERNICE SLOTE AWARD

Prairie Schooner, 123 Andrews Hall, PO Box 880334, Lincoln NE 68588-0334. (402)472-0911. Fax: (402)472-9771. E-mail: jengelhardt2@unl.edu. Website: www.prairieschooner.unl.edu. **Contact:** Kwame Dawes. Offered annually for the best work by a beginning writer published in *Prairie Schooner* in the previous year. Prize: $500. Categories: short stories, essays and poetry. Judged by editorial staff of *Prairie Schooner.* No entry fee. For guidelines, send SASE or visit website. "Only work published in the journal during the previous year will be considered." Work is nominated by the editorial staff. Results announced in the Spring issue. Winners notified by mail in February or March.

KAY SNOW WRITERS' CONTEST

9045 SW Barbur Blvd. #5A, Portland OR 97219-4027. (503)452-1592. Fax: (503)452-0372. E-mail: wilwrite@teleport.com. Website: www.willamettewriters.com. **Contact:** Lizzy Shannon, contest director. Contest offered annually to "offer encouragement and recognition to writers with unpublished submissions." Acquires right to publish excerpts from winning pieces 1 time in their newsletter. Entry fee is $10 for Williamette Writers' members; $15, nonmembers; free for student writers grades 1-12. **Deadline: April 23.** Prizewinners will be honored at the two-day August Willamette Writers' Conference. Press releases will be sent to local and national media announcing the winners, and excerpts from winning entries may appear in our newsletter.

SOUTHWEST WRITERS (SWW) CONTESTS

3721 Morris St. NE, Suite A, Albuquerque NM 87111-3611. (505)265-9485. E-mail: Swwriters@juno.com. Website: www.southwestwriters.com. **Contact:** Contest Chair. The SouthWest Writers (SWW) Contest encourages and honors excellence in writing. There are 14 categories, including Christian Novel. (Please see rules on website for more details.) Prizes: Finalists in all categories are notified by mail and are listed on the SWW website with the title of their entry. First-, second-, and third-place winners in each category also receive cash prizes of $150, $100, and $50 (respectively), as well as a certificate of achievement. First- place winners also compete for the $1,000 Storyteller Award. Winners will be honored at a contest awards banquet (date and time TBA). Categories: Mainstream/Literary Novel, Mystery/Suspense/Thriller/Adventure Novel, Science Fiction/Fantasy/Horror Novel, Historical Novel, Middle Grade or YA Novel, Memoir Book, Memoir Article, Mainstream/Literary Article, Nonfiction Essay/Article, Personal Essay/Column, Nonfiction Book, Children's Fiction or Nonfiction Picture Book, Screenplay, Poetry. Judged by editors and agents (most from New York publishing houses) who are chosen by the contest chairs. Screening panel sends top 15 entries in each category to judges. Judges rank and critique the top three entries in each category. All entries may receive an optional written critique by a qualified consultant. Entry fee: Early deadline with no critique, $20 for members; $30 for nonmembers; Poetry $10 for first poem, $5 for each additional poem; late deadline, an additional $5. Early deadline with critique, $45 for members; $55 for nonmembers; late deadline, an additional $5. Cash, check (made out to SouthWest Writers), money order, or credit card. No cover letter is required; send copy of the SWW Contest Entry Form. Personal information should not appear anywhere on ms. Please follow detailed instructions for submission in Category Specific Guidelines on website. Deadline: May 1; late deadline: May 15. Entries must be unpublished. Open to all writers from around the world. All entries should be submitted in English and follow standard ms format. "Entrants should read the SWW Contest Rules for complete information on the SWW website." Guidelines available in January by SASE, e-mail, on website, or in *SouthWest Sage SWW* newsletter. Accepts inquiries by e-mail, phone. Mail SASE to receive rules, entry form in hard copy. Do not use certified mail to send submissions, as they will be returned unopened; enclose an SASP to verify receipt.

JOHN STEINBECK FICTION AWARD

Reed Magazine, San Jose State University, Dept. of English, One Washington Square, San Jose CA 95192. Website: http://www.reedmag.org/drupal/. **Contact:** Nick Taylor, editor. "Award for an unpublished short story of up to 6,000 words." Annual. Competition/award for short stories. Prize: $1,000 prize and publication in *Reed Magazine*. Receives several hundred entries per category. Entries are judged by a prominent fiction writer; 2007 judge was Tobias Wolff. Entry fee: $15 (includes issue of Reed). **Submission period is June 1-November 1.** Anyone may enter contest. "Do not submit any pornographic material, science fiction, fantasy, or children's literature. The work must be your own, (no translations)." Results announced in April.

SUBTERRAIN ANNUAL LITERARY AWARDS COMPETITION: THE LUSH TRIUMPHANT

subTERRAIN Magazine, P.O. Box 3008 MPO, Vancouver BC V6B 3X5 Canada. (604) 876-8710. Fax: (604) 879-2667. E-mail: subter@portal.ca. Website: www.subterrain.ca. Offered annually to foster new and upcoming writers. Prize: $750 (Canadian) cash prizes in each category, publication, and 1-year subscription to *subTERRAIN*. Categories: short stories, poetry, nonfiction. Judged by an editorial collective. Entry fee: $25. Entrants may submit as many entries in as many categories as they like. All entrants receive a year's subscription. Guidelines on Website. **Deadline: May 15.** Entries must be unpublished. Length: Fiction: 3,000 words maximum; Poetry: a suite of 5 related poems (max 15 pages); creative nonfiction: max 4,000 words. Results announced on Website. "All entries must be previously unpublished material. Submissions will not be returned, so do not send originals."

RONALD SUKENICK AMERICAN BOOK REVIEW INNOVATIVE FICTION PRIZE

FC2, American Book Review University of Houston-Victoria School of Arts and Sciences, 3007 N. Ben Wilson, Victoria TX 77901. (850) 644-2260. Fax: (850) 644-6808. E-mail: FC2@uhv.edu. Website: http://fc2.org/Sukenick%20prize.htm. **Contact:** Carmen Edington, managing editor. "To discover new writers of experimental fiction, and to publish work by writers who have not previously published with FC2." Annual. Competition/award for novels, story collections. Prize: $1000 and publication. Entries are judged by Board of Directors.For the 2007 contest, the final judge was Michael Martone. Each year it will be a different member of the Board. Entry fee: $25. Make checks payable to American Book Review. Guidelines available in June. Accepts inquiries by e-mail. Submission period is August 15-November 1. Entries should be unpublished. Anyone who has not previously published with FC2 may enter contest. Cover letter should include name, address, phone, e-mail, novel/story title. Only the title should appear on the ms, since all mss are read blind by the judges. Writers may submit their own work."Be familiar with our list." Results announced in May. Winners notified by phone, by e-mail. Winners announced in May.

THREE CHEERS AND A TIGER

Website: www.toasted-cheese.com. E-mail: editors@toasted-cheese.com. **Contact:** Stephanie Lenz, editor. Purpose of contest is to write a short story (following a specific theme) within 48 hours. Contests are held first weekend in spring (mystery) and first weekend in fall (sf/f). Prize: Amazon gift certificates and publication. Categories: short stories. Blind-judged by two *Toasted Cheese* editors. Each judge uses his or her own criteria to choose entries. No entry fee. Entries must be unpublished. Contest offered biannually. Word limit announced at the start of the contest. Contest-specific information is announced 48 hours before the contest submission deadline. Open to any writer. Accepts inquiries by e-mail. "Follow the theme, word count and other contest rules. We have more suggestions at our website." Results announced in April and October. Winners notified by e-mail. List of winners on website.

TILIA KLEBENOV JACOBS RELIGIOUS ESSAY COMPETITION

Category in the Soul-Making Literary Competition, National League of American Pen Women, The Webhallow House, 1544 Sweetwood Dr., Broadmoor Village CA 94015-2029. E-mail: pennobhill@aol.com. Website: www.soulmakingcontest.us. **Contact:** Eileen Malone. Estab. 2012. "Call for thoughtful writings of up to 3,000 words. No preaching, no proselytizing. Previously published material is accepted. Indicate category on cover of page and on identifying 3x5 card. Open annually to any writer." Deadline: November 30. Prize: 1st Place: $100; 2nd Place $50; 3rd Place $25.

TOM HOWARD/JOHN H. REID SHORT STORY CONTEST

c/o Winning Writers, 351 Pleasant St., PMB 222, Northampton MA 01060-3961. (866)946-9748. E-mail: johnreid@mail.qango.com. Website: www.winningwriters.com. **Contact:** John Reid. Estab. 1993. Now in its 19th year. Prizes of $3,000, $1,000, $400 and $250 will be awarded, plus six Most Highly Commended Awards of $150 each. Submit any type of short story, essay, or other work of prose. You may submit work that has been published or won prizes elsewhere, as long as you own the online publication rights. $15 entry fee. Submit online or by mail. Early submission encouraged. This contest is sponsored by Tom Howard Books and assisted by Winning Writers. Judges: John H. Reid and Dee C. Konrad. See the complete guidelines and past winners. Make checks payable to Winning Writers (U.S. funds only, please). Guidelines available in July on website. Prefers inquiries by e-mail. **Deadline: March 31, 2011.** "Both published and unpublished works are accepted. In the case of published work, the contestant must own the online publication rights." Open to all writers. Length: 5,000 words max per entry. Cover letter should include name, address, phone, e-mail, story title, place(s) where story was previously published (if any). Only the title should be on the actual ms. Writers may submit own work. "Read past winning entries at www.winningwriters.com/contests/tomstory/ts_pastwinners.php." Winners notified by e-mail. Results made available to entrants on website.

TOMMY AWARD FOR EXCELLENCE IN WRITING

International Book Management Corporation, 3468 Babcock Blvd., Pittsburgh PA 15237-2402. (412)837-2423. E-mail: info@internationalbookmanagement.com; editor@writersnewsweekly.com. Website: writersnewsweekly.com. **Contact:** Christopher Stokum and Sarah Schiavoni. Estab. 2004. The Tommy Award For Writing Excellence recognizes and rewards excellence in full-length literary works in adult fiction and nonfiction. Books must be published in the U.S. between June 1 and May 31 of the following year. Textbooks, e-books, children's books, young adult books, poetry, and audiobooks will not be considered, nor will manuscripts. Judges will select one winner and may designate up to two Honorable Mention books in each of the following categories: fiction, nonfiction, short story collection. Books can be submitted by the publisher or the author. A copy of each book submitted should be mailed directly to: International Book Management Corporation, 3468 Babcock Blvd., Pittsburgh, PA 15237. Please send submissions as soon as possible after publication. No books will be accepted after May 21, 2011. There will be no extensions to this deadline. Winners and honorable mentions will be announced on August 15. The awards are presented in October. Winners receive a certificate and trophy. An author interview and book review of the winning submission will appear on *WritersNewsWeekly*. Entries will not be returned. International Book Management Corp. reserves the right to donate or dispose of entries. No entry fee. More more information contact International Management at: info@internationalbookmanagement.com.

TORONTO BOOK AWARDS

City of Toronto c/o Toronto Protocol, 100 Queen St. W., City Clerk's Office, 2nd floor, West, City Hall, Toronto ON M5H 2N2 Canada. (416)392-7805. Fax: (416)392-1247. E-mail: bkurmey@toronto.ca. Website: www.toronto.ca/book_awards. **Contact:** Bev Kurmey, protocol officer. The Toronto Book Awards honor authors of books of literary or artistic merit that are evocative of Toronto. Annual award for short stories, novels, poetry or short story collections. Prize: $15,000. Each short-listed author (usually 4-6) receives $1,000 and the winner receives the remainder. Categories: No separate categories—novels, short story collections, books of poetry, biographies, history, books about sports, children's books—all are judged together. Judged by jury of five who have demonstrated interest and/or experience in literature, literacy, books and book publishing. No entry fee. Cover letter should include name, address, phone, e-mail and title of entry. Six copies of the entry book are also required. **Deadline: last week of March.** Entries must be previously published. Guidelines available in September on website. Accepts inquires by fax, e-mail, phone. Finalists announced in June; winners notified in September at a gala reception. Guidelines and results available on website.

⊕ TORREY HOUSE CREATIVE LITERARY NONFICTION CONTEST

Creative Literary Nonfiction Contest, Torrey House, Website: www.torreyhouse.com. "Submit great stories of the West that promote appreciation of our beautiful land. Length: 2,000-10,000 words. Show us the power of the Colorado Plateau. Contest submissions must be original and not previously published. Please, no stories written for children for contest entries. Include two title pages: one with your name and contact information and one with the title of your piece only. Double-space your submissions and use a 12-point font, with numbered pages that include the title of the piece as a header. Please e-mail us your material as a document attachment with *Contest: your entry's title* in the subject line and *your entry's title* as the filename. Send your entry to mail@torreyhouse.com. We accept snail mail as well (contact us), though we prefer electronic submissions. The entry fee is $25 per submission and is nonrefundable. You are welcome to enter more than one piece; each will be considered a separate submission and must be accompanied by the $25 fee. Please use the PayPal button "Buy Now" online to make your payment, and be sure to include the same e-mail address you use on your submission so we know you paid. Deadline: May 31, 2011. First prize: $1,000; Second prize: $250; Third prize: $100. All winners published in Torrey House Press annual journal."

"When we accept a submission, we are purchasing first-publication rights. Once we've published your story, you are free to include it in your own collection. Winners will be contacted within 6 weeks of the deadline."

O WAASMODE SHORT FICTION PRIZE

Passages North, NMU 1401 Presque Ilse Ave, Marquette MI 49855. (906) 227-1203. E-mail: passages@nmu.edu. Website: http://myweb.nmu.edu/~passages. Offered every other year—check website for details. Competition/award for short stories. Prize: $1000 first prize; two honorable mentions. Entry fee: $10 per story, includes contest issue. Make checks payable to Northern Michigan University. **Submission period is Oct 15-Feb 15.** Entries should be unpublished. Anyone may enter contest. Length: 7,500 word max. Writers may submit own work. Winners notified by e-mail. Results made available to entrants with SASE.

WILLA LITERARY AWARD

Women Writing the West, 8547 East Arapaho Road, Box J-541, Greenwood Village CO 80112-1436. (801)573-5309. E-mail: alicetrego@mac.com. Website: www.womenwritingthewest.org. **Contact:** Alice D. Trego, contest director.

GARY WILSON SHORT FICTION AWARD

descant, Texas Christian University's literary journal, TCU, Box 297270, Fort Worth TX 76129. Phone: (817)257-6537. Fax: (817)257-6239. E-mail: descant@tcu.edu. Website: www.descant.tcu.edu. **Contact:** David Kuhne, editor. Offered annually for an outstanding story in an issue.

O WISCONSIN INSTITUTE FOR CREATIVE WRITING FELLOWSHIP

University of Wisconsin–Madison, Creative Writing/English Dept., 6195B H.C. White Hall, 600 N. Park St., Madison WI 53706. (608) 263-3374. E-mail: rfkuka@wisc.edu. Website: www.creativewriting.wisc.edu. **Contact:** Ron Kuka, program coordinator. Fellowship provides time, space and an intellectual community for writers working on first books. Receives approximately 300 applicants a year for each genre. Prize: $27,000 for a 9-month appointment. Judged by English Department faculty and current fellows. **Entry fee**: $45, payable to the Department of English. **Deadline: February**. "Candidates must not yet have published, or had accepted for publication, a book by application deadline." Open to any writer with either an MFA or PhD in creative writing. Please enclose a SASE for notification of results. Results announced by May 1. "Send your best work. Stories seem to have a small advantage over novel excerpts."

WORLD FANTASY AWARDS

P.O. Box 43, Mukilteo WA 98275-0043. E-mail: sfexecsec@gmail.com. Website: www.worldfantasy.org.

Contact: Peter Dennis Pautz, president. Awards "to recognize excellence in fantasy literature worldwide." Offered annually for previously published work in several categories, including life achievement, novel, novella, short story, anthology, collection, artist, special award-pro and special award-nonpro. Works are recommended by attendees of current and previous 2 years' conventions and a panel of judges. Prize: Bust of HP Lovecraft. Judged by panel. No entry fee. Guidelines available in December for SASE or on website. **Deadline: June 1.** Entries must be previously published. Published submissions from previous calendar year. Word length: 10,000-40,000 for novella, 10,000 for short story. "All fantasy is eligible, from supernatural horror to Tolkien-esque to sword and sorcery to the occult, and beyond." Cover letter should include name, address, phone, e-mail, word count, title, and publications where submission was previously published, submitted to the address above and the panel of judges when they appear on the website. Results announced November 1 at annual convention. For contest results, visit website.

WORLD'S BEST SHORT SHORT STORY FICTION CONTEST, NARRATIVE NONFICTION CONTEST & SOUTHEAST REVIEW POETRY CONTEST

English Department, Florida State University, Tallahassee FL 32306. E-mail: southeastreview@gmail.com. Website: www.southeastreview.org. Contact: Katie Cortese, acquisitions editor. Estab. 1979. "Annual award for unpublished short-short stories (500 words or less), poetry, and narrative nonfiction (6,000 words or less)." $15 reading fee for up to 3 stories or poems, $15 reading fee per nonfiction entry, fiction, nonfiction, poetry, short stories. Deadline: March 15. Prize: $500 per category. Winners and finalists will be published in the *Southeast Review.*

WRITER'S DIGEST WRITING COMPETITION

Writer's Digest, a publication of F+W Media, Inc., 700 E. State St., Iola WI 54990. (513)531-2690, ext. 1328. E-mail: writing-competition@fwmedia.com; nicole.florence@fwmedia.com. Website: www.writersdigest.com. **Contact:** Nicki Florence. 80th annual. Writing contest with 10 categories: Inspirational Writing (spiritual/religious, maximum 2,500 words); Memoir/Personal Essay (maximum 2,000 words); Magazine Feature Article (maximum 2,000 words); Short Story (genre, maximum 4,000 words); Short Story (mainstream/literary, maximum 4,000 words); Rhyming Poetry (maximum 32 lines); Nonrhyming Poetry (maximum 32 lines); Stage Play (first 15 pages and 1-page synopsis); TV/Movie Script (first 15 pages and 1-page synopsis). Entries must be original, in English, unpublished/unproduced (except for Magazine Feature Articles), and not accepted by another publisher/producer at the time of submission. *Writer's Digest* retains onetime publication rights to the winning entries in each category. $15/first poetry entry; $10/additional poem. All other entries are $20/first ms; $15/additional ms: fiction, poetry, juvenile, scripts, articles, short stories. Deadline: May 2/late entry May 20, additional fee for late entries. Add $5 per manuscript or poem to Entry Fee(s) on all entries submitted between May 3 and May 20. Grand Prize: $3,000 and a trip to New York City to meet with editors and agents; 1st Place: $1,000, ms critique and marketing advice from a *Writer's Digest* editor, commentary from an agent, and $100 of *Writer's Digest* Books; 2nd Place: $500 and $100 of *Writer's Digest* Books; 3rd Place: $250 and $100 of *Writer's Digest* Books; 4th Place: $100 and $50 of *Writer's Digest* Books; 5th Place: $50 and $50 of *Writer's Digest* Books; 6th-10th place $25.

WRITERS-EDITORS NETWORK ANNUAL INTERNATIONAL WRITING COMPETITION

c/o CNW Publishing, Florida Freelance Writers Association, P.O. Box A, North Stratford NH 03590-0167. E-mail: contest@writers-editors.com. Website: www.writers-editors.com. **Contact:** Dana K. Cassell, executive director. Annual award "to recognize publishable talent." Divisions & Categories: Nonfiction (previously published article/essay/column/nonfiction book chapter; unpublished or self-published article/essay/column/nonfiction book chapter); Fiction (unpublished or self-published short story or novel chapter); Children's Literature (unpublished or self-published short story/nonfiction article/book chapter/poem); Poetry (unpublished or self-published free verse/traditional). Prize: 1st Place: $100, plus certificate; 2nd Place: $75, plus certificate; 3rd Place: $50, plus certificate. Honorable Mention certificates will be awarded in each category as warranted. Judged by editors, librarians, and writers. Entry fee: $5 (active or new CNW/FFWA members) or $10 (nonmembers) for each fiction/nonfiction entry under 3,000 words;

$10 (members) or $20 (nonmembers) for each entry of 3,000 words or longer; and $3 (members) or $5 (nonmembers) for each poem. Guidelines for SASE or on website. Deadline: March 15. Open to any writer. Results announced May 31. Winners notified by mail and posted on website. Results available for SASE or visit website.

WRITERS' JOURNAL ANNUAL ROMANCE CONTEST

Val-Tech Media, P.O. Box 394, Perham MN 56573. (218)346-7921. Fax: (218)346-7924. E-mail: writersjournal@writersjournal.com. Website: www.writersjournal.com. Offered annually for previously unpublished works. Cover letter should include name, address, phone, e-mail, word count, and title; just title on ms. Results announced in January/February issue. Winners notified by mail and on website. Enclose SASE for winner's list. Receives fewer than 150 entries.

WRITERS' JOURNAL ANNUAL SHORT STORY CONTEST

Val-Tech Media, P.O. Box 394, Perham MN 56573. (218) 346-7921. Fax: (218) 346-7924. **Contact:** Leon Ogroske. "Offered annually for previously unpublished short stories. Open to any writer. Guidelines for SASE or online." Receives fewer than 250 entries. Needs fiction, short stories. Deadline: May 30. 1st Place: $350; 2nd Place: $125; 3rd Place: $75; plus honorable mentions. Prizewinning stories and selected honorable mentions are published in *Writers' Journal* November/December issue. Winners list published in *Writers' Journal* and on website. Entry fee: $10 reading fee.

O WRITERS' LEAGUE OF TEXAS MANUSCRIPT CONTEST

611 S. Congress Ave., Suite 130, Austin TX 78704. Website: www.writersleague.org. **Contact:** Sara Kocek. Prize: First-place winners meet individually with an agent at the Writers' League of Texas Agents Conference in June. Categories: mainstream fiction, mystery, thriller/action adventure, romance, science fiction/fantasy, historical fiction, narrative nonfiction, children's middle grade, and young adult works. Judged by preliminary judges (first round), then agent or editor reads finalists' manuscripts. **Entry fee**: $50 for score sheet with comments. Open to any writer. Entries must be unpublished. Submit first 10 pages of manuscript, double-spaced. Guidelines available in November by e-mail or on website. **Deadline: March**. Accepts inquiries by e-mail. Results announced at the June conference and on the website.

CONFERENCES & WORKSHOPS

Why are conferences so popular? Writers and conference directors alike tell us it's because writing can be such a lonely business—at conferences writers have the opportunity to meet (and commiserate) with fellow writers, as well as meet and network with publishers, editors, and agents. Conferences and workshops provide some of the best opportunities for writers to make publishing contacts and pick up valuable information on the business, as well as the craft, of writing.

The bulk of the listings in this section are for conferences. Most conferences last from one day to one week and offer a combination of workshop-type writing sessions, panel discussions, and a variety of guest speakers. Topics may include all aspects of writing, from fiction to poetry to scriptwriting, or they may focus on a specific type of writing, such as those conferences sponsored by the Romance Writers of America (RWA) for writers of romance or by the Society of Children's Book Writers and Illustrators (SCBWI) for writers of children's books.

Workshops, however, tend to run longer—usually one to two weeks. Designed to operate like writing classes, most require writers to be prepared to work on and discuss their fiction while attending. An important benefit of workshops is the opportunity they provide writers for an intensive critique of their work, often by professional writing teachers and established writers.

Each of the listings here includes information on the specific focus of an event as well as planned panels, guest speakers, and workshop topics. It is important to note, however, that some conference directors were still in the planning stages for 2012 when we contacted them. If it was not possible to include 2012 dates, fees, or topics, we have provided information from 2011 so you can get an idea of what to expect. For the most current information, it's best to check the conference website or send a self-addressed, stamped envelope to the director in question about three months before the date(s) listed.

FINDING A CONFERENCE

Many writers try to make it to at least one conference a year, but cost and location count as much as subject matter or other considerations when determining which conference to attend. There are conferences in almost every state and province and even some in Europe open to North Americans. The conferences appear in alphabetical order.

To find a conference based on the month in which it occurs, check out our Conference Index by Date at the back of this book.

LEARNING & NETWORKING

Besides learning from workshop leaders and panelists in formal sessions, writers at conferences also benefit from conversations with other attendees. Writers on all levels enjoy sharing insights. Often, a conversation over lunch can reveal a new market for your work or let you know which editors are most receptive to the work of new writers. You can find out about recent editor changes and about specific agents. A casual chat could lead to a new contact or resource in your area.

Many editors and agents make visiting conferences a part of their regular search for new writers. A cover letter or query that starts with "I met you at the Green Mountain Writers Conference," or "I found your talk on your company's new romance line at the Moonlight and Magnolias Writer's Conference most interesting . . ." may give you a small leg up on the competition.

While a few writers have been successful in selling their manuscripts at a conference, the availability of editors and agents does not usually mean these folks will have the time there to read your novel or six best short stories (unless, of course, you've scheduled an individual meeting with them ahead of time). While editors and agents are glad to meet writers and discuss work in general terms, usually they don't have the time (or energy) to give an extensive critique during a conference. In other words, use the conference as a way to make a first, brief contact.

SELECTING A CONFERENCE

Besides the obvious considerations of time, place, and cost, choose your conference based on your writing goals. If, for example, your goal is to improve the quality of your writing, it will be more helpful to you to choose a hands-on craft workshop rather than a conference offering a series of panels on marketing and promotion. If, on the other hand, you are a science fiction novelist who would like to meet your fans, try one of the many science fiction conferences or "cons" held throughout the country and the world.

Look for panelists and workshop instructors whose work you admire and who seem to be writing in your general area. Check for specific panels or discussions of topics relevant to what you are writing now. Think about the size—would you feel more comfortable with a small workshop of eight people or a large group of 100 or more attendees?

If your funds are limited, start by looking for conferences close to home, but you may want to explore those that offer contests with cash prizes—and a chance to recoup your expenses. A few conferences and workshops also offer scholarships, but the competition is stiff and writers interested in these should find out the requirements early. Finally, students may want to look for conferences and workshops that offer college credit. You will find these options included in the listings here. Again, send a self-addressed, stamped envelope for the most current details.

ABROAD WRITERS CONFERENCES

17363 Sutter Creek Rd., Sutter Creek CA 95685. (209)296-4050. E-mail: abroadwriters@yahoo.com. Website: www.abroad-crwf.com/index.html. Conferences are held throughout the year in various places worldwide. See website for scheduling details. Conference duration: 7-10 days. "Instead of being lost in a crowd at a large conference, Abroad Writers' Conference prides itself on holding small group meetings where participants have personal contact with everyone. Stimulating talks, interviews, readings, Q&A's, writing workshops, film screenings, private consultations and social gatherings all take place within a week to ten days. Abroad Writers' Conference promises you true networking opportunities and full detailed feedback on your writing."

"Abroad Writers' Conference is proud to be holding Kolkata, India's first major literary conference in their historic City of Joy. This large literary conference and workshop will take place at the Victoria Memorial Museum and the Oberoi Hotel. We will have 40 authors including two Nobel Prize winners and literary agents. Workshops will be held in fiction, non-fiction, memoir, playwriting and poetry."

COSTS Prices start at $2,750. Discounts and upgrades may apply. Particpants must apply to program no later than 3 months before departure. To secure a place you must send in a deposit of $700. Balance must be paid in full 12 weeks before departure. See website for pricing details.

ADDITIONAL INFORMATION Agents participate in conference. Application is online at website.

ALABAMA WRITERS' CONCLAVE

137 Sterling Dr., Hueytown AL 35023. E-mail: irenelatham@charter.net. Website: www.alabamawritersconclave.org. Contact: Don Johnson, treasurer. Estab. 1923. Last event held July 16-18, 2010. Average attendance: 80-100. **2011 ALABAMA WRITERS' CONCLAVE July 15-17 Huntsville, Alabama Marriott**. Conference to promote all phases of writing. Also offers ms critiques and eight writing contests.

COSTS Fees for conference are $150 (member)/$175 (nonmember), includes 2 meals. Critique fee $25 (member)/$30 (nonmember). Membership $25.

ACCOMMODATIONS Special conference rates.

ADDITIONAL INFORMATION "We have major speakers and faculty members who conduct intensive, energetic workshops. Our annual writing contest guidelines and all other information is available at www.alabamawritersconclave.org."

ALGONKIAN FIVE DAY NOVEL CAMP

2020 Pennsylvania Ave. NW, Suite 443, Washington DC 20006. E-mail: algonkian@webdelsol.com. Website: fwwriters.algonkianconferences.com. Conference duration: 5 days. Average attendance: 12 students maximum per workshop. "During 45+ hours of actual workshop time, students will engage in those rigorous narrative and complication/plot exercises necessary to produce a publishable manuscript. Genres we work with include general commercial fiction, literary fiction, serious and light women's fiction, mystery/cozy/thriller, SF/F, young adult, and memoir/narrative non-fiction. The three areas of workshop emphasis will be PREMISE, PLATFORM, and EXECUTION." Site: "The Algonkian Park is located 30 miles from Washington, D.C. A good map and directions can be found on our website. It is 12 miles from Dulles International Airport (the perfect place to fly into—cab fares from Dulles to Algonkian are about $25.00). The cottages are fully furnished with TV, phones, linens, dishes, central air and heat. All cottages feature fireplaces, decks with grills, equipped kitchens, cathedral ceilings, and expansive riverside views of the Potomac. Participants each have their own room in the cottage. The address of the Algonkian Park Management headquarters is 47001 Fairway Drive, Sterling, Virginia, and their phone number is 703-450-4655. If you have any questions about the cottages or facilities, ask for Lawan, the manager."

COSTS $865.

ACCOMMODATIONS Offers overnight accommodations. Price includes tuition, private cottage room for 5 nights, breakfast and lunch. Transportation to and from the conference and dinner are not included.

ADDITIONAL INFORMATION For brochure, visit website.

ALTERNATIVE PRESS EXPO (APE)

Comic-Con International, P.O. Box 128458, San Diego CA 92112-8458. (619)491-2475. Fax: (619)414-1022. E-mail: cci-info@comic-con.org. Website: www.comic-con.org/ape/. **Contact:** Eddie Ibrahim, director of programming. Annual. Last conference held October 1-2, 2011, in San Francisco. Conference duration: 2 days. "Hundreds of artists and publishers converge for the largest gathering of alternative and self-published comics in the country." Includes panels on graphic novels, Web comics, how to pitch your comic to publishers, and the traditional APE "queer cartoonists" panel. Site: Large conference or expo center in host city. 2011 special guests are Kate Beaton, Daniel Clowes, Craig Thompson, Adrian Tomine, and Shannon Wheeler.

COSTS $7 single day; $10 both days.

ACCOMMODATIONS Does not offer overnight accommodations. Provides list of area hotels or lodging options on website.

ADDITIONAL INFORMATION For brochure, visit website. Editors participate in conference.

AMERICAN CHRISTIAN WRITERS CONFERENCES

P.O. Box 110390, Nashville TN 37222-0390. (800)219-7483. Fax: (615)834-7736. E-mail: acwriters@aol.com. Website: www.acwriters.com. **Contact:** Reg Forder, director. Estab. 1981. Annual. Conferences held throughout the year in over 2 dozen cities, even a Caribbean cruise. Conference duration: 2 days. Average attendance: 30-80. Conference's purpose is to promote all forms of Christian writing. Site: Usually located at a major hotel chain like Holiday Inn.

COSTS $150 for 1 day, $250 for 2 days, plus meals and accommodations.

ACCOMMODATIONS Special rates are available at the host hotel (usually a major chain like Holiday Inn).

ADDITIONAL INFORMATION Send a SASE for conference brochures/guidelines.

AMERICAN INDEPENDENT WRITERS (AIW) AMERICAN WRITERS CONFERENCE

1001 Connecticut Ave. NW, Ste. 701, Washington DC 20036. (202) 775-5150. Fax: (202) 775-5810. E-mail: info@amerindywriters.org; donald@amerindywriters.org. Website: www.amerindywriters.org. **Contact:** Donald O. Graul Jr., Executive Director. Estab. 1975. Annual conference held in June. Conference duration: Saturday. Average attendance: 350. "Gives participants a chance to hear from and talk with dozens of experts on book and magazine publishing as well as meet one-on-one with literary agents." Site: George Washington University Conference Center. Past keynote speakers included Erica Jong, Diana Rehm, Kitty Kelley, Lawrence Block, John Barth, Stephen Hunter, Francine Prose.

ANTIOCH WRITERS' WORKSHOP

c/o Antioch University Midwest, 900 Dayton St., Yellow Springs OH 45387. (937)769-1803. E-mail: info@antiochwritersworkshop.com. Website: www.antiochwritersworkshop.com. **Contact:** Sharon Short, director. Estab. 1986. Annual 1-week conference held in July. Conference duration: July 9-15, 2011. "A la Carte" options include morning-only classes; Focus on Form afternoon seminar, and one-day Saturday seminar on July 9. Average attendance: 80. Workshop concentration: fiction, poetry, personal essay, memoir. Workshop located at Antioch University Midwest and at various sites in the Village of Yellow Springs. 2011 keynoter and morning fiction instructor is Nancy Pickard, author of *New York Times* best-selling novel *The Scent of Rain and Lightning* and co-author of a book for writers, *7 Steps on the Writer's Path*. Visiting Agent: Suzie Townsend (Fine Print Literary Agency). Visiting Editor: Kevin Morgan Watson (Press 53). Other 2011 faculty: poetry—Jim Daniels and Jamey Dunham; nonfiction—Matthew Goodman and Joyce Dyer; fiction—Lucrecia Guerrero, Martha Moody, Rakesh Satyal. Registration for all programs is $125: tuition for Saturday Seminar is covered by registration fee; tuition for morning-only/afternoon-only Focus on Form seminar is $250; tuition for Full Week experience ranges from $450 for Ohio college/university students and faculty; $550 for alumni and local participants; $650 for nonlocal first-time participants. Competitive scholarships are offered. Full Week experience also includes small group lunches with faculty, agent pitch sessions, optional ms critiques. Presented in partnership with Antioch University Midwest. Continuing education and college level credit options available.

COSTS: (registration fee plus tuition) Full week: $735, nonlocal, first time attendees; $675, alumni/locals; $575 for Ohio College/University students and faculty. Optional ms critique is $75 for Full Week attendees. A la carte: $125, Saturday Seminar; $375, Morning Only classes; $375, Afternoon Only Focus on Form seminar.

ACCOMMODATIONS Accommodations are available at local hotels and bed & breakfasts.

ARKANSAS WRITERS' CONFERENCE

600 Interstate 30, Little Rock AR 72227. (501)837-8824; (501)225-0166. E-mail: nlapw1@verizon.net. Website: www.arkansaswritersconference.org. **Contact:** Ellen Withers, Clovita Rice. Estab. 1944. Annual. Conference

held first weekend in June. Average attendance: 175. "We have a variety of subjects related to writing. We have some general sessions, some more specific, but we try to vary each year's subjects." Held June 3-4, 2011. Featured speaker: Jane Friedman.

COSTS Registration: $15; luncheon: $19; banquet: $20; contest entry $10 (2006 rates).

ACCOMMODATIONS "We meet at a Holiday Inn Presidential in Little Rock. Rooms available at reduced rate." Holiday Inn has a bus to bring our attendees from the airport. Rooms average $79.

ADDITIONAL INFORMATION "We have 36 contest categories. Some are open only to Arkansans, most are open to all writers. Our judges are not announced before the conference. All are qualified, many from out of state." Conference information available February 15. For brochures or inquiries send SASE with full mailing address, call or fax. "We have had 226 people attending from 12 states—over 2,000 contest entries from 40 states and New Zealand, Mexico and Canada."

ARTIST-IN-RESIDENCE NATIONAL PARKS

ME E-mail: Acadia_Information@nps.gov. Website: www.nps.gov/archive/volunteer/air.htm. **Contact:** Artist-in-Residence Coordinator. 29 National Parks offer residency programs open to two-dimensional visual artists, photographers, sculptors, performers, writers, composers, video/filmmakers, and others.

ADDITIONAL INFORMATION See website for individual park and contact information.

◐ ART WORKSHOPS IN GUATEMALA

4758 Lyndale Ave. S, Minneapolis MN 55419-5304. (612)825-0747. E-mail: info@artguat.org. Website: www.artguat.org. **Contact:** Liza Fourre, director. Estab. 1995. Annual. Workshops held year-round. Maximim class size: 10 students per class. Workshop titles include: Fiction Writing: check website. Costs (see website) (includes tuition, lodging in a lovely colonial style B&B, and ground transportation, and some pretty interesting field trips).

COSTS See website; includes tuition, lodging, breakfast, ground transportation.

ACCOMMODATIONS All transportation and accommodations included in price of conference.

ADDITIONAL INFORMATION Conference information available now. For brochure/guidelines visit website, e-mail, fax, or call. Accepts inquiries by e-mail, phone.

ASPEN SUMMER WORDS LITERARY FESTIVAL & WRITING RETREAT

Aspen Writers' Foundation, 110 E. Hallam St., #116, Aspen CO 81611. (970)925-3122. Fax: (970)925-5700. E-mail: info@aspenwriters.org. Website: www.aspenwriters.org. **Contact:** Natalie Lacy, programs manager. Estab. 1976. Annual. 2011 conference held June 19-24. Conference duration: 5 days. Average attendance: writing retreat, 150; literary festival, 300+, 1,800 visitors. Retreat includes intensive workshops in fiction (beginning through advanced), creative nonfiction, poetry, writing for young readers, young writers' workshop, magazine writing and food writing, plus a "Readers' Retreat," which will focus on Middle Eastern literature. The literary festival features approximately 18 events (craft talks, author readings, and interviews; publishing panel discussions; agent/editor meeting; and social gatherings) for readers and writers. Festival theme for 2011 retreat is literature of the Middle East. Retreat faculty for 2011; Colum McCann (Advanced Fiction); Ron Rash (Advanced Fiction); Elinor Lipman (Intermediate Fiction); Erica Jong (Memoir); Nikky Finney (Poetry); Derek Green (Beginning Fiction). Randall Kenan (Young Writers Workshop); and Mona Eltahawy. Festival presenters for 2011 are Rabih Alameddine, Firoozeh Dumas, Mona Eltahawy, Khaled Hosseini, Fady Joudah, Daniyal Mueenuddin.

COSTS Check website each year for updates.

ACCOMMODATIONS Discount lodging at the conference site will be available. 2011 rates to be announced. Free shuttle around town.

ADDITIONAL INFORMATION Workshops admission deadline is April 15. Manuscripts for juried workshops must be submitted by April 15 for review and selection. 10-page limit for workshop application manuscript. A limited number of partial-tuition scholarships are available. Deadline for agent/editor meeting registration is May 27. Brochures available for SASE, by e-mail and phone request, and on website.

⊕ ATLANTIC CENTER FOR THE ARTS

1414 Art Center Ave, New Smyrna Beach FL 32618. (386)427-6975. E-mail: shiggins@atlanticcenterforthearts.com. Website: atlanticcenterforthearts.org. **Contact:** program department. Three-week-long residency offered several times a year. "Associates selected will get one-on-one experience with a Master Artist. The Master Artist selects Associate Residents from the applications."

COSTS $850; $25 nonrefundable application fee. Financial aid is available.

ACCOMMODATIONS "Van transportation is provided from ACA two days per week at regularly scheduled times to the shopping center and art supply stores. Many artists do bring their own vehicles and car-pooling may be an option. ACA does provide van transportation to outreaches, when possible. Master Artists are supplied with a car. Bikes are available at ACA." Offers overnight accommodations.

AWP ANNUAL CONFERENCE AND BOOKFAIR

MS 1E3, George Mason Univ., Fairfax VA 22030. (703)993-4317. Fax: (703)993-4302. E-mail: conference@awpwriter.org. Website: www.awpwriter.org/conference; www.awpwriter.org. **Contact:** Anne Le, conference coordinator. Estab. 1967. 2012 AWP Annual Conference & Bookfair, Chicago, IL. February 29-March 3, 2012. Annual. Conference duration: 4 days. AWP holds its Annual Conference in a different region of North America in order to celebrate the outstanding authors, teachers, writing programs, literary centers, and small press publishers of that region. The Annual Conference typically features 350 presentations: readings, lectures, panel discussions, and Forums plus hundreds of book signings, receptions, dances, and informal gatherings. The conference attracts more than 8,000 attendees and more than 500 publishers. All genres are represented. "We will offer 175 panels on everything from writing to teaching to critical analysis." In 2009, Art Spiegelman was the keynote speaker. Others readers were Charles Baxter, Isaiah Sheffer, Z.Z. Packer, Nareem Murr, Marilynne Robinson; 2008: John Irving, Joyce Carol Oates, among others. Contact: Anne Le, conference coordinator.

COSTS Early registration fees: $40 student; $140 AWP member; $160 non-member.

ACCOMMODATIONS Provide airline discounts and rental-car discounts. Special rate at Hilton Chicago & Palmer House Hilton Hotels.

⊕ BACKSPACE WRITERS CONFERENCE & AGENT AUTHOR SEMINAR

P.O. Box 454, Washington MI 48094. (732)267-6449. E-mail: karendionne@bksp.org. Website: http://www.backspacewritersconference.com. **Contact:** Christopher Graham or Karen Dionne, cofounders. Annual. Estab. 2004. 2011 dates: May 31-June 2. Dates for the November 2011 Agent-Author Seminar: Nov. 3rd and 4th. Conference duration: 3 days. Average attendance: 150-200. Conference. "We focus on all genres, from nonfiction to literary fiction and everything in between, covering all popular genres from mysteries, and thrillers to young adult and romance. Formal pitch sessions are a staple at most writers' conferences. However, in planning our Backspace events, we discovered that agents hate conducting pitch sessions almost as much as authors dread doing them. In fact, many of the agents we've talked to are happy to sit on a panel or conduct a workshop, but decline to participate in formal pitch sessions. The goal of the Backspace Agent-Author Seminars is to help authors connect with agents—lots of agents—thereby giving authors the opportunity to ask questions specific to their interests and concerns. We facilitate this through small group workshops of usually no more than 10 writers and 2 agents. Workshops concentrate on query letters and opening pages. That's why we've built so much free time into the program. The full fifteen minutes between panels also allows plenty of opportunity for seminar registrants to talk to agents. Many of the agents will also be available during the noon hour. Remember, agents attend conferences because they want to help authors. They're looking for new talent, and welcome the chance to hear about your work. Instead of a tense, angst-filled pitch session where it's difficult for all but the most confident authors to put their best foot forward, an interesting, relaxed, enjoyable conversation leaves a much more positive impression. And even if authors don't get the chance to mention their project, the pleasant conversation gives the author a point of reference when sending a formal query letter to the agent's office after the seminar is over." 2011 agents in attendance: Jeff Kleinman, Donald Maass, Sharlene Martin, Lois Winston, Jennifer De Chiara, Rebecca Strauss, Kristin Nelson, Kathleen Ortiz, Scott Hoffman, Rachel Vogel, Meredith Barnes, Roseanne Wells, Suzie Townsend, Tamar Rydzinski, April Eberhardt, Diana Fox. Editors: Rachel Griffiths (Scholastic), Brenda Copeland (St. Martin's).

COSTS $200-700; offers member, group, and student discounts along with additional workshops that are priced separately.

ACCOMMODATIONS "We offer a special conference rate at the Radisson Martinique for conference attendees. Average price of $199-279/night, must be booked 30 days in advance." The Radisson Martinique in Manhattan NY is located in Mid-town Manhattan, just a few blocks from Madison Square

Garden/NY Penn Station. See website for more information. Brochures available in January. Accepts inquiries by e-mail and phone. Agents and editors attend conference.

BALTIMORE COMIC-CON

Baltimore Convention Center, One West Pratt St., Baltimore MD 21201. (410)526-7410. E-mail: press@baltimorecomiccon.com. Website: http://baltimorecomiccon.com/. **Contact:** Marc Nathan. Estab. 1999. Annual. August 20-21, 2011. Conference, "promoting the wonderful world of comics to as many people as possible." Jeff Smith returns to Comic-Con. The Baltimore Comic-Con welcomes the return of the Harvey Awards: the Harvey Awards are one of the comic book industry's oldest and most respected awards. The Harveys recognize outstanding achievements in over 20 categories, ranging from Best Artist to the Jack Kirby Hall of Fame. They are the only industry awards both nominated by and selected by the full body of comic book professionals.

COSTS 2-day pass: $25; Saturday or Sunday only: $15.

ACCOMMODATIONS Does not offer overnight accommodations. Provides list of area hotels or lodging options.

ADDITIONAL INFORMATION For brochure, visit website.

BAY TO OCEAN WRITERS' CONFERENCE

P.O. Box 544, St. Michaels MD 21663. (443)786-4536. E-mail: info@baytoocean.com. Website: www.baytoocean.com. **Contact:** Wilson Wyatt, Jr., Coordinator. Estab. 1998. Annual. Conference held last Saturday in February. Average attendance: 150. Approximately 25 speakers conduct workshops on publishing, agents, editing, marketing, craft, the Internet, writing for television and movies, poetry, fiction, nonfiction, and freelance writing. Site: Chesapeake College, Rt. 213 and Rt. 50, Wye Mills, on Maryland's historic Eastern Shore. Accessible to individuals with disabilities.

COSTS $80-100, students $55. Includes choice of 5 of 19 sessions, continental breakfast, and networking lunch.

ADDITIONAL INFORMATION Mail-in registration form available on website in December prior to the conference. Preregistration is required, no registration at door. Conference usually sells out 1 month in advance. Conference is for all levels of writers.

BIG APPLE WRITING WORKSHOPS, MEET THE AUTHORS/MEET THE AGENTS

IWWG, P.O. Box 810, Gracie Station NY 10028. (212) 737-7536. Fax: (212) 737-9469. E-mail: dirhahn@aol.com. Website: www.iwwg.org. **Contact:** Hannalore Hahn, founder & executive director. Estab. 1980. Semiannual. April 2011, October 2011. Conference duration: 2 days. Average attendance: 200. Workshop. "The three-fold purpose entails: 1) A full day writing workshop; 2) A panel discussion with 12 recently published IWWG members about how they became authors, found agents and publishers; 3) An open house with 8 agents for authors to meet." Previous panels include "Fiction and Nonfiction: Writing and Selling on Both Sides of the Aisle" and "The Writer at Work: Writing Adrift/Writing a Draft."

COSTS $10 for members of IWWG/$220 for nonmembers for both days. Individual sections may be selected and paid for if not attending full conference.

ACCOMMODATIONS Does not offer overnight accommodations. Provides list of area hotels or lodging options.

ADDITIONAL INFORMATION For brochure, send SASE, fax request, call, e-mail, visit website. Agents and editors participate in conference. "We've had over 50 Meet the Author/Meet the Agent events. Close to 4,000 books have been published by IWWG members since our inception in 1976."

BLOCKBUSTER PLOT INTENSIVE WRITING WORKSHOPS (SANTA CRUZ)

Santa Cruz CA. E-mail: contact@blockbusterplots.com. Website: www.blockbusterplots.com. **Contact:** Martha Alderson MA, instructor. Estab. 2000. Held 4 times per year. Conference duration: 2 days. Average attendance: 20. Workshop is intended to help writers create an action, character and thematic plotline for a screenplay, memoir, short story, novel, or creative nonfiction. Site: Conference hall.

COSTS $95 per day.

ACCOMMODATIONS Provides list of area hotels and lodging options.

ADDITIONAL INFORMATION Brochures available by e-mail or on website. Accepts inquiries by e-mail.

BLOODY WORDS MYSTERY CONFERENCE

12 Roundwood Court, Toronto ON M1W 1Z2 Canada. Phone/fax: (416)497-5293. E-mail: soles@sff.net.

Website: www.bloodywords.com. **Contact:** Caro Soles, chair. Estab. 1999. Annual. Last conference held June May 28-30, 2010. Average attendance: 300. Focus: Mystery/true crime/forensics, with Canadian slant. Purpose: To bring readers and writers of the mystery genre together in a Canadian setting. Site: 2011: Victoria, BC; Hotel Grand Pacific; June 3-5; Toronto June 1-3— Downtown Hilton Hotel. Conference includes 2 workshops and 2 tracks of panels, one on factual information such as forensics, agents, scene of the crime procedures, etc., and one on fiction, such as "Death in a Cold Climate," "Murder on the Menu," "Elementary, My Dear Watson," and a First Novelists Panel.

COSTS $175 (Canadian include the banquet and all panels, readings, dealers' room and workshop.

ACCOMMODATIONS Offers block of rooms in hotel; list of optional lodging available. Check website for details.

ADDITIONAL INFORMATION Sponsors short mystery story contest—5,000 word limit; judges are experienced editors of anthologies; fee is $5 (entrants must be registered). Conference information is available now. For brochure visit website. Accepts inquiries by e-mail and phone. Agents and editors participate in conference. "This is a conference for both readers and writers of mysteries, the only one of its kind in Canada. We also run 'The Mystery Cafe,' a chance to get to know a dozen or so authors, hear them read and ask questions (half hour each)."

BLUE RIDGE "AUTUMN IN THE MOUNTAINS" NOVEL RETREAT

(800)588-7222. E-mail: ylehman@bellsouth.net. Website: www.lifeway.com/novelretreat. **Contact:** Yvonne Lehman, director. Estab. 2007. Held annually in October. Retreat held October 16-20, 2011. Limited attendance: 55 (register early). For beginning and advanced novelists. Site: LifeWay/Ridgecrest Conference Center, 20 miles east of Asheville, NC. Faculty: Dr. Angela Hunt, Jeff Gerke, Deborah Raney, Ray Blackston, Ann Tatlock, Yvonne Lehman. No editors or agents. Mornings: large group class. Afternoons: writing time and workshops. Evening: discussion and faculty panel.

COSTS Retreat Tuition: $315; Room: $69-89; Meals: $124.

ACCOMMODATIONS Mountain Laurel Hotel on campus

BLUE RIDGE "SUMMER IN THE MOUNTAINS" NOVEL RETREAT

(800)588-7222. E-mail: ylehman@bellsouth.net. Website: www.gideonfilmfestival.com. **Contact:** Yvonne Lehman, Director. Blue Ridge "Summer in the Mountains" Novel Retreat. Held along with the Gideon Media Arts Conference August 6-11, 2011. For beginning and advanced novelists. Faculty: Andrea Boeshaar, Lynette Eason, Eva Marie Everson, Jeff Gerke, Rene Gutteridge, Dr. Dennis Hensley, Yvonne Lehman, Deborah Raney, Rebeca Seitz, Ann Tatlock.

COSTS Tuition $315, Room $69-89, Meals $159.

BLUE RIDGE MOUNTAINS CHRISTIAN WRITERS CONFERENCE

(800) 588-7222. E-mail: alton@ganskycommunications.com. Website: www.lifeway.com/christianwriters. **Contact:** Alton Gansky, director. Estab. 1999. Annual. Last conference held May 9-13, 2011. Average attendance: 380. All areas of Christian writing including fiction, nonfiction, devotionals, women's fiction, romance, suspense, romance, craft of writing, etc. For beginning and advanced writers. Site: LifeWay/Ridgecrest Conference Center, 20 miles east of Asheville, NC. Companies represented May 18-22, 2008 include AMG Publications, B&H, Focus on the Family, Howard Books, The Upper Room, LifeWay Christian Resources, Christian Writers Guild, Living Ink Books, Hensley Publishing, Today's Christian Woman, Benrey Literary Agency, Les Stobbe Agency, Bethan House, Big Idea (Veggie Tales), MacGregor Literary Agency, The Nashville Group, WinePress, William K. Jensen Literary Agency, et al. Faculty includes professional authors, agents and editors.

COSTS 2010: $315, which includes all sessions, breaks, and a special Wednesday evening Awards Ceremony. Additional on-campus meal package available for $98/person.

ACCOMMODATIONS LifeWay Ridgecrest Conference Center. See website for on-campus room rates.

ADDITIONAL INFORMATION The Blue Ridge "Autumn in the Mountains" Novel retreat will be held annually in October at Ridgecrest/Life Way Conference Center (www.lifeway.com/novelretreat). Sponsors contests for unpublished writers. Awards include trophy and $200 scholarship toward next year's conference. See website for critique service and daily schedule—offering keynote sessions, continuing classes, and workshops.

BOOMING GROUND ONLINE WRITERS STUDIO

Buch E-462, 1866 Main Mall, Creative Writing Program, UBC, Vancouver BC V6T 1Z1 Canada. Fax: (604) 648-8848. E-mail: contact@boomingground.com. Website: www.boomingground.com. **Contact:** Jordan Hall, director. Estab. 1998. Average attendance: 30 per session. Online writing mentorships geared toward beginner, intermediate, and advanced levels in novel, short fiction, poetry, nonfiction, and children's writing and more. Open to students. Online mentorship program-students work for 6 months with a mentor by e-mail, allowing up to 120-240 pages of material to be created. Site: Online and by e-mail.

BOUCHERCON

c/o The Mystery Company. E-mail: registration@bouchercon2011.com. Website: www.bouchercon.com. **Contact:** Jon Jordan, Chair 2011. The Bouchercon is "the world mystery and detective fiction event." Held Sept. 15-18, 2011, in St. Louis, MO. See website for details. Special guests are Robert Randisi and John Lutz.

Annual convention held in late September/early October. The Bouchercon World Mystery Convention will be held in St. Louis, MO September 15-18, 2011. . Chair: Jon Jordan. Average attendance: 1,500. Focus is on mystery, suspense, thriller, and true crime novels. Speakers have included Lawrence Block, Jeremiah Healy, James Lee Burke, Ruth Rendell, Ian Rankin, Michael Connelly, Eileen Dreyer, and Earl Emerson. Agents will be speaking and available for informal meetings with attendees.

COSTS $175 registration fee (covers writing workshops, panels, reception, etc.)

ACCOMMODATIONS **The Renaissance St. Louis Grand Hotel** is now taking reservations for Bouchercon 2011. *Room Rate: $161 for a single.* Link on website.

ADDITIONAL INFORMATION Sponsors Anthony Award for published mystery novel; ballots due prior to conference. Information available on website.

BREAD LOAF WRITERS' CONFERENCE

Middlebury College, Middlebury VT 05753. (802)443-5286. Fax: (802)443-2087. E-mail: ncargill@middlebury.edu. Website: www.middlebury.edu/blwc. **Contact:** Noreen Cargill, administrative manager. Estab. 1926. Annual. Conference held August 10-20, 2011. Conference duration: 10 days. Average attendance: 230. For fiction, nonfiction, poetry. Site: Held at the summer campus in Ripton, Vermont (belongs to Middlebury College). The 2011 faculty includes poets Marianne Boruch, Louise Gluck, A. Van Jordan, James Longenbach, Tom Sleigh, Arthur Sze, and Ellen Bryant Voigt; fiction writers Richard Bausch, Charles Baxter, Maud Casey, Peter Ho Davies, Stacey D'Erasmo, Randall Kenan, Chang-rae Lee, Sigrid Nunez, Joanna Scott, and Luis Alberto Urrea; and creative nonfiction writers Jane Brox, Ted Conover, and David Shields. Special guests include nonfiction writer John Elder and poet Philip Levine.

COSTS $2,345 (includes tuition, housing).

ACCOMMODATIONS Bread Loaf Campus in Ripton, Vermont.

ADDITIONAL INFORMATION 2011 Conference Dates: August 10-20. Location: mountain campus of Middlebury College. Average attendance: 230.

BROOKLYN BOOK FESTIVAL

209 Joralemon St., Brooklyn NY 11201. (718)802-3852. E-mail: ekoch@brooklynbp.nyc.gov. Website: www.brooklynbookfestival.org. **Contact:** Liz Koch. Estab. 2005. Annual 1-day festival. "The Brooklyn Book Festival is a huge, free public event presenting an array of local, national, and international literary stars and emerging authors who represent the exciting world of literature today."

ADDITIONAL INFORMATION For brochure visit website.

CALIFORNIA CRIME WRITERS CONFERENCE

cosponsored by Sisters in Crime/Los Angeles and the Southern California Chapter of Mystery Writers of America, No public address available, E-mail: sistersincrimela@gmail.com. Website: www.ccwconference.org. Estab. 1995. Annual. Conference held June 11-12, 2011; following years TBO. Average attendance: 200. Two-day conference on mystery and crime writing. Offers craft, forensic and career-buildings sessions, 2 keynote speakers, author and agent panels and book signings. Breakfast and lunch both days included.

ADDITIONAL INFORMATION Conference information is available on the website. Website might be down temporarily.

CENTRAL OHIO FICTION WRITERS ANNUAL CONFERENCE

P.O. Box 4213, Newark OH 43058. E-mail: KrisBranch@ymail.com. Website: www.cofw.org. **Contact:** Kris Branch, President. Estab. 1990. Annual. Conference held in Worthington, OH. 2011 Conference dates January 22, 2011. Average attendance: 120. COFW is a chapter of Romance Writers of America. The conference focuses on all romance subgenres and welcomes published writers, prepublished writers and readers. Conference theme: celebrates and fosters writers at every stage of their careers. Best-selling authors provide motivation and instruction; workshops, speakers, and materials cover a broad spectrum of topics. Guest speaker: Award winning author, Kara Lennox.

COSTS COFW members—$118, Others—$128. Price includes Friday evening buffet and Saturday lunch. Registration is completely electronic though you can pay by check. There is a $15 late fee for registrations received after Sept. 27.

ACCOMMODATIONS See www.cofw.org for exact location.

ADDITIONAL INFORMATION Registration form and information available on website or by e-mail.

CENTRUM'S PORT TOWNSEND WRITERS' CONFERENCE

P.O. Box 1158, Port Townsend WA 98368-0958. (360)385-3102. Fax: (360)385-2470. E-mail: info@centrum.org; jhartt@centrum.com. Website: www.centrum.org. **Contact:** Jordan Hartt, director of programs. Estab. 1974. Annual. Conference held mid-July. 2011: July 17-24. Average attendance: 180. Conference to promote poetry, fiction, creative nonfiction "featuring many of the nation's leading writers." Two different workshop options: "New Works" and "Works-in-Progress." Site: The conference is held at Fort Worden State Park on the Strait of Juan de Fuca. "The site is a Victorian-era military fort with miles of beaches, wooded trails and recreation facilities. The park is within the limits of Port Townsend, a historic seaport and arts community, approximately 80 miles northwest of Seattle, on the Olympic Peninsula." Guest speakers participate in addition to full-time faculty.

COSTS Tuition for the Conference is $595. Room and board options range from $205 to $515. Admission to afternoon workshops only is $50 per workshop or $275 for unlimited access to all afternoon workshops. Admission to freewrites or morning writing exercises only is $25 per session. All freewrites, morning writing exercises, and afternoon workshops are free for those who are registered for the core morning workshops. Register online at website.

ACCOMMODATIONS "Modest room and board facilities on site." Also list of hotels/motels/inns/bed & breakfasts/private rentals available.

ADDITIONAL INFORMATION Brochures/guidelines available for SASE or on website. "The conference focus is on the craft of writing and the writing life, not on marketing."

CHILDREN'S LITERATURE CONFERENCE

239 Montauk Hwy, Southampton NY 11968-6700. (631)632-5030. Fax: (631)632-2578. E-mail: southamptonwriters@notes.cc.sunysb.edu. Website: www.stonybrook.edu/writers. **Contact:** Adrienne Unger, administrative coordinator. Annual conference held in July. "The seaside campus of Stony Brook Southampton is located in the heart of the Hamptons, a renowned resort area only 70 miles from New York City. During free time, participants can draw on inspiration from the Atlantic beaches or explore the charming seaside towns." Faculty have included Richard Peck, Tor Seidler, Cindy Kane, Gahan Wilson James McMullan, and Mitchell Kriegman. Among the guest presenters currently scheduled are author/illustrator Jules Feiffer, children's literature historian Leonard Marcus, marketing guru Susan Raab, bestselling author and illustrator team Kate and Jim McMullan, and children's literature specialist Connie Rockman.

COSTS Application fee: $15; tuition, room and board: $1270; tuition only $1125 (includes breakfast and lunch).

ACCOMMODATIONS On-campus housing, doubles and small singles with shared baths, is modest but comfortable. Housing assignment is by lottery. Supplies list of lodging alternatives.

ADDITIONAL INFORMATION "Applicants must complete an application and submit a writing sample of original, unpublished work. See Web for details. Brochure available in January by phone, e-mail, and on website. Accepts inquiries by e-mail, phone, and fax."

CLARION SCIENCE FICTION AND FANTASY WRITERS' WORKSHOP

UCSD 9500 Gilman Drive # 0410, La Jolla CA 92097-0410. (858) 534-2115. E-mail: clarion@ucsd.edu. Website: http://clarion.ucsd.edu. **Contact:** Hadas Blinder, Program Coordinator. Estab. 1968. Annual. Conference duration: 6-week residency in summer (late June-early Aug.). Average attendance: 18. Workshop. "Clarion is a short-story writing workshop focused on fundamentals particular to the writing of science fiction, fantasy and horror." Site: The workshop is held at the UC San Diego campus in the beautiful beach town of La Jolla. Participants reside in campus apartments and attend workshop sessions in a seminar room. Beaches and shopping are within easy reach by public transportation. Summer temperatures in San Diego are normally 70-80°F, dry and comfortable. Our 2011 writers in residence are Nina Kiriki Hoffman, John Scalzi, Elizabeth Bear, David Anthony Durham, John Kessel and Kij Johnson. 2011: June 26-August 6.

COSTS The fees for 2009 (application, tuition, room and board) were approximately $4,500. Scholarships were available.

ACCOMMODATIONS Participants make their own travel arrangements to and from the campus. Campus residency is required. Participants are housed in semiprivate accommodations (private bedroom, shared bathroom) in student apartments. The room and board fee includes three meals a day at a campus dining facility. In 2009 the room and board fee for the six-week residency was approximately $2,500 (included in the $4,500 workshop fee).

ADDITIONAL INFORMATION "Workshop participants are selected on the basis of their potential for highly successful writing careers. Applications are judged by a review panel composed of the workshop instructors. Applicants submit an application ($50) and two complete short stories, each between 2,500 words and 6,000 words in length. The application deadline (typically, March 1) is posted on the Clarion website." Information available in September. For brochure, visit website. Agents and editors frequently participate in Clarion as instructors or guest speakers.

CLARION WEST WRITERS WORKSHOP

P.O. Box 31264, Seattle WA 98103-1264. (206)322-9083. E-mail: info@clarionwest.org. Website: www.clarionwest.org. **Contact:** Leslie Howle, Workshop Director. Annual. Workshop usually held in late June through July. Average attendance: 18. "Conference to prepare students for professional careers in science fiction and fantasy writing." Deadline for applications: March 1. Site: Conference held in Seattle's University district, an urban site close to restaurants and cafés, but not too far from downtown. Faculty: 6 teachers (professional writers and editors established in the field). "Every week a new instructor—each a well-known writer chosen for the quality of his or her work and for professional stature—teaches the class, bringing a unique perspective on speculative fiction. During the fifth week, the workshop is taught by a professional editor."

COSTS $3200 (for tuition, housing, most meals). Limited scholarships are available based on financial need.

ACCOMMODATIONS Workshop tuition, dormitory housing and most meals: $3,200. Students stay onsite in workshop housing at one of the University of Washington's sorority houses. "Students write their own stories every week while preparing critiques of all the other students' work for classroom sessions. This gives participants a more focused, professional approach to their writing. The core of the workshop remains speculative fiction, and short stories (not novels) are the focus." Conference information available in Fall. For brochure/guidelines send SASE, visit website, e-mail, or call. Accepts inquiries by e-mail, phone, SASE. Limited scholarships are available, based on financial need. Students must submit 20-30 pages of ms with 4-page biography and $40 fee ($30 if received prior to Feb. 10) for applications sent by mail or e-mail to qualify for admission.

ADDITIONAL INFORMATION This is a critique based workshop. Students are encouraged to write a story every week; the critique of student material produced at the workshop forms the principal activity of the workshop. Students and instructors critique mss as a group. Conference guidelines are available for a SASE. Visit the website for updates and complete details.

⊕ COD WRITERS' CONFERENCE

P.O. Box 408, Osterville MA 02655. (508)420-0200. E-mail: writers@capecodwriterscenter.org. Website: www.capecodwriterscenter.org. **Contact:** Nancy Rubin Stuart, Artistic Director. Annual Conference. Duration: Third week in August, 5 days. Offers workshops in fiction, commercial fiction, nonfiction, poetry, screen writing, digital communications, getting published, manuscript evaluation, mentoring sessions with faculty

COSTS Vary, average for one 5-day class and registration: $200.

⊕ CONFLUENCE

P.O. Box 3681, Pittsburgh PA 15230-3681. (412)344-0456. E-mail: confluence@parsec-sff.org. Website: www.parsec-sff.org/confluence/whatis.html. Estab.

1996. Confluence is about programming that lets fans of science fiction and fantasy hear about the views and visions of some of the leading authors, editors, and critics in the genre. Annual. July 22-24, 2011. Conference. Site: Doubletree Hotel Pittsburgh Airport.

CRESTED BUTTE WRITERS CONFERENCE

P.O. Box 1361, Crested Butte CO 81224. Website: www.crestedbuttewriters.org/conf.php. **Contact:** Barbara Crawford or Theresa Rizzo, co-coordinators. Estab. 2006. Our conference workshops address a wide variety of writing craft and business. Our most popular workshop is Our First Pages Readings—with a twist. Agents and editors read opening pages volunteered by attendees—with a few best-selling authors' openings mixed in. Think the A/E can identify the best sellers? Not so much. Each year one of our attendees has been mistaken for a best seller and obviously garnered requests from some on the panel. Agents attending: Stephen Barr—Writers house, Marisa Corvisiero—L. Perkins Agency, and Helen Breitwieser—Cornerstone Literary. The agents will be speaking. and available for meetings with attendees through our Pitch and Pages system. Editors attending: Holly Blanck—St. Martin's Press—and Mike Braff—Del Rey/Spectra. Award-winning authors: Robin D. Owens, Sophie Littlefield, Juliet Blackwell, and Kaki Warner. Writers may request additional information by e-mail at: coordinator@conf.crestedbuttewriters.org. FAQ page is online at www.crestedbuttewriters.org/conf_faq.php.

COSTS $330 Nonmembers, $300 members, $297 Early Bird, The Sandy Writing Contest Finalist $280, and groups of 5 or more $280.

ACCOMMODATIONS The conference is held at the lovely Elevation Hotel, located at the Crested Butte Mountain Resort at the base of the ski mountain (Mt. Crested Butte, CO). The quaint historic town lies nestled in a stunning mountain valley 3 short miles from the resort area of Mt. Crested Butte. A free bus runs frequently between the two towns. The closest airport is 10 miles away, in Gunnison CO. Our website lists 3 lodging options besides rooms at the event facility. All condos, motels, and hotel options offer special conference rates. No special travel arrangements are made through the conference; however, information for car rental from Gunnison airport or the Alpine Express shuttle is listed on the conference FAQ page.

DESERT DREAMS CONFERENCE: REALIZING THE DREAM

P.O. Box 27407, Tempe AZ 85285. E-mail: desertdreams@desertroserwa.org; desertdreamsconference@gmail.com. Website: www.desertroserwa.org. **Contact:** Conference coordinator. Estab. 1986. Biennial. Last conference held April 16-18, 2010. Next conference Spring 2012. Average attendance: 250. Desert Dreams Writers' Conference provides authors of all skill levels, from beginner to multi-published, with the tools necessary to take their writing to the next level. Sessions will include general writing, career development, genre-specific, agent/publisher spotlights, as well as an agent/editor panel. There will also be one-on-one appointments with editors or agents, a book signing, and keynote addresses. April 27-29, 2012. Site: Chaparral Suites, Scottsdale, Arizona.

COSTS Vary each year; approximately $175-228 for full conference.

ACCOMMODATIONS Hotels may vary for each conference; it is always a resort location in the Phoenix area.

ADDITIONAL INFORMATION Sponsors contest as part of conference, open to conference attendees only. For brochure, inquiries, contact by e-mail, phone, fax, mail, or visit website. Agents and editors participate in conference.

DINGLE WRITING COURSES

Ballintlea, Ventry, Co Kerry Ireland. Phone/Fax: (353)(66)915-9815. E-mail: info@dinglewritingcourses.ie. Website: www.dinglewritingcourses.ie. **Contact:** Abigail Joffe and Nicholas McLachlan. Estab. 1996. Annual. Writing workshops held 3 or 4 weekends per year in September and October. Average attendance: 14. Creative writing weekends for fiction, poetry, memoir, novel, writing for children, etc. Site: "Writer's Retreat on the Dingle Peninsula." Recent tutors included Niall Williams, Paula Meehan and Kate Thompson.

COSTS 420-445 euros. Some bursaries are available from county arts officers.

ACCOMMODATIONS Provides overnight accomodations.

ADDITIONAL INFORMATION Some workshops require material to be submitted in advance. Accepts inquiries by e-mail, phone, and fax.

DRAGON CON

P.O. Box 16459, Atlanta GA 30321. (770)909-0115. Fax: (770)909-0112. E-mail: dragoncon@dragoncon.org. Website: www.dragoncon.org. Annual. Labor Day Weekend, September 2-5, 2011. "Dragon*Con is the largest multi-media, popular culture convention focusing on science fiction and fantasy, gaming, comics, literature, art, music, and film in the US."

EAST TEXAS CHRISTIAN WRITERS CONFERENCE

The School of Humanities, Dr. Jerry L. Summers, Dean, Scarborough Hall, East Texas Baptist Univ., 1209 N. Grove, Marshall TX 75670. (903)923-2269. Fax: (903)923-2077. E-mail: jhopkins@etbu.edu; jcornish@etbu.edu; contest@etbu.edu. Website: www.etbu.edu/News/CWC; www.etbu.edu/News/CWC/default.htm. **Humanities Secretary:** Joy Cornish. Annual Conference held the second weekend in April, Friday and Saturday, April 9-10, 2010. Conference duration: 2 days (Friday & Saturday). Average attendance: 190. "Primarily we are interested in promoting quality Christian writing that would be accepted in mainstream publishing." Site: We use the classrooms, cafeterias, etc., of East Texas Baptist University. Past conference themes were Back to Basics, Getting Started in Fiction, Writers & Agents, Writing Short Stories, Writing for Newspapers, the Significance of Style, Writing Fillers and Articles, Writing Devotionals, Blogging for Writers, Christian Non-Fiction, Inspirational Writing, E-Publishing, Publishing on Demand, and Editor and Author Relations. Past conference speakers/workshop leaders were David Jenkins, Bill Keith, Pete Litterski, Joe Early Jr., Mary Lou Redding, Marie Chapian, Denny Boultinghouse, Vickie Phelps, Michael Farris, Susan Farris, Pamela Dowd, Donn Taylor, Terry Burns, Donna Walker-Nixon, Lexie Smith, Marv Knox, D.D. Turner, Jim Pence, Andrea Chevalier, Marie Bagnull, and Leonard Goss.

COSTS Visit website.

ACCOMMODATIONS Visit website for a list of local hotels offering a discounted rate.

EMERALD CITY COMICON

800 Convention Place, Washington State Convention Center, Seattle WA 98037. (425)744-2767. Fax: (425)675-0737. E-mail: info@emeraldcitycomicon.com; george@emeraldcitycomicon.com. Website: www.emeraldcitycomicon.com. **Contact:** George Demonakos, operations director. Estab. 2002. Site: 800 Convention Place, Washington State Convention Center, Seattle, WA 98037. Emerald City Comicon, 3333 184th St. SW., Suite G, Lynnwood, WA 98037. Annual. 10th Annual ECCC: March 30-April 1, 2012. "The premiere comic book convention of the Pacific Northwest. Includes comic creators and media guests, various creative and publishing panels, exhibitors, dealers and much more." Guests include Jim Cheung, Cully Hamner, Steve McNiven, Yanick Paquette, Pete Woods and many more.

COSTS $15/day or $25/weekend presale, $20/Sat, $15/Sun or $30/weekend on-site. Subject to change.

ACCOMMODATIONS Offers overnight accommdations. Discounted rate at Roosevelt Hotel, Crowne Plaza, and Red Lion in Seattle.

ADDITIONAL INFORMATION For information, visit website. Editors participate in conference.

FESTIVAL OF FAITH AND WRITING

Department of English, Calvin College, 1795 Knollcrest Circle SE, Grand Rapids MI 49546. (616)526-6770. E-mail: ffw@calvin.edu. Website: www.calvin.edu/festival. **Contact:** English Dept. Estab. 1990. E-mail all inquiries about attendance (for registration brochures, program information, etc.). Biennial conference usually held in April of even years. Conference duration: 3 days. Average attendance: 1,800. The Festival of Faith and Writing encourages serious, imaginative writing by all writers interested in the intersections of literature and belief. Site: The festival is held at Calvin College in Grand Rapids, MI, 180 miles north of Chicago. Focus is on fiction, nonfiction, memoir, poetry, drama, children's, young adult, literary criticism, film, and song lyrics. Past speakers have included Annie Dillard, John Updike, Katherine Paterson, Elie Wiesel, Joyce Carol Oates, Leif Enger, Salman Rushdie, and Marilynne Robinson.

COSTS Consult festival website.

ACCOMMODATIONS Shuttles are available to and from local hotels. Shuttles are also available for overflow parking lots. A list of hotels with special rates for conference attendees is available on the festival website. High school and college students can arrange on-campus lodging by e-mail.

ADDITIONAL INFORMATION Online registration opens in October. Accepts inquiries by e-mail and phone

FISHERMAN'S WHARF WRITERS CONFERENCE

Fort Mason, San Francisco CA (800)250-8290. E-mail: algonkian@webdelsol.com. Website: http://algonkian-conferences.com. 2011 dates to be announced. Annual. Conference duration: 5 days. "Using our unique model-and-context method, Algonkian students will study and apply techniques of craft, structure, and style culled from over 20 successful authors (and dramatists) including Ann Patchett, Ken Kesey, Annie Proulx, F. Scott Fitzgerald, Tennessee Williams, Michael Chabon, Gail Godwin, Ernest Hemingway, V. Nabokov, Flannery O'Connor, Barbara Kingsolver, and Robert Graves."

COSTS $495

FLATHEAD RIVER WRITERS CONFERENCE

P.O. Box 7711, Kalispeil MT 59904-7711. E-mail: answers@authorsoftheflathead.org. Website: www.authorsoftheflathead.org. **Contact:** Director. Estab. 1990. Annual. Next general conference October 1-2, 2011. Flathead Valley Community College, Kalilspell, Montana. Recent speakers: Cricket Pechstein (agent) and Sandy Novack-Gottshall (fiction.)

ACCOMMODATIONS Rooms are available at a discounted rate.

ADDITIONAL INFORMATION Come prepared to learn from renowned speakers and enjoy this spectacular area near Glacier National Park. Confirmed presenters for Oct. 1-2, 2011: Agents Deborah Herman of the Jeff Herman Agency, Katharine Sand of the Sarah Jane Freymann Literary Agency, children's book author Kathi Appelt, best-selling memoir author Laura Munson. Watch our website for additional speakers and other details. Register early, as seating is limited.

THE GLEN WORKSHOP

Image, 3307 Third Ave. W., Seattle WA 98119. (206)281-2988. Fax: (206)281-2335. E-mail: glenworkshop@imagejournal.org; jmullins@imagejournal.org. Website: www.imagejournal.org/glen. Estab. 1991. Writing classes. Art classes. A seminar on arts and aesthetics. A retreat option. The Glen Workshop combines an intensive learning experience with a lively festival of the arts. It takes place in the stark, dramatic beauty of the Sangre de Cristo mountains and within easy reach of the rich cultural, artistic, and spiritual traditions of northern New Mexico. Annual. Theme: Creativity from the Margins: Art as Witness. Conference duration: 1 week. Average attendance: 150-200. Workshop focuses on "fiction, poetry, spiritual writing, songwriting, playwriting, painting, drawing, and mixed media. Run by *Image*, a literary journal with a religious focus. The Glen welcomes writers who practice or grapple with religious faith." Site: features "presentations and readings by the faculty." Faculty has included Lauren F. Winner (spiritual writing), B.H. Fairchild and Marilyn Nelson (poetry), Mark St. Germain (playwriting), and Over the Rhine (songwriting).

COSTS See costs online. A limited number of partial scholarships are available.

ACCOMMODATIONS Offers dorm rooms, dorm suites, and apartments.

ADDITIONAL INFORMATION Like *Image*, the Glen is grounded in a Christian perspective, but its tone is informal and hospitable to all spiritual wayfarers. Depending on the teacher, participants may need to submit workshop material prior to arrival (usually 10-25 pages).

GOTHAM WRITERS' WORKSHOP

WritingClasses.com, 555 Eighth Ave., Suite 1402, New York NY 10018. (212)974-8377. Fax: (212)307-6325. E-mail: dana@write.org. Website: www.writingclasses.com. Estab. 1993. "Classes held throughout the year. There are four terms, beginning in January, April, June/July, September/October." Conference duration: 10-week, 6-week, 1-day, and online courses offered. Average attendance: approximately 1,300 students per term, 6,000 students per year. Offers craft-oriented creative writing courses in fiction writing, screenwriting, nonfiction writing, memoir writing, novel writing, children's book writing, playwriting, poetry, songwriting, mystery writing, science fiction writing, romance writing, television writing, documentary film writing, feature article writing, travel writing, creative writing, and business writing. Also, Gotham Writers' Workshop offers a teen program, private instruction, and classes on selling your work. Site: Classes are held at various schools in New York City as well as online at www.writingclasses.com. View a sample online class on the website.

COSTS $395/10-week workshops; $125 for the four-week online selling seminars and 1-day intensive courses; $295 for 6-week creative writing and business writing classes.

ADDITIONAL INFORMATION "Participants do not need to submit workshop material prior to their first class." Sponsors a contest for a free 10-week online creative writing course (value=$420) offered each term. Students should fill out a form online at www.writingclasses.com to participate in the contest. The winner is randomly selected. For brochure send e-mail, visit website, call or fax. Accepts inquiries by e-mail, phone, fax. Agents and editors participate in some workshops.

GREATER LEHIGH VALLEY WRITERS GROUP 'THE WRITE STUFF' WRITERS CONFERENCE

3650 Nazareth Pike, PMB #136, Bethlehem PA 18020-1115. (610)844-2949. E-mail: write@glvwg.org. Website: www.glvwg.org. **Contact:** Donna Brennan, chair. Estab. 1993. Annual. Last conference was March 24-26, 2011. Conference duration: 3 days with pre-conference workshops. Average attendance: 160. This conference features workshops in all genres. Our keynote speaker, Donald Maass, addressed the conference over a delicious hot meal."

COSTS Members, $100 (includes Friday evening session and all Saturday workshops, 2 meals, and a chance to pitch to an editor or agent); nonmembers, $120. Late registration, $135. Pre-conference workshops require an additional fee.

ADDITIONAL INFORMATION "The Writer's Flash contest is judged by conference participants. Write 100 words or less in fiction, creative nonfiction, or poetry. Brochures available in January by SASE, or by phone, e-mail, or on website. Accepts inquiries by SASE, e-mail or phone. Agents and editors attend conference. For updated info refer to the website, and our conference blog http://glvwritersconference.blogspot.com/. Greater Lehigh Valley Writer's Group conference has remained one of the most friendly conferences and gives you the most for your money. Breakout rooms offer craft topics, business of publishing, editor and agent panels. Book fair with book signing by published authors and presenters."

GREAT LAKES WRITERS FESTIVAL

Lakeland College, P.O. Box 359, Sheboygan WI 53082-0359. E-mail: elderk@lakeland.edu. Website: www.greatlakeswritersfestival.org. Estab. 1991. Annual. Last conference held Nov. 4-5, 2010. Conference duration: 2 days. "Festival celebrates the writing of poetry, fiction and creative nonfiction." Site: Lakeland College is a small, 4-yr. liberal arts college of 235 acres, a beautiful campus in a rural setting, founded in 1862. No themes or panels, just readings and workshops. 2011 faculty: Joyce Dyer and Hailey Leithauser.

COSTS Free and open to the public. Participants may purchase meals and must arrange for their own lodging.

ACCOMMODATIONS Does not offer overnight accommodations. Provides list of area hotels or lodging options.

ADDITIONAL INFORMATION All participants who would like to have their writing considered as an object for discussion during the festival workshops must submit it to Karl Elder electronically by Oct. 15. Participants may submit material for workshops in one genre only (poetry, fiction or creative nonfiction). Sponsors contest. Contest entries must contain the writer's name and address on a separate title page, be in type, and be submitted as clear, hard copy on Friday at the festival registration table. Entries may be in each of three genres per participant, yet only one poem, one story, and/or one nonfiction piece may be entered. There are two categories—high school students on one hand, all others on the other—of cash awards for first place in each of the three genres. The judges reserve the right to decline to award a prize in one or more of the genres. Judges will be the editorial staff of *Seems* (AKA *Word of Mouth*), excluding the festival coordinator, Karl Elder. Information available in September. For brochure, visit website.

GREEN LAKE CHRISTIAN WRITERS CONFERENCE

W2511 State Road 23, Green Lake Conference Center, Green Lake, WI 54941-9599 (920)294-3323; (920)294-3848. E-mail: program@glcc.org. Website: www.glcc.org. "Come learn, write and celebrate with us!" "Affordable, inspirational conference for new or well-published writers. May write for the secular or Christian market or both. Workshop leaders are well-published and are experienced teachers. Spend 12 hours of classroom time in any of these areas: fiction, nonfiction, poetry, inspirational, curriculum, publishing for pastors. Special features: writers' contest, manuscript review, one-on-one with leaders, vespers, devotions, music, bookstore, writers' own area for display and sales, Writers' Showcase celebration. A dozen or more optional afternoon seminars and evening panels which cover marketing, internet use, specialized writing, and more." Site: south central WI on the state's deepest lake, with 2½ miles of shoreline and 1,000 acres of land, including outstanding golf course.

ACCOMMODATIONS Hotels, lodges, and all meeting rooms are a/c. Affordable rates, excellent meals.
ADDITIONAL INFORMATION Brochure and scholarship info from website or contact Jan White (920-294-7327). To register, call 920-294-3323.

GREEN MOUNTAIN WRITERS CONFERENCE

47 Hazel St., Rutland, VT 05701 (802)236-6133. E-mail: ydaley@sbcglobal.net. Website: www.vermontwriters.com. Estab. 1999. Annual. Conference duration: 5 days. Average attendance: 40. "The conference is an opportunity for writers at all stages of their development to hone their skills in a beautiful, lakeside environment where published writers across genres share tips and give feedback." Site: Conference held at Tinmouth Pavilion, an old dance pavillion on a 5-acre site on a remote pond in Tinmouth, VT. Past features include Place in Story: the Importance of Environment; Creating Character through Description, Dialogue, Action, Reaction, and Thought; the Collision of Real Events and Imagination. Costs $500 before June 15, $525 after. Fee includes lunch, snacks, beverages, readings. 2010 staff: Yvonne Daley, Stephen Sandy, Joni B. Cole, Chuck Clarino, Tom Smith, Brad Kessler and Verandah Porche. This year, along with these professional authors, several writers who have self-published their books or worked with small publishers will share their experiences and offer advice to those who want to explore this option: Stephen Sandy and Brad Kessler. Both have publishing careers and experience in leading writing workshops.
COSTS $500 before July 1; $525 after July 1. Partial scholarships are available.
ACCOMMODATIONS "We have made arrangements with a major hotel in nearby Rutland and 3 area bed and breakfast inns for special accommodations and rates for conference participants. You must make your own reservations."
ADDITIONAL INFORMATION Participants' mss can be read and commented on at a cost. Sponsors contests. Conference publishes a literary magazine featuring work of participants. Brochures available in January on website or for SASE, e-mail. Accepts inquiries by SASE, e-mail, phone. "We offer the opportunity to learn from some of the nation's best writers at a small, supportive conference in a lakeside setting that allows one-to-one feedback. Participants often continue to correspond and share work after conferences." Further information available on website, by e-mail, or by phone.

HEART TALK

Women's Center for Ministry, Western Seminary, 5511 SE Hawthorne Blvd., Portland OR 97215-3367. (800)517-1800, ext. 1931. Fax: (503)517-1889. E-mail: wcm@westernseminary.edu. Website: www.westernseminary.edu/women. Estab. 1998. Conference duration: 1 day. Average attendance: 100+. Every other year (alternates with speaker's conferences). March 12, 2011 will be next writer's conference. Information will be available on website as it develops. Previous keynote speakers have included Robin Jones Gunn, Patricia Rushford, Deborah Hedstrom-Page, and more. Workshop sessions and 1:1 consultation with professional writers/editors. Topics for new and advanced writers may include: publishing, editing, fiction, market trends, dialogue, screenwriting, websites, book proposals, critique groups, nonfiction, and more. "Heart Talk provides inspirational training for men and women desiring to write for publication and/or speak publicly."
COSTS 2008: $65. See website for more information.
ACCOMMODATIONS Western Seminary has a chapel and classrooms to accommodate various-size groups. The campus has a peaceful, parklike setting with beautiful lawns, trees, and flowers, plus an inviting fountain and pond. Please check website for further details as they become available.
ADDITIONAL INFORMATION Conference infomation is available online, by e-mail, phone, or fax.

HIGHLIGHTS FOUNDATION FOUNDERS WORKSHOPS

814 Court St., Honesdale PA 18437. (570)253-1172. Fax: (570)253-0179. E-mail: contact@highlightsfoundation.org. Website: www.highlightsfoundation.org/pages/current/FWsched_preview.html. **Contact:** Kent L. Brown Jr. Estab. 2000. "Workshops geared toward those interested in writing and illustrating for children, intermediate and advanced levels." Classes offered include: Writing Novels for Young Adults, Biography, Nonfiction Writing, Writing Historical Fiction, Wordplay: Writing Poetry for Children, Heart of the Novel, Nature Writing for Kids, Visual Art of the Picture Book, The Whole Novel Workshop, and more (see website for updated list).
COSTS 2009 costs ranged from $795-1195, including meals, lodging, materials, and much more. "Our scholarship-aid program serves those who may not be able to bear the costs of our programs. In 2009 more

than 100 individuals received scholarships or other financial aid."

ACCOMMODATIONS Coordinates pickup at local airport. Offers overnight accommodations. Participants stay in guest cabins on the wooded grounds surrounding Highlights Founders' home adjacent to the house/conference center.

ADDITIONAL INFORMATION Some workshops require pre-workshop assignment. Brochure available for SASE, by e-mail, on website, by phone, by fax. Accepts inquiries by phone, fax, e-mail, SASE. Editors attend conference. "Applications will be reviewed and accepted on a first-come, first-served basis, applicants must demonstrate specific experience in writing area of workshop they are applying for—writing samples are required for many of the workshops."

HIGHLIGHTS FOUNDATION WRITERS WORKSHOP AT CHAUTAUQUA

814 Court St., Honesdale PA 18431. (570)253-1192. Fax: (570)253-0179. E-mail: contact@highlightsfoundation.org. Website: www.highlightsfoundation.org. Estab. 1985.

COSTS 2009 was $2,400 (includes all meals, conference supplies, gate pass to Chautauqua Institution).

ACCOMMODATIONS We coordinate ground transportation to and from airports, trains, and bus stations in the Erie, Pennsylvania, and Jamestown/Buffalo, New York, area. We also coordinate accommodations for conference attendees.

ADDITIONAL INFORMATION "We offer the opportunity for attendees to submit a manuscript for review at the conference. Workshop brochures/guidelines are available upon request."

TONY HILLERMAN WRITER'S CONFERENCE

1063 Willow Way, Santa FE NM 87505. (505)471-1565. E-mail: wordharvest@wordharvest.com. Website: www.wordharvest.com. **Contact:** Jean Schaumberg, co-director. Estab. 2004. Annual. Conference duration: 3 days. Average attendance: 100. Site: Hotel Santa Fe. First day: Author/teacher Sandi Ault, focuses on the art of writing. Other programs focus on creating memorable plots and the business of writing. We'll honor the winner of the Tony Hillerman Prize for best first mystery at a dinner with keynote speaker Douglas Preston, a New York Times best-selling author. A "flash critique" session, open to any interested attendee, will add to the fun and information.

COSTS Previous year's costs: $395 per registration.

ACCOMMODATIONS Hotel Santa Fe offers $115 single or double occupancy. Nov. 9-13 Book online with the hotel.

ADDITIONAL INFORMATION Sponsors a $10,000 first mystery novel contest with St. Martin's Press and a mystery short story contest with *New Mexico Magazine*. Brochures available in July for SASE, by phone, e-mail, and on website. Accepts inquiries by SASE, phone, e-mail. Deadline for the Hillerman Mystery Competition is June 1; August 15 for the Hillerman Short Story contest.

HOW TO BE PUBLISHED WORKSHOPS

P.O. Box 100031, Birmingham AL 35210-3006. E-mail: mike@writing2sell.com. Website: www.writing2sell.com. **Contact:** Michael Garrett. Estab. 1986. Workshops are offered continuously year-round at various locations. Conference duration: 1 session. Average attendance: 10-15. Workshops to "move writers of category fiction closer to publication." Focus is not on how to write, but how to get published. Site: Workshops held at college campuses and universities. Themes include marketing, idea development, and manuscript critique.

COSTS $49-79.

ADDITIONAL INFORMATION "Special critique is offered, but advance submission is not required." Workshop information available on website. Accepts inquiries by e-mail.

HUMBER SCHOOL FOR WRITERS SUMMER WORKSHOP

3199 Lake Shore Blvd. West, Toronto ON M8V 1K8 Canada. (416)675-6622 ext. 3448. E-mail: antanas.sileika@humber.ca. Website: www.humber.ca/creativeandperformingarts. **Contact:** Antanas Sileika, Artistic Director. Annual. Workshop held second week in July. Conference duration: 1 week. Average attendance: 100. Focuses on fiction, poetry, creative nonfiction. Site: Humber College's Lakeshore campus in Toronto. Panels cover success stories, small presses, large presses, agents. Faculty: Changes annually. 2009 included Martin Amis, Rachel Kushner, Joe Kertes, Alistair Macleod, David Mitchell, Nino Ricci, Wayson Choy, Bruce Jay Friedman, Kim Moritsugu, Olive Senior. Julia Glass and Richard Bausch join us in 2011.

COSTS Workshop fee is $950 Canadian.

ACCOMMODATIONS Provides lodging. Residence fee is approximately $500 Canadian.

ADDITIONAL INFORMATION Participants "must submit sample writing no longer than 15 pages approximately 4 weeks before workshop begins." Brochures available early March by e-mail, phone, fax. Accepts inquiries by e-mail, phone, fax. Agents and editors participate in conference.

INDIANA UNIVERSITY WRITERS' CONFERENCE

464 Ballantine Hall, 1020 E. Kirkwood Ave., Bloomington IN 47405-7103. (812)855-1877. Fax: (812)855-9535. E-mail: writecon@indiana.edu. Website: www.indiana.edu/~writecon. **Contact:** Bob Bledsoe, director. Estab. 1940. Annual. Conference/workshops held in June. Average attendance: 115. "The Indiana University Writers' Conference believes in a craft-based teaching of fiction writing. We emphasize an exploration of creativity through a variety of approaches, offering workshop-based craft discussions, classes focusing on technique, and talks about the careers and concerns of a writing life." 2011 faculty: Dan Chaon, Tony Ardizzone, Patrick Rozal, Lynda Barry, Julia Story, Jill Godmilow, Gary Ferguson.

COSTS 2011 cost: Workshop = $525/week. Classes only = $275/week. Information on accommodations available on website.

ADDITIONAL INFORMATION Fiction workshop applicants must submit up to 25 pages of prose. Registration information available for SASE, by e-mail, or on website. Spaces still available in all workshops and classes for 2011.

INTERNATIONAL COMIC-CON

Comic-Con International, P.O. Box 128458, San Diego CA 92112-8458. (619)491-2475. Fax: (619)414-1022. E-mail: cci-info@comic-con.org. Website: www.comic-con.org/cci/. **Contact:** Gary Sassaman, director of print/publications. Annual. Conference duration: 4 days. Average attendance: 104,000. "The comics industry's largest expo, hosting writers, artists, editors, agents, publishers, buyers and sellers of comics and graphic novels." Site: San Diego Convention Center. "Nearly 300 programming events, including panels, seminars and previews, on the world of comics, movies, television, animation, art, and much more." Legendary comics creator Neal Adams was a special guest for 2010, plus a diverse lineup of special guests. We're also, of course, featuring Golden and Silver Age creators, sf/fantasy writers and artists, and longtime Comic-Con friends. 2006 special guests included Ray Bradbury, Forrest J. Ackerman, Sergio Aragones, John Romita Sr., J. Michael Straczynski, Daniel Clowes, George Perez.

COSTS $50 by April 19, $55 by June 7, $65 at the door. Special discounts for children and seniors.

ACCOMMODATIONS Does not offer overnight accommodations. Provides list of area hotels or lodging options. Special conference hotel and airfare discounts available. See website for details.

ADDITIONAL INFORMATION For brochure, visit website. Agents and editors participate in conference.

INTERNATIONAL MUSIC CAMP CREATIVE WRITING WORKSHOP

111-11th Ave SW, Minot ND 58701. (701)838-8472. E-mail: info@internationalmusiccamp.com. Website: www.internationalmusiccamp.com. **Contact:** Dr. Timothy Wollenzien, camp director. Estab. 1956. Annual. Average attendance: 35. "The workshop offers students the opportunity to refine their skills in thinking, composing and writing in an environment that is conducive to positive reinforcement. In addition to writing poems, essays and stories, individuals are encourgaged to work on their own area of interest with conferencing and feedback from the course instructor." Site: International Peace Garden on the border between the US and Canada. "Similar to a university campus, several dormitories, classrooms, lecture halls and cafeteria provide the perfect site for such a workshop. The beautiful and picturesque International Peace Garden provides additional inspiration to creative thinking." Instructor: Kathy Coudle-King.

COSTS $370, includes tuition, room and board. Early bird registration (postmarked by May 1) $355.

ACCOMMODATIONS Airline and depot shuttles are available upon request. Housing is included in the $355 fee.

ADDITIONAL INFORMATION Conference infomation is available in September. For brochure visit website, e-mail, call, or fax. Accepts inquiries by e-mail, phone and fax.

INTERNATIONAL READERS THEATRE WORKSHOPS

P.O. Box 421262, San Diego CA 92142. (858)277-4274. Fax: (858)277-4222. E-mail: marlene1@san.rr.com. Website: www.readerstheatreinstitute.com. **Contact:** Arlene McCoy. Estab. 1974. Average attendance: 25-35. Workshop on "all aspects of Readers Theatre with emphasis on scriptmaking." Site: Primrose Hill, London.

COSTS $1,975 includes housing for two weeks (twin

accommodations), breakfast, complimentary mid-morning coffee break, and all Institute fees for first-time participants.

ADDITIONAL INFORMATION One-on-one critiques available between writer and faculty (if members). Conference information available now. For reservation form/guidelines, visit website, e-mail, fax, or call. Accepts inquiries by fax, phone, e-mail. Conference offers up to 12 graduate credits. For more information on credit, contact Larisa Kruze, Univ. of Southern Maine, (207) 780-5942.

INTERNATIONAL WOMEN'S WRITING GUILD "REMEMBER THE MAGIC" ANNUAL SUMMER CONFERENCE

P.O. Box 810, Gracie Station, New York NY 10028-0082. (212)737-7536. Fax: (212)737-9469. E-mail: dirhahn@aol.com. Website: www.iwwg.com. **Contact:** Hannelore Hahn, Exec. Director. Estab. 1978. Annual. Conference held in the summer. Conference duration: 1 week. Average attendance: 400. The conference features 40 workshops held every day on every aspect of writing and the arts.

COSTS $1,399 for 7 days; 5-day, weekend, and commuter rates are also available. Includes meals and lodging.

ACCOMMODATIONS Modern, air-conditioned and non-air-conditioned dormitories—single and/or double occupancy. Meals served cafeteria-style with choice of dishes. Variety of fresh fruits, vegetables, and salads have been found plentiful, even by vegetarians. Conference information is available now. E-mail, call, visit website, or fax. "The conference is for women only."

IOWA SUMMER WRITING FESTIVAL

C215 Seashore Hall, University of Iowa, Iowa City IA 52242. (319)335-4160. Fax: (319)335-4743. E-mail: iswfestival@uiowa.edu. Website: www.uiowa.edu/~iswfest. Estab. 1987.

COSTS $560 for full week; $280 for weekend workshop. Housing and meals are separate. Housing and meals are separate. See registration info online.

ACCOMMODATIONS Accommodations available at area hotels. Information on overnight accommodations available by phone or on website.

ADDITIONAL INFORMATION Brochures are available in February. Inquire via e-mail or on website.

IWWG ANNUAL SUMMER CONFERENCE

International Women's Writing Guild "Remember the Magic" Annual Summer Conference, International Women's Writing Guild, P.O. Box 810, Gracie Station, New York NY 10028. (212)737-7536. Fax: (212)737-9469. E-mail: iwwg@iwwg.org. Website: www.iwwg.org. **Contact:** Hannelore Hahn, executive director. Writer and illustrator workshops geared toward all levels. Offers over 50 different workshops—some are for children's book writers and illustrators. Also sponsors other events throughout the U.S. Annual workshops. "Remember the Magic" workshops held every summer for a week. Length of each session: 90 minutes; sessions take place for an entire week. Registration limited to 500. Cost of workshop: $1,399 (includes complete program, room and board). Write for more information. "This workshop takes place at Yale University, New Haven, CT."

COSTS $1,399 (includes complete program, room and board)

IWWG EARLY SPRING IN CALIFORNIA CONFERENCE

International Women's Writing Guild, P.O. Box 810, Gracie Station, New York NY 10028-0082. (212)737-7536. Fax: (212)737-9469. E-mail: iwwg@iwwg.org. Website: www.iwwg.org. **Contact:** Hannelore Hahn, Exec. Director. Estab. 1976. Annual conference held the second week in March. Average attendance: 50. Conference promotes creative writing, personal growth, and voice.

COSTS $350/members; $380/nonmembers for weekend program with room and board; $125 for weekend program without room and board.

ACCOMMODATIONS All participants stay at the conference site or may commute.

ADDITIONAL INFORMATION Brochures and guidelines are available online or for a SASE. Inquire via e-mail or fax.

JACKSON HOLE WRITERS CONFERENCE

PO Box 1974, Jackson WY 83001. (307)413-3332. E-mail: nicole@jacksonholewritersconference.com. Website: www.jacksonholewritersconference.com. Estab. 1991. The Jackson Hole Writers Conference draws a wide range of participants, from beginners to published writers. Site: Center for the Arts. The conference is directed toward fiction, poetry, travel/adventure magazine, young adult playwriting, and creative nonfiction, offering programs relevant to all 5 disciplines: story structure, character development, narrative thrust, work habits, and business techniques. In addition, separate sessions deal with skills particular to each specialty. "We offer three one-on-one manuscript critiques to each participant." Featuring Janet Fitch, Winifred Gallagher, Jeff Chu, and Tim Cahill.

COSTS $355-385, includes all workshops, speaking events, cocktail party, BBQ, and goodie bag with dining coupons. $75 spouse/guest registration; $50 ms evaluation; $75 extended ms evaluation. "You must register for conference to be eligible for manuscript evaluation."

ADDITIONAL INFORMATION Held at the Center for the Arts in Jackson, Wyoming, and online.

JAMES BONNET'S STORYMAKING: THE MASTER CLASS

P.O. Box 7484, Santa Monica CA 90406. (310)451-5418. E-mail: bonnet@storymaking.com. Website: www.storymaking.com/seminars. **Contact:** James Bonnet. Estab. 1990. Intensive weekend seminars held February and October. 7-day writer's workshop retreats held in April and September. Website: www.storymaking.com//seminarandworkshopretreat/ and www.storymaking.com/maryland-writers-workshop. Conference duration: 2 days. Average attendance: 25. Conferences focus on fiction, mystery, and screenwriting. "Seminars focus on mastery of the novel and screenplay arts through an understanding of story and guides writers from inspiration to the final draft. Topics include The Hidden Structures All Great Stories have in Common, The Essence of Story- That Without Which There Would be No Story, The Creative Unconscious, Metaphor, Creating Great Dialogue and Charismatic Characters, The Fundamentals of Plot, Structure, Genre, Conflict, Suspense, and more. Workshops/Retreats include weekend seminar plus 5 days working one-on-one with James Bonnet. James Bonnet will be the speaker."

COSTS $375 for weekend seminar. $1,650 for 7-day workshop/retreat.

ACCOMMODATIONS Provides a list of area hotels or lodging options.

ADDITIONAL INFORMATION For brochure, e-mail, visit website, or call. Accepts inquiries by SASE, e-mail, phone, and fax. "James Bonnet is the author of *Stealing Fire from the Gods: The Complete Guide to Story for Writers and Filmmakers.*"

KENTUCKY WOMEN WRITERS CONFERENCE

232 E. Maxwell, Lexington KY 40506. E-mail: kentuckywomenwriters@gmail.com. Website: www.uky.edu/wwc/. **Contact:** Julie Wrinn, Director. Estab. 1979.Annual. Conference held in March. Conference duration: 3 days. Average attendance: 300-400. Conference covers all genres: poetry, fiction, creative nonfiction, academic. The KWWC highlights a theme every year and considers both creative and academic reflections on this theme. Site: Held at the University of Kentucky and several historic downtown Lexington locations, including the Carnegie Center for Literacy and Learning.

COSTS $120 for 3 days. Some snacks included. Meals and accommodations are not included.

ADDITIONAL INFORMATION Sponsors fiction-writing contest. Length: 10 pages double-spaced. Prize: $100, publication on website, reading at conference. Judged by board members, authors, and student interns. Brochures available in December by phone, e-mail, or on website. Inquiries also accepted by SASE. "The KWWC is always a life-changing event. Authors and participants consistently rave about the quality of programming and level of energy."

KENYON REVIEW WRITERS WORKSHOP

The Kenyon Review, Kenyon College, Gambier OH 43022. (740) 427-5207. Fax: (740) 427-5417. E-mail: writers@kenyonreview.org. Website: www.kenyonreview.org. **Contact:** Anna Duke Reach, director. Estab. 1990. Annual. Workshop held mid to late June. Conference duration: 8 days. Average attendance: 60-70. Participants apply in poetry, fiction, or literary nonfiction, and then participate in intensive daily workshops that focus on the generation and revision of significant new work. Workshop leaders have included David Baker, Ron Carlson, Rebecca McClanahan, Meghan O'Rourke, Linda Gregorson, Dinty Moore, Tara Ison, Jane Hamilton, Lee K. Abbott, and Nancy Zafris.

COSTS $1,995 includes tuition, room and board.

ACCOMMODATIONS The workshop operates a shuttle to and from Gambier and the airport in Columbus, Ohio. Offers overnight accommodations. Participants are housed in Kenyon College student housing. The cost is covered in the tuition.

ADDITIONAL INFORMATION Application includes a writing sample. Admission decisions are made on a rolling basis. Workshop information is available online at www.kenyonreview.org/workshops in November. For brochure send e-mail, visit website, call, fax. Accepts inquiries by SASE, e-mail, phone, fax.

KILLER NASHVILLE

P.O. Box 680686, Franklin TN 37068-0686. (615)599-4032. E-mail: contact@killernashville.com. Website: www.killernashville.com. **Contact:** Clay Stafford. Estab. 2006. Annual. Next events: August 24-26, 2012. Nashville, TN. Conference duration: 4 days. Average attendance: 200+. "Conference designed for writers and fans of mysteries and thrillers, including authors (fiction and nonfiction), playwrights, and screenwriters. 2011 Guest of Honor is Donald Bain. 2012 Guest of Honor to be announced. Sponsors include Middle Tennessee State Univ., Barnes & Noble Booksellers, Mystery Writers of America, Sisters in Crime, First Tennessee Bank, Landmark Booksellers, and the *Nashville Scene*. Law enforcement workshop parters include the Federal Bureau of Investigation (FBI), the Tennessee Bureau of Investigations (TBI), Alcohol, Tobacco, & Firearms (ATF), Franklin Police Department, Brentwood Police Department, and Wilson County Sheriff's Department. Agents, editors and industry professionals have included Jill Marr (Sandra Dijkstra Agency), Carey Nelson Burch (William Morris Agency), Lucienne Diver (the Knight Literary Agency), Miriam Kress (Irene Goodman Literary Agency), Deni Dietz (Five Star/Cengage) and Maryglenn McCombs (Oceanview Publishing). Event includes book signings and panels." Past panelists included authors Michael Connelly, Carol Higgins Clark, Bill Bass, Gregg Hurwitz, Hallie Ephron, Chris Grabenstein, Rhonda Pollero, P.J. Parrish, Reed Farrel Coleman, Kathryn Wall, Mary Saums, Don Bruns, Bill Moody, Richard Helms, Alexandra Sokoloff, and Steven Womack.

Early bird discount sale ends March 1, 2011.

COSTS Signings events are free; current prices for events available on website.

ADDITIONAL INFORMATION "Additional infomation about registration is provided at www.KillerNashville.com."

LEAGUE OF UTAH WRITERS' ANNUAL ROUNDUP

P.O. Box 18430, Kearns UT 84118. E-mail: ediddy.luw@gmail.com; writerscache435@gmail.com. Website: www.luwriters.org/index.html. **Contact:** Edwin Smith, president; Tim Keller, president elect.

COSTS Early bird registration (Deadline August 26) is $120 for members; or $150 after August 26. Cost for nonmembers is $180. Price includes 3 meals, all workshops, general sessions, a syllabus, handouts, and conference packet.

ACCOMMODATIONS Roundup will be held at the Riverwoods Conference Center with lodging available at the Marriott Springhill Suites, (adjacent to the Conference Center) phone 435-750-5180 in Logan, Utah, September 16-17, 2011.

ADDITIONAL INFORMATION Check website www.luwriters.org for updates and specifics.

LEDIG HOUSE INTERNATIONAL WRITERS RESIDENCY

55 Fifth Ave., 15th Floor, New York NY 10003. (212)206-6114. Website: www.artomi.org/ledig. Residency duration: 2 weeks to 2 months. Average attendance: Up to 20 writers per session. Residency. Site: "Up to 20 writers per session—10 at a given time—live and write on the stunning 300 acre grounds and sculpture park that overlooks the Catskill Mountains." Deadline: October 20, 2011.

ACCOMMODATIONS Residents provide their own transportation. Offers overnight accommodations.

ADDITIONAL INFORMATION "Agents and editors from the New York publishing community are invited for dinner and discussion. Bicycles, a swimming pool, and nearby tennis court are available for use."

THE MACDOWELL COLONY

100 High St., Peterborough NH 03458. (603)924-3886. Fax: (603)924-9142. E-mail: admissions@macdowellcolony.org. Website: www.macdowellcolony.org. Estab. 1907. Open to writers and playwrights, composers, visual artists, film/video artists, interdisciplinary artists and architects. Site: includes main building, library, 3 residence halls, and 32 individual studios on over 450 mostly wooded acres, 1 mile from center of small town in southern New Hampshire. Available up to 8 weeks year-round. Provisions for the writer include meals, private sleeping room, individual secluded studio. Accommodates variable number of writers, 10 to 20 at a time.

COSTS Travel reimbursement and stipends are available for participants of the residency, based on need. There are no residency fees.

MARK TWAIN CREATIVE WRITERS WORKSHOPS

5101 Rockhill Rd., Kansas City MO 64110-2499. (816)235-1168. Fax: (816)235-2611. E-mail: BeasleyM@umkc.edu. Website: www.newletters.org. **Contact:** Betsy Beasley, admin. associate. Estab. 1990. Annual. Held 3 weeks of June, from 9:30 to 12:30 each weekday morning. Conference duration: 3 weeks. Average attendance: 40. "Focus is on fiction, poetry and literary nonfiction." Panels planned for next conference include the full range of craft essentials. Staff includes Robert Stewart, editor-in-chief of *New Letters* magazine and BkMk Press, and Michael Pritchett, director of creative writing and English professor.

Submit for workshop 6 poems/1 short story prior to arrival. Conference information is available in March by SASE, e-mail, or on website. Editors participate in conference.

COSTS Fees for regular and noncredit courses.

ACCOMMODATIONS Offers list of area hotels or lodging options.

MONTEVALLO LITERARY FESTIVAL

Sta. 6420, University of Montevallo, Montevallo AL 35115. (205)665-6420. Fax: (205)665-6422. E-mail: murphyj@montevallo.edu. Website: www.montevallo.edu/english. **Contact:** Dr. Jim Murphy, Director. Estab. 2003. Annual. Last festival held: April 15, 2011. Average attendance: 60-100. "Readings, panels, and workshops on all literary genres and on literary editing/publishing. Master class workshops in fiction and poetry." Site: Several sites on a bucolic liberal arts university campus. The 2011 lineup of creative writers included workshop leaders Peter Guralnick (prose), Greg Williamson (poetry), and T.J. Beitelman (pedagogy), as well as A.M. Garner, Carrie Jerrell, Matthew Pitt, Jorge Sanchez, and Elizabeth Wetmore. 2010 fiction workshop leader was Lorraine López. Past fiction workshop faculty included Anthony Grooms, Inman Majors, Patricia Foster, Tom Franklin, Sheri Joseph, Sena Jeter Naslund, Brad Vice, Brad Watson, and John Dufresne. See website for 2012 dates and speakers.

COSTS In 2010: $45 for festival, including meals; $95 for festival, including meals and workshop.

ACCOMMODATIONS Offers overnight accommodations at Ramsay Conference Center on campus; rooms $40/night. Call (205)665-6280 for reservations. Free on-campus parking. Additional information available at www.montevallo.edu/cont_ed/ramsay.shtm.

ADDITIONAL INFORMATION To enroll in a fiction workshop, contact Bryn Chancellor (bchancellor@montevallo.edu). Information for upcoming festival available in February For brochure, visit website. Accepts inquiries by mail (with SASE), e-mail, phone, and fax. Editors participate in conference. "This is a friendly, relaxed festival dedicated to bringing literary writers and readers together on a personal scale." Poetry workshop participants submit up to 5 pages of poetry; e-mail as Word doc to Jim Murphy (murphyj@montevallo.edu) at least 2 weeks prior to festival.

MONTROSE CHRISTIAN WRITERS' CONFERENCE

218 Locust St., Montrose PA 18801. (570)278-1001 or (800)598-5030. Fax: (570)278-3061. E-mail: info@montrosebible.org. Website: www.montrosebible.org. Estab. 1990. Annual conference held in July. Average attendance: 85. "We try to meet a cross-section of writing needs, for beginners and advanced, covering fiction, poetry and writing for children. It is small enough to allow personal interaction between conferees and faculty. We meet in the beautiful village of Montrose, Pennsylvania, situated in the mountains. The Bible Conference provides hotel/motel-like accommodation and good food. The main sessions are held in the chapel with rooms available for other classes. Fiction writing has been taught each year."

COSTS In 2009 registration (tuition) was $155.

ACCOMMODATIONS Will meet planes in Binghamton, NY, and Scranton, PA. On-site accommodations: room and board $285-330/conference; $60-70/day including food (2009 rates). RV court available.

ADDITIONAL INFORMATION "Writers can send work ahead of time and have it critiqued for a small fee." The attendees are usually church related. The writing has a Christian emphasis. Conference information available in April. For brochure send SASE, visit website, e-mail, call, or fax. Accepts inquiries by SASE, e-mail, fax, phone.

MOONLIGHT AND MAGNOLIAS WRITER'S CONFERENCE

3741 Casteel Park Dr., Marietta GA 30064. Website: www.georgiaromancewriters.org. **Contact:** Sally Kilpatrick. Estab. 1982. Georgia Romance Writers, Sept. 29th-Oct. 2nd. E-mail: info@georgiaromancewriters.org. Annual. Last conference held October 1-3, 2010, in the Holiday Inn Decatur. Average attendance: 200. "Conference focuses on writing of women's fiction with emphasis on romance. Includes agents and editors from major publishing houses. Previous workshops have included: beginning writer sessions, research topics, writing basics and professional issues for the published author; plus specialty sessions on writing young adult, multicultural, paranormal, and Regency. Speakers have included experts in law enforcement, screenwriting and research. Literary raffle and advertised speaker and GRW member autographing open to the public. Please note the Maggies are now 100% electronic. Published authors make up first round, editors judge final."

COSTS Approximately $170 GRW member/$199 nonmember for conference registration. Check website for current conference fees, hotel rates, and registration forms.

ACCOMMODATIONS Holiday Inn Decatur, 130 Clairemont Ave., Decatur GA 30030

ADDITIONAL INFORMATION Maggie Awards for Excellence are presented to unpublished writers. The Maggie Award for published writers is now open to all PAN-eligible published members of RWA. Deadline for published Maggie is May 8. Deadline for unpublished Maggies is June 18. Entry forms and guidelines available on website. Published authors judge first round, editors judge final. Guidelines available for SASE in Spring.

⊙ MOUNT HERMON CHRISTIAN WRITERS CONFERENCE

37 Conference Drive, Mount Hermon, CA 95041. (831)335-4466 or (888)642-2677. E-mail: info@mounthermon.org. Website: www.mounthermon.org/writers. Annual. Held Palm Sunday weekend, Friday through Tuesday. "A working, how-to conference with over 10 major morning tracks and 70 options afternoon workshops about the craft of writing fiction, children's books, poetry, nonfiction, articles, and educational curriculum, with varying levels of writing proficiency addressed." Site: "The conference is sponsored by and held at the 440-acre Mount Hermon Christian Conference Center near San Jose, California, in the heart of the coastal redwoods. The faculty/student ratio is about 1:6 or 7. Faculty is made up of editors and publisher representatives from major Christian publishing houses nationwide."

COSTS Registration fees include tuition, all major morning sessions, keynote sessions, and refreshment breaks. Room and board varies depending on choice of housing options. See website for current costs.

ACCOMMODATIONS Registrants stay in hotel-style accommodations. Meals are buffet-style, with faculty joining registrants. See website Nov. 1 for cost updates.

ADDITIONAL INFORMATION "The residential nature of our conference makes this a unique setting for one-on-one interaction with faculty/staff. There is also a decided inspirational flavor to the conference, and general sessions with well-known speakers are a highlight. Registrants may submit 2 works for critique in advance of the conference, then have personal interviews with critiquers during the conference. All conference information is online by December 1 of each year. Send inquiries via e-mail. Tapes of past conferences are also available online."

NANCY SONDEL'S PACIFIC COAST CHILDREN'S WRITERS WORKSHOP

P.O. Box 244, Aptos CA 95001. Website: www.childrenswritersworkshop.com. Estab. 2003. "Our seminar serves semi-advanced through professional-level adult writers. A concurrent, intergenerational workshop is open to students age 14 and up, who give adults target-reader feedback. Intensive focus on craft as a marketing tool. Team-taught master classes (open clinics for manuscript critiques) explore such topics as 'Envision and Edit Your Whole Novel' and 'Story Architecture and Arcs.' Continuous close contact with faculty, who have included literary agent Andrea Brown and Dial Books senior editor Kate Harrison. **Next seminars:** October 7-9, 2011 and October 5-7, 2012. Registration limited to 12 adults and 6 teens. "For the most critique options, submit sample chapters and synopsis with e-application by mid-May; open until filled. **Content:** Character-driven novels with protagonists ages 11 and older. Collegial format; 90 percent hands-on, with dialogues between seasoned faculty and savvy, congenial peers. Our faculty critiques early as well as optional later chapters, plus synopses. Our pre-workshop anthology of peer manuscripts maximizes learning and networking. Several enrollees have landed contracts as a direct result of our seminar. **Details:** visit our website and e-mail us via the contact form.

COSTS Approx $450 (teens) to $600; includes lodging, most meals, and up to 2 in-person faculty critiques of partials. Optional: whole-novel critiques, plus 2 consults with editor or agent, for additional $400-$600. Limited work scholarships.

ACCOMMODATIONS Our venue, Pajaro Dunes

Conference Center and Resort, offers free use of business center with DSL Internet access in enrollees' beachfront townhomes.

NATIONAL WRITERS ASSOCIATION FOUNDATION CONFERENCE

P.O. Box 4187, Parker CO 80134. (303)841-0246. Fax: (303)841-2607. E-mail: natlwritersassn@hotmail.com. Website: www.nationalwriters.com. **Contact:** Sandy Whelchel, executive director. Estab. 1926. 10940 S. Parker Rd. #508, Parker CO 80138. (303) 841-0246. Fax: (303) 841-2607. E-mail: conference@nationalwriters.com. Website: www.nationalwriters.com. Annual. Workshop held in June. Workshop duration: 1 day. Average attendance: 100. For general writing and marketing.

COSTS Approximately $100.

ADDITIONAL INFORMATION Awards for prevous contests will be presented at the conference. Brochures/guidelines are online, or send a SASE.

NEW YORK COMIC BOOK MARKETPLACE

401 Seventh Ave. 33rd St., New York NY 10001-2062. (347)581-6166. E-mail: mikecarbo@gmail.com. Website: www.nycbm.com. **Contact:** Michael Carbonaro, director. "Annual comic book show."

Formerly known as Big Apple Con.

NIMROD ANNUAL WRITERS' WORKSHOP

University of Tulsa, 800 S. Tucker Dr., Tulsa OK 74104. (918)631-3080. Fax: (918)631-3033. E-mail: nimrod@utulsa.edu. Website: www.utulsa.edu/nimrod. **Contact:** Eilis O'Neal, managing editor. Estab. 1978. Annual. Conference held in October. Conference duration: 1 day. Average attendance: 150-200. Workshop in fiction and poetry. "Prize winners (Nimrod Prizes) conduct workshops as do contest judges and other selected writers." Past judges: Rosellen Brown, Stanley Kunitz, Toby Olson, Lucille Clifton, W.S. Merwin, Ron Carlson, Mark Doty, Anita Shreve, and Francine Prose.

COSTS Approximately $50. Lunch provided. Scholarships available for students.

ADDITIONAL INFORMATION *Nimrod International Journal* sponsors *Nimrod* Literary Awards: the Katherine Anne Porter Prize for fiction and the Pablo Neruda Prize for poetry. Poetry and fiction prizes: $2,000 each and publication (1st prize); $1,000 each and publication (2nd prize). Deadline: must be postmarked no later than April 30.

NORTH CAROLINA WRITERS' NETWORK FALL CONFERENCE

P.O. Box 954, Carrboro NC 27510-0954. (919)251-9140. Fax: (919)929-0535. E-mail: mail@ncwriters.org. Website: www.ncwriters.org. Estab. 1985. Average attendance: 350. "The NCWN Fall Conference is a weekend of workshops, discussions, readings, and community-building. The Network's Fall Conference serves writers at all levels of skill and experience, from novices to published professionals. We offer workshops in fiction, nonfiction, poetry, drama, children's writing, journalism, and the publishing business. We make available agents and editors for one-on-one sessions with prospective authors." Site: "The Fall Conference is held at a different hotel conference center each year, so that it reaches all regions of North Carolina."

COSTS Approximately $250 (includes 2 meals).

ACCOMMODATIONS Special rates are usually available at the Conference Hotel, but conferees must make their own reservations.

ADDITIONAL INFORMATION Brochures/guidelines are available online or by sending your street address to mail@ncwriters.org. You can also register online.

THE NOVEL WRITERS WORKSHOP

PO Box 392, Langley WA 98260. Website: www.bobmayer.org. P.O. Box 392, Langley WA 98260. E-mail: bob@bobmayer.org. Website: www.bobmayer.org. **Contact:** Bob Mayer. Estab. 2002. Conference duration: 2 days. Average attendance: limit of 8 attendees.

COSTS $250 in 2010.

ACCOMMODATIONS Does not include overnight accommodations. Provides list of area hotels or lodging options.

ADDITIONAL INFORMATION Participants submit cover letter, 1-page synopsis, and first 15 pages of ms. For brochure, visit website.

NYC PITCH AND SHOP CONFERENCE

Ripley Greer studios, 520 Eighth Avenue, 16th Floor, New York, NY. (800)250-8290. E-mail: algonkian@webdelsol.com. Website: http://nycpitchconference.com/index.htm. Conference duration: Thursday through Sunday. Average attendance: maximum 60 writers; workshops divided into 15 writers each. "The NYC Pitch and Shop promotes aspiring authors writing in the genres of commercial and literary fiction, serious and light women's fiction, historical fiction, mystery/thriller and detective, high-concept young adult, as well as memoir and narrative nonfiction. The conference provides writers with the skills and knowledge necessary to stand a realistic chance of success in today's tough novel market." Site: All NYC Pitch and Shop conferences take place at the Ripley Greer studios located near Madison Square Garden and Penn Station.

COSTS "Following successful application, the registration fee for the conference is $595. This fee covers all conference pitch sessions and workshops."

ACCOMMODATIONS Does not offer overnight accommodations. Provides list of area hotels or lodging options.

ADDITIONAL INFORMATION Upon registration, writers will receive pre-conference pitch assignments. For brochure, visit website. Agents and editors participate in conference.

⊙ ODYSSEY FANTASY WRITING WORKSHOP

P.O. Box 75, Mount Vernon NH 03057. E-mail: jcavelos@sff.net. Website: www.odysseyworkshop.org. Estab. 1996. Saint Anselm College 100 Saint Anselm Drive, Manchester, NH, 03102. (603)673-6234. Annual. Last workshop held June 7 to July 16, 2010. Conference duration: 6 weeks. Average attendance: limited to 16. "A workshop for fantasy, science fiction and horror writers that combines an intensive learning and writing experience with in-depth feedback on students' manuscripts. The only six-week workshop to combine the overall guidance of a single instructor with the varied perspectives of guest lecturers. Also, the only such workshop run by a former New York City book editor." Site: conference held at Saint Anselm College in Manchester, New Hampshire. Previous guest lecturers included: George R.R. Martin, Harlan Ellison, Ben Bova, Dan Simmons, Jane Yolen, Elizabeth Hand, Terry Brooks, Nancy Kress, Patricia McKillip, and John Crowley.

COSTS In 2010: $1,900 tuition, $775 housing (double room), $1,550 (single room); $35 application fee, $400-600 food (approximate), $450 processing fee to receive college credit.

ADDITIONAL INFORMATION Students must apply and include a writing sample. Application deadline April 10. Students' works are critiqued throughout the 6 weeks. Workshop information available in October. For brochure/guidelines send SASE, e-mail, visit website, call, or fax. Accepts inquiries by SASE, e-mail, fax, phone.

PACIFIC NORTHWEST WRITER ASSN. SUMMER WRITER'S CONFERENCE

PMB 2717, 1420 NW Gilman Blvd., Ste. 2, Issaquah WA 98027. E-mail: staff@pnwa.org. Website: www.pnwa.org. Writer conference geared toward beginner, intermediate, advanced, and professional levels. Meet agents and editors. Learn craft from renowned authors. Uncover new marketing secrets. PNWA's 56th Annual Conference will be held August 4-7, 2011, at the Hyatt Regency, Bellevue, WA 98004.

PHILADELPHIA WRITERS' CONFERENCE

P.O. Box 7171, Elkins Park PA 19027-0171. (215)619-7422. E-mail: dresente@mc3.edu. Website: www.pwcwriters.org. Estab. 1949. Annual. Average attendance: 160-200. Conference covers many forms of writing, novel, short story, genre fiction, nonfiction book, magazine writing, juvenile, poetry. Holiday Inn, Independence Mall, Fourth and Arch Streets, Philadelphia, PA 19106-2170.

COSTS 2011: Advance registration postmarked by April 8 is $205; After April 8 and walk-in registration is $225. The banquet and buffet are $40 each.

ACCOMMODATIONS "Hotel offers discount for early registration."

ADDITIONAL INFORMATION Sponsors contest. "Length generally 2,500 words for fiction or nonfiction. First prize in addition to cash and certificate gets free tuition for following year." Also offers ms critique. Brochures available usually in January for SASE, by e-mail, and on website. Accepts inquiries by e-mail and SASE. Agents and editors attend conference. 2011 guest editors and agents included Fran Collin, agent with Frances Collin Literary Agency; Stacia Decker, agent with Donald Mass; Juliet Grames, editor at Soho Press; Julie Will, editor with Rodale Press; and Sarah Yake, agent with Frances Collin Literary Agency. Visit us on the web for further agent and speaker details.

PIMA WRITERS' WORKSHOP

Pima Community College, 2202 W. Anklam Road, Tucson AZ 85709-0170. (520)206-6084. Fax: (520)206-6020. E-mail: mfiles@pima.edu. **Contact:** Meg Files, director. Estab. 1998. Annual. Average attendance: 300. "For anyone interested in writing—a beginning or experienced writer. The workshop offers sessions on writing and publishing fiction, nonfiction, poetry, and stories for children." Past speakers include Michael Blake, Ron

Carlson, Gregg Levoy, Nancy Mairs, Linda McCarriston, Jerome Stern, Connie Willis, Larry McMurtry, Barbara Kingsolver, and Robert Morgan.

COSTS $100 (can include ms critique). Participants may attend for college credit. Meals and accommodations not included.

ACCOMMODATIONS Information on local accommodations is made available, and special workshop rates are available at a specified hotel close to the workshop site (about $70/night).

ADDITIONAL INFORMATION Participants may have up to 20 pages critiqued by the author of their choice. Manuscripts must be submitted 3 weeks before the workshop. Conference brochure/guidelines available for SASE. Accepts inquiries by e-mail. "The workshop atmosphere is casual, friendly and supportive, and guest authors are very accessible. Readings and panel discussions are offered as well as talks and manuscript sessions."

THE PUBLISHING GAME

Peanut Butter & Jelly Press, P.O. Box 590239, Newton MA 02459. E-mail: alyza@publishinggame.com. Website: www.publishinggame.com. **Contact:** Alyza Harris, manager. Estab. 1998. Conference held monthly, in different locales across North America: Boston, New York City, Washington DC, Boca Raton, San Francisco, Los Angeles, Seattle, Chicago. Conference duration: 9 a.m. to 4 p.m. Maximum attendance: 18 writers. "A one-day workshop on finding a literary agent, self-publishing your book, creating a publishing house and promoting your book to bestsellerdom!" Site: "Elegant hotels across the country. Boston locations alternate between the Four Seasons Hotel in downtown Boston and The Inn at Harvard in historic Harvard Square, Cambridge." Fiction panels in 2005 included Propel Your Novel from Idea to Finished Manuscript; How to Self-Publish Your Novel; Craft the Perfect Book Package; How to Promote Your Novel; Selling Your Novel to Bookstores and Libraries. Workshop led by Fern Reiss, author and publisher of The Publishing Game series.

COSTS $195.

ACCOMMODATIONS "All locations are well-known hotels easily accessible by public transportation." Offers discounted conference rates for participants who choose to arrive early. Offers list of area lodging.

ADDITIONAL INFORMATION Brochures available for SASE. Accepts inquiries by SASE, e-mail, phone, fax, but e-mail preferred. Agents and editors attend conference. "If you're considering finding a literary agent, self-publishing your book or just want to sell more copies of your book, this conference will teach you everything you need to know to successfully publish and promote your work."

ROBERT QUACKENBUSH'S CHILDREN'S BOOK WRITING AND ILLUSTRATING WORKSHOP

460 E. 79th St., New York NY 10075-1443. (212)744-3822; (212)861-2761; Fax: (212)861-2761. E-mail: rqstudios@aol.com. Website: www.rquackenbush.com. **Contact:** Robert Quackenbush, director. Estab. 1982. Annual. Workshop to be held during second week of July. Conference duration: Four days. Limited to 10 people. Workshops to promote writing and illustrating books for young readers. "Focus is generally on picture books, easy-to-read and early chapter books. Come prepared with stories and/or illustrations to be developed into a finished state ready to present to a publisher and be ready to meet a lot of nice people to help you." Site: Held at the Manhattan studio of Robert Quackenbush, author and illustrator of more than 200 books for children. All classes led by Robert Quackenbush.

COSTS $750 tuition covers all the costs of the workshop but does not include housing and meals. A $100 nonrefundable deposit is required with the $650 balance due three weeks prior to attendance.

ACCOMMODATIONS A list of recommended hotels and restaurants is sent upon receipt of deposit to applicants living out of the area of New York City.

ADDITIONAL INFORMATION Class is for beginners and professionals. Critiques during workshop. Private consultations also available at an hourly rate. "Programs suited to your needs; individualized schedules can be designed. Write or phone to discuss your goals and you will receive a prompt reply." Conference information available 1 year prior to conference. For brochure, send SASE, e-mail, visit website, call, or fax. Accepts inquiries by fax, e-mail, phone, SASE.

SAGE HILL WRITING EXPERIENCE

Writing Children's & Young Adult Fiction Workshop, Box 1731, Saskatoon SK S7K 3S1 Canada. Phone: (306) 652-7395. Fax: (306)244-0255. E-mail: sage.hill@sasktel.net. Website: www.sagehillwriting.ca. Annual. Workshops held in July and May. Conference duration: 10-14 days. Average attendance: Summer, 30-40; Spring, 6-8. "Sage Hill Writing Experience offers a special working and learning opportunity to writers at different stages of development. Top quality instruction, low instructor-student ratio and the beautiful Sage Hill setting offer conditions ideal for the pursuit of excellence in the arts of fiction, and poetry." Site: The Sage Hill location features "individual accommodation, in-room writing area, lounges, meeting rooms, healthy meals, walking woods and vistas in several directions." Various classes are held: Introduction to Writing Fiction & Poetry; Fiction Workshop; Fiction Colloquium, Poetry Workshop; Poetry Colloquium; Writing for Young Adults Lab.

COSTS Summer program: $1,095 (includes instruction, accommodation, meals). Fall Poetry Colloquium: $1,375. Scholarships and bursaries are available.

ACCOMMODATIONS Located at Lumsden, 45 kilometers outside Regina.

ADDITIONAL INFORMATION For Introduction to Creative Writing, send a 5-page sample of your writing or a statement of your interest in creative writing and a list of courses taken. For workshop and colloquium programs, send a résumé of your writing career and a 12-page sample of your work, plus 5 pages of published work. Guidelines are available for SASE. Inquire via e-mail or fax.

SAN DIEGO STATE UNIVERSITY WRITERS' CONFERENCE

SDSU College of Extended Studies, 5250 Campanile Dr., San Diego State University, San Diego CA 92182-1920. (619)594-2517. Fax: (619)594-8566. E-mail: sdsuwritersconference@mail.sdsu.edu. Website: www.ces.sdsu.edu/writers. **Contact:** Rose Brown, facilitator. E-mail: brownz@mail.sdsu.edu. Estab. 1984. Annual conference held in January. Conference duration: 2 days. Average attendance: 375. Covers fiction, nonfiction, scriptwriting, and e-books. Held at the Doubletree Hotel in Mission Valley. Each year the conference offers a variety of workshops for beginning, intermediate, and advanced writers. This conference allows the individual writer to choose which workshop best suits his/her needs. In addition to the workshops, editor reading appointments and agent/editor consultation appointments are available for additional fees, so attendees can meet with editors and agents one-on-one to discuss specific issues. A reception is offered Saturday immediately following the workshops, offering attendees the opportunity to socialize with the faculty (editors, agents, speakers) in a relaxed atmosphere. Last year, about 70 faculty attended.

COSTS Approximately $365-485 (2012 costs will be published with a fall update of the website).

ACCOMMODATIONS Doubletree Hotel (800)222-TREE. Attendees must make their own travel arrangements.

SAN FRANCISCO WRITERS CONFERENCE

1029 Jones St., San Francisco CA 94109. (415)673-0939. Fax: (415)673-0367. E-mail: Barbara@sfwriters.org; sfwriters@aol.com. Website: www.sfwriters.org. **Contact:** Barbara Santos, marketing director; Elizabeth Pomada. Estab. 2003. Annual. President's Day weekend. Conference duration: 3 days. Average attendance: 350-400. "Focus is on WRITING and PUBLISHING. Attendees learn from bestselling authors, literary agents, and editors. The emphasis is on producing the best possible work and finding the most effective way to get it published from traditional (major publishers to specialty houses are always at the event) to self-publishing (iUniverse is a sponsor) and cutting edge venues (including Web sites/blogging)." The event is held at the Mark Hopkins Hotel in San Francisco. "It is an elegant and historic venue at the top of Nob Hill. General sessions, keynotes and luncheons are in the Ballroom with breakout sessions in smaller rooms at the hotel." Previous panels include A Conversation on Writing (Gail Tsukiyama and Karen Joy Fowler) and Writing for Children (Lemony Snickett). Previous topics include: Romance (Passion on the Page), How to Write a Fiction Query Letter, Workshops on Plot/Dialogue/Characterization, The Art of Literary Fiction, The Perfect Murder. The founders of SFWC are Elizabeth Pomada (fiction and nonfiction literary agent) and Michael Larsen (agent and author of many writing related books including Guerrilla Marketing for Writers). Presenters for 2009 included Sheldon Siegel (*The Confession*), Richard Paul Evans (*The Christmas Box*), Jane Smiley, dozens of literary agents and editors from top publishing houses including St. Martin's, Penguin, Random House, John Wiley & Sons, and New World Library. (Nearly 100 presenters.)

COSTS $600+ with price breaks for early registration (includes all sessions/workshops/keynotes, Speed Dating with Editors, opening gala at the Top of the Mark, 2 continental breakfasts, 2 lunches). Optional Speed Dating for Agents is $50.

ACCOMMODATIONS The Intercontinental Mark

Hopkins Hotel is a historic landmark at the top of Nob Hill in San Francisco. Elegant rooms and first-class service are offered to attendees at the rate of $159/night. The hotel is located so that everyone arriving at the Oakland or San Francisco airport can take BART to either the Embarcadero or Powell Street exits, then walk or take a cable car or taxi directly to the hotel.

ADDITIONAL INFORMATION "Present yourself in a professional manner and the contact you will make will be invaluable to your writing career. Brochures and registration are online."

⊕ SANTA BARBARA WRITERS CONFERENCE

27 West Anapamu St., Suite 305, Santa Barbara CA 93101. (805)568-1516. E-mail: info@sbwriters.com. Website: www.sbwriters.com. Annual. June 18-23, 2011. Conference duration: 5 days. Conference. See website for more details.

⊕○ SCBWI—NEW JERSEY; ANNUAL SUMMER CONFERENCE

SCBWI-New Jersey: Society of Children's Book Writers & Illustrators, New Jersey NJ. Website: www.newjerseyscbwi.com. **Contact:** Kathy Termean, Regional Advisor. This weekend conference is held in the beginning of June in Princeton, NJ. Multiple one-on-one critiques; "how to" workshops for every level, first page sessions, agent pitches, and interaction with the faculty of editors, agents, art director, and authors are some of the highlights of the weekend. On Friday attendees can sign up for writing intensives or register for illstrators' day with the art directors. Published authors attending the conference can sign up to participate in the book fair to sell and autograph their books; illustrators have the opportunity to display their artwork. Attendees have the option to participate in group critiques after dinner on Saturday evening and attend a mix and mingle with the faculty on Friday night. Meals are included with the cost of admission. Conference is known for its high ratio of faculty to attendees and interaction opportunities.

SCBWI SOUTHERN BREEZE SPRINGMINGLE CONFERENCE

Springmingle '12. P.O. Box 26282, Birmingham AL 35260. E-mail: jskittinger@gmail.com. Website: www.southern-breeze.net. **Contact:** Jo Kittinger, co-regional advisor. Estab. 1992. Annual. Conference held the last full weekend each February (Friday PM—Sunday AM). Average Attendance: 160. This is a seminar designed to educate and inspire creators of quality children's literature.

COSTS About $200; SCBWI nonmembers pay about $30 more. Some meals are included.

ACCOMMODATIONS Individuals make their own reservations. Ask for the Southern Breeze group rate in the conference site's hotel.

ADDITIONAL INFORMATION Manuscript and portfolio critiques available for an additional fee. Mss must be sent ahead of time. Visit website for details. Accepts inquiries by SASE, e-mail.

SCBWI—VENTURA/SANTA BARBARA; FALL CONFERENCE

Simi Valley CA 93094-1389. E-mail: alexisinca@aol.com. Website: www.scbwisocal-org/calendar. **Contact:** Alexis O'Neill, Regional Advisor. Estab. 1971. Writers' conference geared toward all levels. Speakers include editors, authors, illustrators, and agents. Fiction and nonfiction picture books, middle grade and YA novels, and magazine submissions addressed. Annual writing contest in all genres plus illustration display. Conference held November 5, 2011, at California Lutheran University in Thousand Oaks, California in cooperation with the CLU School of Education. For fees and other information, e-mail or go to website.

SCBWI WINTER CONFERENCE ON WRITING AND ILLUSTRATING FOR CHILDREN

(formerly SCBWI Midyear Conference), Society of Children's Book Writers and Illustrators. 8271 Beverly Blvd., Los Angeles CA 90048. (323)782-1010. Fax: (323)782-1892. E-mail: scbwi@scbwi.org. Website: www.scbwi.org. **Contact:** Stephen Mooser. Estab. 2000. Annual. Conference held in February. Average attendance: 1,000. Conference is to promote writing and illustrating for children: picture books; fiction; nonfiction; middle grade and young adult; network with professionals; financial planning for writers; marketing your book; art exhibition; etc.

COSTS See website for current cost and conference information.

ADDITIONAL INFORMATION SCBWI also holds an annual summer conference in August in Los Angeles. Visit website for details.

SCWG CONFERENCE

Holiday Inn, 1300 North Atlantic Ave., Cocoa Beach FL 32931. (321)956-7193. Website: scwg.org/conference.asp. **Contact:** Joyce Henderson. Annual. Conference duration: 2 days. Conference held the fourth weekend in January.

COSTS $185 for guild members; $205 nonmembers. One day rates are available; see website for rates.

ADDITIONAL INFORMATION Agents and editors participate in conference.

SEACOAST WRITERS ASSOCIATION SPRING AND FALL CONFERENCES

59 River Rd., Stratham NH 03885-2358. (603)742-1030. E-mail: patparnell@comcast.net. Website: www.seacoastwritersassociation.org. **Contact:** Pat Parnell, conf. coordinator. Annual. Conferences held in May and October. Conference duration: 1 day. Average attendance: 60. "Our conferences offer workshops covering various aspects of fiction, nonfiction and poetry."

COSTS Approx. $50.

ADDITIONAL INFORMATION "We sometimes include critiques. It is up to the workshop presenter." Spring meeting includes a contest. Categories are fiction, nonfiction (essays), and poetry. Judges vary from year to year. Conference and contest information available for SASE November 1, April 1, and September 1. Accepts inquiries by SASE, e-mail, and phone. For further information, check the website or visit us on Facebook: Seacoastwritersassociation.

SEWANEE WRITERS' CONFERENCE

735 University Ave., 123 Gailor Hall, Stamlor Center, Sewanee TN 37383-1000. (931) 598-1654. E-mail: kewilson@sewanee.edu; swc@sewanee.edu. Website: www.sewaneewriters.org. **Contact:** Kevin Wilson. Estab. 1990. Annual. Conference sessions held each July. Average attendance: 150. "We offer genre-based workshops in fiction, poetry, and playwriting along with a full schedule of readings, craft lectures, panel discussions, talks, Q&A sessions along and the like." Site: "The Sewanee Writers' Conference uses the facilities of Sewanee: The University of the South. Physically, the University is a collection of ivy-covered Gothic-style buildings, located on the Cumberland Plateau in mid-Tennessee. Invited editors, publishers, and agents structure their own presentations, but there is always opportunity for questions from the audience." 2008 faculty included fiction writers John Casey, Tony Earley, Randall Kenan, Margot Livesey, Jill McCorkle, Erin McGraw, Tim O'Brien, and Christine Schutt; poets Daniel Anderson, Claudia Emerson, Andrew Hudgins, Mark Jarman, Mary Jo Salter, Brad Leithauser, Mark Strand, and Greg Williamson; and playwrights Romulus Linney and Arlene Hutton. The faculty changes from year to year.

COSTS $1,700 (includes tuition, board, single room, sports and fitness center access).

ACCOMMODATIONS Participants are housed in single rooms in university dormitories. Bathrooms are shared by small groups. Motel or B&B housing is available, but not abundantly so.

ADDITIONAL INFORMATION "Complimentary chartered bus service is available from the Nashville Airport to Sewanee and back on the first and last days of the conference. We offer each participant (excepting auditors) the opportunity for a private manuscript conference with a member of the faculty. These manuscripts are due 1 month before the conference begins. Brochures/guidelines are free. The conference provides a limited number of fellowships and scholarships; these are awarded on a competitive basis."

SHEVACON 19

PO Box 7622, Roanoke VA 24019. (540)248-4152. E-mail: Shevacon@shevacon.org. Website: www.shevacon.org. **Contact:** Lynn Bither, chairperson. Estab. 1993. Average attendance: 400. "We are one of the smaller conventions in the SF/F genre, but we have a lot of big convention qualities." Conference focuses on writing (science fiction and fantasy, some horror), art (science fiction and fantasy), gaming (science fiction and fantasy). Past fiction-related panels have included Stolen Stories: The Use of Historical Models; Blood on the Bulkhead: Is New Fiction Too Graphic?; Bad Guys We Want to Win: Writing Good Villians; Scare Me, Thrill Me: Is Horror More Difficult to Write than Fiction?"

COSTS See website for rates.

ACCOMMODATIONS There is a special rate at the Sheraton Roanoke Hotel & Conference Center, Virginia. "Shuttles from the airport are available; we do not have airline discounts." Offers overnight accomodations; "individuals must make their own reservations." For brochure send SASE or visit website. Accepts inquiries by mail, e-mail, or phone.

ADDITIONAL INFORMATION "SheVaCon is celebrating it's 19th year as the largest Multi-Media Science

Fiction & Fantasy convention in Southwestern Virginia. We offer many fun events and great programming focusing on sci-fi, fantasy, and horror. Workshops, panel discussions, art show & artist alley, dealer's room, costumed fandom groups, auctions, computer and console gaming, RPG/LARP gaming, Video and Anime screenings . . . and so much more!" Confirmed guests are listed on the website and we are updating regularly."

SITKA CENTER FOR ART AND ECOLOGY

P.O. Box 65, Otis OR 97368. (541)994-5485. Fax: (541)994-8024. E-mail: info@sitkacenter.org. Website: www.sitkacenter.org. **Contact:** Jalene Case, program manager. Estab. 1970. Workshop program is open to all levels and is held annually from late May until early October. We also have a residency program from October through May. Average attendance: 10-14/workshop. A variety of workshops in creative process, including book arts and other media. Site: The Center borders a Nature Conservatory Preserve, the Siuslaw National Experimental Forest, and the Salmon River Estuary, located just north of Lincoln City, OR.

COSTS "Workshops are generally $60-500; they do not include meals or lodging."

ACCOMMODATIONS Does not offer overnight accommodations. Provides a list of area hotels or lodging options.

ADDITIONAL INFORMATION Brochure available in February of each year by SASE, phone, e-mail, fax, or visit website. Accepts inquiries by SASE, e-mail, phone, fax.

⊕ SOAPSTONE: A WRITING RETREAT FOR WOMEN

622 SE 29th Ave., Portland OR 97214. (503)233-3936. E-mail: retreats@soapstone.org. Website: www.soapstone.org. Duration: 1-4 weeks. Average attendance: 30 writers/year. Retreat/residency. "Soapstone provides women writers with a stretch of uninterrupted time for their work and the opportunity to live in semi-solitude close to the natural world. In addition to that rare but essential commodity for a writer—a quiet space away from jobs, children, and other responsibilities—Soapstone provides something less tangible but also invaluable: the validation and encouragement necessary to embark upon or sustain a long or difficult writing project." Site: Located in Oregon's Coast Range, 9 miles from the ocean, the retreat stands on 22 acres of densely forested land along the banks of Soapstone Creek and is home to much wildlife. The writers in residence enjoy a unique opportunity to learn about the natural world and join us in conscious stewardship of the land.

COSTS $3 per day. $20 nonrefundable application fee.

ACCOMMODATIONS Residents must provide all of their own transportation. See website for more information. Offers overnight accommodations.

ADDITIONAL INFORMATION Application materials required include 3 copies of the completed application, a writing sample (no more than 3 pages of poetry or 5 pages, double-spaced, of prose), and application fee. Applications must be postmarked July 1-August 1 each year. For brochure, visit website.

THE SOUTHAMPTON WRITERS CONFERENCE

Stony Brook Southampton, 239 Montauk Highway, Southampton NY 11968. (631) 632-5030. Fax: (631)632-2578. E-mail: southamptonwriters@notes.cc.sunysb.edu. Website: www.stonybrook.edu/writers. **Contact:** Christian McLean, conference coordinator. Estab. 1975. Annual. Conference held in July. Conference duration: 12 days. Average attendance: 120. The primary work of the conference is conducted in writing workshops in the novel, short story, poem, play, literary essay, and memoir. Site: The seaside campus of Stony Brook Southampton is located in the heart of the Hamptons, a renowned resort area only 70 miles from New York City. During free time, participants can draw inspiration from Atlantic beaches or explore the charming seaside towns. Faculty has included Frank McCourt, Billy Collins, Mark Doty, Roger Rosenblatt, Ursula Hegi, Meg Wolitzer, David Rakoff, Alan Alda, and Jules Feiffer, Melissa Bank, and Matt Klam.

COSTS Application fee: $25; tuition, room and board: $2,445; tuition only: $1,775 (includes breakfast and lunch).

ACCOMMODATIONS On-campus housing—doubles and small singles additional cost for singles with shared baths—is modest but comfortable. Housing assignment is by lottery. Supplies list of lodging alternatives.

ADDITIONAL INFORMATION Applicants must complete an application form and submit a writing sample of unpublished, original work up to 20 pages (15 pages for poetry). See website for details. Brochures available in January by fax, phone, e-mail, and on website. Accepts inquiries by SASE, e-mail, phone, and fax.

SOUTH COAST WRITERS CONFERENCE

Southwestern Oregon Community College, P.O. Box 590, 29392 Ellensburg Avenue, Gold Beach OR 97444. (541)247-2741. Fax: (541)247-6247. E-mail: scwc@socc.edu. Website: www.socc.edu/scwriters. Estab. 1996. Annual. Conference held President's Day weekend. Workshops held Friday and Saturday. Average attendance: 100. "We try to cover a broad spectrum: fiction, historical, poetry, children's, nature." Site: "Friday workshops are held at The Event Center on the Beach. Saturday workshops are held at the high school."

COSTS $60 before January 31; $70 after. Friday workshops are an additional $55. No meals or lodging included.

ADDITIONAL INFORMATION See website for cost and additional details.

SOUTHEASTERN WRITERS ASSOCIATION

161 Woodstone Dr., Athens GA 30605. Website: www.southeasternwriters.com. Contact: Sheila Hudson, registrar. Estab. 1975. Annual. Conference held third week of June every year. Average attendance: 75 (limited to 100). Conference offers classes in fiction, nonfiction, juvenile, inspirational writing, poetry, etc. Site: Epworth-by-the-Sea, St. Simons Island, GA. Estab. 1975.

COSTS Costs 2011 costs: $399; $150 daily tuition. Three days' tuition required for free manuscript conferences. Conference tuition includes $35 annual membership fee.

ACCOMMODATIONS Offers overnight accommdations. 2010 rates were approximately $675/single to $475/double and including motel-style room and 3 meals/day per person. Off-site lodging also available.

ADDITIONAL INFORMATION Sponsors numerous contests in several genres and up to 3 free ms evaluation conferences with instructors. Agents and editors participate in conference panels and/or private appointments. Group critique sessions are available, and authors can bring books for sale. Complete information is available on the website in March of each year, including registration forms. E-mail or send SASE for brochure.

⊕ SOUTHERN EXPRESSIONS AUTHOR CONFERENCE

P.O. Box 10294, Gulfport MS 39505-0294. (228)239-3575. E-mail: writerpllevin@gmail.com. Website: www.gcwriters.org/se.html. **Contact:** Philip L. Levin. Estab. 2010. Annual conference held October 14, 15, 16; 3 days. Average attendance: 120. Southern Expressions includes 18 speakers, including 4 literary agents, special demonstrations, keynotes by famous published authors, a Friday night cocktail party with silent auction, a Sunday morning brunch and author signing. The conference is sponsored by the IP Casino, Resort and Spa.

COSTS $200 with $25 GCWA discount for members.

ACCOMMODATIONS Room block reserved at the IP Casino, Resort and Spa. Shuttle provided between the IP and the conference. In addition, the city of Ocean Springs is providing transportation from designated parking spots to the art fair, which is two blocks from the conference.

ADDITIONAL INFORMATION Brochures are avaiable online or for SAE. Inquire via e-mail.

SOUTHWEST WRITERS CONFERENCE

3271 Morris NE, Albuquerque NM 87111. (505)265-9485. Fax: (505)265-9483. E-mail: swwriters@juno.com. Website: www.southwestwriters.com. **Contact:** Conference Chair. Estab. 1983. Annual. Conferences held throughout the year. Average attendance: 50. "Conferences concentrate on all areas of writing and include appointments and networking." Workshops and speakers include writers, editors, and agents of all genres for all levels from beginners to advanced.

COSTS $99 and up (members); $159 and up (nonmembers); includes conference sessions and lunch.

ACCOMMODATIONS Usually have official airline and discount rates. Special conference rates are available at hotel. A list of other area hotels and motels is available.

ADDITIONAL INFORMATION Sponsors an annual contest judged by authors, editors, and agents from New York, Los Angeles, etc., and from other major publishing houses. Many categories. Deadline, fee structure on website. For brochures/guidelines send SASE, visit website, e-mail, call. "An appointment (10 minutes, one-on-one) may be set up at the conference with the editor/agent of your choice on a first-registered/first-served basis."

☺ SPACE (SMALL PRESS AND ALTERNATIVE COMICS EXPO)

Back Porch Comics, P.O.Box 20550, Columbus OH 43220. E-mail: bpc13@earthlink.net. Website: www.backporchcomics.com/space.htm. Contact: Bob Corby. Conference duration: 2 days. "The Midwest's largest exhibition of small press, alternative and creator-owned comics." Site: Held at the Aladdin Shrine Complex multipurpose room in Columbus, Ohio. Over 150 small press artists, writers, and publishers. Admission: $5 per day or $8 for weekend.

ADDITIONAL INFORMATION For brochure, visit website. Editors participate in conference.

SQUAW VALLEY COMMUNITY OF WRITERS

P.O. Box 1416, Nevada City CA 95959-1416. (530)470-8440. E-mail: info@squawvalleywriters.org. Website: www.squawvalleywriters.org. **Contact:** Brett Hall Jones, executive director. Estab. 1969. Annual conference held in August. Conference duration: 7 days. Average attendance: 124. "Writers workshops in fiction, nonfiction and memoir assist talented writers by exploring the art and craft as well as the business of writing." Offerings include daily morning workshops led by writer-teachers, editors, or agents of the staff, limited to 12-13 participants; seminars; panel discussions of editing and publishing; craft colloquies; lectures; and staff readings. Past themes and panels included Personal History in Fiction, Narrative Structure, Promise and Premise: Recognizing Subject; The Nation of Narrative Prose: Telling the Truth in Memoir and Personal Essay, and Anatomy of a Short Story.

Covers fiction, nonfiction, and memoir. Held in Squaw Valley, California—the site of the 1960 Winter Olympics. The workshops are held in a ski lodge at the foot of this spectacular ski area. Literary agent speakers have recently included Julie Barer, Michael Carlisle, Henry Dunow, Theresa Park, B.J. Robbins, Janet Silver, and Peter Steinberg. Agents will be speaking and available for meetings with attendees. The airport shuttle is available for an additional cost. Brochures are available online or for a SASE in March. Send inquiries via e-mail.

COSTS Tuition is $800, which includes 6 dinners.

ACCOMMODATIONS The Community of Writers rents houses and condominiums in the Valley for participants to live in during the week of the conference. Single room (one participant): $725/week. Double room (twin beds, room shared by conference participant of the same sex): $350/week. Multiple room (bunk beds, room shared with 2 or more participants of the same sex): $210/week. All rooms subject to availability; early requests are recommended. Can arrange airport shuttle pick-ups for a fee.

ADDITIONAL INFORMATION Admissions are based on submitted ms (unpublished fiction, one or two stories or novel chapters); requires $35 reading fee. Submit ms to Brett Hall Jones, Squaw Valley Community of Writers, P.O. Box 1416, Nevada City, CA 95959. Brochure/guidelines available March by phone, e-mail, or visit website. Accepts inquiries by SASE, e-mail, phone. Agents and editors attend/participate in conferences.

STEINBECK FESTIVAL

1 Main Street, Salinas CA 93901. (831)796-3833. Fax: (831)796-3828. Website: www.steinbeck.org. Estab. 1980. Annual. Annual festival held August 4-7, 2011. Average attendance: 1,000 "over a 4-day period." This year's theme (Friends & Foes) will explore the creative fallout when ideas collide, the pleasure of partnership, the creative clash. It will celebrate friends in letters and dish up the dirt on some literary feuds. It will serve unlikely pairings and pit X against Y. Festival events will reach out and reach across, celebrate our adversaries and allies, and the creative spark between them. This 4-day festival of books, talks, food, tours, and visual and performing arts will be based in Salinas, with International Fringe events taking place in cities throughout the world. Site: National Steinbeck Center, "a multi-million dollar, multi-sensory museum located in California's Central Coast which includes a permanent exhibit that brings to life the world of Nobel Prize-winning author, John Steinbeck, the Rabobank Agricultural Museum, which shares the stories of Salinas Valley agriculture 'from field to fork,' through interactive displays, film and hands on exhibits, and two changing art galleries featuring a variety of art and cultural exhibits."

COSTS Range from $17 to $40 per person, depending on the programs offered. Daily and festival passports are also offered.

ACCOMMODATIONS A list of accommodations and area hotel and lodging options provided.

STELLARCON

Box F4, Brown Annex, Elliott University Center, UNCG, Greensboro NC 27412. (336)294-8041. E-mail: info@stellarcon.org. Website: www.stellarcon.org. **Contact:** Mike Monaghan, convention manager. Estab. 1976. Annual. Last conference held March 13-15, 2009. Average attendance: 500. Conference focuses on "general science fiction and fantasy (horror also) with an emphasis on literature." Site: Hotel High Point, High Point, NC. See website for 2009 speakers.

SUMMER WRITING PROGRAM

Naropa University, 2130 Arapahoe Ave., Boulder CO 80302. (303)245-4600. Fax: (303)546-5287. E-mail: swpr@naropa.edu; clesser@naropa.edu. Website: www.naropa.edu/swp. **Contact:** Julie Kazimer, registration manager. Estab. 1974. Annual. Workshops held: June 13-July 19. Workshop duration: 4 weeks. Average attendance: 250. Offers college credit. "With 13 workshops to choose from each of the four weeks of the program, students may study poetry, prose, hybrid/cross-genre writing, small press printing, or book arts." Site: All workshops, panels, lectures and readings are hosted on the Naropa University main campus. Located in downtown Boulder, the campus is within easy walking distance of restaurants, shopping and the scenic Pearl Street Mall. Prose-related panels include Ecology, Poetics of Prose, Telling Stories, The Informant "Other." 2010 faculty included Samual R. Delany, Linh Dinh, Dolores Dorantes, Penny Arcade, Bhanu Kapil, Akilah Oliver, Selah Saterstrom, Steven Taylor, Bob Holman, Anne Waldman, Xi Chuan, and many others.

COSTS In 2011: $475/week, $1,800 for all four weeks (non-credit students); $1,275/week (BA students); $1,700/week (MFA students).

ACCOMMODATIONS Offers overnight accommdations. Housing is available at Snow Lion Apartments. Single room is $45/night or $315/week, single bedroom apartment is $64/night or $448/week.

ADDITIONAL INFORMATION If students would like to take the Summer Writing Program for academic credit, they must submit a non-degree-seeking academic credit student application, transcripts, a letter of intent, and 5-10 pages of their creative work. Information available in January. For catalog of upcoming program, fill out catalog request form on website. Accepts inquiries by e-mail, phone.

TAOS SUMMER WRITERS' CONFERENCE

Department of English Language and Literature MSC03 2170, 1 University of New Mexico, Albuquerque NM 87131-0001. (505)277-5572. Fax: (505)277-2950. E-mail: taosconf@unm.edu. Website: www.unm.edu/~taosconf. **Contact:** Sharon Oard Warner, director. Estab. 1999. Annual. Held each year in July. Average attendance: 180. Workshops in novel writing, short story writing, screenwriting, poetry, creative nonfiction, publishing, and special topics such as yoga and writing. Master classes in novel, memoir, and poetry. For beginning and experienced writers. "Taos itself makes our conference unique. We also offer daily visits to the D.H. Lawrence Ranch, and other local historical sites." Site: Workshops and readings are all held at the Sagebrush Inn Conference Center, part of the Sagebrush Inn, an historic hotel and Taos landmark since 1929.

COSTS $325/weekend; $625/week; discounted tuition rate of $275/weekend workshop with weeklong workshop or master class registration.

ACCOMMODATIONS $69-109/night at the Sagebrush Inn; $89/night at Comfort Suites.

TEXAS CHRISTIAN WRITERS' CONFERENCE

7401 Katy Freeway, Houston TX 77092. (713)686-7209. E-mail: dannywoodall@yahoo.com. **Contact:** Danny Woodall. First Baptist Church, 6038 Greenmont, Houston TX 77092. (713)686-7209. E-mail: martharogers@sbcglobal.net. Estab. 1990. Annual. Conference held in August. Conference duration: 1 day. Average attendance: 60-65. "Focus on all genres." Site: Held at the First Baptist Church fellowship center and classrooms. 2011 faculty: Diann Mills, Keynote Speaker; Lisa Ludwig; Terry Burns of Hartline Literary Agency; Janice Thompson; Anita Higman; Martha Rogers.

COSTS $65 for members of IWA, $80 nonmembers, discounts for seniors (60+) and couples, meal at noon, continental breakfast and breaks.

ACCOMMODATIONS Offers list of area hotels or lodging options.

ADDITIONAL INFORMATION Open conference for all interested writers. Sponsors a contest for short fiction; categories include articles, devotionals, poetry, short story, book proposals, drama. Fees: $8-15. Conference information available with SASE or e-mail to Danny Woodall, dannywoodall@yahoo.com. Agents participate in conference. (For contest information contact patav@aol.com.)

THRILLERFEST

PO Box 311, Eureka CA 95502. E-mail: infocentral@thrillerwriters.org. Website: www.thrillerfest.com. **Contact:** Shirley Kennett. Estab. 2006. Grand Hyatt New York. 109 E. 42nd St. New York, NY 10017. E-mail: infocentral@thrillerwriters.org. Website: www.thrillerfest.com. Annual. July 7-10 in Manhattan. Conference duration: 4 days. Average attendance: 700. Workshop/conference/festival. "A great place to learn the craft of writing the thriller. Classes taught by NYT best-selling authors. A fabulous event for fans/readers to meet and spend a few days with their favorite authors and packed with terrific programming." Speakers have included David Morrell, James Patterson, Sandra Brown, Ken Follett, Eric Van Lustbader, David Baldacci, Brad Meltzer, Steve Martini, R.L. Stine, Steve Berry, Kathleen Antrim, Douglas Preston, Gayle Lynds, Harlan Coben, Lee Child, Lisa Scottolini, Katherine Neville, Robin Cook, Andrew Gross, Kathy Reichs, Brad Thor, Clive Cussler, Donald Maass, MJ Rose, and Al Zuckerman. Two days of the conference are CraftFest, where the focus is on the craft of writing, and two days are ThrillerFest, which showcase the author-fan relationship. Also featured: AgentFest—a unique event where authors can pitch their work face-to-face to over 40 top literary agents, and the International Thriller Awards and Banquet.

COSTS Price will vary from $200 to $1,000 dollars depending on which events are selected. Various package deals are available offering savings, and Early Bird pricing is offered beginning August of each year.

ACCOMMODATIONS Grand Hyatt in New York City.

THUNDER ARM WRITING RETREAT WITH NORTH CASCADES INSTITUTE

810 Highway 20, Sedro-Wooley WA 98284-9394. Website: www.ncascades.org. Estab. 1999. Thunder Arm Writing Retreat with Tim McNulty, Ana Maria Spagna, and Langdon Cook, September 8-11 (Thurs eve-Sun) North Cascades Environmental Learning Center Cost ranges from $305-545 depending on accommodations Under the mentorship of Tim McNulty, Ana Maria Spagna and Langdon Cook—talented writers with experiences in a wide diversity of genres—you'll learn techniques for crisp, powerful writing inspired by nature. We strive for an inspiring, friendly and supportive atmosphere where student groups rotate through instructors each day, enjoying a combination of presentations, discussions, readings and individual writing activities. Throughout the weekend, our kitchen staff will prepare delicious, nourishing meals with local and organic ingredients, and you'll retire each night to comfortable accommodations in guest lodges. Cost ranges from $305-545 depending on accommodations. Past faculty includes: Barbara Kingsolver, Rick Bass, Robert Michael Pyle, William Kittredge, Ann Zwinger, Gary Ferguson, Kathleen Dean Moore, and William Dietrich. Annual. Conference duration: 4 days. Average attendance: 35.

COSTS 2007 costs were $325 (triple occupancy), $475 (double), $695 (single). All options include meals.

ADDITIONAL INFORMATION For conference information, visit Web Site, e-mail, or call.

TMCC WRITERS' CONFERENCE

5270 Neil Road, Reno NV 89502. (775)829-9010. Fax: (775)829-9032. E-mail: wdce@tmcc.edu. Website: wdce.tmcc.edu. Estab. 1991. Annual. Average attendance: 125. Conference focuses on strengthening mainstream/literary fiction and nonfiction works and how to market them to agents and publisher. Site: Truckee Meadows Community College in Reno, Nevada.

COSTS $99 for a full-day seminar; $15 for 15-minute one-on-one appointment with an agent or editor.

ACCOMMODATIONS The Nugget offers a special rate and shuttle service to the Reno/Tahoe International Airport, which is less than 20 minutes away.

ADDITIONAL INFORMATION "The conference is open to all writers, regardless of their level of experience. Brochures are available online and mailed in the fall. Send inquiries via e-mail."

UCLA EXTENSION WRITERS' PROGRAM

10995 Le Conte Ave., #440, Los Angeles CA 90024. (310)825-9415 or (800)388-UCLA. Fax: (310)206-7382. E-mail: writers@uclaextension.edu. Website: www.uclaextension.org/writers. Estab. 1891. **Contact:** Cindy Lieberman, program manager. Courses held year-round with 1-day or intensive weekend workshops to 12-week courses. Writers Studio held in February; 9-month master classes are also offered every fall. "The diverse offerings span introductory seminars to professional novel and script completion workshops. The annual Writers Studio and a number of 1-, 2- and 4-day intensive workshops are popular with out-of-town students due to their specific focus and the chance to work with industry professionals. The most comprehensive and diverse continuing education writing program in the country, offering over 550 courses a year, including screenwriting, fiction, writing for the youth market, poetry, nonfiction, playwriting and publishing. Adult learners in the UCLA Extension Writers' Program study with professional screenwriters, fiction writers, playwrights, poets and nonfiction writers, who bring practical experience, theoretical knowledge and a wide variety of teaching styles and philosophies to their classes." Site: Courses are offered in Los Angeles on the UCLA campus, in the 1010 Westwood Center in Westwood Village, at the Figueroa Courtyard in downtown Los Angeles, as well as online.

COSTS Depends on length of the course.

ACCOMMODATIONS Students make their own arrangements. Out-of-town students are encouraged to take online courses.

ADDITIONAL INFORMATION Some advanced-level classes have ms submittal requirements; see the UCLA Extension catalog or see website.

⊕ UNIVERSITY OF NORTH FLORIDA WRITERS CONFERENCE

12000 Alumni Dr., Jacksonville FL 32224-2678. (904)620-4200. E-mail: sharon.y.cobb@unf.edu. Website: www.unfwritersconference.com. **Contact:** Sharon Y. Cobb, conference director. Estab. 2009. Annual conference held in August. Next conference held August 5-7, 2011 (also August 3-5, 2012). Conference duration: 3 days. Average attendance: 200. Short workshops in craft, genre, marketing and getting published. Workshops include fiction, young adult, children's, nonfiction, romance, and screenwriting held at the University Center on campus at the University of North Florida. See website for current registration fees. Nearby accommodations with special conference discounts are listed on website. There is free parking provided at the University Center. Writers may submit pitches to agents, editors, and film producers through the conference's *Writers Pitch* Book.

COSTS : See website for current registration fees. Full conference attendees receive: workshops, critiques by faculty and fellow students, lunches, Friday wine/cheese reception, and book signings.

ACCOMMODATIONS Nearby accommodations are listed on website. There is free parking provided at the University Center.

ADDITIONAL INFORMATION Brochures and guidelines available for SASE and on website, or by e-mail.

VERMONT STUDIO CENTER

P.O. Box 613, Johnson VT 05656. (802)635-2727. Fax: (802)635-2730. E-mail: info@vermontstudiocenter.org. Website: www.vermontstudiocenter.org. **Contact:** Gary Clark, writing program director. Estab. 1984. Ongoing residencies. Conference duration: 2-12 weeks. Average attendance: 55 writers and visual artists/month. "The Vermont Studio Center is an international creative community located in Johnson, Vermont, and serving more than 600 American and international artists and writers each year (50 per month). A Studio Center Residency features secluded, uninterrupted writing time, the companionship of dedicated and talented peers, and access to a roster of two distinguished Visiting Writers each month. All VSC Residents receive three meals a day, private, comfortable housing and the company of an international community of painters, sculptors, poets, printmakers and writers. Writers attending residencies at the Studio Center may work on whatever they choose—no matter what month of the year they attend." Visiting writers have included Ron Carlson, Donald Revell, Jane Hirshfield, Rosanna Warren, Chris Abani, Bob Shacochis, Tony Hoagland, and Alice Notley.

ACCOMMODATIONS "The cost of a 4-week residency is $3,750. Generous fellowship and grant assistance available." "Accommodations available on site." "Residents live in single rooms in ten modest, comfortable houses adjacent to the Red Mill Building. Rooms are simply furnished and have shared baths. Complete linen service is provided. The Studio Center is unable to accommodate guests at meals, overnight guests, spouses, children or pets."

ADDITIONAL INFORMATION Fellowships application deadlines are February 15, June 15, and October 1. Writers encouraged to visit website for more information. May also e-mail, call, fax.

VIRGINIA FESTIVAL OF THE BOOK

Virginia Festival of the Book Foundation for the Humanities, 145 Ednam Dr., Charlottesville VA 22903-4629. (434)982-2983. Fax: (434)296-4714. E-mail: vabook@virginia.edu; spcoleman@virginia.edu. Website: www.vabook.org. **Contact:** Nancy Coble Damon, Program Director. Estab. 1995. Annual. Festival held in March. Average attendance: 22,000. Festival held to celebrate books and promote reading and literacy.

COSTS See website for 2012 rates. Most events are free and open to the public. Two luncheons, a breakfast, and a reception require tickets.

ACCOMMODATIONS Overnight accommodations available.

ADDITIONAL INFORMATION "The festival is a five-day event featuring authors, illustrators, and publishing professionals. Authors must apply to the festival to be included on a panel. Preferred method of application is by use of online form. Information is available on the website and inquiries can be made via e-mail, fax, or phone."

WESLEYAN WRITERS CONFERENCE

Wesleyan University, 294 High St., Room 207, Middletown CT 06459. (860)685-3604. Fax: (860)685-2441. E-mail: agreene@wesleyan.edu. Website: www.wesleyan.

edu/writers. Estab. 1956. Annual. Conference held the third week of June. Average attendance: 100. For novel, short story, fiction techniques, poetry, short- and long-form nonfiction, journalism, memoir, multimedia work, digital media. Site: The conference is held on the campus of Wesleyan University, in the hills overlooking the Connecticut River. Features daily seminars, readings, lectures, panels, workshops, mss consultations, publishing advice; faculty of award-winning writers and guest speakers.

ACCOMMODATIONS Meals are provided on campus. Lodging is available on campus or in town.

ADDITIONAL INFORMATION Ms critiques are available, but not required. Scholarships and teaching fellowships are available, including the Joan Jakobson Awards for fiction writers and poets; and the Jon Davidoff Scholarships for nonfiction writers and journalists. Inquire via e-mail, fax, or phone.

WESTERN RESERVE WRITERS & FREELANCE CONFERENCE

Lakeland Community College, 7700 Clocktower Dr., Kirtland OH 44094. (440) 525-7812. E-mail: deencr@aol.com. Website: www.deannaadams.com. **Contact:** Deanna Adams, director/conference coordinator. Estab. 1983. Biannual. Last conference held September 25, 2010. Conference duration: 1 day. Average attendance: 120. "The Western Reserve Writers Conferences are designed for all writers, aspiring and professional, and offer presentations in all genres—nonfiction, fiction, poetry, essays, creative nonfiction and the business of writing, including Web writing and successful freelance writing." The Fall 2010 conference featured top-notch presenters from newspapers and magazines, along with published authors and freelance writers. Presentations included how to draft a standout book proposal and novel synopsis, creating credible characters, contracts/copyrights, public speaking, tips on storytelling for both fiction and nonfiction writers, and when and how to get an agent. Included throughout the day are one-on-one editing consults, Q & A Panel, and book sale/author signings.

COSTS Fall all-day conference, includes lunch: $95. Spring half-day conference, no lunch: $69.

ADDITIONAL INFORMATION Brochures for the conferences are available by January (for spring conference) and July (for fall). Also accepts inquiries by e-mail and phone, or see website. Editors and agents often attend the conferences.

WILLAMETTE WRITERS CONFERENCE

2108 Buck St., Portland OR 97068. (503)305-6729. Fax: (503)452-0372. E-mail: wilwrite@willamettewriters.com. Website: www.willamettewriters.com. **Contact:** Bill Johnson, office manager. Estab. 1968. Annual conference held in August. Conference duration: 3 days. Average attendance: 600. "Williamette Writers is open to all writers, and we plan our conference accordingly. We offer workshops on all aspects of fiction, nonfiction, marketing, the creative process, screenwriting, etc. Also we invite top notch inspirational speakers for keynote addresses. Recent theme was 'The Writers Way.' We always include at least one agent or editor panel and offer a variety of topics of interest to both fiction and nonfiction writers and screenwriters." Recent editors, agents and film producers in attendance have included: Andrea Brown, Marilyn Allen, Angela Rinaldi, Tony Outhwaite.

COSTS Pricing schedule available online.

ACCOMMODATIONS If necessary, arrangements can be made on an individual basis. Special rates may be available.

ADDITIONAL INFORMATION Brochure/guidelines are available for a catalog-sized SASE.

WILLIAM PATERSON UNIVERSITY SPRING WRITER'S CONFERENCE

Atrium 250, 300 Pompton Rd., Wayne NJ 07470-2103. (973)720-3567. E-mail: liut@wpunj.edu. Website: http://euphrates.wpunj.edu/WritersConference. **Contact:** John Parras, professor of English. Annual. Conference held in April. Conference duration: 1 day. Average attendance: 100-125. The 2005 conference focused on "writing the world." Several hands-on workshops were offered in many genres of creative writing, critical writing and literature. Included reading by nationally recognized author. Site: William Paterson University campus. 2005 keynote speaker: poet Linda Gregg. Past faculty has included Yusef Komunyakaa, Joyce Carol Oates, Susan Sontag, and Jimmy Santiago Braca.

COSTS $40 (2005) includes 2 workshops, plenary readings, meals.

ADDITIONAL INFORMATION Conference information is available November/December. For brochure send e-mail, visit website, call. Accepts inquiries by SASE, e-mail, phone. Agents and editors participate in conference.

WINCHESTER WRITERS' CONFERENCE, FESTIVAL AND BOOKFAIR, AND WEEKLONG WRITING WORKSHOPS

University of Winchester, Winchester Hampshire WA S022 4NR United Kingdom. 44 (0) 1962 827238. E-mail: Barbara.Large@winchester.ac.uk. Website: www.writersconference.co.uk. **Contact:** Barbara Large. The 31st Winchester Writers' Conference, Festival, and Bookfair will be preceded by the In-depth Weeklong Writing Workshops, at the University of Winchester, Winchester, Hampshire S022 4NR. Sir Terry Pratchett OBE, internationally famed for his Discworld series, will give the Keynote Address and will lead an outstanding team of 65 professional writers who will offer during 13 mini courses, 43 workshops, 60 lectures and 500 one to one appointments to help writers harness their creative ideas into marketable work. Participate by entering some of the 18 writing competitions, even if you can't attend. Over 100 writers have now reported major publishing successes as a direct result of their attendance at past conferences. This leading literary event offers a magnificent source of information and network of support from tutors who are published writers and industry specialists, a support that continues throughout the year with additional short courses. Enjoy a creative writing holiday in the oldest city in England, yet within an hour of London. Tours planned to Jane Austen's home and Study Centre, the haunts of Keats and the 12th-century Winchester Bible. To receive the 66-page conference programme including all the competition details please contact us.

WINTER POETRY & PROSE GETAWAY IN CAPE MAY

18 N. Richards Ave., Ventnor NJ 08406. (888)887-2105. E-mail: info@wintergetaway.com. Website: www.wintergetaway.com. **Contact:** Peter Murphy. Estab. 1994. Conference duration: 3 days. Average attendance: 200 (10 or fewer participants in each workshop). "Now in its 19th year, the Winter Poetry and Prose Getaway is not your typical writers' conference. Energize your writing with challenging and supportive workshops that focus on starting new material. Advance your craft with feedback from our award-winning faculty, including Pulitzer Prize and National Book Award winners. But the focus isn't on our faculty, it's on helping you improve and advance your skills." Offers a variety of poetry and prose workshops, each with 10 or fewer participants. Featured workshops include Finishing Your Novel, Focusing Your Fiction, Revising a Short Story Toward Publication, Writing and Publishing New Fiction, Writing for the Children's Market, The Art and Craft of Creative Nonfiction, Turning Memory into Memoir, and Reimagining Memoir. Previous faculty has included Renee Ashley, Julianna Baggott, Christian Bauman, Anndee Hochman, Laura McCullough, Sondra Perl, Carol Plum-Ucci, Robbie Clipper Sethi, David Schwartz, Mimi Schwartz, Terese Svoboda, Richard K. Weems, and many more.

ACCOMMODATIONS Please see website or call for current fee information.

ADDITIONAL INFORMATION Previous faculty has included Julianna Baggott, Christian Bauman, Laure-Anne Bosselaar, Kurt Brown, Mark Doty (National Book Award Winner), Stephen Dunn (Pulitzer Prize Winner), Carol Plum-Ucci, James Richardson, Mimi Schwartz, Terese Svoboda, and more.

WISCONSIN REGIONAL WRITERS' ASSOCIATION CONFERENCES

E-mail: vpresident@wrwa.net. Website: www.wrwa.net. Estab. 1948. 9708 Idell Ave., Sparta WI 54656. (608)269-8541. E-mail: registration@wrwa.net. Website: www.wrwa.net. **Contact:** Nate Scholze, Fall Conference Coordinator; Roxanne Aehl, Spring Conference Coordinator. Estab. 1948. Annual. Conferences held in May and September "are dedicated to self-improvement through speakers, workshops and presentations. Topics and speakers vary with each event." Average attendance: 100-150. "We honor all genres of writing. Fall conference is a two-day event featuring the Jade Ring Banquet and awards for six genre categories. Spring conference is a one-day event."

COSTS $40-75.

ACCOMMODATIONS Provides a list of area hotels or lodging options. "We negotiate special rates at each facility. A block of rooms is set aside for a specific time period."

ADDITIONAL INFORMATION Award winners receive a certificate and a cash prize. First place winners of the Jade Ring contest receive a jade ring. Must be a member to enter contests. For brochure, call, e-mail, or visit website in March/July.

WOMEN WRITERS WINTER RETREAT

Homestead House B&B, 38111 West Spaulding, Willoughby OH 44094. (440)946-1902. E-mail: deencr@aol.com. Website: www.deannaadams.com. **Contact:** Deanna Adams, director. Estab. 2007. Annual. Conference duration: 3 days. Average attendance: 35-40. Retreat. "The Women Writers' Winter Retreat was designed for aspiring and professional women writers who cannot seem to find enough time to devote to honing their craft. Each retreat offers class time and workshops facilitated by successful women writers, as well as allows time to do some actual writing, alone or in a group. A Friday night dinner and Keynote kick-starts the weekend, followed by Saturday workshops, free time, meals, and an open mic to read your works. Sunday wraps up with one more workshop and fellowship. All genres welcome. Choice of overnight stay or commuting." Site: Located in the heart of downtown Willoughby, this warm and attractive bed-and-breakfast is easy to find, around the corner from the main street, Erie Street, and behind a popular Arabica coffee house. Door prizes and book sale/author signings throughout the weekend.

COSTS Single room: $299. Shared Room: $225 (includes complete weekend package, with B&B stay and all meals and workshops); weekend commute: $150; Saturday only: $125 (prices include lunch and dinner).

ADDITIONAL INFORMATION "Brochures for the writers retreat are available by December. Accepts inquiries and reservations by e-mail or phone. See website for additional information."

WRANGLING WITH WRITING

Society of Southwestern Authors, (520)546-9382. Fax: (520)751-7877. E-mail: Mike_Rom@hotmail.com. Website: www.ssa-az.org/conference.htm. **Contact:** Mike Rom. Estab. 1972. Phone: (520)296-5299. Fax: (520)296-0409. Website: www.ssa-az.org. 36 Writer workshops geared to all genres. "Limited scholarships available." One-on-one interviews with agents prescheduled prior to conference at an additional cost of $20 for a 15-minute meeting. "Three children's books agents interested in meeting with children's writers." Annual conferences held in September; watch website ssa-az.org. Registration limited to 400. Hotel rooms have data ports for Internet access. Tentative cost: $350 nonmembers, $275 for SSA members; includes selections from all workshop sessions—and individual appointments with keynoters, authors, agents, and teachers. Hotel accommodations are not included. Write for more information. SSA has put on this conference for over 36 years now. "It's hands-on, it's friendly, and every year writers sell their manuscripts."

COSTS See website for costs. Five meals included.

ADDITIONAL INFORMATION Brochures/guidelines are available as of July 15 by e-mail address above. Two banquets will include editor and agent panels for all attendees, and Saturday evening winning plays from contestants will be presented.

WRITE FROM THE HEART

9827 Irvine Avenue, Upper Lake CA 95485. (800)738-6721. E-mail: Halbooks@HalZinaBennet.com. Website: www.HalZinaBennet.com. **Contact:** Hal. Offered 4 to 6 times a year. Conference duration: 3-5 days. Average attendance: 15-30. Online course and individual coaching available. "Open to all genres, focusing on accessing the author's greatest gifts, experiences and areas of expertise; shaping the work for successful publication." Site: Northern California and Midwest; Instructor: Hal Zina Bennett.

COSTS $350 and up.

ACCOMMODATIONS No arrangements for transportation. Provides list of area hotels.

ADDITIONAL INFORMATION By e-mail, phone, fax, or on website. Editors participate in conference. "Hal is the author of 30-plus books, with more than 1.2 million copies in print and has helped over 200 authors develop successful books, including several national bestsellers."

WRITE IT OUT

P.O. Box 704, Sarasota FL 34230-0704. (941)359-3824. E-mail: rmillerwio@aol.com. Website: www.writeitout.com. **Contact:** Ronni Miller, director. Estab. 1997. Workshops held 2-3 times/year in March, June, July, and August. Conference duration: 5-10 days. Average attendance: 4-10. Workshops retreats on "expressive writing and painting, fiction, poetry, memoirs. We also offer intimate, motivational, in-depth free private conferences with instructors." Past facilitators included Arturo Vivante, novelist. Acquisitions: Ronni Miller, director. "Critiques on work are given at the workshops." Conference information available year-round. For brochures/guidelines e-mail, call, or visit website. Accepts inquiries by phone, e-mail. Workshops have "small groups, option to spend time writing and not attend classes, with personal appointments with instructors."

COSTS 2011 fees: Bermuda $757. Italy, $1,300; Cape Cod, $575, Woodstock, NY $375. Price includes tuition, private conferences and salons. Room, board, and airfare not included.

WRITE ON THE SOUND WRITERS' CONFERENCE

Edmonds Arts Commission, 700 Main St., Edmonds WA 98020. (425)771-0228. Fax: (425)771-0253. E-mail: wots@ci.edmonds.wa.us. Website: www.ci.edmonds.wa.us/ArtsCommission/wots.stm. Estab. 1985. Annual. Last conference held October 1-2, 2011. Conference duration: 2.5 days. Average attendance: 180. "Conference is limited to 200 participants, good for networking, and focuses on the craft of writing." Site: "Edmonds is a beautiful community on the shores of Puget Sound, just north of Seattle. View brochure at www.ci.edmonds.wa.us/artscommission/wots.stm."

COSTS See website for more information.

ADDITIONAL INFORMATION Brochures are available in July. Accepts inquiries via phone, e-mail, and fax.

WRITERS IN PARADISE

Eckerd College, 4200 54th Ave South, St. Petersburg FL 33711. (727) 864-7994. Fax: (727) 864-7575. E-mail: cayacr@eckerd.edu. Website: www.writersinparadise.com. **Contact:** Christine Caya, conference coordinator. Estab. 2005. Annual. January. Conference duration: 8 days. Average attendance: 84 max. Workshop. Offers college credit. "Writers in Paradise Conference offers workshop classes in fiction (novel and short story), poetry and nonfiction. Working closely with our award-winning faculty, students will have stimulating opportunities to ask questions and learn valuable skills from fellow students and authors at the top of their form. Most importantly, the intimate size and secluded location of the Writers in Paradise experience allows you the time and opportunity to share your manuscripts, critique one another's work and discuss the craft of writing with experts and peers who can help guide you to the next level." Site: Located on 188 acres of waterfont property in St. Petersburg, Florida, Eckerd College is a private, coeducational college of liberal arts and sciences. "In 2011, lectures were given on the craft of writing by Richard Russo, Michael Koryta, Dennis Lehane, and Sterling Watson. Faculty also led discussions during morning sessions of informal roundtables and formal panel discussions on craft. 2011 faculty and guest faculty included: Richard Russo (*Empire Falls*), Michael Koryta (*So Cold the River*), Dennis Lehane (*The Given Day*), Laura Lippman (*I'd Know You Anywhere*), Lisa Gallagher (Literary Agent), Johnny Temple (Akashic Books), Sterling Watson (*Sweet Dream Baby*), Julianna Baggott (*The Anybodies*), Les Standiford (*Bringing Adam Home*), Tom Perrotta (*Little Children*), Ann Hood (*The Read Thread*), John Dufresne (*Requiem Mass*), and Jane Hamilton (*The Book of Ruth*) and more."

COSTS 2010 tuition fee: $675.

ACCOMMODATIONS Does not offer overnight accommodations. Provides list of preferred conference hotels and lodging options.

ADDITIONAL INFORMATION Application materials are required of all attendees. Acceptance is based on a writing sample and a letter detailing your writing background. Submit 1 short story (25 pg max) or the opening 25 pages of a novel-in-progress, plus a 2-page synopsis of the book. Deadline for application materials is December 1. "Writers in Paradise is a conference for writers of various styles and approaches. While admission is selective, the admissions committee accepts writers with early potential as well as those with strong backgrounds in writing." Sponsors contest. "At the final Evening Reading Series Event, Co-directors Dennis Lehane and Sterling Watson will announce 'The Best of' nominees of the Writers in Paradise Conference. Winners will be published in *Sabal—A Review Featuring the Best Writing of the Writers in Paradise Conference at Eckerd College*. One winner and one honorable mention will be selected from each workshop based on the material brought into the workshop for discussion. Selection will be made by the faculty member leading the workshop. There are no additional fees or entry forms needed." Information available in October 2011. For brochure, send SASE, call, e-mail. Agents participate in conference. Editors participate in conference. "The tranquil seaside landscape sets the tone for this informal gathering of writers, teachers, editors and literary agents. After 8 days of workshopping and engagement with peers and professionals in your field, you will leave this unique opportunity with solid ideas about how to find an agent and get published, along with a new and better understanding of your craft."

WRITERS' INSTITUTE

21 North Park St., Room 7331, Madison WI 53715. (608)265-3972. Fax: (608)265-2475. E-mail: lscheer@dcs.wisc.edu. Website: www.uwwritersinstitute.org. **Contact:** Laurie Scheer. Estab. 1989. Annual. Conference usually held in April. Site: Pyle Center. Average attendance: 200.

COSTS $245 includes materials, breaks.

ACCOMMODATIONS Provides a list of area hotels or lodging options.

ADDITIONAL INFORMATION Sponsors contest. Submit 1-page writing sample and $10 entry fee. Conference speakers are judges. For brochure send e-mail, visit website, call, fax. Accepts inquiries by SASE, e-mail, phone, fax. Agents and editors participate in conference.

WRITERS' LEAGUE OF TEXAS SUMMER WRITING RETREAT

611 S. Congress Ave., Suite 130, Austin TX 78704. (512)499-8914. Fax: (512)499-0441. E-mail: wlt@writersleague.org. Website: www.writersleague.org. **Contact:** Sara Kocek, Program Coordinator. Retreat: Annual Summer Writing Retreat in Alpine, TX, is a weeklong writing intensive with 5 tracks. Instructors include Scott Wiggerman, Carol Dawson, Debra Monroe, Jennifer Ziegler, and W.K. Stratton.

COSTS $299 WLT members/$359 nonmembers.

ADDITIONAL INFORMATION Available at website.

WRITERS STUDIO AT UCLA EXTENSION

1010 Westwood Blvd., Los Angeles CA 90024. (310) 825-9415. E-mail: writers@uclaextension.edu. Website: www.uclaextension.edu/writers. **Contact:** Katy Flaherty. Estab. 1997. Annual in February. Conference duration: 4 days; 10 a.m. to 6 p.m. Average attendance: 150-200. Intensive writing workshops in the areas of creative writing (fiction and nonfiction), screenwriting, and television writing. Site: Conducted at UCLA Extension's 1010 Westwood Center.

COSTS Fee is $775 after December 4, 2010.

ACCOMMODATIONS Information on overnight accommodations is available.

ADDITIONAL INFORMATION For more information, call (310)825-9415 or send an e-mail to writers@uclaextension.edu.

THE WRITERS WORKSHOP

PO Box 329, Langley WA 98260. E-mail: bob@bobmayer.org. Website: www.bobmayer.org. **Contact:** Bob Mayer. Estab. 2002. Held every 3 months. Last conference: January 2010. Conference duration: 2 days. Site: various locations around the country.

COSTS varies depending on venue

ADDITIONAL INFORMATION Limited to 8 participants and focused on their novel and marketability.

WRITERS WORKSHOP IN SCIENCE FICTION

English Department/University of Kansas, Wesoce Hall, 1445 Jayhawk Blvd., Room 3001, Lawrence KS 66045-7590. (785)864-3380. Fax: (785)864-1159. E-mail: jgunn@ku.edu. Website: www.ku.edu/~sfcenter. Estab. 1985. Annual. Workshop held in late June to early July. Conference duration: 2 weeks. Average attendance: 10-14. The workshop is "small, informal and aimed at writers on the edge of publication or regular publication." For writing and marketing science fiction and fantasy. Site: "Housing is provided and classes meet in university housing on the University of Kansas campus. Workshop sessions operate informally in a lounge." Past guests included Frederik Pohl, SF writer and former editor and agent; John Ordover, writer and editor; George Zebrowski, Pamela Sargent, Kij Johnson and Christopher McKittrick, writers; Lou Anders, editor. A novel workshop in science fiction and fantasy is also available.

COSTS See website for tuition rates, dormitory housing costs, and deadlines.

ACCOMMODATIONS Housing information is available. Several airport shuttle services offer reasonable transportation from the Kansas City International Airport to Lawrence.

ADDITIONAL INFORMATION Admission to the workshop is by submission of an acceptable story. Two additional stories should be submitted by the middle of June. These 3 stories are distributed to other participants for critiquing and are the basis for the first week of the workshop. One story is rewritten for the second week. Send SASE for brochure/guidelines. This workshop is intended for writers who have just started to sell their work or need that extra bit of understanding or skill to become a published writer.

WRITE-TO-PUBLISH CONFERENCE

WordPro Communication Services, 9118 W. Elmwood Dr., Suite 1G, Niles IL 60714-5820. (847)296-3964. Fax: (847)296-0754. E-mail: lin@writetopublish.com. Website: www.writetopublish.com. **Contact:** Lin Johnson, director. Estab. 1971. Writer workshops geared toward all levels. **Open to students.** Conference is focused for the Christian market and includes classes on writing for children. Annual conference held June 6-9, 2012. Cost of conference approximately: $480; includes conference and banquet. For information e-mail brochure@writetopublish.com. Conference takes place at Wheaton College in the Chicago area.

COSTS approximately $480.
ACCOMMODATIONS In campus residence halls or discounted hotel rates. Cost approximately $270-350.
ADDITIONAL INFORMATION Optional ms evaluation available. College credit available. Conference information available in January. For details, visit website, or e-mail brochure@writetopublish.com. Accepts inquiries by e-mail, fax, phone.

WRITING FOR THE SOUL

Jerry B. Jenkins Christian Writers Guild, 5525 N. Union Blvd., Suite 200, Colorado Springs CO 80918. (866)495-5177. Fax: (719)495-5181. E-mail: leilani@christianwritersguild.com. Website: www.christianwritersguild.com/conferences. **Contact:** Leilani Squiers, admissions manager. Writing for the Soul. www.christianwritersguild.com/conferences. Annual conference held in February. Workshops and continuing classes cover fiction, nonfiction and magazine writing, children's books, and teen writing. Appointments with more than 30 agents, publishers, and editors are also available. The keynote speakers are nationally known, leading authors. The conference is hosted by Jerry B. Jenkins.
COSTS $649/Guild members; $799/nonmembers.
ACCOMMODATIONS $159/night at the Grand Hyatt in Denver.

THE HELENE WURLITZER FOUNDATION

P.O. Box 1891, Taos NM 87571. (505)758-2413. Fax: (575)758-2559. E-mail: hwf@taosnet.com. Website: www.wurlitzerfoundation.org. **Contact:** Michael A. Knight, executive director. Estab. 1953. Residence duration: 3 months. "The Foundation's purpose is to provide a quiet haven where artists may pursue their creative endeavors without pressure to produce while they are in residence."
ACCOMMODATIONS "Provides individual housing in fully furnished studio/houses (casitas), rent and utility free. Artists are responsible for transportation to and from Taos, their meals, and the materials for their work. Bicycles are provided upon request."

YADDO

The Corporation of Yaddo Residencies, Box 395, 312 Union Ave., Saratoga Springs NY 12866-0395. (518)584-0746. Fax: (518)584-1312. E-mail: chwait@yaddo.org; Lleduc@yaddo.org. Website: www.yaddo.org. **Contact:** Candace Wait, program director. Estab. 1900. Two seasons: large season is in mid-May-August; small season is October-May (stays from 2 weeks to 2 months; average stay is 5 weeks). Average attendance: 220/year. Accommodates approximately 34 artists in large season, 16 in the small season. "Those qualified for invitations to Yaddo are highly qualified writers, visual artists, composers, choreographers, performance artists and film and video artists who are working at the professional level in their fields. Artists who wish to work collaboratively are encouraged to apply. An abiding principle at Yaddo is that applications for residencies are judged on the quality of the artists' work and professional promise." Site: includes 4 small lakes, a rose garden, woodland, swimming pool, tennis courts.
COSTS No fee is charged; residency includes room, board and studio space. Limited travel expenses are available to artists accepted for residencies at Yaddo.
ACCOMMODATIONS No stipends are offered.

GENERAL INDEX

B

C

D

E